So̶u̶...̶c̶a̶

Caribbean Sea

PANAMA

Caracas
Maracaibo
TRINIDAD
Orinoco

V E N E Z U E L A
Georgetown
GUYANA
Paramaribo
Cayenne
SURINAME
*French
Guiana*

Medellín
G U I A N A   *HIGHLANDS*

Bogotá
(Santa Fé)
C O L O M B I A
Branco

Cali
Negro
Marajó I.

Quito
Japur
Belém

ECUADOR
Amazon
Manaus

Guayaquil
Marañón
Madeira
Tapajós
Fortaleza

Juruá
Purus
Xingu
Tocantins
Recife
(Pernambuco)

A
N
Ucayali
B R A Z I L
São Francisco

Lima

P E R U

Salvador
(Bahia)

B O L I V I A
Brasília
BRAZILIAN HIGHLANDS

D
La Paz

E
Sucre

Belo Horizonte

S
Paraguay

C H I L E
P A R A G U A Y
São Paulo
Rio de Janeiro

Paraná

Asunción

Pacific
Paraná

Pôrto Alegre

Ocean
Córdoba
Uruguay

Valparaíso
Rosario
URUGUAY

Santiago
Buenos Aires
Montevideo

Concepción
A R G E N T I N A

Bahía Blanca

Atlantic

Ocean

P A T A G O N I A

*Falkland Islands
(Islas Malvinas)*

Punta Arenas

Tierra del Fuego

500 miles

805 kilometers

ENCYCLOPEDIA OF

LATIN AMERICAN HISTORY AND CULTURE

ADVISORY BOARD

ENCYCLOPEDIA OF

LATIN AMERICAN HISTORY AND CULTURE

BARBARA A. TENENBAUM

EDITOR IN CHIEF

Georgette Magassy Dorn
Mary Karasch
John Jay TePaske
Ralph Lee Woodward, Jr.
ASSOCIATE EDITORS

VOLUME 2

Charles Scribner's Sons

MACMILLAN LIBRARY REFERENCE USA

SIMON & SCHUSTER MACMILLAN

NEW YORK

SIMON & SCHUSTER AND PRENTICE HALL INTERNATIONAL

LONDON   MEXICO CITY   NEW DELHI   SINGAPORE   SYDNEY   TORONTO

An imprint of Simon & Schuster Macmillan
866 Third Ave.
New York, NY 10022

Library of Congress Cataloging-in-Publication Data

Encyclopedia of Latin American history and culture / Barbara A.
    Tenenbaum, editor in chief ; associate editors, Georgette M. Dorn
    . . . [et al.].
        p.   cm.
    Includes bibliographical references and index.
    ISBN 0-684-19253-5 (set : alk. paper). — ISBN 0-684-19752-9 (v. 1
: alk. paper). — ISBN 0-684-19753-7 (v. 2 : alk. paper). — ISBN
0-684-19754-5 (v. 3 : alk. paper). — ISBN 0-684-19755-3 (v. 4 :
alk. paper). — ISBN 0-684-80480-8 (v. 5 : alk. paper).
    1. Latin America—Encyclopedias.   I. Tenenbaum, Barbara A.
F1406.E53   1996   95–31042
980'.003—dc20   CIP

1   3   5   7   9   11   13   15   17   19   V/C   20   18   16   14   12   10   8   6   4   2

PRINTED IN THE UNITED STATES OF AMERICA

The paper used in this publication meets the minimum requirements of American National Standard for Information Sciences—Permanence of Paper for Printed Library Materials. ANSI Z3948-1984.

USING THE ENCYCLOPEDIA

This encyclopedia contains nearly 5,300 separate articles. Most topics appear in English alphabetical order, according to the word-by-word system (e.g., Casa Rosada before Casals). Persons and places generally precede things (Roosevelt, Theodore, before Roosevelt Corollary). Certain subjects are clustered together in composite entries, which may comprise several regions, periods, or genres. For example, the "Slavery" and "Mining" entries contain separate articles for Brazil and Spanish America. "Art" embraces separately signed essays on pre-Columbian, colonial, nineteenth-century, and modern art, as well as folk art.

NATIONAL TOPICS are frequently clustered by country, under one or more of the following subheadings:

> *Constitutions*
> *Organizations* (administrative, cultural, economic, labor, etc.)
> *Political Parties* (listed under the English name and including former revolutionary movements that have entered the political system)
> *Revolutionary Movements*
> *Revolutions*

Note that an event with a distinctive name will be found under that term, whereas a generic name will appear under the appropriate country. Thus, the Chibata Revolt appears under *C* and the Pastry War under *P*, but the Revolution of 1964 appears under "Brazil: Revolutions."

MEASUREMENTS appear in the English system according to United States usage. Following are approximate metric equivalents for the most common units:

$$1 \text{ foot} = 30 \text{ centimeters}$$
$$1 \text{ mile} = 1.6 \text{ kilometers}$$
$$1 \text{ acre} = 0.4 \text{ hectares}$$
$$1 \text{ square mile} = 2.6 \text{ square kilometers}$$
$$1 \text{ pound} = 0.45 \text{ kilograms}$$
$$1 \text{ gallon} = 3.8 \text{ liters}$$

BIOGRAPHICAL ENTRIES (numbering nearly 3,000) are listed separately in an appendix in volume 5, where a rough classification is offered according to sex and field(s) of activity.

CROSS-REFERENCES appear in two forms: SMALL CAPITALS in the text highlight significant persons, concepts, and institutions that are treated in their own entries in the encyclopedia. *See also* references at the end of an entry call attention to articles of more general relevance. Cross-referencing is selective: obvious sources of information (such as most country, state, and city entries) are not highlighted. For full cross-referencing consult the index in volume 5.

ENCYCLOPEDIA OF

LATIN AMERICAN HISTORY AND CULTURE

CASA GRANDE, the main house or family residence on a plantation during Brazil's colonial era and the Empire. Architectural style varied by region, era, and degree of wealth of the planter. The more elaborate homes were grand, two-story dwellings with separate sitting, dining, and ball rooms; numerous bedrooms; a kitchen and a pantry, and sometimes even a chapel. Family living quarters occupied the upper floor; the ground floor was divided into locked areas for storage of supplies, tools, and the products of the plantation. Rather than being set apart in a spacious garden, the *casa grande* typically formed one of a cluster of buildings—workshops, mill or waterwheel, storage sheds, and slave quarters—that made up the living and administrative core of a plantation. Sociologist Gilberto FREYRE used the term *casa grande* in his famous study of slavery and race relations, *Casa grande e senzala*, published in 1933 and subsequently translated into English as *The Masters and the Slaves* (1946), to connote the constellation of cultural assumptions that characterized the patriarchal family and relations between masters and slaves, describing both the institutionalized brutality of slavery and the contributions of Afro-Brazilians to the larger patterns of Brazilian culture.

SANDRA LAUDERDALE GRAHAM

See also **Senzala.**

CASA MATA, PLAN OF, a political proposal leading to the establishment of a federal republic in Mexico. After independence, conflict ensued between the executive and legislative branches of the new government. Em-peror Agustín de ITURBIDE jailed dissenting legislators and ultimately dissolved Congress on 31 October 1822. The generals sent to crush the opposition instead "pronounced" against the emperor, issuing the Plan of Casa Mata on 1 February 1823. The plan, which insisted on the election of a new constituent congress, did not contemplate fundamental change. Indeed, it did not even seek the emperor's removal. But the plan proved revolutionary because it included a provision granting authority to the Provincial Deputation of Veracruz. That offered the provinces an opportunity for home rule, something they pursued immediately. When Iturbide abdicated on 19 March 1823 rather than provoke a civil war, the provinces insisted upon the election of a new congress and ultimately established a federal republic in 1824.

NETTIE LEE BENSON, "The Plan of Casa Mata," in *Hispanic American Historical Review* 25 (February 1945): 45–56; WILLIAM SPENCE ROBERTSON, *Iturbide of Mexico* (1952), esp. pp. 221–260; TIMOTHY E. ANNA, *The Mexican Empire of Iturbide* (1990), esp. pp. 189–216; JAIME E. RODRÍGUEZ O., "The Struggle for the Nation: The First Centralist-Federalist Conflict in Mexico," in *The Americas* 49 (July 1992): 1–22.

JAIME E. RODRÍGUEZ O.

CASA ROSADA (the Pink House), the presidential palace and seat of the executive branch in Argentina. Located in the Plaza de Mayo near the Río de la Plata, its construction began during the presidency of Domingo SARMIENTO (1868–1874) and was completed in 1882, during the presidency of Julio A. ROCA (1880–1886; 1898–1904). Its name, which intentionally evokes its North American antecedent, came as a result of

Casa Rosada and Plaza de Mayo, ca. 1895. Buenos Aires. SOCIEDAD FOTOGRÁFICA ARGENTINA DE AFICIONADOS, COLECCIÓN CRISTIAN FAVIER DUBOIS.

1

Sarmiento's decision to paint it with a blend of the Federalists' red and the Unitarians' white—the colors of the two major political factions that competed for power in Argentina after its break from Spain in 1810.

JAMES R. SCOBIE, *Argentina: A City and a Nation,* 2d ed. (1971), pp. 163, 165.

DANIEL LEWIS

CASADO, CARLOS (*b.* 16 March 1833; *d.* 29 June 1899). Born in Valencia, Spain, Casado emigrated to Argentina in 1857 and opened a business in the city of Rosario in Santa Fe Province. He also established a private bank that became one of the foundations for the offices of the Bank of London and the Río de la Plata that opened in Rosario in 1868. In 1870 he set up the Candelaria agricultural colony, promoting the immigration of European agricultural workers and realizing the first major export shipment of wheat to Europe. Casado organized a company of wheat mills, promoted the construction of docks in the Rosario port, and was a founder and president of the Banco de Santa Fe, a leading commercial bank. He was also elected counselor of the city government of Rosario.

WILLIAM PERKINS, *Las colonias de Santa Fe: Su orígen, progreso y actual situación* (1864); MICHAEL MULHALL, *Handbook of the River Plate* (1885); EZEQUIEL GALLO, *La pampa gringa: La colonización agrícola en Santa Fe* (1984).

CARLOS MARICHAL

CASAL, JULIÁN DEL (*b.* 7 November 1863; *d.* 21 October 1893), Cuban poet who used the pseudonyms the Count of Camors, Hernani, and Alceste at times during his literary career. Casal was born in Havana and showed a great talent for poetry from an early age. His first poems were published in *El Estudio,* an underground publication that he founded with a group of friends. He began studies for a career in law in 1881 at the University of Havana but never finished them. Instead, he became finance minister while writing articles and working in diverse capacities for newspapers and literary publications, among them *La Discusión, El Fígaro,* and *La Habana Literaria.* Casal published a series of articles on Cuban society in the magazine *La Habana Elegante.* The first, a derogatory piece about the Spanish captain-general Sabas Marín, cost him his government post. In his short life Casal earned a place as one of the great poets in Cuban history. Along with three other poets, fellow Cuban José MARTÍ, Colombian José Asunción SILVA, and Mexican Manuel GUTIÉRREZ NÁJERA, he was an initiator of modernism, the first literary movement to originate in Spanish-speaking America.

Some of the most notable of Casal's contemporaries, including Martí, José Lezama Lima, Ramón Mesa, Enrique Varona, and Cintio Vitier, have written about Casal and his poetry. See

EMILIO DE ARMAS, *Casal* (1981). An excellent study in English is ROBERT J. GLICKMAN, *The Poetry of Julián del Casal,* 3 vols. (1976–1978).

ROBERTO VALERO

CASALDÁLIGA, PEDRO (*b.* 1928), bishop of São Félix do Araguaia, Brazil. Casaldáliga was born in Barcelona and raised on his family's cattle ranch in Catalonia. In 1952 he was ordained into the Claretian order, and sixteen years later he arrived in Brazil. By 1971 he had attracted the attention of Brazilian authorities by writing a critical report titled "Feudalism and Slavery in Northern Mato Grosso." In the following year Casaldáliga was consecrated as the first bishop of São Félix do Araguaia, a large but remote region in the states of Goiás and Mato Grosso.

In subsequent years, however, the prolific writer and poet found himself in direct conflict with the landowners of Goiás and Mato Grosso, the Brazilian government, and the Catholic hierarchy because of his emphasis on developing community leadership among the peasants within his diocese, providing health care and education, and resisting the continued expansion of ranches at the expense of peasants' rights. In 1973, the same year that the Missionary Council to Indigenous Peoples was founded in Brazil, Francisco Jentel, a priest under Casaldáliga's authority, was tried under Brazil's National Security Law for inciting class warfare as the government sought resolutions to continuing conflicts at Santa Terezinha. In October 1976 Casaldáliga was present when Brazilian authorities shot and killed a Jesuit missionary, João Bosco Penido Burnier, for interfering with the interrogation and torture of two women. After 1973 public criticism began to surface from Archbishop Sigaud and Cardinal Joseph Ratzinger about Casaldáliga's pastoral work as well as his theological convictions.

In 1985 Casaldáliga began traveling extensively throughout Central America, including Nicaragua, El Salvador, and Cuba, in "a ministry of borders and consolation." As a result of criticism for these trips, as well as for his writings supportive of liberation theologians and his characterization of Archbishop Oscar Romero as a martyr, in 1988 the Vatican issued an order that Casaldáliga not speak publicly, publish any further writings, or leave his diocese without explicit permission.

TEÓFILO CABESTRERO, *Mystic of Liberation: A Portrait of Pedro Casaldáliga* (1981); PENNY LERNOUX, *Cry of the People,* rev. ed. (1982); SCOTT MAINWARING, *The Catholic Church and Politics in Brazil, 1916–1985* (1986); KEVIN NEUHOUSER, "The Radicalization of the Brazilian Catholic Church in Comparative Perspective," in *American Sociological Review* 54, no. 2 (1989): 233–244; PEDRO CASALDÁLIGA, *In Pursuit of the Kingdom,* translated by Philip Berryman (1990).

CAROLYN E. VIEIRA

See also **Catholic Church; Liberation Theology.**

CASALS, FELIPE (*b.* 28 July 1937), Mexican film director. Born in Zapopán, Jalisco, Casals studied film in Paris. He is one of the leading directors of the generation of 1968, which contributed greatly to a brief flowering of Mexican cinema in the 1970s. Among the most celebrated of his films are *Canoa* (1974), *El apando* (1975), *Las poquianchis* (1976), *El año de la peste* (1978), *Bajo la metralla* (1982), *Los motivos de Luz* (1985), and *El tres de copas* (1986). Casals' films are characterized by hard-hitting, violent portrayals of Mexican national issues, particularly social strife and the underclass. Most of his films have been produced by the state. He received the Ariel from the Mexican film academy for best director for *El año de la peste* and *Bajo la metralla*. He has filmed other minor features for the video market, such as *Las abandonadas* and a musical biography of the popular singer Rigo Tovar, entitled *Rigo es amor.*

LUIS REYES DE LA MAZA, *El cine sonoro en México* (1973); E. BRADFORD BURNS, *Latin American Cinema: Film and History* (1975); CARL J. MORA, *Mexican Cinema: Reflections of a Society: 1896–1980* (1982); and JOHN KING, *Magical Reels: A History of Cinema in Latin America* (1990).

DAVID MACIEL

CASANARE, an intendancy of Colombia located in the eastern plains (Llanos Orientales) and occupying an area of 17,169 square miles, it is bounded on the west by the Cordillera Oriental, on the north by the Casanare River, and on the south and east by the Meta River. Mostly low-lying grassland, it has a tropical climate with alternating wet and dry seasons.

In the sixteenth century Spanish and German conquistadores explored Casanare in a futile search for EL DORADO. Later, *encomenderos* and missionaries competed for control of the Indians. Before their expulsion in 1767, the Jesuits established eleven missions and eight haciendas in Casanare, an empire second in size only to their reductions in Paraguay. By this time, cattle raising—the principal economic activity—had produced a mestizo subculture of *llaneros* (cowboys).

Casanare was a major theater in the War of Independence. After royalists reconquered the new Granada highlands, Simón BOLÍVAR sent Francisco de Paula SANTANDER to the plains to forge the fiercely patriotic *llaneros* into a new army. In June 1819, Bolívar led this force in an epic march over the Andes to defeat the Spanish in the battle of BOYACÁ (7 August 1819).

The ravages of war and systematic neglect precipitated Casanare's decline in the nineteenth century from a modestly self-sufficient region to an isolated, forgotten province. Until recently, subsistence agriculture and ranching predominated, but since 1983 large-scale extraction of petroleum near the capital of Yopal promises a more prosperous future.

JAMES J. PARSONS, "Europeanization of the Savanna Lands of Northern South America," in *Human Ecology in Savanna Environments*, edited by David R. Harris (1980), pp. 267–289; JANE

M. RAUSCH, *A Tropical Plains Frontier: The Llanos of Colombia, 1531–1831* (1984); HÉCTOR PUBLIO PÉREZ ÁNGEL, *La participación de Casanare en la guerra de independencia, 1809–1819* (1987).

JANE M. RAUSCH

CASANOVA Y ESTRADA, RICARDO (*b.* 10 November 1844; *d.* 14 April 1913), archbishop of Guatemala (1886–1913). Casanova was born in Guatemala City and studied law at the University of San Carlos. He served in governmental positions until 1874, when he angered President Justo BARRIOS by deciding a case in favor of an abolished religious community. Being forced by Barrios to parade through the city in a cassock convinced the lawyer to become a priest. Ordained in 1875 and consecrated archbishop in 1886, he issued several pastoral letters defending the church against the Liberals. He was exiled by President Manuel BARILLAS in 1887 and returned to Guatemala in 1897, spending the rest of his life guiding the church during the dictatorship of Manuel Estrada Cabrera. Casanova was also a poet, writing under the pseudonym of Andrés Vigil.

JOSÉ M. RAMÍREZ COLÓM, *Reseña biográfica del ilustrísimo y reverendísimo señor arzobispo de Santiago de Guatemala don Ricardo Casanova y Estrada* (1896); AGUSTÍN ESTRADA MONROY, *Datos para la historia de la iglesia en Guatemala*, vol. 3 (1979), pp. 199–308.

EDWARD T. BRETT

See also **Anticlericalism.**

CASAS GRANDES, an archaeological site in north-central Chihuahua state in Mexico. Although it has a number of Mesoamerican features, it is separated from the northernmost Mesoamerican sites in Zacatecas by many miles and really belongs in the southernmost part of the Southwestern Culture area.

The earliest occupation at Casas Grandes is called the Medio period (1060–1340), although for half a millennium earlier a Mogollon-like population occupied the area, lived in pit houses, and made red pottery. During the earliest part of the Medio period, the Buena Fé phase (1060–1205), a large town was built, featuring twenty or so house clusters around plazas enclosed by a fortification wall. The houses were made of "mud concrete poured" walls, had T-shaped doorways, and were usually one story. The people made polychrome pottery and kept breeding boxes for macaws imported from Mesoamerica. Charles Di Peso interpreted this entire construction as built by the *pochteca* traders from central Mexico who invaded and ruled Casas Grandes.

During the next phase, the Paquimé (1205–1261), the town blossomed. Four- or five-story adobe apartment complexes were built, as well as effigy mounds and pyramids. A complex irrigation system and a road system were constructed, features attributable to Mesoamerican influences. The amount of Mexican imports—

copper bells, armlets, rings, pendants, shells, and perhaps obsidian—also increased.

Almost as fast as the Paquimé rise was the decline in the Diablo phase (1261–1340). The multistoried apartments fell into disrepair and the ceremonial structures ceased to be used, although fine polychrome pottery continued to be made and the population may have increased. By the 1350s, however, the site was abandoned, and the Casas Grandes culture ceased to exist.

CHARLES C. DI PESO, *Casas Grandes: A Fallen Trading Center of the Gran Chichimeca*, 7 vols. (1974), and *Casas Grandes and the Gran Chichimeca* (n.d.).

RICHARD S. MacNEISH

CASASOLA, AGUSTÍN (b. 1874; d. 1928), Mexican photographer. Born in Mexico City, Agustín Casasola worked as a reporter for numerous periodicals, including the Porfirian daily *El Imparcial*. There he began to collect illustrations, documents, books, and photographs which would eventually become the Casasola Archives, containing nearly one million photographs, the richest pictorial documents of twentieth-century Mexican history. The most prolific Mexican photographer of his day, Casasola captured the last years of the Porfiriato, the revolutionary struggle, and its aftermath. Like Matthew Brady, distinguished photographer of the American Civil War, he witnessed and recorded history; his photographs include figures such as Pancho Villa and Emiliano Zapata, rebels hanged from trees or executed by firing squads, and *soldaderas* riding atop boxcars and shouldering rifles. A collection of his photography, including some of what he collected from others, was published by his son Gustavo in *Historia gráfica de la Revolución Mexicana: 1900–1940*, edited by Luis González Obregón and Nicolás Rangel.

Diccionario Porrúa de historia, biografía y geografía de México, 5th ed. (1986); VICTOR SORELL, "Mexposición 2: Images of the Revolución, Casasola" (1976); JACOBO WIEBE, "Hazañas fotográficas de Casasola," in *Contenido* 152 (January 1976): 82–87.

MARY KAY VAUGHAN

See also **Photography.**

CASÁUS Y TORRES, RAMÓN (b. 1765; d. 10 November 1845), archbishop of Guatemala (1811–1845). Born in Jaca, Huesca, Spain, Casáus entered the DOMINICAN order in Saragossa and later earned his doctorate in Mexico City. He was bishop of Oaxaca when appointed archbishop of Guatemala in 1811. As archbishop, he worked to improve educational facilities and donated his library to the University of SAN CARLOS. He was especially interested in Indian languages and arranged for teaching Quiché and Cakchiquel at the university and the seminary. He opposed independence from Spain and Mexico and became closely associated with conservative political interests in the civil wars following independence. He strongly resisted establishment of a separate diocese for El Salvador.

Liberal victory in 1829 resulted in Casáus's exile from Central America by Francisco MORAZÁN. He spent the remainder of his life in Havana. The state of Guatemala declared him a traitor on 13 June 1830. After Rafael CARRERA came to power, in 1839, the Guatemalan government invited him to return, but the continuing turmoil on the isthmus deterred the archbishop from returning to his see before his death. His remains were brought to Guatemala for burial in 1846.

FRANCISCO FERNÁNDEZ HALL, "Historiadores de Guatemala posteriores a la independencia nacional: El Doctor don Francisco de Paula García Peláez," in *Anales de la Sociedad de Geografía e Historia* 15, no. 3 (1939): 261–278; MARY P. HOLLERAN, *Church and State in Guatemala* (1949); CARLOS C. HAEUSSLER YELA, *Diccionario general de Guatemala*, vol. 1 (1983), p. 323.

RALPH LEE WOODWARD, JR.

CASEROS, BATTLE OF, a conflict on 3 February 1852 that ended the long rule of the Argentine dictator Governor Juan Manuel de ROSAS of Buenos Aires and opened the way for the organization of the Argentine Confederation. Rosas assumed command of the *porteño* (Buenos Aires) army of 23,000 on 22 January and was defeated at Caseros by the Ejército Grande Libertador, 24,000 strong, commanded by Governor Justo José de URQUIZA of Entre Ríos. Brazil, Corrientes, Entre Ríos, and the government of Montevideo, in alliance, had organized the Ejército Grande Libertador for the purpose of overthrowing Rosas. Brazil gave financial support to Urquiza. Paraguay declined to participate in the alliance. The provinces of Córdoba and Tucumán, although they approved of Urquiza's plans after he had crossed the Paraná River from Entre Ríos to the province of Santa Fe, and thus removed the likelihood of an attack on the army from the rear, did not participate in the campaign. Urquiza's generals included Benjamín Virasoro and Juan Madariaga of Corrientes. Virasoro was chief of staff, and his aides were men from Corrientes who spoke primarily in Guaraní.

According to Urquiza's official battle report, written by Domingo SARMIENTO and Bartolomé MITRE, the battle lasted from 9 A.M. to 2 P.M. Rosas himself left the battlefield for Buenos Aires, and on the way, at Hueco de los Santos, he wrote his resignation as governor and sent it to the provincial legislature. In the city he hid with his daughter, Manuela Rosas de Terrero, in the home of the British minister, Robert Gore. He later sought safety aboard the British frigate *Locust*. On 10 February he and his daughter sailed for Southampton, England.

On the eve of the battle there were numerous unsubstantiated rumors that Angel Pacheco, one of Rosas's generals, was allied with Urquiza. There were pro-

Urquiza plots within Buenos Aires, *porteño* troops were deserting before the battle, and on 2 February Rosas's officers unanimously voted against confrontation. That Rosas had only lukewarm support was made apparent when his officers quickly endorsed Urquiza after the battle. The people, tired of war, were not pro-Urquiza, but Urquiza's proclamations had made it clear that the war was against Rosas and not Buenos Aires. What upset *porteños* after the battle was the looting of the city by fleeing soldiers and Urquiza's decision to send 800 prisoners and most of the provincial arsenal to Entre Ríos. The nucleus of Urquiza supporters was augmented by the return of 93 families whom Rosas had exiled.

The battle of Caseros meant the end of Buenos Aires's monopoly of its customhouse's revenues, the opening of the rivers to foreign trade, and the peopling of the country.

DOMINGO F. SARMIENTO, *Obras de D. F. Sarmiento*, vol. 14, *Campaña en el ejército grande* (1897); JULIO HORACIO RUBE, *Hacia Caseros, 1850–1852* (1975); BEATRIZ BOSCH, *Urquiza y su tiempo*, 2d ed., rev. (1980); ALBERTO J. MASRAMÓN, *Urquiza, libertador y fundador* (1982). In English, see YSABEL F. RENNIE, *The Argentine Republic* (1945), pp. 61, 81; JOSÉ LUIS ROMERO, *A History of Argentine Political Thought*, translated by Thomas F. McGann (1963), pp. 130, 149, 151, 156; JOHN LYNCH, *Argentine Dictator: Juan Manuel de Rosas, 1829–1852* (1981) pp. 331, 332, 333, 334, 348, 353, 357.

JOSEPH T. CRISCENTI

CASHEW INDUSTRY. Before the arrival of the Portuguese, the TUPI Indians used the ripened fruit of the cashew (*acajou*) to mark the passage of time. Portuguese explorers soon discovered this fruit, which they called *cajú*, and by the 1550s, they were exporting its nuts to other parts of their empire. Ranging in color from off-white to red, the fruit is shaped like an upside-down, shiny-skinned pear with a nut growing from its top. Brazilians now value the *cajú* more for its fruit than the cashew nut, which they export. Although cashew trees can be found throughout Brazil, they are prevalent in the Amazonian rain forest.

Cajús ripen in November, when the Brazilians use the fruit to make pies and jellies and its juice for alcoholic liqueurs, or *suco de cajú*. The nut can only be eaten after roasting it to eliminate the poisonous oil found between the nut's inner and outer shells. Starting in World War II, the oil from the shell, which contains insulating and protective properties, was essential in arms production. Since that time, the cashew industry uses 600,000 tons of nuts annually in wood preservation, waterproofing paper, plastics, varnishes, paints, printing ink, and candy. Realizing the growth potential of the cashew market, the Brazilian government encouraged settlers participating in the Polonoroeste development plan of the 1970s to plant cashew trees, and has continued to press for mass production of *cajú* products since that time.

CLARA INÉS OLAYA, ''Cajú/Marañón/Merey/Acaiu/Cashew Nut,'' in *Americas* 42, no. 3 (1990): 52–53.

CAROLYN JOSTOCK

See also **Forests.**

CASIQUIARE CANAL, a remarkable stream in southern Venezuela that provides a permanent, natural link between the ORINOCO River and the Río NEGRO (a major tributary of the Amazon River). Originating at the bifurcation of the Orinoco into separate rivers, the Casiquiare is about 222 miles long. It flows across a relatively smooth plain, picking up velocity as its volume increases. Most of this water is supplied by three large tributaries, rather than by the Orinoco itself.

By the mid-seventeenth century some Europeans, probably Spaniards traveling the upper Orinoco, knew of the Casiquiare's existence and must have been surprised to encounter Portuguese-speaking people who had come entirely by water from the Brazilian Amazon in search of slaves. Native Americans had long been using this route. By the 1740s information on the Casiquiare had reached Europe, arousing the interest of scholars there. Among Alexander von HUMBOLDT's goals when he came to America in 1799 were to see and measure the Casiquiare. Even though Humboldt mapped it correctly nearly two centuries ago, some cartographers still cannot bring themselves to draw the Casiquiare as a natural, navigable link between the Orinoco and the Amazon rivers. That is because at a fork in a stream, cartographers assume one is joining the other, not leaving it. So some depict the Casiquiare as disconnected from either the Orinoco or the Río Negro.

The Casiquiare is generally believed to represent an example of stream capture, in which the Amazon Basin is growing at the expense of the Orinoco Basin. Because the capture has been so slow, the Casiquiare is an important route for the dispersal of numerous types of plants and animals, including freshwater dolphins.

U.S. ARMY CORPS OF ENGINEERS, *Report on Orinoco-Casiquiare-Negro Waterway Venezuela-Colombia-Brazil* (1943); DOUGLAS BOTTING, *Humboldt and the Cosmos* (1973).

WILLIAM J. SMOLE

CASO Y ANDRADE, ALFONSO (*b.* 1 February 1896; *d.* 30 November 1970), Mexican archaeologist, intellectual, and public figure who wrote numerous works on Middle American indigenous populations. From 1931 to 1943 he directed the explorations of Monte Albán, one of Mexico's major archaeological sites.

The son of the engineer Antonio Caso y Morali and Maria Andrade, brother of the distinguished intellectual Antonio CASO Y ANDRADE, and the brother-in-law of a leading intellectual and labor leader, Vicente LOMBARDO TOLEDANO, Caso was part of a significant generation of

Mexican intellectuals. A longtime professor at the National University, he directed the National Preparatory School and, in 1944, after directing the National Institute of Anthropology and History, became rector of the National University. Caso briefly served (1946–1948) in Miguel Alemán's cabinet as the first secretary of government properties and in 1949 he founded and became director of the National Indigenous Institute, a position he held until his death. A member of the National College, an honorary society of distinguished Mexicans, Caso was awarded the National Prize in Arts and Sciences for his intellectual contributions.

ALFONSO CASO, "Discursos," in *Memoria* (1953); LUIS CALDERÓN VEGA, *Los 7 sabios de México* (1961); and ALFONSO CASO, *A un joven arqueólogo mexicano* (1968).

RODERIC AI CAMP

See also **Archaeology.**

CASO Y ANDRADE, ANTONIO (*b.* 19 December 1883; *d.* 6 March 1946), a leading Mexican philosopher who wrote numerous books on values and sociology but is more important for his contribution to the cultural emancipation of the Mexican and the destruction of POSITIVISM. He is also remembered for his notable debates on academic freedom in 1933 and for his impact on dozens of major intellectual and political figures who passed through the National University from 1910 through the 1920s.

The son of engineer Antonio Caso y Morali and Maria Andrade, and brother of Alfonso CASO Y ANDRADE, he became first secretary of the National Treasury in 1910 and was a founding member of the first graduate school in 1913. He was among the members of the distinguished intellectual generation of the Ateneo de la Juventud. Caso directed the National Preparatory School, the School of Philosophy and Letters, and, in 1921–1923, the National University. He served briefly as an ambassador in South America and was an original member of the prestigious National College, an honorary society of distinguished Mexicans.

ANTONIO CASO, *El concepto de la historia universal y la filosofía de los valores* (1933); LUÍS GARRIDO, *Antonio Caso: una vida profunda* (1961); JOHN H. HADDOX, *Antonio Caso: Philosopher of Mexico* (1971); and MARÍA CASO, *20 lecciones de español* (1972).

RODERIC AI CAMP

CASS, LEWIS (*b.* 9 October 1782; *d.* 17 June 1866), U.S. general, secretary of state, diplomat, Democratic presidential candidate in 1848. Characterized as hawkish and anglophobic, Cass was one of the nineteenth century's leading exponents of Manifest Destiny in the United States. Cass backed the annexation of TEXAS and argued in 1847 that the Mexican War offered the United States a great opportunity for westward expansion. He called upon the Senate to approve the military expenditure necessary to force Mexico to surrender all its land north of the Sierra Madre. Cass urged the annexation of the Yucatán Peninsula in 1848, and he was an advocate of U.S. political and economic interests in Central America in the 1850s.

ALBERT K. WEINBERG, *Manifest Destiny: A Study of Nationalist Expansion in American History* (1935); THOMAS D. CLARK, *Frontier America: The Story of the Westward Movement* (1959); THOMAS R. HIETALA, *Manifest Design: Anxious Aggrandizement in Late Jacksonian America* (1985).

HEATHER K. THIESSEN

See also **Mexican-American War; United States–Latin American Relations.**

CASTAÑEDA, FRANCISCO DE PAULA (*b.* 1776; *d.* 12 March 1832), Argentine educator and journalist. Born in Buenos Aires, Castañeda studied at the College of San Carlos, became a Franciscan friar, and was ordained a priest in 1800. He taught moral theology for three years and staunchly supported the May Revolution of 1810. He was a firm advocate of public education and in 1815 founded a school of design and drawing. In the same year he became the superior of the Franciscans.

Castañeda opposed Bernardino RIVADAVIA's anticlerical measures (e.g. abolishing tithes, prohibiting persons under twenty-five from entering monastic life, and limiting the number of monks that could reside in monasteries), for which he was banished from Buenos Aires (1821–1823). He wrote prolifically and energetically against Rivadavia's reforms, characterizing his rule as "insane, heretical, immoral, and despotic." Among his publications are *La verdad desnuda* (1822), *Derecho del hombre*, and *Buenos Aires cautiva*. He founded schools for Indians of Paraná and San José de Feliciano. Castañeda died in Paraná.

RICARDO LEVENE, *A History of Argentina* (1963).

NICHOLAS P. CUSHNER

CASTAÑEDA CASTRO, SALVADOR (*b.* 6 August 1888; *d.* 5 March 1965), general and president of El Salvador (1945–1948). Born in Chalchuapa to a well-connected family, Salvador Castañeda Castro received his education under the Chilean mission to El Salvador and had attained the position of lieutenant by age eighteen. He rose quickly through the ranks and served in a variety of political positions after 1931, the most important being director of the military school, minister of the interior under General Maximiliano HERNÁNDEZ MARTÍNEZ, and governor of various departments. Following the overthrow of Hernández Martínez in 1944, General Castañeda Castro ran unopposed in a presidential election marred by violence and intimidation. His victory represented the supremacy of the army's old guard and a return to *martinista*-style politics without Martínez. In December 1945 a group led by the aged liberal Miguel Tomás Molina invaded El Salvador from Guatemala, but the expected military rebellion against Castañeda Castro never materialized. Less than a year later, popular discontent manifested itself in the general strike of October 1946, which was effectively repressed.

Among the major events of Castañeda's presidency were visits by Chilean and French missions in 1945, the creation of a national tourism commission, and the dedication of both a major thoroughfare in San Salvador and the Pan-American Highway to Franklin Delano ROOSEVELT. During his administration, Castañeda brought the control of notaries under the direction of the Supreme Court and passed a so-called law of social majority designed to tighten the government's control over the population. His most significant undertaking, however, was the passage in 1945 of a new, regressive constitution that alienated even the younger cadres within the military. The latter, led by Colonel Oscar OSORIO, overthrew Castañeda in 1948 when it became clear he would seek to extend his rule through a second term. Castañeda continued to reside in San Salvador until his death.

JORGE LARDE Y LARÍN, *Guía histórica de El Salvador* (1958); MARIA LEISTENSCHNEIDER AND FREDDY LEISTENSCHNEIDER, *Gobernantes de El Salvador* (1980); JAMES DUNKERLEY, *The Long War* (1982); TOMMIE SUE MONTGOMERY, *Revolution in El Salvador* (1982).

KAREN RACINE

CASTE AND CLASS STRUCTURE IN COLONIAL SPANISH AMERICA. During most of the colonial era, Spanish American society had a pyramidal structure with a small number of Spaniards at the top, a group of mixed-race people beneath them, and at the bottom a large indigenous population and small number of slaves, usually of African origin. While the size of these groups varied between regions and fluctuated over the course of three centuries, they comprised the hierarchy of power and social status during most of the colonial period.

SPANIARDS

The upper echelons of colonial society were dominated by Spaniards, who held all of the positions of economic privilege and political power. However, a sharp split existed between those born in Europe, PENINSULARS, and those born in the Americas, CREOLES. While the relationship between these two groups was sometimes friendly, as when peninsular men married into creole families, it could also be antagonistic. Peninsulars sometimes perceived creoles as lazy, mentally deficient, and physically degenerate; while creoles often saw peninsulars as avaricious. In the sixteenth century, rivalries between European-born and American-born friars for

control of the religious orders led to violence that resulted in a formal policy of alternating terms of leadership between creoles and peninsulars. The Spanish crown's preference for European-born Spaniards in government and church posts in the eighteenth century provoked deep resentment among elite creole men over their exclusion from the positions of influence they had come to expect. Their resentment helped fuel anti-Iberian sentiment in the colonies before the wars for independence.

The greed that creoles attributed to peninsulars stemmed from the fact that it was far more possible to make a fortune in the Americas than in Europe. Opportunities were present in retail and transatlantic commerce, in gold and silver mining, and in bureaucratic posts that offered opportunities to trade in native goods and exchange influence for favors. In the sixteenth century many peninsulars made their New World fortunes in order to retire in comfort in Spain. But by the eighteenth century, peninsulars were apt to enmesh themselves in the communities of the Americas.

The numerous opportunities for enrichment made the crown tremendously reluctant to grant titles of nobility to creoles who gained wealth in the Americas. Thus while there were many extraordinarily wealthy creole families, there were comparatively few creole noble titles. This lack of titles created one of the distinctive characteristics of Spanish society in the New World. In Spain a title of nobility clearly indicated an elevated social rank, but in the Americas there were too few titles to identify all the individuals with wealth and power. Nor were all those families ennobled by the crown able to retain their economic position, thus rendering titles uncertain guides to social status. Power and status depended far more upon the recognition of one's peers than upon the external and readily identifiable labels of nobility, while the absence of noble titles contributed to a sense of shared status among all Spaniards. While there were clear, though usually unstated, limits to ideas of equality between elite and nonelite Spaniards, the absence of noble titles and the small size of the European population relative to the indigenous population contributed to sentiments of equality.

Despite the common prejudice against laboring with one's hands, many Spaniards did so, while unskilled labor was performed by Indians. Spanish craftsmen were employed for their skills, even when they were hired out on a daily basis. In rural settings Spaniards were likely to be the managers and foremen over Indians, who did the hard physical labor of planting, weeding, and harvesting crops.

Introduced to the Americas by the Spaniards, horses became symbols of European superiority; they represented wealth (for horses were not cheap), a superior physical vantage point, greater mobility and speed, and the superiority of European society. The horse and iron-based arms were the keys to many military successes during the Conquest, and were broadly held as indicators of the superior social status shared by Spaniards from which all conquered native peoples and slaves were excluded. Weapon-bearing was forbidden to Indians and slaves by Spanish statute for military reasons. And the enforcement of the prohibition was greatly assisted by the popularity of the belief that bearing arms, like riding a horse, was a prerogative of social rank and being Spanish.

CASTAS (RACIALLY MIXED GROUPS)

Members of the intermediate racial groups were called castes or, in Spanish, *castas.* They included the offspring of black and white parents, called mulattoes; of white and Indian parents, called MESTIZOS; and of black and Indian parents, to whom no single term was ever applied. The mestizos, mulattoes, and black Indians themselves intermingled and produced descendants of even greater racial mixture—part Indian, part Spanish, part black. No distinctive name was ever applied to these later residents; they were usually called simply *castas.*

For the first 150 years of Spanish colonial rule the number of *castas* was relatively small, and racially mixed offspring were usually absorbed into the Spanish, Indian, or black groups. During this time only a handful were categorized as *castas,* and these were usually divided into either mestizos or mulattoes. About the middle of the seventeenth century, these groups began to develop an identity of their own. Instead of merely being people who lacked either the tribal affiliation of native peoples or the social prerogatives of Spaniards, they came increasingly to constitute groups in their own right. Women of these intermediate groups were more often employed than their Spanish counterparts, while the men were apt to be artisans, but journeymen rather than masters.

Racially mixed people were officially banned from positions of influence in colonial society. They could not sit on town councils, serve as notaries, or become members of the more exclusive artisan guilds such as the goldsmiths. They were barred from the priesthood and from the universities. Those designated as mestizos were exempt from the tribute payment owed by their Indian relatives, but no such exemption was granted mulattoes; even when freed, they were subject to the traditional payments of conquered peoples to their rulers.

The dramatic growth of the *castas* in the eighteenth century was an increase in sheer numbers of *castas* as well as a proliferation in the number of racial categories. From the simple divisions of mestizo and mulatto emerged categories such as the CASTIZO, an intermediate position between Spaniard and mestizo, and *morisco,* the equivalent between mulatto and Spaniard. And the steady rise of intermarriages among the racially mixed population itself produced an enormous range of physical types, in turn generating a number of novel, often fanciful names for the sheer physical variety apparent for the first time in large numbers during the eighteenth century.

INDIANS

The Indians were a conquered people, and many of the earliest social distinctions regarding them, such as the payment of tribute, stemmed from their initial relationship to the crown as conquered subjects. Spanish rulers exempted indigenous elites from payment of tribute and granted them the honorific "Don," characteristic of the Spanish lesser nobility. But while such titles and exemptions from tribute were hereditary among Spaniards, these titles were held only by Indians who were incumbents. Since the offices they held were rarely hereditary but were passed among members of the community, often by elections, the exemptions from tribute were rarely permanent.

Indigenous communities in the New World were overwhelmingly agricultural. Indians farmed land, either their own or that of Spaniards. Some resided in communities near Spanish settlements, others were forcibly removed and "congregated" near such settlements. In some regions Indians engaged in fishing or hunting. In the urban areas of the Americas, Indians were more apt to be construction workers (bricklayers, stonemasons), day laborers, or vendors of agricultural products.

In the mining regions of Central and South America, Spaniards used Indians to mine the gold and especially the silver found in regions located away from major population centers. Spaniards uprooted Indians, temporarily or permanently, and relocated them in communities near the mines. Slaves were rarely employed in the mines, and never in large numbers. Mining was the labor of Indians.

SLAVES

In the early years of the Spanish conquest a great number of Indians were captured and enslaved on the Caribbean islands and nearby landfalls. SLAVERY was blamed by many for the devastation of indigenous communities, and the practice was outlawed by the NEW LAWS OF 1542, though natives who fought the Spaniards in frontier regions were often enslaved as late as the seventeenth century.

Following the devastation of native peoples in the Caribbean, blacks were introduced as slave labor. The largest number of black slaves arrived in the Spanish colonies between 1550 and 1650. Their arrival corresponded with growth in the cultivation of sugar in Spanish America. But with the surpassing success of sugar production in seventeenth-century Brazil, the Spanish American industry shrank substantially, along with the number of imported slaves. In the nineteenth century, both the number of imported slaves of African origin and the SUGAR INDUSTRY were revived in the Spanish Caribbean. But on the mainland, the numbers of imported slaves fell off sharply after 1650. In addition to the slaves in sugar-growing regions, there were a small number of slaves in the entourages of the wealthy and powerful in Spanish American capitals. These

The Castes, anonymous, eighteenth century. MUSEO DEL VIRREINATO, TEPOTZOTLAN; PHOTO BY BOB SCHALKWIJK.

slaves were often pages, working in the urban homes of the well-to-do.

Between the middle of the seventeenth century and the end of the next century, the slaves of African origin disappeared as a readily identifiable social group in Spanish America. Their integration into the racially mixed population was central to the transformation of Spanish New World society in the eighteenth century.

HISTORICAL CHANGES

The longest running debates over eighteenth-century society in Latin America have concerned the nature of its economic and social transformation. Historians have long noted an increase in economic opportunities during the era. Increased silver production, growing domestic markets for agricultural products and textiles, and increased trade, both licit and illicit, produced unprecedented population and economic growth. This growth allowed many outside the traditional economic and social elites to acquire fortunes. There was a marked increase in the number of prosperous elites, accompanied by an unusual rise in the wealth of traditionally lower-status groups, including those of mixed racial ancestry. Historians have disagreed over whether Spanish society barred entrance to those with new wealth, particularly those of racially mixed origin.

Some historians have argued that there was a rigid social structure known as a society of castes (*sociedad de castas*), and they support their view with reference to the continuing legal and economic disabilities of natives and descendants of African-born people. Furthermore, they point to well-known paintings commissioned in the eighteenth century by wealthy Spaniards showing a proliferation of racial categories. These paintings depict the dress, food, and activity of various racial types in their homes. The paintings are arranged in a series of miniportraits that follow the order of a written or printed page, beginning at the upper left side of the page and depicting a family group sitting down to a meal in a well-appointed home. The label at the top of this miniportrait describes them in genealogical terms: "From Spaniard and Indian comes mestizo." The next portrait portrays in equally favorable terms the intermarriage of mestizo and Spaniard, producing "castizo." The third or fourth portrait begins the sequence all over again portraying a Spanish man and a black woman. But after two or three portraits of Spanish-black unions, reading from left to right, one gradually encounters a profusion of intermediate scenes, depicting various mixtures of Indian and black, often with highly fanciful names, "there you are," or derogatory ones, "wolf." The final portrait is often one of a poor hut, badly furnished, and depicting a woman with a frying pan chasing her husband. Not only is the lowest caste poor, but the paternalism of the Spanish family is inverted, and the woman dominates the man, thus indicating how far they are from the Spanish norm in the upper left. These portraits reveal the prejudice that accompanied the le-

gal liabilities of various categories, and have often been cited as evidence of the difficulties of social mobility in the eighteenth century.

Other historians have focused on the ways in which rigid legal categories and physical distinctions appear to have been overcome. In some cases racial categories were altered on christening records, and a humble origin could be overcome by reputation and wealth. The regional differences of Latin America appear to have had a bearing on such nobility. Some studies suggest that by independence in Mexico several members of the titled nobility were mestizos, while in Peru fewer such examples can be found.

The differences between the term "caste" and "class" have been drawn more commonly by historians in the United States than those in Latin America. Their use as labels to differentiate open and closed societies was first suggested in the 1930s by the U.S. sociologist William Lloyd Warner. On the basis of his work and U.S. sociology of the 1950s and 1960s, the ways of distinguishing between a "caste" and a "class" society have focused on interracial marriage as the key to integration and the definition of an open society. As a result, much of the controversy generated by the dispute has centered on such questions as whether the Spaniards were intermarrying with members of the castes, which racial groups (castes) were marrying members of other groups, and what were the marriage patterns of the black community, which became integrated during the eighteenth century.

Among Latin American historians "class" has been addressed in terms of the emergence of a bourgeoisie, or middle class. The question for many Latin American historians has been whether the individuals who profited from or led the economic revival of the eighteenth century should be considered members of an emerging bourgeoisie. The questions of a class society tend to revolve around the economic attitudes and behavior of the emerging economic elites. Latin American historians, and some U.S. historians of Marxist orientation, have been more apt to use the term "feudal" rather than "caste" to designate a closed society.

The final transformation of caste and class structure in colonial Spanish America came with independence. Peninsular Spaniards were officially expelled by many resentful creole communities. Tribute payments by native communities were suspended throughout Spanish America either at independence or shortly thereafter. Slavery was usually abolished by the new republics within the first two decades of independence, except in the remaining Spanish possessions in the Caribbean, where it endured well into the nineteenth century. Men of mixed racial origin had access to arms and became skilled in using those arms against Spanish troops during the wars for independence. Arms and the horse remained symbols of power, but were no longer identified with Spanish rule and the caste system.

Throughout most of Spanish America the close of the

colonial era removed the rigid racial hierarchy that had lasted for three centuries. The legal distinctions of tribute payers and slaves disappeared, and in many regions, the superiority that automatically accompanied a Spaniard gradually disappeared. In its place emerged a society also stratified by wealth and power, but one where those distinctions were no longer automatically registered by differences of race.

LYLE MC ALISTER, "Social Structure and Social Change in New Spain," in *Hispanic American Historical Review* 43 (1963): 349–370; MAGNUS MÖRNER, *Race Mixture in the History of Latin America* (1967); JOHN K. CHANCE, *Race and Class in Colonial Oaxaca* (1978); PATRICIA SEED, "Social Dimensions of Race: Mexico City, 1753," in *Hispanic American Historical Review* 62, no. 4 (1982): 569–606; PATRICIA SEED and PHILIP RUST, "Estate and Class in Colonial Oaxaca Revisited," in *Comparative Studies in Society and History* 25 (1983): 703–709, 721–724; RODNEY ANDERSON, "Race and Social Stratification: A Comparison of Working Class Spaniards, Indians, and Castas in Guadalajara, Mexico, in 1821," in *Hispanic American Historical Review* 68, no. 2 (1988): 209–243; DOUGLAS COPE, *The Limits of Racial Domination* (1994).

PATRICIA SEED

See also **Class Structure.**

CASTE WAR OF YUCATÁN. Regarded by many as the most militarily successful Indian rebellion in Latin American history, the Guerra de Castas (Caste War) remains the central historical event in the regional popular mind. In fact, many Yucatecans often assume that when one speaks of "the Revolution," one is referring to the great peasant rebellion unleashed in 1847, not the more recent national upheaval that began in 1910.

The rash of agrarian revolts and caste wars that erupted in several key Mexican regions in the aftermath of independence points up both the disintegration of the imperial central state and the political and economic disenfranchisement of Indian minorities during the early national period. In Yucatán, hostilities broke out on the state's southeastern frontier of commercial sugar expansion. Here the MAYA peasantry bitterly resented increased taxation, the loss of their *milpa* (maize lands), and DEBT PEONAGE and physical abuse on the sugar plantations. But unlike their more domesticated counterparts in the older northwestern zone of corn-and-cattle haciendas, the frontier Maya still had the cultural capacity and the mobility to resist white domination. When a series of petty disputes between elite political factions expediently put guns into Indian hands, the frontier Maya turned these guns on the white leaders.

Recent ethnohistorical research, particularly in Maya language sources, has helped to clarify the racial or "caste" nature of the war. A dominant theme in the communications of Indian leaders is that the laws should apply equally to all peoples, whatever their ethnic background. In this sense, the free Maya made a social revolution to erase caste distinctions. On the other hand, the fearful and skittish white elites must bear major re-

sponsibility for redefining a social conflict into a brutal race war. During the earliest days of the rebellion they decided not to honor the distinction that then existed between rich Indian CACIQUES (or *hidalgos*, as they were then called) and the majority of poor, landless Indians. Many of these educated, politically powerful Maya had connections in, and identified closely with, white society. By persecuting and actually lynching members of this privileged class, the whites forced such caciques as Jacinto Pat and Cecilio Chi to identify as Indians and contribute their leadership abilities to the rebel movement. Interestingly, while the war was generally fought along racial lines, many Maya peons tied to the haciendas of northwestern Yucatán remained loyal to their white *patrones*. Indeed, their support may have been crucial in preventing their masters from being killed or driven from the peninsula during the darkest days of the war in 1848. It is the participation of these Maya auxiliaries—as well as the defection of some mestizo and white troops to the rebel Maya side—that has led some historians to argue that the War of the Castes is badly named.

Other nineteenth-century indigenous peasant rebellions would last longer than the Caste War of Yucatán (for example, the Yaqui rebellion in Sonora), encompass a greater geographical area (the Sierra Gorda revolt in central Mexico), or range more freely in their depredations against the dominant white society (the Cora rebellion of Manuel LOZADA). Yet none had as many advantages as the rebel Maya: a homogeneous ethnic base still animated by a vigorous pre-Hispanic cultural tradition; the absence of serious natural obstacles (mountains, rivers, and so forth), which reinforced this ethnic identity and strategically facilitated mobility across the frontier of white settlement; the proximity of British arms and supplies from Belize; and the weak economic, political, and logistical ties between Yucatán and central Mexico, which permitted the revolt to proceed for some time without federal intervention.

It is not surprising, therefore, that the Yucatecan rebellion was the most violent of this turbulent age, nor that its regional consequences were likely the most profound. Estimates of human loss and economic dislocation are staggering: the peninsula's population declined at least 30–40 percent. The southeastern SUGAR INDUSTRY was destroyed; Yucatán's economic and demographic center of gravity would shift from the southeast to the northwest, the site of the future HENEQUEN boom.

But henequen's development would begin only after the northwest had been cleared of rebel Maya. At the point of their furthest advance, in June and July 1848, these "indios bravos" controlled three-fourths of the Yucatán peninsula—and were on the verge of capturing the last two important white strongholds, Mérida and Campeche, before their campaign was interrupted by the economic and cultural imperative to return home for the planting season. In the meantime, the whites were able to regroup—receiving food and ammunition from Havana, Veracruz, and New Orleans, and reinforcements from the federal government. By 1853, the Maya had been driven across the southeastern frontier of settlement into remote portions of Yucatán and what are today the states of Campeche and Quintana Roo. That year a substantial number of the rebels—known henceforth as the *pacíficos del sur*—signed a truce that permitted them a relatively autonomous existence in the Chenes region of Campeche. Meanwhile, however, to the northeast, in the chicle forests of Quintana Roo, a diehard faction of rebel Maya, the Cruzob, would have no truck with the hated whites. Remarkably, they would maintain an independent Maya state centered around a millennarian cult of the Talking Cross until they were finally overrun by a large, combined force of Yucatecan and federal troops in 1901.

NELSON REED, *The Caste War of Yucatan* (1964); VICTORIA R. BRICKER, *The Indian Christ, the Indian King* (1981); GILBERT M. JOSEPH, *Rediscovering the Past at Mexico's Periphery: Essays on the History of Modern Yucatán* (1986); PAUL SULLIVAN, *Unfinished Conversations: Mayas and Foreigners Between Two Wars* (1991).

GILBERT M. JOSEPH

See also **Messianic Movements; Race and Ethnicity.**

CASTELLANOS, AARÓN GONZÁLEZ (*b.* 8 August 1800; *d.* 1 April 1880), commonly regarded as the greatest promoter of agricultural colonization of nineteenth-century Argentina. Born in the city of Salta, as a young man he joined the cavalry forces led by a regional caudillo named Martin Güemes, who fought against the Spanish. After the conclusion of the wars of independence, he went to Peru, where he engaged in trade in the mining center of Cerro de Pasco. Subsequently he became involved in an ambitious colonization scheme on the Río Bermejo but was persecuted by Paraguayan dictator José FRANCIA, who held him prisoner from 1825 to 1830. Later Castellanos established himself in Buenos Aires Province, where he raised cattle. In the late 1830s he sold his properties and went to Paris, where he became known for writing several descriptive publications on Argentina. Castellanos returned to Argentina in 1853 and convinced the provincial government of Santa Fe to support his colonization scheme in the Chaco region. He helped finance the emigration of 200 families of agricultural workers from Dunkirk and Antwerp, then founded the agricultural colony of ESPERANZA in Santa Fe, which is still a prosperous grain-producing town. Castellanos also promoted the construction of docks in the port of Rosario and served in the municipal government of that city.

MARTIN MULHALL, *Handbook of the River Plate* (1885).

CARLOS MARICHAL

CASTELLANOS, GONZALO (*b.* 1926) Venezuelan composer and conductor. Born in Caracas to a musical family, Castellanos studied piano and organ with his father

before apprenticing with the great Vicente Emilio Sojo at the National Modern School. This institution and its graduates initiated a new movement in Venezuelan music that was based on a postimpressionist aesthetic. Castellanos traveled to Paris, where he was active in the Schola Cantorum, and later received training from the European pianist Sergiu Celibidache. Upon his return to Venezuela, Castellanos conducted the Venezuela Symphony Orchestra and served at the collegium of the Museum of Caracas. Among his most famous pieces are *Suite caraqueña, Symphonic Fantasy,* and *Andelación e imitación fugaz.*

HELEN DELPAR, ed., *Encyclopedia of Latin America* (1974); JOSÉ ANTONIO CALCANO, *La ciudad y su música: Crónica músical de Caracas* (1985); LUÍS FELIPE RAMÓN Y RIVERA, *50 Años de música en Caracas, 1930–1980* (1988).

KAREN RACINE

CASTELLANOS, JUAN DE (*b.* 9 March 1522; *d.* 27 November 1607), Spanish poet-chronicler, soldier, and priest. Born to farmers in Alanís (Seville province), Spain, as a teenager with some command of Latin, Castellanos went to Puerto Rico, where he continued his studies. In 1540, he traveled to Cubagua, an island off the Venezuelan coast, to work as a pearl fisherman, then joined the army and traveled to New Granada and Venezuela (1541–1545). From 1545 to 1554 he campaigned in the Bogotá and Pamplona regions, before being ordained a Roman Catholic priest in Cartagena (ca. 1554). Castellanos was curate and diocesan treasurer of Cartagena from 1557 to 1558, when he became curate of Riohacha, a position he served in until 1560. He moved to Tunja, in the highlands, as an assistant curate sometime after 1561; in 1568 he became curate. In Tunja, Castellanos devoted much of his time to writing. His *Elegías y elogios de varones ilustres de Indias* was composed between 1570 and 1590. Its nearly 114,000 verses narrate the discovery, conquest, and settlement of Spanish America, especially New Granada and Venezuela.

ULÍSES ROJAS, *Juan de Castellanos: Biografía* (1958); MARIO GERMÁN ROMERO, *Juan de Castellanos* (1964).

J. LEÓN HELGUERA

CASTELLANOS, ROSARIO (*b.* 25 May 1925; *d.* 7 August 1974), Mexican author and diplomat. Born in Mexico City, Castellanos spent her youth in the state of Chiapas, a region with a high concentration of Indians and a history of conflict between the Tzotzil Indians and the wealthy landowners. In two prize-winning novels, *Balún-Canán* (1957; *The Nine Guardians,* 1960) and *Oficio de Tinieblas* (1962), and in the short stories of *Ciudad Real* (1960), Castellanos depicted the psychology and cosmology of the Chiapas Indians without romanticizing or stereotyping her characters, a marked departure from earlier ''indigenist'' writers.

Castellanos, educated at the National Autonomous University and in Madrid, also pioneered new territory in her exploration of gender relations. Her published master's thesis, *Sobre cultura femenina* (1950), provided the intellectual underpinnings for the contemporary women's movement in Mexico. Her essays, published regularly in Mexican periodicals and compiled in collections such as *Juicios sumarios* (1966) and *Mujer que sabe latín* (1973), as well as her dramatic works, particularly *El eterno femenino* (1975), and some thirteen volumes of poetry, often probed issues relating to the place of women in Mexican culture and history.

Castellanos was also a teacher and diplomat. She taught Latin American literature in Mexico, the United States, and Israel. From 1971 until her accidental death in 1974, she was Mexico's ambassador to Israel.

MAUREEN AHERN and MARY SEALE VÁZQUEZ, eds., *Homenaje a Rosario Castellanos* (1980), contains several excellent critical studies in English of Castellanos's work, as well as a useful bibliography. For an insightful analysis of the relationship between Castellanos's life and works, see OSCAR BONIFAZ CABALLEROS, *Remembering Rosario,* translated and edited by Myralyn F. Allgood (1990). For understanding the intellectual development of Castellanos as a writer, see the interview in ENRIQUE CARBALLO, *Diecinueve protagonistas de la literatura mexicana del siglo XX* (1965).

VIRGINIA M. BOUVIER

See also **Feminism.**

CASTELLI, JUAN JOSÉ (*b.* 19 July 1764; *d.* 12 October 1812), Argentine independence leader. The son of an Italian father and Spanish mother, Castelli was born in Buenos Aires and studied law at the University of Chuquisaca in Upper Peru (modern Bolivia). He practiced in Buenos Aires, where, along with his cousin Manuel BELGRANO and other creoles who had absorbed ENLIGHTENMENT ideas, he worked to promote liberal reforms.

In 1810 Castelli took an active part in the May Revolution and was one of the secretaries of the revolutionary junta. That same year the junta sent him to accompany an expeditionary force to Upper Peru, where he proposed the elimination of monastic houses and other radical religious innovations, while also seeking to enlist the Indian population in the struggle. When Upper Peru was lost in mid-1811, Castelli's rivals sought to make him a scapegoat; he stood trial in Buenos Aires, but before a verdict could be handed down he died of cancer.

JULIO CÉSAR CHAVES, *Castelli, el adalid de mayo,* 2d ed. (1957); JOHN LYNCH, *The Spanish-American Revolutions, 1808–1826* (1973).

DAVID BUSHNELL

See also **Argentina: The Colonial Period.**

CASTELLO BRANCO, HUMBERTO DE ALENCAR (*b.* 20 September 1900; *d.* 18 July 1967), president of Brazil (1964–1967). A *nordestino* (northeasterner) from Fortaleza, Castello Branco was born of a long line of military officers. After studying at the Military Preparatory School of Rio Prado in Rio Grande do Sul from 1912 to 1917, he enrolled as a cadet in the Realengo Military Academy in Rio de Janeiro. Commissioned into the army in 1921, he married Argentina Vianna the next year. Devout Catholics, the couple formed a close union until her death in 1963.

As a young lieutenant devoted to professionalism and the rule of law, Castello Branco declined to participate in the various military uprisings of the 1920s. Instead he fought against the Luís Carlos PRESTES COLUMN in Mato Grosso and Bahia and remained loyal to the government during the Revolution of 1930.

Castello Branco was promoted to captain in 1932, and then named assistant director at Realengo, where he had previously served as an instructor. He was also attached to the French military mission. Subsequently he was sent to Paris to attend the Superior War College, which enhanced his academic reputation.

In 1940 Castello Branco, now a major, was posted to

Humberto de Alencar Castello Branco reviewing troops in 1965. ICONOGRAPHIA.

assist the minister of war, Eurico G. DUTRA, who later became president (1946–1951). In preparation for dispatching the BRAZILIAN EXPEDITIONARY FORCE (FEB), Castello Branco was enrolled in the U.S. Army Command and General Staff College at Fort Leavenworth, Kansas, in 1943. As a lieutenant colonel he embarked the next year for Italy, where he was chief of operations (G-3) of the Brazilian Expeditionary Force. After advancing to colonel in 1945 for his effectiveness during that campaign, he returned to Brazil, where he alternated between general staff and field assignments. In 1952 he was named brigadier general and assumed command of the Tenth Military Region (Ceará). In 1954 he signed the General's Manifesto of 23 August calling for the resignation of President Getúlio VARGAS.

After commanding the army's general staff college in 1954–1955, Castello Branco moved on to the ESCOLA SUPERIOR DA GUERRA (ESG), Brazil's Superior War College, as assistant commandant and director of the armed forces and command course in 1956–1958. As general of division he was transferred in 1958–1960 to head the Amazonia and Eighth Military Region headquartered in Belém, Pará, and went on to assume the directorship of army instruction, which allowed him to remain in close contact with the war college.

The ascension to the presidency of reformist Jânio da Silva QUADROS in 1961 and his subsequent resignation and replacement by populist João GOULART provoked a crisis in the officer corps that polarized into legalist and hard-line factions. In spite of Goulart's pro-Castro stance, nonaligned foreign policy, counterproductive economic policies, and support for a radical syndicalist republic, Castello Branco remained a legalist until early 1964.

Named a four-star general and posted to command the Fourth Army at Recife in 1962, Castello Branco found the Northeast unsettled by Peasant League–provoked turmoil, fomented, he believed, by Pernambuco governor Miguel ARRAES and President Goulart's brother-in-law, Leonel BRIZOLA, leader of one of the socialist parties. Once elevated to army chief of staff in mid-1963, Castello Branco sought to persuade President Goulart to abandon certain of his allegedly unconstitutional actions. Failing to do so, he agreed, in the name of legality, to head a long-prepared military-civilian conspiracy to oust the chief executive.

A well-planned coup led by the army, state governors, and opposition congressmen came off easily, with little loss of life on 31 March 1964. Discussions among the various governors, congressmen, business leaders, politicians, and high-ranking military men resulted in Castello Branco's selection as president. On 11 April 1964, by a wide margin the congress confirmed him as president to complete the remaining two years of Goulart's term. While pledging to respect the Constitution of 1946, Castello Branco appointed coconspirator General Artur da COSTA E SILVA as war minister.

The new chief executive hoped to turn this joint military-civilian coup into a revolution dedicated to controlling inflation, containing Communism, fomenting economic development, and promoting political, social, and educational reform. A team player, Castello Branco selected Roberto CAMPOS as minister of finance and Octavio Bulhões as minister of planning. Together they instituted an indexation system to neutralize economic distortions caused by a high rate of inflation, as well as a tax-reform structure that forced firms and individuals to adopt realistic accounting methods.

A long-term economic policy that endured for some fifteen years was launched under Castello Branco, who sought to promote capital formation, expand the market for durable consumer goods, reduce wages, foster industrial exports, and stimulate foreign capital investment. This growth strategy, however, was designed to perpetuate the country's basic economic and social structure, thereby permitting the traditional agricultural elite to support the regime while the industrial sector expanded. Hence, the nation's potential was developed while its agricultural and industrial sectors retained control. Because foreign as well as domestic stability was deemed essential to development, Brazil avoided being drawn into conflict with the United States, the dominant power in the hemisphere, and sought to associate itself with the United States in global affairs. The latter in turn reciprocated with generous financial aid and investment.

The Castello Branco regime further insured internal order by a series of measures known as INSTITUTIONAL ACTS. The first, promoted by the hard-liners and enacted on 9 April 1964, actually prior to Castello Branco's inauguration, sought to purify the government. Three former presidents—Jânio da Silva Quadros, João Goulart, and Juscelino KUBITSCHEK DE OLIVEIRA—as well as seventy others were stripped of their political rights. In addition, the granting of tenure to civil servants was suspended for six months and military police courts, called IPMs, were established to investigate subversion.

The Second Institutional Act, effective 27 October 1965, was provoked by the reaction of hard-liners to state elections that went against the regime. Under this act all political parties were dissolved, indirect election of the president by congress was mandated, the government's right to dismiss civil servants was reinstated, citizens' political rights were canceled, and the Supreme Court was packed. The next month Brazil's political parties were re-formed. A government party, the National Renovating Alliance (Arena), and an opposition party, the Brazilian Democratic Movement (MDB), were established in congress.

Early in 1966, Castello Branco's presidential term was extended, against his wishes, for another year, to 15 March 1967. Protests against these measures then erupted, led by the National University Students Union and by certain socially sensitive Catholic clergy, notably Hélder CÁMARA, archbishop of Olinda and Recife.

Tensions increased as presidential candidates proliferated. Castello Branco favored a civilian successor. União Democrática Nacional leader Olavo BILAC PINTO, Senator Daniel Krieger of Rio Grande do Sul, and Foreign Minister Juracy Magalhães were his top choices. Nevertheless, the hard-liners prevailed. War Minister Costa e Silva, who was nominated and inaugurated on 15 March 1967, served as president until 1969.

In retirement, Castello Branco continued to exert a moderating influence on national affairs until his untimely death in an airplane accident.

RICHARD BOURNE, *Political Leaders of Latin America* (1970); ROLLIE E. POPPINO, *Brazil: The Land and People* (1973); JOHN W. F. DULLES, *Castello Branco: The Making of a Brazilian President* (1978) and *President Castello Branco, Brazilian Reformer* (1980); HÉLIO VIANNA, "O pensamento militar de Castello Branco," in *Revista do Instituto Histórico e Geográfico Brasileiro* 321 (1978): 242–249; VERNON A. WALTERS, *Silent Missions* (1978); EURICO DE LIMA FIGUEIREDO, *Os Militares e a democracia: Análise estrutural da ideologia do Pres. Castello Branco* (1980).

LEWIS A. TAMBS

CASTILE, sovereign territory of the kings of Spain, united with Aragon by the marriage in 1469 of FERDINAND II OF ARAGON and ISABELLA I OF CASTILE.

The kingdom of Castile was carved out by the Reconquest of Spain, which shaped its enduring political, social, and economic structures, and by the regional division of the Castilian *meseta* (tableland) into a northern area of small land proprietors and villages called Old Castile and a southern area dominated by larger landowners and towns known as New Castile. Superficially united under the crown of Aragon during the region of Ferdinand and Isabella, Castile in the fifteenth century had 80 percent of the population of peninsular Spain, its three largest cities (Seville, Granada, and Toledo), and thriving wool and silk industries. Its superiority in manpower, natural resources, and taxable wealth confirmed Castile's dominant role in forming imperial policy and colonizing the New World. The kings of Castile had absolute legislative authority while Spain's primary representative institution, the Cortes, was restricted to affirming the crown's requests for revenue. Madrid in effect became the capital in 1561, when PHILIP II took the court there.

GERALD BRENAN, *The Spanish Labyrinth* (1943, 2d ed. 1950), esp. pp. 87–130; JOHN H. ELLIOTT, *Imperial Spain, 1469–1716* (1963; repr. 1977), esp. pp. 24–43; RAYMOND CARR, *Spain 1808–1975* (1982), esp. pp. 1–37; HENRY KAMEN, *Spain 1469–1714* (1983), esp. pp. 9–15.

SUZANNE HILES BURKHOLDER

CASTILHOS, JÚLIO DE (b. 29 June 1860; d. 24 October 1903), Brazilian statesman and founder of the "positivist dictatorship" of RIO GRANDE DO SUL. Born into a ranching family in the Serra region of Rio Grande, Castilhos graduated from the São Paulo Law School in 1882. As the director of the Riograndense Republican Party's newspaper *A Federação,* he agitated for a federal republican regime. Following the empire's collapse in 1889, he led the Riograndense delegation at the Constituent Assembly. After imposing an authoritarian state constitution, he was elected governor of Rio Grande do Sul in 1891, but was deposed for supporting President Marechal Deodoro da Fonseca's failed coup in which he closed Congress. In 1892 Castilhos engineered a countercoup and new election, provoking the FEDERALIST REVOLT (1893–1895), which claimed 10,000 casualties. He left office in 1898 but continued to rule through his highly disciplined Republican Party until his untimely death.

The *castilhista* Constitution, inspired by Auguste Comte, remained in effect till 1930 (though modified in 1923). It limited the legislature to budgetary matters, gave the governor decree power on all other issues, and allowed him to serve indefinitely. Despite his authoritarianism, Castilhos's policies on land taxation, public education, and secularization were progressive.

Castilhos's successor in 1898, Antônio BORGES DE MEDEIROS, used the *castilhista* regime to rule the state from Castilhos's death until 1930, serving as governor most of the time.

OTHELO ROSA, *Júlio de Castilhos* (1928); SÉRGIO DA COSTA FRANCO, *Júlio de Castilhos e sua época* (1967); JOSEPH L. LOVE, *Rio Grande do Sul and Brazilian Regionalism, 1882–1930* (1971), chaps. 2–4.

JOSEPH L. LOVE

CASTILLA, RAMÓN (b. 27 August 1797; d. 25 May 1867), military officer and twice president of Peru (1845–1851, 1855–1862), he contributed to the formation of the Peruvian republican state during the nineteenth-century struggle by military strongmen (CAUDILLOS) after independence from Spain. His efforts were aided considerably by the dawn of the GUANO Age, which brought considerable income from export activities to the Peruvian state.

Castilla was born in Tarapacá. During his early military career he was trained by the Spanish colonial army and fought against the forces of independence led by the Argentine general José de SAN MARTÍN in Chacabuco, Chile (1817). Taken prisoner, he escaped to Brazil and then in 1818 to Peru. Castilla switched allegiances only in 1822, when he offered his military services to General San Martín in southern Peru. He fought in the army of Simón BOLÍVAR against the Spanish army in the decisive battle of AYACUCHO (1824), which guaranteed Peruvian independence.

After independence in 1825, Castilla was named subprefect of his native province of Tarapacá. He started his career as a rather conservative and CREOLE-patriotic military caudillo by opposing Bolívar's constitutional designs. In 1829, Castilla rejected General Andrés de SANTA CRUZ's liberal leanings, instead supportingthe protec-

Ramón Castilla. LATIN AMERICAN LIBRARY, TULANE UNIVERSITY; B.F. PEASE.

tionist and conservative General Agustín GAMARRA. In 1833, Castilla fell from grace with Gamarra and transferred his support to generals Luis José de ORBEGOSO and Felipe Santiago SALAVERRY. When Santa Cruz seized power in 1836 for the second time, Castilla traveled to Chile and once again joined Gamarra in a successful Chilean military expedition against Santa Cruz's Peru-Bolivia Confederation. During Gamarra's second administration (1839–1841) Castilla was appointed minister of the treasury and in that capacity arranged the first guano export contracts with native businessman Francisco Quirós. In 1841, Castilla was taken prisoner at Ingaví, Gamarra's failed last adventure against Bolivian forces. Soon, however, Castilla was politically active again in Cuzco.

By 1845, Castilla had surfaced as supreme chief from the complex caudillo struggles that pitted Generals Juan Crisóstomo Torrico, Francisco Vidal, and Manuel Ignacio VIVANCO against each other. During Castilla's first administration his most important measure was the introduction of the first national budget. New contracts for guano marketing abroad were signed with local and foreign merchants. Eventually the British firm Antony GIBBS Y CÍA assumed the distribution of guano to Great Britain and the French firm Montané the distribution to France. Consequently, transportation began to improve (STEAMSHIP lines, the first RAILWAY between Lima and Callao in 1851), and state finances, military facilities, and payroll became organized. Most important, Castilla regularized the service of the internal and external debts, introducing in 1850 the Law of Consolidation (amortization and repayment) of the floating national debt.

Castilla saw in General José Rufino ECHENIQUE a deserving successor and peacefully handed power to him in 1851. However, Echenique's supporters manipulated the consolidation of the internal debt to their own advantage through corrupt means. Politically, the archconservative Echenique began to drift away from Castilla's watchful eye. Sensing growing popular opposition, Castilla decided to lead a motley group of liberals and radicals who fought Echenique in a civil war (1854–1855). To obtain support, Castilla followed the advice of liberals Pedro Gálvez and Manuel Toribio Ureta and abolished SLAVERY and the Indian tribute in 1854. Castilla regained power in 1855 after the battle of La Palma, in which Echenique was finally defeated.

During his second term of office, Castilla initially complied with the liberal faction that had supported him, pressing for the liberal constitution of 1856. However, after the defeat of the conservative reaction led by Vivanco in 1858, Castilla turned against his liberal supporters and promoted instead an executive-biased constitution that was enacted in 1860. His preoccupation with such constitutional matters earned him the name of "Soldier of the Law." A successful short war over boundaries with Ecuador in 1859 enhanced Castilla's conservative constitutionalist and nationalist stand.

At the end of his second term in 1862, Castilla once again peacefully handed power to elected General Miguel de San Román. However, San Román died in office and was succeeded by vice president Juan Antonio PEZET, who, like Echenique before him, disregarded the influential Castilla. The unpopular Pezet was deposed as a result of the nationalist movement led by Colonel Mariano Ignacio PRADO against the Spanish aggression of 1864–1866. Prado, however, was opposed by Castilla, who went into exile in Chile to organize yet another revolution. Castilla died in Tivilichi.

JORGE BASADRE, *Historia de la República del Perú*, vols. 2–3 (1963); ALBERTO REGAL, *Castilla constructor: Las obras de ingeniería de Castilla* (1967); CELIA WU, *Generals and Diplomats: Great Britain and Peru, 1820–40* (1991).

ALFONSO W. QUIROZ

CASTILLA DEL ORO, the name given by a royal decree of 27 July 1513 to Pedro Arias ("Pedrarias") de ÁVILA as governor and captain-general, to "land which until now has been called Tierra Firme, [which] we now order be called Castilla del Oro." The name applies to a long stretch of mainland running west from the Peninsula of

París in Venezuela past the Colombian port cities of Santa Marta and Cartagena into the Gulf of Darién and beyond to that part of Panama known in the early sixteenth century as Veragua.

Even by the rapacious standards of the day, the utter ruin wrought by Pedrarias was remarkable for its swiftness and brutality. The conqueror enlisted under his command such an assortment of wrongdoers that King Ferdinand II wrote to Pedrarias expressing concern, correctly but in vain, about "the quality of the men who have gone with you, soldiers who have been in Italy, [ones] accustomed to very great vices, so that you will have some difficulties." Pedrarias and his men looted and enslaved, torched people as well as property, threw native rulers who could not furnish quantities of gold quickly enough to killer dogs, and generally behaved with such demonic abandon that one official informed the crown that "the land has become so aroused and alarmed by the grave indignities, killings, brutal robbery, and the burning of settlements that all the Castilians maintain themselves only like birds of prey and all the land is lost and desolate." The excesses committed by Pedrarias were never forgotten, even by chroniclers writing decades after his death.

CARL O. SAUER, *The Early Spanish Main* (1966; 2d ed. 1992), tells the sorry tale of Castilla del Oro in all its squalor and sadness. The region's demise also figures in the sixteenth-century account of BARTOLOMÉ DE LAS CASAS, *History of the Indies* (1971), translated and edited by Andrée M. Collard.

W. GEORGE LOVELL

See also **Las Casas, Bartolomé de.**

CASTILLO, JESÚS (*b.* 9 September 1877; *d.* 23 April 1946), Guatemalan composer and student of native Indian music. Castillo was born in San Juan Ostuncalco, near Quezaltenango in the western highlands of Guatemala. As a young man he became interested in traditional Indian music. He composed his "First Indian Overture" based on the Dance of the Little Bulls, a traditional dance at fiestas. Traveling from village to village in the highlands, he collected data about the music of the different Indian groups. Castillo used themes and melodies in a classical tradition to compose his symphonic poems, suites, operas, and ballets. He became a leading authority on Indian music and instruments. His writings include *La música Maya-Quiché* (1941) and *Legado folklórico a la juventud guatemalteca* (1944). He died in Quezaltenango.

DONALD THOMPSON, "Castillo, Jesús," in *New Grove Dictionary of Music and Musicians*, vol. 3 (1980).

DAVID L. JICKLING

CASTILLO, OTTO RENÉ (*b.* 1937; *d.* 19 March 1967), Guatemalan poet. He is the best known of Guatemalan contemporary poets because of his revolutionary militancy and his heroic death. Castillo is one of the "guerrilla poets" who flourished throughout the continent during the 1960s, and is the author of Guatemala's best-known contemporary poem, "Vámonos patria a caminar" ("Let's start walking").

Castillo was born in Quezaltenango, Guatemala's second city. He was a student organizer and led the Association of High School Students. As a result, when the country was invaded in 1954, he was exiled to El Salvador. In 1955 he shared the Premio Centroamericano de Poesía with the Salvadoran poet Roque DALTON. He returned to Guatemala in 1957 and enrolled at the University of San Carlos. In 1959 he left for East Germany, where he studied literature at the University of Leipzig. In the early 1960s he trained as a filmmaker with the well-known Dutch documentary directory Joris Ivens. Castillo returned to Guatemala in 1966 and joined the ranks of the Rebel Armed Forces (FAR). In March 1967, after eating nothing but roots for fifteen days, his guerrilla group was ambushed and captured. Four days of torture ensued, after which Castillo was burned to death. His books are *Vámonos patria a caminar* (1965), *Informe de una injusticia* (1975), and *Sabor de luto* (1976).

OTTO RENÉ CASTILLO et al., *Clamor de América: Antología de poesía latinoamericana* (1970); OTTO RENÉ CASTILLO, *Tomorrow Triumphant: Selected Poems*, edited by Magdaly Fernández and David Volpendesta and translated by Roque Dalton (1984).

ARTURO ARIAS

CASTILLO, RAMÓN S. (*b.* 1871; *d.* 1944), president of Argentina (1942–1943). Born in Catamarca, Castillo was a wealthy landowner, a conservative politician, and a jurist, who served as a criminal judge (1895) and a commercial judge (1905) of the province of Buenos Aires. He was a justice of the criminal court (1910); dean of several law faculties (1923–1928); a member of the Constituent Convention in 1931; senator from Catamarca (1932–1935); minister of justice and public instruction in 1936; minister of the interior (1936–1937); and vice president under President Roberto M. ORTIZ in 1938. Castillo became acting president in 1940 upon the incapacitation of Ortiz, and president when Ortiz resigned in June 1942. During his controversial presidency, Castillo was supported by corrupt members of the oligarchy, disgruntled intellectuals, pro-Fascist elements, and pro-Axis military. While insisting on diplomatic ties with the Axis at the Rio Conference of January 1942 and suppressing pro-Allied demonstrations, he emphasized that the United States would continue to be considered a nonbelligerent. This policy, an attempt to receive military assistance from either side, was not successful. Apprehension about his chosen successor, a wealthy rancher, opposition by pro-Allied and pro-Axis elements, and his inability to secure arms for the military resulted in Castillo's overthrow on 4 June 1943 by General Arturo Rawson, who was replaced three days later by Castillo's minister of war and a member of the right-wing Group of United Officers (GOU), General Pedro Pablo RAMÍREZ.

HUBERT HERRING, *A History of Latin America*, 3d ed. (1968), pp. 746–748, provides domestic background; Castillo's role in foreign relations is covered in ARTHUR P. WHITAKER, *The United States and the Southern Cone: Argentina, Chile, and Uruguay* (1976), pp. 87–88 and 203–205, and MICHAEL J. FRANCIS, *The Limits of Hegemony* (1977), chaps. 2–3 and 5–6.

CHRISTEL K. CONVERSE

See also **Argentina: Organizations.**

CASTILLO ARMAS, CARLOS (*b.* 4 November 1914; *d.* 26 July 1957), president of Guatemala (1954–1957). Born into a provincial LADINO family in the department of Escuintla, Castillo Armas pursued a military career, rising to the rank of colonel and director of the national military academy in 1947.

Obsessed by the July 1949 assassination of army chief and presidential candidate Colonel Francisco Javier ARANA (an act he attributed to Arana's political rival, Lieutenant Colonel Jacobo ARBENZ, who was elected president in November 1950), Castillo Armas launched a five-year rebellion against the Arbenz regime. In November 1949 he led an abortive attack on a Guatemala City military base. He was shot, but he revived while being taken to the cemetery. Sentenced to death, he tunneled out of the Central Penitentiary in June 1951 and took refuge in the Colombian embassy, which granted him political asylum. From Colombia he moved to Honduras, where, with a number of other Guatemalan political dissidents, he launched the National Liberation Movement. Supported by the CENTRAL INTELLIGENCE AGENCY (CIA), this offensive succeeded in overthrowing Arbenz on 2 July 1954 and established Castillo Armas as leader of a five-man governing junta set up in San Salvador under the auspices of U.S. Ambassador John Peurifoy. On 10 October 1954 Castillo Armas was elected president in an unopposed plebescite.

The presidency of Carlos Castillo Armas followed three broad interrelated policies: the dismantling of most of the governmental programs and institutions established by the Cerezo ARÉVALO and Arbenz regimes during the so-called revolutionary decade (1944–1954); a socioeconomic strategy that can be termed "conservative modernization"; and close cooperation with the United States. The "liberationist" regime banned all existing political parties, labor federations, and peasant organizations; disenfranchised three-quarters of the electorate by excluding illiterates; annulled the Arbenz agrarian reform law; and restored the right of the Roman Catholic Church to own property and conduct religious instruction in the public schools.

Seeking to become a "showcase of capitalist development," the regime encouraged foreign investment by granting tax concessions and by repealing laws restricting foreign oil exploration and investments in public utilities. It secured substantial loans and credits from the United States for road building and beef and cotton production. It also sought to stimulate internal investment by maintaining low taxes and wage rates.

The July 1957 assassination of President Castillo Armas by one of his personal bodyguards in the National Palace has been attributed to a power struggle in his political party, the National Democratic Movement.

RICHARD N. ADAMS, *Crucifixion by Power: Essays on Guatemalan National Social Structure, 1944–1966* (1970); THOMAS MELVILLE and MARJORIE MELVILLE, *Guatemala—Another Vietnam?* (1971); STEPHEN SCHLESINGER and STEPHEN KINZER, *Bitter Fruit: The Untold Story of the American Coup in Guatemala* (1982; repr. 1983); JAMES DUNKERLEY, *Power in the Isthmus: A Political History of Modern Central America* (1988).

ROLAND H. EBEL

CASTILLO LEDÓN, AMALIA (*b.* 18 August 1902; *d.* 3 June 1986), prominent early feminist in Mexico. A native of San Jerónimo, Tamaulipas, and daughter of a schoolteacher, Castillo Ledón completed graduate studies in the humanities at the National University. After her marriage to the prominent historian Luis Castillo Ledón, she established herself as an early feminist in United Nations and Mexican organizations. She served as president of the Inter-American Commission of Women in 1949, and in 1953 she addressed the Mexican Senate on women's suffrage, the first woman to do so. The first female Mexican diplomat, she was minister plenipotentiary to Sweden (1953), Finland (1956), and Switzerland (1959). She was the first woman to serve as undersecretary of education (1958–1964).

AURORA M. O'CAMPO and ERNESTO PRADO VELÁZQUEZ, *Diccionario de escritores mexicanos* (1967), pp. 143–144; and *Hispano Americano* 39 (17 June 1986): 41.

RODERIC AI CAMP

CASTILLO Y GUEVARA, FRANCISCA JOSEFA DE LA CONCEPCIÓN DE (*b.* 6 October 1671; *d.* 1742), Colombian nun and author. The daughter of a Spanish official, Francisca Josefa was born in Tunja and entered the convent of Saint Clare in 1689. She remained there until her death, holding various offices in the community, including that of abbess.

Madre Francisca is remembered for two literary works, which she undertook upon the advice of her confessor. The first of these is her autobiography, known as the *Vida*, which was published in 1817. In this work she recounts her physical and spiritual travails, including her conflicts with fellow nuns and her visions of Jesus Christ, the Virgin Mary, and others. The second is the *Afectos espirituales*, also known as *Sentimientos espirituales*, which was published in 1843. The *Afectos* consists of 195 meditations on religious themes that express her longing for union with God. Because of their clear, forceful style and their spirituality, Madre Francisca's writings are often compared to those of other mystics, notably Saint Teresa of Avila.

Obras completas, 2 vols., edited by Darío Achury Valenzuela, (1968). See also MARÍA TERESA MORALES BARRERO, *La madre Castillo: Su espiritualidad y su estilo* (1968); JULIE G. JOHNSON, *Women in Colonial Spanish American Literature* (1985).

HELEN DELPAR

CASTIZO, a term used for a person of mostly Spanish and some Indian ancestry. In the eighteenth century, Spaniards officially described a *castizo* as a person with one-quarter Indian and three-quarters Spanish ancestry, but genealogical investigations were rare, and most assessments of *castizo* status were based on such criteria as physical appearance, occupation, residence, dress, and income. A person of mixed Hispanic and Indian ancestry who appeared darker or was lower in the social or economic order was called a MESTIZO. The term *castizo* was used most frequently in Spanish records during the eighteenth century and appears to have disappeared following independence.

NICHOLÁS LEÓN, *Las castas del México colonial* (1924); LYLE MCALISTER, "Social Structure and Social Change in New Spain," in *Hispanic American Historical Review* 43, no. 3 (1963): 349–370; MAGNUS MÖRNER, *Race Mixture in the History of Latin America* (1967); JOHN K. CHANCE, *Race and Class in Colonial Oaxaca* (1978); PATRICIA SEED, "Social Dimensions of Race: Mexico City, 1753," in *Hispanic American Historical Review* 62, no. 4 (1982): 569–606; PATRICIA SEED and PHILIP RUST, "Estate and Class in Colonial Oaxaca Revisited," in *Comparative Studies in Society and History* 25 (1983): 703–709, 721–724; RODNEY ANDERSON, "Race and Social Stratification: A Comparison of Working Class Spaniards, Indians, and Castas in Guadalajara, Mexico, in 1821," in *Hispanic American Historical Review* 68, no. 2 (1988): 209–243; DOUGLAS COPE, *The Limits of Racial Domination* (1994).

PATRICIA SEED

CASTRO, CIPRIANO (*b.* 12 October 1858; *d.* 4 December 1924), president of Venezuela (1899–1908). Born and raised in Capucho, Táchira, Castro attended schools in Colombia. During the 1880s and 1890s he brought Colombian liberalism to his native Venezuela when he participated in Tachiran politics.

In 1899, Castro launched his Revolution of Liberal Restoration against the government of President Ignacio Andrade, whom he defeated in a campaign that lasted from 23 May to 22 October. He established a coalition government that even included some of the Caracas liberals whom he had overthrown. Basically, Castro attempted to continue the process of centralization begun by Antonio GUZMÁN BLANCO, but financial problems and a series of major conflicts with foreign powers restricted his government. His personal behavior further inhibited his effectiveness as a national leader.

During his reign, Castro adopted a highly nationalistic policy. In 1902, his belligerence led to a blockade of Venezuela by European powers. The intervention of the United States eventually ended the blockade, but Castro remained hostile to foreign governments, including that of the United States. In retaliation for the blockade, Castro closed most Venezuelan ports to trade from the Antilles and imposed a 30-percent surcharge on all goods shipped from the British West Indies.

As a dictator, Castro faced a number of revolts, most notably those led by Manuel Antonio Matos (1902–1903), José Manuel "El Mocho" HERNÁNDEZ (1900), and Antonio Paredes (1907). Over 12,000 died in the fighting. These struggles, and the nation's fiscal difficulties, meant that Castro accomplished very little in the way of reform. He enriched friends and allies through monopoly concessions but did little to improve the nation's transportation, sanitation, or education facilities.

In December 1908, Castro left Venezuela to seek medical treatment in Europe for a urinary tract infection caused by his heavy drinking, use of aphrodisiacs, and venereal disease. Upon his departure, Juan Vicente GÓMEZ seized power. Castro died in exile in Puerto Rico.

WILLIAM M. SULLIVAN, "The Rise of Despotism in Venezuela: Cipriano Castro, 1899–1908" (Ph.D. diss., University of New Mexico, 1974); JOSÉ RAFAEL POCATERRA, *Memorias de un venezolano de la decadencia* (1979); CIPRIANO CASTRO, *El pensamiento político de la Restauración Liberal,* 2 vols. (1983); *La oposición a la dictadura de Cipriano Castro* (1983); CARLOS SISO, *Castro y Gómez: Importancia de la hegemonia andina* (1985); MARIANO PICÓN-SALAS, *Los días de Cipriano Castro* (1986).

For more general treatment, see EDWIN LIEUWEN, *Venezuela* (1961); GUILLERMO MORÓN, *A History of Venezuela,* edited and translated by John Street (1964); JUDITH EWELL, *Venezuela: A Century of Change* (1984).

WINTHROP R. WRIGHT

CASTRO, JOSÉ GIL DE (*b.* ca. 1785; *d.* ca. 1841), Peruvian artist and cartographer. Known as "El Mulato Gil," he was first to paint portraits of the heroes of the South American WARS OF INDEPENDENCE. Born in Lima under Spanish viceroyal rule, he probably apprenticed with a master of the old colonial school. His *Portrait of Fernando VII* (1812) was influenced by Francisco de Goya. He accompanied Bernardo O'HIGGINS in his military campaign for Chilean independence. In Santiago he executed several portraits, including those of General José de SAN MARTÍN, O'Higgins, and their military collaborators. O'Higgins appointed him captain of the engineering corps of the revolutionary army for his expertise in engineering and cartography.

Gil de Castro returned to Peru via Argentina with San Martín's troops and in 1822 was named chamber painter of the Peruvian state. He became the Peruvian aristocracy's favorite portrait painter. In his several portraits of Simón BOLÍVAR, Gil de Castro displayed his fascination with military regalia. His portrayal of sitters in frontal and full-length images recall votive paintings. Craftsmanship, absence of perspective, and the incorporation of inscriptions into framed plaques in his paintings relate Gil de Castro to colonial painting traditions. A provincial neoclassicist, he was the first representative in Latin America of an independent and naive pictorial school.

JAIME EYZAGUIRRE, *José Gil de Castro: Pintor de la independencia americana* (1950); DAWN ADES, *Art in Latin America: The Modern Era, 1820–1980* (1989), pp. 17–21.

MARTA GARSD

CASTRO, JUAN JOSÉ (*b.* 7 March 1895; *d.* 5 September 1968), Argentine composer and conductor. Born in Avellaneda, Buenos Aires Province, Castro began his musical education in Buenos Aires, studying piano and violin under Manuel Posadas, harmony under Constantino Gaito, and fugue and composition under Eduardo Fornarini. As a winner of the Europa Grand Prize, he went to Paris to study composition with Vincent D'Indy at the Schola Cantorum, attending Edouard Risler's piano classes. Returning to Buenos Aires, he founded the Sociedad del Cuarteto in 1926 and performed there as first violin; two years later he started a conducting career with Orquesta Renacimiento. Castro was appointed conductor of the ballet season at the TEATRO COLÓN in 1930 and traveled abroad conducting that ensemble. In 1933 he was named director of the Colón.

Parallel with extensive tours as principal conductor of several Latin American orchestras, Castro began a productive career in composition as a founder-member of the Grupo Renovación; nevertheless, his music was individualistic and he remained independent of group theories. His works exhibit three influences: nationalism, Spanish subject matter, and a free cosmopolitan style, the latter a product of his Parisian years. The last quality applies to the color and sonority of his orchestral works, in which he achieved a sort of American impressionism. He became internationally known when Ernest Ansermet conducted the award-winning *Allegro Lento e Vivace* (1930) at the International Society of Contemporary Music (ISCM) Festival. Among Castro's five stage works there are two operas after Federico García Lorca: *La zapatera prodigiosa* (1943), first performed in Montevideo in 1949, and *Bodas de sangre* (1953), which premiered at the Teatro Colón in 1956. *Proserpina y el extranjero*, a three-act opera, first performed at Milan's La Scala, was the recipient of the first International Verdi Prize in 1951. Among his orchestral pieces is *Corales criollos* No. 3, a first prize winner at the Caracas Interamerican Music Festival (1954). As a teacher, Castro was appointed by Pablo Casals as dean of studies and professor at the National Conservatory in San Juan, Puerto Rico, from 1959 to 1964.

Composers of the Americas, vol. 4 (1958); V. GESUALDO, *Historia de la Música en la Argentina* (1961); R. ARIZAGA, *Juan José Castro* (1963) and *Enciclopedia de la Música Argentina* (1971); JOHN VINTON, ed., *Dictionary of Contemporary Music* (1974); GERARD BÉHAGUE, *Music in Latin America* (1979); STANLEY SADIE, ed., *The New Grove Dictionary of Music and Musicians*, vol. 3 (1980), and *The New Grove Dictionary of Opera*, vol. 1 (1992).

SUSANA SALGADO

CASTRO, JULIÁN (*b.* 1815; *d.* 1875), provisional president of Venezuela from March 1858 to August 1859, during which time the Constitutional Convention of Valencia created the Constitution of 1858. Castro began his career as an officer in the republican army of Venezuela. As a captain he participated in the Revolution of the Reforms in 1835–1836. He joined the Liberal Party at its inception in 1840. Before being chosen as provisional president of the nation, he was governor of the province of Carabobo.

Castro assumed office on 18 March 1858 as the titular head of a coalition of Conservatives and dissident Liberals who conspired to overthrow President José Tadeo MONAGAS. His "gobierno de fusión" was doomed from the start. The only goal the Conservatives and Liberals shared was their desire to remove Monagas from office. Both groups jockeyed for Castro's approval. The Conservatives quickly alienated the Liberals by pushing through Congress a bill making government employees responsible for past embezzlements. The Castro government's refusal to free Monagas and other prominent Liberals who had sought refuge in the French embassy resulted in a blockade of Venezuela's two major ports by the French and British in 1858. Castro's attempts to placate rebellious Liberals through concessions, along with the fact that his government was weak and unpopular, led to the FEDERAL WAR, a civil war that lasted from 1859 to 1864.

On 1 August 1859, Castro was overthrown by a Conservative-led coup known as the Federalist Revolution. He was imprisoned by government troops, then tried and convicted for treason but later absolved. He completed his career as a general in the Liberal armies of Antonio GUZMÁN BLANCO.

GARRIDO MEZGIITA Y COMPANIA, ed., *Diccionario biográfico de Venezuela* (1953); WILLIAM D. MARSLAND and AMY L. MARSLAND, *Venezuela Through Its History* (1954); GUILLERMO MORÓN, *A History of Venezuela* (1964); RAFAEL PÁEZ, *Los hombres que han hecho Venezuela* (1983).

DAVID CAREY, JR.

CASTRO, RICARDO (*b.* 7 February 1864; *d.* 20 November 1907), Mexican pianist and composer. Castro was the leading piano virtuoso in Mexico when that tradition was in full flower at the end of the nineteenth century. After study and a debut in Europe, where his music and his pianistic prowess gained immediate success, he returned to Mexico, propagating a European style marked by his own formidable technique and clarity of expression. His orchestral works (two symphonies and two concertos) and operatic music (*La Légende de Rudel*, 1906) were favorably accepted in his own epoch but have not had the enduring appeal of his works for solo piano.

ROBERT STEVENSON, *Music in Mexico: A Historical Survey* (1952).

ROBERT L. PARKER

CASTRO ALVES, ANTÔNIO DE (*b.* 14 March 1847; *d.* 6 July 1871), Brazilian poet. Castro Alves was the last and the greatest Brazilian romantic poet. He is also remembered as a playwright and an orator. Born on a large plantation in Bahia into a family of slave owners, he developed a passionate opposition to slavery; he is called "the poet of the slaves." Castro Alves is also known as the leader of the *condoreiros* (condor poets), who used the condor, strong and high flying, as their symbol. Their poetry is marked by ardent sentiment and grandiloquence, abounding in daring figures of speech.

Castro Alves led a tragic life. When very young, he fell in love with an actress, Eugênia Câmara. They had an amorous liaison, but after two years Eugênia left him. His mother's early death, the insanity and suicide of his brother, and the amputation of his foot after an accident deeply affected the poet. At sixteen he contracted tuberculosis, which killed him at the age of twenty-four. He loved life and did not want to die: "To die . . . when this world is a paradise," he wrote in "Mocidade e morte" (Youth and Death), which appeared in the collection *Espumas flutuantes* (Floating Foam, 1870). "Mocidade e morte" was written during a critical point in his illness, and it marks the beginning of his great art. Grief awoke in him the supreme accents that he later would extend to the sufferings of humanity.

Castro Alves became known through poems appearing in periodicals and recited at meetings. During his lifetime only one volume of his poetry was published, *Espumas flutuantes,* a collection of erotic, patriotic, and plaintive lyric verses. His antislavery poems appeared posthumously in *A cachoeira de Paulo Afonso* (The Waterfalls of Paulo Afonso, 1876) and *Os escravos* (The Slaves, 1883). The latter contains some of his most celebrated poems, such as "Vozes d'África" (Voices of Africa), an oration from Africa imploring God's justice, and "O navio negreiro" (The Slave Ship), a dramatic composition picturing all the horrors of an African slaver. Additional works include *Obra completa* (1960) and *Gonzaga ou a revolução de Minas* (Gonzaga or the Revolution in Minas, 1875).

JORGE AMADO, *ABC de Castro Alves* (1941); SAMUEL PUTNAM, *Marvelous Journey* (1948); RAYMOND S. SAYERS *The Negro in Brazilian Literature* (1956), pp. 112–117; JON M. TOLMAN, "Castro Alves, poeta amorosa," in *Luso-Brazilian Review* 12 (1975): 241–262; IVAN CAVALCANTI PROENÇA, *Castro Alves Falou* (1979); THOMAS BRAGA, "Castro Alves and the New England Abolitionist Poets," in *Hispania* 67 (1984): 585–593; DAVID T. HABERLY, "Antônio de Castro Alves," in *Latin American Writers,* edited by C. Solé and M. I. Abreu, vol. 1 (1989), pp. 289–297.

MARIA ISABEL ABREU

CASTRO JIJÓN, RAMÓN (*b.* 1915), representative of the navy in the military junta that ruled Ecuador from 11 July 1963 until 1966. Born in Esmeraldas, Castro Jijón received advanced military training in Chile and the United States. He served as a naval attaché in Western Europe. When the military overthrew the government of Carlos Julio AROSEMENA MONROY, Commander Castro was the only member of the junta from the coast. The movement that overthrew Arosemena's government was the first institutional intrusion of the military into politics since the coup of 23 October 1937.

The junta, which had wide public support during its first year, announced that the armed forces had the responsibility to promote new socioeconomic structures that would provide a foundation for true democracy. After suppressing leftist critics and purging the government of Arosemena supporters, the junta began to implement a program of structural reforms, including agrarian and tax reforms, which quickly alienated important civilian groups. The junta created a personal income tax; rationalized taxation by suppressing hundreds of levies that directly financed public agencies and autonomous institutions; and transferred revenue collection from autonomous agencies to the Central Bank. The latter measure prompted widespread public criticism, against which the junta retaliated by imposing martial law. The Agrarian Reform Law of 11 July 1964, which abolished the HUASIPUNGO labor system, and the establishment of maximum limits for the size of landholdings, sought to redress one of the most unequal distributions of land in South America. Although the law was relatively weak and threatened only the most inefficient producers, its passage galvanized sierra elite opposition to the junta.

When the economy began to falter in 1964, government deficits burgeoned. The junta sought to stabilize public finances by increasing import duties, but was forced to back down in the face of widespread public criticism, which culminated in a general strike in Guayaquil. When the junta again sought to increase import duties in early 1966, a second general strike spread throughout the nation and resulted in the resignation of the junta on 29 March 1966.

REPÚBLICA DEL ECUADOR, *Plan político de la Junta Militar de Gobierno* (1963) and *La junta militar de gobierno y la opinión pública* (1964); MARTIN NEEDLER, *Anatomy of a Coup d'État: Ecuador 1963* (1964); JOHN SAMUEL FITCH, *The Military Coup d'État as a Political Process: Ecuador, 1948–1966* (1977), esp. pp. 55–73.

LINDA ALEXANDER RODRÍGUEZ

CASTRO MADRiZ, JOSÉ MARÍA (*b.* 1818; *d.* 1871), president of Costa Rica (1847–1849, 1866–1868). Born in San José, Costa Rica, Castro Madriz studied law in León, Nicaragua. In 1848 he severed Costa Rica's ties with the UNITED PROVINCES OF CENTRAL AMERICA and declared the country's independence. As a result of strong political pressure, he was obliged to leave the presidency in

1849. When reelected in 1866, he supported improvements in the public education system, opened the bay of Limón to trade, and inaugurated Costa Rica's first telegraph. Overthrown in a military coup in 1868, Castro Madriz served as minister in subsequent governments. He was given the title Benemérito de la Patria (National Hero) and is called the founder of the republic.

CLETO GONZÁLEZ VÍQUEZ, *Dos proceres* (1918); RAFAEL OBREGÓN LORÍA, *Dr. José María Castro Madriz, paladín de la libertad y de la cultura* (1949); CLEOTILDE MARÍA OBREGÓN, *Costa Rica: Relaciones exteriores de una república en formación, 1847–1849* (1984).

OSCAR PELÁEZ ALMENGOR

CASTRO POZO, HILDEBRANDO (*b.* 1890; *d.* 1 September 1945), Peruvian intellectual and writer from the northern border state of Piura. Castro Pozo first entered the national arena after he had already written strong essays on the misery and extreme poverty of sharecroppers on the coastal plantations. In 1920, President Augusto LEGUÍA named him to head the section on Indian affairs in the national Ministry of Development, a post he held until 1923. He then became one of the most articulate and forthright defenders of the rights of Indians in the country. Quickly parting with Leguía, he understood INDIGENISMO through the spectacles of socialism; stressing that the exploitative, capitalist plantation agriculture of the coastal valleys of Peru could be ended only by the imposition of socialism. He felt further that the Indians, who had been communal village farmers since Incan times, would be the group in society most likely to carry out such a transformation. With landowners opposing him, he was sent into exile in 1923; he returned in 1924. His *Nuestra comunidad indígena* (1924) is a long essay on the naturally socialist character of indigenous village traditions. This and other writings influenced José Carlos MARIÁTEGUI, his contemporary among Peruvian *indigenistas* and the founder of the Socialist Party. A pragmatic leader, Castro Pozo encouraged party members to take positions in the government to help indigenous villagers. The Socialists hoped the government would introduce technological improvements into the villages, thereby better equipping them to compete with the big landowners. Two years after he died, the government passed a new, comprehensive sharecropping law.

HENRY F. DOBYNS and PAUL L. DOUGHTY, *Peru: A Cultural History* (1976), p. 230; JESÚS CHAVARRÍA, *José Carlos Mariátegui and the Rise of Modern Peru, 1890–1930* (1979), pp. 108, 115.

VINCENT PELOSO

CASTRO RUZ, FIDEL (*b.* 13 August 1926), Cuban revolutionary leader and premier (1959–1976), president, Council of State (since 1976). In 1956 Castro led a small band of revolutionaries in a landing in southeastern Cuba to amass popular support for the overthrow of dictator General Fulgencio BATISTA. Two years later, on New Year's Day 1959, Castro's army marched triumphantly into the Cuban capital of Havana and established a revolutionary regime.

Castro's life can be divided into two distinct periods: his early years as a revolutionary, when he risked all to overthrow the corrupt Batista; and the second, as master politician, successsfully playing off the world's superpowers against each other. This second phase is not over: as the de facto dictator of Cuba since 1959, Castro has shown a remarkable ability to challenge the might of the United States, and even that of his ally, the former Soviet Union, without losing his grip on political and economic control. Castro is one of those rare individuals who has proven to be both a brilliant revolutionary leader and a master politician.

EARLY LIFE

Castro was born in Oriente Province (home of the GRITO DE YARA, which signaled the beginning of the TEN YEARS' WAR of 1868–1878) in the district of Birán to an affluent landowning family. His father, Angel Castro, was a native of Galicia, Spain, while his mother, Lina Ruz Castro, was born in Cuba. Castro attended a Catholic boarding school in Santiago de Cuba and graduated from Belén College, Havana, also a Catholic school. He entered law school at the University of Havana in 1945 and began practicing in 1950. At the university Castro became involved with political factionalism of the campus and even shot a political opponent. In 1947 he took part in a plan to invade the Dominican Republic and overthrow the dictator Rafael TRUJILLO. The invasion was never carried out, however. The following year, 1948, Castro attended an anti-imperialist conference in Bogotá, Colombia, during which the Colombian populist Jorge GAITÁN was murdered and riots broke out. While there, Castro became embroiled in a battle between liberals and conservatives, siding with the liberals. He was arrested for trying to incite mutiny in a police barracks and was released and returned to Cuba only upon the intervention of the Cuban ambassador to Colombia on behalf of him and other students.

While Castro is most often identified with other Communist leaders of the twentieth century, it was anti-imperialist nationalism, not socialism, that served as the driving force of his younger years. His hero was José MARTÍ, not Lenin or Marx. As a student, Castro had amply opportunity to join the Cuban Communist party (Partido Socialista Popular—PSP) as his brother Raúl did, but Castro steered away from socialist politics in favor of the long-suppressed nationalism that influenced so many of Castro's generation. Since Cuba was first subjected to the open imperialism of Spanish rule, and later treated as little more than a colony of the United States, many Cubans had hoped to establish a nation free of the colonialism and neocolonialism under which it had labored for so long. Castro, one such Cuban nationalist, joined the reform-minded Orthodox Party in 1947, and ran for Congress in 1952. In the midst of the campaign, however, Batista headed a coup that suspended the elections and left him dictator of the island. This coup convinced Castro of the futility of trying to transform Cuba's government through legal means and converted him into a revolutionary.

Now firmly committed to a revolutionary course, Castro led a number of attempts that failed to overthrow the U.S.-backed Batista regime before leading his victorious forces into the capital city in 1959. Castro responded to the coup of 1952 by organizing a guerrilla organization to launch attacks against the Batista government. On 26 July 1953, Castro led an assault on the Moncada barracks in Santiago. While this attack was noted mostly for its sheer folly and was easily defeated, Castro nonetheless became a nationally known figure for his prominent role in it. Castro was captured and stood trial, which he skillfully used to his advantage. In his testimony defending the attack, Castro gave his famous "History Will Absolve Me" speech in which he listed, with unique flair, the corruption and shortcomings of the Batista regime as well as his own solutions to the problems besetting Cuba. His message was liberal nationalism, with its call for a democratic government, better education and health care, a more diversified economy, and an end to the overbearing influence of the United States in Cuba's politics and economy. Not only were socialists drawn into Castro's camp but also members of the Cuban middle class resentful of both the alliance of U.S. businesses with Cuba's elite and the uneven development of the Cuban economy.

Castro was jailed for his role in the attack and released as part of a general amnesty two years later. Rather than remaining in Cuba under the watchful eye of Batista's police, Castro went to Mexico to plot his next move. There he joined forces with Ernesto "Che" GUEVARA, an Argentine by birth and a doctor by training. The Argentine's anti-Yankee nationalism quickly led Guevara to embrace Communism after witnessing firsthand a U.S.-backed coup in Guatemala in 1954. Along with Guevara and Castro's brother Raúl, Fidel plotted a new attack on the island nation. On 2 December 1956, eighty-one guerrillas led by Castro landed on the southeastern coast of Cuba in the boat *Granma*. Most of the force was captured or killed, but Castro, Che, and Raúl survived. It was this small, poorly equipped army that would soon rally broad popular support among the Cuban people and overthrow Batista.

As Batista's army continually failed to capture Castro, his image among the Cuban people grew. Starting from his base in the mountains of eastern Cuba, Castro

Fidel Castro addressing cement factory workers, Santiago, Cuba. © 1964, 1994 LEE LOCKWOOD.

quickly made contact with other groups disillusioned with Batista's rule. While most observers, including most of the leaders of the PSP, were startled at Castro's success, he himself never doubted the eventual outcome of his struggle. On 1 January 1959, Castro's forces marched triumphantly into Havana just hours after Batista had fled Cuba.

HEAD OF STATE

Once in power, Castro gained world attention for taking a defiant stand against the United States. As head of the government, Castro made a commitment to nationalizing the Cuban economy, especially the SUGAR INDUSTRY, as well as refusing to bow to U.S. economic and political pressures, which led to a quick cooling of U.S.-Cuban relations. At the same time, the Castro government turned increasingly toward the Soviet Union to counter U.S. pressure.

On 17 April 1961, U.S.-backed Cuban exiles launched an invasion at the BAY OF PIGS on the southern coast of the island. The offensive, ill-conceived and poorly planned during the Eisenhower administration and carried out under the newly elected Kennedy administration, was a conclusive failure. The local police force and militia alone were sufficient to defeat the counterrevolutionaries, and Castro was hailed both at home and abroad as one of the few leaders capable of standing up to the North American giant. It was after the failed invasion, on 2 December 1961, that Castro publicly declared himself a Marxist, a conversion whose sincerity has since been the subject of much debate. The timing of his "conversion" does suggest, however, that Castro's move was more pragmatic than heartfelt. Whatever his motives, Castro was left with little alternative: the U.S. government, which was patently hostile to his rule, would be satisfied only with the continuation of a Batista-style government sans Batista.

In October 1962, U.S. intelligence detected Soviet nuclear missiles on the island, and a tense period known as the CUBAN MISSILE CRISIS followed. For days it appeared that the United States and the Soviet Union were headed toward war, and while the world anxiously waited, Premier Nikita Khrushchev gave an eleventh-hour order to recall the Soviet missiles. This crisis sealed Cuba's fate. From the early 1960s to the present, Castro has led the country, with varied success, on the path of Soviet-style socialism. As had the socialists of Stalinist Russia, the Cuban government nationalized all economic endeavors, no matter how small, in an effort to centralize the economy and the distribution of resources. Absent from Castro's socialism was any hint of the independent workers', peasants', or soldiers' councils argued for by Lenin and the Bolsheviks. Following the model of China and the Soviet Union, all political activities, the press, and education were—and are—closely monitored by the state.

Between 1956 and 1965, when he formally became the head of the Cuban Communist Party, Castro maneu-

vered deftly around the various factions vying for power in revolutionary Cuba. During his march to power, Castro successfully had manipulated varied political groupings within Cuba to help achieve his revolutionary goal without relinquishing any real power. In April 1958 Castro at first supported a general strike planned by the urban wing of the underground TWENTY-SIXTH OF JULY MOVEMENT. This strike was opposed by the PSP and backed by the liberal wing of the movement. But later, when the strike proved unsuccessful, Castro opposed it. From that time forward, Castro was the undisputed leader of the movement to oust Batista. Not only did the failed strike discredit the liberals of the movement, but it also allowed Castro to absorb many PSP members into his twenty-sixth of July Movement. While Castro always mistrusted the party faithful, he nonetheless recognized that their commitment to rank-and-file organization and their well-organized party structure could be useful to his own aims. This would not be the last time Castro would successfully maneuver to exploit the well-organized strength of the PSP.

With the triumph of the revolution, Castro designated Manuel URRUTIA LLEÓ president of the country, a post Castro would take over himself once he had consolidated the necessary power. To do this, he turned again to the well-disciplined PSP, whose members he placed in key positions within the government. Resignations of liberals and moderates quickly followed, accompanied by pro forma protests that Cuba's government was turning too far to the left. But the wave of resignations and dismissals, and the arrest of the popular anti-Communist guerrilla commander Major Hubert Matos, only allowed Castro to consolidate further his political and economic power.

As supreme leader, Castro similarly balanced competing forces in order to maintain his uncontested rule. With the dismissal, exile, and execution of the liberals and moderates of the anti-Batista movement, Castro turned increasingly to his brother Raúl and the charismatic Che Guevara for support. Guevara in particular played a crucial role in government economic planning in the mid-1960s. But while Guevara's lasting contribution as a revolutionary is undeniable, his role as economic planner was largely a failure. Seeking to shift Cuba's traditional reliance away from sugar production, Guevara embarked on a disastrous plan of diversification. When it became clear that sugar was still the only Cuban product of significant value on the world market, he "recruited" armies of workers to get out the sugar harvest. Despite his call for Cubans to build a "new man" (one who would presumably work sixteen-hour days with no days of rest), the sugar harvest continued to falter because of poor economic planning. Yet Castro took little direct blame for the serious economic decline of the middle and late 1960s. Ever the populist caudillo, Castro succeeded in directing most of the responsibility toward Guevara, the unyielding government bureaucracy, and the United States. While events leading up to Guevara's departure are poorly documented and little discussed even today, it is clear that the two revolutionaries had a parting of the ways. Guevara left Cuba, to die in Bolivia in 1967.

Over the years, Castro has relied increasingly on individuals more noted for their loyalty and lack of imagination than their governmental and leadership skills. Second in power to Castro is his brother Raúl, who is general of the army, defense minister, and Fidel's designated successor and second secretary of the Communist Party. Another powerbroker in Castro's ruling circle is Osmani Cienfuegos Gorriarán, a stereotypical bureaucrat as colorless as he is loyal. Conversely, Fidel's rivals, even those who fought with him at the Moncada barracks in 1953, are periodically dismissed. In 1986, Comandante Ramiro Valdés, who served as minister of the interior and a member of the party's politburo, was relieved of his duties. The only top leader besides Fidel to wear the olive-green uniform of the revolution, Valdés is one of only three veterans to carry the title Comandante de la Revolución, a position not even Raúl enjoys.

While Castro's political genius has allowed him to enjoy unchallenged power in Cuba despite tremendous internal and external pressures (the U.S. government has tried every method conceivable to oust Castro, including some, like an attempt to plant a bomb in his cigar, that were simply childish), he has surrounded himself increasingly with sycophants too browbeaten to challenge his decisions. One exception is Carlos Rafael Rodríguez, an experienced politician and Castro's senior by thirteen years. Rodríguez was crucial to the fusion of the guerrillas with the PSP after 1958. A true intellectual, he is vice-president of both the Council of State and the Council of Ministers and enjoys Castro's close friendship.

As Castro has squelched all opposition within the country, so too has he been forced to rely on a charismatic rule that places personality ahead of practical programs. Castro is forever the advocate. A brilliant speaker, he is capable of convincing huge crowds to enthusiastically endorse programs they may have been opposed to minutes earlier. His speeches are legend, both for their length (he has been known to speak for up to nine hours straight) and their ability to persuade. In a country where the citizenry is not consulted on decisions important or otherwise, Castro places great importance on his ability to move massive crowds (and Cuba's television audience) to endorse with their shouts and cheers whatever programs or policy he might be pushing for at the time.

PERSONAL LIFE

While Castro is ever the public figure, there is little known about his private life. In 1948, Fidel married Mirta Díaz-Balart, with whom he had one son before divorcing in 1954. His old comrades have died off, and he lacks close personal friendships with all but a few. He is still in touch with his ex-wife and also keeps in contact with his son, Fidelito, who is married and has two children. Trained as a physicist, Fidelito has taken an increasingly public posture as head of the Cuban Nuclear Commission. Castro maintains varying degrees of cordiality with his siblings. He is closest to his brother Raúl, of course, from their unique shared experiences starting with the attack on the Moncada barracks. One sister, Juana, is actively hostile toward him, however, and attacks him without mercy from self-imposed exile in Miami. (The family landholdings were gradually turned over to government control starting in 1959.)

If Castro has a lover, her identity is unknown, and, since the death of Celia SÁNCHEZ MANDULEY, Castro has shown no interest in elevating another woman to this position. Sánchez was in fact the first lady of Cuba, despite their never marrying. In addition to her role as companion, she exercised considerable political power as secretary of the Council of State and member of the party's Central Committee. Perhaps her greatest role, however, was her courage in standing up to Castro's gigantic ego and bluntly declaring to his face what others had only thought in private—that the great Castro could at times be wrong. After her death in 1980, numerous monuments and parks were erected in her honor.

AN ASSESSMENT

With the collapse of the Soviet bloc, Castro faces still another challenge to his rule and the Cuban state he has built. It is widely accepted that Castro's days are numbered, even that after his death the government will revert to the control of the Cuban exile community based in Miami. Yet the political pundits have never given Castro his due. It was popularly regarded as folly to attack the Moncada barracks and launch a sea invasion of Cuba with the *Granma*, yet Castro silenced his critics. Since the establishment of his socialist regime in Cuba, many have counted by the day or week, not year, the time it would supposedly take for Castro to be ousted, yet he has clung to power for over thirty years.

It is also common to regard Castro as nothing more than a caudillo, and in fact he displays many of the traits associated with such Latin American strongmen. Yet if his only goal had been to replace Batista, certainly a man of Castro's considerable abilities and class background could have reached the pinnacle of power in Cuba through the accepted military and social channels. While Castro's early days in the mountains of eastern Cuba nearly cost him his life, they also established that he was fighting for more than just personal aggrandizement and perpetuation of the old order. From his earliest days as a student, Castro has been an ardent nationalist fighting to rid Cuba of foreign control and the humiliation of poverty and illiteracy. While the foreign influences remain, certainly Cuba enjoyed greater leeway with the Soviet Union than it did in its relations with the United States. And while poverty and illiteracy there have not been eliminated, Cuba far surpasses the rest of Latin America in education and the fulfillment of basic needs. Although he cannot claim sole responsibility for this, Fidel Castro can take partial credit.

LEE LOCKWOOD, *Castro's Cuba, Cuba's Fidel* (1969); CARLOS FRANQUI, *Diary of the Cuban Revolution* (1980); PETER G. BOURNE, *Fidel: A Biography of Fidel Castro* (1986); TAD SZULC, *Fidel, A Critical Portrait* (1986).

MICHAEL POWELSON

See also **Cuban Revolution.**

CASTRO RUZ, RAÚL (*b.* 3 June 1931), Cuban revolutionary and military leader, younger brother of Cuban premier Fidel CASTRO RUZ, and one of the original members of the TWENTY-SIXTH OF JULY MOVEMENT that organized the successful overthrow of Cuban dictator Fulgencio BATISTA in 1959. Castro was born in Oriente Province, in the district of Birán, to an affluent landowning family. His father, Angel, was a native of Galicia, Spain; his mother, Lina Ruz González, was Cuban. As a youth he attended Catholic schools in Oriente Province and went on to study at the University of Havana. Unlike his brother Fidel, Raúl was early attracted to Marxism, and while a student at the university he joined the Socialist Youth Branch of the Partido Socialisto Popular (PSP).

The two brothers found common ground, however, in their hatred of the Batista regime and the pervasive role the United States played in all aspects of Cuban life. Raúl stood alongside his brother during the struggle to overthrow the Batista regime. In 1953 he was imprisoned with Fidel for the attack on the Moncada barracks, and joined his brother in exile in Mexico after Batista declared a general amnesty in 1955. Raúl helped Fidel plan the 1956 landing of a small band of revolutionaries from the boat *Granma* in Oriente Province. This invasion culminated in the ouster of Batista in 1959. When the new revolutionary government took power, Raúl was named minister of Cuba's Revolutionary Armed Forces.

As hostilities with the United States grew after the revolution, both Raúl Castro and Che GUEVARA were instrumental in influencing Fidel Castro to turn increasingly to the Soviet Union for economic and military aid. Whereas Fidel denied he was a Communist until December 1961, Raúl openly courted the Soviets while attacking the United States. With the BAY OF PIGS INVASION in 1961 and the CUBAN MISSILE CRISIS the following year, Raúl played an integral role in moving Cuba from the U.S. to the Soviet sphere of influence.

As a trusted adviser to Fidel, Raúl has increased his power considerably over the years; many have charged the Castro brothers, not without reason, of turning the Cuban government into a family-owned business. Fidel holds the title of Cuban premier; Raúl continues to be vice premier (commander of the armed forces), and was named first vice president of the Council of State and the Council of Ministries during the "institutionalization" process of the 1970s. He is also a member of the Politburo and second secretary of the Cuban Communist Party. He has been president of the Agrarian Reform Institute since 1965, and is responsible for the Council of Ministers, the Ministry of the Interior, the Secretariat of the President, the Ministry of Public Health, and the Children's Institute.

Raúl Castro and his supporters built a modern army capable of protecting Cuba's borders against U.S. aggression and of launching military forays abroad. With the collapse of the Soviet Union and economic crises at home, the Cuban military, led by Raúl, is increasingly prominent in Cuban industries such as manufacturing and TOURISM. Once regarded as an "ideologue" compared to his pragmatic brother Fidel, Raúl Castro has recently shown considerable flexibility, especially in his direction of Cuba's economy. He has endorsed limited capitalist FOREIGN INVESTMENT, as well as market incentives for Cuban producers, as a remedy for the nation's current economic ills. Although Raúl possesses considerable power, he lacks Fidel's charisma, and most Cuba-watchers doubt that he would be able to fill his brother's shoes if Fidel were to die.

While there has been much criticism of Raúl, he and his brother Fidel did lead a successful revolt against both a despised dictator and the overbearing economic and political hegemony of the United States. Although it was widely accepted that Cuba could not survive without massive Soviet military and economic support, since the collapse of the Eastern bloc Cuba shows few signs, so far, of internal turmoil. Raúl Castro can take part of the credit for that.

RAÚL CASTRO and FIDEL CASTRO, *Selección de discursos acerca del partido* (1975); LUIS SUÁREZ, ed., *Entre el fusil y la palabra* (1980); JANE MC MANUS, ed., *From the Palm Tree: Voices of the Cuban Revolution* (1983); FRANK T. FITZGERALD, *Managing Socialism: From Old Cadres to New Professionals in Revolutionary Cuba* (1990); CUBAN STUDIES PROJECT, UNIVERSITY OF MIAMI, *Problems of Succession in Cuba* (1995).

MICHAEL POWELSON

See also **Cuba: Political Parties; Cuban Intervention in Africa; Cuban Revolution.**

CATALONIAN VOLUNTEERS. The Free Company of Catalonian Volunteers was formed in Barcelona in 1767 as part of the BOURBON reorganization of the Spanish military in the Americas. The company participated in the Sonora expedition of 1767–1771, the establishment of California in 1769, the Colorado River Campaign of 1781–1782, the voyage of the *expedición de los limites* to the Pacific Northwest and Alaska during 1790–1793, as well as the royalist effort to quell the movement for Mexican independence. From 1767 to 1815, the Compañía Franca de Voluntarios de Cataluña assisted in Spain's last great push to secure the northwestern portion of its empire in the Western Hemisphere.

JOSEPH P. SÁNCHEZ, *Spanish Bluecoats: The Catalonian Volunteers in Northwestern New Spain, 1767–1810* (1990).

JOSEPH P. SÁNCHEZ

CATAMARCA, capital city of the province of the same name in northwestern Argentina, with 90,000 inhabitants (1980). It was founded in 1558 with the unusual name of London, to commemorate the marriage of Philip II of Spain to Mary Tudor of England, and was destroyed by Diaguita Indians in 1563, 1607, and 1683. Its location today in a well-sheltered valley between Sierra de Ancasti and Sierra de Ambato was chosen by Fernando Mendoza, who was attracted, as were other settlers from Santiago del Estero, by the good soils and by the numerous Indian farming communities that flourished in the valley. On the basis of the region's famed Indian textiles in colonial times, cotton fields and textile mills were established around Catamarca during republican times. However, fruit orchards in the well-irrigated valley dominated the agrarian economy until the late twentieth century.

The hinterland of Catamarca was formerly part of the Diaguita cultural realm extending from Argentina across the Andes into the Norte Chico region of Chile and famous for its fine ceramics. East of the Sierra de Famatina, the interior valley of the Colorado River is still the seat of the traditional Indian-Mestizo agrarian populations, Fiambalá and Tinogasta counting among their centers.

CARLOS VILLAFUERTE, *Catamarca: Camino y tiempo* (Buenos Aires, 1968).

CÉSAR N. CAVIEDES

CATAVI MASSACRE, slaying of Bolivian workers during a miners' strike in 1942. In September 1942, the miners' union in the Catavi tin ore concentration plant presented the Patiño Company with demands for wage increases ranging from 20 percent to 70 percent. The company refused even to negotiate with the union, and union negotiators failed to obtain the support of the government of General Enrique PEÑARANDA. When the union announced a strike for 14 December, the government declared a state of siege in the tin-mining departments, and troops moved into Catavi. When union leaders were arrested on 13 December, the workers mobilized to demand their release, and the police fired on the crowd, killing and wounding several.

The strike continued. On 21 December, workers demonstrating in front of company offices in Catavi were fired on by soldiers, who killed or wounded 35 people. The workers then mobilized some 8,000 people, who descended on the company headquarters in Catavi. Soldiers shot into the crowd and for the next two days roamed through workers' living quarters, beating up and killing miners and members of their families. The government admitted that 19 people were killed—including 3 women—but other sources claimed the deaths were as high as 400.

This incident shocked the country. The Catavi union's secretary general got to La Paz and informed Víctor PAZ ESTENSSORO, leader of the Nationalist Revolutionary Movement (MNR) of what had occurred. MNR deputies then intensively interrogated government ministers, establishing a bond between the MNR and the miners that lasted several decades.

The Catavi massacre provoked wide international protest. The U.S. State Department and the Pan-American Union expressed concern, and the AFL and the CIO sent to Bolivia a joint delegation, roundly denouncing the Peñaranda government.

The Catavi massacre was undoubtedly a major factor undermining the Peñaranda regime, which was overthrown a year later by a coalition of young military men and the MNR.

AUGUSTO CÉSPEDES, *El presidente colgado* (1966); GUILLERMO LORA, *A History of the Bolivian Labour Movement* (1977).

ROBERT J. ALEXANDER

See also **Mining: Modern.**

CATEAU-CAMBRÉSIS, TREATY OF (1559), agreement between France and Spain ending the Hapsburg-Valois wars. The treaty ended four decades (1521–1559) of armed conflict over Navarre, Aragon's borders, Flanders, Artois, Burgundy, and Milan. According to its terms, France kept imperial cities in northern Europe but was almost totally excluded from the Italian peninsula, underscoring the existing balance of power in continental Europe. The reigning monarchs when the treaty was signed on 3 April 1559, PHILIP II of Spain and Henry II of France, were forced by bankruptcy and heresy to make peace. The treaty also marked the end of an Anglo-Spanish alliance that had been crucial in foreign policy during the end of CHARLES I's reign and left Philip II with the problem of defending the Low Countries without an English alliance. The New World was ignored in the treaty by mutual consent and peace was thus limited to the European domain.

WILLIAM S. MALTBY, *Alba: A Biography of Fernando Álvarez de Toledo, Third Duke of Alba, 1507–1582* (1983), esp. pp. 110–116; JOHN LYNCH, *Spain 1516–1598* (1991), pp. 101–137, 251–253.

SUZANNE HILES BURKHOLDER

CATHOLIC ACTION, the generic name for Catholic lay associations that were founded throughout the world in response to Pope Pius XI's call for Catholics to participate more actively in support of the church and to defend Catholicism against the dangers of liberalism, communism, POSITIVISM, and Protestantism. Most Catholic Action national associations in Latin America were founded in the 1930s: Argentina and Chile in 1931, Colombia in 1933, Peru in 1935, and Bolivia in 1938. Based on the Italian model, Catholic Action had branches for men, women, and youths. There were also specialized groups for workers, students, businessmen, secretaries, and rural workers. Many Catholic Action groups had strong ties with the schools run by religious orders, especially the JESUITS. Catholic Action drew its inspiration from the papal social encyclicals and European Catholic intellectuals, such as Jacques Maritain, Gilbert Keith Chesterton, and Hilaire Belloc. Drawing its leadership mainly from the urban upper and middle classes, Catholic Action received a strong impulse from the bishops and papal nuncios. In some cases leading Catholic laymen took the initiative. In Brazil, Jackson de FIGUEIREDO founded the Centro Dom Vital in 1922, and his successor, Alceu Amoroso LIMA, became the most important spokesman for Brazilian Catholic Action.

In many cases the specialized groups had a greater long-term influence than the general association. The most important Catholic Action group among workers was the Young Catholic Workers (Juventud[e] Operaria Católica—JOC). Modeled on the original movement founded in 1925 by a Belgian priest, Joseph Cardijn, JOC aimed to counteract the influence of Communist- or Socialist-run unions. In Chile, Clotario Blest, a Catholic Action leader, was also an important figure in the national union movement. In Cuba the Catholic university student movement, Agrupación Católica Universitaria (ACU), founded in 1931 by the Jesuits, was the most important Catholic Action group on the island. In Brazil, the Catholic University Youth (Juventude Universitária Católica—JUC) numbered many thousands in the 1960s.

Although Catholic Action was officially forbidden to participate in partisan politics, in fact it did serve as a school of political leadership for an entire generation of Catholics. Most of the founders of the Christian Democratic parties began as youth leaders in Catholic Action. Many of the leaders of the CRISTERO movement in Mexico, notably René Capistrán Garza, had their beginnings in the Catholic Student Center, founded by the Jesuits in Mexico City in 1913. Although all members were united in their determination to defend Catholicism, not all shared the same views on politics. Some, such as Jackson de FIGUEIREDO, thought along integralist lines and espoused the creation of a Catholic corporatist state. Most Catholic Action leaders, however, were swayed by Jacques Maritain's concept of a "Christian democracy." By the 1960s some of the university groups had become quite radicalized. The JUC in Brazil took such a leftist and independent course that it was eventually marginalized by the bishops.

By the late 1950s Catholic Action began to decline, to be replaced by other, newer movements. Its most important contribution to Latin American Catholicism was the fostering of a new social awareness among Catholics. It represented the transition from an older, elitist Catholicism to the more modern and pluralistic Catholicism of Vatican II.

HENRY A. LANDSBERGER, ed., *The Church and Social Change in Latin America* (1970); DAVID BAILEY, *¡Viva Cristo Rey! The Cristero Rebellion and the Church–State Conflict in Mexico* (1974); ANA MARÍA BIDEGAIN, *Iglesia, pueblo y política* (1985); EDWARD CLEARY, *Crisis and Change: The Church in Latin America Today* (1985); SCOTT MAINWARING, *The Catholic Church and Politics in Brazil, 1916–1985* (1986); ENRIQUE DUSSEL, ed., *The Church in Latin America, 1492–1992* (1992); JEFFREY KLAIBER, *The Church in Peru, 1821–1985: A Social History* (1992).

JEFFREY KLAIBER

See also **Catholic Church.**

CATHOLIC CHURCH

Colonial Period

The Catholic church in colonial Latin America is often seen as a monolithic institution. In actual fact there were significant divisions within it. The church was divided internally into two basic parts: the secular clergy and the regular clergy. The regular clergy consisted of all priests, friars, and monks who were members of religious orders. Since membership in a religious order called upon the individual to pursue a special rule of life, *regula* in Latin, these clerics were called regulars. The secular clergy was made up of the clerics and priests involved in the day-to-day affairs of parish life. They lived out "in the world," *saeculum* in Latin, from which the term *secular* derives.

The secular clergy in the New World fell under the administrative control of the Iberian monarchs, under the PATRONATO REAL (in Portuguese *Padrado Real*) as developed during and immediately following the discovery and conquest. Each order of the regular clergy, on the other hand, had its own internal organization and leadership, directly under the pope.

Both seculars and regulars existed in Iberian and indigenous societies, and both relied on the gifts, alms, and taxes of the Iberians to help subsidize their work among the Indians.

EARLY SETTLEMENT

In the first phase of the Spanish and Portuguese settlement of the New World, the regulars played a very important role. In each of the major conquering armies one member of a religious order served as the spiritual director of the expedition; in addition, there were also secular clerics involved in the expeditions. Pope Adrian VI empowered the religious orders to engage in missionary activities with his bull *Exponi nobis feciste*, known as *Omnimoda* (1522), which authorized the FRANCISCANS, in particular, to do anything necessary for the conversion of the Indians whenever they were out of the immediate jurisdiction of a bishop (defined as a two-days' ride). Other religious orders eventually received the same or similar powers.

The major effort of conversion fell rather naturally to the religious orders. Structurally they were better suited to the work because they carried with them a sense of institutional direction and oversight, usually arriving in organized groups, normally of twelve, in imitation of the Apostles.

The Iberian powers engaged in an extensive moral debate over the treatment of the natives of the New World. Bartolomé de LAS CASAS, a Dominican friar, and other outspoken critics, decried the harsh treatment which the conquerors had meted out on the natives. In 1537 Pope Paul III, in his bull *Sublimis deus,* declared that the natives were fully human and thus were not to be deprived of their freedom or mastery of their possessions. Another camp, manifest in the work of Juan Ginés de SEPÚLVEDA, argued that the natives were naturally inferior to the Europeans, and thus force could be used against them. Legal provisions were adopted to protect the natives, although in actual application most of these failed.

In confronting the huge indigenous population, which spoke dozens of different and mutually unintelligible languages, the missionaries had to adopt certain operational rules, as there were too many converts and too few clergy. For instance, in administering the sacrament of baptism, the clergy could not engage in a long and complex catechumenate before admitting the Indians to Christianity. It was far more practical to baptize the masses and concentrate later on their spiritual preparation. Clearly it was not practical to teach all of the Indians Spanish or Portuguese in order to then instruct them in Christianity. Consequently the clergy learned the native languages and preached and indoctrinated in them; as a consequence there are scores of books, mostly catechisms and other doctrinal works, printed in native American languages. Many missionaries concentrated on amassing as much knowledge about the native cultures as possible and in the process produced such works as the *Florentine Codex,* a twelve-volume encyclopedia of Aztec life, written in the Aztec language, NAHUATL, by a Franciscan, Friar Bernardino de SAHAGÚN. In Peru one finds the legends of HUAROCHIRÍ collected by the secular priest Francisco de Ávila. Although modern scholars are thrilled to have this wealth of detail about native culture at the time of contact, one must keep in mind the purpose for which it was compiled: to extirpate all vestiges of the pre-Columbian civilization. The need to learn the native languages also produced scores of other books, grammars, and dictionaries of the New World languages, from Floridian TIMUCUA to Chilean ARAUCANIAN, from AYMARA of Bolivia to ZAPOTEC of Mexico and TUPI of Brazil.

The religious orders were the most active in the early phases of European settlement. The first organized missionary expedition to Mexico, a group of twelve Franciscans, arrived in 1524, led by Friar Martín de Valencia. It was followed in 1526 by twelve DOMINICANS led by Friar Tomás Ortiz and in 1533 by seven AUGUSTINIANS under the guidance of Friar Francisco de la Cruz. By 1559 the missionary corps of New Spain had swelled to some 802 religious in some 160 monasteries.

The first missionary efforts in Brazil were conducted principally by Franciscans who accompanied the early voyages of discovery. The first organized missionary effort to Brazil was an expedition of six Jesuits under the leadership of Manuel da NÓBREGA in 1544. By the end of the century there were 128 JESUITS active in Brazil. The secular clergy were active in Brazil from a very early date. The first parishes were erected in 1532, and in 1551 the diocese of Brazil was created. The first convent for nuns was not established until 1665, the second in 1735.

In Peru a similar pattern emerged. The Franciscans were among the first missionaries to arrive, along with Dominicans and MERCEDARIANS, shortly following the Conquest. The Franciscan mission was initially led by Fray Marcos de NIZA, who came down from Mexico with a small expedition but apparently returned home upon reaching what is southern Panama. In 1534–1535 the Franciscans established monasteries in Quito and in Los Reyes (modern-day Lima). In 1540 twelve Dominicans, the second expedition organized by the order, arrived under the leadership of Friar Francisco Toscano. The first Mercedarians appeared in Lima in 1535, and by 1540 they had established four monasteries, in Lima, San Miguel de Piura, Cuzco, and Guamanga.

Although active in Mexico, the Augustinians did not participate in the early missions in Peru. The Mercedarians arrived in Mexico in the late sixteenth century. In 1593 they established a college and a novitiate under the direction of the Guatemalan province. It was not until 1619 that the Mercedarians established an independent Mexican province. In the mid-sixteenth century the Jesuits became active throughout Hispanic America.

THE SECULAR CLERGY

The first dioceses were erected in the Caribbean in 1511, including Santo Domingo, Cuba, Concepción, and Puerto Rico. On the mainland the first diocese, called Carola, was founded in 1519 and inspired by the ongoing conquest of the Aztecs. Following the confusion of the Conquest, the diocese was resurrected as Tlaxcala in 1526. The seat of the diocese later moved to the Spanish city of Puebla de los Ángeles, and thus the diocese is known variously as Tlaxcala, Puebla, or Tlaxcala-Puebla. The diocese of Mexico was erected in 1530 with Friar Juan de ZUMÁRRAGA as first bishop. In South America, the diocese of Cuzco was the first to be erected, in 1537, with Vicente de Valverde, a Dominican and chaplain to Pizarro, as first bishop. Lima was founded in 1541. Both Mexico and Lima became archbishoprics in 1546, along with Santo Domingo.

The church in the Hispanic Americas was divided into three provinces, under the three archdioceses. Each of the three archdioceses had a number of suffragan, or subject, dioceses. The Province of Santo Domingo included all the dioceses erected in the Caribbean. The

The Catholic Church in Colonial Spanish America

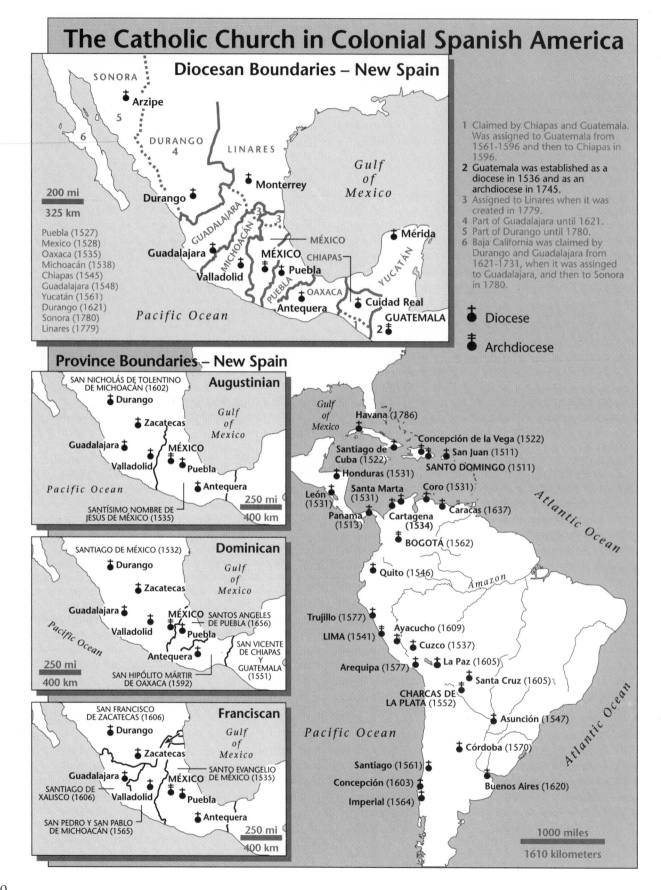

Diocesan Boundaries – New Spain

SONORA

✝ Arzipe

DURANGO 4

LINARES

5

6

200 mi
325 km

✝ Durango

✝ Monterrey

Gulf of Mexico

GUADALAJARA

MICHOACÁN 3 3

MÉXICO

✝ Guadalajara

MÉXICO

CHIAPAS

✝ Valladolid ✝ Puebla

PUEBLA

YUCATÁN

✝ Mérida

OAXACA

Pacific Ocean

✝ Antequera

✝ Cuidad Real

GUATEMALA

2 ⚭

Puebla (1527)
Mexico (1528)
Oaxaca (1535)
Michoacán (1538)
Chiapas (1545)
Guadalajara (1548)
Yucatán (1561)
Durango (1621)
Sonora (1780)
Linares (1779)

1 Claimed by Chiapas and Guatemala. Was assigned to Guatemala from 1561-1596 and then to Chiapas in 1596.
2 Guatemala was established as a diocese in 1536 and as an archdiocese in 1745.
3 Assigned to Linares when it was created in 1779.
4 Part of Guadalajara until 1621.
5 Part of Durango until 1780.
6 Baja California was claimed by Durango and Guadalajara from 1621-1731, when it was assigned to Guadalajara, and then to Sonora in 1780.

✝ Diocese

⚭ Archdiocese

Province Boundaries – New Spain

Augustinian

SAN NICHOLÁS DE TOLENTINO DE MICHOACÁN (1602)

✝ Durango

✝ Zacatecas

Gulf of Mexico

✝ Guadalajara

MÉXICO

✝ Valladolid ✝ Puebla

Pacific Ocean

✝ Antequera

SANTÍSIMO NOMBRE DE JESÚS DE MÉXICO (1535)

250 mi
400 km

Dominican

SANTIAGO DE MÉXICO (1532)

✝ Durango

✝ Zacatecas

Gulf of Mexico

✝ Guadalajara

MÉXICO

SANTOS ANGELES DE PUEBLA (1656)

✝ Valladolid ✝ Puebla

SAN VICENTE DE CHIAPAS Y GUATEMALA (1551)

Pacific Ocean

✝ Antequera

250 mi
400 km

SAN HIPÓLITO MÁRTIR DE OAXACA (1592)

Franciscan

SAN FRANCISCO DE ZACATECAS (1606)

✝ Durango

✝ Zacatecas

Gulf of Mexico

✝ Guadalajara

MÉXICO

SANTO EVANGELIO DE MÉXICO (1535)

SANTIAGO DE XALISCO (1606)

✝ Valladolid ✝ Puebla

SAN PEDRO Y SAN PABLO DE MICHOACÁN (1565)

✝ Antequera

250 mi
400 km

Gulf of Mexico

Havana (1786)

Concepción de la Vega (1522)

Santiago de Cuba (1522) ✝ San Juan (1511)

SANTO DOMINGO (1511)

✝ Honduras (1531)

León (1531)

Santa Marta (1531)

Coro (1531)

Panamá (1513)

Cartagena (1534)

Caracas (1637)

BOGOTÁ (1562)

✝ Quito (1546)

Amazon

Trujillo (1577)

Ayacucho (1609)

LIMA (1541)

✝ Cuzco (1537)

Arequipa (1577)

✝ La Paz (1605)

Santa Cruz (1605)

CHARCAS DE LA PLATA (1552)

Asunción (1547)

Pacific Ocean

✝ Córdoba (1570)

Santiago (1561)

Concepción (1603)

Buenos Aires (1620)

Imperial (1564)

Atlantic Ocean

1000 miles
1610 kilometers

Province of Mexico included all the dioceses of Mexico, Central America, and the Philippines, until 1595, when Manila was elevated to an archdiocese. Later, in 1743 Guatemala became an archdiocese. The Province of Peru included all of South America. In 1564 Santa Fe de Bogotá became an archdiocese, controlling the northern part of the continent and Panama. In 1609, La Plata (modern-day Sucre, Bolivia) was elevated to an archdiocese.

The Portuguese placed all of their overseas possessions into one ecclesiastical province, centered in Funchal, on the island of Madeira. In 1551 the various territories within Brazil were placed under the administrative control of the newly created bishopric of Salvador da Bahia. In 1676 Bahia was made an archdiocese and Rio de Janeiro and Pernambuco were made suffragan dioceses. The African dioceses of São Tomé and Angola were also placed under the administrative control of the archbishop of Bahia. The following year Maranhão became a diocese, followed in 1719 by Pará, and in 1745 São Paulo and Mariana (Minas Gerais).

The secular clergy was organized under the authority of the local bishop; clerics were assigned to the cathedral, to provide it with ecclesiastical staff and to assist the bishop in his administration of the diocese. These clerics were collectively known as the cathedral chapter, or *cabildo eclesiástico*, which had a maximum of twenty-seven clerics, including five dignitaries, ten canons, six *racioneros*, and six *medio-racioneros*. The dignitaries, dean, archdeacon, *chantre* (precentor), *maestrescuelas* (schoolmaster), and treasurer, all received the honorific title *don*, and theoretically oversaw specific areas of the church's life. The canons and *racioneros* both participated in the daily round of religious observations. All these functionaries received stipends from the ecclesiastical tax, the tithe. The terms *racionero* and *medio-racionero* signify that these clerics received either a full or half ration from the tithe.

The organization of the cathedral chapters in Brazil was very similar to that in Spanish America. Yet in addition to the structure seen in the Hispanic world, the Brazilian church was also divided into prelacies. There were territories within established dioceses, which functioned as proto-dioceses. For example, in 1575 the Prelacy of Rio de Janeiro was created by Pope Gregory XIII. The territory was fully subject to the bishop of Bahia, but had its own local prelate. The prelate, often called a vicar, exercised most of the functions of the bishop for the southern territories of Brazil. At the same time a prelacy was created for the far north, in Pernambuco. Both would become independent dioceses in 1676.

The parish priest might fulfill several obligations. His principal responsibility was the spiritual cure of souls. If he enjoyed an income guaranteed by the crown or by some other patron, he would be the beneficiary of that stipend, or *beneficiado*, signifying that he held his office for life. If he served as an ecclesiastical judge, whose power emanated from the bishop, the ordinary ecclesiastical judge of the diocese, he would be known as a *vicario*.

THE REGULAR CLERGY

Just as the secular clergy was divided into dioceses and grouped into provinces, so, too, was the regular clergy divided into provinces. In Mexico, the Franciscans had two. The Province of the Santo Evangelio de México encompassed the central region of the colony, mostly the dioceses of Puebla and Mexico; the Discalced Franciscans administered the Province of San Pedro y San Pablo in the western area, in the dioceses of Michoacán and Guadalajara. The Augustinians likewise had two provinces: in the west was the Province of San Nicolás Tolentino, and in the central zone was the Province of the Santísimo Nombre de Jesús. The Dominicans had a province in the central area, the Province of Santiago. In the south, in the dioceses of Oaxaca and Chiapas, there was another Dominican province, that of San Hipólito. Thus, in each instance the orders established one province in the central area and another in a more distant region. As the church developed, additional provinces were added, especially in Central America.

Likewise in South America the orders divided into provinces. The Dominicans had the Province of San Juan Bautista, serving Peru; the Province of Santa Catalina Mártir for Quito and Popayan; and the Province of San Lorenzo Mártir for Upper Peru and Río de la Plata. The Franciscans had the Province of the Twelve Apostles for Peru, the Province of San Francisco for Quito, the Province of La Santísima Trinidad for Chile, the Province of San Antonio for Upper Peru, and the Province of Santa Fe for Bogotá. Similarly the Mercedarians and Augustinians divided the region into their own provinces.

Several of the religious orders were active in Brazil. The Jesuits and the Franciscans had the longest history in the region, dating from the first decades of Portuguese occupation. Each order had one province to administer their activities in Brazil. In the seventeenth century the BENEDICTINES, Carmelites, and Trinitarians established missions, convents, and monasteries. Other orders had a smaller presence, including the CAPUCHINS, the Discalced CARMELITES, and the Oratorians. The Mercedarians and Augustinians arrived only in the eighteenth century.

NONRELIGIOUS ACTIVITIES

In addition to providing for the spiritual needs of the faithful, the church took an active role in education. While the Dominicans had established some grammar schools, as had the Franciscans, education in Ibero-America came to be dominated by the Jesuits. Three universities were founded in the mid-sixteenth century in Santo Domingo, Mexico, Peru. Most dioceses established seminaries for the secular clergy in the seventeenth century, although these relied heavily on the Jesuits.

In Brazil the Jesuits were also at the forefront of higher education. The Jesuit colleges in Bahia and Rio de Jan-

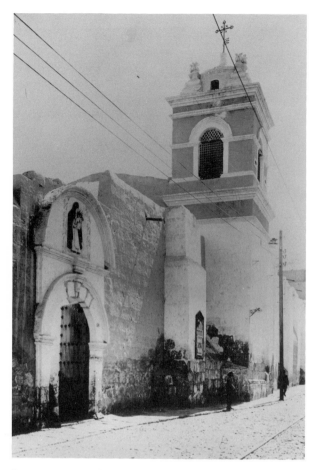

Santa Catarina Church. Arequipa, Peru. LATIN AMERICAN
LIBRARY, TULANE UNIVERSITY.

eiro were the first authorized to grant degrees and prepare students for further study at the University of
Coimbra, in Portugal. Later in the colonial period other
schools were founded by the Jesuits, Oratorians, and
local bishops, yet none was ever granted the title of
university.

The church also acted as a bank. In general, colonial
Hispanic and Portuguese America was cash poor. Many
transactions relied on credit. The principal source of
institutional credit was the church. Through the institution of pious works, and specifically chantries, CAPE-
LLANÍAS, the church acquired significant amounts of
cash which had to be loaned at interest to generate more
income. The church only loaned money when real estate
was used as collateral. The loan took the form of a mortgage or lien. The important difference was that the
church did not want, or expect, the loan to be paid off or
the mortgage amortized. The church needed the constant income to pay for her various ministries and
projects. Thus the impositions became nearly perpetual.
If an individual lacked cash but still wished to found a
capellanía, he could do one of two things: he could give
real estate to the church, which would then rent or sell

the property to generate the needed income; or he could
give part of a piece of property or voluntarily impose a
lien on a free and clear property and begin to pay the
interest, thereby donating money which he did not actually possess. This latter method provided the colonial
economy with a means of capital formation.

The secular clergy and religious orders acquired large
tracts of land. By far the leader in this regard was the
Society of Jesus (Jesuits). The religious orders depended
on the rents and revenues generated by rural and urban
property for their long-term sustenance. The only order
to eschew this practice was the Franciscans. The Franciscans found that the possession of property was antithetical to their ideal of apostolic poverty. Nevertheless,
when taken as a whole, the lands held by the church
constituted a significant portion, some estimates have
even placed it as high as a third, of the arable agricultural land of the Ibero-American colonies.

INTERNAL STRUCTURE

As the religious orders accepted sons of the local elite, a
significant change occurred in their social composition.
By the beginning of the seventeenth century, membership in the religious orders was evenly divided among
those born in Europe (PENINSULARS) and those born in
the New World (CREOLES). As the orders were largely
self-governing on the local level, the social division between peninsulars and creoles led to factionalism whenever elections were held. In order to ameliorate the
effects of this division, a system in which control would
alternate between the two factions was developed. This
system, the *alternativa,* eventually was adopted throughout most of the religious orders and also came to include the European-born Spaniards who had entered
the orders in the New World.

In the seventeenth century there were many conflicts
between the secular and regular clergy. In 1574 PHILLIP
II of Spain had decreed that all parishes would eventually be subject to the control of the seculars, but the
indigenous population was so large and the clerical
population still so small, that it was necessary to keep
the regulars in the parishes. The process through which
parishes passed from the regular to the secular clergy
was usually a bitter one and did not end until the 1740s.

The second area of conflict between the seculars and
regulars concerned the payment of the tithe. The regular clergy claimed to be exempt from payment, since the
church should not rightly tax itself. On the other hand
the local bishops felt that as long as the religious orders
did not recognize the bishop's supervisory power over
their actions in the parishes, the orders were not truly
subject to the bishop. Therefore, they had to pay the
tithe. This conflict came to a head in the diocese of Puebla, in New Spain, during the episcopacy of don Juan de
PALAFOX Y MENDOZA (*d.* 1659), when the Jesuits refused
to tithe. Eventually the religious orders accepted both
the duty to tithe and to subjugate themselves to the local
bishop.

THE CROWN VERSUS THE CLERGY

What had been a series of conflicts between the seculars and the regulars in the seventeenth century turned into an assault by the monarch on ecclesiastical privilege in the eighteenth century. The monarch favored the seculars, since under the *patronato real* he controlled the seculars far more completely. Consequently the monarch attempted to limit the independent action of the regulars or to place them firmly under the control of local bishops. There were several decrees of the early eighteenth century which placed limits on the construction of new monasteries, moratoria on entrance into the religious orders, and limits on bequests to the orders. This pattern came to a dramatic conclusion in 1767, when the crown expelled the Jesuits from the New World. (They had been expelled from Brazil in 1759–1760.) While the expulsion of the Jesuits responded to many concerns emanating from Europe, it can clearly be seen as part of a general royal attempt to bring the orders under royal authority.

The fourth provincial council of Mexico (1771) and the sixth provincial council of Peru (1772) clearly recognized the monarch's rights and privileges as patron of the church and accorded him all deference and honor, in essence making him the pope for the New World. The Mexican decrees were so excessively favorable to the monarch that they were somewhat of an embarrassment in Madrid and received neither royal nor papal approval.

The pattern of increasing royal control over the church culminated in the early nineteenth century. In 1804 the monarch called in all of the loans, liens, and mortgages extended by the church. In a desire for more capital the crown demanded the amortization of the loans and promised to pay the church the annual interest based on royal bonds, or *juros*. In 1812, in the wake of the French invasion of Spain and the flush of liberal power, the ecclesiastical *fuero*, the right of clerics to have their legal cases heard in church courts, was abolished—an act that clearly defined the clergy as just another royal bureaucracy.

MARIANO CUEVAS, *Historia de la iglesia en México*, 5 vols. (1921–1928); LEWIS HANKE, *The Spanish Struggle for Justice in the Conquest of America* (1949); ANTONINE TIBESAR, *Franciscan Beginnings in Colonial Peru* (1953); RUBÉN VARGAS UGARTE, *Historia de la iglesia en el Perú*, vols. 1 and 2 (1953–1959); LEON LOPETEGUI and ANTONIO DE EGAÑA, *Historia de la iglesia en la América española*, 2 vols. (1965–1966); ROBERT RICARD, *The Spiritual Conquest of Mexico* (1966); MICHAEL P. COSTELOE, *Church Wealth in Mexico, 1800–1856* (1967); NANCY M. FARRISS, *Crown and Clergy in Colonial Mexico, 1759–1821* (1968); EDUARDO HOORNAERT ET AL., *História da igreja no Brasil* (1977); JOHN F. SCHWALLER, *Origins of Church Wealth in Mexico* (1985) and *Church and Clergy in Sixteenth-Century Mexico* (1987); ARLINDO RUBERT, *Historia de la iglesia en Brasil* (1992).

JOHN F. SCHWALLER

See also **Anticlericalism.**

The Modern Period

The Catholic church was the most important colonial institution to survive the WARS OF INDEPENDENCE. Throughout the nineteenth and twentieth centuries the church was the principal symbol of tradition and stability in the midst of political and social change. It touched the lives of everyone, but its influence was felt most deeply among the lower classes and the rural peasantry. Religion not only offered consolation, but Sunday morning Mass or the patron saint's feast day were natural occasions to socialize or sell wares in the village plaza. But this most traditional of all institutions, after undergoing a series of prolonged crises in the post-Independence period, experienced a profound transformation in the 1960s. Since that time the church has emerged as an advocate of human rights, democracy, and social change.

INDEPENDENCE

The Wars of Independence produced internal cleavages in the ranks of the clergy. The upper clergy (which consisted of six archbishops, thirty-one bishops, and other dignitaries), most of whom were Spanish, remained loyal to the king, while large sectors of the lower clergy, most of whom were creoles, supported the insurgent movement. When independence was finally achieved, most of the bishops and many priests and religious were obliged to return to Spain. The church also contributed much of its wealth, willingly and sometimes unwillingly, to both sides.

In spite of these difficulties, the church as a whole came out of the wars relatively intact. In Mexico, Miguel HIDALGO, José María MORELOS, and other priests who fought and died for the independence of their country were considered patriots and heroes. Liberal clergymen such as Francisco Javier de LUNA PIZARRO in Peru and Deán Gregorio FUNES in Argentina helped to write the constitutions of their respective nations and played important roles in politics. Most of these liberal priests belonged to the secular clergy.

The religious clergy, which unlike the secular clergy included many Spanish missionaries in colonial times, fared less well. The liberals associated the religious orders with the old regime, and in many countries they confiscated monasteries and enacted laws severely limiting membership in the orders. As a result, the religious way of life for both men and women underwent an institutional crisis from which it did not recover until the end of the century.

RESTORATION AND ROMANIZATION
IN HISPANIC AMERICA

The major post-Independence crisis, however, concerned the episcopal vacancies. The new republican governments attempted to assume control over the church by creating a national patronage in place of the old PATRONATO REAL. But the Holy See refused to recognize these claims of the new governments. As a result, most dioceses of Spanish America remained vacant for lengthy periods. Finally, the different governments and the Holy See entered into formal agreements (concordats) or arrived at informal arrangements by which the state could name bishops, who in turn would have to be approved by Rome. By the middle of the 1830s, the episcopacy had been restored in most countries of Spanish America.

In the process, however, the Latin American church also became "romanized." If before the church was principally a Spanish church, now it became a Roman church, reorganized and centralized under the pope. Although all the new bishops were Latin Americans, Rome preferred men who were obedient to the papacy, and that implied not being sympathetic to liberalism. Allegiance to the papacy strengthened the bishops in their battle against liberalism. But overdependence on Rome also limited the church's ability to deal creatively with Latin American realities.

The bishops reopened the seminaries and standardized them according to criteria laid down in Rome. In 1858 a seminary (known as the South American College) for Latin Americans was founded in Rome. The majority of Latin America's bishops have been drawn from priests who have studied there. At the same time liberal clergymen were marginalized in the church. Rome's ties to Latin America were further strengthened when the Latin American bishops participated in the First Vatican Council (1869–1870), and again, in 1899, when the bishops attended a special plenary council for Latin America, convoked by Pope LEO XIII.

BRAZIL AND CUBA

For different reasons Brazil and Cuba escaped the general pattern for the church that emerged elsewhere in Latin America. When Brazil achieved its independence in 1822, the monarchy assumed control of national patronage of the church. As a result, the Brazilian church did not fall under Rome's direct jurisdiction until the end of the monarchy (1889). Also, liberal clergymen such as Diogo Antônio FEIJÓ, who served as regent of the empire (1835–1837), enjoyed greater freedom from Rome than their counterparts in Spanish America. The otherwise harmonious relations between PEDRO II and the church were interrupted by the "religious question" between the years of 1872 and 1875. The emperor imprisoned two bishops who followed Rome's orders forbidding Catholics to participate in Masonic activities. The provisional republican government separated the church from the state in 1890. For its part, Cuba remained under the church in Spain until its independence in 1898. After that, as in Brazil, it came under Roman jurisdiction.

THE CHURCH-LIBERAL STRUGGLE

After 1850 the liberals enacted more laws to curb the church's influence in society and to transfer its wealth and lands to the state or private hands. The church reacted by organizing the laity into associations such as the "Catholic Union" and by publishing periodicals defending its positions. The church also sought out the protection of conservative caudillos and parties, a factor that further alienated it from the progressive middle classes. The persecution against the church was especially severe in Mexico as a result of the Reform Laws and the liberal struggle for power (1857–1860) and in Ecuador under the Eloy ALFARO DELGADO regime at the turn of the century.

In the midst of the struggle with liberalism the church suffered another, more serious crisis. Beginning in the middle of the nineteenth century the number of vocations to the priesthood declined considerably, especially in countries with a small middle class or with a large indigenous population. The reasons for the decline are varied. The liberal governments cut off economic support to the church, and the conservative image the church projected did not attract vocations from progressive sectors of society. Also, the church required that candidates for the seminaries be able to read and write, a factor that disqualified the Indians and most peasants. In Peru, Bolivia, and Nicaragua, among other countries, close to 60 percent of the clergy remains foreign born.

In the second half of the nineteenth century, concerned over its waning influence in society, the church brought over many different religious orders and congregations from Europe. The Daughters of Charity, the Good Shepherd Sisters, and other similar congregations established many hospitals and charitable institutions for the poor. The JESUITS, the Sacred Heart nuns, the Ursulines, the SALESIANS, the Marists, and other teaching orders and congregations founded numerous schools, usually for the middle and upper classes, throughout all of Latin America.

POPULAR PIETY

Liberalism made many inroads among the middle classes, but it did not touch the lower classes. The church continued to exercise considerable influence among the Indians, peasants, blacks, and MESTIZOS, who made up the lower classes, especially through the many local devotions that nourished popular religiosity. Some of the more famous popular devotions are Our Lady of GUADALUPE in Mexico, The Lord of Miracles in Lima, the Virgin of LUJÁN in Argentina, Our Lady of Copacabana in Bolivia, and the *Dolorosa* of Ecuador. As a result of the spread of liberalism, many middle- and upper-class men ceased to practice their religion. The women, who did continue to practice, virtually became the mainstay of Catholicism in that social milieu.

CATHOLIC ACTION

At the behest of Pope Pius XI, nearly every local church created a national branch of CATHOLIC ACTION in the 1920s and 1930s. Catholic Action was an association of laypeople committed to the task of bringing new life to the church, defending it against its critics, and spread-

Pilgrimage, a common form of popular piety. LIBRARY OF CONGRESS; PHOTO BY JESUS NAZARENO, COLLECTED BY W. G. LELAND.

ing the church's doctrine of social justice. In Brazil, Archbishop Sebastião Leme of Rio de Janeiro became the leading promoter of Brazilian Catholic Action. In Chile, Eduardo FREI MONTALVA helped found the National Phalanx (1938), which drew together many young Christian intellectuals who were dissatisfied with the traditional church. Although not an official church organization, Frei's party (which became the Christian Democratic Party) contributed to the social awareness of Chilean Catholics. Mexico represented a unique case of Catholic Action in response to official government persecution. In reaction to the harsh ANTICLERICALISM of the Plutarco ELÍAS CALLES regime (1924–1928), many peasants led by middle-class Catholics, known as *Cristeros* (from their cry, "Long live Christ the King!"), took up arms against the central government in the CRISTERO REBELLION. But the church disavowed the movement and the *Cristeros* were forced into submission.

Most members of Catholic Action came from the urban middle classes. Some, like Jackson de FIGUEIREDO in Brazil and José de la RIVA-AGÜERO in Peru, harbored integralist and authoritarian solutions to the problems of political unrest and the spread of socialism. But others, like Frei in Chile and Victor Andrés BELAÚNDE in Peru, looked to the Western democracies as models for Latin America. Many of the leaders of Catholic Action became founders of the Christian Democratic parties.

MODERNIZATION

Although the Latin American church in general continued to be very conservative in the post–World War II period, frequently legitimizing anti-Communist dicta-torships, it was nonetheless influenced by the same tendencies and intellectual currents that had begun to affect the church in the First World. In response to the priest shortage, Pope Pius XII and his successor, John XXIII, called for missionaries from Europe and the United States to work in Latin America. Hundreds of priests, nuns, brothers, and lay volunteers from the Western democracies flocked to Latin America in the late 1950s and early 1960s, bringing with them progressive attitudes and plans for development projects. The MARYKNOLL Fathers and Sisters, the best-known American missionary society, had already arrived in Latin America in 1943.

Certain churchmen were especially influential in awakening other Catholics to the need for change. José María Cardinal Caro, archbishop of Santiago (1939–1958), fostered many social works for the poor. Juan LANDÁZURI RICKETTS, the cardinal-archbishop of Lima (1955–1990), built parishes and medical posts to aid the dwellers in the growing shantytowns. The massive migrations of the rural or mountain peasants to the big cities spurred church planners to be more innovative and creative. Other socially progressive churchmen were Dom Hélder CÂMARA of Recife, who won fame for his work among the poor; Bishop Leonidas Proanño of Riobamba, Ecuador, who was noted for his support of the peasants; and Bishop Manuel Larraín of Talca, Chile, who played a key role in preparing the way for the Medellín conference. In 1955 the bishops founded CELAM, the permanent CONFERENCE OF LATIN AMERICAN BISHOPS, for the purpose of coordinating the church's pastoral activities.

The Second Vatican Council (1962–1965) was also instrumental in changing the mentality of many Latin American Catholics. The nearly six hundred bishops of Latin America who attended the council, though they contributed little to the theological discussions, acquired a deeper sense of identity as Latin Americans.

In the wake of the CUBAN REVOLUTION, the church felt the urgency of finding social solutions to Latin America's poverty, preferably by democratic means. In 1966 Camilo TORRES RESTREPO, a Colombian priest, joined a guerrilla movement and was killed shortly afterwards. His action dramatically underlined the fact that practicing Catholics were being subjected to the same dilemmas over the use of peaceful versus violent means that were causing divisions among Latin Americans in general in those years.

MEDELLÍN

In 1968 in MEDELLÍN, Colombia, 130 bishops attended the second general assembly of the Latin American episcopate. The bishops gave the church a mandate to foster social justice and to work in solidarity with the poor. The Medellín conference constituted a dramatic change for the traditionally conservative Latin American church. The bishops were especially influenced by LIBERATION THEOLOGY, which called for the church to help the poor in their struggle to free themselves from unjust social structures. Some of the principal liberation theologians included Gustavo GUTIÉRREZ, Leonardo BOFF, Juan Luis Segundo, and Jon Sobrino. Also, the ideas of

Brazilian educator Paulo FREIRE on education as a tool of liberation influenced many church groups. The basic nucleus in which liberation theology was put into practice was the base ecclesial community. A pastoral innovation created by the Brazilian bishops, a base ecclesial community consists of a small group of people who apply the lessons of the Bible to their everyday lives and to society in general. In the wake of Medellín base ecclesial communities sprang up throughout Latin America. By 1991 in Brazil alone there were more than 150,000 of these communities.

Both Vatican Council II and the Medellín conference encouraged greater lay participation in the church. Besides forming base ecclesial communities, the laity also exercised leadership by becoming adult catechists, or delegates of the word. Other lay movements that flourished after Vatican II were the *Cursillos de Cristiandad* (weekend retreats geared originally for men), the charismatic movement, and Marriage Encounter. Religious women also changed their life-style and diversified their pastoral activities. Before Medellín most religious women taught in schools or worked in hospitals. After Medellín they expanded their activities to include work in the shantytowns, the Andes, or the Amazon jungle as catechists, community organizers, and chaplains in prisons as well as health and social advisers. The church also diversified its educational presence. While it continued to administer many *colegios* and a few universities, it also opened up numerous schools for the poor and sponsored specialized short courses for working

Religious procession in Bahia, Brazil, 1980. ORGANIZATION OF AMERICAN STATES.

adults. The *Fe y Alegría* (Faith and Joy) schools founded by the Jesuits in many Latin American countries are among the more notable of these popular educational centers.

These radical changes led to conflict between the church, on the one hand, and on the other, dictators, the political right, and most of the military regimes that came to power in the 1960s and 1970s. In sharp contrast to the past, when it supported the military and conservative groups, the church, with few exceptions, took a leading role in denouncing violations of human rights and in encouraging democratic popular participation. Relations between the military, their right-wing sympathizers, and the church were very tense, and many bishops, priests, nuns, and laypeople were executed, tortured, or imprisoned in retaliation for their critical stance. Peru and Argentina were exceptions to this rule, for different reasons. In Peru, the military under General Juan VELASCO ALVARADO were reformist and thus were supported by the church. In Argentina, where a right-wing military government (1976–1983) suppressed basic liberties and tortured and killed dissidents, the church hierarchy either sympathized with the military or maintained neutrality.

But the situation in Brazil fit the general pattern more exactly. During the period of military rule (1964–1985), the national bishops' conference fully supported the movement to return to civilian rule. Hélder Câmara, Cardinals Pablo Arns of São Paulo and Aloisio Lorscheider of Fortaleza, and Pedro Casaldáliga, a bishop in the Amazon, stood out especially for their denunciations of police and paramilitary brutality. In Chile, under the Augusto PINOCHET regime, Raúl Cardinal SILVA HENRÍQUEZ of Santiago created the VICARIATE OF SOLIDARITY, an organization intended to protect victims of political persecution and to search for missing persons. He and his successor, Juan Francisco Cardinal Fresno Larrain, were instrumental in organizing civilian opposition to the government. The church played a similar role in Bolivia, especially during the Hugo BÁNZER SUÁREZ and Luis GARCÍA MESA governments, and in Paraguay under Alfredo STROESSNER.

In Central America and in the Caribbean, Catholics also stood out for their progressive positions. Nicaragua provided the most dramatic example of Catholic participation in a revolution. Early on a moderate sector led by Archbishop Miguel OBANDO Y BRAVO of Managua took a critical stance regarding the Anastasia SOMOZA regime, and more radical Catholics from the base ecclesial communities, including many priests, actively fought with the SANDINISTAS to overthrow the dictator. After the revolution, however, the church was sharply divided. A few priests, notably Ernesto CARDENAL, Miguel D'Escoto, and Fernando Cardenal, held important posts in the Sandinista government, much to the displeasure of the pope and Miguel Cardinal OBANDO. In 1980 unknown assassins shot and killed Bishop Oscar ROMERO of El Salvador. Romero, a leading critic of the military's excesses, be-

came the most celebrated martyr bishop in Latin America. In Haiti, Jean-Bertrand ARISTIDE, a priest influenced by liberation theology, was elected president of the country in 1990. After the Cuban revolution, the church vehemently opposed the Castro regime, and many priests went into exile. The government in turn marginalized the church from public affairs. After Medellín, however, the church sought to end its isolation by becoming a part of mainstream life on the island. By the middle of the 1980s, the state and the church had arrived at a mutually acceptable modus vivendi.

During the third general meeting of the bishops in Puebla, Mexico, in 1979, tensions surfaced between progressives and conservatives. Pope John Paul II, elected in 1978, inaugurated the Puebla conference, and during the next decade he visited nearly every Latin American country. Everywhere he was received by enthusiastic crowds. He lent support to the bishops who were critical of liberation theology and other changes in the church. As a result, progressive-conservative tensions have loomed over church discussions since the Puebla conference.

GENERAL STATISTICS
The percentage of Catholics in Latin America averages between 85 percent and 92 percent. In most countries, however, only about 10 percent of Catholics regularly attend church services. In 1988 there were 1,030 Catholic bishops in Latin America, 52,452 priests, 125,895 religious women, and 8,663 religious men (brothers). The average number of Catholics per priest is slightly more than 7,000. At one extreme is Chile (1 to every 4,965), at the other, Nicaragua (1 to every 10,653).

J. LLOYD MECHAM, *Church and State in Latin America*, 2d ed. (1966); ROBERT E. QUIRK, *The Mexican Revolution and the Catholic Church, 1910–1929* (1973); PENNY LERNOUX, *Cry of the People: U.S. Involvement in the Rise of Fascism* (1980); ENRIQUE DUSSEL, *A History of the Church in Latin America* (1981); BRIAN H. SMITH, *The Church and Politics in Chile: Challenges to Modern Catholicism* (1982); PHILLIP BERRYMAN, *The Religious Roots of Rebellion: Christians in Central American Revolutions* (1984); EDWARD L. CLEARY, *Crisis and Change: The Church in Latin America Today* (1985); DANIEL H. LEVINE, ed., *Religion and Political Conflict in Latin America* (1986); SCOTT MAINWARING, *The Catholic Church and Politics in Brazil, 1916–1985* (1986); JOHN M. KIRK, *Between God and the Party: Religion and Politics in Revolutionary Cuba* (1989); SCOTT MAINWARING and ALEXANDER WILDE, eds., *The Progressive Church in Latin America* (1989); JEFFREY L. KLAIBER, *The Church in Peru: A Social History, 1821–1985* (1992).

JEFFREY KLAIBER

CATURLA, ALEJANDRO GARCÍA. *See* **García Caturla, Alejandro.**

CAUCA RIVER, Colombia's second longest river. The Cauca flows northward some 838 miles from its origin south of Popayán to its entrance into the MAGDALENA

RIVER at Pinillos, in the department of Bolívar. The waterway is comprised by three zones. The first, which defines the rich agricultural area of the CAUCA VALLEY, is readily navigable. From here, the river then descends into the largely impassable "Cauca Canyon" (a source of gold in the colonial period) through the departments of Caldas, Risaralda, and Antioquia until reaching the town of Valdivia. Its fertile second valley merges into a vast swamp before joining the Magdalena basin, the third zone, a desolated region until the development of a coffee-based economy in the early twentieth century.

During the colonial period, the upper valley's cattle haciendas and tobacco production supplemented the gold-mining activities of the region's economy, products augmented by sugar and coffee production in the late nineteenth century. The region around CALI contains one of Colombia's most diversified and dynamic economic centers.

DAVID BUSHNELL, *The Making of Modern Colombia: A Nation in Spite of Itself* (1993).

DAVID SOWELL

CAUCA VALLEY, an inland valley of southwestern Colombia between the western and central chains of the Andes. It is the site of one of Colombia's most developed networks of urban centers, with Cartago at the northern end and Cali, the main urban center of the valley, at the southern end. No other area of Colombia can boast such a significant network of middle-sized urban centers.

Considered one of the most fertile plains in Latin America, the region was stagnant economically for centuries and absent from participation in the world market. The opening of the PANAMA CANAL, however, provided the impetus for economic transformation. Growth was further stimulated by the phenomenal sugar cane boom of 1930–1980, which transformed the inefficient haciendas into the large-scale sugar agribusinesses of today—a process that, unfortunately, provoked a certain amount of violence in the 1940s and 1950s. In the 1950s the entrepreneurial elite of Cali provided another economic boost by promoting the creation of a regional development corporation modeled after the Tennessee Valley Authority—the Corporación autónoma regional del Valle del Cauca (CVC)—which has been instrumental in promoting electrification, dam construction, and land reclamation.

RAYMOND E. CRIST, *The Cauca Valley, Colombia: Land Tenure and Land Use* (1952); RICHARD P. HYLAND, *El crédito y la economía, 1851–1880. Vol. IV, Sociedad y economía en el Valle del Cauca* (1983); JOSÉ MARÍA ROJAS, *Empresarios y Tecnología en la Formación del Sector Azucarero en Colombia, 1860–1980. Vol. V, Sociedad y economía en el Valle del Cauca* (1983).

JOSÉ ESORCIA

CAUDILLISMO, CAUDILLO, an authoritarian form of leadership common throughout the history of the Hispanic world. Among the Spanish words for leader is *caudillo*, which derives from the Latin *capitellum*, the diminutive of *caput* (head). Although it is common to think of caudillos in the context of Spanish America, the prototypes are deep in the Iberian past.

Caudillismo is often narrowly interpreted to apply mainly to those leaders who emerged in the newly independent republics. There are, however, so many who deserve the name "caudillo"—from Pelayo (the eighth-century Asturian chieftain) to Augusto PINOCHET—that it is too limiting to direct attention only to an early-nineteenth-century "Age of Caudillos." It is, nevertheless, important to employ qualifiers when dealing with individuals. Although caudillos are often military men, there are civilians like Gabriel GARCÍA MORENO of Ecuador, who might be called "theocratic," and Rafael NÚÑEZ of Colombia, who was a lawyer, career politician, and poet. Many caudillos acquired sobriquets that set them apart. José Gaspar FRANCIA of Paraguay was "El Supremo," Plutarco Elías CALLES of Mexico was called "El Jefe Máximo" (the Ultimate Chief), Juan Vicente GÓMEZ of Venezuela carried the nickname "El Bagre" (the Catfish), and Alfredo STROESSNER was known to his foes in Paraguay as "El Tiranosauro."

The variety of caudillos is practically endless, but certain common qualities help distinguish them from other leaders: a personalist rapport with followers, the ability to create reciprocal advantages between leaders and the led, a combination of charisma and machismo, and access to political and economic power are fundamental characteristics. In a controversial book Glen Dealy argues that "public men" in Catholic societies—particularly in Latin America—surround themselves first with their family and *compadrazgo* (godparent) relations and then concentrically with aggregates of friends, who are more important to them than wealth. The Dominican Republic's Rafael TRUJILLO, "The Benefactor," arranged to be the *compadre* (godfather) at the baptism of thousands of babies to enhance his power.

Some caudillos were actually manipulated by elites, and only seemed to be dominant. Martín GÜEMES of Salta, in what later became Argentina, was a regional caudillo during the Independence wars (1810–1821) who prospered as long as he served the interests of his extended family, and was destroyed when he deviated.

Many caudillos have understood the value of ceremony and the need to look the part of a dominant personality, often in uniform, whether on horseback, in the back of an open limousine, or on a balcony. Part of this theatrical display and attendant propaganda is designed to fill the vacuum of moral authority lost in Spanish America with the end of the empire. From the days of Hernán Cortés to the present, caudillos have sought legitimacy. Peter Smith (whose essay is included in this author's edited work, *Caudillos*) examines Max Weber's criteria for legitimacy—"traditional," "legal," and "charismatic"—and then adds two of his own: "dominance" and "achievement-expertise," or the technical ability to solve a nation's problems. Chile's Augusto Pinochet skillfully manipulated the military's hierarchy and the traditions of the country's presidency to ensconce himself in power for fifteen years (1973–1988) before the democratic process reasserted itself. Many caudillos cleverly utilized rigged elections, plebiscites, and constitutional amendments to extend themselves in power in a process called CONTINUISMO. Anastasio "Tacho" SOMOZA and his two sons were particularly adept at this in Nicaragua, and managed for a time to overcome the problem of political succession that has plagued most caudillos. That such undemocratic maneuvers often succeeded suggests that caudillismo does not necessarily always carry a pejorative connotation within the culture. On the contrary, José de Palafox, a hero of Spanish resistance against the French in 1808, was called "El Caudillo Palafox," and Francisco Franco, the victor in the Spanish Civil War (1936–1939) and autocrat of Spain until his death in 1975, proudly dubbed himself "El Caudillo."

Military dependency has been widespread among caudillos, but it is not universal. Antonio López de SANTA ANNA of Mexico, Francisco Solano LÓPEZ in Paraguay, and Marcos PÉREZ JIMÉNEZ of Venezuela banked heavily on their armies. But adroit politicians like Porfirio DÍAZ in Mexico recognized that a strong army might threaten their power and thus played generals against each other and against civilian factions and corporations. Díaz, for example, expanded a paramilitary force called the RURALES to parry the army's pretensions. Juan PERÓN sought to broaden his support beyond the military in Argentina by cultivating labor.

Caudillos have often been characterized by their violence, intimidation of their enemies, and the use of torture. Resort to such practices is a function of the problem of succession. Caudillos most often have come to power through coups d'état, and are conscious of the fact that the "out" factions are waiting—usually in exile—for an opportunity to repeat the process. Vigilance, oppression, and wealth from Venezuelan oil wells helped the notorious Juan Vicente GÓMEZ to remain in power from 1908 to 1935. He died of old age. One of the most vicious of caudillos was Manuel ESTRADA CABRERA of Guatemala (1898–1920), who became the model for the novel *El señor presidente* by the Nobel laureate Miguel Ángel Asturias.

In historical perspective caudillismo—already well developed in the reconquest of the Iberian Peninsula—arrived in the Americas with the explorers and conquistadores. Bands were almost always centered about leaders like Cortés and Francisco Pizarro. The mutual reliance of followers and their chiefs was always dependent upon *caudillaje*, the essence of close personal ties. These relationships, however, were often tenuous—witness the difficulties that Cortés had with the followers of Governor Diego Velázquez in Cuba and the factional divisions that beset Pizarro. Once the goals of conquest were achieved, the sometime soldiers quickly dispersed and settled down or returned to Spain as civilians to enjoy the fruits of their victories.

As the colonial era developed, it was local political bosses or caciques who tended to characterize leadership. They could be bureaucrats, *hacendados*, miners, merchants, militia officers, or priests as well as bandits and peasant leaders. These frequently formed personalist networks to which they turned after Napoleon's invasion of Spain in 1808 broke down the royal mechanisms to resolve disputes among colonial factions. These caciques moved into the political vacuums everywhere evident in the Independence wars, and some rose to national caudillo status.

New constitutional forms in the early republics lacked the moral authority once associated with the crown. The ambitious caudillos who emerged had their own agendas or *pronunciamientos* in which ideology was less important than the degree of stability and economic control a given leader might guarantee his supporters. Some used liberalism as an excuse to exploit the communal property of indigenous peoples, while others, like José Rafael CARRERA of Guatemala, became what E. Bradford Burns calls "folk caudillos" bent upon preserving traditional patterns of property and institutions.

Weak states and powerful regions so characterized mid-nineteenth-century Spanish America that later caudillos like Rafael Núñez abandoned federalism in favor of recentralizing authority.

Caudillismo since 1900 has been an uneven but persistent phenomenon. Countries like Costa Rica and Venezuela (after Pérez Jiménez left in 1958) have had little recent experience with caudillos. Mexico has developed the dominant party to replace the dominant individual. But Cuba (with Fulgencio BATISTA and Fidel CASTRO), Panama (with Omar TORRIJOS and Manuel NORIEGA), the Dominican Republic (with Trujillo and Joaquín BALAGUER), Paraguay (chiefly with Stroessner), and Argentina (with Perón and a succession of military strongmen), as well as Chile, have had their histories punctuated by caudillos during the middle and later decades of the twentieth century.

For a comprehensive guide to the interpretive and illustrative literature on caudillismo, see HUGH M. HAMILL, ed., *Caudillos: Dictators in Spanish America* (1992), and JOHN LYNCH, *Caudillos in Spanish America, 1800–1850* (1992). Efforts to explain caudillismo include PETER H. SMITH, "Political Legitimacy in Spanish America," in *New Approaches to Latin American History*, edited by Richard Graham and Peter Smith (1974); GLENN CAUDILL DEALY, *The Public Man: An Interpretation of Latin American and Other Catholic Countries* (1977); and TORCUATO S. DI-TELLA, *Latin American Politics: A Theoretical Framework* (1990). ROBERT L. GILMORE makes a useful distinction in his *Caudillism and Militarism in Venezuela, 1810–1910* (1964). A Chilean woman's view of caudillismo is in ISABELLE ALLENDE's novel *The House of the Spirits*, translated by Magda Bogin (1985). JOHN HOYT WILLIAMS treats Francia, Carlos Antonio López, and his son, Francisco Solano López, in *The Rise and Fall of the Para-*

guayan Republic, 1800–1870 (1979). A sample of the massive literature on individual caudillos includes ROGER M. HAIGH, *Martín Güemes: Tyrant or Tool? A Study of the Sources of Power of an Argentine Caudillo* (1968); HOWARD J. WIARDA, *Dictatorship and Development: The Methods of Control in Trujillo's Dominican Republic* (1968); JOHN LYNCH, *Argentine Dictator: Juan Manuel de Rosas, 1829–1852* (1981); JOSEPH A. PAGE, *Perón: A Biography* (1983); JAMES WILLIAM PARK, *Rafael Núñez and the Politics of Colombian Regionalism, 1863–1886* (1985); GENARO ARRIAGADA, *Pinochet: The Politics of Power,* translated by Nancy A. Morris, Vincent Ercolano, and Kristen A. Whitney (1988); SEBASTIAN BALFOUR, *Castro* (1990); and CARLOS R. MIRANDA, *The Stroessner Era: Authoritarian Rule in Paraguay* (1990); RALPH LEE WOODWARD, JR., *Rafael Carrera and the Emergence of the Republic of Guatemala, 1821–1871* (1993).

HUGH M. HAMILL

CAUPOLICÁN (*d.* 1558), ARAUCANIAN warrior and hero. The cacique of Palmaiquén, he was active in the Araucanian resistance to the Spanish conquistadores from

Statue of Caupolicán, Santa Lucía, Chile. ORGANIZATION OF AMERICAN STATES.

early on. He rose to prominence among his people after the death of LAUTARO (April 1557), when he was chosen as TOQUI (chief). He was a principal adversary of the newly arrived Spanish governor García HURTADO DE MENDOZA (1535–1609). Caupolicán's attacks on the new governor's hastily constructed fort near Concepción were repulsed. The Spaniards, now reinforced, defeated the Araucanians at the battles of Lagunillas (or Bío-bío) and Millarapue in November 1557. Caupolicán rejected all Hurtado de Mendoza's offers of peace. In mid-1558 a Spanish captain, Alonso de Reinoso, organized a surprise raid on the *toqui's* encampment at Palmaiquén and succeeded in capturing him. A woman, presumably his wife, revealed his identity to the Spaniards by reproaching him for being taken alive and dashing her infant son to the ground. (The name traditionally given to her, Fresia, is probably an invention of the poet Alonso de ERCILLA Y ZÚÑIGA.) Reinoso took Caupolicán back to the newly founded settlement at Cañete, where he was executed by impalement. He is remembered as second only to Lautaro among the Araucanian heroes of the sixteenth century.

SIMON COLLIER

See also **Araucana, La.**

CAVALCANTI, NEWTON (*b.* 1930), Brazilian engraver and illustrator. Although born in Pernambuco and trained in Europe, Cavalcanti moved in 1952 to Rio de Janeiro, where he met the Brazilian metal engraver Raimudo Cela. In 1954 he studied wood engraving at the National School of Fine Arts in Rio de Janeiro under Oswaldo Goeldi. Along with fellow Pernambucan Gilvan Samico, Cavalcanti dedicated himself to xylography, the art of wood-block printing. Cavalcanti's woodcuts and wood engravings focused mainly upon themes from the legends, myths, and stories of Brazil's Northeast. Lyrical, grotesque, and fantastic animals and saints drift in and out of his nearly monochromatic green and black compositions. Examples of this style include *The System of the Doctor* and *The Counselor.* In 1960 he accepted a position teaching printmaking at the Educational Center in Niterói. Although best known for his graphic art, Cavalcanti has also produced illustrated books and has worked on film projects.

DAWN ADES, *Art in Latin America* (1989), p. 342.

CAREN A. MEGHREBLIAN

CAVALLÓN, JUAN DE (*b.* 1524; *d.* 1565), first conqueror of Costa Rica during the early 1560s. Although largely unsuccessful on his own, his invasion from Nicaragua in 1561 both set in motion the process and established the mechanisms by which subordinates such as Juan Vázquez de CORONADO would conquer the province. Cavallón held a licenciate in law and came from Castillo de Garcimuñoz, Cuenca, New Castile. He married Leonor de Barahona, the daughter of one of CORTÉS's associates in the conquest of Mexico. He was named *alcalde mayor* of Nicoya in the 1550s. From this base he led 80 to 90 men, recruited in Guatemala in 1560, as an expeditionary force to claim the province of Costa Rica.

In January 1561 the force left its base and landed on the coast near the modern port of Puntarenas. They attempted to establish two settlements, Landecho as a port and Castillo de Garcimuñoz further inland, but both soon failed. Relations with the Indians deteriorated quickly as their leader, Garabito, organized resistance to Cavallón's requisitioning of corn supplies. Cavallón financed this expedition in association with the Franciscan priest Juan de Estrada Rávago, a native of Guadalajara, New Castile, long resident in the Salvadoran Indian parishes of the cacao-rich Izalco district. Cavallón claimed to have lost nine thousand pesos of his own funds in the enterprise, and Estrada may have invested six or seven thousand. Estrada also undertook an expedition along the Atlantic coast, in coordination with Cavallón's march from the Pacific side, but with even more dismal results.

Cavallón was named *fiscal* of the AUDIENCIA in Guatemala in 1562 and left Estrada in charge of a rapidly declining force. Estrada also left Costa Rica, returning eventually to Spain, but several members of the conquering band remained to claim positions and ENCOMIENDAS after the more lasting conquest expedition of Vázquez de Coronado in 1563.

The best sources of Cavallón's exploits in Costa Rica are those of CARLOS MELÉNDEZ CHAVERRI: *Conquistadores y pobladores: Orígines histórico-sociales de los costarricenses* (1982), and *Juan Vázquez de Coronado, conquistador y fundador de Costa Rica,* 2d ed. (1972).

LOWELL GUDMUNDSON

CAVIEDES, JUAN DEL VALLE Y (*b.* 1650?; *d.* 1697), Peruvian poet. Very little is known of the early life of this foremost writer except that he was born in Andalusia, migrated to Peru at an early age, and kept a small shop in Lima. Although manuscripts of his work circulated during his lifetime, no printed editions appeared until the nineteenth century.

Caviedes's early work consists primarily of love lyrics and religious and philosophical poems, but his best talent is revealed in his satirical verse, which ridicules the superstitious, irrational Peruvian society and in particular the pretentious pseudoscience of the medical profession, as well as the corruption of the viceregal court. He describes one collection of his poems as a revelation of "deeds of ignorance brought to light by a patient who miraculously escaped from the errors of the physicians," and another as dedicated to social climbers who profess saintliness, learning, or nobility in order to secure status and wealth. The directness of his satire contrasts strongly with the artificiality of most literature of the seventeenth century.

DANIEL R. REEDY, *The Poetic Art of Juan del Valle y Caviedes* (1964); JULIE G. JOHNSON, "Three Dramatic Works by Juan del Valle y Caviedes," in *Hispanic Journal* 3 (1981): 59–71; JAMES HIGGINS, *A History of Peruvian Literature* (1987), esp. pp. 48–54.

JOHN R. FISHER

CAXIAS, DUQUE DE. *See* **Lima e Silva, Luis Alves de.**

CAYENNE, BRAZILIAN INVASION OF. On 22 March 1808, Portuguese forces, aided by the British, invaded the French colony of Cayenne in retaliation for the French invasion of Portugal in 1807. The original purpose of the mission under the count of Linhares was to completely destroy the colony. In May 1809 Dom João (later JOÃO VI) made the decision to keep the colony and to build it up for trade and military purposes. With Manuel Marques serving as intendent and Maciel da Costa as civilian administrator, Portuguese rule was relatively enlightened and accepted by the French colonists. However, European powers at the Congress of Vienna forced the return of Cayenne to the French on 8 November 1817.

PEDRO CALMON, *A história do Brasil*, vol. 4, (1963), pp. 1419–1420; SÉRGIO BUARQUE DE HOLLANDA, ed., *História geral da civilização brasileira*, vol. 1, no. 2, (1963), pp. 283–299; *South American Handbook*, 67th ed. (1991), p. 1125.

ROBERT A. HAYES

CAYMAN ISLANDS, a British dependency in the Caribbean located south of Cuba and northwest of Jamaica. Consisting of the islands of Grand Cayman, Cayman Brac, and Little Cayman, the territory covers an area of about 100 square miles. Sighted by Christopher Columbus in 1503, the island group was named Las Tortugas on account of its native sea turtles. By 1530 the name "Caimanas," or "Caymans," derived from a word meaning crocodile in the language of the Caribs, early island visitors, came into acceptance. Permanent settlers arrived after the Treaty of MADRID (1670), by which Spain recognized English claims to these islands in exchange for restraint of pirates whose haunts included the Caymans. From 1863 to 1959, the Cayman Islands were officially a dependency of Jamaica. Upon Jamaican independence in 1962, they chose to remain a British Crown Colony. Since the Constitution of 1972 was implemented, the Caymans have been internally autonomous under an appointed governor. Aided by government promotion, TOURISM has become a major industry. Offshore finance, another industry of recent prominence, developed in response to banking confidentiality legislation and the absence of direct taxation, making the Caymans an international financial center, host to over 500 banks and trust companies.

GEORGE S. S. HIRST, *Notes on the History of the Cayman Islands* (1910; repr. 1967); H. B. L. HUGHES, "Notes on the Cayman Islands," in *Jamaican Historical Review* 1, no. 2 (1946): 154–158; NEVILLE WILLIAMS, *A History of the Cayman Islands* (1970); BRIAN UZZELL, ed., *The Cayman Islands Yearbook and Business Directory* (annual).

PAULA S. GIBBS

CAYMMI, DORIVAL (*b.* 1914), Brazilian songwriter. Beginning in the 1930s, Salvador-born Caymmi composed a wide variety of highly successful tunes that explored Bahian and Afro-Brazilian culture and were popularized by singers such as Carmen Miranda, Anjos do Inferno, Ângela Maria, João GILBERTO, Elis Regina, Gal Costa, Gilberto Gil, and Caetano Veloso, as well as by foreign interpreters such as Andy Williams and Paul Winter. Caymmi worked in many different musical styles, including SAMBAS, *marchas, toadas, modinhas, canções praieiras* (fishermen's songs), *cocos, sambas de roda,* and *pontos de candomblé* (CANDOMBLÉ invocations). Like novelist Jorge AMADO, with whom he composed "É doce morrer no mar" (It's Sweet to Die in the Sea), he is closely identified with Bahian culture.

Caymmi gained fame with "O que é que a baiana tem?" (What Is It That the Baiana's Got?), sung by Carmen Miranda in the films *Banana da terra* (1938) and *Greenwich Village* (1944); Caymmi recorded a duet with the actress in 1939. Other Caymmi standards include: "Samba da minha terra" (Samba of My Land), "Marina," "Nem eu" (Me Neither), "Saudade de Itapoã," "Oração de mae menininha" (a tribute to a famed *mae-de-santo* in Salvador), "Rosa morena," "Saudade da Bahia," "João Valentão," "Requebre que eu dou um doce," "Doralice," "Das rosas," and "Promessa de pescador" (Promise of a Fisherman). His three children (singer Nana, singer-songwriter Dori, and flutist-composer Danilo) are also musicians.

DORIVAL CAYMMI, *Cancioneiro da Bahia* (1978); RITA CAÚRIO, ed., *Brasil Musical* (1988); CHRIS MC GOWAN and RICARDO PESSANHA, *The Brazilian Sound: Samba, Bossa Nova, and the Popular Music of Brazil* (1991).

CHRIS MCGOWAN

CAZNEAU, WILLIAM LESLIE (*b.* 5 October 1807; *d.* 7 January 1876), a wealthy Texan and supporter of William WALKER's filibustering scheme in Nicaragua. As an expansionist in the 1840s, Cazneau encouraged the annexation of Cuba and Mexico's northern states to the United States. Subsequently, he fought in the MEXICAN-AMERICAN WAR (1846–1848), for which he received the rank of general. In 1853 Secretary of State William L. Marcy appointed Cazneau special minister to Santo Domingo to negotiate a commercial treaty and to obtain Samaná Bay as a coaling station. The mission failed, and Cazneau returned to the United States in 1855. In 1856, he contracted with Walker to send one thousand colonists to Nicaragua within a year to be established in settlements of not fewer than fifty families, each settler to be given title to eighty acres of land. In return, Cazneau was to receive a considerable land grant. The effort failed with Walker's ouster from Nicaragua in May 1857.

SUMNER WELLES, *Naboth's Vineyard: The Dominican Republic, 1844–1924,* 2 vols. (1928); CHARLES C. TANSILL, *The United States and Santo Domingo, 1798–1873* (1938); ROBERT E. MAY, "Lobbyists for Commercial Empire: Jane Cazneau, William Cazneau, and U.S. Caribbean Policy, 1846–1878," *Pacific Historical Review* 48 (1979): 383–412.

THOMAS M. LEONARD

CEARÁ, a state of northeastern Brazil. Covering 58,150 square miles, Ceará has a population of 6,401,000 (1989 est.). Its capital is FORTALEZA. Partly on the sandy coastal plain and partly on semiarid uplands, Ceará suffers periodic droughts. The state is economically reliant upon COTTON, SUGAR, TOBACCO, carnauba wax, and other agricultural products. Rural poverty is widespread.

The French presence among Indian populations inhibited early Portuguese settlement of the area, but ranchers pressed into the interior during the 1600s. Occupied by the Dutch from 1637 until 1654, the region was part of MARANHÃO until 1680, when it became a dependency of PERNAMBUCO. Ceará became an independent captaincy in 1799, a province of the empire in 1822, and a state of the republic in 1889.

In the 1700s, the economy centered on cattle ranching and sugar. In the 1800s, long-staple cotton rose to prominence, particularly during the American Civil War. Ceará's unprecedented prosperity, resulting from a surge in cotton exports, ended with a severe drought in 1877–1879. The drought overwhelmed attempts to provide relief, and an estimated 200,000–500,000 people died of starvation and disease. Roughly 30–50 percent of Ceará's population emigrated or perished.

By 1880, property had been devastated throughout the Northeast, and slaves were virtually the only negotiable commodity. Many slaves were shipped south in exchange for food and in order to conserve local food supplies. Since the 1860s and perhaps earlier, free workers had performed most of Ceará's agricultural labor, but access to southern markets bolstered slave prices. In the early 1880s, laws restricting interprovincial slave trading undercut slaves' value in Ceará. Abolitionism gained momentum, and the province abolished slavery in 1884, four years before the national emancipation law. Ceará's action served a symbolic function for abolitionism elsewhere in Brazil.

Between 1877 and 1915, four major droughts struck Ceará, prompting massive migrations of SERTANEJOS (inhabitants of the interior). Some fled to cities within Ceará, while others were attracted to coffee production in the south and work in the rubber tree forests of Amazonas and Pará. Although Ceará's government collected a head tax on emigrants, the loss of manpower resulted in a chronic labor shortage lasting into the 1920s. Economic hardships of this period also abetted the coalescence of *sertanejos* around Padre Cícero Romão Batista of Joaseiro (now JUAZEIRO DO NORTE). Padre Cícero held sway over much of the state from the mid 1910s until his death in 1934.

Droughts continue to wreak havoc in the region. The federal government has sponsored construction of numerous dams, but irrigation networks remain inadequate. Heavy out-migration to the Amazon Basin and to southeastern commercial and industrial centers continues.

RALPH DELLA CAVA, *Miracle at Joaseiro* (1970); ROBERT CONRAD, *The Destruction of Brazilian Slavery, 1850–1888* (1972).

CARA SHELLY

See also **Messianic Movements: Brazil; Slavery: Brazil; Slave Trade.**

CEDEÑO, JUAN MANUEL (*b.* 1914), Panamanian painter. Cedeño studied under Humberto IVALDI and Roberto LEWIS at the Escuela Nacional de Pintura in Panama and at the Chicago Art Institute (B.F.A., 1948). His role as an educator is one of his greatest contributions to Panama. He was director of his alma mater, in 1952 renamed the Escuela Nacional de Artes Plásticas (1948–1967) and professor at the University of Panama (1967–1978).

In his work with local folklore themes, Cedeño was one of the first Panamanian artists to experiment with the geometrization of forms derived from cubism and futurism, as in *Domingo de Ramos* (1955). Although he also paints landscapes and still lifes, he is best known for his many commissioned portraits, for example, *Octavio Méndez Pereira* (1950).

MÓNICA KUPFER, ed., *Exposición Retrospectiva de la obra de Juan Manuel Cedeño* (1983); P. PADROS, *Exposición Maestros-Maestros* (1987).

MONICA E. KUPFER

CEDILLO MARTÍNEZ, SATURNINO (*b.* 29 November 1890; *d.* 11 January 1939), Mexican politician and rebel leader. An important revolutionary general and the regional boss of the state of San Luis Potosí, Cedillo led the last military rebellion against the government in the post-Revolutionary period and was killed in battle.

Born at Rancho de Palomas, Ciudad del Maíz, San Luis Potosí, the son of landowning peasants, he obtained a primary school education. He joined the Maderistas, but later, with his brothers Magdaleno and Cleofas, he sided with Emiliano ZAPATA and fought against MADERO on the side of Pascual OROZCO in 1912. He was captured and imprisoned. He later joined the Constitutionalists, but abandoned Venustiano CARRANZA to support the Plan of

Agua Prieta in 1920. He remained in the army, holding top military commands, and supported the government against rebel causes in 1923 and 1929. After serving as governor of his home state, he provided decisive peasant support for Lázaro CÁRDENAS's presidential candidacy in 1934, for which he was rewarded with the post of secretary of agriculture (1935). He broke with the president in 1937, leaving the cabinet. He then organized his supporters into a small army and opposed the Cárdenas government.

NATHANIEL WEYL and SYLVIA WEYL, *The Reconquest of Mexico: The Years of Lázaro Cárdenas* (1939).

RODERIC AI CAMP

CÉDULA, legislation signed, at least in theory, by the ruling monarch of Castile. A *cédula* or *real cédula* was a form of legislation issued by the sovereign to dispense an appointment or favor, resolve a question, or require some action. When solicited from America it was a *cédula de parte*. When initiated by the Council of the Indies, it was a *cédula de oficio*. A *cédula* began with the heading *El Rey* or *La Reina* and was signed by the monarch or in his or her name. As a direct communication from the monarch, a *cédula* took precedence over royal decrees or orders issued by the Council of the Indies or royal ministers.

Diccionario de la lengua española, 18th ed. (1956).

MARK A. BURKHOLDER

CEIBO (seibo), *Erythrina crista-galli*, a tree common in well-watered areas of central and northern Argentina. The cockspur coral tree or cockspur coral bean tree is bushy and thorny, with wide, lustrous, dark green leaves about four inches long and three inches wide. It sprouts bright red blooms and beanlike pods. It generally grows to twenty or thirty feet in height but can reach eighty feet. Residents of the Río de la Plata developed many medicinal uses for the tree, including bathing wounds, gargling, and treating hemorrhoids.

FÉLIX COLUCCIO, *Diccionario Folklórico argentino*, vol. 1 (1964), pp. 75–76.

RICHARD W. SLATTA

CELAM. *See* **Conference of Latin American Bishops.**

CELAYA, BATTLES OF, the critical encounters in central Mexico between Venustiano CARRANZA's Constitutionalist forces and Francisco VILLA's Division of the North. The two battles of Celaya turned the course of the revolution in favor of the Carrancistas.

The Constitutionalists, commanded by Álvaro OBREGÓN, met the Division of the North at Celaya, Guanajuato, on 6 April 1915. Villa used his predictable but effective tactic of relentless cavalry assaults against Obregón's fortified positions. After Villa's forces exhausted themselves, Obregón attacked Villa's flanks and repulsed the Division of the North, which suffered heavy casualties and captives. Villa attempted a second assault on Celaya on 13 April. Using the same tactics, he again met defeat with many casualties. As in the first encounter, Obregón's casualties were remarkably light.

Obregón's victories of Celaya are attributed to Villa's poor planning, faulty supply lines, ammunition shortages, and inaccurate and inefficient use of artillery; rain and mud, which slowed Villa's assaults; the professionalism of the Constitutionalist forces and the soundness of Obregón's tactics; and division and dissension among Villa's officers.

After defeating Villa at Celaya, Obregón pushed further north. In May 1915 he defeated Villa's rejuvenated and resupplied army at León. A month later, Obregón routed the Division of the North at Aguascalientes. By July 1915 the once invincible Villistas were reduced to small guerrilla bands in northern Mexico. In contrast, Obregón's popularity and power increased within the Constitutionalist movement.

CHARLES C. CUMBERLAND, *Mexican Revolution: The Constitutionalist Years* (1972), pp. 200–201; ALAN KNIGHT, *The Mexican Revolution.* Vol. 2, *Counter-Revolution and Reconstruction* (1986), pp. 322–325; JOHN MASON HART, *Revolutionary Mexico: The Coming and Process of the Mexican Revolution* (1987), p. 311.

AARON PAINE MAHR

CEMPOALA (Zempoala), one of several Totonac states located near Veracruz Vieja, where Cortés's expedition disembarked to penetrate central Mexico. It contained a large population (20,000–30,000 tributaries) clustered around a ceremonial center. Cempoala had just recently been conquered by the AZTECS, and the people rankled at the empire's tribute demands. Cortés therefore found them willing allies. The Spanish had to protect Cempoala from Aztec retribution. In 1520 Cempoala was swept by a smallpox epidemic that left virtually no survivors. The remaining population was congregated in a neighboring town in 1569.

PETER GERHARD, *A Guide to the Historical Geography of New Spain* (1972).

JOHN E. KICZA

See also **Totonaco.**

CENSORSHIP. To sketch a historical context for understanding censorship in Latin America, we must begin by defining the term. Better yet, by providing competing conceptions of censorship, crucial issues involved in debates concerning freedom of the press will emerge. Essentially, two points of view predominate. On the one hand, the liberal-pluralist stance understands censor-ship in a relatively narrow manner and focuses on whether or not there are any formal impediments to the exercise of free expression by the media. The other view is broader and implies a more nuanced conception of mass communication: regardless of whether the media are privately owned or government-controlled, the notion of censorship is related to the degree of access available to the population, either as individual citizens or as members of interest groups, and to their potential capacity to define public issues. Thus, in addition to legal and formal obstacles to free expression, informal means of restricting access to the public sphere may also be considered forms of censorship.

Both formal and informal censorship practices have existed since early colonial times in what today is Latin America. Actually, in precolonial civilizations, like the Maya and the Inca, the definition of the social order was the exclusive privilege of the ruling elites. But since we are considering censorship in relation to mass communication, whose origin we (somewhat Eurocentrically) associate with the invention of the printing press, then the precolonial era must be left out of our treatment. The Spanish and Portuguese authorities banned books, usually on religious and moral grounds, throughout the colonial empire, thus marking the start of censoring practices in the New World. However, only with the appearance and subsequent prohibition of patriotic *pasquines* (political pamphlets) during the independence period do we begin to see in Latin America the curtailment of press freedom that we currently associate with censorship.

Once the new nations had gained independence, daily newspapers proliferated. This was largely a partisan press, which openly espoused the political views of its publishers. Throughout the nineteenth century, these partisan newspapers ebbed and flowed according to the fortunes of their sponsors. The dominant political tradition of the century was CAUDILLISMO, which entailed a sustained struggle among regional military chieftains, or caudillos, who were constantly vying for national power. They invariably formed shifting alliances with one or another of the political parties of the national oligarchy, which usually divided itself along liberal and conservative lines. All along, it was customary for the party in power to harass and outlaw the partisan press sponsored by its political opponents, in the understanding that, when power shifted, as it often did, that party's own newspapers would be banned from circulation. Such "censorship" was an integral part of the political modus operandi of the times.

This is not to say, however, that the situation was the same for all Latin American countries. In Chile, for example, a country where the volatile caudillo politics of the nineteenth century was less entrenched and eventually gave way to a remarkably stable democratic system in the twentieth century, the first nonsectarian newspaper was founded as early as 1855, thereby paving the way for the establishment of an independent press. In contrast, Venezuela, where *caudillismo* remained strong well into the twentieth century, did not enjoy any semblance of a stable free press until recently. Paradoxically, these two countries underwent a remarkable role reversal. While a 1973 military coup d'état abruptly ended an extended democratic tradition and brought about severe censorship of all mass media in Chile, the Venezuelan media at the time faced virtually no official restrictions and the government was actually pushing for reforms in the direction of greater democratization in mass communication. In many countries even today, the government exerts heavy influence over the press by its release or withholding of newsprint and advertising. In extreme cases, of course, publishers are harassed, imprisoned, or even assassinated, as in the case of Pedro Joaquín CHAMORRO, owner of *La Prensa,* in Managua, Nicaragua, in 1978.

The structure of media ownership, particularly television, is the key factor in determining the subtler forms of censorship that were outlined above in terms of limited access and ability to define issues. Electronic media in Latin America grew on a commercial basis, and the vast majority of television stations are privately owned. Thus, messages tend to favor the worldview of the urban privileged, fostering consumerism and political conservatism.

A critical movement aimed at alleviating this situation took hold in several countries during the 1960s and early 1970s, eventually resulting in a 1976 meeting sponsored by UNESCO, where representatives of twenty Latin American nations discussed communication policies. The recommendations of this conference, which sought to increase popular participation and access to media, were seldom implemented. By the time they were formulated, the political climate that favored government intervention to promote greater media democratization had passed, and a wave of stern dictatorial regimes was sweeping the region, particularly the Southern Cone. In addition, the power of the private broadcasters themselves has become formidable and few governments can afford to antagonize them. In Brazil, for instance, the Globo television network has far more influence and power than any current political force, whereas Mexico's Televisa maintains a cozy symbiotic relationship with the Institutional Revolutionary Party (PRI), which has held a virtual monopoly on power over the course of three generations.

The emerging picture suggests that the concentration of wealth and political power characteristic of most Latin American nations is reflected in media ownership. The values of the privileged few tend to be selectively portrayed to the exclusion of the majority of citizens, who have access to media only as spectators, but not as producers or participants in the definitions of the public representations of their society.

Two major contributions that, from different perspectives, deal with issues of censorship in Latin American twentieth-century media are MARVIN ALISKY, *Latin American Media: Guid-*

ance and Censorship (1981), and ELIZABETH FOX, ed., *Media and Politics in Latin America: The Struggle for Democracy* (1988). On censorship during colonial times, see PABLO GONZÁLEZ CASANOVA, *La Literatura perseguida en la crisis de la colonia* (1986). For a discussion of press harassment in the twentieth century, see MARÍA TERESA CAMARILLO CARBAJAL, *La represión a la prensa en América Latina: Hemerografía, 1978–1982* (1985). Three interesting national studies of Argentina, Brazil, and Chile, respectively, are ANDRÉS AVELLANEDA, *Censura, autoritarismo y cultura: Argentina, 1960–1983* (1986); SILVANA GOULART GUIMARAES, *Sob a verdade oficial: Ideologia, propaganda e censura* (1990); and HERNÁN MILLAS, *Los señores censores* (1985).

OMAR HERNÁNDEZ

See also **Journalism.**

CENTER FOR ADVANCED MILITARY STUDIES (CAEM), a Peruvian institution for specialized higher military education created in 1950 under the rule of the de facto president General Manuel ODRÍA. Its original objectives were to define national war doctrines, train Peruvian colonels aspiring to higher military posts, and relate the issues of national defense to national problems. It was similar in scope to contemporary military centers in France, the United States (Inter-American Defense College), Argentina, and Brazil.

Peruvian military training and education had been modeled since 1896 on the French military school (in part as a reaction to the German model used by the Chilean army at the time). The French model perceived the role of the military in a wider social and administrative dimension. With this perspective the Peruvian general Oscar Torres, President José Luis BUSTAMANTE Y RIVERO's minister of war, called as early as 1945 for the establishment of a specialized military training institution.

The CAEM's graduates and teaching staff began a gradual transformation in the military mentality toward a ''new professionalism.'' They favored institutional military intervention in matters of national development, Indian ''integration,'' and diminished foreign dependency. The CAEM played an important role in the military suppression of the peasant uprisings in Cuzco in the early 1960s through ''civic action.'' In Cuzco the military introduced the first land reform ever executed in Peru in order to avoid further insurrections.

It has been assumed that the CAEM had a decisive influence among those who supported the 1968 military coup led by General Juan VELASCO ALVARADO against constitutional President Fernando BELAÚNDE. While some supporters of Velasco were CAEM graduates (such as General Jorge Fernández Maldonado), recent studies point to the much more important bearing of concepts of strategic internal and external defense (rather than the CAEM's developmental doctrines) expounded by the newly expanded military intelligence.

45

ALFRED STEPAN, *The State and Society: Peru in Comparative Perspective* (1978); DANIEL MASTERSON, *Militarism and Politics in Latin America: Peru from Sánchez Cerro to Sendero Luminoso* (1991).

ALFONSO W. QUIROZ

CENTRAL AMERICA. The term "Central America" is often used to designate the region stretching southeastward from the isthmus of Tehuantepec, in Mexico, to the boundary between Panama and Colombia. Historically, however, it has more often been used with reference to the five states that once made up the Central American federation—GUATEMALA, EL SALVADOR, HONDURAS, NICARAGUA, and COSTA RICA—but also including BELIZE, which has long been claimed by Guatemala. As the Spanish colonial Kingdom of Guatemala also included the area occupied by the present-day Mexican state of CHIAPAS, that state is sometimes included in considerations of Central America. And since its independence from Colombia in 1903, PANAMA has increasingly been thought of politically as well as geographically as a part of Central America.

Before the arrival of the Europeans, Central America, an archaeological bridge between North and South America, was home to a variety of nomadic and sedentary peoples. Mayan civilization occupied much of the isthmus, from Chiapas and Yucatán through Guatemala, Honduras, Belize, El Salvador, and into Nicaragua. Various tribes of Nahuatl origin had moved along the Pacific watershed from central Mexico as far as Nicaragua. Chibcha and other South American Indians occupied lower Central America into Nicaragua. Although the Maya were the most advanced pre-Columbian civilization, they were neither unified nor cohesive. Unlike the Aztecs or Incas, their autonomous city-states remained independent, presaging the political fragmentation that would characterize modern Central America. What unity existed was cultural rather than political.

These Indian peoples suffered greatly under the Spanish military conquest. Efforts to enslave the natives decimated their numbers, but far more destructive were the biological consequences of the conquest. Epidemics of smallpox, plague, syphilis, and other diseases killed millions, perhaps 80 to 90 percent of the population. The population continued to decline until about 1750, then began to grow slightly through the nineteenth century and to rise at an alarming pace in the twentieth century.

Much of the contemporary writing on Central America focuses on individual states, offering rather myopic analyses with little sense of the larger regional issues. Even most of the growing number of works concentrating on the contemporary crises in Central America for the most part deal with the region on a state-by-state basis. This is not, of course, altogether unjustified or unwelcome, for there has been a need for more careful studies of individual states and most of these works contribute to understanding the dynamics of Central American development. At the same time, there is a Central American regional cohesiveness across a broad spectrum of activity. The concept of Central American nationality is deeply ingrained in isthmian history, and although the period since the 1870s has fostered the nationalism of the separate city-states, Central American reunification remains a possibility many Central Americans desire.

THE COLONIAL PERIOD

Central American history reveals a strong thread of unity. Although political union was not a feature of pre-Columbian Central America, there was considerable cultural similarity among the peoples occupying the present-day states of Central America, with extensive commercial relations among them and some sense of common enemies from without. In the early sixteenth century, however, the Spanish imposed political, economic, social, and cultural unity. As the Kingdom of Guatemala, for three centuries the region evolved as a single political unit, governed from Santiago de Guatemala (present-day ANTIGUA). Moved occasionally because of natural disasters, that city became the home of a patrician creole elite and the peninsular bureaucrats who ruled these provinces. Their progeny extended into the provinces and formed the nucleus of the local aristocracy in each provincial capital.

While varying degrees of allegiance and amounts of colonial tribute were paid to the viceregal capital at Mexico City and to Spain, the immediate and real center of the Central American universe was Santiago de Guatemala. Until the very last years of Spanish rule, it contained the only university in the kingdom (the University of SAN CARLOS, founded in 1681), and was the headquarters for every religious order on the isthmus, the center for overseas trade and finance, and, of course, the administrative capital of the kingdom. The cream of the local creole stock came from the provinces to be educated, to enter commerce, to join the bureaucracy, and to establish closer ties with the families at the center of the kingdom.

To be sure, there were centrifugal forces as well. Inadequate transportation facilities caused much of the

Estimates of Central American Population (1500–2025)

Year	Population	Year	Population
1500	2,500,000	1945	8,141,493
1778	805,339	1955	9,155,000
1810	1,000,000	1965	12,515,000
1824	1,287,491	1975	17,670,000
1855	2,000,000	1985	24,218,000
1915	4,915,133	2000	37,178,000
1930	6,018,880	2025	65,113,000

SOURCE: R. L. Woodward, Jr., *Central America, A Nation Divided,* 2d ed. (1985). Panama is not included in these figures.

region to be remote from the capital and its advantages. The kingdom often represented an intrusion on local subsistence, a burden in the form of taxes and service to crown or cross. There was the conflict between the two great socioeconomic systems that have characterized Central America since 1524: feudalism and capitalism. The conquistadores established a kingdom with feudal concepts, institutions, and customs. The vestiges of that kingdom can still be seen in institutions and attitudes in modern Central America, but there also was a Renaissance capitalism carried to Central America that emphasized mineral exploitation, agroexport production, development of infrastructure, and greater unity among the provinces of the kingdom. This capitalist trend slowed during the seventeenth century and, if anything, feudal institutions became stronger then. But as Spain declined economically, her rivals gained strength and the industrial revolution caused them to probe the isthmus for trade and plunder, which contributed ultimately to greater overseas trade. The eighteenth-century Bourbons especially promoted increased agricultural export production in the backwater regions of the Spanish Empire that had been predominantly subsistence-oriented.

In Central America this produced some very substantial changes. Provinces formerly subservient to Guatemala began to gain importance in their own right. Honduras exploited silver mines and, as in Nicaragua, a flourishing ranching community emerged that drove large herds to markets in El Salvador and Guatemala. Costa Rica exported cacao and tobacco. And, most of all, El Salvador's indigo became the major export of the isthmus. This greater economic importance of the provinces contributed to their resentment against the persistent economic and political dominance of Guatemala City, but it also caused some severe economic dislocations. During the final half-century of Hispanic rule, strong divisions began to emerge among the colonial elite regarding economic development, the role of the Roman Catholic church, provincial representation, and, ultimately, the question of independence from Spain.

INDEPENDENCE TO 1850

All the various issues crystallized the educated creole class into two factions that emerged after independence as the conservative and liberal parties. The liberals advocated a continuation of Bourbon policies that promoted liberal capitalism, while the conservatives looked back to the perceived harmony of Hapsburg times, with strong feudal overtones. This would have major consequences for the future of Central American nationalism.

Conservatives looked toward maintenance of the two-class society that had so long characterized Spain and Central America. They favored policies that would preserve the landholding elites in their traditional, dominant roles but also, in noblesse oblige fashion, they assured the peasants of some protection against exploitation by the liberal modernizers. Overcoming initial liberal gains at the outset of independence, these conservatives and their caudillos controlled most of Central America in the mid-nineteenth century. They preserved traditional Hispanic values and institutions, especially the Roman Catholic church, and they rewarded loyal Indian and mestizo peasants with paternalism and respect for their communal lands. They made real, if limited, demands on the peasants, for most of whom subsistence agriculture continued to be the principal activity. In feudal style, they relied on the clergy and local caudillos and landowners for social control, peace, and security. They thus defended states' rights against national unity and were xenophobic toward foreigners who threatened their traditional society with Protestantism, democracy, and modernization.

While the conservatives welcomed expansion of agroexports, they were sensitive to the danger of upsetting native labor and land tenure patterns, and they were forcefully opposed to granting the nation's land and resources to foreigners who generally did not share their religion, language, or social and cultural values, and who might threaten the preeminent place that the conservatives held in the social structure of the provinces. Peasant insurgency against liberal innovators in the 1830s, sometimes instigated by small landlords, was instrumental in the conservative accession to power.

Liberals, on the other hand, represented the segment of the creole elite and an incipient bourgeoisie that wished to modernize Central America by imitating the economic and political success of western Europe and the United States. These "modernizers" rejected traditional Hispanic values and institutions, especially the church. They espoused classical economic liberalism, opposing monopolies while encouraging private foreign trade, immigration, and investment. They emphasized exports and treated the rural masses and their land as the principal resources to be exploited in this effort. Although republican and democratic in political theory, they became much influenced first by utilitarianism and later by positivist materialism, and were contemptuous of, even embarrassed by, the indigenous heritage of their countries. Once in power they often resorted to dictatorship to accomplish their economic goals and to defend their gains.

Thus the professionalization of the military, which became their power base, was an important trend in the late nineteenth and early twentieth centuries. The absence of stronger middle sectors in the traditional two-class Central American society and the persistence of elitist attitudes toward the masses meant, however, that in practice the liberals proceeded very differently than did the industrialized nations. Instead, there emerged elite oligarchies of planters and capitalists who cynically, and without the noblesse oblige of their conservative predecessors, continued to live off the labor of an oppressed rural population that shared little if any of the benefits of the expanded export production. On the contrary, they found their subsistence threatened by

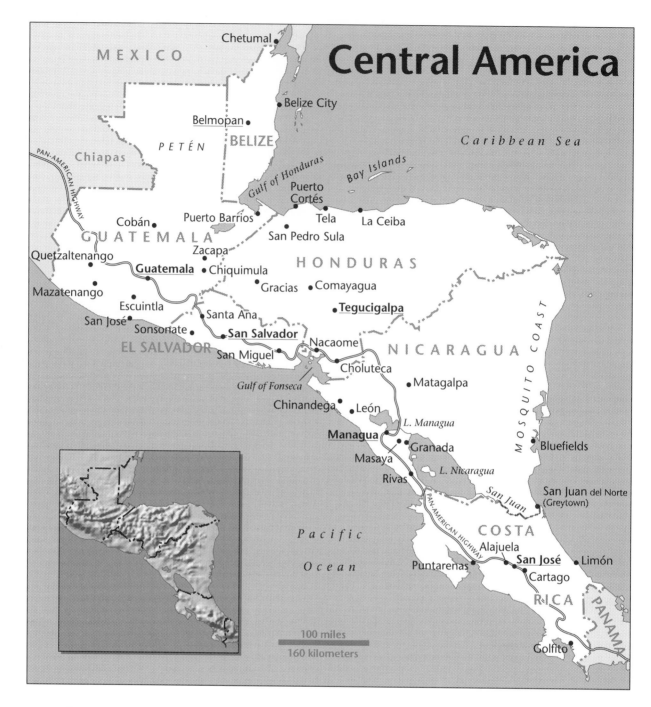

Central America

encroachment on their lands for production of export commodities.

Few Central Americans at the beginning of the nineteenth century envisioned or favored independence for the separate city-states of the Kingdom of Guatemala. But the peculiar circumstances, which Mario Rodríguez has described brilliantly in his *Cádiz Experiment* (1978), brought together both provincial resentment toward Guatemala City and greater local autonomy through the reforms of the Cádiz government in 1810 to 1814. Independence from Spain came through endorsement

of Agustín Iturbide's "Plan of IGUALA" on 15 September 1821, by a council of notables in GUATEMALA CITY. Following the brief continuation of the Kingdom of Guatemala within Iturbide's Mexican Empire (1822–1823), an elected assembly dominated by liberals met in Guatemala City and on 1 July 1823 declared independence from Mexico and organized the UNITED PROVINCES OF THE CENTER OF AMERICA (Provincias Unidas del Centro de América). In 1824 it adopted a republican constitution providing for a loose federation of Guatemala, El Salvador, Honduras, Nicaragua, and Costa Rica. Chiapas had elected to stay with Mexico in 1823, and Panama had become part of Gran Colombia in 1821.

From the outset, the failure of federal leaders to enforce the constitutional provisions led to fragmentation of the union. Provincial jealousies and ideological differences that had emerged in the late colonial period had already sown the seeds of disunion. In the first presidential election (1825) Manuel José ARCE, a liberal Salvadoran army officer, won a disputed election over a moderate Honduran attorney and prominent intellectual, José Cecilio del Valle. The intrigue connected with the electoral process alienated not only conservatives supporting Valle but also extreme liberals, who accused Arce of selling out to conservatives in the congress. Arce did, in fact, ally himself with conservative interests in Guatemala City, and when the liberal Guatemalan state government became hostile toward him, he deposed Governor Juan BARRUNDIA and replaced him with the staunchly conservative Mariano AYCINENA. This act prompted the Salvadoran state government to rebel, touching off a civil war in 1826 that produced animosities throughout the federation that would last beyond the brief life of the United Provinces.

Liberal victory in 1829, under the leadership of Honduran General Francisco MORAZÁN, resulted in a sweeping reform program that included strong anticlericalism, promotion of infrastructure and agroexports, integration of the Indian population, and approval of new judicial and penal codes, notably including trial by jury and, in Guatemala, the ill-advised adoption of the Livingston Codes. Under Morazán's presidency (1831–1839), the liberals exiled prominent conservatives, including the archbishop and other clergy. Morazán also moved the federal capital from Guatemala City to SAN SALVADOR in 1834.

This disintegration of the old kingdom is of crucial importance to Central America's subsequent history. Struggles emerged between conservative and liberal creole elites in every province, as well as between provinces. Fighting was especially bitter between Guatemala City and San Salvador and between the Nicaraguan cities of GRANADA and LEÓN. But nearly as serious were conflicts between Comayagua and Tegucigalpa in Honduras and among the four towns of the Costa Rican central valley, where liberal San José ultimately emerged victorious over traditional Cartago. Quetzaltenango and other towns of western Guatemala also harbored separatist sentiments that surfaced in unsuccessful secession movements in 1839 and in 1848.

Resistance to the liberal reforms arose among the rural masses in El Salvador in the rebellion of the Indian leader Anastasio Aquino, beginning in 1833, but Morazán suppressed this insurrection. Disenchantment with the liberal reforms was also evident in the presidential election at the end of 1833, when opposition candidate José Cecilio del Valle defeated Morazán, but died before taking office. Morazán, as the runner-up, remained constitutionally in office, confirmed by a new

election in February 1835. In Guatemala, opposition to the liberal policies of Governor Mariano Gálvez—including anticlericalism, land grants to foreigners, judicial reform, and imposition of a general head tax—combined with panic caused by a serious cholera epidemic ignited a peasant revolt beginning in 1837. Encouraged by the rural clergy and led by the charismatic Rafael CARRERA, the peasants toppled Gálvez and sharply divided the liberals in Guatemala, allowing the conservatives to gain control.

Meanwhile, western Guatemala, under liberal leadership, seceded and formed a sixth state, called Los Altos. Carrera quickly reconquered these departments in January 1840, however, and when Morazán brought federal troops into the conflict, Carrera defeated him decisively at Guatemala City in March 1840. The federation was already in disarray, as Nicaragua, Honduras, and Costa Rica had seceded in 1838. Morazán fled to Chiriquí in Colombian Panama. He returned two years later and briefly took over the government of Costa Rica, but in this action he not only failed to reunite the states but also inspired a Costa Rican reaction that ended in his own execution before a firing squad on 15 September 1842.

Even at that, conservatives as well as liberals were reluctant to abandon national union. The states formed a conservative alliance in 1842, which served to prevent the liberals from regaining control. Despite their declared preference for reunion, however, the conservative caudillos of the mid-nineteenth century laid the foundations for the modern city-state republics of Central America. Guatemala in 1847 and Costa Rica in 1848, in their fervor to prevent a return of the Morazanistas, declared their "states" to be "republics," and the other states followed their lead within a decade.

1850 TO 1945

Even in the symbolic declarations of independence from the defunct federation, the countries reiterated their hopes for reunion at "a more propitious time." Carrera's stunning defeat of a liberal "National Army" at ARADA, Guatemala, in February 1851 destroyed whatever chances a reunification effort organized by José Francisco BARRUNDIA and other liberals might have had, and a conservative "National Campaign" under the leadership of Costa Rica's Juan Rafael MORA defeated William WALKER's unionist aspirations in 1857. Walker had come to the aid of Nicaraguan liberals and then established himself as president of that state. A strong Costa Rican–Guatemalan axis throughout the midnineteenth century, both before and after the Walker episode, prevented the middle states from returning to liberalism.

That "more propitious time" has come and gone frequently, with more than a hundred attempts at reunification between 1824 and 1965. The liberal resurgence that recovered control of all the states before 1900 appeared propitious to some, especially to liberal caudillos Justo Rufino BARRIOS (1873–1885) of Guatemala and José Santos ZELAYA of Nicaragua (1893–1909), who sought to reunite the isthmus under their respective military leadership.

In reality, the liberal caudillos brought a different kind of unity to the isthmus in their common policies of welcoming foreign, especially United States, capital to the region. In a very real sense, the United States provided the kind of external unity over the region in the twentieth century that Spain had lost at the beginning of the nineteenth century and that Great Britain had only partially achieved in the mid-nineteenth century.

In the early twentieth century, Nicaraguan writer Salvador MENDIETA spearheaded another unionist movement that, although it failed, helped to generate interstate cooperative agencies and laid a foundation for the later integration movement. A Mendieta-inspired Unionist Party won the Guatemalan presidency briefly in 1920, but traditional liberals displaced it a year later.

Central Americans have often charged that foreign nations—Britain in the nineteenth century, the United States in the twentieth—have sabotaged unity, following a "divide and conquer" policy. Certainly there is some truth to the charge with regard to the activities of nationals and diplomats of both English-speaking countries. It was, for example, easier for the giant fruit companies to deal with small, weak states than with a larger, united republic. Yet had there not been substantial internal causes of disunity for foreigners to exploit, Central Americans might still have achieved union.

After World War II foreign aid programs, particularly from the United States but also from international organizations, focused on the need for Central American unity and engendered a spirit of cooperation. Working with the United States Agency for International Development (formerly International Cooperation Administration) and United Nations organizations, the Central American states launched multilateral programs that promoted a spirit of unity at least among the technocrats and politicians associated with them. Cultural and ideological unity came more gradually with programs to eliminate unnecessary duplication in Central American universities and vocational schools.

These foreign assistance programs imposed a kind of unity over the region. Studies made by private corporations and foundations, by national and international governmental agencies, and by academicians in several disciplines encouraged the five states to collaborate in facing common problems. Movement toward economic integration and its accompanying interstate organizations promoted cooperation and unity on the isthmus, as did a rise in interstate investment and the advent of better transportation and communication among the states. Symbolically, the printing of "Centro-América" on the automobile license tags in all five states reflected the new spirit of unity.

Unfortunately, aid programs were often ill conceived and not applicable to the particular problems of Central America. The failure of the United States to support the socioeconomic reforms of Juan José ARÉVALO, the SANDINISTAS, and other progressive forces attached an aura of reaction to United States programs that made them suspect to many Central Americans. At the same time, the military grew and often became the principal beneficiary of aid programs. The refusal of most U.S. aid programs to recognize the need for basic restructuring of the society and economy of the region was at the heart of the failure of the programs to achieve greater change. Many Central Americans saw the programs simply as devices to maintain the region in economic dependence on the capitalists.

FROM 1945 TO 1994

With more progressive governments in Guatemala, Costa Rica, and El Salvador following World War II—and even some spirit of the benefits of cooperation evidence in Honduras and Nicaragua—the movement for unity picked up. Guatemalan and Salvadoran initiatives led to a general meeting of Central American foreign ministers in October 1951, from which came plans for the formation of the ORGANIZATION OF CENTRAL AMERICAN STATES (ODECA), formally founded in 1955. In 1952 economic ministers of the five states met in Tegucigalpa with the United Nations Economic Commission for Latin America, leading eventually to a 1958 treaty for Central American economic integration that included the CENTRAL AMERICAN COMMON MARKET (CACM), a series of trade agreements, and planned industries, which expanded through the 1960s. Costa Rica, the most prosperous state, was reluctant to cooperate fully, fearing competition from countries with cheap labor and especially distrustful of Nicaragua. Thus, a full common market was never achieved, but substantial advances were made, particularly in Guatemala, El Salvador, and Honduras, where new industrial establishments blossomed. Panama also was a limited member of the CACM. Other results of the cooperation included an acceleration in road building and completion of the PAN-AMERICAN HIGHWAY to Panama in 1964. These improvements promoted interstate trade, industry, and tourism, although political instability limited these advances.

The two-week FOOTBALL WAR between El Salvador and Honduras in the summer of 1969 brought a halt to the growth of the CACM and emphasized that without stronger political cooperation, economic union was precarious. The Central American states had settled most disputes amicably since World War II, but the outbreak of this war brought back memories of the frequent civil wars and the meddling in each other's affairs so common earlier. It abruptly interrupted a decade of growth and economic diversification. Although interstate trade soon reached pre-1969 levels and there was modest commercial growth throughout most of the 1970s, in the aftermath of that clash careful analysis revealed not only that economic union could go only so far without closer political confederation but also that the CACM had not been uniformly beneficial for all five states. The Permanent Secretariat for Economic Integration of Central America (SIECA) concluded that if it was truly to benefit the entire region, there would have to be provision for redistribution of the generated wealth that flowed from one region to another as a result of trade patterns.

The worsening economic and social conditions stimulated by rampant inflation and the worldwide oil crisis led to the formation of the High-Level Committee, which drafted a treaty in 1976 that, if adopted, would have extended the integration movement to total trade liberalization, standardization of foreign investment rules, tax harmonization, free movement of labor and capital, a common agricultural policy, a coordinated system of basic industries, and a unified social policy that promoted health, nutrition, housing, support of labor unions, and harmonization of social security and minimum wages. This progressive proposal, however, was rejected by all five states, and the integration movement lost its earlier momentum. The failure of the Central American elites to seize this opportunity was far more damaging than the Football War, reflecting selfish concerns to protect privileged positions within their respective city-states.

The economic problems and political turmoil of the late 1970s fragmented the isthmus and made integration seem remote. The rise of the Sandinistas in Nicaragua and the guerrilla warfare in El Salvador and Guatemala curtailed traffic on the Pan-American Highway, meanwhile the real value of exports fell for all of the states. Yet hope did not die, and the violence and economic decline of the 1980s once again emphasized the desirability of unity. Encouraged especially by Presidents Vinicio CEREZO of Guatemala, Oscar ARIAS SÁNCHEZ of Costa Rica, and Daniel ORTEGA of Nicaragua, this new interest in unity resulted by 1990 in renewed plans for integration and a Central American parliament modeled on that of the European community. Although Costa Rica's legislature kept that state aloof from this initiative, the other four states proceeded to hold elections and organize the Central American Parliament with guarded optimism.

By 1980 political and economic crisis in Central America had made it the focus of an East-West confrontation that brought new manifestations of U.S. hegemony over the region. The pattern of military dictatorship in all of the states except Costa Rica had intensified in reaction to the rise of Fidel CASTRO after 1959. A military phase of the Central American integration movement was the formation, beginning in 1963, by Guatemala, Honduras, El Salvador, and Nicaragua of the CENTRAL AMERICAN DEFENSE COUNCIL (CONDECA) with strong U.S. support. The 1969 war weakened this organization when Honduras pulled out, and in the 1970s it faded into near obscurity, with greater emphasis being placed on economic and social development. After the 1968 Medellín Episcopal Conference, the Roman Catholic church began to promote, with some success, greater attention to the plight of the poor and oppressed, contributing to a new international awareness of the problem of human rights violations and social injustice in Central America. International organizations began to focus on Guatemala, Nicaragua, and El Salvador, and they often scored the United States for its support of repressive regimes in those countries. When Secretary of State Henry Kissinger visited Costa Rica and Guatemala in February 1976, he was greeted with riots and outcries against U.S. support of reactionary regimes in Latin America.

President Jimmy Carter (1977–1981) sought to establish a more humanitarian U.S. policy, but his pro-human rights policy brought stiff opposition from elites in Guatemala and El Salvador, especially after the 1979 overthrow of Anastasio Somoza in Nicaragua. Carter also pushed through treaties under which the U.S. agreed to turn over the Panama Canal to Panama by the year 2000, ending severely strained relations between the U.S. and Panama, and helping the government of strongman Omar TORRIJOS to reverse the unfavorable economic trends in his country. Although the Carter government opposed the Sandinistas in Nicaragua, it accepted their victory gracefully, and in late September 1979 the U.S. Congress approved a Nicaraguan aid package.

The election of Ronald Reagan in 1980, however, brought a sharp reversal of these policies. Reagan had opposed transfer of the Canal Zone, and his administration obstructed implementation of the 1978 treaties, risking deteriorating relations with Panama in a period when that state was undergoing political adjustments following the 1981 death of Torrijos in a plane crash. Reagan cultivated better relations with the Central American armies, however. Soon after taking office he resumed sales of military items to Guatemala, sent military advisers to El Salvador, and suspended aid to Nicaragua. By November 1981 Reagan had begun support of covert operations against the Nicaraguan government, and soon afterward the Nicaraguan CONTRAS emerged to launch a civil war aimed at overthrowing the Sandinistas. He also increased U.S. support against guerrilla opposition forces in El Salvador.

From the outset of his administration, it was clear that Reagan intended to roll back the revolutionary tide in Central America and to make the isthmus a theater in the escalating confrontation with Soviet power. The American presence was most obvious in Honduras, where a massive U.S. military and naval buildup supported the militarization of Honduras and aid to the Nicaraguan contras in an effort to intimidate both the Sandinistas and the Salvadoran guerrillas. In 1983, with the strong backing of the Reagan administration, Honduras, Guatemala, El Salvador, and Panama resurrected CONDECA, with Nicaragua excluded and Costa Rica, emphasizing its neutrality, declining participation. But the Reagan administration played on traditional Costa Rican fear of Nicaragua to encourage a military buildup in that country as well.

As debate over U.S. policy heightened, Reagan named Henry KISSINGER in 1983 to head a bipartisan commission to study Central America. The committee's report, although providing considerable evidence that the basic problems on the isthmus were socioeconomic, concluded with an endorsement of the military policies of the Reagan government. It also called, however, for a massive economic and social aid program, which the Reagan government began to implement. A rapidly deteriorating economic crisis in Nicaragua accompanied continued U.S. support of the contras after 1985. After much negotiation a peace initiative by Costa Rican president Oscar Arias Sánchez finally succeeded in 1989. The U.S. agreed to disband the contras and the Sandinistas agreed to hold free elections, which in 1990 brought to power an anti-Sandinista coalition strongly linked to the old Conservative Party and United States interests under the presidency of Violeta BARRIOS DE CHAMORRO, widow of the slain *La Prensa* editor who had opposed the Somoza dynasty.

Reagan's successor, George Bush (1989–1993), continued the military approach to Central American problems, however. In Panama, General Manuel NORIEGA challenged American interests there after having collaborated with the CIA for years. President Bush cited Noriega's role in drug trafficking as justification for a U.S. invasion of Panama in December 1989 but was obviously concerned about Noriega's ties to Cuba. Noriega was captured and brought to the United States, where he was convicted of violating U.S. drug laws. A successor government under Guillermo Endara, widely regarded as a U.S. puppet government, however, appeared to allow continuation of the drug trafficking at an even higher level than under Noriega. Meanwhile, the col-

lapse of the Eastern bloc, beginning in 1989, ended the perceived Soviet threat in Central America, and U.S. direct interest in the region dropped sharply.

As the twentieth century closed, the middle and working classes were continuing to challenge the power of creole oligarchies that had inherited power at independence. Yet while the Reagan-Bush Central American policy had verbalized a great deal about its support of the "democratization" of Central America, much of the progress was superficial and limited to the supervision of free elections. A 1991 poll of Latin American academic specialists in the United States (the 1991 Fitzgibbon-Johnson Image-Index on Latin American Democracy, conducted by Phil Kelly of Emporia State University) rated Costa Rica as the most democratic of the twenty Latin American republics; Nicaragua placed tenth, and Honduras (seventeenth), Guatemala (eighteenth), and El Salvador (nineteenth) ranked above only Haiti in the poll. While some of the more visible manifestations of military rule in those states have been camouflaged, the serious social and economic obstacles to democracy remain strong.

Chances of Central American reunion now seem more unlikely than at any time since 1839, but the appeal of union remains irresistible. If governments representing a broader segment of the population gain power and can check the self-serving policies of the elites, then the hopes of Francisco Morazán and Salvador Mendieta for a single Central American republic may yet come to fruition. Steve Ropp has written an article entitled "Central America in Search of a Cavour," which notes striking similarities between nineteenth-century Italy and

Central American Conference, 15 June 1990. © JEREMY BOGWOOD / GAMMA LIAISON.

contemporary Central America. Once initiated, a progress toward a rejuvenated Central American republic could come rapidly, and the new Central American Parliament may well be a step in that direction. But for the immediate future, while cooperation at many levels will probably resume, it is just as likely that Central America will remain divided into five sovereign states with strong nationalistic elements that emphasize their unique differences rather than their common problems.

There are useful bibliographical volumes on each Central American country in Clio Press's World Bibliographical Series. RALPH LEE WOODWARD, JR., *Central America, a Nation Divided*, 3d ed. (1993), is a general history of Central America in English; for the post-Independence period JAMES DUNKERLEY, *Power in the Isthmus: A Political History of Modern Central America* (1988), is much more detailed. HÉCTOR PÉREZ BRIGNOLI, *A Brief History of Central America*, translated by Ricardo B. Sawrey and Susana Stettri de Sawrey, 2d ed. (1989), and RODOLFO PASTOR, *Historia de Centroamérica* (1988), offer Central American interpretations. LESLIE BETHELL, ed., *Central America Since Independence* (1991), conveniently provides the pertinent chapters from *The Cambridge History of Latin America*, 10 vols. (1984–1994). Although over a century old, HUBERT HOWE BANCROFT, *History of Central America*, 3 vols. (1883–1887), still has much utility, especially in its presentation of the liberal interpretation. MARY W. HELMS, *Middle America: A Culture History of Heartlands and Frontiers* (1975), surveys isthmian history from an anthropological perspective from pre-Columbian to modern times. For the colonial period, see MURDO J. MACLEOD, *Spanish Central America: A Socioeconomic History, 1520–1720* (1973), and MILES WORTMAN, *Government and Society in Central America, 1680–1840* (1982). SEVERO MARTÍNEZ PELÁEZ, *La patria del criollo* (1971), is an extended interpretive essay by a leading Guatemalan historian that offers a detailed description of the colonial social structure and the formation of the creole mentality. MARIO RODRÍGUEZ, *The Cádiz Experiment in Central America, 1808 to 1826* (1978), is a superb study on the independence period and the influence of the Spanish Constitution of 1812 in Central America; THOMAS L. KARNES, *The Failure of Union: Central America, 1824–1975*, rev. ed. (1976), describes the failure of the Central American federation and surveys attempts to revive it throughout the nineteenth and twentieth centuries. RALPH LEE WOODWARD, JR., *Rafael Carrera and the Emergence of the Republic of Guatemala, 1821–1871* (1993), deals with the first half-century of independence, with particular attention to Guatemala.

LOWELL GUDMUNDSON, *Costa Rica Before Coffee: Society and Economy on the Eve of the Export Boom* (1986), provides an excellent reevaluation of the early development of Costa Rica, including considerable discussion of the myths of Costa Rican history and its historiography. DAVID BROWING, *El Salvador, Landscape and Society* (1971), is an excellent description of land use and tenure in El Salvador, with relevance for understanding the relation between land and history throughout the region. E. BRADFORD BURNS, *The Poverty of Progress: Latin America in the Nineteenth Century* (1980), pays considerable attention to Central America and calls attention to the damage done to folk culture by the liberal economic policies of the nineteenth century. E. BRADFORD BURNS, *Patriarch and Folk: The Emergence of Nicaragua, 1798–1858* (1991), interprets nineteenth-century Nicaragua within that framework. The early-twentieth-century problems of Central America are described in excruciating detail in SALVADOR MENDIETA, *Alrededor del problema unionista de Centro-América*, 2 vols. (1934), and *La enfermedad de Centro-América*, 3 vols. (1910–1934).

VICTOR BULMER-THOMAS, *The Political Economy of Central America Since 1920* (1987), stresses the difficulties created by Central American emphasis on export-led economic development. ROBERT G. WILLIAMS, *Export Agriculture and the Crisis in Central America* (1986), focuses on the cotton and beef industries since World War II, explaining their impact on the social and political crises of the 1980s. WILLIAM DURHAM, *Scarcity and Survival in Central America: Ecological Origins of the Soccer War* (1979), is a superb study that pursues the underlying causes of the 1969 war between El Salvador and Honduras and exposes many of the socioeconomic problems of Central America and their long-term historical consequences. A number of anthologies focus on the crises of the 1980s, but from a historical perspective the most useful include STEVE C. ROPP and JAMES A. MORRIS, eds., *Central America: Crisis and Adaptation* (1984), and RALPH LEE WOODWARD, JR., ed., *Central America: Historical Perspectives on the Contemporary Crises* (1988). See also STEVE C. ROPP, ''Waiting for Cavour: The Current Central America Crisis and Unification,'' in *Proceedings of the Pacific Coast Council on Latin American Studies* 12 (1985–1986): 109–118.

RALPH LEE WOODWARD, JR.

See also **United States–Latin American Relations.**

CENTRAL AMERICA, UNITED PROVINCES OF, a loose confederation of former Spanish colonies that had comprised most of the captaincy general of Guatemala from the middle of the sixteenth century until their independence from Spain in 1821. This CAPTAINCY or ''kingdom,'' as it was popularly known, included present-day Guatemala, El Salvador, Honduras, Nicaragua, and Costa Rica, as well as other jurisdictions, such as Chiapas, no longer considered part of CENTRAL AMERICA. As the United Provinces, they clung together with varying degrees of unity until their complete separation and the disintegration of any semblance of a central government in 1838.

Three centuries of colonial experience provided scant evidence that these provinces might ever become a single nation-state. The Central American region had been conquered by expeditions launched from Panama, Santo Domingo, and Mexico, creating a variety of interests, loyalties, and responsibilities. Poor communications meant that these feelings extended most strongly to the village or town around which settlers tended to cluster. The larger communities, generally greater distances apart, were usually governed by a council or *ayuntamiento* in something of the manner of a city-state. While higher-ranking colonial officials almost always were Spanish-born and Spanish-oriented, the members of the *ayuntamientos* tended to be creoles, American-born persons of Spanish ancestry. With the passage of time, council members in the larger towns often formed a small, tight aristocracy, not democratic but strongly representing local interests of the elite against Spain and forming the nucleus of a growing Americanism.

Such developments were, of course, not Spain's intent.

The Hapsburgs created an elaborate centralism for America, and their Bourbon successors in the eighteenth century attempted to tighten the system even more. Central Americans fell under the jurisdiction of the vast VICE-ROYALTY of New Spain with its capital in faraway Mexico City; one division of the viceroyalty was the AUDIENCIA of Guatemala, whose presiding officer was generally a CAPTAIN-GENERAL. Time, distance, and travel conditions meant that in most administrative matters Mexico City was bypassed by the Central Americans.

By the eighteenth century the capital at Guatemala had become a city of some stature, as effective as a viceroyalty; its aristocratic families carried out their roles in commensurate fashion. But even this "kingdom" could not reach authoritatively to most of Central America; the provincials ran their own affairs as much as possible, and viewed Guatemala as something of an expensive nuisance. Worse, the large city of San Salvador yearned to run more of its own political and religious affairs.

Lacking the mineral wealth of Peru or Mexico, the kingdom of Guatemala never equaled their importance in the Spanish scheme of things. Most of the folk in the kingdom were peasants or small farmers living out their lives in obscure labor; a few others were into the export business and made good profits by working with Europeans. So the decades passed slowly, sometimes peacefully, sometimes in turbulence, but gradually strengthening local feelings.

Although in the backwash of Spanish intellectualism, the Central Americans were not ignorant of the ideas of freedom the ENLIGHTENMENT brought to Europe. NAPOLEON I's invasion of Spain and his overthrow of the monarchy disconnected the metropolitan power from its colonies and forced some rethinking by colonial *ayuntamientos* about their future status. Dreams of a brighter place in the empire's sun died with the return of King FERDINAND VII and his reactionary regime.

Barring a few minor skirmishes, no Central American war of independence took place. But the issue of freedom was argued in every *ayuntamiento*, some colonials favoring a return to the empire and others seeking improved status within the Mexican orbit. Still others demanded "independence from Spain, Mexico, and every other power." In the end, the last group won out, and following a brief annexation to the Mexican Empire of Agustín de ITURBIDE (1822–1823), Central American provinces—and towns—made individual decisions about their sovereignty. The majority agreed upon a consolidated government for Central America, free from Spain *and* Mexico.

The United Provinces of Central America drew up a constitution in 1824, the same five states of Guatemala, El Salvador, Honduras, Nicaragua, and Costa Rica now calling themselves the Federal Republic of Central America. Partially copying several constitutions, including that of the United States and that of Spain (1812), the framers called for a federal type of government with certain powers retained by the states and others granted to the national government. Given time, a nation might have evolved. But there was no time. The rulers of the old "kingdom" wanted a strong governmental presence in Guatemala; the provinces wanted greater rights for the states; the old tax structure had been destroyed and poorly replaced; San Salvador wanted its own bishop; there was electoral fraud, village rivalries, and suspicions—these matters and many others surfaced on the withdrawal of Spain's restraining hands.

A Salvadoran Liberal, Manuel José ARCE, was elected president in 1825, governing from the temporary capital in GUATEMALA CITY. Needing support against the demands—and accusations—of Liberals outside the capital, Arce linked himself with the elite families, frightening his original backers. Salvadorans brought up the bishop question. In each state personalist and ideological issues surfaced. Most states faced local civil war; Costa Rica tried to ignore all the others. A series of battles between 1826 and 1829 resulted in victory for the Liberals, now led by Francisco MORAZÁN, a Honduran who forced the Arce government into exile and assumed the presidency of the federation.

Morazán, reelected in 1835, has since been recognized by most Central Americans as the soul of the federation movement. But his liberal reforms were too broad and too sudden for many of his people, and they caused fear. Secession movements, a cholera epidemic, and a revolt of peasants led by an able caudillo, José Rafael CARRERA, led to Morazán's overthrow. Government reverted to localism, and the federation came to an end. The five states went their own ways.

On twenty-five or more occasions since 1838, groups of Central American states have attempted to reunite in some fashion. Failure followed every effort, even when all five states participated in the attempt. In spite of all the obvious advantages that a greater Central America might bring, the five states still cling tenaciously to their sovereignty.

HUBERT H. BANCROFT, *History of Central America*, vol. 3 (1887); SALVADOR MENDIETA, *Alrededor del problema unionista de Centro-América* (1926); RODRIGO FACIO, *Trayectorio y crisis de la Federación Centroamericana* (1949); ROBERT S. CHAMBERLAIN, *Francisco Morazán, Champion of Central American Federation* (1950); PEDRO JOAQUÍN CHAMORRO CARDENAL, *Historia de la Federación de la América Central* (1951); ALBERTO HERRARTE, *La unión de Centro América* (1955); ANDRÉS TOWNSEND EZCURRA, *Las provincias unidas de Centroamérica* (1958); THOMAS L. KARNES, *The Failure of Union: Central America, 1824–1975*, rev. ed. (1976); RALPH LEE WOODWARD, JR., *Central America: A Nation Divided* (1976).

THOMAS L. KARNES

CENTRAL AMERICA: CONSTITUTION OF 1824.

The Constitution of 1824, the first constitution of the UNITED PROVINCES OF THE CENTER OF AMERICA, was put into effect in November 1824 by the National Constituent Assembly but was not ratified by the first elected congress until August 1825.

The constitution was based heavily on the Spanish CONSTITUTION OF 1812, with some influence from the U.S. Constitution of 1789. José Cecilio del VALLE played a leading role in its formulation as a compromise between liberal and conservative principals. It came to be regarded as the prototype of liberal constitutions in the subsequent Central American republics of Guatemala, El Salvador, Honduras, Nicaragua, and Costa Rica throughout the nineteenth century. It established Roman Catholicism as the state religion, excluding any other public worship, but limited the clergy's participation in government. It outlawed slavery and guaranteed individual liberties and provided for a unicameral congress with a relatively weak executive, except for his command of the armed forces. The constitution also provided for a senate (with two senators from each state) that had to approve all legislation and could veto acts of the congress, which could override senate votes with a two-thirds majority. The senate could not initiate legislation and was actually more of an executive council than part of the legislature. Supreme Court justices were elected for two-year, staggered terms. In providing the framework for a federation of the five autonomous states, a major weakness of the document was the lack of sufficient power at the national level.

The Constitution of 1824 may be found in LUIS MARIÑAS OTERO, *Las constituciones de Guatemala* (1958), as well as in other compilations of the constitutions of the Central American states. JORGE MARIO GARCÍA LAGUARDIA has written extensively on the development of this constitution, most notably in *La génesis del constitucionalismo guatemalteco* (1971); MARIO RODRÍGUEZ has described the importance of the Constitution of 1812 to its formulation in *The Cádiz Experiment in Central America, 1810 to 1826* (1978). For briefer discussions of its relevance to Central American history see THOMAS KARNES, *Failure of Union* (1965); and RALPH LEE WOODWARD, JR., "The Aftermath of Independence, 1821–c. 1870," in *Central America Since Independence*, edited by Leslie Bethell (1991), pp. 10–12.

RALPH LEE WOODWARD, JR.

CENTRAL AMERICA: INDEPENDENCE OF.

At the end of the eighteenth century the captaincy general of Guatemala, also known as the Kingdom of Guatemala, encompassed the five modern-day Central American republics as well as the state of Chiapas y Soconusco, today part of Mexico. At the time, the area had a population of about 1 million. Its urban centers did not boast large populations. Among the most important were Guatemala City, with approximately 20,000 inhabitants, and San Salvador, with fewer than 15,000. Communications among the provinces was difficult. Compared to New Spain and Peru, the captaincy general of Guatemala was of peripheral importance. The chief sources of wealth for its colonizers were land and Indians. Natural dyes were its chief exports.

The turn of the nineteenth century marked the beginning of events that would determine the destiny of the entire captaincy general of Guatemala. First, the Bourbon reforms gave political power to several cities, San Salvador among them, through the creation of Intendancies. Second, Napoleon's invasion of Spain in 1808 broke the economic connections necessary for the commercialization of Central America's prime source of revenue: indigo. Third, there was political upheaval, which brought about the revolt led by Miguel HIDALGO Y COSTILLA and José MORELOS Y PAVÓN in Mexico.

During this period, rash attempts to secure independence occurred in Nicaragua, El Salvador, and Honduras from 1811 to 1813. In 1814 a conspiracy against Spanish power arose in Guatemala City, but the authorities managed to quell it at its beginning. An important figure in these events was Field Marshal José BUSTAMANTE Y GUERRA, who from 1811 to 1818 fought any separatist attempts with a firm hand.

The political atmosphere in Guatemala City began to change in 1820, with the restoration of the liberal Constitution of 1812. On one side, radical professionals, educated at the University of San Carlos and led by Pedro MOLINA, attacked the old colonial system. On the other, a more conservative group, led by José Cecilio del VALLE, kept hope alive for the continuation of Spanish power. Members of the Guatemalan elite sought to break the Spanish commercial monopoly that had brought them serious economic problems.

In 1821 events in Mexico changed the panorama. The Mexican *criollos*, under the leadership of Agustín de ITURBIDE, managed to move without major violence from an absolute to a constitutional monarchy. News of Mexican independence and the PLAN OF IGUALA spread rapidly throughout Central America. Chiapas joined the movement in September of that year. Field Marshal Gabino GAÍNZA yielded to demands for a meeting of the different institutions on 15 September. That day, after a stormy session, Guatemalan political independence was declared. Although control of the government remained in the hands of the Spanish bureaucracy under Gaínza, through a maneuver by conservatives, Guatemala was annexed to the Mexican Empire of Iturbide on 5 January 1822. In July of that same year, Iturbide sent Vicente FILÍSOLA to take possession of the captaincy general.

Rejection of the annexation by several Central American cities resulted in war, particularly against San Salvador. With the destruction of the Mexican Empire, Filísola convoked a constituent assembly that began 24 June 1823. On 1 July 1823 the assembly declared Central America free and independent, adopting the name UNITED PROVINCES OF CENTRAL AMERICA. This put an end to Spanish domination and the annexation to Mexico, and was the definitive beginning of independent life for the region.

MARIO RODRÍGUEZ, *The Cádiz Experiment in Central America* (1978); JULIO CÉSAR PINTO SORIA, *Centroamérica: De la independencia al estado nacional (1800–1840)* (1989); CARLOS MELÉNDEZ, *La independencia de Centroamérica* (1993); RALPH LEE WOODWARD, jr., *Rafael Carrera and the Emergence of the Republic of Guatemala, 1821–1871* (1993).

Oscar G. Peláez Almengor

CENTRAL AMERICAN COMMON MARKET (CACM), an economic agreement among the five Central American countries (Costa Rica, El Salvador, Guatemala, Honduras, and Nicaragua). This movement toward regional economic integration commenced in 1951 with adoption of a resolution by the United Nations economic commission for latin america (ECLA). Years of study and negotiation followed.

In 1958, the five countries, under the tutelage of ECLA, concluded two agreements: the Multilateral Treaty on Central American Free Trade and Economic Integration and the Convention on the Regime of Central American Integration Industries. The former, entered into force on 2 June 1959, provided for limited intraregional free trade, with additional items to be made subject to free trade over a ten-year period. The latter agreement provided for protected regional "integration industries" (those requiring free access, without competition, to the entire Central American market in order to be economically viable). The industries were to be allocated among the five countries.

Costa Rica signed, but did not ratify, the agreements. Its failure to do so rendered the convention inoperational.

In 1960, a three-country (El Salvador, Guatemala, and Honduras) agreement backed by the United States— the Treaty of Economic Association—was signed. It created an expanded and accelerated movement toward integration. Only fifty-five items were exempted from regional free trade. The treaty created a development assistance fund and a set of regional institutions—neither were provided for in the earlier protocols. The free-trade area would become a common market after five years, provided that the signatories had equalized external tariffs. The treaty did not incorporate integration industries.

The Treaty of Economic Association created crisis in the regionwide movement toward economic integration and prompted all five Central American countries to conclude yet another agreement, the General Treaty of Central American Economic Integration, this time under ECLA tutelage, in December 1960. This treaty provided for immediate regional free trade for all except a very small number of products. It stipulated that virtually all exempted products would be freely traded in five years. It also provided for a uniform external tariff and a common market in five years. Integration industries were incorporated. Additionally, the treaty established a set of institutions and provided for the establishment of the Central American Bank for Economic Integration.

The treaty was signed and ratified by all but Costa Rica, which offered economic reasons for its refusal but in reality acted out of a sense of distinctiveness from the rest of Central America. In 1963 it reversed its position.

Under the free-trade provisions, intra–Central American trade grew dramatically—from $8.3 million in 1950 to $32.7 million in 1960 to $213.6 million in 1967. Central America experienced considerable economic growth in the 1960s and into the 1970s, averaging 5.8 percent per year. Most of the growth took place in the urban industrial sector under the stimulus of the common market. The common market, by creating a regional market free of most trade barriers, made feasible a greater degree of industrial development than would have been possible in five separate markets.

The common market's impact was not entirely positive. It did nothing to promote development of the agrarian sector. And because the common market adhered to free-market forces, the bulk of the industrial development that followed its creation was concentrated in El Salvador and Guatemala, already the most developed Central American countries. Much of the industrialization was capital-intensive rather than labor-intensive. The opportunities created by the common market were mainly exploited by foreign investors.

Operation of the common market was disrupted by the 1969 war between El Salvador and Honduras and its aftermath. It was even more seriously disrupted by the economic-political crises of the 1970s and 1980s. Any return to economic dynamism in Central America in the future probably depends on a revival of the economic integration of the region.

Andrew B. Wardlaw, *The Operations of the Central American Common Market* (1966), and *Achievement and Problems of the Central American Common Market* (1969); joseph s. nye, jr., "Central American Regional Integration," in *International Conciliation* 562 (March 1967); james d. cochrane, *The Politics of Regional Integration: The Central American Case* (1969); isaac cohen orantes, *Regional Economic Integration in Central America* (1972); william r. cline and enrique delgado, eds., *Economic Integration in Central America* (1978).

James D. Cochrane

CENTRAL AMERICAN COURT OF JUSTICE, a body created at the Central American Conference held in Washington, D.C., in November and December 1907. Escalating isthmian political turmoil and the threat of international conflict prompted the united states and Mexico—nations with specific interests in central america—to host the meeting. Once the conference began, however, the host powers played a passive role in the proceedings, thus allowing the Central Americans to resolve their outstanding differences without any significant outside interference. Luis Anderson Morúa of Costa Rica, elected president of the conference, advocated the adoption by the Central American nations of the principle of obligatory arbitration of international disputes. With the support of the Salvadoran delegation, Anderson was able to convince the other delegates of the need to establish a Central American Court of Justice.

The court was the first international tribunal requiring mandatory adjudication of international disputes among the contracting parties, and thus represented a precedent-breaking step in international jurisprudence. The promise of the court, however, was never really fulfilled as political partisanship, more often than not, tended to influence the decisions of the judges who represented the various isthmian nations. The court ceased to function in 1918 following Nicaragua's denunciation, in the previous year, of the 1907 WASHINGTON TREATIES. The Nicaraguan action came as the result of the Central American Court's ruling on the BRYAN–CHAMORRO Treaty. The court decreed that Nicaragua, by signing the treaty with the United States, had violated preexisting treaty rights held by Costa Rica and El Salvador. Rather than accept the court's interpretation of the Bryan–Chamorro Treaty, the Nicaraguan authorities chose in effect to destroy the 1907 treaty system, and with it the Central American Court of Justice.

DANA G. MUNRO, *Intervention and Dollar Diplomacy in the Caribbean, 1900–1921* (1964), esp. pp. 152–153, 402–403; CARLOS JOSÉ GUTIÉRREZ GUTIÉRREZ, *La corte de justicia centroamericana* (1978).

RICHARD V. SALISBURY

CENTRAL AMERICAN DEFENSE COUNCIL (CONDECA), a special regional defense organization established in 1965. Its founding member states were Guatemala, Honduras, El Salvador, and Nicaragua. Costa Rica and Panama were offered observer status. Panama accepted observer status but opposed U.S. pressure to upgrade its status to full membership; Costa Rica refused membership at any level. CONDECA was closely linked to the U.S. Southern Command (SOUTHCOM) in Panama and thus enjoyed substantial U.S. backing. Its establishment was considered the military phase of a growing movement toward Central American integration.

CONDECA emphasized development of coordinated military action against guerrilla activity to counter any perceived Soviet penetration of Central America and to foster cooperation between the national armies of the region. CONDECA proved ineffective, and its military coordination was hampered by the withdrawal of Panama in 1968, Honduras in 1973, and Nicaragua in 1979. In 1983, however, CONDECA was revived at the insistence of the Reagan administration that Nicaragua was destabilizing the region. El Salvador, Honduras, and Guatemala, with U.S. backing, reestablished CONDECA. The revival was criticized for being under the influence of Washington and for undermining the CONTADORA peace initiative. Despite the original intention to coordinate regional strategy, CONDECA's revival only served to strengthen the relationship between the Pentagon and the military governments of the region.

ROBERT S. LEIKEN, ed., *Central America: Anatomy of Conflict* (1984); HELEN SCHOOLEY, *Conflict in Central America* (1987); PETER CALVERT, ed., *The Central American Security System: North-South or East-West?* (1988).

HEATHER K. THIESSEN

CENTRAL AMERICAN MISSION (CAM), a nondenominational Protestant "faith mission" based in Dallas, Texas, for the evangelization and proselytization of Central Americans. CAM was founded in 1890 by Cyrus I. Scofield, a businessman and biblical scholar who is best remembered for his authorship of a reference Bible which still bears his name. Scofield, an adherent of "dispensationalist" theology, believed that the conversion of all humanity was a precondition of Christ's second coming, and he founded the CAM with the belief that the conversion of Central America to Protestantism would hasten the fulfillment of biblical prophecy. The CAM organization, while not a true denomination, still adheres to dispensationalist theology.

The first CAM missionaries went to Costa Rica in 1891. Three years later, a missionary couple named Dillon was sent to establish missions in northern Central America; both succumbed to fever outside the Salvadoran port of Acajutla and were buried at sea on the way there. Missions were eventually established in El Salvador and Honduras in 1896. CAM began mission work in Guatemala in 1899, and in Nicaragua in 1900.

Although CAM has always considered its primary purpose to be evangelization, it is involved in many secular projects. Until the 1960s, CAM never attracted many local converts in Central America; however, CAM-run schools and linguistic projects have long given the mission an influence disproportionate to its size. Most CAM projects in Central America are based in Guatemala, where CAM has historically enjoyed the greatest number of native converts, although prior to the 1960s, even there converts numbered less than a few thousand.

CAM first became involved in linguistic work in 1919, when a CAM missionary, Cameron Townsend, developed a grammar and dictionary in the Maya language Cakchiquel in order to translate the New Testament. Townsend eventually left CAM to found the Wycliffe Bible Translators/Summer Institute of Linguistics, a nondenominational organization devoted to translating religious literature into the languages of the indigenous peoples of the Americas. Despite Townsend's departure, linguistic work has remained central to CAM's work to the present day.

CAM also established a number of elementary and secondary schools in the early twentieth century, the largest of which, the Jardín de las Rosas, was founded in Guatemala City in 1914. Today, CAM runs the Theological Seminary of Central America (formerly the Central American Biblical Institute) in Guatemala City, which is the largest and most influential fundamentalist seminary on the isthmus.

WILKINS BOWDRE WINN, "A History of the Central American Mission as Seen in the Work of Albert Edward Bishop, 1896–1922" (Ph.D. diss., University of Alabama, 1964); WILTON M. NELSON, *El protestantismo en Centro América* (1982); DAVID STOLL, *Fishers of Men or Founders of Empire? The Wycliffe Bible Translators in Latin America* (1982); WILTON M. NELSON, *Historia del protestantismo en Costa Rica* (1983); VIRGINIA GARRARD-BURNETT, "A History of Protestantism in Guatemala" (Ph.D. diss., Tulane University, 1986).

VIRGINIA GARRARD-BURNETT

See also **Missions; Protestantism.**

CENTRAL AMERICAN PARLIAMENT, Guatemalan proposal approved in 1986 by the Central American presidents during a summit at ESQUIPULAS, Guatemala, which was held to negotiate peace in Central America. The articles were approved in 1987 by mandatories (leaders) from Guatemala, El Salvador, Honduras, Nicaragua, and Costa Rica. As of 1994, the Congress of Costa Rica had not yet ratified it.

As envisioned in the Declaration of Esquipulas, the parliament would seat twenty representatives from each country, and would develop "strategies, analyses and recommendations" on Central America's political and economic problems. Its headquarters, as designated by the declaration, is Esquipulas. Former presidents and vice presidents are, ex officio, representatives of the parliament. Among its powers would be advising the *buena vecindad* and the Central American Common Market, the entities of Central American integration. The European Community supported the initiative, offering financial support for its realization.

By 1994, Guatemala, El Salvador, and Honduras had elected parliaments; Nicaragua had yet to hold elections.

Tratado constitutivo del parlamento centroamericano y otras instancias políticas (1988); M. S. GLORIA ABRAHAM, *El parlamento centroamericano: Su incidencia en el desarollo futuro del istmo* (1989).

FERNANDO GONZÁLEZ DAVISON

CENTRAL INTELLIGENCE AGENCY (CIA). The history of the Central Intelligence Agency is inseparable from that of U.S. cold war relations with Latin America. Established by the 1947 National Security Act only to collect, coordinate, and evaluate intelligence, the new agency got off to an inauspicious start. Rioting at the 1948 Inter-American Conference held in Bogotá, Colombia, elicited charges that the CIA had failed to forewarn the State Department. Although the first director (DCI), Rear Admiral Roscoe H. Hillenkoetter, successfully fended off Capitol Hill critics, he failed to convince bureaucratic rivals, especially J. Edgar Hoover and the Federal Bureau of Investigation (FBI), that they should cede their responsibilities in Latin America to the fledgling CIA.

The CIA's reputation improved, and it overcame its competitors' opposition when, empowered by a series of secret National Security Council (NSC) directives, it became progressively more involved in covert activities. It scored some immediate successes, and the selection of the respected General Walter Bedell Smith as DCI in 1950 solidified the Agency's standing. Three years later the CIA's golden era began. Bringing to the White House an enthusiasm for clandestine operations and psychological warfare developed during his World War II military command, President Dwight D. Eisenhower increased the CIA's authority and resources. To succeed Smith as DCI, he appointed Allen W. Dulles, Office of Strategic Services (OSS) veteran, principal author of the 1949 report that granted the CIA exclusive aegis over covert projects, and Smith's deputy director for plans. Eisenhower named Smith chief deputy to Secretary of State John Foster Dulles, Allen's brother.

Within Eisenhower's first year in office, the CIA rewarded the president by orchestrating the ouster of Iran's prime minister, Muhammad Mussadegh, and the shah's return to the Peacock Throne. It was in GUATEMALA the next year, however, that the Agency achieved legendary status. Since Guatemala's 1944 revolution, the United States had become increasingly concerned with the perceived leftward drift of presidents Juan José ARÉVALO BERMEJO and Jacobo ARBENZ GUZMÁN. These concerns escalated when the Arbenz government enacted agrarian reform legislation in 1952 that appropriated some 400,000 acres held by Guatemala's largest landowner, the UNITED FRUIT COMPANY. CIA analysts ascribed this behavior to the influence on Arbenz of Guatemalan Communists. Unless checked, these presumed agents of the Kremlin would, it was believed, promote Soviet penetration of the Western Hemisphere, thereby confronting the United States with a strategic nightmare.

Recent scholars have rejected the CIA's estimate of the threat. Eisenhower never questioned it; he instructed the Agency to develop plans to rid the hemisphere of the menace. After the CIA failed to prevent the arrival in Guatemala of Czech-manufactured arms, Eisenhower approved Operation Success. On 18 June 1954, under the leadership of Carlos CASTILLO ARMAS, the U.S.-sponsored "Army of Liberation" invaded Guatemala from Honduras. Its progress, however, was less a determinant of the outcome than was the CIA's intensive program of psychological warfare that all but paralyzed Arbenz and his military. On 27 June, Arbenz resigned and left the country. Guatemala's next president was Castillo Armas. Subsequently many North and South American commentators have judged the United States culpable for Guatemala's internal strife and dismal record of human rights abuse.

The Eisenhower administration basked in the glory of the Guatemalan success. Predictably, therefore, notwithstanding CIA failures during the ensuing years, when Fidel CASTRO embraced the Soviet Union after overthrowing Cuba's longtime caudillo Fulgencio BA-TISTA, Eisenhower again asked the Agency to eradicate a hemispheric cancer. Dulles delegated primary responsibility for planning to Richard M. Bissell, Jr., who had joined the CIA just in time to play an important role in Operation Success, and by masterminding the U-2 overflights program had become Dulles's heir apparent. Bissell modeled the plan to depose Castro after the Guatemalan venture and assigned many of the same personnel to it. By the time Operation Zapata took its final form, it had grown in size and degree of risk. Moreover, John F. Kennedy had become U.S. president.

Kennedy was never comfortable with Bissell's scheme, and many of his advisers were hostile to it. But Bissell gave assurances that when confronted with a brigade of Cuban exiles spread across three beachheads along the BAY OF PIGS, Castro would suffer the same loss of nerve as Arbenz and his military had. In the worst-case scenario a stalemate would result that the ORGANIZATION OF AMERICAN STATES (OAS) would resolve in favor of the United States. On 17 April 1961, Kennedy sanctioned the operation's implementation, but he curtailed the concomitant air strikes to reduce U.S. exposure. Castro's fighter planes retained air superiority, and his forces either killed or captured the defenseless invaders stranded on the beach. The Bay of Pigs fiasco strengthened Castro in Cuba and ended Dulles's and Bissell's careers in the CIA.

Its early warning of Soviet missile emplacements in Cuba in 1962 and the 1967 assassination of Castro's lieutenant Ernesto "Che" GUEVARA in Bolivia helped restore some of the CIA's lost luster. But after Operation Mongoose failed to eliminate Castro, and as it became increasingly preoccupied in Southeast Asia, the Agency in the 1960s and 1970s confined most of its Latin American enterprises to assisting the counterinsurgency efforts of U.S. clients. The major exception came in Chile, where the CIA expended great energy and resources to prevent the socialist Salvador ALLENDE from securing the presidency. In 1970 he did so nonetheless. Debate continues over the extent of the CIA's direct involvement in the military coup three years later that ended in Allende's death. What is unambiguous is that between 1970 and 1973 the CIA distributed millions of dollars among Allende's opponents, and that it knew about and encouraged the successful plot against him.

Ronald Reagan's election in 1980 and his appointment of OSS veteran William Casey as DCI brought a revival of CIA activism, in Central America above all. The fundamental objectives were to bring about the collapse of Nicaragua's leftist Sandinista regime and to bolster the government of El Salvador in its battle against the guerrilla forces associated with the Farabundo Martí National Liberation Front (FMLN). Assuming that the FMLN depended on the Sandinistas, the administration concentrated on the Nicaraguan front. Reagan proclaimed the indigenous opposition to the Sandinistas to be "freedom fighters," and Casey,

aided by White House staffers and private citizens who had participated in the CIA's "secret war" in Laos, funneled human, financial, and material support to CONTRA units operating inside Nicaragua and across neighboring borders. Often this assistance required circumventing congressional prohibitions, the most notorious case of which led to the Iran–Contra scandal. The combination of Casey's sudden death, grants of immunity to key witnesses, the Sandinistas' electoral defeat, and the negotiated end to the Salvadoran insurrection has left many details of the CIA's operations in Central America unclear. The greater openness that has accompanied the end of the Cold War holds the promise that additional information will be forthcoming. Until then, the CIA's checkered record during the 1980s and throughout its history will remain incomplete.

General histories of the CIA include JOHN RANELAGH, *The Agency: The Rise and Decline of the CIA* (1986); LOCH JOHNSON, *America's Secret Power: The CIA in a Democratic Society* (1989); and RHODRI JEFFREYS-JONES, *The CIA and American Democracy* (1989). Equally insightful are biographies of the two most influential DCIs: THOMAS POWERS, *The Man Who Kept the Secrets: Richard Helms and the CIA* (1979); and PETER GROSE, *Gentleman Spy: The Life of Allen Dulles* (1994). The most comprehensive survey of the CIA's covert operations is JOHN PRADOS, *Presidents' Secret Wars: CIA and Pentagon Covert Operations Since World War II* (1986). For the project in Guatemala, see RICHARD IMMERMAN, *The CIA in Guatemala: The Foreign Policy of Intervention* (1982); STEPHEN SCHLESINGER and STEPHEN KINZER, *Bitter Fruit: The Untold Story of the American Coup in Guatemala* (1982); and PIERO GLEIJESES, *Shattered Hope: The Guatemalan Revolution and the United States, 1944–1954* (1991). The best studies of the Bay of Pigs are PETER WYDEN, *Bay of Pigs: The Untold Story* (1979); and TRUMBULL HIGGINS, *The Perfect Failure: Kennedy, Eisenhower, and the CIA at the Bay of Pigs* (1987). GREGORY TREVERTON, *Covert Action: The Limits of Intervention in the Postwar World* (1987), is excellent on the CIA and Allende. Starting points for examining CIA activity in Central America in the 1980s are BOB WOODWARD, *Veil: The Secret Wars of the CIA, 1981–1987* (1987); ROBERT A. PASTOR, *Condemned to Repetition: The United States and Nicaragua* (1987); and WALTER LA FEBER, *Inevitable Revolutions: The United States in Central America* (1993).

RICHARD H. IMMERMAN

See also **Cuban Missile Crisis; Nicaragua: Political Parties.**

CENTRO DE ALTOS ESTUDIOS MILITARES. *See* **Center for Advanced Military Studies.**

CENTROMÍN, state-owned Peruvian mining company. After prolonged and sometimes acrimonious negotiations from 1971 to 1973 between the CERRO DE PASCO CORPORATION and the Peruvian State for the purchase of the company, the government of Juan VELASCO ALVARADO finally nationalized it, as well as its huge copper mining complex in the central highlands. Cerro was one of the oldest foreign companies operating in Peru and long a nationalist target; its takeover set off a country-wide celebration in December 1973. The nationalized company became Centromín-Perú, a branch of Minero-Perú, which comprised all state mining operations.

PETER F. KLARÉN

CENTURIÓN, CARLOS R. (*b.* 1902; *d.* 1969), Paraguayan historian. Born into an old and established family, Centurión chose to enter the legal profession but also spent many years in academic pursuits. His first literary undertaking, a two-volume account of the Gran Chaco dispute, *El conflicto del Chaco: Gestiones diplomáticas*, published in 1937, was well received, and a year later, he produced a detailed examination of Paraguay's first constitutional convention, *Los hombres de la convención del 70* (1938).

These two early works gave Centurión excellent preparation for his magnum opus, *Historia de las letras paraguayas*. This study, which appeared in three volumes between 1947 and 1951, has long been regarded as the most complete and best-researched intellectual history of Paraguay. Perhaps its only rival is Efraím Cardozo's *Historiografía paraguaya*, which addresses only the colonial period. Centurión's work received considerable acclaim when it first appeared. Subsequent critics have nonetheless charged that it avoids in-depth analysis of Paraguayan writers in favor of a superficial thoroughness. Even these critics, however, have failed to duplicate Centurión's efforts.

CARLOS CENTURIÓN, *Historia de la cultura paraguaya*, 2 vols. (1961); CHARLES J. KOLINSKI, *Historical Dictionary of Paraguay* (1975).

THOMAS L. WHIGHAM

CENTURIÓN, JUAN CRISÓSTOMO (*b.* 1840; *d.* 12 March 1903), Paraguayan diplomat, journalist, and author. Born in Itauguá in 1840, Centurión received his early education in Asunción, where he studied literature with European tutors. In the late 1850s, the government selected him as one of several young Paraguayans sent abroad for further education at state expense. He went to Britain, where he learned English and French and studied international law. He returned to Paraguay in 1863 and immediately became a key adviser to President Francisco Solano LÓPEZ. Two years later, when his country became deeply involved in a war with Argentina and Brazil, Centurión contributed his part, acting as a military officer, magistrate, and state propagandist. Faithful to López to the end, he fought at Itá-Ybaté and, in 1870, was with his commander at Cerro Corá, where he suffered a painful face wound. His Brazilian captors took him to Rio de Janeiro after the war.

Released a few months later, Centurión made his way to London, where he married a Cuban acquaintance. He and his wife then moved to Cuba, where he practiced law. In 1877 he published a short memoir in New York. In 1878 he returned to Asunción, where he edited a key newspaper, *La Reforma*, served as attorney general under President Bernardino CABALLERO, and began writing another set of memoirs. Centurión joined General Caballero in organizing the Partido Colorado in 1887 and served as foreign minister under Patricio Escobar. In 1895, Centurión was elected senator, a post he held until his death in Asunción. His three-volume *Memorias o reminiscencias históricas sobre la guerra del Paraguay* (Buenos Aires, 1894–1897) is still regarded as the best war memoir from the Paraguayan side.

CHARLES KOLINSKI, *Historical Dictionary of Paraguay* (1973), p. 49; HARRIS G. WARREN, *Rebirth of the Paraguayan Republic: The First Colorado Era, 1878–1904* (1985), p. 292.

THOMAS L. WHIGHAM

CENTURIÓN, ROQUE MIRANDA (*b.* 1900; *d.* 1960), Paraguayan dramatist. Born in Carapeguá, Centurión completed his secondary education at the National College in Asunción and began his theatrical career in the capital city in 1926 as an actor in Félix Fernández's *Mborayjhú pajhú*. That same year, his first play, *Cupido sudando*, was performed. From 1926 to 1928, he lived in France and Spain. In 1932, he collaborated with Josefina PLÁ in the Spanish-Guarani play *Episodios chaqueños*. In 1933, his play *Tuyú*, in Guarani, was performed, and in 1942 and 1943, he again collaborated with Plá in *Desheredado* and *Sobre en blanco*.

Centurión was the founder of the Escuela Municipal de Declamación y Arte Escénico, which he directed until 1960. He was one of the founders of the ACADEMIA DE LA LENGUA Y CULTURA GUARANÍ. A radio pioneer, in 1936, Centurión promoted "La Peña," a broadcast created to provide the airways with cultural programs. In 1939, with Plá, he initiated the radio series "Proal," and he created the program "La Voz Cultural de la Nación."

CARLOS R. CENTURIÓN, *Historia de la cultura paraguaya*, vol. 2 (1961).

THOMAS E. CASE

CEPEDA, BATTLES OF, two conflicts at the *cañada* (ravine) of Cepeda in Buenos Aires Province in 1820 and 1859. The first of the two battles, over the issue of centralism versus federalism, took place on 1 February 1820. It was fought by the Federalist army under General Francisco RAMÍREZ of Entre Ríos, and the Buenos Aires army, headed by General José RONDEAU. Rondeau failed to secure assistance from José de SAN MARTÍN and Manuel BELGRANO—as they were busy elsewhere—and the *porteño* (Buenos Aires) army was dispersed at the first cavalry attack.

Porteño officers convinced the Buenos Aires *cabildo* to disband the directorate, Congress dissolved itself, and on 19 February 1820, the *cabildo* was replaced by a junta. On 23 February, Manuel de SARRATEA, head of the Buenos Aires junta, met with Estanislao LÓPEZ and Ramírez at the Capilla del Pilar, Buenos Aires Province, to sign a peace treaty, which the junta approved the following day. The public portion of the treaty provided for the security of the provinces of Buenos Aires, Entre Ríos, and Santa Fe and, anticipating the federal pact of 1831, accepted the principle of federation as the basis for national organization. Sixty days after the ratification, freely elected provincial representatives were to meet in San Lorenzo to form a constitutional convention. Entre Ríos and Santa Fe were to withdraw their forces from Buenos Aires, and free trade on the rivers bordering those provinces would resume. The national Congress would settle all boundary disputes. The treaty's secret portion stipulated that Ramírez would ask José ARTIGAS to ratify the treaty for the Banda Oriental, to join them, and to suspend military operations against Brazil. Ramírez entered Buenos Aires on 15 February and left it on 12 April, when he learned that Artigas, who disapproved of the Pilar treaty, had invaded Entre Ríos. The arrangements made at Pilar broke down when López and Juan Manuel de ROSAS signed a treaty at Benegas on 24 November 1820, in order to isolate Ramírez.

The second battle of Cepeda was fought 23 October 1859 over the tariff war between Buenos Aires and the Argentine Confederation, the refusal of Buenos Aires Province to join the union, and the national Congress's decision to authorize President-General Justo José de URQUIZA to bring a recalcitrant Buenos Aires into the union. Urquiza commanded the confederation's army, and Governor Bartolomé MITRE, the army of Buenos Aires. Fighting alongside the *porteños* was a Uruguayan division under General Venancio FLORES. The Buenos Aires forces were dispersed, and Mitre withdrew. Urquiza then negotiated an armistice at San Nicolás, mediated by Francisco Solano LÓPEZ of Paraguay.

Cepeda ended a war that the international community had tried to avoid. The Pact of the Union was signed on 11 November 1859, and Buenos Aires became a member of the Argentine Confederation. In accordance with the treaty, Buenos Aires proposed amendments to the national constitution that were accepted in 1860.

RAMÓN J. CÁRCANO, *Del sitio de Buenos Aires al campo de Cepeda*, 2d ed. (1921); DIEGO LUIS MOLINARI, *"¡Viva Ramírez!" El despotismo en las provincias de la Unión del Sur (1816–1820)* (1938); BEATRIZ BOSCH, *Urquiza y su tiempo*, 2d ed., rev. (1980). In English see JOSÉ LUIS ROMERO, *A History of Argentine Political Thought*, translated by Thomas F. McGann (1963), pp. 88, 89, 108; JOHN LYNCH, *The Spanish-American Revolutions, 1808–1826* (1973), pp. 69, 100, and *Argentine Dictator: Juan Manuel de Rosas* (1981), p. 26; LESLIE BETHELL, ed., *Spanish America After Independence, c. 1820–c. 1870* (1987), pp. 331, 352.

JOSEPH T. CRISCENTI

CERDO GORDO, BATTLE OF, an engagement on 18 April 1847 in which the Mexican Army was decisively defeated by the United States Army at a mountain pass between Veracruz and Mexico City. Following the indecisive engagement at BUENA VISTA, Antonio López de SANTA ANNA rushed south to deal with political problems in Mexico City and to confront the U.S. Army led by General Winfield SCOTT. Santa Anna chose to meet Scott at a narrow pass named Cerdo Gordo just east of Jalapa. He blocked the road with 25 pieces of artillery and 4,000 of his best troops and fortified the nearby heights of El Telégrafo and La Atalaya, holding 8,000 troops in reserve.

On 12 April, General David Twiggs, commanding some 2,500 men, ordered a precipitous attack on the Mexican position but escaped disaster by the overeagerness of the Mexican gunners. Scott arrived the following day with 6,000 men and ordered a reconnaissance of the formidable Mexican position. Engineer officers Captain Robert E. Lee and Lieutenant George Derby discovered a path around the Mexican position, which was unknown to Santa Anna.

Early on the morning of 18 April, Scott opened his assault with an artillery barrage. While part of the U.S. Army engaged the Mexicans along their front, Twiggs advanced along the path in order to cut off the Mexican line of retreat. Before reaching the Mexican rear as ordered, Twiggs prematurely attacked El Telégrafo and La Atalaya. After three hours of fighting, the Mexican Army broke and fled in disarray; Santa Anna barely escaped capture. The Mexicans lost approximately 3,000 men, and a like number were captured along with a large quantity of munitions. The United States suffered 64 dead and 353 wounded.

The victory at Cerdo Gordo allowed the U.S. Army to escape the unhealthy lowlands at the beginning of the yellow fever season. Also, the Mexicans lost most of their remaining better-trained units. Although the MEXICAN-AMERICAN WAR continued for another year, the Mexican Army was no longer capable of executing offensive maneuvers.

HUBERT HOWE BANCROFT, *History of Mexico* (1883); JOSÉ FERNANDO RAMÍREZ, *Mexico During the War with the United States*, edited by Walter V. Scholes and translated by Elliott B. Scherr (1950).

ROBERT SCHEINA

CERÉN, a small Late Classic (A.D. 650–900) residential site that was buried during the eruption of the Laguna Caldera volcano in the sixth or seventh century. Located in the Zapotitán Valley in central El Salvador, Cerén consists of two houses, outbuildings, activity areas, and a *milpa* (cornfield). The descending cloud of volcanic ash and gases burned palm-thatch roofs and wooden supports in walls, and blanketed the surfaces of all structures. The thirteen-foot-thick blanket of ash insulated site remains from erosion and decay, and the high temperatures of ash and gas at deposition fired the architectural features to nearly indestructible hardness.

Cerén appears to represent part of a dispersed settlement pattern of farmers living near their fields. Besides two houses, excavations have revealed storehouses containing storage pots for chiles, corn, and beans; a sweat house; a kitchen; and workshop areas. The house most fully excavated had *bajareque* (mud-and-pole) walls and floors made of a thick layer of clay. Thatch-roof construction resembled that in modern Maya houses.

Evidence of domestic activities that occurred in sections of the house were preserved. Behind a dividing wall on the raised floor were four large pots and a maul, much like modern kitchens in traditional areas of El Salvador. In the central portion of the house were a spindle whorl, for spinning cotton thread, and a miniature ceramic vessel, perhaps made by a child learning the craft. The southeastern end of the house had the vestiges of a grass floor mat, probably used for sleeping.

The *milpa* at Cerén had parallel cultivation ridges with intervening furrows, a method very different from that used by modern traditional Maya agriculturalists. The plant casts indicate that the Cerén site was buried by ash shortly after the onset of the growing season, in May or early June.

PAYSON D. SHEETS, "Maya Recovery from Volcanic Disasters: Ilopango and Cerén," in *Archaeology* 32 (1979):32–42; PAYSON D. SHEETS, ed., *Archaeology and Volcanism in Central America: The Zapotitán Valley of El Salvador* (1983); PAYSON D. SHEETS et al., "Household Archaeology at Cerén, El Salvador," in *Ancient Mesoamerica* 1 (1990):81–90; PAYSON D. SHEETS, *The Cerén Site: A Prehistoric Village Buried by Volcanic Ash in Central America* (1992).

KATHRYN SAMPECK

CEREZO ARÉVALO, MARCO VINICIO (*b.* 26 December 1942), president of Guatemala (1986–1991). Vinicio Cerezo was born in Guatemala City into a politically prominent family. His grandfather was murdered for opposing Jorge UBICO (1931–1944) and his father served on the Guatemalan Supreme Court. In 1954 Cerezo's political inclinations were awakened by the U.S.-sponsored overthrow of Jacobo ARBENZ (1951–1954). He joined the Christian Democratic Party (DCG) while a law student at the University of San Carlos. After completing his degree in 1968, he studied at Loyola University in New Orleans, Louisiana, and in Chile, Venezuela, West Germany, and Italy. He was elected to the congress in 1974. During the repressive regime of General LUCAS GARCÍA (1978–1982), he survived at least three attempts on his life.

In 1986 Vinicio Cerezo became the first elected civilian president since 1970 and only the second since Juan José ARÉVALO (1945–1951). Cerezo faced a difficult situation in 1986: a troublesome insurgency on the left, an intransigent military on the right, an increasingly mo-

bilized peasantry, and an economy in a state of crisis (declining GNP, escalating inflation, 40 percent unemployment, and scarce foreign exchange). To address these problems Cerezo launched a neoliberal program of export diversification, currency devaluation, removal of price controls, and increased taxes. The results were generally favorable for the national economy, but living standards for most people were reduced. This led to a series of massive strikes in 1987, 1988, and 1989.

Although supported by the military high command, Cerezo was opposed by field commanders who thought that domestic concerns were taking precedence over the government's counterinsurgency efforts. Coup attempts by disgruntled officers were launched in May 1988 and again in 1989.

In January 1987 Cerezo renewed the diplomatic relations with Britain that had been ruptured in 1981 by the granting of independence to Belize. In 1986 and 1987, he hosted the Central American peace talks in ESQUIPULAS which led to the successful implementation of the Arias peace plan, whose goal was the settlement of the insurgency wars in Central America.

Although elected on a platform to bring peace to Guatemala, Cerezo made little progress in ending the leftist insurgency or improving the country's human rights record. The coalition of four major guerrilla groups, the Guatemalan National Revolutionary Union (URNG), expanded its operations, and the number of assassinations by alleged right-wing death squads increased in Guatemala City. The problem was exacerbated by the massacre of fourteen men and boys in the Indian village of Santiago Atitlan in December 1990, which resulted in the cutoff of U.S. military aid.

Plagued by charges of corruption and drug trafficking, Cerezo was unable to secure the election of his handpicked successor, but he did preside over the first successive democratic presidential election in 151 years. Jorge SERRANO ELÍAS (*b.* 1945) was inaugurated in January 1991.

STEPHEN KINZER, "Walking the Tightrope in Guatemala," in *New York Times Magazine*, 9 November 1986; INFORPRESS CENTROAMERICANA, *Guatemala—1986, The Year of Promises* (1987); JAMES PAINTER, *Guatemala: False Hope, False Freedom: The Rich, The Poor, and the Christian Democrats* (1987); STEPHEN KINZER, "What Has Democracy Wrought," in *New York Times Magazine,* 26 March 1989; ROLAND H. EBEL, "Guatemala: The Politics of Unstable Stability," in *Latin American Politics and Development,* edited by Howard J. Wiarda and Harvey F. Kline (1990).

ROLAND H. EBEL

CERNA, VICENTE (*b.* ca. 1810; *d.* 27 June 1885), field marshal and president of Guatemala (1865–1871). A military officer who became by 1847 a close associate of the dictator Rafael CARRERA (1840–1865), Cerna played an important role at the battle of ARADA (1851). This battle established Carrera as the dominant military figure in Central America and as president for life (formally so in 1854). Outside Carrera's family no military man was closer to the dictator than Cerna, who was politically and militarily dependable and a devout Catholic, as was Carrera. Cerna later received the rank of field marshal for his performance in the difficult 1863 campaign against El Salvador's Liberal president Gerardo BARRIOS. Shortly before his death in April 1865, Carrera named Cerna to succeed him. In the close presidential election that followed in May this endorsement gave Cerna his margin of victory.

Carrera's regime had been in large measure reactionary but provided peace and encouraged development of coffee culture. Cerna continued most of Carrera's policies, seeking sufficient modernization for economic development under traditional institutions such as monopoly franchises (ESTANCOS) and the Consulado de Comercio, which favored a restricted circle of landowners, entrepreneurs, and merchants. Under Cerna Guatemala became more closely connected with the world trading system, which favored free trade. Cerna's regime improved the infrastructure of transportation and communication: the Pacific port of San José was built up; some roads and highways were improved; railroads were commissioned, though not built; and the telegraph was introduced, although it would not become effective until after 1871. In 1870–1871 an ambitious currency reform was introduced, a reform of land tenure sought, and a modern public market, which would stand for a century, was completed.

Despite some successes, pressures on the regime grew. A series of insurrections began in 1867 and Cerna's church-dominated government had poor relations with Benito JUÁREZ's victorious Liberal regime in Mexico. Both foreign and Guatemalan entrepreneurs associated with the expanding coffee culture became impatient with Cerna's policy. His reelection in 1869 involved manipulation, and in 1870 political repression ended parliamentary debate. Miguel GARCÍA GRANADOS, leader of the opposition, was forced into exile, from whence both Guatemalan and Mexican allies aided his organization of the Liberal revolution of 1871. Joined by those impatient for modernization in Guatemala, García Granados and Justo Rufino BARRIOS defeated Cerna's army on 29 June 1871 and took control of the government the next day.

JORGE SKINNER KLEE, *Revolución y derecho: Una investigación sobre el problema de la revolución en el derecho guatemalteco* (1971), esp. pp. 65–74; WAYNE M. CLEGERN, "Transition from Conservatism to Liberalism in Guatemala, 1865–1871," in *Hispanic-American Essays in Honor of Max Leon Moorhead*, edited by William S. Coker (1979), pp. 98–110; RALPH LEE WOODWARD, JR., *Central America: A Nation Divided*, 2d ed. (1985), and *Rafael Carrera and the Emergence of the Republic of Guatemala, 1821–1871* (1993); CAROL A. SMITH, ed., *Guatemalan Indians and the State, 1540–1988* (1990), esp. pp. 52–136; WAYNE M. CLEGERN, *Origins of Liberal Dictatorship in Central America* (1994).

WAYNE M. CLEGERN

CERRADO, tropical savanna of the Brazilian central plateau covering more than 700,000 square miles, or 22 percent of Brazil. *Cerrado* is rolling terrain with deep sandy soils of low fertility. Rainfall is heavy in the summer (November to March), while there is little precipitation the rest of the year. Vegetation consists of grasses, low bushes, and scattered trees. *Cerrado* has supported a cattle industry since the seventeenth century and is now the most important ranching region of Brazil. It also hosts vast soybean agribusinesses.

Cerrado was probably formed and maintained by the action of fire. Since the arrival of humans, it has been exposed to seasonal burning first by Indians and later by ranchers. Fire combined with overgrazing has caused severe erosion in some areas and the replacement of native grasses by tough invader species that first entered Brazil in explorer and slave ships. Several species of plants and animals in this region are on the endangered list due to habitat pressure.

Cerrado native peoples have also suffered significant population loss over the last century due to the expansion of permanent settlement originating in more populated regions of Brazil. The national capital city of BRASÍLIA is located in the middle of *cerrado*. The government and the region are often referred to by the term *planalto* (plateau).

KURT HUECK, "A primitividade dos 'campos cerrados' brasileiros e novas observações em seu limite meridional," in *Boletim Geográfico* (Rio de Janeiro) 31, no. 230 (set/out 1972): 215–225. LINDALVO BEZERRA DOS SANTOS, "Campo cerrado," in *Tipos e aspectos do Brasil*, 10th ed. (1975), pp. 469–470; G. EITEN, "Brazilian 'Savannas,'" and L. M. COUTINHO, "Ecological Effect of Fire in Brazilian Cerrado," in *Ecology of Tropical Savannas*, edited by B. J. Huntley and B. H. Walker (1982), pp. 25–47, 273–291; G. SARMIENTO, "The Savannas of Tropical America," in *Tropical Savannas*, edited by François Bourlière (1983), pp. 245–288.

ROBERT WILCOX

CERRO CORÁ, BATTLE OF, the final engagement of the WAR OF THE TRIPLE ALLIANCE on 1 March 1870. The remnants of the Paraguayan army under Field Marshal Francisco Solano LÓPEZ had been in flight for nearly a year when Brazilian cavalry units closed in on them at a spot along the Aquidaban-Nigui creek in northeastern Paraguay. In the battle, really more of a skirmish, the Brazilians quickly overwhelmed the defenders. The Paraguayan vice president, several ministers, and high military officers were all killed. So was Field Marshal López, who, when called upon to surrender, purportedly refused in the most florid terms, crying, "Muero con mi patria!" (I die with my country!). Extremist writers and hagiographers later converted that expression into a virtual national slogan for Paraguay. In reality, López's demise at Cerro Corá ended a bloody war that had taken the lives of at least 100,000 people.

CHARLES A. WASHBURN, *The History of Paraguay, with Notes and Personal Observations* (1871), vol. 2, *passim*; CHARLES J. KO-

LINSKI, "The Death of Francisco Solano López," *The Historian* 26, no. 1 (1963): 75–91, and *Independence or Death! The Story of the Paraguayan War* (1965).

THOMAS L. WHIGHAM

CERRO CORPORACIÓN. *See* **Gran Minería.**

CERRO DE PASCO CORPORATION, foreign-owned Peruvian mining company. Cerro was founded in 1902 by an American syndicate composed, among others, of J. P. Morgan, Henry Clay Frick, and Darius Ogden Mills. It shortly came to control the majority of mines in Cerro de Pasco and Morococha, spearheading a general trend toward the denationalization of the Peruvian mining industry during the first three decades of the twentieth century. The labor force at Cerro was recruited from the surrounding peasantry and, at its peak prior to the depression, amounted to some 13,000 workers, or about 30 percent of the total mining proletariat in the country. Between 1916 and 1937 Cerro's gross earnings amounted to some $375 million, of which $207 million or (55 percent) was returned to the local economy and $169 million (45 percent) went abroad to pay for imports and as profits. As one of the largest multinational corporations operating in Peru during the twentieth century, Cerro not only had a huge impact on the national and local economy but also intervened directly and indirectly in both internal and external affairs, leading it to become a source of deep resentment to the Peruvian people prior to its nationalization in 1973 as CENTROMÍN.

DIRK KRUIJT and MENNO VELLINGA, *Labor Relations and Multinational Corporations: The Cerro de Pasco Corporation in Peru (1902–1974)* (1979).

PETER F. KLARÉN

CERRO NARRÍO, an important archaeological site in the south-central highlands of Ecuador. Stratigraphic excavations conducted at the site in the 1940s have produced some of the earliest known pottery in the highlands and have yielded a lengthy ceramic sequence that has been used as a baseline for interpreting the regional archaeology. The site is also significant for the evidence it has produced of early connections between the sierra, coastal Ecuador, and the Amazonian lowlands.

The site of Cerro Narrío is situated on a hilltop across the river from the modern town of Cañar, at an elevation of 10,230 feet. The surface of this barren hilltop is literally paved with ceramic potsherds. In the early 1920s, a find of several gold objects at Cerro Narrío induced indiscriminate looting of the site on a massive scale. For all the activity, very little gold was actually recovered and the site of Cerro Narrío was all but destroyed.

Twenty years later, two North American scholars, recognizing the archaeological significance of the site, undertook limited excavations in the remaining undisturbed areas. Their excavations produced enormous quantities of sherds, the principal variety being that which the excavators classified as Narrío Red-on-Buff. This pottery type, most often a jar form decorated with painted red bands, is found in all occupation levels at the site. Almost as common numerically, though confined to the lower levels, is the spectacularly thin-walled pottery identified as Narrío Red-on-Buff Fine. This was the index ware (the pottery type that marks or indicates a specific chronological period) for the archaeological culture or phase known as Chaullabamba. In addition to the local pottery, exotic styles and influences identified at Cerro Narrío include Valdivia and Chorrera elements from coastal Ecuador, the "Group X" components possibly deriving from the eastern Andean slopes or lowlands, Puruhá and Tuncahuán wares from further north, Kotosh styles from the Peruvian MONTAÑA, and Chimú pieces from Peru's north coast.

Based on the relative changes in the percentages of these wares found in different stratigraphic levels, the occupational history of the site was divided into an earlier and a later phase. Though work at the site was conducted prior to the advent of radiocarbon dating, subsequent assays of charcoal collected from the lower levels of the site gave a date of 1978 B.C. This and other carbon 14 dates from sites in the Cañar Valley having an Early Cerro Narrío component associate this phase with the Early Formative period of Ecuadorian prehistory. Cross-referencing of exotic styles found primarily in the upper levels of the site associate the Late Cerro Narrío phase with the Late Formative period (about 1500–500 B.C.).

In addition to pottery, occupational debris found at the site includes stone beads, bone awls and whistles, shell beads and figurines, copper objects, and cylindrical pottery "drums." Charred remnants provide direct evidence of maize cultivation, while numerous deer and rabbit bones indicate that hunting continued to be an important subsistence activity. Postholes encountered in some excavation units indicate that the dwellings constructed by the site's inhabitants were both circular and rectangular in form, with the latter type perhaps postdating the former. The burials encountered were simple and generally lacking in funerary offerings.

The ceramic sequence at Cerro Narrío and the crosscorrelation of exotic styles found at the site with other regions have been taken as evidence of early contact between the southern Ecuadorian highlands, coast, and eastern lowlands; of trade with the north coast of Peru; of indirect links with the civilizations of Central America; and of possible influences from the Middle Horizon cultures of southern Peru. Cerro Narrío is thus considered a key site in the reconstruction of Ecuadorian prehistory.

BETTY J. MEGGERS, *Ecuador* (1966), especially pp. 53–55, 108–111; DONALD COLLIER and JOHN V. MURRA, *Survey and Excavations in Southern Ecuador,* Field Museum of Natural History,

Anthropological Series, Publication 523, vol. 35 (1943); and ROBERT BRAUN, "The Formative as Seen from the Southern Ecuadorian Highlands," in *Primer simpósio de corelaciones antropológicas Andino-Mesoamericano*, edited by Jorge Marcos and Presley Norton (1982), pp. 41–53.

TAMARA L. BRAY

CERROS, a Late Preclassic (300 B.C.–A.D. 250) Maya site located in Belize on a narrow spit of swampy land where the New River empties into Chetumal Bay. Cerros underwent a dramatic transformation from an egalitarian fishing and trading community to a cosmopolitan political capital during the Late Preclassic period.

Inhabitants fished in fresh and salt water and also worked wood extensively, probably making dugout canoes. Raised agricultural fields were located both at the site center and near the river's mouth. A large, low platform bordering the nucleated village's shoreline appears to have been a dock. Imported ceramics and foreign stylistic affinities indicate that Cerros was a trading community.

The initial phase of settlement (300–200 B.C.) was a nucleated village. Slightly later, an elaborately decorated pyramid was built. The south side and lower terraces flanking the stairway of the pyramid were decorated with polychrome painted panels and modeled stucco masks. The use of this pyramid and the nucleated settlement ended in an elaborate ritual, evinced by ceramics and jade that were smashed and left in place. Elite residences and ceremonial structures were subsequently erected over this same area.

From 200 to 50 B.C., residential settlement gradually became more dispersed. The transition from nucleated to dispersed settlement and additions to ceremonial architecture at the center were completed by A.D. 150. An elaborate system of artificial drainage was used during this period, probably to help compensate for the seasonal availability of fresh water. A massive artificial canal bordered the dispersed settlement zone and drained the central precinct. This hydraulic system rapidly deteriorated following the Late Preclassic collapse of Cerros as a political capital. Settlement at Cerros persisted after A.D. 250, but the site never regained the political, economic, or religious importance it had during the Late Preclassic.

DAVID A. FREIDEL, "Maritime Adaptation and the Rise of Maya Civilization: The View from Cerros, Belize," in *Prehistoric Coastal Adaptations*, edited by Barbara L. Stark and Barbara Voorhies (1978), pp. 239–265; ROBIN A. ROBERTSON, *Archaeology at Cerros, Belize, Central America*, vol. 1, *An Interim Report* (1986); DAVID A. FREIDEL and LINDA SCHELE, *A Forest of Kings: The Untold Story of the Ancient Maya* (1990), esp. pp. 96–129.

KATHRYN SAMPECK

CERRUTO, ÓSCAR (*b.* 13 June 1912; *d.* 10 April 1981), Bolivian poet, novelist, and storyteller. One of the most important figures of contemporary Bolivian literature,

Cerruto wrote his first group of poems, *Cifra de las rosas* (1957), within the aesthetics of modernism. This poetical composition is followed by *Patria de sal cautiva* (1958), *Estrella segregada* (1973), and *Reverso de la transparencia* (1975), wherein Cerruto explores the possibilities of avant-gardism. His imagery is harsh and in harmony with the high plateau landscapes of Andean Bolivia. Of great intensity and linguistic precision, Cerruto's works denounce the excesses of power and examine the topics of hate, solitude, fear, and death. His poetry, embedded in the Judeo-Christian notion of guilt, dissociates itself from his early revolutionary ideals of social transformation, admirably set forth in his novel *Aluvión de fuego* (1935). The absence of social redemption can be perceived in his later narrative, particularly in *Cerco de penumbras* (1958), a volume of short stories.

A brief but excellent study of Cerruto's poetry may be found in EDUARDO MITRE, *El árbol y la piedra: Poetas contemporáneos de Bolivia* (1988). Two major contributions on Cerruto are LUIS H. ANTEZANA, "Sobre 'Estrella segregada' de Óscar Cerruto," in his *Ensayos y lecturas* (1986); and ÓSCAR RIVERA-RODAS, "La poesía de Óscar Cerruto," in *Cuadernos Hispanoamericanos* 417 (1985): 146–154.

JAVIER SANJINÉS C.

CERUTI, ROQUE (*b.* ca. 1683; *d.* 6 December 1760), Italian composer active in Peru. Born in Milan, then under Spanish rule, Ceruti studied the violin there until 1706. When the Marquis Castell dos Ríus, viceroy of Peru, appointed him director of music, Ceruti settled in Lima, where he conducted the premiere of his opera *El mejor escudo de Perseo* at the viceroyal palace on 17 September 1708. In 1720 he moved to Trujillo and was named *maestro de capilla* of the cathedral there (1721–1728). In 1728 Ceruti succeeded Tomás de TORREJÓN Y VELASCO as *maestro de capilla* of the Lima cathedral, remaining in that position until his death. During Ceruti's tenure the cathedral continued to be an active music center. Ceruti composed and published numerous works: mythological operas and pastorals, secular and religious music, some in Spanish, others on Latin texts. His manuscripts are kept in the Lima Archives, in the San Antonio Abad Seminary in Cuzco, in Sucre cathedral, in Santa Clara Conventín Cochabamba, in private collections, and at the archive of the church of San Francisco de Asís in Montevideo. He died in Lima.

ROBERT M. STEVENSON, *The Music of Peru* (1960) and *Renaissance and Baroque Musical Sources in the Americas* (1970); *New Grove Dictionary of Music and Musicians*, vol. 4 (1980).

SUSANA SALGADO

CERVANTES, VICENTE (*b.* 1755; *d.* 26 July 1829), distinguished botanist of Bourbon Mexico. Born in Zafra, Badajoz, Spain, Cervantes began his career as an apprentice to an apothecary, studying pharmacy part-time. After passing the pharmacist's examination, he served as chief pharmacist at the general hospital in Madrid until Charles III chose him as a member of the royal botanical expedition to New Spain. The expedition arrived in New Spain in 1787; Cervantes, appointed professor of botany at the University of Mexico, began teaching the following year. His popular courses, which emphasized Linnaean principles, introduced a generation of Mexican creoles to the modern study of botany.

Cervantes also was a founder of the Royal Botanical Gardens, located in the viceregal palace, and its head from 1802. There, he and his assistants cultivated some 1,400 species of plants; the New World flora came mostly from central Mexico, though some species were imported from as far away as Havana. Cervantes, who remained in Mexico when the rest of the expedition departed, faced difficulties after 1810. The hard-pressed viceregal government progressively slashed the Royal Botanical Gardens' budget, and Cervantes was unable to prevent the institution's gradual deterioration. He died in Mexico City.

The most complete study of Cervantes and the Royal Botanical Gardens is HAROLD WILLIAM RICKETT, *The Royal Botanical Expedition to New Spain, 1788–1820* (1947). For a more general treatment of botanical studies under the Bourbons, see ARTHUR R. STEELE, *Flowers for the King: The Expedition of Ruíz and Pavón and the Flora of Peru* (1964), esp. pp. 3–49.

R. DOUGLAS COPE

CERVANTES KAWANAGH, IGNACIO (*b.* 31 July 1847; *d.* 29 April 1905), pioneer of Cuban musical nationalism. Cervantes, a native of Havana, was not the first Cuban nationalist musician, but it was in his *contradanzas* that this musical genre found its fullest expression. He benefited from the friendship of the American composer Louis M. Gottschalk, who in 1865 advised Cervantes's parents to send him to study in Paris, where he won numerous awards. Like José WHITE, another Cuban musician, he was forced by the Spaniards to leave Cuba (to which he had returned in 1870) during the TEN YEARS' WAR (1868–1878). He later became a friend of José MARTÍ, whom he assisted in his revolutionary activities. As a composer his magnum opus was his series of Cuban dances (some forty of which are extant). Because of their richness and complexity, they became concert music. They have been described as "the soul of Cuba in full bloom." He died in Havana.

JOSÉ I. LASAGA, *Cuban Lives: Pages from Cuban History* (1984), vol. 1, pp. 223–231. See also ALEJO CARPENTIER, *La música en Cuba* (1946).

JOSÉ M. HERNÁNDEZ

CERVETTI, SERGIO (*b.* 9 November 1940), Uruguayan composer. Born in Dolores, Cervetti studied piano in Montevideo with Hugo Balzo and counterpoint and harmony with Carlos ESTRADA and Guido Santórsola. He then studied composition at the Peabody Conserva-

tory in Baltimore under the direction of Ernst Krenek and Stefan Grové. Later he worked in electronic music under the guidance of Mario DAVIDOVSKY, Vladimir Ussachevsky, and Alcides LANZA. He received the composition prize at the Caracas Festival in 1966. In 1968 he was artist-in-residence with the DAAD (German exchange program) for the city of Berlin and received important commissions from Baden-Baden and the Art Academy in Berlin. His music for ballet includes *Transatlantic Light* (1987) for the Dance Company of Nina Wiener and *40 Second/42 Variations* (1979) for the Holland Festival.

Until 1971 Cervetti's work was characterized by dodecaphonic tendencies with some incursions into aleatoric languages. Following his move to New York City, he became part of the minimalist movement. Even if his aesthetics separated him completely from other Latin American musical schools modeled after the European, particularly Polish, composers, Cervetti created his own version of minimalism, producing works with strong lyrical lines, thick counterpoint, and a hypnotic atmosphere.

Other important works by Cervetti include Five Episodes for chamber ensemble (1965); *Divertimento* for woodwinds (1964); *Plexus* for orchestra (1970), commissioned by the Fifth Inter-American Music Festival, Washington, D.C.; *Zinctum* for string quartet (1967); *The Bottom of the Iceberg* for solo guitar (1975); *Transatlantic Light* for electronic keyboard (1987); *Lucet in Tenebris* for choir (1970); *Bits and Pieces and Moving Parts* for chamber ensemble and tape (1970); Trumpet Concerto (1977); *4 Fragments of Isadora* for soprano and piano (1979); *Wind Devil* for electronic tape (1983); *Llanto, muerte y danza* for harpsichord (1984); *3 Estudios australes* for piano (1989); Concerto for harpsichord and eleven instruments (1990); *Leyenda* for soprano and orchestra (1991); and *Las indias olvidadas*, a concerto for harpsichord and chamber group (1992), commissioned by the Festival of Alicante, Spain.

JOHN VINTON, ed. *Dictionary of Contemporary Music* (1974), p. 134; GÉRARD BÉHAGUE, *Music in Latin America: An Introduction* (1979), pp. 341–342; *Octavo festival internacional de música contemporánea* (1992), pp. 46–47, 110–111.

ALCIDES LANZA

CÉSAIRE, AIMÉ (*b.* 25 June 1913), West Indian writer. Born in Martinique, Césaire graduated from the well-known Lycée Victor Schoelcher in Fort-de-France in 1931. He later studied in Paris at the Lycée Louis-le-Grand, where he met Léopold Sédar Senghor from Senegal and many other young black students from African and Caribbean countries. In 1934 Césaire invented the neologism NÉGRITUDE as an expression of pride in the African cultural heritage. Césaire helped found the black magazine *L'Étudiant Noir* (1934–1936). In 1939, the same year that his now classic epic poem *Cahier d'un retour au pays natal* (1939; Notebook of a Return to the Native Land) came out in Paris, Césaire returned to Martinique.

During World War II, Césaire worked as a teacher and founded the magazine *Tropiques* (1941–1945) in order to maintain contact with French-language literature. In spring 1941, the famous surrealist poet André Breton payed Césaire a visit. This historic encounter not only confirmed the strong identification Césaire felt with the antirationalism of the surrealist movement but also inspired Bretón to write a preface to a new edition of the *Notebook* (1947), in which he described Césaire as the "Great Black Poet." In the meantime, Césaire, who had written about the Haitian hero of independence Toussaint L'OUVERTURE in his *Notebook*, undertook a trip to Haiti, where he remained from May to December of 1944.

Although Césaire's poetry is highly regarded, he is better known for his polemical essays and plays. In 1945 he was elected mayor of Fort-de-France and, after denouncing the French Communist Party in 1956, he founded his own independent socialist party, the Martinican Progressive Party, or PPM, two years later. His political ideas are reflected in his essay against colonialism, *Discours sur le colonialisme* (1950); the letters against communism, *Lettres à Maurice Thorez* (1956); and a historical interpretation of *Toussaint L'Ouverture* (1960). In his plays—such as *La Tragédie du roi Christophe, Une saison au Congo* (1967), and *Une tempête* (1969)—he concentrates on the problems of newly independent African countries against the background of Caribbean history.

An extensive biographical and critical overview is provided by two African scholars: MBAWIL A MPAANG NGAL, *Aimé Césaire: Un homme à la recherche d'une patrie* (1975), and ALIKO SONGOLO, *Aimé Césaire, un poétique de la découverte* (1985). JEAN-CLAUDE BAJEUX, *Antilia retrouvée* (1983), compares Césaire's work with the poetry of Claude McKay and Luis Palés Matos from Puerto Rico. JOSAPHAT B. KUBAYANDA in *The Poet's Africa: Africanness in the Poetry of Nicolás Guillén and Aimé Césaire* (1990), links Césaire's poetry to the work of the Cuban poet Nicolás Guillén. Also in English is JANIS PALLISTER, *Aimé Césaire* (1992).

INEKE PHAF

CÉSPEDES, CARLOS MANUEL DE (THE ELDER)

(*b.* 18 April 1819; *d.* ca. 22 March 1874), nineteenth-century Cuban revolutionary. Son of a sugar planter in Cuba's Oriente Province, Céspedes received his baccalaureate degree in Havana in 1840. He then went to study law in Spain where he was exposed to the ideas of FREEMASONRY, participated in revolutionary activities for which he was exiled to France, and committed himself to opposing colonial repression. When he returned to Cuba, Céspedes joined with other like-minded eastern planters and cattle ranchers, including Ignacio AGRAMONTE, Salvador Cisneros Betancourt, Bartolomé Masó, Pedro Figueredo, and Francisco Vicente Aguilera, who were convinced that Cuba would only win its freedom through the military defeat of Spain. Hence, in the isolated and less-developed corners of the Oriente, Céspedes and the other conspirators used Masonic lodges to organize and coordinate their activities.

On 10 October 1868, without consulting the other leaders, Céspedes held a public meeting at his plantation, La Demajagua, at which he freed his slaves. He then encouraged his listeners to follow the path of such Latin American freedom fighters as Simón BOLÍVAR and José de SAN MARTÍN. Finally, he issued the GRITO DE YARA, in which he proclaimed Cuban independence from Spain.

But despite their commitment to independence, Céspedes and his co-conspirators envisioned independence as a transitional step in the process of union with the United States. Only weeks after the independence proclamation, Céspedes led a delegation of Cuban revolutionaries to Washington, D.C., to petition the American secretary of state to consider Cuba's admission to the Union. A year later the revolutionary Constituent Assembly of Guáimaro explicitly proclaimed annexation as the ultimate purpose of the Cuban rebellion.

Despite an initial setback, by 1869 Céspedes was the acknowledged leader of the insurrection and on 10 April he was chosen to be president of the republic declared by the Constituent Assembly. However, divided by petty regionalism, class origins, and conflicts over military strategy, the revolutionaries lacked the unity and discipline essential for victory. Céspedes's authoritarian disposition only intensified the centrifugal forces of the revolutionary movement. In 1873 Céspedes was deposed in absentia as president, and on 22 March of the following year he was killed in a skirmish with Spanish forces.

CHARLES E. CHAPMAN, *History of the Cuban Republic* (1927); TERESITA MARTÍNEZ VERGNE, "Politics and Society in the Spanish Caribbean during the Nineteenth Century" (1989); LOUIS A. PÉREZ, JR., *Cuba: Between Reform and Revolution* (1989), and *Cuba and the United States* (1990); LESLIE BETHELL, *Cuba: A Short History* (1993).

WADE A. KIT

CÉSPEDES Y QUESADA, CARLOS MANUEL DE

(*b.* 1871; *d.* 1939), Cuban diplomat and writer. Céspedes y Quesada was the son of Carlos Manuel de CÉSPEDES, the Elder, the Cuban revolutionary who was elected president in 1869 and who was killed in battle during the TEN YEARS' WAR. As a child he studied in the United States, France, and Germany, and in 1901 he received a degree in public and civil law from the University of Havana.

Like his father, Céspedes y Quesada played an active role in the movement for Cuban independence. He was among the leading participants of the 1895 Cuban Revolution. Prior to American involvement in the war, he served as governor of Oriente Province, representative of the Second Army Corps, secretary of the Assembly of La Yaya, colonel of the General Staff of the Inspector General, and secretary of the "junta consultiva."

During the two American interventions (1899–1902, 1906–1909), Céspedes y Quesada withdrew entirely from political life. But upon the creation of the republic, he initiated a long and fruitful diplomatic and political career that lasted for more than thirty years. Among the most important posts he occupied were congressional representative from Oriente; president of the Commission on Tariffs and Codes; ambassador successively to Italy (1909–1912), to Argentina (1912–1913), and to the United States (1913–1922); secretary of state (1922–1926); and ambassador to France (1930–1933). While minister in Washington he negotiated the sale of the Cuban sugar crops of 1917 and 1918 to the United States and the Allies. Upon the overthrow of Cuban dictator Gerardo MACHADO Y MORALES in 1933, Céspedes y Quesada, by virtue of his brief tenure as secretary of state, became president of the republic, a position he held from 12 August until 5 September.

Besides being a member of numerous learned societies and the recipient of countless Cuban and foreign honors, he also was a renowned writer. Among the many works he authored, the most noteworthy are *Cuba y el derecho de la fuerza*, *El problema de la haciendas comuneras*, *La oración fúnebre del Mayor General Bartolomé Masó*, and *Carlos Manuel de Céspedes y Loynaz*.

LOUIS A. PÉREZ, *Cuba Under the Platt Amendment, 1902–1934* (1986), and *Cuba: Between Reform and Revolution* (1989); LESLIE BETHELL, *Cuba: A Short History* (1993).

WADE A. KIT

CEVALLOS, PEDRO ANTONIO DE (*b.* 29 June 1715; *d.* 24 December 1778), governor of Buenos Aires (1756–1766); viceroy of Río de la Plata (1777–1778). Born in Cádiz, the son of the general superintendent of customs of that city, Cevallos studied for a military career at the Seminario de Nobles in Madrid. Promoted to field marshal by 1747, Cevallos arrived in the Río de la Plata in 1756 as governor and chief of a sizable military expedition charged with containing the Portuguese. During his tenure as governor, Cevallos traveled extensively in the Misiones area. He returned to Spain in 1767, but in 1776 was again called upon to confront the Portuguese. Proving himself to be a fine strategist, he successfully ousted the Portuguese from Colonia in 1777, proceeding to Buenos Aires as first viceroy of the Río de la Plata. During his brief term of office, Cevallos promulgated free-trade ordinances. Shortly after taking office, he fell ill on a trip to Córdoba and died. A lifelong bachelor, Cevallos left at least one illegitimate son in Buenos Aires, born shortly after his father's death.

ENRIQUE UDAONDO, *Diccionario biográfico colonial argentino* (1945), pp. 249–252; HIALMAR EDMUNDO GAMMALSSON, *El virrey Cevallos* (1976); ENRIQUE M. BARBA, *Don Pedro de Cevallos*, 2d ed. (1978).

SUSAN M. SOCOLOW

CHACABUCO, BATTLE OF (12 February 1817), a clash between the Spanish Royalists and the pro-independence Army of the Andes. Chacabuco was an important military encounter in Chile's struggle to win independence from Spain. The rebel force, raised in Mendoza by the Argentine general José de SAN MARTÍN

Bernardo O'Higgins in the battle of Chacabuco. PHOTOGRAPHIC ARCHIVE, UNIVERSIDAD DE CHILE.

and Chilean patriot Bernardo o'HIGGINS, crossed the Andes at Uspallata and Los Patos, surprising and defeating the troops of Francisco Casimiro Marcó del Pont before he could mass his soldiers. Although some Spanish troops remained in Chile, requiring additional mopping up, the insurgent victory at Chacabuco constituted the first successful step in the struggle which culminated in Chile's independence.

LUIS GALDAMES, *A History of Chile* (1941), pp. 195, 209; STEPHEN CLISSOLD, *Bernardo O'Higgins and the Independence of Chile* (1968), pp. 144–146, 148.

WILLIAM F. SATER

CHACARA. *See* **Land Tenure: Brazil.**

CHACMOOLS. A *Chacmool* (literally, "red" or "great jaguar paw") is a Mesoamerican human figural sculpture in a distinctive semireclining position, with legs flexed, chest raised at an incline, head looking toward the viewer, and holding a receptacle on its stomach. Twelve *chacmools* have been discovered at CHICHÉN ITZÁ, eight are known from Tula, Hidalgo, and many others have been found at Tenochtitlán and sites in Veracruz, Tlaxcala, Michoacán, Querétaro, and Central America. They date from the Terminal Classic to Early Postclassic periods (ca. 800–1521).

The *chacmool* generally has been considered a TOLTEC sculptural form, introduced at Chichén Itzá from Tula between about 900 and 1000. Some scholars question this view, however, since no pre-Toltec central Mexican prototype exists, and since a greater number come from Chichén Itzá. Mary Ellen Miller (1985) proposed that the *chacmool* derives from recumbent captives depicted in Classic MAYA art.

Chacmool, Chichén Itzá, Yucatán. ORGANIZATION OF AMERICAN STATES.

The functions and cult associations of the *chacmool* may have varied over time. Late versions have been associated with fertility deities such as Tezcatzoncatl, a México pulque god, or the rain god Tlaloc. Earlier *chacmools* from Tula and Chichén Itzá lack distinctive deity associations but hold platelike receptacles for sacrificial offerings, suggesting they served as divine messengers.

ENRIQUE JUAN PALACIOS, "El simbolismo del chac-mool: Su interpretación," in *Revista Mexicana de Estudios Antropológicos* 4, nos. 1–2 (1940): 43–56; CÉSAR LIZARDI RAMOS, "El Chacmool mexicano," in *Cuadernos Americanos* 14 (March–April 1944): 137–148; J. CORONA NÚÑEZ, "Cual es el verdadero significado del Chac Mool?" in *Tlatoani* 1, nos. 5–6 (1952): 57–62; ALFREDO CUELLAR, *Tezcatzoncatl escultórico: El "Chac Mool" (el dios mesoamericano del vino)* (1981); MARY ELLEN MILLER, "A Reexamination of the Mesoamerican Chacmool," in *Art Bulletin* 67, no. 1 (1985): 7–17.

JEFF KARL KOWALSKI

CHACO REGION (El Gran Chaco), a vast alluvial plain, shaped like a cone, in the interior of South America. The Chaco region occupies more than 100,000 square miles of western Paraguay, eastern Bolivia, and northern Argentina. It is extremely flat, rising only gently from the Paraná-Paraguay river system in the east to western Argentina and the lowlands of eastern Bolivia. It is divided by rivers into three sections: the Chaco Austral between the Salado and Bermejo rivers, the Chaco Central between the Bermejo and Pilcomayo rivers, and the Chaco Boreal from the Pilcomayo to just north of the Paraguay-Bolivia border.

During the summer, many areas are drenched with rain, leaving lagoons, swamps, and rivulets overflowing in every direction. In winter these same areas are arid wastelands cut irregularly by thorn forests. The region is home to a vast array of fauna, including jaguars, tapirs, parrots, and a species of peccary long thought to be extinct. Usually cited as one of the continent's last great wildernesses, much of it remains sparsely settled and infrequently visited, although it produces timber, livestock, and cotton.

In pre-Columbian times the Chaco region was synonymous with the unknown. The Indians of the Altiplano simply called it *chacu,* a Quechua word meaning "great hunting ground." GUARANI Indians from Paraguay and Brazil crossed it to trade with Andean peoples. Sixteenth-century Spanish explorers followed the Guaranis across the Chaco to Peru; but after the Chaco peoples, including the MOCOBÍS, ABIPONES, and Tobas, acquired horses and resisted Spanish incursions, the Spaniards forgot the route and rarely ventured into the region.

In the eighteenth century Spanish ranchers and timber merchants penetrated the Chaco. Late in the century, government expeditions probed the interior, and minor missions were sent to the Abipones and Mocobís. During the late nineteenth century, venture capitalists from Argentina and Europe sought to open the Chaco to commercial exploitation. They focused primarily on the region's hardwoods—lapacho, curupay, petereby, and especially QUEBRACHO (a source of tannin for curing leather). Their efforts were hampered by the climate, terrain, and Indian resistance. The Indians of the Argentine Chaco were finally subdued in the 1880s, those of the Bolivian Chaco in the 1890s. Only MENNONITE farmers, who came from eastern Europe to the Paraguayan Chaco in the beginning of the twentieth century seemed to make the land thrive. They raised cattle and grew cotton.

Border disputes—and a lingering rumor that the region possessed sizable reserves of petroleum—led to the CHACO WAR (1932–1935), in which Paraguay bested Bolivia, gaining most of the Chaco Boreal, at the cost of tens of thousands of lives.

After the war, colonization increased, especially in the eastern part of the Chaco. Ranches and farms gradually replaced military posts. The Chaco Indian groups—Chiriguanos, Makas, Nivaklés, Lenguas, Ayoreos, and others—hired out as wranglers or day-laborers chiefly on Mennonite lands. National and foreign companies exploited the Argentine Chaco. Oil companies explored the Chaco without success. By the late 1980s, stockraising, dairy farming, and cotton growing had transformed the Argentine Chaco and the eastern Paraguayan Chaco. The traditional isolation and backwardness of these areas were becoming things of the past. Daily commuters from Asunción now crossed a new bridge over the Paraguay River to Chaco communities, and Chaco products traveled to Asunción. Nevertheless, vast stretches of the Chaco, especially in the center and west, were still nearly empty of human population.

MARTIN DOBRIZHOFFER, *An Account of the Abipones: An Equestrian People of Paraguay*, 3 vols., translated by Sara Coleridge (1822; repr. in 1 vol., 1970); PEDRO LOZANO, *Descripción corográfica del Gran Chaco Gualambra* (1941); ALFRED MÉTRAUX, "Ethnography of the Chaco," and JUAN BELAIEFF, "The Present-Day Indians of the Gran Chaco," in *Handbook of South American Indians*, vol. 1, edited by Julian H. Steward (1946), pp. 197–370, 371–380; DAVID H. ZOOK, *The Conduct of the Chaco War* (1960); HARRY ROBINSON, *Latin America: A Geographic Survey* (rev. ed., 1967), pp. 432–435, 464–466; LUIS JORGE FONTANA, *El Gran Chaco: Estudio Preliminar de Ernesto J. A. Maeder* (1977); ANDREW NICKSON, *Historical Dictionary of Paraguay* (rev. ed., 1993), pp. 111–123.

JAMES SCHOFIELD SAEGER
THOMAS L. WHIGHAM

CHACO WAR, a conflict that began in June 1932 when Bolivian and Paraguayan outposts clashed at a brackish lake in the northern Chaco Boreal, a territory over which the two nations disputed sovereignty. This spark began a bloody war that lasted until 1935.

The Chaco War front, 14 June 1934: Paraguayan regiments get last orders before leaving to do battle with the Bolivian army. BETTMANN ARCHIVE.

The Chaco Boreal was a vast, inhospitable, and sparsely populated area bordering the two countries. In the summer (November–February) the sun parched the hot, dry earth, and in the rainy season (March–October) heavy rains created huge marshes that bred disease-carrying insects. Both Bolivia and Paraguay looked upon the Chaco as a potential site of development and wealth. Some Bolivians believed that they could regain their access to the sea, which they had lost in the WAR OF THE PACIFIC (1879–1883), by developing a port on the PARAGUAY RIVER at the northeastern corner of the disputed territory. Much of Paraguay's foreign exchange was earned by exports of quebracho bark and cattle hides from the Chaco. In order to improve their claims to the territory, both countries had accelerated exploration and the establishment of outposts.

Although both sides had been preparing for this war for decades, neither really appreciated the logistical obstacles that they would face. As a result, prewar operational plans were useless and soon abandoned. Bolivia's situation was made significantly more difficult by the differences in strategy and priorities between President Daniel SALAMANCA and the country's military leaders, whose antagonism grew as the war progressed. In contrast, General José ESTIGARRIBIA emerged as the de facto commander of the Paraguayan Army and won the unconditional support of recently elected President Eusebio AYALA.

Following the fighting at Lake Pitiantuta, the Bolivian army conducted a limited offensive in the east-central Chaco, capturing a number of *fortines* (small forts), the most important being Boquerón. Salamanca then ordered the army to suspend operations, fearing that Argentina might intervene on the side of Paraguay. Estigarribia immediately attacked Boquerón, and after a stout defense by the Bolivians, the Paraguayans captured it on 29 September. Each side sustained some 3,000 casualties.

The Bolivian public was shocked at this defeat and demanded the recall of General Hans Kundt from exile. Kundt had headed a German military mission to Bolivia prior to World War I, and following the war he returned, became a Bolivian citizen, and resumed command of the army. During the late 1920s he had been exiled for political activity. Many Bolivians believed that, as the creator of the modern army, he could win the day. In December 1932 Kundt launched a series of offensives against Paraguayan *fortines*, focusing on Nanawa in the east-central Chaco. Time and time again, Kundt unsuccessfully threw masses of infantry against well-prepared defensive positions. Nanawa earned the nickname the Verdun of South America. After a year of unimaginative, costly tactics, Kundt was relieved by General Enrique PEÑARANDA.

In October 1932 Estigarribia began his offensive, driving the Bolivians from *fortín* to *fortín* across the central Chaco. He was finally halted before Fortín Ballivián on the bank of the PILCOMAYO RIVER in the southwest corner of the Chaco. Although the *fortín* had no special military significance, it had become the symbol of Bolivia's presence in the Chaco. Nonetheless, General Peñaranda ordered General David TORO to abandon the *fortín* in order to shorten Bolivia's overstretched defenses. Toro refused to obey and Peñaranda acquiesced.

By July 1934 a large Paraguayan force commanded by Colonel Rafael FRANCO had driven across the central Chaco north of Ballivián and into undisputed Bolivian territory. Estigarribia realized that Franco had outdistanced his supply system and ordered him to fall back slowly. Toro, on his own initiative, decided to attempt to cut off Franco's retreating force, so he marched north with a significant part of Fortín Ballivián's garrison.

Estigarribia perceived the Bolivian move and ordered Franco to fight a delaying action against Toro's superior numbers. Toro attempted to circle Franco's force but failed. Slowly, Toro was enticed farther and farther into the Chaco by the retreating Franco. Finally, in December 1934, Estigarribia rushed significant reinforcements to Franco's aid. The Paraguayans captured the wells supplying water to the Bolivians. A significant part of Toro's force was surrounded and captured. Of approximately 11,000 Bolivians, perhaps only half escaped the Paraguayan trap. In the meantime, the Paraguayans captured the now weakly defended Fortín Ballivián.

By early 1935 the Paraguayans had won almost all of the disputed Chaco and were besieging the Bolivian town of Villa Montes. But the balance of power had begun to shift in favor of the Bolivians as the Paraguayans overextended their supply lines. Also, Bolivia finally declared a general mobilization, thus taking advantage of its significantly larger population. Both sides were exhausted and nearly bankrupt. On 12 June 1935 they agreed to a cease-fire, which took effect on the 14th, and the war was formally ended in 1938.

Paraguay won most of the entire Chaco during the war and was awarded most of it during the peace negotiations. Bolivia sustained about 57,000 dead and Paraguay some 36,000. The war destroyed the fragile democratic governments in both countries: Salamanca was overthrown on 27 November 1934 and Ayala on 17 February 1936.

ANGEL RODRÍGUEZ, *Autopsia de una guerra* (1940); PABLO MAX YNSFRÁN, ed., *The Epic of the Chaco: Marshal Estigarribia's Memoirs of the Chaco War, 1932–1935* (1950); DAVID H. ZOOK, *The Conduct of the Chaco War* (1960); RAMÓN CÉSAR BEJARANO, *Síntesis de la guerra del Chaco* (1982).

ROBERT SCHEINA

CHACÓN, LÁZARO (*b.* 27 June 1873; *d.* 1931), president of Guatemala (1926–1930). Lázaro Chacón was born in Teculután, Zacapa. His grandfather was a military officer and his father was a cattle rancher. A career army officer, General Chacón assumed the presidency of Guatemala on 27 September 1926, the day following the fatal heart attack of General José María ORELLANA, his boyhood friend. Chacón's critics charged that the new president "was a man of very little intelligence, less education and no experience in government affairs."

Upon assuming the presidency, Chacón committed his government to the continuation of the policies of his predecessor. Also, with the country in the midst of a remarkable economic boom, Chacón announced his intention to prevent all forms of social and political unrest. Supported by a large majority of Guatemalan liberals, Chacón easily won the December 1926 presidential election. From most reports, the outcome of the election was never in doubt. Most of Guatemala's traditionally powerful landed elite had little reason to oppose Chacón's promises of prosperity and stability. While the opposition Progressive Party candidate, future president Jorge UBICO Y CASTAÑEDA, ran a campaign that was vaguely reformist, Chacón capitalized on his links to the Guatemalan military and on the economic prosperity enjoyed by the nation's coffee elite to secure an easy victory.

When the Guatemalan economy was crippled by the effects of a worldwide depression in the late 1920s, Chacón's government was already unpopular with the Guatemalan upper and middle classes. Accused of mismanagement, corruption, and inept administration, the Chacón government appeared to be on the verge of anarchy. In December 1930, Chacón suffered a massive stroke. With Chacón incapacitated, the government wallowed in a sea of indecision until Jorge Ubico was elected president in early February 1931.

JOSEPH A. PITTI, "Jorge Ubico and Guatemalan Politics in the 1920's" (Ph.D. diss., University of New Mexico, 1975); WADE KIT, "Precursor of Change: Failed Reform and the Guatemalan Coffee Elite, 1918–1926" (Master's thesis, University of Saskatchewan, 1989).

WADE A. KIT

CHACRA, a small plot of land for market gardening. The specific meaning of *chacra* varies by locale and time. Generally it denotes modest plots of land devoted in part to the production of agricultural goods for household consumption, and in part to small surpluses for sale in local markets. As such, *chacras* are important sources of household income, usually tended by women and children while men work on nearby estates or in cities for wages. They flourish particularly in agrarian zones around cities, for which they are important sources of foodstuffs. In some regions and times, the *chacra* may produce for market more than for subsistence and provide full employment for all household members.

JEREMY ADELMAN

CHACRINHA (José Abelardo de Barbosa Medeiros; *b.* 1918; *d.* 1989), Brazilian television variety show host. Born in Pernambuco, he was one of the longest-running stars of radio, starting in 1943, then of television, with a leading show on TV Rio by 1958. He was considered very innovative in developing one of the two major Brazilian television entertainment forms, the live variety show (*show de auditório*). (The other major form is the TELENOVELA.) His programs were characterized by his dressing in a flamboyant clown costume, an outrageous style of comedy, and close interaction with his audience. His shows relied on amateur performances, comedy, music, guests, dancers, and games. His two best-known shows were *Buzina de Chacrinha* (Chacrinha's Horn) and *Discoteca de Chacrinha*. In the 1960s and 1970s, Chacrinha was identified with the movement, known as *tropicalismo*, to revive authentic Brazilian popular culture, particularly in music. He was mentioned in Gilberto GIL's salute to Brazilian tropical culture, the song "Alegria, Alegria" (Joy, Joy). While Chacrinha was considered in dubious taste by some, including TV Globo's management, which fired him in 1972, many popular culture experts, both Brazilian and foreign, considered his shows the best forum for authentic Brazilian popular culture. He was called one of Brazil's best communicators for his rapport with his audience. His programs, along with other live programs, were banned by the military governments from 1972 to 1979 because they were too difficult to control. In the 1980s, Chacrinha appeared on several competing Brazilian networks.

JOSEPH STRAUBHAAR, "Brazilian Television Variety Shows," in *Studies in Latin American Popular Culture* 2 (1983): 71–78.

JOSEPH STRAUBHAAR

CHADBOURNE PLAN. During the Great Depression, New York lawyer Thomas L. Chadbourne supervised two agreements to alleviate the problem of stockpiled Cuban sugar. The 1930 Cuban Stabilization Law imposed production controls on the SUGAR INDUSTRY. The following year, the Chadbourne Plan established international guidelines for sugar production and marketing.

The continuing depression and concomitant autarky, however, ended the plan's hope that world consumption would climb as sugar tariffs ended. By imposing the largest production reduction on Cuba, the plan benefited only U.S. banks holding stockpiled sugar, while hurting Cuban sharecroppers and cane cutters. Therefore, it only added anticapitalist fuel to Cuban nationalism, already inflamed by the PLATT AMENDMENT.

HARRY F. GUGGENHEIM, *The U.S. and Cuba: A Study in International Relations* (1934); BORIS SWERLING, *International Control of Sugar, 1910–1941* (1949); JULES BENJAMIN, *The United States and Cuba: Hegemony and Dependent Development, 1880–1934* (1977).

EDMOND KONRAD

CHAGAS, CARLOS RIBEIRO JUSTINIANO (b. 9 July 1879; d. 8 November 1934), Brazilian medical scientist. Chagas is remembered for discovering a new human disease, *Trypanosomiasis americana,* commonly known as Chagas' disease, which to this day afflicts millions of people in South America.

Chagas was born in Minas Gerais and trained in medicine in Rio de Janeiro, where he obtained his medical degree in 1902. In 1907 he joined the staff of the OSWALDO CRUZ INSTITUTE, which later sent him to Lassance, 300 miles from Rio, to organize an antimalaria campaign. It was while he was in Lassance that Chagas took up the study of a biting insect commonly known as the *barbeiro* (a *triatoma*), which lived in the walls and thatched roofs of the local dwellings. Finding a trypa-

nosome in the gut of the insect, he suspected that it might produce disease and that humans might be its natural host. Therefore, Chagas proceeded to test its pathogenic effects in animals. He went on to discover trypanosome in the heart and brain tissues of patients whose diverse clinical symptoms had escaped understanding until that time.

The announcement of a new human disease in 1909 initiated years of research into its insect vectors; the life cycle of the causative agent, the *Trypanosoma cruzi* (named after Oswaldo CRUZ, Chagas's friend and director of the Oswaldo Cruz Institute); and its clinical symptoms. The disease has acute and chronic forms and causes cardiac, gastrointestinal, and neurological symptoms.

In 1917, Chagas took over the direction of the Oswaldo Cruz Institute; in 1919 he also became director of the federal public health program, where he oversaw the extension of public health campaigns into the rural areas of Brazil. Nevertheless, Chagas was primarily known as a medical scientist. His work on *Trypanosomiasis americana* gave him an international reputation in medicine; he received the Schaudinn prize for protozoology in 1913 and several honorary degrees.

The *Annals of the International Congress of Chagas' Disease,* 5 vols. (1960), contains a complete bibliography of Chagas's writings; his career is described in NANCY STEPAN, *Beginnings of Brazilian Science: Oswaldo Cruz, Medical Research, and Policy, 1890–1920* (1976).

NANCY LEYS STEPAN

See also **Diseases.**

CHALCATZINGO, an archaeological site located in the modern state of Morelos, Mexico, approximately 60 miles southeast of Mexico City. It was one of the earliest and largest ceremonial centers and one of the first complex chiefdom societies to develop in central Mexico.

Chalcatzingo is located at the base of a large mountain known as Cerro Chalcatzingo. Between 1000 and 100 B.C. terraces were constructed across the hillside where household gardens were planted adjacent to individual residences. A large upper terrace immediately adjacent to Cerro Chalcatzingo was the focus of the site's elite and ritual activity. A large platform (77 feet long by 33 feet wide by 3 feet high), a large public plaza, and an elite residential area were the center of the community's ritual life. After 700 B.C. the ceremonial zone expanded and ritual architecture was constructed on adjacent terraces, which included rectangular stone-faced platforms with one or more carved stelae (stone monuments) and an enclosed patio with a tabletop altar.

Chalcatzingo is famous for its Olmec-style rock carvings, many of which are located on the talus above the site's ceremonial core. These carvings reflect Chalcatzingo's role as a major ritual center and its participation in long-distance trade networks throughout MESOAMER-

ICA. Chalcatzingo grew to its greatest size between 700 and 500 B.C., when it covered slightly more than 88 acres and had a population of between four hundred and one thousand people. During this period Chalcatzingo brought the Amatzinac region under its direct political control and developed perhaps central Mexico's first chiefdom-level society based on social ranking, the inheritance of status, and differential access to wealth.

DAVID GROVE, et al., "Settlement and Cultural Development at Chalcatzingo," in *Science* 192 (1976): 1203–1210; *Chalcatzingo, Excavations on the Olmec Frontier* (1984); *Ancient Chalcatzingo* (1987); KENNETH HIRTH, "Interregional Trade and the Formation of Prehistoric Gateway Communities," in *American Antiquity* 43 (1978): 35–45.

KENNETH HIRTH

CHALCHUAPA, BATTLE OF. On 28 February 1885, the president of Guatemala, Justo Rufino BARRIOS, issued a declaration calling for the establishment of a Central American Union. As the self-proclaimed supreme military commander of Central America, Barrios asked each of the Central American states (Costa Rica, Honduras, El Salvador, Nicaragua, and Guatemala) to recognize the union and to send delegates to Guatemala City to create the institutions of the new government.

The governments of Costa Rica, Nicaragua, and El Salvador opposed the union immediately. As a result, on 31 March 1885, Barrios initiated a military campaign against El Salvador to crush the resistance of Salvadoran president Rafael Zaldívar. Two days later, on 2 April 1885, Barrios was killed in battle and the Guatemalan army was soundly defeated at Chalchuapa, El Salvador. Following the defeat, the Guatemalan forces dispersed and the war with El Salvador came to a rapid conclusion. In subsequent weeks, Barrios's proclamation recognizing the creation of the Central American Union was revoked and his dream of unity thwarted.

THOMAS L. KARNES, *The Failure of Union, Central America, 1824–1960* (1961), pp. 152–162.

WADE A. KIT

CHALMA (or Chalmita), a renowned pilgrimage site in Mexico and symbol of folk Catholicism, combining elements of indigenous and European faiths. According to legend, in 1539, Augustinian friars found an idol (possibly representing Tezcatlipoca) and evidence of sacrifices to it in a cave at Chalma. Later, when they went to replace the idol with a cross, they reputedly found the image broken in pieces and a crucifix already in its place. The idol had been the object of pilgrimages in pre-Hispanic times; subsequent treks were made from great distances to worship the miraculous new god and the nearby town's new patron, St. Michael, who also came to occupy a place at the sacred shrine. Which deity Oztoteotl (the "cave god"), as the idol came

to be called, truly represented, and whether his attributes were transferred to Christ and/or St. Michael in the hearts of the indigenous people, are unresolved questions. Modern pilgrimages are lively events marked by floral displays, song, dance, and fireworks.

ERNA FERGUSSON, *Fiesta in Mexico* (1934), pp. 47–67, and ALEJANDRA GONZÁLEZ LEYVA, *Chalma: Una devoción agustina* (Toluca, 1991), provide an example of the folklore surrounding the shrine at Chalma. GILBERTO GIMÉNEZ offers details of a modern pilgrimage to Chalma in his *Cultura popular y religión en el Anáhuac* (1978).

STEPHANIE WOOD

CHAMBI, MARTÍN (*b.* 5 November 1891; *d.* 1973), Peruvian photographer. Although all biographical facts about Chambi are currently under scrutiny, it is safe to say that he was born into a modest peasant family of Indian stock in the village of Coaza, near Lake Titicaca, in the southern highlands of Peru. His first experience with photography occurred when his father was working for the British Santo Domingo Mining Company, near Carabaya. The curious boy eagerly sought to help the company photographer, who was taking survey views of the area. Around 1908, Chambi moved to Arequipa, where he allegedly pursued a high school education and until 1917 was an apprentice at the studio of the then famous photographer Max T. Vargas. That same year he married Manuela López Viza; they had six children.

In 1917, seeking to establish his own business, Chambi moved to the thriving town of Sicuani. Some three years later he moved on to Cuzco, where he sought out Juan Manuel Figueroa Aznar, a former pupil of Vargas. For a while Chambi and Figueroa shared a studio in Cuzco. At the time, that ancient capital of the Incas was undergoing a cultural renaissance and the beginning of an economic recession. INDIGENISMO became a major intellectual and political force in Cuzco. Chambi befriended such leading *indigenista* intellectuals as José Uriel García, Luis Valcárcel, Gamaliel Churata, Roberto Latorre, and Luis Valesco Aragón. Chambi's work was published in illustrated magazines like *Variedades*. Politically, he sympathized with the early APRA party and contributed to the radical avant-garde magazine *Kosko* by taking ads for his studio in it.

During the 1920s Chambi's prestige as a photographer peaked, and his clientele included wealthy families such as the Lomellinis and the Montes. Some of his most memorable images are commissioned portraits to which he added a social commentary. Yet, his ethnographic work and documentation of Cuzco's colonial and Inca architecture is probably his most systematic. Many of the images for which he is famous today were never shown in the exhibitions curated by Chambi himself. The American photographer Edward Ranney, largely responsible for Chambi's "rediscovery" in 1977,

Photo by Martín Chambi depicting the Andes in Peru. COURTESY OF JULIA CHAMBI.

has played an important role in the appreciation and perception of his work.

RODERIC AI CAMP, "Martín Chambi: Photographer of the Andes," in *Latin American Research Review* 13, no. 2 (1978): 223–228, and "Martín Chambi: Pioneer Photographer of Peru," in *Américas* 30, no. 3 (March 1978): 5–10; EDWARD RANNEY, "Martín Chambi: Poet of Light," in *Earthwatch News* 1 (Spring–Summer 1979): 3–6; FERNANDO CASTRO, *Martín Chambi: De Coaza al MoMA* (1989); JOSÉ CARLOS HUAYHUACA, *Martín Chambi, fotógrafo* (1991); *Martín Chambi: Photographs, 1920–1950*, translated by Margaret Sayers Peden (1993).

FERNANDO CASTRO

See also **Photography.**

CHAMIZAL CONFLICT. From 1864 to 1963, the United States and Mexico claimed sovereignty over the El Chamizal tract ("the thicket"), located between El Paso, Texas, and what is now Ciudad Juárez, Chihuahua. Changes in the course of the Rio Grande caused this land, formerly on the Mexican side of the river, to shift to the U.S. side, thereby altering the international boundary. Both nations claimed the Chamizal. The dispute was submitted to international arbitration in 1911. The

United States rejected the arbitral tribunal's award, which divided the area between the claimants.

Settlement of problems between the United States and Mexico was impeded by the continued Chamizal conflict. For instance, the petroleum expropriation controversy of the 1930s could not immediately be resolved because Mexico distrusted the intentions of the United States and refused to submit the matter to arbitration.

In 1963 President John F. Kennedy agreed to settle the dispute on the basis of the 1911 arbitration award. This action eliminated a source of propaganda directed against United States imperialism and allayed Mexican fears about further U.S. expansion into its territory.

SHELDON B. LISS, *A Century of Disagreement: The Chamizal Conflict, 1864–1964* (1965); ALAN C. LAMBORN and STEPHEN P. MUMME, *Statecraft, Domestic Politics, and Foreign Policy Making: The El Chamizal Dispute* (1988).

SHELDON B. LISS

See also **United States–Mexico Border.**

CHAMORRO, FRUTO (*b.* 20 October 1804; *d.* 12 March 1855), first director of state and first president of Nicaragua (1853–1855). Chamorro is considered one of the most influential and significant figures in the political life of Nicaragua. He restored order to the republic after the chaos of the incessant postindependence wars caused by friction between Conservatives and Liberals.

Born in Guatemala to a Nicaraguan father, Pedro José Chamorro, Fruto Chamorro left his homeland for Nicaragua in early 1827. Soon realizing that Nicaragua suffered from anarchy, factionalism, and militarism, he focused his energy on the fight for liberty and order. In 1836 Chamorro was elected deputy to the Granada state legislature, a position he used to establish public education in that state. He considered education basic to social progress and saw it as a way to mend the fatal localism afflicting the country. Chamorro also was instrumental in the establishment of elections to create a Constituent Assembly that would reform the constitution of 1838. From 1839 to 1842 he was a senator.

By the end of 1842 Chamorro was managing the first newspaper in Granada, *Mentor Nicaragüense,* an organ of the Universidad de Oriente in whose pages he revealed his moral personality. He was an intensely faithful Christian, a staunch supporter of public education, an enemy of ignorance, a concerned political activist, and a dedicated public servant who devoted himself to the preservation of order in Nicaragua. The maintenance of order was Chamorro's major objective upon his assumption of the office of supreme director on 1 April 1853. The new constitution, promulgated on 4 March 1854, provided that the State of Nicaragua be renamed the Republic of Nicaragua and that the title supreme director be changed to president of the republic; thus, Chamorro served as the first and only supreme director and the first president of Nicaragua.

On 1 June 1855, U.S. adventurer William WALKER landed fifty-seven men at Realjo in order to take over Nicaragua. After initial military setbacks, Walker captured Granada in October 1855 and was appointed armed forces chief. Patricio RIVAS served as a figurehead president. Although Walker himself was elected president in June 1856, Honduras, El Salvador, and Guatemala allied against him. Nicaraguan forces ousted Walker in May 1857, and he spent the next three years trying to incite other revolutions. British marines eventually captured Walker in Honduras. He was executed in Trujillo on 12 September 1860. Nicaragua returned to peace, which the Conservative presidents who followed Chamorro maintained until 1893.

Chamorro's legacy, then, rests on the fact that his administration provided the foundation for the orderly succession of mainly civilian Conservative presidents. In addition, Chamorro was responsible for the formation of political clubs that evolved into the Conservative Party. His family has been an active and integral element in the Conservative Party ranks for generations. The Conservatives posthumously honored Chamorro as the founder of their party in 1859.

SARA LUISA BARQUERO, *Gobernantes de Nicaragua, 1825–1947* (1945), esp. pp. 81–85; PEDRO JOAQUÍN CHAMORRO ZELAYA, *Fruto Chamorro* (1960); FRANCISCO ORTEGA ARANCIBIA, *Cuarenta años (1838–1878) de historia de Nicaragua* (1975); RICARDO PAÍZ CASTILLO, *Breve historia del Partido Conservador de Nicaragua y estampas conservadoras* (1984), esp. pp. 29–31, 109–119.

SHANNON BELLAMY

See also **National War; Nicaragua: Political Parties.**

CHAMORRO, VIOLETA. *See* **Barrios de Chamorro, Violeta.**

CHAMORRO CARDENAL, PEDRO JOAQUÍN (*b.* 23 September 1924; *d.* 10 January 1978), Nicaraguan political activist. Chamorro came from a prominent Nicaraguan family with a long history of participation in partisan politics (four of his ancestors held the Nicaraguan presidency). Chamorro's father, Pedro Joaquín Chamorro Zelaya, had founded the daily newspaper *La Prensa* in 1926; upon his father's death in 1952, Chamorro became editor in chief and owner of the paper, which became a vehicle for his opposition to the dictatorship of the SOMOZA family. Chamorro also condemned the government in a number of books he wrote. In 1948 he cofounded the short-lived National Union of Popular Action and Justice (UNAP). In 1954 he was a member of the Internal Front, which attempted to overthrow Somoza García. He participated in an invasion of Nicaragua from Costa Rica in 1959, the first air invasion in Latin American history and another failed attempt to overthrow the Somoza dictatorship. In 1974 he brought together much of the middle-class opposition to Somoza in the Democratic Union of Liberation (UDEL).

Chamorro paid a high price for his activism. He suffered repeated imprisonment, torture, house arrest, and exile before his assassination in 1978. The public response to his death was a series of general strikes leading to mass insurrection. His death closed off the option of a negotiated end to the Somoza dictatorship. Instead, guerrillas of the Sandinista Liberation Front (Frente Sandinista de la Liberación Nacional—FSLN) overthrew the dictatorship in July 1979.

Chamorro's legacy is still debated. His widow, Violeta BARRIOS DE CHAMORRO (who was elected president of Nicaragua in 1990), and two of his children, Pedro Joaquín and Cristiana, all favor a conservative interpretation of that legacy. They argue that Chamorro was a nationalist devoid of Communist leanings, and that he was a staunch and traditional Catholic. They believe he would have struggled against the Sandinistas, just as they have done.

But his brother Xavier and two other of Pedro Joaquín's children, Carlos Fernando and Claudia, claim that his legacy was far more radical. They note that his nationalism led him to oppose the imperialist aggression of the United States and that his Catholicism led him to work for social justice through what he called "Christian revolution." They claim he would have been a Sandinista revolutionary as they are.

PEDRO JOAQUÍN CHAMORRO, *Estirpe Sangrienta: Los Somoza* (1980), and *Diario de un Preso* (1981); PATRICIA TAYLOR EDMISTEN, *Nicaragua Divided: La Prensa and the Chamorro Legacy* (1990).

KAREN KAMPWIRTH

See also **Nicaragua: Political Parties.**

CHAMORRO VARGAS, EMILIANO (*b.* 11 May 1871; *d.* 26 February 1966), president of Nicaragua (1917–1921; 1926). The Nicaraguan who led more revolutions than any other began his military career in 1903, when he commanded an uprising against the Liberal dictator José Santos ZELAYA. Although unsuccessful, this armed rebellion catapulted the Conservative Emiliano Chamorro into the forefront of Nicaraguan politics. Chamorro's animosity toward Zelaya seemingly stemmed not only from party politics and personal ambition but also from Zelaya's mistreatment of Chamorro's father. Chamorro became Zelaya's primary military rival when he joined forces with Juan José ESTRADA and José María MONCADA to overthrow the dictator. By 1909, Zelaya had resigned under pressure from Conservative and anti-Zelaya Liberal forces. Chamorro not only proved himself through this success but also solidified his position as leader of the Conservative Party, a position he maintained until his death.

After Zelaya's ouster, Chamorro served as head of the Constituent Assembly. He returned to the battlefield in 1912, when Minister of War Luis Mena revolted against President Adolfo DÍAZ. After Chamorro defeated Mena, he expressed his own presidential ambitions. The United States, however, supported Díaz and offered Chamorro the position of envoy to the U.S., thereby eliminating any potential challenge to its old friend Díaz.

As envoy, Chamorro negotiated and signed the controversial BRYAN–CHAMORRO TREATY, which gave the U.S. the option on a canal through Nicaragua. After the completion of the PANAMA CANAL, the U.S. wanted to ensure that no other country would build a canal in Nicaragua. Besides the canal option, the U.S. received a ninety-nine-year lease on the Corn Islands in the Caribbean and on a naval base in the Gulf of Fonseca that would be under U.S. jurisdiction. In turn, the U.S. agreed to pay $3 million in gold to Nicaragua upon ratification. William Jennings Bryan, the U.S. secretary of state under President Woodrow WILSON, and Chamorro signed the treaty in 1914, and the U.S. Senate ratified it in 1916.

The treaty met with strong opposition, particularly from Costa Rica, El Salvador, and Colombia. Costa Rica argued that Nicaragua had violated an arbitral award

by U.S. President Grover Cleveland (1888) that bound Nicaragua not to make a canal grant without consulting Costa Rica, because of their common San Juan River boundary. El Salvador expressed outrage at the casual treatment of its territorial rights in the Gulf of Fonseca. Colombia protested Nicaragua's usurpation of the Corn Islands because Colombia claimed sovereignty over them. Chamorro maintained that the treaty provided the best means of solving Nicaragua's economic woes. Not until 1938 did he recognize his mistake in supporting and signing the treaty, for it jeopardized the sovereignty not only of other Latin American countries but also of Nicaragua itself.

Chamorro resigned his position as envoy in 1916 and returned to Nicaragua in order to seek the presidency. The U.S. had previously expressed doubts about Chamorro's military background—it preferred civilian leaders—but after his service as envoy, the U.S. supported Chamorro during the 1916 election, which he won. Upon assuming the presidency, he faced an empty treasury, a national debt, and a foreign debt outstanding since the days of Zelaya. He therefore focused his efforts on obtaining payment of the $3 million in gold promised to Nicaragua upon ratification of the Bryan–Chamorro Treaty. The U.S., however, tied its payment to the settlement of Nicaragua's foreign debt; consequently, Chamorro spent most of his term embroiled in lengthy negotiations.

Chamorro was elected president a second time in 1926, after he overthrew the Conservative government of Carlos SOLÓRZANO. Ostensibly, the coup was intended to neutralize the Liberal influence of Vice President Juan Bautista SACASA, but Chamorro's own desire for the presidency was widely known. Once again, Conservatives and Liberals waged war against one another. Although Chamorro's forces performed well at first, he had fallen out of favor with the U.S. He therefore resigned on 30 October 1926.

During the dictatorship of Anastasio SOMOZA GARCÍA, Chamorro continued his political machinations in the form of abortive uprisings and assassination attempts against the Liberal dictator. Nonetheless, in 1950 Chamorro and Somoza signed the Pact of the Generals, which guaranteed Conservatives one-third of the seats in Congress and one seat on the Supreme Court. Thus, the Conservatives obtained positions within the government while Chamorro's action, as leader of the Conservative Party, gave a boost to the regime's image. These benefits, however, were reaped at great cost, for the Conservative Party ultimately became a mere appendage of the Somoza dictatorship. The consequences were monumental: younger Conservatives who were disenchanted with their party and its leadership sought new avenues for political expression. Their quest led to the creation of the Frente Sandinista de Liberación Nacional, which overthrew the Somoza dynasty on 19 July 1979.

Chamorro, as head of the Conservative Party during

this period, failed to provide true leadership, for in reality he represented only his personal ambitions and the interests of a small, elite class. The perennial revolutionary was merely an opportunist.

CALVIN B. CARTER, "The Kentucky Feud in Nicaragua: Why Civil War Has Become Her National Sport," in *The World's Work* 54 (July 1927): 312–321; SARA LUISA BARQUERO, *Gobernantes de Nicaragua, 1825–1947* (1945); WILLIAM KAMMAN, *A Search for Stability: United States Diplomacy Toward Nicaragua, 1925–1933* (1968); EMILIANO CHAMORRO, *El último caudillo: Autobiografía* (1983); LESTER D. LANGLEY, *The Banana Wars: United States Intervention in the Caribbean, 1898–1934* (1983).

SHANNON BELLAMY

See also **Nicaragua: Political Parties.**

CHAN CHAN, the capital of the CHIMÚ Empire. Located in the Moche valley of Peru's north coast, the city of Chan Chan was founded between A.D. 850 and 900. As the imperial capital of the Chimú, it eventually grew to be one of the largest pre-Columbian cities in South America.

The city, constructed of adobe bricks, covered nearly ten square miles. Ten huge palacelike structures, called *ciudadelas,* which are believed to correspond to the ten rulers of the Chimú dynasty, dominate the city. Surrounded by walls thirty feet or more in height, these structures contained rooms and corridors in a complex labyrinthine arrangement. Architecturally, they were a radical break with the earlier MOCHE tradition of ceremonial centers dominated by pyramids. Whereas Moche monumental architecture was principally religious, the most complex Chimú structures seem to have been rulers' residences, which suggests that the rulers had become divine. The form of the *ciudadela* probably derived from earlier HUARI architecture, which was widely distributed throughout ancient Peru and would have provided a model for prestigious imperial buildings.

These *ciudadelas* have been interpreted as the residence and treasure vault of the reigning emperor and, after his death, his mortuary monument, for they include kitchens, wells, shrines, living quarters, numerous storerooms, and burial platforms. The many storerooms are thought to have housed the accumulated valuables of the ruler, such as fine cloth, gold and silver objects, *spondylus* shells, and other high-status goods.

Between the large *ciudadelas,* lesser compounds housed the nobles and lower-ranking elite. These were simpler versions of the great compounds and housed many of the same functions on a reduced scale. The city also contained residential districts for artisans and their workshops; these buildings were much smaller and lacked the elaboration of the elite buildings.

The principal sources on the city of Chan Chan are ROGGER RAVINES, *Chan Chan metrópoli Chimú* (1980); and MICHAEL MOSELEY and KENT C. DAY, eds., *Chan Chan: Andean Desert City* (1982). See also JOHN H. ROWE, "The Kingdom of Chimor," *Acta Americana* 6 (1948): 26–59; and MICHAEL MOSELEY and ALANA CORDY-COLLINS, *The Northern Dynasties: Kingship and Statecraft in Chimor* (1990). For a discussion of the architectural origins of Chan Chan, see GORDON F. MC EWAN, "Some Formal Correspondences Between the Imperial Architecture of the Wari and Chimú Cultures of Ancient Peru," *Latin American Antiquity* 1, no. 2 (1990): 97–116.

GORDON F. MCEWAN

CHANCAY, culture of ancient Peru that developed in the central coast valleys of Chancay and Chillón at the southern end of CHIMÚ territory. This culture, which appears to have originated after the HUARI collapse (ca. A.D. 900), was incorporated by the Chimú Empire and ultimately was conquered by the Incas around 1470.

Chancay culture is defined archaeologically by a distinctive and homogeneous ceramic style. These ceramics are known from extensive cemeteries in the Chancay region, where they were included in burials as grave goods. They are generally mold-made of a peculiarly gritty clay that leaves an unpolished matte surface, sometimes as rough as sandpaper. Over this is painted a white slip, decorated with black or dark brown designs, in a style known as Chancay Black on White. Vessel forms included both single- and double-chambered bottles, face-neck jars, ring-based plates, and open bowls. Clay figurines representing humans and animals also were produced. These often had yarn hair attached to a row of holes along the top of the head and were clothed in miniature textiles. One theory is that the llamas and human figurines were sacrificial surrogates for living animals and people, and as such were interred to accompany the dead.

The major artistic achievement for which the Chancay are known is their mastery of textiles. They produced plain weave, brocade, and openwork textiles in which open spaces were deliberately woven into the cloth as part of the decorative design. Plain woven cloth was also decorated with painted designs. Chancay weavers specialized particularly in delicate gauze work. Cloth was produced for clothing and decoration, and no doubt served the typical pre-Columbian function as a medium of value and prestige. Curious small dolls or human figurines made of cloth were included in burials. These figurines were sometimes arranged in scenes of activities perhaps suggesting the daily life of the deceased.

Beyond their art, little is known of the Chancay people; they seem to have left no cities nor great architectural monuments. Like all peoples of the dry desert coast, however, they must have been irrigation farmers and must have derived part of their living from the sea as well. They probably exploited the same food crops as

Chancay-style male and female ceramic figurines. Central Coast, Peru. COURTESY OF DEPARTMENT OF LIBRARY SERVICES, AMERICAN MUSEUM OF NATURAL HISTORY.

other coastal peoples, growing cotton and importing wool for textiles.

Sources on the Chancay are few. See EDWARD P. LANNING, *Peru Before the Incas* (1967); and LUIS G. LUMBRERAS, *The Peoples and Cultures of Ancient Peru*, translated by Betty J. Meggars (1974).

GORDON F. McEWAN

See also **Archaeology.**

CHANGADOR, a term for a person who herded cattle raised for the tanning of leather in the eighteenth-century BANDA ORIENTAL (the former name of Uruguay). Similar expressions with slight nuances are *corambrero, faenero, gauderío,* and *gaucho,* the last of which became the most widespread and enduring. The raising of beef cattle was introduced to the Banda Oriental by Governor Hernandarias of Asunción (Paraguay) at the beginning of the seventeenth century. The abundance of water and good pasture and a mild climate allowed the practice to spread rapidly. Leather became the region's first product to be traded in the world market.

JUAN E. PIVEL DEVOTO, *Raíces coloniales de la revolución oriental de 1811*, 2d ed. (1957); WASHINGTON REYES ABADIE et al., *La Banda Oriental: Pradera, frontera, puerto* (1965).

JOSÉ DE TORRES WILSON

CHAPALA, LAKE, Mexico's largest lake. It lies in a long depression 5,000 feet above sea level in the state of Jalisco. The lake is part of the Lerma-Chapala-Santiago system in which the LERMA RIVER empties into, and the Santiago River flows out from, Chapala. The lake has experienced numerous oscillations in its shoreline. By 1954 a combination of drought and water diversion caused Chapala to recede 2.5 miles, a deficit from which the lake has never fully recovered.

Farmers exploit the exposed lake-bed soils, and small, informal restaurants dot the shores. Increased demands by Mexico City on the Lerma and diversions from Chapala to supply Guadalajara with water are again threatening the viability of the lake. Still, Chapala's beautiful setting and recreational attractions draw many Mexican visitors, and it is a favorite retirement site for a growing colony of North Americans.

DAVID BARKIN and TIMOTHY KING, *Regional Economic Development: The River Basin Approach in Mexico* (1970), esp. pp. 113–115; JOSÉ ROGELIO ALVAREZ, ed., *Encyclopedia de México*, 3d ed., vol. 5 (1978), pp. 265–268; ROBERT C. WEST and JOHN P. AUGELLI, *Middle America: Its Lands and Peoples*, 3d ed. (1989).

MARIE D. PRICE

CHAPULTEPEC, ACT OF. *See* **Pan-American Conferences: Mexico City Conference.**

CHAPULTEPEC, BOSQUE DE, a centrally located park in Mexico City and the oldest recreational space in the Americas. The park takes its name from the hill called *Chapulín* on which Chapultepec Castle was constructed in the 1780s. In the park are found the presidential residence (Los Pinos), the National Museum of Anthropology, the Tamayo Museum, the Museum of Modern Art, the National Auditorium, a renovated ZOO, athletic fields, recreational areas, and several lakes. It was once a forest of giant cypress (*ahuehuete*), but these have almost disappeared due to the loss of lands that surrounded their marshy habitat.

In about 1250 a roving tribe of AZTECS settled in Chapultepec. Upon gaining power in the Valley of Mexico and consolidating TENOCHTITLÁN as the capital of their confederacy with TEXCOCO and Tlacopán, they made it a sacred place and alternative residence of their emperors. NEZAHUALCÓYOTL, king of Texcoco, designed it as a park in about 1450 and constructed an aqueduct that supplied drinking water first to Tenochtitlán and

later to the colonial city. It is believed that the hill was the burying place of the Aztec emperors, some of whose effigies are preserved as rock carvings.

During the siege of 1521, Chapultepec was heroically defended by the Aztecs. Hernán CORTÉS added it to his possessions. Carlos V took it from Cortés's estate and gave it back to Mexico City. The viceroy Bernardo de GÁLVEZ began construction of the Castle as a summer residence in 1786 and had finished a great part of it the following year when he died. It was finished in 1842, when the Military Academy occupied it. During the battle for the capital in 1847, 200 cadets defended it to the death against the forces of Winfield Scott. (See NIÑOS HEROES.) MAXIMILIAN and Carlota made the castle their imperial palace from 1864–1867. Porfirio DÍAZ divided it for use as the presidential residence, often called El Alcázar, and the Military Academy. Almost every postrevolutionary president resided in it until Lázaro CÁRDENAS moved to Los Pinos in 1936. In 1944 the castle was opened as the National Museum of History.

Between 1898 and 1910 the ancient forest was converted to a French park in the style of the Bois de Boulogne in Paris. From that time until the completion of the subway in 1969 it was the preferred promenade of the middle class. Today it is overwhelmed by the public for recreation. Visits are free, and each week more than 1.5 million people pass through it. The construction of freeways and public buildings around its perimeter have caused the park to suffer devastating consequences. Lying in the middle of a city of 20 million inhabitants, with an excessive number of factories and automobiles, it shows evidence of damage from pollution. As an attempt to alleviate this problem, the central part has been closed to vehicular traffic. The zoo is the only one in the world where pandas and sea lions have reproduced in captivity.

Most books about Mexico City discuss Chapultepec as well. See, for example, JONATHAN KANDELL, *La Capital* (1988).

J. E. PACHECO

CHARCAS, AUDIENCIA OF, the high court of Charcas, which had its seat in the city of La Plata (now Sucre), in the eastern Andes in what is now Bolivia. It was often known as the Audiencia of La Plata and sometimes as that of Chuquisaca, another name for the same town. Proposals for its foundation date back to 1551, inspired in part by the great silver strike in 1545 at Potosí, 50 miles to the southwest. The resultant rise of local population called for a firmer royal presence. Final arrangements were made in 1558–1559, and the first set of four *oidores* (judges) took office in 1561.

After 1570 the northern limit of the audiencia's district was set 120 miles south of Cuzco and ran down on the Pacific coast to the Copiapó River valley in Chile. Inland the district extended east to a vague line in the interior, but a projection southward covered Tucumán, Paraguay, and the settlements along the Río de la Plata.

Buenos Aires, after its refounding in 1580, became the district's southeastern extremity. This was the largest AUDIENCIA jurisdiction in South America, and it remained little changed until 1783, when an *audiencia* was permanently set up in Buenos Aires to take cases from Tucumán, Paraguay, and Buenos Aires Province.

The Audiencia of Charcas, like others in colonial Spanish America, combined judicial and administrative functions. Constant dispute over the exercise of *gobierno* (adminstration) took place, however, between the audiencia and the viceroy in Lima, in whose broad adminstrative domain it resided (until 1776, when it passed to the new Viceroyalty of the Río de la Plata). The Audiencia's district, in its reduced post-1783 form, was the direct ancestor of the territory of modern Bolivia.

ERNESTO SCHÄFER, *El Consejo Real y Supremo de las Indias; Su historia, organización y labor adminstrativa hasta la terminación de la casa de Austria* (1947); INGE WOLFF, *Regierung und Verwaltung der Kolonialspanischen Städte in Hochperu, 1538–1650* (1970); HERBERT S. KLEIN, *Bolivia: The Evolution of a Multi-Ethnic Society* (1982).

PETER BAKEWELL

CHARLES I OF SPAIN (*b.* 24 February 1500; *d.* 21 September 1558), king of Spain (1516–1556) and Holy Roman emperor (as Charles V, 1519–1558). The grandson of FERDINAND II and ISABELLA I as well as the emperor MAXIMILIAN I, Charles inherited an empire that stretched from Germany to the Americas. Throughout his reign he struggled to keep his inheritance intact in the face of Protestant threats in Germany, French threats in Italy, and Turkish threats on the Mediterranean coast. Despite tremendous military expenditures, Charles was unable to check all three forces simultaneously. The war against France kept him, for instance, from giving the necessary attention to the spread of Lutheran doctrine in Germany. Charles's solution there was to delegate authority to his brother, Ferdinand (king of Bohemia and Hungary), who ultimately negotiated a religious settlement in the Peace of Augsburg (1555). Toward the end of his reign Charles began a division of the Hapsburg inheritance by giving to his son PHILIP II the territories of Naples, Milan, the Netherlands, and Spain (1554–1556) and relinquishing his imperial title (1556–1558) to his brother, who reigned as Emperor Ferdinand I.

Because of his Burgundian origins, Charles I was initially not well received in Spain. He faced his first political crisis in 1519 with the revolt of the *comuneros* (Castilian rebels) who demanded that he exclude foreigners from high positions at court and give the Cortes a greater role in government. When Charles granted the participating cities a general pardon, he inaugurated a more favorable relationship with his Spanish subjects.

Charles respected the autonomy of his widespread domains and ruled through a system of viceroys or regents (often family members, to preserve his personal rule). The viceroys acted as liaisons with his various councils. The central governing institution and highest administrative body was the Council of Castile, staffed largely by nonaristocratic jurists. Grandees served on an advisory council of state. To these bodies were added councils of finance (1523) and the Indies (1524). Charles's main sources of royal revenue were Castile, Aragon, the church, and America, although he also drew upon resources in the Netherlands and Italy.

Charles maintained a Eurocentric attitude toward his New World possessions, and for most of his reign European mines produced greater quantities of silver than those in the colonies. On the other hand, he capitalized on the influx of American silver to secure monetary loans from European financiers.

KARL BRANDI, *The Emperor Charles V* (1939; repr. 1980); RAMÓN CARANDE THOBAR, *Carlos V y sus banqueros*, 3 vols. (1943–1967); MANUEL FERNÁNDEZ ÁLVAREZ, *Charles V* (1975).

SUZANNE HILES BURKHOLDER

CHARLES II OF SPAIN (*b.* November 1661; *d.* 1 November 1700), king of Spain, Naples, and Sicily (1665–1700). Chronically ill throughout his life, Charles II ruled early on through his mother, as regent, and a five-member government junta, which was an aristocratic faction headed by his illegitimate brother, Don John of Austria. Toward the end of his reign, he ruled through titled prime ministers. Charles's reign was marked by increasing governmental decentralization accompanied by a resurgence of aristocratic influence in government and a revival of provincial liberties.

During Charles's tenuous rule, Spain fought the French to retain the Spanish Netherlands but lost strategic territory at considerable cost to the ailing economy. In addition to this costly war, Castile suffered a number of natural disasters—harvest failures caused by a drought-and-deluge cycle, locusts, an earthquake, and epidemics—all of which exacerbated the effects of monetary depression. Yet Castile's very weakness forced its ministers to recognize the need for administrative and economic reforms and to act upon it, a policy that characterized the reigns of Charles's Bourbon successors.

JOHN LYNCH, *Spain Under the Habsburgs*, vol. 2, *Spain and America 1598–1700* (1964–1969), esp. pp. 229–280; HENRY KAMEN, *Spain in the Later Seventeenth Century, 1665–1700* (1980).

SUZANNE HILES BURKHOLDER

CHARLES III OF SPAIN (*b.* 20 January 1716; *d.* 14 December 1788), king of Spain (1759–1788) and Naples and Sicily (1734–1759). Often termed an "enlightened despot," Charles III is chiefly known for the administrative and economic reforms during his reign and for the expulsion of the JESUITS (1767). He brought to the Spanish throne twenty-five years of experience as the king of Naples. Charles was a proponent of royal absolutism whose main concern was the welfare of the state, which he intended to strengthen through domestic reforms, imperial defense, and stringent colonial control. He attempted neutrality in the SEVEN YEARS' WAR but was drawn into the losing side of the conflict by a desire to fortify Spanish land and sea power with a French alliance. In 1779, Charles entered into the war between America and Britain to regain control over the Gulf coast and the Mississippi and destroy British colonial power in Central America. His rewards for this effort were Florida and Minorca.

Charles's domestic and foreign policies were influenced by a succession of enlightened ministers who pressed for varying degrees of reform within a framework of absolute monarchy. His first administration was dominated by such Italians as Leopoldo de Gregorio Squillace and Grimaldi, who supported the reforms of CAMPOMANES, which infringed on the privileges of the clergy and aristocracy. Initial reforms sparked riots in Madrid and other cities (1766) and led to the dismissal of Squillace, the minister of finance. The count of Aranda dominated the second administration as president of the Council of Castile (1766–1773). Aranda's political rival, the count of Floridablanca, later served as secretary of state (1776–1792) and essentially ran the government during the latter years of Charles's reign.

In centralizing control over colonial affairs, Charles III created new administrative units, reduced the political power of the creoles, expelled the Jesuits, and expanded the army with American-born recruits. However, his increased taxation and new colonial inspections (*visitas*) were met with rebellions in the early 1780s. These uprisings in turn led to tighter control under the secretary of the Indies, José de GALVÉZ (1776–1787), who favored the introduction of the intendant system of royal administrators as a link between the districts and the central authorities. In 1765 the crown began to reduce the restrictions on colonial trade so as to expand commerce within the empire, while at the same time reinforcing the Spanish monopoly. By 1789 this system of free trade within the empire encompassed all of Spain's New World colonies.

Despite much talk about increasing state revenues through tax reforms, the reincorporation of noble estates (*señoríos*), and confiscation of church property, there was little opportunity for structural change during the reign of Charles III. In addition to resistance from privileged groups, the king and his ministers had limited resources and often deferred domestic investment to meet the costs of war.

VICENTE RODRÍGUEZ CASADO, *La política y los políticos en el reinado de Carlos III* (1962); ANTHONY H. HULL, *Charles III and the Revival of Spain* (1980); JAVIER GUILLAMÓN ÁLVAREZ, *Las reformas de la administración local durante el reinado de Carlos III* (1980); JOHN LYNCH, *Bourbon Spain, 1700–1808* (1989), esp. pp. 247–374.

SUZANNE HILES BURKHOLDER

CHARLES IV OF SPAIN (*b.* 12 November 1748; *d.* 19 January 1819), king of Spain (1788–1808). Charles IV had neither experience nor interest in government when he came to the throne. Although he began his rule with ministers inherited from his father, he soon handed the reins of government to Manuel de GODOY, whose rapid rise to power earned him widespread unpopularity in both Spain and the colonies. Distracted by revolutionary events in France, Charles and Godoy presided over the demise of the old regime while doing little to acknowledge or avert it.

War and the threat of state bankruptcy determined Charles's foreign and domestic policy. The Spanish monarch's decision to intercede on behalf of his cousin, the king of France, led to war (1793–1795), a subsequent alliance with France (1796), and costly conflicts with England (1796–1802 and 1804–1808). In the Indies, what was left of the Spanish monopoly eroded during the reign of Charles IV with the legalization of neutral trade.

Quests for further sources of state revenue dominated domestic policy during the reign of Charles IV. The few reforms generated by the crown's fiscal needs were lost amid the demands of wartime conditions and did little to improve Godoy's popularity. Opposition to him as the court favorite ultimately manifested itself in aristocratic support for the king's heir, FERDINAND VII, and in a revolt at Aranjuez (1808) demanding that Charles abdicate in favor of his son. Shortly thereafter, NAPOLEON I lured Charles and Ferdinand to France, where he forced them to abdicate in favor of his brother, Joseph BONAPARTE.

CARLOS CORONA, *Revolución y reacción en el reinado de Carlos IV* (1957); JOHN LYNCH, *Bourbon Spain, 1700–1808* (1989).

SUZANNE HILES BURKHOLDER

CHARQUI, term for sun-dried salted meat used in Chile and other Andean regions. Throughout the colonial period and well into the twentieth century, *charqui*, beef or horse meat cut into strips, salted and dried, was a food staple for rural peasants in Chile as well as for the MAPUCHES. *Charqui* was prepared for consumption by pounding or grinding the dried meat into a coarse meal to be served in stews, accompanied by toasted wheat. *Charqui* became increasingly important in the native Chilean economy in the early nineteenth century, when it was exported north for use in the mines.

RODOLFO LENZ, *Diccionario etimológico* (1910).

KRISTINE L. JONES

CHARREADA, Mexican roping and riding contest. The precursor of the American rodeo, a *charreada* is a contest consisting of the *suertes* (events) of *charrería*, the national sport of Mexico. Such *suertes* as *coleadero* (downing a bull by twisting its tail) and *jaripeo* (bull riding) originated in sixteenth-century *corridas*. Others developed from cattle ranching: *jineteo* (riding wild mares and young bulls), *paso de la muerte* (death pass: jumping from a tame horse to the back of a wild horse), *piales* (roping the hind legs of a running mare), *manganas* (roping the forelegs of a running mare), and *terna en el ruedo* (team roping: one CHARRO ropes the bull's head and the other, the hind legs). *Charreadas* reached their greatest popularity as part of nineteenth-century hacienda fiestas during roundups and branding. This popularity was enhanced by Ponciano Díaz, an exceptionally skilled *charro* and bullfighter who organized the first professional shows and made several international tours.

The MEXICAN REVOLUTION and the breakup of the haciendas ended the heyday of the *charro*. To preserve the cultural heritage, a group of former *charros* in 1921 wrote standard rules, making *charreadas* team contests among members of amateur *charro* clubs. Held in special arenas known as *lienzos*, contemporary *charreadas* include the events of the past four centuries, as well as the *cala de caballo*, a form of dressage, and *escaramuza charra*, precision sidesaddle riding by women's teams. As in the nineteenth century, *charreadas* end with the *jarabe tapitío* (Mexican hat dance). Since 1933 *charrería* has been regulated by the Federacíon Nacional de Charros. In 1991 fifty U.S. clubs broke away and formed the rival Federacíon de Charros, U.S., Inc.

HIGINIO VÁZQUEZ SANTA ANA, *La charrería mexicana* (1950); ENRIQUE GUARNER, *Historia del toreo en México* (1979); MARY LOU LE COMPTE, "The Hispanic Influence on the History of Rodeo, 1823–1922," in *Journal of Sport History* 23 (1983): 21–38; JOSÉ ALVAREZ DEL VILLAR, *La charrería mexicana* (1987); KATHLEEN SANDS, *Charrería Mexicana: An Equestrian Folk Tradition* (1993).

MARY LOU LeCOMPTE

CHARRO, Mexican horseman skilled in roping and riding. The first *charros* were elite Spaniards who perpetuated *jineta* (Moorish-style riding) on their New World *encomiendas*. The group subsequently included mestizos, many of whom were landowners or hacienda overseers. Over time they combined *jineta* with events derived from cattle ranching and developed the whole into a sport called *charrería*, which became the national sport of Mexico. Always known for their distinctive riding style and flamboyant costumes, *charros* gained fame in the MEXICAN REVOLUTION because they formed a great part of the insurgent groups. Both Pancho VILLA and Emiliano ZAPATA were *charros*. Since 1921, most *charros* have been members of one of over 800 amateur *charro* clubs in Mexico and the United States. Unlike their rural predecessors, contemporary *charros* usually live in cities, and many follow professions like law or medicine. Clubs regularly compete against one another in CHARREADAS, which are somewhat like American rodeos except that competition is team rather than individual, with rules and events more like those of earlier centuries.

CARLOS RINCÓN GALLARDO, *El charro mexicano* (1939); ALFONSO RINCÓN GALLARDO, "Contemporary Charrería," in *Artes de México* 14, no. 99 (1967): 41–42 (entire issue is devoted to *charrería*); JAMES NORMAN SCHMIDT, *Charro: Mexican Horseman* (1969); JOSÉ ALVAREZ DEL VILLAR, *Men and Horses of Mexico:*

Charros. COLLECTION OF MARTHA DAVIDSON; PHOTO BY OSUNA.

History and Practice of "Charrería," translated by Margaret Fischer de Nicolin (1979); KATHLEEN M. SANDS, "Charreada: Performance and Interpretation of an Equestrian Folk Tradition in Mexico and the United States," in *Studies in Latin American Popular Culture* 13 (1994): 77–100.

MARY LOU LeCOMPTE

See also **Sports.**

CHARRY LARA, FERNANDO (*b.* 1920), Colombian poet, born in Bogotá. His love poetry is erotic and characterized by a sense of mystery inspired by the night. Charry Lara's importance lies in his occupying a transitional position between the poets of the Piedra y Cielo group and those of the Mito group, which is known for its universalist poetry. The members of Piedra y Cielo, following the style of Spanish poetry, concentrated on purity of forms, whereas the members of Mito, influenced by existentialism, worried less about form and meditated on reality, love, and poetry itself. Charry Lara became famous with the publication of his first poems in 1944 in the poetry magazine *Cántico*. In the 1950s he was a part of the Mito group, whose magazine is notable for its criticism of the Colombian literary and social situation. Charry Lara's poetry collections are *Nocturnos y otros sueños* (1949), *Los adioses* (1963), and *Pensamientos del amante* (1981). Of the Mito group members, Charry Lara contributed the most to the criticism of Colombian poetry with his essay collection *Lector de poesía* (1975). His poetry was influenced by such Spanish poets as Vicente Aleixandre, by Pablo NERUDA and Jorge Luis BORGES, and by the German Romantic poets.

FRANCISCO AGUILERA and GEORGETTE MAGASSY DORN, *The Archive of Hispanic Literature on Tape* (1974); RAFAEL GUTIÉRREZ GIRARDOT, "Poesía y crítica literaria en Fernando Charry Lara," in *Revista Iberoamericana* 50 (1984): 839–852; ARMANDO ROMERO, "Fernando Charry Lara o la obsesión de la noche," in his *Las palabras están en situación* (1985), pp. 86–96; JUAN GUSTAVO COBO BORDA, *Poesía colombiana 1880–1980* (1987), pp. 172–178; JAIME GARCÍA MAFFLA, *Fernando Charry Lara* (1989).

JUAN CARLOS GALEANO

CHARTERED COMPANIES. *See* **Companies, Chartered.**

CHATFIELD, FREDERICK (*b.* 6 February 1801; *d.* 30 September 1872), key British agent in Central America (1833–1840, 1842–1852).

A native of London, Chatfield had already outlined British policy in Central America before his arrival as minister plenipotentiary. But the territorial question of BELIZE (British Honduras) stirred up nationalistic reactions that frustrated England's political and economic objectives. The 1839 takeover of Roatán (one of the Bay Islands) and the promotion of protectorate status for the MISKITO Shore further complicated relationships.

Although Chatfield had pursued a constructive line with the UNIONIST PARTY, assisting the Central American Federation in making financial and customs reforms, the Roatán takeover forced him into a negative stance. Having become the leader of the States' Righters, he devised favorable "doctrines" and employed financial claims to bring on blockades for political objectives. Aiming at establishing a British protectorate in Central America before North Americans took control of a trans-isthmian interoceanic route, he seized Tigre Island (Honduras) on 16 October 1849. War with "Brother Jonathan" (North Americans) seemed inevitable. Lord Palmerston's parliamentary enemies defeated the aggression by signing the CLAYTON–BULWER TREATY (1850). Palmerston's dismissal in 1851 and Chatfield's recall in 1852 underscored the reversal in British policy.

MARY WILHELMINE WILLIAMS, *Anglo-American Isthmian Diplomacy, 1815–1915* (1916); RICHARD W. VAN ALSTYNE, "The Central American Policy of Lord Palmerston, 1846–1848," in *Hispanic American Historical Review* 16, no. 3 (1936): 339, 359, and "British Diplomacy and the Clayton–Bulwer Treaty, 1850–60," in *Journal of Modern History* 11, no. 2 (1939): 149–183; THOMAS KARNES, *Failure of Union: Central America, 1824–1860* (1961); MARIO RODRÍGUEZ, *A Palmerstonian Diplomat in Central America: Frederick Chatfield, Esq.* (1964).

MARIO RODRÍGUEZ

CHAUVET, MARIE VIEUX (*b.* 16 September 1916, *d.* 19 June 1973), Haitian novelist and playwright. Chauvet is the most widely known Haitian woman novelist, and yet her audience has remained restricted. She received early recognition for her first novel, *Fille d'Haïti* (1954; Prize of the Alliance Française). In *Danse sur le volcan* (1957), she brought a feminist perspective to bear on the Haitian Revolution, at a moment when women's movements were virtually nonexistent in Haiti. *Fonds des Nègres* (1960) depicts a young city woman who regains the taste for traditional culture when she is caught in a small town (France-Antilles Prize). *Amour, colère et folie* (1968) has received high critical acclaim for the combination of a lucid style and unadorned insights into the fearful grip of François DUVALIER and his TONTON MACOUTES on the Haitian bourgeoisie and intellectuals. It was banned in Haiti, however, and the Chauvet family bought back all rights. *Les rapaces* (1986) was published posthumously after the fall of Jean-Claude Duvalier.

Although the Haitian political situation and a faltering literary establishment have kept Chauvet from gaining wide readership, she is increasingly recognized as a powerful writer and an early Haitian advocate of women's rights.

Works by Marie Vieux Chauvet include: *La légende des fleurs* (theater, 1947); *La danse sur le volcan* (novel, 1957), translated by Salvator Attanasio as *Dance on the Volcano* (1959); and *Fonds des Nègres* (novel, 1960).

MARYSE CONDÉ, *La parole des femmes: Essais sur les romancières des Antilles de langue française* (1979), pp. 98–110; JOAN DAYAN, "Reading Women in the Caribbean: Chauvet's *Love, Anger, and*

Madness," in *The Politics of Tradition*, edited by JOAN DE JEAN and NANCY MILLER (1990).

CARROL F. COATES

CHAVES, FEDERICO (*b.* 1882; *d.* 24 April 1978), Paraguayan political leader and president (1949–1954). The son of Portuguese immigrants, Federico Chaves spent his early life as a lawyer and judge in Asunción and other locales. His affiliation with the Asociación Nacional Republicana (or Partido Colorado) in the 1930s and 1940s brought him some national prominence, and by 1946, he was vice president of the party. In that year, the dictator Higínio MORÍNIGO brought Chaves into the government as a concession to the Colorados. This coalition regime did not last, however, and in the 1947 civil war that followed, Chaves clarified his position as chief of the "democratic" wing of the party. By so doing, he had placed himself in opposition to the violent Guión Rojo faction, led by Juan Natalicio GONZÁLEZ. In 1948 a coup d'état gave Chaves the chance to ally himself with the new president, Felipe Molas López, with whom he purged the government of González followers.

This housecleaning paved the way for Chaves's own accession to the presidency in 1949. During his administration the Paraguayan economy was plagued by inflation, which Chaves sought to relieve through a close economic union with Perón's Argentina. At home, his policies were repressive, but his arbitrary use of police power failed to curb the opposition of former Guionistas and army officers, one of whom, General Alfredo STROESSNER, launched a revolt in May 1954. After some fierce fighting, Chaves stepped down. A year later, Stroessner rewarded his predecessor's noninterference in the new government by making him ambassador to Paris. He died in Asunción.

LEO B. LOTT, *Venezuela and Paraguay: Political Modernity and Tradition in Conflict* (1972); PAUL H. LEWIS, *Paraguay Under Stroessner* (1980), esp. pp. 28–60; ALFREDO M. SEIFERHELD, comp., *La caída de Federico Chaves: Una visión documental norteamericana* (1987); RIORDEN ROETT and RICHARD S. SACKS, *Paraguay: The Personalist Legacy* (1991), esp. pp. 51–54.

THOMAS L. WHIGHAM

CHAVES, FRANCISCO C. (*b.* 7 June 1875; *d.* 1961), Paraguayan educator and statesman. Chaves was born in the city of Asunción in the period in which Paraguay was recovering from the disastrous WAR OF THE TRIPLE ALLIANCE. His well-connected family was involved in the country's reconstruction at many levels and contributed several sons and grandsons to serve in high office. Chaves was educated at the Colegio Nacional, graduating with a bachelor's degree in 1895, and at the National University, from which he received a doctorate in law in 1901. He spent the rest of his career teaching law to young students.

After receiving his doctorate, the government named him a justice of the Superior Court and a professor of civil law at the university. Over the next ten years, he held numerous offices, including minister of justice, national deputy, minister to Brazil, and rector of the university.

Chaves taught a generation of lawyers in Paraguay and added a great deal to the professionalization of that field within the country. In later life, he became special envoy to a dozen international conferences while simultaneously serving as a national senator and president of the central bank. He capped his legal career by being named president of the Supreme Court.

WILLIAM BELMONT PARKER, *Paraguayans of To-Day* (1921), pp. 189–190; CHARLES J. KOLINSKI, *Historical Dictionary of Paraguay* (1975), p. 54.

THOMAS L. WHIGHAM

CHAVES, JULIO CÉSAR (*b.* 1907; *d.* 20 February 1988), Paraguayan historian and diplomat. Born into an old and distinguished Asunción family, Chaves spent his early years in the Paraguayan capital, where he later studied international law. After receiving his law degree from the National University in 1929, he went on to hold various educational and diplomatic posts. Chaves was ambassador to Bolivia after the conclusion of the CHACO WAR (1932–1935), and in 1940 he became President José Félix ESTIGARRIBIA's ambassador to Peru. Two years later, political conditions at home forced him to leave the diplomatic service, and he relocated to Buenos Aires, where he remained eleven years.

In Argentina, Chaves began to pursue his interest in historical topics. He eschewed the blind nationalism of many of his contemporaries and made every effort to give his investigations a measure of empirical depth. To this end, he conducted extensive research in South American and European archives and incorporated his findings in many publications. These included *Historia de las relaciones entre Buenos Aires y el Paraguay* (1938), *Castelli: El Adalid de Mayo*, 2d ed. (1957), *San Martín y Bolívar en Guayaquil* (1950), *El presidente López: Vida y gobierno de Don Carlos* (1955), *La conferencia de Yataity-Corá* (1958), and *Descubrimiento y conquista del Río de la Plata y el Paraguay* (1968). By common consent, however, Chaves's greatest work was *El supremo dictador* (1942), the first modern biographical treatment of the nineteenth-century Paraguayan dictator Dr. José Gaspar Rodriguez de FRANCIA.

After his return to Asunción in the mid-1950s, Chaves resumed his teaching career. His good relations with the STROESSNER government (his brother was longtime president of the Colorado Party) assured him freedom of action in the country as well as considerable prestige. He became an unofficial spokesman for his country's intellectuals, traveling to scores of international scholarly conferences and acting as head of the Paraguayan PEN Club and of the Academia Paraguaya de la Historia.

JULIO CÉSAR CHAVES, *El Supremo Dictador*, 3d ed. (1958); LUIS G. BENÍTEZ, *Historia de la cultura en el Paraguay* (1976), pp. 239–240.

THOMAS L. WHIGHAM

CHÁVEZ, CARLOS (*b.* 13 June 1899; *d.* 2 August 1978), Mexican composer, conductor, educator, and administrator. Chávez began piano studies with his brother and continued with Manuel Ponce and Luis Ogazón. His penchant for improvisation led him to begin composing at an early age. He wrote his first symphony at age sixteen, but most of his early works were miniatures derivative of European styles or drawn from the Mexican song tradition. A concert of his works in 1921 brought public awareness of a new creative voice in Mexico. Travels in 1922 left him discouraged over the conservative state of music in Europe. Back in Mexico he produced new music concerts, but impatient for a better response, he moved to New York City (1926–1928) and received professional encouragement from the new music establishment, notably Aaron Copland, Roger Sessions, and Edgard Varèse. Chávez returned to Mexico in 1928 and was appointed director of the Symphony Orchestra of Mexico (remaining twenty-one years). Quick success led to directorships of the National Conservatory and fine arts department in the Ministry of Education. His conducting reputation grew rapidly through engagements with the New York Philharmonic and NBC Orchestras (1937–1938). In 1947 President Miguel Alemán named him founding director of the National Institute of Fine Arts with sweeping authority over all of the arts. Chávez was an active and productive writer, lecturer, conductor, teacher, and statesman, but claimed these activities were no more than a means for him to compose. His most widely accepted composition was the nationalistic work employing Mexican Indian themes, *Sinfonía india* (1935). His more abstract and cerebral style in later years signaled a move away from nationalism.

ROBERT L. PARKER, *Carlos Chávez: Mexico's Modern-Day Orpheus* (1984).

ROBERT L. PARKER

CHÁVEZ, MARIANO (*b.* 1808; *d.* ca. 1845), president of the New Mexico Assembly and interim governor (1844). Like many of the political actors of the Mexican period, Chávez became wealthy through his participation in the trade between Santa Fe and Missouri during the 1830s. His wealth and elevated social status brought Chávez the opportunity to demonstrate his leadership during the popular revolt of northern New Mexicans in 1837 against the centralist governor, Albino PÉREZ. Chávez exhorted those who chose to show their allegiance to SANTA ANNA and his centralist government to follow the leadership of General Manuel ARMIJO. The Plan de Tomé denounced the rebel governor, José González, and named Armijo as the New Mexican leader and Chávez as his lieutenant. Together Armijo and Chávez defeated the rebels, reoccupied Santa Fe, and apprehended and executed González.

Chávez's status as a *rico* and his family connections to Manuel Armijo aided his election in 1844 as president of the New Mexican Assembly and explains his appointment as interim governor shortly afterward by Armijo, who became ill. As Assembly president, Chávez swore loyalty to Santa Anna and his recently promulgated BASES ORGÁNICAS while protesting the neglect of New Mexico by the central government.

During his brief tenure as governor, Chávez distinguished himself by becoming involved in a feud between Father Antonio José Martínez of Taos and Charles Bent and his business associates. In 1844, in response to a petition by Martínez, Chávez revoked the enormous Beaubien-Miranda grant made by Armijo, thereby adding to its already complicated history. The year before, the governor's brother, Antonio José Chávez, had been robbed and murdered by American bandits. Agreeing with Martínez that increasing foreign influence and interest in New Mexico threatened Mexican sovereignty, Chávez sought to enforce a ban on foreigners holding an interest in Mexican land grants, apparently believing that Charles Bent held a share of the Beaubien-Miranda grant. On 15 May 1844, Chávez was replaced by a Santa Anna appointee, General Mariano Martínez.

Known as a wealthy and educated political operator during his short career, Chávez used his moment in power to diminish the growing political and economic power that American expatriates were gaining in New Mexico. Just before sending his son José Francisco to school in Saint Louis in 1841, Chávez apparently said to him: "The heretics are going to overrun all this country. Go and learn their language and come back prepared to defend your people."

ANGELICO CHÁVEZ, *Origins of New Mexico Families* (1954); HOWARD ROBERTS LAMAR, *The Far Southwest, 1846–1912: A Territorial History* (1966); MARC SIMMONS, *The Little Lion of the Southwest: A Life of Manuel Antonio Chaves* (1973); DAVID J. WEBER, *The Mexican Frontier, 1821–1846: The American Southwest under Mexico* (1982); VICTOR WESTPHALL, *Mercedes Reales: Hispanic Land Grants of the Upper Rio Grande Region* (1983).

ROSS H. FRANK

CHÁVEZ MORADO, JOSÉ (*b.* 4 January 1909), Mexican painter and educator. Born in Siloa, Guanajuato, Mexico, Chávez Morado belongs to the "second generation" of Mexican mural painters. He studied engraving and lithography at San Carlos Academy in Mexico City. In 1937, together with Feliciano Peña, Francisco Gutiérrez, and Olga Costa, he painted the murals of the Escuela Normal. In one year alone (1948) he painted over fifteen public buildings, using various techniques. Later he painted frescoes at the Alhóndiga de Granaditas and the Exhacienda Minera (now called Pastita) in Guanajuato. He has exhibited his easel paintings in important galleries and museums throughout Latin America, Europe, Asia, and the United States.

BÉLGICA RODRÍGUEZ

CHÁVEZ SÁNCHEZ, IGNACIO (*b.* 31 January 1897; *d.* 12 July 1979), Mexican educator and cardiologist. Member of a distinguished generation of intellectuals and politicians from the Colegio Nacional de San Nicolás, Morelia, Michoacán, Chávez became one of the youngest figures ever to direct a major Mexican university, the Colegio Nacional de San Nicolás, in 1920. After obtaining medical and Ph.D. degrees from the National University, he studied in Europe. He served as dean of the National Medical School (1933–1934) and in 1944 founded the National Institute of Cardiology, which he directed for many years. He was rector of the National University from 1961 to 1966, a period of student unrest. Personal physician to many presidents, Chávez left an important legacy in institutionalizing Mexican heart research. He was awarded Mexico's National Prize of Arts and Sciences in 1961.

IGNACIO CHÁVEZ, *México en la cultura médica* (1947) and "Discurso," in *Colegio Nacional, Memoria,* vol. 6 (1967–1968), pp. 249–256.

RODERIC AI CAMP

CHAVÍN, the first of the widespread, great art styles of the Andes. Chavín is named for the archaeological site of CHAVÍN DE HUÁNTAR in the northern Peruvian highlands, a temple complex that exhibits the greatest formal expression of this style. Its widespread distribution corresponds generally to the Early Horizon of the Andean chronological sequence (ca. 1400–400 B.C.).

Around 1400 B.C. a religious movement began to spread across northern Peru that archaeologists term the cult of Chavín. It incorporated elements from older prehistoric Andean coastal religions represented by temples with sunken circular courts and later U-shaped temples, and combined them with elements from the tropical forests of the Amazon basin. Many of the images most commonly represented in Chavín art are wild animals found in the tropical jungle of the Amazonian lowlands. Prominent are the cayman, the JAGUAR, the serpent, and raptorial birds such as hawks or harpy eagles. Features of these animals, especially fangs and claws, are used even on nonanimal and human representations in Chavín art, probably as a sign of divinity. These features occur in a great variety of contexts even on a single image. Hair is represented as snakes, limbs end in feet with large raptorial bird claws or jaguar claws, junctions of the limbs with the trunk of the body are often shown as snarling, fanged feline or cayman mouths, as is the waist, or even the knees. Feathers may end in eyes, snakes' heads, or feline mouths. It has been

suggested that the constant use of these features represents a system of visual metaphors. These are thought to be analogous to kenning, or comparison by substitution. The audience for Chavín art would have understood the references, so that, for example, as a result of an artist's consistently substituting snakes for hair in an image, snakes would eventually come to symbolize hair or represent the qualities of hair. It would also be possible to make kennings of well-known kennings and thus add more complexity to the images.

Chavín art conformed to a specific set of canons. In addition to the use of kennings, the principles of Chavín art include bilateral symmetry, reversible images, and double-profile heads. Bilateral symmetry was extensively used but was rarely perfect, for compositions often have at least one unsymmetrical element, typically a face looking to one side in the center. Many Chavín compositions also contain reversible imagery, whereby a work rotated side to side and/or inverted will still present a right-side-up image. This is usually achieved by clever and careful use of mouth and eye images in kennings on the major intersections of body parts, typically at the junction of the legs, arms, and head with the trunk of the figure. Double-profile heads are achieved through careful placement of two profile heads. Facing

El Lanzón, Chavín culture. LATIN AMERICAN LIBRARY, TULANE UNIVERSITY; PHOTO BY FERNANDO LA ROSA.

each other, the elements of the two heads can be visually combined and read as a single face.

By 1300–1200 B.C. temples and artworks associated with this cult had been built in the north highlands of Peru and on the Peruvian north coast. In the highlands, the temples were built of stone and decorated with low-relief carvings of Chavín deities and icons. The coastal temples were built of adobe and embellished with sculpted mud friezes that were painted in bright colors. By 1000 B.C. Chavín influence had appeared as far south as the area near the modern city of Lima. The cult continued to expand, and by 500 B.C., Chavín influence extended from the modern cities of Cajamarca in the north to Ayacucho in the south. Enduring for centuries, the Chavín cult was enormously successful, but by about 400 B.C. it seems to have disappeared, as a number of new regional traditions asserted themselves.

An excellent synthesis of archaeological research on Chavín can be found in RICHARD L. BURGER, "Unity and Heterogeneity within the Chavín Horizon," in *Peruvian Prehistory*, edited by Richard W. Keatinge (1988), pp. 99–144. See also RICHARD L. BURGER, *The Prehistoric Occupation of Chavín de Huantar, Peru* (1984). For a discussion of kenning in Chavín art, see JOHN H. ROWE, "Form and Meaning in Chavín Art," in *Peruvian Archaeology: Selected Readings*, edited by John H. Rowe and Dorothy Menzel (1967), pp. 72–103. See also PETER G. ROE, *A Further Exploration of the Rowe Chavín Seriation and Its Implication for North Central Coast Chronology* (1974); and RICHARD L. BURGER, *Chavín and the Origins of Andean Civilization* (1992).

GORDON F. McEWAN

See also **Archaeology.**

CHAVÍN DE HUÁNTAR, an archaeological site in the Mosna Valley in Peru's northern highlands. From 900 B.C. until 200 B.C. Chavín de Huántar was an important religious and economic center. At its height, it played a key role within a sphere of interaction that included cultures distributed nearly to the current Ecuadorian border on the north and to the highlands of Ayacucho and the coast of Ica in southern Peru.

In 1919 the pioneering Peruvian archaeologist Julio C. TELLO initiated investigations at Chavín de Huántar. Over the next three decades he argued that the developments there had provided the cultural matrix out of which later Andean civilization developed. More recent investigations have demonstrated that many of the distinguishing features of the site's art and monumental architecture had been based on earlier cultural traditions from the coast and highlands. Nevertheless, the distinctive blend of these older styles constitutes a major artistic accomplishment, and the Chavín style is considered by many to have been among the greatest artistic achievements of indigenous South America.

The public constructions consist of a series of pyramid-platforms arranged in a U-shaped ground plan. Their exteriors were faced in cut and polished masonry, and decorated with stone carvings of tropical forest animals like the jaguar, caiman, harpy eagle, and anaconda. The largest of these structures reached a height of 52.5 feet. They were catacombed with subterranean passageways and chambers, some of which were used for religious rituals. The principal cult object, a large granite sculpture of a fanged anthropomorphic figure (known as the Lanzón), can still be found in situ in the center of the oldest temple structures. While many of the religious rites were held on building summits and in the subterranean chambers, most of the ceremonial activities probably took place in the open-air, semisubterranean, rectangular and circular courts built at the foot of the platforms.

At the outset, a small residential population was associated with Chavín's ceremonial complex, but after 400 B.C. this settlement grew to a considerable size (104 acres, including the public architecture), and the population may have reached two thousand or more. Located at the intersection of two natural routes of communication, the center at Chavín de Huántar became an important focus of interregional trade and religious pilgrimage. While the local subsistence economy was based on a mixed agro-pastoral system of high-altitude crops (such as potatoes), maize, and llama herding, substantial amounts of exotic utilitarian items and ritual goods were acquired from distant sources. There is evidence of socioeconomic stratification at Chavín de Huántar by 300 B.C., and it is likely that the center of Chavín de Huántar served as the focus of one of the first complex societies to develop in the Central Andes.

A synthesis on the archaeology of Chavín de Huántar and its significance for Andean prehistory may be found in RICHARD L. BURGER, *Chavín and the Origins of Andean Civilization* (1992). More detailed descriptions of excavations in the temple sector are provided in JULIO C. TELLO, *Chavín: Cultura Matriz de la Civilización Andina* (1960), and LUIS LUMBRERAS, *Chavín de Huántar en el Nacimiento de la Civilización Andina* (1989). The best-known studies of the Chavín art style are JOHN H. ROWE, *Chavín Art: An Inquiry into Its Form and Meaning* (1962), and PETER ROE, *A Further Exploration of the Rowe Chavín Seriation and Its Implications for North Central Coast Chronology* (1974).

RICHARD L. BURGER

See also **Cupisnique Culture; Kotosh.**

CHAYANTA, REVOLT OF (1777–1781), an indigenous insurrection in Chayanta Province of Upper Peru (modern Bolivia). It began earlier than the more famous 1780–1781 revolt of TÚPAC AMARU, with which it became associated.

In 1777 the AYMARAS in Macha began protesting the colonial government's failure to protect traditional land practices and rights to *cacicazgo* (chieftainship). A *corregidor* (provincial governor), Nicolás Usarinqui, appointed as a *cacique* (chief) of Macha a mestizo, who had no legitimate claim to leadership within the *ayllu* (kinship unit). Among other duties the cacique allocated *ayllu* lands, but this one did so to his own rather than to the community's advantage. By so doing he harmed the villagers, who depended on their agricultural production to pay tributes and provide food and other things for their ill-paid *mitayos* drafted for the mines of Potosí. To protect his people, Tomás Catari, the rightful cacique, protested this corruption and abuse to royal treasury officials in Potosí, who decreed the false cacique's removal. Nonetheless, the new *corregidor,* Joaquín Alós, disregarded the ruling.

Between early 1778 and January 1781, Catari appealed four times to the Potosí officials and four times to the royal Audiencia of Charcas. Seeking redress, he also traveled by foot to Buenos Aires, where he met with the viceroy. The colonial bureaucracy repeatedly approved his petitions but did not force local officials to comply. For his troubles, Catari suffered beatings, five arrests, and ten months in jail. Threats and riots by his followers secured his release. Violence mounted, and disturbances spread to neighboring provinces. The *audiencia* and Alós conspired to eliminate Catari, who was murdered during the night of 15 January 1781.

The insurrection in Chayanta intensified following Catari's death, with his brothers Dámaso and Nicolás helping lead the movement. Chayanta was crucial in spreading rebellion throughout Upper Peru, where dissatisfaction with *repartos* (forced distribution of merchandise to Indians), the MITA (forced labor), and the colonial system generally was explosive. Although the Spanish suspected that the revolts of Tomás Catari and Túpac Amaru were linked, and in fact there was correspondence between the two, the causes of the Chayanta revolt were peculiar to its Aymara peasantry.

An excellent analysis of the revolt's causes is SERGIO SERUL-NIKOV, *Reivindicaciones indígenas y legalidad colonial: La rebelión de Chayanta (1777–1781)* (1989). Also see LILLIAN ESTELLE FISHER, *The Last Inca Revolt, 1780–1783* (1966), esp. pp. 53–94; and MARÍA CECILIA CANGIANO, *Curas, caciques, y comunidades: Chayanta a fines del siglo XVIII* (1988).

KENDALL W. BROWN

CHAYANTA, REVOLT OF (1927), one of the largest peasant rebellions in twentieth-century Bolivian history, in which up to 10,000 Indians attacked HACIENDAS and towns throughout the central highlands between Potosí, Sucre, and Oruro. The uprising lasted about a month, and although it was violently suppressed by the army, the revolt effectively ended the period of hacienda expansion at the expense of highland Indian communities. During the early 1920s community Indians of south-central Bolivia, who had previously fought the alienation of their lands primarily through nonviolent means, became radicalized as legal methods and passive resistance failed. Organized around new leaders, including Manuel Michel, a monolingual Quechua-speaking MESTIZO, the movement attempted to incorporate not only community Indians but also hacienda

peons and urban intellectuals (including the Bolivian Socialist Party). The leaders' principal goals were to fight for the establishment of schools in the communities and for a redistribution of hacienda lands to Indians, whether peons or community members. Shortly after the revolt broke out on 25 July 1927, the rebels took control of a number of haciendas in the Chayanta area (northern Potosí). They killed a landowner but caused few other fatalities. Indian communities elsewhere attempted to rise up but were quickly suppressed. The government mobilized the army and by mid-August had brought the rebellion under control after killing hundreds of Indians. Hundreds more were jailed and the leaders exiled. Armed conflict continued in the countryside at much lower levels of violence for some years thereafter.

The most thorough general description of the revolt is contained in RENÉ ARZE AGUIRRE, *Guerra y conflictos sociales: El caso rural boliviano durante la campaña del Chaco* (1987), pp 11–25. See also OLIVIA HARRIS and XAVIER ALBO, *Monteras y guardatojos: Campesinos y mineros en el norte de Potosí,* rev. ed. (1984), pp. 59–71; and ERICK D. LANGER, "Andean Rituals of Revolt: The Chayanta Rebellion of 1927," in *Ethnohistory* 37, no. 3 (1990): 227–253.

ERICK D. LANGER

CHE GUEVARA. *See* **Guevara, Ernesto "Che."**

CHESS. *See* **Sports.**

CHIAPA DE CORZO, an important Mesoamerican site because of its occupation from 1400 B.C. to the present. It is located on the Grijalva River, in the central section of the Isthmus of Tehuantépec near the modern town of Tuxtla Gutiérrez, Chiapas, Mexico. This location has a tropical lowland environment but the surrounding hills are arid and lack similar pre-Columbian occupations. The site is important for its long ceramic sequence and its location, which facilitates comparisons with regions to the east and west.

The earliest evidence of occupation in the Cotorra phase consists of adobe plaster from a construction and pottery jars and bowls. This pottery was decorated with a variety of surface techniques: punctation, stamping, and appliqué. By 550 B.C. there were pyramids and civic buildings, and by 150 B.C. there was social differentiation, indicated by palaces of cut stone and polished stucco. Tomb 1 of this period held an important personage. Built of unfired brick, it contained a burial with an obsidian-bladed lance, unusual pottery vessels, and jade jewelry. Bones and sculptures were carved in the Izapan style. Mound 5 of the same period was notable for large quantities of pottery in great variety.

GARETH W. LOWE, *Research in Chiapas, Mexico,* New World Archaeological Report no. 2 (1959); NEW WORLD ARCHAEOLOGICAL FOUNDATION, *Excavations at Chiapa de Corzo, Mexico,* papers 8–11

(1960); *Mound 5 and Minor Excavations, Chiapa de Corzo, Chiapas, Mexico*, 12 (1962); and "Archaeological Chronology of Eastern Mesoamerica," in *New World Chronologies*, edited by Royal Ervin Taylor and Clement Woodward Meighan (1973).

EUGENIA J. ROBINSON

See also **Mesoamerica.**

CHIAPAS, southernmost state of Mexico, bounded on the southwest by the Pacific Ocean, on the east by Guatemala, on the north by the state of Tabasco, and on the west by the states of Veracruz and Oaxaca. The 1986 population was 2,435,000, most of them mestizos but about one-third Indians of Maya descent. The capital is Tuxtla Gutiérrez. Much of its area of 28,724 square miles is traversed by the Chiapas-Guatemala Highlands. Its rugged terrain is divided into four distinct geographic regions: the Meseta Central, to the east, with altitudes ranging from 5,000 to 8,000 feet; the Valle Central (Central Valley of Chiapas), drained by the Grijalva River (Río Grande); the Sierra Madre, to the west, a range of mountains with altitudes of 9,000 feet within 20 miles of the Pacific Ocean; and the low coastal plain along the Pacific, an area called Soconusco during the colonial period. This uneven landscape produces extreme variations in climate and vegetation: the lowlands are hot and humid; the valley is relatively dry and hot; the higher parts of the plateau are quite cold, with heavy seasonal (May–October) rains and a good deal of forest.

Chiapas was a flourishing center of the great Maya civilization, the remnants of which may be seen in such important archaeological sites of the Classic period as PALENQUE, YAXCHILÁN, and TONINÁ. At their first contact, the Spaniards found in Chiapas a variety of ethnic states which occupied distinctly different territories and environments. Among the most important were the Zoque, the Chiapanecos, the Tzotzil, the Tzeltal, and the Coxoh. To the east were the Chol and the unsubdued Lacandones. The Pacific littoral was inhabited by people who spoke a Zoquean dialect, Huehuetlatecan. Native society in Chiapas was stratified, with a nobility, commoners, and slaves.

On his way to Guatemala, Pedro de ALVARADO conquered SOCONUSCO in 1524. In the highlands the definitive conquest was carried out by a larger group of Spaniards and native Mexicans under Diego de Mazariegos in 1527–1528. Mazariegos established the first Spanish township, Villa Real (present-day SAN CRISTÓBAL DE LAS CASAS), and distributed the first ENCOMIENDAS (land grants) in the province. By the 1540s, excepting the wild Chol-Lacandón country to the east, the province was generally under Spanish control.

Initially Chiapas was attached to the government of New Spain. From 1549 onward, the highland districts functioned as an *alcaldía mayor*, an administrative subdivision of the Captaincy-General of Guatemala, while Soconusco was organized as an autonomous *gobierno*. In 1786 the Spanish government eliminated both administrative units and established the intendancy of Chiapas, under the jurisdiction of an intendant, whose seat was at Ciudad Real.

The early *encomenderos* found little mineral wealth in the region, so they turned instead to the Indian tribute and agriculture as their chief sources of income. In Soconusco cash crops such as cotton, dyestuffs, and especially cacao proved most lucrative for a while. Foreign competition, however, together with the drastic decline of the laboring population, brought the cacao boom to an end.

In addition to SLAVERY and the collapse of political authority, the Conquest was responsible for a demographic disaster among the native population of Chiapas, chiefly through epidemic diseases. The population of Soconusco was virtually wiped out, and the highlands lost about 90 percent of its estimated population within the first century of colonization.

The first bishop was Bartolomé de LAS CASAS. Thanks in part to his activism on behalf of the Indians, the crown promulgated the NEW LAWS OF 1542, which were intended to eliminate slavery and *encomiendas*. The crown also sent missionaries to establish Indian pueblos (townships) in an effort to further protect the natives from abusive officials and colonists. In these pueblos, Maya traditions showing European influences have survived to this day.

In 1821, led by friar Matías de Córdoba, Ciudad Real and Comitlán were among the first Central American townships to declare their independence. The province proceeded to join Agustín de ITURBIDE's Mexican Empire, becoming a Mexican state in 1824. Soconusco was annexed by Mexico in 1842, and the boundaries with Guatemala were finally settled in 1882.

After independence, liberal policies in Chiapas drastically altered both the region's economy and social relations. The aggressive drive toward modernization through agricultural exports deprived most native communities of their land while transforming highland families into hacienda peons, and compelling those who remained in towns to pay rent and a head tax (*capitación*). Increased international demand for tropical products prompted both Mexican and foreign capitalists to invest in such lucrative cash crops as sugar, cotton, indigo, rice, rubber, and, most notably, coffee, which remain the mainstay of the state's economy.

The 1910 revolution brought agrarian reform and political as well as social change. Ranchers and coffee planters learned to live with the new regime, however, and thus retained their control. At the same time political activists and labor organizers founded socialist parties and peasant unions which called for improvement of the peasants' standard of living.

Since 1936, the expansion of the economy has resulted in the emergence of new social classes in Chiapas. Traditional ethnic differences have tended to become submerged beneath more fundamental differences of wealth, property, and power. The extension of the Pan American Highway, together with the Inter-American Railway built in the 1950s, integrated Chiapas into the national market. The extraction of oil from the eastern highlands increased greatly in economic importance during the late 1970s.

In the late 1980s, there was greater economic liberalization and modernization as well as increasing integration of Mexico into the global capitalist system. This trend reached a climactic point with the inclusion of Mexico as part of the North American Free-Trade Agreement (NAFTA), which went into effect on 1 January 1993. The accelerating expansion of the export sectors of the economy caused further erosion of the standard of living for the majority of the Maya population in Chiapas, as most of the benefits tended to accrue to non-Indian landowners and entrepreneurs. There emerged a variety of radical peasant political organizations, among them the Revolutionary Worker's and Peasant's Party of Popular Unity and the Party of the Poor, calling for land reform, better living conditions, and basic political rights for the Indian peoples. Drawing inspiration from Emiliano ZAPATA, a hero of the 1910 Mexican Revolution, who defended the right of peasants to take over land, these organizations appeared to have coalesced into the Zapatista Army of National Liberation by the early 1990s. This group staged an armed uprising just hours into the new year of 1993, seizing temporarily the state capital of San Cristóbal de las Casas as well as three other neighboring towns. The rebel leaders, citing as their principal motive the participation of Mexico in NAFTA, an agreement which they called a "death certificate for the Indian peoples of Mexico," vowed to fight on until they reached Mexico City. Following heavy fighting, government troops succeeded in forcing the rebel troops to retreat into the hills. The clashes left more than 145 people dead and many wounded. The government of Carlos SALINAS DE GORTARI appointed a negotiating commission which managed to work out a cease-fire on 12 January 1994 by promising to comply with some of the rebels' demands. Tensions remained high, however. In December, shortly after the inauguration of the new President, Ernesto Zedillo, the Zapatista army resumed hostilities, accusing the government of failing to adhere to the terms of the cease-fire. Prospects for a peaceful solution to the conflict appeared bleak, as Mexico entered a new cycle of troubled economic times.

GEORGE A. COLLIER, *Fields of the Tzotzil: The Ecological Bases of Tradition in Highland Chiapas* (1975); PETER GERHARD, *The Southeast Frontier of New Spain* (1979); ROBERT WASSERSTROM, *Class and Society in Central Chiapas* (1983), and "Spaniards and Indians in Colonial Chiapas, 1528–1790," in Murdo MacLeod and Robert Wasserstrom, eds., *Spaniards and Indians in Southeastern Mesoamerica: Essays on the History of Ethnic Relations* (1983).

JORGE H. GONZÁLEZ

CHIARI, RODOLFO E. (*b.* 15 November 1870; *d.* 16 August 1937), Panamanian politician, president (1924–1928), and businessman. Born in Aguadulce, he held many government posts before and after the country's separation from Colombia. He was a deputy to the National Convention in 1904, treasurer of Panama City (1905–1906), deputy secretary of the treasury in the national government (1908), and manager of the national Bank (1909–1914). In 1910 he was elected third designate to the presidency, and in 1912 he briefly took charge of the executive. In 1914 he became the secretary of government and justice, and in 1922 he was appointed director general of the telegraph service. Chiari was a prominent member of the Liberal Party, perhaps second only to Belisario PORRAS. Following his election in 1924, Chiari substituted Porras's populist style with a more business-oriented administration, which led to a quarrel and ultimately to a split in the party.

In 1925 Chiari faced two serious crises. The first was a rebellion by the Cuna Indians on the San Blas Islands, which he quelled successfully. Then, the TENANTS REVOLT (MOVIMIENTO INQUILINARIO) paralyzed the city for two days. The strike was defeated only after Chiari requested the help of U.S. troops stationed in the Canal Zone.

Chiari negotiated a new treaty with the United States in 1926, but it was never ratified by the National Assembly because of concern over one article that made Panama an instant ally of the United States whenever the latter became involved in an armed conflict.

MANUEL MARÍA ALBA, *Cronología de los gobernantes de Panamá, 1510–1967* (1967); MANUEL OCTAVIO SISNET, *Belisario Porras o la vocación de la nacionalidad* (1972); WALTER LA FEBER, *The Panama Canal: The Crisis in Historical Perspective* (1978); JORGE CONTE PORRAS, *Diccionario biográfico ilustrado de Panamá*, 2d ed. (1986).

JUAN MANUEL PÉREZ

CHIARI REMÓN, ROBERTO FRANCISCO (*b.* 2 March 1905; *d.* 1981), Panamanian president (1949, 1960–1964). A liberal and popular politician, he was the son of Roberto CHIARI, who had been president of Panama from 1924 to 1928. Before becoming president he was deputy to the National Assembly (1940–1945) and minister of health and public works (1945). In 1948 he was elected second vice president, and in the following year he was president for five days (20–24 November 1949) after the overthrow of Daniel Chanis. Chiari resigned after the Supreme Court declared him ineligible for the presidency. In 1952 he was the presidential candidate of a popular coalition called the Civilista Alliance, whose victory was not recognized because of the opposition's imposition of Colonel José Antonio ("Chichi") REMÓN CANTERA.

Chiari was elected president in 1960 as the candidate of a four-party coalition, the first opposition candidate to win an election in Panama. He entered office with a reformist attitude and was intent on breaking the oligarchy's grip on power. However, most of his reform measures were blocked by the National Assembly. Seeking better relations with the United States, Chiari traveled to Washington, D.C., and won some concessions from the Kennedy administration, including the right to fly the Panamanian flag at certain sites in the Canal Zone. However, as a result of the 1964 flag riots, Chiari broke diplomatic relations with the United States and demanded the abrogation of the 1903 treaty. He was succeeded in 1964 by Marcos Aurelio ROBLES.

WALTER LA FEBER, *The Panama Canal: The Crisis in Historical Perspective* (1978); *Panama: A Country Study* (1989).

JUAN MANUEL PÉREZ

See also **Panama: Flag Riots.**

CHIBÁS, EDUARDO (*b.* 26 August 1907; *d.* 5 August 1951), founder of the Cuban Orthodox Party. Born in Oriente, Chibás was one of the founders of the Directorio Estudiantil at the University of Havana in the mid-1920s. He studied law and then lived in exile in Miami, Florida (1927–1933), because of his sharp criticism of Gerardo MACHADO's government (1925–1933). Following Machado's downfall, Chibás returned to Cuba to support the candidacy of Ramón GRAU SAN MARTÍN, who became president on 10 September 1933. On 14 January 1934, Fulgencio BATISTA orchestrated Grau's removal from power. Chibás became strongly critical of the series of governments headed by puppet presidents, and particularly of Batista. In 1938, he joined the Authentic Party and in 1940 again backed Grau for the presidency. After Grau was elected president in 1944, Chibás became disillusioned with his nepotism and governmental corruption.

In 1947, Chibás broke away from the Authentic Party and founded the Orthodox Party. He was a candidate for the presidency in 1948, finishing third in the race. During Carlos PRÍO SOCARRÁS's tenure (1948–1952), Chibás used weekly radio broadcasts to attack government policies and corruption.

Chibás committed suicide by shooting himself during an emotional radio broadcast on 5 August 1951. His death created a political vacuum and rift in the Orthodox Party, facilitating Batista's coup on 10 March 1952.

HUGH THOMAS, *Cuba: The Pursuit of Happiness* (1971); JAIME SUCHLICKI, *Historical Dictionary of Cuba* (1988) and *Cuba: From Columbus to Castro*, 3d ed. (1990).

JAIME SUCHLICKI

CHIBATA, REVOLT OF THE, Brazilian sailors' mutiny (1910). Brazil began an ambitious naval expansion program in 1907, purchasing two dreadnoughts, the *Minas Gerais* and the *São Paulo*, in 1908–1909, then the world's largest battleships. Soon Brazil had the world's fifth largest navy in tons displaced. An enormous gulf sep-

arated officers from seamen. Serving fifteen-year tours, seaman were mostly black and often forcibly recruited. Officers were white and aristocratic. Despite abolition (1888) and the naval prohibition of flogging with the *chibata* on the second day of the Republic in 1889, the practice continued.

A week after Marshal Hermes da FONSECA was inaugurated as president in November 1910, the squadron in the waters of Rio de Janeiro, the capital, revolted. Four officers were killed as the crews of the two dreadnoughts and lesser ships mutinied. The immediate cause was a brutal whipping of a sailor aboard the *Minas Gerais*. The command of the squadron and 2,400 rebel sailors passed to a thirty-year-old black, semiliterate seaman.

João Candido Felisberto, the son of a slave, directed the ships, coordinating their movements and loading coal, ammunition, and provisions. He demanded the abolition of corporal punishment and an amnesty for all mutineers. When Congress tarried, he fired on the capital. The president and naval authorities wanted to punish the rebels, but feared destruction of the city and loss of the costly warships. Congress capitulated to the demands.

In December a revolt of marines broke out, but João Candido and his dreadnought crew remained loyal to the government, even after officers had abandoned his ship. The revolt was quelled, and some participants in the second uprising were shot, while others were sent to Amazonian rubber plantations. The previously amnestied rebels of the first rebellion were put into prison, where sixteen suffocated. João Candido, who nearly suffocated, was tried for participation in the second revolt, but was acquitted. The first rebellion was the world's only mutiny in which a common sailor led a squadron, and one containing the most powerful war machines of its time. The *chibata* became a symbol of black and lower-class resistance.

EDMAR MOREL, *A Revolta da Chibata*, 2d ed. (1963); ROBERT L. SCHEINA, *Latin America: A Naval History, 1810–1987* (1987), pp. 80–86, 105–107; HÉLIO LEÔNCIO MARTINS, *A revolta dos marinheiros: 1910* (1988).

JOSEPH L. LOVE

CHIBCHAS. *See* **Muisca.**

CHICAGO BOYS, a group of nonliberal economists who formulated and implemented the economic policy of General Augusto PINOCHET from 1975 through the early 1980s. Most did postgraduate studies in economics at the University of Chicago through a cooperative program established in 1955 with the Faculty of Economics at the Universidad Católica at Santiago. Strongly influenced by monetarist economists Milton Friedman and Arnold Harberger, most returned to Chile and disseminated these ideas to a new generation of economists at the Universidad Católica. The free-market approach that they promoted stressed restrictive monetary policy, encouragement of foreign investment, reduction of the public sector, and minimal state intervention in the economy. The approach contrasted sharply with the structuralist/import-substitution industrialization model of economic development predominant in Latin America since the 1950s. The orthodox monetarist policies of these technocrats brought inflation under control and led to strong rates of growth, but resulted in an extreme concentration of economic assets, unemployment, and the increasing misery of the poorer classes. After the economic crisis of the early 1980s, the direct influence of the Chicago Boys waned, but the concepts they introduced remain pertinent to the economic debate in Chile today.

JUAN GABRIEL VALDÉS, *La escuela de Chicago: Operación Chile* (1989); SEBASTIAN EDWARDS and ALEJANDRA COE EDWARDS, *Monetarism and Liberalization: The Chilean Experiment* (1991); PATRICIO SILVA, "Technocrats and Politics in Chile: From Chicago Boys to the CIEPLAN Monks," in *Journal of Latin American Studies* 23, no. 2 (May 1991): 385–410.

J. DAVID DRESSING

CHICANOS, Americans of Mexican descent. Chicanos represent an extension of Mexico within the borders of the United States and possess a unique history combining both old and new experiences. While many Chicanos can trace their history to the early encounters of Spanish conquerors, missionaries, and settlers with the indigenous populations of what later would become known as the American Southwest, others derive from continuous immigration from Mexico.

Originally Chicanos became part of the United States after the MEXICAN-AMERICAN WAR (1846–1848). Following the conflict, the victorious United States annexed territories stretching from present-day Texas to California that had been held first by Spain and then by Mexico. This "Conquered Generation," as subjects of a new government, often lost their land, became second-class citizens, and suffered cultural degradation.

The Mexican population in the Southwest started to grow considerably at the turn of the twentieth century because of new mass immigration from Mexico facilitated by the building of railroads and flight from the MEXICAN REVOLUTION (1910–1917). The labor of this "Immigrant Generation" largely sparked the region's economic development in transportation, agriculture, mining, and smelting.

By the 1930s, a generation calling itself Mexican American came of age, despite the deportation of thousands of Mexicans because of the Great Depression. This group used new organizational strategies as well as its mass participation in World War II to struggle for

Portrait of the Artist as the Virgin of Guadalupe. Oil pastel on paper by the Chicana artist Yolanda M. López, 1978. PHOTO BY THE ARTIST.

greater integration into American life. Nevertheless, despite certain gains in civil rights, these Mexican Americans still represented a marginalized population in the postwar period.

In the 1960s and 1970s the Chicano movement launched a new period of intense political struggle. This generation responded more militantly than ever before to racial and ethnic inequality. It stressed self-determination for Chicanos as well as a new cultural pride in its heritage. In the 1990s Chicanos continued to occupy an ambivalent position in U.S. society. Progress and poverty, as well as acculturation and cultural preservation, characterize Chicano life.

ALBERT CAMARILLO, *Chicanos in a Changing Society: From Mexican Pueblos to American Barrios in Santa Barbara and Southern California, 1848–1930* (1979); MARIO T. GARCÍA, *Desert Immigrants: The Mexican of El Paso, 1880–1920* (1981); VICKI L. RUIZ, *Cannery Women, Cannery Lives: Mexican Women, Unionization, and the California Food Processing Industry, 1930–1950* (1987); MARIO T. GARCÍA, *Mexican Americans: Leadership, Ideology, and Identity, 1930–1960* (1989); CARLOS MUÑOZ, JR., *Youth, Identity, Power: The Chicano Movement* (1989); DOUGLAS MONROY, *Thrown Among Strangers: The Making of Mexican Culture in Frontier California* (1990); RAMÓN A. GUTIÉRREZ, *When Jesus Came, the Corn Mothers Went Away: Marriage, Sexuality, and Power in New Mex-*

ico, 1500–1846 (1991); ZARAGOSA VARGAS, *Proletarians of the North: A History of Mexican Industrial Workers in Detroit and the Midwest, 1917–1933* (1993).

MARIO T. GARCÍA

CHICHÉN ITZÁ, a major pre-Hispanic MAYA site (A.D. 850–1250) in the northern Maya lowlands in the modern Mexican state of Yucatán. In its masonry, fresco art, and architecture it bears a striking resemblance to TULA, Hidalgo, Mexico, home of the Toltecs north of Mexico City. Chichén Itzá participated in extensive canoe trade around the peninsula through a port at Isla Cerritos. The site was used for ritual pilgrimages long after its abandonment, and was described by Bishop Diego de LANDA in the sixteenth century (1566).

Architecture includes a large stepped pyramid with symmetric stairways up all four sides, one of the largest ritual ball courts in MESOAMERICA, and a round astronomical observatory. The southern part of the site contains structures with fanciful mosaic veneer façades strongly resembling those of the Puuc region to the southwest, while structures in the northern part more closely resemble those in central Mexico.

The largest pyramid (Castillo), with carved references to Kukulcán (the feathered serpent QUETZALCOATL), is aligned to cause rays of the setting equinoctial sun to cast the shadow of an undulating serpent's body along the northern stairway. The shadow joins with the heads of masonry serpents that lay, disembodied through the year, at the foot of the stairs. The stairway faces a *sacbe* (causeway) leading to a large ceremonial *cenote* (natural well), from which numerous artifacts (jade, gold, wood, fabric), sacrificial objects (bowls, copal incense), and skeletons of all ages and both sexes have been recovered. The mouth (*chi*) of the well (*chen*) and the Maya tribe (Itza) gave the site its name in pre-Conquest times. The Castillo covers a smaller, similar pyramid that contained a red jaguar throne, with spots of jade and eyes of ivory, and a sacrificial CHACMOOL, a reclining stone figure holding a plate for the hearts of sacrificial victims.

The observatory (CARACOL), a rare, round Maya building, has narrow observation ports aligned with the setting sun, moon, and Venus. The ball court has carved stone rings high on the mid-court walls and extensive bas-reliefs of the Maya ritual BALL GAME, players' attire, and ritual beheading of (losing?) players with an obsidian knife. A large columned temple with a courtyard of carved warrior columns also covers a smaller, similar structure (Temple of the Warriors, Court of a Thousand Columns).

Chichén Itzá still guards several major puzzles. Its relationship with Tula is not clear. (Which came first, or did both derive from some third area along the Gulf Coast?) Nor is it known if the obvious central-Mexican influences are due to invasion, colonization, or cultural interaction and trade. Also unclear is whether the mural fresco battle scenes refer to events at Chichén Itzá or to mythical earlier battles. The site had just begun its long ascendance to power at the time of the Maya collapse in the southern lowlands. Though a major tourist destination and the subject of much research, the site is not securely dated, nor have its environs been well studied.

See SYLVANUS G. MORLEY and GEORGE W. BRAINERD, *The Ancient Maya,* 4th ed. (1983), esp. pp. 348–357. See also KARL J. RUPPERT's work in the Carnegie Institution of Washington Publications (nos. 403, 454, 546, and 595 from 1931–1952); and ALFRED M. TOZZER, *Chichén Itzá and Its Cenote of Sacrifice,* vols. 11 and 12 (1957).

WALTER R. T. WITSCHEY

CHICHIMECS, a term for various groups of nomadic, warlike Indians to the north of Mexico City. From the Nahuatl *chichi* (dog) and *mecatl* (lineage) the term may have been pejorative, or it may have had totemic significance. Long before the Spanish Conquest, the term was applied to succeeding waves of invading bands of Anahuac peoples. In the sixteenth century it encompassed the Guachachiles, Guamares, Pames, and Zacatecos, all of whom lived to the north of Mexico City. With the great silver discoveries of mid-century, the Chichimecs resisted the Spanish advance to the north. Because of the Chichimecs' ferocity and successful resistance, the colonists consistently called for a total war of extermination or enslavement. The proposed war was roundly condemned by the bishops of the Third Mexican Council (1585). Eventually, the Chichimecs were pacified by a combination of PRESIDIO and MISSIONS that were directed by the Jesuits.

PHILIP WAYNE POWELL, *Soldiers, Indians, and Silver: North America's First Frontier War* (1952, repr. 1975); STAFFORD POOLE, C.M., "War by Fire and Blood: The Church and the Chichimecas in 1585, in *The Americas* 55 (1965): 115–137.

STAFFORD POOLE, C.M.

CHICLE INDUSTRY, the extraction of resin from chicle trees for use as a base in the manufacture of chewing gum. The chicle tree (*Achras sapota* or *Manikara sapota*) is a broadleaf evergreen found in the tropical lowlands of several Latin American countries. In some regions chicle is also known as *níspero* or *tuna.* The primary sources of chicle are Mexico, Belize (formerly British Honduras), and the Petén region of northern Guatemala. Although the export of chicle never assumed great national importance, the industry was and remains significant to local economies.

John Curtis of the United States is credited with the first commercial production of chewing gum in 1848. Curtis used spruce resin as a base but by the 1870s manufacturers had come to prefer chicle resin. Commercial interests from the United States began their chicle operations in Mexico in 1869. A dramatic increase in chewing gum consumption took place during World War I. Advertising campaigns by the Wrigley Company promoted chewing gum for soldiers and civilians to relieve tension and satiate thirst. The growth of chewing gum sales led to the expansion of the chicle industry. By 1930 the United States imported 15 million pounds of chicle resin a year, a boom that lasted until the 1940s, when synthetic substitutes came on the market. Chicle production continues, but the industry is threatened. Competition from synthetics and deforestation are major problems. Attempts to cultivate chicle trees on commercial plantations have failed.

The backbone of the industry is the individual *chiclero* (chicle gatherer). Although they operate out of a common base camp for several months, *chicleros* work alone in the jungle to locate chicle trees, tap them, and collect the sap. A *chiclero* might locate and tap ten trees on an average day. A single tree can yield from 1 to 5 pounds of resin, depending on its age and the number of times it has been tapped. The same tree cannot be tapped successfully for another four to eight years. Tapping requires that the *chiclero* climb the tree and cut a vertical line of V-shaped notches along the trunk. At the base of this line a bucket is placed to catch the resin. The accumulated resin will be returned to camp, where it is boiled down to reduce its water content and then poured into molds. A contractor pays the *chiclero* according to the weight and water content of the resin molds.

ROBERT HENDRICKSON, *The Great American Chewing Gum Book* (1976); HERMAN W. KONRAD, "Una población chiclera: Contexto histórico-económico y un perfil demográfico," in *Boletín de la Escuela de Ciencias Antropológicas de la Universidad de Yucatán* 8 (December 1981): 2–39; NORMAN B. SCHWARTZ, *Forest Society: A Social History of Petén, Guatemala* (1990).

STEVEN S. GILLICK

CHICO ANÍSIO (Francisco Anísio de Oliveira Paulo Filho; b. 1931 or 1932), Brazilian television personality and fiction writer. Chico Anísio created a variety of memorable television characters, including Santelmo, Coronel Limoeiro, and the Mayor of Chico City. His style of humor has been equally successful in his fiction. Chico Anísio aims for the jugular through satire and social critique presented in a direct, oral, and truly popular language and style. A predominant theme in his work is the desperation of society's marginalized population. The stories in *Feijoada no Copa* (1976) censure the upper classes for their insensitivity toward the reality surrounding them. The collection of stories *Teje preso* (1975) focuses on his own Northeastern roots and the region's traditions.

IRWIN STERN, "Anísio, Chico," in *Dictionary of Brazilian Literature* (1988).

IRWIN STERN

CHIHUAHUA, the largest state in Mexico, with an area of 95,400 square miles and a population of 2.44 million (1990). The state lost territory as a result of the Treaty of GUADALUPE HIDALGO (1848) and increased in size slightly with the Chamizal Agreement of 1963. Bounded on the north by Texas and New Mexico and on the west, south, and east by Sonora, Sinaloa, Durango, and Coahuila, the region has long been a sparsely populated frontier zone characterized by mining and large landed estates dedicated to livestock raising. Chihuahua is divided into three basic geographical zones: the Sierra Madre Occidental, cut by deep canyons, in the west; the eastern slopes of the mountains with their basins, ranges, and valleys; and the huge desert depression in the east known as the Bolsón de Mapimí. These geographical features, an arid climate, the absence of water, isolation from the rest of Mexico, and a history of endemic violence have led historians to describe Chihuahua as a harsh and violent land.

The region has a long record of human habitation. Twenty-five to thirty thousand years ago, hunters entered the area. New arrivals from the north about A.D. 900, linked to the Mogollon culture in southern Arizona and New Mexico and influenced by the Anasazi, built and inhabited the site of Casas Grandes (Paquimé) in northwestern Chihuahua between 1060 and 1340. This cultural and trading center also displayed probable Toltec influences, including L-shaped ball courts. By the sixteenth century, the region of Chihuahua was inhabited principally by Tarahumares, or Raramuri, estimated to number twenty thousand at the time of contact with the Spaniards, as well as Conchos, Tobosos, Sumas, Mansos, Jumanos, Warihios, and various Apache bands in the far north. Spanish settlement and demands for mine labor, combined with mission activity, led to rebellions and the eventual disappearance of Amerindian peoples, except the Raramuri and Apache. Endemic violence and the lack of a large, sedentary Indian population limited race mixture, weakened the hold of the Catholic Church, encouraged the development of labor forms characterized by mobility and wage relationships, and fostered the creation of PRESIDIOS and ranches for defensive purposes.

The Spaniards first settled the mining district of Santa Bárbara, founded in 1567. The discovery of silver ore at Parral in 1631 and nearby Nuevas Minas (now Villa Escobedo) in 1634 prompted governors to run the province of Nueva Vizcaya from Parral for the next hundred years. Later, a similar find converted Santa Eulalia (1708) and the newly founded San Felipe el Real de Chihuahua into mining, commercial, and administrative centers and the headquarters of the newly organized Commandancy General of the Internal Provinces after 1776.

Although political factionalism, war with the United States, Indian raids, drought, and epidemic laid waste to much of newly independent Chihuahua, with economic activity reaching a low point in the mid-nineteenth century, after 1880 foreign investment in railroads, mining, forestry, and land made for rapid economic expansion. After the defeat of the Apache in 1880 and the construction of the Mexican Central Railroad in 1884, U.S. companies took over the state's mining industry and foreigners controlled the largest commercial firms. At the same time, a local oligarchy, the Terrazas-Creel family, monopolized economic power, becoming one of the largest landowners in the country, and centralized political power. This pattern of economic development, resentment of the Terrazas-Creel oligarchy, and the loss of village lands prompted mountain communities, political "outs," the middle-class, and displaced artisans to revolt in 1910, leading, subsequently, to the identification of Chihuahua as "the cradle of the Revolution."

Despite the changes ushered in by the MEXICAN REVOLUTION, including the demise of the great estate, restriction in the power of the church, land reform, and labor legislation, subsequent developments in Chihuahua have continued previous patterns. Beginning with the creation of a free-trade zone in 1885 (eliminated in 1905) and Mexican migration to the United States in the late nineteenth century, the border, not regulated until 1929, has drawn people and investment. The Bracero Program (1942–1964) and an accompanying illegal movement of an even larger magnitude, along with the Border Industrialization Program, established by the Mexican government in 1965, and the import of many commodities duty-free (*artículos ganchos*) since 1971 have contributed to phenomenal population growth in Ciudad Juárez (population 800,000 in 1986), as well as to the establishment of assembly plants known as MAQUILADORAS. Such plants, allowing the tariff-free importation of parts and equipment and return of finished goods to the United States with tariffs charged only on the value added, numbered 281 in 1990 and employed 126,657 workers, mostly young women. The *maquiladoras* have stimulated migration and consequent overcrowding and have increased the region's dependence on inputs from the United States.

The economic and cultural influence of the United States combined with a long history of resistance to the centralizing Mexican state (the area was a bastion of federalism, liberalism, and anticlericalism in the nineteenth century) have made Chihuahua a center of organized political opposition and popular antipathy to the central government. An opposition party, the National Action Party (PAN), made significant gains in municipal elections in 1983 and the gubernatorial elections in 1986.

FRANCISCO R. ALMADA, *Resumen de la historia del estado de Chihuahua* (1955); MARVIN D. BERNSTEIN, *The Mexican Mining Industry, 1890–1950: A Study of the Interaction of Politics, Economics, and Technology* (1964); FLORENCE C. LISTER and ROBERT H. LISTER, *Chihuahua: Storehouse of Storms* (1966); MARK WASSSERMAN, *Capitalists, Caciques, and Revolution: The Native Elite and Foreign Enterprise in Chihuahua, Mexico, 1854–1911* (1984); OAKAH L. JONES, JR., *Nueva Vizcaya: Heartland of the Spanish Frontier* (1988).

WILLIAM FRENCH

See also **North American Free Trade Agreement (NAFTA).**

CHILAM BALAM, a MAYA priestly class whose members' predictions form the basis for local historiography. Literally translated from Classical Yucatecan Maya, *Chilam Balam* means "spokesmen of the jaguar." The *Books of Chilam Balam* are a set of Yucatecan Maya documents that were compiled during the seventeenth to nineteenth centuries covering events of the seventh to nineteenth centuries. Several types of documents have been titled *Chilam Balam*. The most widely recognized are fourteen manuscripts (twelve survive) that are named after the community of the YUCATÁN Peninsula of southern Mexico where they were found.

Although the term *Chilam Balam* implies priests who could foretell the future, only five of the books (those from Chan Kan, Chumayel, Kaua, Mani, and Tizimin) include prophetic texts. They are histories of the past and at the same time predictions of the future. These books are grounded in the belief that events occurring during certain periods of time will recur in particular future periods. Specifically, *katuns*, or cycles of 20 tuns (the 360-day Maya civil year), that end on days with the same name and coefficient will contain analogous events. In the books containing the prophetic texts, close attention is given to historical and calendrical accuracy; a reliable picture of what the future held was at stake.

Topics covered in the nonprophetic books include astrology, calendrics, and medicine. *The Book of Chilam Balam of Nah* contains the greatest amount of medical information, including descriptions of ailments, etiology, and various means of treatment.

The Chilam Balam of Chumayel, because of multiple translations, is the most widely known. The book reveals many details of everyday life including cuisine. It also offers a glimpse of the indigenous view of the Spanish: certain passages suggest that the Maya understood the arrival of Christianity as the fulfillment of calendrical predictions.

The *Books of Chilam Balam* have been and will continue to be important documents for understanding the present and future Maya of Yucatán.

RALPH L. ROYS, trans. *The Book of Chilam Balam of Chumayel* (1913); EUGENE R. CRAINE and REGINALD C. REINDORP, *The Codex Pérez and the Book of Chilam Balam of Mani* (1979); MUNRO S. EDMONSON, trans. *The Ancient Future of the Itza: The Book of Chilam Balam of Tizimin* (1982).

MATT KRYSTAL

CHILDREN in Latin America have been deeply influenced by the impact of race, economic and social status, and a shift in ideas regarding the roles of family and government in the education and socialization of children. From the time of the Conquest, families, especially fathers, were invested with extensive powers over and responsibilities for their children. Gradually governmental authorities, as well as mothers, began to share the responsibility. Severe economic, political, and racial differences, however, have resulted in the inability or unwillingness to care for children. The result has been periodic surges in the numbers of abandoned or homeless children.

The basic unit of Latin American society is the legally and religiously sanctioned biological family. The offspring of these unions historically have transmitted familial economic, social, political, and religious status. During the colonial era, legitimate children perpetuated the patriarchal name as well as the material fortunes of both parents. In the case of upper-class families, this meant that the child inherited their social status, and efforts were made to prepare that child to perpetuate or enhance the family's reputation. Often selected children were promised to the Catholic church as an indication of family piety. If the child were female, upon marriage she would assume the status of her husband's family.

Most Latin American children, however, were born to poor families who rarely were sanctioned by either the state or the Catholic church. Furthermore, racial miscegenation (*mestizaje*) and poverty usually prevented offspring from improving family status by marriage or by service to the church. Instead of property and social status, children born to African or Afro-Latin American slave women inherited the stigma of slavery, regardless of the status of the father.

Indian mothers faced other realities. If the father was Indian, the children inherited the burdens of the family's tribute payments in the form of labor, produce, or money. The children, particularly the young women who learned how to weave and embroider, also helped celebrate indigenous identity through custom and clothing. If the father was not Indian, the mestizo offspring of Indian women lost both their Indian identity and their obligation to pay tribute.

From the Independence era onward, Latin American governments began to revise the significance of both children's legal birthrights and (thus) their political, social, and economic value. From the nineteenth century on, governments began to insist on greater involvement in education, public health, and the development of the economy. Consequently, many patriarchal privileges, such as the right to select an occupation and provide an education for offspring, were limited. There was also a weakening of economic responsibility for children through the decline of the dowry for young brides, and child abandonment. The inability of an unmarried mother to force the father to recognize his paternity, along with development of religious and secular institutions designed to care for unwanted children, exacerbated these conditions. By the twentieth century a father's patriarchal privileges over his children (*patria potestad*) were further restricted by laws regarding parents accused of abandonment, maltreatment, or moral turpitude. In practice, however, governments rarely enforce the laws and have been unwilling to pay the financial costs of rearing most of the children involved.

Thus, from the Conquest to the present, the social and emotional value that society has placed on children has been highly contradictory. At the same time that childbirth was often a welcome event, illegal abortions were common, and high infant mortality and popular Catholicism led to the belief that the death of young, baptized children transformed them into angels. There are patterns of ritualized celebration of infant death through portraiture and, by the nineteenth century, of photographs of the child. Examples of the *angelito* (*anjinho* in Portuguese) phenomenon are still common in Mexico and Brazil. The children, regardless of economic status, are adorned with a crown of flowers and often dressed in white.

During the same time periods, parents who could not afford the social stigma or the economic burden of illegitimate children gave them to better-off families or abandoned them on a *turno* (*roda* in Portuguese; foundling wheel), usually at a convent, or left them at the doorsteps of churches or town council halls, or in the doorways of families they believed would take pity on the child. These traditions dated from European medieval times and allowed children to be taken into new homes without the stigma of their birth. Despite this Catholic tradition, the strength of blood ties was so strong that fostered children could never share equal inheritance with legitimate offspring unless their identities were falsified. The practice of legal adoption reached many Latin American countries only in the twentieth century. Reforms of the Civil Codes authorizing adoption occurred in Brazil in 1917; Peru in 1936; Chile in 1934; Uruguay in 1868, 1934, and 1945; and Argentina in 1948. The enactment of these laws took place in the midst of debates regarding the right of parents to have legal heirs as well as the right of orphaned or abandoned children to have parents. Adoption laws have been reexamined after military antiterrorist campaigns in the 1970s and 1980s in Central and South America left significant numbers of orphans who were illegally adopted after their parents were executed.

The formation in the late nineteenth and early twentieth centuries of a cadre of physicians specializing in public health took up the challenge of infant mortality by providing new technologies of childbirth, inoculations against childhood diseases, and improved water and sewage services, and by advocating programs for infant nutrition. Initially breast-feeding was the recommended strategy to save children of poor mothers, and campaigns against the sale of breast milk by wet nurses were launched. Until 1888 and the end of slavery, Brazilian doctors diverged from their counterparts elsewhere due to their belief in the superior qualities of black women's breast milk. By the early twentieth century, the availability of reliable sources of pasteurized milk in urban areas, along with the development of powdered milk and prepared baby formulas, created new opportunities for physicians to teach mothers how to feed their children. Some of these campaigns were influenced by principles of eugenics.

Elite women also had a significant role to play in the

campaign against infant mortality. The Sociedad de Beneficiencia, for example, in 1823 was authorized by the Argentine government to care for sick women and children. By the 1880s it fed and provided shelter for hundreds of orphaned or abandoned children in Buenos Aires. Eventually, through government subsidies and private donations, it built children's homes throughout the province of Buenos Aires. Similar organizations were founded in Chile, Uruguay (1857), Costa Rica (1887), Cuba, and Mexico. Feminist women, often of upper- and middle-class origins, as well as socialist women in many Latin American countries encouraged *puericultura* (the scientific study of child rearing) and persuaded their male counterparts to enact legislation to help both women and their children. In addition to these organizations, municipal Defensores de Menores and the Patronato de la Infancia in Argentina (1892), the Mexican Asociación Nacional de Protección a la Infancia (1925), Gotas de Leche (Chile, Cuba, Argentina), the Asociación Uruguaya de Protección a la Infancia (1925), the Comisión Nacional de Protección de la Maternidad e Infancia (Cuba), and the Patronato de la Infancia (Costa Rica, 1930) worked to aid orphans or abused and neglected children.

Latin American child specialists began to meet in scientific and politically sponsored congresses. The Pan-American Union, predecessor of the Organization of American States, sponsored children's congresses from 1916 to 1984. In addition, Argentina hosted one in 1913, as well as a congress on abandoned and delinquent children in 1933. Mexico held one in 1923 and then another in 1925. Costa Rica's congress took place in 1931, and Venezuela held its first Congreso Nacional del Niño in 1936. Among the topics discussed were the need for special legislation to establish appropriate forms of re-education for delinquent children and juvenile courts, and ways to enable government authorities to intervene in what had previously been considered family matters.

These meetings resulted in the enactment of significant legislation in several Latin American nations. In 1919 Argentine legislators enacted the Ley Agote. For the first time judges had clear guidelines as to when the courts could remove the right of *patria potestad* from parents who were considered immoral or irresponsible, or who had abandoned their children. It identified the degree of responsibility for a child's crime by age and authorized expansion of reform schools for delinquent children so that they would not have to be jailed with adult prisoners, but provided no funds to accomplish this. (A newer, more comprehensive, version of this legislation, called Códigos del Niño, was promulgated in Uruguay in 1933.) It also created juvenile courts. Colombia already had the beginning of a juvenile court system in 1946, when the Estatuto Orgánico del Niño was promulgated. In 1934 Venezuela established its Código del Niño, which was superseded by the Estatuto de Menores in 1950.

Despite the early efforts to promote a scientific yet

Elementary school recess. Caracas, Venezuela, 1992. ULRIKE WELSCH.

caring governmental policy dealing with children, recent economic and political events have made it difficult for Latin American nations to live up to both the spirit and the letter of the law. Extreme poverty, militarism, and the burdens of governmental debt have led to the abandonment of strong state intervention in the needs and care of children, and have relegated much of the social assistance to children to nongovernmental organizations. Impoverished children in the 1990s face the challenge of survival on the streets, often because of the actions of government elements. For example, in Brazil, in recent years, death squads of the military police have been murdering *meninos da rua* (street children).

Memorias del VII Congreso panamericano del niño reunido en la Ciudad de México del 12 al 19 de octubre de 1935, 2 vols. (1937); *Actos y trabajos del Primer Congreso nacional de puericultura, 7–11 de octubre de 1940,* 2 vols. (1941), for Argentina; CARLOS BUENO-GUZMAN,"The Child in the Civil Law of the Latin American States," in *The Child and the Law* (1975); SILVIA M. ARROM, "Changes in Mexican Family Law in the Nineteenth Century: The Civil Codes of 1870 and 1884," in *Journal of Family History* 10, no. 3 (1985): 305–317; DONNA J. GUY, "Lower-Class Families, Women and the Law in Nineteenth-Century Argentina," in *Journal of Family History* 10, no. 3 (1985): 318–331; PATRICIA SEED, *To Love, Honor, and Obey in Colonial Mexico: Conflicts over Marriage Choice, 1574–1821* (1988); JOHN BOSWELL, *The Kindness of Strangers: The Abandonment of Children in Western Europe from Late Antiquity to the Renaissance* (1990); EMILIO GARCÍA MÉNDEZ and ELÍAS CARRANZA, eds., *Infancia, adolescencia y control social en América Latina: Argentina, Colombia, Costa Rica, Uruguay, Venezuela* (1990); MARY DEL PRIORE, ed., *Historia da criança no Brasil* (1991); JOSEPH M. HAWES and N. RAY HINER, eds., *Children in Historical and Comparative Perspective: An International Handbook and Research Guide* (1991); ELIZABETH ANNE KUZNESOF, "Sexual Politics, Race, and Bastard-Bearing in Nineteenth-Century Brazil: A Question of Culture or Power?" in *Journal of Family History* 16, no. 3 (1991): 241–260; NANCY STEPAN, *"The Hour of Eugenics": Race, Gender, and Nation in Latin America* (1991).

DONNA J. GUY

See also **Family.**

CHILE. [Coverage begins with a three-part survey of Chilean political history. There follow a variety of entries on specialized topics: **Constitutions; Geography; Junta del Gobierno; Organizations** (civic, cultural, labor, etc.); **Parliamentary Regime; Political Parties; Revolutions; Socialist Republic of 100 Days;** and **War with Spain.**]

Foundations Through Independence

COLONIAL FOUNDATIONS

Perched on one of the remotest edges of the Spanish American empire, the captaincy-general of Chile was never counted among the richest or most developed territories of the Spanish crown. Isolation was a keynote of Chilean history from the outset. Until the advent of the steamship, the territory was rarely less than four months by sea from Europe. Yet from the first, Spaniards arriving in Chile were attracted by its fertile soil and its usually moderate climate: "This land is such that for living in and perpetuating ourselves in there is none better in the world," wrote Pedro de VALDIVIA (ca. 1498–1553) to Emperor Charles V (1500–1558) on 4 September 1545. Valdivia was the first conquistador to establish permanent settlements in Chile; his first "city" was SANTIAGO (founded 12 February 1541), the hegemonic focus of Chilean life from that day forward.

The first decades of the new colony's existence were dominated by warfare. Resistance to the invading Spaniards was fiercest in the south, in the lands beyond the Bío-bío River, where the MAPUCHE proved more than able to hold their own. The Spaniards came to refer to the native Chileans as ARAUCANIANS; their military prowess was generously eulogized by Alonso de ERCILLA Y ZÚÑIGA (1533–1594), the soldier-poet whose epic LA ARAUCANA narrated the early phases of the prolonged struggle of the Spaniards and Mapuche.

After extending the colony to the south of the Bío-bío, Valdivia himself was killed by the Mapuche in December 1553. His successors as governor were obliged to give most of their attention to warfare. By the end of the sixteenth century, it was clear that the colony was impossibly overextended: its Spanish-creole population at that point was less than eight thousand. In 1599 the point was proved by a major Araucanian offensive that drove the invaders from their settlements south of the Bío-bío—Valdivia's "seven cities"—and confined them to the northern half of the Central Valley.

For the rest of the colonial period and well beyond, the Bío-bío became a frontier zone. From the early seventeenth century a small standing army (financed by the Viceroyalty of Peru) was based in the south to protect the frontier, but Chile was not important enough to the empire to warrant a full-scale military assault on Araucania. The Mapuche preserved their political independence until the mid-nineteenth century. Their culture and society, however, undoubtedly were altered as a result of contact with Spanish Chile, an observation supported by developments in both agriculture and cross-frontier trade. Warfare continued at regular intervals throughout the seventeenth century. In 1723, however, an Araucanian offensive was curtailed because of the disruption it was causing to trade, and there was only one further serious flurry of warfare (1766) in colonial times. Missionaries tried more peaceful methods of winning over the Mapuche, but with no conspicuous success.

As a result of the Araucanians' success in defending their trans-Bío-bío homeland, the dimensions of colonial Chile were fairly compact, the main nuclei of population concentrated in the northern section of the Central Valley and in the adjacent Aconcagua Valley (or Vale of Chile). A few small clusters of population existed further north, toward the desert, and by the second half of the eighteenth century, the mining town of Copiapó marked the rough northern limit of Spanish settlement. South of "indomitable Araucania" there were diminutive outposts at Valdivia and on the island of Chiloé, remote appendages of the captaincy-general that counted for very little in colonial times. Colonial Chilean life thus developed in a relatively limited area. Geographical isolation contributed to the formation of a distinctive and increasingly homogeneous culture.

The evolving social structure of the colony resembled that of other parts of the Spanish Empire, but was also marked by certain local differences. The basic shapes and forms of Chilean life were developed during the sixteenth and (especially) seventeenth centuries, and consolidated in the eighteenth. During this period the population became increasingly less diversified: mestizos were already a conspicuous group by 1600, and continued miscegenation meant that 200 years later they were the numerically dominant component in the Chilean population of 700,000 or so. Native Chilean numbers north of the Bío-bío declined rather sharply as European pathogens took their toll. (How many natives made their way to the free redoubt of Araucania is impossible to say, although some did.) The Spanish-creole elite was not rich enough to constitute a market for African slaves: in 1800 there were approximately five thousand of these.

The Chile that developed in colonial times essentially

consisted of a largely mestizo majority and a small upper class of Spaniards and creoles. Upper-class culture was basically Spanish. Mestizo culture reflected both Spanish and native influences, observable in such things as games, diet, vocabulary, and popular superstitions. By the end of colonial times, however, mestizos tended where possible to pass themselves off as "Spaniards." Their names, language, and religion were all Spanish.

Societies built on brutal conquest are often sharply stratified. In the Chilean case, economic imperatives reinforced stratification. The main aim of the conquistadors themselves was to mobilize native labor through the ENCOMIENDA for washing gold from the rivers and for ranching and agriculture. In theory the *encomienda* was not a grant of land but an allocation of natives. In practice many natives were assigned a place in the large seigneurial landholdings that grew up after the Conquest. With the decline of the native population, the *encomienda* lost its importance, though surviving in outlying areas like Chiloé and the north until the 1780s. Alternative sources of labor (the enslavement of Mapuche captured in war, or the transfer of natives from Cuyo across the Andes) proved unsatisfactory. A more stable rural labor system was needed and one gradually evolved.

The seventeenth century is often described as Chile's "tallow century." Tallow, *charqui* (jerked beef), and cattle hides were exported to Lima and Potosí, while Chilean mules were sent to the great annual fair at Salta. Ranching helped to consolidate the great estate, a process that was enhanced at the end of the century by the growth of a demand for wheat both domestically (as mestizos developed European dietary preferences) and in the Peruvian market. HACIENDAS, as Chilean estates were now usually called, began to adopt cereal cultivation. The mestizos and "poor Spaniards" who had been enticed onto the earlier ranches as "renters" (given a small plot in exchange for help with the livestock) were gradually transformed into a permanent class of tied peasants, known in Chile as *inquilinos*. (Use of this term became customary in the second half of the eighteenth century, by which time the classic Chilean hacienda was more or less fully formed.) The stable hacienda population of *inquilinos* was complemented, in the countryside, by a large mass of casual and frequently itinerant peons, whose lack of opportunities often forced them into vagabondage and petty banditry—a phenomenon that was especially noticeable in the area between the Maule and Bío-bío rivers.

Though overwhelmingly dominant in the Chilean countryside, haciendas were never universal. In the vicinity of the townships, fruit and vegetables were often grown on small farms called *chacras* (often owned by hacendados), while numerous subsistence plots were worked by peons wherever they were able to squat. The position of the great estate, however, was enhanced over the years. Ownership of a hacienda was one of the clearest marks of upper-class status. Agriculture was the

principal motor of the eighteenth-century colonial economy, with wheat usually accounting for 50 percent of Chile's exports to Peru. At the end of the colonial period, the mining of gold, silver, and copper in the thinly populated north (the area Chileans now refer to as the NORTE CHICO) assumed a new importance, prefiguring its spectacular nineteenth-century profile. There were hundreds of mines in the semi-desert north, mostly very shallow, worked with primitive technology, and rich in high-grade ores. The new salience of mining was acknowledged in 1787 by the creation of a mines administration on the model of Mexico's.

EIGHTEENTH-CENTURY GROWTH

By the end of colonial times, metals were becoming increasingly important in the colony's trading pattern. In the seventeenth century, the captaincy-general was no more than an economic appendage of Peru and, because of the highly regulated imperial system, at the end of a long commerical chain that extended through Lima and Panama to Spain. This made European merchandise impossibly expensive. The eighteenth-century Bourbon reforms had a notably stimulating effect on Chilean trade. From 1740 ships were permitted to sail directly from Spain to Chile, and trade with the RÍO DE LA PLATA provinces was finally legalized. Thus the colony could now trade directly with Spain, with the Río de la Plata (whence came the YERBA MATÉ so popular in Chile), and with Peru. The powerful Consulado (merchant guild) of Lima tried to resist such developments, but in vain. Chile shook free from its irksome dependence on the Viceroyalty: after 1750 the colony could mint its own coins, and in 1796 a separate consulado was set up in Santiago. The only real advantage now enjoyed by Peru was control of the shipping that carried Chilean wheat to Lima. This enabled Peruvian merchants to fix the wheat price—a long-running Chilean grievance.

While it is important not to exaggerate the scale of Chile's eighteenth-century commercial expansion, it is undeniable that new opportunities attracted a flow of Spanish immigrants into the colony—some twenty-four thousand Spaniards between 1700 and 1810. Roughly half of these were Basque or Navarrese. The most enterprising immigrants accumulated sufficient capital (usually in trade) to insert themselves into the creole upper class by marriage and by the purchase of haciendas. Some of these newcomers founded impressive family networks. The so-called Basque-Castilian aristocracy thus formed played a dominant part in Chilean affairs until the twentieth century. Taking *mayorazgos* (strict entails) and titles of nobility as a fairly reliable indicator, this Chilean creole elite looks much less impressive than its counterparts in the viceroyalties. In 1800 there were only seventeen *mayorazgos* and twelve titles (seven *marqueses* and five *condes*) held by Chilean families. Very few creoles were really well-to-do; not until the trade booms of the nineteenth century did agriculture and mining yield large fortunes.

Nevertheless the creoles, old and new, were clearly the leaders of colonial society by the second half of the eighteenth century. High political office was generally denied them, a practice which in due course became a grievance. Chile's political status was that of a captaincy-general, formally subordinate to the Viceroyalty of Peru (until 1798), but for all practical purposes ruled separately by a governor and an AUDIENCIA (operating temporarily in 1567–1575 and permanently after 1609). As part of the Bourbon overhaul of imperial administration, the colony was divided in 1786–1787 into two INTENDANCIES, Santiago and Concepción, under a governor acting as the senior intendant. These changes do not seem to have impinged as negatively on creoles as may have been the case elsewhere in the empire. In any case, the Chilean elite was adept at exerting informal pressure on colonial officials.

It is difficult to find evidence of serious disaffection from the imperial political system. This perhaps became more likely with the rising educational level of creoles: the University of San Felipe opened in 1758, and by 1813 nearly two thousand students had passed through it. In the same period the university conferred 299 doctorates: 128 in law, 106 in theology.

THE BREAK WITH COLONIAL RULE

However isolated and remote, the colony could not remain entirely cut off from the new trends of thought then emanating from the outside world. A number of educated creoles assimilated the ideas of the Enlightenment. Those few who traveled to Europe were especially exposed to its influence. Some of them developed a strong interest in economic reform. Manuel de SALAS (1754–1841), a conspicuous member of this group, wrote a classic account of the colony's economy and society (1796), in which he contrasted the material backwardness of the territory with its abundant physical potential. Such feelings fueled a growing sense of creole patriotism. Salas and similar figures were neomercantilists, impressed by movements for enlightened reform in Spain itself, and they placed a good deal of faith in the imperial state. However, it is also clear that they deeply desired improvements, and this stance doubtless inclined them to favor creole-run national governments when the time came.

A much smaller group of creoles, probably no more than a handful, was enthused by the Enlightenment, by the anticolonial struggle in British North America, and (less straightforwardly) by the French Revolution, and aspired to complete independence and the creation of a Chilean republic. Representative of this group was Bernardo O'HIGGINS (1778–1842), a frontier landowner who had been educated in England, where he had met Francisco de MIRANDA (1750–1816) and had been converted to Miranda's separatist vision. All that radicals like O'Higgins could do was bide their time and wait for an opportunity that might never come. It came sooner than they could have imagined possible.

Napoleon's invasion of Spain in 1808 caused consternation in Chile, as everywhere else. Creole leadership had already been perturbed by the attempted British conquest of the Río de la Plata in 1806–1807. The initial feelings of loyalty to Spain expressed by the *cabildo* (municipal government) of Santiago lasted several months, but soon lost ground to the notion of establishing an autonomous (and creole-directed) government, if only to preserve the colony for the dethroned King FERDINAND VII (1784–1833). The governor, Francisco Antonio García Carrasco (1742–1813), a military man with little political subtlety, interpreted creole aspirations as subversive, an attitude also taken by the Audiencia. In what it saw as a preemptive move against the creole-dominated CABILDO, the Audiencia prevailed on García Carrasco to resign in favor of a rich and well-respected creole, Mateo de TORO ZAMBRANO (1727–1811). Emboldened by the news of the May Revolution in Buenos Aires, the *cabildo* responded by invoking colonial precedent and calling for a *cabildo abierto*, an open meeting of leading citizens. Toro Zambrano eventually agreed, and the assembly was convened on 18 September 1810 with about four hundred people in attendance. A national JUNTA of seven members was chosen, and the governor himself installed as president. The stated aim of the junta was to preserve Chile for the "unfortunate" monarch Ferdinand VII. But the promise to convene a national congress (which met, to no great effect, in July 1811) owed nothing to colonial precedent and was a revolutionary step toward dismantling colonial rule.

It may be doubted whether more than a small minority of creoles yet favored outright independence. In fact none of the "patriot" governments of the next four years—the period Chileans call the PATRIA VIEJA (old homeland)—made a formal declaration of independence. And in any case, divisions within the patriot leadership soon emerged. These were not merely the predictable divisions between moderates and radicals, but a serious rivalry between the powerful (and highly extended) Larraín family and its adversaries, whose self-appointed leader was an ambitious army officer returning from Spain—José Miguel CARRERA (1785–1821). In November 1811 Carrera used his sway over the military to seize power, dissolving the first national congress and, over the next few months, neutralizing his opponents, who had entrenched themselves in the south. With the Carrera dictatorship, the impetus for reform gained momentum. Chile's first newspaper, *La Aurora de Chile*, did much to spread new revolutionary doctrines. Yet Carrera made no real move toward a final break with Spain.

This ambiguous stance did not deter the Viceroy of Peru, José Fernando de ABASCAL Y SOUSA (1743–1821) from sending three successive task forces to Chile to form the nucleus of royalist armies (1813–1814). So began Chile's WAR OF INDEPENDENCE. Carrera's lack of success against the royalists weakened his position. Power in Santiago passed into the hands of a series of juntas. Carrera's successor as commander-in-chief, Bernardo O'Higgins, was neutralized by the second major royalist offensive, and a short-lived peace treaty ensued (May 1814).

On 23 July 1814 Carrera once again seized power in Santiago, and civil war between O'Higginistas and Carreriños seemed unavoidable, but a third royalist army, commanded by General Mariano OSORIO, swept up the Central Valley from the south and overwhelmed the patriot forces at RANCAGUA (1–2 October 1814). O'Higgins, Carrera, and many other patriots fled to Argentina, and Chile reverted to colonial rule. This "Spanish reconquest" lasted two years and four months, and was an unhappy time of persecutions and occasional atrocities. This in itself weaned most creoles from the idea of colonial rule.

INDEPENDENCE AND THE NEW STATE
It fell to the great Argentine general José Francisco de SAN MARTÍN (1778–1850) to effect the final liberation of Chile. He saw this as an essential step in his plan for a seaborne invasion of the Viceroyalty of Peru. At the start of 1817, San Martín's Army of the Andes (more than four thousand men) crossed the high passes of the Cordillera and won a decisive victory over the royalists at CHACABUCO (12 February 1817). O'Higgins, by this stage a close associate of San Martín, was selected as supreme director of the new Chilean state. A massive royalist counterattack, led once again by Osorio, was finally checked at the very bloody battle of MAIPÚ on 5 April 1818, by which time O'Higgins had formally proclaimed the independence of Chile (February 1818).

The patriots then created a small Chilean navy, which was placed in the command of the redoubtable Scottish admiral-adventurer Lord Thomas COCHRANE (1775–1860), whose audacious forays cleared the seas of Spanish shipping and enabled San Martín's Chilean-financed (and largely Chilean-manned) expedition to set off for Peru in August 1820. The rest of the South American war of independence was waged far from Chile, whose part had been both decisive and heroic. In Benjamín Vicuña Mackenna's great phrase, "free, she freed others."

Independence enabled the creoles of the Basque-Castilian aristocracy to assume their place as the governing class of the new state. It was more than a decade, however, before they found an adequate form of government. Meanwhile the apparatus of separate nationality was adopted with enthusiasm, and reforms were enacted: O'Higgins abolished titles of nobility and the display of coats of arms (1817), and reestablished institutions such as the Instituto Nacional (National Institute of Higher Education) and the National Library, abolished under the Spanish reconquest. Slavery was abolished in 1823.

Commercial reforms—four ports were thrown open to international trade in 1811—stimulated mild economic expansion: the value of Chile's external trade nearly tripled between 1810 and 1840 (from 5 million pesos to 14 million pesos). Agriculture, it is true, was seriously disrupted by the wars of independence, especially in the south, where recovery did not come much before the 1840s. But the mining zone, unaffected by fighting, benefited immediately from the increase in commercial traffic. Silver production may have doubled between 1810 and 1830, while the export of copper showed a threefold rise between the 1810s and the 1830s. Imports also flooded into the country, though the limited market was quickly saturated. Overall, Chile's economic capacity was appreciably heightened by independence, even if it took several decades for genuine commerical booms to set in, as they did in the later 1840s and again in the 1860s.

Politically, the search for an appropriate framework was by no means easy. O'Higgin's regime was essentially a war dictatorship until 1820 and, as such, brilliantly successful. With the tide of war receding, however, he was less able to handle domestic political pressures. His abdication on 28 January 1823 was followed by several years of makeshift constitutional experiment, with the main role assumed by Liberal politicians. A weirdly idiosyncratic constitution devised by Juan EGAÑA in 1823 was soon jettisoned. A brief flirtation with "federalist" ideas in the mid-1820s proved similarly fruitless. In 1828, under President Francisco Antonio PINTO (1775–1858), the Liberals succeeded in enacting yet another constitution, and for a while the prospects for stable Liberal government seemed promising. Unfortunately, certain Liberal actions and a mild tendency toward anticlericalism provoked hostility from the Conservative opposition. A clear-cut differentiation of Liberals and Conservatives, however, is difficult: the Conservative "Party" probably included the best-established section of the elite, whereas the Liberals had a greater share of professional men, intellectuals, and so forth. In the Chile of the 1820s the influence of the Conservatives was always potentially stronger.

The Conservative rebellion of 1829–1830, captained by the remarkable and resolute Diego PORTALES (1793–1837), ended the Liberal phase and inaugurated a long period of political stability with the new Constitution of 1833 as its legal framework. The new regime was at times repressive: it depended on strong presidential power and the systematic manipulation of elections, a practice that did not cease until after 1891. With all its blemishes, however, the "Conservative Republic" gave Chile internal tranquillity and provided the basis for commercial expansion, and it was flexible enough to allow an eventual transition to Liberal-dominated politics in the 1860s and 1870s.

In political terms, the aftermath of Chile's struggle for independence was the most unusual story in nineteenth-century Spanish America. It was due in part to the strength of the colonial legacy: isolation, separate cultural development, and relative homogeneity were all factors that influenced the Chile that emerged from the colonial chrysalis into the light of freedom.

LOUIS DE ARMOND, "Frontier Warfare in Colonial Chile," in *Pacific Historical Review* 23 (1954): 125–143; SIMON COLLIER, *Ideas and Politics of Chilean Independence, 1808–1833* (1967); H. R. S. POCOCK, *The Conquest of Chile* (1967); MARIO CÓNGORA, *Orígen de los 'inquilinos' de Chile central*, 2d ed. (1974); ARNOLD J. BAUER, *Chilean Rural Society from the Spanish Conquest to 1930* (1975), chap. 1; MARY LOWENTHAL FELSTINER, "Kinship Politics in the Chilean Independence Movement," in *Hispanic American Historical Review* 56 (1976): 58–80; JACQUES A. BARBIER, *Reform and Politics in Bourbon Chile, 1755–1796* (1980); ARMANDO DE RAMÓN and JOSÉ MANUEL LARRAÍN, *Orígenes de la vida económica chilena, 1659–1808* (1982); BRIAN LOVEMAN, *Chile: The Legacy of Hispanic Capitalism*, 2d ed. (1988), chaps. 2–3.

SIMON COLLIER

The Nineteenth Century

The defeat of the Spanish at CHACABUCO on 12 February 1817 marked a milestone on, but not the end of, Chile's quest for liberty. Since Chileans fought for both the Royalists and the *independistas*, their struggle to end Madrid's rule was both a civil war and a rebellion. The defeat of the Spanish army did not end conflict; it simply permitted the latent tensions which had riven Chilean society to surface. Thus, the end to the struggle against Spain set the stage for a more prolonged civil war.

AFTER CHACABUCO

Following Chacabuco, three groups vied for power: the followers of José Miguel CARRERA, who sought radical economic and social change; Bernardo O'HIGGINS's supporters, who hoped to introduce mild reforms; and the traditionalists, who wished to limit change by substituting the Chilean elite for the old colonial bureaucracy. O'Higgins enjoyed certain advantages: he had led the triumphant army and hence had won some personal popularity. Unlike his rivals, moreover, he already wielded power. However, the traditional elements disliked O'Higgins because he revoked their titles of nobility, thereby diminishing their social status, and because he abolished the entailed estate, thus threatening their economic base. But as much as they loathed O'Higgins, the traditionalists dared not move against him, fearful that the more radical Carrera might take over.

The execution of Carrera and his brothers in 1821 and the expulsion of the Spanish from the south emboldened O'Higgins's foes. Consequently, the opposition forced the Supreme Director to enact a constitution. Presumably undertaken to ensure popular sovereignty, this document in fact sought to limit O'Higgins's power. Although O'Higgins's social, political, and economic policies were somewhat restrained by the new constitutional strictures, they continued to alienate, especially the most powerful. Even nature seemed to turn on him: poor harvests, which produced a famine, and a terrible earthquake ravaged O'Higgins's Chile. The combination proved too much; discontent finally blossomed into

unrest. Rather than fight a fratricidal civil war, O'Higgins resigned on 28 January 1823 and fled to Peru.

O'Higgins's premature departure from office initiated a period of political turmoil that lasted until 1830. For approximately seven years, Chileans embraced, then rejected, different leaders, constitutions, and political systems, and even established a federal republic. Chile's presidential palace, the MONEDA, became a way station. First Ramón FREIRE ruled, as both president and dictator, until 1826. Next, Manuel BLANCO ENCALADA and his associate Agustín Eyzaguirre lasted until 1827, when Freire briefly returned to power. Then he gave way first to Francisco Antonio PINTO and then to Francisco Ramón VICUÑA.

While turbulent, this period was not without accomplishments. The new republic won U.S. and British diplomatic recognition; it abolished slavery in 1823; and three years later it finally drove out the last Spanish garrison, although Madrid waited until 1844 before belatedly acknowledging the existence of its former colony. Yet, despite these achievements, the economic elite and the landholding aristocracy had tired of the unrest. In 1829, after seeing their candidate unfairly denied victory, these elements rebelled as southern aristocrats, who resented Santiago's rule, raised an army under General Joaquín PRIETO, who marched on the capital. At the LIRCAY River, on 17 April 1830, Prieto's troops defeated the government's forces under the leadership of general and former president Ramón Freire.

THE 1830s: NEW STABILITY

The victory brought to power the conservatives, men who wanted to restore to Chile many of the colonial system's institutions. Under the guiding genius of Diego PORTALES, a new state emerged, authoritarian by nature, albeit republican in name. The Constitution of 1833 created a political system that restricted the vote and the right to hold public office to less than 10 percent of the nation. While clearly undemocratic, the constitution recognized the reality of Chile: the wealthy were in control, and unless they could dominate the political system, unrest would roil the nation. But in return for receiving control of the state, the oligarchy had to submit to its authority.

This social contract worked. From 1831 to 1871, only four men—Joaquín Prieto (1831–1841), Manuel BULNES (1841–1851), Manuel MONTT (1851–1861), and José Joaquín PÉREZ (1861–1871)—governed Chile. In contrast to nearby nations, which seemed to change presidents with each new season, Chile's political life seemed staid, if not stodgy. Thus, while Santiago's potentially richer neighbors wallowed in seemingly perpetual political turmoil, Chile could devote its energies to developing its economy, instead of squandering its treasure and blood maintaining internal order.

The passage of the Constitution of 1833 alone did not guarantee order. Diego Portales made sure that it worked, by purging the military and the bureaucracy of

The Palacio de la Moneda, by Becquet. A mint that later became the presidential palace. PHOTOGRAPHIC ARCHIVE, UNIVERSIDAD DE CHILE.

anyone whom he suspected of harboring treasonous thoughts. His policies were brutal but efficient: by the late 1830s, Chile had become strong enough to fight a war to destroy the PERU-BOLIVIAN CONFEDERATION. True, the president did have to rule by extraordinary decree—which meant that he could suspend the precious few civil liberties remaining—but he managed to quell domestic as well as foreign foes. Indeed, it was a tribute to the strength of the state that it could survive the loss of its progenitor when Portales died in an abortive coup (1837). Hence, Chile emerged from the decade of the 1830s stronger domestically and, after forcing the dissolution of the confederation, more powerful internationally.

Economic prosperity seemed to follow in the wake of Chile's political stability. During the 1830s, and particularly in the 1840s, Chilean farmers thrived by exporting their foodstuffs first to hemispheric customers and later to England. Chile's real wealth, however, lay not in the agrarian central valley but in the arid NORTE CHICO. The discovery of silver—as well as copper—first in LA SERENA and then in Chañarcillo, provided the state with a generous source of income in the form of export taxes. Trade also buttressed Chile's prosperity. By constructing an enormous complex of warehouses and wharf facilities that allowed foreigners to store their cargoes for minimal fees and by providing repair facilities and victualing for vessels arriving from Europe or the United States, Portales's minister of economics, Manuel RENGIFO CÁRDENAS, made Valparaiso into the hemisphere's most important Pacific entrepôt.

THE 1840s: DISCOVERY AND DEVELOPMENT
The 1840s proved a decade of development for Chile. Its new president and hero of the war against the defunct Peru-Bolivian Confederation, General Manuel Bulnes, ruled in a relatively benign fashion, attempting to reconcile the nation politically. Economically, Chile hummed. The discovery of gold in California proved a boon to the nation's farmers, who grew rich feeding the Forty-Niners, as did the merchants of Valparaíso, who revictualed the California-bound ships. The discovery of additional silver deposits in the north, in conjunction with the development of domestic coal pits in Lota, increased the vitality of the MINING sector. Chile's first railroad, connecting the port of Caldera with the northern center of Copiapó, began to function.

The state invested many of its new revenues in developing the nation's infrastructure, creating the University of Chile and a normal school as well as various other cultural and technical institutions. To protect the country's trade routes to Europe, Chile occupied the Strait of Magellan and founded the city of Magallanes (later Punta Arenas). It also encouraged German immigrants to settle in the country's virgin forests in the south.

The influence of foreign political refugees—Argentines like Domingo Faustino SARMIENTO and the Venezuelan Andrés BELLO—as well as European ideas, particularly those associated with the revolutions of 1848, became more pronounced. Chilean thinkers like José Victorino LASTARRIA, Francisco BILBAO, Santiago ARCOS, and Eusebio Lillo spread these ideas, along with many of their own, throughout the nation.

MID-CENTURY: GROWING POLITICAL MATURITY

The growing social and intellectual diversity in Chile's elites eventually undermined the nation's monolithic political system. A squabble between two former ministers of the interior, Manuel Montt and Camilo Vial, erupted into a schism in the Conservative Party. Political dissidents, whom Portales had driven underground, surfaced, joining the supporters of Vial to form the Liberal Party. The new organization demanded a more open political environment: abolition of the Senate, an end to presidential succession, an extension of suffrage, local autonomy (including the right to select local officials), and greater personal freedom. The demise of the old consensus might, many feared, signal a return to political unrest.

The pessimists proved right: revolution did follow liberalization. In 1851, Chileans rebelled for the first time, opposing Bulnes's attempt to select Manuel Montt as his successor. The son of impoverished gentry, Montt rose to occupy several important governmental positions. But although he was an extremely competent and hard-working man, the prospect of Montt's presidency managed to fuse traditionally disparate groups into a solid phalanx of hate. Rebellions erupted throughout the country when it became clear that Montt would indeed become president. Violence spread from the mining north even as far south as Magallanes. The government was unable to restore order until early 1852.

Initially, Montt reacted vindictively, sentencing many of the rebels to death. Although he subsequently commuted these sentences, he still held tight to the reins of power: for almost half of his ten-year regime, Montt governed either under a state of siege or under the rubric of his extraordinary presidential powers.

Even this formidable authority could not assure Montt a tranquil administration. He became involved in a series of fruitless struggles with the Roman Catholic church when its hierarchy under Archbishop Rafael Valentín Valdivieso y Zañartu challenged his authority to regulate the clergy. The president became so infuriated with the church that he broke with the ultramontane Conservatives to found a new political bloc, the National Party, or the Montt-Varistas, which would rule Chile for the next several decades. Except for its repudiation of ultramontane ideals, the Nationals shared many of the old Conservative ideologies. Montt's decision to create his own political party drove the Liberal and Conservative opposition elements to form an alliance to oppose him.

Despite a turbulent beginning, Montt ruled well. He modernized the economy by abolishing the entailed estates, or MAYORAZGOS, in 1852. He initiated the construction of a rail line between SANTIAGO and VALPARAÍSO, as well as another connecting the capital with the agrarian south. Montt established telegraph service connecting Santiago with Valparaíso and Talca. Of equal importance, his government published a new commercial code, organized a mail service, founded a credit bank, and authorized the creation of private lending institutions and public corporations.

A downturn in the economy turned Montt's second term sour. The agricultural boom generated by gold rushes in the United States (1849) and Australia (1853) evaporated when these areas became self-sufficient in food production. The loss of the Californian and Australian markets caused economic dislocation in Chile, whose farmers and millers suffered even more when exports of American farm surplus began to drive down prices for Chile's agricultural commodities. Mineral production also fell when the mines of Chañarcillo began to peter out. The downturn in the fields and mines reduced the flow first of exports, then of imports, and finally of the states' revenues, impoverishing both the commercial sector and the government.

Montt, like his predecessors, tried to handpick the man who would replace him as president. His choice was his alter ego, Antonio VARAS, whose career and ideals seemed a mirror image of his mentor's. The political parties, however, would no longer tolerate the old ways. In 1859 rebellions erupted in the north as well as the south. Although the government's troops crushed the uprisings, the rebels made their point: the political system would have to become more open. Rather than perpetuate the existing venomous feelings by accepting Montt's support for the presidency, Varas bowed out of the race for president. In his stead Montt selected José Joaquín Pérez, a jovial, benign politician whose presence neither antagonized nor frightened anyone. Pérez immediately amnestied all those involved in the 1851 and 1859 rebellions. He ruled Chile during a ruinous war with Spain. Santiago joined the hemispheric outrage when Madrid, in 1862, seized the CHINCHA ISLANDS, off the coast of Peru. The Spanish fleet eventually retreated, but before leaving Chilean waters it cannonaded Valparaíso, devastating the port and the nation's economy.

Happily, Chile's domestic political scene seemed more placid. Helped by the affable Pérez, who included members of the Liberal-Conservative Fusion in his government, Chile's political system continued to evolve. In the early 1860s, a group of dissident Liberals created the Radical Party. Its ferocious name notwithstanding, this new group sought not to change the political system drastically but to secularize society by stripping the Roman Catholic church of its special privileges. Eventually, four political parties proclaimed that they would not tolerate operating under the old strictures.

In 1865, with the election of an antigovernment majority, the Congress enacted laws that guaranteed increased religious freedom, particularly for Protestants. Five years later the legislature revised the election laws, including mechanisms intended to prevent vote fraud. The culmination of the reform movement was an 1870 constitutional amendment limiting the president to a single five-year term.

The first man elected under this new law was Federico ERRÁZURIZ, who, like many of his contemporaries, had been jailed for opposing the Montt regime. The standard bearer of the Liberal Party, Errázuriz was also a friend of Archbishop Rafael Valdivieso, whose support he cultivated in order to win the 1870 presidential election, defeating a candidate of the National and Radical Parties. Errázuriz, however, would turn against his Conservative allies.

Perhaps this political split was inevitable, for what united the Liberals and Conservatives was not a shared ideology but a hatred of the National Party. Once Errázuriz came to power, he had to deal with the Conservative agenda. The new president increasingly disliked the fact that various Roman Catholic institutions seemed to enjoy certain extralegal prerogatives such as controlling the rite of marriage and the use of cemeteries. In 1872 the Catholic minister of education, Abdón Cifuentes, ordered the University of Chile to admit students who had passed entrance exams administered not by the university but by church schools. Cifuentes's edict unleashed a political firestorm. Subjected to fierce parliamentary questioning, Cifuentes and his Conservative colleagues resigned their cabinet posts.

With the Conservatives gone, Errázuriz moved to the left, thus accelerating the pace of reform and the secularization of society. In 1873 and 1874, for example, the congress liberalized the constitutional requirements for legislative quorums and for naturalization, extended the right of free association, required that senators be elected directly from specific districts—previously they had been selected at large—and created a joint congressional committee that could, under certain conditions, request the president to convoke an extraordinary legislative session.

The impetus to convert Chile's government into a quasi-parliamentary system accelerated: it became easier for the legislature to challenge ministers, and harder for the president to declare a state of siege. Changes were also made in the electoral process. Henceforth, the local communities' most affluent people would maintain the voting rolls, and the state eliminated the provision that individuals must possess property in order to vote. The congress also passed a law enhancing the ability of minority parties to win office.

Theoretically, these measures prevented the government from manipulating the political process. In fact, they made it only slightly more difficult while permitting local oligarchies, particularly rural landowners, a free hand in influencing elections. Other significant reforms included the promulgation of a new criminal code, which among its provisions restricted the powers of the clergy, and a mining code.

THE 1870s: GROWTH AND DECLINE

Chile had changed dramatically by the mid-1870s. The population numbered 2 million and the number of urban centers had increased, as had the population of Santiago and Valparaíso. The nation's economy, based on a mix of mining, commerce, and agriculture, became increasingly diversified. But a more significant shift took place.

Although the nation had flirted with free trade beginning in the 1870s, the legislature began, on a piecemeal basis, to pass laws protecting national industries as they began producing consumer goods like textiles or shoes. The manufacture of agricultural tools as well as heavy machinery began. Chileans constructed mineral refineries in the south where, using local coal, they smelted imported and domestic ores into ingots of pure silver and copper. Linked by an ever-expanding rail system and a merchant marine, and backed up by telegraph and mail service, Chile's economy became integrated into that of the world. Cereals were exported not merely to Latin America but to England, and metals were sold everywhere.

Blessed with increasing revenues, particularly from the development of the CARACOLES silver mines in Bolivia, the government constructed various public-works projects and even purchased two ironclad warships for its navy. Then the good times came to a halt. Beginning in 1873, a series of unrelated events short-circuited Chile's economy. First, various European nations adopted the gold standard, depreciating the value of silver, by then Chile's most lucrative export. And roughly at the same time that the silver mines in Chile and Bolivia became less productive, copper output also declined. In the interim, a depression enveloped both the United States and Europe. Hence, Chile simultaneously lost both its markets and its principal source of income.

Errázuriz's term of office expired in 1876. His handpicked successor, Aníbal PINTO, however, needed massive intervention by Errázuriz to force the Liberal Party to nominate him. After his election, Pinto almost did not take office. Elements within the army considered launching a coup and imposing Pinto's rival, Benjamín VICUÑA MACKENNA, on the nation. The government, however, managed to crush the potential putsch, exiling the conspirators.

During the ensuing years, Pinto might have wished that Vicuña Mackenna had triumphed. The year Pinto took office, floods destroyed the crops in Chile's south while drought devastated them in the north. The enormous drop in agricultural output not only reduced exports but drove up domestic food prices. The following year brought no respite. Famine became widespread, forcing people into the cities in a futile search for food. Desperate people turned to crime or fled the nation in search of work.

Pinto initially attempted to deal with the crisis by reducing government expenditures. When that measure failed to balance the budget, he and the congress passed a tax on income and inheritances as well as gifts. While not substantial, these imposts nevertheless represented a milestone in Chile's economic history. This was the first time the government had imposed direct taxes on its citizens and the first time the levies were designed to fall mainly upon the affluent.

The combination of the declines in mining and agriculture continued to devastate Chile. By 1878 it became clear that virtually all but one of the nation's financial institutions were bankrupt. Fearing a panic, the government decreed that the public could no longer convert the banks' paper money into specie. Not just the financial institutions suffered. The Moneda, literally without gold or silver, had to print paper money.

As Pinto attempted to confront this economic Armageddon, his nation became embroiled in a bitter border dispute with Argentina over the ownership of Patagonia and control of the Strait of Magellan, which threatened to plunge Chile into war. No sooner had Pinto temporarily resolved this problem, when Bolivia initiated a series of steps that would push not only Chile but also Peru into war.

In late 1878, Bolivia's president, Hilarión DAZA, increased taxes on NITRATES, or *salitre*, mined by a Chilean corporation operating in Bolivia's ATACAMA DESERT. This tax increase violated an earlier treaty under which Chile had ceded to Bolivia control of the desert in return for its promise not to raise taxes on any Chilean corporation operating in that area.

Pinto did not wish a confrontation with La Paz. His decision to negotiate with Argentina, however, infuriated his domestic enemies. Fearing that his political opponents might use the dispute with Bolivia to their advantage, Pinto recognized that he had to defend strenuously Chile's interests in Bolivia. Thus, in February 1879 Pinto acted, ordering his troops to occupy the territory that Santiago had earlier ceded to La Paz in return for its concessions to the Chilean mining interests. Daza responded by declaring war.

Six years earlier, Peru and Bolivia had signed a secret military alliance binding both nations to support each other in case either one became involved in a war with Chile. Chile knew of the treaty's existence but had never reacted. Pinto demanded to know officially whether Peru had signed an alliance with Bolivia and, if so, whether Lima would join in the war against Chile. Faced with an ultimatum, Peru's envoy admitted that it would honor its military commitment to Bolivia. Hence, in April 1879 Chile declared war on both Peru and Bolivia.

THE WAR OF THE PACIFIC

The ensuing struggle, known as the WAR OF THE PACIFIC, lasted for four years. Although Chile eventually triumphed, its victory was neither easy nor guaranteed. Indeed, outnumbered and geographically smaller than its enemies, Chile seemed to be at great risk. Santiago, however, managed to win control of the sea lanes, allowing it to launch an attack. By late 1879, Chile had driven the combined Peruvian and Bolivian armies from the nitrate-rich province of TARAPACÁ. The next year Pinto's army tortuously invaded TACNA and ARICA, eventually capturing the area. In January 1881 the victorious army seized Lima.

The fall of Lima did not end the war, however, since Peru's leader, Nicholás de PIÉROLA, refused to cede territory to Chile in return for a peace treaty. Instead he and other zealots organized centers of resistance in Peru's interior. Faced with this resistance, Santiago tried to form a rump government that would sign a peace treaty. It required two years of diplomatic badgering and bloody fighting before Peru capitulated, granting Chile Tarapacá as well as the right to occupy Tacna and Arica for a period of ten years. Bolivia quickly followed suit, agreeing to an armistice allowing Chile to occupy the Atacama.

AFTERMATH OF THE WAR OF THE PACIFIC

The War of the Pacific severely taxed Chile's economic, military, and political resources. Not until the conquest of Tarapacá, which permitted the Chilean government to export nitrates, did the Moneda receive a more constant source of income. The Chilean public had quickly tired of war. Faced with a lack of volunteers, the army began impressing society's less fortunate—drunks and vagrants—and eventually peasants and urban workers. Pinto also had problems with his professional military. Too many officers proved incapable of directing the war, causing the president to send civilians to help prod the army into action and to take charge of plotting strategy as well as provisioning the army.

Finally, the war threatened Chile's political system. The capture of a transport ship, the *Rimac*, in the winter of 1879 unleashed a series of riots in Santiago which threatened Pinto's regime and required force to quash. Had the war not shifted in Santiago's favor, the Chileans might have turned their president out of office. Pinto enjoyed only slightly less support within the Congress. The president's enemies used every opportunity to harass Pinto, unsuccessfully trying to use the war to force him to form a cabinet of national unity.

Having surmounted the earlier crisis, Pinto managed to finish his term of office. His successor, Domingo SANTA MARÍA (1881–1886), was, like Pinto, handpicked. Given his lack of broad support, Santa María encountered even more political problems than had Pinto. The intense partisan bickering that would characterize the PARLIAMENTARY REGIME had begun in the latter days of the Pinto government and came into full flower during Santa María's administration. The Conservative opposition, for example, delayed the passage of a budget—even though the nation was at war—in hopes of forcing the government to invite them to join the cabinet. Santa María refused. Instead of capitulating, he solved this problem by shamelessly manipulating the 1882 congressional elections so that none of the opposition Conservatives won.

With a relatively tame legislature, Santa María achieved one of his most cherished goals: secularizing Chilean society. In the mid-1880s the president prodded the legislature into passing measures that made marriage a civil, not a religious, contract and gave the state control over the civil registry and cemeteries. (The latter measure had particularly ghoulish results as the pious, rather than allowing their deceased loved ones to lie beside possible nonbelievers or, even worse, Protestants, clandestinely disinterred them to rebury them in consecrated ground.) The ultramontanes and the Catholic church accused Santa María of launching a *Kulturkampf* against them, but to no avail; short of complete separation, the Moneda had effectively curtailed the church's power.

Santa María's greatest achievement was Chile's victory over Peru and Bolivia. In 1883, Lima signed the Treaty of ANCÓN, which ceded Tarapacá to Chile. A year later, Bolivia reluctantly permitted Santiago to take ANTOFAGASTA. Regrettably, the status of two additional provinces, Tacna and Arica, as well as a final resolution of the War of the Pacific, remained to vex the belligerents for decades.

Now one-third larger, Chile had incorporated the nitrate-rich northern provinces into the nation, thereby creating a market for locally produced consumer goods as well as giving the state control over the world's nitrate supply. Rather than operate these mines itself, the government sold the mines (called *salitreras*) to private interests. Many have subsequently lamented that the Chilean state did not retain ownership of the *salitreras*. However, had Santiago opted to operate the mines, it would have had to liquidate an enormous debt before it could own them outright. Thus, rather than indenturing itself and assuming the responsibility for running the mines—a task for which it was unsuited—the state preferred to levy a heavy tax on the export of nitrates.

Nitrates, which at first blush appeared to be a boon to the Chilean economy, eventually poisoned the country. The easy money from nitrates encouraged congress to abandon the earlier taxes on land, income, and estates—levies which obviously fell upon the wealthy—and instead place the economic burden on the foreign consumer. Chileans preferred to invest their capital in nitrate shares, which guaranteed them a high rate of return, rather than in national industries. Hence, the country's revenues and its economy, which earlier had been so diversified, increasingly depended upon the good fortune of the *salitreras*.

These problems did not surface immediately. On the contrary, Chile seemed to have entered the promised land. The newly rich government launched numerous public-works projects, erected palatial *belle époque* public buildings, expanded the bureaucracy, and extended the railroads deeper into the south. The Moneda dedi-

cated substantial sums to modernizing the army, which had finally vanquished the ARAUCANIAN Indians, as well as to the navy, which possessed some of the world's finest warships.

The man destined to follow in Santa María's footsteps was his former minister of the interior, José Manuel BALMACEDA. The new president, who like so many of his predecessors achieved office through chicanery if not brute force, took his oath of office in September 1886.

When Balmaceda became president, he controlled a vast source of revenue, which he hoped to use to fund numerous public-works projects. Unfortunately, many members of the president's own party, as well as the opposition, vied with him for control of the purse strings. Balmaceda resented their intrusions, preferring to retain power so that he alone could dispense patronage. He also objected to the fact that congress had become obstreperous. Like his predecessor, Balmaceda manipulated the congressional elections to pack the legislature with his supporters. Balmaceda's intervention incensed not only those who lost but also some Liberals, who increasingly disliked this policy. They also disliked the fact that Balmaceda often acted without winning their prior approval.

As his opposition grew and coalesced, Balmaceda's own followers became divided over the issue of presidential succession. Balmaceda wished to select his successor, but his Liberal colleagues opposed his choice. It became clear that Balmaceda would have to act in consort with the legislature, in effect making Chile a de facto parliamentary republic, if he wished to govern effectively. The strong-willed Balmaceda, who before he became president had spearheaded a drive to weaken the president's power, refused to accept this possibility.

In late 1890 the Congress refused to approve Balmaceda's budget unless he agreed to form a cabinet which enjoyed the legislature's approval. The president refused, declaring that he would use the 1890 budget for 1891 as well. Outraged at this violation of the 1833 Constitution, the congressional forces rebelled.

Backed by the Chilean navy, Balmaceda's opposition, the congressionalists, fled to Iquique, where they established their headquarters. Better equipped, and apparently better led, the rebels defeated the loyalist army at the battles of Placilla and Concón, then seized the capital. Although Santiago was declared an open city, the victorious congressional forces looted the homes of Balmaceda's supporters and murdered some of his officials. Balmaceda wisely took refuge in the Argentine embassy, where he remained until his term of office expired. The following day, he committed suicide.

THE PARLIAMENTARY REGIME
The death of Balmaceda ushered in the Parliamentary Regime, which would rule, but not govern, Chile until 1924. The passage of new legislation transferred the supervision of elections from the central to the local gov-

ernments. Presumably designed to prevent fraud, the new law merely changed the malefactors. Henceforth, corrupt provincial officials, under the thumb of the landed aristocracy or urban political bosses, rather than the president's minions, perverted the electoral process. Thus, instead of having to appeal to the electorate, candidates needed only to satisfy the aspirations of the power elite.

Chile's rampant corruption perpetuated a political order that remained insensitive, if not deaf, to the nation's pressing social and economic ills. In fairness, it should be noted that new political parties appeared. The Democratic Party, in 1887, became Chile's first avowedly working-class political party, and the Balmacedistas, after futilely attempting to overthrow the Parliamentary Regime, eventually joined it in the 1890s by creating the Liberal Democratic Party. Eventually, both the Democrats and the Balmacedistas compromised their principles, moving from opposing the regime to joining it.

The parliamentary regime marked the beginning of Chile's decline. The existence of so many parties—six, competing for the votes of 150,000 people, or less than 10 percent of the nation's total population—virtually guaranteed political instability and hence administrative paralysis. An indication of potential problems was the fact that during the government of Federico Errázuriz Echaurren (1896–1901) alone, there were more cabinet changes than had occurred between 1830 and 1851. Unfortunately, since the president could not fill the political vacuum precipitated by so much parliamentary shuffling, the nation seemed inert.

At the same time, Chile was no longer the Southern Cone's principal political force. Argentina, which had finally put its house in order, was larger, wealthier, and more populated. Using the revenues generated by its pastoral and cereal economy, Buenos Aires purchased a navy that successfully challenged Santiago's hegemony on the seas.

OVERVIEW

At the end of the nineteenth century, Chile's future seemed to have taken a turn for the worse. When the century began, Chile had indeed been an oligarchic republic. Still, as it matured it had become more open, permitting the dissemination of new ideas and the creation of new political parties. This openness created a climate that, while maintaining order, permitted the economy to grow. Indeed, the economy seemed to represent as many different economic interests as the nation's political parties did ideologies. The nation, which owed its success to the development of a diversified economy, became addicted to nitrates. Then the Revolution of 1891 unleashed latent forces that had existed for years, if not decades, mortally wounding the domestic political process at precisely the time when it would have to confront foreign enemies and internal social problems.

The references have been selected because they are in English and for the most part readily available. A good place to begin a study of this era is two important essays in the *Cambridge History of Latin America*: SIMON COLLIER, "Chile from Independence to the War of the Pacific," vol. 3 (1985), pp. 583–613, and HAROLD BLAKEMORE, "Chile from the War of the Pacific to the World Depression, 1880–1930," vol. 5 (1986), pp. 449–551.

Diplomatic studies: FREDRICK B. PIKE, *Chile and the United States, 1880–1962* (1963); ROBERT N. BURR, *By Reason or Force* (1965); and WILLIAM F. SATER, *Chile and the United States: Empires in Conflict* (1990).

Economic topics: STEFAN DE VYLDER, *From Colonialism to Dependence: An Introduction to Chile's Economic History* (1974); MARKOS MAMALAKIS, *The Growth and Structure of the Chilean Economy: From Independence to Allende* (1976); C. CARRIOLA and O. SUNKEL, "Chile," in Roberto Cortés Conde and Stanley J. Stein, eds., *Latin America: A Guide to Economic History, 1830–1930* (1977); LUIS ORTEGA, "Economic Policy and Growth in Chile from Independence to the War of the Pacific," in Christopher Abel and Colin Lewis, *Latin America, Economic Imperialism, and the State* (1985); CRISTÓBAL KAY, "The Development of the Chilean Hacienda System," in KENNETH DUNCAN et al., *Land and Labour in Latin America* (1977), pp. 103–139; JOHN MAYO, *British Merchants and Chilean Development, 1851–1886* (1987); WILLIAM F. SATER, "Economic Nationalism and Tax Reform in Nineteenth-Century Chile," in *The Americas* 22 (1976): 311–335.

For different aspects of mining, see LELAND R. PEDERSON, *The Mining Industry of the Norte Chico, Chile* (1966); LUIS ORTEGA, "The First Four Decades of the Chilean Coalmining Industry, 1840–1879," in *Journal of Latin American Studies* 14, no. 1 (1982): 1–32; WILLIAM CULVER and CORNEL REINHART, "The Decline of a Mining Region and Mining Policy: Chilean Copper in the Nineteenth Century," in *Miners and Mining in the Americas*, edited by Thomas Greaves and William Culver (1985), 68–81. Specifically on nitrates, see THOMAS O'BRIEN, *The Nitrate Industry and Chile's Crucial Transition, 1870–1891* (1982).

On railroad development, see ROBERT OPPENHEIMER, "Chile's Central Valley Railroads and Economic Development in the Nineteenth Century," in *Proceedings of the Pacific Coast Council on Latin American Studies* 6 (1977–1979): 73–86.

Intellectual, political, and social history: FREDRICK B. PIKE, "Aspects of Class Relations in Chile, 1850–1960," in *Hispanic American Historical Review* 43, no. 1 (1963): 14–33; SIMON COLLIER, *Ideas and Politics of Chilean Independence, 1808–1833* (1967); SOLOMON LIPP, *Three Chilean Thinkers* (1975); ALLEN WOLL, *A Functional Past: The Uses of History in Nineteenth-Century Chile* (1982). The War of the Pacific is covered in WILLIAM F. SATER, *Chile and the War of the Pacific* (1986). For the postwar period, see HAROLD BLAKEMORE, *British Nitrates and Chilean Politics, 1886–1896: Balmaceda and North* (1974); KAREN L. REMMER, "The Timing, Pace, and Sequence of Political Change in Chile, 1891–1925," in *Hispanic American Historical Review* 57, no. 2 (1977): 205–230.

WILLIAM F. SATER

The Twentieth Century

Chile's elites greeted the twentieth century with confidence and optimism. Victory in the WAR OF THE PACIFIC had validated Chileans' feelings of regional ethnic and institutional superiority, and while the 1891 civil war caused some introspection, the reestablishment of peace soon restored the buoyancy of the elites. Prosperity, political stability, and social tranquillity reigned as Chile observed the century mark.

THE ARISTOCRATIC REPUBLIC, 1900–1919

The economic model that underpinned the Chilean system at the turn of the century was basically unaltered since its emergence in the early 1880s. After annexing the provinces of Tarapacá from Peru and Antofagasta from Bolivia, Chile entered its nitrate age (1880–1930). Although British-dominated and geographically remote from national population centers, the NITRATE INDUSTRY was more than an export enclave. Numerous Chilean entrepreneurs participated directly in nitrate production; overall, the Chilean share of ownership in nitrates grew from 36 percent in 1882 to 56 percent in 1920. Central Valley landowners prospered from the growth of northern demand for agricultural production, which doubled between 1895 and 1920. After the protectionist 1897 tariff, domestic manufacturers and processors also found outlets in the nitrate provinces. Chilean owners of merchant houses, shipping fleets, and coal mines likewise reaped benefits from this expanded commerce. The tax on nitrate exports, which supplied more than half of all government revenues between 1900 and 1930, financed an extensive railroad network, roads and ports, and Latin America's premiere system of public education. Chile thus was able to harness the nitrate economy, albeit inconsistently and erratically, for national economic development.

While benefiting Chile's elites and fueling development, nitrates also subjected Chile to the vicissitudes of the world economy and established a pattern of dependency that persisted through the twentieth century. The periodic international financial crises of the late nineteenth and early twentieth centuries reduced European demand for nitrates, causing unemployment, restricting imports, and disrupting government income. As Chile's integration into the world economy increased, so did the secular pattern of currency devaluation and constant inflation that plagued the country in the twentieth century. These problems, along with the elites' refusal to tax property and wealth as long as nitrates covered basic governmental expenses, limited the impact of the nitrate economy on national development.

Presiding over the prosperous years of the early twentieth century was an oligarchy that a U.S. political scientist described in 1909 as "the only aristocracy in the world which still has full and acknowledged control of the economic, political, and social forces of the state in which they live" (Paul S. Reinsch, "Parliamentary Government in Chile," in *American Political Science Review* 3 [1909]: 508). The Chilean oligarchy was a fluid, economically hybrid, and substantive elite that was divided by party affiliation, business interests, and philia for different European countries but was united in fundamental

values and in defense of its privileges. Typical elite extended families owned rural land, urban real estate, commercial ventures, and stock in banks, mining companies, and the new manufacturing sector; marriage into established families, purchase of prestigious country estates, and entry into the Club de la Unión provided means of social integration for the parvenus, both Chilean and foreign.

Direct control of the state apparatus gave the elites opportunities for further enrichment and the means of defending their gains. Elite domination had been solidified in the 1891 civil war when the congressional faction defeated the forces loyal to President José Manuel BALMACEDA and the proponents of presidential supremacy. The "autonomous commune" law of 1891, which placed the electoral machinery under the control of the municipalities, ended sixty years of presidential dominance and laid the basis for Chile's Parliamentary Republic (1891–1924). The historic Conservative and Liberal parties served the oligarchy's interests, while the defeated Balmacedists reappeared as the National Party and some elites joined the stridently anticlerical Radical Party. Most of the ideological issues dividing Liberals and Conservatives—primarily matters of church-state and presidential-legislative relations—had been resolved in the nineteenth century, leaving these dominant parties as electoral machines serving individual and family clients. Access to office in congress or the ministries meant the opportunity to further personal and local economic interests through patronage and apportionment of the normally robust national budget. Congress, filled with men of impeccable aristocratic credentials, dominated the republic's political life while the president's role was largely ceremonial.

Beneath the veneer of prosperity, social peace, and constitutional rule, the new realities of the twentieth century began to appear. Foremost was the growth of Chile's working class in the nitrate mines, ports, railroads, and incipient industrial centers and of an urban lumpen proletariat, which was housed in teeming CONVENTILLOS (tenements). The working class had begun to organize in the late nineteenth century; by 1920, tens of thousands of workers were affiliated with unions of various kinds, from mutual aid societies to anarchist cells. Protesting working conditions, inflation, periodic unemployment, government corruption, and electoral fraud, workers staged major strikes or protests in Valparaíso (1903), Santiago (1905), Antofagasta (1906), and Iquique (1907), to which the authorities responded with violent repression. These manifestations of discontent elicited considerable attention from the elites and brought forth a host of university theses on "the social question" as well as exposés such as Alejandro Venegas's *Sinceridad: Chile íntimo en 1910*. Congress appointed several commissions to investigate conditions underlying the strikes and radicalization of labor, but it was unable to agree on concrete steps to ameliorate them. These new national problems and the failure to address them began to erode the superlative self-confidence and sense of national superiority with which Chile's elites had greeted the twentieth century, and they gave rise to dire analyses and predictions.

THE ADVENT OF COPPER AND MASS POLITICS, 1919–1941

The Parliamentary Republic was mortally wounded in 1919, when a profound economic crisis resulting from WORLD WAR I revealed the extent of Chile's vulnerability to world-market fluctuations and precipitated mass mobilization on a scale unprecedented in Chile. The repercussions of wartime disruptions spread from the nitrate sector, where a majority of the labor force became unemployed, throughout the economy, creating a dual crisis of unemployment and inflation. Focusing on food price inflation as a rallying point, labor and student leaders in late 1918 formed the Workers' Assembly of National Nutrition, which mobilized hundreds of thousands of people throughout the country. Radicalized by the government's inertia, the protest movement adopted a fifty-point program of general social and political demands. The 1920 presidential election, held against the backdrop of continuing economic crisis and political mobilization, split the oligarchy into two factions: those opposed to concessions and those, led by Arturo ALESSANDRI PALMA who were willing to implement preemptive reforms to defuse the political crisis.

Alessandri's narrow victory did not resolve matters; rather, it deepened the political instability that would characterize Chile in the 1920s and 1930s as the country adjusted to mass politics. Intransigents controlled Congress, blocking Alessandri's proposed social legislation, while the emerging Left continued to organize demonstrations and strikes, even penetrating the countryside to proselytize among agricultural workers. The impasse was resolved in 1924 by military intervention, which prompted the president's resignation; this also led to the enactment of his social program as well as the Constitution of 1925, which restored presidential supremacy over Congress and established a state commitment to social welfare. However, continuing economic problems and political disarray opened the way for a career army officer, Carlos IBÁÑEZ DEL CAMPO, to assume the presidency in 1927. During his four-year rule, he packed and controlled Congress, experimented with corporatist organization, and launched the developmentalist and social welfare state.

The Great Depression undermined the Ibáñez government and led to a series of short-lived regimes that included a military-led, self-styled Socialist Republic (1932). Aided by a gradual economic recovery, selective repression, and moderate social reforms, the second Arturo Alessandri government (1932–1938) guided the country back toward the political stability and constitutional order that had been Chile's hallmark from the 1830s onward.

The 1930s also marked the completion of a fundamen-

tal realignment from elite to mass politics. By the mid-1930s, the Chilean political system had effectively incorporated the urban and mining working classes through legislation legalizing unions and the appearance and growth of Marxist political parties. The Communist Party, founded in 1922, and the Socialist Party, formed in 1933 from several factions, provided the working class with political representation and established the core of a Left bloc in Congress. The leftward movement of the historic Radical Party, founded in 1863, in the 1920s and 1930s made it a thoroughly middle-class organization and placed it in the center of the new political spectrum; the Radicals were essential to the formation of congressional majorities at most times from 1933 to the 1960s. The growth of the Left and center presented a permanent challenge to the traditional Conservative and Liberal parties, which nonetheless remained overrepresented in Congress by virtue of landowners' economic and electoral supremacy in rural Chile. Yet, by the 1930s, the Chilean political system that emerged from a decade and a half of instability and institutional disruption was arguably Latin America's most open, competitive, and democratic.

The 1938 presidential election illustrated the extent of political change since World War I. Responding to the USSR's call for Popular Front governments to fight Fascism, the Communists and Socialists backed Radical Pedro AGUIRRE CERDA and, for the first time in Chile, raised the specter of Marxists in government (Salvador ALLENDE served as minister of health from 1939 to 1942). The Popular Front victory was tempered, however, by the president's moderate inclinations. While supporting legislation favoring working-class and middle-class interests and establishing the Chilean Development Corporation (CORFO) to promote industrialization, Aguirre Cerda, a landowner himself, forbade the extension of union and leftist party activity into the countryside. This decision preserved landowners' control of the rural vote and their veto power in national politics until the 1960s and, by keeping labor costs low in agriculture, subsidized the provisioning of cities at the expense of rural labor. At the close of its first cycle of political reform (1919–1941), Chile had progressed remarkably, but the rural masses remained on the margin of national life.

Chile's political evolution had paralleled a substantial economic transformation, which was propelled by changes in the international economy and by new policies adopted by the governments of the 1920s and 1930s. During the 1920s, the United States supplanted Great Britain as Chile's primary trading partner and supplier of capital; this change reflected the general post–World War I pattern throughout South America, where the retreat of European capital was followed by a flood of U.S. loans and direct investment. Of equal significance, the nitrate economy, hurt by the development of synthetic nitrates, stagnated and collapsed in the two decades following World War I. Meanwhile, beginning early in the

century, U.S. mining corporations purchased copper mines and expanded production tenfold between 1906 and 1929. In the conversion from a nitrate- to a copper-based export economy, Chile lost ground in the control of its basic national asset, for while Chilean ownership of nitrates increased in the long run, copper from the onset of its ascendancy was almost exclusively foreign-owned. Nor did copper relieve Chile of its dependence on world-market conditions over which it had no control.

Governmental responses to the crises of World War I and the Great Depression further affected the national economy. Most fundamentally, in common with other Latin American countries, Chile adopted tariff protection and complementary policies to foster industrial development in order to reduce the country's dependence on export income and hence its vulnerability to world market fluctuations. The Ministry of Development, established by Ibáñez in 1927, pursued economic diversification, and CORFO was used to direct industrial development by providing infrastructure and investment of state funds in essential sectors such as steel and communications. The initiatives of the 1920s and 1930s launched Chile on the path that gave it one of Latin America's most state-dominated economies by the 1960s.

ECONOMIC FRUSTRATION AND POLITICAL DEADLOCK, 1941–1964

Chile's economic development in the 1940s and 1950s was substantial but uneven. The GRAN MINERÍA (large-scale producers) of copper confirmed its dominance in the export sector, accounting for the bulk of Chile's export earnings and a substantial portion of government income during those decades. While investment and production increased, copper price fluctuations, such as those bracketing the Korean War, affected employment and government revenues. Reflecting a growth of economic nationalism and of the need for revenue, the governments of the period progressively raised the tax on copper until it surpassed 70 percent of profits at one point in the 1950s before falling somewhat.

Led by CORFO and highly protective tariffs, Chile industrialized steadily, with the steel plant established in 1950 at Huachipato symbolizing the country's determination to achieve economic independence. By the late 1950s, however, import-substitution industrialization slowed as Chile's small population and its skewed income distribution began to limit the growth of markets for consumer goods, causing stagnation in the industrial belts of Santiago, Valparaíso, and Concepción. The Achilles heel of national development was agriculture, where the growth of production lagged behind Chile's relatively modest population growth, making the *fértil provincia* a net importer of foodstuffs. Debate raged over the causes of agricultural stagnation, pitting monetarists, who faulted government price and trade policy, against structuralists, who targeted the hacienda-dominated land-tenure system. By the 1950s, consensus had been

Cathedral, Santiago de Chile. © PETER MENZEL / STOCK, BOSTON.

reached that the country must take measures to improve agricultural production.

Between the censuses of 1907 and 1930, Chile's population had grown from 3.0 to 4.4 million; by 1960 it had reached 7.6 million. Santiago grew from 333,000 to 1.9 million between 1907 and 1960, while the overall urban population increased from 43 to 68 percent of the total. Industrialization and rural-to-urban migration augmented the working class, but restrictive labor legislation kept union membership relatively low. The new style of suburban slums, called *callampas* (mushroom villages) or *poblaciones* (towns), made their appearance as the inner-city *conventillos* proved inadequate to absorb the flood of migrants. Chile's middle class expanded steadily, becoming one of Latin America's largest by percentage, as the result of economic development, urbanization, and the country's excellent system of public and university education that created a highly educated but underemployed white-collar sector. Chilean intellectuals attained a well-deserved stature within Latin America, and two poets, Gabriela MISTRAL (in 1945) and Pablo NERUDA (in 1971), won Nobel prizes for literature.

In politics, the two decades following Aguirre Cerda's death and the dissolution of the Popular Front were essentially a period of deadlock favoring the right and cur-

tailing reform. After achieving major goals such as social security, a compensatory mechanism to protect salaries against institutionalized inflation, and enhanced educational opportunities, the Radical Party dropped its alliance with the left and opted for a working relationship with the Liberal Party. Radical presidents Juan Antonio RÍOS MORALES and Gabriel GONZÁLEZ VIDELA pursued moderate programs featuring development over reform, and González Videla outlawed the Communist Party in 1948. Dissatisfaction with party politics contributed to the election of former president Carlos Ibáñez to a second term in 1952. In a crowded field, Conservative Jorge ALESSANDRI RODRÍGUEZ, son of the former president, drew only 33,500 votes more than Socialist Salvador ALLENDE, out of 1,236,000 cast, to win the 1958 presidential election.

The 1958 election revealed the emergence of forces that would soon propel Chile into a second cycle of reform—this one much more radical than the initial phase of 1919–1941. High copper prices during the Korean War could not offset the combination of economic stagnation and accelerating inflation during the Ibáñez years that heightened popular discontent. Introduction of the Australian ballot, relegalization of the Communist Party, and a renewal of leftist proselytization in the countryside began to erode landowners' hold over the rural vote and, hence, their essential veto power in national politics. To these domestic developments was added the sweeping influence of the CUBAN REVOLUTION (1959), which, by its example, ignited mounting demands for change throughout Latin America. The greatest rallying cry from Cuba was land reform, and in Chile the long-repressed rural work force joined the continentwide demand for land. In response to rising pressures, the Alessandri administration instituted a mild agrarian reform in 1962, but its timid use of preemption could not stem the rising demands for change. Chile thus entered a decade that would make that country the world's laboratory for radical social and economic reform within a democratic, constitutional setting.

THE SECOND CYCLE OF REFORM, 1964–1973

By 1964, Chile was one of the most modern, progressive countries in Latin America. Its political system stood out within the region as a paragon of stability and democracy, but underlying these traits were two important weaknesses: an underdeveloped, dependent economy and the continued marginalization of the agricultural labor force and the shantytown-dwelling urban masses. Both factors would render Chile vulnerable to the winds of change that blew across Latin America in the 1960s and 1970s.

The established Marxist parties and the new Christian Democratic Party (PDC), founded in 1957, led the renewed push for reform. Ideologically grounded in the work of Jacques Maritain and European Christian Democracy, the PDC embraced structural reform as a means of creating a "communitarian society." In the radicalized climate of the early 1960s, the PDC quickly supplanted the Radical Party as the voice of Chile's large middle class and secured a strong base among peasants and urban marginals as well as some labor unions. Amid signs of a collapse of conservative voting strength, the Conservative and Liberal parties opted to support PDC candidate Eduardo FREI in the 1964 presidential election, rather than field their own candidate, in order to thwart Socialist Salvador Allende, then making his third run at the presidency. Frei's attractive program and personality, the Right's vote, and heavy, clandestine U.S. financing assured Frei's victory with 56 percent of the vote.

Frei had promised a "revolution in liberty" featuring the "Chileanization" of the U.S. copper companies, an agrarian reform to create 100,000 new landowners, tax reform, major investment in worker housing and education, and aggressive economic development measures. His government received considerable U.S. aid and became a showcase for the U.S.-sponsored ALLIANCE FOR PROGRESS; along with the government of Venezuela, it was the leading reformist alternative to the Cuban Revolution. Among Frei's accomplishments were a 1966 law acquiring 51 percent of foreign-owned copper holdings for the Chilean state, minimum wage and unionization laws for agriculture, and substantial progress in educa-

tion and housing. Under a progressive 1967 agrarian reform law, the government began dismantling the hacienda system but was able to create less than a third of the promised new family farms.

Despite an impressive record of reform, Frei was unable to satisfy the heightened aspirations of Chile's lower classes for change and improved living conditions. This was most visibly the case in the rural sector, where the very success of Frei's union law had given workers the means of pressing their growing demands for land, with which agrarian reform did not keep pace. At the same time, the government that was too moderate for the Left alarmed the Right by its advocacy of redistributive measures, mobilization of mass organizations, and apparent lack of firm commitment to capitalist private property. Reacting sharply to the Frei reforms, the National Party, formed in 1966 of the decimated Liberal and Conservative parties, opted to contest the 1970 presidential election by running its own candidate.

The 1970 election offered clear choices. Allende was the candidate of Unidad Popular (UP), a coalition of the Radical Party, three small non-Marxist groups, and the dominant Communist and Socialist parties. He promised an acceleration of the reforms already under way and extensive nationalizations to propel Chile toward socialism. As in 1964, the United States spent millions of dollars to stop Allende. The Right backed former president Jorge Alessandri, a respected and pragmatic conservative. PDC candidate Radomiro TOMIC of the party's left-center bloc called for a significant deepening of reform, including the nationalization of copper, completion of agrarian reform, and expropriation of substantial parts of the economy. Allende won with 36.5 percent of the vote to Alessandri's 35.2 percent and Tomic's 28.0 percent. Allende's victory, with a narrow margin and a minority of votes cast, was a normal outcome of Chilean elections involving multiple parties and candidates and lacking a runoff provision; but the stakes in 1970 were far higher than usual. Despite a mandate for accelerated change manifested in the combined UP-PDC vote, Allende faced a host of problems from the outset because of his Marxism, his commitment to ending large-scale capitalism in Chile, and his quest for independence in foreign relations.

Allende's first challenge came from the Richard Nixon administration, supported by elements of the Chilean Right. Having spent millions and employed various covert actions over the years to prevent Allende's election, the United States now turned to blocking his installation as president. An approach known as Track I involved heavy pressure on the Chilean Congress, which formally elected the president in the absence of a major winner, to refuse to ratify the candidate who received the most votes. This was an action without precedent. The Christian Democrats' refusal to cooperate closed the legal loophole. Washington concurrently pursued Track II, a desperate and unlikely effort to generate a military coup. Allende's inauguration two months after the general election thus represented a victory in itself.

Once inaugurated, Allende faced the challenge of implementing an ambitious reform program while controlling only one branch of government. Lacking a congressional majority, he relied on elastic definitions of presidential powers and existing law to push UP goals. In doing so, he faced the dogged opposition of an unsympathetic judiciary wedded to capitalist law. Finally, there was the ultimate arbiter of politics, the armed forces. Despite Chile's long history of rarely interrupted civilian government, the military was certain to face unprecedented pressure from anti-UP forces to save the nation from "communism."

Despite the obstacles facing his administration, Allende's first year in office was characterized by an atmosphere of enthusiasm and optimism within the government and a broad spectrum of the population. The president combined old-fashioned pump priming with creative use of presidential powers to redistribute income toward the working and middle classes and to make significant progress in agrarian reform and nationalizing the economy. Extensive expropriations and buyouts in banking, insurance, communications, transportation, textiles, cement, and other manufacturing sectors, combined with the complete nationalization of copper, gave the state control of the "commanding heights" of the economy (as Lenin called them) within Allende's first year. Chile also reestablished diplomatic relations with Cuba, thus becoming the first Latin American nation to resume ties severed as the result of a 1964 ORGANIZATION OF AMERICAN STATES (OAS) action to isolate Cuba. The April 1971 municipal elections, in which the UP received a slight majority, reflected the success of Allende's first five months as president.

By the end of his first year, mounting economic and political problems overshadowed these successes. Expensive nationalizations and social expenditures had consumed a large portion of Chile's foreign currency reserves and a U.S.-orchestrated credit boycott had been established. By early 1972, Chile's chronic inflation was accelerating, and by September 1973 had reached a 300 percent annual rate. The PDC and the National Party established a formal anti-Allende alliance, and Senator Carlos Altamirano of the Socialist Party's extreme left wing—a bloc that flirted with insurrection even while participating in the government—became secretary-general of Allende's own party. The power struggle between the president and Congress reached a new plane in January 1972 with the first of several congressional impeachments of cabinet ministers. A visit by Fidel CASTRO and a scandal involving the government's clandestine importation of Cuban arms exacerbated tensions. The Nixon administration, firmly committed to Allende's overthrow, used the Central Intelligence Agency (CIA) and millions of dollars in pursuit of its objective.

Underlying the increasing confrontation and polarization were a growing mass mobilization and the government's ambivalent attitude toward controlling it. Throughout rural Chile, unauthorized worker occupations of estates, often orchestrated by UP groups and the Movimiento de Izquièrda Revolucionaria (MIR), a party to the government's left, led to chaos and frequent violence as landowners organized and armed themselves to defend their properties. In Santiago and other cities, similar extralegal expropriations proceeded apace, especially in the industrial belts of the capital, where workers and leftists seized dozens of factories. This "hypermobilization" of the rural and urban working class posed a difficult dilemma for the Allende administration. On one hand, Allende acknowledged his constitutional responsibility to enforce the law, which of course guaranteed private ownership rights until a valid expropriation order was given. On the other hand, the workers were Allende's constituency, and for ideological as well as practical reasons he was understandably loath to use the force of a "people's" government against the people.

The inconsistency of government responses to the wave of unauthorized seizures of factories and haciendas reflected Allende's schizophrenia over property rights and the rule of law. It also reflected the deep division within the UP coalition and within Allende's own Socialist Party over strategy and tactics for making the revolution. On the left, a strong minority of the UP and its allies advocated pushing ahead with all speed, ignoring legal restraints, to break the back of capitalism before the opposition could regroup and react. The more conservative UP majority, consisting of the Communists, the Allende Socialists, and most of the non-Marxist groups, advocated moving vigorously toward socialism, primarily through legal means, so as to avoid provoking an armed reaction against the government. They preferred consolidation of gains at a certain point, if necessary, over continual confrontation. These deep divisions within the UP remained unresolved to the end of the Allende government.

The government's vacillation on the rule of law was a major factor in the UP's political failure. Chile's large middle class was crucial to Allende's success; he needed their votes to achieve a congressional majority in the 1973 election, and he needed their tolerance to keep the military, led by a largely middle-class officer corps, on the sidelines. Yet rising levels of violence, governmental vacillation on law enforcement, accelerating inflation, shortages of food and consumer goods, and the leveling tendencies in UP policy progressively eroded middle-class tolerance of the UP government. Substantial parts of the middle class revealed their antigovernment sentiments in October 1972, when a truck owners' strike, called to protest a government plan to nationalize the trucking sector, precipitated action by Chile's economic and professional associations, or *gremios* (GUILDS).

The *gremio* movement had been formed during the latter Frei years by the historic, elite-dominated, interest associations, including the Sociedad Nacional de Agricultura and the Sociedad de Fomento Fabril. These groups sought an alliance with middling and small farmers, shopkeepers, professionals, and even artisans as a means of offsetting the decline of rightist electoral strength. Beginning with the truckers' strike, these hundreds of thousands of organized, largely middle-class Chileans allied themselves with the elites and played a central role in the overthrow of Allende and of Chile's political institutions. The October strike—a full-scale business and service shutdown accompanied by housewives' MARCH OF THE EMPTY POTS—was settled after four weeks, but only with the incorporation of military men into the cabinet—the beginning of the armed forces' overt politicization.

The March 1973 congressional elections, which gave the opposition 56 percent to the UP's 44 percent, did nothing to relieve tensions. Beset by runaway inflation, declining production, shortages, decapitalization, and mounting deficits, the economy was near collapse by mid-1973. Rising street violence, growing incidents of assassination and sabotage, the arming of workers and of the right-wing organization Patria y Libertad, and the establishment of neighborhood vigilance patrols reflected the growing insecurity and instability that were rapidly undermining Chile's institutional foundations. An aborted military coup on 29 June 1973 forecast the breakdown of the armed forces neutrality, and a second, larger, national strike by the *gremios* in late July thrust Chile into full crisis. Reports of UP-inspired subversion in the navy were the final provocation that pushed the armed forces to mount a coup.

THE MILITARY GOVERNMENT, 1973–1990
The military insurrection of 11 September 1973 ended Chile's distinctive tradition of civilian government. Given the extreme deterioration of political and economic conditions, the coup surprised few observers, but the brutality with which it was executed was shocking even to its advocates. President Allende was but one victim of the thousands who overwhelmed the capacities of jails, hospitals, and morgues. Expectations of a surgical, short-term intervention followed by new elections quickly evaporated as the armed forces, led by army commander Gen. Augusto PINOCHET moved to consolidate their power by dissolving Congress, banning or recessing parties and labor unions, and establishing a curfew, strict censorship, and a state of siege.

The regime set forth the essence of the new order in a March 1974 Declaration of Principles that announced that the armed forces "do not set timetables for their management of the government, because the task of rebuilding the country morally, institutionally, and economically requires prolonged and profound actions." The moral rebuilding involved the extirpation of Marxism and its doctrine of class struggle and their replacement with the values of conservative Catholicism, class harmony, and Chilean nationalism; it entailed "changing the mentality of Chileans" by such measures as the

complete revision of school curricula, strict control of the media, and strategic placement of symbols such as that of the authoritarian "founder of the nation," Diego PORTALES. The reconstruction of institutions implied not only the proscription of Marxism but the creation of a political system that, unlike liberal democracy, would guarantee its permanent exclusion. The military attempted to legitimize its rule in a 1980 plebiscite on a new constitution that essentially codified the status quo, described as a "protected democracy" based on the ongoing exclusion of political parties and the military's "guardianship" role. The document also sanctioned the continuation of existing dictatorial institutions until at least 1989, with a provision for an extension of eight more years. Ratified by an announced 68 percent of the vote after a campaign in which opposition was prohibited, the 1980 Constitution legalized not only military control but also the personal power that General Pinochet had been building over the years.

The country's economic reconstruction was based on the neoliberal model of the Chicago School and Milton Friedman, approved by the International Monetary Fund, and largely financed by foreign private banks. The so-called CHICAGO BOYS set out to strip away half a century's accretion of government regulation and ownership by reducing tariffs, lifting price controls, devaluing the currency, selling off state industries, cutting government spending, guaranteeing foreign investment, and establishing good relations with U.S. lenders who had boycotted the Allende government. Through the application of this "shock" therapy, the Chilean economy was thoroughly transformed and integrated into the world economy as the state's share of total investment fell from 77 percent in Frei's last year to under 30 percent in 1980. After nurturing industry for half a century, Chile deindustrialized under competition from imports and became increasingly a raw-material exporter. It supplemented its traditional copper exports with fishery and forest products and out-of-season fruits for Northern Hemisphere markets. After an initial contraction, the neoliberal model took hold and the economy experienced what was called a "miracle" of rapid growth between 1977 and 1981. A deep recession in 1982 forced some modifications, but the Chicago model remained largely intact throughout the life of the military government.

The poor and middle classes paid the price of the Chicago Boys' radical experiment. Lacking union and political representation, they were defenseless against policies that at least tripled unemployment and cut workers' real wages by half while reducing the social welfare programs they needed to survive the crisis. In the countryside, the government set out to reverse one of Latin America's most far-reaching agrarian reforms by returning some land to former owners and reducing aid to new smallholders, forcing many to sell. To sustain these economic policies, the Pinochet government refined the apparatus of state terror that it had used effectively to destroy the Left in the aftermath of the coup. The Dirección de Inteligencia Nacional (DINA), the backbone of the repressive forces, operated torture centers, detained and interrogated at will, and thoroughly intimidated potential opponents. Army and police sweeps of slums became routine, and residents of worker neighborhoods were sent to detention centers as hostages for the good behavior of family and friends made ever more desperate by government economic policies. Under international prodding, the regime periodically released political prisoners and gradually moved toward limited tolerance of mild dissent, but it never altered the essence of the terrorist state.

The economic decline beginning in 1982 brought forth for the first time an incipient civil opposition movement. The outlawed parties, the church, and labor leaders issued a Democratic Manifesto in March 1983 and called for monthly "national days of protest" featuring rallies, sick-outs, boycotts, and the banging of empty pots—the hallmark of the *gremios'* opposition to Allende. By 1985 a "national dialogue" had begun as the end of hard-line military regimes in Argentina, Uruguay, and Brazil fueled the debate on Chile's future. Pinochet's 1980 Constitution stipulated a 1988 plebiscite on the extension of military rule until 1997, whether by Pinochet himself, another officer, or a puppet civilian. The upcoming election forced the general for the first time to act like a politician and cultivate public support. Accordingly, the government authorized the return of most exiles, legalized non-Marxist parties, and allowed some opposition press to publish, while continuing selective repression. The opposition won the plebiscite by 55 to 43 percent after an intense campaign for the "no," opening the way for the first presidential election in nineteen years. In December 1989, Christian Democrat Patricio AYLWIN AZÓCAR, the candidate of a broad center-left "Concertación de Partidos por la Democracia," won 55 percent of the vote against two conservative candidates.

CHILE IN THE 1990s
Economically, Aylwin's four-year administration benefited from the painful adjustments imposed during the dictatorship, which by 1990 had placed Chile in the vanguard of the neoliberal order in Latin America. Driven by international market forces for nearly two decades, Chile drew praise for its economic efficiency, its austere policies, its relatively low international debt, and its ability to attract foreign loans and investment. Official statistics indicated that Chile's high incidence of poverty, a legacy of the conversion to a market economy, began to decline in the early 1990s. Reconciliation among Chileans, however, proved elusive. The 1991 report of the National Commission on Truth and Reconciliation (Rettig Commission) established beyond a doubt the extent of human-rights violations under the military, but the courts continued to protect the accused and thwart justice, with the notable exception of the 1993 sentencing of former DINA head Manuel Contreras Sepúlveda to

prison for the 1976 assassination of former UP minister Orlando LETELIER SOLAR in Washington, D.C. The armed forces continued to exercise close oversight through constitutional provisions, including the president's inability to appoint and remove service commanders and dominance of the National Security Council by military appointees, and by occasional overt intimidation of elected officials.

The December 1993 election essentially ratified the political status quo. Receiving 58 percent of the vote in a field of six candidates, Christian Democrat Eduardo Frei Ruiz-Tagle, son of former president Eduardo Frei Montalva, confirmed the continuing popularity of the center-left Concertación. The congressional election, by contrast, demonstrated the efficacy of the electoral code bequeathed by Pinochet, which, by a combination of weighted districting and a binomial system of list voting, assured overrepresentation of the Right. The electoral outcome, fortified by the presence of eight militarily-appointed senators, gave conservative interests veto power over reform of the constitution and the electoral code and the ability to block even ordinary legislation. The 1993 election demonstrated that, despite the return of civilian government, Chile in many ways was still the "protected democracy" that Pinochet had established with his 1980 Constitution.

Chile in the 1990s was a country radically transformed after sixteen and a half years of military rule, as the thousands of returning exiles discovered. The entrepreneurial ethic and the neoliberal model were firmly rooted, the "renovated" Left had adapted to the existing political and economic framework, and the military's success in creating a materialistic and politically apathetic generation was plainly visible. The new society had contrasting faces: Businessmen in imported suits carrying cellular phones passed former industrial workers and professionals reduced to street hawking, car watching, or similar marginal activities. Yet families of the disappeared continued to seek justice, unions pressed for recognition of their former rights, many aspired to rebuild the shattered public education and health systems, and a majority of the political establishment demanded a return to full-scale democracy. The greatest challenge for the Frei administration, elected to serve until the year 2000, would be to balance a formidable range of conflicting interests and demands: the requirements of the new economic model with the need for social investment, the competing claims of victims and perpetrators of repression, and the popular sentiment for full democracy against the military's and the Right's fear of it. The outcome of this balancing act will largely determine whether Chile enters the twenty-first century with the confidence and optimism that marked the country a hundred years earlier.

FREDERICK B. PIKE, *Chile and the United States, 1880–1962* (1965); FREDERICK M. NUNN, *Chilean Politics, 1920–1931: The Honorable Mission of the Armed Forces* (1970); ARNOLD J. BAUER, *Chilean Rural Society from the Conquest to 1930* (1975); BRIAN

LOVEMAN, *Struggle in the Countryside: Politics and Rural Labor in Chile, 1919–1973* (1976); MARKOS MAMALAKIS, *The Growth and Structure of the Chilean Economy: From Independence to Allende* (1976); IAN ROXBOROUGH, PHILIP O'BRIEN, and JACKIE RODDICK, *Chile: The State and Revolution* (1977); PAUL SIGMUND, *The Overthrow of Allende and the Politics of Chile, 1964–1976* (1977); STEFAN DE VYLDER, *Allende's Chile: The Political Economy of the Rise and Fall of the Unidad Popular* (1978); PAUL W. DRAKE, *Socialism and Populism in Chile, 1932–1952* (1978); BARBARA STALLINGS, *Class Conflict and Economic Development in Chile, 1958–1973* (1978); ARTURO VALENZUELA, *The Breakdown of Democratic Regimes: Chile* (1978); GONZALO VIAL CORREA, *Historia de Chile, 1891–1973*, 4 vols. (1981–1987); BRIAN H. SMITH, *The Church and Politics in Chile* (1982); THOMAS C. WRIGHT, *Landowners and Reform in Chile: The Sociedad Nacional de Agricultura, 1919–1940* (1982); PETER DE SHAZO, *Urban Workers and Labor Unions in Chile, 1902–1927* (1983); MICHAEL FLEET, *The Rise and Fall of Chilean Christian Democracy* (1985); SERGIO BITAR, *Chile: Experiment in Democracy* (1986); J. SAMUEL VALENZUELA and ARTURO VALENZUELA, eds., *Military Rule in Chile: Dictatorship and Oppositions* (1986); BRIAN LOVEMAN, *Chile: The Legacy of Hispanic Capitalism*, 2d ed. (1988); PAMELA CONSTABLE and ARTURO VALENZUELA, *A Nation of Enemies: Chile Under Pinochet* (1991); and PAUL W. DRAKE and IVÁN JAKSIĆ, eds., *The Struggle for Democracy in Chile, 1982–1990* (1991).

THOMAS C. WRIGHT

CHILE: CONSTITUTIONS. Two seminal constitutions provided the legal framework for ruling Chile from 1833 until 1973.

CONSTITUTION OF 1833

Chile's 1833 Constitution, while not the nation's first, was the most durable, lasting until 1925. By initially insisting that only men at least twenty-one years old, literate, and affluent could vote, it sought to empower only the most conservative. Predictably, the requirements for becoming legislators were substantially more demanding than those for mere voters: the indirectly elected senators, who served for nine years, had to be at least thirty-five years old and own more property than the popularly elected deputies, who served for three years and had to be at least thirty years old. The president, who had to be older and wealthier than any of the legislators, enjoyed enormous powers. He appointed men to the judiciary, provincial office, and the cabinet; he could veto laws and could, if needed, declare a state of siege, thereby suspending an already limited number of political freedoms. Initially, the legislature could do little to restrain the president. Every eighteen months it could deny him the right to collect taxes, refuse to pass his budget, and limit the size of the armed forces.

The 1833 Constitution successfully restored order to Chile. As the nation's political system became less monolithic, demands for change became more vocal. As early as 1846, the legislature won the right to interpolate ministers; eleven years later the congress threatened to withhold funds unless President Manuel MONTT changed the composition of his cabinet. The proliferation of parties,

all of which wanted a chance to participate in the political system, increased the pace of change. In the 1860s the legislature passed laws granting increased religious freedom to non-Catholics and preventing the president from succeeding himself in office. Within a few years congress altered the requirements on legislative quorums, liberalized the naturalization process, granted the right of free association, increased the number of deputies, established electoral districts for senators—who previously had been elected at large—limited the president's right to rule by decree or to invoke his extraordinary powers, created a panel to protect civil liberties, and increased the legislature's right to question ministers. Subsequent measures extended suffrage by reducing the voting age and eliminating property requirements. During the 1880s the constitution was altered to end the church's control over cemeteries and the civil registry while making marriage a civil contract.

The 1891 revolution that forced President José Manuel BALMACEDA FERNÁNDEZ from power decisively altered the 1833 Constitution. After 1891 a hybrid parliamentary system ruled Chile. As in other parliamentary democracies, the ministry remained in power only as long as it enjoyed the confidence of the legislature. Unfortunately, it became increasingly difficult for anyone to govern. From 1891 to 1924, 121 separate cabinets attempted to rule, and there were more than five hundred ministerial changes. This instability resulted from the fact that widespread bribery, intimidation, and simple fraud permitted candidates to win office without having to appeal to the electorate. The combination of proportional representation and vote fraud led to a proliferation of political parties, which virtually required the formation of coalition governments. Insulated from the electorate's legitimate wrath, congress ignored the country's pressing social problems and the widening economic gap separating the oligarchy from the rest of the country. Finally, the post–World War I collapse of the NITRATE markets forced Chile to confront the political debacle. In 1925, following two rebellions and the resignation of Arturo ALESSANDRI PALMA, Chileans abandoned the 1833 Constitution in favor of a new charter.

CONSTITUTION OF 1925

Politically, the 1925 Constitution restored the presidential form of government, allowing the people to elect the chief executive directly for a single term of six years. Following the legislature's approval, the cabinet would serve at the president's pleasure, although the Chamber of Deputies could impeach a minister for cause.

Chile remained a highly centralized nation. The president appointed virtually all the members of the judiciary as well as provincial officials (except for city councilmen), initiated the budget, and still retained the power to declare a state of siege. The president also enjoyed the right to authorize certain laws and expenditures by decree.

The 1925 Constitution retained a bicameral legislature in which the term for senators fell from nine to eight years and that for congressmen rose from three to four. Reflecting the experience of the PARLIAMENTARY REGIME, the legislature's ability to influence the budgetary process was diminished from that enjoyed under the 1833 Constitution. Under the 1925 Constitution, the president could put the budget into effect if congress failed to act within four months.

While guaranteeing civil liberties and the right of private property, the 1925 Constitution empowered the state to guarantee its citizens' right to work and to provide them with certain minimum benefits for themselves and their families. In addition, the constitution called for the government to stimulate agriculture, mining, and industrialization. To accomplish these and other goals, the central government enjoyed the right to subordinate private property to the public good.

Despite its dual commitment to the preservation of political freedoms as well as the promotion of social and economic change, the 1925 Constitution suffered from certain defects. For one thing, it adopted the complicated d'Hondt system of proportional representation, which effectively denied minority parties their fair share of legislative representation while seating individuals who often had not won a majority of the votes. The new constitution also perpetuated the political parties that had long outlived their rationale. Thus, presidents still had to build fragile coalitions, which resulted in some of the same political instability that characterized the Parliamentary Regime. The constitution, moreover, enfranchised neither women, who finally received the right to vote in 1949, nor illiterates. Because it did not call for reapportioning legislative districts, rural precincts enjoyed more political power than industrial urban centers. Political corruption remained quite common. Landowners often either cajoled or forced their workers to vote for their candidates, and in the cities the parties resorted to buying votes or stuffing the ballot boxes. It was not until the passage of reform laws in 1958 and 1962 that many of these abuses ended.

Still, the 1925 Constitution served Chile well, advancing efforts to protect its citizens' political rights and promoting the cause of social justice. Under its aegis, Chileans implemented sweeping economic changes like agrarian reform while enjoying ample political freedom. Unfortunately, the constitution could not settle the intensely partisan conflicts that arose during the ALLENDE years, nor prevent the 1973 coup. In 1980 the PINOCHET government submitted a substitute for the 1925 Constitution to the Chilean public which, following a referendum of questionable value, approved the new document.

PAUL V. SHAW, *The Early Constitutions of Chile, 1810–1833* (1930); LUIS GALDÁMES, *A History of Chile* (1941); JULIO HEISE GONZÁLEZ, *La Constitución de 1925 y las nuevas tendencias político-sociales* (1951); FERNANDO CAMPOS HARRIET, *Historia constitucional de Chile* (1956); JULIO HEISE GONZÁLEZ, *150 años de evolución institucional* (1960); FREDRICK B. PIKE, *Chile and the United States, 1880–1962* (1963), pp. 182–185; FEDERICO G. GIL, *The Political System of Chile* (1966); KAREN L. REMMER, *Party Competition in Argentina and Chile* (1984).

WILLIAM F. SATER

CHILE: GEOGRAPHY. With 13,386,000 inhabitants (1990), Chile stretches from tropical (17 degrees south) to subantarctic (56 degrees south) latitudes. Between the high summits of the Andes and the shores of the Pacific Ocean, Chile occupies a narrow fringe of land with a minimum width of 7 miles and a maximum width of 220 miles. Despite the fact that most of the country's northern segment lies within the tropical belt, the influence of the cold HUMBOLDT CURRENT (Peruvian Current) lowers temperatures considerably, so that most of the country has a temperate climate. Rainfall, however, varies from almost none in the extremely arid and always sunny climate of the north to quite a bit in the humid areas of the south. Toward the central part of the country the humidity is moderate, caused mostly by winter rains. As one progresses southward, the rainy season grows longer and includes a good part of autumn, all of winter, and most of spring. Finally, in the high latitudes, it rains all year long as the humid air masses are carried to the continent by the constantly blowing westerly winds.

The great variability in rainfall means that there is a corresponding variability in vegetation. In the northern segment of the country, desert conditions dominate. Along the coast, the desert climate is mitigated by fogs, but they never render any real precipitation. The desert extends into the interior, with the exception of some piedmont oases that are fed by ground water generating from the snowmelt of numerous volcanoes. Advancing south, shrubs and cacti dominate the landscape as humidity increases. In central Chile, the mediterranean region of the country, the winter rains and constant snowmelt from the ANDES contribute to maintain a vegetation consisting of hardwoods, shrubs, and winter grass. Farther south, with more rainfall, the hardwoods give way to the evergreen and deciduous trees of the temperate rain forests. In the southern extreme of the country, cooler temperatures and perennial rains favor the growth of large coniferous trees that are interspersed with dense rain forest.

Given the extensive desert regions, the high mountains, and the boggy land under the southern rain forests, only 27 percent of the territory is considered habitable. In this area, which stretches between latitudes 27 and 42 degrees south, 90 percent of the national population is concentrated. Even within this ecumene there are considerable variations: Metropolitan Santiago is home to nearly 39 percent of the Chilean population; another 13 percent live in the neighboring region of Valparaíso and Viña del Mar. Eighty-four percent of all Chileans live in urban centers. This increasing urbanization of the population is probably responsible for the relatively modern demographic character of the country. The rate of intercensal growth is 2.8 percent, fertility is 2.5 children per woman, life expectancy is 72 years, and infant mortality is 17 per thousand—the lowest in Latin America.

The national economy depends on two major activities, mining and agriculture, which provide 23 percent and 19 percent of the gross national product, respectively. The highest percentage (32 percent) of employment is in the service sector, but its contribution to GNP is only 23.5 percent. Manufactures employ 16.6 percent of the active population. Mining hinges on the production of copper (Chuquicamata, Salvador, Río Blanco, and El Teniente), iron ore (Romeral), and nitrate (mines in the provinces of Tarapacá and Antofagasta). The agricultural activities are concentrated in the temperate Central Valley, where grapes and wine are the main export commodities. They are followed closely by fruit and timber. In the 1980s, with 232,935 acres of planted pine forests (and 14,875,812 of natural forests), Chile was the leading exporter of timber and paper pulp in Latin America. Fishing is a dominant activity in the north, yielding about 5.5 million tons of sardines, anchovies, and jack mackerel annually; most of them go into the production of fish meal and fish oil for export. These are indicators of the strong export economy initiated by General Augusto PINOCHET during his rule (1973–1990).

Traditionally Chile has been divided into six regions: (1) the NORTE GRANDE (Great North), the region of deserts, mining settlements, and coastal towns dedicated mostly to fishing and the shipping of minerals; (2) the NORTE CHICO (Little North), a transitional region in which greater precipitation allows the growing of fruit but where mining is still a strong supporter of the economy; (3) the Central Region, which encompasses most of mediterranean Chile (the core of the temperate zone), the capital city, and the large conurbations of Valparaíso–Viña del Mar and Concepción–Talcahuano, where most of the industrial establishments are concentrated; (4) La Frontera (the Frontier), a region of predominantly Mapuche ethnic composition, which was incorporated and colonized only after 1881; (5) Los Lagos (the Lakes Region), a territory mostly colonized by Europeans, where dairy products, sugar beets, and grains are the main commodities and tourism is one of the major assets; and (6) the Great South, which comprises the islands, fjords, channels, and rain forests of the Strait of Magellan, Chilean Patagonia, and Tierra del Fuego, formerly inhabited by ALAKALUF and Fuegino Indians.

The central valley of Chile is the name given to a central depression extending between the Andes and the Coastal Range (Cordillera de la Costa), latitudes 33 to 41.5 degrees south. This tectonic trench has been filled by volcanic, fluvial, and glacial materials carried from the Andes by numerous torrential rivers, among them, the Mapocho, Maipo, Cachapoal, Maule, Ñuble, Bío-bío,

and Toltén. Owing to its good soils and adequate irrigation facilities, the Central Valley is the core of the agricultural region, which specializes in grapes, wine, dry fruits, wheat, cattle, and vegetables. In colonial times a string of agricultural settlements—Rancagua, Curicó, Talca, Linares, Los Ángeles, Temuco, and Osorno—was established and in 1921 was connected by a railway line that runs between Santiago and Puerto Montt, at the southern extreme of the Central Valley. Originally the region was occupied by large haciendas and was considered the cradle of the landowning aristocracy. In the 1960s large landed estates were expropriated, and most of the land was given to the workers by the agrarian reform implemented by presidents Eduardo FREI and Salvador ALLENDE. The best wines are produced in the Maipo, Cachapoal, and Teno river valleys. In the Bío-bío segment, sandy volcanic soils are excellent for growing pine trees, which support the paper pulp and lumber industries. The southern portion of the Central Valley is predominantly dedicated to dairy farming.

Historically, Chile was the name given by Peruvians to the country between the Aconcagua and Maule rivers settled by friendly Indians. To the south lies Araucania, the territory of the belligerent MAPUCHES. Just after the conquest of the country, colonization efforts by Spaniards incorporated Cuyo, on the east side of the Andes. The Governancy of Chile also claimed jurisdiction over the Strait of Magellan and Terra Australis (the name given to Tierra del Fuego and the lands thought to expand to the south). After the WAR OF THE PACIFIC (1879–1884) against Bolivia and Peru, Chile occupied the Bolivian segment of the Pacific coast and the southern Peruvian department of Tarapacá. In the South Pacific, Easter Island became a dependency in 1889, after three decades of French missionary presence on the remote island.

CÉSAR N. CAVIEDES, *The Politics of Chile: A Sociogeographical Assessment* (1979); HUGO ROMERO, "Fundamentos geográficos del territorio nacional," in Instituto Geográfico Militar, *Geografía de Chile* (1984); JORDI FUENTES, ET AL. *Diccionario histórico de Chile*, 8th ed. (1984); PEDRO CUNILL, *Geografía de Chile* (1986); BRIAN LOVEMAN, *Chile: The Legacy of Hispanic Capitalism* (1988); JOSEPH L. SCARPACI, *Primary Medical Care in Chile* (1988). On the Central Valley, see EUGENE E. MARTIN, *La división de la tierra en Chile Central* (Santiago, 1960); and DIONISIO VÍO, "Geografía de la actividad agropecuaria," in *Geografía de Chile*, vol. 17 (Santiago, 1987).

CÉSAR N. CAVIEDES

See also individual features and regions.

CHILE: JUNTA DEL GOBIERNO, military council that ruled Chile after the overthrow of President Salvador ALLENDE GOSSENS in 1973. The leaders of the armed forces, comprising Augusto PINOCHET UGARTE (army), General Gustavo Leigh (air force, replaced with General

Fernando Matthei in 1978), Admiral José Toribio Merino (navy), and General César Mendoza (*carabineros*, replaced with General Rodolfo Stange in 1985), ousted President Allende on 11 September. The junta cited as justification for the coup what it said was President Allende's imminent plan to assassinate senior military officials and other prominent figures. This alleged plot, known as "Plan Z," was fabricated by the military with the assistance of the U.S. Central Intelligence Agency.

After the junta took control, Congress was closed. Elections, including those of private associations, were eliminated or severely curtailed. Military officials headed educational and other institutions. During the initial "state of internal war," Chile was purged of all "leftists," beginning with the political parties of the Left and their collaborators. The military tyrannized poor neighborhoods and arrested thousands; many were killed or disappeared. Periodically the junta declared a "state of siege." Decree Law 527 of June 1974 established Pinochet as the supreme chief of the nation. Although legislative and constitutional powers were assigned to the junta, Pinochet could function without it. Once in power, the junta's quasilegal government, supported by business and middle-class conservatives, was upheld by the Supreme Court. On 11 September 1980, Pinochet became de jure president under a constitution drafted by his regime and adopted by popular plebiscite. In August 1988 the junta selected Pinochet for the 1989–1997 term. But in the 5 October 1988 plebiscite, 55 percent of Chileans voted against him. On 30 July 1989 the electorate approved constitutional reforms. The democratic election of Patricio AYLWIN AZÓCAR on 14 December 1989 and his subsequent inauguration on 11 March 1990 ended the rule of the junta del gobierno.

PAUL E. SIGMUND, *The Overthrow of Allende and the Politics of Chile, 1964–1976* (1977); PAMELA CONSTABLE and ARTURO VALENZUELA, *A Nation of Enemies: Chile under Pinochet* (1991).

CHRISTEL K. CONVERSE

CHILE: ORGANIZATIONS

Chilean Nitrate Company
Compañía de Salitre de Chile—COSACH

Owned by the government of Chile and private interests, this mining company was founded to produce NITRATE. In the 1920s, the Guggenheim family interests introduced a new technique to refine nitrate. Although more economical, the natural nitrates, or *salitre,* had difficulty competing with synthetics, particularly those produced by German chemical firms using the Haber-Bayer process. In hopes of lowering production costs and thus the price, the Guggenheims requested that the government of Carlos IBÁÑEZ rescind the export tax on nitrates, but the government needed money and could not grant the concession. As a compromise, the Guggenheims and Ibáñez created COSACH in 1931. Since the

new corporation virtually controlled the mining and marketing of natural nitrates, the U.S. and Chilean interests hoped that COSACH could maintain prices. In return for the abolition of the export tax, the Guggenheims gave the Chilean government $80 million over a four-year period. From then on, the Chilean government and the corporation agreed to share equally in COSACH's profits or losses. Consistent with Ibáñez's policy of economic nationalism, Chileans would have to constitute at least 80 percent of COSACH's work force.

COSACH never fulfilled the expectations of either the government or the Guggenheims. Although the new technology did increase production, it also dramatically cut—by more than 85 percent—the number of people working in the nitrate mines. What was worse, the onset of the Great Depression reduced world demand so that the price of nitrates fell and even the more efficient COSACH could not make a profit. Arturo ALESSANDRI abolished COSACH in 1933, heavily in debt and denounced by nationalists who claimed that Ibáñez had sold out to the Guggenheims. It was replaced in 1934 by COVENSA (Corporaton for the Sale of Nitrate and Iodine), a solely government-owned company that produced and marketed nitrates.

FREDERICK M. NUNN, *Chilean Politics: The Honorable Mission of the Armed Forces 1920–1931* (1970), pp. 157–158, 169, 171–172; THOMAS O'BRIEN, "Rich beyond the Dreams of Avarice: The Guggenheims in Chile," in *Business History Review* 63 (1989):122–159.

WILLIAM F. SATER

Corporation of Agrarian Reform
Corporación de la Reforma Agraria—CORA

Created during the government of Jorge ALESSANDRI (1958–1964), this Chilean land-reform agency oversaw the agrarian reform process by buying land and dividing it into parcels for individual or cooperative development, as well as by providing these new agricultural units with technical assistance and funding. CORA, representing a commitment by the state to provide assistance to the rural poor, initially concentrated on converting largely government-owned property into individual plots. The enabling legislation granted CORA the right to pay for expropriated property in a combination of cash and long-term government bonds, which repesented a radical departure from earlier laws, as well as the power to take land that was abandoned or inefficiently operated. The government charged CORA with ensuring that landlords respected the rights of agrarian workers.

Although CORA was accused of being paternalistic and failing to provide needed technical assistance, during the administration of Eduardo FREI (1964–1970) it still expropriated 18 percent of Chile's irrigated land and 12 percent of its nonirrigated property, converting this property either into individual holdings, cooperatives, or temporary communal farms called *asentamien-*

tos. Despite its failures, which included creating a largely unneeded bureaucracy, CORA did achieve certain reforms until its demise in 1978. More significantly, it constituted the first agency to deal in a realistic fashion with the problem of agrarian reform in Chile.

ROBERT B. KAUFMAN, *The Politics of Land Reform in Chile, 1950–1970: Public Policy, Political Institutions and Social Change* (1972); BRIAN LOVEMAN, *Struggle in the Countryside: Politics and Rural Labor in Chile, 1919–1973* (1976), pp. 233–240, 268–272.

WILLIAM F. SATER

Development Corporation
Corporación de Fomento—CORFO

This Chilean development agency was begun as a government entity to supervise the reconstruction of Chile's south following a disastrous 1939 earthquake that inflicted enormous damage and took approximately 30,000 lives. The Pedro AGUIRRE CERDA regime (1938–1941) subsequently gave CORFO the task of developing the Chilean economy, particularly by increasing the country's power supplies and creating basic industries. Funded initially by special taxes, particularly on largely U.S.-owned copper mines, and by foreign loans, this government agency grew. CORFO has also financed private ventures, as well as state enterprises, if they seemed to lead to import substitution and to produce products that might improve the nation's standard of living.

As one of its many achievements, CORFO succeeded in developing hydroelectric projects as well as a state-owned steel mill, and in discovering petroleum in Magallanes. CORFO often acted as a minority stockholder in privately owned corporations. During the Salvador ALLENDE regime (1970–1973), CORFO received additional funds which it used to purchase shares of public corporations, in effect transferring them from the private to the public sector. Then, consistent with its economic philosophy, the Augusto PINOCHET administration (1973–1990) sold many of CORFO's assets to private individuals. CORFO not only has provided significant assistance to Chile's industrial sector but also has demonstrated the role of the state in fostering economic development.

HERMAN FINER, *The Chilean Development Corporation* (1947); P. T. ELLSWORTH, *Chile: An Economy in Transition* (1954); MARKOS MAMALAKIS, "An Analysis of the Financial and Investment Activities of the Chilean Development Corporation: 1939–1964," in *Journal of Development Studies* 5 (Jan. 1969): 118–137; LUIS ORTEGA M., ET AL., *Corporación de Fomento de la Producción, 50 años de realizaciones, 1939–1989* (1989).

WILLIAM F. SATER

Federation of Chilean Students
Federación de Estudiantes de Chile—FECH

Founded in 1906 as the official student organization of the University of Chile, FECH was the first, largest, and politically most powerful student federation in Chile until 1973. Because the university was the largest institution of higher education in the country and the source of much of Chile's political and professional elite, FECH exercised strong influence on national affairs. Since its inception, FECH has contributed significantly to political change through alliances with unions and political parties, or through massive mobilizations that have affected policy at the national or university levels. In 1931, for example, it contributed to the demise of General Carlos IBÁÑEZ DEL CAMPO. In 1957 FECH again challenged Ibáñez during his second administration. During the 1960s and early 1970s, it became part and parcel of political struggles at the national level and mobilized the student population to an unprecedented degree. During this period, FECH secured a 25 percent representation in rectorship elections, thus achieving the university reform ideal of *co-gobierno* (co-government). In 1973, FECH was banned and its leaders driven underground. In conjunction with the resurrection of other democratic forces in the mid-1980s, FECH once again entered the political fray, but this time in a weakened and less ideological position, reflecting the overall decline of the university.

FRANK BONILLA and MYRON GLAZER, *Student Politics in Chile* (1970); CARLOS HUNEEUS MADGE, *La reforma en la Universidad de Chile* (1973); DANIEL C. LEVY, *Higher Education and the State in Latin America: Private Challenges to Public Dominance* (1986); IVÁN JAKSIĆ and SONIA NAZARIO, "Chile," in *Student Political Activism: An International Reference Handbook*, edited by Philip G. Altbach (1989).

IVÁN JAKSIĆ

See also **Universities.**

Federation of Chilean Workers
Federación Obrera de Chile—FOCH

A Chilean labor union created in 1909, FOCH was originally a mutual-aid organization of railroad workers who contributed small sums monthly to provide members with medical assistance. Named FOCH in 1917, it was reorganized in 1919 into a confederation of skilled and unskilled workers who called for unions to operate the factories and who opposed capitalism. FOCH initially included socialists, anarchists, nonpolitical Social Democrats, and even bourgeois Radicals as well as Communists. Eventually the Communist members purged the non-Communists from positions of leadership within the federation. By the mid-1920s, FOCH was identifying itself as part of the Communist Party and tending to recruit its members from among the nitrate and coal miners, with whom the Communists had made the most inroads. At its height, FOCH's membership may have numbered as many as 150,000. The federation eventually collapsed during the late 1920s as the result of government oppression, particularly during the IBÁÑEZ period (1927–1931), and declining economic conditions in FOCH's most important constituencies, the nitrate mines.

ALAN ANGELL, *Politics and the Labour Movement in Chile* (1972), pp. 32–38; PETER DE SHAZO, *Urban Workers and Labor Unions in Chile, 1902–1927* (1983).

WILLIAM F. SATER

Grupo Cruzat-Larraín

The Grupo Cruzat-Larraín was one of the largest of the *grupos económicos* (economic conglomerates) that came to dominate the Chilean financial system under the neoliberal economic policies implemented in the mid-1970s. Led by financiers Manuel Cruzat Infante and Fernando Larraín Peña, the group purchased controlling interests in virtually every sector of the Chilean economy during the privatization of public enterprises in the early years of the Pinochet regime. Liberalization of the domestic financial markets, an absence of government regulation, and easy access to international credit allowed for their spectacular growth. Their growth was also facilitated by close relations with key economic policymakers, some of whom periodically took positions with the groups. At its peak the Grupo Cruzat-Larraín had a virtual monopoly in petroleum distribution and owned at least 109 companies. The free-market policies of the CHICAGO BOYS seemed to encourage this extreme economic concentration, further exacerbating the uneven distribution of wealth. The economic crisis of 1981–1982 resulted in the bankruptcy and liquidation of both the Grupo Cruzat-Larraín and the Grupo Vial, and led to a reform of the banking system. Popular discontent and street protests stemming from this economic crisis challenged the survival of the Pinochet regime.

FERNANDO DAHSE, *El mapa de la extrema riqueza* (1979); LOIS HECHT OPPENHEIM, *Politics in Chile: Democracy, Authoritarianism, and the Search for Development* (1993); DAVID E. HOJMAN, *Chile: The Political Economy of Development and Democracy in the 1990s* (1993).

J. DAVID DRESSING

Movimiento Pro Emancipación de la Mujer Chilena—MEMCH

Founded in 1935 by members of the Asociación de Mujeres Universitarias under the leadership of the lawyer Elena Caffarena, MEMCH advocated full legal rights and equal work and pay opportunities for women and pursued a broad-based agenda of social concerns as it attacked poverty, prostitution, and the high rate of infant mortality. MEMCH's involvement in women's health issues led it to support the use of contraceptives and, within limits, access to abortion. MEMCH organized women in many provinces into local committees and laid the groundwork for the Federación Chilena de Instituciones Femeninas (FECHIF). MEMCH's organizational tactics, strategies, and membership base later served as the sustaining force of FECHIF. MEMCH's petitions and street demonstrations were instrumental in gaining for women the right to vote in 1949. In addition to pursuing women's rights, MEMCH supported the families of strikers and victims of political oppression. Though nonpartisan, MEMCH had a leftist orientation that led to its marginalization in the cold war climate of the late 1940s.

Named for the original MEMCH, MEMCH83 was founded in 1983 as an umbrella group to coordinate the activities of Chilean feminist and nonfeminist women's groups working to restore democracy to the nation. Though at first women's issues were not addressed,

Members of the Movimiento Pro-Emancipación de la Mujer Chilena. Elena Caffarena and Olga Poblete, founders of the Women's Movement. PHOTO BY JUAN MANDELBAUM.

MEMCH83's first large-scale demonstration, on 28 November 1983, not only opposed the Pinochet government but called for peace and women's rights. Beginning in 1987 partisan splits, sectarian conflict, and shifting political alliances resulted in changes in the groups claiming or disclaiming affiliation with MEMCH83.

PATRICIA M. CHURCHRYK, "Feminist Anti-Authoritarian Politics: The Role of Women's Organizations in the Chilean Transition to Democracy," in *The Women's Movement in Latin America*, edited by Jane S. Jaquette (1989); CORINNE ANTEZANA-PERNET, "Peace in the World and Democracy at Home: The Chilean Women's Movement in the 1940s," in *Latin America in the 1940s*, edited by David Rock (1994).

CORINNE ANTEZANA-PERNET
FRANCESCA MILLER

See also **Feminism and Feminist Organizations.**

Sociedad Nacional de Agricultura—SNA

The SNA is a voluntary association of landowners in Chile. Since its founding in 1869, the SNA has been dominated by the large landowners of the Central Valley, many of them also members of the national social and political elites. During the nineteenth century its primary mission was to promote the modernization of agricultural practices. By 1900, the organization had become more explicitly political in response to the creation of competing economic interests. With the rise of working-class organizations and militance following World War I, the SNA became increasingly identified with the defense of landowners on social issues, including food price controls, unionization of agricultural workers, and, by the 1930s, land reform. To meet these challenges, the SNA reached beyond its elite core by recruiting smaller landowners and founding the Confederación de la Producción y del Comercio, a multisectoral business pressure group, in 1934.

With the renewal of political challenges in the 1960s, the SNA became the most visible symbol of elite resistance to reform, but its efforts could not forestall the Eduardo FREI government's rural unionization and agrarian reform legislation that began dismantling the traditional rural estate in 1964. Defeated in the legislative arena, the SNA was instrumental in forming the *gremio* (GUILD) movement that began in the late 1960s and mushroomed after the 1970 election of Salvador ALLENDE. A broad-based, militant coalition of large entrepreneurial associations with their smaller counterparts, the *gremio* movement used "bosses' strikes" and street demonstrations to weaken the Allende government in preparation for its overthrow. The SNA subsequently collaborated with the Augusto PINOCHET government in reversing the previous decade's rural reforms and shaping Chile's dynamic new agricultural export sector.

GONZALO IZQUIERDO FERNÁNDEZ, *Un estudio de las ideologías chilenas: La Sociedad de Agricultura en el siglo XIX* (1968); and THOMAS C. WRIGHT, *Landowners and Reform in Chile: The Sociedad Nacional de Agricultura, 1919–1940* (1982).

THOMAS C. WRIGHT

See also **Agrarian Reform.**

Society of Equality
Sociedad de la Igualdad

The Society of Equality was a radical political organization formed in Chile on 14 April 1850 by Santiago ARCOS (1818–1874), Francisco BILBAO (1823–1865), and others. Originally intended as an organization for educating artisans (and for making them aware of their political rights), the Sociedad quickly became associated with the growing opposition to the presidential candidacy of Manuel MONTT (1809–1880). It had a membership of several hundred, including many artisans, though it cannot be regarded as a genuinely spontaneous artisan movement. Its meetings sometimes attracted more than a thousand participants. Enrolling members were asked to accept the three principles of "popular sovereignty," "the sovereignty of reason," and "love and universal fraternity." *Escuelas populares* (people's schools) organized by the Sociedad held classes in Spanish, English, music, mathematics, history, and drafting.

Highly unusual in the quiet Santiago of the period, the marches and processions of the *igualitarios* dismayed the authorities. On 19 August 1850 the Sociedad's premises were assaulted by a group probably hired by the police. In November 1850 the imposition of a state of siege brought the dissolution of the Sociedad, without popular protest. Politically, the effect of the Sociedad's agitation caused the ruling Conservative Party to accept the controversial candidacy of Montt, the consequence of which was two civil wars (1851, 1859).

CRISTIÁN GAZMURI, *El "48" Chileno: Igualitarios, reformistas, radicales, masones y bomberos* (1992).

SIMON COLLIER

Vicariate of Solidarity
Vicaría de la Solidaridad

The vicariate was the principal human rights organization in Chile during the military government of General Augusto PINOCHET (1973–1990). Established by the Catholic church in January 1976, the vicariate took over the activities of the ecumenical Committee of Cooperation for Peace, which had been formed after the 11 September 1973 coup that overturned the Socialist government of Salvador ALLENDE. The brutality of the new regime had caused Catholic, Protestant, and Jewish leaders to establish this humanitarian relief agency for the victims and their families. When the committee was closed in 1975, due in part to government pressure, Cardinal Raúl SILVA HENRÍQUEZ established the Vicariate of Solidarity as part of the archdiocese of Santiago.

The vicariate focused on providing legal, medical, and humanitarian assistance to Chileans throughout the country. Its legal department became renowned for its creativity in using existing national and international law to defend political prisoners, secure the release of those illegally detained, and investigate assassinations, torture, and disappearances. It also provided technical assistance to human rights organizations in other countries.

In addition to its legal work, the vicariate established medical services, communal kitchens, consumer and producer cooperatives, and basic educational and job training programs, and provided technical assistance and credit, particularly to poor communities. In one year, its facilities provided 5 million meals for children. By the 1980s, public opinion surveys indicated that the vicariate was the most trusted institution in Chile.

With the return of elected civilian government in March 1990, the vicariate began scaling down its human rights activities on the grounds that civic and other organizations could assume such tasks. The Vicariate of Solidarity closed in December 1992.

JUAN IGNACIO GUTIÉRREZ FUENTE, *Chile: La Vicaría de la Solidaridad* (Madrid, 1986); HANNAH W. STEWART-GAMBINO, *The Church and Politics in the Chilean Countryside* (1992).

MARGARET E. CRAHAN

CHILE: PARLIAMENTARY REGIME, the political system under which Chile was ruled from 1891 to 1925. The 1891 Revolution effectively destroyed the presidential form of government that had been in effect in Chile since 1833. Henceforth, the chief executive acted as a figurehead while the Congress, under the leadership of the minister of the interior, the Chilean equivalent of a prime minister, dictated national policy.

While not intrinsically defective, Chile's parliamentary system suffered significant flaws. In order to ensure honest elections, the Law of Municipalities (1891) shifted control of the electoral system from the central government to the provinces. This transfer of power, however, merely permitted urban bosses and rural landowners to control the political process. Consequently, these individuals selected their own candidates, ensuring their electoral triumph through bribery, intimidation, or fraud. Since the candidates no longer had to court voters but merely the power brokers, they could safely ignore the needs of the nation. Dishonest elections also preserved parties that possessed no distinctive ideologies or rationales for existing, other than the egos of their own members.

Chile's extremely limited electorate divided their votes between an increasing number of parties. One of the results of the dishonest electoral system was that no one party could achieve a parliamentary majority. Hence, coalition politics became the standard. Regrettably, the creation of parliamentary majorities became increasingly complicated: politicians demanded high prices in terms of patronage for their cooperation, and even members of the same party would sometimes not cooperate with each other. The number of complete cabinet changes accelerated from eight during the government of Jorge MONTT (1891–1896) to seventeen under Juan Luis SANFUENTES (1915–1920). During the period of 1891–1920, more than eighty cabinets attempted to rule the nation. Since few ministries retained power long enough to formulate and implement a coherent program, the nation foundered.

Meanwhile, Chile's problems in this period desperately needed attention. The process of urbanization was crowding the nation's poor into filthy and unhealthy housing, where they perished at a higher rate than in India. Working conditions were equally perilous: men and women were injured or even died laboring in the nation's ill-ventilated factories and *salitreras*. The fortunes of Chile's domestic economy ebbed and flowed according to the price of nitrates. When revenues were high, the government prospered, but when they declined the nation retrenched. In bad times, the state made up its deficits by borrowing or selling off nitrate lands to private interests.

For decades, Chile's working class endured poor pay, wretched living and working conditions, and an inflation that eroded their purchasing power. Eventually, when they demanded change, the political elites, depending upon their beliefs, either could or would not respond. The post–Word War I collapse of the nitrate economy so distorted Chile's economy in conjunction with this inept political system that it forced radical change. In 1925 the nation ratified a new constitution which restored a presidential system to Chile and guaranteed the need of the state to intervene in order to address the nation's social and economic needs.

KAREN L. REMMER, "The Timing, Pace and Sequence of Political Change in Chile, 1891–1925," in *Hispanic American Historical Review* 57, 2 (1977): 205–230, and *Party Competition in Argentina and Chile* (1984), pp. 23–24, 85–86.

WILLIAM F. SATER

CHILE: POLITICAL PARTIES

Christian Democratic Party
Partido Demócrata Christiano—PDC

The Christian Democratic Party was Chile's largest single political force most of the time from its establishment in 1957 to the mid-1990s. The product of several progressive offshoots of the country's once-powerful Conservative Party, its multiclass following ranges from wealthy Catholic industrialists through professionals, small businessmen, and other middle-sector elements to industrial workers, miners, peasants, and agricultural laborers. The party claims to be an alternative to traditionally defined right- and left-wing political forces, although its own ranks have long contained factions or tendencies that lean in both of these directions. Much of its growth and development comes from its association with Eduardo FREI MONTALVA, a founding father, long-time leader, and one of the more successful and popular presidents (1964–1970) in modern Chilean history.

During the early 1970s, the party joined its erstwhile rightist adversaries in opposing the government of Salvador ALLENDE. It also welcomed his overthrow by the Chilean military, apparently expecting that power would revert to civilian hands after a not-too-lengthy interval. As it became clearer that army General Augusto PINOCHET was not going to relinquish power soon, and as his government adopted socially regressive economic policies and continued to violate the human rights of actual and potential adversaries, the party became increasingly critical of the military government, albeit circumspectly at first and independently of the Communists and more radical Socialists.

With the downturn in the Chilean economy that began in mid-1981 and continued through 1985, the PDC became the nucleus of an increasingly broad and assertive opposition movement that combined strikes and protest marches with calls for dialogue and a negotiated end to military rule. Although these efforts failed to dislodge Pinochet any sooner than 1989, the date called for by the 1980 Constitution, they did bring democratic parties of the left, center, and right together in support of a common program and antiregime strategy. This consensus won the support of a majority of Chilean voters in both the 1988 plebiscite and 1989 general elections.

In the 1989 elections, the party's Patricio AYLWIN AZÓCAR won 55 percent of the presidential vote, easily defeating two right-wing rivals. Christian Democratic candidates, running on the same ticket with candidates of other democratic parties, won 12 of the 37 contested Senate seats and 50 of the 120 seats in the Chamber of Deputies. As at previous times, the party included both progressive and more conservative, technocratic factions, with the latter in a dominant position. Its divisions seemed less troublesome than previously, however, given the willingness of most political forces to proceed cautiously in the initial postmilitary period. Another reason for this new, cooperative spirit was the crisis into which Marxist parties fell throughout the world beginning in the late 1980s and the willingness of the left to make the construction of a socialist society and economy an ultimate, rather than an immediate, objective.

MICHAEL FLEET, *The Rise and Fall of Chilean Christian Democracy* (1985); TIMOTHY R. SCULLY, *Rethinking the Center: Party Politics in Nineteenth- and Twentieth-Century Chile* (1992).

MICHAEL FLEET

Christian Left
Izquierda Cristiana

A breakaway faction of Chile's Christian Democratic Party (PDC), the Christian Left was active during the regime of Salvador ALLENDE (1970–1973). Comprised of the more leftist members of the PDC and under the leadership of Senator Renán Fuentealba, these elements demanded that Eduardo FREI and his followers support Allende's economic policies. Hoping to remain politically potent, many of the PDC initially supported many of the Christian Left's positions. In a 1971 Christian Democratic Party meeting, the leaders of what became the Christian Left submitted a proposal suggesting that the PDC cease cooperating with the conservative National Party (PN). When their motion failed, those who believed it not inconsistent for Christians to support Allende's struggle to bring socialism to Chile broke with the PDC, forming the Christian Left. While the new party, which included six former PDC deputies, attracted some of the members of the United Movement of Popular Action, or MAPU (another PDC splinter group), it failed to bolster the Allende coalition. As just one of many leftist parties, the Izquierda Cristiana won only 1.1 percent of the vote in the 1973 congressional elections, indicating its lack of popular support. Banned by the PINOCHET government, it continued to operate clandestinely, joining the Movimiento Democrático Popular to try to restore democracy in Chile.

PAUL E. SIGMUND, *The Overthrow of Allende and the Politics of Chile, 1964–1976* (1977), p. 135; CARMELO FURCI, *The Chilean Communist Party and the Road to Socialism* (1984).

WILLIAM F. SATER

Communist Party
Partido Comunista

The Communist Party of Chile traces its origins to the left wing of the Democratic Party and its successor, the Partido Obrero Socialista (POS). In 1922, after six years of its independent existence, Luis Emilio RECABARREN led the POS into the Communist International. Persecuted by the Carlos IBÁÑEZ government, it also suffered from internal schisms. Politically isolated even after Ibáñez's 1931 overthrow, it agreed to cooperate with other parties, largely by order of the Communist International, which commanded its members to work with progressive elements to stop the spread of FASCISM. Although the Communist Party proved instrumental in the creation and triumph of the Popular Front (Frente Popular), it would not accept any ministerial posts in that government, apparently not wishing to suffer a possible loss of prestige if the Front should fail.

The Soviet Union's 1939 nonaggression pact with Germany and struggle for control of the unions led the Communists to quit the Front until the Nazi invasion of Russia forced a reconciliation between the Communists and their old allies. The Communists' support of the Radical candidate Gabriel GONZÁLEZ VIDELA led to their participation in his government. Apparently fearing that the Communists were becoming too powerful, and encouraged by the British and Americans, González Videla expelled the party from his cabinet. When the

Communists retaliated by launching a series of deadly strikes, González Videla banned the party and struck its members from the voting rolls. As political repression slowly eased, the party reappeared under the new name of the Democratic Party, and much of its literature became available. Although it still remained clandestine, the Communist Party announced in 1956 at its tenth congress that it would use peaceful means to achieve its goals of ending U.S. imperialism; promoting state ownership of all industries, land, and credit institutions; and empowering the working class. Following the Ibáñez government's 1958 rescinding of the Law for the Defense of Democracy, which had outlawed them, the Communists returned to political life.

The Communists helped create Popular Action Front (FRAP), which supported Salvador ALLENDE's presidential aspirations in 1958 and 1964. The party also played a significant role in the 1970 Popular Unity (Unidad Popular) government, a coalition of the Communist, Socialist, and Radical Parties that again nominated Allende. Unlike the Socialists, the Communists were willing to cooperate with bourgeois political parties or individuals regardless of their class. These differences between parties became more pronounced during Allende's regime, when the Communists urged the government to consolidate its gains rather than press for more drastic change. With the adoption of this position, the party appeared less hostile to the interests of small property owners and the middle class. Conversely, the Socialists urged Allende to become more radical.

Well-disciplined, cohesive, and possessed of a history of operating successfully underground, the Communists survived the 1973 PINOCHET coup. Within a relatively short period, the party was meeting clandestinely and publishing its journals. In 1980, after studying Chile's political situation, the party announced that it would use force to overthrow the Pinochet government. Although it denied any involvement, the Communists organized the Frente Patriótico Manuel Rodríguez (FPMR), described as the armed vanguard of the resistance movement. This group's most audacious act was an attempted assassination of General Pinochet. While initially refusing to cooperate with other antigovernment forces, the Communists subsequently did go along with the measures that ultimately led to the 1989 plebiscite which brought Patricio AYLWIN to power. Although the Communists failed to elect anyone to the Congress, the party remains viable, and the FPMR continues to use violent means to remind people of its existence.

ERNEST HALPERIN, *Nationalism and Communism in Chile* (1965); HERNÁN RAMÍREZ NECOCHEA, *Origen y formación del Partido Comunista de Chile* (1965); FEDERICO G. GIL, *The Political System of Chile* (1966), pp. 277–283; CARMELO FURCI, *The Chilean Communist Party and the Road to Socialism* (1984); JULIO FAÚNDEZ, Marxism and Democracy in Chile (1988), pp. 94–95, 168–169, 174–175, 195–196, 201–202.

WILLIAM F. SATER

Concentración Nacional

The Concentración Nacional was a post–World War II Chilean political alliance. Following his 1946 election, Gabriel GONZÁLEZ VIDELA initially created a government that included members of the Communist Party. In 1947, however, he reshuffled his cabinet, this time excluding the Communists, who he felt had become too popular. Infuriated, the Communists launched a series of strikes, some of which became violent. Claiming that the Communists were threatening Chile's political stability, González Videla created a new cabinet, the Concentración Nacional, which consisted of the Radical, Conservative, Democratic, and Liberal parties. In 1948 this coalition cabinet passed a measure called the Law for the Permanent Defense of Democracy, which outlawed the Communist Party. The Concentración Nacional lasted until 1950, when a split over labor and prices led to the cabinet's resignation.

CÉSAR CAVIEDES L., *The Politics of Chile: A Sociogeographical Assessment* (1979), pp. 184–185; JULIO FAÚNDEZ, *Marxism and Democracy in Chile* (1988), p. 75.

WILLIAM F. SATER

Conservative Party
Partido Conservador

Other than possessing a commitment to maintaining social order and preserving property rights, the original Conservative Party did not hold its first convention until 1878. Lacking an ideology for their first forty years of existence did not seem to trouble the Conservatives. Emerging victorious from the Battle of Lircay (1830), the Conservatives happily turned power over to Diego Portales, who created a strong centralized government wielding enough power to keep order. Once the Conservatives lost control of the Moneda (government house), they tried to reduce the power of the central government and enhance political liberties. Paradoxically, they still insisted that the state support the Catholic church's desire to deny Protestants religious freedom. Even after losing the presidency, the Conservatives continued to hold ministerial posts. In the 1870s, however, the Conservatives broke with the other parties over the issue of the role of the Roman Catholic church and did not participate in government until after the 1891 revolution.

Although numerically small, the Conservative Party remained highly disciplined. It managed to preserve its share of the seats in the legislature largely because most of its members were large landowners who cynically forced their *inquilinos* (tenant farmers) to vote for Conservative candidates. The so-called reforms produced by the 1891 revolution enhanced the Conservatives' power base by permitting local governments, not the Moneda, to supervise the electoral process. This power, plus the fact that rural communities were overrepresented in the legislature, breathed new life into the Conservative cause.

127

At its 1901 party convention some Conservatives, under the influence of Pope Leo XIII's 1891 encyclical *Rerum Novarum*, began to advocate social and economic reforms: the construction of housing for the poor, improvement of working conditions, and increased educational opportunities. Social and economic reform continued to be one of the party's concerns.

The party managed to survive, but when it turned to the right, in the early 1930s, it lost several of its brightest members, some of whom bolted to form what became the Christian Democratic Party (PDC). After 1945, those who remained within the Conservative Party split into two groups: the Social Christian wing and the traditionalists. Later the Social Christians would join the PDC. The party managed to retain wide support, often outpolling the Left. Changes in the election process and a refusal of the *inquilinos* to accept passively their patrons' control led to a collapse of the Conservative Party's base of support. In 1965, for example, the Conservatives won only 5 percent of the vote in the congressional elections, losing all its places in the Senate and retaining only three places in the lower house. In order to unify the right wing and not dissipate their power, the Conservatives, in league with the Liberals, formed the National Party in 1966.

The Conservative Party retains its faith in the teachings of the Roman Catholic church. While it does not question democracy, it wishes to reduce the power of the central government. Economically, it favors the free-enterprise system, but admits that private property rights can be subordinated to the needs of society. It remains an elitist, upper-class party, whose members are large provincial property owners. Needless to say, these elements resisted attempts at agrarian reform, which they often denounced as a U.S. plot.

The National Party continued its opposition to the Allende administration, working in league with the Christian Democrats in crucial by-elections and in supporting various antigovernment labor actions. The Nationals fielded candidates in the 1989 congressional elections but elected none.

FREDRICK B. PIKE, *Chile and the United States, 1880–1962* (1963), pp. 250–256; FEDERICO G. GIL, *The Political System of Chile* (1966), pp. 245–252; GERMÁN URZÚA VALENZUELA, *Los partidos políticos chilenos* (1968), pp. 102–134; BEN BURNETT, *Political Groups in Chile: The Dialogue Between Order and Change* (1970), pp. 161–170, 178–181; KAREN L. REMMER, *Party Competition in Argentina and Chile* (1984), pp. 12–15, 72–74, 76–80, 117–120.

WILLIAM F. SATER

Democratic Party
Partido Demócrata

The Partido Demócrata was the first Chilean political party dedicated to advancing the cause of the workers. Created in 1887 by an offshoot of the Radical Party, the Democrats held their first convention two years later. This party was the first in Chile seeking to protect the economic and political interests of the lower classes, calling for honest elections, laws to provide decent housing and improved working conditions, a return to the gold standard, and economic nationalism.

Unlike other political organizations, the Democratic Party's directors included professionals and intellectuals like lawyer Malaquías Concha and physician Alejandro Bustamante, but more significantly, it also included workers, such as printer Luis Emilio RECABARREN. Not surprisingly, this party, which seriously challenged Chile's status quo, encountered difficulties. Its support of José Manuel BALMACEDA during the 1891 revolution led to the persecution of its leaders at the hands of the congressionalist victors. Perhaps because it included various political extremists such as anarchists, the party initially refused to participate in any of the parliamentary political coalitions. It also provided leadership in organizing various strikes and demonstrations, such as the 1905 Santiago Meat Riots.

Eventually, anxious to participate in government, and perhaps in patronage as well, the Democrats abandoned their principles of noncooperation, often supporting extremely reactionary candidates such as those of the Conservative Party, in return for ministerial portfolios. This willingness to cooperate with bourgeois parties, which gained the Democrats a ministerial post, precipitated various schisms. The conflict between the traditionalists and those advocating socialism ultimately led, in 1912, to the creation of the Socialist Workers Party (Partido Obrero Socialista—POS).

Electing its first deputy to the national Congress in 1894, the Democratic Party continued to win additional victories. In 1904 six Democratic congressmen and, for the first time, a senator, won legislative seats. Triumph at the polls, however, did not always translate into political power, as the Congress sometimes refused to seat Democratic legislators. The party nevertheless enjoyed increasing popularity, particularly in the nitrate pampas and among urban workers. The Democrats seemed to reach their political zenith in 1932, when the party elected thirteen deputies. Too conservative for the Left and too radical for the Right, the party began to lose support, particularly when some of its more progressive members, like Recabarren, left the party. Even those who remained seemed without direction: in the 1958 presidential election the members of the Democratic Party supported each of the three candidates. By this time the party had won but 5 percent of the vote, and by 1965 it had ceased to be of any real importance.

Although it eventually went out of existence, the Democratic Party nonetheless fulfilled an important function. It was one of the first of Chile's parties to articulate such ideas as creating a labor section and providing social security, worker compensation, and accident insurance to protect the nation's working class.

HECTOR DE PETRIS GIESEN, *Historia del partido democrático* (1942); GERMÁN URZÚA VALENZUELA, *Los partidos políticos chilenos* (1968), pp. 53–55; BEN G. BURNETT, *Political Groups in Chile*

(1970), pp. 161–170, 178–181; PETER DE SHAZO, *Urban Workers and Labor Unions in Chile, 1902–1927* (1983), pp. 90–92, 109–113, 119–122, 126, 139–140, 175, 177; KAREN L. REMMER, *Party Competition in Argentina and Chile: Political Recruitment and Public Policy, 1890–1930* (1984), pp. 67–70, 85–86, 118–120.

WILLIAM F. SATER

Feminine Party
Partido Femenino de Chile

Founded in 1946 by María de la Cruz, this party joined the umbrella group FECHIF (Federación Chilena de Instituciones Femeninas) the same year. De la Cruz was influenced by Juan and Eva PERÓN, and the Feminine Party platform stressed "justice and social harmony." The party reflected de la Cruz's beliefs about women's moral superiority, defended traditional gender roles and femininity, and argued that female "emotionality" was a necessary counterweight to male "rationality." Journalist Georgina Durand and lawyer Felícitas Klimpel were on the Feminine Party board of directors. In 1951 the party split over de la Cruz's personalist leadership, but both factions supported the successful independent presidential candidacy of Carlos Ibáñez in 1952. Running as the Feminine Party candidate, de la Cruz was the first woman to be elected to the Chilean Senate in 1952; the party disintegrated following her expulsion from the Senate in 1953.

FELÍCITAS KLIMPEL, *La mujer chilena (el aporte femenino al progreso de Chile) 1910–1960* (1962); CORINNE ANTEZANA-PERNET, "Peace in the World and Democracy at Home: The Chilean Women's Movement in the 1940s," in *Latin America in the 1940s*, edited by David Rock (1994).

CORINNE ANTEZANA-PERNET

See also **Feminism and Feminist Organizations.**

Liberal-Conservative Fusion
Fusión Liberal-Conservadora

The Fusion grew out of a Chilean political alliance formed in January 1858 to fight against President Manuel MONTT (1851–1861) and his National Party (founded December 1857) in the congressional elections of that year. It consisted of the Liberals, who had been in opposition since 1830, and those Conservatives (probably a majority) then defecting from Montt, partly provoked by his handling of the QUESTION OF THE SACRISTAN. This alliance of old enemies was more resilient than its opponents suspected it would be: it lasted fifteen years. In 1859 the Fusion mounted unsuccessful armed rebellions against Montt. His tolerant successor, José Joaquín PÉREZ (1861–1871), invited the alliance into the cabinet in July 1862. Though opposed by the now-displaced Nationals and also by the "unreconstructed" Liberals known as Radicals, the Fusion retained its power, and in 1871 elected its own president, Federico ERRÁZURIZ

ZAÑARTU (1871–1876). It finally broke up in 1873 over a contentious dispute about private education, when the Conservatives went into opposition.

SIMON COLLIER

Liberal Party
Partido Liberal

The first Liberal Party of Chile consisted of a group of men who shared vague ideals rather than a cohesive ideology. Crushed by the Conservatives at the battle of LIRCAY in 1830, the party dissolved, and its supporters went to ground. The Manuel BULNES administration (1841–1851) proved more benign than its predecessor, permitting a more open political atmosphere. A split in Conservative ranks provided the impetus and the leadership for the creation of the Liberal Party. The dissident Conservatives attracted the support of pre-1830 Liberals as well as a new generation of political mavericks, such as Francisco BILBAO and José Victorino LASTARRIA, who were strongly influenced by events in Europe, particularly the various revolutions of 1848. Together they founded the Liberal Party in 1849.

The newly created Liberals did not fare well. Twice, in 1851 and 1859, they participated in rebellions intended to bring political change to Chile. Displeased by the Manuel MONTT administration (1851–1861), the Liberals began to side with Conservatives to form an antigovernment opposition. The conclusion of the Montt regime, however, brought the Liberals into increasing prominence and even into the José Joaquín PÉREZ administration's cabinet. Under their aegis the legislature gave rights to non-Catholics, reduced the powers of the president to suspend the Constitution, and limited his tenure to one term.

From 1871 to 1891, Liberal presidents ruled Chile, initiating legislation that amplified civil rights, reduced the power of the government, enfranchised more people, and secularized many institutions. The party, however, suffered on various occasions from numerous splits, which limited its effectiveness, often forcing it to forge coalitions in order to rule.

Like the Conservative Party, the Liberal Party did not hold its first convention until late: in September 1892, when it announced its support for the parliamentary system and free elections. Because of its propensity for internal disputes and lack of organization, the party lost much of its effectiveness during the first half of the parliamentary period. The Liberal Party rarely lived up to its name: other than calling for separation of church and state, it tended to concentrate on political change rather than demand substantive socioeconomic reforms. Even the Conservatives were more liberal.

The Liberals continued to splinter after 1925, with each faction often supporting different candidates. Periodically, Liberals participated in various cabinets, even working with Communists on one occasion, thereby indicating that political consistency was not their strong suit. Despite its problems, the Liberal Party still elected candidates largely from rural areas where it could control the peasant vote. For the same reasons the Conservatives lost congressional power—changes in the electoral law and an end to election fraud—the Liberals lost as well. By 1965 they had attracted but 7.3 percent of the congressional vote, electing only six deputies and five senators. Increasingly, the Liberal Party functioned as part of a coalition. Its last experience, working with Conservatives and Radicals to elect a congressional candidate, failed dismally. Recognizing the problems confronting it, in 1966 the Liberals joined the Conservatives, once their mortal foes, to create the National Party which continues to function.

SERGIO GUILISASTI, *Partidos políticos chilenos* (1964), pp. 71–128; FEDERICO G. GIL, *The Political System of Chile* (1966), pp. 231–243, 252–256, 308–309; JAMES O. MORRIS, *Elites, Intellectuals, and Consensus: A Study of the Social Question and the Industrial Relations System in Chile* (1966), pp. 9, 101, 144–171, 180–184, 187, 217, 233–234; BEN G. BURNETT, *Political Groups in Chile* (1970), pp. 161–170, 178–181; KAREN L. REMMER, *Party Competition in Argentina and Chile: Political Recruitment and Public Policy, 1890–1930* (1984), pp. 12–19, 23, 74–76, 80, 82, 85, 117–120.

WILLIAM F. SATER

Movement of National Unity
Movimiento de Unión Nacional—MUN

In late 1983 the Movement of National Unity was formed by traditional and younger-generation rightists who were critical of the military government's economic policies and of restrictions on political activity. Projecting itself as a civilian alternative capable of consolidating General Augusto PINOCHET's work, it signed the 1985 National Accord that called for a more rapid return to democratic rule. In 1987 the group joined with other right-wing movements to form the National Renovation Party (RN), which supported Pinochet in the 1988 plebiscite and campaigned on a pro-regime platform in the 1989 election. Although the MUN supported some early initiatives of the government of Patricio AYLWIN AZÓCAR, it subsequently opposed him and worked closely with the more stridently rightist Independent Democratic Movement (UDI).

A. CAVALLO et al., *La historia oculta del regimen militar* (Santiago, 1989); P. W. DRAKE and I. JAKSIC, eds., *The Struggle for Democracy in Chile, 1882–1990* (1991).

MICHAEL FLEET

Movement of the Revolutionary Left
Movimiento de la Izquierda Revolucionaria—MIR

The Movimiento de la Izquierda Revolucionaria is an extremist Marxist political organization founded in the 1960s largely by young, middle-class students who accused both the Socialist and the Communist parties of lacking sufficient revolutionary zeal. Influenced by Régis Debray and the Cuban experience, the MIR believed that the working class should eschew cooperation with the bourgeoisie and take power immediately. In 1969, just prior to the presidential elections, the MIR went underground and began a series of assaults and bank robberies to finance their activities. While refusing to participate in the political process, the MIR nonetheless supported Salvador Allende's 1970 candidacy for the presidency. Upon his election, members of the MIR organized illegal seizures of farmland called *tomas*, as well as organize urban centers of political support called *cordones industriales* (industrial zones), which they ran. Apparently, the organization also helped plan the abortive 1973 naval mutiny that immediately preceded the fall of Allende's government.

Although most of the MIR's leadership escaped the repression following the September 1973 coup, taking refuge in foreign embassies and ultimately leaving Chile under safe-conduct passes, some clandestinely reentered Chile to launch a series of urban assaults, assassinations, and attempts to create a guerrilla base in Chile's south. Operating from abroad, the MIR maintained close relations with various terrorist organizations, publishing a newsletter and in a few cases joining other groups such as the Argentine People's Revolutionary Army (ERP).

The Pinochet government that followed Allende's seemed to enjoy some success running to ground leaders of the MIR. Eventually, the group seemed to lose its enthusiasm for continuing the revolutionary struggle and was replaced in large part by the Communist-backed (Frente Patriótico) Manuel Rodríguez. Since the late 1980s, the MIR has faded from the public eye.

CARMELO FURCI, *The Chilean Communist Party and the Road to Socialism* (1984), pp. 98–100, 120, 124, 137–139, 150–152, 155, 157–162, 164, 166–167; WILLIAM F. SATER, *The Revolutionary Left and Terrorist Violence in Chile* (1986).

WILLIAM F. SATER

National Party
Montt–Varista Party

The National Party, a Chilean political organization which functioned between 1857 and 1932, was the creation and the vehicle of President Manuel MONTT and his protégé Antonio VARAS. Initially conservative, it was distinguished from other contemporary parties by its predilection for authoritarian methods—not all that unusual at the time—and an intense hostility toward the Roman Catholic church. In truth, the party owed its existence as much to a fight between Montt and his political opponents on both the Right and the Left as to a clash between the hierarchy and the Moneda, or administration, over the right of the civil government to assert jurisdiction over clerics. Still, the new organization became known as the National Party presumably because it sought to protect national interests from Chilean ultramontanes who wished to subordinate Santiago to the will of Rome.

Once in power, the Nationals, whose motto was "liberty within order," enjoyed only a brief place in the political sun. When it became clear that Montt could not impose Varas as his successor, the party began to lose its power. The Montt–Varistas lost their parliamentary majority in 1864, and a coalition including the Nationals proved unable to elect its candidate in the 1871 election. After President José Joaquín PÉREZ, the Nationals would not win the Moneda, although numerous Montt–Varistas held ministerial portfolios and the party supported the election of Aníbal PINTO and Domingo SANTA MARÍA GONZÁLEZ. The Nationals were among the last to abandon José Manuel BALMACEDA. Perhaps because of this fact, they suffered heavy losses in the 1894 parliamentary elections. The party, however, did enjoy a resurgence during the parliamentary period of the 1890s and saw its founder's son, Pedro Montt, become president in 1906. It also elected a total of sixteen deputies in 1909. After that date, however, the Nationals again began to lose ground slowly, though often backing winning candidates in ensuing presidential elections. In return for their support, the Nationals occupied, however briefly, various cabinet posts.

Fundamentally the brainchild of Manuel Montt, the Nationals initially lacked any clear ideology beyond a willingness to adhere to their founder's wishes. Once it lost control of the Moneda, the party, like many of those which no longer dominated the government, advocated reducing the powers of the chief executive, expanding individual liberties, and restricting the power of the church. While it was perhaps not politically unique, the National Party did provide a vehicle for the emerging Chilean middle class, particularly those involved in the civil service and later commerce as well as finance.

Insulted by the Chilean political system, the party continued to function even after its political rationale had ceased to exist. Moreover, the party began to fracture, thus accelerating its decline. After 1925 the National Party lost its appeal. Although in it participated in selecting the Thermal Congress (1930–1932), the National Party ceased to exist. In 1932 it joined with various Liberals and some long-time supporters of Balmaceda to form the United Liberal Party.

LUIS GALDAMES, *A History of Chile* (1941), pp. 294–298; GERMÁN URZÚA VALENZUELA, *Diccionario político institucional de Chile* (1979), pp. 103–104.

WILLIAM F. SATER

National Phalanx
Falange Nacional

The Falange Nacional, a Chilean political party, was the precursor of the Christian Democratic Party. Influenced by Christian Socialism, the Falange broke from the Conservative Party in 1938. It advocated domestic social and economic reforms, espousing a neutralist foreign policy which included supporting the refusal of Juan Antonio Ríos to declare war on the Axis powers and opposing Chile's alignment with the United States during the Cold War. The Falange continued to function during the 1940s, reaching its political high point in 1957, when it elected fourteen deputies and a senator. Consistent with its centrist tendencies, its members served as ministers in the government of Juan Antonio RÍOS, Alfredo Duhalde, and Gabriel GONZÁLEZ VIDELA. In 1957 the Falange merged with the Social Christian Conservative Party to form the Christian Democratic Party.

FEDERICO G. GIL, *The Political System of Chile* (1966), pp. 67, 71, 266; CÉSAR CAVIEDES L., *The Politics of Chile: A Sociogeographical Assessment* (1979), pp. 57–59.

WILLIAM F. SATER

Popular Action Unitary Movement
Movimiento de Acción Popular Unitaria—MAPU

MAPU was formed in 1969 by radical Christian Democrats unhappy with the slow pace of reform under the government of Eduardo FREI MONTALVA (1964–1970) and with their party's unwillingness to work with Marxists and other leftists in the construction of a socialist society. It joined the Popular Unity coalition that backed Salvador ALLENDE for president in 1970, and several of its members served in his cabinet. Some *mapucistas* wanted to create a distinctively Christian socialist party, and in 1971 they formed the Christian Left movement (IC) with other dissident Christian Democrats. Those who remained moved further left, embracing orthodox, and increasingly secular, Marxist-Leninist positions and either abandoning or setting aside their Christian faith.

During the next year, two wings emerged in MAPU: the more moderate (Gazmuri) wing, aligned with the Chilean Communist Party and committed to the development of a national political force, and the more radical (Garretón) wing, which favored the Socialist Party and stressed the development of social movements at the local level. A formal split occurred early in 1973, with the moderates forming MAPU Obrero-Campesino (MAPU—OC or MOC) and the radicals continuing to function as MAPU.

During the years of military rule, most *mapucistas* abandoned their radical Leninist positions. Those associated with the MOC, such as Manuel Antonio Garretón and José Antonio Viera-Gallo, were particularly influential in critical discussions of the Popular Unity experience and the future of Chilean socialism. They were active in promoting the reunification of the Socialist Party, with whose moderate Nuñez wing most were identified, and to which many of their erstwhile MAPU comrades were later attracted. A smaller number of *mapucistas*, most of whom were younger, Christian community activists, were active in the paramilitary MAPU-Lautaro, which carried out armed attacks against the military government.

RICARDO ISRAEL, *Allende's Chile* (1989); CARLOS BASCUNAN EDWARDS, *La izquierda sin Allende* (1990).

MICHAEL FLEET

Popular Action Front
Frente de Acción Popular—FRAP

A left-wing political alliance, the Popular Action Front was formed in 1956. The coalition was composed of Socialists, Popular Socialists, the Laborites, the People's Democratic and Democratic parties, as well as the outlawed Communists. The FRAP represented the first time that the Socialists and Communists, who were permitted to return to public life in 1958, formed a cohesive unit. FRAP's 1958 presidential candidate, Salvador ALLENDE GOSSENS, called for the empowerment of workers, nationalization of the country's basic industries and financial institutions, agrarian reform, and the adoption of a neutralist, if not overtly anti-American, foreign policy.

Though Allende lost to Jorge ALESSANDRI RODRÍGUEZ, the Conservative candidate, the FRAP's popularity increased. Because of changes in the electoral law, the coalition did well in predominantly agricultural districts. Thus the FRAP won 31 percent of the popular vote in the 1961 congressional contest, virtually doubling its seats in the Chamber of Deputies while increasing, by 50 percent, its power in the Senate; three years later FRAP won almost 40 percent of the vote.

In 1964, the FRAP again nominated Allende, who advocated extending suffrage, increasing social benefits, and calling for the state to take a more active role in developing the economy. Eduardo FREI MONTALVO, the Christian Democratic candidate, easily defeated Allende, who lost the heavily populated cities of Santiago and Valparaíso as well as the rural areas. Although the FRAP was dissolved in 1969, it constituted the first movement that successfully welded Chile's Marxist parties into a formidable political bloc.

FEDERICO G. GIL, *The Political System of Chile* (1966), pp. 204–205, 229–243, 276–277, 299–307; JAMES PETRAS, *Politics and Social Forces in Chilean Development* (1969), pp. 174–196, 209, 245–246, 262, 266–269, 276–283.

WILLIAM F. SATER

Popular Front
Frente Popular

The Popular Front was a political coalition of the Communist, Socialist, Democratic, Radical-Socialist, and Radical parties, as well as the Chilean Confederation of Workers, that ruled Chile from 1938 until 1941. Fearing the rise of Fascism and Nazism in Europe, the Communist International ordered its members to cooperate with democratic elements in order to achieve progressive programs. The Chilean Communist Party complied, forming an alliance, the Popular Front, with the Socialist Party and the more powerful Radicals. The front sought to strengthen democratic government as well as civil rights; institute reforms to redistribute the wealth, stimulate the economy, and foment national industries; and regulate working and living conditions as well as encourage education.

The Popular Front's slate of congressional candidates did so well that it agreed to run a candidate, Pedro AGUIRRE CERDA, a member of the Radical Party, for the presidency in 1938. A surprise victor, Aguirre Cerda won the presidency by a scant nine thousand votes, and the Popular Front ruled Chile until infighting between the Communists and Socialists, in part precipitated by Stalin's signing of a nonaggression pact with Hitler, destroyed the fragile coalition.

During its brief tenure, the Popular Front passed legislation favoring unionization, increased social benefits for the nation's needy, and called for increased government intervention in Chile's economic development.

JOHN R. STEVENSON, *The Chilean Popular Front* (1942); RICHARD SUPER, "The Chilean Popular Front Presidency of Pedro Aguirre Cerda, 1938–1941," (Ph.D. diss., Arizona State University, 1975).

WILLIAM F. SATER

Popular Unity
Unidad Popular—UP

The Popular Unity Chilean political coalition ruled Chile from 1970 to 1973. The successor to Popular Action Front (FRAP), the Unidad Popular was founded in 1969. Initially it consisted of Marxist and progressive parties—the Socialists, the Communists, the Social Democrats, the Movimiento de Acción Popular Unida (MAPU), Acción Popular Independiente (AP), and the Radicals—but later it added the Izquierda Cristiana, while losing some elements of the Radical Party. The Popular Unity party provided ministerial portfolios to its members, but the Socialists and Communists dominated the coalition.

Calling for radical economic change—nationalization of the mines, a neutralist foreign policy, an accelerated program of agrarian reform, state control of the banks and insurance companies and major means of production—the party nominated Salvador ALLENDE as its candidate in the 1970 presidential election. Given its eclectic composition, the UP suffered from internal schisms, with the Communists favoring consolidation of its gains and the Socialists demanding yet more radical change. The extreme Left often refused to cooperate with the government and adopted various policies, such as sponsoring illegal seizures of land and factories, assassinating Edmundo Pérez Zujovic, pushing for an ideological education program, and attempting to politicize the military, that alienated elements who might have been willing to support the Allende government. Moreover, establishing a quota system that accorded each UP faction a share of the government's appointments based upon a party's importance within the coalition handicapped the Unidad Popular's performance. Riven by internal disputes and under increasing pressure, the Unidad Popular government succumbed to a coup in 1973.

ARTURO VALENZUELA, *The Breakdown of Democratic Regimes, Chile* (1978), pp. 64–68, 83, 89, 109, 123; JULIO FAÚNDEZ, *Marxism and Democracy in Chile* (1988), pp. 154, 159, 170–171, 174, 176, 191–194, 199–200, 203–204, 221–223.

WILLIAM F. SATER

Radical Party
Partido Radical

The Radical Party began in the early 1850s, influenced by European ideas as well as those of the radical Francisco BILBAO, when various members of the Liberal Party objected to cooperating with the Conservative Party. In 1857 these men, many of whom were identified with the newly emerging mining elites, split from the Liberals to form the Radical Party. Their commitment to a secular state and, more significantly, their opposition to an authoritarian central government attracted the attention of the Manuel MONTT government, which exiled many of the new party's leaders. Within ten years, the Radicals had elected members to the Congress. After 1875 they served in the cabinets of Federico ERRÁZURIZ ZAÑARTU, Aníbal PINTO, and Domingo SANTA MARÍA GONZÁLEZ. The Radicals joined the anti-Balmaceda forces during the 1891 Revolution.

The party did not hold its first convention until 1888, when it called for municipal autonomy; the separation of church and state; an expansion of individual liberties; state support for a free, obligatory secular education; and improved conditions for workers and women. In 1906, at its third convention, the Radical Party confronted the issue of growing social and economic inequality. Valentín LETELIER MADARIAGA advocated that the party adopt a program calling for state-sponsored social reforms to end the nation's endemic poverty. His main opposition came from Enrique MAC-IVER RODRÍGUEZ, who argued that a lack of moral fiber, not economic deprivation, was what was causing Chile's social problems. Letelier carried the day, and, henceforth, the Radical Party sponsored various pieces of social legislation.

From 1912 to 1921 the Radicals doubled their number of seats in the legislative branch, but electoral fraud prevented them from winning the presidency. Over the years, the party's composition changed as the urban middle class, professionals, and the bureaucracy joined its ranks. Rhetorically, it seemed to become more left wing as it competed with the Democratic Party for votes. In fact, this political change was more cosmetic than real.

In 1931, either in response to the economic dislocations of the Great Depression or to undercut the increasing popularity of the leftist parties, the Radical Party denounced capitalism, advocating instead a collectivization of the means of production. Despite this switch, the Radicals did not get a chance to direct the nation until the Popular Front's 1938 triumph brought Pedro AGUIRRE CERDA to power. Aguirre Cerda did institute certain social programs and create basic industries, but, fearing political retaliation, he refused to deal with the more vexing issue of agrarian reform. His Radical successors, Juan Antonio RÍOS MORALES and Gabriel GONZÁLEZ VIDELA, seemed incapable of successfully instituting political and economic reforms or ending a crippling inflation. By 1958, when it had become clear that the Radicals were more interested in preserving their political position than in instituting significant change, the public became disenchanted with the party, and by 1963 the Christian Democrats were outpolling them. Anxious to retain some share of power, the Radicals became the handmaiden of the Unidad Popular (UP). This opportunistic policy proved disastrous. The party began to suffer defections, with many people bolting to join the anti-UP forces. By 1971, many of the party's most senior leaders had quit to form a new party, the Radical Left Party. In the 1973 congressional elections the Radicals won a paltry 3.7 percent of the popular vote. The Radical Party had become a shadow of its once-powerful self.

PETER G. SNOW, *The Radical Parties of Chile and Argentina* (1963); SERGIO GUILISASTI, *Partidos políticos chilenos* (1964), pp. 129–197; FEDERICO G. GIL, *The Political System of Chile* (1966), pp. 42–43, 67–69, 231–243, 257–266, 308–309; LUIS PALMA, *Historia del Partido Radical* (1967); KAREN L. REMMER, *Party Competition in Argentina and Chile: Political Recruitment and Public Policy, 1890–1930* (1984), pp. 14–17, 63–67, 85–86, 118–120.

WILLIAM F. SATER

Socialist Party
Partido Socialista

A conglomeration of various Marxist groups—the Nueva Acción Pública, the Acción Revolucionaria Socialista, the Partido Socialista Marxista, the Orden Socialista, and the Partido Socialista Unificado—became the Socialist Party on 19 April 1933. Created to fill a political vacuum caused by the collapse of the Carlos IBÁÑEZ government and the failure of the SOCIALIST REPUBLIC OF 100 DAYS, the party endured repression at the hands of the Arturo ALESSANDRI PALMA government, which exiled many of its leaders, including Marmaduke GROVE VALLEJO. The Socialists created a special niche for themselves: they favored the class struggle and the dictatorship of the proletariat, and opposed capitalism and imperialism, particularly that of the United States. But while ideologically akin to the Communists, they refused to accept the domination of Moscow.

Initially acting alone, the Socialists urged an alliance

with other left-wing parties to form the Bloque de Izquierda in 1935. Two years later, the Communists joined the Socialists and other elements, including the Radical Party, to establish the Popular Front. Although they held various ministerial portfolios in the AGUIRRE CERDA government, some dissidents accused the party's leaders of betraying Socialist principles by supporting the reformist, but hardly revolutionary, Aguirre Cerda government.

This dispute, which led to the creation of the Socialist Workers Party (Partido Socialista de Trabajadores), constituted the first of many splits which shattered the party's cohesion. Grove later led another splinter group out of the Socialist fold and into the Partido Socialista Auténtico when radicals criticized his support of the Ríos regime. Given the party's eclectic composition, it is not surprising that schisms appeared. By 1946 the Socialists had formed three parties, and not surprisingly, their collective fortunes declined in the elections. Two years later, the party coalesced into just two factions: the Partido Socialista de Chile and the Partido Socialista Popular.

The Partido Socialista Popular unexpectedly supported the candidacy of Carlos Ibáñez, a former dictator associated with conservative policies. Although the party attempted to rationalize this policy, its decision represented an attempt to jump on the Ibáñez bandwagon in order to win back some of its former supporters. This opportunistic policy bore fruit when the party won certain ministerial posts and increased its congressional representation. But when Ibáñez's policies began to misfire, the Socialist faction withdrew its support. In 1957 the Socialists managed to reconcile their two factions. Earlier, in 1956, the Socialists had joined the Communists to create the Popular Action Front (FRAP), which would nominate Salvador ALLENDE as its presidential candidate in 1958 and 1964. They also participated in the 1970 Popular Unity government.

The largely working-class Socialists sought to establish a broad-based authoritarian government to reorder drastically the nation's economic, social, and political priorities. Unlike the Communists, the Socialists believed that Chile's own experience should shape the revolutionary process. The Socialists became more vociferous during the Allende period, advocating armed revolution, seeking the abolition of the bourgeois state, and refusing to compromise with the Christian Democrats. Many believe that Socialist intransigence prevented Allende from compromising on certain essential issues, thus hastening the collapse of his government.

Since 1973, the party has split into various factions, including one led by Ricardo LAGOS, which appeared willing to compromise with non-Marxists, and another under the control of the more radical Clodomiro Almeyda Medina, which was not. Despite these differences, the Socialists cooperated with the anti-Pinochet forces, helping to elect Patricio AYLWIN in 1989 and electing representatives to both houses of Congress.

JULIO CÉSAR JOBET BURQUEZ, *El socialismo chileno a través de sus congresos* (1965) and *El partido socialista de Chile,* 2 vols. (1971); MIRIAM R. HOCHWALD, ''Imagery in Politics: A Study of the Ideology of the Chilean Socialist Party'' (Ph.D. diss., UCLA, 1971); PAUL W. DRAKE, *Socialism and Populism in Chile, 1932–52* (1978); BENNY POLLACK and HERNÁN ROSENKRANZ, *Revolutionary Social Democracy—The Chilean Socialist Party* (1986).

WILLIAM F. SATER

CHILE: REVOLUTIONS

Revolutions of 1851 and 1859

Two political upheavals during the Manuel MONTT regime both cost Chile dearly in treasure and blood. Each had its roots in deep-seated economic causes and, in some cases, conflicting ideologies. Fundamentally, a loathing of Montt and the system he represented drove two politically and geographically disparate elements into rebellion.

THE REVOLUTION OF 1851
Manuel Montt, best described as the law personified, came to power in 1851, threatening to perpetuate a highly centralized government that would limit the opposition parties' access to the political system. As a result, even before Montt took office a rebellion erupted in two areas: LA SERENA, in the nation's north, and CONCEPCIÓN, Chile's third most important city.

The northern rebellion was spearheaded by mainly middle-class liberal intellectuals, many of whom were members of the Society of Equality (a reform group influenced by European liberalism), but it was supported by various lower-class elements as well. The 1851 insurgency, which began on 7 September, was organized by José Miguel Carrera's son, José Miguel Carrera Fontecilla, who became the provincial intendant. CARRERA organized a militia, which eventually numbered about 1,000 men to defend the fledgling revolution.

While successfully occupying various cities, the northerners committed a crucial mistake in seizing a British ship, the *Fire Fly,* which was anchored in Coquimbo. The administration in the Moneda requested and received naval assistance from the British, who blockaded the port. Meanwhile, Montt ordered his troops to attack the insurgents, who were advancing toward the Central Valley and Santiago, where they hoped to link up with southern rebels. These elements, however, proved unequal to the regular troops, who destroyed the insurgent army of approximately 2,000 men at the battle of Petorca in October 1851.

Suffering heavy casualties, the rebels withdrew to La Serena, where, reinforced by the arrival of numerous miners, they prepared for a siege. The government troops first had to quash an abortive uprising in Coquimbo, but having wiped out this pocket of insurgents, they joined the units that had vanquished the rebels at Petorca to attack La Serena.

Surprisingly, the inexperienced rebels repelled three infantry assaults. When it became clear that the insurgents could not survive, their leaders offered to capitulate, but the popular elements refused. Unfortunately, discipline among the rebels collapsed, leading to widespread looting and allowing the regular army to capture the city. The last rebel units, led by Bernardino Barahona, a miner from Huasco, held out until routed by the troops of Victorino Garrido at the battle of Linderos on 8 January 1852.

The southern rebels, who began their uprising on 13 September, seemed the ideological opposites of their northern brethren. This insurgency was fundamentally rooted in a colonial-era rivalry between Concepción and Santiago. The old landholding elites rallied to the cause of General José María de la Cruz, a dissatisfied officer who had been relieved of both his command and the post of intendant of Concepción. After raising an army of 4,000, de la Cruz planned to attack the loyalist army under General Manuel BULNES. Unfortunately for him, however, various units which had promised to support the rebellion either could not join his troops or changed their minds about siding with the insurgents.

Bulnes created a 3,000-man army composed of militia and regular units. Outnumbered and running low on ammunition, he had to retreat. On 8 December 1851, he decided to make his stand near the banks of the Loncomilla River. De la Cruz, who early in the battle had foolishly lost his cavalry, could not repel Bulnes's infantry, which, after outflanking the rebel commander, attacked his rear. Under deadly fire, de la Cruz had to withdraw while Bulnes kindly ceased fire in order to spare the lives of his opponents. De la Cruz managed to escape but was cornered by Bulnes on the banks of the Purapel River, where, on 14 December 1851, he capitulated.

While the extreme north and the south constituted the main thrusts of the 1851 rebellion, an uprising also occurred in VALPARAÍSO. The fall of this city could have proven fatal for the central government, since it would have prevented the Bulnes administration from reinforcing its garrisons. Fortunately for President Montt, the local intendant, Admiral Manuel BLANCO ENCALADA, drove the rebels from their positions.

Inspired by the activities in the central part of Chile, some officers under the leadership of José Miguel Cambiazo rebelled on 21 November, supporting de la Cruz's candidacy for the presidency. Cambiazo evacuated the city and set sail for Europe, using a captured merchant vessel. The crew managed to seize the rebel ship, turning the leaders over to the authorities, who tried and executed them.

THE REVOLUTION OF 1859

The agreements ending the 1851 Revolution should be seen as more an armistice than a definitive solution. Many of the forces that precipitated the earlier upheaval caused the second: a political system that purported to represent if not the will of the people then at least that of the oligarchy, but which existed merely so that Manuel Montt could continue to rule. Thus, many of the same Liberals who had rebelled in 1851 did so again eight years later. Curiously, the Conservatives also joined the anti-Montt forces. Since they no longer controlled the government, they refused to allow the secular National Party to enjoy the same unlimited power it had once wielded. The Conservative Senate tried to hamstring Montt by refusing to ratify his budget unless he would shuffle his cabinet. Although he agreed to do so, thus opening the door to an incipient parliamentary system, the Liberals demanded more. These elements published a journal called *La asamblea constituyente*, which sought to revamp the 1833 Consitution. When the supporters of this drive met, government forces arrested them and later exiled them, declaring a state of siege. Aware that the opposition could not legally obtain power, the anti-Montt forces rebelled.

As before, the focus of the revolt was the mining north, Copiapó. Pedro León GALLO, who had become rich mining silver in Chañarcillo, organized a coup and seized the city on 5 January 1859. The rebel chieftain formed a 1,500-man army with which he hoped to capture Santiago.

The rebels had planned for uprisings to follow in Valparaíso, Concepción, Talca, and San Felipe. Unfortunately for their cause, those outbreaks that did erupt lacked the intensity of those of the northern insurgents. Most of the rebel groups consisted of small bands, some under the protection of local landed barons who disliked the Montt government for a variety of reasons. These units sought to harass the central government and to cut its lines of communication with the Concepción region. Rebel bands also captured the towns of Talca and San Felipe, while their compatriots organized guerrilla bands in the south.

In the 1859 Revolution the army, unlike that of 1851, remained loyal to the central government. De la Cruz, who had been asked to lead the rebellion, refused. First blood went to the rebels, who, on 14 March 1859, defeated the regular troops at Los Loros. An outraged Montt then raised another army under Juan Vidaurre, the same general who had put down the 1851 rebellion.

Vidaurre, at the head of a substantial expeditionary force, sailed north from Valparaíso, landed at Tongoy, and marched overland, with the cavalry in tow, to Cerro Grande, where Gallo's forces had taken up positions defending La Serena. Vidaurre's troops, enjoying naval support from the *Esmeralda,* attacked Gallo's men, half of whom had no weapons. On 29 April the regular troops easily vanquished the rebels, who took flight, occupying La Serena the next day.

While Vidaurre was mounting his northern campaign, the rest of the regular army was eradicating pockets of rebel resistance, including Valparaíso, in the Central Valley. Most of these cities surrendered, although it took twenty-two days before Talca capitulated. Various rebel leaders, including José Miguel Carrera, organized guerrilla bands in the south. One of these units, composed in part of Araucanian Indians and numbering more than 2,000 men, attacked Chillán. Although Montt's army vanquished the rebels, peace was not restored to the south until mid-April. The rebels' final stand occurred on 18 September 1859, when an armed band attacked Valparaíso. Vidaurre, who had been appointed intendant of the province, successfully organized a bayonet charge, which ended the rebellion. Ironically, Vidaurre died in this skirmish, shot during this afterthought of the 1859 Revolution.

BENJAMÍN VICUÑA MACKENNA, *Historia de la jornada del 20 de abril de 1851* (1878); PEDRO PABLO FIGUEROA, *Historia de la Revolución Constituyente* (1889); LUIS GALDAMES, *A History of Chile* (1941), pp. 288, 298–299; DANIEL RIQUELME, *La revolución de 20 de abril de 1851* (1966); LUIS VITALE, *Interpretación marxista de la historia de Chile* (1969), pp. 223–287, and *Las guerras civiles de 1851 y 1859 en Chile* (1971); *Historia del ejército de Chile* (1981), vol. 4, pp. 67–158; MAURICE ZEITLIN, *The Civil Wars in Chile* (1984).

WILLIAM F. SATER

Revolution of 1891

In 1891 a seminal civil war dramatically altered the nature of Chilean political life. José Manuel BALMACEDA, who became chief executive in 1886, tried to rule in an authoritarian manner. Times had changed, however. The legislature now demanded to participate in the decision-making process, particularly to dispense political patronage, and it resented Balmaceda's attempt to select his successor. After months of bickering, the two sides collided when the Congress refused to approve Balmaceda's budget for 1891 until he reshuffled his cabinet. The president responded by unilaterally declaring that he would simply use the authorization for the 1890 budget for 1891. At this, a faction of the legislature, the congressionalists, rebelled. Having won the support of the navy, they sailed for the north and eventually established their seat of government in the nitrate port of Iquique.

The capture of Iquique provided the insurgents with crucial economic support with which to finance the rebellion. Their control of the fleet ensured that the army, most of which had remained loyal to Balmaceda, could not attack the rebel stronghold. His lack of a fleet—Balmaceda's forces consisted of but two torpedo boats and a converted transport—gave the congressionalists the time to raise and equip an army.

In addition to the navy, Balmaceda's foes enjoyed certain other key advantages: they possessed unlimited funds to purchase arms and, thanks to the defections of various high-ranking army officers, including that of a German-born military adviser, Emil KÖRNER, excellent leaders. Finally, the Balmaceda government's clumsy crushing of a nitrate strike so alienated the miners that they flocked to join the congressionalist army at the outbreak of the revolution.

In mid-August, the rebel forces under Körner's direction, landed north of VALPARAÍSO and moved inland toward the vital port. Better equipped—the insurgents had the more rapid-firing Mannlicher rifles—and better led, the congressionalist forces defeated Balmaceda's army first at the battle of Concón on 21 August 1891, then at Placilla a week later. The loyalist army suffered enormous casualties, including the loss of their generals, whose bodies were mutilated after they were brutally murdered. Valparaíso, though not a battle site, nonetheless suffered substantial property damage and loss of life when the congressionalist victory turned into an opportunity for looting and vengeance.

Fearful that the capital would suffer a similar fate, the Balmaceda government declared Santiago an open city and turned its administration over to the hero of the WAR OF THE PACIFIC, General Manuel BAQUEDANO. Despite his sometimes desultory efforts to preserve order, the homes of various Balmaceda supporters were looted. Balmaceda himself took refuge in the Argentine embassy, where he remained until 19 September 1891, the day after his term of office had legally ended. Then the former president committed suicide.

The 1891 Revolution marked the culmination of a movement begun decades before to limit the power of the presidency. Until 1924 it would be the Congress, not the chief executive, that ruled Chile.

MAURICE HERVEY, *Dark Days in Chile* (1891); JAMES H. SEARS and B. W. WELLS, JR., *The Chilean Revolution of 1891* (1893); JULIO BAÑADOS E., *Balmaceda, su gobierno y la revolución de 1891*, 2 vols. (1894); HAROLD BLAKEMORE, "The Chilean Revolution of 1891 and Its Historiography," in *Hispanic American Historical Review* 44, 3 (1965): 393–421; and *British Nitrates and Chilean Politics, 1886–1896: Balmaceda and North* (1974).

WILLIAM F. SATER

CHILE: SOCIALIST REPUBLIC OF 100 DAYS, a radical political regime which ruled Chile from 4 June 1932 to 13 September of that year. Juan Esteban MONTERO, elected president in late 1931, could not revive Chile's Depression-devastated economy. In June 1932, the Chilean Air Force, under the command of Marmaduke GROVE, rebelled, forced Montero from power, and established the Socialist Republic. In truth, this "republic" was a series of juntas which had seized power illegally and hence ruled without the consent of the nation.

The first junta consisted of General Arturo Puga, Socialist politician Eugenio Matte, and former ambassador to the United States Carlos DÁVILA. This junta dissolved the Congress Carlos IBÁÑEZ had appointed, declared a moratorium on the collection of all debts, and returned all goods held in pawn at the government-owned Banco de Crédito Popular. On 16 June, Dávila forced Matte from power, exiling him with Grove to Easter Island.

The second junta, firmly under Dávila's control, while less socialist than its predecessor, nonetheless passed various laws giving the state more power to intervene in the economic process, including the right to establish prices and to seize and operate any private business. Eventually, in July, Dávila seized power for himself, only to be deposed in September by General Bartolomé Blanche, who, although tempted to remain in power, held elections which restored democracy to Chile and put Arturo ALESSANDRI back into the presidency.

The Socialist Republic did accomplish some things. For one, it led to the creation of the Socialist Party, which would emerge as one of the nation's most powerful political blocs. It also enacted some laws which, while not sanctioned by a popularly elected congress, allowed the ALLENDE administration (1970–1973) to attempt to seize control of Chile's industrial sector.

PAUL W. DRAKE, *Socialism and Populism in Chile: The Origins of the Leftward Movement of the Chilean Electorate, 1932–52* (1971), pp. 71–83, 91, 94, 96, 149–152; MANUEL DINAMARCA, *La república socialista chilena: Orígenes legítimos del partido socialista* (1987), pp. 159–218.

WILLIAM F. SATER

See also **Chile: Political Parties.**

CHILE: WAR WITH SPAIN, a late-nineteenth-century conflict between Chile and Peru and Spain. In the early 1860s, Spain seized Peru's Chincha Islands, which, by virtue of their enormous deposits of GUANO, constituted the mainstay of Lima's economy. When Peru called upon its hemispheric neighbors for support, Chile responded by forbidding Chileans from selling the Spanish fleet fuel or supplies and by joining an inter-American conference to stop Spanish aggression. Madrid turned on Chile for permitting its citizens to make what it considered scurrilous remarks about the Spanish queen and for placing an embargo on Spanish ships. As compensation for the insults, Spain demanded that Chile pay a large indemnity as well as fire a twenty-one-gun salute to the Spanish flag. When the Chileans refused, Spain instituted a naval blockade. The government in Santiago responded by declaring war on 24 September 1865.

During the conflict, which was essentially a naval contest, the larger Spanish flotilla quickly asserted control of Chile's coast, blockading VALPARAÍSO. After suffering some minor losses, the Spanish fleet warned the Chileans that unless they paid damages and fired a twenty-one-gun salute, its fleet would fire on the port. Although nearby American and British fleets could have protected Valparaíso from the Spanish, they elected not to do so.

On 31 March 1866, the Spanish ships opened fire on a virtually defenseless Valparaíso, inflicting substantial damage. The Spanish fleet remained in the area until mid-April, when it sailed for Callao, where it subsequently suffered a major defeat at the hands of Peruvian coastal batteries.

Because the United States chose not to invoke its MONROE DOCTRINE to protect Chile from a European aggressor, relations between Santiago and Washington

suffered. The war with Spain also demonstrated to the Chileans their need both to fortify its principal ports and to acquire a fleet to defend its frontiers.

LUIS GALDAMES, *A History of Chile* (1941), pp. 306–310; W. C. DAVIS, *The Last Conquistadores: The Spanish Intervention in Peru and Chile, 1863–1866* (1950).

WILLIAM F. SATER

CHILES (or, in English, chilies), hot peppers that are indigenous to the New World and are one of the significant food contributions to the world following the Columbian period. Members of the *Capsicum* genus number over two hundred, with over one hundred Mexican species. Chiles vary in shape, size (from the huge *chile de agua* to the half-inch-long *pequín*), and color (common green and red to unusual black, yellow, and white). They are used fresh, dried, pickled, and smoked in various CUISINES, especially in Mexican cooking.

Known for their spicy character, each variety has a distinctive taste and piquancy, from mild to hot. Chile aficionados rely on Scoville units, devised by Wilbur L. Scoville, to measure the hotness of the capsaicin (an enzyme) contained in the peppers. The scale ranges from the hottest, rating 10 (100,000 to 300,000 Scoville units), of the *habanero* (from Yucatán) and Scotch bonnet (from Jamaica), to the mildest, rating 0 (0 Scoville units) of bell, pimiento, and sweet banana peppers. The well-known *jalapeño* has a 5 ranking (2,500–5,000 Scoville units).

Besides their use as a spice, chiles have also been an essential ingredient in numerous folk remedies of the Americas. Medical science today acknowledges that chiles are higher in vitamin A than carrots and higher in vitamin C than most citrus fruits. Chiles are used as a decongestant and expectorant, and as an aid in weight loss and pain relief. Promising experiments are under way by arthritis and rheumatism researchers using capsaicin in lotions that reduce pain and inflammation in joints. Other capsaicin creams have been successfully used to treat severe itching that affects many patients who undergo kidney dialysis.

The most widespread use of chiles is in the production of *salsa*, or hot sauce, which has become so popular in the United States that it has surpassed the rather bland catsup in consumer purchases.

DIANA KENNEDY, *The Cuisines of Mexico* (1972); JANET LONG-SOLÍS, *Capsicum y cultura: La historia del chilli* (1986); *Dallas Morning News*, 7 December 1992, sec. C, pp. 3–4, and 9 June 1993, sec. F, pp. 2, 4.

WILLIAM H. BEEZLEY

CHILOÉ, province of 112,430 inhabitants encompassing several islands in southern Chile. On the largest of them the Spaniards established several fortified settlements (Castro, Ancud, Curaco de Vélez) to protect the southern flank of the Viceroyalty of Peru from English and Dutch corsairs sailing into the Pacific after crossing the Strait of Magellan or Cape Horn. With strong attachments to Spain, Chiloé was Chile's loyalist stronghold during the WARS OF INDEPENDENCE. Today the area is extremely depressed: young people leave for Argentine PATAGONIA or the Chilean province of MAGALLANES.

RENATO CÁRDENAS, *Apuntes para un diccionario de Chiloé* (Castro, 1978); and PHILIPPE GRENIER, *Chiloé et les chilotes* (Aix-en-Provence, 1984).

CÉSAR N. CAVIEDES

CHILPANCINGO, CONGRESS OF, Mexico's first political assembly. The need for military and political organization prompted the principal leaders of the insurgents, particularly Ignacio RAYÓN (1773–1832) and José María MORELOS Y PAVÓN (1765–1815), to form a governing junta. Their first effort, the *Junta de Zitácuaro*, proved unsuccessful. The divisions among its members convinced Morelos to accept Carlos María de BUSTAMANTE's (1774–1848) proposal to convene a Congress, the Supremo Congreso Nacional Americano, with representatives from the provinces, at Chilpancingo in September 1813. Because elections could not be completed in all provinces, only two deputies, José Manuel de Herrera (c. 1776–1831) and José María Murguía y Galardi, were elected. Morelos named three other proprietary deputies, López Rayón, José María Liceaga (c. 1780–1818), and José Sixto Verduzco, and three substitutes, Bustamante, José María COS Y PÉREZ (d. 1819) and Andrés QUINTANA ROO (1787–1851). The *Reglamento* (the regulations) for its organization was issued on 11 September, and Morelos's views on government, the *Sentimientos de la Nación*, were read at its inauguration on 14 September. Once installed, Congress selected Morelos for the executive and determined how the judiciary should be established. On 6 November the Congress issued its *Acta solemne de la declaración de independencia*, the declaration of national independence.

The establishment of the Congress, however, did not resolve the divisions among the insurgents, and the conflicts between the military leaders and the lawyers resulted in a decline of the movement. Pursued by the royalists, Congress wandered in search of safety. It increased its number of deputies early in 1814, but functioned in an irregular manner. In October 1814 it issued the APATZINGÁN constitution, the *Decreto constitucional para la libertad de la América mexicana*. After Morelos was captured by the royalists (November 1815), Manuel MIER Y TERÁN (1789–1832) dissolved Congress in Tehuacán on 15 December 1815.

ERNESTO LEMOINE, "Zitácuaro, Chilpancingo y Apatzingán. Tres grandes momentos de la insurgencia mexicana," in *Boletín del Archivo General de la Nación*, 2d series, vol. 4, no. 3 (1963); ERNESTO LEMOINE, ed., *Manuscrito Cárdenas, Documentos del Congreso de Chilpancingo hallados entre los papeles del caudillo José*

María Morelos, sorprendido por los realistas en la acción de Tlacotepec el 24 de febrero de 1814 (1980); VIRGINIA GUEDEA, "Los procesos electorales insurgentes," *Estudios de Historia Novohispana* 11 (1991): 201–249.

VIRGINIA GUEDEA

CHIMALPAHIN (*b.* 26 May 1579; *d.* 1660), premier writer of NAHUATL prose. Don Domingo Francisco de San Antón Muñón Chimalpahin Quauhtlehuanitzin, who was born in Amecameca, Mexico, and was most active in the first two decades of the seventeenth century, produced a mass of historical writings on indigenous Mexico. Although he never lost his close identification with his homeland, his career unfolded in Mexico City. Chimalpahin wrote copiously about both Chalco and Mexico TENOCHTITLÁN, covering both pre-conquest and post-conquest periods. His annals represent a large range of Nahuatl thought and expression.

SUSAN SCHROEDER, *Chimalpahin and the Kingdoms of Chalco* (1991).

JAMES LOCKHART

CHIMÚ, Between A.D. 900 and 1460 the north coast of Peru was dominated by an empire controlled by an ethnic group called the Chimú. This empire, called by the Spanish "the Kingdom of Chimor," controlled at its maximum extent more than 620 miles of the Peruvian coast. The Chimú Empire is the only pre-Columbian Peruvian state other than the INCAS for which there exists ethnohistoric information. The Incas had conquered the Chimú between 1460 and 1470, only sixty to seventy years before the European invasion. As a result, Spanish chroniclers were able to record a limited amount of information about the Chimú culture as it existed before the Inca conquest. Unfortunately, only a few fragments of this information from the chronicles have survived. These bits of information, together with Spanish legal documents of the early colonial period and recent archaeological studies, have shed some light on the Chimú culture.

Chimú origin stories collected as oral histories by the Spaniards name Taycanamu as the legendary founder of the first Chimú dynasty. He is said to have arrived in the Moche valley after having traveled by sea on a balsa raft. Saying he was sent by a great lord across the sea to govern this land, he established a settlement in the lower valley. The son and the grandson of Taycanamu, whose names were Guacricaur and Ñançenpinco, established control over the entire valley. Archaeological and ethnohistoric data suggest that the Chimú then began a two-phase expansion.

Ñançenpinco, having completed the conquest of the Moche valley, began the first phase of imperial expansion around 1350. His conquests extended to the Jequetepeque valley in the north and the Santa valley in the south. Following a series of unnamed successors,

Ceremonial Chimú knife. Peru, ca. 1100–1300. Peru Museum, Lima. PHOTO BY GUILLERMO DE ORBEGOSO.

the seventh or eighth king, Minchancaman, continued a second phase of imperial expansion. Completed by about 1450, the second expansion brought the empire to its maximum extent, from the Chillón valley in the south to Tumbes in the north. Shortly thereafter, the Chimú fell to the invading Inca armies. By 1470 the Inca had conquered Chimor and carried off Minchancaman (whom the Incas called Chimú Capac) to Cuzco as a royal hostage.

The economy of the Chimú Empire was based primarily on AGRICULTURE, but fishing and shellfish gathering were also important. Highly complex irrigation systems were used to bring water to the vast number of fields in the Chimú domain. These enormous networks of canals were the largest ever created in ancient Peru. The construction and maintenance of the canals and the proper distribution of water required an extensive administrative bureaucracy. Archaeological studies have identified a hierarchy of provincial administrative centers throughout the empire that provided state control over production. These centers carried out the will of the emperor, who governed from the imperial capital at CHAN CHAN. State construction projects such as canals, roads, and cities, and staffing of the imperial army, were

accomplished by the citizens of the empire paying their taxes in labor.

Chimú society was a rigid hierarchy of social classes. The most powerful class, the hereditary nobility, exercised complete control over the production, storage, and redistribution of the wealth of the state. Luxury goods seem to have been concentrated in the hands of the elite. Class distinction was so absolute that kings were held to be divine. Kings and nobles were believed to have had a separate origin from that of commoners. Beyond the distinction between nobles and commoners, people were ranked by their occupation. In a society with an economy based on complex hydraulic works, people having technical knowledge were especially valued. Artisans, working for the elite, had special status and special privileges: they could wear ear spools and live next to the nobility.

Ethnohistoric accounts give some insight into the Chimú legal system. Society was regulated by strict laws with severe punishments for offenders. Chimú society seems to have been especially concerned about theft, which may have been regarded as an offense against the gods as well as against humans. Although artistic expression was standardized in terms of the motifs used, the Chimú were superb artisans and craftsmen. They particularly excelled in the arts of weaving and metalwork. Chimú goldsmiths were carried off to work for the Incas, and much of the golden treasure captured from the Inca by the Spanish was of Chimú origin.

The classic source of the Chimú is JOHN H. ROWE, "The Kingdom of Chimor," *Acta Americana* 6 (1948): 26–59. See also MICHAEL MOSELEY and KENT C. DAY, eds., *Chan Chan: Andean Desert City* (1982); and MICHAEL MOSELEY and ALANA CORDY-COLLINS, *The Northern Dynasties: Kingship and Statecraft in Chimor* (1990).

GORDON F. McEWAN

See also **Archaeology.**

CHINA POBLANA, a style of dress worn by Mexican women in Puebla from the sixteenth through the late nineteenth century. The word *china* has little to do with China. *China poblana* was originally the name given to domestic servants but also was used to refer to a pulque seller, a woman who wrapped cigars, a laundress, or a prostitute. A *china poblana* was distinguished by her ornate style of dress, which was distinct from indigenous and European upper-class modes. Her skirt of colorful, sturdy wool was dotted with sequins of gold and silver. Cinched at the waist and very wide at the bottom, it covered billowing petticoats and was complemented by ribbons, silk stockings, and satin slippers. Her finely embroidered blouse was immaculately white. She wrapped a rebozo around her arms and coiffed her abundant hair in thick braids, interwoven with colored ribbons and gathered on the top of her head by a fine comb. She completed her costume with long gold earrings and fine bracelets. She did not merely walk. She sauntered with elegance and arrogance along the streets.

During the Wars of the Reform, the *china poblana* became a national symbol, accompanying her husband into battles and adorning her costume with tricolor ribbons. Although her dress fell into disuse in Puebla in the 1880s, it has preoccupied writers and poets as material for legend and folkloric color since the colonial period. Stylizations of the dress are still used in festivals, especially in central Mexico. The tricolor skirt with an eagle embroidered in sequins is one of the best-known versions.

R. CARRASCO PUENTE, *Bibliografía de Catarina de San Juan y de la china poblana* (1950); FRANCISCO J. SANTAMARÍA, *Diccionario de Mejicanismos* (1959); ENRIQUE CORDERO Y TORRES, *Historia compendiada del estado de Puebla*, vol. 2 (1965).

MARY KAY VAUGHAN

CHINAMPAS, a term from the Nahuatl *chinámitl* that refers to an indigenous method of agriculture used to promote the high yields required to support a dense population. By extending strips of land (*chinampas*) into the shallow lakes and wetlands of Mesoamerica, the farmers have the benefit of year-round irrigation. Best known in the Basin of Mexico and dating there from as early as 1100, *chinampas* are still extant in, for example, XOCHIMILCO. Some sources employ the Spanish term *camellones* as a synonym for *chinampas*. Recent archaeological and historical research may be broadening the temporal and spatial framework for this type of agriculture, pointing to the importance of "raised fields" as a means of sustaining state formation in the Maya sphere.

For centuries foreign observers have mistaken chinampas for "floating gardens," possibly because *chinampas* often have woven reed structures fortifying their banks. Alternatively, the confusion may be owing to some movable nurseries that were towed about Lake Chalco-Xochimilco.

S. L. CLINE, *Colonial Culhuacán, 1580–1600: A Social History of an Aztec Town* (1986), pp. 132–135, provides data derived from indigenous sources on *chinampas*. See also JEFFREY R. PARSONS, "The Role of Chinampa Agriculture in the Food Supply of Aztec Tenochtitlán," in *Cultural Change and Continuity: Essays in Honor of James Bennett Griffin*, edited by Charles E. Cleland, (1976), pp. 233–257, and PEDRO ARMILLAS, "Gardens on Swamps," in *Science* 174 (1971), pp. 653–661, for a discussion of the importance of this type of farming for the support of a large population.

STEPHANIE WOOD

CHINANDEGA, an important agricultural center in western Nicaragua. In 1842 Chinandega served as the site of unsuccessful Central American unification talks among Honduras, El Salvador, and Nicaragua, and it subsequently was often mentioned as a possible capital of a new Central American Union. In 1855 it served as one of the bases for William WALKER's invasion of Nicaragua. In February 1927 an aerial bombardment of Chinandega was carried out by two U.S. pilots as part of the effort to control Liberal insurrectionists who were located there. Several hundred women and children were killed, and widespread destruction resulted from what was considered to be the first tactical use of air power in warfare. In 1978–1979 heavy fighting took place around Chinandega between the Sandinistas and government troops. Today it is a prosperous commercial and agricultural processing center. Traditionally, the region was famous for corn, coffee, and oranges. Cotton production was expanded in the 1950s, but there have been difficulties in controlling pests. Sugarcane continues to be grown. The largest sugar refinery in the country is near Chinandega. The city is estimated to have a population of 37,000 people (1990).

JEFFREY L. GOULD, *To Lead As Equals: Rural Protest and Political Consciousness in Chinandega, Nicaragua, 1912–1979* (1990).

DAVID L. JICKLING

CHINCHA, one of the most important pre-Inca kingdoms in Peru. It ruled the Chincha valley, about 130 miles south of Lima, but the exact dates of the kingdom are unknown. It probably controlled the valley by A.D. 1300 and was incorporated into the Inca Empire about 1450. Relations between Chincha and the INCA were cordial. The lord of Chincha was traveling with the Inca ATAHUALPA at the time the Inca was captured by the Spanish at Cajamarca in 1532. The archaeological site known as LA CENTINELA, near modern Chincha Baja, apparently served as the Chincha capital.

The Chincha valley, shallow but very wide at its mouth, is probably the richest Peruvian coastal valley south of Lima. María Rostworowski's studies of early colonial documents have provided evidence of a population divided into specialized economic groups of farmers, fishermen, and long-distance traders. These traders were the most intriguing feature of Chincha social and economic organization. It is believed that they sailed hundreds of boats on the ocean and had a virtual monopoly on trade with the area that is modern Ecuador. While there is no certainty of the nature of this trade, it is believed that it mainly involved an exchange of metals from inland regions to the south and east for the highly valued spondylus shell from the warm waters off the Ecuadorian coast. The Pacific coast of Peru is influenced by the cold Humboldt current, which fosters one of the richest regions of marine plant and animal life in the world. However, this region does not include the spondylus, or spiny oyster, which appeared in the south only during the periods of EL NIÑO events, when cold currents were displaced by a southward movement of warmer water. The rare appearances of spondylus corresponded with rains on the Peruvian desert coast. The association between rains and spondylus apparently resulted in the belief that the spondylus brought rain. The red shells became sacred and extremely valuable. It is believed that Chincha dominated the trade that brought the shells from the north by boat, supplying large areas of the Andean highlands.

Archaeological studies have not yet located installations used by the traders. Evidence of the fisherfolk referred to in the written sources has been identified at a seaside site called Lo Demas. Numerous sites of various sizes in the inland heart of the well-irrigated valley were probably related to agricultural activities. These sites include Huacarones and Las Huacas. While the most dense occupation of the Chincha valley dates to the period between 1300 and 1532, its occupation and use began in the early periods of Andean prehistory. Archaeological sites dating to the time of the PARACAS and Nazca cultures are prominent in the valley, demonstrating that the great wealth and large populations documented by both the archaeological and written sources for the immediately pre-Columbian periods extended back for more than a millennium.

DOROTHY MENZEL and JOHN ROWE, "The Role of Chincha in Late Pre-Spanish Peru," in *Ñawpa Pacha* 4 (1966): 63–79; MARÍA ROSTWOROWSKI DE DÍEZ CANSECO, "Mercaderes del valle de Chincha en la época prehispánica: Un documento y unos comentarios," in *Revista Española de Antropologia Americana* 5 (1970): 135–177; CRAIG MORRIS, "Más allá de las fronteras de Chincha," in *La frontera del estado Inca*, edited by Tom D. Dillehay and Patricia Netherly (1988), pp. 131–140; DANIEL H. SANDWEISS, *The Archaeology of Chincha Fishermen: Specialization and Status in Inka Peru* (1992).

CRAIG MORRIS

See also **Archaeology; Indians.**

CHINCHA ISLANDS, the best-known group of some thirty major islands and scores of islets and rock outcrops located off the coast of Peru. Under the administration of Ramón CASTILLA in the 1850s, the GUANO-rich islands assumed increased importance in the economic history of Peru. Guano, the excrement from the guanay (Peruvian cormorant) and other seabirds, was in increased demand as a fertilizer for agriculture around the world. This led to increased foreign investment and immigration, much of it forced Chinese labor, and to the systematic exploitation of the islands. Production has been erratic in the twentieth century, but the islands remained commercially important producers of guano.

ROBERT CUSHMAN MURPHY, *Bird Islands of Peru* (1925); EMILIO ROMERO, *Perú: Una nueva geografía*, 2 vols. (1973).

JOHN C. SUPER

CHINCHULÍN, PACT OF (Pork-Barrel Pact), an October 1931 power-sharing agreement between two of the principal party factions in Uruguay. Under the 1919 Constitution, executive authority was divided between the president and a nine-member National Council of Ad-

ministration. Reflecting votes cast in the 1928 elections for the council, the Colorado Party had five seats (of which three went to the Batllist faction) and the Blancos, four. The Batllists sought support for their proposal to create a new public corporation Ancap (National Administration of Fuel, Alcohol, and Cement). The urban-oriented, elitist *principista* faction of the Blancos agreed to enter the pact with the Batllists on the condition that the directorates of all public corporations reflect the party composition of the National Council of Administration. The Blancos thus secured an enhanced share of patronage in the public sector. The pact was opposed by the Herrerist Blancos, who supported the overthrow of the constitution by Gabriel TERRA in 1933.

GÖRAN G. LINDAHL, *Uruguay's New Path: A Study in Politics During the First Colegiado, 1919–1933* (1962); GERARDO CAETANO and RAÚL JACOB, *El nacimiento del terrismo, 1930–1933* (1989).

HENRY FINCH

CHINESE LABOR (PERU). Imports of Chinese labor into Peru began when social and diplomatic pressure to end black slavery by 1854 forced coastal export planters to seek substitute cheap labor. They began contracting peasant labor from Macao. Between 1849 and 1874, nearly 100,000 men were kidnapped or lured from wharfside taverns, shackled on ships, and traded at Peruvian ports for about 300 pesos apiece in groups of fifty or more. The purchasers legally had contracted the labor of each man for eight years, after which he would return to China. The men worked in the guano fields, on the railroads, and in the sugar and cotton fields. On the plantations, housed in former slave barracks, they received meager food rations—a pound of rice and some vegetables once or twice a day. Ill-clothed and housed, the men lacked good medical care. Uric acid in the guano dust undoubtedly infected the lungs of many. Overwork also plagued the indentured men. Workdays were fourteen to sixteen hours long, and holidays were few and far between. Public officials rarely intervened between contract owners and contractees. Disease, poor nutrition, neglect, and overwork took their toll. One estimate places the death rate before 1865 in all venues at about 50 percent.

After 1860 the previously sluggish demand for indentured Chinese resumed when the market for cotton grew with the havoc wrought by the Civil War in the United States. Without legal recourse and not understanding Spanish, many men resisted indenture by fighting—often with one another in the barracks at night—attacking their overseers, fleeing, and in some cases committing suicide. Owners sought to dull resistance by distributing opium and cheap liquor in the barracks, to little avail. The guano mines, rail construction sites, and plantation fields were dangerous and volatile areas subjected to high security. Nevertheless, some men fled successfully, hiding in forests and no doubt aided on occasion by sympathetic local peasants despite offers of rewards. Those who were caught were returned to the work sites, where they underwent severe public whippings, time in the stocks, and other humiliations. They also were isolated from their fellow workers. Suicide occurred rarely enough among the contractees that there is reason to believe that their worldview was largely informed by Confucius, who celebrated the sanctity of all life, and perhaps they became fatalistic. They also may have realized that landlords in Peru were not much different from landlords in China. There is some speculation that suicides were prompted by the conviction that death would mean transportation of the soul back to China. But few of those who outlived indenture ever returned to their homeland.

By 1874 the reorganized Chinese government demanded the abolition of indenture in Peru. Peruvian leaders acceded to the demand with the proviso that the contracts for labor be resolved locally. This method allowed the contract owners to demand a resolution of debts incurred over the life of the contracts. Many men had incurred debts that plantation owners could document for days of work missed due to illness and flight, breakage of tools, personal loans at interest, unpaid purchases of clothing and "luxuries" (firecrackers and candles to celebrate religious holidays), and the like. In these cases contract owners could claim labor for years into the future. Indenture thus was prolonged in some cases into the 1890s, but the importation of new Chinese labor ended in 1874.

As indenture waned and agricultural labor remained scarce, itinerant Chinese plantation labor gangs bargained for wages along with other workers. Competition between ethnic work gangs became common, and by the end of the century indigenous Andean highlanders joined in. Fear of the Chinese may have stirred jealousies within the Afro-Peruvian and indigenous populations. Ethnically divided conflict occurred periodically on the coastal plantations until the War of the Pacific (1879–1883), when conflict between Asians and Peruvians reached new heights with massive attacks on Chinese peasants. After the war Chinese workers once more joined the ethnically mixed plantation labor force. By the early twentieth century a new wave of Chinese and Japanese emigrated voluntarily to Peru. Many were petty merchants and shopkeepers. A Chinese community arose in Lima, and gradually Chinese foods and cooking styles joined the indigenous and European influences in making up a diverse Peruvian cuisine.

PETER BLANCHARD, *The Origins of the Peruvian Labor Movement, 1883–1919* (1982), esp. pp. 123–125; MICHAEL GONZÁLES, *Plantation Agriculture and Social Control in Northern Peru, 1875–1933* (1985); HUMBERTO RODRÍGUEZ PASTOR, *Hijos del celeste imperio en el Perú (1850–1900): Migración, agricultura, mentalidad y explotación* (1989).

VINCENT PELOSO

See also **Asians; Plantations.**

CHINESE–LATIN AMERICAN RELATIONS. Traces of the first Chinese in Mexico can be found as far back as 1585. The MANILA GALLEONS (1571–1814) that crossed the Pacific, bringing to Mexico and other Spanish colonies in the Western Hemisphere silk, brocades, linen, tea, and spices from China and other Asian lands, also brought many Chinese sailors and merchants, some of whom stayed in the New World. In 1810, the Portuguese contracted with several hundred Chinese workers to plant tea in the capital of Brazil. (*Chá*, the Portuguese word for tea, is a transliteration of the Chinese word for tea.) To remedy the labor shortage in Peru, Mexico, and the Caribbean toward the end of the nineteenth century, more than 300,000 Chinese "coolies" were imported. Since the early twentieth century, there have been few new Chinese arrivals in Latin America due to restrictive immigration laws. Today, Chinese are found in all Latin American countries, assimilated into their societies. Apart from the Manila galleon trade, early contact between China and Latin America arose from emigration.

With the founding of the People's Republic of China (PRC) in 1949, relations between China and Latin America were strained by complex ideological and political factors. During the pre–CUBAN REVOLUTION period, Beijing (Peking) had neither the opportunity nor the incentive for involvement in Latin America. The Cuban Revolution in 1959 gave the PRC an opportunity to break the American policy of "containing China," and to establish relations with Latin American countries. However, except for Cuba, China made no diplomatic breakthroughs in the Western Hemisphere in the 1960s. By the 1970s, most of the trade and cultural exchanges between China and Latin America were concentrated on Cuba.

After the PRC's joining the United Nations and the U.S.–China rapprochement, Chinese diplomatic representation in Latin America increased, and by 1978 China had embassies in twelve Latin American countries. This paralleled the growth of Chinese economic activities in Latin America. Nonetheless, the political and economic ties between the two regions were very limited before China adopted an "open-door" policy in 1978.

Since the late 1970s, however, Chinese–Latin American relations have undergone a radical change. Economic interactions have intensified; financial, commercial, investment, and technical ties have been formed where, in general, few existed before. By the end of 1993, China had established diplomatic relations with most of the countries in the region. Taiwan maintains diplomatic and close economic ties with several Central American and the Caribbean countries.

China's 1992 trade volume with Latin American countries reached nearly $3 billion, an all-time high, compared with only $2 million in 1950. Chinese import volume accounted for nearly $1.9 billion, a 21.5 percent increase over the previous year. Export volume climbed to $1.1 billion, a rise of 35.3 percent over 1991. In 1991, Cuba was the only country in the region to which China's exports exceeded $100 million. In 1992, imports of Mexico, Panama, Chile, and Argentina from China also exceeded this figure. Enormous changes have also taken place in the composition of Chinese exports to Latin America. Prior to the 1990s, China's exports to the region were confined to textiles and some raw materials. In recent years, alongside sustained increases in exports of textiles, those of machinery, motor vehicles, airplanes, ships, electrical appliances, and farm machinery rose rapidly. Under the Chinese policy of modernization, imports from Latin America, such as copper, lumber, lead, and zinc are of prime importance. Latin American agricultural exports of wheat, fish meal, and maize have been long-term staples for Chinese consumption.

ANITA BRADLEY, *Trans-Pacific Relations of Latin America* (1942); CECIL EARLE JOHNSON, *Communist China and Latin America, 1959–1967* (1970); LEONARDO RUILOVA, *China Popular en América Latina* (1978); ROMER CORNEJO BUSTAMENTE, "El comercio exterior de China con América Latina," in *Comercio Exterior* 35, no. 7 (July 1985): 714–720; SHA DING et al., *Zhongguo he ladinmeizhou guanxi jianshi* (1987); HUMBERTO RODRÍGUEZ PASTOR, *Hijos del Celeste Imperio en el Perú (1850–1900): Migración, agricultura, mentalidad y explotación* (1989); HE LI, *Sino–Latin American Economic Relations* (1991); MARISELA CONNELLY and ROMER CORNEJO BUSTAMENTE, *China–América Latina* (1992).

HE LI

See also **Asians in Latin America.**

CHIQUINHA. *See* **Gonzaga, Francisca Hedwiges.**

CHIQUINQUIRÁ, a city of about 70,000 in Colombia's Boyacá Department, is the seat of the shrine of the Virgin of the Rosary of Chiquinquirá. The painting of the Chiquinquirá Virgin, showing her between Saint Anthony of Padua and Saint Andrew, has been dated at about 1550. After being neglected for some years, it was restored to its pristine state, according to witnesses, on 26 December 1586. Custody of the miracle-working image was given to the DOMINICANS, and an increasingly larger shrine was constructed over the centuries by the order. Until recently the Chiquinquirá region specifically and Boyacá in general were the major source of novices for the Dominicans in Colombia. Since 1919, the Virgin of Chiquinquirá has been the patroness of Colombia. She has devotees in Venezuela as well.

ANDRÉS MESANZA, O.P., *Nuestra Señora de Chiquinquirá: Y monografía histórica de esta villa* (1913); PEDRO DE TOBAR Y BUENDÍA, O.P., *Verdadera histórica relación del origen, manifestación y prodigiosa renovación por sí misma y milagros de la imagen de la Sacratíssima Virgen María . . . de Chiquinquirá*, 2d ed. (1986).

J. LEÓN HELGUERA

CHIRIGUANOS, the descendants of the TUPI-GUARANÍ Indians who migrated in the fifteenth century from what is now Brazil to the foothills of the southeastern Bolivian Andes, where they conquered and intermingled with the resident Chané Indians. Superb warriors, the Chiriguanos presented a threat to the INCAS, who constructed numerous fortresses to defend themselves, not always successfully. When the Spanish conquered the Andean peoples, the Chiriguanos raided deep into the highlands, almost reaching the silver-mining center of Potosí. Viceroy Francisco TOLEDO mounted a large expedition against the Chiriguanos, but was forced to retreat. He then adopted the Inca strategy of creating a number of fortress-towns to contain the Indians. Chiriguano demographic growth in the seventeenth century and a society organized for war made it possible to resist Spanish encroachment.

By the end of the century, the Chiriguano population may have approached 250,000. A highly decentralized system of government, based on consensual politics under village-level chiefs who accepted the loose leadership of regional chiefs, remained a distinguishing feature of Chiriguano politics. JESUIT attempts at missionizing the Chiriguanos in the eighteenth century failed, but between 1780 and 1810 the FRANCISCANS were able to establish a string of missions in the region. The WARS OF INDEPENDENCE led to the destruction of the mission system, and participation on the patriots' side by Chiriguano groups under the leadership of Cumbay helped them to reconquer much of the territory lost earlier.

In the second half of the nineteenth century CREOLES were able to regain the initiative when the Bolivian mining economy improved and cattle ranching, the main creole economic activity, became lucrative. Creole settlers drove their cattle onto the Indians' cornfields and, with better weapons, were able to subjugate the Chiriguanos. A sharp demographic decline set in; whereas the Chiriguanos numbered around 100,000 at the beginning of the nineteenth century, by the early twentieth those remaining in Bolivia numbered only 26,000. By this time, many Indians had migrated to Argentina. At the same time a new Franciscan mission system, in which Chiriguano groups sought refuge from the exactions of the settlers, helped in the conquest of the region. In an effort to avoid the onerous living conditions on HACIENDAS or the restricted environment of the missions, many Chiriguanos left their homes and, through labor contracts mediated by their chiefs, became migrant laborers on the SUGAR plantations of Jujuy in northern Argentina. Valued very highly for their hard work, the Chiriguanos were the most important workers on the plantations from the late nineteenth century to the 1930s.

The CHACO WAR (1932–1935) brought about the destruction of the Franciscan missions and the dispersal of the Chiriguanos into Paraguay and especially Argentina. Because they spoke Guaraní like many Paraguayans, the Bolivian military saw the Chiriguanos as traitors and often refused to permit them to return to their homeland. As a result, Chiriguano groups are dispersed throughout southeastern Bolivia, the Salta province of Argentina, and the Paraguayan Chaco, living as hacienda peons or in independent villages.

The most inclusive histories of the Chiriguanos are FRANCISCO PIFARRÉ, *Los Chiriguano-Guaraní: Historia de un pueblo* (1989); and GIUSEPPE CALZAVARINI, *Nación chiriguana: Grandeza y ocaso* (1980). A collection of brilliant essays spanning much of Chiriguano history is THIERRY SAIGNES, *Ava y karai: Ensayos sobre la frontera chiriguana: Siglos XVI–XXX* (1990). HERNANDO SANABRIA FERNÁNDEZ, *Apiaguaiqui Tumpa* (1972), and ERICK D. LANGER, *Economic Change and Rural Resistance in Southern Bolivia: 1880–1930* (1989), treat the nineteenth and twentieth centuries.

ERICK D. LANGER

CHIRINO, JOSÉ LEONARDO (d. 10 December 1796), leader of the 1795 slave uprising in Coro, Venezuela. Chirino was a ZAMBO, the freeborn son of a male slave and an Indian woman. He worked for a rich Coro trader named José Tellería, whom Chirino had accompanied on one of his commercial ventures to Haiti. While there, Chirino became aware of the early black and mulatto insurrectionary movements. In 1795, he and fellow conspirator José Caridad González, an African slave who had fled Curaçao for Coro, instigated an uprising of blacks in which they favored the establishment of a republic based on French law and proclaiming social equality and the abolition of privileges. Chirino was pursued, imprisoned, and condemned to death by hanging. He was executed in the central plaza of Caracas. His head was hung in a cage at the door of the city, and his severed hands were displayed in two towns in the area of Falcón.

PEDRO MANUEL ARCAYA, *Insurrección de los negros de la serranía de Coro* (1949).

INÉS QUINTERO

CHIRIPÁ. GAUCHOS of the Río de la Plata adopted many elements of Indian culture, including clothing. Indians developed the *chiripá* (a word of probable Quechua origin), a rectangular cloth worn like a diaper. After passing the cloth between his legs, the Indian or gaucho secured it around his waist with a stout belt (*tirador*). The seamless garment provided great comfort while riding. Underneath the *chiripá*, gauchos sometimes wore white, lace-fringed leggings called *calzoncillos blancos*. During the late nineteenth century, the traditional *chiripá* gave way to imported *bombachas*, bloused (usually black) pants taken in at the ankle.

MADALINE WALLIS NICHOLS, *The Gaucho* (1968), p. 13; RICHARD W. SLATTA, *Gauchos and the Vanishing Frontier* (1983), p. 73.

RICHARD W. SLATTA

CHISPAS. *See* **Violencia, La.**

CHOCANO, JOSÉ SANTOS (b. 14 May 1875; d. 13 December 1934), Peruvian poet. Acclaimed as Poet of America, Chocano was born in Lima to a father whose origin can be traced to Don Gonzalo Fernández de Córdoba, a famous Spanish soldier known as the "Great Captain"; his mother was a wealthy miner's daughter. Nevertheless, Chocano was not a happy child; he made the motto of his family coat of arms his own: Either I find a way, or I make one. On entering the University of San Marcos, at age 16, he began three careers: student, poet, and politician. In politics he learned that in Peru, family name means more than personal skills. His success as a poet was outstanding: he began writing before the age of ten and published his first book at twenty. His *Poesías completas* was published in Spain in 1902. King Alfonso XIII received from Chocano's hand the book *Alma América* (1906); Spanish American countries demanded his presence and applauded his recitals; and, in 1922, the Peruvian nation crowned him National Poet.

Chocano did not achieve political power because his creed accepted the so-called organizational dictatorships. But as a diplomat, he scored resounding victories arbitrating disputes between Guatemala and El Salvador, Colombia and Peru, and Peru and Ecuador. Twice Chocano escaped the firing squad. Once he eluded an angry mob in Guatemala, and on another occasion, after receiving a slap in the face, he fatally shot his adversary. One biographer characterized Chocano's adventurous and colorful life as a "mixture of vigor, audacity, and the picaresque." Disheartened, he moved with his young wife, Margarita, and their son to Chile. The Chileans welcomed Chocano, who continued writing, reciting, and trying his hand at business ventures. He died when an assassin fatally stabbed him on a streetcar. One of his verses inadvertently became a prophecy: "He who took a life by assault/could only die by a sword thrust."

AUGUSTO TAMAYO Y VARGAS, "J.S.C.," in *Latin American Writers*, edited by Carlos A. Solé and Maria Isabel Abreu, vol. 2 (1989), pp. 543–549.

BALBINA SAMANIEGO

CHOCÓ, a department in northwestern Colombia, comprising approximately 18,000 square miles. One of the most isolated and least developed regions of Colombia, the Chocó is covered by dense tropical vegetation and is cut off from the interior of the country by the Western Cordillera. It is one of the rainiest places on earth, with an average annual rainfall of 420 inches. In 1985 the department had a population of 234,000, 90 percent of whom were blacks and mulattoes, concentrated along the San Juan and Atrato rivers. The capital, Quibdó, which is located on the Atrato, had a population of more than 74,000 in 1985.

In the sixteenth century the region was inhabited by the Chocó and CUNA Indians, who resisted Spanish occupation. Spaniards were eager to exploit the rich gold deposits of the Chocó, but it was not until the late seventeenth century that the Indians were subdued and MINING could begin on a large scale. Blacks were used increasingly as laborers and by 1778 accounted for 60 percent of the population.

The Chocó was part of the state (later department) of Cauca in the nineteenth century but became a separate department in 1947. The mining of gold and platinum remained the basis of the economy, but individual miners rarely prospered because of the primitive methods used and the large share of the profits taken by intermediaries. As a result, the Chocó remained one of Colombia's poorest departments; a 1980s government study found that 83 percent of the population lacked the basic necessities of life.

ROBERT C. WEST, *The Pacific Lowlands of Colombia: A Negroid Area of the American Tropics* (1957); WILLIAM FREDERICK SHARP, *Slavery on the Spanish Frontier: The Colombian Chocó, 1680–1810* (1976); PETER WADE, *Blackness and Race Mixture: The Dynamics of Racial Identity in Colombia* (1993), esp. pp. 94–148.

HELEN DELPAR

CHOCRÓN, ISAAC (*b.* 25 September 1932), Venezuelan playwright, director, actor, critic, and novelist, was trained in the United States and England as an economist. One of the moving forces in the contemporary Venezuelan theater, along with José Ignacio Cabrujas and Román Chalbaud, Chocrón, a native of Maracay, founded the Nuevo Grupo in 1967 and pioneered a vanguard, independent theater in Caracas that set the standards of quality for a new generation. The Nuevo Grupo offered an international repertoire as well as original plays by Venezuelan authors.

Chocrón's theater is varied and polemical. His first play, *Mónica y el florentino* (1959), focused on problems of alienation and communication within an international guest house. His popular *Asia y el lejano oriente* (1966), about the selling of a nation, was revived in 1984 for the grand opening of the Venezuelan National Theater Company, which Chocrón was invited to head. Chocrón dealt with consumerism in *O.K.* (1969) and with homosexuality in *La revolución* (1972). Other plays include *El acompañante* (1978) and *Mesopotamia* (1979). *Simón* (1983) presents Simón Bolívar and his mentor Simón Rodríguez in a challenging encounter between the would-be hero and his wiser master, who obliges him to face up his potential and to the promise of his leadership. Chocrón has written a major book on American playwrights of the twentieth century.

KIRSTEN F. NIGRO, "A Triple Insurgence: Isaac Chocrón's *La revolución*," *Bulletin of the Rocky Mountain MLA* 35, no. 1 (1981): 47–53; EDWARD H. FRIEDMAN, "The Beast Within: The Rhetoric of Signification in Isaac Chocrón's *Animales feroces*," *Essays on Foreign Languages and Literatures* 17 (1987): 167–183; JOYCE LEE DURBIN, *La dramaturgia de Isaac Chocrón.* Dissertation Abstracts International 50, no. 6 (Dec. 1989), 1673A.

GEORGE WOODYARD

CHOLERA. *See* **Diseases.**

Cholo women in Bolivia, ca. 1980s. PHOTO BY PETER MC FARREN.

CHOLO, term used in Ecuador, Peru, small parts of northern Argentina, and especially Bolivia as a synonym for MESTIZO, specifically a person of mixed Andean Indian and white heritage, usually a white father and an Indian mother. The Indian element is generally AYMARA or QUECHUA. The term can be derogatory but also can express ethnic pride.

What mainly identifies *cholos* is their life-style as well as their occupational and educational status. They are fluent in Spanish and the Indian languages (Quechua, Aymara). Most are engaged in petty trade, small farming, and herding. *Cholas* dress colorfully in rich material, with several full petticoats, embroidered blouses, and hats that vary by locality (such as a stylish derby). A change in life-style, a university education, Western dress, and speaking Spanish nearly always move them into the Europeanized middle class. Sometimes the middle class uses the term *cholo* to characterize undignified behavior. Since the 1950s, when the social revolution gained power in Bolivia, and increasingly in the 1980s and 1990s, many *cholos* were elected to political office, including the vice presidency in 1993. Therefore the derogatory use of the term has become improper, and the ethnic pride of many *cholos* is noticeable. This change in attitude is also occurring in Ecuador and Peru, but to a lesser extent.

DANIEL PÉREZ VELASCO, *La mentalidad chola en Bolivia* (1928); JOSÉ VARALLANOS, *El cholo y el Perú* (1962); ANTHONY VETRANO, *The Ecuadorian Indian and Cholo in the Novels of Jorge Icaza: Their Lot and Languages* (1974); PAULOVICH [Alfonso Prudencio Claure], *Diccionario del cholo ilustrado* (1978); HERNÁN BARRA, *Indios y cholos* (1992).

CHARLES W. ARNADE

CHOLULA (Cholula de Rívadabia), city in the state of Puebla, Mexico. A city of approximately 25,000 inhabitants, situated at an altitude of 7,095 feet, Cholula is 72 miles southeast of Mexico City and 8 miles west of the state capital, Puebla. Founded on 27 October 1537, Cholula is primarily an agricultural and commercial center, a tourist site, and increasingly a bedroom community of the nearby state capital; however, it is best known for its pre-Columbian history, its role in the Spanish conquest of Mexico, and its many colonial-era churches.

Cholula ("place from which one jumps or flees" in NAHUATL) was one of the principal centers of pre-Columbian civilization. Its origins are obscure, but probably it was occupied by migrating Nahuatl-Olmec peoples. In the seventh century, TOLTECS conquered the area, turned Cholula into an important religious site, and built what would become the largest pyramid in the Americas. It was here that the high priest QUETZAL-COATL stayed after fleeing from Tula and before the fall of the Toltec civilization in 1116. The Spanish conquerer Hernán CORTÉS stopped in Cholula on his march from Veracruz to TENOCHTITLÁN (Mexico City) in October 1519. Fearing an ambush, Cortés ordered a preemptive attack that resulted in the deaths of perhaps as many as ten thousand Indians.

LUZ MARÍA JOSEFINA WALLES MORALES, *Cholula* (1971); GUILLERMO BONFIL BATALLA, *Cholula: La Ciudad sagrada en la era industrial* (1973); MICHAEL C. MEYER and WILLIAM L. SHERMAN, *The Course of Mexican History*, 4th ed. (1991), esp. pp. 24, 36, 39, 108–110.

DAVID LaFRANCE

CHOLULA (PRE-COLUMBIAN), ancient city near Puebla, Mexico. Inhabited since about 1000 B.C., Cholula is probably one of the longest continuously occupied cities in the country. Three enormous pyramids rise within its limits; the largest, the Great Pyramid, is the biggest building ever constructed. Called Tlachihual-tépetl (Mountain Made by Hand) in NAHUATL, it measures over 1,419 feet on a side, is over 210 feet high, and consists of superimposed structures built between about 200 B.C. and A.D. 800. The oldest structure was a west-facing temple that measured 325 feet on a side and was about 55 feet high. It was later decorated with murals depicting grasshoppers with human skull faces. Later structures within the Great Pyramid were also decorated with murals, the most famous being the Bebedores (Drunkards) murals depicting persons engaged in ritual pulque drinking. Excavations around the Great Pyramid have revealed a large plaza (Patio of the Altars) with carved stone altars and stelae.

By about A.D. 1000 the Great Pyramid was left in ruins and a "new" center of the city, called the Great Square, was built to the northwest. It included the Temple of QUETZALCOATL, the council hall, the *calmécac* (school for priests), and the residences of the high priests and noble rulers. When the Spaniards arrived in Cholula in 1519, they reported that it was a holy city, like Rome, to the Indians of Mesoamerica. It had a population of about 55,000 and was the capital of a kingdom independent from the AZTEC state. A fine polychrome pottery produced in Cholula was among the dinnerware used by the Aztec emperor MOTECUHZOMA I. The Spaniards, told there was a conspiracy to ambush them, assembled the nobles of Cholula in the Great Square and proceeded to carry out one of their most infamous massacres (18 October 1519).

ADOLPHE FRANCIS BANDELIER, *Report of an Archaeological Tour in Mexico in 1881* (1884); IGNACIO MARQUINA, *La arquitectura prehispánica*, 2d ed. (1964), pp. 115–129; GEORGE KUBLER, *Art and Architecture of Ancient America*, 3d ed. (1984), pp. 57–59; DAVID A. PETERSON, "The Real Cholula," in *Notas mesoamericanas*, no. 10 (1987): 71–118.

MICHAEL D. LIND

CHONCHOL, JACQUES (*b.* ca. 1926), Chilean political leader and agrarian reform expert. A member of the Christian Democratic Party (PDC), Chonchol advocated the creation of a communitarian society as the way to solve Chile's economic problems and to avoid the excesses of socialism and capitalism. A member of the PDC's left wing, he served as a functionary of Eduardo FREI's agrarian reform program. In 1968, distressed by what he considered Frei's conservative policies, he broke with the PDC, creating the United Movement of Popular Action (MAPU). Chonchol later served as Salvador Allende's minister of agriculture, accelerating the pace of agrarian reform. He subsequently bolted from MAPU, which he claimed had become too Marxist, to form the Christian Left. Later he resigned from Allende's cabinet over political differences.

BRIAN LOVEMAN, *Struggle in the Countryside* (1976), pp. 280, 285–286, 291–292, 296–300; PAUL SIGMUND, *The Overthrow of Allende and the Politics of Chile, 1964–1976* (1977), pp. 52–53, 62–63, 72, 79, 84, 89, 91, 130, 139, 151–152.

WILLIAM F. SATER

See also **Chile: Political Parties.**

CHONG NETO, MANUEL (*b.* 1927), Panamanian artist. Chong Neto studied painting at the San Carlos Academy in Mexico (1963–1965). He began his professional career as a high school art teacher and, after 1970, he also taught at the Casa de la Escultura, the Escuela Nacional de Artes Plásticas, and the National University.

A figurative artist, Chong Neto's compositions are characterized by formal balance and the contrast of darks and lights. His early renderings of human characters and urban landscapes show the influence of Mexican social realism. He is best known for the large, sensuous, and enigmatic woman who appears in most of his paintings. She is often accompanied by men, voyeurs, and symbolic birds or owls, as in his dramatic drawings series *Poemas Eróticos* (1976).

R. OVIERO, "Chong Neto y el tema como pretexto estético," in *La Prensa* (Panama) (June 1982); MÓNICA KUPFER, ed., *Manuel Chong Neto: Visión Retrospectiva, 1955–1985* (1986).

MONICA E. KUPFER

146

CHORO, CHORINHO, a small Brazilian urban band or the kind of music performed by such a band; a word literally meaning "to cry." A *choro* ensemble typically includes flute, clarinet, trombone, trumpet, large and small guitars, *cavaquinhos* (Brazilian ukulelelike instruments), and a few percussion instruments.

Appearing as a musical genre in the late 1880s, *choro* was at first strictly an instrumental style, and was marked by its improvisational character and the virtuosity of its solos. Thus it has often been compared with ragtime and early-twentieth-century New Orleans–style jazz. Formally, its structure is in three parts in the pattern A-B-A-C-A. Vocal forms of *choro* in which the voice substitutes for a solo wind instrument began to appear in the 1920s and 1930s. Among notable examples of the genre are "Urubu," by PIXINGUINHA, and "Sai faísca."

ONEYDA ALVARENGA, *Música popular brasileira* (1982); MÁRIO DE ANDRADE, *Dictionário musical brasileiro*, coordinated by Oneyda Alvarenga and Flávia Camargo Toni (1982–1989); CHARLES A. PERRONE, *Masters of Contemporary Brazilian Song* (1989).

ROBERT MYERS

See also **Lundu; Maxixe; Música Popular Brasileira; Samba.**

CHORRERA, a pre-Columbian culture located in western Ecuador, also called Engoroy by some archaeologists. Scarcely investigated, Chorrera's existence has been dated variously from 1500 to 500 B.C.E to as recently as 800 to 100 B.C.E. These temporal differences may in fact date occupations in different geographical areas. Chorrera is known principally for technically innovative and aesthetically pleasing ceramics, often depicting the local fauna and the wild and cultivated plants of the Pacific coast, savanna, and tropical forests of western Ecuador.

Chorrera existed during the Late Formative period of Ecuadorian prehistory. Archaeologists describe Formative period cultures as initiating many of the developments that later became the foundations of "high" civilization in the Central Andes, culminating in the Inca empire-state. These novel developments included settled life in permanent villages, highly productive agricultural systems, the invention and elaboration of pottery, social-status differences reinforced by differential access to exotic goods, and the beginnings of monumental constructions undertaken through corporate labor projects.

Two contrasting views have been proposed to explain the origins of Chorrera culture. One view argues for strong links between Chorrera and Formative cultures in MESOAMERICA, with the latter region as the proposed place of origin. The presence of ceramic traits such as iridescent painting and napkin-ring ear spools in both areas suggests to some that long-distance contacts existed. Mesoamerica is seen as the more precocious region, and therefore as the donor of many cultural traits

to the Andean region. According to the opposing view, many purported Mesoamerican traits in Chorrera ceramics occurred earliest in Ecuador, and therefore its origins were elsewhere, either in the forested eastern Andes or southern highlands of Ecuador. The representations of plants and animals in Chorrera pottery are seen as indications of a well-established tropical-forest cultural pattern, similar to ethnographically known groups from present-day Amazonia.

Much of the information archaeologists use to reconstruct Chorrera culture comes from the carefully crafted naturalistic depictions on Chorrera pottery. Chorrera bottles, jars, and bowls often incorporate a variety of forest mammals and reptiles, as well as numerous species of birds. The depiction of marine animals suggests the exploitation of maritime resources. Chorrera pottery also offers information about agricultural practices. Various types of squashes and tropical fruits appear on bottles. Botanical analyses from archaeological excavations indicate that maize and root crops were cultivated. In addition, many wild plants from the forests appear to have played an important role in subsistence.

Ceramic human figurines were also made by Chorrera potters. The fronts of figurines appear to have been fashioned using molds, while the backs were modeled by hand. Although neither the archaeological context nor the use of these figurines is known, they do provide clues as to possible clothing and hair styles, and may reflect the practice of tattooing or body painting.

Archaeologists have recovered little information regarding Chorrera mortuary practices. Excavations at a cemetery site in southwestern Ecuador uncovered several burials. Individuals were sometimes accompanied by grave goods, including stone beads, ceramic bowls, and effigy bottles. Other perishable items may have been included in burials, but did not preserve over time. Also recovered were secondary collective burials documenting the practice of reburying the disarticulated bones of several individuals together in circular pits.

CLIFFORD EVANS and BETTY J. MEGGERS, "Formative Period Cultures in the Guayas Basin, Coastal Ecuador," in *American Antiquity* 22 (1957): 235–247; EMILIO ESTRADA, *Las culturas preclásicas: Formativas o arcaicas del Ecuador* (1958); CARLOS ZEVALLOS MENÉNDEZ, "Informe preliminar sobre el Cementerio Chorrera, Bahía de Santa Elena, Ecuador," in *Revista del Museo Nacional* 34 (1965–1966): 20–27; BETTY J. MEGGERS, *Ecuador* (1966); DONALD W. LATHRAP, *Ancient Ecuador: Culture, Clay, and Creativity, 3000–300 B.C.* (1975); HENNING BISCHOF, "La fase Engoroy—períodos, cronología y relaciones," in *Primer Simposio de Correlaciones Antropológicas Andino-Mesoamericano* (1982), pp. 135–176.

EVAN C. ENGWALL

See also **Art: Pre-Columbian Art of Mesoamerica.**

CHOTUNA, a major archaeological site located in the lower part of the Lambayeque Valley of northern Peru. It is thought to have been associated with a legendary dynasty, founded by Naymlap, that came to this valley centuries before European contact in the early sixteenth century. According to the legend, Naymlap came by sea on a fleet of balsa rafts, bringing with him many concubines, a chief wife named Ceterni, and many people who followed him as their captain and leader. Among the latter were forty officials who served in his royal court.

Naymlap and his followers are said to have beached their boats at the mouth of a river, and then followed that river approximately one-half mile inland. Naymlap built a palace for his principal wife, and nearby, at a place called Chot, he built a palace for himself where he lived for many years. When he was about to die, he had his trusted servants bury him in a room and spread the word among his people that he had grown wings and flown away. Chotuna is thought to be Chot of the Naymlap legend, and Chornancap, another archaeological site approximately one-half mile west of Chotuna, is thought to be where Naymlap built the palace for Ceterni.

Today, the site of Chotuna consists of a series of pyramids, palaces, and walled enclosures scattered over an area of approximately 50 acres. In 1941 grave robbers looting at Chotuna uncovered walls with elaborate low relief friezes. Their designs were so similar to friezes at Dragon, an archaeological site in the Moche Valley, approximately 110 miles to the south, that it was thought that the two sites were somehow related. Major excavation at Chotuna between 1980 and 1982 revealed that the site was first inhabited approximately A.D. 700, and continued to be occupied until 1100, when a major period of flooding destroyed much of the ancient architecture. After 1100 the site was reoccupied by people with different ceramics who lived there until the early part of the Colonial Period, around 1650. If Naymlap was a real person, his story probably relates to the founding of the site, and the period prior to the flooding. The friezes date to the period after the flooding, probably between 1100 and 1250.

ALFRED L. KROEBER, *Peruvian Archaeology in 1942* (1944); CHRISTOPHER B. DONNAN, ''An Assessment of the Validity of the Naymlap Dynasty'' and ''The Chotuna Friezes and the Chotuna-Dragon Connection,'' in *The Northern Dynasties: Kingship and Statecraft in Chimor*, edited by Michael E. Moseley and Alana Cordy-Collins (1990).

CHRISTOPHER B. DONNAN

CHRIST OF THE ANDES, monument, also known as Cristo Redentor (Christ the Redeemer), standing on Uspallata Pass (13,860 feet) on the old dirt road from Mendoza (Argentina) to Los Andes (Chile). It was erected in 1904 to commemorate the peaceful solution of long and bitter boundary disputes by the treaty signed in 1902 after British arbitration. Made from the bronze of melted-down cannons, the 25-foot-high statue is of

Christ standing on a globe, holding a cross in his right hand and raising his left arm in the sign of peace. The inscription at the base reads ''Let these mighty mountains turn to dust before two sister nations wage war against each other.''

SALVATORE BIZZARRO, *Historical Dictionary of Chile* (1987).

CÉSAR N. CAVIEDES

CHRIST THE REDEEMER. *See* **Corcovado.**

CHRISTIAN BASE COMMUNITIES (Comunidades Eclesiales de Base—CEB), groups of twenty to thirty members within a parish, who meet regularly for Bible study, led by a priest or nun; who elect their own leaders; and who decide democratically with what other activities the community should be concerned. At their inception, CEBs were seen as a mechanism by which the liberal Catholic doctrine developed during the Second Vatican Council (1962–1965) and the Bishops' Conference held at Medellín, Colombia (1968), could be implemented. The goal was to bring the laity into the life of the church, to teach that the church is a community of equals before God in which everyone has obligations to each other and responsibilities to share. CEBs reflect a rupture with the past, when the church was allied with wealth and power, and demonstrate a new commitment to a ''preferential option for the poor.'' It is not surprising, therefore, that CEBs have flourished in poor parishes across Latin America but are virtually unknown in middle- and upper-class parishes.

Lay leaders are known as catechists and delegates of the Word. They are chosen by the community for their leadership qualities, moral rectitude, Christian commitment, and willingness to serve. Catechists prepare parishioners for baptism, first communion, and marriage. Delegates lead the community in worship services; in many countries they are also authorized to give communion, to perform marriages, and to conduct burial services. Both catechists and delegates receive training from clergy and nuns and/or attend short courses at lay training centers.

The content of Bible study courses rejects the church's traditional message, preached from the Conquest onward, that one should accept one's lot on earth and wait patiently for one's reward in heaven. Through the CEBs (in line with Medellín documents), the people receive a different message: that God, who is a God of justice, has acted throughout human history on behalf of the poor and oppressed; that it is not God's will that they be poor; that, before God, they are equal to the rich; that they have a basic human right to organize and take control of their own lives; and that the church has responsibility to ''accompany'' them in that journey.

The impact of this process is profound. More than one peasant has commented that when the priest or nun came to organize CEBs, it was the first time anyone had asked what she or he thought about anything. Nuns report observing their parishioners' traditional fatalism change over a few months to a new sociopolitical awareness: "It's 'God's will' when a child dies becomes 'The system caused this.' " Religious workers also report that CEB members change physically: "They walk upright, their heads high, with self-confidence," rather than shuffling along with heads bowed.

CEBs can continue for years and develop in different ways. All, however, share four characteristics. First, the CEBs provide an organization, a means by which the people can meet together on a regular basis. Since the poor have been unorganized in most societies, this is usually the first experience of its kind for CEB members. Furthermore, the form and function of each CEB are determined by the members of the community, not by the priest or nun, whose role is that of facilitator, resource, and occasionally advocate. It is the people who decide what they want and who organize themselves to get it, whether "it" be literacy classes, an agricultural cooperative, or paramedical training for a member of the community.

Second, the CEBs produce grass-roots leadership by selecting their own catechists and delegates. Among people who have been treated as objects for almost five centuries, the opportunity to develop local leadership has meant that for the first time since the Conquest, the poor have their own spokespeople who are willing and able to advocate on behalf of their communities.

Third, CEBs are working models of participatory democracy. The lay leaders never have the right to impose their will on the community; if they try to do so, they will be removed by the people. The same applies to priests. Traditionally it is unheard of for parishioners, especially peasants, to talk back to a priest. But two CEBs stopped a priest cold in one Central American country when he tried to discredit the nun who had been working with them for years, accusing her of "political work." The people told him he was wrong and refused to entertain the priest's charges.

Fourth, together with the Mass, CEBs provide the means by which the people reflect on God's word in the Bible, which contributes to *concientización* (or *consentização*, a word coined by Brazilian educator Paulo FREIRE), the process by which the people become aware (conscious) of the interconnectedness of God's Word, their lives, and their world.

The growth of CEBs has been explosive in some countries and virtually nonexistent in others. In still other countries there are great variations among dioceses. The data suggest two critical variables. First, there appears to be a correlation between the extent of poverty in a country and the number of CEBs. CEBs are few and far between in Argentina, Uruguay, Chile, and Costa Rica, countries that have enjoyed a relatively higher standard of living than the rest of Latin America. Second, there is

a clear and even stronger correlation between the support a bishop gives the development of CEBs in his diocese and the number of CEBs that are organized. Brazil, with well over a hundred thousand CEBs, best illustrates both variables: widespread poverty and the most progressive bishops of any national church in the world. At the other end of the theological spectrum, Colombia, with equally widespread poverty and one of the most conservative hierarchies in Latin America, has relatively few CEBs. El Salvador, Guatemala, and Mexico also qualify on both points, but the development of CEBs in each of these countries has been highly erratic: in dioceses with progressive bishops large numbers of CEBs flourish, while dioceses headed by conservatives have few.

It should not be surprising that conservative episcopal reaction echoes in the larger society. CEBs have come to be regarded as "subversive" by elites bent on maintaining the economic and political status quo. Dozens of priests and nuns involved with CEBs have been harrassed, exiled, tortured, or murdered. Hundreds of catechists and delegates and even some bishops have met the same fate.

Still, the development and growth of CEBs continues. They represent the most significant development in the Latin American church since the Conquest. They are likely to endure into the next century, and to continue changing the institutional church out of which they come, the people who create them, and the societies into which they are born.

ERNESTO CARDENAL *The Gospel in Solentiname,* 4 vols. (1979); PENNY LERNOUX, *Cry of the People* (1980); PHILIP BERRYMAN, *The Religious Roots of Rebellion: Christians in Central American Revolutions* (1984); GUILLERMO COOK, *The Expectation of the Poor: Latin American Base Ecclesial Communities in Protestant Perspective* (1985); PABLO GALDÁMEZ, *Faith of a People: The Life of a Basic Christian Community in El Salvador,* translated by Robert R. Barr (1986); SCOTT MAINWARING and ALEXANDER WILDE, eds., *The Progressive Church in Latin America* (1988); W. E. HEWITT, *Base Christian Communities and Social Change in Brazil* (1991); CECILIA LORETO MARIZ, *Coping with Poverty: Pentecostals and Christian Base Communities in Brazil* (1994).

TOMMIE SUE MONTGOMERY

See also **Catholic Church; Liberation Theology.**

CHRISTIE AFFAIR, a series of reprisals taken by the British Navy against Brazilian merchantmen from December 1862 to 5 January 1863. Named for William Christie, the British ambassador to Brazil at the time, it brought to a head thirty-five years of growing animosity between the two governments concerning slavery in Brazil. In 1861, the British ship *Prince of Wales* sank off the coast of Brazil. The British suspected foul play because the Brazilian government would not, or could not, produce the bodies of any of the last crewmen or any of the ship's cargo, which had been stolen by local inhabitants. A year later, three out-of-uniform British sailors were arrested in Brazil for drunkenness and disorderly conduct. The British government viewed these arrests as deliberate provocation and demanded an apology for the arrests and immediate restitution for the *Prince of Wales*. It authorized Christie to use reprisals if these demands were not met. Christie subsequently ordered British naval vessels to blockade Rio de Janeiro harbor; during a six-day blockade the British seized five Brazilian ships. Thereupon, the Brazilian government agreed to pay for the *Prince of Wales* and put the matter of the sailors' arrests to an arbitrator.

The arbitrator decided in favor of Brazil, ruling that no insult to Great Britain had been intended. Brazil then demanded restitution for its five ships. The British refused, and the Brazilians severed diplomatic relations with Great Britain. Although the British never paid for the seized Brazilian ships, Brazil restored diplomatic relations five years later for economic reasons.

Since William Christie and the British government were keenly interested in the abolition of slavery in Brazil, this affair was seen in Brazil as a warning that Britain was willing to use force, if needed, to push Brazil toward the abolition of slavery.

RICHARD GRAHAM, "Causes for the Abolition of Negro Slavery in Brazil: An Interpetive Essay," *HAHR* 46, no. 2 (1966): 123–137, and *Britain and the Onset of Modernization in Brazil, 1850–1914* (1968), pp. 169–183; BRADFORD E. BURNS, *Nationalism in Brazil: A Historical Survey* (1968).

MICHAEL J. BROYLES

CHRISTMAS, LEE (*b.* 22 February 1863; *d.* 24 January 1924), North American soldier of fortune in Honduras. Christmas was probably the most famous of a generation of North American adventurers and FILIBUSTERS who migrated to Central America from the 1890s until World War I. He left New Orleans in 1894 and got a job railroading on the north Honduran coast. From then until his return to the United States after World War I, he was involved in the political turmoil of Honduras and Guatemala. He served as national police chief of Honduras, fought in the Honduran-Nicaraguan war of 1907, and plotted with former Honduran president Manuel BONILLA and Guy "Machine-Gun" MOLONY to restore Bonilla to power, a plan that culminated in the attack on La Ceiba in January 1911. Christmas was rewarded with a sinecure at Puerto Cortés, and Sam "The Banana Man" ZEMURRAY gained valuable concessions for his CUYAMEL FRUIT COMPANY on the north Honduran coast. In 1915 Christmas lost favor with the Honduran regime and joined Manuel Estrada Cabrera's secret service in Guatemala. He returned virtually penniless to the United States in March 1922 and died of tropical sprue.

HERMANN DEUTSCH, *The Incredible Yanqui: The Career of Lee Christmas* (1931).

LESTER D. LANGLEY

CHRISTOPHE, HENRI (*b.* 6 October 1767; *d.* 8 October 1820), president of the State of Haiti (1806–1811) and king (1811–1820). In the inky darkness of a mountain night, an exhausted entourage of royalty and servants led by Queen Marie-Louise reached the outer gates of the fortress of CITADELLE LA FERRIÈRE. Once inside the compound, two royal aides hurriedly looked for shovels and a place to dispose of their cargo, an unshrouded body in a hammock. Finally, unable to inter the cadaver in suitable fashion, they simply dumped their cargo into a pile of quick lime and left. Later Haiti would entomb the remains on this site with the occupant's own prepared epitaph: "I shall be reborn from my ashes."

Always the showman, Henri Christophe left Haitians with the fear that he just might return. He had cleverly built a personal mythology to buttress his tyrannical rule of the northern State of Haiti. Historian James Leyburn called Christophe Haiti's best nineteenth-century ruler, which he was. And Simon BOLÍVAR might have been thinking of Christophe when he stated in his Jamaica Letter (1815) that Latin America needed strong, paternalistic rulers who would govern for life and who would educate and guide their people to assume democratic responsibilities.

Born a slave on Grenada, Christophe became the property of a ship captain and then the chattel of Saint-Domingue sugar planter Master Badechi, who soon put him to work at Couronne, a hostelry in Le Cap François. In 1778 Christophe served as a slave orderly for the French at Savannah, Georgia, where he suffered injury. In 1790 in northern Saint-Domingue he rode with a dragoon unit that suppressed the rebellion of Vincent Ogé (1755?–1791). It is probable that by this time Christophe had become a free black. He cherished his British origins, always gave the English spelling, "Henry," and chose George III for hero worship.

When Toussaint L'OUVERTURE joined the French in 1794, Christophe's military career had been languishing, as he had attained only the rank of captain of the infantry at the garrison of Le Cap François. But Toussaint recognized in the young officer the qualities of good leadership. Christophe served his commander well in the La Petite-Anse district, where he and Colonel Vincent introduced the *fermage* (system of forced labor and government management) to maintain the plantation system. Under this profit-sharing plan, laborers had to surrender a great deal of personal freedom and submit to corporal punishment. Toussaint was impressed and used the scheme widely across Saint-Domingue. In 1799 Christophe, by then a colonel, commanded the garrison at Le Cap François and would later join Toussaint in crushing the Moyse Rebellion (October 1801).

When the expedition of General Charles Leclerc reached Haiti from France, Christophe at first fought well by torching Le Cap François and moving to the interior. But then came an unexpected event, Christophe's surrender to the French on 26 April 1802, and his agreement to command a French unit under General Jean Hardy. Ralph Korngold has argued that Christophe betrayed Toussaint, but his belief is not shared by biographer Hubert Cole. Christophe himself defended his action by saying that he was tired of living like a savage. In October 1802, he deserted the French and joined the rising tide of black rebels opposed to the restoration of slavery.

In February 1807, Christophe was angered when the mulatto-dominated assembly at Port-au-Prince handed him a weakened presidency. There followed a civil conflict in which Christophe ruled the State of Haiti in the north and Alexandre PÉTION and a mulatto clique governed the Republic of Haiti in the south.

From the beginning of his rule, Christophe pursued an effective social policy. He hired English teachers to establish a system of national schools. He demanded that his subjects have church marriages. On this issue he often wandered about the countryside looking for wayward lovers. If they suffered his apprehension, their fate was an altar and a priest. He even tried to impose desirable personal habits upon his people. The Royal Dahomets, his special African police force, inspected Haitians for neatness and honesty. They tested this second quality by dropping a wallet and other valuables in a public place, hiding, and then arresting any culprit who found the items without making a police report. Public awe of Christophe grew as his subjects often sighted him attended by an aide with a telescope. Popular rumor maintained that Christophe saw all and punished all.

Economically, Christophe followed Toussaint's maintenance of the plantation system without slavery. But Christophe did break up some of the large estates late in his rule and sold the parcels to small farmers, a point Hubert Cole believes other historians may have missed. To further his economic plans, Christophe became King Henry I on 28 March 1811. Surrounding his crown was a new Haitian nobility. To them he gave generous land grants and pompous titles. To him they gave loyalty and maintained prosperous plantations.

On 8 October 1820 a dying Christophe committed suicide at his plush palace, Sans Souci. Faithful followers carried his body to Citadelle La Ferrière, the great monument to black work skills, which Christophe had constructed during his rule. Their monument was fittingly his last resting place.

W. W. HARVEY, *Sketches of Haiti* (1827); C. L. R. JAMES, *The Black Jacobins* (1938); JAMES LEYBURN, *The Haitian People* (1941); RALPH KORNGOLD, *Citizen Toussaint* (1944); HUBERT COLE, *Christophe: King of Haiti* (1967); THOMAS O. OTT, *The Haitian Revolution, 1789–1804* (1973); DAVID NICHOLLS, *From Dessalines to Duvalier: Race, Colour, and National Independence in Haiti* (1979).

THOMAS O. OTT

CHUBUT, southern province of Argentina drained by the Chubut and Chico rivers, at whose confluence lies the capital city of Rawson (population 34,000). Once an unpopulated region of PATAGONIA, it caught the attention of Welsh Captain M. Elsewood in 1852 as an area of possible colonization. In 1855 Henry L. Jones attempted to establish a settlement but failed owing to the harshness of the climate. Ten years later, under the sponsorship of the Argentine statesman Guillermo RAWSON, a group of Welsh families settled in Golfo Nuevo, near present-day Puerto Madryn. In 1865 the permanent settlement of Rawson was founded at the mouth of the Chubut River, and Welsh scouts explored the upper course of the river for new lands to open. Their contacts with the Indians were friendly, assuring the survival of the sparse settlements during the years of the Indian wars. Subsequently, the establishment of Salesian missions helped pacify the area and draw in new settlers.

Chubut became a national territory in 1884, and the central government began to promote the populating of remote areas of northern Patagonia. Welsh colonists established themselves along the Chubut River, cultivating grain and raising sheep. In 1901 the coastal town of Comodoro Rivadavia was founded near petroleum deposits, and in 1906 the establishment of the town of Esquel assured the Argentine presence in the eastern foothills of the Andes. By 1991 the population had grown from a few thousand at the turn of the century to 356,587. The growth in population and the wealth of natural resources, particularly oil and gas deposits in the vicinities of Sarmiento and Comodoro Rivadavia, led to the establishment of Chubut as a province. Today the port cities of Puerto Madryn and Rawson as well as the river oasis towns of Las Plumas and Trelew are bustling with activities connected to the oil and natural gas industries. These resources are shipped to northern Argentina from Caleta Córdoba, along with wool, mutton, and summer fruits from farms in the Chubut valley. Otherwise, the flat regions of central Patagonia are inhospitable, continually battered by the cold subantarctic winds.

JUAN MEISEN, *Relatos del Chubut viejo* (Buenos Aires, 1989).

CÉSAR N. CAVIEDES

See also **Petroleum Industry.**

CHUCUITO, a province in the department of Puno, Peru. Juli is its capital. Bordered by Lake TITICACA to the east and Bolivia to the south, the province's elevations range from 12,500 to 13,200 feet. The region was an important center of pre-Hispanic cultures. The published official inquiry (*visita*) by Garci Diez de San Miguel in 1567 describes in great detail the Lupaca people of the region, thus constituting a crucial source on the precolonial and early Conquest periods. Commerce with Bolivia and livestock raising are the province's major economic activities today.

GARCI DIEZ DE SAN MIGUEL, *Visita hecha a la provincia de Chucuito por Garci Diez de San Miguel en al año 1567*, edited by Waldemar Espinoza Soriano (1964); PEDRO FELIPE CORTÁZAR, *Department del Puno*, vol. 21 of *Documental del Perú*, 2d ed. (1972).

CHARLES F. WALKER

CHUMACERO, ALÍ (*b.* 9 July 1918), Mexican poet, editor, and essayist. Early in his career Chumacero was associated with the literary journals *Tierra Nueva* (1940–1942) and *El Hijo Pródigo* (1943–1946) and subsequently with *México en la Cultura* and *La Cultura en México*, among others. He has held important positions with the publisher Fondo de Cultura Económica, has edited works of nineteenth-century Mexican Romantic poets and of Alfonso REYES and Xavier VILLAURRUTIA, and has collaborated with Octavio PAZ, José Emilio PACHECO, and Homero ARIDJIS in the preparation of the influential anthology *Poesía en movimiento* (1966). His essays range across the fields of poetics, literary history and criticism, and contemporary Mexican art. Chumacero's poetry, almost all of it written before 1956, is a very carefully crafted, subtle exploration of existential desolation, solitude, and the inadequate consolations of love. The earlier poems (*Páramo de sueños* [1944] and *Imágenes desterradas* [1948]) are quite hermetic, bearing traces of his predecessors, the CONTEMPORÁNEOS (most notably José GOROSTIZA and Villaurrutía). The later poems (*Palabras en reposo* [1956]) are more accessible, though no less complex.

MARCO ANTONIO CAMPOS has edited the *Poesía completa* (1980). MIGUEL ANGEL FLORES presents a fine selection of Chumacero's essays in *Los momentos críticos* (1987). For an extended discussion of the poetry and additional bibliography, see FRANK DAUSTER, *The Double Strand* (1987).

MICHAEL J. DOUDOROFF

CHUMASH INDIANS, an Indian group that inhabited an extensive south-central California territory that stretched from the southern Salinas Valley in the north to the Santa Monica Mountains in the south. The Chumash territory also included the Santa Barbara Channel Islands. They numbered an estimated 18,500 when the Spaniards came to Alta California in 1769.

The Chumash had a sophisticated tribal government and were, at the time of Spanish arrival, in the process of a social evolution that was leading to social differentiation. They practiced food-resource management and utilized a variety of food sources from the diverse ecologies found within their territory. They used burning to maximize seed production and selectively promoted the growth of certain grasses that produced more seeds. Fish, marine mammals, and shellfish were also exploited.

The Franciscan missionaries established five MISSIONS in Chumash territory: San Luis Obispo (1772), San Buenaventura (1782), Santa Barbara (1786), La Purísima (1787), and Santa Ynez (1804). During the course of some fifty years, the FRANCISCANS resettled the bulk of the Chumash in these five missions, where life proved unhealthy for them because of disease, the stress of cultural change, and crowded living conditions. The rate of population decline reached about 85 percent from contact population levels, so that by 1832, there were only 2,259 Chumash converts living in the five missions. Infant mortality was particularly high—about two-thirds of all children died before reaching age five, and only one-fourth reached puberty. A small number of Chumash survive today in the Santa Barbara–San Luis Obispo county areas and preserve much of their culture.

ALFRED L. KROEBER, *Handbook of California Indians* (1925, repr. 1976); JOHN R. JOHNSON, "The Chumash and the Missions" in DAVID H. THOMAS, ed., *Columbian Consequences*, vol. 1, *Archaeological and Historical Perspectives on the Spanish Borderlands West* (1989), pp. 365–375.

ROBERT H. JACKSON

CHUQUICAMATA MINE, world's largest open-pit copper mine, located in the northern Atacama Desert in Chile, approximately 150 miles northeast of the port city of Antofagasta. At 9,500 feet above sea level, it measures 2 miles in length, 1.5 miles in width, and almost half a mile in depth. With estimated reserves of 600 million to 1 billion tons of 1.6 percent copper content, the mine produced 667,000 metric tons in 1991, almost half of Chile's copper output and 13 percent of its foreign revenues. Operated by the state-owned Chile Copper Corporation, it employed 10,000 workers in 1992. Originally purchased by the Guggenheim interests, the mine began operation in 1915. It was sold to the Chile Exploration Company, a subsidiary of U.S.-based Anaconda, in 1923. In the 1920s bitter strikes, led by the leftist Federation of Chilean Workers, and harsh retaliation by the mine's management led to demonstrations of Chilean nationalistic sentiment and to congressional inquiries. In spite of persistent disturbances, Chuquicamata yielded consistently higher profits than Anaconda's domestic operations. The Christian Democratic government of Eduardo FREI MONTALVO (1964–1970) "Chileanized" the mine, putting 51 percent of its stock under state control with compensation paid to Anaconda over a twelve-year period. During the Popular Unity government of Salvador ALLENDE GOSSENS (1970–1973), Congress unanimously approved full nationalization. Charging Anaconda with excess profits in the past, the Allende government denied compensation, further provoking the United States opposition to his regime. In 1974 the Augusto PINOCHET UGARTE government prom-

Chuquicamata Copper Mine, Chile. PHOTO BY MARCELO MONTECINO.

ised compensation of $253 million; the claim was settled in 1975.

MARCIAL FIGUEROA, *Chuquicamata: La tumba del chileno* (1928); FREDRICK B. PIKE, *Chile and the United States, 1880–1962* (1963), esp. pp. 161, 234, and 409 for the early period; THEODORE H. MORAN, *Multinational Corporations and the Politics of Dependence: Copper in Chile* (1975) for the post-1945 era; PAUL W. DRAKE, *Socialism and Populism in Chile 1932–1952* (1978), esp. pp. 19, 44, 200, 287, 319, 355.

CHRISTEL K. CONVERSE

See also **Copper Industry.**

CHUQUITANTA. *See* **El Paraíso.**

CHURCH-STATE CONFLICTS. *See* **Anticlericalism.**

CHURRASCO, chunks of beef or mutton roasted over a wood or charcoal fire. GAUCHOS and other rural inhabitants of the Río de la Plata region relished fresh beef cooked in this way. In some cases, the cook wrapped the meat in a hide and laid it on a bed of hot coals. This technique better retained the meat's flavor and juices.

Gauchos could seemingly subsist on a diet consisting largely of *churrasco* and their favorite beverage, MATE. A gaucho used only his long knife (FACÓN) to slice and eat the meat. Traditionalists in the Río de la Plata region continue to prepare *churrasco, carne asado,* and other beef delicacies.

FÉLIX COLUCCIO, *Diccionario folklórico argentino,* vol. 1 (1964), p. 121.

RICHARD W. SLATTA

CHURRIGUERESQUE, a style of architectural decoration of eighteenth-century Mexico. Named after José Benito Churriguera (1665–1725) of Madrid, its origin and character in Mexico are actually based on the work of Jerónimo de BALBÁS, whose Retablo de los Reyes (1718–1737) in the cathedral of Mexico City is the first Churrigueresque work in New Spain. Academic neoclassicism put an end to Churrigueresque by around 1790. Its identifying feature is the *estípite* (a pillar whose lower section is an elongated and inverted truncated pyramid), but just as significant are the changes in proportions and, consequently, in compositional principles. Freestanding figure sculpture and a more naturalistic style of ornament with rococo elements also accompany the *estípite.* The historical inaccuracy of the word "Churrigueresque" has led many scholars to reject or limit its use. Alternatives

Retablo de los Reyes showing Churrigueresque style, cathedral of Mexico City. BENSON LATIN AMERICAN COLLECTION, UNIVERSITY OF TEXAS AT AUSTIN.

are "ultrabaroque," "balbasiano," or, simply and most commonly now, "*estípite* baroque."

JUSTINO FERNÁNDEZ, *El Retablo de los Reyes* (1972), pp. 279–282.

CLARA BARGELLINI

See also **Architecture.**

CHURUBUSCO, BATTLE OF. *See* **Mexican-American War.**

CÍBOLA. *See* **Seven Cities of Cíbola.**

CÍCERO, PADRE. *See* **Batista, Cícero Romão.**

CIELITO, a traditional folk dance of the rural Río de la Plata region and Chile, also called *cielo.* The slow, stately dance, dating from colonial days, is performed by couples who dance around one another. Partners do not touch each other. Over time, the rural lower classes enlivened the dance with variations, such as snapping their fingers. *Cielito* shared some similarities with the nineteenth-century *pericón,* which came to be considered the most patriotic and typical dance of Argentina.

CARLOS VEGA, *Las danzas populares argentinas* (1952); FÉLIX COLUCCIO, *Diccionario folklórico argentino,* vol. 1 (1964), p. 77.

RICHARD W. SLATTA

CIENFUEGOS, CAMILO (*b.* 1931; *d.* October 1959), Cuban revolutionary and chief of staff of the rebel army. Born to a poor family in the Layanó district of Havana, Camilo Cienfuegos nevertheless had a happy childhood. He managed to secure an eighth-grade education while selling shoes to support his family, and he displayed his social conscience at an early age, collecting money in 1937 to aid the orphans of the Spanish Civil War. Cienfuegos's father resisted formal education for his children, preferring instead that Camilo and his older brother Osmany receive private lessons from an old Communist acquaintance. Nevertheless, Camilo was drawn to more social forms of activity and joined the anti-Fascist student paper *Lídice* in 1945. He was a handsome, popular, and athletic young man with red hair and a quick laugh. In 1947 Cienfuegos won the national *pelota* championships and was the pride of his family.

After ending his formal education for good, Cienfuegos worked at odd jobs in Havana and took up sculpting. The on-air suicide of political activist and radio personality Eddy Chibás in 1951 prompted Cienfuegos to leave Cuba for the United States, where he hoped to make his fortune. In 1955 he was back in Cuba and participating in demonstrations against BATISTA and the police on behalf of Fidel CASTRO'S TWENTY-SIXTH OF JULY MOVEMENT. With his forceful personality, Camilo Cienfuegos quickly caught Castro's eye, and he joined the exile group in Mexico that was preparing for an invasion of Cuba. He was one of the eighty-one men who set out with Fidel Castro in November 1956 on the *Granma* to start a revolution.

After the initial landing, Cienfuegos became one of the *comandantes* of the rebel forces. He appears to have been an avowed Marxist at a time when the revolutionaries had not yet declared an official ideology; in his districts Cienfuegos set up schools that taught literacy and socialist doctrine.

After the rebels' victory on 1 January 1959, Cienfuegos was appointed chief of staff of the armed forces and became the second most popular figure of the revolution after Castro himself. He disappeared mysteriously on a solo flight from Camagüey to Havana in October 1959; no trace of the wreckage was ever found, and the disappearance remained controversial.

ERNESTO "CHE" GUEVARA, *José Martí, Antonio Guiteras, Antonio Maceo, Camilo Cienfuegos* (1977); WILLIAM GÁLVEZ, *Camilo, señor de la vanguardia* (1979); Carlos Franquí, *Diary of the Cuban Revolution,* translated by Georgette Felix et al. (1980); and TAD SZULC, *Fidel: A Critical Portrait* (1986).

KAREN RACINE

See also **Cuban Revolution.**

CIENTÍFICOS, Mexican political faction in the Porfiriato. Supporters of the dictatorship of Porfirio DÍAZ (1876–1910), the *científicos* were a group of young lawyers and journalists who, in the periodical *La Libertad,* articulated a theory of "scientific" politics based upon the POSITIVISM of Auguste Comte and Herbert Spencer as an alternative to "doctrinaire" and "metaphysical" liberalism. They advocated strong government marked by technocratic management and were concerned less with rights and liberties than they were with issues of order, peace, and economic growth. The original group included Justo Sierra, Telesforo García, Francisco Cosmes, Francisco BULNES, Pablo Macedo, and José Yves LIMANTOUR.

In 1892, these powerful tenured public servants in the Díaz government formed the Liberal Union to advocate a third term for Díaz. With a developmentalist platform, they called for a money-saving reorganization of the ministry of war, rationalization of the tax system, and a commercial and fiscal policy to accelerate foreign investment. They also sought constitutional amendments that would create institutional safeguards against persistent dictatorial rule. To strengthen the separation of powers, they advocated a vice presidency independent of the supreme court and the irremovability of judges. In the debate over these reforms, the group was dubbed "Científicos."

Only partially successful in their constitutional reform proposals, the *científicos* were more effective with their developmentalist agenda. As minister of finance, José Yves Limantour created a budget surplus after repaying the foreign debt; reorganized finances and credit; suppressed the *alcabala,* or internal sales tax; lowered tariffs on imports; negotiated foreign loans; put Mexico on the gold standard; and succeeded in enacting new mining and land legislation to encourage unfettered growth through foreign investment.

In 1903 the *científicos* once again organized the reelection of Díaz through a second Liberal Union convention and at the same time sought constitutional safeguards for institutionalizing the transfer of power. As Díaz's

Mexico City–centered power group, the *científicos* were clearly one of the two major contending political factions. Opposed to their European-oriented development policy to offset U.S. penetration were the *reyistas,* supporters of the Nuevo León governor Bernardo Reyes, who were more closely allied with the military and with peripheral, regional bases of power. The political contention between these two factions gave rise to the crisis of succession and the Revolution of 1910.

After the Revolution of 1910, *científico* became a derogatory term applied to those most closely associated with the dictatorship who had accumulated capital, wealth, and power at the expense of the Mexican people and their development.

Interpretations of the *científicos* vary among historians. François Javier Guerra and Charles Hale see them as constitutionalists. Guerra, however, believes that they clearly distinguished themselves from liberalism after 1893. Hale sees their liberal derivation as always fundamental. Friedrich Katz sees them as a key political faction motivating the crisis of succession in 1910. Leopoldo Zea and Arnaldo Córdova see them as ideologues and administrators of the Mexican bourgeoisie and managers of dictatorship for capitalist development.

DANIEL COSÍO VILLEGAS, *Historia moderna de México,* vol. 9 (1955–1972); Jesús Reyes Heroles, *El liberalismo mexicano,* 3 vols. (1957–1961); LEOPOLDO ZEA, *El positivismo en México* (1968); ARNALDO CÓRDOVA, *La ideología de la revolución mexicana: La formación del nuevo régimen* (1974); FRIEDRICH KATZ, *The Secret War in Mexico* (1982); FRANÇOIS JAVIER GUERRA, *Mexico, del antiguo régimen a la revolución,* 2 vols. (1988); CHARLES HALE, *The Transformation of Liberalism in Late Nineteenth Century Mexico* (1989).

MARY KAY VAUGHAN

CIEZA DE LEÓN, PEDRO DE (*b.* ca. 1520; *d.* 2 July 1554), "prince of the Peruvian chroniclers." Born in Llerena, Spain, the son of Lope de León and Leonor de Cazalla, Pedro had at least three sisters and one brother. Little is known of his early years. On 3 June 1535 he set sail for the Indies, heading for Santo Domingo. He first entered South America via Cartagena on the north coast of present-day Colombia and participated in minor expeditions in search of riches, some of which were little more than grave-robbing episodes. In 1536 he joined the ENTRADA of Juan de Vadillo to explore the Gulf of URABÁ; the next year he followed the same leader in the discovery of the province of Abibe—both were financial disasters. In 1539 he set out to explore the Cauca and Atrato basin with a new force under Jorge Robledo that later founded Ancerma and Cartago (1540) in the rich Quimbaya region. It was in Cartago in 1541 that Cieza first began to keep copious notes on what he saw and experienced. The following year he was representing Jorge Robledo in the Audiencia of Panamá, where he probably met for the first time those escaping the conflict in Peru. The same year he helped found the city of Arma and received an ENCOMIENDA for his efforts.

With the rising of Gonzalo PIZARRO in Peru, Cieza traveled to serve the royalists under Pedro de la GASCA, president of the Audiencia of Lima. In September 1547 he crossed the Pacasmayo Valley with the king's forces, continued into highland Jauja, and marched southward toward Cuzco. He fought at the battle of Jaquijahuana (9 April 1548) and witnessed the execution of the rebels Gonzalo Pizarro and Francisco de Carvajal. Gasca must have been impressed by young Cieza's scholarly capabilities, for he seems to have appointed Cieza official chronicler of events in Peru. During 1549 the young chronicler traveled into southern Charcas (modern Bolivia) under the president's orders. For a few months in 1550 he resided in Cuzco, where he took oral testimony about the INCA past from several Indians, including Cayu Tupac, descendant of the ruler HUAYNA CAPAC. Cieza completed the first part of his multivolume history in Lima on 8 September 1550.

In 1551 Cieza voyaged back to Spain and was in Toledo by mid-1552 to present PHILIP II with a copy of the manuscript. Following his return to Spain, Cieza married Isabel López de Abreu, daughter of Maria de Abreu and the prosperous merchant Juan de Llerena. Cieza died before he could complete his massive narrative and was buried in Seville in the Church of San Vicente alongside his wife, who died at age thirty-four only two months earlier.

Cieza de León intended to publish a four-part history of Peru. Part one, the only section printed during the author's lifetime, was a geographical and ethnological account of South America's Andean region; part two, the "Señorío de los Incas," was a history of the Incas; part three was the account of the Spanish discovery and conquest of the realm; and part four, made up of five book-length manuscripts, examined the civil wars: Las Salinas, Chupas, Quito, Huarina, and Jaquijahuana. Cieza became a sixteenth-century "best-seller" with the 1553 Seville edition of part one, which was quickly followed by three Spanish editions in Amberes in 1554 and seven Italian translations between 1555 and 1576.

PEDRO DE CIEZA DE LEÓN, *The Incas of Pedro de Cieza de León* (1959); FRANCESCA CANTU, ed., *Pedro de Cieza de León e il "Descubrimiento y Conquista del Perú"* (1979).

NOBLE DAVID COOK

CIHUATÁN, a large Early Postclassic (A.D. 900–1250) settlement located atop a hill with a commanding view of the Acelhuate River floodplain in the Paraíso Basin of central El Salvador. This site has yielded unequivocal evidence of the intrusion and dominance of Mexican (PIPIL) or Mexicanized populations in central El Salvador during the Early Postclassic period.

Strong contrasts in settlement pattern and material

culture distinguish the preceding Late Classic (A.D. 550–900) Fogón phase from the Early Postclassic Guazapa phase. Fogón settlements near Cihuatán are tightly nucleated clusters arranged in *plazuela* groups and located on river terraces. Guazapa settlements at the site are in a dispersed pattern, surrounding a central zone of monumental public buildings and elite residences. Guazapa settlements occur on the floodplain, on relict terraces, and atop hills. Mexican architectural traits, such as the *talud-tablero* form, I-shaped ball courts, and T-shaped temple platforms, characterize the public buildings at Cihuatán.

Unlike Maya-looking Fogón ceramics, the Guazapa ceramic complex emphasizes forms and decorative techniques from central Mexico and the southern Gulf Coast area. Large spiked censers are very similar to those from Tula. Life-sized modeled effigies of Mexican deities such as Tlaloc and Xipe Totec are very much like those from central Mexico and central and southern Veracruz. Mold-made, wheeled figurines are almost identical to those from TULA and the Veracruz Gulf Coast. These new traits that emerged during the Early Postclassic had antecedents not in any nearby region but in central and southern Mexico, indicating that Cihuatán was occupied by a foreign population during the Early Postclassic.

The fall of Cihuatán may be linked to struggles among recently arrived and established populations in El Salvador and Guatemala. It was destroyed by fire around A.D. 1250.

WILLIAM R. FOWLER, JR., "The Pipil-Nicarao of Central America (Ph.D. diss., University of Calgary, 1981); WILLIAM R. FOWLER, JR., and HOWARD H. EARNEST, JR., "Settlement Patterns and Prehistory of the Paraíso Basin of El Salvador," in *Journal of Field Archaeology* 12 (1985):19–32; WILLIAM R. FOWLER, JR., *The Cultural Evolution of Ancient Nahua Civilizations: The Pipil-Nicarao of Central America* (1989).

KATHRYN SAMPECK

CIMARRÓNES. *See* **Maroons.**

CINCHONA, a genus of thirty-eight species of trees and shrubs found on the western slopes of the Andes, from Colombia to Peru. Although some of these plants are known for their fever-reducing properties, there is no evidence that the Incas were aware of their medicinal value. The earliest recorded use of cinchona was in 1630, when JESUITS treated the viceroy of Peru for fever with the bark of the plant. This bark, in pulverized form called "Jesuit powder," proved to be extremely popular as a preventive and cure for malaria for Europeans in the tropics. Linnaeus named the plants in 1742 after the Countess of Chinchón, who was said to have recovered from malaria after being treated with the powdered bark. Although the story was without factual basis, the name stuck.

The active ingredients in the bark of the cinchona are any one of four alkaloids, cinchonine, cinchonidine, quinidine, and QUININE, this last being the most important of the four. As the amount of quinine in each species varies greatly, efforts were made to separate the drug from the bark. In 1820 French chemists Pierre Pelletier and Joseph Caventou successfully produced crystallized quinine from cinchona.

After 1821, the Jesuit practice of planting five trees for every one cut was discontinued by the governments of the newly liberated countries, a decision that led to the destruction of most of the cinchona in Peru and Colombia. From 1844 to 1851 Bolivia passed laws regulating the export of cinchona bark and forbidding the export of cinchona seeds. These policies resulted in an insufficient European supply, which spurred efforts to smuggle the seeds out of South America. Clements R. Markham, an Englishman, safely brought plant seeds of the *succirubra* and *oficialis* varieties of cinchona to Europe in 1858, and seven years later, Charles Ledger arrived in Europe with seeds of *c. ledgeriana,* a superior variety. Ledger learned about the different kinds of cinchona plants and their properties from a Bolivian Indian, Manuel Incra Mamani, who pointed out the red-bark cinchona as having the greatest curative powers. It is this variety that bears Ledger's name.

The Dutch were the most successful in establishing cinchona plantations. Their East Indies properties yielded enough quinine for European needs until World War II interrupted production. Synthetic quinine, such as atebrin, which was developed by I. G. Farbenindustrie in 1930, then became an important substitute for the natural product. Today, synthetics remain the major source of quinine, while cinchona is used mostly for flavoring tonics, such as quinine water.

JAIME JARAMILLO ARANGO, *The Conquest of Malaria* (1950); GABRIELE GRAMICCIA, *The Life of Charles Ledger* (1988).

SHEILA L. HOOKER

See also **Medicinal Plants; Medicine.**

CINCO DE MAYO, a Mexican national holiday commemorating the triumph of the Mexican army over the French on 5 May 1862, the battle of PUEBLA. General Ignacio ZARAGOZA led the Mexican army, consisting of about 2,000 conscript soldiers, to victory over a French force of some 6,000 well-equipped professional soldiers commanded by General Charles Latrille, count of Lorencez. The battle was part of a campaign by the French to place the Austrian archduke MAXIMILIAN on the Mexican throne and to establish an American empire. Although the French were ultimately successful in defeating the Mexicans and imposing Maximilian, the Mexican victory at Puebla, in the face of inadequate manpower and weaponry, inspired the Mexican nation to fight with new determination. Mexico, in honor of the victory, made Cinco de Mayo a holiday and an important

national symbol. Cinco de Mayo has been celebrated for many years in the United States, especially in the Southwest and other areas with substantial communities of Mexican origin. It is often confused with Mexican Independence Day (16 September).

JACK AUTREY DABBS, *The French Army in Mexico, 1861–1867: A Study in Military Government* (1963); LILIA DÍAZ LÓPEZ, *Versión francesa de México: Informes diplomáticos (1853–1858)* (1963); ERNESTO DE LA TORRE VILLAR, *La intervención francesa y el triunfo de la república* (1968); FRANCISCO P. TRONCOSO, *Diario de las operaciones del sitio de Puebla en 1863* (1972); DAVID G. LAFRANCE, "A Battle for Nationhood," *Vista* 5 (6 May 1990): 8–10, and "Dashed Ambition," *Vista* 6 (5 May 1991): 12–13, 18.

PAUL GANSTER

CINEMA has played a vigorous role in shaping Latin American popular culture and in portraying Latin America to the world. Its economic history has been influenced by the role of the state, positively and negatively, through nationalization, subsidies, government development corporations, exhibition quotas, and censorship. In the last years of the nineteenth century, from the capitals of Mexico and Argentina to the highlands of Bolivia, entrepreneurs trucked film equipment and novelty shorts. In clubs, cafés, and theaters, audiences watched comedy routines, advertisements, images of great rural estates, and scenes of military and political pomp.

SILENT FILM
Silent films became entertainment staples in urban Latin America, accompanying immigration and industrialization. Production remained, however, artisanal, complementing the burgeoning products of European and U.S. studios, which occupied 90 to 95 percent of screen time. World War I, which limited European film production, benefited U.S. producers. U.S. distributors offered U.S. films, which had recouped costs at home, at rates far lower than those Latin American producers could afford to charge for their films. Latin American productions often mimicked competing products from Europe or the United States. In Brazil, for example, directors making "Westerns" even took Anglo-Saxon pseudonyms. Nonetheless, an indigenous film culture was born. In Mexico, silent-film actresses became national icons; in Brazil, the "golden age" (1898–1912) was marked by romantic, even idyllic versions of the countryside and portraits of fashionable society.

Documentary subjects predominated, with some filmed theater and occasional fiction, such as the wildly successful Mexican *María* (1922), drawn from the romantic novel by Colombian Jorge ISAACS. Censorship honored the power of the documentary as early as 1913; newsreels in many places, already flickering reflections of the powerful, came to have something of an officialist character. Sometimes fiction subjects were drawn from headlines, such as the murder tale *El pequeño heroe del arroyo de oro* (The Little Hero of the Arroyo de Oro [Uruguay, 1929]) or the Mexican crime story *La banda de automóvil gris* (The Gray Car Gang [1919]). Religious and historical subjects were also popular.

Working-class culture gradually became a theme of popular silent film. The Argentine José Agustín ("El Negro") Ferreyra made films about the life of the *arrabales* (working-class suburbs) such as *La muchacha de Arrabal* (Neighborhood Girl [1922]), which incorporated a tango played by an orchestra. The Brazilian Humberto Mauro explored the relationship between country and city in several films, including *Braza dormida* (Dying Embers [1928]). Rarely was film a medium for the fine arts, with the notable exception of Mario Peixoto's *Limite* (Limit [1929]).

SOUND FILM

When sound film was introduced in 1929, U.S. studios produced simultaneous remakes in Spanish and later dubbed (in hilariously heterogenous Spanish) versions in response to audiences' clamor to see the original stars. The U.S. GOOD NEIGHBOR POLICY in the 1930s vigorously fostered free-trade agreements backed strongly by U.S. industry groups, establishing a diplomatic tradition of U.S. cultural export. Latin American sound-film production thus was low throughout the 1930s.

National industries in Mexico and Argentina were fostered by corporatist states in the 1930s. There, as in lesser production centers such as Brazil, Peru, and Cuba, radio provided an important source of stars, plots (especially from soap operas and series), themes, styles, and soundtracks. The studio model was borrowed from the United States, often with integrated exhibition. One indication of U.S. dominance was Brazil's first sound film, *Broadway Melody* (1929; original title in English), which was about Brazilians backstage in New York.

In Argentina, sound films started early. The TANGO generated a popular musical genre that developed within a decade from vigorously populist to cloying cliché as the cinema sought a middle-class audience. The star Carlos GARDEL made several tango movies before continuing his career in Europe. Some productions went beyond populist celebration, for instance Mario Soffici's 1939 *Prisioneros de la tierra* (Prisoners of the Land), about the exploitation of maté workers, and the psychological dramas of Leopoldo Torres Ríos, such as *La vuelta al nido* (Return to the Nest [1938]), about a family in crisis. Import-substitution policies, urbanization, and cutbacks in Spanish-language competition because of the Spanish Civil War fueled the business. However, Argentina's neutrality in World War II caused the United States to suspend shipments of raw stock, further intensifying national filmmakers' demands for state protection. After 1946, Juan Domingo PERÓN introduced quotas, government loans, and an admissions tax; production was boosted, but *churros* ("quota quickies," low-quality films made simply to fill mandatory screen time) were also common.

In Mexico, the Lázaro CÁRDENAS government established a tradition of heavy state involvement, bankrolling studios, and establishing loan policies as well as quotas from 1935 on. U.S. support during World War II, quotas, and state financing—including the purchase of some distribution companies in 1947—garnered 15 percent of the home market for Mexican production. A studio system flourished, complete with major stars such as María FÉLIX, Pedro ARMENDÁRIZ, and Dolores DEL RIO, and the 1940s became the "golden age" of Mexican commercial cinema. Genre films arose, such as the *cabaretera* (brothel) films, *comedias rancheras* (cowboy films), historical films of the Revolution, and redolent melodramas playing on the virgin/whore female image. Among the best-known directors of the period was Emilio ("El Indio") FERNÁNDEZ, who produced a trilogy on the Mexican Revolution and has been compared to John Ford for his creation of a national iconography. CANTINFLAS, the comedian whose character and films have had enduring popularity throughout the region, rose to celebrity in the late 1930s. As the system consolidated, state support for studios also entrenched a group of veteran filmmakers and, along with the international market, encouraged filmic clichés. Centralized distribution after 1953 fostered the production of *churros*.

The uncompleted epic work of Soviet filmmaker Sergei Eisenstein in Mexico in 1930–1931 acquainted several Mexican filmmakers, including the renowned cinematographer Gabriel FIGUEROA, with his vision and style. (By contrast, the Spanish exile Luis Buñuel's postwar stay in Mexico, while resulting in some remarkable films, had little stylistic impact except on the work of his associate Luis ALCORIZA.)

In Brazil, whose major trading partner was the United States, and whose options to control film production were correspondingly reduced, mild quotas from 1930 on encouraged entrepreneurs. They produced films that sentimentally celebrated the lives of the poor and disenfranchisesd, such as Humberto Mauro's *Ganga bruta* (Thugs [1933]) and *Favela dos meus amores* (Slum of My Desires [1935]), and also films that transformed radio musical tradition into the *chanchada* musical. A clutch of production companies, including Cinédia—started by the self-styled nationalist entrepreneur Adhémar Gonzaga—were formed, featuring carnivalesque films that were precursors to *chanchadas*. The Rio production company Atlántida, later to become a foremost producer of *chanchadas*, was founded in 1941 to produce films involving themes of daily life; *Moleque Tião* (Kid Tião [1943]) featured the great black comedian and actor Grande Otelo. Vera Cruz was started by a São Paulo industrialist in 1949 to upgrade Brazilian cinema and appeal to an international audience. It produced the internationally acclaimed *O cangaceiro* (The Bandit, [1953]), a film about backlands bandits that showed the influence of the U.S. Western genre, but also treated a national subject that would be well worked in CINEMA NOVO. However, the U.S. studio Columbia Pictures owned international distribution rights to Vera Cruz, and it calculatedly failed to find the international audience. The company went bankrupt in 1954, a year after *O cangaceiro* won a prize at the Cannes film festival.

In the late 1930s and 1940s, Mexican cinema became preeminent throughout Latin America, and Mexicans both produced and influenced production in other countries, such as Guatemala, Colombia, Venezuela, and Cuba. Argentine cinema—both its capital and talent—spread to Chile and Uruguay. The forms pioneered by both cinemas became models, even to the extent that Brazilian movie music sometimes had a Caribbean flavor. Censorship affected the choice of subject and tone. For instance, *Manuel García* (Cuba [1941]) was censored in Cuba for its Robin Hood–like theme. Mexican censorship forced a happy ending in the first of Fernando de Fuentes's films about the Revolution, *El prisionero trece* (Prisoner Number Thirteen [1933]).

NUEVO CINE

In the 1950s, studio production declined and an energetic wave of film production developed on completely different terms, for a variety of reasons. It came to be called Nuevo Cine Latino Americano after a film festival in Viña del Mar, Chile, in 1967. U.S. wartime support for national production did not continue, and the trade association Motion Picture Export Association zealously guarded distribution networks for U.S. films. Film audiences declined and film studios collapsed for other reasons as well. Latin American government production policies all too often produced low-quality films, and admission prices set by the state limited capital. Television proved a fierce rival for cinema.

At the same time, political forces—the rise of postcolonial nations in Africa and Asia, the Cuban Revolution international lending policies for development, and U.S. diplomacy—fostered nationalist and populist rhetoric. Culturally, Italian neorealists and the French New Wave variously demonstrated the creative power of the socially engaged or dissident artist.

In Latin America, middle-class, mostly male youths typical of the international youth and student culture of the 1950s—both political and individualistic, in opposition to and yet part of the nation's cultural elite—established film clubs, film magazines, and cinematheques. In Argentina in 1956, Fernando Birri, who like several other Latin American filmmakers had studied with the Italian neorealists, founded a production center at the National University of the Littoral in Santa Fe, soon known as the Documentary Film School of Santa Fe and inspiring among others a center called Cine Experimental at the University of Chile.

Some strove to be missionaries of "cultured cinema" and to produce personal artistic statements within the dramatic conventions of international feature film. Argentine Leopoldo Torre Nilsson's Bergmanesque elaborations on middle- and upper-class alienation; Argentine Fernand Ayala's *Paula la cautiva* (The Captive

Paula [1963]), portraying a decadent aristocracy; the Brazilian Anselmo Duarte's *O pagador de promessas* (The Given Word [1962]), a tale of a backlands simpleton who comes to the city to fulfill a promise to an Afro-Brazilian saint; and several Mexican adaptations of Gabriel GARCÍA MÁRQUEZ stories, including Arturo Ripstein's *Tiempo de morir* (A Time to Die [1965]), each demonstrate a simultaneous search for indigenous themes, a personal style, and a conformity to existing conventions of feature cinema.

Many strove to both reflect and to affect social reality, while also reaching mass audiences. This goal took many expressive forms. Films such as Venezuelan Margot Benacerraf's *Araya* (1958); the early films of the Argentine Santa Fe film school, such as the documentary *Tire dié* (Throw Me a Dime [1956–1958]) and the fiction feature *Los inundados* (The Flooded Ones [1961]); the early films of Brazilian *cinema novo* leader Nelso Pereira dos Santos, including *Vidas secas* (Barren Lives [1963]); Argentine Leonardo Favio's *Crónica de un niño solo* (Tale of an Orphan [1964]); Chilean Aldo Francia's *Valparaíso mi amor* (Valparaiso My Love [1968]); and Chilean Miguel Littin's *El chacal de Nahueltoro* (The Jackal of Nahueltoro [1969]), refracting the mandate of Italian neorealism, plunged with documentary or documentary-like realism into long-hidden social realities. In some cases film served as exposé and testament, as in the Mexican Central University of Film Studies *El Grito* (1968), the chronicle of the Mexican student movement whose clash with authorities resulted in the Tlatelolco massacre of 1968.

"Militant cinema" called for a divorce both from studio and art cinema and from traditional lowest-common-denominator goals of entertainment, aiming instead to provoke heightened political awareness. Aesthetic polemics ensued over what was variously called "the cinema of hunger" (the Brazilian Glauber Rocha), "imperfect cinema" (the Cuban Julio García Espinosa), "revolutionary cinema" (the Bolivian Jorge Sanjinés), and "third cinema" (the Argentines Fernando Solanas and Octavio Getino). Stylistically innovative films, whose formal challenge was motivated by a desire to break through social clichés and stereotypes, included Jorge Sanjinés and Oscar Soria's *Revolución* (1964); Glauber Rocha's astonishingly rich opus *Deus e o diabo na terra do sol* (Black God/White Devil [1964]); Fernando Solanas and Octavio Getino's *La hora de los hornos* (Hour of the Furnaces [1968]); Argentine Raymundo Gleyzer's *México: La revolución congelada* (Mexico, the Frozen Revolution [1970]); Cuban Manuel Octavio Gómez's *La primera carga al machete* (First Charge of the Machete [1969]); Cuban Tomás Gutiérrez Alea's abundant and brilliant opus, including his early *Memorias de subdesarrollo* (Memories of Underdevelopment [1968]); and the early work of Chilean Raúl (later Raoul) Ruíz.

This spectacular flourishing of cinematic creativity was heralded in film festivals and international retrospectives worldwide. This recognition also made possible some international coproductions, such as those

Scene from *Memories of Underdevelopment* by Tomás Gutiérrez Alea, Cuba, 1968. NEW YORKER FILMS.

between Italian national television and Jorge Sanjinés in the production of *El Coraje del Pueblo* (The Courage of the People [1971]). The Latin American audience, however, was always sparse for such films, partly because they were often formally challenging and partly because of political suppression, especially in the Southern Cone. Governments increasingly censored, exiled, and even "disappeared" filmmakers. Works of distinction were produced in exile, including the remarkable three-part documentary of the Allende regime *Batalla de Chile* (Battle of Chile [1975, 1976, 1979]). In a few cases institutions endured, such as the Cinemateca Uruguaya, which resisted censorship and kept open doors throughout military rule.

FILM INSTITUTIONS
Even governments that found the Nuevo Cine Latinoamericano profoundly threatening sought to promote quality cinema. In Argentina, the National Institute of Cinema, offering loans to filmmakers from box-office taxes, was responsible for a rise in cinematic production in the mid-1970s, including Héctor Olivera's internationally acclaimed *La Patagonia rebelde* (Rebellion in Patagonia [1974]). In Brazil, Embrafilme was launched in the early 1970s, the result of filmmakers' lobbying, and thereafter perpetually reorganized until its abolition in 1990. In the mid-1970s it controlled some distribution, produced up to half the Brazilian films made, and exercised a screen quota. Brazilian commercial production tended to be raucous and rowdy, with the *pornochanchada*, a debased form of the earlier musical genre, flourishing along with slapstick comedy.

In Mexico, the state continued to play a powerful, controversial, and erratic role. In the early 1960s a corrupt and financially stagnant industry produced low-quality films with a virtual government guarantee of profitability. Independent filmmakers of the Nuevo Cine generation agitated and developed projects. Begin-

ning in 1970, the Luis ECHEVERRÍA ALVAREZ government founded new film institutions and supported many independent filmmakers, including Arturo Ripstein, Jaime Hermosillo, Felipe Cazals, Luis Alcoriza, and Paul Leduc, but his successor, José LÓPEZ PORTILLO, quickly reversed much of this policy. The presidency of Miguel de la MADRID HURTADO reinstated the goal of producing quality cinema by creating the Mexican Institute of Cinema (IMCINE), which coordinated state roles in production, distribution, and exhibition. Occasional works of quality have emerged, although most Mexican movies have been low-quality features aimed at a Mexican and U.S.-Hispanic audience.

Other governments throughout Latin America supported cinema as a tool of cultural self-discovery, with mixed results. In 1952 a nationalist military government in Bolivia established the Bolivian Film Institute, which lasted for more than a decade and involved Bolivia's major film producers, Antonio Eguino, Oscar Sonia, and Jorge Sanjinés, who headed it briefly. After a tempestuous history, the institute was shut down by a military government in 1967. In 1968 Peru's nationalist military government stimulated film production, mostly in shorts, by invoking quotas and lifting import fees on equipment. Francisco Lombardi's 1977 *Muerte al amanecer* (Death at Dawn) was a rare box-office success; he later enjoyed several others. In Colombia, entertainment taxes were targeted from 1971 to support cinema, in combination with mandated screen time, and in 1978 a development company, Focine, was established. Several interesting Colombian films resulted, including Carlos Mayolo's *Carne de tu carne* (Flesh of Your Flesh [1983]) and Luis Ospina's *Pura sangre* (Pure Blood [1982]), both obliquely referencing Colombian politics through vampire metaphors. In Venezuela, where oil profits were fueling cultural policy, state film financing and required exhibition of national films promoted cinema from 1975 on. Additional support came from the Venezuelan development company Focine, a mixed public-private corporation founded in 1981 that was responsible for an uneven record of commercial production. In Panama, the left-leaning Torrijos government established in 1972 the Grupo Experimental de Cine Universitário, which produced several shorts and maintained a magazine and film exhibition center. The Chilean national film institute did not survive the 1973 coup.

The Cuban government's Institute of Cinematic Art and Industry (ICAIC), established months after the revolution, was a uniqe institution, with profound effects for Nuevo Cine. Growing from an aggressively experimental documentary and newsreel base—one that drew heavily on the montage tradition of early Russian formalists—the small industry soon began producing fiction features on themes of revolutionary life. After a censorship controversy in 1961, Fidel Castro described the industry's role with the dictum, "Within the Revolution, everything; against the Revolution, nothing"—a phrase that did not inhibit a vigorous internal history of conflict over aesthetics and politics at ICAIC.

ICAIC became an important coproduction and post-production site for Latin American left filmmakers under pressure at home by the late 1960s. By 1979, Cuba was ready to offer an international showcase for Latin American film in its annual Festival of New Latin American Cinema. For a decade, before Cuba began suffering from the collapse of its socialist allies, it flourished as the premier Latin American film festival and became a major marketplace as well (although the Latin American marketplace for Latin cinema continued to be poor). In 1986 an international school of cinema and television, headed by Nuevo Cine veteran and visionary Fernando Birri, was founded in Cuba to foster a new generation of socially conscious filmmakers. By 1990, it had weathered several crises, some caused by the clash of expectations between teachers and highly diverse students, but had an uncertain future. At the same time the Foundation for Latin American Cinema, an international organization headed by Gabriel García Márquez and also based in Cuba, experimented with international coproduction with mild success. On the model of ICAIC, the Nicaraguan Sandinista government established in 1979 a national film institute, INCINE, which produced some provocative documentaries and newsreels with ample help from ICAIC and international media makers, but was crippled by lack of resources and the gradual collapse of the Sandinista government.

AFTER THE MILITARY

As civilian rule was restored in the Southern Cone in the 1980s and film clubs revived, Nuevo Cine veterans began making films with a social edge and high production values, such as Brazilian Ruy Guerra's *Eréndira* (1982) and Argentine Fernando Solanas's *Tangos: El exilio de Gardel* (Tangos [1985]). Others who had trained in advertising also made films that offered social criticism along with entertainment, including Marcos Zurinaga's *La gran fiesta* (The Grand Ball, Puerto Rico [1986]) and Argentine Luis Puenzo's *La historia oficial* (The Official Story [1985]). Women met internationally, formed production units, and produced documentary and fiction work. Among the leading female directors were Brazilian Suzana Amaral (*A hora da estrela* [Hour of the Star, 1985]), Argentine María Luisa Bemberg (*Camila* [1984]), and Mexican María Novaro (*Danzón* [1991]).

Although European television programmers created funding possibilities for filmmakers, satellite signal piracy also fostered the growth of low-cost television services throughout Latin America. Movie attendance shrank dramatically with hard times, unrenovated theaters, and the threat of street crime at night. The collapse of the socialist bloc, long a dependable if not lucrative venue, especially for documentaries, also affected the market. International coproductions often lacked a distinctive style. Throughout Latin America, national film boards and institutes were battered by eco-

nomic crises in the late 1980s. Argentina's INC was repeatedly threatened with abolition under sweeping and draconian economic measures; Brazil's Embrafilme was abolished in 1990, and with it much of Brazil's production.

Some of the producer/distributor cooperatives begun in the 1970s, including the Colombian Cine Mujer, the Mexican Zafra, and the Peruvian Grupo Chaski, seized on the grassroots potential of video. Left-wing media makers increasingly turned to video as a mode of communication. The Brazilian Workers' Center, part of a large metallurgical union, launched ambitious grassroots video production, and grass-roots video burgeoned in Colombia, Ecuador, and elsewhere. In some areas, particularly lowlands Brazil, indigenous groups experimented with video. In El Salvador, video became a propaganda weapon.

For some filmmakers, the advent of portable video and digital editing, combined with economic recession and the high cost of film, suggested the end of film making as they had known it. But some of the old guard of Nuevo Cine held out hope that video makers of tomorrow would continue the social inquiry of new Latin American film. As Paul Leduc said to his colleagues at the Havana film festival in 1987, "Cinema, the cinema we always knew, is a dinosaur becoming extinct; but the lizards and salamanders that survived the catastrophe are beginning to appear.... Dinosaur cinema is extinct! Long live the salamander cinema!"

JORGE A. SCHNITMAN, *Film Industries in Latin America: Dependency and Development* (1984); PAULO PARANAGUA, *Cinema na América Latina: Longe de Deus e perto de Hollywood* (1985); TIM BARNARD, ed., *Argentine Cinema* (1986); JULIANNE BURTON, ed., *Cinema and Social Change in Latin America: Conversations with Filmmakers* (1986); RANDAL JOHNSON, *The Film Industry in Brazil: Culture and the State* (1987); PETER. B. SCHUMANN, *Historia del cine latinoamericano* (1987); PATRICIA AUFDERHEIDE, ed., *Latin American Visions* (1989); CARL. J. MORA, *Mexican Cinema: Reflections of a Society*, rev. ed. (1989); JORGE SANJINES and the UKAMAU GROUP, *Theory and Practice of a Cinema with the People* (1989); JULIANNE BURTON, ed., *The Social Documentary in Latin America* (1990); JOHN KING, *Magical Reels: A History of Cinema in Latin America* (1990).

PATRICIA AUFDERHEIDE

CINEMA NOVO, a movement that marks the beginning of modern cinema in Brazil. Although Cinema Novo ceased to exist as a unified movement by the early 1970s, virtually every significant Brazilian film made since the late 1950s has been directly or indirectly influenced by the movement and its critical vision of Brazilian society.

Cinema Novo arose in the late 1950s and early 1960s as part of a broad, heterogeneous movement of cultural transformation that involved theater, popular music, and literature as well as the cinema. It evolved through a number of discernible phases, each corresponding to a specific sociopolitical conjuncture. Between 1960 and 1964, the year of the military coup d'état that overthrew the government of João GOULART, questions such as agrarian reform and social transformation were debated at almost every level of society. The films of this period attempted to contribute to the debate with films about the country's lower classes.

Initially, Cinema Novo sought to reveal the truth about the country's underdevelopment, in the hope that the Brazilian people would gain a critical consciousness and then participate in the struggle for national liberation. As Glauber Rocha wrote in his 1965 manifesto, "An Aesthetic of Hunger," "Cinema Novo is . . . an evolving complex of films that will ultimately make the public aware of its own misery."

In their attempt to raise the Brazilian people's level of consciousness, filmmakers initially set their stories in areas of Brazil where social contradictions were most apparent: poor fishing villages, urban slums, and the country's impoverished Northeast. Glauber Rocha's *Barravento* (1962; The Turning Wind) denounces Afro-Brazilian religion as a form of alienation while at the same time affirming its value as a means of preserving cultural identity and as a potential site of collective resistance. Nelson Pereira dos Santos's *Vidas secas* (1963; Barren Lives), based on the Graciliano RAMOS novel, outlines the plight of a peasant family during a period of drought, including its conflict with an absentee landowner. Ruy Guerra's *Os fuzis* (1964; The Guns) concerns soldiers who guard a landowner's food warehouse to keep its contents from starving peasants. Rocha's *Deus e o diabo na terra do sol* (1964; Black God, White Devil) indirectly discusses the feudal structures that impede a more just distribution of land in the Northeast.

From 1964 until 1968, the year of the military government's Fifth Institutional Act, which inaugurated a period of extremely repressive military rule, political liberties were restricted and censorship increased, but there was still a degree of space for discussion and debate. During this period, the focus of Cinema Novo shifted from rural to urban Brazil as filmmakers turned their cameras on the urban middle class, and more specifically on intellectuals like themselves, in an attempt to understand the failure of the Left in 1964.

Paulo César Saraceni's *O desafio* (1966; The Challenge) deals with a young, anguished, and socially impotent journalist in the period immediately following the coup. Glauber Rocha's *Terra em transe* (1967; Land in Anguish) dissects the populist arrangements that have long dominated Brazilian politics by tracing the trajectory of a poet as he moves between Left and Right and his final, suicidal option for individual armed struggle. Gustavo Dahl's *O bravo guerreiro* (1968; The Brave Warrior) focuses on the futile struggle of an idealistic young congressman, and ends with a scene in which he looks into a mirror and points a gun into his mouth. In Nelson Pereira dos Santos's *Fome de amor* (1968; Hunger for Love), the revolutionary leader is deaf, dumb, and blind. These films express the pessimism, disillusion, and despair of many intellectuals after 1964.

The final phase of Cinema Novo ran from 1968 until around 1972. During this period of extremely harsh military rule, it was difficult for filmmakers to express opinions directly, so allegory became the preferred mode of cinematic discourse of what is known as TROPICALISMO in Brazilian cinema. Glauber Rocha's *O dragão da maldade contra o santo guerreiro* (also called *Antônio das Mortes*, 1968) uses a highly allegorical, quasi-operatic style to portray a metaphysical struggle between good and evil that shifts, at the end of the film, to a struggle against imperialism. Joaquim Pedro de Andrade's adaptation of Mário de Andrade's modernist novel *Macunaíma* (1969) develops cannibalism as a metaphor for exploitative social relationships. Nelson Pereira dos Santos's *Como era gostoso o meu francês* (1972; How Tasty Was My Little Frenchman) uses the same metaphor for the often conflictive relationship between Brazilian and European cultures and the development of a national cultural identity in Brazil.

The period since 1972 has been characterized by stylistic and thematic diversity, and Cinema Novo's legacy has continued to be one of its major driving forces. Its practitioners have remained in the forefront of Brazilian cinema with films such as Joaquim Pedro de Andrade's *O homem do pau-brasil* (1982; The Brazilwood Man), Carlos Diegues's *Bye bye Brasil* (1980), Ruy Guerra's *A queda* (1978; The Fall), Leon Hirszman's *Eles não usam black-tie* (1981; They Don't Wear Black-Tie), Arnaldo Jabor's *Tudo bem* (1978; All's Well), Glauber Rocha's *A idade da terra* (1980; Age of the Earth), and Nelson Pereira dos Santos's *Memórias do cárcere* (1984; Prison Memoirs).

Following Cinema Novo's lead, the best of Brazilian cinema has continued to express certain historical moments as few other art forms have been able to do. The influence of the movement's critical vision of Brazilian society is evident in films such as Hector Babenco's courageous *Lúcio Flávio* (1977), the first film to depict police torture, and the same director's *Pixote* (1980), a brutal portrait of street kids. It is also clear in Roberto Farias's *Pra frente Brasil* (1982; Onward Brazil), which deals with the torture and murder of an innocent man by the military police on a day when the nation's attention was turned toward the 1970 World Soccer championship in Mexico, and in Tizuka Yamasaki's *Patriamada* (1984; Beloved Country), which is set during the 1984 campaign for direct elections. *Patriamada* combines fiction and documentary sequences with highly original effects. With its highly creative films and its continuing rich legacy, Cinema Novo is virtually synonymous with modern Brazilian cinema.

JEAN-CLAUDE BERNARDET, *Brasil em tempo de cinema*, 2d ed. (1977), and *Cinema brasileiro: Propostas para uma história* (1979); ISMAIL XAVIER, *Sertão mar: Glauber Rocha e a estética da fome* (1983); RANDAL JOHNSON, *Cinema Novo × 5: Masters of Contemporary Brazilian Film* (1984) and *The Film Industry in Brazil: Culture and the State* (1987); RANDAL JOHNSON and ROBERT STAM, eds., *Brazilian Cinema* (1988).

RANDAL JOHNSON

CIRANDA, a round dance of Portuguese origin found throughout Brazil in both children's and adult versions. The children's *ciranda* is a round game with sung verses. The adult version is a group dance performed in a circle around a small ensemble of musicians and a singer. In one common form, dancers hold hands facing the center as they collectively take several steps to the right and one back to the left so that the circle slowly moves counterclockwise. The ensemble usually includes a trumpet or saxophone, a snare drum, a *bombo* (tenor drum), and a *mineiro* (metal shaker). The songs are performed in call-and-response form between the *mestre* (lead singer) and the dancers.

EVANDRO RABELLO, *Ciranda: Dança de roda, dança da moda* (1979); ONEYDA ALVARENGA, *Música popular brasileira*, 2d ed. (1982), esp. pp. 195–197.

LARRY N. CROOK

See also **Music: Popular Music and Dance.**

CÍRCULO MILITAR, a social club for officers in the Argentine army. Founded in 1881, the Círculo Militar has been a focal point of political activity within the Argentine armed forces since the 1920s. It is located in the Retiro district of Buenos Aires, near the Plaza San Martín. Chartered as a social club for army officers, it soon became a center for discussion and debate of the role that the armed forces should play in politics. President Hipólito YRIGOYEN's promotion of loyal officers to command positions during his first administration (1916–1922) angered traditionalists within the army's high command. Members of a secret organization, the Logia General San Martín, took control of the club and used it to organize support within the army.

Corporate concerns evolved into broader political differences after 1928. Club presidents José Agustín JUSTO and Arturo Rawson challenged popular government and championed the army as a defender of nationalism. As a result, the leadership of the Círculo Militar became deeply involved in the Revolution of 1930, the first of a series of military interventions that have plagued Argentina since World War I.

ROBERT A. POTASH, *The Army and Politics in Argentina, 1928–1945: Yrigoyen to Perón* (1969); ISAÍAS JOSÉ GARCÍA ENCISO, *Los 100 años del Círculo Militar* (1981).

DANIEL LEWIS

CISNEROS, BALTASAR HIDALGO DE (*b.* 12 June 1755; *d.* 9 June 1829), viceroy of Río de la Plata (1809–1810). A military man and the last viceroy of the Río de la Plata, Cisneros was born in Cartagena, Spain, the son of a high-ranking naval officer. Following in his father's footsteps, Cisneros entered the navy, progressing through the ranks and serving in the Pacific, in Algeria, and in the Spanish campaigns against the revolutionary

government of France. He arrived in Buenos Aires in June 1809, sent by the Seville junta that was ruling Spain in the name of the deposed king. His nine months in office were marked by a disintegration of the political scene and a worsening of economic conditions. He also was unable to bring the local militia, emboldened by their victories in repelling two British invasions (1804, 1806–1807), under his control. By May 1810, forced into an emergency created by the fall of Seville to the French, Cisneros decided to call an open town council meeting (*cabildo abierto*). Although the viceroy believed that he would be called upon to form a new government, the *cabildo abierto* voted to depose Cisneros; however, he was allowed to return to Spain.

Able to absolve himself of any blame for the loss of Buenos Aires, Cisneros was successively named commandant general of Cádiz, minister of the navy, and director general of the fleet. Appointed captain-general of Cartagena by the Constitutionist government during the 1820 uprising, he held this post until his death.

ENRIQUE UDAONDO, *Diccionario biográfico colonial argentino* (1945), pp. 442–443.

SUSAN M. SOCOLOW

CISNEROS, FRANCISCO JAVIER (*b.* 28 December 1836; *d.* 7 July 1898), transportation developer in Colombia. Cisneros was educated in his hometown of Santiago de Cuba and in Havana, where he received his civil engineering degree (1857). He studied at Rensselaer Polytechnic Institute in Troy, New York, then engaged in railway construction in Cuba from 1857 to 1868. His pro-independence activities (1868–1871) forced him into exile in New York City. Cisneros attempted to work in Peru but in 1873 left for Colombia. There, the Antioquia Railroad (upon which he labored intermittently until 1885), the Cauca Railroad (1878–1883), the Barranquilla Railroad (1885–1895), plus dock construction at Puerto Colombia and the placement of steamboats on the Magdalena River (1877–1885; 1889–1898) all testify to Cisneros's developmental vision. Colombia's unsettled politics and weak economy were structural liabilities that Cisneros found insurmountable. He died in New York City.

ALFREDO D. BATEMAN, *Francisco Javier Cisneros* (1970); HERNÁN HORNA, *Transport Modernization and Entrepreneurship in Nineteenth Century Colombia* (1992).

J. LEÓN HELGUERA

See also **Railroads.**

CISNEROS BETANCOURT, SALVADOR (*b.* 10 October 1828; *d.* 28 February 1914), Cuban independence leader and legislator. Cisneros Betancourt was born in Camagüey, central Cuba, to a wealthy and noble family. After independence, people affectionately continued to

163

call him by his title, Marqués of Santa Lucía. As a young man, he was imprisoned in Spain for his conspiratorial activities. Cisneros Betancourt was involved in Cuba's two wars of independence and was president of the insurgent provisional government in both. He also participated in the framing of the insurgent constitutions and was a delegate to the constituent assembly that approved Cuba's first constitution as an independent nation (1900–1901). Cisneros Betancourt strongly urged the rejection of the PLATT AMENDMENT, accusing the United States of exercising "the power of the strong over the weak." He was a member of the Cuban Senate from 1902 until his death. Cisneros Betancourt died in Havana.

For Cisneros Betancourt's role in the wars of independence, see JOSÉ M. HERNÁNDEZ, *Cuba and the United States: Intervention and Militarism, 1868–1933* (1993); for his opposition to the Platt Amendment, see PHILIP S. FONER, *The Spanish-Cuban-American War and the Birth of American Imperialism* (1972), vol. 2, pp. 534–632.

JOSÉ M. HERNÁNDEZ

CISPLATINE CONGRESS, a meeting convened by the Portuguese in Montevideo, Uruguay (15 July–8 August 1821), after having defeated the resistance led by José ARTIGAS. At this congress, the Provincia Oriental was incorporated into the United Realm of Portugal, Brazil, and Algarve as the State of Cisplatine. King JOÃO VI of Portugal had returned to Lisbon after residing in Río de Janeiro since 1808. Liberal ideas predominated in Portugal. One leader who espoused them was Chancellor Silvestre Pinheiro Ferreira, who believed that the people of the Provincia Oriental themselves should decide their fate. Nevertheless, Carlos Federico Lecór, baron of Laguna and commander of the invading army, had a decisive influence on the outcome of the congress.

JUAN E. PIVEL DEVOTO, "El Congreso Cisplatino (1821)," in *Revista del Instituto Histórico y Geográfico del Uruguay* 3 (1936): 111–409; JOHN STREET, *Artigas and the Emancipation of Uruguay* (1959); ALFREDO CASTELLANOS, *La Cisplatina: La independencia y la república caudillesca, 1820–1838* (1974).

JOSÉ DE TORRES WILSON

CISPLATINE PROVINCE, the buffer territory of the eastern bank of the Uruguay River. In 1821 a weak and subservient Uruguayan congress formally annexed the BANDA ORIENTAL to Portuguese Brazil as the Cisplatine Province. Between 1825 and 1828 the region was a battleground between Argentina and Brazil. Argentina regarded the area as her east bank; Brazil considered it her Cisplatine Province, or Estado Cisplatino. Great Britain, anxious to enlarge her trade in the Plata region, persuaded Brazil to end the conflict. The Cisplatine Province was recognized as the independent state of Uruguay in 1828.

MARVIN ALISKY, *Uruguay: A Contemporary Survey* (1969), pp. 19–20; JEAN L. WILLIS, *Historical Dictionary of Uruguay* (1974), pp. 101–102; RODERICK J. BARMAN, *Brazil: The Forging of a Nation* (1988).

ORLANDO R. ARAGONA

CISPLATINE WAR, struggle between Uruguayan patriots and the Brazilian army of occupation between 1825 and 1828. In April 1825, thirty-three Uruguayan patriots, led by Juan Antonio LA VALLEJA, crossed the river from Buenos Aires at night to rally their countrymen against the Brazilian army. In an effort to enlarge their efforts, the band of thirty-three leaders gathered around them groups of fighting GAUCHOS. For three years, a few thousand Uruguayans successfully harassed the Brazilian regiments in Uruguay. In 1828 British mediation brought Brazilian recognition of independent Uruguay and an end to the war.

RODERICK J. BARMAN, *Brazil: The Forging of a Nation* (1988).

ORLANDO R. ARAGONA

CITADELLE LA FERRIÈRE, a Haitian fortress situated atop Pic La Ferrière at 3,100 feet. The structure was begun by Jean Jacques DESSALINES in 1804 and completed by Henri CHRISTOPHE (King Henry I) in 1817. Access to this huge granite fortress in northern Haiti is by a precipitous road from the king's plush palace of Sans Souci at the foot of the mountain. The fortress itself has walls up to 140 feet high and 13 feet thick. In area it is 10,750 square yards and could house 15,000 soldiers. Protecting the citadel's outer walls were three galleries of 365 cannons. Two huge roof cisterns provided an internal water supply.

Dessalines began the fortress as a final place of retreat should France reinvade Haiti, and Christophe shared this purpose in completing it. But Christophe had additional motives. He wanted to show the world that blacks were capable of a grand construction—even with severe human loss. Further, it made him more mysterious and powerful in the eyes of the masses. For enraging the king, an errant duke or baron or even the monarch's own son might find himself sentenced there to hard labor among the granite. Fittingly, Christophe is buried inside the fortress with an epitaph boasting that he would rise to life from his ashes.

W. W. HARVEY, *Sketches of Haiti* (1827); JAMES LEYBURN, *The Haitian People* (1941); HUBERT COLE, *Christophe, King of Haiti* (1967).

THOMAS O. OTT

CITIES AND URBANIZATION

URBANIZATION PRIOR TO THE CONQUEST
When Spanish conquistador Bernal DÍAZ DEL CASTILLO first saw TENOCHTITLÁN, the capital of the Aztec empire, in central Mexico, he exclaimed, "With such wonderful

sights to gaze on, we did not know what to say or if this was real that we saw before our eyes." The cities encountered by the conquistadores—Tenochtitlán, and CAJAMARCA and CUZCO in Peru—were the latest products of a centuries-old tradition of urbanism. As with their modern counterparts, pre-Columbian cities emerged as a result of processes in which political, religious, residential, and economic functions were centralized and society became increasingly complex. Some of these processes set so-called New World cities apart from those in the Old World, calling into question the applicability of European definitions of urbanism to the Western Hemisphere. For example, archaeoastronomers point out that sophisticated planners constructed cities such as TEOTIHUACÁN in Mexico and Cuzco in Peru, among others, to accommodate horizon markers that determined specific periods in the sacred year. Debate has been especially heated in recent years concerning definitions of pre-Columbian urban traditions in MESOAMERICA. Some scholars favor the term "regal-ritual city" as a replacement of the dated concept of the "ceremonial center" where, it was once believed, the theocracy lived, and to which people came from small disparate rural settlements on special occasions for worship and celebrations. Strenuous objectors also challenge the minimizing of the densely populated, administrative urbanism that may have characterized such Maya sites as TIKAL, with perhaps 55,000 people at its height (ca. A.D. 600–830), or CARACOL, with 35,000 to 60,000 residents (ca. A.D. 700). The "ceremonial center" concept still appears in the literature on Andean settlement patterns, associated, for example, with places such as HUARI and TIAHUANACO. Andean variation defies a neat typology, however, as illustrated in the example of Cahuachi, of the NASCA culture, on the south coast of Peru. Scholars once believed it to be a city at its height (A.D. 1–700), but recent excavations show much of the "resident" population was transient, visiting during periodic pilgrimages. Yet there were also clear city formations such as at CHAN CHAN, with 50,000 or more residents, and numerous "towns" with approximate populations of 10,000.

Teotihuacán, approximately 12 miles from modern MEXICO CITY, was the largest pre-Columbian city in the Classic Period with perhaps 100,000 people ca. A.D. 500. Some 2,000 apartment complexes have been mapped for this city, where one compound could house 60 to 100 individuals of greatly varying social status. Teotihuacán also had neighborhoods of people from the Gulf Coast and Oaxaca. Its many markets and artisanal workshops indicate that it functioned as a true production and distribution center. The scale of its monumental architecture embodied in the two principal pyramids are indicative of the emergent power of secular elites and the priesthood during that period.

As was the case with many Mesoamerican cities, Teotihuacán experienced a puzzling, drastic decline in the eighth century, when its central buildings suffered a fiery destruction. A more modest city arose shortly afterwards at the same site. The dramatic so-called collapse of Classic Lowland Maya cities in the eighth century, still something of a mystery, is attributed now largely to environmental deterioration and a shift to the northern lowland Puuc region and CHICHÉN ITZÁ. There cultural florescence continued, extending the Classic Period to the fall of Chichén Itzá (ca. A.D. 1200), while the considerably depopulated southern cities remained in crisis and the culture underwent changes in settlement patterns and economic organization.

Among Postclassic cities, one of the largest and best documented is the Aztec capital, Tenochtitlán, which may have had a population of 300,000. Destroyed by Cortés in 1521, this island city, with its numerous canals and heavy water traffic, struck the Spaniards as another Venice.

CONQUEST AND COLONIAL URBANIZATION

Following their subjugation of indigenous societies, conquistadores razed existing structures and superimposed new religious and administrative buildings in their place. Elsewhere, they built military garrisons as the frontier of conquest turned into a frontier of colonization. This ushered in a new period of urbanization as towns became the instrument and vehicle for the shipment of agricultural and mineral wealth to Europe. By 1580, Spaniards had established 225 populated cities; by 1630 there were 331. Nearly every major urban center of Latin America had been founded by 1600; by 1620 Mexico City boasted 100,000; SALVADOR da Bahia in Brazil, 21,000; LIMA, 9,500 propertied residents; 8,000 in RECIFE; and 4,000 in the mining town of POTOSÍ. Nevertheless, these cities grew unevenly—slowly in some cases, because of indigenous depopulation, which was not reversed until after 1750, but rapidly in others, as in the case of the mining center of Potosí, with 160,000 by 1650. If cities survived their first thirty years, they generally prevailed for the entire colonial period.

Urban structures during the colonial period tended to vary according to the specific objective of town formation. While a defensive function spawned military garrisons or "way stations" (e.g., LA PAZ between Cuzco and Potosí), political jurisdiction over a hinterland often led to a more functional and differentiated urban fabric. The discovery of a mineral strike generated a haphazard and precarious urban settlement in contrast to port cities that funneled primary resources to Spain and Portugal while distributing manufactured and other European imports.

Spaniards had already founded many cities before the 1573 Ordinances of the Laws of the Indies provided some 149 technical criteria for their organization. These included appropriate site conditions, the downwind location of dumps and slaughterhouses, the street widths and block sizes, and the positioning of the jail, the treasury, and the town council on the central square. The street layout was invariably one of a grid running off the central plaza, which was dominated by a large church. Indeed, these planning guidelines, together with the fact that many cities grew very slowly during the colonial period, guaranteed that this basic structure often remains widely visible today, especially in center-city ground plans.

Some scholars have argued that the Portuguese too issued town-planning legislation for Brazil beginning from the establishment of Salvador da Bahia in 1549. Further, the discovery of gold in the interior of Brazil in the 1690s advanced this process as Portuguese officials sought ways to exert control over spontaneous settlements and impose Enlightenment views on the colonization of the indigenous population. Subsequently from 1716 on, officials insisted that new communities conform to a plan with straight-street, well-marked town plazas (often surrounded by trees) with similar buildings.

Until 1778 towns were barred from developing an independent productive and commercial base, since all trade had to go through Spain and Portugal. This policy undoubtedly "stunted" urban development and meant that the emerging structure was very weakly articulated, thanks also to enormous physical distances and barriers. Even at this early stage there is some evidence of urban "primacy," in which a single city like Mexico City or Lima dominated the urban structure disproportionately. But almost everywhere else, the formation of towns was precarious, since they were often settled according to the whim of an individual, or a rationale that all too quickly could become redundant (e.g., a military or mining venture), and were often threatened by physical destruction from earthquakes (Antigua, Guatemala), volcanic eruption, or floods (Lima, Peru). Moreover, many cities began as mining camps, and if the strike was a rich one, then these settlements grew quickly and haphazardly. The mining towns of MINAS GERAIS in Brazil (e.g., OURO PRÊTO) and Potosí in Bolivia are prime examples, as are cities such as GUANAJUATO, TAXCO, and ZACATECAS in Mexico. In these cities, too, the topography does not make for a neat urban settlement pattern, but rather for one that is growing and unorganized.

INDEPENDENCE AND DIFFERENT URBAN STRUCTURES AND SYSTEMS

It was not until the mid-eighteenth century that population in the Latin American region began to increase markedly, growing from between 10 and 12 million in 1750 to 22 million in the early 1820s, by which time almost all countries had won their independence from Spain and Portugal. This increase was due to continued European immigration, the influx of slaves into plantation economies, improved export markets, and greater resistance to diseases. Some argue that independence stimulated the growth and influence of national capital cities while others suggest that rural-based creole elites filled in gaps left by defeated Iberian elites. In Mexico

TABLE 1   Absolute Population Data for Seven Latin American Cities, 1800–1930 (figures in 000's)

	1800	1850	1870	1890	1910	1930
Bogotá	28	27	41	120	121	330
Buenos Aires	38	91	216	663	1,576	2,178
Caracas	31	44	49	72	80	203
Lima	53	85	100	104	170	273
Mexico City	137	200	230	326	471	1,049
Rio de Janeiro	53	186	275	523	975	1,701
Santiago	35	65	150	256	391	696

SOURCES: Data taken from JORGE ENRIQUE HARDOY and MARÍA ELENA LANGDON, "Analisis estadístico preliminar de la urbanización de América Latina entre 1850 y 1930," *Revista Paraguaya de Sociología* (1978), table 41, pp. 115–173; RICHARD MORSE, *The Urban Development of Latin America, 1750–1920* (1971); LOUISA SCHELL HOBERMAN and SUSAN MIGDEN SOCOLOW, eds., *Cities and Society in Colonial Latin America* (1986).

City and CARACAS population rebounded from previous losses. RIO DE JANEIRO grew significantly when the Portuguese court migrated there in 1808 to escape from Napoleonic troops. The city grew substantially both in terms of new building and new population, only to decline after 1849 due to yellow fever and cholera epidemics. The cities of BOGOTÁ and Lima showed much slower growth (see table 1). Indeed, some reported a "primacy dip" (i.e., a reduction in the dominance of the largest city) as new lands were cultivated to produce export commodities (e.g., coffee in Brazil and Venezuela).

The success of the post-Independence economy virtually determined the urbanization process. Mineral-based economies, together with tropical agricultural systems built around plantations like coffee in Brazil and sugar, tended to create urban enclaves rather than a broader system of urban centers. The exportation of coffee, conversely, led to the expansion of both São Paulo and Santos. Other forms of agriculture, although labor intensive, were often organized into small holdings and thereby generated greater multiplier effects for other associated activities. The requirements for different types of infrastructural development in each case also accentuated this process. Mining initially required the mule routes to the coast to get raw materials out of the country. Later these were superseded by railways linking the mines to the port-heads. Temperate agriculture in Argentina, for example, also required railways to bring produce to market, but Argentina developed a much more integrated network with a hierarchy of central places dedicated to a wide variety of wholesale and retail functions and a broader urban structure.

Income distribution also influenced urbanization. Where an economy was dominated by a small number of families (e.g., the Patiño family in Bolivia), few other activities developed. Similarly, the size of the population engaged in the principal sector shaped the form and dynamism of the urban process: where it was relatively small and narrow (as in the case of Bolivian tin), then urbanization was stunted; where it was large and more broadly based (e.g., coffee in Brazil, or the sequence of agricultural products in Argentina), then urbanization moved ahead rapidly, and towns were more dispersed.

THE URBAN EXPLOSION: FROM PLAZA
TO SUBURB TO MEGACITY

The first four decades of the twentieth century saw fundamental changes throughout Latin America, as the continent's economic base shifted from agriculture to industry and services, and as its population shifted from rural to urban centers. In 1900 BUENOS AIRES contained around 800,000 people, and Rio de Janeiro almost 690,000; twelve other cities had more than 100,000. By 1920, São Paulo had become the manufacturing center of Brazil. Table 2 shows that between 1950 and 1990 only Argentina, Chile, and Brazil show a sharp rise in population brought about in large part by immigration from Southern Europe. Latin American demography conspired to increase dramatically the absolute size of national populations as the reduction in crude death rates from over 40 per 1,000 early in the century to below 10 per 1,000 since 1970 led to a sharp rise in natural increase, especially from the 1940s onward as fertility rates rose. Although no one knows whether urban areas are intrinsically healthier than rural ones, it seems likely that morbidity rates are lower in cities due to higher levels of vaccination, better diets, and servicing levels available in cities, although all are subject to important intracity variations in morbidity.

While national population growth rates of nearly 3 percent per annum have been commonplace, urban growth has often proceeded at twice that speed because of rural migration. While migration may account for up to 70 percent of the decennial increase during the early period of rapid urbanization, a large portion of these newcomers are in their early child-rearing years, so that natural increase takes over and eclipses the relative importance of migration.

Initially scholars argued that limited economic opportunities and life chances in rural areas and the relative attractions of city life drew such migration; now they argue that urban migration was a direct outcome of the new demand for (cheap) labor as countries industrialized from the 1950s onward. These new urban citizens included drought refugees forced to leave the Brazilian Northeast as well as rural workers forced off the land due to mechanization and land concentration/monopoly. They were closely tied into the economic process, but on terms that left them poorly paid and unable to qualify for housing credit or access to legal dwellings.

Obelisk on the Avenida 9 de Julio commemorating the fourth centenary of the founding of Buenos Aires. Designed by Alberto Prebisch, completed in 1936. PHOTO BY VICTOR ENGLEBERT.

TABLE 2 Population Growth in Seven Latin American Cities, 1950–1990

	1950		1970		1990	
	Population in 000's	% of National Population	Population in 000's	% of National Population	Population in 000's	% of National Population
Bogotá	680	5.9	2,370	11.4	5,590	17.6
Buenos Aires	5,130	29.9	8,310	34.7	11,580	34.8
Caracas	680	13.6	2,050	19.3	3,960	20.1
Lima	1,010	13.2	2,840	21.5	6,500	29.1
Mexico City	2,880	10.3	8,740	16.6	19,370	21.9
Santiago	1,330	21.9	2,840	29.9	4,700	35.7
São Paulo	2,584	4.9	8,060	8.4	18,420	12.2

SOURCE: JAMES W. WILKIE et al., eds., *Statistical Abstract of Latin America*, vol. 30, part 1, tables 633 and 634 (1993).

Industrialization and urbanization went together when countries sought to develop the import-substituting industrialization strategy that underpinned the economic "miracle" experienced in countries like Brazil and Mexico. This strategy tended to accentuate the growth of the existing large urban centers. Since the late 1970s, however, the industrialization strategy in many countries has moved toward an export-oriented manufacturing growth model as a new range of urban centers developed in tax havens, around ports and air freight facilities, and around new industrial growth points in the provinces. These "intermediate" cities often experience the fastest growth rates today, and the direction of migration flows appears to be shifting toward those centers and away from the largest metropolitan regions.

During the 1940s and 1950s, the labor force successfully incorporated the most enterprising and able migrants, who melded into the same environment as those city born. With the slowdown in job creation, and the decline in the "positive selection" of migrants from rural regions, new arrivals to the city have begun to experience difficulties in obtaining jobs and housing, and have to depend on networks of friends and family who migrated before them for important lifelines and mechanisms for adapting to and integrating into urban life today.

Today the majority of Latin America's population is urbanized (taking a population center threshold of 10,000 people). City growth rates of 5 percent per annum, although common in the 1950s and 1960s, have begun to turn down significantly, except in certain newly industrializing centers. Often, however, urban structures remain imbalanced. A disproportionate number of many nations' urban dwellers reside in the two or three largest cities, while a vast number of tiny population settlements, often highly dispersed in remote regions, have difficulty receiving essential services. In 1992 four of the world's thirteen "megacities" (defined as cities with over 10 million people) were in Latin America: SÃO PAULO, Greater Rio de Janeiro, Buenos Aires, and Mexico City. By the end of the century, demographers predict that Mexico City and São Paulo will

be the largest cities in the world with 26.3 and 24 million, respectively, and the total urban population in the region will have increased by 160 million since 1985. Planning, therefore, faces a challenge of achieving a more balanced and integrated national system.

Some analysts have argued that this formerly highly polarized (and sometimes "primate") structure is beginning to break down, as intermediate cities become the principal attraction points of investment and population growth. They predict that "polarization reversal" might, therefore, lead to a more evenly distributed urban system in the future, but the cities growing most rapidly are often located very near the established metropolitan centers. Viewed regionally, therefore, the process may be one of increasing polarization, not less. Urban decentralization policies have had little effect. Proposals to move the locus of decision-making power away from traditional capitals (such as from Rio de Janeiro to a newly built city in the interior, BRASÍLIA), or to decentralize some public-sector activities to provincial centers, are expensive to implement and have not led to a significant decentralization of population and activities away from the principal population centers and megacities.

Cities themselves have changed dramatically during the twentieth century. From 1900 on, the elite were beginning to move away from their traditional residential location around congested and purportedly unhealthy plazas in favor of suburban neighborhoods easily reached as public and private transportation systems developed. This shift occurred in almost all Latin American cities, although in some cases just since the 1950s. Although some downtown areas have been subject to large-scale redevelopment programs, the inner city mostly comprises mixed residential and commercial land uses with modern commerce and business, government offices, small businesses and workshops, and working-class rental housing all present. The elite, the middle classes, and the major shopping malls, meanwhile, have moved out into the suburbs, conforming increasingly to the pattern of the United States. Suburban growth has also included the self-help irregular settlements that have burgeoned throughout most Latin American cities. From the 1950s on, irregular settlements began to form the largest tracts of the built-up area, with growth rates sometimes doubling those of the rest of the city. After living with family or in rental tenements elsewhere—*cortiços* or *favelas* (Brazil), *callejones* (Peru), *conventillos* (Argentina), and *vecindades* (Mexico)—city born and migrants alike who decide that they want to set up on their own would begin to look to "own" a home in the suburbs, albeit through illegal land acquisition. Yet, there are exceptions to this pattern, too, as in São Paulo, where residents begin in a *favela* on the periphery and then move to an apartment or shared house in the city. Residents' self-help, combined with increasing government intervention to provide basic services, often upgrade these neighborhoods into the working-class *barrios* or *bairros* that today dominate the urban fabric of most cities.

The problems facing city populations today are relatively similar to those that have existed since the pre-Columbian period and relate to sustainability, access to resources to meet basic needs, the optimum forms of social organization, the satisfaction derived from urban residence, and so on. The patterns of urban growth and the evolution of urban structures, the rising importance of "locality" and the orientation of social groups toward their neighborhood and community, the innovativeness and tenacity of city populations themselves, and the greater sophistication and sensitivity of government intervention, all suggest that Latin American cities will survive, and may even thrive, in the future.

For pre-Columbian America, see RICHARD P. SCHAEDEL, JORGE E. HARDOY, NORA SCOTT KINZER, ed., *Urbanization in the Americas from Its Beginning to the Present* (1978); ANTHONY AVENI, *Skywatchers of Ancient Mexico* (1980); DIANE Z. CHASE, ARLEN F. CHASE, and WILLIAM A. HAVILAND, "The Classic Maya City: Reconsidering the 'Mesoamerican Urban Tradition,'" *American Anthropologist* 92:2 (June 1990): 499–506; JANET CATHERINE BERLO, ed., *Art, Ideology, and the City of Teotihuacán: A Symposium at Dumbarton Oaks, 8–9 October 1988*; JEREMY A. SABLOFF, "Interpreting the Collapse of Classic Maya Civilization: A Case Study of Changing Archaeological Perspectives," in Lester Embree, ed., *Metaarchaeology: Reflections by Archaeologists and Philosophers* (1992), pp. 99–119.

On the growth of cities the classic is DAN STANISLAWSKI, "Early Spanish Town Planning in the New World," in *Geographical Review* 37 (1947): 94–105. PETER JOHN BAKEWELL provides a detailed account of city growth in a mining town, *Silver Mining and Society in Colonial Mexico: Zacatecas 1546–1700* (1971). Population dynamics of the late colonial and independent periods are discussed in RICHARD MC GEE MORSE, MICHAEL CONNIF, and JOHN WIBEL, eds., *The Urban Development of Latin America, 1750–1920* (1971). JAMES SCOBIE provides a rich historical geography of Buenos Aires growth at the turn of the century, *Buenos Aires: Plaza to Suburb, 1870–1910* (1974). For more recent treatments, see ROBERTA MARX DELSON, *New Towns for Colonial Brazil. Spatial and Social Planning of the Eighteenth Century* (Ph.D. diss., Syracuse University, 1979); and LOUISA

SCHELL HOBERMAN and SUSAN MIGDEN SOCOLOW, eds., *Cities and Society in Colonial Latin America* (1986).

One of the first (and best) accounts of the relationship between the nature of a primary export commodity and the resulting urban structure is the specific case study discussed in the text from ALAN GILBERT, et al., eds., *Urbanization in Contemporary Latin America* (1982). See also RICHARD M. MORSE and JORGE E. HARDOY, *Rethinking the Latin American City* (1992).

On the links between industrialization and urbanization, see ROBERT GWYNNE, *Industrialization and Urbanization in Latin America* (1985). ALAN GILBERT and PETER M. WARD provide a comparative account of irregular settlements and urban political economy in *Housing, the State and the Poor: Policy and Practice in Three Latin American Cities* (1985); see also FRANCIS VIOLICH, *The Challenge of Metropolitan Growth* (1987). Decentralization policies are discussed in ARTHUR S. MORRIS and STELLA S. LOWDER, eds., *Decentralization in Latin America: An Evaluation* (1992). DOUGLAS BUTTERWORTH and JOHN K. CHANCE provide a comprehensive overview of the literature of Latin American migration in *Latin American Urbanization* (1981).

PETER M. WARD

CIUDAD BOLÍVAR, Venezuelan city situated on the Orinoco River some 250 miles from its mouth and the capital of the state of Bolívar. Founded in 1764 as Santo Tomé de la Nueva Guayana, it took on the name of Angostura in 1768 because of its location at a narrows. In 1849, it was renamed Ciudad Bolívar in honor of Venezuela's liberator.

During the WARS OF INDEPENDENCE, Simón BOLÍVAR established his headquarters at Angostura and on 15 March 1819 convened the Congress of Angostura, the ruling body of his loyalist government. Ciudad Bolívar suffered from the war in the region and never fully recovered its prewar prosperity because of local struggles for power that followed the independence movement.

Ciudad Bolívar always provided an important link in Venezuela's waterway system. Its principal exports included gold, cattle, cacao, horses, mules, tobacco, rubber, bitters, hides, timber, and other forest products.

JOHN V. LOMBARDI, *People and Places in Colonial Venezuela* (1976), and *Venezuela: The Search for Order, the Dream of Progress* (1982); JUDITH EWELL, *Venezuela: A Century of Change* (1984).

WINTHROP R. WRIGHT

See also **Angostura, Congress of.**

CIUDAD DEL ESTE (originally known as Puerto Presidente Stroessner), settlement in Paraguay founded on the former site of Puerto Aguirre, on the PARANÁ RIVER, facing Foz do Iguaçu (Brazil). The construction of the ITAIPÚ Dam and the city's location on the route from Asunción to Curitiba have contributed to its growth. The 85,000 inhabitants and those of the neighboring towns of Hernandarias (34,500) and Puerto Presidente Franco (26,000) are mostly engaged in the informal sector and in trade, with little employment in the hydro-electric station. In light of its modernized infrastructure and active trade with Brazil, the city is expected to become the main service center for ongoing colonization of eastern Paraguay by Brazilian natives. After the fall of the Stroessner regime on 3 February 1989, Puerto Presidente Stroessner became Ciudad del Este.

EDGAR L. YNSFRAN, *Un giro geopolítico: El milagro de una ciudad* (Asunción, 1990).

CÉSAR N. CAVIEDES

CIUDAD REAL. *See* **San Cristóbal de las Casas.**

CIUDAD TRUJILLO, official name given to the city of SANTO DOMINGO, Dominican Republic, on 8 January 1936, in honor of President Rafael Leónidas TRUJILLO MOLINA. On 21 November 1961, almost six months after Trujillo's assassination, the city was renamed Santo Domingo, as it had been called since its founding in 1496. During Trujillo's domination (1930–1961) the city grew from a population of less than 100,000 to nearly 400,000 and experienced considerable modernization.

GERMÁN E. ORNES, *Trujillo: Little Caesar of the Caribbean* (1958); ROBERT D. CRASSWELLER, *Trujillo: The Life and Times of a Caribbean Dictator* (1966); HOWARD WIARDA, *Dictatorship, Development, and Disintegration: Politics and Social Change in the Dominican Republic* (1975); JACINTO GIMBERNARD, *Historia de Santo Domingo*, 7th ed. (1978).

RALPH LEE WOODWARD, JR.

CIUDADELA, LA. *See* **La Ciudadela.**

CLAIR, JANETE (*b.* 1925; *d.* 1983), Brazilian *telenovela* author, was born in Minas Gerais. She was the most prominent scriptwriter of *telenovelas* (prime-time serial dramas) for TV Globo from the late 1960s to 1983. She started as a radio actress in 1943 for Rádio Tupi in São Paulo, and turned to writing after she married playwright Dias Gomes, who also became a prominent scriptwriter for TV Globo. Clair's first major success came in 1956 with the *radionovela Perdão, meu filho* for Radio Nacional. She wrote a few TELENOVELAS, such as *Paixão proibida* (Prohibited Passion), for TV Tupi in the mid-1960s, then moved to TV Globo in 1967, at the time it began to invest heavily in *telenovela* production, including hiring all the best talent available. After 1968, TV Globo began to dominate the market for *telenovelas*, in part due to Clair's writing. She was the most popular author for the most watched *telenovela* time slot, 8 P.M. Her personal popularity contributed to an unusual phenomenon in popular television: some of the major scriptwriters for Brazilian *telenovelas* became major public figures, as popular and well known as the most prominent actors and actresses. Clair wrote nineteen

telenovelas for TV Globo from 1967 to 1983. Her first was *Anastácia, a mulher sem destino* (Anastasia, the Woman Without a Destiny, 1967). Two of her more popular *telenovelas* were for *Selva de pedra* (Jungle of Stone, 1972) and *Pecado capital* (Mortal Sin, 1975–1976). After her death in 1983, her writing style and popular touch remained standards by which *telenovelas* were judged by critics and public. The TV Globo Center for Production (Casa da Criação) was named for her.

JOSEPH STRAUBHAAR, "The Rise of the *Telenovela* as the Preeminent Form of Popular Culture in Brazil," in *Studies in Latin American Popular Culture* 1 (1982): 138–150; NIKO VINK, *The Telenovela and Emancipation* (1990).

JOSEPH STRAUBHAAR

CLARK, LYGIA (*b.* 1920; *d.* 1988), Brazilian painter and sculptor. Clark began her artistic training in the late 1940s at the school of Fine Arts in Belo Horizonte, where she was born. Her first teachers were the painter Alberto da Veiga Guignard and the landscape architect Roberto BURLE MARX. Upon graduating, she traveled to Europe and studied in Paris for two years with Ferdinand Léger. In 1952 she returned to Rio de Janeiro, where she began to experiment with the geometric abstract language common to constructivist and concrete art. In 1954, with the concrete movement in full swing, Clark joined Lygia PAPE, Hélio OITICICA, Decio Vieira, and other concrete artists as members of Grupo Frente. Eschewing representation, these artists opposed the imitation of nature as well as lyrical nonfigurative art.

By 1959, with the fragmentation of the concrete movement, Clark, Ferreira Gullar, Lygia Pape, Hélio Oiticica, and others formed the neoconcrete group. In their manifesto they declared that the neoconcrete movement had "emerged out of the need to express the complex realities of modern man with a new plastic language." They rejected the scientific and POSITIVIST attitudes permeating the concrete movement and called for the incorporation of "new verbal dimensions" in art. Through painting and sculpture, Clark sought to create "real," kinetic space. Toward this end, she extended her canvases beyond the confines of the frame, searching for an organic dimension within geometry so that the spectator could enter the painting and participate, such as in *Animals,* a sculpture formed of metal surfaces, which the spectator can manipulate.

In the 1960s Clark experimented with other tactile artistic projects such as short films and body art. By the 1970s her interests ventured away from art into the psychological implications of spectator participation and in 1976 led her to declare herself a "nonartist."

LYGIA CLARK, "O homem como suporte vivo de una arquitetura biológica imanente," in *Arte Brasileira Hoje,* edited by Ferreira Gullar (1973), pp. 159–160; DAWN ADES, *Art in Latin America* (1989), esp. pp. 264–265.

CAREN A. MEGHREBLIAN

CLARK MEMORANDUM (1930), a statement written by Undersecretary of State Joshua Reuben Clark during the administration of Herbert Hoover. The Clark Memorandum was a restatement of the MONROE DOCTRINE made necessary by rising Latin American criticism of U.S. interventionist policy, especially in Nicaragua, in the 1920s. Theodore ROOSEVELT had expanded the scope of the Monroe Doctrine in the ROOSEVELT COROLLARY (1904), justifying U.S. intervention in Latin America in order to protect the region from European interference. Latin American governments had condemned this interpretation as self-serving. The Clark Memorandum did not repudiate intervention but declared that the United States had the right to safeguard its national security under international law, and thus did not require the Roosevelt Corollary. Nonetheless, scholars contend that the memorandum helped to lay the groundwork for the noninterventionist declaration of Franklin D. Roosevelt.

ALEXANDER DE CONDE, *Herbert Hoover's Latin American Policy* (1951); DEXTER PERKINS, *A History of the Monroe Doctrine,* rev. ed. (1963).

LESTER D. LANGLEY

See also **Big Stick Policy; Good Neighbor Policy; United States–Latin American Relations.**

CLASS STRUCTURE: COLONIAL. *See* **Caste and Class Structure.**

CLASS STRUCTURE IN MODERN LATIN AMERICA. The class structures of Latin America are determined by the social relationships of basic ECONOMIC activities. These relationships include property ownership, LABOR arrangements, forms and sources of INCOME, and patterns of supervision and subordination, among others. In addition, some groups of people may be confined to certain jobs or discriminated against on the basis of GENDER, RACE, ethnicity, and so on. All of these factors contribute to the formation and characteristics of contemporary social classes. Given the great diversity among Latin American countries, the following discussion should be considered mainly as a portrayal of general regional patterns.

CLASS STRUCTURE IN HISTORICAL PERSPECTIVE

To understand contemporary class structures, it is imperative to review the historical forces that have shaped them since the mid-nineteenth century. Between roughly 1850 and 1930, national governments pursued an "outward-looking" development model based on the export of primary agricultural and mineral commodities and the import of manufactured goods from Europe (and later the United States). The creation of large-scale export economies entailed profound transformations of class relations.

In the countryside, landholding patterns were altered, legally and/or forcibly, to facilitate the creation of large enterprises devoted to export crops, such as COFFEE in Central America, northern South America, and Brazil, and WHEAT in the Southern Cone. Estate labor needs were met by transforming peasants into full-time or part-time laborers. Where labor was scarce, as in Argentina and southern Brazil, European immigrants were contracted. In the Caribbean, meanwhile, growth was driven by the creation of a BANANA export economy and the revival of SUGAR, mainly on foreign-owned plantations. Labor forces were largely recruited from among ex-slaves and their descendants.

In highland regions, the rise or resurgence of mining export economies reflected new demands for industrial minerals. Copper and tin mining altered the course of development in Chile, Bolivia, and Peru, while oil discoveries transformed Venezuela and Mexico. The organization of mining economies followed that of plantation AGRICULTURE in their dependence on foreign capital and permanent wage labor forces.

These developments had several important effects on social structures. Landowning classes were greatly empowered, politically as well as economically. The industrial-style organization of plantation and mining economies facilitated the emergence of the first large labor unions in the region. In the cities, the largest urban merchants linked to export-import trade began to emerge among national elites. Manufacturing remained relatively small and largely artisanal in nature. Middle classes were weak, although by the turn of the century they were expanding in the larger countries with the growth of public sector employment.

The export-import national development model was highly vulnerable to the shifting fortunes of the international economy, and the narrow distribution of benefits impeded the creation of dynamic domestic markets. Consequently, the Great Depression of the 1930s and the drastic downturn in international trade, which persisted until after World War II, created a general sense of crisis throughout the hemisphere.

One response to this crisis was populism, such as the movements led by Juan Perón in Argentina, Víctor Raúl HAYA DE LA TORRE in Peru, Getúlio VARGAS in Brazil, and Lázaro CÁRDENAS in Mexico. Populist governments shared such features as anti-imperialism and hostility to foreign capital, mass-based appeals to play off against traditional elites, support for labor unions, and a new emphasis on state intervention in the economy. Elsewhere in the region, authoritarian regimes clamped down on popular unrest in response to the crisis. These governments, however, also felt compelled to take a more active role in economic management. Thus one far-reaching outcome of the crisis of the old model was a dramatic expansion of Latin American states.

The new economic model of the period was import-substituting industrialization (ISI), defined by the replacement of manufacturing imports with the output of domestic industries. Where local private investment was inadequate to sustain this process, the state was assigned a leading role in building an industrial base. After 1945, protectionist policies were adopted to shield the new industries from European and North American competition. In the larger countries of the region (and later in the smaller ones, following the implementation of regional integration schemes), the protected domestic markets proved attractive to new foreign investment, chiefly by U.S.-based firms.

The growth of industry and expansion of the state ignited a rapid process of urbanization. With both working class and middle-class employment growing, the major Latin American CITIES proved irresistible magnets for migrants from smaller towns and the countryside. Rural-urban migration was also spurred by the transformation of agrarian economies. New postwar export opportunities, as well as the growing urban demand for food, generated a renewed expansion of large-scale agriculture. This development generally was unfavorable to peasants, as new employment opportunities were offset by reduced access to good farmland and the effects of labor-saving technologies. Combined with high rates of POPULATION growth, these changes swelled the cityward exodus.

Class structures were profoundly altered by these developments. Dominant class interests were diversified to incorporate domestic and transnational manufacturing sectors alongside the traditional export and mercantile groups. A growing middle class was nurtured by the rapid growth of state bureaucracies, as well as opportunities among larger private firms. And industrial working classes were expanding as well. By 1960, the majority of Latin America's economically active population was employed in non-agricultural work, and the proportion in manufacturing had reached as high as 34 percent in Argentina, 30 percent in Chile, and around 20 percent in Mexico, Peru, and Brazil.

Nonetheless, this expansion was outpaced by high population growth and migration. Consequently, Latin American cities witnessed the proliferation of the INFORMAL SECTORS. Growing numbers of residents were forced to improvise their livelihoods as street vendors, providers of personal services, and part-time or temporary wage laborers. Characterized by myriad subsistence strategies, the informal sectors were largely unregulated by the state and bereft of benefits or security for workers. Their most visible manifestation was the sprawling shantytowns and squatter settlements that spread across Latin American cities during the 1950s and 1960s.

In the countryside, as small farms became more difficult to sustain, peasants were increasingly forced to depend on seasonal wage labor and non-agricultural employment. Remittances from family members in the cities came to play an important role in many rural communities. Most Latin American governments undertook to shore up peasant agriculture and rural employment with AGRARIAN REFORM programs during the

1960s, but in general these programs were hampered by dominant class opposition and government inability to provide support (such as credit, technical assistance, and market access) for reform projects.

Agrarian reform did serve to mobilize peasants politically, however, and the 1960s saw rising working class protests linked to both populist and socialist political movements. Growing elite resistance to reforms fueled an increasing willingness on the left to embrace revolutionary alternatives. The resulting confrontational spiral was brought to a violent halt by the authoritarian, military-led regimes which swept across the region beginning with Brazil in 1964.

The advent of repressive military regimes in the 1960s and 1970s did not greatly alter the state-centered, ISI-based development model. During the 1970s military governments presided over major state initiatives drawing on cheap, easily obtained credit from international banks. In the early 1980s, however, debt repayment and interest obligations began to mount just as a global recession reduced new capital inflows and depressed Latin America's trade balances. Most governments were compelled to rely on the assistance (and policy prescriptions) of the International Monetary Fund (IMF) and other global financial institutions. Facing rising popular opposition, decreasing support from dominant groups, and economic crisis, military leaders were forced to restore executive office to civilian hands.

The new civilian leaders faced the daunting challenge of strengthening democracy while pursuing the reactivation of their economies within the context of IMF restrictions. Thus, since the mid-1980s, diverse governments have pursued similar economic strategies. They have opened up their economies by removing protectionist tariffs and other trade barriers, promoting foreign investment, privatizing state enterprises, and reducing subsidies for public services. This "neo-liberal" approach has generated substantial popular resistance, but remains the predominant development model in the late 1990s and an important determinant of contemporary class structures.

CONTEMPORARY RURAL CLASS STRUCTURES

The traditional relationships of landlord and peasant that helped to define Latin American societies have all but disappeared in the 1990s. Large estates are no longer so large, in many cases having been curtailed by agrarian reform in the 1960s, and farms devoted to exports are more likely to be run according to strictly capitalistic criteria. Moreover, rural society in general is much more closely linked to the major urban centers and national economic and political forces. The incidence of poverty, however, remains high—about 60 percent of the rural population for Latin America as a whole.

Agrarian elites are less easily characterized as oligarchies. Large farms are likely to be run by managers, while owners may be impersonal corporations or city-dwellers with diversified economic interests. Rural elite

Demonstration against special privileges, Montevideo, 1930s. OAS.

interests tend to be promoted through professional associations and political parties, rather than through the direct exercise of coercive power. This evolution has fundamentally altered rural class relations; peasants now deal with entrepreneurs, commercial intermediaries, and state agencies rather than traditional large landowners.

Peasants have both gained and suffered as a result of these changes. On the one hand, they are freer to organize themselves, pursue political alliances, and negotiate with state agencies. The disappearance of military regimes has also contributed to the rise of organized peasant activism in countries such as Brazil, Bolivia, and Peru. Rural educational levels and access to basic services have risen as well. On the other hand, the advancing "modernization" of agriculture has reduced employment opportunities. In the context of continuing population growth, the migratory outflow from the countryside has continued.

A further challenge to peasants since 1980 has been the elimination of the agrarian reform policies that had sought to shore up peasant agriculture. Even where such policies had not been suspended earlier by MILITARY DICTATORSHIPS, the prescriptions of economic liberalization have been to curtail state efforts to redistribute land and organize production, relying instead on market forces to drive rural development.

The net effect of these changes has been to accelerate both the differentiation of Latin American peasantries and their integration into larger social structures. Viable small farms persist in some regions, especially where proximity to urban centers guarantees a stable demand for food crops. The largest farm enterprises still provide permanent wage employment for a significant group of workers. The majority of peasant families, however, are pursuing diversified subsistence strategies that may combine cultivation of tiny plots, occasional wage labor on larger farms, and off-farm sources of income. Among the most important sources of the latter are non-

agricultural employment (for instance, in rural food-processing or manufacturing assembly plants) and remittances from family members who have moved to the city, or even out of the country. Many rural communities in Mexico, El Salvador, and the Dominican Republic, for example, are now sustained by family remittances from the United States.

CONTEMPORARY URBAN CLASS STRUCTURES

The dominant classes are a very small proportion of the economically active population in modern Latin American societies. Their ranks are characterized by diverse interests, however, including the traditional export and mercantile sectors, transnational and domestic manufacturing, SERVICES (BANKING in particular), and even large state-owned enterprises. The crisis of the 1980s and the ascendance of neo-liberalism have altered the dominant class profile. PRIVATIZATION policies are gradually doing away with state enterprises; transnational firms have acquired many of them. Among private firms, those best able to cope with prevailing economic conditions have been those least reliant on the domestic market and more geared toward non-traditional exports, as well as those with the capacity to spread their resources across borders and foreign currencies. Increasingly, transnational capital refers not just to U.S.-, European-, or Asian-based firms operating in Latin America, but also to Latin American firms and investors who have looked abroad for greater security or greater returns.

The middle classes include professionals, mid-level managerial and technical personnel, and career-oriented government employees. While these groups remain considerably better off than the working classes, the economic downturn of the 1980s represented a blow, as the expectations of upward mobility and increased consumer buying power that earlier had accompanied economic growth were suddenly dashed. Emigration has become a more attractive option among these groups, as has that of abandoning work in large firms to start small businesses.

PUBLIC SECTOR employees have been especially affected. By the 1980s, the public sector accounted for between 15 and 30 percent of total urban employment in most Latin American countries. The curtailment of government spending resulting from the debt crisis and readjustment policies has signified a major decrease in real wages and living standards for public sector employees, although the number of jobs has generally remained stable. The incidence of poverty has risen to encompass around one-fourth of all civil servants in Brazil, Mexico, and Venezuela.

The formal working class, or proletariat, has been perhaps the hardest hit of all classes by recent economic trends. During the 1980s, employment in manufacturing throughout the region declined sharply relative to services, and in several cases declined in absolute terms as well. The number of workers in manufacturing in Argentina declined by 29 percent from 1980 to 1990;

Peru and Brazil experienced drops of 19 percent and 13 percent, respectively. Open unemployment rates soared in most major cities. For those that kept their jobs, incomes headed downward. Over the same decade, real wages in the manufacturing sector fell by 45 percent in Venezuela, 24 percent in Argentina, 18 percent in Brazil, and 8 percent in Mexico.

Workers have found it difficult to defend their interests. Labor unions, weakened during the years of repression and military rule, have been further affected by declining employment in some of the industries where they were once strongest, notably mining. A related factor has been the shrinking electoral fortunes of socialist and communist political parties, once devoted to the cause of organized labor, but now forced to seek compromise in electoral coalitions. Both on the right and on the left, an important political shift has occurred, as traditional class-based strategies have been replaced by coalition-building and cross-class appeals.

One noteworthy exception to the pattern of declining industrial employment has been the phenomenal growth of MAQUILADORAS, best known in Mexico but also expanding in countries like Guatemala and Colombia. These are export processing plants established under special concessionary regulations; textiles and clothing, food processing, and electronics are the typical industries. In Mexico, employment in this sector more than quadrupled during the 1980s. Perhaps the most significant contribution of the *maquiladora* industries to the changing class structure of Latin America has been their heavy reliance on female labor.

The evolution of the informal sectors since 1980 has been complex. On the one hand, many informal workers have experienced deteriorating living standards. Contributing factors include the swelling of the informal labor force by those displaced from formal employment, the further overcrowding of housing in the shantytowns and poor neighborhoods, the decline in part-time or casual wage labor (in such fields as construction), and the reduction in state services, subsidies, and other programs aimed at the poor. On the other hand, the same downturn produced new economic opportunities. Depressed earnings of middle and working class consumers have translated into greater demand for goods produced cheaply by informal businesses and street vendors. Other informal entrepreneurs are producing inputs needed by large formal sector firms through "piece-rate work" and "home work" arrangements, replacing inputs previously produced by formal sector firms.

Thus increasing urban poverty levels have masked some informal success stories. In Otavalo, Ecuador, Indian entrepreneurs have established small weaving operations, in which workers turn out jeans and shirts for the national market and luxury woolen items for export. Using machinery acquired from failed textile mills and doing their own marketing, these firms have turned into profitable operations. In another case, Uruguayan

women working in cooperatives have also developed a thriving garment industry. The co-ops are linked in *Manos*, an umbrella organization that operates wholesale outlets in the capital city of Montevideo, supplying both domestic and export markets. Democratic openings have also provided more space for neighborhood and cooperative associations to become active. Organizations such as these are often at the forefront of protests against neo-liberal economic policies.

THE SIGNIFICANCE OF OTHER SOCIAL CLEAVAGES
It is important to recognize that other social divisions cut across class structure and help to determine the specific characteristics and identities associated with social classes. The most important of these distinctions are gender and race/ethnicity.

During 1950–1980, Latin America witnessed a slow but steady expansion of women's participation in the labor force. This was largely the consequence of broader patterns of social change, including urbanization, higher educational achievement, evolving labor markets, and associated changes in cultural values. Women's employment was highly segmented, however, with jobs concentrated in the areas of personal (including domestic) services, office services, and sales.

As with the informal sector as a whole, women experienced contradictory developments during the crisis of the 1980s. Unemployment rates for women generally increased faster than those of men, reflecting a relative decline in formal employment opportunities. At the same time, however, younger women were entering the labor force at an accelerated rate, given family needs for additional workers to offset the declining incomes of those already working. Much of this additional labor was absorbed in small-scale informal sector activities.

New opportunities arose with the appearance of nontraditional export industries. In the countryside, large firms producing commodities like cut flowers in Colombia or fresh fruit in Chile hired women to do the processing or packing. This gender-based preference was mirrored in the *maquiladora* industries. Finally, women were also hired preferentially for "home work" jobs, in which parts of production processes (such as for shoes and clothing) are subcontracted to individual workers to carry out in their homes. These opportunities have carried a cost, however—women workers have been consistently subject to discriminatory wage rates (relative to men), extreme job insecurity, and difficult work environments. The persistence of discriminatory practices, along with other gender-based issues, has helped spark the rapid growth of women's organizations. These movements represent an increasingly active presence in the Latin American political arena.

Racial and ethnic divisions represent a defining aspect of Latin American and Caribbean class structures. The colonial reliance on native Americans and African slaves as a labor force for European conquerors has been an enduring legacy. Despite the vast changes that have since occurred, it remains true that throughout the hemisphere, to be identifiably Indian or black is to rank lower in economic, political, and social status than non-Indians or non-blacks. There is great variation across countries and regions in how these inequalities are expressed, but a few major trends are worth noting.

Indigenous groups generically categorized as "Indians" have been largely assimilated or confined to remote areas in many countries of the region, but remain a substantial component of the population in Mesoamerica (especially Mexico and Guatemala) and the Andean countries. Long concentrated in peasant communities that provided the basis for maintaining separate ethnic identities, these groups by the mid-twentieth century had joined migration streams toward the cities, where their ethnic identities inevitably underwent significant change. Indian ethnicity, however, has proven remarkably resilient. In many cases urban migrants have maintained community-based identities through the social networks that led them to settle in the same neighborhoods as their family and friends.

More recently, confronting economic crisis, some Indian city dwellers have strengthened linkages with rural regions through exchanges of food production, job contacts, and other resources. In Peru, for example, this has led to the emergence of regional ethnic identities, more inclusive than community ties. In Guatemala, on the other hand, a pan-Maya identity has begun to spread as a result of the revolutionary upheavals and violent repression of the 1980s, which destroyed many traditional communities and threw together Indians from disparate linguistic and cultural backgrounds. These examples show both the resilience and malleability of ethnic identities as a crucial element of modern class structures.

The relationship between class and race has been no less complex. In the Caribbean, the demise of the plantation system, with its sharply defined racial hierarchy, has produced varied outcomes. On the smaller islands, where white elites never constituted more than a tiny minority, blacks and mulattoes have acquired greater political and economic status. In the larger countries, like Cuba or the Dominican Republic, where the white population was considerably larger, racial stratification has been more persistent. In general, the evolution of social and political movements based on racial awareness has been more marked by selective strategies than polarization on the U.S. model. Movements centered on black self-awareness, for instance, have focused at various times on achieving national independence, resisting U.S. interventions, or opposing transnational corporations—but rarely on opposition to whites in general. In other instances, once-racial distinctions are now expressed more in ethnic terms, as with black and mulatto populations in Haiti, or black and Asian Indian groups in Trinidad and Guyana.

Brazil offers yet another pattern. There the discriminatory heritage of slave plantations was reinforced until

the mid-twentieth century by the spatial concentration of blacks in the economically depressed Northeast, while the white population (enlarged by European migration) inhabited the more prosperous South. Despite increasing black migration from the Northeast to the South, however, racial inequality has not lessened. During the "economic miracle" of the 1970s, despite general gains for Brazilian workers, the black and mulatto populations remained concentrated in the most disadvantaged educational categories and occupations. One result has been, since the late 1980s, the rise of social movements and organizations articulating a distinct Afro-Brazilian identity.

While there are many references for analyses of class structures in specific Latin American countries, there are very few recent works that treat social class from a regional perspective. The publications of the U.N. Economic Commission for Latin America and the Caribbean (ECLAC) constitute good sources of data or analyses of social structure and inequality across the region. See, for example, MARTINE DIRVEN, "Rural Society: Its Integration and Disintegration," in *CEPAL Review*, No. 51 (December 1993): 69–87; ECLAC, *Social Panorama of Latin America* (Santiago, 1993) and *Major Changes and Crisis: The Impact on Women in Latin America and the Caribbean* (Santiago, 1992); ENZO FALETTO, "The History of the Social Stratification of Latin America," in *CEPAL Review*, No. 50 (August 1993): 163–180; MARSHALL WOLFE, "Social Structures and Democracy in the 1990s," in *CEPAL Review*, No. 40 (April 1991): 53–68.

A rigorous sociological approach to the topic can be found in ALEJANDRO PORTES, "Latin American Class Structures: Their Composition and Change during the Last Decades," in *Latin American Research Review*, vol. 20, No. 3 (1985): 7–40. Older but still useful standard references in the field are FERNANDO HENRIQUE CARDOSO and ENZO FALETTO, *Dependency and Development in Latin America* (Univ. of California Press, 1979); FLORESTAN FERNANDES, *Capitalismo dependente e clases sociais na América Latina* (Rio de Janeiro, 1973); GINO GERMANI, *Política y sociedad en una época de transición* (Buenos Aires, 1962); and TORCUATO DI TELLA, *Clases sociales y estructuras políticas* (Buenos Aires, 1974).

A. DOUGLAS KINCAID

See also **African Brazilians; Brazil: Economic Miracle; Slavery.**

CLAVÉ, PELEGRÍN (*b.* 17 June 1811; *d.* 13 September 1880), painter. Trained in his native Barcelona and in Rome, Clavé was in Mexico between 1846 and 1867 as director of the reestablished ACADEMIA DE SAN CARLOS. In Rome he studied with Tommaso Minardi and, like the sculptor Manuel VILAR, he was sympathetic to the Nazarenes (a group of German artists who sought to revitalize Christian art). While in Mexico he executed many portraits reminiscent of those of Jean Auguste Dominique Ingres, with which he must have become familiar in Rome; these are considered his most significant work. With his pupils Clavé decorated the interior of the dome of the church of the Profesa (1860–1867; destroyed by fire in 1914). He was instrumental in the formation of the collection of colonial paintings in the galleries of the Academia de San Carlos. Political difficulties led Clavé to return to Barcelona in 1868. There he lectured and wrote about Mexican painting, and worked on plans to decorate the dome of the church of the Merced.

SALVADOR MORENO, *El pintor Pelegrín Clavé* (1966).

CLARA BARGELLINI

CLAVER, PEDRO (*b.* 26? June 1580; *d.* 8 September 1654), Catalan Jesuit missionary in Colombia who became a saint. Born in Verdú, Spain, Claver joined the Jesuits in 1602. He arrived in Cartagena in 1610, then quickly went on to Bogotá and Tunja, where he studied until 1615. Ordained in Cartagena in 1616, Claver worked among the black slaves as a protégé of Father Alonso Sandoval. In 1622 he signed his final vows as "Pedro Claver, slave of the negroes forever." For the next three decades he met the slave ships coming to Cartagena, the main slave emporium in Spanish America, and ministered to the needs of their human cargo. Claver had black translators fluent in African languages who questioned, instructed, and aided the slaves in religious and health matters. He also sought out the destitute in hospitals and jails and provided them with medicine, food, and clothes. When asked how many he had baptized, he answered, "more than three hundred thousand." Claver died in Cartagena. He was beatified by Pius IX in 1851 and canonized by Leo XIII in 1888.

A good survey is ANGEL VALTIERRA, S.J., *Pedro Claver: El santo redentor de los negros*, 2 vols. (1980); the earlier edition (1954) is available in English as *Peter Claver: Saint of the Slaves*, translated by Janet H. Perry and L. J. Woodward (1960). A succinct account can be found in JUAN MANUEL PACHECO, S.J., *Historia extensa de Colombia*, vol. 13; *Historia eclesiástica*, Tomo 2, *La consolidación de la iglesia, siglo xvii* (1975), esp. pp. 633–637.

MAURICE P. BRUNGARDT

CLAVIGERO, FRANCISCO JAVIER (Clavijero; *b.* 9 September 1731; *d.* 2 April 1787), historian and promoter of the Mexican Enlightenment. Clavigero, a native of Veracruz, is noted for his role in introducing modern PHILOSOPHY into Mexico (a modified Aristotelian cosmology influenced by eighteenth-century sciences with an emphasis on empirically based critical analysis). He taught in the Jesuit *colegios* in Valladolid (modern-day Morelia) and in Guadalajara, where he was residing when the Jesuits were expelled from the Spanish Empire in 1767. Exiled to Bologna in the Papal States, Clavigero turned to history to consolidate the record of pre-Hispanic Mexico and also to refute the so-called theory of American degeneracy that some European writers, like Corneille de Pauw, were propagating to the effect that America and her native inhabitants were far inferior to Europe because of America's wretched climate and other factors. The outcome was

his *Storia antica del Messico* (1780–1781) that not only accomplished his purpose but also fostered a spirit of regionalism and neo-Aztecism among certain Mexican patriots which they used to justify their revolt against Spain. Noteworthy also is his posthumously published *Storia della California* (1789), written to counteract charges against the JESUITS and their California MISSIONS and to acquaint Europe with that peninsula and its inhabitants. He died in Bologna.

ANTONELLO GERBI, *The Dispute of the New World: The History of a Polemic, 1750–1900*, rev. and enl. ed., translated by Jeremy Moyle (1973), pp. 196–211; CHARLES E. RONAN, S.J. *Francisco Javier Clavigero (1731–1787)* (1977).

CHARLES E. RONAN, S.J.

CLAY, HENRY (*b.* 12 April 1777; *d.* 29 June 1852), U.S. statesman who served as secretary of state (1825–1829). Clay was one of the country's great political leaders before the Civil War. A native of Virginia, Clay achieved success as a lawyer and state legislator in Kentucky before entering the Senate in 1806. He was an unsuccessful presidential candidate in 1832 and 1844. Although Clay identified the movements for Latin American independence with the U.S. colonial struggle against the British, he wanted the United States to remain neutral during the conflict because he thought it would hinder the U.S. effort to acquire the Floridas from Spain. Anticipating commercial opportunities and wanting to secure the Caribbean region from European interlopers, by 1818, Clay urged the granting of recognition to the independent South American nations. Clay's advocacy of an American system of independent states to counterbalance the European Holy Alliance led to his support of the MONROE DOCTRINE, which proclaimed the western hemisphere off limits to foreign intruders, and his hope that the Panama Congress (1826) would declare its support for the doctrine. Subsequently, Clay lost his fraternalistic spirit with the South American nations as more information about their corruption surfaced following their independence. To secure the U.S. position in Latin America, Clay encouraged the signing of favorable treaties of amity and commerce, illustrated by the treaty signed in 1825 with the Federation of Central America. Late in his career, Clay opposed the annexation of Texas over the slavery issue, but he supported the MEXICAN-AMERICAN WAR once it had begun (1846).

H. L. HOSKINS, "The Hispanic American Policy of Henry Clay, 1816–1828," *Hispanic American Historical Review* 7, no. 4 (1927): 460–478; GLYNDON G. VAN DEUSEN, *The Life of Henry Clay* (1937); CLEMENT EATON, *Henry Clay and the Art of American Politics* (1957).

THOMAS M. LEONARD

CLAYTON-BULWER TREATY (1850), an agreement between Britain and the United States codifying Anglo-American relations with regard to Central America. The treaty was signed 19 April 1850 by U.S. Secretary of

State John M. Clayton and Sir Henry L. Bulwer, British minister to the United States. Seeking to end a dangerous rivalry, the treaty prohibited colonization, fortification, or the exercise of exclusive influence in Central America by either side and provided joint Anglo-American protection for any interoceanic canal built on the isthmus. It remained in effect until superseded by the HAY-PAUNCEFOTE TREATIES of 1901, which granted the United States exclusive rights to build and operate an isthmian canal.

The treaty was the diplomatic meeting ground of British "informal" colonialism in mid-nineteenth-century Central America and the Caribbean phase of U.S. Manifest Destiny. Historians have variously claimed the treaty as a victory for both sides, but it appears to have been a compromise in which the interests of both benefited, although no canal was realized. As Mary W. Williams pointed out early in this century, however, the treaty was arrived at by avoiding certain basic questions, namely, what to do with existing British holdings in the region: Belize, the Bay Islands, and the Mosquito Protectorate. Belize was excluded from the treaty's provisions by a subsequent exchange of diplomatic notes. The Bay Islands question, however, was muddled by the British Colonial Office's proclamation of the Bay Islands Colony in 1852 without consulting the British Foreign Office. British efforts to relinquish the Mosquito Protectorate were frustrated first by Nicaragua's defiance and then by its collapse amidst civil war and FILIBUSTER invasion. British absorption in the Crimean War (1853–1856) and the bellicose posturing of the Pierce administration (1853–1857) postponed an Anglo-American rapprochement over Central America and threatened to undermine the treaty itself.

The treaty (and the mutually self-denying compromise it represented) was finally preserved by a series of British treaties signed in 1859 and 1860 with Guatemala, Honduras, and Nicaragua, relinquishing or otherwise clarifying British holdings in the region to the satisfaction of the United States, and by the Buchanan administration's (1857–1861) formal repudiation of filibustering. Ultimately, the U.S. Civil War slowed the momentum of Caribbean Manifest Destiny, thereby removing the most serious challenge to the 1850 treaty until the end of the nineteenth century.

LESTER D. LANGLEY, *Struggle for the American Mediterranean: United States-European Rivalry in the Gulf-Caribbean, 1776–1904* (1976), pp. 81–106, provides an excellent introduction to the Anglo-American rivalry in Central America. WILBUR D. JONES, *The American Problem in British Diplomacy, 1841–1861* (1974) gives an excellent account of the British side, while MARY W. WILLIAMS, *Anglo-American Isthmian Rivalry, 1815–1915* (1916) remains extremely useful. A recent view of the "Clayton-Bulwer process" is provided in RICHMOND F. BROWN, "Charles Lennox Wyke and the Clayton-Bulwer Formula in Central America, 1852–1860," in *The Americas* 47 (April 1991): 411–445.

RICHMOND F. BROWN

See also **British-Latin American Relations.**

CLEMENTE WALKER, ROBERTO (*b.* 18 August 1934; *d.* 31 December 1972), Puerto Rican baseball player. Born in Carolina, P.R., near San Juan, Clemente signed out of high school with the Los Angeles Dodgers (1954) but played his entire major league career, beginning in 1955, with the Pittsburgh Pirates. In his 2,433 Pirate games, he had 3,000 hits and a .317 batting average; he won four batting titles and twelve Golden Gloves, was named his league's Most Valuable Player in 1966, as well as World Series MVP in 1971, and appeared in twelve Major League All-Star Games. Until 1971 he likewise repaid his countrymen by playing in the Puerto Rican winter league. To achieve all this and earn deserved praise in the United States, he had to overcome racism and prejudice against blacks and Hispanics and persistent physical ailments that hampered him and brought cruel accusations that he was a hypochondriac and malingerer. He died in a plane crash while trying to deliver relief aid that he had raised for earthquake victims in Managua, Nicaragua. In 1973 a special election made him the first Latin to enter baseball's Hall of Fame. In life, as on the field, Clemente displayed a capacity for toughness and tenderness, aggressiveness and compassion, as appropriate for the situation. In Puerto Rico his widow Vera and others still operate the youth sports center named in his honor.

BILL CHRISTINE, *Roberto!* (1973); PHIL MUSICK, *Who Was Roberto? A Biography of Roberto Clemente* (1974); KAL WAGENHEIM, *Clemente!* (1984); MICHAEL M. OLEKSAK and MARY ADAMS OLEKSAK, *Béisbol: Latin Americans and the Grand Old Game* (1991).

JOSEPH L. ARBENA

CLEMENTINA. *See* **De Jesus, Clementina.**

CLIMATE. *See* **Environment and Climate.**

CLOSED CORPORATE PEASANT COMMUNITY (CCPC), an organizational framework for analysis of peasant communities developed by anthropologist Eric Wolf in the 1950s. Wolf applied his typology of peasant organization to communities in Central Java and Mesoamerica, specifically Mexico and Guatemala. The CCPC, according to Wolf, is a "relatively autonomous economic, social, linguistic, and politico-religious system." The community is corporate because it maintains a body of rights and membership, and closed because it limits its benefits to members and discourages participation with the larger society. Wolf believes the development of the closed corporate peasant community was a result of the serious social and cultural crises of indigenous communities brought on by the Spanish Conquest of Latin America. Peasant communities closed into themselves in response to the economic and social changes wrought by colonization. Thus the CCPC can be understood as a protective device of peasant and indigenous communities to ensure their self-preservation in light of such radical change.

ERIC WOLF, "The Closed Corporate Peasant Communities in Mesoamerica and Central Java," in *Southwestern Journal of Anthropology* 13, no. 1 (1957): 1–18, and "The Vicissitudes of the Closed Corporate Peasant Community," in *American Ethnologist* 13 (May 1986): 325–329.

HEATHER K. THIESSEN

CLOUTHIER DEL RINCÓN, MANUEL J. (*b.* 13 June 1934; *d.* 1 October 1989), leading Mexican opposition politician and 1988 presidential candidate. A native of Culiacán, Sinaloa, Clouthier attended high school in the United States at the Brown Military Academy in San Diego, and graduated from Monterey's Institute of Higher Studies with a degree in agricultural engineering. A successful local businessman, he became active in a variety of regional business-interest groups, including the United Fresh Fruit and Vegetable Association and the Businessman's Coordinating Council. In 1981–1983, he presided over the national Businessman Coordinating Council, one of Mexico's most influential private-sector organizations. Known for his hard-line defense of powerful agricultural interests, Clouthier became politically involved in the National Action Party (PAN). After losing as a PAN candidate for Congress, he led the party's opposition by running against Carlos SALINAS in the 1988 presidential election, during which he ran an aggressive and charismatic campaign, endearing himself to many voters. He lost the election, but helped many congressional candidates from his party to win. Clouthier was killed in an auto accident in Sinaloa under disputed circumstances.

ABRAHAM NUNCIO, *El PAN* (1986); WAYNE CORNELIUS et al., *Mexico's Alternative Political Futures* (1989); *New York Times*, 2 Oct. 1989, sec. D, p. 12, col. 1.

RODERIC AI CAMP

See also **Mexico: Political Parties.**

CLUZEAU-MORTET, LUIS [RICARDO] (*b.* 16 November 1889; *d.* 28 September 1957), Uruguayan composer, violist, and pianist. Born in Montevideo, Cluzeau-Mortet studied piano, harmony, and composition with his maternal grandfather, Paul Faget, a winner of the Grand Prix of the Paris Conservatory. Later he studied violin and viola with María Visca. In 1914 he joined the Asociación Uruguaya de Música de Cámara, for whom he played viola until 1931, when he accepted the position as first viola in the Uruguayan state orchestra (OS-SODRE), where he remained until his retirement in 1946. Cluzeau-Mortet received an invitation from the British Council to visit London in 1938, to which he responded by giving concerts of his vocal and piano works there and in Paris.

Cluzeau-Mortet's musicial output comprises nearly two hundred works. His career can be divided into three periods: a brief romantic-impressionist phase that produced songs based on French poetry; a nationalist period; and a universalist phase. It is for his nationalist works that he is best known; indeed, Cluzeau-Mortet, with Alfonso BROQUA and Eduardo FABINI, is considered a progenitor of Uruguayan nationalism. About half of his output, which includes several orchestral pieces, is made up of chamber music works. Among them the vocal and piano compositions are the masterpieces of his career. *Pericón* for piano (1918), premiered by Artur Rubinstein, and *Canto de chingolo* for voice and piano (1924), recorded by RCA Victor in 1930, are the most well-known and representative works from his nationalist period. Other important works are: *Llanuras* (1932); *Soledad campestre* (1936); *Rancherío* (1940), premiered by Jasha Horenstein in 1947 and winner of a SODRE composition competition; and *Sinfonía Artigas* (1951), all for orchestra. He died in Montevideo.

Composers of the Americas, vol. 14 (1968), pp. 47–64; *New Grove Dictionary of Music and Musicians*, vol. 4 (1980); SUSANA SALGADO, *Breve historia de la música culta en el Uruguay*, 2d ed., (1980), and *Cluzeau-Mortet* (1983).

SUSANA SALGADO

COAHUILA, third largest state in Mexico. With a population (1990) of 1,971,300 and an area of 58,522 square miles, Coahuila lies south of TEXAS along the big bend of the RIO GRANDE known to Mexicans as the Río Bravo. The Spanish settlement of Coahuila, known as Nueva Extremadura, began in the late sixteenth century, and in 1577 the present-day capital of Saltillo was founded. Due to its scarcity of water, fertile land, and valuable minerals, and because of the presence of nomadic and often hostile native groups, Coahuila remained a sparsely occupied ranching, farming, and mining frontier during the colonial era. As part of Spain's administrative reorganization of the northern frontier during the eighteenth century, Coahuila was incorporated into the Interior Provinces, and in 1785 it became part of the Commandancy of the East, along with Texas, NUEVO LEÓN, and TAMAULIPAS. In 1824, after Mexico had gained its independence, Coahuila and Texas (and for a brief time, Nuevo León) were established as one state. The union of Coahuila and Texas was challenged in 1836 by the Texas declaration of independence, and again in 1845 with the annexation of Texas by the United States. As a result of the Mexican-American War, Coahuila lost all of its territory north of the Río Bravo, and U.S. soldiers occupied Saltillo and other areas of the state.

During the Reform period of the mid-nineteenth century, Coahuila was annexed to the neighboring state of Nuevo León (1856–1864). It regained independent status by order of President Benito JUÁREZ, who briefly sojourned in Saltillo during the French intervention in

Mexico (1862–1867). The era of Porfirio DÍAZ (1877–1911) and the relatively peaceful conditions of the late nineteenth century encouraged the growth of Coahuila's agriculture, ranching, and mining sectors. The construction of railroads added to the state's prosperity and promoted the development of a manufacturing sector. During the MEXICAN REVOLUTION, Coahuila played a prominent role, producing several leaders and serving as an important strategic base. Francisco MADERO's revolt against Porfirio Díaz began in Coahuila, and the later Constitutionalist revolution was led by another native son, Venustiano CARRANZA. The state suffered severe destruction during the revolution, as competing armies struggled for control of this important northern area. Coahuila emerged from the revolution with a depressed economy, and during the 1920s and 1930s it continued to experience periodic unrest, including two minor manifestations of the CRISTERO REBELLION. During the 1940s, Coahuila began a slow economic recovery, visible in the growth of industry and an increase in population.

Generally speaking, economic development has been very important, and Coahuila has remained a center of foreign, especially American, investment. The Saltillo-Ramos Arizpe industrial "corridor" is home to two large auto plants operated by Chrysler and General Motors, and Coahuila is the site of Mexico's largest steel plant, Altos Hornos de Mexico.

Throughout the twentieth century as well, Coahuila has remained a center of the Mexican workers' movement. In 1918, Saltillo hosted the conference that gave rise to the Confederación Regional de Obreros Mexicanos (CROM), and the governor at that time, Gustavo Espinosa Mireles, played a key part in its organization. Workers in Coahuila's coal-mining region have always been especially active, and in the 1950s they struck against the American Smelting and Refining Company, which operated mines in the areas of Nueva Rosita and Cloete. Miners' demands for better working conditions were met with repression by the government and the mining company, which tried to starve workers into submission (blocking supplies of food sent by union sympathizers in the Laguna region), thereby precipitating the "Caravan of Hunger"—a protest march of some 5,000 workers from Coahuila to Mexico City, where workers were repressed, and many thrown in jail.

VITO ALESSIO ROBLES, Coahuila y Texas, desde la consumación de la independencia hasta el tratado de paz de Guadalupe Hidalgo, 2 vols. (1945–1946); ILDEFONSO VILLARELLO VÉLEZ, Historia de la revolución mexicana en Coahuila (1970); PABLO CUÉLLAR VALDÉS, Historia de la ciudad de Saltillo (1975), and Historia del estado de Coahuila (1979); EDUARDO ENRÍQUEZ TERRAZAS and JOSÉ LUIS GARCÍA VALERO, Coahuila: una historia compartida (1989); EDUARDO ENRÍQUEZ TERRAZAS and MARTHA RODRÍGUEZ GARCÍA, comps., Coahuila: Textos de su historia (1989); RITA FAVRET TONDATO, Tenencia de la tierra en el estado de Coahuila (1880–1987) (1992).

SUZANNE B. PASZTOR

COATEPEQUE, BATTLE OF (22–24 February 1863, near Santa Ana, El Salvador). At Coatepeque, Salvadoran forces under Gerardo BARRIOS and Liberal Nicaraguans under Máximo JÉREZ stopped the Guatemalan army of Rafael CARRERA. Carrera invaded El Salvador in an effort to crush the Liberal government of Barrios. He occupied Santa Ana with little resistance on 21 February. Hoping to end the war quickly, the next day he marched his troops to Coatepeque without sufficient provision for food and water. Well-entrenched Salvadorans engaged the Guatemalans in a twelve-hour artillery duel on 23 February. On the following day Barrios's forces repulsed the hungry and thirsty Guatemalans. Heavy losses, however, prevented the Liberals from pursuing Carrera, who retreated into Guatemala with only moderate losses. Instead, joined by Honduran forces who entered the war as a consequence of the Liberal victory at Coatepeque, Barrios and Jérez marched into Nicaragua in an unsuccessful effort to take León.

Carrera launched a new, more cautious offensive in June 1863, leading to his capture of San Salvador in October, ending the war. Barrios escaped to La Unión and sailed to Costa Rica.

FEDERICO HERNÁNDEZ DE LEÓN, El libro de las efemérides, vol. 5 (1963), pp. 307–312; PEDRO ZAMORA CASTELLANOS, Vida militar de Centro América, 2d. ed. (1967), vol. 2, pp. 193–206.

RALPH LEE WOODWARD, JR.

COATLICUE, Aztec deity, mother of the Mexica patron and war god HUITZILOPOCHTLI. Coatlicue is one of a complex of Aztec female supernaturals associated with the earth, reproduction, and sacrificial death. According to myth, Coatlicue (Serpent-skirt) was magically impregnated by a ball of down while sweeping the temple atop the mythical mountain of Coatepec (Serpent Mountain). Her 400 sons and her daughter, Coyolxauhqui, shocked that their mother had become pregnant while engaged in temple service, plotted to murder her and the unborn child. One of the sons revealed the plot to the unborn Huitzilopochtli. After Coatlicue was beheaded by her daughter, Huitzilopochtli burst from the womb armed with the Fire Serpent and vanquished his sister and brothers.

The southern portion of the Great Temple in Tenochtitlán was intended to replicate Coatepec. The colossal stone sculpture of Coatlicue, discovered in 1790, probably originally stood in that temple. A masterpiece of Aztec art, the statue presides over the Mexica Hall of Mexico's National Museum of Anthropology. It depicts the deity dressed in a skirt of intertwined serpents and a necklace of human hearts and hands. Blood flows from her severed neck in the form of two serpents, whose adjoined profiles create a monstrous face.

ESTHER PASZTORY, Aztec Art (1983); BERNARDINO DE SAHAGÚN, Florentine Codex: General History of the Things of New Spain, bk. 3, translated by Arthur J. O. Anderson and Charles E. Dib-

Coatlicue, mother of the Aztec gods. PHOTO BY BRADLEY SMITH / LAURIE PLATT WINFREY, INC.

ble (1978); JOHANNA BRODA, DAVÍD CARRASCO, and EDUARDO MATOS MOCTEZUMA, *The Great Temple of Tenochtitlán* (1987); INGA CLENDINNEN, *Aztecs: An Interpretation* (1991).

LOUISE M. BURKHART

See also **Aztecs; Mesoamerica.**

COATZACOALCOS RIVER, a relatively small river that drains a basin of 8,448 square miles. It forms on the north slope of the Sierra Atravesada, flows northward across the Isthmus of Tehuantepec, and empties into the Gulf of Mexico near its namesake city. A major tributary, the Jaltepec, rises on the northern side of the Sierra de Oaxaca.

Despite its size, the river always has been important because of its association with transisthmian communications. In 1521 Hernán CORTÉS sent Gonzalo de Sandoval to explore it as a potential route to the Pacific. During the colonial period, goods were carried by boat to an upriver landing on the Coatzacoalcos and thence over-land to Tehuantepec on the Pacific side of the isthmus.

In 1774, the viceroy of New Spain, Antonio María de BUCARELI ordered a survey of the isthmus for construction of a canal through the mountains to connect the upper reaches of the Coatzacoalcos with the Pacific. Almost a century later, in 1870, as interest in a U.S. canal developed after the Civil War, Admiral Robert W. Shufeldt surveyed the Coatzacoalcos and recommended that it be built there. Proposals for a railway that would carry fully laden ships across the isthmus were advanced in 1880 (by James B. Eads) and again in the 1940s (by the Mexican engineer Modesto Rolland), but neither of these remarkably ambitious projects got beyond the planning stage.

The earliest petroleum finds on the Gulf side of the isthmus were in 1907, but it was not until additional discoveries were made in the 1970s that the region became an important center of petroleum production. The Coatzacoalcos River is navigable for more than 100 miles and is the port for the city of Coatzacoalcos. Mexico's busiest port, Pajaritos, which serves a massive Pemex complex, is adjacent to the river.

EDWARD B. GLICK, *Straddling the Isthmus of Tehuantepec*, School of Inter-American Studies, Latin American Monograph Series no. 6 (1959); JORGE L. TAMAYO, *Geografía general de Mexico*, 2d ed., vol. 2 (1962), pp. 326–328; ROBERT COOPER WEST, ed., *Handbook of Middle American Indians*, vol. 1 (1964), pp. 87–88, 92–93.

JOHN J. WINBERRY

See also **Petroleos Mexicanos.**

COBÁ, an ancient MAYA metropolis in central Quintana Roo, Mexico, less than 12 miles from the eastern coast of the Yucatán peninsula. During the eighth century an estimated forty thousand people lived at the site, making it one of the largest urban centers anywhere in MESOAMERICA at that time. Cobá also figures prominently in the traditional Maya histories of the late pre-Hispanic period, with legendary ties to many of the city-states and royal lineages that dominated Yucatán at the time of contact with the Spanish. At the height of its power, this lowland city probably dominated much of the northeastern Yucatán peninsula and competed with other regional centers at Tizimín, Izamal, UXMAL, and EDZNA.

Cobá is probably best known for its radiating *sacbeob*, wide causeways that connected the city's monumental core to residential neighborhoods, nearby towns, and more-distant centers up to 60 miles away. At the core of the city were four major pyramid and palace complexes linked by *sacbeob* and dispersed around four large, shallow lakes. Minor temples, the residences of lesser nobility, and countless walled commoners' compounds packed the surrounding urban sprawl, which covered an additional 28 square miles around the core.

Researchers believe that from A.D. 600 to 800, Cobá was a diversified city of residential wards and craft guilds at the center of a powerful regional state. By the time the great center of CHICHÉN ITZÁ (A.D. 1000–1200) had risen a little more than 60 miles to the east, Cobá had declined to a less important shrine center where the magnificent stelae (thirty-one presently located) and temples of an earlier age were probably revered and maintained as powerful symbols of the postclassic nobility's links to a more glorious past.

WILLIAM J. FOLAN, ELLEN R. KINTZ, and LARAINE A. FLETCHER, *Cobá: A Classic Maya Metropolis* (1983); LINDA MANZANILLA, *Cobá, Quintana Roo: Análisis de dos unidades habitacionales mayas* (1987).

THOMAS W. KILLION

COBO, BERNABÉ (*b.* 1580; *d.* 1657), Spanish Jesuit scholar of the New World. Father Bernabé Cobo arrived in Lima from Spain in 1599. He spent the rest of his life in different locations in Peru and Mexico, working as a missionary, teacher, and writer. Of the original forty-three books making up his *Historia del nuevo mundo* (History of the New World, finished 1653, published 1890), seventeen are extant. The first fourteen comprise a study of New World natural history and the history of the INCAS; the last three treat the foundation of Lima.

Cobo, like other historians of his era, based his writing on personal observations, interviews with native informants, and the chronicles of other Spanish historians. His views on Inca beliefs and practices are highly judgmental, condemning native religion as diabolical. He provides excellent information on many Inca monuments as they were in the early seventeenth century. The *Historia* also contributes to our knowledge of the customs of everyday life in Peru before and after the Conquest. The prose is straightforward and clear, tending toward observation and description rather than interpretation.

There are two volumes of Cobo's *Historia* in English translation; each one includes two books of the original Spanish manuscript. They also offer short, useful introductions to the author and his work. See BERNABÉ COBO, *History of the Inca Empire* (1979) and *Inca Religions and Customs* (1990), both translated and edited by Roland Hamilton.

KATHLEEN ROSS

COBOS, FRANCISCO DE LOS (*b.* ca. 1477; *d.* 10 May 1547), official under King CHARLES I. The son of an impoverished noble family of Ubeda, Francisco de los Cobos devoted his career to government service. Aided by Lope Conchillos, who in 1507 was given substantial authority over New World affairs, Cobos's fortunes rose and he ultimately became secretary, and thus a leading adviser, to King Charles I (Emperor Charles V). In the 1520s Cobos served as secretary of a number of councils, including the new COUNCIL OF THE INDIES. He remained influential until his death.

Cobos used his position to advance relatives and clients and to build a fortune. He amassed numerous royal favors, including grants from Indies' revenues, and gifts from persons, including the conquistador Hernán CORTÉS, who sought royal favor. Cobos invested in commerce in the Indies, participating with conquistador Pedro de ALVARADO in sending black slaves to Guatemala. To guarantee the perpetuation of his fortune, Cobos established an entailed estate (MAYORAZGO). His career vividly illustrates the rewards available to a trusted servant of the monarch.

HAYWARD KENISTON, *Francisco de los Cobos: Secretary of the Emperor Charles V* (1959).

MARK A. BURKHOLDER

COCAINE. *See* **Drugs and Drug Trade.**

COCHABAMBA, city and department in Bolivia.

THE CITY
Cochabamba City is the capital of its department and the third largest city in Bolivia. The estimated 1993 population of the city and its immediate environs was 580,000. Although its population has more than quadrupled since 1963, it has lost its position as the second largest city of Bolivia to the even faster growing Santa Cruz, in the eastern lowlands.

Cochabamba was founded in 1574 by Sebastián Barba de Padilla, who named it Villa de Oropeza (Oropesa). In 1783 the name was changed to the Quechua *Kochapampa* (eventually *Cochabamba*), meaning "a plain with small ponds." The creator and first president of Bolivia, Simon BOLÍVAR, wanted Cochabamba to be the new nation's capital, but he failed to convince the colonial elite.

The city is located in a fertile valley, about 15 miles long and 6 miles wide at an altitude of 8,400 feet, facing the Tunari range, which in the winter is covered with snow. The valley has a moderate climate, with an average temperature of 66 degrees Fahrenheit. Considered the granary of Bolivia, it produces a variety of fruits, and has considerable herding. Cochabamba has some small industries and an oil refinery. It is an active trade center with a large and colorful weekly market (La Cancha). The University of San Simón has a fine medical school.

Although modernization has destroyed some of the colonial residences, Cochabamba still has a number of architectural treasures, such as the cathedral, the municipal palace, churches, and a cloistered convent with paintings by Goya. There are also notable nineteenth-century buildings, including the mansion of the late tin magnate Simón PATIÑO, which is now a museum and conference center.

Ancient Totora village, Cochabamba, Bolivia. PHOTO BY JULIA VARGAS WEISE. COURTESY OF THE BOLIVIAN EMBASSY.

THE DEPARTMENT

One of the nine departments of Bolivia, Cochabamba has sixteen provinces. Under the nation's unitary form of government, the head of the department (*prefecto*) is appointed by the president. Cochabamba is the most centrally located department in Bolivia; it covers 23,300 square miles. In December 1993 its population was estimated at 1,110,000, slightly more than double that of 1973.

The department has a varied topography. The famous eighteenth-century German naturalist Thaddeus Haenke, author of a classic account of Cochabamba, described the region as a continuous descent from the high peaks of the Andes in the west to the tropical plains in the east, from over 16,000 feet to 500 feet. The western and central parts, the most populated, have large, fertile valleys with a year-round temperate climate. The capital of the department, the city of Cochabamba, is located in the largest valley. In the north is the continuation of the YUNGAS, subtropical forested valleys that are accessible from La Paz. East of the Cochabamba Valley is the subtropical Chaparé region, which is well suited for the cultivation of coca. Although it is a traditional crop, the increased production of coca since the 1960s, much of it for illegal export, has become a focus of intense controversy and international attention (*see also* DRUGS).

The population is heavily MESTIZO and Quechua with a Europeanized urban sector. In the rural areas Quechua is the predominant language. There is a modern airport in the city of Cochabamba. The only railroad link is with the city of Oruro, where it connects with railroads to La Paz (the de facto capital of Bolivia), Argentina, and Chile. An all-weather highway goes to Santa Cruz. All the rivers of the department join the vast eastern Bolivian fluvial system, which connects with the Amazon system.

The main production is agricultural, especially cereals and fruits in the fertile valleys. There is also considerable herding and some small industry, mostly in the city of Cochabamba and its surroundings.

For both city and department, see AUGUSTO GUZMÁN, *Cochabamba: Panorama geográfico, proceso histórico* (1972), and *Geografía de Cochabamba* (1978); S. R. L. VIAJES TEJADA, *Cochabamba: Su belleza y sus riquezas* (1974). For the city, see JOSÉ BENITO GUZMÁN, *Crónica de la villa de Oropesa* (1884); JOSÉ MACEDONIO URQUIDI, *El orígen de ''la noble villa de Oropesa,''* Cochabamba (1950); RICARDO ANAYA, *La ciudad de Cochabamba* (1959); FERNANDO CALDERÓN G., *La Cancha: Un gran feria campesina en la ciudad de Cochabamba* (1984). For the department, see GUILLERMO URQUIDI, *Monografía del departamento de Cochabamba* (1954); THADDEUS HAENKE, *Taddeo Haenke, su obra en los Andes y la selva boliviana* (1974); CENTRO DE INVESTIGACIÓN Y DESARROLLO REGIONAL, *Monografía del trópico del departamento de Cochabamba* (1990); HUMBERTO SOLARES SERRANO, *Historia, espacio y sociedad de Cochabamba, 1550–1950* (1990).

CHARLES W. ARNADE

COCHASQUÍ, an important archaeological site in Ecuador located approximately 30 miles north of the capital city of Quito in Pichincha province. Excavated in the mid-1960s by a team of German archaeologists, Cochasquí remains the best studied of a class of sites found in the equatorial Andes comprising earthen mounds, or *tolas* as they are locally known. The distribution of these mound sites is coterminous with the territory of the ethnic group known as the Caranqui, who occupied the northern Ecuadorian highlands at the time of the Spanish invasion. Mound sites in this region date to the late prehistoric period, approximately A.D. 1000 to A.D. 1500, and represent pre-Columbian centers of political power. Ethnohistoric accounts of the Inca invasion of the Caranqui region suggest that Cochasquí was an important center of local resistance.

The number of *tolas* per site varies greatly, ranging from a few to well over one hundred. At Cochasquí, there may have originally been forty-five mounds, though less than two-thirds of that number still remain. Two basic types of mounds are found at Cochasquí and elsewhere in the region: the round, hemispherically shaped variety and the truncated pyramidal forms, which may or may not have associated ramps. The former range from 20 to 132 feet in diameter and represent both mortuary features and house sites. The largest of the truncated pyramidal mounds at Cochasquí is 264 by 297 feet at the base and 66 feet tall. These quadrilateral mounds are generally thought to have served as house platforms for elite residences and are also often assigned a ceremonial function. The hemispherical habitation mounds tend to predate the quadrilateral mounds, with the construction of the latter thought to signal fundamental changes in the level of sociopolitical organization.

The primary reference works are those of the German archaeologists who directed excavations: UDO OBEREM, *Cochasquí: Estudios arqueológicos* (1981), and UDO OBEREM and WOLFGANG WURSTER, *Excavaciones en Cochasquí, Ecuador, 1964–1965* (1989). LUIS LUMBRERAS, *Cronología arqueológica de Cochasquí* (1990), offers a critical evaluation of the work conducted at Cochasquí and considers the site in its regional context. For a more general study of mound sites in the northern highlands, see J. STEPHEN ATHENS, "Ethnicity and Adaptation: The Late Period–Cara Occupation in Northern Highland Equador," in *Resources, Power, and Interregional Interaction,* edited by Edward Schortman and Patricia Urban (1992), pp. 193–219.

TAMARA L. BRAY

COCHINEAL (*grana cochinilla*), a bright red dye made from the bodies of small insects found on the nopal cactus. The production of cochineal dates to pre-Hispanic times. The Indians of southern Mexico and Guatemala traded cochineal extensively and used it as a dye for textiles. The process of extracting cochineal was extremely tedious and required great skill. It took approximately 25,000 live insects to make one pound of dye, and 70,000 dried ones to make the same amount.

Although indigenous peoples harvested the cochineal insect from wild plants, the Spaniards raised and produced cochineal on commercial estates or *nopalerías.* In pre-Hispanic times, cochineal grew in great quantities in the Mixteca region, in Oaxaca, and around Puebla in Mexico, and these areas continued to be important centers of production after the Conquest. By 1600, Spaniards shipped between 250,000 and 300,000 pounds of Mexican cochineal annually from Veracruz to Spain, where it was usually sold to textile makers in the Netherlands. During the colonial period, cochineal was worked almost exclusively by Indian labor.

The successes of the Mexican cochineal trade encouraged Spaniards in Central America to cultivate the dye, particularly after the profitable cacao market collapsed in the early seventeenth century. In 1611, the arrival of an ambitious governor, the Conde de la Gómara, signaled the beginning of a brief boom in the cochineal industry in Central America. With his encouragement, *nopalerías* appeared in the western highlands of Guatemala, in Totonicapán, Suchitepequez, Guazacapán, and south of Lake Atitlán, as well as throughout northern Nicaragua. The boom lasted until 1621 and then ended abruptly, possibly due to plagues of locusts which ravaged the crop in 1616 and 1618.

After 1621, the production of cochineal was centered almost completely in Mexico, which had always remained the primary producer of the crop. Although a lack of skilled Indian labor hampered the industry's expansion during the seventeenth century, the rich red dye was in such demand by Flemish, Dutch, and English textile weavers that it remained a vital commodity for Mexico throughout the entire colonial period. By the early eighteenth century, the growing textile industry in Europe and expanded economic policies under the Bourbon rulers of Spain greatly enhanced cochineal's popularity as an export commodity. In the 1760s, the Portuguese attempted to cultivate cochineal with limited success in Rio Grande de São Pedro and the island of Santa Catarina, but New Spain remained Europe's main supplier of the dye. By the mid-eighteenth century, cochineal had become Mexico's second most valuable export, after silver. It was grown mainly in Oaxaca, where as many as thirty thousand Indians were employed in the industry. Cochineal remained a vital export for Mexico into the nineteenth century, until the international textile industry converted to the use of cheaper synthetic red dyes.

WILLIAM B. TAYLOR, *Landlord and Peasant in Colonial Oaxaca* (1972); MURDO J. MAC LEOD, *Spanish Central America: A Socioeconomic History 1520–1720* (1973); MILES L. WORTMAN, *Government and Society in Central America 1680–1840* (1982); MICHAEL MEYERS and WILLIAM SHERMAN, *The Course of Mexican History* (3d ed., 1987); RICHARD J. SALVUCCI, *Textiles and Capitalism in Mexico: An Economic History of the Obrajes* (1987).

VIRGINIA GARRARD-BURNETT

See also **Indigo.**

COCHRANE, LORD THOMAS ALEXANDER (*b.* 14 December 1775; *d.* 30 October 1860), naval commander in wars for Latin American independence. A member of the Scottish nobility with a distinguished record in the Royal Navy during the Napoleonic Wars, Cochrane came to South America in 1818, at the invitation of the independent Chilean government, which gave him command of its fledgling navy. Consisting of odds and ends of warships and heavily dependent on foreign adventurers for skilled seamen, this force under Cochrane's leadership harassed Spanish-held ports along the Pacific coast and was instrumental in the capture of the key fortress of Valdivia in southern Chile (1820). In 1820 Cochrane convoyed the army of José de SAN MARTÍN on its way to invade Peru. But he soon quarreled with San Martín over questions of strategy as well as over what he considered inadequate support of his naval forces.

Cochrane's pursuit of Spanish shipping in the Pacific took him as far north as Mexico before he finally returned in 1822 to Chile, where he had an estate. He did not stay there long, for in 1823 he accepted an invitation from the new Brazilian monarchy to head its naval forces in the struggle for independence from Portugal. Once again he had a heterogeneous collection of ships and a large number of foreign sailors, including British seamen whom he induced to desert their own ships. However, when Cochrane sailed against Bahia in mid-1823, the fear inspired by his reputation, quite as much as the forces he commanded, led the Portuguese military entrenched there to depart without a struggle—and Cochrane harassed their fleet all the way to the coast of Portugal. He next helped evict the Portuguese from ports they still held on the north coast of Brazil. In 1825, however, he had a falling out with the Brazilian government and returned to Europe. There he volunteered his services to help in the Greek struggle for independence from Turkey in 1827, and was reinstated in the Royal Navy in 1832.

Basic sources on Cochrane are his own *Narrative of Services in the Liberation of Chili* [sic], *Peru, and Brazil from Spanish and Portuguese Domination*, 2 vols. (1859), and his *Autobiography of a Seaman*, 2 vols. (1869). For his Chilean and Peruvian service, see DONALD E. WORCESTER, *Sea Power and Chilean Independence* (1962). His contribution to Brazilian independence is covered in NEILL MACAULAY, *Dom Pedro: The Struggle for Liberty in Brazil and Portugal, 1798–1834* (1986), chap. 5.

DAVID BUSHNELL

COCKFIGHTING. *See* **Sports.**

CÔCO, a popular northeastern Brazilian form of song and dance of African and Amerindian origin, found especially in Alagoas. *Côco* songs consist of choruses and refrains that are both traditional and improvised. As the name suggests, the earliest *côcos* were work songs of the Afro-Brazilians of Palmares, who would harvest and break coconuts to a rhythmic beat. The form now goes by a variety of names, such as *côco de ganzá, côco de zambê, côco de usina,* and *côco da praia.* It was also danced in the salons of Alagoas and Paraiba under the names *samba, pagode, zambê,* and *bambelô.*

In a common form of the dance, men and women form a circle with a soloist in the center who sings and performs a ritual dance, inviting the next soloist into the center with an *umbigada* (belly bounce) or courteous bow. Most of the instruments driving this lively exchange are percussion, namely *ingonos, cuícas, pandeiros, ganzás,* or wooden boxes.

DAVID P. APPLEBY, *The Music of Brazil* (1983); LUIS DA CAMARA CASCUDO, *Dicionário do folclore brasileiro,* 5th ed. (1984); CHRIS MC GOWAN and RICARDO PESSANHA, *The Brazilian Sound: Samba, Bossa Nova, and the Popular Music of Brazil* (1991).

BERNADETTE DICKERSON

See also **Musical Instruments.**

CODAZZI, AGUSTÍN (*b.* ca. 12 July 1793; *d.* 7 February 1859), military officer and cartographer. Born in Lugo, on the northeastern coast of Italy near Ravenna, Codazzi was a veteran of the Napoleonic armies and one of the European volunteers who joined Simón BOLÍVAR's troops in the War of Independence. However, his main contribution to both Venezuela and New Granada was as a geographer, by charting the maps of both countries and by actually visiting many unknown territories of both nations. After the war he remained in the Venezuelan Army as a geographer and cartographer for almost three decades.

In 1848, Codazzi became involved in one of the many civil wars between Páez and Monagas. Ending up on the losing side, he was exiled to New Granada, where he was put in charge of the Comisión Corográfica, a group that studied in detail most of the Colombian provinces and territories known and unknown, producing maps and descriptions of the local economies and advising how to build needed roads. Codazzi died in Colombia in a town on the Caribbean coast. The town and the National Geographic Institute of Colombia now bear his name.

JOSÉ MANUEL RESTREPO, *Historia de la Nueva Granada,* tomos I, II (1952–1963); MARIO LONGHENA, *Memorias de Agustín Codazzi* (1973).

JOSÉ ESCORCIA

CODESIDO, JULIA (*b.* 5 August 1883; *d.* 8 May 1979), Peruvian artist. Codesido, known as one of the *indigenistas sabogalinos* (close followers of painter José SABOGAL) was born in Lima. She, like other *indigenistas,* aimed at creating a Peruvian school of painting based on the exploration of native themes and the depiction of Andean local scenes and customs. She studied at the National

School of Fine Arts, in Lima, where she later taught. In 1935, she visited Mexico to study the muralist movement. After this visit, the influence of SIQUEIROS became evident in her work.

Codesido abstracted some pictorial elements in her paintings—trees, architecture—although she always stayed within the boundaries of realism.

In 1936, Codesido participated in the First Congress of American Artists, held in New York City. She exhibited in Mexico City and New York (1935 and 1936). When in 1943 Sabogal was relieved of his position as director of the National School of Fine Arts over artistic differences, Codesido resigned in solidarity with him. Subsequently, she dedicated herself to forming, with other members of the *indigenista* movement, a collection of popular art and artisanal work for the National Museum of Peruvian Culture.

JUAN ACHA, *Art in Latin America Today: Perú* (1961); GILBERT CHASE, *Contemporary Art in Latin America* (1970), p. 101.

MARTA GARSD

CODICES, a term that is applied to sixteen diverse native-style documents produced in the pre-Hispanic and early colonial period by the indigenous peoples of central Mexico, the MIXTECS of southern Mexico, and the MAYA of Yucatán. Earlier examples have been discovered, but were too fragile to survive excavation. Most postclassic native books were destroyed by the Spanish, and the extant corpus probably represents a small fraction of the total number produced in the New World.

These documents are mistakenly called codices, although none of the pre-Hispanic books is actually a volume bound on one side of the page. Instead, they are screenfold manuscripts that were painted on strips of animal hide in the highlands and on native paper among the Maya. The strips were cut to the same width, sewn or glued together, and folded in accordion pleats into pages. Pigments were derived from mineral and vegetable sources. Some examples are painted on only one side. When both sides are painted, one side is des-

ignated as the obverse and the other as the reverse. Several have protective covers.

The manuscripts have no consistent starting point. Some are read from right to left, some from left to right, and some from the bottom to the top of the page. Genealogical manuscripts are usually read one page at a time, while divinatory information frequently stretches across two or more pages. Red or black guidelines divide sections and subjects or establish a meandering reading pattern.

Information is conveyed through conventionalized pictures that illustrate actions, gestures, and rituals; figures of speech; and complex linguistic puns in the indigenous language of a manuscript's patron. Pictographic, ideographic, and phonetic signs may be used in a single document. In Mexican examples, pictorial forms indicate basic outlines of a story or ritual, and the pre-Hispanic reader drew from his or her store of knowledge for details. The Mayan manuscripts also employ extensive hieroglyphic inscriptions. Europeans sometimes added glosses to identify ceremonies or the name of an owner, but frequently these glosses have no relationship to the pre-Hispanic pictorial information.

The codices are an elite art describing dynastic histories of rulers and records of ritual, calendrical, and divinatory matters. Genealogical manuscripts may have been recited to affirm or assert claims of dynasties to territories, while ritual and divinatory manuscripts may have been consulted on less public occasions for their guidance. In the decades soon after contact, the manuscripts were sent to Europe, presumably as curios to inform various sacred and secular authorities about native books. Their exact New World provenances are generally unknown, and they are named for the collections and libraries in which they have been deposited, or for the family or individuals who owned or made them known to the public.

The Borgia Group manuscripts, named for one member of the group, Codex Borgia, also include Codices Vaticanus 3773, Laud, Fejéváry-Mayer, and Cospi. All are concerned with ritual and divinatory matters, in-

Mixtec Codex Vaticanus, with calendar of 260-day religious year. LEE BOLTIN.

cluding the 260-day ritual calendar, the dispensations of repeating cycles of twenty- and thirteen-day periods, prognostications for auspicious and inauspicious days for traveling, auguries for marriage, and predictions about years with good and lean harvests. They may be deciphered to some extent through information in central Mexican chronicles. Nevertheless, they are not a unified group in style or emphasis. Various provenances have been suggested, but a Mixteca-Puebla origin may be correct for some of them.

Only four Mayan manuscripts survived the Conquest: the Codices Dresden, Madrid, Paris, and Grolier (the last of which came to light only in 1971). Mayan manuscripts are concerned with ritual and astronomical matters, including tables of the movements of the planet Venus, eclipses, the 260-day count, rituals concerned with rain, agriculture, and prophecies for individual years and larger cycles of time.

The Mixtec manuscripts include Codices Selden 3135 (A.2), Bodley 2858, Colombino-Becker I (two fragments of a single document), Becker II, Sánchez-Solís, and Vindobonensis Mexicanus I. The first six are concerned primarily with dynastic histories that describe the marriages, offspring, wars, and occasionally the deaths of rulers of small city-states in southern Mexico. Codex Vindobonensis is a ritual manuscript that describes the beginning of the world, first performances of rituals, and the establishment of Mixtec territories.

Most of the manuscripts have been published in photographic facsimiles with accompanying commentaries by the Akademische Druck- und Verlagsanstalt of Graz, Austria. See also KARL ANTON NOWOTNY, *Tlacuilolli* (1961); MARY ELIZABETH SMITH, *Picture Writing from Ancient Southern Mexico* (1973); JOHN GLASS, "A Survey of Native Middle American Pictorial Documents," in *Handbook of Middle American Indians* 14 (1975): 3–80; JOHN GLASS in collaboration with DONALD ROBERTSON, "A Census of Native Middle American Pictorical Manuscripts," in *Handbook of Middle American Indians* 14 (1975): 81–252; THOMAS A. LEE, JR., *Los Códices Mayas* (1985).

JILL LESLIE MCKEEVER-FURST

COELHO, JORGE DE ALBUQUERQUE (*b.* 23 April 1539; *d.* 23 April 1601), third lord-proprietor of PERNAMBUCO (1582–1601). Albuquerque was born in Olinda in the captaincy of Pernambuco, a younger son of Duarte COELHO PEREIRA, Pernambuco's first lord-proprietor. He and his older brother, Duarte Coelho de Albuquerque, were sent for their education to Portugal, where Jorge soon gained a reputation for his military skills. In 1560, he accompanied his brother, second lord-proprietor of Pernambuco, to Brazil to deal with Native American threats to the family's CAPTAINCY. Albuquerque was placed in charge of the Portuguese offensive. After almost five years of fierce warfare, he managed to remove hostile Indians from the coastal region south to the Rio São Francisco as well as from much of the fertile inte-

rior. His task completed, he left RECIFE for Portugal in mid-1565 on the 200-ton *Santo Antônio*, never to return to the land of his birth. This four-and-a-half-month voyage, described by Frei Vicente do Salvador as "one of the worst and most dangerous seafarers had seen," was the subject of a famous Portuguese shipwreck narrative. By 1601, an account written by Afonso Luís had gone through at least two printings of a thousand copies each.

After recovering from the effects of the voyage, Albuquerque served at the court of young King SEBASTIAN. In 1574 he was a participant in the first of that monarch's two expeditions to North Africa. In late November of that year, he returned to Sagres in the company of Dom Antônia, prior of Crato. The following year, he was captain of a galley patrolling the Algarve coast. He also served with his future father-in-law, Dom Pedro da Cunha, on a mission to Flanders. In June 1578, Albuquerque and his brother (who had returned from Pernambuco six years earlier) were part of King Sebastian's ill-fated second expedition to North Africa. Celebrated by chroniclers for offering his horse to the hapless king during the battle of Alcácer Quibir, Albuquerque was captured. Wounded badly, he and his brother, who was also a captive, were among the eighty nobles ransomed at great expense. He was back in Portugal by 1579. His brother, however, died in 1581 in Morocco on the journey home. Permanently crippled, Albuquerque officially succeeded him as lord-proprietor of Pernambuco in 1582.

By the mid-1580s, because of revenues from his captaincy, Albuquerque was considered one of the wealthiest of those men who gained their riches from Portuguese America. His captaincy of Pernambuco continued to prosper, especially from SUGAR. In 1591 a crown official reported that there were sixty-three sugar mills in that captaincy and tithes of 28,500 cruzados. Albuquerque encouraged the religious life of the captaincy and was generous to the Franciscans, the Benedictines, and the Carmelites. He was, however, an absentee lord-proprietor, and in his absence there were charges of corruption. From 1593 to 1595 a visitor from the INQUISITION was stationed in Olinda taking testimony from the inhabitants. In 1595, the English pirate James Lancaster seized Recife, sacking the port for several months before sailing on. As a result, Albuquerque suffered great financial losses as well as the loss of confidence of Pernambuco's inhabitants in the security of their port city.

After the death of his first wife, Albuquerque married the daughter of Dom Alvaro Coutinho, commander of Almourol. From this union there were two sons. The first, born in 1591, was Duarte de Albuquerque Coelho, who became fourth lord-proprietor of Pernambuco and author of *Memorias diarias de la guerra del Brasil* (1654), the eyewitness account of the early years (1630–1638) of the struggle against the Dutch in Pernambuco. The second, Matias de ALBUQUERQUE, born in 1595, later became *capitão-mor* of Pernambuco and governor-general of Brazil. Jorge de Albuquerque Coelho died in Lisbon and was buried in the Church of São Nicolau.

CHARLES R. BOXER has translated the "Shipwreck Suffered by Jorge d'Albuquerque Coelho, Captain and Governor of Pernambuco" and provided a useful introduction to the subject. See *Further Selections from the Tragic History of the Sea, 1559–1565* (1968), pp. 108–157 and 12–21, respectively. New information on the lord-proprietor's life and death can be found in FRANCIS A. DUTRA, "Notas sobre a vida e morte de Jorge de Albuquerque Coelho e a tutela de seus filhos," in *Studia,* 37 (December 1973): 261–286.

FRANCIS A. DUTRA

COELHO NETO, HENRIQUE (*b.* 21 February 1864; *d.* 28 November 1934), Brazilian writer. Born in Caxias, in the state of Maranhão, he was a prolific novelist as well as a journalist, essayist, short-story writer, and playwright. Some of his chief novels are *Miragem* and *O rei fantasma,* both published in 1895, *Inverno em flor* (1897) and *A capital federal* (1893). His principal work, *Turbilhão,* was published in 1906. He is best known for his narratives, in which he employed many innovative literary techniques for which Brazilian letters would become known following the introduction of its modernist movement to the world during MODERN ART WEEK, held in São Paulo in 1922. His work, however, is classified as premodernist, for it exhibits many Parnassian and symbolist characteristics. He also proposed a return to Brazilian nationalistic themes and sentiments. In fact, according to critics, Coelho Neto spoke vehemently against the modernist direction Brazilian letters was taking during the last years of his life. Coelho Neto also had an active political career. He was a public lecturer, and in 1909 he was elected as a federal deputy. He was subsequently reelected to two more legislatures. In addition, he occupied several diplomatic and other government posts. In 1926, he was elected president of the BRAZILIAN ACADEMY OF LETTERS.

CLAUDE HULET, *Brazilian Literature,* vol. 2 (1974); ASSIS BRASIL, *O livro de ouro da literatura brasileira* (1980); LEMUEL A. JOHNSON, "The *Romance Bárbaro* as an Agent of Disappearance: Henrique Coelho Neto's *Rei Negro* and Its Conventions," in *Voices from Under: Black Narrative in Latin America and the Caribbean,* edited by William Luis (1984).

ROSÂNGELA MARIA VIEIRA

COELHO PEREIRA, DUARTE (*b.* latter part of the fifteenth century; *d.* 1553 or 1554), first lord-proprietor of PERNAMBUCO (1534–1553/54). Coelho was one of the most important figures in sixteenth-century Brazil. The circumstances surrounding his birth and early career are shrouded in mystery. It is known, however, that he was the illegitimate son of a certain Gonçalo Coelho and that a brother, João de Azevedo, was a priest and chaplain. In 1509, Coelho joined an armada going to India under the leadership of Dom Fernando Coutinho. During the next twenty years, Coelho's actions in the Far East earned him deserved praise and mention in almost all the chronicles of the period. He also amassed an immense fortune that later served him well in his efforts to colonize Brazil. In 1521 he was made a fidalgo in the king's household. Sometime around 1529, he arrived back in Portugal. In the latter part of 1530, Coelho was sent on a diplomatic mission to France. He returned to Portugal by late April or early May of 1531 and shortly thereafter was named CAPITÃO-MOR of the annual armada sent to the African fortress of São Jorge de Mina. On the return voyage, he rendezvoused in the Azores with ships arriving from India. Later in the year 1532, he was again in charge of an armada, this one on coast guard duty along the Malagueta Coast. On this voyage, Coelho captured a French galleon. Toward the end of January 1533, he and his armada were ordered to the Azores to await that year's armada from India. He was back in Portugal by the end of July or early August of 1533.

By 1534, Coelho was married to Dona Brites de Albuquerque, niece of Jorge de Albuquerque, twice captain of Malacca and a former comrade-in-arms. In that year he was one of twelve men awarded captaincies in Brazil. Because of his exploits in Asia and as one of King JOÃO III's most trusted and dependable military men, Coelho received the choicest grant of land in Brazil: territory with fertile soil, a good port, previous settlement, and proximity to Portugal. On 10 March 1534, he was granted sixty leagues of land, roughly the area from the Rio São Francisco northward to the southern banks of the Rio Igaraçu (including all of present-day Alagoas and most of Pernambuco) and a vast number of powers and privileges. On 24 September 1534, the king issued Coelho's charter (*foral*), a statement of the obligations of the lord-proprietor (DONATÁRIO) and his settlers. Like the other lords-proprietor, Coelho was granted extensive administrative, fiscal, and judicial powers by the crown in exchange for settling and defending at his own cost the land granted him.

Early in 1535, with his wife and her brother, Jerónimo de Albuquerque, plus a good-sized armada of personnel and supplies, Coelho left Lisbon for Pernambuco. The lord-proprietor took firm hold of his CAPTAINCY and brought it order and prosperity by leading the fight against hostile Indians and French interlopers and by providing the blueprint for a stable agrarian colony. Even though BRAZILWOOD had been the region's most important product before the era of the captaincies and continued to play a major role during the first lord-proprietor's lifetime, it was soon supplanted by SUGAR as the chief money crop. Exactly when the first sugarcane was planted in Coelho's colony is not known, but by April of 1542 the lord-proprietor was reporting to the king that much cane had been planted and that a large sugar mill was almost ready for operation. At the same time, Coelho requested permission to import black slaves from Guiné (Guinea). Eight years later, in 1550, there were five *engenhos* (sugar mills) in use and many others under construction. Thus, in less than twenty years, Coelho had set his captaincy on a path of agro-industrial development that it would follow for the remainder of the Portuguese colonial era and well into the national period of Brazilian history.

Coelho, who had been granted his own coat of arms in 1545, reacted strongly to the crown's program in 1548 to cut back on donatarial prerogatives and establish a system of royal and centralized government in Brazil. As he informed King João III in 1550: "All the people of this Nova Lusitania were and are very much upset with these changes" (Dutra, 438). In mid-1553 or 1554, Coelho returned a second time to Portugal to plead his case personally but died shortly after his arrival. He was buried in the tomb of Manuel de Moura in Lisbon's church of São João da Praça. He left as his heirs two teenage sons, Duarte Coelho de Albuquerque and Jorge de Albuquerque COELHO, who succeeded him as second and third lords-proprietor of Pernambuco.

The best edition of Duarte Coelho Pereira's correspondence is JOSÉ ANTÔNIO GONSALVES DE MELLO and CLEONIR XAVIER DE ALBUQUERQUE, eds., *Cartas de Duarte Coelho a el rei* (1967). New archival materials are used in FRANCIS A. DUTRA, "Duarte Coelho Pereira, First Lord-Proprietor of Pernambuco: The Beginning of a Dynasty," in *The Americas* 29, no. 4 (1973): 415–441. Also useful is the narrative by COSTA PORTO, *Duarte Coelho* (1961). For the years separating Coelho's Asian and Brazilian experiences, see A. TEIXEIRA DA MOTA, "Duarte Coelho, Capitão-Mor de Armadas no Atlântico (1531–1535)," a *separata* (offprint) of the *Revista de Ciências do Homem* 4, series A (1971). An important new work on the *donatarios* (lords-proprietors) of Portuguese America (as well as other parts of the Portuguese Empire) is ANTÔNIO VASCONCELOS DE SALDANHA, *As capitanias. O regime senhorial na expansão ultramarina portuguesa* (1992).

FRANCIS A. DUTRA

See also **Albuquerque, Matias de.**

COFFEE, VALORIZATION OF (BRAZIL), the government's efforts to prop up (valorize) the price of COFFEE by reducing the world supply. The first valorization (1906–1914) was occasioned by an unusually large crop that threatened to decimate coffee prices. The governors of São Paulo, Minas Gerais, and Rio de Janeiro agreed to reduce production and remove coffee stocks from the market. The valorization did not raise coffee prices, but it successfully prevented prices from falling further, since Brazil controlled 80 percent of world coffee production.

The success of the first program convinced the federal government to finance another valorization program in 1917, when coffee prices again slumped. Undertaken only with Brazilian funds, it enjoyed great success because a severe frost in 1918 reduced production and ended the threat of glut. The last stocks were sold off two years later. In 1921 the federal government along

with São Paulo intervened again to prevent low prices. European and U.S. lenders and exporters provided the funds to sustain prices until 1924.

In the 1920s São Paulo, Rio de Janeiro, and Minas Gerais established state institutes to finance and regulate coffee's flow to market. In 1931 the new government of President Getúlio VARGAS created the National Coffee Council (changed to the National Department of Coffee in 1933) to control coffee marketing and financing. This arrangement was effective as long as Brazil produced most of the world's coffee, but after the late 1920s its share declined. In 1946 the Brazilian government signed the Inter-American Coffee Agreement to stabilize prices within the Americas through a quota system. This program was expanded to producers in the rest of the world in 1962 with the signing of the International Coffee Agreement, which made coffee one of the most closely state-controlled commodities in the world. The agreement remained in effect until 1989, when Brazil abandoned it in a dispute over quotas and at the same time, abolished the National Department of Coffee. The next year Brazil lost its place as the world's leading coffee producer to Colombia, though it subsequently regained its preeminence.

CARLOS MANUEL PELAEZ, "Análise econômica do programa brasileiro de sustentação do café, 1906–1945," in *Revista Brasileira de Economia* 25, no. 4 (1971): 5–211; THOMAS HOLLOWAY, *The Brazilian Coffee Valorization of 1906: Regional Politics and Economic Dependence* (1975); ANTÔNIO DELFIM NETTO, *O problema do café no Brasil*, 2d ed. (1979); STEVEN TOPIK, *The Political Economy of the Brazilian State, 1889–1930* (1987).

STEVEN TOPIK

COFFEE INDUSTRY, major economic activity of several Latin American countries, with consequent influence on patterns of land use, population distribution, and social relations. Native to northeast Africa, coffee was introduced into the Caribbean and the Guianas in the eighteenth century, but it became a major commercial crop only in the nineteenth century, as demand grew in Europe and North America and transportation technology connected remote producing areas to seaports. Coffee requires a frost-free, temperate climate with well-distributed rainfall and fairly rich soils—conditions met by the interior uplands of southeast Brazil as well as the highland areas of Colombia, Central America, southern Mexico, and the larger Caribbean islands. While it is a perennial shrub with a normal life span of twenty to forty years, yields can vary markedly from one year to the next. Aggregate world demand changes only slowly, but abrupt fluctuations in supply, and consequently prices, make coffee a risky business. Nations heavily dependent on coffee for foreign exchange earnings and government revenue have gone through cycles of boom and bust, mitigated somewhat since World War II by a series of international coffee agreements intended to regulate production levels and even out price swings.

TABLE 1 Export trends for principal coffee-producing countries (in thousands of 132-pound bags) and percentage of total world exports

	1909–1913		1939–1943		1979–1983	
	Bags	%	Bags	%	Bags	%
Brazil	12,668	69.0	11,422	49.9	13,333	20.7
Colombia	773	4.2	4,132	18.1	9,750	15.2
El Salvador	489	2.7	881	3.9	2,813	4.4
Guatemala	656	3.6	755	3.3	2,293	3.6
Mexico	371	2.0	484	2.1	2,460	3.8
Costa Rica	215	1.2	352	1.6	1,597	2.5
Ecuador	62	0.3	193	0.9	1,137	1.8
Haiti	581	3.2	374	1.6	307	0.5
Nicaragua	144	0.8	234	1.0	877	1.4
Honduras	8	0.1	28	0.1	1,097	1.7
Peru	8	0.1	30	0.1	830	1.3
Dominican Republic	27	0.1	178	0.8	557	0.9

SOURCES: *Tea and Coffee Trade Journal;* WORLD BANK, *Commodity Trade and Price Trends.*

In Brazil coffee replaced sugar as the most important export by 1830, holding that position until superseded by soybeans in about 1980. When leaf-rust disease decimated coffee groves in Ceylon and Java in the 1870s, Brazil became the world's primary producer. Coffee spread south and west from Rio de Janeiro, with African slaves providing the labor force on large plantations. That pattern extended into western São Paulo with the construction of railroads connecting the port of Santos to the interior. In the late 1880s, during a decade of high prices and rapid growth, European immigrants replaced slaves as the mainstay of the labor force in São Paulo, just before the final abolition of slavery in 1888. In the first two decades of the twentieth century, Brazil produced three-quarters of the world's coffee, with the state of São Paulo accounting for fully half the world's supply. A bumper crop in 1906 of 20 million 132-pound bags, the highest recorded in Brazil for many years, prompted a government program of price supports and market controls that became a recurring feature of Brazilian coffee policy. During the 1930s such policies included the purchase and destruction of large quantities in the face of depressed world prices. The coffee trade brought mass immigration from Europe, high govern-

Coffee pickers. Colombia, 1900. PHOTO BY MELITÓN RODRÍGUEZ / FOTOGRAFÍA RODRÍGUEZ.

TABLE 2   Percentage contribution of coffee exports to the total value of exports from each country

	1960	1970	1980
Brazil	56	34	10
Colombia	72	57	60
El Salvador	69	50	57
Guatemala	66	34	30
Costa Rica	49	32	25
Ecuador	15	23	6
Haiti	56	38	34
Nicaragua	34	13	37
Honduras	19	15	24
Dominican Republic	13	14	4

SOURCE: WORLD BANK, *Commodity Trade and Price Trends.*

ment revenues, and complementary economic activity—all fundamental in the eventual emergence of São Paulo as South America's largest industrial center.

Colombia first exported small quantities of coffee in 1835, and by the early twentieth century was exporting about 500,000 bags per year (at a time when Brazilian exports averaged some 12 million bags annually). The formation of the National Federation of Coffee Growers in 1927 institutionalized a system whereby the coffee of many medium and small farms was marketed through what became a powerful political and financial organization controlling the country's principal export. By specializing in higher-quality varieties and astute marketing, Colombia's production expanded steadily after World War II, so that by the 1980s the aggregate value of its coffee exports rivaled that of Brazil (whose large internal market absorbs about half of its total production).

Cultivation began in the highland areas of Central America also in the nineteenth century, as newly consolidating national elites encroached on indigenous village lands through privatization laws and usurpation, and many formerly autonomous peasants were forced or drawn into the labor force of the new export sector. German planters and trading firms were important from the 1870s to World War I in some areas of Guatemala and Chiapas, Mexico. Costa Rica's coffee sector, like that of Colombia, has had a greater proportion of small

TABLE 3   Average value of annual coffee exports from principal producers, 1979–1983 (in millions of U.S. dollars)

Brazil	$1,974	Ecuador	$157
Colombia	1,779	Haiti	51
El Salvador	504	Nicaragua	137
Guatemala	377	Honduras	162
Mexico	453	Peru	140
Costa Rica	255	Dominican Republic	97

SOURCE: WORLD BANK, *Commodity Trade and Price Trends.*

and medium-sized producing units than was the case in Guatemala and El Salvador, where larger plantations have been the norm. Although coffee became dominant in the profile of exports in several countries, none rivaled Brazil in total production, and the vagaries of Brazil's annual crop continued to influence world price levels. Since World War II, production in central Africa also expanded, led by Ivory Coast, Uganda, and Kenya, so that by the 1980s Latin America accounted for 55 to 60 percent of world exports, down from nearly 90 percent in the early 1900s.

VERNON D. WICKIZER, *The World Coffee Economy, with Special Reference to Control Schemes* (1943); STANLEY STEIN, *Vassouras, a Brazilian Coffee County, 1850–1900* (1957); BART S. FISHER, *The International Coffee Agreement: A Study in Coffee Diplomacy* (1972); THOMAS H. HOLLOWAY, *Immigrants on the Land: Coffee and Society in São Paulo, 1886–1934* (1980); MARCO PALACIOS, *Coffee in Colombia, 1850–1970* (1980); LAIRD BERGAD, *Coffee and the Growth of Agrarian Capitalism in Nineteenth-Century Puerto Rico* (1983); WILLIAM ROSEBERRY, *Coffee and Capitalism in the Venezuelan Andes* (1983); CHARLES BERGQUIST, *Coffee and Conflict in Colombia* (1986); ANTHONY WINSON, *Coffee and Democracy in Modern Costa Rica* (1989).

THOMAS H. HOLLOWAY

See also **Colombia: National Federation of Coffee Growers.**

COFRADÍA, a religious sodality, also known as a confraternity. The *cofradía* was an ecclesiastical institution of the laity based on the veneration of a specific image or religious attribution, such as the Blessed Sacrament (*Santísimo Sacramento*), Saint Peter, or the Virgin Mary. The *cofradía* was popular among all racial and caste groups, although the individual sodalities were not ethnically integrated. The institution provided spiritual security and collective identity through common acts of piety, such as sponsoring processions, celebrations, and masses. At the very minimum it was a burial society in which members paid dues to offset the costs of burial. The very largest and wealthiest *cofradías* owned large tracts of land and controlled vast amounts of capital. Among native communities the *cofradía* came to form part of a civil-religious hierarchy in which males in the community would advance by assuming a series of increasingly important offices in the *cofradía* and municipal government during the course of their life. In Spanish and mixed communitites the *cofradía* often came to serve as an extension of the guild, or GREMIO, fostering social cohesion and reinforcing common values.

ASUNCIÓN LAVRÍN, "La Congregación de San Pedro: Una cofradía urbana del México colonial, 1640–1730," in *Historia Mexicana* 29 (1980): 562–601; RICHARD GREENLEAF, "The Inquisition Brotherhood: Cofradía de San Pedro Mártir of Colonial Mexico," in *The Americas* 40 (1983): 171–208.

JOHN F. SCHWALLER

See also **Brotherhoods; Catholic Church.**

COHEN PLAN, an Integralist Party forgery that alleged plans for a Communist overthrow of the Brazilian government. The Cohen Plan was used to justify the imposition of the ESTADO NOVO. The plan, "discovered" in September 1937, was actually authored by a Brazilian Army captain, Olympio Mourão Filho, head of the Integralist propaganda section.

The fictitious plan was passed to Army chief of staff and Getúlio VARGAS confidant General Góes Monteiro. It became public on September 29 when War Minister Eurico DUTRA, while speaking on a national radio program, urged a renewal of previous national emergency decrees. This request was overwhelmingly approved by Congress. The Cohen Plan was widely accepted by the press and the public as legitimate, and its publication was followed by an executive decree that suspended many of the personal rights granted by the Constitution of 1934.

The "Cohen" part of the plan's title was deliberately chosen to create a linkage between Judaism and communism, a false linkage, but one held to be true by many associated with the Vargas regime. According to Mourão Filho, he originally signed the document with the name of the Hungarian Communist Bela Kun as a joke. Later, he recalled, "I remembered that one of our leaders always referred to Kun as Cohen [so I] crossed out the surname Kun and wrote Cohen." The forgery, when released, appeared to be authorized by the nonexistent Cohen, presumably a Jew and a Communist.

ROBERT LEVINE, *The Vargas Regime: The Critical Years, 1934–1938* (1970), esp. pp. 138–158; HELGIO TRINDADE, *Integralismo: O fascismo brasileiro na década de 30* (1979); HÉLIO SILVA, with MARIA CECÍLIA RIBAS CARNEIRO and JOSÉ AUGUSTO DRUMMOND, *A ameaça vermelha: O Plano Cohen* (1980).

JEFFREY LESSER

COICOU, MASSILLON (*b.* 9 October 1867; *d.* 15 March 1908), Haitian writer. Coicou became secretary of the cabinet of President Tirésias Sam in 1897. He later served as secretary and chargé d'affaires of the Haitian legation in Paris from 1900 to 1903. Several of his plays were produced in Paris, and he became known in literary circles. Several volumes of his poetry were also published in Paris. After returning to Port-au-Prince, Coicou founded the journal *L'oeuvre.* He taught philosophy at the Lycée Pétion from 1904 on and founded the "Théâtre Haïtien" during this period. After becoming involved in clandestine opposition to President Nord Alexis, Coicou was arrested and summarily executed with his two brothers and eight other persons.

Coicou was the author of numerous plays—tragedies, comedies, and one-act plays—most of them unpublished. The historical drama *Liberté* (produced in Haiti, 1894; in Paris, 1904), on the Haitian revolution, was highly praised by Parisian reviewers. While his surviving dramas have been criticized for weak structuring, Coicou was a master of French versification, and his poem "L'alarme" was memorized by most Haitian secondary students.

Poésies nationales (1892); *Impressions* (1903); *Passions* (1903); *Poésies nationales* (1904); *La noire* (novel, published in the newspaper *Le soir*, 1905); *L'empereur Dessalines* (drama, 1906); and *Le génie français et l'âme haïtienne* (essay, 1904).

See also NAOMI M. GARRET, *The Renaissance of Haitian Poetry* (1963), pp. 35–37; ROBERT CORNEVIN, *Le théâtre haïtien des origines à nos jours* (1973), pp. 110–115; F. RAPHAËL BERROU and PRADEL POMPILUS, *Histoire de la littérature haïtienne illustrée par les textes,* vol. 1 (1975), pp. 423–492.

CARROL F. COATES

COIMBRA, UNIVERSITY OF, Portuguese institution created in 1290 with four schools: canons, law, medicine, and arts. The school of theology was added about 1400. From 1537 to 1538 approximately three hundred students attended the lectures; between 1764 and 1769 twenty thousand scholars were educated at the university. University reform was initiated in 1772 by the Marqués of POMBAL (1699–1782), prime minister during the reign of King JOSÉ I. From 1772 until Brazil's independence in 1822, 866 Brazilian-born students received their degrees at Coimbra. Most of them came from the most populated and developed captaincies of Bahia, Rio de Janeiro, and Pernambuco.

Francisco de Lemos was the dean of the university when the Pombaline reform was instituted. He was born in Brazil, and his family was well established in the captaincy of Rio de Janeiro. Other famous Brazilians who studied at Coimbra were José Bonifácio de ANDRADA E SILVA (1763–1838), whose scientific work was so highly esteemed by the Portuguese government that it opened the civil service to him until he became a politician and mentor of Brazilian independence; and Francisco de Melo Franco (1757–1823), a renowned author of medical books to whom a satirical work on academic life is credited by some scholars.

After the university reform, natural sciences attracted the best students, while the school of theology suffered a severe crisis; in 1800 just one student attended its lectures. One explanation for this decline was given by the vice-dean: Those who had chosen the priesthood preferred to study canons because that school prepared them for all ecclesiastical jobs. The new spirit of the university was more visible in the organization of the medical school as well as the schools of philosophy and mathematics. Henceforth, the practical side of medical studies was stressed with the establishment of a hospital where Luso-Brazilian students could learn anatomy and a pharmacy where they could master the manipulation of medicines. Practice had replaced medical theories on the origins of diseases.

ANTÔNIO FERRÃO, *A reforma pombalina da Universidade de Coimbra* (1926); LAERTE RAMOS DE CARVALHO, *As reformas pombalinas da instrução pública* (1978).

MARIA BEATRIZ NIZZA DA SILVA

See also **Education.**

COINAGE (COLONIAL SPANISH AMERICA). With gold and silver dominating the export economy of the Spanish Indies, not surprisingly, the minting of gold and silver coins became a significant colonial enterprise. Apparently, the first coins appeared in Española in 1497—crude gold specie fashioned in Santo Domingo as a convenience for the growing population and trade on the island. As the Spanish presence expanded in the Caribbean and elswhere, so too did the stamping of gold coins in Santo Domingo. In fact, by 1520 over 14,000 kilograms of gold in bars and specie reached Seville from the Indies. Moreover, until about 1535, the standard monetary unit in the Indies was the *peso de oro,* also called a *castellaño* or *peso de minas,* with a value of 450 *maravedís,* a weight of 4.6 grams, and a fineness of 22.5 carats, jor one-fiftieth of a mark (*marco*) of gold.

In 1535, with the successful conquest of Mexico, Peru, and New Granada, CHARLES I ordered the founding of mints (*casas de moneda*) in Mexico City, Lima, and Santa Fe de Bogotá. Set up ten years later at POTOSÍ was a Temporary mint, which functioned until a permanent structure was erected in 1572. In Mexico the first coins issued by the Casa de Moneda in 1536 were gold *pesos de tupuzque,* valued at 272 maravedís. Appearing in 1537, the first silver peso (also called the *peso fuerte, patacón, duro,* or piece of eight by the English), became a standard monetary unit in the Indies for the next three centuries. Royal edicts also called for the minting of silver coins of a quarter, half, one, two, three, four (*tostones*), and eight reales, in addition to the peso. The two-real coin was the most commonly used.

Pesos of eight reales oscillated in size between 33 and 40 millimeters. Although they varied somewhat in their inscriptions, during the sixteenth and seventeenth centuries most coins were circular, with one side depicting castles and lions, separated into four parts by a cross, and carrying an inscription of the value of the coin. On the reverse side were two columns representing the pillars of Hercules with the inscription *plus ultra* in the middle; on the edge were the name of the monarch in Latin and a name or letter designating the site of the mint—M for Mexico, L for Lima, P for Potosí, and so forth.

Until the seventeenth century coins were fashioned crudely by stamping pieces of silver bars (*trozos*) with a round-mold hammer, but the coins were seldom perfect circles or of the proper weight or fineness. By 1600, however, better technology, more precise assay methods, and more stringent oversight of mint empresarios by royal officials established the Spanish American piece of eight as one of the most reliable monetary units in the world. In fact at the end of the sixteenth century, merchant contracts in faraway Turkey often specified payment in pesos of Potosí.

Despite the spate of gold discovered or seized during the early years of the Conquest, silver quickly replaced gold as the only metal being minted in Mexico, Lima, and Potosí. In the late sixteenth and seventeenth centuries, only the gold coins of Spain circulated in these placs, at least until 1675, when CHARLES II once again authorized mintage of gold. In New Granada, however, where gold output vastly overshadowed silver production, crude gold coins stamped in Bogotá or Cartagena and gold dust circulated as a means of exchange in the sixteenth century. By 1627 Turillo de Yebra, a royal treasurer in Bogotá, had begun minting both gold and silver coins, an enterprise which continued in New Granada through the WARS OF INDEPENDENCE.

The wide variety of specie circulating in Spain and the Indies during the sixteenth and seventeenth centuries led to the establishment of imaginary monetary units of account to ensure reduction of the myriad currencies to a single common denominator. For this purpose the crown used the maravedí with a real valued at 34 maravedís, a peso of eight reales at 272 maravedís, and a *peso de oro* at 450 maravedís. In Peru and Upper Peru the *peso ensayado* of 450 maravedís was another common, imaginary unit of account which existed until about 1735. This imaginary *peso ensayado* reflected the traffic in silver bars valued at 2,250 maravedís from which 5 pesos of 450 maravedís could be coined. Still another imaginary monetary unit used primarily in the sixteenth century, the *ducado,* or ducat, valued at 375 maravedís, provided another conversion unit more convenient than the tiny maravedí. Unlike Spain, where copper coins called *moneda de vellón* circulated widely in various denominations of maravedís, no copper money or maravedís were coined in America, preserving the integrity of the *peso de ocho* and reales both in the Indies and worldwide.

Despite their continual debasement or devaluation of the currency in Spain, the Hapsburgs did not pursue a similar policy in the Indies. From 1535 to 1728 the piece of eight was valued at 272 maravedís, had a silver content of 25.561 grams, and weighed 27.468 grams. In 1728, however, PHILIP V lowered the silver content to 24.809 grams. Then later in 1772, CHARLES III decreased it still further to 24.433 grams, and finally in 1786 to 24.245 grams. Thus, the fine silver content of a peso decreased by about 5 percent over the course of the eighteenth century, or expressed another way, the amount of fine silver contained in one *peso de ocho* was 0.9306 from 1535 to 1728, 0.9167 from 1728 to 1772, 0.9028 from 1772 to 1786, and 0.8958 from 1786 to 1825.

At the same time the Bourbon regime began reducing the silver content of American coins, it transformed the mintage system in the Indies. Bourbon monarchs set up new mints in Santiago de Chile, Guatemala, Guanajuato, Guadalajara, and Popayán. Later, during the Wars of Independence, *casas de moneda* emerged in Mexico at Durango and Zacatecas and at Cuzco in Peru. Moreover, throughout the Indies, private mint operators, formerly supervised by royal assayers and treasury officials, gave way to royal control and management of all mint activity.

In another reform, the crown also ordered mintage of new coins with ridged edges and with the bust of the king inscribed on the specie. Although silver specie was issued in the same denominations as before, the Bourbon bureaucracy hoped that the new silver coins with the ridged edges would stop the practice of shaving or clipping. In Bogotá and Popayán, mint officials began stamping gold *escudos* of eight, four, two (*doblón*), or one *escudo* (*escudo sencillo*). At the same time, mints at Potosí, Lima, and Mexico City increased their output of gold coins. In still another move to tighten metropolitan control of colonial coinage in the late eighteenth century, mint officials in the Indies were required to send samples of their coins to Spain every six months for inspection and assay.

During the Wars of Independence (1808–1825) royal *casas de moneda* continued to operate, at least until they fell to rebel forces, but mint activity declined sharply. In 1812 the mint in Lima, for example, coined 3,876,000 pesos (456,000 marks) of silver and 575,000 pesos (4,228 marks) of gold; in 1821 the same Casa de Moneda minted approximately 476,000 pesos (56,000 marks) of silver and 272,000 pesos (2,000 marks) of gold. In Mexico in 1808 various mints stamped almost 25 million pesos in silver coins and a bit over 1 million pesos in gold; in 1821, however, mint output amounted to only 5,600,000 pesos in silver and 300,000 pesos in gold, evidence of the devastation wrought by the struggle for independence.

HUMBERTO BURZIO, "El 'peso de oro' hispanoamericano," in *Historia* 1, no. 4 (1956):9–24, and "El 'peso de plata' hispanoamericano," in *Historia* 3, no. 12 (1958): 21–52; A. M. BARRIGA VILLALBA, *Historia de la Casa Moneda*, 2 vols. (1969); JULIO BENAVIDES M., *Historia de la moneda en Bolivia* (1972); MANUEL MOREYRA PAZ SOLDÁN, *La moneda colonial en el Perú* (1980).

JOHN JAY TePASKE

See also **Mining.**

COLEGIO MILITAR (ARGENTINA), the Argentine Military Academy, which traces its origins back to 1810 through numerous institutions. On 19 August 1810 the revolutionary government established the Military Academy of Mathematics. In order to extend educational opportunity, the Mathematics Academy, which also taught military art, was founded on 20 January 1816 for cadets and volunteers, including private citizens.

In January 1815, Father Francisco de Paula Castañeda organized in the Convent Recoletos the Academy of Design, whose students included military officers. On 3 December 1817 a permanent academy for infantry and cavalry cadets was created in Buenos Aires, and on 1 May 1823 the Union College and the Natural Sciences College for officers was created. The former changed its name to Moral Sciences and on 26 January 1824 created an annex of military studies. In 1829–1830 the college moved to the province of Buenos Aires. On 5 August 1826 Governor Manuel Dorrego created the Theoretical and Practical Academy of Artillery.

Following the unification of Argentina, the National Military Academy was created by President Domingo SARMIENTO on 11 October 1869. Its first site was at San Benito de Palermo. In 1892 it was transferred to the current site of the General San Martín Military School in Buenos Aires Province. Since 1940 the Military Academy has been located at El Palomar, also in Buenos Aires Province. Following the FALKLANDS/MALVINAS WAR in 1982, the academy changed from a strict military curriculum to one that includes other disciplines, such as liberal arts.

"El Colegio Militar de la Nación," in *Ejercito Argentino* 1 (1979); *Cronología militar argentina, 1806–1980* (1982).

ROBERT SCHEINA

COLEGIO NACIONAL DE BUENOS AIRES, a secondary school established on 14 March 1863 as part of president Bartolomé MITRE's policy for improving public instruction. Its five-year program of studies was developed under the minister of justice and public instruction, Eduardo Costa. The curriculum consisted of humanities and letters (languages and literature), moral sciences (philosophy and history), and natural sciences (mathematics and science). The school occupied the site of the early Jesuit headquarters in Argentina. Its prestigious location, only a few blocks from the central Plaza de Mayo and bounded by Alsina, Bolívar, Moreno, and Peru streets, was the site of several previous schools, including Colegio Máximo de San Ignacio (1767), the Colegio Convictorio y Universidad Máxima de San Carlos (1768), Real Colegio de San Carlos (1783), and Real Colegio de la Unión del Sur (1817). In 1821 the new Universidad de Buenos Aires opened on this site.

The Colegio's first rector in 1863 was Eusebio Agüero. Later that year he was replaced by Amadeo Jacques, who served until his death in 1865. In 1911 Argentine president Roque SÁENZ PEÑA placed the Colegio under the administration of the Universidad de Buenos Aires as the Colegio Nacional Central. From 1919 to 1945 it was called Colegio Nacional San Carlos. In 1945 it returned to the name Colegio Nacional de Buenos Aires.

DIEGO ABAD DE SANTILLÁN, ed., *Gran enciclopedia Argentina*, vol. 2 (1951), pp. 330–331. For additional facts on the early history of the school, see IONE S. WRIGHT and LISA M. NEKHOM, *Historical Dictionary of Argentina* (1978).

JAMES A. BAER

See also **Education.**

COLÉGIOS (BRAZIL), literally "schools," a term that refers to a range of secondary educational institutions in Brazil, from the earliest times to the present. During the first two centuries of colonization, the JESUITS, who held almost a monopoly over education, established eleven *colégios*, stretching from Pará to São Paulo. The teaching comprised classes on the humanities (but with the native Indian language in place of Greek), philosophy, mathematics, and, in Salvador and Rio de Janeiro, theology. In the eighteenth century, the Oratorians also held classes in Bahia and Pernambuco, but the episcopal seminaries in Rio de Janeiro (1739) and Minas Gerais (1750) were the only new institutions that could properly be called *colégios*. All the Jesuits' activities, however, collapsed in 1759, when the Marquês de POMBAL expelled the order from the realm and began a far-reaching educational reform. The buildings of the *colégios* were neglected, and they were replaced by a small number of *aulas régias* (royal classes) throughout the territory. Ecclesiastics retained a strong influence on education, however, and in 1800 a new episcopal seminary was founded at Olinda. Conceived after the reform of Coimbra University by POMBAL, it was intended to train a skilled colonial elite to share in the administration of the overseas dominions. *Aulas avulsas* (loose classes, each conducted by a different teacher at a different address) and private tuition continued to flourish. But the Olinda Seminary represented a return to a systematic educational policy and became an important model for the *colégios* of the first half of the nineteenth century. In 1821 Lazarist priests created the Colégio do Caraça in Minas Gerais. A few years later Pernambuco became the first province to have its public *colégio*, the Liceu Pernambucano (1826).

With the ADDITIONAL ACT (1834), the provinces were granted authority over local educational matters, but it was an enterprise from the central government that looms largest in this period. The imperial Colégio Pedro II (1837) was designed to be the exemplar for Brazilian secondary education and to provide the nation with bureaucrats. Moreover, it proclaimed to the local elites the primacy of Rio de Janeiro as the intellectual capital of an empire beset by regional strife. The intent of secondary education, however, remained above all to prepare students for matriculation in the law, medical, and engineering schools that had been created since 1827. In this objective, private institutions, which enjoyed their golden age between 1860 and 1890, were much more successful than the public, provincial *colégios* and normal schools. Among the former, some established prominent reputations, such as the Colégio do Dr. Kopke, Colégio Briggs, Colégio Abilio, and the Externato (half-day school) Aquino, all in the Rio de Janeiro area. Besides the Colégio do Caraça, which was then in full bloom, the BENEDICTINES founded a *colégio* in Rio de Janeiro (1858), and the Jesuits regained a role in the educational field, although they were not as prominent as before. Even a few Methodist and Presbyterian *colégios* were created.

Colégios for women were rare, and only in the last quarter of the century did coeducational institutions emerge. With the republic (1889), a large-scale educational reform was undertaken, but it was unable to change the narrow scope of secondary education in Brazil.

FERNANDO DE AZEVEDO, *A cultura brasileira*, 4th ed. (1964); LAERTE RAMOS DE CARVALHO, "A educação e seus métodos," and MARIA JOSÉ GARCIA WEREBE, "A educação," in *História geral da civilização brasileira*, edited by Sérgio Buarque de Holanda and Pedro Moacyr Campos, vol. 2, 3d ed. (1973), pp. 78–87, and vol. 6, 2d ed. (1974), pp. 366–383; MANOEL DA SILVEIRA CARDOZO, "The Modernization of Portugal and the Independence of Brazil," in *From Colony to Nation* (1975), by A.J.R. Russell-Wood, pp. 185–210; JOSÉ RICARDO PIRES DE ALMEIDA, *História da instrução pública no Brasil, 1500–1889*, translated by Antonio Chizzotti (1989).

LÚCIA M. BASTOS P. NEVES
GUILHERME PEREIRA DAS NEVES

See also **Education.**

COLL Y TOSTE, CAYETANO (*b.* 30 November 1850; *d.* 19 November 1930), Puerto Rican physician, politician, historian. Born in Arecibo, Puerto Rico, Coll y Toste was educated in both Puerto Rico and Barcelona, Spain. Although he practiced medicine and wrote articles in that field, Coll y Toste is best known for his historiographical contributions. After retiring from the practice of medicine, he wrote numerous biographies of distinguished Puerto Ricans, compiled legends, and published the *Boletín histórico de Puerto Rico*, a multivolume collection of documents on the island's history. In 1913 he was given the title of official historian of Puerto Rico. Coll y Toste died in Madrid, Spain.

Biographical sketches of Coll y Toste appear in ADOLFO DE HOSTOS, *Diccionario histórico bibliográfico comentado de Puerto Rico* (1976), pp. 275–277; ISABEL CUCHÍ COLL, Introduction to *Puertorriqueños ilustres* (1978); DONALD E. HERDECK, ed., *Caribbean Writers: A Bio-Bibliographical-Critical Encyclopedia* (1979).

OLGA JIMÉNEZ DE WAGENHEIM

COLLOR, LINDOLFO (*b.* 4 February 1890; *d.* 21 September 1942), Brazilian statesman. Born in RIO GRANDE DO SUL of German descent, Collor received a pharmacy degree in 1909, but his first professional endeavors involved journalism and literature. His career in politics began when Antônio Augusto BORGES DE MEDEIROS, virtual dictator of Rio Grande, asked him to direct the state Republican Party newspaper in 1919. Thereafter, Collor rose rapidly in Riograndense politics and entered congress in 1925. After fellow Riograndense Getúlio VARGAS was defeated for the presidency in 1930, Collor participated in the October revolution of that year, a movement which overthrew the Constitution of 1891. One of the first acts of Vargas's provisional government was to create a labor ministry, headed by Collor.

Collor legalized those unions approved by the labor ministry, which could also intervene in their internal operation. In addition, he introduced the so-called two-thirds law, which required that two-thirds of the work force of all industrial enterprises be Brazilian nationals. He also set up conciliation boards to settle labor disputes, regulated working conditions of women, and established a minimum wage.

Collor's labor system has expanded and survived all the regimes since 1930. Fundamentally corporative, it was also eclectic, inspired by Catholic social doctrine (though Collor was Protestant), the welfarism of Uruguayan José BATLLE Y ORDOÑEZ, the Comtian paternalism of Julio de CASTILHOS, and Vargas's new commodity syndicates in Rio Grande.

Collor resigned his ministry in 1932, protesting Vargas's continuing dictatorship, and remained an opponent of his former colleague. A grandson, Fernando COLLOR DE MELLO, became president of Brazil in 1990 but resigned at the end of 1992 following impeachment.

JOHN W. F. DULLES, *Vargas of Brazil* (1967), pp. 1–116; JOSEPH L. LOVE, *Rio Grande do Sul and Brazilian Regionalism, 1882–1930* (1971), chaps. 10–11; EDGARD CARONE, *A república nova (1930–1937)* (1974), pp. 98–151; ROSA MARIA BARBOZA DE ARAUJO, *O batismo do trabalho: A experiencia de Lindolfo Collor* (1981): ISRAEL BELOCH and ALZIRA ALVES DE ABREU, eds., *Dicionário histórico-biográfico brasileiro, 1930–1983* (1984), pp. 2142–2151.

JOSEPH L. LOVE

COLLOR DE MELLO, FERNANDO AFFONSO (*b.* 12 August 1949), president of Brazil (1990–1992). Collor was born in Rio de Janeiro. His father, Arnon de Mello, was a journalist, senator, and governor of Alagoas. His mother, Leda Collor de Mello, was the daughter of Lindolfo Collor, who served as minister of labor in the first administration of Getúlio VARGAS. After attending the Padre Antônio Vieira, São Vicente de Paulo, and São José schools in Rio de Janeiro, in 1966 he transferred to the Centro Integrado de Ensino Médio (CIEM) in Brasília. He studied economics at the University of Brasília, then attended the Federal University of Alagoas, and returned to Brasília to obtain a degree in social communication. In his youth, Collor was an avid athlete and attained a black belt in karate. In 1975, Collor married Celi Elizabeth Monteiro de Carvalho, with whom he had two sons. They divorced in 1981, and the following year he married Rosane Malta, a member of a prominent family from Alagoas and manager of Rosane Enterprises.

In 1979, the National Renovating Alliance (ARENA), a government party, named Collor mayor of Maceió, where he served until 1982, when he was elected federal deputy by the Social Democratic Party (PDS). After changing his party affiliation to the Brazilian Democratic Movement Party (PMDB), he was elected governor of Alagoas (1987–1989). As governor and an outspoken critic of then President José SARNEY, he attracted national attention for his anticorruption measures aimed at public servants who received exorbitant salaries, often without working full time. Collor fought against powerful sugar-mill owners who refused to pay their debts to the state bank, Produban, which was eventually closed by the federal government.

Rejected by the PMDB, Collor launched his presidential campaign almost single-handedly, preaching the need for a crackdown on political corruption and promising a clean, efficient government. For months he remained third in the national polls, but eventually began to take the lead. In November 1989, among twenty-one candidates, he received the highest number of votes during the first round of elections, and he went on to the second round in a two-way contest against Luís Inácio (Lula) da Silva. On 17 December 1989, Collor was elected president with 43 percent of the vote to Lula's 38 percent. At age forty, he became the youngest president in Brazilian history.

During his inauguration speech, Collor declared that the federal government could no longer continue to subsidize a bloated bureaucracy. Breaking with Sarney's Cruzado Plan II, the newly elected president announced economic policies of austerity and cutbacks. In May 1991 he revamped his economic team and formulated new economic policies signaling a greater flexibility in negotiations with international banks. In the spring of 1992, Collor again made major ministerial changes. During that year, Brazil hosted the United Nations Conference on Environment and Development (Earth Summit), which won praise from the international community. By that time, however, the president had become the target of corruption charges. Following Collor's impeachment by the Chamber of Deputies, Vice President Itamar FRANCO was named acting president on 2 October 1992. Collor was officially removed from office by the Senate on 29 December and was charged with corruption in June 1993.

Isto é Senhor, 27 December 1989; RONALD M. SCHNEIDER, *Order and Progress: A Political History of Brazil* (1991).

IÊDA SIQUEIRA WIARDA

COLMÁN, NARCISO (*b.* 1876; *d.* 1954), Paraguayan poet and anthologist. Born in poor circumstances in the interior town of Ybytymí, Colmán relocated to Asunción in the late 1880s to study at the Escuela Normal. In search of better opportunities, he went to Buenos Aires, where for several years he worked as a telegraphist for the Argentine National Railways. He finally returned to Paraguay in 1901 to assume the post of chief telegrapher with the postal administration, and spent a good part of the rest of his life in that position and in various juridical posts.

Colmán's true interest, however, lay in developing a

public interest in GUARANI, the native Indian language of Paraguay. He collected folklore in the *campo* (countryside) and popularized it for the generation of the 1920s and 1930s. Writing under the pen name Rosicran, he published his own poetry in Guarani, including *Ocara Poty* (Wild Flowers), in two volumes, and, more important, *Ñande Ypy Cuera* (Our Forefathers), an evocation of Guarani myths. In many ways, Colmán could take credit for rescuing Guarani from the ignominy to which it had been relegated by Paraguayan writers who worked exclusively in Spanish and who, disdaining the Indian tongue, produced simple imitations of European styles.

WILLIAM BELMONT PARKER, *Paraguayans of To-Day* (1921), pp. 212–214; RAFAEL ELADIO VALÁZQUEZ, *Breve historia de la cultura en el Paraguay* (1980), pp. 259–260.

THOMAS L. WHIGHAM

COLOMBIA. [Coverage begins with a two-part survey of Colmbian political history. There follow a variety of entries on specialized topics: **Constitutions; Great Banana Strike; Organizations** (civic, cultural, labor, etc.); **Pacific Coast; Political Parties;** and **Revolutionary Movements.**]

From the Conquest Through Independence

DISCOVERY AND CONQUEST

Spanish discovery of Colombian territory began in 1499, when Alonso de OJEDA, accompanied by Juan de la Cosa and possibly Amerigo VESPUCCI, sailed the northern shores of South America from Guyana to the Guajira Peninsula. In 1500 Rodrigo de BASTIDAS mounted another voyage to that area, known as Tierra Firme. With Juan de la Cosa, he sailed from Cabo de la Vela to the Gulf of Urabá, thus traversing virtually the entire length of Colombia's Caribbean shoreline. They left Urabá with a cargo of Indian treasure, and the prospect of taking gold and slaves lured further expeditions to the region in the years that followed. Juan de la Costa returned in 1505, capturing Indians for slaves at CARTAGENA, raiding Indian settlements on the Sinú coast, and seizing Indian towns at Urabá and Darién before sailing back to Hispaniola.

In 1508, Ojeda and Cosa jointed in another expedition, this time with a view to establishing a settlement at Cartagena. Repelled by a native attack which killed Cosa and many others, Ojeda moved west to the Gulf of Urabá, where he established Spain's first permanent settlements in Colombian territory. The first was at San Sebastián de Urabá, founded in 1510. It was quickly superseded by Santa María de la Antigua, based on the Indian town of Darién on the western side of the Gulf of Urabá. For a time, Santa María was the main base for exploration in Tierra Firme; when it was abandoned in 1524, Spanish settlement had spread to other points on the South American coast, all of which were to act as springboards for conquest and colonization in the interior. One was on the Isthmus of Panama, in the land known to Spaniards as Castilla del Oro (Golden Castile); another was at Santa Marta, founded by Bastidas in 1526; a third focus was Cartagena de Indias, established by Pedro de HEREDIA in 1533. Settlements in Panama were to be stepping-stones to the Pacific and thus to western Colombia and Peru; those at Santa Marta and Cartagena became bases for exploring and conquering the Colombian interior.

Spanish exploration of the Colombian core began in earnest after Francisco PIZARRO's conquests of Peru in 1533. Excited by the possibility of finding new riches in the lands which lay between the Caribbean coast and Peru, bands of adventurers entered Colombia's interior from several directions. Penetration from the south was spearheaded by Sebastián de BELALCÁZAR, the conqueror of Quito. In 1535, his agents, Pedro de Añasco and Juan de Ampudia, entered the Pasto region and passed into the CAUCA Valley; they were shortly followed by Belalcázar, who founded CALI in 1536 and POPAYÁN in 1537.

After briefly returning to Quito, Belalcázar reentered Colombian territory in 1538 and from Popayán headed northward along the Magdalena River toward the Eastern Cordillera. There, in 1539, Belalcázar converged with other Spaniards who had entered the interior from the north and had discovered the rich and populous lands of the CHIBCHAS. These expeditions came from two bases on the northern coasts. The first, led by Gonzalo Jiménez de QUESADA, started out from Santa Marta in October 1536 and found the rich Chibcha civilization in the mountains of Colombia's Eastern CORDILLERA. In April 1537, Quesada entered the main Chibcha town of BOGOTÁ, extracted a large booty in gold and emeralds from the natives, and claimed the surrounding territory for Spain, calling it the Nuevo Reino de Granada (Kingdom of New Granada) after his native city. The other expedition that entered Chibcha lands from the north came from Coro in Venezuela and was led by the German, Nicholas FEDERMANN. Federmann's arrival coincided with Belalcázar's, and in March 1539 the two leaders joined with Jiménez de Quesada to found Santa Fe de Bogotá; they also pooled their forces to strengthen the Spanish presence in the area and agreed to have the crown adjudicate their conflicting claims to rights of conquest.

Meanwhile, Spaniards at Cartagena and Urabá were active in exploring central and western Colombia. From 1534, Pedro de Heredia ranged over the Sinú and Ayapel regions, ransacking Indian tombs for gold; in 1535, he mounted an expedition southward on the river Atrato, an initiative that was soon followed by others in search of gold in the Central and Western Cordilleras. The most important of these was organized by Juan de Vadillo, who left Urabá in 1538, crossed the Central Cordillera and followed the river Cauca south to Cali,

Cartagena, Colombia. Reproduced from John Ogilby, *America, Being an Accurate Description of the New World* (London, 1670). BY PERMISSION OF THE HOUGHTON LIBRARY, HARVARD UNIVERSITY.

where he met with Spaniards commanded by Lorenzo de Aldana. While Vadillo returned to Cartagena via Quito and Santo Domingo, Aldana sent Jorge de Robledo northward, initiating the conquest and colonization of Antioquia.

COLONIZATION

By the mid-sixteenth century Spaniards had carved out the major spaces within which colonial society was to develop in Colombia and had established rudimentary forms of communication between them. On the Caribbean coast stood Santa Marta and Cartagena; of these Cartagena soon became the more important, emerging as the principal point of entry into the interior and the major port for trade with Spain. In the center of the country, Jiménez de Quesada's Kingdom of New Granada became another key area for colonization, attracting Spaniards who fanned out from Bogotá in search of Indians and gold. By mid-century Spanish settlement had extended from Bogotá throughout Colombia's Eastern Cordillera and beyond.

To the north, settlement reached through Vélez, TUNJA, and Málaga to Pamplona; westward, Spaniards crossed the river MAGDALENA, founding towns at Ibagué, Mariquita, and Honda; eastward, they moved down the slopes of the Andes to the fringes of the LLANOS, establishing strongholds at Medina de las Torres, Santiago de las Atalayas, and San Juan de los Llanos. To the south, the towns founded at Neiva, Timaná, and La Plata facilitated contact with Belalcázar's sphere of influence in Popayán, first by the Guanacas trail, which led to Popayán by way of Neiva and Ti-

maná, and then, from 1550, through the Quindío Pass across the Central Cordillera into the Cauca Valley. There lay the heart of Belalcázar's great province of Popayán, which extended over a vast area of southern and western Colombia. For some years, it seemed that Popayán would become a separate dominion, independent of both Peru to the south and New Granada to the north; this possibility finally disappeared in 1563, when Antioquia was removed from its jurisdiction and brought under the Audiencia of Santa Fe de Bogotá.

Conquest Colombia was, then, a fragmented entity. Spanish settlements were widely dispersed, and their tendency toward autonomy was accentuated by difficulties of communication over long distances and rugged terrain. The development of the colonial population is difficult to ascertain, but it was still small in the mid-sixteenth century. Contemporary estimates suggest that by 1560 there were probably between 6,000 and 8,000 colonists scattered over the country, with small clusters of Spaniards living in rudimentary towns that usually held no more than about 100 Spanish *vecinos* (householders) and their families. The largest urban center was Santa Fe de Bogotá, with a core of about 600 *vecinos*, while Cartagena and Tunja had about 200 and 250 respectively. There was also a growing population of blacks and people of mixed race, between 5,000 and 7,000 in 1560, and a surviving Indian population of around 1.26 million. Of course, the Indian population was greatly diminished, as within a few decades of the Europeans' arrival, almost all native peoples were adversely affected by the consequences of war, epidemic disease, and exploitation.

197

INDIGENOUS CULTURES

Many different native cultures inhabited Colombia at the time of the Spanish invasions. At one extreme were the simple hunting and gathering bands which lived in the tropical rain FORESTS of the Pacific coast and in the great plains crossed by the tributaries of the ORINOCO and AMAZON rivers. At the other extreme stood two great cultural complexes: the TAIRONAS of the Sierra Nevada de Santa Marta and the Chibchas of the Eastern Cordillera. Both were at a relatively advanced stage of social and political organization, uniting densely populated federations of villages under leaders who combined political and religious roles. Between these extremes, most native peoples were organized in the tribal groups which Spaniards called *cacicazgos*. In the Central Cordillera, these tribes were frequently at war with each other, and according to Spanish commentators, they routinely practiced ritual cannibalism. On the Caribbean coast, intertribal warfare was less common, and the *cacicazgos* seem to have organized more for religious than military purposes. Whatever their differences, Colombia's native peoples shared a common fate after the Conquest; within half a century, the Indian population had been severely depleted, beginning a decline that was never fully reversed.

It is difficult to gauge the full extent of indigenous demographic decline after the Conquest, because the size of the native population before the arrival of Europeans cannot be fixed with any certainty. Some historians believe that Colombia's pre-Conquest native population was about 850,000; others estimate that it was at least 3 million and possibly over 4 million. Indeed, a recent calculation suggests that over a million people lived in the Eastern Cordillera region, another million in the Cauca Valley, at least half a million on the Caribbean coast, and between 300,000 and 400,000 in the upper and middle Magdalena Valley and its central slopes and in the southern ALTIPLANO region around PASTO. If the size of the pre-Conquest population is still in dispute, there is no doubt that in the decades after the arrival of the Spaniards, most indigenous communities experienced catastrophic reductions and some were completely obliterated.

ECONOMY

Decimation of indigenous societies, sudden and violent in some areas, more gradual in others, was paralleled by the formation of new types of social and economic organizations designed to meet Spanish needs and aspirations. Two basic patterns emerged. One was a rural economy in which arable farming was combined with extensive cattle raising. The other was a MINING economy that extracted gold, essential for trade with Europe. These economies were established in the same general pattern which Spaniards employed throughout the Americas. They founded towns from which to dominate and exploit the local native population and used the institution of ENCOMIENDA to obtain the goods and labor needed to support nascent settler communities, while also seeking sources of precious metals in order to pay for imports from Europe.

The discovery of gold and the development of gold mining played a central role in shaping Colombia's colonial economy. In the early years of settlement, Spaniards acquired gold by looting native communities of their ornaments and mortuary regalia; then, as permanent Spanish towns were founded in the interior, plunder gave way to mining the underground veins and gold alluvions found through Colombian territory. Some gold was found in New Granada, at Pamplona, and on the western banks of the Magdalena River; however, the richest and most enduring sources were in the south and west of the country, in the provinces of Popayán, ANTIOQUIA, and later, the CHOCÓ. The most important mining districts of the sixteenth century were developed along the course and slopes of the river Cauca, at Cáceres and Santa Fe de Antioquia in the north, around Arma, Anserma, and CARTAGO to the south, and in the headwaters of the Cauca near Popayán. To these gold fields, others were added during the second half of the sixteenth century when Spaniards pushed into the Pacific lowlands and found the gold-rich rivers of the lower Chocó.

The first great cycle of Colombian gold mining was roughly between 1550 and 1640. It started with the exploitation of gold deposits in Pamplona and the western slopes of the Magdalena, mostly mined by Spaniards from Bogotá. Gold production in the south and west was also underway in these years but was less stable and less valuable, partly because of the scarcity of Indian labor. Around 1580, mining suffered a temporary crisis as the Indian workforce declined dramatically in the districts controlled from Bogotá. However, gold production recuperated as new mines opened in western Colombian after 1580, mainly in Cáceres and Zaragoza. There, deposits were so rich that miners could afford to buy black slaves to work them, and so production soared, reaching its highest point in 1595–1599 with an average production equivalent to about 1.8 million pesos per year. The boom then tailed off as miners reached the limits of their technical capacity until, between 1640 and 1644, gold output fell to a fraction of late-sixteenth-century levels.

The second major cycle of gold production began at the close of the seventeenth century and lasted until the end of the colonial period. It was based on fresh discoveries of gold, found chiefly in the alluvions of the Pacific lowlands (in Chocó province and in Raposo, Iscuandé, and Barbacoas) and the Central Cordillera (in the province of Antioquia). Unlike the first mining boom, this late colonial phase of mining expansion used very little Indian labor. The gold frontier of the Pacific lowlands relied heavily on imported African slaves, while growing gold output in Antioquia depended mainly on the activities of individual prospectors and miners with small slave gangs. The value of gold production during the eighteenth century is, again, impossible to measure accurately from official records. Contemporary statistics do nonetheless suggest a powerful upward trend: in 1700 gold to the value of just over 250,000 silver pesos was minted at Bogotá; by 1800, the mints of Bogotá and Popayán were producing 2 million pesos.

Gold mining was vital to colonial society because it both supplied the means to buy European imports and stimulated the development of internal trade and production. Colonial Colombia was nonetheless an overwhelmingly agrarian society which provided for its own basic needs from agricultural holdings of many different types. In the early years of colonization, Spaniards relied for subsistence on products and services supplied by natives as tribute, channeled through the encomienda system. *Encomenderos* and other settlers also appropriated Indian land, and in the core regions of colonization they created large estates on which to raise cattle and cultivate commercial crops such as WHEAT, barley, and SUGAR. Before the end of the sixteenth century, landholdings of this kind were replacing the encomienda as a major source of wealth, as the latter was undermined by the falling Indian population. However, early in the seventeenth century, the prosperity of agriculture diminished when mining declined, stunting the growth of domestic markets. As poor whites and MESTIZOS found it increasingly difficult to live in the dwindling economy of the *encomenderos* and mineowners, they spread into the countryside and created farming settlements which later became Spanish parishes. Such, for example, were the origins of the villages and towns of the SAN GIL and SOCORRO regions north to Tunja, and the MEDELLÍN area of Antioquia, all of which subsequently became important centers of population.

As gold mining contracted during the seventeenth century, the Spanish provinces in the Colombian region showed a tendency toward ruralization and greater domestic self-sufficiency. This was not necessarily a sign of generalized retreat into economic decline. Depleted though it undoubtedly was, the output of gold continued to fuel the regional interchange of foodstuffs and basic manufactures. Indeed, interregional trade was fostered after 1620 by the establishment of a mint in Santa Fe de Bogotá and by the introduction of a silver COINAGE which facilitated trade within the domestic economy. Information on internal trade during the seventeenth century is scarce, but competition over the farming of river port revenues around mid-century suggests that internal commerce in domestic products was reasonably buoyant. There were also signs that the colony was developing rudimentary manufactures.

In the final decade of the sixteenth century, the president of the Audiencia of Santa Fe de Bogotá called upon the CORREGIDORES of his jurisdiction to organize Indian labor in workshops for producing woolen cloth, coarse woolen skirts, blankets, and hats. By 1610 there were eight such *obrajes* in the city of Tunja, and during the seventeenth century the city became the hub of a flourishing trade conducted with other regions in Colombia and with neighboring Venezuela. The growth of interregional trade was further reinforced during the late seventeenth century by the development of farming communities in the San Gil and Socorro regions, producing crude COTTON textiles both for domestic use and sale in regional markets. Thus, the colonial economy went through a long phase of change and consolidation, during which it became self-sufficient in basic foodstuffs and crude textiles and less dependent on gold mining and imports from Spain.

Throughout the colonial period, Cartagena de Indias was the region's chief port for overseas trade, providing colonial Colombia with a direct connection into the Spanish commercial system through the Tierra Firme fleet which supplied Spanish South America. Fueled by gold, this trade declined when the mining sector contracted in the mid-seventeenth century and revived when growth in gold output resumed during the eighteenth century. Bourbon monarchs introduced a succession of measures to guarantee Spain's monopoly of such trade, beginning with the 1720 *Proyecto para Flotas y Galeones* (Project for Fleets and Galleons), which sought to rebuild the system of annual fleets between Spain and America, proceeding to the abolition of the galleons in 1739, and culminating in *comercio libre,* or imperial free trade, which was decreed in 1778. The deregulation allowed by *comercio libre* stimulated a short phase of vigorous growth during the 1780s, but per capita exports remained relatively small compared to other areas in Spanish America and, despite official efforts to encourage diversification, continued to consist largely of gold remittances. At the turn of the nineteenth century, Spanish commerce with the region declined dramatically. Disrupted by the Anglo-Spanish wars of 1796–1802 and 1804–1808, it was finally ended by the break with Spain in 1810.

SOCIETY

Colombian colonial society was built on three ethnic groups. At first, European invasion created a dual society of conquering Spaniards and conquered Indians. Later, the growing importation of African slaves added an additional ethnic component, and miscegenation produced intermediate groups of people of mixed race, known to Spaniards as the *castas*. Over the colonial period as a whole, two major demographic trends stand out: a steep fall in the native population, and a gradual increase in the numbers of whites, blacks, and people of mixed race. According to one estimate, there were roughly 50,000 whites, 60,000 blacks, 20,000 mestizos, and 600,000 Indians in the region in 1650, giving a total population of about 730,000. By the late eighteenth century, this population had increased to about 850,000 people, and the *castas* had become the single largest group. The first countrywide census, taken in 1778–1780, shows that people of mixed race made up 46 percent of the population, whites about 26 percent, Indians 20 percent, and black slaves 8 percent. The preponderance of mestizos is striking, as is the decline of native peoples. At the end of the eighteenth century, the only areas where Indians were still a local majority were in the province of Pasto, in the Llanos of Casanare, and in frontier areas along the Pacific and Caribbean coasts where Indians had successfully resisted or evaded white encroachments. Elsewhere, Indians had become a minority in their own land, outnumbered by whites and mestizos in a demographic structure which contrasted sharply with those of the Andean lands to the south in Ecuador, Peru, and Bolivia.

Colombia's conversion into an essentially mestizo society had important implications for its development. The dual society of Indian and Spanish ''republics'' envisaged by early Spanish law had been almost completely undermined by *mestizaje*, (miscegenation between whites and Indians), and compared to the Andean territories to the south, Indian communities made only a small contribution to the Hispanic state and economy, whether in labor, markets, or taxes. There were, of course, regional variations within Colombia, but generally the absence of large native populations, based in the corporate ownership of land and standing in a special relationship to the Spanish state, had produced a social order different from those regions of the empire where Indians were in the majority. Racial divisions reinforced by economic inequalities stratified society as they did in other parts of Spanish America, but colonial Colombia was in many ways a less rigid society than those where Indian cultures had remained strong, as in the highlands of Quito, the southern Andean regions of Peru and Upper Peru, or southern Mexico.

GOVERNMENT AND POLITICS

The earliest forms of Spanish political authority in Colombia were the leaders of conquering expeditions. Having contracted with the crown to bring new territories under Castilian sovereignty in return for political and economic privileges, the captains of conquest were usually the original royal governors. Thus, Bastidas was first governor of Santa Marta, while Heredia held the same post in Cartagena, Belalcázar in Popayán, and Jiménez de Quesada in New Granada. By establishing towns, these men also implanted a second pillar of Spanish political authority, the CABILDO, or municipal council. Its members were originally chosen by the governor from amongst the powerful *encomenderos*; members then chose new officers from among their peers, setting a pattern in which *cabildos* tended to become self-perpetuating oligarchies, dominated first by *encomenderos* and later by leading landowners, miners, and merchants.

Royal authority was strengthened in the later sixteenth century by the creation of the Audiencia of Santa Fe. Installed at Bogotá in 1550, the audiencia was established after the abortive efforts of Juan Díaz de Armen-

dáriz to impose the New Laws of CHARLES I (1542). With the audiencia in place, the crown commissioned a series of *visitas* (official inspections) with a view to improving government, imposing a regulated system of tribute on the Indians, and providing the natives with protection from unrestrained exploitation by settlers. In practice, relatively little was achieved in any of these spheres. For while the presence of royal judges signaled the crown's determination to centralize authority, the audiencia failed to exert close control over Spanish settlers and their creole descendants, even when it was led by strong and active presidents such as Andrés Venero de Leiva (1563–1574) or Antonio González (1590–1597).

At the start of the seventeenth century, the crown sought to enhance the audiencia's authority in two ways. First, it endowed the audiencia president with military powers and duties, appointing Juan de Borja as the first Presidente de Capa y Espada in 1605. Borja proved to be an unusually energetic and effective official, and in the twenty-two years that he held the office (1605–1628), he strengthened the royal government in several ways. Borja brought new areas under its jurisdiction, oversaw the establishment of a Tribunal de Cuentas (a supreme court of audit for the royal treasury), and put the royal mint into operation at Bogotá. In his war against the Pijaos and in other anti-Indian campaigns, Borja crushed important redoubts of native resistance to Spanish rule and thereby extended the frontier for colonial settlement.

The appointment of his successor, Sancho Girón, marquis of Sofraga (1630–1637), saw a second innovation designed to enhance the authority of New Granada's audiencia: the appointment to the presidency of members of the Spanish nobility. This did not guarantee good or effective government, however. At the end of the seventeenth century, the *visita* conducted by Carlos Alcedo y Sotomayor (1695–1698) revealed that royal authority, while acknowledged in principle, was flouted in practice. Administered by corrupt officials acting in collusion with local elites, colonial government was undermined by widespread tax evasion, fraud, and graft.

Defenses against foreign attack and territorial encroachment also weakened in the later seventeenth century. In 1697, Cartagena de Indias fell to a French naval attack led by Baron de Pointis, and in 1698 a Scots colony was established at Darién, threatening Spanish sovereignty in a strategic frontier area. Thus, when Hapsburg rule finally ended with the death of CHARLES II in 1700, Spanish control over the provinces subject to the Audiencia of Santa Fe had become highly attenuated. Provincial governments run by venal governors, frequently ignored orders from Bogotá; the audiencia judges were themselves invariably concerned more with private than public business; royal finances were in a shambles; and colonial resources, particularly gold, were being diverted by contrabandists into the hands of foreigners.

The Bourbon succession to the Spanish throne, guaranteed by the Treaty of Utrecht in 1713, prepared a way for changes in these conditions. In 1717 the crown sent Antonio de la PEDROSA Y GUERRERO to New Granada with orders to investigate and overhaul the region's administration, finances, and defenses and to prepare the territory for government by a viceregency based in Santa Fe de Bogotá. The Viceroyalty of New Granada (also known as the Viceroyalty of Santa Fe, after its capital) was duly created but did not survive long. The first VICEROY, Jorge de VILLALONGA (1719–1723), was an inept politician and poor administrator, and when he proved unable to protect Spanish fleets against fierce competition from foreign contraband on Colombia's Caribbean shores, he was sacked and the experiment with viceregal government ended. A quarter century later, the viceroyalty was revived when the crown again decided that such a structure was essential if it was to tighten its control of New Granada's government and finances and to harden its defenses against foreign attack.

Reestablishment of the Viceroyalty of New Granada in 1739 inaugurated a distinctive period in Colombia's colonial history. The viceroys exercised jurisdiction over a huge area (equivalent to the modern republics of Colombia, Ecuador, Panama, Venezuela, and the Guayanas), but in practice they focused their authority mainly on the provinces of New Granada and Popayán (an area roughly coterminous with modern Colombia). In so doing, successive viceroys strengthened government finances, brought previously autonomous provincial governments under closer supervision, and strengthened Bogotá's role as a center for a more integrated system of government.

On these foundations, CHARLES III (1759–1788) intensified reform of the region's government and commerce during the 1770s and 1780s. As part of its wider program for revitalizing the empire, the crown opened the region's ports to imperial free trade in 1778 and, at the same time, sent a visitor-general to Bogotá with orders to increase tax yields and to make government more responsive to central command. These plans met with strong opposition. When visitor-general Juan GUTIÉRREZ DE PIÑERES took steps to restructure administration and taxation, he alienated sectors of both patrician and plebeian society and triggered the COMUNERO REVOLT of 1781. This great regional uprising mobilized a force of 20,000 people at its height, and under the slogan "Long live the king and down with bad government," merged the discontents, ideas, and aspirations of more than one social group. Some historians have portrayed it as a protonationalist movement and precursor of Colombian independence; some have regarded it as an aborted social revolution which revealed underlying conflicts between rich and poor; others have seen it as an essentially "constitutionalist" movement defending customary procedures and practices in government and CREOLE rights to consultation in important matters of policy. Whatever the causes of the Comunero revolt, its con-

sequences were clear. The authorities were forced temporarily to retract tax increases and permanently to abandon plans to introduce the system of government by INTENDANTS favored by Minister of the Indies José de GÁLVEZ and widely implemented elsewhere in the empire. Charles III's program of colonial reform was, therefore, less fully and effectively implemented in Colombia than in other parts of Spanish America.

After the Comunero revolt, other signs of opposition to colonial government appeared within the ranks of the creole elite. In 1794, the authorities arrested a number of creoles in Bogotá on charges of sedition, alleging that, inspired by North American and French republican ideas, they had plotted to overthrown Spanish rule. Among those arrested was Antonio NARIÑO, who admitted translating and printing the French Assembly's Declaration of the Rights of Man and who, after escaping from Spanish custody, began a career as a revolutionary which was eventually to lead him to a prominent role in the struggle for independence. At the time, however, Nariño and the tiny group of dissidents arrested in 1794 (mostly young men drawn together by a common interest in modern science, philosophy, and political ideas) were not a significant threat to the established order, since they were poorly organized and politically isolated. Their dislike of colonial government did nonetheless reflect an emerging creole consciousness, in which enthusiasm for the ideas of the ENLIGHTENMENT blended with resentment toward Spain for its discrimination against creoles. So long as Spanish authority remained intact, creole criticism of the parent power was contained within the colonial political system; when the monarchy faltered, such criticism was used as justification for breaking with the system.

INDEPENDENCE

The movement toward Colombian independence was initially triggered by crisis in Spain, caused by NAPOLEON's capture of the Spanish throne in 1808 and the subsequent war of national liberation against France. Without a legitimate monarch at the center of the empire, the colonies were left in a political vacuum; while Spanish government was weak and discredited, creole dissidents seized opportunity for self-government. The first revolt in the Viceroyalty of New Granada occurred in Quito in August 1809 and was suppressed by force. The second came in Caracas in April 1810 and established a junta which soon sought independence from Spain. In Colombia the first effective move to overthrow Spanish colonial authority took place in Cartagena de Indias, which replaced its royal governor with a junta of local notables on 14 June 1810. Similar moves were made in the first half of July at Cali, Pamplona, and Socorro. Most important, Bogotá followed on 20 July 1810. There, the overthrow of viceregal government was achieved by a small group of creole conspirators who, by manipulating urban crowds and neutralizing the local garrison, succeeded in replacing Viceroy Antonio

Amar y Borbón with a "Supreme Junta" which claimed to hold authority in the name of King FERDINAND VII.

Overthrowing the viceroy proved easier than creating an alternative government. In December 1810, the junta convoked a congress of representatives from all provinces in the viceroyalty, but only six representatives attended. Even this small group failed to agree, and in February 1811 the congress dissolved itself, having achieved nothing. Thus, the first attempt to create a central government failed, as the country split into competing provinces, each dominated by urban elites determined to pursue their local interests. In March 1811, centralists in Bogotá created the state of Cundinamarca, which recognized the authority of Ferdinand VII; through it they hoped to impose their authority over the rest of the country. It was led first by Jorge Tadeo Lozano, then by Antonio Nariño. Other provinces joined in the rival Federation of New Granadan Provinces, with Tunja as its capital and Camilo Torres as its first president, while Cartagena declared itself an independent and sovereign state. When the state of Cundinamarca itself became an independent republic in 1813, there were three rival patriot governments in Colombia. Tension between them eventually led to war, and in December 1814, Cundinamarca was defeated by the Federation and Nariño's government was overthrown.

While the autonomous provinces fought amongst themselves, royalist forces in Popayán, Pasto, and Santa Marta were regrouping and regaining territory. In 1813 and 1814, they came to dominate a large area of the Caribbean coast and gained ground in both the south, at Pasto, and in the Magdalena Valley. This prepared the way for the reestablishment of Spanish rule. In July 1815, a military expedition from Spain led by Pablo MORILLO landed at Santa Marta and from there began the successful reconquest of New Granada.

Reimposition of Spanish rule by military force did not bring a permanent reconstruction of the colonial order. Weariness with civil conflict and regional disunion facilitated Spanish reconquest in 1815–1816, but the savage repression which followed rekindled opposition to the colonial regime. In some regions, rebels mounted an anti-Spanish insurgency which, if it could not create a nation, did harass the royalists and keep alive the idea of independence. In 1818, when Morillo withdrew some of his troops for deployment against rebels in Venezuela, Simón BOLÍVAR sent the New Granadan Francisco de Paula SANTANDER into the Casanare plains where he rallied resistance to Spain. Then, in mid-1819, Bolívar led his own forces out of the Venezuelan plains and across the Andes to defeat Spanish forces near Bogotá at the battle of BOYACÁ (7 August 1819). With this decisive victory, Bolívar retook central new Granada and laid the foundations of the Republic of Colombia. In December 1819, the Congress of Angostura formally established the republic, which was to be based on the erstwhile Viceroyalty of Santa Fe. Known to historians as GRAN COLOMBIA, this state was essentially the brain-child of Bolívar who became and remained its first president while continuing the war of liberation against Spain throughout South America.

The constitution of the new state, drawn up at the Congress of CÚCUTA in 1821, was centralist and conservative. It united the colonial territories of New Granada, Panama, Venezuela, and Quito under a single government in Bogotá, endowed the president with greater power than the legislature, and limited the franchise to propertied and literate members of society. But Bogotá's domination of such a huge area could not endure. Even before Bolívar had completed the task of liberating South America from Spain, underlying regional and ideological divisions fractured Gran Colombian unity. In Bogotá, liberals resented Bolívar's authoritarianism and federalists disliked his centralism; in Venezuela, separatists led by the caudillo José Antonio Páez wanted their own government and in 1826 broke away from Bogotá; and finally, in 1830, Ecuador also seceded from the remains of Gran Colombia, leaving Bogotá to govern the old Audiencia of Santa Fe and the adjoining province of Popayán. Reconstituted in 1832 as the Republic of New Granada, this territory formed the basis of the modern Republic of Colombia.

An indispensable introduction to early Spanish activity in Colombia is CARL ORTWIN SAUER, *The Early Spanish Main* (1966). A clear and concise account of conquest and colonization during the sixteenth century is given by JORGE ORLANDO MELO, *Historia de Colombia*, vol. 1, *La dominación española* (1977). THOMAS GÓMEZ, *L'envers de L'Eldorado: Économie coloniale et travail indigène dans la Colombie du XVIème siècle* (1984), provides a vivid view of the consequences of conquest for the native population, while JULIÁN B. RUÍZ RIVERA, *Encomienda y mita en Nueva Granada en el siglo XVII* (1975), traces the trends and implications of Indian demographic decline.

An excellent study of a settler society during the same century is Peter Marzahl, *Town in the Empire: Government, Politics, and Society in Seventeenth-Century Popayán* (1978), while GERMÁN COLMENARES, *Historia económica y social de Colombia*, vol. 1, *1537–1719* (1973), and vol. 2, *Popayán: Una sociedad esclavista, 1680–1800* (1979), are indispensable contributions to colonial economic and social history. The fundamental study of colonial gold mining is ROBERT C. WEST, *Colonial Placer Mining in Colombia* (1952); highly informative regional studies are WILLIAM F. SHARP, *Slavery on the Spanish Frontier: The Colombian Chocó, 1680–1810* (1976); Ann Twinam, *Miners, Merchants, and Farmers in Colonial Colombia* (1982); and JANE RAUSCH, *A Tropical Plains Frontier: The Llanos of Colombia, 1531–1831* (1984).

On government and political developments during the eighteenth century, see JOHN LEDDY PHELAN, *The People and the King: The Comunero Revolution in Colombia, 1781* (1978), and RENÁN SILVA, *Prensa y revolución a finales del siglo XVIII: Contribución a una análisis de la formación de la ideología de independencia nacional* (1988). Economic and political developments throughout the late colonial period are surveyed in ANTHONY MC FARLANE, *Colombia Before Independence: Economy, Society, and Politics Under Bourbon Rule* (1993).

A clear and reliable account of the first stage of independence is given by SERGIO ELÍAS ORTÍZ, *Génesis de la revolución de 20 de julio de 1810* (1960); the career of a revolutionary leader can be traced in THOMAS BLOSSOM, *Nariño, Hero of Colombian*

Independence (1967), while the years of the first republic are detailed in DAVID BUSHNELL, *The Santander Regime in Gran Colombia* (1954). Useful essays on colonial Colombia can be found in JAIME JARAMILLO URIBE, *Ensayos sobre la historia social colombiana* (1968), and in JOHN R. FISHER et al., eds., *Reform and Insurrection in Bourbon New Granada and Peru* (1990).

ANTHONY MCFARLANE

See also **Agriculture; Commercial Policy; Independent Republics; Wars of Independence.**

Since Independence

THE INDEPENDENCE MOVEMENT

Leading citizens of Cartagena, Pamplona, Socorro, Bogotá, and other provincial towns initiated the movement toward Colombian independence in 1810. The power struggle of the *Patria Boba* (Foolish Fatherland) period (1810–1816) foreshadowed the nineteenth-century disputes surrounding the issue of regional autonomy (FEDERALISM) versus centralized rule. Miguel Pombo and Camilo Torres RESTREPO drew upon Enlightenment thought and the example of the United States in their defense of federalism within the United Provinces of NEW GRANADA—a governmental model well suited to the starkly divided Colombian topography, though not, perhaps, to Colombian political dispositions. The "precursor" Antonio NARIÑO, however, insisted on a centralized structure for reasons of military expediency and political authority. The conflict between these factions facilitated the 1816 Spanish reconquest by General Pablo MORILLO, whose pacification techniques included the execution of Torres and some three hundred other patriots. After Morillo's 1816 capture of Bogotá, patriot forces retreated to the plains of Casanare, where they joined the *llanero* (plainsman) chief José Antonio PÁEZ. Francisco de Paula SANTANDER, a Cúcuta-born lawyer who served as the administrator of Casanare, helped Simón BOLÍVAR plan the march over the Andes that led to victory at the Battle of BOYACÁ on 7 August 1819. Shortly thereafter the Congress of ANGOSTURA unified Colombia, Venezuela, and Ecuador into the Republic of Colombia, which is generally known as GRAN COLOMBIA.

The Congress of CÚCUTA in 1821 established a constitutional framework that shaped the subsequent Colombian constitutions of 1832 and 1843. These centralized regimes allowed for the division of authority among the executive, legislative, and judicial branches, with a clause providing the executive with "emergency" authority. Bolívar was selected as president, although Vice President Santander gave the new government administrative shape and direction while Bolívar led the independence struggle further to the south. The regime instituted the standard reforms, including the elimination of the Inquisition, Indian tribute, and the ALCABALA (sales tax); the opening of ports; the assertion of patron-

age over the church; and the gradual emancipation of slaves. A moderately protective tariff was retained for fiscal purposes, as were monopolies on tobacco and *aguardiente*.

Regional tensions doomed the Gran Colombian experiment. The 1826 federalist revolt by José Antonio Páez drew Bolívar back to Gran Colombia from Peru. Bolívar achieved an uneasy unity until 1828, when "the Liberator" imposed a "dictatorship" upon the country. Opponents failed in their attempt to assassinate Bolívar in September, a failure that earned Santander a European exile and others death. Gran Colombia collapsed two years later as both Venezuela and Ecuador charted their own national destinies. Santander was selected as president of the Republic of New Granada in 1832.

REGIONALISM

Six major regions, shaped by geography, patterns of economic and social development, and political jurisdiction have profoundly influenced Colombian history. These early national regions included: the Cauca, centered at Popayán but with secondary towns at Pasto and Cali; Antioquia, with the urban center of Medellín; the coast, centered at Cartagena, with urban nodes at Santa Marta and Panamá; the Central Highlands, centered at Bogotá and Tunja; the northeast, with the multiple nodes of Vélez, Socorro, and Pamplona; and the llanos to the east of the Andes.

Separation from Spain did not stimulate a rapid expansion of the Colombian economy. Agriculture remained the most important activity in a regionally dispersed economy, with larger estates (often dedicated to cattle raising) more prevalent in the Cauca, coastal, and central highland regions and smaller peasant production dominant elsewhere, especially in areas around Socorro–San Gil, Pasto, and Medellín. Estates to the north of Popayán, which had relied upon slave labor, suffered a significant decline as wartime emancipation and flight of enslaved peoples stimulated the emergence of widespread subsistence activities (as well as social strife). As the most important export earner until well into the century, gold from the Pacific lowlands and the Antioquia slopes continued to sustain substantial mercantile activity. Manufacturing remained in the hands of multitalented rural and urban artisans, with the Socorro–San Gil region containing a well-developed domestic textile industry. Efforts by the New Granadan government to stimulate manufacture industry through a system of privileges in the 1830s proved largely unsuccessful, although they did sustain a fledgling iron industry in the central highlands.

The early national social structure is poorly understood, but several characteristics are apparent. An elite bound by kinship ties dominated regional social hierarchies, drawing their strengths from large landholdings and positions in the civil bureaucracy, church, or mercantile communities. Most members of rural societies, especially those of the central highlands and Cauca

Colombia

Caribbean Sea

Santa Marta
Barranquilla
Cartagena
Colón
Panamá
PANAMA
CHOCO
CORDOBA
SUCRE
BOLIVAR
MAGDALENA
GUAJIRA
CÉSAR
NORTE DE SANTANDER
Lake Maracaibo
Cúcuta
Pamplona
Barrancabermeja
Bucaramanga
Arauca
ANTIOQUIA
SANTANDER
ARAUCA
Medellín
Vélez
Quibdó
Manizales
Tunja
Honda
BOYACÁ
CASANARE
Meta
VENEZUELA
Orinoco
VICHADA
Pacific Ocean
Ambalema
Santa Fe de Bogotá
Ibagué
Villavicencio
META
Buenaventura
Cali
Neiva
Guaviare
GUAINÍA
CAUCA
Magdalena
Cauca
Popayán
NARIÑO
Florencia
VAUPÉS
Pasto
PUTUMAYO
CAQUETÁ
Quito
Caquetá
BRAZIL
ECUADOR
AMAZONAS
Leticia
Amazon
PERU

200 miles
325 kilometers

1	ATLÁNTICO
2	CALDAS
3	CUNDINAMARCA
4	DIST. ESPECIAL
5	HUILA
6	QUINDIO
7	RISARALDÁ
8	TOLIMA
9	VALLE DEL CAUCA

regions, were highly deferential, bound by tradition and dependence upon landholders. Native inhabitants of the *resguardos* (common lands) maintained more independent lives and defended themselves against efforts to abolish their corporate privileges. Small farmers and artisans of the northeast and central highlands had even more social, economic, and political autonomy. Antioqueño society was dominated by large landholders, the church, and mining elite, but also contained numerous independent small farmers.

The degree of autonomy enjoyed by these social sectors shaped both patterns of political affiliation and social strife. More rigid patron-client relations produced long-term partisan loyalties and more stable social hi-

erarchies, patterns evident, for example, in the Boyacá region around Tunja. By contrast, Socorreño craftsmen, Antioqueño freeholders, and the newly liberated slaves of the Cauca valley resisted the reimposition of elite control. Urban artisans, especially those of Bogotá, exercised considerable social and political independence.

Regionalism manifested itself in the initial bipartisan alignment of the Conservative and Liberal parties. Men with ready access to centers of authority, education, religion, and political position during the late colonial and early national periods aligned themselves into the Conservative Party by the late 1840s. By contrast, the elite and middling sectors of secondary provincial centers such as Vélez or Socorro aligned themselves into the Liberal Party at the same time. Other issues affected party alignment, such as the Bolívar-Santander division of the 1820s or alliances during the WAR OF THE SUPREMES, but social location seems to have been a key factionalizer. After the 1830s, members of the Conservative and Liberal parties dominated the system of formal politics until well into the twentieth century, engaging in numerous civil wars shaped more by party loyalty than by any other factor.

EARLY NATIONAL POLITICS

The presidential election of 1837 and the War of the Supremes (1839–1842) revealed these sociopolitical divisions. Santander wished that General José María OBANDO succeed him as president, but Obando's military background, ambiguous social station in the aristocratic Popayán region, and alleged involvement in the assassination of Antonio José de SUCRE embittered other groups, who supported José Ignacio MÁRQUEZ, the eventual winner. In the aftermath of the election, both sides mobilized urban middle sectors, especially artisans, in the attempt to expand their bases of popular support, a critical step in the development of the party system. In 1839 the National Congress ordered the closing of several minor convents in the highly religious community of Pasto, a move that sparked the War of the Supremes, in which Obando played an important role as the alleged protector of religion and federalism. Several other pro-Santander leaders declared themselves in revolt, which the government did not suppress until 1842.

By the mid-1840s, the promises of independence had proved illusory, leaving political leaders ready for significant reforms. The liberal reforms that began with the presidency of the nominal Conservative Tomás Cipriano de MOSQUERA (1845–1849) included the reduction of tariff rates and the abolition of the tobacco monopoly, antecedents to the widespread reforms undertaken by the Liberal José Hilario LÓPEZ (1849–1853). The latter's government abolished slavery, expelled the Jesuits, decentralized the nation's fiscal structure, declared absolute freedom of the press, and began political decentralization. The Constitution of 1853 established the separation of church and state, allowed for civil marriage and divorce, extended suffrage to all male citizens over the age of twenty-one, instituted the popular election of governors and many other officials, and weakened executive powers. Several years later, in the wake of the civil war of 1859–1861, a final set of reforms privatized corporate properties for public sale and outlawed convents and monasteries.

Despite basic agreements on economic issues, serious conflicts erupted over several reforms, especially those concerning social order and public morality. Conservatives tended to view the church as the proper foundation, whereas Liberals placed their faith in an educated and self-reliant citizenry. The abolition of slavery threatened vested interests in both the Cauca and Antioquia regions, a primary factor in the unsuccessful Conserv-

ative revolt of 1851. Reduction of tariff rates inspired Bogotá's craftsmen to mobilize politically into the DEMOCRATIC SOCIETY OF ARTISANS, and eventually to align themselves with moderate (Draconiano) Liberals who, like Obando, opposed the reduction of executive powers and the threats to the military contained within the Constitution of 1853. This alignment of forces, generally drawn from the middle sectors of rural and urban society, produced General José María MELO's 1854 coup d'état, a movement whose defeat by a Conservative-Liberal elite alliance paved the way for the election of Conservative Mariano OSPINA RODRÍGUEZ as president in 1857.

The Constitution of 1863 established a federalist system of quasi-independent state governments within the "United States of Colombia." States were allowed their own armies and all nine had to agree upon constitutional revisions. A president served for two years without opportunity for reelection, a system that ensured near-continual campaigning and political strife throughout the thirty some years of Liberal hegemony.

The economic liberalization undertaken during the reform era thrust the country into a world market in which Colombian commodities enjoyed only sporadic success. Exports earned an estimated $1.88 per capita in the 1830s and $4.77 in 1880, figures which suggest a general increase in value, but which ranked Colombia's export economy among the least important in nineteenth-century Latin America. Furthermore, the fate of exports caused serious political and social instability. Tobacco boomed in the lowland Ambalema region after demonopolization, but declined in the 1870s due to inconsistent quality and Javanese competition. Cotton, cinchona bark (a source of quinine), Panama hats, indigo, and coffee experienced similar booms (and busts), with only the last surviving in the export mix as, of course, did gold.

DEMOGRAPHIC, SOCIAL, AND POLITICAL TRANSFORMATIONS

The great southward migration of Antioqueños to the frontiers of south-central Colombia constitutes perhaps the most important nineteenth-century social and economic phenomenon. The movement gained force in the 1830s and 1840s, fueled by a rate of demographic increase substantially above that of the rest of the country. Pioneer farmers (colonos) sought freehold for subsistence crops on the forested slopes of what were largely unclaimed public lands, or land whose claims were disputed by inheritors of earlier grants, who were more often than not men of considerable economic and social prestige. Tremendous amounts of litigation accompanied the colonization of the frontier, most of it around access to land and control of the labor for the production of coffee, a pattern of conflict that persisted well into the 1930s. Through decades of struggles, thousands of colonos established small, family farms that sustained the twentieth-century coffee industry.

Most migrants came from the north as opposed to the south, despite seemingly favorable conditions to spur migration from that direction as well. A significant demographic pool of mulattoes, blacks, and mestizos existed in the central Cauca, but these groups pursued subsistence farming and relative autonomy on abandoned lowlands and slopes and the establishment of medium-sized farms. These "dangerous" social sectors were at the center of numerous social tensions, as when Obando utilized them in support of his cause during the War of the Supremes or in the protests against large landholders near Cali in the early 1850s. Conflicts over access to land and the social order played roles in both the 1851 Conservative rebellion and in the Melo coup of 1854.

The Conservative intellectual and Cauca political leader Sergio Arboleda decried this lack of order in the early 1870s, suggesting that a combination of Catholic social restraint and capitalist economic development could save the region from social and political disorder. The failure of Conservatives and Catholic leaders to achieve the political authority to legislate public order led to the civil war of 1876–1877, perhaps the only armed conflict in Colombia with a genuine religious core. Importantly, that conflict sealed the Liberal Party division between Radicals and Independents.

THE REGENERATION AND BIPARTISAN RULE
Economic, political, and social tensions forced a fundamental realignment of the Colombian polity in the 1880s. The failure of export commodities undermined the fiscal resources of the state and engendered social unrest. Rafael NÚÑEZ's 1880 and 1884 Independent Liberal presidential victories propelled Radical Liberals to rebellion in 1885. Conservatives joined with Independents to repress the Radicals, thereby allowing Núñez to undertake the REGENERACIÓN (Regeneration) of the country. With the crucial assistance of Conservative philosopher and politician Miguel Antonio CARO, Núñez engineered passage of the Constitution of 1886, which swept aside the tenets of mid-century liberalism and established a centralized state with departments instead of sovereign states. Núñez accepted both the first six-year presidency and the increased executive authority, which included enhanced power to direct economic policy through a national bank. Núñez, who had increased tariffs in 1880, did so again. He also initiated state support for industrial development and soon took advantage of the government's ability to print paper money by numerous large issues, with disputed economic effect. Caro's concern for a "proper" social hierarchy restored Roman Catholicism as the state religion, reestablished its strong role in public education, and helped produce a concordat with the Vatican in 1887.

Independents and Conservatives cooperated in the establishment of the bipartisan National Party, whose purpose was to end partisan contention in support of the new regime. Núñez's preference for his native city of Cartagena to the highland capital made this mission impossible. (Núñez's absence from the capital meant that executive power rested in the hands of the vice president.) Both the dogmaticism and heavy-handedness of Caro's vice presidency alienated many Regeneration leaders, especially those "historical" Conservatives, led by *antioqueño* Marceliano Vélez, who were less willing to cooperate with Independents. The 1892 presidential election formalized this split, as both Caro and Vélez contended for the vice presidential position, the latter unsuccessfully. The Liberal Party attempted to regain its political voice in 1893, only to face arrest and overt repression.

Partisan political strife escalated through the 1890s, culminating in the WAR OF THE THOUSAND DAYS (1899–1902). Inflationary pressures from the release of paper money and the sporadic performance of coffee called into question the fiscal leadership of Caro's government. The more aggressive "war liberals," who had failed in an 1895 insurrection, redoubled their efforts after the inefficacious presidential election of 1897 placed the feeble, eighty-three-year-old Manuel A. Sanclemente at the head of the government. Economic and political crises merged into war in October 1899. The "gentlemen's war" soon gave way to bitter conflict between Liberal guerrillas and government forces, who were assisted by their own guerrillas. Although the zones of coffee agriculture in present-day Huila (then belonging to the department of Tolima) and in Cundinamarca, the Cauca, and Santander were the targets of conflict, few regions of the country were spared before the struggle came to a merciful conclusion in 1902. The estimated one hundred thousand deaths fail to reveal the bitter social animosities engendered by the conflict, many of which persisted as social vendettas for decades. Nor does the human loss reflect the traumatic national impact, which created conditions for the successful separation of the department of Panama from the mountainous mainland.

The Conservative General Rafael REYES emerged victorious in the suspiciously corrupt 1904 presidential election. The well-born Reyes favored cooperative politics and named several Liberals to his cabinet. Reyes practiced the interventionist style of the Mexican dictator Porfirio Díaz and instituted reforms intended to restore stability to the fiscal system, improve the country's rail infrastructure, boost industrial activity through protective tariffs, and increase the production of coffee. Reyes mirrored Díaz's penchant for personal rule, dismissing the Congress in 1905 in favor of a handpicked "national assembly," which immediately extended the president's term in office. Reyes sought to restore the friendly relations with the United States that had been disturbed by the latter's role in the independence of Panama. The proposed treaty to resolve outstanding issues required the approval of the national assembly, which, when called back into session, sided with popular opinion and rejected Reyes's proposal in March

1909. The president resigned his position and left the country several months later.

Most presidents in the years 1910–1946 shared Reyes's tendency toward bipartisan rule, though not his predilection toward strong-handedness. The constitutional reform of 1910 mandated minority representation and reduced the presidential term to four years. Carlos E. RESTREPO, a Conservative who headed the bipartisan Republican Union Party, assumed the presidency in 1910. The increased social polarization that marked his rule and that of his successors represented the diverging interests of conservative church reformers, organized labor, peasants, and an emerging middle class. The Liberal Rafael URIBE URIBE symbolized some of these sentiments, abandoning his party's commitment to dogmatic theory in his call for state socialism. Uribe Uribe's 1914 assassination blunted this tendency within his party until the emergence of Jorge Eliécer Gaitán.

COFFEE, INDUSTRY, AND URBANIZATION

Coffee is central to an understanding of twentieth-century Colombia. Production boomed after the War of the Thousand Days as Antioqueño colonization pushed the coffee frontier southward. One million 60-kilogram (132-pound) bags were exported in 1913: 32.8 percent from Santander, 20.0 percent from Cundinamarca, and 16.1 percent from Antioquia. By the early 1930s, when exports had surpassed 3 million bags and constituted almost 70 percent of the country's exports, Santander counted for just over 10 percent of production, Cundinamarca perhaps 13 percent, and Antioquia about 20 percent, while the "new" zones of production in the departments of Caldas, Risaralda, Quindío, Tolima, and Valle del Cauca accounted for well over half of the exports. National exports topped 5 million bags in 1943 and 6 million bags ten years later—a level of production maintained through the 1990s.

Family-owned-and-operated farms accounted for three-fourths of the 150,000–200,000 coffee farms in the 1930s–1950s. These small farmers tended toward economic and social conservativism in defense of their relative social autonomy, generally resisted efforts to mobilize their collective energies in labor struggles, and aligned themselves with either local Conservative or Liberal patrons. Although they produced the vast majority of the country's coffee, the product has been marketed since 1927 by the National Federation of Coffeegrowers (Fedecafe), which itself is dominated by large producers. Large producers supplanted the output of small producers in the 1950s through the planting of a coffee tree more conducive to large-scale labor and harvesting, and came to dominate the industry through their control of marketing, credit, and distribution systems.

Coffee produced large quantities of capital that helped stimulate rapid changes in the Colombian economy and polity. Annual export earnings increased from the average $26 million level of the Reyes period to the $200 million average of the late 1920s. Industrial entrepreneurs, especially in the Medellín region, created an industrial base, most significantly in textiles. A $25 million indemnification from the United States for its role in the separation of Panama (stipulated by the 1922 Urrutia-Thomson Treaty) opened the way for $260 million of foreign loans, much of which was invested in infrastructural and municipal development. Foreign loans accompanied foreign investment, which included the establishment of a UNITED FRUIT COMPANY banana enclave near Santa Marta, oil extraction and refining by the Tropical Oil (Jersey Standard, now Exxon) Company near Barrancabermeja, and the Barco concession to Gulf and Socony (now Mobil) south of Lake Maracaibo. Railways, highways, maritime traffic, and other infrastructural improvements knitted much of central-western Colombia into a single economic unit.

Urbanization and population growth further transformed Colombian society. From an urban total of perhaps 5 percent of the nation's 3.89 million people in 1900, the number of urbanites increased sixfold by 1930, when the total population approached 8 million. The national population reached 17.5 million (54 percent urban) in 1964 and 33 million (70 percent urban) in 1990. Bogotá led the urban increase, from about 150,000 in 1918 to 355,000 in 1938; 1,697,311 in 1964 to just under 3 million in 1973 and 4.2 million in 1985. Medellín, Cali, Barranquilla, and Cartagena mirrored this pattern shortly thereafter, with only the latter under 1 million in the 1985 census. Smaller towns such as Manizales, Ibagué, and Bucaramanga grew as well, with rates of growth exceeding those of the largest urban centers after 1973. Total population increase has hovered at just over 2 percent since the 1970s, which should bring the national total to about 38 million by the year 2000.

Slightly over one-half of the 8.7 million people counted in the 1938 census were considered "economically active," with 75 percent of them involved in the production of primary materials, including coffee. Barely 10 percent of the population labored in industrial activities, three-quarters of which were cottage industries of under five people that produced just over one-third of all manufacturing output. Although numbering only 3 percent of the total laboring population, larger industrial shops doubled the output of the smaller, artisanal establishments. The larger shops received significant import-substitution support during the Great Depression. Oil workers, transportation workers, and industrial laborers were numerically few but of critical economic importance. Urbanization, increased commercial activity, and industrialization created service and professional occupations that provided the foundation for the middle class, which became increasingly important after World War II.

This recast social spectrum combined with the new economic structure to change the nature of Colombian politics. Protests by transportation and dock workers on the coast shook the nation in 1918. The initial government response to labor militancy was to institute a right-to-work law, force mediation, and ban strikes in strategic sectors, including transportation. Strikes in the oil enclave of Barrancabermeja (1924 and 1927) and in the banana enclave of Santa Marta (1928) resulted in mass arrests and violent repression. Fledgling left-wing groups such as the Socialist Revolutionary Party (PSR) attempted to mobilize these social forces under the leadership of dynamic orators such as María de los Ángeles CANO, "the revolutionary red flower." However, most workers tended to channel their political energies into the Conservative or Liberal parties. The young Liberal Jorge Eliécer GAITÁN emerged as a prominent national figure in leading the investigation of the 1928 "banana massacre," which revealed the intimate relationship between Conservative politicians and foreign investors. Foreign loans began to dry up in 1927 and government revenues declined, undermining the Conservative presidency of Miguel ABADÍA MÉNDEZ. The economic foundation of the Colombian state suffered a serious blow with the 1929 collapse of the world economy. The resulting conditions enabled the Liberal Enrique OLAYA HERRERA to win the 1930 presidential election as Conservatives split their votes between two of their own candidates.

THE *REVOLUCIÓN EN MARCHA* AND *LA VIOLENCIA*

Olaya Herrera's administration proved to be the calm before the partisan political storm. The Liberal president appointed Conservatives to both national and regional offices, resuming a pattern of bipartisan representation and dialogue. Nevertheless, armed strife broke out between local Liberals and Conservatives over the spoils of office. Gaitán used the short-lived Unión Izquierdista Revolucionaria (UNIR) Party to rail against the *país político* in favor of the *país nacional*, populist rhetoric which disturbed many in the upper class. UNIR and Communist organizers attempted to mobilize disgruntled coffee farmers in favor of assertive land and labor reforms.

The presidency of Alfonso LÓPEZ PUMAREJO (1934–1938) moderated the tensions surrounding land, labor, and foreign investment by asserting the role of the state in social management in the REVOLUTION ON THE MARCH (1934–1938). The constitutional reform of 1936 stipulated that property had a social function and that ineffective use of property could lead to its expropriation by the state. Law 200 of the same year applied this principle to land, favoring squatters and others who had occupied land as opposed to "landlords" with dubious and unverifiable titles. The López regime tended not to use the power of the state in support of capital in disputes and to overtly support labor in the establishment of the Federation of Colombian Workers (CTC), the first such nationwide organization. The state expanded its support for education, removing its control from local officials and lessening the influence of the church. Finally, taxes were increased somewhat and collection improved, especially those on foreign firms.

The effects of these reforms were generally more symbolic than revolutionary, but they called Liberal opponents to action, even as they drew new workers and the urban middle class into the Liberal ranks. Even Liberal leaders such as President Eduardo SANTOS (1938–1942) found the resulting tenor to be unsettling and assumed a more moderate stance. A decidedly less reformist López returned to office in 1942, reversing some of the land and labor policies initiated in his first administration.

Conservative Laureano GÓMEZ CASTRO served as the intellectual and political counterweight to these Liberal leaders. Gómez seized control of the party in the early 1930s, using it as forum to analyze the failures of Liberalism in favor of traditional, principled Conservatism. Gómez criticized the reduction of Catholic authority in the 1936 constitutional reform and the role of Communists in the first López government. Gaitán, too, criticized López, but in the name of the "small capitalist" and members of the middle class who lacked political authority. These critics so weakened the second López regime (which suffered from an unsuccessful Conservative military revolt in 1944) that López resigned in favor of Alberto LLERAS CAMARGO in 1945.

The presidential election of 1946 spurred a wave of partisan bloodshed that initiated La VIOLENCIA (The Violence). Gaitán and the moderate Liberal Gabriel TURBAY split the Liberal vote, enabling the moderate Conservative Mariano OSPINA PÉREZ, an Antioqueño industrialist and former head of Fedecafe, to emerge victorious. The first stage of the violence began in rural areas with the transferral of power, just as it had in 1930, even though the president named Liberals to his regime. Ospina Pérez shifted government support of organized labor to the newly founded and more conservative Union of Colombian Workers (UTC). When Gaitán gradually convinced moderate Liberals of the futility of their cooperation with Ospina Pérez, they withdrew from the government in March 1948.

Gaitán's assassination on 9 April 1948 led to a massive riot that ravaged Bogotá, leaving hundreds of people dead and much physical damage, and initiated the second stage of La Violencia. Liberals throughout the country joined in the outrage against Conservatives, so frightening the party leadership that they rejoined the Ospina Pérez regime to calm partisan tensions. Indeed, violence soon ebbed, but did not disappear. Gómez won the uncontested presidential election of late 1949, sparking a sharp increase in violence, to which his regime responded with brutal repression. Partisan civil war soon ravaged the countryside. Gómez responded in 1952 with an unsuccessful attempt to create a corporatist constitution to impose his ideology upon the Colombian polity. By 1953, with an estimated 160,000 people dead since 1946, the Colombian political framework was in shambles.

General Gustavo ROJAS PINILLA came to power in a coup sponsored by moderate Conservatives in June

1953. Partisan violence had scarred most of rural Colombia, especially the coffee zones and llanos, sparing only the coast and department of Nariño from its ravages. An amnesty reduced the level of violence, which unfortunately resumed by 1954 in widespread political banditry with increased social and class undertones. An additional 17,000 people died during the Rojas regime (1953–1957) and some 16,000 more before 1966, an unofficial end to the violence.

THE *FRENTE NACIONAL*

While Rojas Pinilla succeeded in restoring relative order to the country, his populist leanings and increasingly independent actions inspired Conservative and Liberal leaders to set aside their differences in the Frente Nacional (National Front), a unique Latin American political experiment. In mid-1956 Lleras Camargo and Laureano Gómez initialed a power-sharing formula—an antecedent to the "general strike" that drove the general from power in May 1957. The eventual National Front agreement stipulated that the presidency would alternate between the Conservative and Liberal parties for sixteen years, during which time appointed and elective positions would be shared on an equal basis. A national plebiscite approved these terms by an overwhelming majority. Lleras Camargo once again assumed the presidency in August 1958.

Two notable "successes" can be properly claimed by the National Front: the end to partisan violence and modernization of the nation's economy. Conservative Guillermo León Valencia (1962–1966) and Liberal Carlos LLERAS RESTREPO (1966–1970) dutifully took office according to the National Front formula. In 1970 the Conservative Party split its votes for the last guaranteed Conservative presidency of the National Front among several candidates in an election that was complicated by the presidential candidacy of Rojas Pinella. Drawing strength from his Conservative roots and dissident Liberal supporters, Rojas had helped the Popular National Alliance Party (ANAPO) to win one-fifth of the congressional seats in 1966. The extremely close election on 19 April 1970 generated charges of vote fraud by the government, which allowed Conservative Misael PASTRANA BORRERO to emerge victorious. The urban guerrilla Movement of 19 April (M-19) emerged to challenge the oligarchic control of the government in 1973, a year before Alfonso LÓPEZ MICHELSEN, former head of the dissident Movement of Revolutionary Liberals, became the first non-National Front president (1974–1978).

Various organizations saw in the National Front agreement the opportunity to assume a more active role in national economic development. The National Association of Industrialists (Andi), Fedecafe, the Colombian Bankers Association (Asobancaria), and other producers' groups, all bipartisan in nature and elite in leadership, supported the new regimes. So, too, did international bodies such as the World Bank, the AGENCY FOR INTERNATIONAL DEVELOPMENT (AID), and the Rocke-

feller Foundation, which served the anti-Communist agenda of the ALLIANCE FOR PROGRESS.

Despite some differences, most domestic and international groups supported development and political reform initiatives. These included the implementation of an agreement with Renault to develop a national automobile industry, the establishment of the ANDEAN COMMON MARKET, and further import-substitution industrialization. The Colombian Agricultural Society (SAC), by contrast, opposed the 1961 land-reform program of Lleras Camargo, leaving Lleras Restrepo the task of putting some teeth (however small) into land reform. Restrepo, however, did help organize the National Association of Peasants (ANUC), which asserted itself quite forcefully in the 1970s. He also oversaw reforms that strengthened the executive's hand in economic development and allowed for the gradual dismantling of shared offices in the National Front, which eventually ended in 1978. President Misael Pastrana's administration (1970–1974) helped launch "Operation Colombia," which stimulated housing construction, promoted nontraditional exports, increased agricultural productivity, and supported effective taxation. Pastrana, however, capitulated to landowning groups by undercutting much of the strength of earlier land-reform measures.

The National Front, though effective at ending partisan violence, did not sponsor political democratization. Numerous guerrilla groups rose to challenge the oligarchic control of politics during this period, including the Colombian Revolutionary Armed Forces (FARC), the Castro-inspired National Liberation Army (ELN), the Maoist Popular Liberation Army (SPL), and the M-19. Though the guerrillas were contained by an increasingly professionalized military, social inequalities, popular support, and inhospitable terrain have prevented their elimination. Guerrilla groups attracted considerable national attention as a possible alternative to bipartisan rule, but none gained sufficient power to challenge the Colombian state effectively.

CONTEMPORARY COLOMBIA

The period from the 1970s to the mid-1990s is open to widely varied interpretations. Seen from the past, the continued strife associated with the bipartisan political structure, the economic importance of coffee, and the violence associated with social inequality emerge as an important analytical signpost.

Colombia's export economy is perhaps the most balanced and profitable in Latin America. While most Latin American economies stagnated in the 1980s, Colombia's export-led economy grew at an annual rate of 3.5 percent. In 1990, Colombia exported $6.76 billion worth of goods and imported goods valued at $5.69 billion, leaving a healthy balance of trade among multiple nations. Colombia's primary trading partner, the United States, purchases 37 percent of its exports and supplies 45 percent of its imports. Colombia imports just over one-quarter of its goods from, and exports one-fifth to, the European Community. About 20 percent of Colombian imports come from South America and the Caribbean nations, which purchase 14 percent of its exports. Japan is a minor trading partner, supplying 9 percent of Colombian imports and purchasing 4 percent of its exports, primarily coal. While coffee's share of export earnings had hovered around 50 percent through the 1970s, by the late 1980s it fell to less than one-third. Noncoffee commodities, led by petroleum and coal, produce almost 40 percent of the country's export earnings. Colombia is Latin America's largest producer of coal and third largest producer of petroleum, with newly discovered fields of over 2 billion barrels yet to be put into production. A highly diversified mix of minor exports surpasses coffee's total.

Perhaps surprisingly, the minifundia and nontraditional exports constitute the most dynamic agricultural sectors. Agricultural imports have declined since the 1950s as the efficiency of domestic producers has increased. Cut-flowers, a semi-industrialized agricultural product from the high plains around Bogotá, employs about 140,000 people, mostly women. (Flower workers are exposed to large amounts of pesticides and are said to be among the most abused in the country.) African palms, cacao, sorghum, and bananas are increasingly important exports. Although the peasant-to-consumer ratio has increased from 1 to 11.3 in 1951 to 1 to 21.8 in 1988, small-scale agriculturalists continue to produce sufficient supplies of the potatoes, yucca, beans, corn, fruits, and plantains so important to the Colombian diet. This improvement is due to increased prices for these basic goods, increased productivity, and the intensive labor that is characteristic of minifundio production.

Independence Day parade in Cali, 1971. NICHOLAS SAPIEHA / STOCK, BOSTON.

The Colombian social structure has changed along with its economic activities. Since 1960 the agricultural labor force has declined from just over one-half of the population to about 31 percent; the industrial share has risen from 19 to about 22 percent; and the service sector now includes over 56 percent of the population. Urban workers comprise 65 percent of the labor force, two-thirds of whom are in the formal sector. The remaining third are outside the coverage of state social and legal jurisdiction in the "informal sector," working in occupations ranging from street traders, domestics, small producers, to junk collectors. This informal sector, whose growth has mirrored that of the cities, particularly since the 1960s, is subject to considerable poverty and social stress.

The tremendous demand for marijuana and cocaine from drug-consuming societies (chiefly the United States) has had profound and mostly negative impacts upon the country. High-quality marijuana, grown mostly on small farms on the northern coast in the early 1970s, stimulated regional economic activity and increased the standard of living before U.S. pressures upon the Julio César TURBAY AYALA regime (1978–1982) led to extensive spraying of defoliants (chemicals, it might be noted, that were banned in the United States). In the 1980s the processing of cocaine by a limited number of producer cartels resulted in widespread social and political violence as well as an influx of dollars to the Medellín and Cali regions. Bribes to politicians and military officials undermined the authority and perceived legitimacy of the state, leading reformist politicians, including Luis Carlos GALÁN and Rodrigo Lara Bonilla, to assume a decidedly antitrafficker stance. Drug lords responded with a wave of assassinations, including that of Lara Bonilla in 1984 and Galán in 1989, which precipitated years of war between the state and drug lords. By the early 1990s, the human cost of the drug violence had reached staggering proportions and resulted in a series of agreements to reduce assassinations and violence in exchange for judicial leniency. One author comments that "narcotrafficking has acted as a catalyst of the crisis of the political regime, exacerbating its political, economic, and social factors."

Colombia's political crisis has led to remarkable departures from earlier patterns. In particular, the peace process initiated by Conservative Belisario BETANCUR CUARTAS (1982–1986) could end the bipartisan control of the Colombian polity. Overtures to the M-19, FARC, and SPL eventually produced peace accords that would bring those groups into the political mainstream. Some of their members formed the Patriotic Union Party, which, despite attacks from right-wing death squads, has received considerable regional political support. Spurred by an overwhelming popular vote in December 1990, a constituent congress produced a new constitution in 1991. Under the new constitution the executive loses considerable power to the legislature, which itself is democratized and less beholden to regional party bosses. The judicial system has been overhauled and extradition to foreign states banned. Elections to the initial congress revealed a fundamental schism in the venerable Conservative Party, the decline of the Liberal Party to a mere plurality, and the emergence of Democratic Alliance M-19 as the country's second largest political association (at least temporarily). It remains to be seen whether these developments represent a true departure from historic patterns or a momentary disruption in the two-party domination of the Colombian state. Insofar as César Agusto GAVIRIA TRUJILLO has joined the Pan-American economic liberalization movement, economic growth seems likely to continue, as do social tensions stemming from maldistribution of income and wealth.

The single best overview of Colombian history is DAVID BUSHNELL, *The Making of Modern Colombia: A Nation in Spite of Itself* (1993). JOHN LYNCH, *The Spanish American Revolutions, 1808–1826* (1986), provides a succinct account of the Independence period. The early national period is introduced in DAVID BUSHNELL, *The Santander Regime in Gran Colombia* (1970).

Economic patterns are detailed in LUIS OSPINA VÁSQUEZ, *Industria y protección en Colombia, 1810 a 1930* (1959); WILLIAM PAUL MC GREEVEY, *An Economic History of Colombia, 1845–1930* (1971); JOSÉ ANTONIO OCAMPO, *Colombia y la economía mundial, 1830–1910* (1984); and ANTHONY MC FARLANE, ''The Transition from Colonialism in Colombia, 1819–1975,'' in *Latin America, Economic Imperialism, and the State,* edited by Christopher Abel and Colin Lewis (1985), pp. 101–124. The late-nineteenth-century political scene is covered by CHARLES BERGQUIST, *Coffee and Conflict in Colombia, 1886–1910* (1978); HELEN DELPAR, *Red Against Blue: The Liberal Party in Colombian Politics, 1863–1899* (1981); and JAMES W. PARK, *Rafael Núñez and the Politics of Colombian Regionalism, 1863–1886* (1985). For coffee, see MARCO PALACIOS, *Coffee in Colombia, 1850–1970: An Economic, Social and Political History* (1980); and CHARLES BERGQUIST, *Labor in Latin America: Comparative Essays on Chile, Argentina, Venezuela, and Colombia* (1986).

JONATHAN HARTLYN, *The Politics of Coalition Rule in Colombia* (1988) is a valuable survey of twentieth-century politics, as are VERNON LEE FLUHARTY, *Dance of the Millions: Military Rule and the Social Revolution in Colombia, 1930–1956* (1971); and JAMES HENDERSON, *Conservative Thought in Twentieth Century Colombia: The Ideas of Laureano Gómez* (1988). Social strife and La Violencia can be examined in PAUL OQUIST, *Violence, Conflict, and Politics in Colombia* (1980); and HERBERT BRAUN, *The Assassination of Gaitán (1985).*

Valuable insights on the rural sector can be gleaned from CATHERINE LEGRAND, *Frontier Expansion and Peasant Protest in Colombia, 1830–1936* (1986); LEON ZAMOSC, *The Agrarian Question and the Peasant Movement in Colombia* (1986); and NOLA REINHARDT, *Our Daily Bread: The Peasant Question and Family Farming in Colombia* (1988). On labor history, see MIGUEL URRUTIA, *The Development of the Colombian Labor Movement* (1969); and CHARLES BERGQUIST, *Labor in Latin America* (1969).

Other important facets of contemporary Colombian history can be examined in VIRGINIA GUTIÉRREZ DE PINEDA, *Familia y cultura en Colombia: Tipologías, funciones y dinámica de la familia* (1977); DANIEL H. LEVINE, *Religion and Politics in Latin America: The Catholic Church in Venezuela and Colombia* (1981); *Journal of Inter-American Studies—World Affairs* 30, nos. 2–3 (1988); and

PETER WADE, *Blackness and Race Mixture: The Dynamics of Racial Identity in Colombia* (1993).

DAVID SOWELL

See also **Banana Industry; Coffee Industry; Drugs and Drug Trade.**

COLOMBIA: CONSTITUTIONS

Overview

On 4 July 1991 Colombia officially adopted a new constitution, which replaced the Constitution of 1886, one of the world's oldest. Through its independent history the nation functioned under a number of charters, but after the early years there developed patterns more stable than in neighboring countries. An Act of Federation signed on 27 November 1811 created a federation known as the United Provinces of NEW GRANADA, but meaningful independence came only after the victory by patriot forces at the battle of BOYACÁ in August 1819, which established the state of GRAN COLOMBIA under the Constitution of Cúcuta (1821). Providing for a strong executive, a bicameral legislature, an appointed judiciary, and indirect elections, it also recognized departments, provinces, cantons, and parishes.

Criticized as being too centralized, it was replaced by a new document following the 1830 breakup of Gran Colombia, when Venezuela and Ecuador went their own ways. The 1832 charter recognized the Republic of New Granada as a decentralized entity, and the conflict between centralism and federalism remained at the center of politics throughout the nineteenth century. The centralist impulse was enshrined in the Constitution of 1843, which represented in part a reaction to the 1832 document. A strong president was granted unlimited power of appointment plus the authority to initiate legislative debates, while provincial assemblies were subordinated to the national government. Within a few years, however, the trends were in the direction of decentralization, leading to the constitutions of 1853, 1858, and 1863.

The first of these documents was notable for a wide range of liberal reforms, including the abolition of slavery, separation of church and state, recognition of press freedom, trial by jury, and a strengthening of provincial legislatures. Five years later the Constitution of 1858 renamed the nation the Granadine Confederation. Eight sovereign states were recognized, each with residual powers. The national government's authority was restricted largely to foreign affairs and defense.

It was the Constitution of 1863, adopted on 8 May by a convention of delegates assembled in Rionegro, that carried the federalist approach to its extreme. Nine states established the United States of Colombia, the central government of which was prohibited from interference in state affairs. Each of the federated states enjoyed sovereignty and was permitted to have its own army. Individual liberties were virtually unlimited, and capital punishment was abolished. The presidential term was shortened from four to two years, with immediate reelection prohibited. The Rionegro constitution was among the most extreme federalist documents ever known. In practice, its decentralization of authority was such that more than fifty uprisings broke out in the next quarter century, accompanied by a cavalcade of state constitutions.

An eventual alliance between Conservatives and so-called Independent Liberals in 1885 supported Rafael NÚÑEZ as president and moved for a change of the system. The Constitution of 1886 created the Republic of Colombia along unitary lines. Strong centralism was restored, while the authority of the provinces was subordinated to Bogotá. Governors were to be appointed, rather than elected, to serve four-year terms. Reelection was permitted after one term out of office. A bicameral legislature was to be elected for four-year terms. This charter proved to be Colombia's most durable and was amended in 1936, 1945, 1957, and 1968.

The most far-reaching of these amendments came in 1957, legitimizing a sixteen-year period of controlled rule by the Conservative-Liberal hegemony known as the National Front. Parity of representation, along with alternation in executive power, constituted the cornerstone of the arrangement, as further modified by reforms in 1968. This arrangement served to stabilize the system, while also assuring unchallenged control by traditional party elites.

By the 1980s, rising political pressures called for major reforms, as was manifested by a popular vote in 1990 approving the convening of a constitutional assembly, the body that subsequently wrote the Constitution of 1991. Popular participation was encouraged, congressional privilege was restricted, electoral procedures were democratized, the judicial system was reorganized, and party clientelism was reduced. Individual rights—socioeconomic as well as political—were spelled out in detail. The presidential term remained four years, but reelection was ruled out, while the office of vice president was created for the first time. The management and organization of fiscal and economic policy were also restructured.

The new constitution was lengthy, and many reforms were outlined in considerable detail. The intention of opening up the constitutional and political system had carried the constitutional assembly further than had been expected. The impact on the Colombian political system can be judged only with the passing of time. However, the constitutional changes from 1886 to 1991 were unquestionably extensive and destined to have a powerful impact on Colombia. The stability of the traditionalist framework that had endured for a full century can no longer be taken for granted.

JESÚS MARÍA HENAO and GERARDO ARRUBLA, History of Colombia, translated by J. Fred Rippy (1938); HELEN DELPAR, Red Against Blue: The Liberal Party in Colombian Politics, 1863–1899 (1981); HARVEY F. KLINE, Colombia: Portrait of Unity and Diversity (1983); ROBERT H. DIX, The Politics of Colombia (1987); JORGE PABLO OSTERLING, Democracy in Colombia: Clientelist Politics and Guerrilla Warfare (1989).

JOHN D. MARTZ

See also Cúcuta, Congress of.

Constitution of 1863
(Rionegro Constitution)

In effect from 1863 to 1885, the constitution, produced by an all-Liberal assembly at Rionegro, Antioquia, was the maximum expression of Colombian federalism, outstripping its already federalist predecessor of 1858. Colombia's nine "sovereign states" were permitted to raise armies, set electoral laws, and do most anything else of consequence; the federal president was limited to a nonrenewable two-year term, and he was indirectly elected by the states. The document's libertarian bent, providing for absolute freedom of the press (including libel) and unrestricted traffic in arms, led the French novelist Victor Hugo to deem it a constitution for a "nation of angels." Conservatives, and many Liberals, blamed the document for Colombia's persistent instability and underdevelopment. In January 1886 President Rafael NÚÑEZ, after crushing a Liberal revolt, declared that the 1863 constitution had "ceased to exist"; its successor, in force until 1991, reverted to a centralist and quasi-authoritarian model.

SALVADOR CAMACHO ROLDÁN, "La convención de Rionegro," in his Memorias (1923); WILLIAM M. GIBSON, The Constitutions of Colombia (1948); JAMES WILLIAM PARK, Rafael Núñez and the Politics of Colombian Regionalism, 1863–1886 (1985).

RICHARD J. STOLLER

See also Mosquera, Tomás Cipriano de.

COLOMBIA: GREAT BANANA STRIKE, a violent labor dispute in 1928. The target of the strikers was the UNITED FRUIT COMPANY, which controlled banana production and marketing in the coastal department of Magdalena. In mid-November 1928 about twenty thousand workers went on strike against United Fruit and Colombian growers. The strikers' main demand was that they be recognized as company employees so that they might receive benefits guaranteed by law. To avoid providing these benefits, the company used labor contractors in hiring and firing. The strikers also sought wage increases and collective contracts. Intransigence on both sides prolonged the strike, and as tension mounted, the government declared martial law on 5 December. Early the next morning General Carlos Cortés Vargas ordered a crowd of 1,500 strikers and family members camped in the plaza of Ciénaga to disperse. When the order was ignored, his soldiers fired, killing thirteen. Strikers then attacked and burned company buildings in Sevilla, where soldiers killed twenty-nine. A wave of repression that followed produced additional deaths. The total number of victims is not known, but a historian has estimated the total between sixty and seventy-five. Many strike leaders were also jailed.

The Conservative government's handling of the strike, and especially the use of the army in defense of a foreign enterprise, provoked outrage and contributed to the Liberal victory in 1930. Jorge E. GAITÁN, then a Liberal member of Congress, excoriated the government in an inflammatory debate that solidified his reputation as a friend of labor. The strike occupies an important place in Colombian national consciousness. It is the focal point of Álvaro Cepeda Samudio's novel *La casa grande* (1962) and the subject of a key episode in Gabriel GARCÍA MÁRQUEZ's *Cien años de soledad* (1967).

MIGUEL URRUTIA, *The Development of the Colombian Labor Movement* (1969), esp. pp. 99–109; JUDITH WHITE, *Historia de una ignominia* (1978); ROBERTO HERRERA SOTO and RAFAEL ROMERO CASTAÑEDA, *La zona bananera del Magdalena* (1979); CARLOS ARANGO Z., *Sobrevivientes de las bananeras* (1981).

HELEN DELPAR

See also **Banana Industry.**

COLOMBIA: ORGANIZATIONS

Colombian Indigenist Institute

This organization was established in 1942 to promote the founding of indigenist groups to advise governments on official Indian policy. Formed in response to the call of the First Inter-American Indigenist Congress (at Pátzcuaro, Mexico), the institute was a private entity founded by leading Colombian intellectuals, including Gregorio Hernández de Alba, Antonio García, Juan Friede, Gerardo Reichel Dolmatoff, and Alfredo Vásquez Carrizosa. Its objectives included the publication of cultural, historical, and socioeconomic studies of Colombian Indians as well as the promotion of applied anthropology projects aimed at the rational integration of Indians into the national life of Colombia. The Colombian Indigenist Institute was active in confronting official policies, and it was critical of the liquidation of indigenous communities and government support of Catholic missions among indigenous people. The institute was incorporated into the National University of Colombia in 1947, but was dissolved during the VIOLENCIA of the following decade.

ROBERTO PINEDA CAMACHO, "La reivindicación del indio en el pensamiento social colombiano (1850–1950)," in *Un siglo de investigación social: Antropología en Colombia,* edited by Jaime Arocha and Nina S. de Friedemann (1984).

JOANNE RAPPAPORT

Colombian Institute for Agrarian Reform—INCORA

This organization was created as a result of the Agrarian Social Reform Law of 1961 to redistribute land to peasants, support colonization movements, provide technical assistance, and promote peasant cooperatives. Its earliest tasks in the wake of the VIOLENCIA were the redistribution of land in areas of conflict and the provision of assistance for colonization of the eastern lowlands by families displaced by the violence. An attempt in 1968 to legislate compulsory redistribution of lands in haciendas where sharecropping was the norm was met with fierce opposition, which effectively curbed the return of peasants to the countryside.

Less than 15 percent of potential beneficiaries obtained land through INCORA, and land redistribution was most successful when driven by peasant protest. The agrarian landscape was more successfully transformed by the appearance of agrarian capitalism; INCORA was most successful in providing a reserve of temporary labor for agro-industry.

LEON ZAMOSC, *The Agrarian Question and the Peasant Movement in Colombia* (1986); PIERRE GILHODES, "La cuestión agraria en Colombia (1958–1985)," in *Nueva historia de Colombia,* vol. 3, edited by Alvaro Tirado Mejía (1989).

JOANNE RAPPAPORT

Confederation of Colombian Workers Confederación de Trabajadores de Colombia—CTC

The CTC was the first national labor confederation in Colombia. The return of the Liberal Party to power in 1930 was followed by extensive unionization, culminating in the establishment of the CTC in 1935 to represent all unionized workers. Transportation workers were the backbone of the CTC, which was weakened by bitter rivalry between Communist and Liberal factions. In exchange for supporting Liberal candidates the CTC received government funds, yet it could not shed its image as a radical organization of the extreme left.

The Liberal government crushed a major strike by river dockworkers in 1945 because it felt that the CTC had become too powerful. In 1947 the CTC had 109,000 members, who belonged to 427 affiliated unions. When the Conservative Party returned to power in 1946, it supported, at the urging of the Catholic church, a rival confederation, the Union of Colombian Workers (UTC). By 1950, the UTC had replaced the CTC as the largest labor organization. Defections from the CTC to the UTC and the growing ranks of unaffiliated unions further weakened the CTC, which by 1959 represented only 27 unions.

Following the Cuban Revolution the U.S. government, through the CIA, convinced the CTC to expel remaining Communist members. In return, the CTC received funds and backing to revive itself as an attractive alternative for those workers not comfortable with the Catholic and Conservative ideas of the UTC. The expelled Communists set up the Syndical Confederation of Colombian Workers (CSTC) in 1964, while the CTC, with support from the Colombian and U.S. governments, was able to push its membership figures back above 100,000. In 1979 the CTC claimed to have more than 400,000 members, almost the same number as the rival UTC. By then the CTC was a hollow organization whose corrupt leaders had lost contact with the rank and file. Many unions defected to the new Unified Central of Workers (CUT). By the early 1990s, the CTC represented less than 13 percent of unionized workers in Colombia; its membership had dropped below 80,000; and its very survival was in doubt.

EDGAR CAICEDO, *Historia de las luchas sindicales en Colombia* (1982); RENÉ DE LA PEDRAJA, "Colombia," in *Latin American Labor Organizations*, edited by Gerald Greenfield and Sheldon L. Maram (1987), pp. 179–212; FERNANDO LÓPEZ-ALVES, "Explaining Confederation: Colombian Unions in the 1980s," in *Latin American Research Review* 25 (1990): 115–133.

RENÉ DE LA PEDRAJA

See also **Labor Movements.**

Democratic Society of Artisans
Sociedad Democrática de Artesanos

The Democratic Society of Artisans played an often contradictory role within the mid-nineteenth-century liberal reform era in Colombia. The society emerged in 1849 from the Society of Artisans, which had been founded by craftsmen to reverse the tariff reduction of 1847. Helping to establish hundreds of chapters throughout the country, Gólgotan Liberals manipulated the nonelite organization to serve the interests of the Liberal Party until 1852. Some chapters, however, became involved in local contentious issues, such as the question of *ejido* (public commons) lands around Cali or the construction of a republican polity in San Gil. Artisans and disgruntled Draconiano Liberals regained control of the capital's chapter in 1851, after which it became closely aligned with the administration of General José María OBANDO (1853–1854). Its earlier myopic focus on higher tariff rates had evolved into a potent criticism of the liberal reform process by 1854, when the Bogotá, Cali, and San Gil chapters supported the *golpe de estado* of José María MELO.

GUSTAVO VARGAS MARTÍNEZ, *Colombia 1854: Melo, los artesanos y el socialismo* (*La dictadura democrático-artesanal de 1854, expresión del socialismo utópico en Colombia*) (1972); DAVID SOWELL, " '*La teoría i la realidad*': The Democratic Society of Artisans of Bogotá, 1847–1854," in *Hispanic American Historical Review* 67 (1987): 611–630.

DAVID SOWELL

National Association of Industrialists
Asociación Nacional de Industriales—Andi

Founded 18 November 1944 in Medellín at a meeting of several of the country's largest manufacturers, Andi is one of the best-organized and most powerful producer groups (*gremios*) in Colombia. Its emergence reflected not only the rapid growth of Colombian industry at the time but also the desire of industrialists, led by the Echavarría clan and other wealthy capitalists from Medellín, to promote their interests by urging the government to pursue protectionist economic policies. Speaking for major sectors of Colombian business, the group has had an impact through its outspoken support of the free-enterprise system, as well as the work of its economists and the advice of its consultants.

HARVEY KLINE, *Colombia: Portrait of Unity and Diversity* (1983), pp. 79–80; EDUARDO SÁENZ ROVNER, "The Industrialists and Politics in Colombia, 1945–1950" (Ph.D. diss., Brandeis University, 1989).

PAMELA MURRAY

National Federation of Coffee Growers
Federación Nacional de Cafeteros—Fedecafé

An organization that seeks to represent domestic producers and sellers of coffee, Colombia's primary export commodity. It was founded in 1927 by prominent landowners and politicians who have played a vital role in the development of the Colombian COFFEE INDUSTRY. Supported by a government tax on coffee exports, Fedecafé has stimulated coffee productivity by disseminating information on modern farming methods, improving marketing, and promoting trade policies to make Colombia's crop competitive worldwide. Despite its claim to speak for both small and big growers, the federation has mainly represented Colombia's largest coffee interests, including some of the oldest and wealthiest landowning families in the country. Its leadership has included members of the political elite, such as Mariano OSPINA PÉREZ, who served as the federation's first president (1927–1934) before becoming president of Colombia. This connection explains the federation's quasi-governmental influence not only on the coffee industry but on national economic policies as well.

BENNETT E. KOFFMAN, "The National Federation of Coffee Growers of Colombia" (Ph.D. diss., University of Virginia, 1969); MARCO PALACIOS, *Coffee in Colombia, 1850–1970: An Economic, Social, and Political History* (1980).

PAMELA MURRAY

National School of Mines of Medellín

Colombia's first school for mining engineers, founded 11 April 1887 in Medellín, is also one of the oldest and most prestigious academic bodies within the country's national university system, to which it was annexed in 1939. It has achieved fame for its traditionally high academic and professional standards and for the vital role its graduates play in the industrialization of MEDELLÍN, particularly in the development of the mining, railway transportation, and manufacturing industries, which fueled Medellín's notable growth during the first half of the twentieth century. As of the early 1990s the school continued to supply the country with a variety of engineers (concentrating in nine different areas), industrial entrepreneurs and administrators, and leaders of government. Thus, the school remains a key source of the country's technocratic elite.

ALBERTO MAYOR MORA, *Ética, trabajo y productividad en Antioquia* (1984); PAMELA MURRAY, "Forging a Technocratic Elite in Colombia: A History of the Escuela Nacional de Minas of Medellín, 1887–1970" (Ph.D. diss., Tulane University, 1990).

PAMELA MURRAY

Unified Central of Workers
Central Unitaria de Trabajadores—CUT

The largest labor confederation in Colombia since 1986, the CUT has at various times represented from 50 to possibly 80 percent of unionized workers. The creation of the CUT reflected the growing disenchantment of the rank and file with the corrupt and ineffective leadership of the two traditional labor confederations, the Union of Colombian Workers (UTC) and the Confederation of Colombian Workers (CTC). When, starting in 1980, employers launched an antiunion campaign to drastically slash wages, the workers became militant and began to sympathize with the Communist organization, the Syndical Confederation of Colombian Workers (CSTC), itself reeling from a combined government–employer offensive.

To preempt the Communists, in 1985 President Belisario BETANCUR appointed a union leader, Jorge Carrillo Rojas, as minister of labor. Carillo Rojas decided to merge the four existing labor confederations into a new one, the CUT. This unwieldy coalition survived while he remained as minister but disintegrated as soon as he resigned to become the head of the CUT in 1986. Most unions stayed in the CUT, however, so that it continued to represent at least half of the unionized workers. Likewise, many unaffiliated unions joined the CUT. When the CSTC merged with the CUT, the CTC and UTC leaders charged that the new confederation was under Communist control. Against the advice of Carrillo Rojas, militants voted to participate in two general strikes, in 1987 and 1988, both of which ended in failure.

Employers and the government had wanted the CUT to end Communist influence but not to become an independent force. In an attempt to undermine support for the CUT, the government funded and supported the nearly moribund CTC and UTC. Since 1988 the CUT has concentrated on backing workers in specific struggles, such as those on banana plantations and in government agencies threatened with privatization.

RENÉ DE LA PEDRAJA, "Colombia," in *Latin American Labor Organizations*, edited by Gerald Greenfield and Sheldon L. Maram (1987), pp. 179–212; FERNANDO LÓPEZ-ALVES, "Explain-

ing Confederation: Colombian Unions in the 1980s," in *Latin American Research Review* 25 (1990): 115–133.

RENÉ DE LA PEDRAJA

See also **Labor Movements.**

Union of Colombian Workers
Unión de Trabajadores de Colombia—UTC

The UTC was the most important labor confederation in Colombia from 1950 to 1980. It was created in 1946 at the urging of the Catholic church to counter the leftist Confederation of Colombian Workers (CTC). The strong religious tendency within the early UTC (Jesuit advisers remained active until the 1960s) made the confederation acceptable to female workers and traditional factory owners. During the wave of industrialization in Colombia after 1945, the UTC organized the new industrial workers, and by 1950 it had replaced the CTC as the largest confederation.

During its early years, the UTC had tried to avoid partisan issues, but in 1963 a new UTC president, Tulio Cuevas, linked the UTC with the Conservative Party. Backing and funds from the Colombian and U.S. governments fueled the expansion of the UTC, whose membership reached half a million workers in 1971. The rank and file became disenchanted with the corrupt and autocratic leadership, and in 1980 the 100,000 members from CUNDINAMARCA bolted from the UTC. Other unions followed, many of which later joined the new Unified Central of Workers (CUT). By 1986, the UTC's membership had dropped to 80,000, representing barely 13 percent of unionized workers in Colombia. The UTC has continued to decline, and its future survival is seriously in doubt, as is that of the CTC. The obsession of leaders with preserving their plush posts, however, has blocked attempts to merge the former rivals, which have been eclipsed by the CUT.

HERNANDO GÓMEZ B. et al., *Sindicalismo y política económica* (1986); RENÉ DE LA PEDRAJA, "Colombia," in *Latin American Labor Organizations*, edited by Gerald Greenfield and Sheldon L. Maram (1987), pp. 179–212; FERNANDO LÓPEZ-ALVES, "Explaining Confederation: Colombian Unions in the 1980s," in *Latin American Research Review* 25 (1990): 115–133.

RENÉ DE LA PEDRAJA

See also **Labor Movements.**

Union Society of Artisans
Sociedad Unión de Artesanos

The Union Society of Artisans, a labor organization, culminated twenty years of political activities by Bogotá's artisans during the liberal reform era. Founded in 1866 in the aftermath of the 1859–1862 civil war, amidst a serious economic recession, it attempted to forge a nonpartisan alliance of artisans. Membership in the society ranged from perhaps 300 to 500 artisans during its first year, before partisan upheaval caused by Tomás Cipriano de MOSQUERA's abortive coup divided the organization. The society finally dissolved after the November 1868 overthrow of the Cundinamarcan state government. The society's newspaper, *La Alianza* (The Alliance), articulated an ideology of "artisan republicanism," based in part on a labor theory of value. It advocated the return to centralized government, a restitution of clerical temporal authority, a biparty government, and protection of native industries. José Leocadio Camacho, Antonio Cárdenas, Saturnino González, and Felipe Roa Ramírez were the most visible leaders of the society.

DAVID SOWELL, *The Early Colombian Labor Movement: Artisans and Politics in Bogota, 1832–1919* (1992).

DAVID SOWELL

COLOMBIA: PACIFIC COAST, a geographic unit between the Pacific shore and the western highlands of Colombia. In terms of ARCHAEOLOGY, knowledge remains so scant that processes of social development in the area can only be described in the most general terms. Even today major interpretations still claim migrations and diffusion as the most important variables shaping the societies that the Spaniards described in the region upon their arrival early in the sixteenth century.

Colombia was probably occupied by human societies coming from lower Central America about 10,000 to 12,000 B.C. Thus, early preceramic occupation along the Pacific coast is important for the understanding of the very early human societies that settled South America. Early human presence in the region is inferred from tools that have been found in surface collections without pottery. Two projectile points found in the Golfo de Urabá, not far from the border with Panama, suggest hunting activities around 8000 B.C. Very little is known in terms of other economic activities, settlement patterns, and cultural features.

Knowledge improves somewhat for much later periods, when pottery and goldwork were introduced in the area. Early radiocarbon dates have been obtained for sites in the Tumaco area, close to the Colombia-Ecuador border. About 325 B.C. human societies in this region elaborated fine pottery and used gold adornments. Other sites this old have been found farther north, in the Lower Calima and near the Munguidó river. Pottery from Tumaco shows similarities with pottery excavated along the Pacific coast of Ecuador (CHORRERA) and sites in the CALIMA region near Cali (the Ilama period). In Tumaco one of the main features in pottery manufacture is the elaboration of fine figurines. This period is also known for the construction of mounds locally known as *tolas*. Economic activities included fishing and the exploitation of mangroves, hunting, and agriculture. It seems that intensive cultivation of maize was present in some areas from about 200 to 100 B.C., although earlier dates in the neighboring Calima region to the east

would suggest maize was known long before its consumption became important. Other plants seem to have been at least as relevant as maize during early times.

Later periods in Tumaco are described as a sequence of changes in pottery styles, including the progressive modification of figurines that become more and more rudimentary. Construction of *tolas* disappears about A.D. 1000. Nonetheless, social changes in the region do not suggest a decadence in social organization or economic activities. Between A.D. 800 and 1500 there is evidence of agricultural progress, including labor-intensive practices of fertilization. Also, the elaboration of metal adornments continued to the time of the Spanish Conquest. Trade activities along the Pacific coast were described during the sixteenth century and there is some speculation that long-distance trade networks linked the Pacific coast with Ecuador and Panama. Archaeological evidence of this trade, however, remains scant.

A summary of archaeological research in the area is provided by LEONOR HERRERA, "Costa del Pacífico y vertiente oeste de la cordillera occidental," in *Colombia Prehispánica-Regiones Arqueológicas* (1989). Excavations in Tumaco are reported by FRANCOIS BOUCHARD, "Excavaciones arqueológicas en la Región de Tumaco, Nariño, Colombia," in *Revista Colombiana de Antropología* (1985). Also see DIÓGENES PATIÑO, *Asentamientos Prehispánicos en la Costa Pacífica Caucana*. A description in English of archaeological research in the area is WARWICK BRAY, "Across the Darien Gap: A Colombian View of Isthmian Archaeology," in *The Archaeology of Lower Central America*, edited by Frederick W. Lange and Doris Z. Stone (1984). For a general overview of Colombian archaeology see CARL HENRIK LANGEBAEK, *Noticias de Caciques muy Mayores: Orígen y desarrollo de sociedades complejas en el nororiente de Colombia y norte de Venezuela* (1992).

CARL HENRIK LANGEBAEK R.

COLOMBIA: POLITICAL PARTIES

Overview

Colombia's party system is the oldest in Latin America. Its two traditional parties, the Liberals and Conservatives, date back to the late 1840s and have dominated national politics. While historically the parties have been divided over significant policy issues, these divisions have faded since the middle of the twentieth century. At the same time, elitist control was established at the very beginning, and mass participation discouraged. The parties have facilitated the domination of public affairs by a small group of national leaders.

Following the breakup of the GRAN COLOMBIAN Federation in 1830, major issues centered on questions of constitutional structure, church-state relations, and basic economic policies. Conservatives favored a strong centralized state in contrast to the Liberals' preference for a federal association of individually powerful states. Conservatives advocated close ties between church and state; the Liberals did not. And Conservatives wanted government involvement in economic policy-making, while Liberals championed a nineteenth-century view of laissez-faire economics. These differences, along with regional rivalries and personalistic ambitions, characterized party conflict for a century.

While the parties were organizations of "notables" rather than forces for mass political participation, the leadership built strong support and loyalties that were strengthened by patron-client relationships. Liberal and Conservative leaders generated substantial backing for the succession of civil wars and uprisings that took place in the nineteenth century. The struggle for power was often violent. Not until the 1880s was the situation stabilized, when Rafael NÚÑEZ MOLEDO moved toward establishing a strong central government. It was legitimated by the Constitution of 1886, which drastically reduced the authority of individual states while also recognizing Catholicism as Colombia's official religion. By the time of Núñez's death in 1894, structures had been erected that would strengthen Conservative domination.

Civil strife was by no means ended: there was a brief insurgency in 1895 and then the WAR OF THE THOUSAND DAYS (1899–1902). Yet Conservative rule continued until the Liberals returned to power in 1930. Four years later, when Alfonso LÓPEZ PUMAREJO won the presidency and instituted a number of reforms, the level of partisan debate rose. López and his Liberal followers sought an expansion of the state, greater activity in labor and welfare policy, and a redefined relationship with the CATHOLIC CHURCH. He met with fierce opposition from within his own party as well as from the Conservatives. These differences eventually led to a Liberal division in 1946, permitting the Conservatives to regain power under Mariano OSPINA PÉREZ. The next few years saw a progressive deterioration of the party system, fueled by growing violence in the countryside. This situation in turn brought a collapse of political civility and reluctant intervention by the armed forces in 1953.

Party leaders—notably Alberto LLERAS CAMARGO for the Liberals and Laureano Gómez for the Conservatives—negotiated in exile a series of agreements that were adopted by constitutional plebiscite following the 1957 collapse of the military regime. The resultant National Front assured sixteen years during which congressional, ministerial, and other major positions would be divided equally between the two parties, while the presidency would alternate between them. These measures guaranteed that third parties were relegated to a minor position in the system, while traditional Conservative and Liberal elites could retain control of public policy. With the return of competitive elections, the Liberals proved to be the majority party. From 1974 to the early 1990s, they lost the presidency only once—in 1982 when two Liberal candidates divided the vote. At the same time, amendments to the original National Front provisions adopted in 1968 called for continuing participation in government by both the majority and minor-

ity parties. Not until 1986, under the Liberal Virgilio BARCO, was an administration formed without significant representation of both parties.

Meanwhile, the two party organizations had weakened internally, with national leaders increasingly relying upon local and regional bosses for votes and services. Customary elitist control over the traditional parties diminished. National Front rules also discouraged participation in elections, and abstention rates were high. Levels of public cynicism rose, increasing pressure for reforms and political modernization. In 1990 the Liberals again won comfortably, and César GAVIRIA TRUJILLO became president. He backed the movement that eventually led to the new constitution of 1991. It promised to weaken traditional party domination, with new electoral regulations sharply limiting the old control mechanisms of local leaders. Elections for the Constituent Assembly had been notable for the rise of M-19 (Movimiento 19 de Abril), previously an insurgent organization, which had agreed to adopt nonviolent measures. Its leader, Antonio NAVARRO WOLFF, was influential in the Assembly, and the party constituted a new element in politics.

For the Liberals and Conservatives (rechristened Social Conservatives in 1986), the challenge from M-19 and other budding parties was accompanied by their own serious internal divisions. President Gaviria himself, the central figure in constitutional reformism, was barred from a second term once he left office. And while the Liberals reacted to the new political environment, the Social Conservatives were split between the factions headed by former President Misael PASTRANA BORRERO and by former presidential candidate Alvaro Gómez Hurtado. The reforms of the 1990s constitute a serious threat to the traditional domination of the two historic parties and may well lead to a democratization of long-standing patterns of party power and authority.

R. ALBERT BERRY, RONALD G. HELLMAN, and MAURICIO SOLAÚN, eds., *Politics of Compromise: Coalition Government in Colombia* (1980); HARVEY F. KLINE, *Colombia: Portrait of Unity and Diversity* (1983); ROBERT H. DIX, *The Politics of Colombia* (1987); JONATHAN HARTLYN, *The Politics of Coalition Rule in Colombia* (1988); JENNY PEARCE, *Colombia: Inside the Labyrinth* (1990).

JOHN D. MARTZ

Conservative Party
Partido Conservador

One of Colombia's two traditional political parties, the Conservatives date back to a statement of principles authored by José Eusebio CARO and Mariano OSPINA RODRÍGUEZ (1849). Like conservatives in neighboring states, they advocated a strong central government and cooperation with the CATHOLIC CHURCH. Dominant during the early years of the twentieth century, they have held power only infrequently in recent times. The National Front arrangement (1958–1974) called for a sharing of power, and two Conservatives reached the presidency. The only victory under competitive conditions, however, came when Belisario BETANCUR won office against a divided Liberal Party (1982). Since then the party has been weakened by the split between former President Misael PASTRANA BORRERO and two-time candidate Alvaro Gómez Hurtado. Pastrana Borrero changed the party's name to Social Conservative in 1986, while Gómez later withdrew to create the Movimiento de Salvación Nacional (MSN), which outpolled the Social Conservatives in 1990.

HARVEY F. KLINE, *Colombia: Portrait of Unity and Diversity* (1983); JONATHAN HARTLYN, *The Politics of Coalition Rule in Colombia* (1988).

JOHN D. MARTZ

Liberal Party
Partido Liberal

One of Colombia's two traditional parties, the Liberals trace their origins back to the 1840s. Opposed to the clericalism and statism of the Conservative Party, they alternated with the Conservatives in power during the nineteenth century, went into opposition, and returned in 1930. They have been the majority party since that time, although they often collaborate with the Conservatives in government. The two parties worked together to establish the system of shared government through the National Front. During the Front's years (1958–1974) the Liberals held the presidency twice. Since then their only loss was in 1982, when the party split. In both 1986 and 1990 the Liberals won resounding victories in the presidential races. The new constitution of 1991 has opened the party system to broader participation, but the Liberals remain more popular than the Conservatives and are likely to retain a dominant position well into the 1990s.

HARVEY F. KLINE, *Colombia: Portrait of Unity and Diversity* (1983); JONATHAN HARTLYN, *The Politics of Coalition Rule in Colombia* (1988).

JOHN D. MARTZ

See also **Radical Olympus** (below).

National Front
Frente Nacional

The National Front was a coalition between Colombia's two main political parties, in force between 1958 and 1974. In 1956 Liberal leader Alberto LLERAS CAMARGO and exiled Conservative leader Laureano GÓMEZ started discussions on a long-term accord to end the partisan VIOLENCIA that had claimed 200,000 lives since the 1940s, and to replace the military regime in power since 1953. The final accord, ratified in the plebiscite of December 1957, provided for alternation of the presidency between the two parties; parity in the cabinet, the judiciary, and in all elected bodies; and the requirement for a two-thirds

majority to pass important legislation. (This last provision was amended in 1968.) The Frente regimes were successful in controlling the *Violencia* and in redefining its remnants as apolitical or subversive. The Frente's social and economic record was generally mediocre; politically, the Frente's provisions increased the level of intraparty conflict and eventually encouraged abstentionism. The Frente lapsed in 1974, its mission completed; a residual provision for "equitable participation" by the opposition party in the cabinet was abolished in the 1991 constitution.

R. ALBERT BERRY, RONALD G. HELLMAN, and MAURICIO SOLAUN, eds., *Politics of Compromise: Coalition Government in Colombia* (1980); JONATHAN HARTLYN, *The Politics of Coalition Rule in Colombia* (1988).

RICHARD J. STOLLER

National Popular Alliance
Alianza Nacional Popular—ANAPO

The National Popular Alliance was founded in 1961 by former President Gustavo ROJAS PINILLA of Colombia to help him stage a political comeback. It was initially a movement sponsoring candidates under Conservative and Liberal factional labels, which were the only ones permitted under the National Front (1958–1974). In 1970, Rojas Pinilla ran for the presidency as a Conservative and was narrowly defeated. Many claimed that he was fraudulently deprived of victory by political elites alarmed by his antiestablishment, populist rhetoric.

In 1974, ANAPO, by now constituted as a party, chose Rojas's daughter, María Eugenia Rojas de Moreno, as its presidential candidate, but she ran a poor third behind the Liberal and Conservative contenders. Thereafter the party declined, partly because of internal divisions and the death of the elder Rojas in 1975. In 1982, ANAPO endorsed the victorious Conservative candidate, Belisario BETANCUR, who appointed María Eugenia Rojas director of an important housing agency.

R. ALBERT BERRY et al., eds., *Politics of Compromise: Coalition Government in Colombia* (1980), pp. 31–179.

HELEN DELPAR

Radical Olympus

Radical Olympus was a name applied to leaders of the Radical wing of Colombia's Liberal Party in the late nineteenth century. Among the principal members of the group were three presidents of the period: Manuel MURILLO TORO (1864–1866, 1872–1874), Santiago Pérez (1874–1876), and Aquileo PARRA (1876–1878). Admirers used the name as a tribute to the integrity and devotion to principle they found characteristic of the gods of Mount Olympus. Critics referred instead to a Radical "oligarchy" which held the national government in an iron grip. Most members of the Olympus came from eastern Colombia. They were generally identified with the federalist constitution of 1863, a belief in limited government, and anticlericalism, but in reality they held a wide range of positions on these issues. After 1878 the Radicals lost control of the national government but remained active in opposition.

EDUARDO RODRÍGUEZ PIÑERES, *El Olimpo Radical: Ensayos conocidos e inéditos sobre su época, 1864–1884* (1950); HELEN DELPAR, *Red Against Blue: The Liberal Party in Colombian Politics, 1863–1899* (1981).

HELEN DELPAR

COLOMBIA: REVOLUTIONARY MOVEMENTS

Army of National Liberation
Ejército de Liberación Nacional—ELN

One of Colombia's leftist guerrilla groups, the ELN was founded in 1964 by a group of mostly college-educated activists, some with Communist or dissident Liberal antecedents. The ELN was (and remains in the 1990s) strongly Castroite both in its goal of socialist revolution and in its strategy of establishing zones of dominance (*focos*). The ELN's first action was the seizure of Simacota, Santander, on 7 January 1965, but it first came to public attention when Father Camilo TORRES RESTREPO, organizer of the United People's Front movement in Bogotá, died in combat in February 1966, shortly after joining the ELN. The movement was weakened by a brutal purge in 1966–1967; an army assault in August 1973 nearly finished it off. In the 1980s the ELN returned to prominence under the defrocked Spanish priest Manuel Pérez, first as the lone holdout during the peace initiative of President Belisario BETANCUR (1984), and, since 1986, for its attacks on eastern Colombia's oil production and pipeline network.

JAIME ARENAS, *La guerrilla por dentro: Análisis del E.L.N. colombiano* (1971); JORGE P. OSTERLING, *Democracy in Colombia* (1989), pp. 307–313.

RICHARD J. STOLLER

Army of Popular Liberation
Ejército Popular de Liberación—EPL

A guerrilla group active from 1967 to 1991, the EPL had its origins in the Partido Comunista Colombiano Marxista-Leninista (PCC-ML), a pro-Chinese party founded in 1964. It was most active in the northwestern department of Córdoba, a zone of conflict between peasant settlers and expanding cattle interests. The EPL, which numbered perhaps 600 fighters at its peak, made little progress in the face of army pressure. Attempts to organize an urban front in Cali in the mid-1970s also failed. In 1984 it signed a cease-fire accord with the Belisario BETANCUR regime; but after the assassination of Oscar William Calvo Ocampo, EPL negotiator and one of the group's founders, the group returned to armed struggle in November 1985. The EPL's Córdoba

base was seriously threatened by the army's new aggressiveness in 1990. A new round of negotiations led to the group's demobilization in March 1991 and a political alliance with the Alianza Democrática M-19. A hardline faction of the EPL has rejected the demobilization and now operates in league with the Army of National Liberation (ELN).

FABIOLA CALVO OCAMPO, *EPL: Díez hombres, un ejército, una historia* (1985); JORGE P. OSTERLING, *Democracy in Colombia* (1989), 314–317.

RICHARD J. STOLLER

M-19
Movimiento 19 de Abril

Active from 1974 to 1990, the M-19 guerrilla group was an offshoot of the National Popular Alliance (ANAPO) of former dictator Gustavo ROJAS PINILLA; its name comes from the date in 1970 when electoral fraud allegedly deprived him of the presidency. Unlike Rojas himself, M-19 was decidedly leftist (though not Marxist) in its populism and "anti-imperialism." Its early actions, under Jaime Bateman Cayón (*d.* 1983), were highly theatrical, such as the theft of Simón Bolívar's sword in January 1974; the 1979 arms theft from the main army depot; and the 1980 seizure of the Dominican Republic Embassy were high points of the group's visibility and prestige. A truce with the government in 1984 collapsed after several attacks on M-19 leaders and continued extortion by the guerrillas. In late 1985, M-19 suffered critical defeats at the Palace of Justice in Bogotá and in Cali's Siloé neighborhood; many of the group's remaining leaders were killed. After renewed negotiations, M-19 demobilized in early 1990, and as the Alianza Democrática M-19 it has garnered significant electoral support under the leadership of Antonio NAVARRO WOLFF, one of the few surviving leaders of the armed movement.

PATRICIA LARA, *Siembra vientos y recogerás tempestades* (1982); OLGA BEHAR, *Noches de humo* (1988); JORGE P. OSTERLING, *Democracy in Colombia* (1989), pp. 300–307.

RICHARD J. STOLLER

Revolutionary Armed Forces of Colombia
Fuerzas Armadas Revolucionarias de Colombia—FARC

The largest of Colombia's guerrilla groups, FARC was officially founded in 1964. It originated with the Communist guerrillas of the VIOLENCIA period, who escaped from the Sumapaz region to southern Tolima in the late 1950s. The group's formal founding occurred during the army assault on its redoubt in Marquetalia, Tolima; its base has since moved several times, always in the Tolima-Meta region. Much of the current FARC leadership, including commander Manuel Marulanda Vélez (alias Tirofijo; *b.* 1928), are Marquetalia veterans. More than other Colombian insurgencies, FARC has pursued a rural-based strategy designed to gain and hold territory; this it has done in several departments, sometimes over several years. In 1984, FARC participated in President Belisario BETANCUR CUARTAS's peace process but quickly pulled out, leaving many to doubt its sincerity about negotiations; by the late 1980s the group was larger—perhaps 6,000 fighters—and operated on more fronts—over forty—than before the truce. Once solidly linked to the legal Partido Comunista Colombiano, FARC has been politically autonomous for several years; its links to the Unión Patriotica, the leftist party founded during the Betancur period, remain a matter of speculation and polemic. In November 1990 the army destroyed FARC's seat at La Uribe, Meta, and the group retaliated with stepped-up attacks throughout the country. There seems little prospect of a settlement, leaving FARC as one of the few guerrilla groups in the world whose leaders (such as the ideologist Jacobo Arenas, *b.* 1924; *d.* 1991) die of old age, still in the field.

CARLOS ARANGO Z., *FARC: Veinte años de Marquetalia a la Uribe* (1984); ARTURO ALAPE, *Las vidas de Pedro Antonio Marín— Manuel Marulanda Vélez—Tirofijo* (1989); JORGE P. OSTERLING, *Democracy in Colombia* (1989).

RICHARD J. STOLLER

COLOMBRES, JOSÉ EUSEBIO (*b.* 16 December 1778; *d.* 11 February 1859), ecclesiastic and signer of the Argentine Declaration of Independence. Colombres was born in Tucumán, received his doctorate from the University of Córdoba in 1803, and was ordained a priest the same year. He served as a parish priest in Catamarca and supported the May Revolution of 1810. Colombres was elected to the Congress of Tucumán (24 March 1816) and was a signer of the Declaration of Independence of the United Provinces of La Plata on 9 July 1816, by which the political bonds with Spain were broken. While the leaders of the United Provinces were busy establishing their independence, Spain had reasserted its rule in the surrounding areas and overthrown the newly established regime.

Colombres played an active political role in Tucumán, but he is also known for reintroducing sugarcane cultivation there. Sugarcane had been introduced in the 1550s and fostered by the Jesuits on their estates, but at their expulsion in 1767 the industry collapsed. Colombres planted extensive fields and built ox-driven mills to crush the cane. In 1831, however, Juan Facundo Quiroga's forces burned the fields, and Colombres was imprisoned.

Colombres became a government minister under Governor Bernabé Aráoz. He supported the formation of the Coalition of the North, but when the unitarist forces were defeated, he went into exile in Bolivia. After the fall of Juan Manuel de ROSAS (1852), Colombres

returned and held ecclesiastical positions in Salta. He died in Tucumán.

TULIO HALPERÍN-DONGHI, *Politics, Economics, and Society in Argentina in the Revolutionary Period,* translated by Richard Southern (1975).

NICHOLAS P. CUSHNER

COLONIA, department of Uruguay with 112,800 inhabitants and city of 19,102 (1985) inhabitants west of Montevideo, on the shores of the RÍO DE LA PLATA. This historical emplacement was founded in 1680 by the governor of Río de Janeiro, Manuel de Lobo, according to instructions from the Portuguese crown to occupy for Brazil the northern shore of the estuary to counteract the influence of Buenos Aires on the southern shore. Because there had been no significant Spanish presence on the northern shore since Captain Juan Romero's colonization attempt had been foiled by the ferocious Charrúa Indians in 1552, the Portuguese established a colony and fortified a small town overlooking the estuary. The threat of a Portuguese enclave in the middle of the Spanish Río de la Plata, aggravated by the active smuggling of French and English merchandise, called for immediate action from Buenos Aires. Since repeated attempts to forcefully dislodge the invaders failed, Colonia del Sacramento was put under siege by Pedro Antonio de CEVALLOS in 1762. It was not until the signing of the Treaty of SAN ILDEFONSO (1777) that the Spanish regained control of the settlement and Portugal withdrew its claims on the Río de la Plata.

Today, Colonia is a picturesque and pleasant town, an active station on the route between Montevideo and Buenos Aires via a hydrofoil that crosses the 25-mile-wide estuary, and a vacation spot for residents of Montevideo. Vineyards, fruit groves, and vegetable gardens dot the route connecting Colonia with Montevideo, 95 miles away.

OMAR MOREIRA, *Colonia del Sacramento* (Montevideo, 1984).

CÉSAR N. CAVIEDES

COLÔNIA DO SACRAMENTO. *See* **Sacramento, Colônia do.**

COLONO, a term that in Spanish and Portuguese refers to a class of rural workers tied to the land, often with a status similar to that of sharecroppers in U.S. history. As a general rule, *colonos* provide their labor in exchange for either access to land or for a portion of the harvest on large LATIFUNDIA. In Argentina the term *colono* simply implies a member of a colony of agricultural immigrants.

The actual practice of *colonage* varies widely by region, but generally it is associated with the rise of debt peonage and dependent labor that accompanied the consolidation of the large landed estates in Latin America. This solution to labor shortages offered the laborer a minimum of basic needs in exchange for the land-owners' guarantee of work during harvests and other peak labor demand periods.

In Brazil, *colono* generally refers to a small (tenant) farmer. In the nineteenth century it was associated with foreign immigrants whom planters introduced to work their estates as an alternative to slave labor. Private and public sources financed the transatlantic transportation and settlement of tenant farmers under contract arrangements that stipulated the number of coffee trees to cultivate, process, and harvest. The *colono* received half of the profits from the sale of the coffee he harvested after processing, transport, and other expenses were deducted. Payment might be made at the termination of the harvest or on an annual basis.

Initial experiments with colonization plans involving immigrant *colonos* proved a costly and, in the long run, unfeasible labor alternative. They faced large debts and tropical illnesses, lacked clergymen and legal counsel, and were subject to the disciplinary measures of local planters and police authorities. A second wave of European immigration to Brazil introduced contract farm laborers into the expanding coffee areas of São Paulo in the 1880s and 1890s. In Rio de Janeiro, Minas Gerais, and Espírito Santo, where postemancipation labor needs were met mostly with Brazilian labor, *colonos* referred to foreigners and Brazilians who were contracted individually or in family units as sharecroppers, tenants, and in some cases part-time salaried laborers on rural estates.

WARREN DEAN, *Rio Claro* (1976); EMÍLIA VIOTTI DA COSTA, *Da senzala a colónia*, 2d ed. (1982).

TODD LITTLE-SIEBOLD
NANCY PRISCILLA SMITH NARO

COLORADO RIVER, waterway arising in the high ANDES (36 degrees south latitude) just past the confluence of the Río Grande and the Barrancas in Argentina. The Colorado River follows a 530-mile course to the southeast that ends in a wide delta at Bahía Anegada, south of BAHÍA BLANCA. Fed by the snow of the Andes and by short-lived summer rains, this stream crosses large segments of the arid PAMPA without vanishing in the sand, as do other regional rivers. Not many significant settlements are located along its course, with the exception of Colonia Catriel, in the province of Neuquén, where natural gas is extracted and sent to the city of Neuquén for processing and shipping. The inhospitable and arid riverine lands attracted no colonists during the past century and constituted the roving grounds of Mapuche Indians, who periodically raided military outposts. The Colorado River was the frontier from which Argentine forces pushed the Indians southward into the Andes during the CAMPAIGN OF THE DESERT (1860–1881).

CÉSAR N. CAVIEDES

COLOSIO MURRIETA, LUIS DONALDO (*b.* 10 February 1950, *d.* 23 March, 1994), assassinated Mexican political leader. Born in Magdaleno de Kino, Sonora, he graduated from the Instituto de Estudios Superiores in Monterrey. He received an MA in economics from the University of Pennsylvania and spent a year in Vienna before taking a position at the Secretaría de Programación y Presupuesto in 1979. In 1985 he was elected a federal deputy from Sonora, and during the presidential campaign of Carlos SALINAS, he served as Oficial Mayor of the Institutional Revolutionary Party (PRI). After a brief stint as senator in 1988, Colosio became party president and presided over the 1991 congressional elections and internal party returns. In 1992, President Salinas made him the first secretary of the newly reconstituted Social Development Secretariat, where he presided over the Solidarity program before he was designated by Salinas as the PRI's candidate for president. It was expected that he would win the August 1994 presidential elections, but he was assassinated in Tijuana in mid-campaign. Colosio's murder produced numerous consequences for the political system, and coming so soon after the indigenous uprising in CHIAPAS, contributed to political instability. President Salinas was forced to select a replacement candidate, Colosio's campaign manager Ernesto Zedillo, who did not generate equal support within the party. Although the Salinas administration claimed Colosio was killed by a single, deranged gunman, President Zedillo later reopened the investigation, which alleges a wider plot, involving the chief of security, a general in the army.

RODERIC AI CAMP

See also **Mexico: Political Parties.**

COLTEJER. The Compañía Colombiana de Tejidos, one of the oldest and largest textile firms in Colombia, was founded in 1907 in Medellín by the wealthy Echavarrías family of merchants. Developed initially as an extension of Alejandro Echavarría's cloth import and retail business, Coltejer grew to become the country's single largest industrial enterprise within the next half century. Most of the company's growth occurred in the 1930s and 1940s, when the worldwide economic depression and World War II disrupted the supply of foreign-made goods and gave Colombian manufacturers a chance to fill the breach. Besides expanding plant size and acquiring modern equipment, such as the two hundred automated looms imported from England in 1932, Coltejer also took the lead in technological innovations. With the help of machines imported from Czechoslovakia in the early 1930s, it became the first manufacturer of printed cloth in Colombia, setting the pace for other Colombian textile companies.

By 1940 Coltejer was able to compete with foreign producers in the production of fine fabrics, and its merger with the Rosellón company in 1942 marked the peak of its expansion in this period. Acquisition of Rosellón, third or fourth largest producer in the country at the time, doubled Coltejer's plant size and capital reserves. By 1943 the company had 1,900 looms and close to 4,000 workers. Its labor force had also changed, from all female in the early years to virtually all male after 1945. Coltejer has prided itself on its paternalistic policies toward workers, which, in the late 1940s and 1950s, began to include provisions for social security, annual paid vacations, overtime compensation, low-interest home loans, and various other services that preceded national legislation on these matters.

ENRIQUE ECHAVARRÍA, *Historia de los textiles en Antioquia* (1943); FERNANDO GÓMEZ and ARTURO PUERTA, *Biografía económica de las industrias de Antioquia* (1945); FERNANDO BOTERO HERRERA, *La industrialización en Antioquia: génesis y consolidación, 1900–1930* (1984); ALBERTO MAYOR MORA, "Historia de la industria colombiana 1930–1968," in *Nueva historia de Colombia,* vol. 7, edited by Jesús Antonio Bejarano (1989).

PAMELA MURRAY

COLUMBUS, BARTHOLOMEW (Bartolomé Colón: *b.* ca. 1454; *d.* 1514). A wool carder in his youth in Genoa, Bartholomew played a key role in the achievements of his more famous brother, Christopher. A skilled chartmaker and a superb navigator, he preceded Christopher to Lisbon, where he endured poverty while making charts and planning the "great enterprise." Sharing his brother's hardships and suffering the same indignities, Bartholomew remained steadfast and resolute during the many years of frustration. Sent by Christopher in 1488 to seek the aid of Henry VII of England, he was unsuccessful; and though he fared no better at the court of Charles VIII of France in 1490, he was at least consoled by the king's sister Anne de Beaujeu, at Fontainebleau. Meanwhile, unknown to Bartholomew, Christopher had reached the Indies. By the time he learned of the feat and made his way to Spain (1493), Christopher had already sailed on his second voyage. Bartholomew was sent with three ships to Hispaniola, where he served as captain-general from 1494 to 1496 and founded the city of Santo Domingo. In the absence of Christopher from the island, he acted as governor until 1498, then as captain-general again until 1500, after which he returned to Castile. In recognition of Bartholomew's services, Christopher conferred on him the prestigious rank of ADELANTADO of the Indies.

A brave and bold leader, in 1497 Bartholomew faced a violent rebellion led by Francisco ROLDÁN because he enforced strict and unrealistic rules on the colonists and meted out severe punishment. When Indians defiled sacred Christian religious images, the *adelantado* burned some of the natives at the stake. Continuing disorder in the colony resulted in the sending in 1500 of a royal agent, Francisco de BOBADILLA, who arrested the Columbus brothers and shipped them in chains to Spain. Later Bartholomew was sorely tested when he accom-

panied Christopher on the disastrous fourth voyage (1502–1503) to Central America. With Christopher ill much of the time, Bartholomew explored Veragua, finding some gold and bravely fighting off Indians and mutineers, suffering two wounds in the process. Bartholomew returned to Spain but sailed again to Hispaniola with his nephew Diego in 1509. He continued to serve the crown until his death in Santo Domingo.

The most important work in English on the Columbus family is SAMUEL ELIOT MORISON, *Admiral of the Ocean Sea: A Life of Christopher Columbus,* 2 vols. (1942). See also FERNANDO COLÓN, *The Life of the Admiral Christopher Columbus by His Son Ferdinand,* edited and translated by Benjamin Keen (1959), and TROY FLOYD, *The Columbus Dynasty in the Caribbean, 1492–1526* (1973).

WILLIAM L. SHERMAN

COLUMBUS, CHRISTOPHER (*b.* ca. 1451; *d.* 1506), Genoese explorer.

EARLY LIFE IN GENOA AND PORTUGAL
Christopher Columbus was born in the republic of Genoa. His father, Domenico Colombo, was a wool weaver, wool merchant, tavern keeper, and political appointee. Columbus's early education was limited, although he read widely after reaching adulthood. He went to sea at an early age and sailed the Mediterranean on merchant vessels, traveling as far east as the island of Chios. In the mid-1470s, he settled in Portugal, joining other Italian merchants in Lisbon. Columbus sailed north to England and Ireland, and possibly as far as Iceland. He also visited the MADEIRA and CANARY ISLANDS and the African coast as far south as the Portuguese trading post at São Jorge da Mina (in modern Ghana).

In 1478 or 1479, Columbus married Felipa Moniz, member of a prominent Italian-Portuguese family. Her father and brother were hereditary captains of the island of Porto Santo, and her mother came from a noble family. In 1480 Felipa bore Columbus a son named Diogo (Diego in Spanish), who would later have a bureaucratic career in the lands his father claimed for Spain. Columbus's marriage provided connections to the Portuguese court, important ties to Madeira and Porto Santo, and at least some wealth.

THE ENTERPRISE OF THE INDIES
Columbus based his ideas about the size of the world and the possibility of a westward voyage to the fabled riches of Asia on rumors of unknown Atlantic islands, unusual objects drifting ashore from the west, and wide reading of academic geography in printed books. He was also influenced by the Italian humanist-geographer Paulo del Pozzo Toscanelli, who described the feasibility of a westward route to Asia. Although Columbus knew that the world was spherical, he underestimated its circumference and believed that Asia stretched some 30 degrees farther east than it really does, and that Ja-

Christopher Columbus. Reproduced from Paulus Jovius, *Eulogia Vivorum Illustrium* (Basel, 1575). COURTESY OF THE JOHN CARTER BROWN LIBRARY AT BROWN UNIVERSITY.

pan lay 1,500 miles east of the Asian mainland. Columbus estimated that the Canary Islands lay only 2,400 nautical miles from Japan, instead of the actual distance of 10,600 nautical miles. Neither Columbus nor anyone else in Europe suspected that two vast continents lay in the way of a westward passage to Asia.

Probably in 1485, on the basis of his miscalculations, Columbus tried to interest Dom JOÃO II of Portugal in his scheme for a westward passage to Asia, his "enterprise of the Indies." After assembling a learned committee to examine Columbus's ideas, the king turned him down, for unrecorded reasons, although he licensed other westward probes.

SPAIN BACKS COLUMBUS

Columbus left Portugal for Spain in 1485. After meeting Columbus early in 1486 at Alcalá de Henares, ISABELLA I of Castile and her husband, FERDINAND II of Aragon, appointed a commission to investigate the details of Columbus's plan. The spherical shape of the world was never in question. Although the commission disputed Columbus's flawed geography, the monarchs suggested that they might support him once they conquered Muslim Granada, and they even provided him with periodic subsidies.

During his years of waiting, Columbus established a liaison with a young woman in Córdoba, Beatriz Enríquez de Arana. In 1488, they had a son named Hernando, whom Columbus later legitimized. Hernando accompanied Columbus on his fourth transatlantic voyage and ultimately wrote a biography of his father.

In January 1492, during the final siege of Granada, Queen Isabella summoned Columbus to court. In the CAPITULATIONS OF SANTA FE, signed in April, the monarchs contracted to sponsor a voyage and to grant Columbus noble status and the titles of admiral, viceroy, and governor-general for any islands or mainlands he might discover.

THE FIRST VOYAGE, 1492–1493

Columbus secured the use of two caravels, the *Pinta* and the *Niña*, and a larger *nao*, the *Santa María*. With the help of Martín Alonso PINZÓN, a prominent local mariner and captain of the *Pinta*, Columbus gathered a crew of around ninety men, including three from the local jail. The three ships sailed from Palos on 3 August 1492. After repairs and reprovisioning in the Canaries on 6 September 1492, the fleet headed west into the open ocean, propelled by the northeast trade winds. The voyage went smoothly, with fair winds and remarkably little grumbling among the crew. On 12 October, at 2 A.M., the lookout on the *Pinta* saw a light; shortly after dawn the fleet dropped anchor at an island in what are now the Bahamas that local people called Guanahaní and that Columbus renamed SAN SALVADOR. Believing they were in Asia, the Europeans called the islanders "Indians."

The fleet sailed through the Bahamas and visited CUBA, seeking the vast commerce and rich ports of Asia. From Cuba, Martín Alonso Pinzón, without permission, sailed off in the *Pinta* to explore on his own. The two ships remaining with Columbus sailed to the island they named HISPANIOLA and explored its northern coast. On Christmas Eve 1492, the *Santa María* ran aground and broke up. Columbus founded a settlement, Villa de la Navidad, for the thirty-nine men he had to leave behind. Afterward Pinzón rejoined Columbus, and on 16 January the *Niña* and *Pinta* set sail for home with six captured Indians.

Columbus first tried a course directly east, but contrary winds forced him northward until he found winds blowing from the west. After a stormy passage, during which the caravels were separated, and a stopover in the AZORES, the *Niña* reached Lisbon on 4 March. Columbus paid a courtesy call to Dom João II and departed for Spain on 13 March 1493, arriving in Palos two days later. Pinzón brought the *Pinta* into port later that same day, having first landed at Bayona, on the northwest coast of Spain.

Isabella and Ferdinand received Columbus warmly in Barcelona in mid-April. They confirmed all his privileges and gave him permission for a second voyage. Columbus asserted that the Asian mainland lay close to the islands he had found.

THE SECOND VOYAGE, 1493–1496

The Spanish monarchs facilitated Columbus's colonizing effort, and the queen ordered that the native islanders be treated well and converted to Christianity. Columbus found 1,200 men to accompany him as settlers. On 3 November 1493, the fleet of seventeen vessels reached an island in the Caribbean that Columbus named Dominica, then sailed through the Lesser Antilles and the Virgin Islands, past Puerto Rico, to Hispaniola.

They found that the men left in La Navidad the previous January were all dead, most of them killed by the islanders. Columbus founded a new settlement, named Isabella for the queen, on a poor site without fresh water. He then began to enslave some of the islanders. According to Spanish law, if the local people peacefully accepted takeover by the Europeans, they were protected against enslavement as subjects of the Castilian crown, but if they made war, they could be seized as slaves. Some islanders were certainly at war against the Europeans, and Columbus used their resistance as a justification for outright conquest. He and his men marched through the island with horses, war dogs, and harquebuses, seeking gold through barter but conquering and taking captives when they met opposition.

In April 1494, leaving Hispaniola under the control of his brother Diego, Columbus took an expedition to explore the southern shore of Cuba, which he believed was part of the Asian mainland. He even made his crew members sign a document to that effect. Columbus's brother Bartholomew had arrived on Hispaniola during Columbus's absence and found the colony in chaos. Disappointed colonists returned to Spain on a fleet dispatched by Columbus in 1494 and spread stories about the Columbus brothers' misdeeds and ineptitude as administrators. The Spanish rulers sent out an investigator named Juan Aguado, who observed many deaths among the Amerindians, and disease and desertions among the Europeans. To defend his administration in person, Columbus departed for Spain on 10 March 1496, leaving Bartholomew in charge on Hispaniola. He reached Cádiz on 11 June.

THE THIRD VOYAGE, 1498–1500

Despite reports about Columbus's failings as an administrator, the monarchs confirmed his previous grants and gave him permission for a third voyage, with a *nao* and two caravels for exploration and three more caravels to carry provisions to Hispaniola, plus 300 men and 30 women as additional colonists, including 10 pardoned criminals.

Departing from Spain on 30 May 1498, Columbus took his three ships south to the CAPE VERDE ISLANDS before heading west, reaching the island of Trinidad on 31 July. He then sailed to the mainland of South America, realizing from the vast flow of water from the Orinoco River that he had encountered an enormous landmass, which he believed to be in Asia and near the Garden of Eden described in the Bible. After briefly exploring the coast of Venezuela, Columbus sailed on to Hispaniola.

Although Bartholomew had moved the main settlement from Isabella to Santo Domingo, the situation was in crisis. Some of the colonists had mutinied, the Indians were increasingly hostile, and neither Bartholomew nor Diego Columbus had been able to maintain order. Columbus himself had little better luck. Ferdinand and Isabella sent out Francisco de BOBADILLA to investigate and restore authority. He arrested the three Columbus brothers, seized their money, and sent them home in chains in December 1500. Columbus was summoned to court in Granada, but the monarchs delayed granting his request for reinstatement to his official posts.

Eventually Ferdinand and Isabella allowed Columbus to keep some of his titles and all of his property, but the titles were thereafter empty of authority. They also delayed granting him permission for another voyage. Instead, they began to establish a bureaucratic structure outside Columbus's control, appointing Nicolás de OVANDO governor of Hispaniola and dispatching a large colonization fleet. In March 1502 Ferdinand and Isabella finally granted Columbus permission for a fourth voyage.

THE FOURTH VOYAGE, 1502–1504

With Columbus and his son Hernando sailing on the flagship, a fleet of four rickety caravels with second-rate crews left Spain on 11 May 1502. Departing the Canaries on 25 May, they arrived at Hispaniola on 29 June, even though Columbus was specifically forbidden to land there. Columbus knew that Governor Ovando was about to send a fleet home and saw that a hurricane was brewing. He warned Ovando of the approaching storm and asked to anchor in the harbor. Ovando refused and ordered the fleet to depart, just before the hurricane struck. Twenty-five of the fleet's ships were sunk.

Thereafter, Columbus and his men spent much of the voyage sailing along the coast of Central America. Bad weather and adverse currents and winds kept the crews from learning much about the lands and peoples, and the hostility of local Indians forced them to abandon plans for a settlement in Panama. Unable to reach Hispaniola, Columbus landed in northern Jamaica and awaited rescue for a year. He sailed back to Spain, broken in health, and reached Seville on 7 November 1504, never again to return to the Indies.

LAST YEARS

Columbus struggled to have all his grants and titles restored. He remained a wealthy man, but he felt betrayed and slighted by his royal patrons. For their part, the Spanish sovereigns justified their withdrawal of support on the basis of Columbus's mismanagement. Colonial settlement had grown too complex for any one person to manage.

Surrounded by family and friends, Columbus died in

Valladolid in 1506, rich but dissatisfied. With the perspective of five centuries, we can recognize the extraordinary changes that resulted from his voyages. Instead of finding a new route to Asia, Columbus made the lands and peoples of the Western Hemisphere known to Europeans and set in motion a chain of events that altered human history on a global scale. The origin of many characteristics of the modern world, including the interdependent system of world trade, can be traced directly to his voyages.

COLUMBUS IN HISTORY AND MYTH

The myths surrounding Columbus make it difficult to put his accomplishments into their proper context. Often he is depicted as a perfect hero in advance of his time who conceived the idea of a spherical earth and had to fight traditional religious beliefs and prejudice before succeeding, and who died poor and alone. None of this is true. A product of his times, Columbus was strongly influenced by the powerful religious and economic currents of his day. In pursuit of profits, he established a slave trade in Caribbean natives, arguing that such slavery would allow them to be converted and reformed. Far from being oppressed by Christian beliefs, he hoped that some of the profits from his ventures would be used to recapture Jerusalem from the Muslims, in fulfillment of Christian prophecy. Neither the simple hero portrayed by generations of textbook writers nor the unredeemable villain depicted by some recent writers, Columbus was a complex human being who exemplified the virtues and the flaws of his time and place in history.

The most important primary sources dealing with Columbus are BARTOLOMÉ DE LAS CASAS, *Historia de las Indias*, edited by Agustín Millares Carlo, 3 vols. (1951); FERDINAND COLUMBUS, *The Life of the Admiral Christopher Columbus by His Son Ferdinand*, translated by Benjamin Keen (1959); CRISTÓBAL COLÓN, *Textos y documentos completos*, edited by Consuelo Varela, 2d ed. (1984); and OLIVER C. DUNN and JAMES E. KELLEY, JR., eds. and trans., *The Diario of Christopher Columbus's First Voyage to America, 1492–1493, Abstracted by Fray Bartolomé de las Casas* (1989). For a half century, the standard English-language biography, stressing the maritime facets of Columbus's career, was SAMUEL ELIOT MORISON, *Admiral of the Ocean Sea: A Life of Christopher Columbus,* 2 vols. (1942). A Spanish-language biography of the same period deserves to be better known: ANTONIO BALLESTEROS BERETTA, *Cristóbal Colón y el descubrimiento de América,* 2 vols. (1945). Since the 1940s, numerous scholars have added important new interpretations. A detailed biography on Columbus's life up to 1492 is provided by the Genoese historian and Italian senator PAOLO EMILIO TAVIANI, *Christopher Columbus: The Grand Design,* translated by William Weaver (1985).

ANTONIO RUMEU DE ARMAS has written many studies clarifying particular aspects of the Columbus story, including *Nueva luz sobre las Capitulaciones de Santa Fe de 1492* (1985). JUAN MANZANO MANZANO provides a detailed but not totally convincing study of Columbus in Spain before the first voyage, *Cristóbal Colón: Siete años decisivos de su vida, 1485–1492,* 2d ed. (1989); and, with ANA MARÍA MANZANO FERNÁNDEZ-HEREDIA, a lengthy study of Columbus's Spanish collaborators: *Los Pinzones y el descubrimiento de América,* 3 vols. (1988). MARVIN LUNENFELD, ed., *1492: Discovery, Invasion, Encounter: Sources and Interpretations* (1991), serves as an excellent introduction to the heated controversies surrounding the quincentenary. Based on the documents and recent scholarship, WILLIAM D. PHILLIPS, JR., and CARLA RAHN PHILLIPS place the actions of Columbus and the consequences of his voyages in the broad context of world history in *The Worlds of Christopher Columbus* (1992). *The Christopher Columbus Encyclopedia,* edited by SILVIO A. BEDINI, 2 vols. (1992), offers an array of articles on Columbus and his times.

WILLIAM D. PHILLIPS, JR.

COLUMBUS, DIEGO (Giacomo Colombo; *b.* ca. 1468; *d.* before 20 February 1515), youngest brother of Christopher COLUMBUS. He left Genoa to join Christopher in Spain and sailed with him on the second voyage to America. Described as amiable, virtuous, and peaceful, Diego had no instincts for seamanship, warfare, or administration. Nevertheless, Christopher's devotion to his brother led to Diego's appointment as president of a ruling council for Hispaniola during Christopher's absence on another voyage, a heavy responsibility for the young man. Francisco ROLDÁN, the ALCALDE MAYOR, offended at Diego's superior position, led the island's malcontents in rebellion. Christopher returned to find the colony in anarchy. He sought to bring about order by removing the hapless Diego, who was sent to Spain in February 1495 to defend Christopher against their enemies at court. Months later Diego returned to Hispaniola, endeavoring as best he could to assist his beleaguered brothers against rebellious colonists. In 1500 the concerned sovereigns sent Francisco de BOBADILLA as chief justice to pacify the island. Diego, by then governing in the port city of Santo Domingo, with uncharacteristic backbone defied Bobadilla, who clapped Diego in irons, along with his brothers, and shipped him to Spain. The same year Diego finally found his true vocation when he took holy orders. Although Christopher sought to obtain a bishopric for Diego from the queen, the request was denied on grounds of his foreign birth. In 1509 Diego made a brief visit to Santo Domingo, then returned to Seville, where he died.

FERNANDO COLÓN, *The Life of the Admiral Christopher Columbus by His Son Ferdinand,* edited and translated by Benjamin Keen (1959); TROY FLOYD, *The Columbus Dynasty in the Caribbean, 1492–1526* (1973).

WILLIAM L. SHERMAN

COLUMBUS, DIEGO (Diego Colón; *b.* ca. 1480; *d.* 1526), eldest son of Christopher Columbus. Following the death in 1485 of his mother, Felipa Perestrello, a Portuguese noblewoman, Diego was left by his father at the Franciscan friary of La Rábida (Spain) for education. In 1494, he began court life, attached to the infante Don

225

Juan, at whose death he became a page to Queen ISA-BELLA II, and later a member of her bodyguard. When Isabella died in 1504, Diego continued in crown favor, owing in part to his marriage to María de Toledo, a cousin of the king. At his father's urging, Diego endeavored for years to secure titles and financial rewards for the family, but with little success. In 1505, he sought appointment as governor and viceroy of Hispaniola, but having spent his years as a privileged courtier, and being still a young man who had not seen military action, he was judged too inexperienced to govern the ruffians in the Indies. On his father's death in 1506, Diego inherited the title Admiral of the Indies, and in 1509 the sovereign conferred on him the governorship he sought. In 1511, he was appointed viceroy of the islands as well, but not "of the Indies," as he had hoped. For fifteen years, Diego served as a capable governor of the turbulent islands. Though he continued to press for further honors and compensation for the Columbus family, he died with his hopes unfulfilled.

TROY FLOYD, *The Columbus Dynasty in the Caribbean, 1492–1526* (1973), contains many references to Diego. See also SAMUEL ELIOT MORISON, *Admiral of the Ocean Sea: A Life of Christopher Columbus,* 2 vols. (1942).

WILLIAM L. SHERMAN

COLUNJE, GIL (*b.* 1831; *d.* 1898), Panamanian jurist who spent most of his life in Colombia, where he became a senator. In his writings he often speaks against government corruption and injustice, which gained the admiration and respect of the people. He was repeatedly harassed by the government because of his ideas. Colunje held many government posts throughout his life. He served as minister of foreign relations, member of the Supreme Court, president of the Bank of Bogotá, and rector of the Colegio Mayor del Rosario. In 1865 he occupied briefly the presidency of the Sovereign State of Panama.

ERNESTO DE JESÚS CASTILLERO REYES, *Historia de Panamá,* 7th ed. (1962); JORGE CONTE PORRAS, *Diccionario biográfico ilustrado de Panamá,* 2d ed. (1986).

JUAN MANUEL PÉREZ

COMALCALCO, one of the westernmost Late Classic Maya sites, located near the coast of the Gulf of Mexico in the state of Tabasco, Mexico. Comalcalco is a huge site with many buildings, often set on platforms and noted for their corbeled roof vaults. These and other architectural features reveal a relationship to PALENQUE, to the east. Like Palenque, Comalcalco has elaborate tombs, one with 4-foot-high stucco figures of humans on each of its three walls, three figures per wall. Although some archaeologists have suggested these figures might represent rulers or aristocrats, Mayan customs suggest they represent the nine lords of the night and the underworld.

Although much of the art and architecture in the period 800–950 indicates Comalcalco was under the influence of Palenque, some features suggest northern Mexican, non-Maya influence. One of these is its gray or orange pottery with a distinctive fine paste and firing technique. This pottery, known as Fine Orange and Slate Ware, is a time marker for the period and seems to have been manufactured throughout the general region from Tampico in the north of Guatemala and Honduras in the south.

Although its architecture resembles that of Palenque in format and construction, Comalcalco has one very distinctive architectural feature—the use of flat, fired clay bricks. These bricks have a characteristic red color, and some have incised geometric designs, including possible hieroglyphs—a unique feature in the Maya lowland region.

F. J. SANTAMARÍA, *Las ruinas occidentales del Viejo Imperio Maya* (1933); GEORGE F. ANDREWS, *Comalcalco, Tabasco, Mexico: Maya Art and Architecture,* 2d ed. (1989).

RICHARD S. MacNEISH

COMANCHES, a Shoshonean tribe that migrated southward to the plains of Texas and New Mexico in the late seventeenth century. They represented the epitome of Plains Indian culture: they were master warriors and hunters on horseback. Comanche raids against northern Mexican settlements, missions, and the pueblos of New Mexico began in the mid-1700s; by the 1820s the Comanches were attacking towns and ranches as far south as Zacatecas. In 1786 a peace was negotiated between the Spanish and the Comanches that lasted into the late colonial era and in some cases through Independence. The fragmented nature of Comanche social organization, however, prevented the general observance of any peace treaty, and different bands continued to raid in northern Mexico.

The Comanches became valuable allies to the New Mexicans and some Texan settlements in the wars (ca. 1750s) against certain Apache groups, and the Comanches often allied with the Kiowas in their wars against the Apaches. Men known as *comancheros* traded between the New Mexicans and the Comanches and developed a lively commerce in guns, ammunition, supplies, stolen horses, and captives on the plains. However, as Anglo-Americans pushed into Texas in the 1860s, the Comanches raided deeper into Mexico. Ultimately, the increased number of westward-migrating Anglo settlers and ranchers prompted renewed Comanche warfare on the southern plains. As a result of the Red River War of 1874 between the U.S. Army and the Comanches and their Kiowa allies, the Comanches were forced to settle on small reservations in Oklahoma.

CHARLES L. KENNER, *A History of New Mexico-Plains Indians Relations* (1969); ELIZABETH A. H. JOHN, "Nurturing the Peace: Spanish and Comanche Cooperation in the Early Nineteenth Century," in *New Mexico Historical Review* 59, no. 4 (1984):

345–369; WILLIAM B. GRIFFEN, *Utmost Good Faith: Patterns of Apache-Mexican Hostilities in Northern Chihuahua Border Warfare, 1821–1848* (1988), chap. 9.

AARON PAINE MAHR

COMANDANTE ZERO. *See* **Pastora, Eden.**

COMARCA, a judicial district. A territorial subdivision within the Brazilian captaincies, the *comarca* was a judicial district composed of two or more counties. Ordinarily the *comarca* incorporated a district larger than a municipality. Usually there were two *comarcas* per captaincy. In the colonial period and the early empire, they were often sizeable. The *comarca* of São Francisco represented more than half of the territory of Pernambuco before it was ceded to Bahia. In 1720 Brazil was divided into three *comarcas*, with centers in Paraíba, Bahia, and Rio de Janeiro, each of which was headed by a *corregidor*. Pernambuco and all of Brazil north of it was under the jurisdiction of Paraíba, which served as a court of appeals for all the cases before the judges and *ouvidores* of Pernambuco, with further appeals and matters outside of Paraíban jurisdiction going to the Relação (High Court) in Lisbon. After the discovery of gold and diamonds in the interior, new *comarcas* were set up in Minas Gerais, Goiás, and Mato Grosso to see that the king's justice moved westward. Sudden shifts of population as a result of new mining discoveries made a visible judicial presence desirable. By the nineteenth century *juízes de direito*—district judges—were under central control. As instruments of royal justice and control, the *comarcas* brought law and order to frontier areas and contributed to the administrative incorporation of Brazil.

CAIO PRADO, JR., *The Colonial Background of Modern Brazil* (1967); FRANCIS A. DUTRA, "Centralization *vs.* Donatorial Privilege: Pernambuco, 1602–1639," in *Colonial Roots of Modern Brazil*, edited by Dauril Alden (1973); ROBERT M. LEVINE, *Historical Dictionary of Brazil*, translated by Suzette Macedo (1979), p. 59; *The Cambridge History of Latin America*, edited by LESLIE BETHELL, vol. 2 (1984).

PATRICIA MULVEY

COMAYAGUA, the former capital of Honduras (1985 est. pop. 30,700), located on a plain bearing the same name in a central valley. An agricultural center for cattle, sugarcane, and food staples as well as an economic link for the western portion of the country, Comayagua is also the name of the department, one of the first seven departments established in 1825. It boasts a broad agricultural valley as well as extensive pre-Columbian ruins.

Founded in 1537 as Valladolid de Santa María de Comayagua, the city participated in a celebrated rivalry with Tegucigalpa after silver deposits led to an expansion of the latter after 1578. Political and economic rivalry continued between the two cities throughout the colonial period, independence, annexation to Mexico, membership in the Central American federation, and the national period until the triumph of more Liberal Tegucigalpa over more Conservative Comayagua during the presidency of Marco Aurelio SOTO (1876–1881). Soto moved the capital to Tegucigalpa in 1880, after it had alternated several times between the two cities. The older Camino Real was replaced in 1970 by a highway linking the cities of San Pedro Sula, Comayagua, and Tegucigalpa and providing needed transportation infrastructure to an economy historically plagued by regional isolation.

JOSÉ REINA VALENZUELA, *Comayagua antañona, 1537–1821* (1968); STEVEN J. REIF, *Comayagua: A City in Central Honduras* (1980); LUIS MARIÑAS OTERO, *Honduras* (1983).

JEFFREY D. SAMUELS

COMECHINGONES, an ethnic group that, until the middle of the sixteenth century, occupied the mountainous region in what are now the central Argentine provinces of Córdoba and San Luis. The economy of the Comechingones was based on agriculture using irrigation. Their chief crops were corn, squash, beans, and chili peppers. The ALGARROBO (genus *Prosopis*), whose fruit they collected, served as another important resource. They also tended *auchenidos* (llama, alpaca, vicuña, and guamoco). The two most common linguistic variants of the Comechingones were Camiare and Henia, although different dialects existed. They lived in settlements consisting of as many as forty pit-dwellings, the bottom half of which were constructed underground. As protection, the settlement was surrounded by an enclosure made of thorny plants. Each settlement was home to a kinship group (probably similar to the Andean *ayllu*) and under the authority of a chief (*curaca*). There is almost no information available on the religious life of the Comechingones, except that during ceremonies they consumed cebil (genus *Anadenanthera*). Ceremonial dances took place inside branch enclosures that contained animal figures carved in wood. Documents testify that by the end of the sixteenth century the population, spread among some six hundred settlements, was perhaps 30,000. One hundred years later, due either to demographic shift, cultural homogenization, or interbreeding, Comechingones culture no longer existed.

CATALINA TERESA MICHIELI, *Los Comechingones según la crónica de Gerónimo de Bibar y su conformación con otras fuentes* (1985).

JOSÉ ANTONIO PÉREZ GOLLÁN

COMIBOL, the Mining Corporation of Bolivia (Corporación Minera de Bolivia). On 2 October 1952 the government of Víctor PAZ ESTENSSORO established Comibol as an autonomous public corporation. The government's objective was to centralize control over approximately

163 mines and mineral properties nationalized by the April 1952 revolution. In a short span, Comibol became the single most important source of foreign exchange for Bolivia. However, while Comibol subsidized nearly every other bureaucracy and allowed for spending in education and other areas, the government did not reinvest in the enterprise, thus allowing it to suffer a severe process of decapitalization.

Under the Nationalist Revolutionary Movement (MNR), the mine workers federation (Federación Sindical de Trabajadores Mineros de Bolivia—FSTMB) enjoyed worker comanagement in Comibol, a fact that accounted for slight improvements in working conditions but also both politicized the institution and eroded its finances. Efforts to end worker comanagement often led to violent confrontations between workers and the state. In 1964 the military coup that ended the MNR's twelve-year revolutionary experiment also terminated worker comanagement through outright repression. Over the course of the next eighteen years, several military governments attempted to downsize Comibol through the use of force, periodically stationing troops in mining districts to prevent worker unrest.

Military repression failed to bring Comibol workers under control. Paradoxically, in 1985 Paz Estenssoro, the very person who had established Comibol, accomplished what years of coercion had not. In launching his New Economic Policy (NPE) he downsized Comibol considerably, firing 23,000 mineworkers and closing nonproductive mines. The NPE also called for the privatization and decentralization of Comibol.

MELVIN BURKE, *The Corporación Minera de Bolivia* (*Comibol*) *and the Triangular Plan: A Case Study in Dependency* (1987).

EDUARDO A. GAMARRA

See also **Mining.**

COMINTERN. *See* **Communism.**

COMMERCIAL POLICY

Colonial Brazil

From the beginning of its expansion down the coast of Africa in 1420, the Portuguese crown always drew a clear distinction between the free access it granted to foreign ships coming to the metropolis and adjacent islands (Madeira, Azores) via seas that had "long been open to all," and its prohibition on their entry into seas and adjacent coasts that it had recently discovered; unlicensed ships found there were subject to seizure. The coast of Brazil fell into the latter category; thus its commerce was, from the beginning, a monopoly reserved for the crown and its subjects.

Shortly after the discovery of Brazil in 1500, the Portuguese crown decided to lease out its monopoly rights there to a group of merchants led by Fernão de Loronha,

a naturalized Portuguese of Italian ancestry. This original lease lasted for three years, with the crown taking, in the final year, 25 percent of the proceeds. In 1506 the lease was renewed for another ten years upon payment of a lump sum, after which Brazilian trade was "royalized" and conducted by the crown for its own account via salaried *comisários* (agents).

With the definite decision in 1532 to settle Brazil, royal trade policy changed. Portuguese settlers, as well as metropolitan and foreign merchants, were allowed to trade freely with Brazil on condition of paying a 10 percent duty and securing royal licenses for the cargoes. Nonetheless, foreigners were compelled to channel their trade through the Portuguese inhabitants, who were the only persons authorized to deal directly with the Indians. Control was further tightened circa 1550 with the creation of *alfândegas* (customs houses) in most of the captaincies to collect crown duties.

Trade was conducted through a variety of ports both in Portugal (such a Lisbon, Oporto, Viana do Castelo, and Aveiro) as well as in Brazil (such as Recife, Bahia, Porto Seguro, Vitória, Rio de Janeiro, and São Vicente), although some commodities, such as brazilwood, had to go through the *Casa da Índia* (India House) in Lisbon, which acted as the crown agency for its monopoly trades. Varying duties, too complex to describe in detail, were levied on both exports and imports at points along the way: this was the primary benefit derived by the crown from the trade. Additional duties were added (and sometimes subtracted) from time to time. For example, in 1592, all import and export trade with Brazil carried a 3 percent ad valorem duty (the CONSULADO) to defray the expense of an armada to protect shipping to and from Brazil.

Portugal's primary problem during the sixteenth century and the first half of the seventeenth was the growth of illegal (unlicensed) trading in its empire by other European nations: primarily the French in the sixteenth century; the Dutch in the period 1590–1600; and the English intermittently throughout. After 1580, when PHILIP II of Spain became king of Portugal, the latter found itself swept up into the world conflicts of the House of Hapsburg. At war with the Dutch and the English, Philip closed all the ports of the Iberian Peninsula to their merchants (laws of 1591 and 1605). This drove the Dutch, in particular, to increase their direct trade with Brazil in order to secure the sugar that they had previously been able to acquire in Lisbon. After a short truce (1609–1621) the Dutch renewed their attack on Brazil with the occupation of BAHIA in 1624–1625 and the conquest of PERNAMBUCO in 1630–1654, which they gradually extended to all the other northern captaincies. Coupled with these losses, the Dutch also seized Portuguese slave stations in Africa. PIRACY at sea also increased after 1625, leading to severe losses until Portugal finally severed its connection with Spain in 1640 and signed a truce with the Dutch in 1641, leading to peace in 1661.

In 1649 the Portuguese crown chartered, on the Dutch

model, a joint-stock company that was to control trade and protect commerce via a system of fleets between Portugal and its colony. About the same time, a series of commercial treaties was negotiated with the nations that had been the main interlopers in Portugal's imperial trade monopoly—with the English in 1642, the Dutch in 1661, and the French in 1667. Due to the ambiguous language used, these treaties permitted those nations extensive, though ill-defined, rights to trade within the Portuguese Empire.

During the next century, Portugal attempted to control and profit from its Brazilian commerce more via the establishment of monopoly companies than through the earlier policy of a blanket prohibition on unlicensed foreign shipping. In 1755 a company was created to monopolize the trade with the northern area of Brazil (Grão-Pará and Maranhão), and in 1759 a similar company was established to revitalize the SUGAR trade with Pernambuco and PARAÍBA.

Throughout the colonial era Portugal used the products of its empire to balance its trade with the exterior. It achieved this in the period up to 1570 with pepper from India and, from circa 1570 to 1670, with sugar exports from Brazil. The decline in the latter near the end of the seventeenth century, at least partly due to the establishment of competing plantations by the English, French, and Dutch in the Caribbean, forced the crown to initiate a policy of industrialization to lessen Portugal's dependence on foreign imports. The discovery, however, of gold in Brazil circa 1690 again permitted Portugal to balance its trade with a colonial commodity, and the industrial policy was scrapped only a couple of decades after it was begun. When gold gave out at the end of the 1750s, Portugal once again turned to an industrial policy to lessen its dependence upon imports. In the sixteenth and seventeenth centuries, Portugal had not made any attempt to stifle the development of industry in Brazil; in fact, it had encouraged sugar refining there by prohibiting it in the homeland (1559), fearful that the process might consume so much wood that it would deforest the kingdom. At the end of the eighteenth century, however, Brazilian industry was seen as a threat to the exports of a newly industrialized Portugal, and was generally prohibited. Nonetheless, Brazil after 1770 found a new prosperity in a revived and diversified agriculture, much of which benefited Portugal itself, and the colonial period closed on a note of a general prosperity both in Brazil and in Portugal.

JOEL SERRÃO, ed., Dicionário de História de Portugal (1963). V. M. GODINHO, Ensaíos II: Sobre a história de Portugal (1978), pp. 295–315; JOSE GONÇALVES SALVADOR, Os Cristãos-Novos e o comércio no Atlântico meridional (1978), pp. 195 passim; LESLIE BETHELL, ed., The Cambridge History of Latin America (1984); FRÉDÉRIC MAURO, Portugal, o Brasil e o Atlântico, vol. 2 (1989), pp. 183–248.

HAROLD B. JOHNSON

See also **Captaincy System; Trade.**

Colonial Spanish America

The essential characteristic of Spanish commercial policy toward Spanish America throughout the colonial period was the firm belief that the benefits of commercial intercourse between metropolitan Spain and its empire should be reserved for Spaniards alone. The definition of "Spaniards" included American as well as peninsular Spaniards, but the needs and interests of the former were considered to be secondary to those of the Spanish monarchy and peninsular producers and exporters. This general policy was articulated in different ways, and with variable success, throughout the three centuries of Spanish rule in America. In the Hapsburg period it was built around the formal restriction of transatlantic trade to a single peninsular port (first Seville, subsequently Cádiz), and to a limited number of American ports in the Caribbean basin. (Moreover, intercolonial trade which might compete with that from Spain was restricted and sometimes prohibited.) In the eighteenth century the gradual introduction of free trade in the period 1765–1789 eventually permitted the major ports of Spain and Spanish America to trade directly with each other. Even in the late eighteenth century, however, the formal policy of excluding foreign ships from direct participation in the commercial exchange between the metropolis and its American dependencies was breached (by the grudging grant of permission for neutral ships to enter Spanish American ports) for only limited periods during the long French revolutionary wars, when Spanish ships were kept in port by British naval blockades. This monopoly, although undermined in practice by both CONTRABAND and the inefficiency of peninsular industry, was consistent with the commercial policies also implemented by Portugal, France, England, and Holland in their overseas empires, and thus reflected the general mercantilistic view that the ideal economic relationship between a European imperial power and its overseas territories was one in which the dependencies provided fiscal surpluses and raw materials for processing in the factories of the metropolis (and for re-export to third parties), and protected markets for its manufactured goods. In reality, for most of the colonial period the actual commercial relationships between Spain and Spanish America deviated considerably from this notional norm, partly because of the preponderance of bullion in exports from America (even in the late eighteenth century, when Spain first sought to exploit systematically America's agricultural potential, precious metals constituted almost 60 percent of the value of exports), and partly because of the related problem that the majority of the manufactured goods exported from Spain to America were produced not in the peninsula but in other European countries.

THE HAPSBURG COMMERCIAL SYSTEM

Spanish Mercantile Communities During the first five decades of Spanish discovery and exploration in America, the nature and the value of trade was determined in large measure by the rhythm of conquest, the seizure of the accumulated treasure stocks of native civilizations, and the steady export from Seville of the basic commodities (primarily flour, oil, and wine) that the settlers required for their subsistence, together with tools, weapons, animals, and building materials. Short-term fluctuations in the value of this trade were caused primarily by the availability of gold as a return cargo and by the state of Spain's relations with France. By the 1540s, the bonanza of native gold was over, and the more farsighted colonists were turning from looting and barter to the development of SILVER MINING, which was well-established at both POTOSÍ (in modern Bolivia) and ZACATECAS (Mexico) by 1550.

The decade of the 1550s was one of depression in the Indies trade, primarily as a consequence of Franco-Spanish hostilities. At the onset in the early 1560s there was a prolonged period of growth that gathered pace in the 1580s and 1590s and soared to its apex in the first decade of the seventeenth century before entering a period of gradual but inexorable decline that continued until the end of the seventeenth century. During the half-century of expansion up to about 1610—in 1608, the record year for westbound sailings, over two hundred ships left for America, and the two years that followed also saw very large fleets dispatched from Seville—despite occasional interruptions caused by, for example, the diversion of merchant ships to carry the ill-fated Spanish invasion force to England in 1588 and Francis Drake's attack on Cádiz in 1596, imports of American bullion reached record levels, averaging almost 7 million pesos a year in the 1590s, and, although tailing off slightly in the first quarter of the sevententh century, remained above 5 million pesos a year until 1630. Thereafter, for both external and internal reasons, including a clear tendency for a greater proportion of the output of the American mines to be retained in the empire to meet the soaring costs of defense, remittances fell sharply to an estimated average of 3.3 million pesos in the 1630s, 2.6 million pesos in the 1640s, and 1.7 million in the 1650s, before plunging to truly insignificant levels in the last two decades of the seventeenth century.

The Spanish Crown In the short term the Spanish crown was somewhat better protected from commercial decline in the seventeenth century than were the mercantile communities of Spain and America, for it was in the advantageous position of being able to increase taxation. In the long term, of course, resort to this device merely intensified the crisis by encouraging both fiscal fraud at the Spanish end of the system and outright contraband in the Americas. It is important to stress, however, that throughout the sixteenth century and for a substantial part of the seventeenth, the crown could rely upon the receipt of a secure, significant income from America, and succeeded in protecting both the sources of that wealth, its American possessions, and the commercial system that conveyed it to Spain from

the hostile attentions of emerging imperial rivals and their agents, both official and unofficial.

Throughout this period Seville served as the only port for trade to and from America. Although strongly criticized by eighteenth-century reformers, its monopoly (which was definitively transferred in 1717 to Cádiz, primarily as a consequence of the silting-up of the Guadalquivir River) reflected not an artificial privilege but a natural concentration of both administrative and commercial authority in the principal city of southwestern Spain, whose natural advantages included a secure port, a rich agricultural hinterland, and a sophisticated commercial-financial-artisan infrastructure capable of satisfying the needs of the rapidly developing American enterprise.

Casa de Contratación The defense of Spain's monopoly of American trade, and in the process the control of emigration, was based initially upon the administrative control over trade provided by the creation in Seville in 1503 of the CASA DE CONTRATACIÓN, or House of Trade. This powerful body combined a variety of commercial, political, scientific, and judicial functions, the majority of which it retained even after the formal establishment of the COUNCIL OF THE INDIES in 1524. The Casa registered every ship sailing to and from the Indies, organized convoys, trained pilots, made maps and charts, functioned as a post office and a receptory for royal treasure, and fulfilled important legal functions. From 1543 it worked closely with the CONSULADO, or incorporated merchant guild, of Seville, whose members—drawn from the city's leading commercial families—received from the crown a grant of a formal monopoly of the Indies trade in the form of an obligation to organize the financing and defense of periodic fleets.

Convoy System The organization of shipping into convoys protected by warships was a further key feature of the Hapsburg imperial commercial system that those instrumental in the BOURBON REFORMS were wont to criticize as a hindrance to commercial freedom and flexibility. The system again represented, at least in its origins, an institutionalization from 1564 of two natural devices for the protection of Indies shipping from both privateers and the naval forces of other European powers rather than the imposition from above of an artificial structure. From this date the *Carrera de las Indias,* or Indies trade, assumed the configuration that it was to retain until the WAR OF THE SPANISH SUCCESSION, without any significant structural modification other than an increasing practical inability to dispatch fleets on time, particularly in the second half of the seventeenth century, when there were frequently gaps of several years between them.

In principle two fleets a year sailed from Seville: the *flota,* which left in April for Veracruz (see FLEET SYSTEM), and the GALEONES, intended primarily to trade indirectly with the viceroyalty of Peru, which departed in August for Nombre de Dios—(superseded in 1598, after Sir Francis DRAKE and John HAWKINS sacked it, by

PORTOBELO) on the isthmus of Panama. The principal armed escort, the Armanda de la Guardia de la Carrera de las Indias, usually consisting of at least two and more commonly up to eight large, well-armed vessels, was never able to prevent attacks upon isolated ships or those involved in local Caribbean trade. The returning *galeones* were never plundered in their entirety, however, and the treasure of the New Spain *flota* was lost only once, when the Dutch privateer, Piet Heyn, captured it at Matanzas, on the north coast of Cuba, in 1628. The Armada de Barlovento, a separate squadron based in Puerto Rico, paid for by an increase in the rate of ALCABALA (sales tax) levied in New Spain and consisting of ships built in Havana, was established in principle in 1636. It succeeded in preventing another Matanzas but was incapable of curbing both the settlement of uninhabited islands and widespread contraband by Dutch, English, and French intruders. Similarly, the ARMADA DE LA MAR DEL SUR, although established too late to prevent Drake from seizing bullion worth 450,000 pesos off the coast of Peru during his 1577–1580 circumnavigation, succeeded thereafter in ensuring the security of silver fleets in the Pacific.

If on the whole the FLEET SYSTEM functioned effectively in its prime task of protecting transatlantic shipping and the subsidiary Pacific convoys that carried silver from ARICA (Peru) to CALLAO (Peru) and on to Panama, it also had the negative effects of constricting trade, both geographically and structurally, and failing to provide the commercial flexibility necessary to respond to the changing needs of American consumers and producers, particularly in the late seventeenth and early eighteenth centuries. In part, this inflexibility resulted from the restriction of transatlantic trade at the American end of the system to VERACRUZ, the isthmus of Panama, and to a lesser extent SANTO DOMINGO.

Contraband Trade Although both historical and geographical considerations made Panama, for example, the natural supply route for Peru and the return of its silver to Spain in the sixteenth century, the consequent failure of the crown and merchants alike to respond in the later Hapsburg period to the growth of contraband trade in the RÍO DE LA PLATA by legalizing trade with Buenos Aires starkly demonstrated the inflexibility of vested commercial interests. To a large extent this rigidity derived from not only legal restrictions but also the monopoly of trade within the American system enjoyed by the *consulados* of Mexico and Lima, incorporated in 1592 and 1593, respectively, along similar lines to that of Seville, with whose members the Mexican and Peruvian merchants enjoyed extremely close ties of business, friendship, and often family. For these merchants, whose capital and influence controlled the dispatch of fleets from Seville, the conduct of the trade fairs of Veracruz and Portobelo, and the subsequent transfer of merchandise to the warehouses of Mexico and Callao for distribution throughout New Spain and Peru, shortages of goods did not necessarily constitute a problem,

for scarcity guaranteed high prices and easy profits. In fact, the fundamental economic problem of the Hapsburg commercial system was that the merchandise required by American consumers increasingly could not be supplied in adequate quantities and at acceptable prices, not only because of the restrictionist attitudes of the monopolists but also because by the end of the Hapsburg period Spain possessed neither the productive capacity nor the initiative to satisfy even the basic needs of the American market.

Throughout America the perennial shortage of goods supplied through official channels, and the exorbitant prices charged for those which did arrive, induced American producers and consumers, particularly in areas remote from the viceregal capitals, to indulge in contraband with foreign ships, which sailed into the many unguarded harbors open to them along the Atlantic and Caribbean coasts, and local officials to turn a blind eye to and even participate in their illegal practices. Not surprisingly, Spain's clear inability to preserve the commercial integrity of its American possessions encouraged its imperial rivals to go beyond mere contraband to engage in selective territorial expansion, acquiring in the course of the seventeenth century Caribbean bases such as Jamaica and Saint Domingue, which built their prosperity upon both the smuggling and the production of sugar and tobacco for the European market.

THE BOURBON ERA

The advent of the Bourbon dynasty in 1700 brought the question of the reform of the American commercial system to the forefront of discussions about national regeneration from late-Hapsburg decline and the ravages of the War of the Spanish Succession (1702–1713). During the war only one trade fair was held at Portobelo (in 1708)—like that of 1713 it was a commercial flop, largely because licensed French merchantmen and contrabandists had saturated the market—although the five *flotas* dispatched in the same period to Veracruz enjoyed more success. In the short term the prospects for postwar commercial recovery were not strong, partly because of the grant in 1713 to the English South Sea Company by the *asiento* (contract) to supply slaves to Spanish American ports, and the supplementary right to send a merchant ship to each of the trade fairs attended by the *galeones* and *flotas*. Before their abolition in 1750, these privileges provided a smokescreen for widespread contraband activity. In the meantime, despite the clamor of influential writers such as José del Campillo y Cossío (1693–1744), minister of finance under PHILIP V, for a more liberal commercial structure, the crown—under pressure from the *consulados* of Cádiz, Mexico City, and Lima—limited structural change to the formal abolition in 1740 of the Portobelo fairs (the last of which was held in 1731) in favor of the use of individual register ships, an increasing number of which sailed to Pacific ports.

During the first half of the eighteenth century, registered Spanish trade with America grew modestly, primarily as a consequence of economic growth in America: the index of tonnage increased from a base figure of 100 at the beginning of the century to 160 in the period 1710–1747, and to 300 in the period 1748–1778. Despite this encouraging trend many commentators argued that the need for the abolition of the fleet system and the Cádiz monopoly remained urgent if contraband were to be curbed and major commercial growth secured. The crown considered further radical reform in 1754, but, under pressure from conservative forces, confirmed that biennial fleets would continue to be dispatched from Cádiz to New Spain: in fact, only six fleets sailed in the 1757–1776 period, and the majority found it very difficult to sell their cargoes in a market saturated by contraband goods. In the meantime, a new king, CHARLES III (1759–1788), and his advisers moved gradually in the wake of Spain's humiliating defeat in the final stages of the SEVEN YEARS' WAR (1756–1763) toward genuine structural reform, which culminated in the famous "Decree of Free Trade" of 1778.

Free Trade The principal features of the new Bourbon commercial policy were the decision in 1765 to open the Spanish islands in the Caribbean to direct trade with nine peninsular ports; the 1778 FREE TRADE ACT, which increased the peninsular ports licensed to trade to thirteen, and extended the new system to all of Spanish America except Venezuela and New Spain; and, finally, in 1789, the definitive admission of all Spanish America to the free trade system. Although these changes were radical, the slowness of their introduction reflects the durability of the Hapsburg system and the timidity of the Bourbon reformers. However, there is no doubt that the new system (which allowed Spanish and Spanish American ports to trade freely with each other but not with foreigners) ushered in a fourfold increase in the value of Spanish exports to America in the period 1782–1796, and an elevenfold increase in the value of the return trade. It was less successful in breaking the practical monopoly of Cádiz—which controlled 80 percent of this trade—and in promoting significant industrial growth in the peninsula: although there was some expansion in textile production in Catalonia, the principal beneficiaries of free trade in Spain were the agricultural and viticultural sectors.

In America, the results were more spectacular: although bullion continued to dominate exports to Spain (in the late eighteenth century its share fell from 76 percent of the value to 56 percent), the agricultural and pastoral economies of formerly neglected regions such as Venezuela, the Río de la Plata, and Cuba grew rapidly, as did that of New Spain.

This economic and commercial growth ground to an abrupt halt in 1797, following Spain's 1796 entry into what turned out to be a prolonged war against Britain. The crown's reluctant decision in November 1797 to allow trade to be conducted in the ships of neutral nations encouraged some vessels to test the British blockade of Cádiz, but the principal beneficiaries were North American merchants who brought foreign manufactures and foodstuffs to Spanish American ports, and returned directly to their home ports with silver, sugar, and other products rather than taking them to Spain. Aware of this abuse, the crown revoked the general grant of neutral trade in 1799, although it was subsequently forced to endorse its partial restoration, as local officials simply flouted the prohibition, citing wartime necessity as their excuse. Official Spanish trade made a brief recovery in 1802–1804, with the suspension of hostilities in Europe, and again picked up marginally in 1809–1810 and 1815–1816.

During the period 1797–1820 as a whole, however, the average value of exports from Spain to America was only 9 percent higher than in 1778. Throughout the last two decades of imperialism, CHARLES IV and FERDINAND VII refused consistently to introduce genuine free trade. The result was that the quest for the right to trade freely with the world at large was a major factor in persuading many Spanish Americans by 1810 that real commercial freedom could not be secured without political emancipation from Spain.

HUGUETTE CHAUNU and PIERRE CHAUNU, *Séville et l'Atlantique,* 8 vols. (1955–1956); VALENTÍN VÁZQUEZ DE PRADA, "Las rutas comerciales entre España y América en el siglo XVIII," in *Anuario de Estudios Americanos* 25 (1968): 197–237; ANTONIO GARCÍA-BAQUERO GONZÁLEZ, *Cádiz y el Atlántico (1717–1778),* 2 vols. (1976); GEOFFREY J. WALKER, *Spanish Politics and Imperial Trade, 1700–1789* (1979); LUTGARDO GARCÍA FUENTES, *El comercio español con América, 1650–1700* (1980); ENRIQUETA VILA VILAR, "Las ferias de Portobelo: Apariencia y realidad del comercio con Indias," in *Anuario de Estudios Americanos* 39 (1982): 275–340; JOHN R. FISHER, *Commercial Relations Between Spain and Spanish America in the Era of Free Trade, 1778–1796* (1985); JOSEP FONTANA and ANTONIO MIGUEL BERNAL, eds., *El "comercio libre" entre España y América (1765–1824)* (1987); PETER T. BRADLEY, *The Lure of Peru: Maritime Intrusion into the South Sea, 1598–1701* (1989); HECTOR R. FELICIANO RAMOS, *El contrabando inglés en el Caribe y el Golfo de México (1748–1778)* (1990).

JOHN R. FISHER

COMMUNISM. Virtually from its inception, the Communist International (Comintern) had affiliates in Latin America. The International Socialist Party (Partido Socialista Internacionalista) of Argentina—a dissident group that had broken away from the Argentine Socialist Party in January 1918—although unable to send a delegate to the founding congress of the Comintern, authorized the Italian Socialist Party to speak on its behalf at that meeting. It therefore regarded itself as a founding member of the International, and in 1920, in conformity with the requirement laid down by the Second Comintern Congress, changed its name to Partido Comunista.

Two years later, the Socialist parties of Chile and Uruguay joined the Comintern. At about the same time, a group of young anarchist trade unionists and intellectuals launched the Partido Comunista do Brasil. Former anarchists played a major role in founding the Cuban Communist Party. In the meantime, a Communist party had been organized in Mexico (1919), largely by foreigners, including Americans who had fled the World War I draft, the young Indian nationalist M. N. Roy, and the Japanese Socialist Sen Katayama. Roy represented that party at the Second Congress of the Comintern in 1920.

By the early 1930s, there were Communist parties in virtually all of the Latin American republics. In some cases, particularly in Central America, they were driven deep underground and virtually disappeared, to be revived in the somewhat more hospitable atmosphere of the mid-1940s.

The Latin American Communist parties followed all of the twists and turns of the line of the Comintern. When the Comintern adopted its "third period" position of extreme isolation and sectarianism, the Latin American parties followed suit. One result of this was the formation of separate, Communist-controlled trade union groups in each country where the Communists had any influence in the organized labor movement. In 1929 these groups were brought together in a congress to found the Latin American Trade Union Confederation (Confederación Sindical Latino Americana—CSLA).

When, after 1934, the Comintern switched from extreme isolation to support formation of "popular fronts," the Latin American parties again followed its lead. The best-known Latin American popular front was that established in Chile in 1936; it won the 1938 presidential election—although the Communists chose not to participate in the new government of Pedro AGUIRRE CERDA. In Mexico, the Communists regarded the coalition administration of President Lázaro CÁRDENAS as a version of the popular front. In Cuba, alliance with the dictator Fulgencio BATISTA was that island republic's version of popular frontism.

One important result of the adoption of the popular front line was liquidation of the CSLA and formation in 1938 of the Latin American Workers Confederation (CONFEDERACIÓN DE TRABAJADORES DE AMÉRICA LATINA—CTAL). It brought together union groups under the control of Communist, Socialist, and various other parties. By the Second Regular Congress of the CTAL in December 1944, the Communists dominated the organization.

When the Comintern line again veered toward isolation with the signing of the pact between the Soviet Union and Germany in 1939 and the beginning of World War II, the Latin American parties again adhered to the new line. Between September 1939 and June 1941, all the parties argued strenuously that World War II was an "imperialist" conflict in which the workers had no interest.

Then, after the Nazi invasion of the Soviet Union, the war suddenly changed its character for the Latin American Communists, as for the Comintern. In some instances, the sudden switch in line was embarrassing—the Uruguayan party suddenly had to change the theme of a large public meeting it had called for the day after the attack on the Soviet Union from one of opposition to the war to one picturing it as a crusade in which all workers were bound to support the Allies. During this second phase of World War II, the Communists gained much ground. Their policy of discouraging all trade-union militancy in the name of aiding the Soviet Union and its allies conformed to the policies of most of the governments of the area. They developed close relations with such pro-Allied dictators as Anastasio SOMOZA in Nicaragua and Manuel PRADO of Peru. Friendly relations with Fulgencio Batista continued.

During the latter part of World War II and the years immediately following, Communist influence reached its apogee in Latin America. The Stalinists were the largest group in the organized labor movement in the area, and Communists entered governments for the first time in Cuba, Ecuador, and Chile. However, during the most intense years of the Cold War, in the decade after 1948, Communist influence declined drastically in Latin America in general. Many workers and intellectuals who had earlier worked with or supported the Stalinists, turned against them. The Communists generally lost control of the labor movements of the various countries, and the Inter-American Regional Organization of Workers (Organización Regional Interamericano de Trabajadores—ORIT), with which the American Federation of Labor (AFL) and Congress of Industrial Organizations (CIO), then the AFL-CIO, were affiliated, and a Catholic-oriented regional group gathered most of the national union groups into their ranks, far surpassing the CTAL, which finally disappeared in the late 1950s.

One exception to the general decline of the Communists in the 1950s was Guatemala. There, during the administration of President Jacobo ARBENZ (1950–1954), the Communists, with the aid of the government, won complete domination of the labor movement, and Communists and their sympathizers held key posts in major government agencies, such as the Agrarian Reform Institute and the social security system.

One area of expansion of communism in the 1950s and for some time thereafter was the anglophone West Indies. As the countries of that area approached independence, Communist parties appeared in several of them. Most notable was the People's Progressive Party of Guyana, led by Cheddi Jagan, who was prime minister for some years preceding independence and remained in the opposition for a quarter of a century thereafter.

The advent of the Castro regime in Cuba early in 1959 opened a new chapter in the history of communism in Latin America. On the one hand, that government soon evolved into a self-proclaimed Communist regime and developed very close ties with the Soviet Union. On the other hand, the CUBAN REVOLUTION provoked the appearance of more or less serious rivals to the left of the orthodox Communists in a number of Latin American countries.

For a period in the 1960s, Fidel CASTRO courted and sought to bring together these far Left groups while snubbing most of the old Communist parties. To this end, he sponsored establishment of the Organization of Latin American Solidarity (Organización Latino Americana de Solidaridad—OLAS). At the same time, the far left groups followed Castro's lead and had his help in trying to organize guerrilla movements in several Latin American countries, including Argentina, Peru, Bolivia, Ecuador, Brazil, and Venezuela. Such guerrilla activities ran very much against the line then being followed by the Soviet regime, to which the old Communist parties remained loyal. Only in Venezuela did the orthodox Communists join the guerrilla effort; their withdrawal after a few years provoked a bitter polemic between them and Castro. Subsequently, virtually all the Communist Youth and a majority of the Communist Party members split away to form the Movement to Socialism (Movimiento a Socialismo), which forswore Marxism-Leninism.

The most notable of these Marxist-Leninist groups was the Sandinista National Liberation Front (Frente Sandinista de Liberación Nacional—FSLN) in Nicaragua, formed by dissident Communists in 1961, with the

Socialist poster from Havana. CENTER FOR THE STUDY OF POLITICAL GRAPHICS.

encouragement and aid of Castro. After years of desultory guerrilla efforts, it finally led the overthrow of the Somoza regime in 1979. It dominated the government from then until 1990, when it was defeated in an election. The FSLN professed Marxism-Leninism but was quite unorthodox. The traditional Communist party, the Nicaraguan Socialist Party (Partido Socialista Nicaragüense), was in the opposition throughout the Sandinista period in power.

During the 1960s, the old-line Communists faced another type of leftist rival, the Maoists. With the break between the Soviet Union and China, which began during the government of Nikita Khrushchev and was intensified for a time under Leonid Brezhnev, splits developed within a number of Latin American Communist parties—most notably in Bolivia, Peru, Brazil, Colombia, and Paraguay, and on a smaller scale in several other countries. These dissident parties preached—and sometimes practiced—a much more militant revolutionary policy than that being followed by the orthodox Communist parties. For several years they had strong encouragement from Mao Zedong and other Chinese leaders.

The zigzags of Chinese Communist Party and government policies in the 1970s, and the loss of interest by the Chinese party in fostering groups in its own image in other countries, largely deflated the Maoist movement. The most important survivors of it were the Partido Comunista do Brasil, which proved to have more influence with organized labor and the electorate than did the orthodox party following reestablishment of a democratic regime in the mid-1980s, and the Shining Path (Sendero Luminoso) in Peru, an offshoot of the original Maoist group there, which has been carrying on a violent guerrilla struggle since the early 1980s.

A third element that, by its own proclamation, is to the left of the orthodox Communists and has its origins in the Comintern is the Trotskyites. In several countries, Trotskyite parties of some significance had appeared in the 1930s, notably in Cuba, Bolivia, Mexico, Chile, and Brazil. Subsequently they languished, but since the 1960s, and particularly after the trend toward more democratic regimes in the 1980s, there has been a recrudescence of Trotskyism in Latin America. Parties capable of electing members of parliament appeared in Mexico, Bolivia, Peru, and Argentina; in Brazil, Trotskyites, working largely within the Workers Party (Partido dos Trabalhadores), have gained some trade-union influence and have elected state and local legislators.

The more democratic atmosphere that emerged in most Latin American countries in the 1980s made it possible for the Communist parties to operate much more freely than in the recent past. However, events in the Soviet Union and eastern Europe after the advent of Mikhail Gorbachev to power in the Soviet Union had a drastic negative impact on the Latin American old-line Communist parties. The Brazilian Communist Party declared that it had repudiated Marxism-Leninism, ran a national television program featuring its principal leaders explaining this shift (interspersed with pictures of the tearing down of the Berlin Wall), and called for formation of a new party of the democratic Left. The Uruguayan party ex post facto declared that it had been too subservient to the Soviet Union and had been wrong not to criticize negative situations there. Meanwhile, the Communist Party of Mexico had lost its independent identity, merging with other groups to form the Mexican Socialist Party (Partido Socialista Mexicano—PSM). The PSM itself merged with several other groups to form the Party of the Democratic Revolution (Partido de la Revolución Democrática) after the 1988 election.

Among the most decimated of Latin American Communist parties is that of Chile, long considered the Latin American Communist party most loyal to Moscow, which suffered not only from reverberations of Soviet events but also from its own misjudgments. Until the penultimate moment, the Chilean Communists isolated themselves from the united political forces seeking to end the dictatorship of General Augusto PINOCHET. As a consequence, for the first time since the early 1920s, the Communists failed to win even a single seat in the 1989 parliamentary election. Subsequently, the party suffered a major split, with many of its secondary leaders and major leaders of the Communist Youth abandoning not only the Communist Party but also the Marxist-Leninist ideology for which it stood.

By 1991, orthodox communism in Latin America was at a low ebb. Although the Cuban Communist Party and regime still professed strong loyalty to classical Marxism-Leninism in theory and practice, the movement was in crisis in the other countries of the area. The only country in which the Communist Party clearly dominated the labor movement was Uruguay, and the only other nations in which Communist trade-union influence was still appreciable were Chile, Peru, Bolivia, and Guyana. Although the People's Progressive Party finally returned to power in Guyana in 1993, with Cheddi Jagan as president of the Republic, the PPP had lost whatever Stalinist orthodoxy it originally may have possessed. Only in Bolivia, Peru, Venezuela, Costa Rica, and Guyana were clearly identified Communists elected to parliament. Most important of all, none of the orthodox Communist parties had been able adequately to explain to themselves and to their followers how the model that for more than six decades they had been following and trying to emulate, the Soviet Union, had collapsed so completely.

ROBERT J. ALEXANDER, *Communism in Latin America* (1957); ROLLIE POPPINO, *International Communism in Latin America: A History of the Movement 1917–1983* (1964); ROBERT J. ALEXANDER, *Organized Labor in Latin America* (1965), *Trotskyism in Latin America* (1973); BARRY CARR and STEVE ELLNER, *The Latin American Left from the Fall of Allende to Perestroika* (1993).

ROBERT J. ALEXANDER

See also **Labor and Labor Movements; Political Parties** under individual countries.

COMODORO RIVADAVIA, city of 128,837 (1991) inhabitants located on the Gulf of San Jorge, along the southern coast of CHUBUT province in Argentina. Named after the navy officer Martín Rivadavia, who charted the waters of PATAGONIA, it was founded in 1901 by Francisco Petrobelli as the port of exit for the products of Colonia Sarmiento, a settlement established a few years earlier on Lake Colué. Since 1907 petroleum extraction has transformed the small, isolated town into a major focus of population growth in Patagonia. The Argentine oil company YPF lodges most of its technical personnel in this city, and oil and gas production from the surroundings accounts for nearly 60 percent of Argentina's total. The petrochemical plant Petroquímica has developed heavy industries connected with oil in the suburb of General Mosconi, and Caleta Córdoba is the terminal from which petroleum is shipped to central Argentina. Comodoro Rivadavia also exports wool from the numerous sheep ranches (*estancias*) stretching over southern Patagonia and zinc and cement produced in the vicinity. In addition, Comodoro Rivadavia is an important defense center in southern Argentina and the site of the renowned Salesian college of San Juan Bosco.

LINO M. BUDINO, *Comodoro Rivadavia: Sociedad enferma* (Buenos Aires, 1971).

CÉSAR N. CAVIEDES

COMONFORT, IGNACIO (*b.* 1812; *d.* 13 November 1863), president of Mexico (1855–1858). Born in the state of Puebla, he pursued a military career from the period of the 1830s onward. After the war against the United States (1846–1848), he became the chief customs official in Acapulco and a close associate of Juan ÁLVAREZ, the CAUDILLO of Guerrero. Comonfort was one of the authors of the PLAN OF AYUTLA (1 March 1854), which began the military movement to oust Antonio López de SANTA ANNA from the presidency and put in place a Liberal government. He then traveled to the United States to raise funds for the war effort.

Returning to Mexico, Comonfort became the general in charge of operations in Jalisco and Michoacán. His mentor, Juan Álvarez, led the Ayutla Revolution to victory, became president in late 1855, and appointed his protégé his minister of war. Álvarez governed only briefly; Comonfort replaced him on 11 December 1855. A moderate Liberal, Comonfort tried to harmonize the demands of the radicals for rapid implementation of a reform program with the more gradual approach advocated by the moderates. He signed and promulgated the famous LEY LERDO (25 June 1856) calling for the alienation of church and municipal properties, written by his treasury minister Miguel LERDO DE TEJADA. He vigorously crushed a Conservative revolt in Puebla in early 1856 and he also promulgated the Constitution of 1857. By late 1857, however, he was concerned that the radicals were too influential and were leading Mexico into a civil war. He then conspired with Conservatives to bring them to power, an act that started the war he had hoped to avoid, the War of the Reform (1858–1860).

Comonfort left the presidency in early 1858, remained in exile in the United States until 1861, and then returned to Mexico. He was rehabilitated by the Liberals, given a commission, served in President Benito JUÁREZ's cabinet, and took an active role in confronting the FRENCH INTERVENTION. He was killed in a skirmish.

The following works are all by RAY F. BROUSSARD: "Ignacio Comonfort: His Contributions to the Mexican Reform, 1855–1857" (Ph.D. diss., University of Texas at Austin, 1959); "Comonfort y la revolucíon de Ayutla," in *Humanitas* 8 (1967): 511–528; "El regreso de Comonfort del exilio," in *Historia Mexicana* 16, no. 4 (1967): 516–530; and "Viduarri, Juárez, and Comonfort's Return from Exile," in *Hispanic American Historical Review* 49 (1969): 268–280. In addition, see ROSAURA HERNÁNDEZ RODRÍGUEZ, *Ignacio Comonfort: Trayectoría política, documentos* (1967).

CHARLES R. BERRY

COMPADRAZGO, a special bond between two social equals. Rooted in personal trust, *compadrazgo* is a relationship between individuals who rely upon one another for mutual support in times of need. *Compadrazgo* is not defined by social hierarchy (as in patron-client relations) or even necessarily blood or affinal relationship (birth or marriage); rather it is a "ritual" kinship.

Originally the term referred to the relationship between the sponsor and the candidate at the Catholic sacraments of baptism and confirmation. Medieval Catholic doctrine treated this ritually instituted kinship as identical to blood kinship and labeled marriages between participants "incestuous." Today only the sense of an intimate bond remains, not necessarily one created by a ritual or joint participation in a rite of passage. Sometimes used for in-laws, this bond is secondary to the primary pact of mutual help and trust.

SIDNEY W. MINTZ and ERIC R. WOLF, "An Analysis of Ritual Co-Parenthood (Compadrazgo)," in *Southwestern Journal of Anthropology* 6, no. 4 (1950):341–368; JULIAN PITT-RIVERS, *The People of the Sierra* (1954).

PATRICIA SEED

COMPADRESCO, a godparent relationship. *Compadresco* is a form of religious kinship in Luso-Brazilian Catholic society whereby a person acquires one or two godparents at baptism, confirmation, and marriage. By acting as a spiritual sponsor at baptism, the godparents (*padrinho* and *madrinha*) become coparents, assuming the responsibility of watching over the child's spiritual life and material well-being. In Brazil, as in other Catholic countries, the godparent relationship is taken very seriously and involves lifelong obligations including adopting godchildren in case of the death of their parents and awarding dowries. The *compadrio* ties allow families to strengthen and enlarge kinship links with wealthy individuals of higher social class. The *parentela* (kinship network) thus created is a vital institution in Brazilian society and politics. Since family counts for everything, a lone individual could be included in family groups by a favorable marriage alliance and godparent relationships. In colonial times the *compadrio* relationships helped ambitious families to secure favorable political positions and alliances with wealthy landowning and merchant families, thereby strengthening and reinforcing the existing *parentelas*. Social linkages were vital in colonial times, when the cycles of boom and bust could reduce even the wealthiest families to poverty. Slaves commonly sought godparents for their children from the free population and among their owners to aid in freeing their children.

SIDNEY W. MINTZ and ERIC R. WOLF, "An Analysis of Ritual Co-Parenthood (Compadrazgo)," in *Southwestern Journal of Anthropology* 6, no. 4 (1950): 341–368; A. J. R. RUSSELL-WOOD, *Fidalgos and Philanthropists: The Santa Casa da Misericordia of Bahia, 1550–1755* (1968); STEPHEN GUDEMAN, "The *Compadrazgo* as a Reflection of the Natural and Spiritual Person," in *Proceedings of the Royal Anthropological Institute* (1971), pp. 45–71; STEPHEN GUDEMAN and STUART B. SCHWARTZ, "Baptismal Godparents in Slavery: Cleansing Original Sin in Eighteenth-Century Bahia," *Kinship, Ideology, and Practice in Latin America*, edited by RAYMOND T. SMITH (1984), pp. 35–58.

PATRICIA MULVEY

See also **Compadrazgo.**

COMPADRITO, one of the most colorful figures in Argentine literature and music of the early twentieth century, the flashy urban dandy mentioned in TANGO lyrics. Usually of lower-class origin, the *compadrito* was familiar with the language and habits of the denizens of *la mala vida*, the easy—and often criminal—life of Buenos Aires. He rarely had a job, often bragged about exploits in which he had never participated, and tried to dress as if he were affluent.

Many Argentine intellectuals identify the *compadrito* as emblematic of the deleterious consequences of the urban transformation that made Buenos Aires unique. There, men no longer dressed as gauchos (cowboys) but instead put brilliantine on their hair, dangled cigarettes from their lips, wore hats that obscured their eyes, donned flashy scarves, and wore shoes with thick heels. This uniform separated these urban men from their rural counterparts and indicated their integration into a Europeanized modern city. The *compadrito*'s female counterpart was the dance-hall girl, often a prostitute. To middle- and upper-class critics of lower-class culture both social types were considered immoral. In fact, what the *compadrito* and the music-hall girl represented was the most marginal, yet visible, group of lower-class inhabitants: those who responded to the poverty and lack of well-paid work in Buenos Aires by turning to more remunerative, but less socially acceptable, activities.

ANDRÉS M. CARRETERO, *El compadrito y el tango* (1964); JORGE LUÍS BORGES and SILVINA BULLRICH, *El compadrito: Su destino, sus barrios, su música* (1968); FERNANDO GUIBERT, *The Argentine Compadrito*, translated by Eric Gibson (1968).

DONNA J. GUY

COMPANHIA GERAL. *See* **Trade: Colonial Brazil.**

COMPANHIA VALE DO RIO DOCE (CVRD), Brazil's state-owned iron-ore mining company, the world's largest such firm. In 1942 the first Getúlio VARGAS government (1930–1945) founded the Companhia Vale do Rio Doce to produce iron for the country's industrialization program. The founding charter restricts its operation to the exploration, extraction, beneficiation (turning minerals into metals), and marketing of iron ore. To become self-sufficient in industrial raw materials and reduce Brazil's reliance on external sources, the government chose to go into the mining business on its own. To that end, it founded the country's newest iron-ore reserve, in the Rio Doce valley in Minas Gerais, from which the company got its name.

One of the world's most profitable mining companies, CVRD has had a distinguished record of efficient management. It has successfully developed several mining projects, including Carajás, the world's largest iron mine, in southern Pará, in the Brazilian Amazon. With its ultramodern facilities, including a 450-mile railroad tying Carajás to the port of São Luís do Maranhão, CVRD exports its products to Western Europe, Asia, and the United States. Minerals from Minas Gerais are sent out through CVRD's Tubarão port of Espírito Santo, a world-class loading and unloading facility. Late in 1991, CVRD bought part of the privatized steel mill, Usiminas, thus diversifying its activities into downstream business.

WERNER BAER, *The Development of the Brazilian Steel Industry* (1969); JANET KELLY ESCOBAR, "Comparing State Enterprises Across International Boundaries: The Corporación Venezolana de Guayana and the Companhia Vale do Rio Doce," in *Public Enterprise in Less-Developed Countries*, edited by Leroy P. Jones (1982), pp. 103–127.

EUL-SOO PANG

COMPAÑÍA GUIPUZCOANA, a company established for the monopoly control of commerce between Spain and the province of Venezuela (1728–1785). From the beginning of the Spanish presence in America, commercial activity with the overseas provinces was controlled by the House of Contracts in Seville. After two centuries this system had not yielded successful results. Bureaucratic red tape, smuggling, conflicts of interest, supply problems, and diverse restrictions all led many subjects to propose the creation of private companies to deal with trade. It was not until the beginning of the eighteenth century and the ascendancy of the Bourbon dynasty to the Spanish throne that the lessons of the French concerning the benefits of a commercial monopoly began to be applied. The idea of creating a company responsible for commerce with the province of Venezuela grew in favor when Pedro José de Olavarriaga visited it from 1720 to 1721 and made a report on the conditions of commerce there, including the boom in Venezuelan cocoa and the obvious deterioration of trade between the province and Spain.

The Compañía Guipuzcoana was created with broad powers by the royal decree of 25 September 1728. In 1730 its first ships sailed, and its business was rapidly established. Three years later it declared a dividend, and its volume of trade was steadily rising. The *compañía* extended its area of activity to include Maracaibo in 1752. It achieved a substantial reduction in the price of cocoa, increased production, extended areas of cultivation, and increased the crown's revenues.

The formation of the *compañía* and its success caused great uneasiness in the province, however. ANDRESOTE's uprising in Yaracuy occurred between 1730 and 1733, and later the displeasure of the creole elite would be felt with greater force, since the *compañía*'s activities destabilized the business that the local merchants and harvesters had with other Spanish colonies.

In 1749 Juan Francisco de León, backed by a great number of notables and important cocoa growers, led a revolt against the *compañía*. Added to the discontent were accusations that the directors were benefiting illicitly by making private deals, by not paying dividends to shareholders, and by rendering inadequate accounts to the crown. All of this resulted in the convocation of a general junta to investigate the *compañía* and the imposition of severe restrictions upon it. A price-regulating junta was formed; the *compañía* was obliged to reserve up to one-sixth of its ships' capacity for use by the shippers of Caracas; and it was required to take on shareholders from Caracas and Maracaibo. When the intendancy was created in 1776, the *compañía*'s activities were subject to the control of the intendant, José de ABALOS. And in 1779, when war with England broke out, its business declined. By 1780 the *compañía* had lost its privileges, and in 1785 it was finally dissolved by the royal decree of 10 March.

ROLAND DENNIS HUSSEY, *The Caracas Company, 1728–84* (1934); EDUARDO ARCILA FARÍAS, *Economía colonial de Venezuela* (1946); RAMÓN DE BASTERRA, *Una empresa del siglo XVIII, los navíos de la ilustración: Real Compañía Guipuzcoana de Caracas y su influencia en los destinos de América* (1954); VINCENTE DE AMEZAGA ARESTI, *Hombres de la Compañía Guipuzcoana* (1963); and MERCEDES MARGARITA ÁLVAREZ FREITES, *Comercio y comerciantes, y sus proyecciones en la independencia venezolana*, 2d ed. (1964).

INÉS QUINTERO

COMPANIES, CHARTERED. Corporations formed through a grant by a sovereign power for the purposes of foreign trade. Proposals for the formation of trading companies within the Spanish empire abounded during the eighteenth century, and companies reached their heyday at mid-century. Principally directed at expanding trade between Spain and her American kingdoms, companies were established with varying degrees of success for trade with Honduras (1714); Caracas (1728); the Philippines (1733); Cuba (1740); Portugal (1746); Buenos Aires, Cartagena, Veracruz, and Panama (1747); and the islands of Santo Domingo, Puerto Rico, and Marguerita (1755). After negotiation between merchants and the crown, the king would typically issue a charter (*cedula real*) directing formation of a company for either exclusive or privileged trade with specific American ports. The charter would establish a starting capital and sometimes designate the number of years for which the contract was valid. Shares would then be sold and when the company had attained sufficient funds, business would begin.

The establishment of trading companies was influenced by Colbertian mercantilism, the philosophy and practice of state sponsorship of factories and monopolies to stimulate production, with two primary intentions in the Americas: to support a growing state apparatus and to keep out imperial rivals. The companies were an alternative to the fleet system, by which once a year, each of two treasure ship convoys left Spain at different times, one to Veracruz and the other to Terra Firme. By the early eighteenth century the fleet system was generally acknowledged to be seriously outmoded to the needs of empire. It was slow, costly, and because of its predictability, highly susceptible to PIRACY. Compounding these ills, the fleet system prevented Spain from maximizing the profits of empire, kept the colonies undersupplied, restrained the development of industry in Spain, encouraged contraband, and created powerful interest groups antithetical to the Bourbon, absolutist ideal.

Company formation was intended to increase trade in areas peripheral to traditional Spanish interests where contraband had flourished. These regions typically did not produce precious metals, but rather cash crops such as indigo, tobacco, and cacao. At the same time, companies theoretically would reduce the influence of merchant monopolies in Cádiz, Mexico, and Lima by expanding the number of ports open to trade. Companies further provoked opposition in the Americas by obliging colonists to sell produce for less and to buy imported goods for more than they had been accustomed to.

Despite opposition on several fronts, the monarchy was encouraged by the early success of the Compañía Guipuzcoana, or CARACAS COMPANY, which drove out foreign trade and eliminated the need for an annual subsidy from New Spain. Trade between Spain and the Americas did increase under chartered companies, but the success of the Caracas Company, which was created in 1728 and endured until 1784, was not repeated. Several companies never began trade after receiving char-

ters. Even those that achieved early success fell apart by the century's final quarter, because of internal dissension, corruption, and the beginnings of intercolonial free trade introduced in 1765.

ROLAND D. HUSSEY, *The Caracas Company, 1728–1784* (1934); CARMELO SAENZ DE SANTAMARÍA, "La Compañía de Comercio de Honduras, 1714–1717" in *Revista de Indias* 40 (January–December 1980); JORGE PINTO RODRÍGUEZ, "Los Cinco Gremios Mayores de Madrid y el comercio colonial en el siglo XVII," in *Revista de Indias* 51 (May–August 1991).

PHILIPPE L. SEILER

See also **Commercial Policy.**

COMPOSICIÓN, a procedure used in the Spanish Indies to settle legal disputes by payment of fees to the royal treasury. Initially, *composición* was used to legitimize or revoke titles to guardianships (ENCOMIENDAS) over the Indians in cases where the original title could not be produced by the holder (*composición de encomiendas*). Later it was used to validate landownership in cases of land seized, often illegally, from Indian communities by Spaniards or land occupied by colonizers as squatters for farming or cattle raising. Usually, after residing on the land for an appropriate time, the claimant asked authorities for a *composición* to validate his land title in return for a payment of a fee (*composición de tierras*).

The procedure was useful to Spaniards wishing to acquire native lands, particularly as Indian communities were decimated by disease or were moved to other areas away from their villages to be Christianized and thus unable to challenge the *composición*. Moreover, it provided the REAL HACIENDA (royal treasury) with revenues, and it also allowed foreigners to remain in Spanish America despite strong prohibitions against their presence there. In return for payment of a yearly assessment, approved aliens were permitted to remain in the Indies (*composición de extranjeros*) Foreign women and foreign priests were exempt from this levy.

Recopilación de leyes de los reynos de las Indias, 4 vols. (1681; repr. 1973), libro IV, título XII; leyes XV–XXI; libro IX, título XXVII: leyes XI–XXXI.

JOHN JAY TEPASKE

COMPUTER INDUSTRY. During the 1960s governmental agencies, banks, and large businesses became the first in Latin America to use U.S.-produced mainframe computers for internal control applications. By the early 1980s, over a dozen computer firms had established plants in Mexico by means of different business arrangements: Mexican majority ownership (e.g., Apple, Burroughs, Hewlett Packard, Honeywell), agreements with local manufacturers (NCR, Sperry), or retention of complete control, as IBM had in exchange for exporting 90 percent of production and distributing software in Spanish.

Brazil attempted to develop its own computer hardware industry in the early 1970s when potential computer manufacturers, including major banks and "frustrated nationalist technicians," lobbied the Brazilian military government to foster a national industry. They founded the Comissão Coordenodora dos Atividados de Processamento Electronico (CAPRE) in April 1972 and in July 1974 the first national company, Computadores e Sistemas Brasileiros, S.A. (COBRA), was formed to manufacture minicomputers. Beginning in 1977 the government prohibited imports of mini- and microcomputers, terminals, printers, other peripherals, and software, and severely limited foreign investment in these areas. In 1979 a new regulatory body, the Special Informatics Secretariat (SEI) replaced CAPRE and in 1984 the Informatics Law formalized the strict prohibitions already in effect. Beginning with the election of Fernando COLLOR in 1989, however, the government removed import prohibitions and lowered tariffs on foreign computers, peripherals, and software. In 1992, Brazil permitted the entry of foreign technology and capital, easier formation of joint ventures, and the establishment of wholly owned subsidiaries of foreign manufacturers, allowing the construction of American, European, and Asian plants.

The Brazilian experiment failed for the very reasons most Latin American nations have not tried to develop their own industries outside of implementing equipment import conditions and setting research and training standards to encourage local development. Domestic technology generation could not keep pace with global changes in the industry; neither national entrepreneurs nor the government could provide adequate resources for local technology and software development; computer users and manufacturers needed access to up-to-date technology at lower cost; and foreign manufacturers and governments, particularly the United States, exerted pressure to end piracy and copyright violation.

The advent of the microcomputer in the 1980s made computing affordable to smaller businesses and educational institutions in Latin America and created a market for locally produced software, as well as for the cheaper Asian personal computer (PC) "clones." Latin American computer users, especially those in rural areas, still contend with unreliable power supplies, the lack of trained support personnel, systems and documentation available only in English, difficulties in getting supplies and spare parts, and expensive imported equipment. Still, these problems have not prevented the adoption of computers; the few studies and reliable statistics show that in 1993, there were approximately 13 computers per 1,000 Mexicans, 6 per 1,000 Brazilians, and 2 per 1,000 Guatemalans, while the United States counted 265 computers per 1,000 citizens.

In 1990, the small Latin American market represented only 3.2 percent of the international revenues for U.S. software producers that dominate the PC-based systems software and programming markets worldwide. Brazil and Mexico are the two most important sources of software demand, followed by Argentina, Venezuela, and Chile. Since unauthorized copying of software by users and computer dealers is rampant, U.S. software producers have brought successful cases against dealers in Argentina and Mexico, and will probably bring tougher sanctions on a regional level in the mid-1990s. Meanwhile, on the applications side, there are hundreds of small software development companies that serve the needs of local clients according to demand in each country's marketplace.

Latin American telecommunications services are intimately related to regional computer software and hardware industries. Creating links to worldwide computer networks has been a slow process, mainly because of difficulties in obtaining reliable and cost-effective communications links from government-owned telephone companies. By the late 1980s, most of the traffic was email, based on personal computers and carried mainly on direct dial-up connections. The APC (Association for Progressive Communications), for example, established nodes in Brazil (Alternex), Ecuador, Nicaragua, and Uruguay. By the early 1990s, a growing number of countries (including Brazil, Argentina, Peru, Mexico, Costa Rica, and Chile) were linking up to the Internet and developing networks within their borders. In 1991, the Organization of American States launched its Hemisphere Wide Inter-University Scientific and Technological Information Network to foster the interconnection of academic computer systems throughout Latin America and the Caribbean, supporting efforts in the Caribbean (CUNet), Jamaica (JAMNet), Central America (RedCACyT), Argentina, Chile, and the Andean countries.

The information revolution is ending Latin American isolation, and has already affected revolutions of a different sort there. In 1995 it was widely reported that Sub-Comandante Marcos, leader of the Zapatista revolt in Chiapas, Mexico, plugs his laptop computer into cigarette lighter outlets in Jeeps to send messages worldwide. Cries for help, complete with President Ernesto Zedillo's FAX number, were spread through the Internet during an army crackdown, resulting in a deluge of communications at the Presidential Palace and perhaps a suspension in hostilities.

JUAN F. RADA, *The Impact of Microelectronics and Information Technology: Case Studies in Latin America* (1982); PAULO B. TIGRE, *Computadores brasileiros* (1984); LUIS CASTELAZO-MORALES, *The Microcomputer Industry in the U.S. and Opportunities in Mexico Professional Report*, The University of Texas at Austin, Graduate School of Business (August 1985); PETER B. EVANS, "State, Capital, and the Transformation of Dependence: The Brazilian Computer Case," in *World Development* 14, no. 7 (1986): 791–808; EMANUEL ADLER, *The Power of Ideology: The Quest for Technological Autonomy in Argentina and Brazil* (1987).

GRETE PASCH
JOSEPH STRAUBHAAR

COMUNERO REVOLT (NEW GRANADA), large-scale rebellion (March–October 1781) against colonial authority in what is now northeastern Colombia. On 16 March 1781, a crowd in SOCORRO, led by Manuela BELTRÁN, tore down an edict on new sales tax (*alcabala*) rates, one of a package of fiscal measures promulgated by the royal VISITADOR, Juan Francisco GUTIÉRREZ DE PIÑERES. Similar disturbances occurred in other towns in the region, and on 16 April leading figures of the Socorro elite endorsed the movement. One of them, Juan Francisco BERBEO, was named leader (*capitán*). The rebellious towns quickly organized a force of between 10,000 and 20,000 men to march on Santa Fe de BOGOTÁ, and in late May they arrived at Zipaquirá, just north of the viceregal capital. Viceroy Manuel Antonio FLORES was in Cartagena, and Gutiérrez fled the capital, leaving a junta under Archbishop Antonio CABALLERO Y GÓNGORA in charge.

Caballero traveled to Zipaquirá to parley with the rebels (and to exploit the substantial differences among them), and on 5 June Caballero and Berbeo agreed to a set of thirty-four articles—the CAPITULATIONS OF ZIPAQUIRÁ. These articles dealt with the full range of the northeasterners' complaints against the fiscal and administrative aspects of Bourbon reformism, including sales tax and head tax increases, restrictions on tobacco cultivation (the region's only viable cash crop), abuses of the liquor monopoly, the one-way flow of public monies to Bogotá, and others. Several of the articles called for improvements in the lot of Indians and free blacks, two groups whose numbers were insignificant in the movement's mestizo heartland—although Indians were more numerous in the neighboring provinces of Pamplona to the north and Tunja to the south, which were nominally part of the rebellion. (The Comunero revolt, it should be noted, was unrelated to the far more threatening and violent TÚPAC AMARU insurrection in Peru in 1780.)

After Berbeo and most of the *comuneros* returned home, Caballero and Flores promptly denounced the *capitulaciones* as null and void. After granting amnesty to the vast majority of the *comuneros*, including Berbeo and other elite leaders, Caballero then spent six months in the northeast, preaching obedience to royal authority and restoring many (though not all) of Gutiérrez's fiscal measures. Berbeo and other patricians were happy to avoid punishment for their involvement; plebeians, however dissatisfied, had to return to their precarious livelihoods. Only a small core of *comuneros*, led by José Antonio Galán, a small farmer from Charalá, continued the armed struggle. They were captured in October 1781, and Galán was executed along with three of his lieutenants in February 1782. The visible long-term consequences of the rebellion were slight, though subsequent viceroys took care to draw up defensive plans lest Bogotá again find itself threatened by *socorranos*.

For many decades the Comunero episode was practically unknown outside the Socorro region; only in 1880 did Manuel Briceño publish his study *Los comuneros* and a version of the *capitulaciones*. Like many Colombian historians after him, Briceño saw the movement as a precursor to independence, not just chronologically but programmatically as well. This idea has been effectively refuted by recent studies, which note that elites and plebeians gladly invoked the figure of the king against the abuses of his officials, a typical colonial gambit. However, authors differ as to the overall import of the demands codified in the *capitulaciones*.

John L. Phelan, in *The People and the King* (1978), argues that the rebellion reflected societal rejection of centralizing Bourbonist infringements upon local autonomy, whereas Mario Aguilera Peña, in *Los comuneros: guerra social y lucha anticolonial* (1983), emphasizes the importance of agrarian and other socioeconomic conflicts in Socorro. Given the dominant characteristics of Socorro society circa 1781—the relative autonomy of the region's smallholder/artisan majority, their increasingly tenuous economic situation, and the role of the fiscal system in ensuring the elite's viability—the power of a literalist view that takes the *capitulaciones* at face value should not be underestimated.

Besides the works cited above, see ANTHONY MC FARLANE, *Colombia Before Independence* (1993).

RICHARD STOLLER

See also **Bourbon Reforms.**

COMUNERO REVOLT (PARAGUAY, 1730–1735). The revolt originated in the long-standing hostility of Paraguayans to the Society of Jesus. Paraguayans coveted JESUIT lands, commercial privileges, and the monopoly on GUARANI labor in Jesuit MISSIONS. This hostility first appeared in the violence of the 1640s, when Bishop Bernardino de CÁRDENAS articulated Paraguayan grievances; it surfaced again during the incendiary governorship of José de ANTEQUERA Y CASTRO. Under Antequera, in 1724, Paraguayans routed a Guarani army from the missions, expelled Jesuits from their Asunción *colegio*, and remained largely unchastised when Antequera fled in 1725.

Although Paraguayans were relatively quiescent during the governorship of Martín de Barúa, resentment smoldered. Paraguayans disliked but accepted the return of the Jesuits to Asunción. In 1730 the appointment as governor of Ignacio de Soroeta, a client of Viceroy José de ARMENDÁRIZ, marqués de Castelfuerte, the jailer of Antequera and the restorer of the Jesuits to their properties in Asunción, roused Paraguayans to renew their resistance. Soroeta's pro-Jesuit associations goaded Paraguayans past the boundaries of good sense and overcame the counsels of local moderates and Jesuit partisans.

Bishop José de Palos, a Franciscan who supported the Jesuit position, was unable to soothe tempers. A shadowy figure named Fernando MOMPOX DE ZAYAS, a fugitive from Lima, encouraged rebellion. An acquaintance of Antequera's and a fellow prisoner in the viceregal jail in Lima, Mompox was a person to whom Jesuit writers and other critics of the rebellious Paraguayans ascribed inordinate influence. Modern Paraguayan patriots have suggested that he was a premature antimonarchist. The theory of natural rights that Mompox supposedly revealed to Paraguayans held that political authority was vested in the people, or *común* (thus *comuneros*), and they delegated it to the monarch. This view of the limited powers of kingship was reactionary, not revolutionary. It was an approach to monarchy predating eighteenth-century absolutism, and it flourished in provincial Asunción, where men treasured the exploits of the heroes of the sixteenth century.

Paraguayans in 1731 expelled Soroeta from the province, incidentally condemning to death Antequera in Lima. Some Paraguayans, whose leadership centered on the Asunción *cabildo*, created the *junta gobernativa*, a

Engraving by Rodríguez after a drawing by Urdaneta, representing a comunero of 1781.

committee that hoped to direct the province. Although offensive to royal authority, this body was not a truly revolutionary creation. Its aim was to rival the city council. Direction of the insurrection came from the Asunción elite. For a time, the *alcalde ordinario* José Luis Barreiro, who expelled Mompox from the province, directed local affairs. Leadership then fell to Miguel de Garay and the former Antequera partisan Antonio Ruíz de Arellano. In 1732, Paraguayans again expelled the Jesuits from Asunción, showing the continuity between earlier uprisings and the 1730s. In July 1733, Governor-designate Manuel Agustín de Ruiloba y Calderón, another Castelfuerte appointee, arrived in Paraguay. Paraguayans shot him. The elderly bishop of Buenos Aires, Juan de Arregui, who was visiting the province, then served briefly as governor. Unable to command respect, he departed. Cristóbal Domínguez de Obelar, a Paraguayan *encomendero* and local magistrate, took charge of the government until 1735, when pacification of the province again fell to Buenos Aires governor Bruno Mauricio de Závala, who was more repressive than when he had suppressed the earlier insurrection in 1725. He sentenced to death four leaders of the uprising, ordered thirteen exiles, removed municipal officials from their posts, and prohibited public meetings.

Later interpreters have followed the argument of Father Pedro LOZANO, the Jesuit chronicler of the revolt, who wished to discredit Paraguayans by picturing them as radicals. Many twentieth-century authors have also seen the rebellion as a precursor to modern revolutions, which it was not. Its leaders never pursued revolutionary goals. They saw themselves as patriots loyal to the Spanish monarchy. Nevertheless, present-day Paraguayans cherish the memory of the *comuneros* and consider them patriots and precursors of independence.

ANTONIO ZINNY, *Historia de los gobernantes del Paraguay* (1887); PEDRO LOZANO, *Historia de las revoluciones de la provincia del Paraguay*, 2 vols. (1905); CARLOS ZUBIZARRETA, *Historia de mi cuidad: Etopeya de la Asunción colonial* (1964); JAMES SCHOFIELD SAEGER, "Origins of the Rebellion of Paraguay," in *Hispanic American Historical Review* 52, no. 2 (1972): 215–229; ADALBERTO LÓPEZ, *The Revolt of the Comuneros, 1721–1735: A Study in the Colonial History of Paraguay* (1976).

JAMES SCHOFIELD SAEGER

CONCEPCIÓN, CHILE, capital of the central Chilean province of the same name and of the BÍO-BÍO region. With a population of 306,464 (1990) inhabitants, including the sister port city of Talcahuano, it is the third-largest urban center of the country after Greater Santiago and Valparaíso–Viña del Mar. Concepción was founded by Pedro de VALDIVIA in 1550 as a stronghold against the MAPUCHE Indians of the Bío-bío region. After being repeatedly destroyed by earthquakes, tidal waves, and Indian attacks, the city was established in its present location on the northern margin of the Bío-bío River in the eighteenth century. During colonial times it developed into a strong, independent power that used its strategic location and proximity to the sea to challenge Santiago for its position as capital city. Between 1858 (when coal was discovered in Lota) and 1940, Concepción and its surroundings became a bustling industrial center (textiles, steel mill, glass factories). It is also the location of the University of Concepción. During the 1960s and 1970s the active militancy of students and workers converted Concepción into the most powerful political stronghold of the Left.

INSTITUTO GEOGRÁFICO MILITAR, "La región del BioBio," in *Geografía de Chile,* vol. 30 (Santiago, 1986).

CÉSAR N. CAVIEDES

CONCEPCIÓN, PARAGUAY, city founded 31 May 1773 by Spanish colonel Agustín Fernando de Pinedo y Valdivieso on the east bank of the Paraguay River, 193 miles north of Asunción, to dominate the MBAYÁ INDIANS, to contain the Portuguese, and to explore the *yerbales* (agricultural prospects) between the rivers Jejúi and Apa. It remained a small town, with the population increasing from 44 families and three military companies in the 1780s to 2,768 in 1846, 14,640 in 1950, 18,232 in 1962, and 22,866 in 1982.

Although Concepción was laid out in the Spanish rectangular pattern, its commerce was concentrated around the port. The town was a center of the yerba trade in the eighteenth century, and by 1864 it boasted lime and brick factories, several general stores, and half a dozen *pulperías* (grocery stores). It exported YERBA MATÉ, QUEBRACHO, lumber, and cattle, and it protected the northern frontier with Brazil. From 1826 to 1831 the town served as a place of exile for Europeans, Corrientinos, and Paraguayans who questioned the authority of dictator José Gaspar de FRANCIA. Although the region lost population during the War of the TRIPLE ALLIANCE (1864–1870), its northern position protected it from destruction, though not from declining prosperity after the war. Because Concepción opposed General HIGÍNIO MORÍNIGO in the 1947 civil war, it suffered neglect from both General Alfredo Stroessner and the Colorado Party.

NATALICO OLMEDO, *Album gráfico de Concepción* (1927), deals with both the province and the city between 1870 and 1925. GUILLERMO A. CABRAL GIMÉNEZ, *Semblanzas de Concepción* (1970), while including historical material from the colonial period to 1970, is inclined to concentrate on political issues post-1870. See also JOHN HOYT WILLIAMS, *The Rise and Fall of the Paraguayan Republic, 1800–1870* (1979), esp. pp. 12, 56, 60, 67, 77, and 217–218, the best available nineteenth-century history.

VERA BLINN REBER

CONCHA, ANDRÉS DE LA (*b.* ca. 1554; *d.* after 1612), painter and architect. Born in Seville and trained there in the mannerist style, possibly under Peter Kempeneer, Concha went to New Spain in 1567, with a contract to execute the main RETABLO at Yanhuitlán. Among the many works by Concha referred to in documents, numerous paintings and altarpieces were for the Dominican order in Oaxaca and Mexico City. A good number survive, such as the panels at Yanhuitlán, Coixtlahuaca, and Tamazulapán. In addition, the paintings that were formerly attributed to the "Master of Santa Cecilia" are now credited to Concha. Concha was named *maestro mayor* of the cathedral of Mexico City in 1601, and most of his activity after that year was architectural. This lends weight to a recent hypothesis that there were two artists of the same name, one a painter and the other an architect.

JOSÉ GUADALUPE VICTORIA, "Sobre las nuevas consideraciones en torno a Andrés de la Concha," in *Anales del Instituto de investigaciones estéticas* 50, no. 1 (1982): 77–86.

CLARA BARGELLINI

CONCHA, JOSÉ VICENTE (*b.* 21 April 1867; *d.* 8 December 1929), president of Colombia (1914–1918). A member of the Conservative Party's traditionalist, or "Historical" wing, Concha, a native of Bogotá, became a critic of the Nationalist regime of Miguel Antonio CARO (1892–1898). In 1900 he conspired with fellow Historicals and with members of the Liberal Party to overthrow Nationalist President Manuel Antonio Sanclemente. The plotters replaced Sanclemente with José Manuel MARROQUÍN, who headed the government until 1904. Concha served as Marroquín's minister of war, and in 1902 was sent to Washington, D.C., to conclude negotiations on the HAY–HERRAN TREATY.

Concha was a leader in the struggle against the authoritarian regime of President Rafael REYES, whose five-year term (1904–1909) is known in Colombian history as El Quinquenio. Concha's term as president coincided with World War I, during which Colombia remained neutral in the face of U.S. pressure to declare war on Germany. Philosophically committed to administrative decentralization, to laissez-faire economics, and to a nonpartisan political style, Concha was frequently praised by leaders of the opposition Liberal Party.

Following his presidency, Concha served in the Colombian Senate, taught university courses, wrote literary essays, and authored legal treatises, especially in the areas of penology and constitutional law. He served as Colombia's minister to the Vatican under President Miguel ABADÍA MÉNDEZ (1926–1930). He died in Rome.

See the essay by JUAN LOZANO Y LOZANO on José Vicente Concha in Lozano's *Ensayos críticos* (1934). For additional information see DAVID BUSHNELL, *The Making of Modern Colombia, a Nation in Spite of Itself* (1993).

JAMES D. HENDERSON

See also **Colombia: Political Parties.**

CONCILIAÇÃO, the program of conciliation and unity adopted by the ministry of the Marquês de PARANÁ

(1853–1856). Two developments motivated the concili-ação program. First, party politics established in Brazil during the 1840s generated a factionalism that polarized and corrupted public life while stultifying the administrative system. Second, industrialization and the growth of infrastructure in Europe and the United States had created a sense of backwardness among educated Brazilians. Abolition of the slave trade with Africa and a burgeoning coffee economy generated a sense of optimism and a willingness to experiment. As interpreted by the Paraná ministry, *conciliação* meant a government willing to employ all men of talent, regardless of previous party allegiance. The associated term *melhoramentos* (improvements) referred to the construction of a modern infrastructure both physical (e.g., railroads) and social (e.g., mass education). This twofold program proved difficult to implement. The political goals were too vague to generate broad and solid support, while the creation of a national infrastructure required a mobilization of resources and a reordering of society more sweeping than the ministry could accept. The personal prestige and authority of the Marquês de Paraná alone kept the cabinet and its policies functioning, so that his death in September 1856 effectively ended this experiment in conservative reformism.

RODERICK J. BARMAN

CONCORDANCIA (1931–1943). Formed in the wake of the Revolution of 1930, the Concordancia was a coalition of three political factions that shared power during Argentina's Infamous Decade: the National Democratic Party, the Independent Socialist Party, and the Anti-Personalist wing of the Radical Civic Union. The most important of the three was the Anti-Personalists, who had two of their members—José Agustín JUSTO (1932–1938) and Roberto ORTIZ (1938–1940)—elected president. During the Concordancia, opposition groups faced electoral fraud, censorship, and repression. With opponents effectively blocked from national politics, coalition members pursued policies that protected the conservative interests of the Argentine elite. Through the Great Depression and into World War II, its governments used a blend of economic orthodoxy and pragmatism, including reduced spending, exchange controls, and trade promotions, to protect agriculture and preserve Argentina's foreign markets. When political divisions and economic challenges crested during World War II, the military removed the coalition from power in June 1943.

MARK FALCOFF and RONALD H. DOLKART, eds., *Prologue to Perón: Argentina in Depression and War, 1930–1943* (1975); MARÍA DOLORES BÉJAR, *Uriburu y Justo: El auge conservador, 1930–1935* (1983).

DANIEL LEWIS

See also **Argentina: Political Parties.**

CONCORDAT OF 1887, a treaty (31 December 1887) between the Colombian government and the Vatican that regulated church-state relations in that country for more than five decades. It gave the Roman Catholic church a privileged position in the religious and educational life of Colombia.

The negotiation of a concordat was authorized by the Constitution of 1886, which established a regime dominated by Conservatives eager to undo the anticlerical policies of their Liberal predecessors. Ratified by the Colombian Congress in 1888, the concordat declared Catholicism the religion of the nation. While public authorities were to protect the Catholic church and ensure that it be respected, the church was to enjoy complete freedom and independence from the state, including the right to own property. The president of Colombia was given a major voice in the nomination of archbishops and bishops, however. The concordat also stipulated that religious instruction was to be compulsory in all educational institutions and that marriage in accordance with the Catholic rite was to be valid for civil purposes. Subsequent conventions (1892, 1902) regulated the power of the church in other areas, such as the control of cemeteries and mission fields.

After 1930 the slow but perceptible waning of Catholic influence in Colombia led to limitations on the powers of the church through constitutional reform (1936) and the signing of new concordats (1942, 1973). Further erosion of the church's position was made likely by the adoption of the Constitution of 1991, which guaranteed the equality of all religions before the law and forbade compulsory religious instruction in public schools.

J. LLOYD MECHAM, *Church and State in Latin America*, rev. ed. (1966), esp. pp. 115–138.

HELEN DELPAR

CONCRETISM, a term incorporating a broad panoply of Brazilian neovanguardist movements in the plastic arts and in literature launched in the 1950s and active through the 1970s. The term "concrete," drawing on "concrete music" of the early European musical vanguards, refers in Brazilian poetics to a rigidly simplified and exteriorized structure of composition based on the mathematical, graphic, and spatial awareness of artistic language as object. It also came to refer to a syncretic tradition of literary innovation in the art of representation, exemplified by certain modernist writers such as Stéphane Mallarmé and Ezra Pound. Brazilian concretism is largely circumscribed and defined by the Poesia Concreta (Concrete Poetry) movement of São Paulo, with its international and universalizing dimensions, that has proved to be highly influential on subsequent literary theory and production.

The constructivist, rationalist, and mathematical structures in the geometrical abstractionism of Max Bill and Eugen Gomringer at the I BIENAL DE SÃO PAULO in 1951 influenced the formative phase of Brazilian neovanguard groups in the plastic arts. Abstract Brazilian art was exhibited by the Grupo Ruptura at the São Paulo Museum of Modern Art in 1952, followed by the I Exposição Nacional de Arte Abstrata (Petrópolis, 1953), the Grupo Frente de Artistas Plásticos (Instituto Brasil-Estados Unidos/Rio de Janeiro, 1954), and the first Exposição Nacional de Arte Concreta at the Museum of Modern Art (São Paulo, 1956). The definitive launching of the concrete aesthetic as a polemical, experimental movement occurred at the Exposição Nacional de Arte Concreta at the Ministry of Education in Rio de Janeiro (4–11 February 1957). Later concretist groups include the short-lived neoconcretism of Rio de Janeiro, Mário Chamie's "poema praxis," and Waldimir Dias Pino's "poema processo."

The concrete poems of São Paulo provided concretism with an extensive theoretical apparatus and many literary works published in their magazines *Invenção* and *Noigandres* in the 1950s and later codified in *Teoria de poesia concreta* (1965; Theory of Concrete Poetry). Viewing their work as a continuation of experimentalism and aesthetic modernization, of which João CABRAL DE MELO NETO's *O engenheiro* (1945; The Engineer) is a credible predecessor, the Paulista concrete poets—Décio Pignatari, Haroldo de Campos, and Augusto de Campos, with the participation at different times of Ronaldo de Azeredo, Edgar Braga, José Lino Grünewald, José Paulo Paes, Dias Pino, Ferreira Gullar, and others—defined concrete works as the "tension of word-objects in space-time" and sought to relate concrete poetry to international graphic and representational trends. Supporting theory includes a synthetic chronology of texts by such diverse figures as Mallarmé, Pound, James Joyce, Paul Klee, e. e. cummings, William Carlos Williams, Anton von Webern, and Karlheinz Stockhausen.

At the same time, through its rejection of discursive writing and its radical revision of artistic form through semiotics, concrete poetry took a position in the open debate of the early 1960s on national literary values, particularly the role of experimental art in underdevelopment. Poetry was to embody the constructive rationality and the aesthetic sensibilities of the concrete city. After 1968, concrete poetry sought association with the Tropicália counterculture movement in popular music and with the anthropophagic critical metaphors of modernist writer Oswald de ANDRADE. Critical dimensions are present in many of the most widely read and cited poems: Pignatari's "Beba Coca Cola" (Drink Coca Cola set to music by composer Gilberto MENDES); Augusto de Campos's "Luxo lixo" (Luxury garbage); and Haroldo de Campos's "Servidão de passagem" (Passageway).

Recovery of a Brazilian literary tradition of innovation and translation of world poetry are two complementary areas of concretist production. The poetry of Oswald de Andrade, Sousândrade, and Pedro Kilkerry was republished with critical studies, while selected works of Joyce, Pound, cummings, William Blake, and troubadour poets, Dante, and others were translated into Portuguese.

Brazilian concrete works can be found in such English anthologies as MARY ELLEN SOLT, ed., *Concrete Poetry: A World View* (1968), and EMMET WILLIAMS, ed., *An Anthology of Concrete Poetry* (1967). For scholarly views, see DOUGLAS THOMPSON, "Pound and Brazilian Concretism," *Paideuma* (Winter 1977): 279–294; CLAUS CLÜVER, "Languages of the Concrete Poem," in *Transformations of Literary Language in Latin American Literature,* edited by K. David Jackson (1987), pp. 32–43. The theoretical texts are reunited in AUGUSTO DE CAMPOS, DÉCIO PIGNATARI, and HAROLDO DE CAMPOS, *Teoria da poesia concreta,* 2d ed. (1975). Summaries of concretist movements can be found in the Concretism issue of *Revista de cultura: Vozes,* no. 1 (1977), and in IUMNA MARIA SIMON and VINICIUS DANTAS, *Poesia concreta* (1982).

K. DAVID JACKSON

See also **Art; Literature; Modernism.**

CONDÉ, MARYSE (née Boucoulon; *b.* 11 Feb. 1937), Guadeloupean writer and teacher. After studying in Guadeloupe and Paris, Condé taught in Guinea, Ghana, and Senegal for twelve years. Returning to Paris in 1972, she began a doctoral thesis and helped produce her first play, "Le morne de Massabielle." Condé complained that her early novels were badly received in the Caribbean and Africa, but she enjoyed wide success with the first volume of her trilogy, *Ségou,* distributed by a French book club in 1984. *Moi, Tituba sorcière . . .* received the Grand Prix Littéraire de la Femme in 1987.

Condé writes of the search for Caribbean identity. She has become an influential commentator on questions of the triple colonization of Caribbean women in sexist, racist, and colonialist cultures. She also writes novels for young people.

The Hills of Massabielle (theater, 1972), translated by Richard Philcox (1991); *La mort d'Oluwémi d'Ajumako* (theater, 1972); *Hérémakhonon* (novel, 1976), translated by Richard Philcox (1982); *La civilisation du bossale* (essay, 1978); *La parole des femmes: Essai sur des romancières des Antilles de langue française* (essay, 1979); *Ségou,* vol. 1, *Les murailles de terre* (1984), translated by Barbara Bray as *Segu* (1987); *Ségou,* vol. 2, *La terre en miettes* (novel, 1985), translated by Linda Coverdale as *The Children of Segu* (1989); *Moi, Tituba sorcière . . .* (novel, 1986), translated by Richard Philcox as *I, Tituba, Black Witch of Salem,* 1992; *La vie scélérae* (novel, 1987), translated by Victoria Reiter as *Tree of Life* (1992); *Pension des Alizés* (theater, 1988); *Traversée de la mangrove* (novel, 1989); *Les derniers rois mages* (novel, 1992).

See also VÈVÈ CLARK, "I Have Made Peace with My Island: An Interview with Maryse Condé," in *Callaloo* 12:1 (1989), 85–133; ANN ARMSTRONG SCARBORO, *I, Tituba, Black Witch of Salem,* pp. 187–227; *Callaloo* 15:1 (1992), special issue on the literature of Guadeloupe and Martinique, edited by Condé.

CARROL F. COATES

CONDE D'EU. *See* **Gastão d'Orléans.**

CONDOR, large vulture that feeds mainly on carrion. *Gymnogyps Californicus,* the California condor, is found in the mountains of southern California. It is extremely endangered, with only eighty-eight individuals surviving as of 1994. Its body is about 50 inches long, and it has a bald yellow head. The bare, reddish neck is circled by a black feathered ruff. There are white feathers on the underside of the wings.

Vultur gryphus, the Andean condor, found in the Andes from Venezuela to the Strait of Magellan, is threatened with extinction. The body length varies from 52 to 63 inches, and the wingspan can be up to 10 feet. A bald, reddish, crest-crowned head tops a bare, reddish neck circled by a white feathered ruff. There are white feathers on the wings.

Both species have long, powerful, hooked beaks. Their bodies and wings are covered by dark gray feathers. All species of condor are strictly protected.

ERWIN PATZELT, *Fauna del Ecuador* (1989), pp. 60, 61; FRANCESCO B. SALVATORI, *Rare Animals of the World* (1990), p. 156.

RAÚL CUCALÓN

CONFEDERACIÓN DE TRABAJADORES DE AMÉRICA LATINA (CTAL), a regional labor organization that was formed by union delegates from twelve Latin American nations in Mexico City in September 1938. Vicente LOMBARDO TOLEDANO, the Marxist leader of the Confederación de Trabajadores de México (CTM), served as president throughout the life of the organization. The CTAL sought to end exploitation of the working class, promote democracy, obtain political and economic autonomy for Latin America, and join the popular front movement against international FASCISM. The CTAL brought together national labor organizations of diverse political orientations, including Communists, socialists, Auténticos, and Apristas.

The CTAL's influence and hemispheric labor unity deteriorated in the postwar period. Argentina's Confederación General de Trabajadores (CGT) withdrew in 1944 to create a rival, Peronist regional labor organization Agrupación de Trabajadores Latinoamericanos Sindicalistas (ATLAS). The CGT's withdrawal and the heightened influence of Communists in several national labor confederations led to Marxist domination by the time of the CTAL's December 1944 Congress. The CTAL joined the leftist World Federation of Trade Unions (WFTU) in 1945. Noncommunist labor groups abandoned the CTAL to join the Confederación Inter-Americana de Trabajadores (CIT), established in 1948 with support from the American Federation of Labor. Even Toledano's own CTM left the CTAL and expelled Toledano from the CTM in 1948. CTAL influence waned throughout the 1950s, and the confederation officially dissolved in 1962.

MOISÉS POBLETE TRONCOSO and BEN G. BURNETT, *The Rise of the Latin American Labor Movement* (1960), pp. 134–139; ROBERT J. ALEXANDER, *Organized Labor in Latin America* (1965), esp. pp. 246–248; VICTOR ALBA, *Politics and the Labor Movement in Latin America* (1968); HOBART A. SPALDING, JR., *Organized Labor in Latin America* (1977), pp. 255–256.

STEVEN S. GILLICK

See also **Labor and Labor Movements.**

CONFEDERATES IN BRAZIL AND MEXICO. After the American Civil War, thousands of former rebels fled the South, seeking new homes in Latin America. Because of proximity and a welcome from Emperor MAXIMILIAN, Mexico attracted many settlers, among them a number of well-known ex-Confederates, including oceanographer Matthew Fontaine Maury; Generals Joseph Shelby, Sterling Price, J. B. Magruder, and Thomas C. Hindman; and former governors Isham G. Harris of Tennessee and Henry W. Allen of Louisiana. Confederate émigrés scattered across Mexico, but Córdova and the Tuxpan region were the two most important areas of settlement. For most emigrants, settlement in Mexico was of brief duration because of the political turmoil attendant upon Maximilian's overthrow in 1867, the hardships of pioneering, and the lack of capital. British Honduras (now Belize) and Venezuela also attracted ex-Confederates, but the country which received the most Confederate emigrants, a conservatively estimated 2,500 to 4,000, was Brazil.

Former rebels who settled in Brazil feared the onset of a harsh Reconstruction in the United States and dreamed of rebuilding their plantation way of life. Prior to the war, Matthew Fontaine Maury had propagandized for the settlement of fertile lands in Brazil. In 1865 and 1866 emigrant agents toured Brazil, made arrangements to purchase land and bring settlers, and wrote enthusiastic books and letters on the prospects of settlement. Former leaders of the Confederacy and the Southern press were hostile, however, viewing emigration as abandonment of the South.

The peak years of emigration were 1867 and 1868. Since most *confederados* lacked adequate means for settlement, Brazil's attraction was a liberal immigration policy with good land offered at prices as low as twenty-two cents an acre and mortgages payable in five equal installments. Equally important was the presence of SLAVERY and cheap labor in general. There were four distinct areas of rural settlement: 200 pioneers located at SANTARÉM on the Amazon River 500 miles from the coast; 50 or more families settled at Lake Juparana (the Rio Doce settlement) 30 miles from the coast and 300 miles north of Rio de Janeiro; 150 families formed a community on the Juquiá River near Iguape, some 100 miles south of São Paulo; and some 75 families located in a cluster of communities (Retiro, Campo, and Villa Americana) in the Santa Barbara area, 80 to 100 miles northwest of São Paulo. After clearing land and planting, most settlers soon failed because of their remoteness from markets and lack of transportation and capital. Disillusioned, they moved on to São Paulo and Rio, or returned to the United States. By the mid-1870s most had abandoned rural life, and Brazil's two largest cities had the greatest numbers of remaining *confederados*, the most successful of whom were doctors, dentists, and engineers.

The only successful rural settlement was Americana. Located 30 miles from a rail line to São Paulo, Estação or Villa Americana, as it was first called, was initially a cotton-growing settlement; settlers later switched to other crops, among them the Georgia rattlesnake watermelon, which they introduced to Brazil. The *confederados* of Americana tried to maintain a ''Southern way of life,'' but by the third generation they had become Brazilianized. Today Americana is a city of 160,000 where descendants of the first settlers still celebrate the Fourth of July and the Fraternidade Descendência Americana meets quarterly at the American Cemetery to remember the past.

PETER A. BRANNON, ed., ''Southern Emigration to Brazil: Embodying the Diary of Jennie R. Keyes, Montgomery, Alabama,'' in *Alabama Historical Quarterly*, 1 (Summer 1930): 74–75, (Fall 1930):280–305, (Winter 1930): 467–488; LAWRENCE F. HILL, ''The Confederate Exodus to Latin America,'' in *Southwestern Historical Quarterly*, 39, no. 2 (October 1935): 100–134, no. 3 (January 1936):161–199, no. 4 (April 1936):309–326; BLANCHE HENRY CLARK WEAVER, ''Confederate Emigration to Brazil,'' in *Journal of Southern History*, 27, no. 1 (February 1961):33–53; ANDREW R. FOLLE, *The Lost Cause: The Confederate Exodus to Mexico* (1965); BELL J. WILEY, ''Confederate Exiles in Brazil,'' in *Civil War Times Illustrated*, 15 (January 1977):22–32; EUGENE C. HARTER, *The Lost Colony of the Confederacy* (1985); WILLIAM CLARK GRIGGS, *The Elusive Eden: Frank McMullan's Confederate Colony in Brazil* (1987).

CARL OSTHAUS

CONFEDERATION OF THE EQUATOR, a separatist movement in Northeast Brazil in 1824. Reaction by provinces in Brazil's Northeast to the dissolution of the 1823 Constituent Assembly by Dom PEDRO I is usually cited as the main cause for the rebellion, although others point to the political ambitions of rebel leaders, especially Manuel de Carvalho Pais de Andrade. Andrade, a member of the governing junta in 1824, issued a series of proclamations renouncing Dom Pedro's control and establishing a republic called the Confederation of the Equator. Royal troops commanded by Brigadier Francisco de Lima e Silva, supported by a five-ship armada under Lord Thomas COCHRANE, attacked the port city of Recife, Pernambuco. The revolt, however, spread to the provinces of Paraíba, Rio Grande do Norte, and Ceará, provoking further fighting in those areas. Several principal leaders, including the famous Frei Joaquim do Amor Divino Rabelo e CANECA, editor of the newspaper, *O Tífis Pernambucano*, were captured, tried, and executed. Others, including Pais de Andrade, who took

refuge aboard a British naval vessel, escaped to the exterior. Order was reestablished in the area by Francisco de Lima e Silva by 1 December 1824. Andrade later (7 March 1825) was permitted to swear allegiance to the Imperial Constitution and reenter public life with an appointment as senator from Pernambuco.

SÉRGIO BUARQUE DE HOLANDA, ed., *Historia geral da civilzaçao brasileira*, vol. 1, pt. 1 (1962), pp. 227–237; *Dicionário de história do Brasil* (1973), pp. 474–475; E. BRADFORD BURNS, *A History of Brazil*, 2d ed. (1980), pp. 168–169.

ROBERT A. HAYES

CONFERENCE OF LATIN AMERICAN BISHOPS (CELAM) emerged in 1955 as an initial step toward modernizing the structures of Latin American Catholicism. The major function of its various departments has been to promote communication across national lines by means of conferences, training institutes, and publications. The General Conferences of CELAM held at Medellín, Colombia (1968), and Puebla, Mexico (1979), are important milestones in the recent history of the Latin American church.

The Medellín conference, the agenda of which was heavily influenced by a small group of progressive Latin American clergy and by the modernizing tendencies of the Second Vatican Council (1962–1965), began an effort to apply the principles of Vatican II to Latin America. Medellín established the importance of the church's addressing contemporary socioeconomic realities, endorsed new pastoral practices, and marked the emergence of the new, distinctly Latin American ''theology of liberation.'' These changing perspectives had a great impact on the religious and political life of Latin America. First, they reoriented a significant part of the Catholic clergy and hierarchy away from its former preoccupation with the needs of the elite and the preservation of the status quo. Second, they promoted the power and participation of the lay Catholic masses in both religious and political affairs.

The 1979 Puebla conference reflected the influence of more conservative forces, which had assumed control of CELAM in 1972. While there was some slowing of the process of change associated with Medellín, the bishops nevertheless reaffirmed their earlier positions and stressed their commitment to a ''preferential option for the poor.''

A General Conference held in 1992 in Santo Domingo, Dominican Republic, generally reaffirmed the positions taken at Medellín and Puebla. Most notably, the bishops emphasized the ''preferential option for the poor,'' singling out the needs of indigenous groups, African Americans, and peasants. They also focused energy on new concerns, including the role of women in the church, ecology, and the rapid expansion of fundamentalist Protestantism in Latin America.

No single book is devoted to CELAM. EDWARD L. CLEARY, *Crisis and Change: The Church in Latin America Today* (1985), and PHILLIP BERRYMAN, *Liberation Theology* (1987), both do an excellent job of presenting CELAM and its work.

BRUCE CALDER

See also **Liberation Theology.**

CONGADA (also called congado or congo), a Brazilian folk dance and music form of African, Portuguese, and Spanish origin. First observed among African slaves during the late seventeenth century, the congada is a processional dance, fusing elements of Iberian popular drama and Catholicism with African indigenous ceremonies. Dressed as members of the royal court, the participants of the congada enact such themes as military victory and the crowning of Queen Nginga Nbandi of Angola.

While the congada is indigenous to central and southern Brazil, the congo is found in the northern sections of the country. Because women were historically excluded from participating in the congo, the coronation theme has centered around King Henrique. In the congo procession dancers sing to the sounds of drums, *chocalhos*, *pandeiros*, and violas.

Congadas are observed during the Christmas season and are often enacted throughout the year depending upon region and symbolic significance. Although the congada originated among African slaves, it has been known to include Indian participants who have incorporated their own native dances. According to scholars the congada, despite its distinctly African thematic and stylistic influences, is a uniquely Brazilian art form; no performances of the congada have been found on the African continent.

GILBERT CHASE, *The Music of Spain*, 2d rev. ed. (1959); DAVID P. APPLEBY, *The Music of Brazil* (1983); CHRIS MC GOWAN and RICARDO PESSANHA, *The Brazilian Sound: Samba, Bossa Nova, and the Popular Music of Brazil* (1991).

JOHN COHASSEY

CONGREGACIÓN, a forced resettlement program, also known as *reducción*. As a result of the pestilence and population mobility unleashed by the Spanish conquest of the Americas, many previously densely populated regions were depopulated. As the system of colonial administration developed in the sixteenth century, the Spanish recognized the need to consolidate widely scattered native populations in nucleated villages for ease of control. Thus, from the decade of the 1570s throughout the rest of the colonial period the Spanish regularly instituted *congregación* programs.

Three resettlement programs have received considerable scholarly attention. The earliest of these was the program initiated by don Francisco de TOLEDO, viceroy of Peru, in the 1570s. Later, from 1599 to 1604, there was an extensive program in New Spain. The last was initiated by JESUIT missionaries in the region of modern-day Paraguay in the eighteenth century.

The *congregaciones* aided Spanish missionaries and crown officials. Yet the policy had serious disadvantages for the Indians, including loss of land, disruption of traditional political and social ties, and an increased susceptibility to disease. On the positive side, some have argued that the Jesuit settlements protected the natives of Paraguay from mistreatment at the hands of colonists and slave raids of the Portuguese.

HOWARD F. CLINE, "Civil Congregations of the Indians of New Spain, 1598–1606," in *Hispanic American Historical Review* 29 (1949): 349–369; GUILLERMO FURLONG CARDIFF, *Misiones y sus pueblos de Guaraníes* (1962); FRANCISCO SOLANO, "Política de concentración de la población indígena: Objetivos, proceso, problemas, resultados," in *Revista de Indias* 36, nos. 145–146 (1976): 7–29.

JOHN F. SCHWALLER

See also **Aldeias; Missions, Jesuit.**

CONGRESS OF APRIL 1813, an important meeting convened in the headquarters of José ARTIGAS on 5, 6, 13, and 20 April 1813, during the second siege of Montevideo, at which for the first time Artigas fully expressed his federalist ideas. Artigas had returned from his "Exodus," that is, the emigration that resulted from the Montevideo and Buenos Aires peace accord. The Constituent Assembly that was meeting in Buenos Aires to determine the fate of the provinces that had belonged to the Viceroyalty of Río de la Plata solicited Artigas to send delegates. As requested, he convened the Congress of April, also known as the Congress of Three Crosses, for the place near Montevideo where it was held (near the present-day Hospital Británico).

Artigas maintained that the Constituent Assembly must be recognized "by agreement" and not "out of obedience." The conditional clauses for recognizing the provinces in question were drawn up, along with a set of instructions the six delegates were to take to the Assembly. The delegates were rejected by the Assembly on technicalities, the real reason perhaps being the federalist character of their proposals, which ran contrary to the "unitarism" or "centralism" of Buenos Aires. Despite Artigas's efforts to appeal, the delegates were again rejected. The opposition of unitarism and federalism remained a clearly defined cause of the revolution in Río de la Plata. Artigas attempted to reach an agreement with General José RONDEAU, commander of the forces of Buenos Aires in the second siege of Montevideo, but the confrontation between the two factions was by then inevitable.

JOHN STREET, *Artigas and the Emancipation of Uruguay* (1959); WASHINGTON REYES ABADIE, *Artigas y el federalismo rioplatense* (1974); WASHINGTON REYES ABADIE and ANDRÉS VÁZQUEZ ROMERO, *Crónica general del Uruguay,* vol. 2 (1984).

JOSÉ DE TORRES WILSON

CONI, EMILIO R. (*b.* 1854; *d.* 3 July 1928), one of Argentina's pioneer public-health physicians. Born in Corrientes in 1854, he attended medical school at the University of Buenos Aires during the 1870s and became well known in the medical community for his many statistical articles about diseases and mortality rates. Coni also published numerous books, including his autobiography, *Memorias de un médico higienista* (1918), and a study of Buenos Aires's public and private social assistance agencies, *Asistencia y previsión social Buenos Aires caritativo y previsor* (1918). Coni was particularly interested in the control of venereal disease through medically supervised prostitution, the establishment of tuberculosis treatment centers, the regulation of wet nurses and milk supplies of all types, the treatment of alcoholics, and the creation of municipal medical facilities to shelter the indigent. He was also involved in efforts to improve sanitation in Buenos Aires. Many of these programs were implemented as a result of Coni's determination to have the medical facilities of Buenos Aires rival those found in contemporary Europe.

EMILIO R. CONI, *Asistencia y previsión social Buenos Aires caritativo y previsor* (1918) and *Memorias de un médico higienista* (1918); OSVALDO LOUDET, *Figuras próximas y lejanas, al margen de la historia* (1970); DONNA J. GUY, "Emilio and Gabriela Coni: Reformers, Public Health, and Working Women," in *The Human Tradition in Latin America: The Nineteenth Century,* edited by Judith Ewell and William H. Beezley (1989), pp. 233–248.

DONNA J. GUY

CONI, GABRIELA LAPERRIÈRE DE (*b.* 1866; *d.* January 1907), Argentine feminist and health-care activist. The public career of Gabriela Laperrière de Coni was intense but brief. Little is known about her early life except that she was born in Bordeaux, France, in 1866 and published a novel about a woman's efforts to help sick children. In her career, fiction mirrored reality. Once Laperrière became active in Argentina, she campaigned as a feminist socialist for improved working and health conditions for poor families. Her marriage in 1899 to Dr. Emilio R. Coni, a noted public-health physician, reinforced her commitment to health issues. One manifestation of this concern was the extensive lectures she gave about the dangers of tuberculosis.

Laperrière's Argentine career began in 1900, when she served as the press secretary for the Argentine National Council of Women. Two years later she was appointed Buenos Aires's first factory inspector by the city's mayor, Adolfo Bullrich. Her research led in April 1902 to recommend that legislation to protect workers be enacted. Such a law was enacted by the Argentine Congress in 1907.

A popular speaker on public-health issues, Laperrière also helped found the Centro Socialista Femenino (Socialist Women's Feminist Center). In one of her last public appearances she helped mediate a dispute between factory owners and working women in a shoe factory. Her death in January 1907 terminated her brief career, but her concerns about health and working conditions were implemented by others.

ENRIQUE DICKMANN, *Recuerdos de un militante socialista* (1949); DONNA J. GUY, "Emilio and Gabriela Coni: Reformers, Public Health, and Working Women," in *The Human Tradition in Latin America: The Nineteenth Century,* edited by Judith Ewell and William H. Beezley (1989), pp. 233–248.

DONNA J. GUY

CONQUEST OF THE DESERT, the final Argentine defeat of the Indians of the PAMPA (1879–1880). General Julio A. ROCA brought together the commitment, technology, planning, and manpower to accomplish a centuries-old goal, frontier security against Indian attack. Roca mobilized five divisions of 8,000 men. He commanded the first division, Nicolás Levalle the second, Eduardo Racedo the third, Napoleón Uriburu the fourth, and Hilario Lagos the fifth. Preliminary operations began in mid-1878, with expeditions targeted on specific caciques.

The Argentine military completed its mission with multipronged attacks that swept across the pampa in 1879. They quickly captured five important caciques and nearly 1,300 braves, and wounded or killed another 2,362. Argentina's navy participated with forces on the Río Negro and Lake Nahuel Huapi.

Technology played a decisive role in the Indians' defeat. Thanks to the nation's growing telegraph system, commanders had timely intelligence and could coordinate their actions. This counterbalanced the Indians' tactical advantage and better knowledge of the pampas terrain. Argentina's expanding railroads permitted better, quicker logistical support for Roca's troops. Modern arms technology favored the army. Armed with a repeating Remington rifle, one soldier could take on five Indians.

Roca practiced a hard-line policy "to break the spirit of the Indians, and to inspire them with fear, in order that they might think only of escaping." Roca leveled villages and sent Indians to reservations or exiled them to Chile. Sporadic Indian raids followed in the 1880s, but whites, not Indians, now controlled the vast pampas.

The conquest brought a windfall of land to Roca's political cronies. An estimated 49.4 million hectares of Indian land went to 500 of Roca's supporters. His military victory paved the way to the presidency in 1880.

Conquest of the Desert. Anonymous painting. ARCHIVO GENERAL DE LA NACIÓN, BUENOS AIRES.

ALFRED HASBROUCK, "The Conquest of the Desert," in *Hispanic American Historical Review* 15 (1935):195–228; JUAN CARLOS WALTHER, *La conquista del desierto* (1964).

RICHARD W. SLATTA

CONQUISTADORES, the conquerors of a New World empire for Spain in the sixteenth century. The conquistadores were men who participated in the conquest of MEXICO, PERU, and other regions of what became the Spanish Empire from the early sixteenth century to approximately 1570. They went to the New World seeking a better life for themselves and their families, and often endured incredible hardships in their pursuit of this dream. While the vast majority were laymen, a number of dedicated clerics also participated in the conquests, adding a spiritual dimension to the military ventures.

The conquistadores represented every segment of Spanish society except the high nobility. The early conquistadores and their most celebrated leaders—Hernán CORTÉS, Francisco PIZARRO, Francisco de MONTEJO, Hernando de SOTO, and others—were born in Spain, frequently in Estremadura, and arrived in the New World as young men. Typically they led privately financed expeditions and shared any booty with their men. Most initially saw their exploits as a means to provide wealth which would enable them to return to Spain and live a life of leisure. Except for some participants in the capture and ransom of the Inca ATAHUALPA, however, few realized their dream, for the rewards of conquest were typically ENCOMIENDAS, land, and offices, commodities not transferable to Spain. Most conquistadores remained in the New World, some moving every few years in pursuit of "another Peru."

As a group, the conquistadores shared the desire to own a big house and a horse; marry a Spanish wife; be able to entertain family, retainers, and friends lavishly; and live off the labor of natives held in *encomienda*. Those who were successful diversified their investments and engaged in stock raising, farming, mining, commerce, and officeholding. They and their heirs were a central part of the early colonial aristocracy.

BERNAL DÍAZ DEL CASTILLO, *The True History of the Conquest of New Spain, 1517–1521,* 5 vols. in 4, translated by Alfred P. Maudslay (repr. 1967); JAMES LOCKHART, *The Men of Cajamarca: A Social and Biographical Study of the First Conquerors of Peru* (1972).

MARK A. BURKHOLDER

CONSELHEIRO, ANTÔNIO (*b.* 13 March 1830; *d.* October 1897), a late-nineteenth-century Brazilian Catholic mystic and lay missionary. His career is immortalized in Euclides da CUNHA's *Os sertões* (1902; *Rebellion in the Backlands*).

António Vicente Mendes Maciel was born in Santo António de Quixeramobim, deep in the Ceará backlands. His grandparents were *vaqueiros* (cowboys). His father, Vicente's, first marriage ended disastrously; he deserted his wife after cudgeling her so savagely that she nearly died. Vicente's common-law second wife, Maria Maciel, was the boy's stepmother during his formative years. Known in the village as Maria Chana, she compensated by imposing strict religious discipline within her household and meting out frequent punishments to her children and slaves. Gradually, Vicente's fortunes as a merchant and property owner began to slip away. He grew morose and sullen, and was frequently inebriated.

As a child, Antônio was unobtrusive and studious. The boy's complexion was tawny (*moreno*), later attributed to partial Calabaça Indian ancestry. His birth certificate listed him as *pardo* (dark), but chroniclers who saw him generally referred to him as "white." His first formal instruction came from his father, who wanted him to become a priest. He was then enrolled in a school taught by Professor Manuel Antônio Ferreira Nobre, where he studied arithmetic, geography, Portuguese, French, and Latin. Some of his schoolmates later took their places in the regional elite as police chiefs, newspapermen, and lawyers.

The Mendes Maciel clan was a "good family" in the eyes of local inhabitants and, in the language of the day, part of the "conservative classes" although not particularly wealthy. At the age of twenty-five Antônio found himself responsible for four unmarried younger girls (two of them half sisters). He took over his father's business and filed papers to back the outstanding loans with a mortgage. In 1857, when he was twenty-seven, he married his fifteen-year-old cousin, Brasilina Laurentina de Lima, the daughter of Francisca Maciel, his father's sister. When she ran away with a soldier, Maciel sold his house and struck off to wander the backlands. He dressed austerely, fasted, and spent weeks and even months in small backlands towns, rebuilding dilapidated churches and cemetery walls. By the 1880s he began to acquire a reputation as a *conselheiro*, or religious counselor.

His wanderings took him through the backlands of Ceará, Pernambuco, Sergipe, and Bahia, in the heart of Brazil's Northeastern drought region. In 1887 he reached the seacoast, at Vila do Conde; he then turned back toward the semiarid interior. He wore a blue tunic tied with a sash, a turned-down hat to protect him from the sun, and sandals. He carried a leather bag with pen and ink, paper, and two prayer books.

Antônio lived on alms and slept in the back rooms of houses and in barns, always on the floor. His nightly orations from makeshift podiums in public squares entranced listeners, although he was not a particularly forceful speaker. The sophisticated called him a buffoon, laughing at his mixture of dogmatic counsels, vulgarized precepts from Christian morality, Latinate phrases, and prophecies. But he exerted a charismatic hold on the humble, many of whom began to follow him as he walked from place to place. In 1893, after a skirmish between his disciples and troops sent from the coast to arrest him, he set out for a remote abandoned cattle ranch on the banks of the Vasa-Barris River in the state of Bahia, a hamlet of 500 or so mud-thatched wooden shanties. Here, protected by a ring of mountains surrounding the valley (and by friendly landowners in the region as well as some local priests), he established a religious community called Canudos, or Belo Monte. As many as 25,000 pilgrims of all racial and economic groups (most of them impoverished backlands CABOCLOS of mixed origin) took up residence there, making it Bahia's second most populous urban center by 1895.

Conselheiro's theological vision inverted the harsh and austere reality of the impoverished backlands: the weak, strengthened by their faith, would inherit the earth. Nature would be transformed: rains would come to the arid *sertão*, bringing forth the earth's bounty. Canudos would be a "New Jerusalem." As community leader, he retained his personal asceticism and humility. He dissuaded others from calling him a saint, and he never assumed the powers of the clergy. Although he borrowed from a Catholic apocalyptic missal used widely during the late nineteenth century (*A missão abreviada*), his teachings never strayed from traditional church doctrine. Conselheiro admonished his disciples to live austerely, to renounce luxury, and to await the imminent coming of the Day of Judgment at the millennium. He was a misogynist, and avoided eye contact with women. But he was no religious fanatic. His preachments fell squarely within the tradition of backlands popular Catholicism, which, cut off from church influence by the paucity of available clergy, always had emphasized the presence of sin, the need for penitence, and the personal role of saints and other intermediaries.

Politically, he opposed the (1889) Republic because he revered the exiled emperor PEDRO II and because Brazil's Constitution of 1891, influenced by POSITIVIST ideas, ceded jurisdiction over the registry of births, marriages, and deaths to the state. His enemies accused him of sedition and of advocating the violent restoration of the monarchy, presumably with aid from monarchists elsewhere in Brazil as well as from monarchies in Europe. Opposition to Conselheiro and his community was led by backlands landowners threatened by the loss of their traditionally docile labor force as thousands abandoned their residences and streamed to Canudos.

Conselheiro's community at Canudos was destroyed by a massive and bloody assault by the Brazilian army in October 1897, following four attacks over the space of more than a year. He had died, probably of dysentery, some days before, and had been buried by pious villagers. His body was disinterred, the head severed and mounted on a pike, and displayed at the head of military parades in Salvador and in other cities on the coast.

RONALD H. CHILCOTE, *Power and the Ruling Classes in Northeast Brazil* (1990); *Luso-Brazilian Review,* special issue on messianism and millenarianism (Summer 1991); ROBERT M. LEVINE, *Vale of Tears: Revisiting the Canudos Massacre in Northeastern Brazil* (1992).

ROBERT M. LEVINE

See also **Canudos Campaign.**

CONSELHO DA INDIA. *See* **Portuguese Overseas Administration.**

CONSELHO DA FAZENDA (Treasury Council), founded in 1591 after Spain's annexation of Portugal as part of PHILIP II's attempt to centralize the state bureaucracy. The Conselho da Fazenda exercised jurisdiction over all matters pertaining to the crown's royal revenues. During the Portuguese Restoration, the Conselho assumed the appearance it would maintain throughout the early modern era. After 1642 it consisted of three *vedores* (inspectors), who were noblemen; four *conselheiros* (counselors), all of whom were university-trained lawyers (LETRADOS) and who by 1700 were judges (DESEMBARGADORES); and four scribes. Several subordinate tribunals worked under the Conselho, including customs (*alfândega*), mint, *Casa da India,* and *Casa dos Contos* (exchequer).

In addition to the collection and management of royal revenues, the Conselho dealt with wide-ranging problems affecting commerce at home and in the colonies. Apart from the daily management of the royal revenues, it is difficult to judge how much power the Conselho da Fazenda, or most of the other councils, actually wielded. Portuguese kings had no obligation to heed its decisions. Because noblemen frequently sat on several councils at the same time, the crown increasingly came to rely on a small group of advisers for important decisions. In 1761 the marquês de POMBAL stripped most of the Conselho's authority by turning it into a voluntary claims tribunal and severely narrowing its jurisdiction. In 1790 the Conselho was consolidated with the royal exchequer and effectively dissolved.

PADRE ANTÔNIO CARVALHO DA COSTA, *Corografia portuguesa, e descrição topográfica do famoso reyno de Portugal,* 3 vols. (1706–1712); JOEL SERRÃO, ed., *Dicionário de história de Portugal,* 6 vols. (1979).

WILLIAM DONOVAN

CONSELHO ULTRAMARINO. *See* **Overseas Council.**

CONSERVATIVE PARTIES

OVERVIEW

Latin American conservative parties have been important political forces throughout the region since their formation during the 1830s and 1840s. Organized in response to the exigencies of republicanism, and in opposition to social, economic, and political reform, they struggled for power against rival liberal parties during the middle decades of the nineteenth century. Toward the end of the century, conservative and liberal elites achieved a modus vivendi in most parts of Latin America, first because their frequently bloody struggles had clearly harmed national interests, and second because leaders of both parties believed civil order would lead to progress.

Conservatives described the era of consensus as one of "national" or "progressive" conservatism. Liberals termed it a time of "conservative liberalism." In both instances all but the most doctrinaire found they could compromise ideological differences on a platform accentuating economic progress and social order.

Elite accommodation prevailed in Latin America until the early twentieth century, when a traditionally quiescent citizenry began to demand both a meaningful voice in political affairs and substantive social reform. The awakening of a constituency that historically had been passive, respectful of authority, and accepting of elite governance, destroyed conservative-liberal consensus and brought with it political ferment and partisan realignment. Conservatives were especially hard-pressed to recast their political message so as to maintain their constituencies.

The modernization of traditional party platforms came too late in Mexico, Brazil, and Argentina, where revolutionary change either destroyed the old parties or rendered them powerless. Elsewhere conservative parties either passed out of existence or shrank to insignificance. Only Colombia's and Nicaragua's Conservative parties retained their traditional platforms and remained important forces in national politics. In several countries, notably Chile and Venezuela, young conservatives formed new parties founded on conservative principles but aggressively promoting social reform. In so doing they heeded the call of Pope Pius XI, who in his 1931 encyclical *Quadragesimo Anno* gave motive force to what would become the Christian Democratic movement.

Over the following decades, Christian Democratic parties appeared in most Latin American nations, and where they did not—in Colombia and Nicaragua, for example—existing conservative parties eventually adopted Christian Democratic–like platforms.

Twentieth-century social change thus produced an inexorable shift in the orientation of Latin America's conservative parties. In that they came to embrace reform programs, they stood poles apart from the hidebound organizations of earlier times. But in that their platforms and ideologies were rooted in Roman Catholic social and philosophic teachings, they proclaimed their descent from Latin America's original conservative parties.

CONSERVATIVE PARTY EVOLUTION

The motive force for conservative party formation in Latin America came from liberals who, following European and North American models, proposed ambitious programs of economic and social reform in decades following the wars of independence (1810–1824). Liberals sought to free their respective countries from traditional social constraints of every sort. In economics they pursued free-trade policies; in politics they endorsed a broadening of democracy; and in the social sphere they struck at limitations to individual freedom. Rational, utilitarian-minded liberals were especially intent on lessening the power of the Roman Catholic church, which they perceived as the chief obstacle to national progress. The church enjoyed special legal privileges, or FUEROS, inherited from colonial times, and owned considerable property, which liberals believed should be placed at the disposal of individual citizens.

These policies and beliefs did violence to conservative interests and values at every point, driving adherents to organize politically. By 1850, conservative parties had been constituted in virtually all Latin American nations. Party leaders were united in both interest and ideology. Many of them were descended from landowning families favored by economic policies derived from Spanish mercantilism. At the same time, they viewed economic liberalism as a self-serving device promoting the interests of an upwardly mobile creole commercial elite. They saw liberal egalitarianism and democratic premises as both politically motivated and potentially disruptive of social tranquility. And conservatives were scandalized by liberal attacks on the church, which they viewed as both the repository of divinely inspired moral values and a vital social institution in its own right. Confessional Catholics almost to a man, Latin America's first conservatives could not but see liberal reforms as perverse—even atheistic—disruptions of national social hierarchies, and hence productive of social dissolution. Proponents of strong, even monarchical state leadership, they likewise viewed the extreme federalism endorsed by liberals as wrongheaded and antinational.

Conservative attempts to preserve the closed, inegalitarian system of earlier times, and liberal efforts to open it by striking at traditional institutions and beliefs, formed a common theme in civil wars fought throughout Spanish America during the middle decades of the nineteenth century. Notable figures emerged to orient and lead the traditionalists. Some, like Rafael CARRERA in Central America, José Antonio Páez in Venezuela, and Juan Manuel de ROSAS in Argentina, were military leaders. Others, like Lucas ALAMÁN in Mexico, Mariano OSPINA RODRÍGUEZ in Colombia, Gabriel GARCÍA MORENO in Ecuador, and Diego PORTALES PALAZUELOS

in Chile, left the fighting to others, concentrating instead on providing their partisans with political, intellectual, and moral leadership. Only Brazil, which existed under a constitutional monarchy until 1889, managed to avoid bloodshed produced by conservative-liberal struggles.

As elites fought over issues of principle and self-interest, Latin America fell farther behind Europe and the United States in economic development. By the latter nineteenth century, the backwardness of the region had become galling to national leaders. Sensitivity to their backwardness, coupled with the appearance of new commercial elites, drove conservatives and liberals to reconcile their differences. For their part, conservatives became convinced that the masses would remain tractable. Having diversified their economic interests, they were no longer threatened by the freeing of national markets to international trade. Meanwhile, the liberals had softened their ANTICLERICALISM and had embraced the notion that social order demanded strong, even authoritarian rule. As Spanish America entered the new century, peace springing from elite accommodation reigned everywhere in the region. The bourgeois calm prevailed in Brazil, too, where coffee-based prosperity and the positivist slogan "order and progress" united the new republic's political arbiters.

Latin America's social tranquility did not last past the first decade of the twentieth century. Economic progress had frequently been achieved at the expense of the rank and file, who continued to be, in overwhelming numbers, uneducated peasants having little or no voice in political affairs. Beginning in Mexico in 1910, where rural-based revolution destroyed the political establishment, Latin America woke abruptly from its premodern slumber. Economic change produced increased industrialization and urbanization, which gave rise to new social groups whose members demanded political representation. Their calls produced a plethora of new political parties, most of which employed radical, frequently revolutionary, messages to win constituents.

Conservative party leaders reacted to social and political change in several ways. Some, like Colombia's Laureano GÓMEZ CASTRO and Chile's Alberto Edwards Vives, resisted it; they based their political messages on a defense of elitist rule and attacks on liberalism and socialism alike. Elsewhere, in Ecuador, Peru, and Argentina, conservatives joined coalition movements or entered dominant political movements, such as Peru's APRA and Argentina's Peronist Party, coming to constitute right-wing factions in them.

In Nicaragua the Conservatives steadily lost ground to the Liberals over the course of the 1920s, prior to establishment of the Somoza dynasty (1933–1979). Throughout Somoza's regime the Conservative Party remained the leading official opposition in the country, although it splintered into several factions. In the upheavals of the late 1970s Conservatives, led by the editor of *La Prensa*, Pedro Joaquín CHAMORRO CARDENAL, eventually joined with the Sandinistas to end the Somoza regime. The assassination of Chamorro on 10 January 1978 was a major catalyst in the popular uprising that brought an end to the dynasty.

Most Conservatives broke with the Marxist Sandinistas after 1979. While some joined the CIA-backed CONTRAS, most formed the nucleus of the opposition coalition within Nicaragua that eventually triumphed against the Sandinistas in the 1990 election, when Pedro Chamorro's widow, Violeta BARRIOS DE CHAMORRO, was elected president.

The most significant conservative response to social change during the twentieth century lay in the formation of Christian Democratic parties. Young conservatives like Eduardo FREI MONTALVA in Chile and Rafael CALDERA RODRÍGUEZ in Venezuela rejected the authoritarianism of the extreme right, the threat to private property posed by the extreme left, and the secularism of doctrinaire liberals. They sought and found theoretical and practical inspiration for an alternative path to social change in the encyclical *Rerum Novarum,* issued by Pope Leo XIII in 1891 and commemorated by Pius XI forty years later in *Quadragesimo Anno.* For Frei and the others, *Rerum Novarum* showed Latin Americans a way of addressing social problems while remaining faithful to their oldest cultural value and moral precepts. In that regard the Christian Democrats remained squarely in the tradition of early-day conservatives such as Lucas Alamán, Mariano Ospina Rodríguez, and Gabriel García Moreno.

Through Christian Democracy, Latin American conservatives found they could embrace nontraditional, progressive solutions of social problems, all the while remaining steadfast in their fundamental political principles.

MODERN PARTY PLATFORMS
At the end of the twentieth century, Latin American conservative parties frequently won presidential elections on political platforms with populist, liberal, and even socialist overtones. Yet on close analysis, those platforms bore clear signs of their conservative character. Party platforms called for social reform within a nonrevolutionary context, whether articulated by Colombia's Social Conservative Party; Ecuador's National Front conservative coalition, which bore Belisario BETANCUR and León FEBRES-CORDERO to victory during the 1980s; Nicaragua's anti-Somoza and later anti-Sandinista Conservative coalition; Costa Rica's Social Christian Unity Party; or Chile's Christian Democratic Party, whose leaders Rafael CALDERÓN GUARDIA and Patricio AYLWIN AZÓCAR won national elections during the early 1990s. Those platforms stressed harmonious change on behalf of the "common good," a phrase, rooted in Roman Catholic social organicism conveying the belief that societies governed in accord with divine law are harmonious ones in which human beings enjoy justice of a distributive character. Modern conservative party platforms endorsed the notion that the social function of property takes precedence over its private function—a reversal of earlier conservatives' intransigent defense of the individual's right to private property.

A final, notable plank in modern conservative party platforms permitted them to support social order while opposing authoritarian or quasi-authoritarian forms of government. That opposition was justified through the principle of subsidiarity, which is rooted in corporatist theory and which holds that individuals and groups have a natural right to autonomy within the state. Mexico's Partido de Acción Nacional (PAN) bases its opposition to the hegemonic Partido Revolucionario Institucional (PRI) on the principle of subsidiarity.

Late-twentieth-century conservative party politicians employed the idiom of religion, morality, and virtue, coupled with explicit or implicit condemnation of relativism, moral laxness, and the loss of ethical standards. In so doing they presented to their respective electorates a modern version of the historic conservative condemnation of secularism, which they blamed for the decline of public and private virtue.

HAROLD E. DAVIS touches on Conservative Party development in his *Latin American Thought: A Historical Introduction* (1972), as does JAMES D. HENDERSON in *Conservative Thought in Twentieth Century Latin America* (1988). A useful anthology of writings by Latin American conservatives is *Pensamiento conservador, 1815–1898* (1978), edited by José Luis Romero. Romero's *El pensamiento político de la derecha latinoamericana* (1970) stands as the only attempt to survey nineteenth-century Latin American conservatism. HAROLD E. DAVIS, *Latin American Social Thought: The History of Its Development Since Independence, with Selected Readings* (1963), contains samples of nineteenth- and twentieth-century conservative writing in English translation. The process of late-nineteenth-century conservative-liberal accommodation is treated in CHARLES A. HALE, "Political and Social Ideas, 1870–1930," in *The Cambridge History of Latin America,* vol. 4 (1986), edited by Leslie Bethel. Hale also deals extensively with conservative-liberal reconciliation in *The Transformation of Liberalism in Late Nineteenth-Century Mexico* (1989). EDUARDO FREI MONTALVA, *Aún es tiempo* (1942), is an early statement of progressive conservativism. Venezuelan Christian Democratic leader RAFAEL CALDERA suggests the progressive thrust of most modern conservative thought in his *Idearo: La democracia cristiana en América Latina* (1970). HEINRICH A. ROMMEN, *The State in Catholic Thought: A Treatise in Political Philosophy* (1969), is an excellent starting point for those wishing to understand the ideological foundations of Latin American political conservatism, while NOËL O'SULLIVAN, *Conservatism* (1976), treats the subject within the context of post-Enlightenment Western politics.

JAMES D. HENDERSON

See also **"Political Parties" under individual countries.**

CONSOLIDACIÓN, LAW OF. The Spanish crown decreed the law of *consolidación* on 26 December 1804. The law, or more exactly collection of laws and implementing decrees, required that officials of the church's Juzgado de Capellanías recall all funds that had been invested by the court. The principal of the loans was to be handed over to royal officials, and the crown would pay the court 3 percent annual interest on the principal. Over the course of the Spanish colonial period, very large sums of money had been given to the church for the establishment of pious works. Those funds were normally invested in mortgages on real estate, both urban and rural. Many authors writing at the time believed that more than half of the available capital of the colonies was tied up in these loans. Many borrowers had held these loans for several generations and were hard put to come up with the cash necessary to pay them off, in accordance with the royal decree, and their recall posed an immediate and dire threat to the economic stability of the colonies. In the archdiocese of Mexico, within four years a total of over 2.5 million pesos was collected.

MICHAEL P. COSTELOE, *Church Wealth in Mexico: A Study of the "Juzgado de Capellanías" in the Archbishopric of Mexico 1800–1856* (1967).

JOHN F. SCHWALLER

See also **Catholic Church: The Colonial Period.**

CONSPIRACY OF THE TAILORS. *See* **Inconfidência dos Alfaiates.**

CONSTANT BOTELHO DE MAGALHÃES, BENJAMIN (*b.* 18 October 1836; *d.* 22 January 1891), one of the founders of the Brazilian Republic. The son of a schoolteacher and a seamstress, Constant was instrumental in Brazil's transition from monarchy to republic. The army gave him the opportunity to rise above his humble birth. Trained as an engineer at Rio de Janeiro's Military Academy, Constant later taught mathematics at his alma mater. In 1866 he participated briefly in the WAR OF THE TRIPLE ALLIANCE, but illness forced his return to Rio de Janeiro.

A more successful teacher than soldier, Constant nonetheless was part of the new military that emerged from the Paraguayan war committed to more active participation in political affairs of the empire. He became a convert to positivist doctrines and was influential in spreading them among his students at the Military Academy and later at the War College. By the late 1880s Constant demonstrated vocal support for republicanism and conspired to bring down the empire in 1889. His prestige among students brought many cadets to support the republican cause. In November 1889, as vice president of the Military Club, he urged its president, General Manuel Deodoro da FONSECA, to lead the military against the Emperor PEDRO II and proclaim the republic.

Under the Republican administration, Constant served first as minister of war, then as minister of public instruction and postmaster in 1890. The positivist slogan, "Order and Progress," emblazoned on the Brazilian flag is attributed to him.

JOÃO CRUZ COSTA, *A History of Ideas in Brazil,* translated by Suzette Machado (1964), esp. pp. 143–148; HEITOR LYRA, *História da queda do império,* 2 vols. (1964); RONALD SCHNEIDER, *"Order and Progress": A Political History of Brazil* (1991), esp. pp. 56–57.

JOAN MEZNAR

See also **Positivism.**

CONSTITUTIONS. *See under individual countries.*

CONSULADO. The Spanish-American *consulados* (merchant guilds) had their roots in medieval Mediterranean institutions formed to protect merchant interests after the breakdown of the Roman Empire. Their central feature was a tribunal to hear commercial litigation. Although rooted in Greco-Roman legal precedents, the Spanish merchant guilds derived more directly from Italian sea consulates, which were highly organized by the end of the twelfth century at Genoa, Pisa, Siena, Bologna, and elsewhere. From Italy the institution spread northwestward through Provence and Languedoc to several towns along the Aragon coast from Perpignan to Valencia as well as to Majorca. The most important of these came to be Barcelona's Council of One Hundred (Concell de Cent), which James I authorized in 1249. In the foreign ports with which Barcelona traded, it appointed consuls who could govern, judge, and punish all the subjects of the Crown of Aragon who resided in those ports. The fourteenth-century *Libre del Consolat de mar* of the Barcelona guild thus became one of the earliest codes of maritime and commercial law. This Barcelona sea consulate (consolat de mar), although not officially chartered until 1347, became the model for those which followed in the Spanish world. By that date it had a commercial court elected by the merchants that heard commercial cases.

By 1450 eight towns in the Kingdom of Aragon had similar commercial courts. These courts eliminated the expense of lawsuits and strife in mercantile litigation because they circumvented the legalism and obstruction encountered in the ordinary courts. In addition, the merchants usually elected a junta to represent them in negotiations with other organizations and at trade fairs, to administer the finances of the guild, and to enforce trade regulations within the area of the *consulado*'s jurisdiction. The early *consulados* were closely allied to the municipal administration of their respective cities and played important roles in the economic and political structure of eastern Spain by 1450.

After the union of Aragon and Castile in 1479, Catalonian commercial customs influenced those of Castile as the Spanish Empire began to take shape. There had been merchant guilds in Burgos, Bilbao, and other northern Castilian towns for half a century before the union with Aragon, but it was not until after unification that the judicial court privileges were granted in Castile. Burgos (1494) and Bilbao (1511) were the first Castilian towns to receive royal sanction for *consulados*. In 1543 the crown authorized a *consulado* to the merchants of Seville (Universidad de los Cargadores de las Indias), where it held a monopoly on the trade with America. To supervise the colonial trade, the crown had established the CASA DE CONTRATACIÓN (Board of Trade) in Seville in 1503, after the pattern of the Board of Trade established in Barcelona to supervise Mediterranean commerce in the fourteenth century. The Casa de Contratación controlled every detail of trade, and the *consulado* established in Seville in 1543 worked closely with it to protect the merchants of the city, strenuously resisting any curtailment of the monopoly they held on the trade with the Indies. The *consulado* of Seville supervised the FLEET SYSTEM that channeled legal trade with the Indies through the annual fairs at Portobelo for Peru and Veracruz (or Xalapa) for New Spain.

Establishment of *consulados* in Mexico and Lima extended the control of the Seville merchant guild. Patterned after those in the Spanish towns, they were composed of the chief importers, mostly representatives of Seville merchants. These first Latin American *consulados* thus served to strengthen the Seville merchant monopoly over trade with the Indies. Agitation for a Mexican *consulado* began as early as 1580; it was authorized on 15 June 1592 and was formally established in Mexico City in 1604. The crown authorized the Peruvian *consulado* on 29 December 1593, but its organization was not completed until February 1613. In the seventeenth century these two *consulados* enjoyed great power as the institution of the European residents, serving as a sympathetic tribunal to hear disputes over contracts, bankruptcy, shipping, insurance, and other commercial matters. They established consular deputations in towns throughout their respective viceroyalties and developed large funds that came to be an important source for development of public works and loans to the viceregal governments.

The merchants in the viceregal capitals jealously guarded their privileged monopolies and successfully opposed any new *consulados* in America for two centuries, despite petitions for such institutions from other cities from the mid-seventeenth century forward. With the exception of a *consulado* in Bogotá, which functioned between 1694 and 1712, outside of Lima and Mexico City the only mercantile organization permitted in Spanish America consisted of some commercial deputies who exercised limited functions as commercial judges and tax collectors in an ill-defined system that frequently led to confusion, delay, and sizable backlogs of cases.

Under Charles III and Charles IV, late in the eigh-

teenth century, the efforts to liberalize commercial activity and to reduce the Seville-Cádiz monopoly finally led to formation of several new *consulados*. Manila gained a *consulado* in 1769, with jurisdiction over the Philippines. Then, between 1793 and 1795, the crown erected new *consulados* in Caracas, Guatemala, Buenos Aires, Havana, Veracruz, Santiago de Chile, Guadalajara, and Cartagena. Several of these had already been operating limited commercial courts as consular deputations of the *consulados* of Mexico or Lima. Although apparently never formally chartered by the crown, consular deputations in Montevideo and San Juan also evolved into institutions operating as *consulados* in the early nineteenth century. All these new *consulados* had as their "principal duty" the protection and advancement of commerce. In addition to their judicial functions, these newer *consulados* came to have an important role in the development of the economic infrastructure of the colonies. There were also new *consulados* formed during the struggle for independence, including one at Puebla in Mexico and at Guayaquil, Cuenca, and Angostura in South America, all of them short-lived. At least one *consulado*, in Valparaíso, Chile, was established after independence.

Because of their close association with Spanish peninsular interests, most of the *consulados* were abolished during or soon after independence. The Spanish government abolished the institution in 1829, although Valencia revived its *consulado* in 1934. In Latin America, however, a few *consulados* survived well into the nineteenth century, notably in Chile until 1875, in Guatemala until 1871, and in Argentina until 1862. Representing the principle of commercial monopoly, however, all of them eventually fell before the dominance of classical liberal economic philosophy in the nineteenth century.

ROBERT SIDNEY SMITH, *The Spanish Guild Merchant: A History of the Consulado, 1250–1700* (1940; repr. 1972), provides the best overview of the institution of the *consulado* in the Spanish world; ROBERT SIDNEY SMITH, "Research Report on Consulado History," in *Homenaje a don José María de la Peña y Cámara* (1969), pp. 121–140, provides a useful survey of much of the literature on the topic. On the origins of the institution, STANLEY S. JADOS, *Consulate of the Sea and Related Documents* (1975), is useful; and on the Seville merchant society, RUTH PIKE, *Aristocrats and Traders: Sevillean Society in the Sixteenth Century* (1972), is the best introduction.

Several of the Latin American *consulados* have received treatment. C. NORMAN GUICE, "The Consulado of New Spain, 1594–1795" (Ph.D. diss., University of California, 1952) surveys the Mexican *consulado*. See also LOUISA SCHELL HOBERMAN, *Mexico's Merchant Elite, 1590–1660: Silver, State, and Society* (1991); DAVID A. BRADING, *Miners and Merchants in Bourbon Mexico, 1763–1810* (1971); and JAVIER ORTIZ DE LA TABLA DUCASSE, *Memorias políticas y económicas del consulado de Veracruz, 1796–1822* (1985). On the Peruvian *consulado* see LAWRENCE A. CLAYTON, "Sources in Lima for the Study of the Colonial Consulado of Peru," in *The Americas* 33 (1977): 457–469; and JOHN MELZER, *Bastion of Commerce in the City of Kings: The Consulado de Comercio of Lima, 1593–1887* (1991). On Caracas, see MANUEL NUNES DIAS, *El real consulado de Caracas (1793–1810)* (1971), and

HUMBERTO TANDRÓN, *El real consulado de Caracas y el comercio exterior de Venezuela* (1976); on Guatemala, RALPH LEE WOODWARD, JR., *Class Privilege and Economic Development: The Consulado de Comercio of Guatemala, 1793–1871* (1966); on Buenos Aires, GERMÁN O. TJARKS, *El consulado de Buenos Aires y sus proyecciones en la historia del Río de la Plata* (1962). See also SUSAN MIGDEN SOCOLOW, *The Merchants of Buenos Aires, 1778–1810* (1978). On the brief history of the *consulado* in Bogotá, see ROBERT S. SMITH, "The Consulado de Santa Fe de Bogotá," in *Hispanic American Historical Review* 45, no. 3 (1965): 442–451.

RALPH LEE WOODWARD, JR.

See also **Commercial Policy.**

CONTADORA, an effort to achieve a peace treaty between the Central American nations of Guatemala, El Salvador, Honduras, Nicaragua, and Costa Rica in the late 1980s. The sponsoring countries were Mexico, Panama, Colombia, and Venezuela, with a support group consisting of Argentina, Brazil, Peru, and Uruguay. Contadora was so named for an island off the western coast of Panama where the first meeting took place in 1983. The principal objectives were to stop the war between the Sandinista government in Nicaragua and the U.S.-backed counterrevolutionary force based in Honduras, and to remove foreign military influence from Central America.

Daniel ORTEGA, representing Nicaragua, signed the first draft of Contadora in September 1984, but the other Central American executives balked. New language was inserted to pressure Nicaragua to adopt more democratic institutions. In June 1986, Ortega and Guatemalan president Vinicio CEREZO were ready to sign, but the United States achieved the abstention of Costa Rica, Honduras, and El Salvador. In February 1987, Costa Rican president Oscar ARIAS presented a new plan based on the original Contadora provisions. On 7 August 1987, all five countries signed the Arias Peace Plan (for which Arias received the 1987 Nobel Peace Prize).

The Contadora sponsors and support group have provided teams for the International Corps of Inspectors and the Verification Commission which have monitored various phases of the Arias Plan. In 1993 the functions of Contadora were absorbed by the UNITED NATIONS and the ORGANIZATION OF AMERICAN STATES.

MORRIS BLACHMAN et al., eds. *Confronting Revolution: Security Through Diplomacy in Central America* (1986); CENTER FOR INTERNATIONAL POLICY, "Contadora Primer," in *International Policy Report* (November 1986); JIM MORRELL, "The Nine Lives of the Central American Peace Process," in *International Policy Report* (February 1989), pp. 1–7.

MARK EVERINGHAM

See also **Esquipulos II.**

CONTADURÍA, a general term refering to accounting procedures in Spain and the Indies. Throughout Span-

ish America royal accountants (*contadores*) kept records for the royal treasury (*caja*) in their district. In Lima and Mexico City similar officials labored over the ledgers of the viceregal matrix treasuries along with a host of other accountants who were responsible for keeping track of one specific tax category (*ramo*) such as tribute, indulgences, mercury, stamped legal paper, and sales taxes. In 1605, to strengthen the colonial accounting system, Philip III established in Bogotá, Mexico City, and Lima auditing bureaus (Tribunales de Cuentas) whose task was to audit the myriad of ledgers generated by regional and viceregal accountants. After the audits, the *tribunals* forwarded the accounts to the contaduría of the COUNCIL OF THE INDIES in Spain. Here, more accountants subjected these books to still another vigilant review, before sending them to the archives—after 1783 to the General Archive of the Indies in Seville.

Recopiliacíon de leyes de los reynos de las Indias, 4 vols. (1681; repr. 1973), libro II, título XI; libro VIII, título II; libro IX, título VIII; GASPAR DE ESCALONA Y AGÜERO, *Gazofilacio Real del Perú*, 4th ed. (1941).

JOHN JAY TEPASKE

CONTEMPORÁNEOS, LOS, a group of Mexican artists and writers in the 1920s who opposed the dogmatic character of the Escuela Mexicana (Mexican School) and disseminated the ideas of the European avant garde. Among its most important members were the writers Xavier VILLAURRUTÍA, Salvador NOVO, Jaime TORRES BODET, and the artist and critic Agustín Lazo. Originally gathered around Antonieta Rivas Mercado and the first experimental theater in Mexico, Teatro Ulises, these writers and artists went on to form the group called Los Contemporáneos in 1927. They founded an important journal devoted to art and literature titled *Contemporáneos* (1928–1931). Often attacked by the members of the Escuela Mexicana for being overly concerned with European modernism, Los Contemporáneos nevertheless were important promoters of a number of lesser-known Mexican artists, including Abraham Angel, Manuel Rodríguez Lozano, Carlos MÉRIDA, and Julio Castellanos. In 1935 they organized an exhibition of the work of Rufino TAMAYO at the Galería de Arte Mexicano. Although Los Contemporáneos were condemned for not being fervent nationalists, they wrote extensively about Mexican art and literature.

OLIVIER DEBROISE, *Figuras en el trópico, plástica mexicana 1920–1940* (1984), esp. p. 141; JORGE ALBERTO MANRIQUE, "Rompimiento y rompimientos en el arte mexicano," in Museo de Arte Alvar y Carmen T. de Carrillo Gil, *Ruptura 1952–1965* (1988), pp. 25–42, and "Otras caras del arte mexicano," in Museo Nacional de Arte de Mexico, *Modernidad y modernización en el arte mexicano 1920–1960* (1991), pp. 131–143.

ILONA KATZEW

See also **Literature: Spanish America.**

CONTESTADO REBELLION, which pitted some 25,000 millenarian rebels against two-thirds of the Brazilian army (7,000 men) between 1912 and March 1916, was the last of three great millenarian movements (along with rebellions at CANUDOS and JUAZEIRO) that shook Brazil at the turn of this century. The rebellion was fought in the contested border region between the Brazilian states of Paraná and Santa Catarina ("the Contestado"). Rebels who followed the teachings of the "prophet" José Maria created "holy cities" for believers, attacked skeptics, and called for the return of the Brazilian monarchy (overthrown in 1889). An army scorched-earth campaign eventually starved the rebels into submission.

Rapid socioeconomic change at the beginning of the twentieth century prompted the rebellion. Before that time small-scale cattle ranching dominated the Contestado economy. Landowners secured their large, undefined holdings via usufruct land grants to AGREGADOS (combination ranch hands and sharecroppers). An unequal, yet reciprocal, relationship developed between landowners and *agregados,* one maintained not only by material exchanges but also by the establishment of ritual kinship ties between the landowner, the *agregado,* and the latter's family.

But turn-of-the-century colonization projects and railroad construction transformed life in the Contestado. Between 1890 and 1912 thousands of new European immigrants colonized lands donated by state governments. In 1906 the American-owned Brazil Railway Company began construction of the first railroad through the region, at the same time promoting the colonization of thousands of hectares of Contestado land it had received as part of a federal government concession. Local landowners subsequently sold large portions of their holdings because of the booming real estate market, thereby dispossessing their *agregados* and their families.

The actions of "faceless" North American capitalists and local landowners threatened peasant subsistence in the Contestado. What emerged was not only a material crisis but also a spiritual crisis of values, for the profit-hungry landowners, the godfathers of *agregados* and their families, had broken their religiously sanctioned subsistence guarantees. By calling for landowners and peasants to live together in holy cities the millenarian movement led by José Maria promised to heal both the internal crisis of values and the material threat of peasant subsistence. It was this powerful dual message that fueled and inspired one of the largest popular rebellions in the history of Brazil.

DUGLAS TEIXERIA MONTEIRO, *Os errantes do novo século* (1974); MARIA ISAURA PEREIRA DE QUEIROZ, *O messianismo no Brasil e no mundo,* 2d ed. (1976); BERNARD J. SIEGEL, "The Contestado Rebellion, 1912–1916: A Case Study in Brazilian Messianism and Regional Dynamics," in *The Anthropology of Power,* edited by Raymond D. Fogelson and Richard N. Adams (1977), pp. 325–336; MAURÍCIO VINHAS DE QUEIROZ, *Messianismo e conflito social,* 3d ed. (1981); PATRICIA PESSAR, "Unmasking the Politics of Religion," in *Journal of Latin American Lore* 7, no. 2 (1981): 255–278; TODD A. DIACON, *Millenarian Vision, Capitalist Reality: Brazil's Contestado Rebellion, 1912–1916* (1991).

TODD A. DIACON

See also **Batista, Cícero; Conselheiro, Antonio.**

CONTINUISMO, the practice of maintaining a president in office beyond his legal term. Because most Latin American constitutions contain one-term limitations for the president, a variety of devices have been used by resourceful chief executives to continue in office. Among the more common have been: (1) constitutional revision (Juan Domingo PERÓN [Argentina] in 1951 and Alfredo STROESSNER [Paraguay] in 1954), (2) legislative enactment (Jorge UBICO [Guatemala] in 1941), (3) plebiscite (Carlos CASTILLO ARMAS [Guatemala] in 1954 and Marcos PÉREZ JIMÉNEZ [Venezuela] in 1958), (4) internal coup (Getúlio Dornelles VARGAS [Brazil] in 1938), (5) imposition of a weak candidate to serve as a figurehead while the outgoing president rules behind the scenes (Plutarco Calles's [Mexico] choice of Emilio PORTES GIL to succeed him in 1928 and Luis SOMOZA's [Nicaragua] decision to install René SCHICK GUTIÉRREZ in the presidency in 1963), (6) conferral of the title President for Life to François DUVALIER in 1964 by the Haitian legislature, and (7) maintenance of a leader's power by a political movement or hegemonic political party (Fidel CASTRO [Cuba]).

Based on these practices, a number of types of *continuista* regimes can be identified. First is classical *continuismo,* which is the manipulation of the constitutional or legal system by a personal dictator to perpetuate himself in power. The "depression dictatorships" of Central America and the Caribbean, such as that of Maximiliano HERNÁNDEZ MARTÍNEZ of El Salvador, are of this type. Second, dynastic *continuismo* is the passing of power from father to son (for example, the Duvaliers [Haiti] and the Somozas [Nicaragua]), from husband to wife (Juan Perón to Isabel PERÓN [Argentina] through the vice presidency in 1974), and, potentially, between brothers (Raúl CASTRO is generally considered to be Fidel Castro's heir apparent). A third type, institutional *continuismo,* is the perpetuation of a ruler in office or the naming of his successor by a hegemonic party (Mexico and Cuba). Finally, there is a type of military *continuismo,* which is the circulation of power among a succession of military rulers by the general staff, a practice evident in the bureaucratic-authoritarian regimes in Brazil, Argentina, and Uruguay.

"Continuismo," in *Latin American Political Dictionary,* edited by Ernest E. Rossi and Jack C. Plano (1980).

ROLAND H. EBEL

CONTRABAND (COLONIAL SPANISH AMERICA), external trade and trade goods that flowed outside the bounds of formal Spanish taxation, regulation, and national monopoly.

Contraband and its economic cousins—smuggling, fraud, illicit commerce, and illegal trade—were integral elements in the economies of colonial Spanish America. Technically, each term referred to a specific element of the multifaceted phenomenon. Fraud, for example, consisted of trade that, although legal per se, occurred at levels disallowed by license or law. Trade of Spanish or Spanish American origin expressly forbidden by law was considered contraband. The illegal direct trade of foreigners with Spanish America was categorized as illicit commerce. But as Pedro González de Salcedo generalized in his *Tratado jurídico-político del contra-bando* (1654, 1729), and as the king of Spain, CHARLES III, reaffirmed in 1770, contraband was understood also to include all trade prohibited by law or ruled by the monarch to damage the public good. Generally, this economic interplay between restrictions and lawbreaking called "contraband" applied to descriptions of external commerce. However, illegal trade and tax fraud also marked internal commerce and created economic problems and opportunities in the interior similar to those afforded by smuggling in coastal regions of Spanish America.

Coastal contraband occurred throughout the empire, but it was especially prevalent in northern South America from Portobelo, in present-day Panama, to Cumaná, in present-day northern Venezuela, and in the Río de la Plata delta. Its practice, well-established by the 1590s, surged in the seventeenth century with the Dutch seizure of Curaçao in 1634, the British capture of Jamaica in 1655 and the subsequent suppression of piracy in the 1680s, and the Portuguese establishment of Colonia del Sacramento in 1680. The Treaty of Utrecht (1713) and the international wars of the eighteenth century furthered illegal trafficking through Spanish American ports. These developments reflect the general regionalism of Spanish American contraband. While England had merchants throughout the Americas, the Dutch primarily worked the southern Caribbean, the Portuguese the Río de la Plata basin, and the French the Pacific coasts.

There were two distinctly divergent points of view regarding contraband within the Spanish Empire. On one hand, peninsulars blamed illicit commerce on inordinate American consumer demands and insufficient American regard for law and custom. Americans, on the other, focused on the failure of the metropolis to appreciate sufficiently American needs and to service properly its American dominions. But, in either case, Spaniards—and foreigners, too—recognized the illegality of smuggling.

Contrary, then, to official will and purpose and to the principles of mercantilist theory, contraband trafficking in Spanish American colonies represented to policy-making elites and peninsular monopolists a serious threat to imperial well-being. They commonly called contraband a "cancer" that ate away at legitimate royal revenues, sapped the economic vitality of the empire, and eroded the moral fiber of Spanish vassals. Consequently, the Spanish crown sought to curb, if not eliminate, contraband. At times, it merely took a necessary public position. Smuggling could not go unchallenged without undermining the power and influence of Spanish law, royal authority, and the assertion of hegemonic economic dominance in Spanish America. At other times, however, the metropolis addressed the problem of contraband with significant and creative measures, including the creation of the viceroyalties of New Granada (1717 and 1739) and Río de la Plata (1776), the formation of the monopolistic CARACAS COMPANY in 1728, and the formulation of "free trade" policies in the late eighteenth century. More often than not, however, all of these efforts fell short of their goal, because imperial realities constrained them. Unwieldy Spanish bureaucracies, metropolitan commercial weaknesses, American consumer demands, the difficulties of law enforcement, official corruption, international war, unpacified Indian groups, the commercial interest of European rivals in Spanish American wealth, the smugglers' ingenious and practical methods of hiding their activities, and the long coastlines of the colonies all limited, if not undid, the effectiveness of these initiatives.

Given the inconstancies of legal Spanish commerce, smuggling also represented logical economic behavior and so complemented formal trade. In the absence of licensed Spanish shipping, only illicit commerce kept ports (including important entrepôts like Portobelo in present-day Panama) active and their respective markets supplied. Contraband provided American consumers with a wide variety of goods—new and used clothing; textiles of all sorts; common items such as scissors, toys, and candles; foodstuffs, including wheat flour and spices; and slaves—at prices that undercut those of licit goods. In return, Spanish Americans supplied silver, gold, gems, tobacco, cacao, livestock, hides, yerba, and dyewoods, according to local availability. Even local treasuries occasionally relied on the capture, sale, and taxation of contraband goods for major funding during the year.

Because contraband trade was illegal and therefore largely unrecorded, it is difficult to measure its volume, value, and movement and so to know fully its actual role in Spanish colonial economies. Both contemporary observers and modern scholars agree, however, on its importance. The openness with which smugglers sold their wares in the marketplaces of Cartagena and Buenos Aires testifies to the commercial prominence of contraband. So does the number of smuggling vessels that called on Spanish American ports. In 1706, for example, sixty Dutch ships called on Portobelo customers; and when the galleons arrived in 1708, twenty British merchantmen were in the harbor. Contemporary estimates of the value of contraband point as well to its vigor. In 1800, José Ignacio de Pombo, one of the most astute merchants and economic thinkers of viceregal New Granada, set the annual value of illegal Jamaican imports alone to Cartagena at 1 million pesos.

Contraband, furthermore, cut across social lines, employing high government officials and slaves; priests, soldiers, merchants, and Indians (especially Guajiros, Cunas, and Osage); males and females; outlaws and law-enforcement agents; and Spaniards and foreigners alike. So, albeit illegal, contraband played a significant role in the economic life of colonial Spanish America.

Significant monographic studies of Spanish American contraband include SERGIO VILLALOBOS R., *Comercio y contrabando en el Río de la Plata y Chile, 1700–1811* (1965); CELESTINO ANDRÉS ARAÚZ, *El contrabando holandés en el Caribe durante la primera mitad del siglo XVIII* (1984); CORNELIS CH. GOSLINGA, *The Dutch in the Caribbean and in the Guianas, 1680–1791* (1985); MICHEL MORINEAU, *Incroyables gazettes et fabuleux métaux: Les retours des trésors américains d'après les gazettes hollandaises (XVIe–XVIIIe siècles)* (1985); ZACARÍAS MOUTOUKIAS, *Contrabando y control colonial en el siglo XVII: Buenos Aires, el Atlántico, y el espacio peruano* (1988); and HÉCTOR R. FELICIANO RAMOS, *El contrabando inglés en el Caribe y el Golfo de Mexico, 1748–1778* (1990).

Three pioneering articles in English are VERA LEE BROWN, "Contraband Trade: A Factor in the Decline of Spain's American Empire," in *Hispanic American Historial Review* 8, no. 2 (1928): 178–189; ALLAN CHRISTELOW, "Contraband Trade Between Jamaica and the Spanish Main, and the Free Port Act of 1766," in *Hispanic American Historical Review* 22, no. 2 (1942): 309–343; and GEORGE H. NELSON, "Contraband Trade Under the Asiento," in *American Historical Review* 51, no. 1 (1945): 55–67.

LANCE R. GRAHN

CONTRAS, an anti-Sandinista military force supported by the administration of President Ronald Reagan during the 1980s. Conceived in 1981 as an armed force to interdict arms supplies shipped from Nicaragua to anti-government guerrillas in El Salvador, the contras grew from a five-hundred-man force to an estimated twelve thousand men with the objective of ousting the Sandinistas from political power. The contras eventually represented Nicaragua's diverse political factions: ex-Somocistas, Miskito Indians and disgruntled Sandinistas, and members of Nicaragua's upper, middle, and lower social sectors. U.S. congressional discontent with the contras' attacks upon civilian targets and their continued human rights violations led in 1984 to the Boland Amendment, which cut military aid to them. The Reagan administration then turned to the National Security Council, where Lieutenant Colonel Oliver North solicited money from leaders of oil-rich nations and generated funds from missile sales to Iran. Operating from base camps in Honduras, the contras conducted forays into Nicaragua but never controlled any territory inside the country, nor did they ever gain popular support. As Reagan's Central American policy came under increasing criticism at home, Central American peace initiatives took hold. In 1989, first at Tesoro Beach, El Salvador, in February and then at Tela, Honduras, in August, the Central American presidents forged an agreement that provided for free elections in Nicaragua and the disbanding of the contras. Under these conditions, the U.S. Congress appropriated $49.7 million in humanitarian aid for the contras pending the results of the February 1990 elections. When Violeta BARRIOS DE CHAMORRO defeated Daniel ORTEGA SAAVEDRA for the Nicaraguan presidency, the justification for the exis-

Contra and Sandinista troops meet near Quilalí, 1988. © CINDY KARP / BLACK STAR.

tence of the contras disappeared. Under the supervision of a United Nations peacekeeping force, the contras were disbanded by June 1990, but not all returned to Nicaragua. Some remained scattered throughout Central America, while the wealthier supporters resided in the United States.

ROBERT A. PASTOR, *Condemned to Repetition: The United States and Nicaragua* (1987); BOB WOODWARD, *Veil: The Secret Wars of the CIA, 1981–1987* (1987); U.S. CONGRESS. HOUSE OF REPRESENTATIVES SELECT COMMITTEE TO INVESTIGATE COVERT ARMS TRANSACTIONS WITH IRAN AND SENATE SELECT COMMITTEE ON SECRET MILITARY ASSISTANCE TO IRAN AND THE NICARAGUAN OPPOSITION, *Iran-Contra Affair.* 100th Congress, 1st session, House Report No. 100–433, Senate Report No. 100–216 (1987); ROY GUTMAN, *Banana Diplomacy: The Making of American Policy in Nicaragua, 1981–1987* (1988).

THOMAS M. LEONARD

See also **Nicaragua: Political Parties.**

CONTRERAS BROTHERS (Hernando [*b.* ca. 1529; *d.* 1550] and Pedro [*b.* ca. 1531; *d.* 1550]), sons of Rodrigo de Contreras, governor of Nicaragua (1534–1544), and grandsons of Pedro Arias de ÁVILA; in 1550 they led one of the most serious revolts against Spanish royal authority during the colonial period. Their father, from a prominent Segovian family, was accused, among other abuses, of misappropriating to himself, his family, and his friends the best ENCOMIENDAS in Nicaragua. When he was relieved of office, his sons and supporters faced the reduction or loss of their pueblos, along with diminished social and political influence. Emboldened by sulking *encomenderos* and malcontents from Peru, the brothers rebelled with some three hundred followers, a majority of the residents in Nicaragua.

In León, Hernando and others murdered Bishop Antonio de Valdivieso, a persistent critic of Rodrigo, after which other rebels proceeded to destroy livestock and crops, as well as surplus sailing vessels. They aimed to capture the silver fleet from Peru, commanded by the formidable Pedro de la GASCA, and take control of the city of Panama. Thereafter they planned to establish rule in Peru under Hernando Contreras, the "prince of liberty," spuriously claiming that kingdom because initial Spanish expeditions to the general region had sailed under the aegis of Ávila and that, accordingly, certain proprietary rights accrued to his grandsons.

Because of overconfidence, poor planning, and inept leadership, the uprising failed. Reared in luxury and enjoying the favor of the colonists, the leaders were inexperienced; Hernando, though a licentiate, was only twenty-one, and Pedro nineteen. They understood strategy very poorly, making the mistake of dividing their forces into small groups. After a clumsy attack on Panama City, the residents there fought back with unexpected skill and resolution. In disarray, the hapless rebels fled for their lives. Pedro was lost at sea, and

Hernando drowned in a river. His head was displayed as a warning to would-be traitors.

The most complete study of the Contreras family is MARQUÉS DE LOZOYA (JUAN DE CONTRERAS), *Vida del segoviano Rodrigo de Contreras, gobernador de Nicaragua (1534–1544)* (1920), although the author, a descendant of Rodrigo, is biased in his presentation. In English, see HUBERT HOWE BANCROFT, *History of Central America,* vol. 2 (1883). See also ANTONIO DE REMESAL, *Historia general de las Indias Occidentales y particular de la gobernación de Chiapa y Guatemala,* 2 vols. (1966), first published in 1619. A more recent publication of interest is TEODORO HAMPE-MARTÍNEZ, *Don Pedro de la Gasca (1493–1567): Su obra política en España y América* (1990).

WILLIAM L. SHERMAN

CONVENTILLO, a term applied to substandard urban housing in Chile around the turn of the twentieth century. As dispossessed agricultural and mining families migrated to large cities, they crowded into these substandard living quarters not unlike North American tenements. Generally one-story buildings, *conventillos* were without running water, electricity, and often windows, and usually faced each other across an open sewer. Given these squalid living conditions, the inhabitants of *conventillos,* who lived in extreme overcrowding, suffered enormously from various communicable diseases such as smallpox, cholera, bubonic plague, and typhoid. Not surprisingly, the mortality rate in Santiago was higher than in Bombay or Alexandria.

PETER D. SHAZO, *Urban Workers and Labor Unions in Chile, 1902–1927* (1983), pp. 56–64; LUIS ROMERO, "Condiciones de vidas de los sectores populares en Santiago de Chile, 1840–1895," in *Nueva Historia* 3, no. 9 (1984): 3–87.

WILLIAM F. SATER

COOKE, JOHN WILLIAM (*b.* 14 November 1920; *d.* 19 September 1968), principal Argentine theoretician of revolutionary Peronism, or *justicialismo.* Cooke was elected to Argentina's Congress in 1946 as a member of the Radical Party. He quickly gravitated to the charismatic Juan Domingo PERÓN, whom he supported in the pages of *De Frente,* a publication that to many Peronists became the political and moral conscience of the movement. With Perón's ouster in September 1955, Cooke developed a plan of resistance that had as its focus guerrilla warfare followed by general insurrection. Arrested in October 1955, he clandestinely directed from prison the Peronist resistance against both military and civilian governments. A dramatic escape in 1957 was followed in 1959 by exile in Cuba, where he arranged for the training of Argentine guerrillas.

By 1962 Cooke, still in Cuba, and Perón, in exile in Spain, had moved to different political positions and adopted different strategies. Cooke remained on the violent extreme left of the Peronist movement and felt that Perón had become little more than a symbolic mem-

A conventillo in Buenos Aires, ca. 1906. ARCHIVO GENERAL DE LA NACIÓN, BUENOS AIRES.

ory. Perón considered Cooke "too Cuban" and unrepresentative of *justicialismo*, Perón's political and social philosophy. Cooke returned to Argentina in the mid-1960s, where he died of cancer.

DANIEL JAMES, "The Peronist Left, 1955–1975," in *Journal of Latin American Studies* 8, no. 2 (1976):273–296; RICHARD GILLESPIE, *John William Cooke: El peronismo alternativo* (1989); DONALD C. HODGES, *Argentina's "Dirty War": An Intellectual Biography* (1991), pp. 73–4, 78–9.

PAUL GOODWIN

COPACABANA FORT, REVOLT OF (1922). Cannon fire shook Brazil's capital during the early morning of 5 July 1922, initiating a rebellion that became the epicenter of a series of military insurrections known as the *tenente* (lieutenant) revolts. Mutinies orchestrated by army coconspirators quickly ensued in other Carioca (Rio de Janeiro) garrisons, but legalist officers were forewarned and easily crushed these subsequent uprisings. Organized primarily by junior officers, the revolt included common soldiers, noncommissioned officers, cadets, and a handful of civilians. Incensed by the civilian government's corruption and the arrest of former president and army spokesman Marshal HERMES DA FON-

SECA, the junior officers acted to depose President Epitácio PESSOA.

The rebels of Copacabana Fort learned of the revolt's failure outside their battlements but refused to surrender, despite heavy bombardment. On 6 July the acting commander, Lieutenant Antônio de Siqueira Campos, allowed all soldiers not prepared to fight to the death to leave the fort. The eighteen troops and officers who remained sallied forth with shreds of the fort's Brazilian flag in their breast pockets. Eleven of them confronted loyalist forces in a suicidal gun battle on the beachfront Avenida Atlântica. This audacious act captured popular attention, providing martyrs and inspiration for succeeding *tenente* revolts.

For a narrative account of the revolt, consult GLAUCO CARNEIRO, *História das revoluções brasileiras*, 2d ed. (1989). A recent analysis of this insurrection can be found in JOSÉ AUGUSTO DRUMMOND, *O movimento tenentista* (1986). Sources in English deal with this initial *tenente* revolt only in passing. A standard reference that focuses on the subsequent uprisings is NEILL MACAULAY, *The Prestes Column: A Revolution in Brazil* (1980).

PETER M. BEATTIE

See also **Tenentismo.**

261

COPÁN, a major pre-Hispanic MAYA center on the western border of Honduras near Guatemala. It marks the eastern boundary of Maya territory and undoubtedly controlled trade between the Maya area and Central America during its time of major activity, the Late Classic Period. The earliest and latest dated monuments show 9.1.0.0.0 (A.D. 455) on stela 20 and 9.18.10.0.0 (A.D. 790) on altar 61. The site has been known since reported by Don Diego García de Palacios in 1576.

The site center consists of a large open plaza to the north, bounded by modest structures, in which stand numerous ornately carved stone stelae of the rulers of Copán. Many have burial caches beneath. In the southeast corner of the plaza are an elegant ball court and a

Stela H, Copán, Honduras. PHOTO BY IAN GRAHAM.

hieroglyphic stairway with the longest known carved Maya inscription (1,500–2,000 glyphs), with details of Copán's long dynastic history. The southern half of the site center consists of a large elevated (120-foot) platform, the Acropolis, with multiple construction phases and numerous elite ceremonial buildings. The Copán River eroded away a portion of the east side of the Acropolis, exposing an archaeological cross-section noted for its size (900 feet long by 120 feet high). (The river has been rechanneled to protect the site.) From the northeast, a *sacbe* (causeway) leads to an area of elite residences with richly carved, full-figure hieroglyphic inscriptions. Recent studies show that wide areas of the Copán valley surrounding the site center were occupied. The site has several astronomical alignments and carved evidence of a new Maya method for finding the length of a lunar month.

The carved dynastic monuments, in concert with the stelae of nearby QUIRIGUA, record the capture of Copán's ruler, 18 Rabbit, in A.D. 737. Though two additional rulers are recorded, Copán's peak had passed and major activity ended abruptly after A.D. 800. The site shows its own emblem glyph on monuments, and also mentions TIKAL, PALENQUE, and CALAKMUL.

Active field research was continuing at the site in 1991. See SYLVANUS G. MORLEY and GEORGE W. BRAINERD, *The Ancient Maya*, 4th ed. (1983), pp. 320–328; PROYECTO ARQUEOLÓGICO COPÁN (Instituto Hondureño de Antropología e Historia), *Introducción a la arqueología de Copán, Honduras,* 3 vols. and detailed maps (1983).

WALTER R. T. WITSCHEY

COPARTICIPACIÓN (Coparticipation), the doctrine under which the government administration in Uruguay was shared by the two traditional political parties, the Blancos and the Colorados. During the nineteenth century this system took the form of a territorial division, with departments under the control of one party or the other, but under President José BATLLE Y ORDÓÑEZ (1903–1907, 1911–1915), who favored a one-party government, the institutions of the central government were shared. Coparticipation was redefined to mean the right of the minority party to representation in Parliament, and under the 1919 Constitution the opposition participated in the National Council of Administration and secured rights of patronage.

GÖRAN G. LINDAHL, *Uruguay's New Path: A Study in Politics During the First Colegiado, 1919–1933* (1962).

HENRY FINCH

COPPER INDUSTRY. Early Andean copper mining was prompted by the need to develop symbolic objects that served political power, the display of social status, and communication of religious belief. Gold-plated and alloyed copper objects were common in the pre-Inca

Metalworkers inspect newly cast cakes of copper, Chile. LIBRARY OF CONGRESS.

CHAVÍN culture of about 1000 B.C. Electrochemical replacement and depletion silvering and gilding on copper surfaces were devised in pre-Columbian times to give a precious-metal appearance. The first known Andean example of copper-silver alloy is a Peruvian bead from the Lurin valley site of Malposo. Tumbaga, a gold-copper alloy, was first produced in the central Andes, but later became common to many parts of pre-Columbian South America and as far north as Mexico. In 1494, Columbus reportedly initiated gold mining with a copper by-product in the Dominican Republic. The Spanish CONQUISTADORES valued copper for use in armaments.

The first European copper mine in Latin America opened in 1522 at TAXCO, Mexico. Mexico produced a total of 8,000 tons of copper by 1890, averaged about 65,000 tons annually by 1905, and more than 200,000 tons per year by the early 1970s. The most important Mexican deposits are located at Cananea and Nacozari (La Caridad) in Sonora and, formerly, at El Boleo in Baja California.

The nineteenth century was a time of political turmoil in Chile, and copper mining became increasingly important. The WAR OF THE PACIFIC, involving Chile, Bolivia, and Peru (1879–1883) resulted in the incorporation of the copper-rich Regions I and II into northern Chile. Copper mining expanded in Chile following the introduction of the first reverberatory furnace in 1842, which permitted smelting of copper sulfide minerals. Chile

was the foremost world producer until 1882, when the United States took the lead. A new era for Chilean copper evolved in the early 1900s through U.S. investment and mining technology. Using the U.S.-developed froth flotation for concentration of copper ores and large-scale open-pit mining methods, low-grade Chilean copper porphyries could be exploited. The Chilean Cordillera possesses several major copper porphyry deposits at Chuquicamata, El Salvador, Potrerillos, Rio Blanco, El Teniente, and now, La Escondida and La Candelaria. Chile's largest, the CHUQUICAMATA MINE (600,000 tons per year), began large-scale production in 1912. La Escondida Mine (300,000 tons per year) started production in late 1990. The mostly U.S.-owned large Chilean copper mines were nationalized on 16 July 1971. The government-owned copper company, Corporación Nacional del Cobre de Chile (CODELCO-Chile), is the largest copper mining and refining company in the world. Today, Chile is the world's largest copper producer, having regained that position in 1982, when it surpassed the United States. Chile's annual copper production currently is more than 1.6 million tons of copper.

Peruvian production is about 400,000 tons of copper per year, but Peru's copper industry did not grow significantly until after the War of the Pacific, aided by the completion of the central railway, and between 1940 and 1960, by the significant exploration and mining development efforts of U.S.-owned companies. Though significant reserves are known in the Carajas District of

263

Brazil, mines of the Rio Grande do Sul area have been the most important and currently produce about 46,000 tons of copper per year. Copper also has been mined in Argentina, Bolivia, Colombia, Cuba, Ecuador, Guatemala, Haiti, Honduras, Nicaragua, Panama, and Venezuela, but although some countries have undeveloped resources, the amount mined has been small. Between 1800 and 1926, the copper mines in the Bolivian province of Pacajes near the Chilean border had an annual production of about 20,000 tons of copper per year. Argentina, Bolivia, Honduras, and Ecuador currently produce less than 600 tons per year of copper each. Cuba has produced copper from the Pinar del Río Province near Matahambre since the end of the nineteenth century. Copper has been mined near Caracas, Venezuela, and from deposits near the port of Cabello in the state of Yaracuy since the early sixteenth century. Copper mining in Haiti began in 1728, and with development of the Meme copper deposit in the late 1950s, continued through 1971.

In 1991 the countries of Latin America contributed 25 percent of the world copper mine production of about 9.1 million tons, and held 35 percent of the total world copper ore reserve base of 543 million tons of copper. Chile possesses 21.7 percent, Peru 6 percent, and Mexico 4 percent of the world's copper reserve base, according to the U.S. Bureau of Mines.

ALBERTO Q. BENAVIDES, "Exploration and Mining Ventures in Peru," in *Economic Geology* 7 (November 1990): 1296–1302; HEATHER LECHTMAN, "Pre-Columbian Surface Metallurgy," in *Scientific American*, Spring 1984, pp. 56–63; A. B. PARSONS, *The Porphyry Coppers* (1933), pp. 320–354; "The Caribbean Island Arc—a Major Storehouse," in *Northern Miner* 61, no. 27 (September 1975): 52–53; JENARO GONZÁLEZ REYNA, *Riqueza minera y yacimientos minerales de México* (1947), pp. 173–183; U.S. BUREAU OF MINES, "Copper," in *Minerals Yearbook* vol. I, 1900–1989 issues.

JANICE L. W. JOLLY

See also **Mining.**

CORCOVADO. Part of the Gavea-Tijuca Massif, Corcovado (the "Hunchback") stands near the entrance to Guanabara Bay in RIO DE JANEIRO (see illustration). During the nineteenth century, Corcovado was the site of early coffee plantations and a refuge for runaway slaves, who lived in *quilombos* (huts) on its slopes. A cog railway, built in 1884 by engineer Pereira Passos, afforded easy access to the peak, which had long been a tourist attraction. Guglielmo Marconi designed an electrical system to light the mountain, which began operating in 1912, further enhancing the area's appeal.

The mountain is best known for the 98-foot concrete and soapstone statue of Christ the Redeemer, which stands at its peak. The statue, planned and directed by Brazilian engineer H. Silva Costa, was completed in 1931. It was designed by French sculptor Paul Landowski and funded by contributions from the people of Rio.

BRUCE WEBER "On High," in *The New York Times Magazine*, 22 July 1990, p. 46.

SHEILA L. HOOKER

CORDEL, LITERATURE OF THE. Originally presented in oral form in the tradition of epic and other popular literature in the world, these "ballads," primarily of northeastern Brazil, were eventually printed as *folhetos* (pamphlets or "little books") and sold dangling from a *cordel* (string). The cover, usually in pastel colors, has a photograph or print not always related to the text. The reader, often illiterate, may recognize a familiar tale and be persuaded to buy according to its cover design. A picture of the author and some information are often found on the back cover. Contemporary storytellers, frequently well-known writers, continue to develop the tradition. Read now rather than recited, and without musical accompaniment (both hands are needed to turn pages), the ballads usually consist of high dramatic dialogue as befits the customary content.

The traditional *cordel* is a collection of folktales in verse (usually *sextilhas*, six lines of seven syllables each, rhymed *a b c b d b*) on a wide variety of subjects that express the strict morality of the extended community of the Northeast. To name but a few, there are *cordel* versions of news events; the lives and exploits of famous bandits, cowboys, saints, and other historical personages; as well as of Romeo and Juliet, Sleeping Beauty, and numerous other European, Asian, and African figures. Fabled animals, such as mysterious bulls, are part of the vast body of *cordel* material.

A carefully balanced trial between good and evil, in which the former always clearly wins, is a constant theme in the *cordel*. Most of the personages are either saints or sinners. The protagonist generally undergoes a test of character which he or she may fail, but usually passes. In narratives of actual or would-be incest, for example, the besieged daughter ascends into heaven at the end, while the father who has assailed or tempted his child descends into hell. In a formula usually resembling a court trial comprising an opposition between honor and dishonor, an initial pact is tested, after which there is a response and a counterresponse, followed by a judgment and a final confirmation of the pact.

The stories are offered to the people as models of how daily life should be lived ideally. The traditional pattern is both a literary convention and a means of reasserting a code of ethics. Their authors do not merely protest or chide the dominant class from the point of view and in the language of the proletariat, however, but express politicized and ideological struggles in terms that may not always be literary.

CANDACE SLATER, *Stories on a String: The Brazilian Literatura de Cordel* (1982).

RICHARD A. MAZZARA

See also **Literature: Brazil.**

CORDERO, JUAN (*b.* 10 June 1822; *d.* 28 May 1884), Mexican painter. After having attended the ACADEMIA DE SAN CARLOS during what was probably its most difficult period, Cordero went in 1844 to Rome, where he came into contact with the Nazarenes (a group of German artists who sought to revitalize Christian art) and executed religious and historical canvases as well as portraits. On his return to Mexico in 1853, Cordero was disappointed at not being named director of painting at the Academia de San Carlos, a post then occupied by Pelegrín CLAVÉ. Nevertheless, he produced numerous fine portraits and received important commissions. Contrasts in lighting characterize a good number of his works, and a realistic bent informs even his most idealized portraits. Cordero painted the vaults and dome of the Church of Santa Teresa and the dome of the Church of San Fernando. An allegorical mural for the Escuela Nacional Preparatoria, known only through a copy, has been considered an antecedent of twentieth-century muralism by nationalist historians.

ELISA GARCÍA BARRAGÁN, *El pintor Juan Cordero* (1984).

CLARA BARGELLINI

CORDERO, ROQUE (*b.* 16 August 1917), Panamanian composer and pedagogue. Born in Panama City, Cordero studied composition at Hamline University in St. Paul, Minnesota, and orchestral conducting at Tanglewood. Among his teachers were Ernst Krenek, Leon Barzin, and Dimitri Mitropoulos. He was the director of the National Institute of Music in Panama from 1953 until 1964 and artistic director and conductor of the National Orchestra of Panama from 1964 to 1966. He then became professor of composition at the Latin American Music Center at Indiana University. Cordero's compositional style evolved from a guarded nationalistic approach near the beginning of his career to an atonal language with twelve-tone procedures. His own version of a serially organized atonal language became his most prevalent compositional technique from 1950 on. It is applied to pitch classes and intervals but also determines the evolution of his complex rhythmic structures and the overall form of the piece. In 1976 he received the First Inter-American Composition Prize in Costa Rica. Cordero has been music adviser to Peer International Corporation in New York City and has been invited to judge many international composition competitions.

His more nationalistic works include *Capricho interio-rano* (1939), *Sonatina rítmica* (1943), *Obertura Panameña* (1944), and *Rapsodia campesina* (1953). Those early works show Cordero expressing himself through elaborations of typical Panamanian dance rhythms, such as the *mejorana* and the *tamborillo*. His first twelve-tone composition is his 1946 Sonatina for violin and piano. Other important works are the Symphony no. 2 (1956); String Quartet no. 1 (1960); *Mensaja fúnebre* for clarinet and string orchestra (1961), written in memory of Dimitri Mitropoulos; Violin Concerto (1962), written in a virtuoso style and full of intricate rhythms; Soliloquies for alto sax; Sonata for cello and piano (1963); Symphony no. 3 (1965), a work with one theme and five variations, commissioned by the Third Music Festival in Caracas, Venezuela; *Sonata breve* for piano (1966); *Circumvolutions and Mobiles* for fifty-seven instruments (1967); String Quartets no. 2 and no. 3 (1968, 1973); Cantata (1974); *Permutaciones* (1974); *Variations and Theme for Five* (1975); and *Paz, Paix, Peace* for chamber ensemble (1970).

JOHN VINTON, ed. *Dictionary of Contemporary Music* (1974); GÉRARD BÉHAGUE, *Music in Latin America: An Introduction* (1979); *New Grove Dictionary of Music and Musicians* (1980); *Octavo festival internacional de música contemporánea* (1992), pp. 47–48, 122.

ALCIDES LANZA

CORDERO CRESPO, LUIS (*b.* 6 April 1833; *d.* 30 January 1912), president of Ecuador (1892–1895). Born into a prominent family of Azuay, Luis Cordero Crespo studied law at the University of Quito but chose to devote himself to letters and politics rather than jurisprudence. As a man of letters he was most noted for his *Poesías serias* (1895), *Poesías jocosas* (1895), and a Spanish-Quechua dictionary. He founded several newspapers, was a professor of literature at the National College in Cuenca, and helped to inaugurate the universities of Guayaquil and Cuenca. He served as rector of the University of Cuenca from 1911 to 1912.

In 1883, Cordero helped found the Republican Party. After serving in Congress as a deputy and then as a senator, he was elected president in 1892. He attempted unsuccessfully to conciliate warring Liberals and Conservatives. His declaration that church interests were superior to those of the state turned Liberals against him. Revelation of his government's secret involvement in the sale of a Chilean warship to Japan aroused public indignation and forced Cordero to resign. The fall of the government brought the Liberal general Eloy ALFARO to power, thus ending twelve years of civilian rule.

REMIGIO CRESPO TORAL, *Luis Cordero* (1917); LUIS ROBALINO DÁVILA, *Diez años de civilismo* (1968), pp. 437–701; FRANK MACDONALD SPINDLER, *Nineteenth-Century Ecuador: An Historical Introduction* (1987), pp. 137–147.

MARK J. VAN AKEN

CÓRDOBA, FERNÁNDEZ/HERNÁNDEZ DE. *See* Fernández/Hernández de Córdoba.

CÓRDOBA, JOSÉ MARÍA (also Córdova; *b.* 8 September 1799; *d.* 17 October 1829), Colombian military hero. Born in La Concepción, Antioquia, the son of the alcalde, Córdoba joined the patriots in 1814. His valor brought him a captaincy in 1817; he was named lieutenant colonel in 1819 and, after the battle of BOYACÁ (7 August 1819), commandant of ANTIOQUIA (1819–1820). He proceeded to eliminate royalist remnants from Chocó and the northern Cauca and Magdalena basins (1820–1821), and was promoted to colonel. He joined General Antonio José de SUCRE ALCALÁ in Ecuador, distinguished himself at PICHINCHA (24 May 1822), and became a general (3 January 1823). In Peru, Córdoba went on to win further laurels. He led the Colombian infantry's decisive charge at AYACUCHO (9 December 1824), the apex of his career.

Although Córdoba had killed one of his sergeants at Popayán on 28 December 1823, and had threatened the lives of two other subordinates in 1824, he was acquitted by a court-martial for murder and threats to murder (1827). Then he became engaged to Fanny Henderson, daughter of James Henderson, the British consul general in Bogotá. Although Córdoba was BOLÍVAR's minister of war (1828), the two men became estranged over Bolívar's flirtation with monarchy. Falsely accused of disloyalty by Tomás Cipriano de MOSQUERA, he rebelled against the government and attempted to raise Antioquia. Wounded and a prisoner, with his little force routed, he was cut down at El Santuario by Colonel Rupert Hand.

PILAR MORENO DE ÁNGEL, *José María Córdova* (1977); and "Córdoba, José María," in *Historical Dictionary of the Spanish Empire, 1492–1975*, edited by James S. Olson.

J. LEÓN HELGUERA

See also **Wars of Independence.**

CÓRDOBA

THE PROVINCE

The central province of Argentina, Córdoba encompasses 65,161 square miles and has a population of 2,748,000 (1991). Located between the Río Dulce in the north and the Río Quinto in the south, the province of Córdoba stretches across three physiographic units: the eastern pampa, the Sierra de Córdoba, and the interior pampa. Its center is occupied by the Sierra de Córdoba, a crystalline-metamorphic massif rising to a maximum height of 9,817 feet in the Cerro Champaquí. Among the minerals extracted from this sierra and adjacent ranges are manganese, beryl, bismuth, and wolfram. Air purity and cooler temperatures have converted many mountain villages (especially in the Punilla Valley) into spa resorts, frequented by Córdobans and residents of the pampa during the hot summers. In the humid pampa plains east of the sierra, the dominant activity is raising cattle for either meat or dairy production. However, owing to the relatively ample water supply from the Sierra de Córdoba, large areas along the eastern slope and the pampa have specialized in the production of wheat (the main agricultural commodity of the province), rye, maize, flax, peanuts, millet, and alfalfa. Recently, the land dedicated to soybean production has increased to the same degree that the land producing wheat has decreased. Of lesser agricultural significance is the segment of the pampa between the western slope of the sierra and the foothills of the Andes. Excessive aridity and lack of water have created a semidesert landscape; the salt flats of Salinas Grandes and Pampa de Salinas are the most significant examples.

THE CITY

The city of Córdoba (1989 population 969,000) was founded on 6 July 1573 by Jerónimo Luis de Cabrera, governor of TUCUMÁN, in order to facilitate the transit between Alto Perú and Santa María del Buen Aire (now BUENOS AIRES) on the RÍO DE LA PLATA estuary. The city lies on the banks of the Río Primero, at the eastern slopes of the Sierra de Córdoba. By 1584 forty landholders with trusted Indians settled in the peaceful town to practice agriculture and cattle ranching, and in 1599 the Jesuits opened a mission there. In 1623 Bishop Fernando de Trejo y Sanabria founded the University of Córdoba on the site of what had been a Jesuit academy (1613), and several administrative services were established in the growing town as agricultural activities developed and wealth accumulated. Soon Córdoba competed with Tucumán as a major trading center in the Río de la Plata hinterland: in 1622 an inland custom was instituted to stop the smuggling of European merchandise from the estuary into the interior.

When it was declared the seat of the Intendancy of Córdoba in 1783, with jurisdiction over the provinces of Córdoba, La Rioja, Mendoza, San Juan, and San Luis, the city of Córdoba gained in prestige as one of the most prosperous, cultured, aristocratic, and Spain-oriented settlements in the Río de la Plata region. In the seventeenth and eighteenth centuries, religious orders flocked to the city. The numerous churches, such as the cathedral and the Church of the Compañía de Jesús, are testimony to their presence and influence. At the time independence was declared by the Buenos Aires junta on 25 May 1810, the authorities of Córdoba voted to remain faithful to the king of Spain. A split from and rivalry with Buenos Aires ensued, and Córdoba became one of the most stubborn supporters of the autonomy of the Platine provinces. Rulers of Buenos Aires, such as Bernardino RIVADAVIA, Juan Manuel de ROSAS, Manuel DORREGO, Juan Galo LAVALLE, Juan QUIROGA, and Manuel LÓPEZ, tried to subdue the rebellious interior province, which in the process was torn apart by internal strife. It was not until 1868 that Governor Félix de la Peña was able to establish order and harmony in the province.

In 1870 a railway line was opened between Córdoba and the capital city of Buenos Aires, accelerating the integration of the region into the national mainstream and promoting active colonization of the interior PAMPA. Yet occasional outbursts of dissension continued to perpetuate the traditional enmity between Córdoba and Buenos Aires: in 1880 conservative and Catholic sectors of Córdoba strongly opposed the laicist laws discussed in the congress of Buenos Aires, and throughout republican times the city's elites were at odds with the political leaders of Buenos Aires over accepting foreigners without a patriarchal family background. As recently as the 1950s, Juan PERÓN was resisted not only because of his attacks against the Catholic hierarchy but also because of his plebeian origin, and in 1955 the army uprising that overthrew Perón was started by General Eduardo Leonardi in the artillery barracks of Córdoba.

Nonconformism and rebelliousness have not been the hallmark exclusively of the conservative circles of Córdobans. In 1969 workers and students from that city initiated the CORDOBAZO, a massive rebellion that brought an end to the rule of General Juan C. ONGANÍA. During subsequent military governments, *montonero* guerrillas effectively attacked military and government targets in the city of Córdoba, keeping military rulers at bay.

The metropolitan perimeter of Córdoba stretches over a gentle slope between 1,320 and 1,650 feet. Originally the settlement spread out from the left bank of the Río Primero. Later, it expanded along the river into the General Paz and San Vicente boroughs. Early in the twentieth century the city grew toward the western slope, where today most military garrisons are established. After World War II the most accelerated development took place along the highway leading to Buenos Aires and Rosario. Along this artery are located most of the industrial establishments of the city: automobile factories, chemical and fertilizer plants, factories of electromechanical equipment, and food-processing plants.

Since colonial times, Córdoba has benefited from good communications with neighboring and distant regions. Railway lines of the General Belgrano and Bartolomé Mitre systems connect the city with Rosario and Buenos Aires to the southeast; with Tucumán, La Rioja, and San Juan to the north and west across the Sierra de Córdoba; and with Mendoza to the southwest, after connecting with the General San Martín railway at Mercedes. Airport Coronel Olmedo secures communications with the nation's capital and with major cities in western Argentina.

The main cultural center is the University of Córdoba, supported by the Catholic University of Córdoba. The observatory established in 1869 is credited with producing the first star atlas of the Southern Hemisphere, in the early 1900s.

ALFREDO TERZAGA, *Geografía de Córdoba* (Córdoba, 1963); EFRAÍN BISCHOFF, *Historia de la provincia de Córdoba* (Buenos Aires, 1968); RAÚL J. ARIAS, *Córdoba: Cuatro siglos* (Buenos Aires, 1973); and MARÍA C. VERA, *Córdoba: Una historia para los argentinos* (Buenos Aires, 1989.)

CÉSAR N. CAVIEDES

CÓRDOBA, TREATY OF (1821), an agreement that recognized Mexico's independent sovereignty and arranged for the withdrawal of remaining Spanish forces. Arriving at Veracruz in 1821 after most of Mexico had fallen to Agustín de ITURBIDE's Army of the THREE GUARANTEES, Captain-General Juan O'DONOJÚ, a liberal and Mason who had served as Spanish minister of war under the Constitution of 1812, entered negotiations with Iturbide at Córdoba rather than unnecessarily prolong the revolutionary war. Recognizing that the PLAN OF IGUALA sought to maintain the Bourbon dynasty and strong links between Spain and Mexico, O'Donojú signed the Treaty of Córdoba on 24 August 1821. The sixteen articles of the treaty followed the spirit of the Plan of Iguala. For most Mexicans, the fact that the Spanish government later repudiated the treaty was irrelevant. After assisting with the transition of power, O'Donojú died in Mexico City of a disease contracted during his stay at Veracruz.

JAIME DELGADO, *España y México en el siglo XIX,* 3 vols. (1950); WILLIAM SPENCE ROBERTSON, *Iturbide of Mexico* (1968); TIMOTHY E. ANNA, *The Mexican Empire of Iturbide* (1990).

CHRISTON I. ARCHER

CÓRDOBA, UNIVERSITY OF Argentina's oldest university, established in 1613 by the JESUITS, and the center of the city's civic and cultural life from colonial times to well into the twentieth century. The university remained under the control of the Jesuits until their expulsion from the Spanish colonies in 1767, at which point it came under the direction of the FRANCISCANS. In 1858, the national government of Justo José URQUIZA officially assumed control of its administration. But almost two and a half centuries of church control of education, as well as isolation from the secularizing influences to be found in Buenos Aires, imbued the city with a strong Catholic ethos, and the church retained a preponderant influence in the university, with the clergy continuing to hold the majority of faculty and administrative positions well into the twentieth century.

From early in its history, the city's aristocratic families developed a close relationship to the university and the title of "doctor" was considered the highest social distinction. Throughout the nineteenth and early twentieth centuries, the university was a bastion of traditionalism, with a curriculum heavily weighted in favor of a scholastic education in law and theology. Because of its hidebound conservatism and social influence, it became the target of an important reform movement in 1918. In the wake of the Radical Party's 1916 electoral victory, middle-class students organized boycotts and an eventual occupation of the university, demanding a series of reforms, most notably university autonomy, student participation in the election and administration of university councils, modernization of the curriculum, and the competitive selection and periodic review of all professors. To coordinate the reform campaign, students established the Federación Universitaria de Córdoba (FUC), an organization that would dominate student university politics for the next half century.

International influences such as the Mexican and Russian revolutions fired the young minds of the student reformers and radicalized the movement, bringing support from both the Socialist Party and the labor movement and leading to demands for free university education and the establishment of university extension courses for the working class. University issues again found common cause with social unrest in the 1969 uprising known as the CORDOBAZO. International influences included the Cuban Revolution and the events in Paris of May 1968. The alliance of the university with the trade unions led to an even more explosive social protest, highlighting once again that the university was a central part of public life in Córdoba.

RICHARD J. WALTER, *Student Politics in Argentina: The University Reform and Its Effects, 1918–1964* (1968); EFRAIN U. BISCHOFF, *Historia de Córdoba* (1979).

JAMES P. BRENNAN

See also **Universities: Modern.**

CORDOBAZO, EL, a social protest in the Argentine industrial city of Córdoba that took place 29–30 May 1969. The city's militant trade union movement found common cause with student protesters and the general citizenry in an uprising directed against the dictatorship of Juan Carlos ONGANÍA and the provincial government. The independent structures and combative practices of the Peronist unions, together with a radicalized local political culture, permitted a broad alliance in the uprising and an exceptionally violent protest in which symbols of both the government and imperialism were attacked. Fourteen persons were killed. The Cordobazo was the seminal political event of the 1960s, fatally weakening the Onganía dictatorship and serving as a powerful symbol for the Peronist and Marxist left in the following years.

JAMES P. BRENNAN, *The Labor Wars in Córdoba, 1955–1976: Ideology, Work, and Labor Politics in an Argentine Industrial City* (1994); JAMES P. BRENNAN and MÓNICA B. GORDILLO, "Working Class Protest, Popular Revolt, and Urban Insurrection in Argentina: The 1969 Cordobazo," in *Journal of Social History* 27, no. 3 (Spring 1994): 477–498.

JAMES P. BRENNAN

CÓRDOVA, ARTURO DE (*b.* 8 May 1908; *d.* 1973), Mexican film actor. Born Arturo García Rodriguez in Mérida, Yucatán, Córdova studied in Argentina. Upon his return to Mexico in 1930, he worked in radio. He made his cinematic debut in Hollywood with a small part in the film *For Whom the Bell Tolls*. In Mexico, his first acting part was in *Celos* (1936). By the 1940s, he had become one of the most sought-out and popular leading men of the "golden age" of the Mexican cinema. He starred in over 300 films in Mexico, Hollywood, Brazil, Spain, and Venezuela, and received three Ariels from the Mexican film academy for best performance by an actor for the films *En la palma de tu mano* (1950), *Las tres perfectas casadas* (1952), and *Feliz año amor mío* (1955).

LUIS REYES DE LA MAZA, *El cine sonoro en México* (1973); E. BRADFORD BURNS, *Latin American Cinema: Film and History* (1975); CARL J. MORA, *Mexican Cinema: Reflections of a Society: 1896–1980* (1982); and JOHN KING, *Magical Reels: A History of Cinema in Latin America* (1990).

DAVID MACIEL

CÓRDOVA, JORGE (*b.* 1822; *d.* 23 October 1861), president of Bolivia (1855–1857). Córdova's parents remain unknown. He joined the army of Andrés de SANTA CRUZ as an ordinary soldier and rose rapidly in rank. Córdova's marriage to the daughter of President Manuel Isidoro BELZÚ facilitated his entrance into politics.

Córdova succeeded his father-in-law as president. The transferral of power from Belzú to Córdova was the first peaceful one in Bolivia's history. Although Córdova was elected, he was overthrown by a military revolt and escaped to Peru. He returned to Bolivia several years later as a private citizen and died violently in the Massacre de Yáñez, which marred the presidency of José María ACHÁ.

Córdova had a reputation as a man of pleasure. As president he was fair and unpretentious and desperately tried to foster internal peace, tolerance, and cooperation among the political factions. These activities consumed so much of his time that little of substance was accomplished during his tenure.

MOISÉS ASCARRUNZ, *De siglo a siglo: Hombres célebres de Bolivia* (1920); ALCIDES ARGUEDAS, *La plebe en acción*, in *Obras Completas*, vol. 2 (1959).

CHARLES W. ARNADE

CÓRDOVA RIVERA, GONZALO S. (*b.* 15 July 1863; *d.* 13 April 1928), president of Ecuador. Born in Cuenca, Córdova Rivera completed a law degree at the Universidad de Cuenca. He served as deputy from Cañar Province from 1892 to 1897 and as governor of that province from 1898 to 1902. He was minister of the interior from 1903 to 1906. In 1912 he served as senator from Carchi Province and as vice president of the senate. He was Ecuador's minister to Chile, Argentina, and the United

States in the period 1911–1913, and minister to Venezuela in 1922. He was popularly elected to the presidency in 1924. On July 9, 1925, a group of young lieutenants overthrew the Córdova government.

Linda Alexander Rodríguez, *The Search for Public Policy: Regional Politics and Government Finances in Ecuador, 1830–1940* (1985), esp. pp. 51–52, 123–129.

LINDA ALEXANDER RODRÍGUEZ

CORNEJO, MARIANO H. (*b.* 1873; *d.* 25 March 1942), one of a group of POSITIVIST social scientists in late-nineteenth-century Peru. In 1896 he was appointed to the first chair of sociology at the National University of San Marcos. Cornejo relied upon precepts and convictions learned from European thinkers and adapted them to the society around him. He expressed optimism that an open-ended Peruvian aristocracy that admitted "new blood," together with the nation's scientists, could discover the sociological laws necessary to carry out the task of national progress. He scorned revolutionary change, favoring universal education and gradualism as the keys to national improvement. He denied that either race or class antagonisms governed history and foresaw utilitarian cooperation as a more useful framework of analysis.

FREDRICK B. PIKE, *The Modern History of Peru* (1967), pp. 162–164; and THOMAS M. DAVIES, JR., *Indian Integration in Peru, 1900–1948* (1974).

VINCENT PELOSO

CORN ISLANDS, two small islands about 40 miles off of the east coast of Nicaragua, near the coastal town of BLUEFIELDS. Little Corn and Great Corn islands have become increasingly important tourist destinations in recent years. Their historical significance, however, derives from their location rather than their beaches. As part of its attempts to construct a canal linking the Atlantic and Pacific oceans, the United States sought and gained the right to fortify these islands to protect the approach to a potential canal across Nicaragua. The concession was part of a much broader struggle between Britain and the United States for control of potential canal routes as well as political and economic dominance throughout the Caribbean Basin in the late nineteenth and early twentieth centuries. The islands also were considered as a possible resort by the dictator of Nicaragua, Anastasio SOMOZA, who invited U.S. millionaire Howard Hughes to Nicaragua to discuss plans for the islands in 1972.

TODD LITTLE-SIEBOLD

CORONA, RAMÓN (*b.* 1837; *d.* 11 November 1889), Liberal military commander and governor of Jalisco. Born to a family of modest social position in the southern Jaliscan village of Tuxcueca, Corona was the administrator of some mining operations near the Sinaloa–Tepic border when the REFORM war began in 1858. Over the next decade, he emerged as the leader of the migrants driven from Tepic who sought to restore white and MESTIZO dominance over that territory and its Indians, whom Manuel LOZADA had united and allied with the imperialist cause. Rising to command the Tepic Brigade, and then the Army of the West during the Intervention (1862–1867), Corona became the dominant military and political figure in west-central Mexico in the postwar years. His career culminated in his defeat of Lozada in 1873. After serving as ambassador to Spain and Portugal for twelve years, Corona returned as the elected governor of Jalisco in March 1887. An activist who promoted infrastructure and education, he acquired a growing national reputation and became a leading presidential candidate. Corona was assassinated in Guadalajara.

DANIEL COSÍO VILLEGAS, *Historia moderna de México: La República restaurada—la vida política* (1955) and *Historia moderna de México: El Porfiriato—la vida política interior,* 2 vols. (1970); STUART F. VOSS, *On the Periphery of Nineteenth Century Mexico: Sonora and Sinaloa, 1810–1877* (1982).

STUART VOSS

CORONADO, JUAN VÁZQUEZ DE (*b.* 1523; *d.* October 1565), conquistador and governor of Costa Rica (1562–1565). Founder of the Costa Rican city of Cartago (1564), Coronado headed a series of expeditions that brought most of Costa Rica under Spanish control by 1565.

Born in Salamanca, Spain, of noble parents, Coronado left Spain in 1540 to seek his fortune. He traveled to Mexico, joining his uncle, conquistador Francisco Vázquez de CORONADO. In 1548, Juan Vázquez de Coronado departed for Guatemala with a *cedula real* (royal letters patent) recommending him to the *audiencia.* Upon his arrival he was named *alcalde mayor* (royal governor) of El Salvador and Honduras. In subsequent years Coronado distinguished himself as a capable administrator and an adept conquistador. He was made *alcalde mayor* of Nicaragua in 1561. One of his first acts in this post was to subvert a rebellion of Spanish soldiers led by Lope de AGUIRRE.

In 1562, King PHILIP II designated him *alcalde mayor* of the provinces of Nueva Cartago and Costa Rica. Coronado began an extended campaign, tending to administrative problems in the cities of León, Nicoya, and Garcimuñoz, and pursuing the rebel *cacique* (local ruler) Garabito. In interactions with caciques, he proved to be a skillful negotiator and was far more moderate in his treatment of the Indians than were many of his contemporaries.

Coronado journeyed to Quepo and through the Guarco Valley in 1563, encountering strong Indian resistance in the town of Cuoto. A prolonged and bloody battle there ended in a Spanish victory. Coronado remained in the valley briefly, negotiating a peace with neighboring caciques and founding the city of Cartago, which became the capital of Costa Rica. After overseeing the provisioning and settlement of the city, he headed north, taking possession of the valley of Guaymi and the provinces of Texbi and Duy. He discovered gold in the Estrella River and in 1564 organized a registry of mines to facilitate the exploitation of the river's wealth.

In 1565, Coronado traveled to Spain to give Philip II a personal account of his progress. The Spanish monarch named him *adelantado* (governor) in perpetuity of the province of Costa Rica. In addition, Coronado received an annual salary, royal recognition of Cartago, and a three-year appointment as governor of Nicaragua. He was never to enjoy these privileges, however; on the return voyage, his ship, the *San Josepe*, was wrecked in a storm, leaving no survivors.

ACADEMIA DE GEOGRAFÍA E HISTORIA DE COSTA RICA, *Juan Vázquez de Coronado: Cartas de relación sobre la conquista de Costa Rica* (1964); CARLOS MELÉNDEZ CHAVERRI, *Juan Vázquez de Coronado: Conquistador y fundador de Costa Rica* (1966); VICTORIA URBANO, *Juan Vázquez de Coronado y su ética en la conquista de Costa Rica* (1968); *Revista del Archivo Nacional de Costa Rica* 33, nos. 1–12 (January–December 1969): 13–17, 45–64; RICARDO FERNÁNDEZ GUARDIA, *El descubrimiento y la Conquista* (1975), pp. 107–127.

SARA FLEMING

CORONEL, PEDRO (*b.* 25 May 1923; *d.* 23 May 1985), Mexican painter and sculptor. Born in Jerez, Zacatecas, Coronel left in 1940 for Mexico City, where he studied at the National School of Painting and Sculpture (La Esmeralda) until 1945. He taught sculpture there in 1945–1946. In 1946, Coronel traveled to Europe. While living in Paris he studied painting in the studio of Victor Brauner and sculpture with Constantin Brancusi. In later years he was a friend of Sonia Delaunay, the Ukrainian-born painter and designer who was married to Robert Delaunay. Throughout his life Coronel traveled extensively in Mexico, Europe, Africa, and Asia, assembling collections of artifacts from these countries. Coronel returned to Mexico in 1952 and in 1954 had his first important exhibition in the Proteo Gallery, Mexico City, which was very well received and reviewed. From that point on he exhibited regularly in Mexico, the United States, and Europe, most notably in Mexico City at the Gallery of Mexican Art.

Coronel's mature work draws heavily upon the tenets of abstraction while incorporating figural imagery derived from ancient artifacts of Mexico, Europe, Africa, and Asia. His works on canvas are heavily textured and aggressively colored. Sculptures are executed in marble, onyx, and bronze. In 1959, Coronel received the National Prize of Painting; in 1984, he was awarded the National Prize of Plastic Arts.

JUSTINO FERNÁNDEZ, *Pedro Coronel: Pintor y escultor* (1971), and *Exhibition of Paintings by Pedro Coronel: Lunar Poetics* (1972); SERGIO PITOL et al., *El universo del Pedro Coronel* (1981); ERIKA BILLETER, ed., *Images of Mexico* (1988).

CLAYTON KIRKING

CORONEL URTECHO, JOSÉ (*b.* 28 February 1906), except for Rubén DARÍO considered to be Nicaragua's most important writer. Born in Granada and educated at the Colegio Centroamérica, Coronel Urtecho studied for several years in the United States before returning to Nicaragua in 1925, bringing back a passionate interest in the "new American poetry" of Ezra Pound and others. With Luís Alberto Cabrales in 1931 he founded the *vanguardia* movement, which included Pablo Antonio CUADRA, Luís Downing, Joaquín Pasos, and others, most of them disaffected from their conservative upper-class Granada families. Taking as a motto "Beside our ancestors we go against our fathers," the iconoclastic *vanguardistas* reacted against Darío's imitators, bourgeois culture, the academy, and U.S. intervention in Nicaraguan political affairs. They proclaimed support for the patriotism of Augusto César SANDINO and fomented a rediscovery of "lo nicaragüense" (that which is Nicaraguan). The best work of the *vanguardistas* revitalized interest in the indigenous roots of national culture, introduced vigorous new North American and European literature (much of which they translated into Spanish) into Nicaragua, and produced an influential body of innovative writing in a variety of genres. Unfortunately, their paradoxical fascination with the elitist and antidemocratic ideals of emerging European fascism led them into a naive attempt to put their ideas into practice by supporting and taking part in the embryonic Somoza dictatorship.

Coronel Urtecho's own writing has embraced many genres: short stories and short novels, poetry, essays, translations, literary criticism, political commentary, and history. Loath to write books, he left the task of collecting his widely dispersed writings mostly to others. Major collections are *Rápido tránsito (al ritmo de norteamérica)* (1953), an account of his North American sojourn; *Pól-la d'ananta katánta paránta: Imitaciones y traducciones* (1970), a collection of his poetry edited by Nicaraguan poet Ernesto Gutiérrez; *Prosa* (1972), edited by Carlos Martínez Rivas; and *Prosa reunida* (1985), which includes portions of his influential *Panorama y antología de la poesía norteamericana* (1949). A major historical work is *Reflexiones sobre la historia de Nicaragua* (3 vols., 1962–1967). Both Coronel Urtecho's writings and his politics have evolved continuously. In *Mea máxima culpa* (1975), he publicly regretted having served in the Somoza regime, as subsecretary of external relations, from the 1930s into the 1950s. In the 1970s, he moved into sympathy with the emerging Sandinista movement, writing *exteriorista* poetry in the manner of Ernesto CARDENAL. His *Conversación con Carlos* (1986) praises FSLN

(Sandinista National Liberation Front) founder Carlos FONSECA AMADOR.

An excellent biographical source is MANLIO TIRADO, *Conversando con José Coronel Urtecho* (1983).

DAVID E. WHISNANT

CORONEL, CORONELISMO, a rural political boss during the predominantly agrarian phase of Brazilian history (ca. 1870–1940); *coronelismo* is the phenomenon of local and regional political rule by one or more *coronéis*.

A coronel was a member of the local economic and social elite, generally a landowner, merchant, lawyer, or even a priest, who rose to political prominence in his region because of his status in society. The title of coronel, or colonel, a military rank, was frequently associated with Brazil's National Guard (1834–1917). Prominent citizens took part in guard activities and held military rank. The use of military titles became pervasive in rural Brazil, where the elite seldom had formal higher education. Many influential political coronels never held official rank in the guard, however.

By using his economic and social resources, the coronel controlled a large dependent population, whose well-being was his concern. In return, the common folk obeyed their coronel. The First Republic (1889–1930) observed the rituals of the electoral process, however fraudulent and manipulated, and coronéis came to play the role of vote producers for state and national politicians, exchanging votes for favors.

By the 1910s, intricate alliances of coronéis and state and national politicians emerged. Influential coronéis were able to bring in public works—frequently roads, dams, and even railroads—which opened up backward agricultural enclaves to urban and export centers. Attentive national and state politicians made sure that key coronéis got what they wanted. The coronéis in turn appointed all local and state officials in their towns and exacted absolute loyalty from them. Many important coronéis never held public office.

This system of personal parallel governance especially thrived in the north, northeast, and far west, the country's agrarian bastion and backwaters. In the center-south, coronéis were often loyal members of regional parties. After 1930 *coronelismo* as an informal form of government for rural Brazil began to wane as the country experienced intensive urbanization, industrialization, and political centralization.

MARIA ISAURA PEREIRA DE QUEIROZ, *O mandonismo local na vida política brasileira e outros ensaios* (1976); VICTOR LEAL NUNES, *Coronelismo: The Municipality and Representative Government in Brazil*, translated by June Henfrey (1977); EUL-SOO PANG, *Bahia in the First Brazilian Republic: Coronelismo and Oligarchies, 1889–1934* (1979).

EUL-SOO PANG

See also **Caudillo; Patronage.**

CORRAL VERDUGO, RAMÓN (*b.* 10 January 1854; *d.* 10 November 1912), Mexican politician and vice president (1904–1911). Influential figure in Sonoran state politics and a fixture of the Porfirio DÍAZ administration from 1900 to 1911, he was a prototypical political-financial leader of the Porfiriato.

Corral was born in the mining town of Álamos, Sonora, on the Hacienda de Las Mendes, where his father operated a small store in the Palmarejo mines and later became mayor of Chinipas. Sharing his father's interest in politics, Corral wrote for opposition newspapers in an attempt to oust a succession of governors. In 1876 he joined the political faction of Luis E. Torres, serving as vice-governor, then governor (1895–1899) of Sonora. Although Corral was responsible for many public works in Sonora, thousands of Yaqui Indians were killed or deported to Yucatán during his administration. In 1900 he served in cabinet-level posts, beginning with governor of the Federal District (1900–1903), and in the key agency of secretary of government (1903–1911) while simultaneously holding office as vice president. Corral had many financial investments in Sonora. He died in exile in Paris.

JESÚS LUNA, *The Public Career of Don Ramón Corral* (1979); DELMAR LEON BEENE, *Sonora in the Age of Ramón Corral, 1875–1900* (1972); STUART F. VOSS, *On the Periphery of Nineteenth-Century Mexico: Sonora and Sinaloa, 1810–1877* (1982); and MANUEL R. URUCHURTU, *Apuntes biográficos de don Ramón Corral 1854–1900* (1984).

RODERIC AI CAMP

CORREA, JUAN (*b.* ca. 1645; *d.* 3 November 1716), Mexican painter. An almost exact contemporary of Cristóbal de VILLALPANDO, Correa is more sober and conservative but equally productive and uneven. His works are found throughout Mexico and even in Europe. His first known painting is *Saint Rose of Lima* (1671). Notable are the two great canvases for the sacristy of the cathedral of Mexico City (1689–1691) and many devotional images. The catalog of his work lists nearly 400 paintings. A mulatto, Correa had a large and successful workshop and numerous followers, many of them relatives. The extensive and detailed knowledge of this workshop gained through recent studies sheds much light on the practice of painting in colonial Mexico.

ELISA VARGAS LUGO et al., *Juan Correa, su vida y su obra* (1985–).

CLARA BARGELLINI

CORREA, JULIO MYZKOWSKY (*b.* 1890; *d.* 14 July 1953), Paraguayan dramatist, poet, and short-story writer. Son of a Brazilian who fought against Paraguay in the WAR OF THE TRIPLE ALLIANCE and grandson of a Polish immigrant who fought for Paraguay in the same war, Correa was raised in the GUARANÍ-speaking countryside. He became known as the creator of the Guaraní theater as it is known today. At the time of the CHACO WAR, he began to write down his plays, and to perform them with the help of his actress wife. He also did the staging, costuming, and training of the actors. Although Correa did not have a formal education in the theater and his works are crude and lacking in technique, his powerful characterizations of national types and his ability to dramatize the political feelings of his countrymen in Guaraní guaranteed his success. A prevalent theme in his works is the injustice of the LATIFUNDIA and the deprivation of land and opportunity for the Paraguayan peasant. His bold and poignant satire landed him in jail more than once. He also defended the poor Guaraní-speaking peasant in his poetry and short stories.

JULIO CORREA, *Ñame mba' era' în. sainete en tres actos* (1964), and *Sombrero Ka'a y cuentos* (1969); HUGO RODRÍGUEZ-ALCALÁ, *Historia de la literatura paraguaya* (1971), pp. 113–116.

CATALINA SEGOVIA-CASE

CORREGIDOR, administrator of a territorial unit known as a *corregimiento* in Peru and some other parts of the Spanish Empire. His judicial, administrative, military, and legislative responsibilities were indistinguishable from those of ALCALDES MAYORES in New Spain. There were eighty-eight corregidores in Peru in 1633.

The post of corregidor was introduced in the sixteenth century both to provide sustenance for Spaniards and to expand royal authority from the urban centers into the countryside and over the indigenous population. Most corregidores served a single term of five years or less. The crown preferred men with military, or at least militia, backgrounds.

From the stabilization of the position until 1677, most corregidores were named by viceroys or other regional chief executives. The crown's decision to sell corregidor appointments in 1677 reduced the viceroys' patronage. In addition, the sales, which continued until at least 1750, forced corregidores to increase their pressure on the native populations of their districts in order to recoup their investment and make a profit.

Working closely with wholesale merchants, corregidores routinely required the natives to purchase animals and merchandise from them (*repartimiento de mercancías* or *bienes*) at inflated prices, and in some cases they forced the natives to sell their produce to them at below market prices. These abuses led to repeated local rebellions in the Andes and, in some cases, to the death of the corregidor. The TÚPAC AMARU II Revolt in Peru (1780–1783) was provoked in part by the exactions of corregidores and one of its objectives was to end the hated *repartimiento de mercancías*.

To correct the abuses of the corregidores and their lieutenants, the crown replaced them with intendants in most of the empire during the late eighteenth century.

CLARENCE H. HARING, *The Spanish Empire in America* (1947); JOHN ROBERT FISHER, *Government and Society in Colonial Peru: The Intendant System, 1784–1814* (1970).

MARK A. BURKHOLDER

See also **Intendancy System.**

CORREIA, DIOGO ÁLVARES. *See* **Caramurú.**

CORREOSO, BUENAVENTURA (*b.* 1831; *d.* 1911), Panamanian educator and journalist. In 1856 he headed the investigation of an incident in Panama City known as the WATERMELON RIOT, which was caused by a dispute between a white American and a black Panamanian watermelon vendor that led to a riot between Americans and Panamanians in which seventeen people died. He was a populist leader, greatly admired by the lower classes. In 1868, with the support of the people of the lower-class neighborhoods in the capital, he led a successful uprising against the government. He was chief of state three times. Correoso founded numerous schools and the first public library in the country.

ERNESTO DE JESÚS CASTILLERO REYES, *Historia de Panamá*, 7th ed. (1962); JORGE CONTE PORRAS, *Panameños ilustres* (1978), *Diccionario biográfico ilustrado de Panamá*, 2d ed. (1986).

JUAN MANUEL PÉREZ

CORRIDO, a type of song presented by a traveling storyteller, narrating a lengthy tale of heroic or tragic deeds, noteworthy events, and interesting (often satirical) anecdotes. Although the *corrido* has Spanish antecedents and developed in various Latin American nations, it is most closely associated with northern Mexico and its frontier, where it may have appeared as early as the seventeenth century. During the 1800s it was commonly used as a vehicle for the lampoon of public figures and for the description of technological progress. The revolution against Porfirio Díaz caused an outpouring of *corridos* that recounted battles, endurance of hardship, feats of bravery, and deeds of treachery. Several leaders had personal *corrido* singers, such as Pancho Villa's Samuel Lozano, who continued composing after the war.

The standard song was in 2/4 or 3/4 time, with verses of four lines and four beats to the line over which a musical statement of verse length was repeated. The song's content was stated at the beginning, and a finale somewhat formally bade the listener "good-bye." The record industry required that *corridos* be shortened to fit the length of a 78-rpm disc. Radio and singing stars widely popularized the form, and new songs, such as Victor Cordero's "Juan Charrasqueado" became popular. The widely known "Adelita" is actually a popular song. During the Tlatelolco uprising in 1968, student protests appeared in *corrido* form, and national competitions in the 1970s helped stimulate its revival. *Corridos* such as "Gregorio Cortez" are a vital part of Mexican-American culture.

See listing under "Mexico" in *New Grove Dictionary of Music* (1980), and record series, "Corrido," released by Arhoolie, with extensive notes.

GUY BENSUSAN

CORRIENTES, capital city of the province of the same name in Argentina. With 181,000 inhabitants (1981), it is located on the eastern bank of the PARANÁ RIVER south of the confluence with the PARAGUAY RIVER. The settlement was founded by Spanish scouts from Asunción, Juan Torres de Vera y Aragón and Alonso de Vera y Aragón, on 3 April 1588 and was given the name San Juan de Vera de las Siete Corrientes, indicating the number of streams that converge into the Paraná River. The purpose of this outpost was to secure the southern edge of the Paraguayan governance from Indian attacks and facilitate communications between Asunción and Santa María del Buen Aire (now Buenos Aires). The development of the settlement was not easy: not only did the city have to fight off the fierce GUARANÍ Indians, but it was also a favorite raiding post of Brazilian slave hunters (*bandeirantes*), not to speak of its frictions with the authorities of both Asunción and Buenos Aires. In 1782 Corrientes became an integral part of the Intendancy of Buenos Aires, but during the struggle for independence it was a bone of contention among independents from Uruguay, federalists from Buenos Aires, and annexists from Paraguay. Not until 1852 did Corrientes become a full-fledged Argentine province.

The city of Corrientes is mainly a service hub for the agricultural hinterland, which focuses on the production of beef and the cultivation of cotton, tobacco, rice, and yerba maté. Until recent times Corrientes exported timber products, among them *quebracho* wood, which was shipped on ocean vessels expressly equipped to reach the fluvial port of Corrientes. The city is the center of a cultural region known as *El Litoral* (The Riverfront), famed for its indigenous musical folklore (the *chamamé*), and its inhabitants proudly call themselves *correntinos*. Decay of the traditional agrarian activities in the province has led to massive migration downriver to the industrial cities of Rosario and Buenos Aires.

CRISTINA M. SONSOGNI, *La población de la ciudad de Corrientes a mediados del siglo XIX* (Corrientes, 1980); and JAMES R. SCOBIE, *Secondary Cities of Argentina: The Social History of Corrientes, Salta, and Mendoza, 1850–1910* (1988).

CÉSAR N. CAVIEDES

CORTÁZAR, JULIO (*b.* 26 August 1914; *d.* 12 February 1984), Argentine novelist, short-story writer, poet, and essayist. Born in Brussels, Cortázar returned with his family to Argentina when he was four. In 1951 he moved to Paris, where he lived until his death. With BORGES, SÁBATO, and BIOY CASARES, he was instrumental in renovating Argentine narrative. Although considered a writer of fantastic literature, Cortázar illuminated problems of the Argentine middle class as well as the metaphysical anguish of modern man. His works have aesthetic and metaphysical dimensions, but also social and political ones, since he was an ardent defender of the Cuban and Nicaraguan revolutions. Throughout his texts, Cortázar always sought "an exactness of expression that would enhance creative freedom." To that effect, he employed words from different languages, diverse linguistic styles, and even invented a jargon (*glíglico*) composed of phonetic analogies. He played "phonosemantic tricks" with words, parodied linguistic clichés, and used semiphonetic graphemes to make his discourse as "nonaesthetic" as possible.

Modern language has a transcendent, creative, even magical function, according to Cortázar. Chiefly in his famous novel *Rayuela* (1963; Hopscotch, 1966), but also in *62: Modelo para armar* (1968; 62: A Model Kit, 1972), he subverted the very structure of the novel. In an almost surrealistic vein, Cortázar substituted imagination and desire for inefficient "reason." He perceived the search for man's essence as an ascesis or a mandala and there-

Julio Cortázar in the 1930s. ORGANIZATION OF AMERICAN STATES.

fore his literary creations assumed the character of an ontological peregrination: "To write is to draw my mandala and, at the same time, to travel over it, to invent purification purifying myself; the task of a poor white shaman with nylon underwear." He rejected limiting taxonomies and everything conventional and academic, and focused his interest on the exceptional, singular, and disconnected. These ideas determined the apparent disorder and fragmentation in his fiction. Nevertheless, he tended to a totality that goes beyond consciousness and permits one to discover what he called the "figures," the constellation of which one is part without knowing it. In Cortázar's creations, times, places, and people are mysteriously related to each other in nonlogical associations. These "figures" were a culmination of the theme of the doppelgänger, a sort of "bridge" or "passage" (key words in his work) between the distant and different beings who form the figures. All this compelled Cortázar to demand that his reader become his "accomplice." Through dreams, absurd situations or characters, Jungian coincidences, premonitions, eroticism, humor, and gratuitous acts, Cortázar was fighting life's absurdity and a dehumanizing world.

JAIME ALAZRAKI and IVAR IVASK, eds., *The Final Island: The Fiction of Julio Cortázar* (1978); *The Review of Contemporary Fiction* 3, no. 3 (1983); E. D. CARTER, JR., *Julio Cortázar: Life, Work, and Criticism* (1986); MALVA E. FILER, "Spatial and Temporal Representation in the Late Fiction of Julio Cortázar," in *The Centennial Review* 30, no. 2 (1986): 260–268; JOHN H. TURNER, "Sexual Violence in Two Stories of Julio Cortázar: Reading as Psychotherapy," in *Latin American Literary Review* 15, no. 30 (1987): 43–56; *Canadian Fiction Magazine* 61–62 (1987); TERRY J. PEAVLER, *Julio Cortázar* (1900).

ANGELA B. DELLEPIANE

CORTÉS, HERNÁN (Fernando, Hernando; *b.* ca. 1484; *d.* 2 December 1547), conqueror of Mexico. Hernán Cortés was born in Medellín, Spain, in the province of Extremadura. Best known for his conquest of the AZTECS (Mexica) of central Mexico, he is also renowned for his famous *Cartas de relación*. Cortés was often depicted as a psychological and tactical master, but his greatest achievement was neither military nor literary; instead, it lay in his understanding that successful conquest was dependent upon successful colonization.

Cortés studied law at the University of Salamanca. While he probably did not become a *bachiller*, his activities and writings betray legal knowledge, especially of the SIETE PARTIDAS, which aided him in the process of conquest.

Seeking wealth and power, Cortés sailed for HISPANIOLA in 1504. After briefly serving as a notary in Hispaniola, he joined Diego VELÁZQUEZ in the conquest of Cuba, where he assumed the position of *alcalde* and in about 1515 married Catalina Suárez Marcaida. By 1517, he had acquired both an ENCOMIENDA and several gold mines. Having shown little interest in the early explor-

Hernán Cortés. Portrait by Christoph Weiditz, 1529.
GERMANISCHES NATIONALMUSEUM, NÜRNBERG.

atory voyages of Hernández de CÓRDOBA and Juan de GRIJALVA, he was nevertheless chosen to lead an expedition to find Grijalva in late 1518. By the time Cortés was ready, Grijalva had returned. Cortés, nevertheless, set forth on what became a mission of trade and exploration to the Yucatán in November 1519.

With an army of 508 soldiers, Cortés set out on an expedition that was primarily intended for trade, but he also was instructed to evangelize the Indians and to take possession of any new lands discovered, two tasks he undertook with zeal. He was not instructed to colonize, however. In April 1519 Cortés reached what is now Veracruz, where he learned of a rich and powerful ruler, MOTECUHZOMA II, who was located inland but who held domain over a vast area extending to the coastal region. The subsequent events of Cortés's conquest of the Aztec king's domain were defined by Cortés's unshakable desire to deliver that empire to the kingdom of Castile.

Cortés also learned that Motecuhzoma and his army had many enemies who might be turned against the Mexica. But to carry out such a project, both to find Motecuhzoma and to make alliances with native groups, would take time and material resources. Expanding upon the orders of Pánfilo de NARVÁEZ, an ally of Velázquez, Cortés established a town with a *cabildo* (Villa Rica de la Vera Cruz) and placed the town directly under the king's authority.

Now in open rebellion against Velázquez, Cortés and his army destroyed their own ships to cut their means of connection to Cuba. Meanwhile, envoys carrying gold and examples of elaborate Mexica featherwork had been dispatched to Spain, seeking royal sanction of Cortés's actions. Velázquez sent a representative to Spain to brand Cortés a traitor and organized an army to move against him. By August 1519, Cortés and most of his army had set forth, moving west to find Motecuhzoma and the capital of his empire, the island city TENOCH-TITLÁN. By September, Cortés had reached Tlaxcala. He may have heard that the Tlaxcalans were longtime enemies of the Mexica and thus been motivated to find and make allies of them. It took fierce fighting to subdue the Tlaxcalans, but by late September, Cortés had formed a critical alliance with Tlaxcala. After next pacifying Cholula, Cortés was ready to march into the heart of the Valley of Mexico. Having negotiated with emissaries of Motecuhzoma several times during the march west, Cortés could not be persuaded against entering the heart of Mexica territory, and Cortés and Motecuhzoma met in early November.

While we can never know precisely what occurred during the first meetings of the representatives of these two very different societies, the ultimate outcome was the imprisonment of Motecuhzoma by the Spaniards. Cortés decisively beat back the forces of Pánfilo de Narváez sent by Velázquez and thereby gained needed reinforcements. The entire conquest project, however, was almost ruined by the slaughter at the Great Temple by Pedro de ALVARADO, Cortés's lieutenant, and his forces. Cortés, meanwhile, released Motecuhzoma's brother, CUITLAHUAC, who immediately rallied the Mexica in violent opposition to the Spanish.

The situation deteriorated so badly that Cortés decided that retreat was necessary. On the so-called NO-CHE TRISTE many Spanish soldiers lost their lives. Revealingly, Cortés's accounts also lament the gold that was lost that night. Retreating to Tlaxcala in July 1520, Cortés prepared for a final siege of Tenochtitlán. He ordered the building of thirteen brigantines to blockade the island capital, and set forth for Texcoco on 28 December. Over the next months, the Spanish soldiers conducted a series of assaults on Indian towns surrounding Tenochtitlán to pacify the area and to increase the size of their allied Indian forces. Once the ships were ready, Cortés undertook the final assault, which was achieved by blockade, massive force, and great destruction of life and property. Tenochtitlán fell in August 1521.

Salvador de Madariaga, one of Cortés's biographers, says that he was conquered by his own conquest; the events of the sixteen years after it bear this out. While he was consolidating his leadership of NEW SPAIN, he received official recognition as its legitimate conqueror and governor. But many of his soldiers nursed grievances, other Spaniards were jealous and resentful, and his wife died under mysterious circumstances.

Cortés embarked on further territorial expansion, sending Pedro de Alvarado to conquer Guatemala and

The March to Tenochtitlán-Mexico

Cristóbal de OLID to conquer Honduras. Alvarado succeeded but with little gain; Olid, with Velázquez's encouragement, rebelled against Cortés's authority. Olid's betrayal prompted Cortés to set off on an ill-fated expedition to Honduras. Royal authorities became disturbed by his willingness to take the law into his own hands, and his absence from Mexico City provided an opening for his enemies to move against his followers, thus strengthening the royal conviction to bring New Spain under its own firm control.

In 1529, after personal entreaties from Cortés, who had traveled to Spain, Charles V granted him the title marqués del Valle de Oaxaca, twenty-two *encomienda* towns, and the right to entail his estate. While he returned again to Mexico in the mid-1530s, he never again held the governorship. Thus to others fell the task of solidifying the territorial gains and administrative structures Cortés had put in place. Dogged by lawsuits and investigations, the marqués spent much of his latter years defending himself. Brilliant, active, and cruel, Cortés was the conqueror of the largest single community pacified in the New World. He died in Spain still seeking the status and riches he believed he had been denied.

SALVADOR DE MADARIAGA, *Hernan Cortés, Conqueror of Mexico* (1942); HENRY R. WAGNER, *The Rise of Fernando Cortés* (1944); EULALIA GUZMÁN, *Relaciones de Hernán Cortés a Carlos V sobre la invasión de Anáhuac* (1958); BERNAL DÍAZ DEL CASTILLO, *The Conquest of New Spain*, translated by J. M. Cohen (1963); FRANCISCO LÓPEZ DE GÓMARA, *Cortés: The Life of the Conqueror by His Secretary*, translated and edited by Lesley B. Simpson (1966); HERNAN CORTÉS, *Letters from Mexico*, translated and edited by Anthony Pagden (1971), pp. xiff.

SUSAN KELLOGG

CORTÉS, MARTÍN (*b.* 1532/1533; *d.* 13 August 1589), legitimate son of the conquistador Hernán CORTÉS and Juana de Zúñiga, born in Cuernavaca. Not to be confused with his stepbrother, also named Martín (son of Cortés and MALINCHE), this Martín was the second marqués del Valle de Oaxaca. In 1540, he went to Spain, where he joined Charles V's royal service and later became a favorite in the entourage of Philip II. His return to Mexico in 1562 to claim his father's titles and property coincided with the Spanish crown's attempt to revoke the extension of the ENCOMIENDA to the sons and grandsons of conquistadores. Indignant at the crown's assertiveness and eager to protect their inheritance, the criollos naturally looked to Martín Cortés for leadership. Don Martín, however, had an arrogant disposition and had an ostentatious lifestyle that offended many; more important, he seemed to lack the natural leadership abilities of his father. Though he tacitly agreed to their plan to make him king of Mexico, he never fully pledged his support for criollo plans to assassinate royal officials and overthrow the government. The plot failed, and the leaders were severely punished. Cortés was apprehended and sent to Spain to face trial in 1567; he was

fined and sentenced to military duty. Though pardoned by the crown in 1574, Cortés never returned to Mexico. This failed uprising represented the last serious challenge to the crown's authority in Mexico by the early conquistadores and their families. Cortés died in Madrid.

IRVING ALBER LEONARD, *Baroque Times in Old Mexico* (1966); MICHAEL C. MEYER and WILLIAM L. SHERMAN, *The Course of Mexican History* (1991).

J. DAVID DRESSING

CORTÉS CASTRO, LEÓN (*b.* 8 December 1882; *d.* 2 March 1946), president of Costa Rica (1936–1940). After receiving a law degree from the School of Law in San José, León Cortés Castro held many elected and appointed positions beginning with his appointment by the military dictator President Federico Tinoco Granados (1917–1919), to the post of commander of the Alajuela Garrison (Comandante de Plaza de Alajuela). Cortés served as president of the National Assembly (1925–1926), as minister of education (1929–1930), and as minister of public works (1930; 1932–1936). His tour as minister of public works under president Ricardo JIMÉNEZ OREAMUNO consolidated Cortés's reputation as a no-nonsense and frugal administrator, which prompted the leaders of the National Republican Party to choose him as their standard-bearer in 1936.

During his administration Cortés was a proponent of fiscal responsibility, extending the nation's highway network and embarking on an ambitious construction program. His brick, mortar, and asphalt approach provided employment that helped ameliorate setbacks due to the Great Depression. He founded the National Bank of Costa Rica in 1936.

Although generally accredited even by his detractors with being an effective administrator, Cortés frequently was charged with arbitrary actions. While president he intervened in the 1938 and 1940 elections preventing opposition candidates from being elected; he also meddled in the presidential candidacy of three-time president Ricardo Jiménez.

Shortly after Rafael Angel CALDERÓN GUARDIA's inauguration in 1940, Cortés, as the most prominent leader of the opposition forces, openly broke with Calderón and formed a rival party. When Cortés lost the 1944 election to Teodoro PICADO MICHALSKI (1944–1948), there were widespread charges that Calderón had used his executive power to perpetrate electoral fraud on a grand scale.

Cortés remained the leader of the opposition until his sudden death following a heart attack in 1946.

WILLIAM KREHM, *Democracies and Tyrannies of the Caribbean* (1984), discusses Cortés as president and presidential candidate; JOHN PATRICK BELL, *Crisis in Costa Rica* (1971), discusses Cortés's role in the turbulent events leading to the 1948 revolution; FRANKLIN D. PARKER, *The Central American Republics* (1964), provides a succinct general history; CARLOS CALVO

GAMBOA, *León Cortés, y su tiempo* (1969), deals with Cortés and the politics of the period.

JOHN PATRICK BELL

See also **Costa Rica: Political Parties.**

CORTÉS DE MADARIAGA, JOSÉ (*b.* 8 July 1766; *d.* March 1826), priest and political activist in the Venezuelan independence movement. A native of Chile, Cortés de Madariaga was ordained in 1788. He arrived in Venezuela by chance in 1802 and obtained a canonry in the Cathedral of Caracas. He played an active role in the events of 19 April 1810 in Caracas and was a member of the JUNTA SUPREMA OF CARACAS. Cortés de Madariaga traveled to New Granada in 1811 and signed the first treaty of alliance and federation between Cundinamarca and Venezuela. At the fall of the republic in 1812, he was sent to the military prison at Ceuta, in Africa, from which he escaped two years later. When Venezuela regained its independence in 1817, he returned and promoted the founding of a representative, federal government. This plan was disclaimed and condemned by Simón BOLÍVAR. Cortés de Madariaga later traveled to Jamaica, where he again worked for independence. In 1823 the Congress of Colombia granted him a pension for his services in the cause of independence.

DANIEL ARIAS ARGAEZ, *El canónigo don José Cortés y Madariaga* (1938); and NICOLÁS PERAZZO, *José Cortés de Madariaga* (1972).

INÉS QUINTERO

CORTES OF CÁDIZ. The placement of Joseph BONAPARTE on the throne of Spain in 1808 by his brother Napoleon resulted in widespread resistance to the French organized by provincial juntas of Spanish patriots. With French troops occupying nearly all of the country by January 1810, the Central Junta of resistance at Seville turned authority over to a five-member regency to rule in the name of the captive Spanish Bourbon, FERDINAND VII. This regency, however, lacked the legitimacy of the popular resistance juntas, and thus it called for election of deputies to a General and Extraordinary Cortes that convened in Cádiz beginning on 24 September 1810. While British forces attacked the French in Spain through Portugal, the Cortes (Congress) of Cádiz directed loyalist guerrilla resistance to the French and sought to maintain the loyalty of Spain's American dominions.

The Cortes of Cádiz claimed legitimacy as the sole representative of Spanish sovereignty, assuming administration of the American dominions and granting them representation in the Cortes. In fact, colonial deputies to the Cortes played an important role in its deliberations, even though many did not reach Cádiz for some time. The Cortes supervised elections in the Cádiz region (the only area of Spain not held by the French) and throughout Spanish America for municipal offices and for the Cortes of 1812. These elections established an influential precedent for the subsequent political history of Spanish America. Many of the Cortes's actions reflected compromise between conservative and liberal deputies, but the Cortes had a discernible liberal tone, and its CONSTITUTION OF 1812 became the fundamental charter of nineteenth-century liberalism in Spain and Spanish America. Colonial representation in the Cortes and the attack on aristocratic privilege and monopolies were especially important liberal advances. Although the Cortes retained the Roman Catholic church as the established church, it suppressed the Holy Office of the INQUISITION and limited the regular orders. The American representatives pressured their peninsular counterparts on free trade, on ending restrictions on agriculture and manufacturing in the colonies, and on granting them a guaranteed percentage of bureaucratic appointments.

With the defeat of Napoleon in 1814, Ferdinand VII replaced Joseph Bonaparte as king of Spain. He immediately dissolved the Cortes and nullified all of its acts with a single decree on 4 May 1814. He refused to recognize the constitution or the Cortes, beginning a period of strong repression that lasted until the Riego Revolt of 1820, which forced Ferdinand to accept restoration of the constitution.

The primary sources for research on the Cortes are *Actas de las Cortes de Cádiz*, 2 vols. (1964) and *El Perú en las Cortes de Cádiz*, 2 vols. (1974). Among secondary works, MARIO RODRÍGUEZ, *The Cádiz Experiment in Central America, 1808 to 1826* (1978), is especially perceptive. See also CESAREO DE ARMELLADA, *La causa indígena americana en las Cortes de Cádiz* (1959); DANIEL A. MORENO, *Las Cortes de Cádiz y la Constitución de 1812* (1964); NETTIE LEE BENSON, ed., *Mexico and the Spanish Cortes, 1810–1822* (1966); DARDO PÉREZ GUILHOU, *La opinión pública española y las Cortes de Cádiz frente a la emancipación hispanoamericana, 1808–1814*; (1981); RAYMOND CARR, *Spain 1808–1975*, 2d ed. (1982); MARÍA TERESA BERRUEZO, *La participación americana en las Cortes de Cádiz, 1810–1814* (1986); JORGE MARIO GARCÍA LA GUARDIA, *La Constitución de Cádiz y su influencia en América (175 años 1812–1987)* (1987).

HEATHER THIESSEN

CORTES, PORTUGUESE, politico-administrative bodies that, according to some historians, had their roots in national councils of the Visigoth monarchy. The word *cortes* is derived from the Latin *cohors*, meaning assembly or party. From the thirteenth to the nineteenth century, the *cortes* had a significant influence on Portuguese politics. They were composed of members of the clergy, nobles, and lawyers of the towns and cities. They represented the country and legitimized the king's power. Convened by the sovereigns, they discussed economic and financial matters and heard protests brought before the crown by the religious orders. Besides being a primarily consultive body, they acted as mediators, serving to mete out royal power along classic absolutist lines. With the revolution of Pôrto in 1820, however, the *cortes* were convened by the Provisional Junta of the

Supreme Government of the Realm rather than by the king. Although the liberals affirmed they were seeking the reestablishment of the former fundamental laws of the monarchy, the General and Special Cortes had quite a different character. They rejected the old representation by orders and established equitable representation for all citizens. Therefore they became the sole supreme constitutional authority expressing the will of the nation.

ALBERTO MARTINS DE CARVALHO, "Cortes," in *Dicionário de história de Portugal*, vol. 1 (1963), pp. 711–715; FERNANDO PITEIRA SANTOS, *Geografia e economia da revolução de 1820*, 3d ed. (1980); RODERICK J. BARMAN, *Brazil: The Forging of a Nation, 1798–1852* (1988), pp. 64–96.

LÚCIA M. BASTOS P. NEVES

CORVALÁN LEPE, LUIS (*b.* 1916), politician and secretary general of Unidad Popular, the Chilean Communist Party. A professor by education, Corvalán worked his way up in the party to serve as a senator representing the south. Then, selected by his predecessor, he became head of the party in 1957. Always a supporter of Moscow, he was nevertheless willing to cooperate with progressive elements. Corvalán rationalized the Unidad Popular's policies, arguing that it was possible to achieve socialism in Chile without revolution. Captured in the 1973 coup that overthrew Allende, Corvalán suffered torture at the hands of the PINOCHET government. In 1976 he was exchanged for the Soviet political prisoner Vladimir Bukovsky.

CARMELO FURCI, *The Chilean Communist Party and the Road to Socialism* (1984), pp. 19, 37, 56, 85–88, 153, 167; JULIO B. FAÚNDEZ, *Marxism and Democracy in Chile* (1988), p. 172.

WILLIAM F. SATER

CORZO, EL. *See* **Ruiz, Antonio.**

COS, MARTÍN PERFECTO DE (*b.* 1800; *d.* 1854), Mexican general. A native of Veracruz, Cos joined the Veracruz regiment in 1820. He became a lieutenant under Augustín de ITURBIDE during 1821, but supported the formation of a Mexican republic by 1823. After Cos became a general in 1833, President Antonio Lopéz de SANTA ANNA sent him to control unrest in the North. In December 1835 he lost San Antonio to the Texans. Cos fought at the ALAMO (1836) before being captured at SAN JACINTO in early 1836. Federalists defeated him in battle at Tampico in 1838 and at Tuxpan in 1839. During 1847 he fought against the U.S. army at Tuxpan. Cos acted as government leader for TEHUANTEPEC before his death.

WALTER LORD, *A Time to Stand* (1961); JOSEPH MILTON NANCE, *After San Jacinto: The Texas-Mexican Frontier, 1836–1841* (1963);

"Cos, Martín Perfecto de," in *Diccionario Porrúa de historia, biografía y geografía de México* (1986); ALWYN BARR, *Texans in Revolt: The Battle for San Antonio, 1835* (1990).

ALWYN BARR

COS Y PÉREZ, JOSÉ MARÍA (*d.* November 1819), Mexican insurgent ideologue. Born in Zacatecas, he studied in Guadalajara, where he entered the Seminario Tridentino. A doctor of theology, he opposed the insurrection in 1810. When suspected of sedition, he joined Ignacio LÓPEZ RAYÓN (1773–1832) and became a writer and ideologue for the insurgency. In 1812 he wrote the *Plan de paz y plan de guerra*, and published the insurgent papers *Ilustrador Nacional* and *Ilustrador Americano*. He served as vicar general of the army and deputy for Zacatecas in the insurgent Congress. A signer of the Constitution of APATZINGÁN (1814), he became a member of the executive branch. When Congress reprimanded him for directing troops while serving in the executive, he disavowed that body in 1815. Although first condemned to death and later to life imprisonment, he was released by Rayón and later received amnesty from the colonial regime in 1817. He died in Pátzcuaro.

ALEJANDRO VILLASEÑOR Y VILLASEÑOR, *Biografías de los héroes y caudillos de la Independencia*, vol. 2 (1910), pp. 1–12; JOSÉ MARÍA MIQUEL I VERGÉS, *La Independencia mexicana y la prensa insurgente* (1941) and *Diccionario de insurgentes* (1969), pp. 151–154.

VIRGINIA GUEDEA

See also **Chilpancingo, Congress of.**

COSIATA, LA (1826), a politico-military movement for the secession of Venezuela from GRAN COLOMBIA. When Gran Colombia was formed in 1821, conflicts arose in the territory of Venezuela over political and administrative difficulties resulting from the location of the center of power in Bogotá. Rejection of the conscription system imposed by the government of Bogotá was widespread. Also, there were outright confrontations between entities of civil and military power, stemming both from their insufficiently defined powers and the lack of institutionalized authority.

Several factors contributed to the restless climate leading up to Venezuela's eventual decision to ignore Bogotá's authority and to the Municipality of Caracas's appointment of José Antonio PÁEZ as chief of the department of Venezuela in 1826. One was the imprecision as to the authority and jurisdiction of the various local, departmental, and national entities of power. A second was the great distances between the various political and administrative bodies. A third was the newness of the Gran Colombia experiment, and a fourth involved tensions between political factions and problems brought about by the war.

The series of events that comprise La Cosiata began in the city of Valencia on 27 April 1826, when the municipal council expressed its regret over the suspension of Páez as military commander in chief of the department of Venezuela earlier in the year. Discontent spread rapidly throughout most of the territory formerly known as the captaincy general of Venezuela. An assembly of Venezuelan municipalities called for a convention and the adoption of a federal system. General Francisco de Paula SANTANDER declared Páez a rebel and deployed troops. In December, Simón BOLÍVAR entered Venezuela, declared an amnesty, and named Páez chief civil and military leader of Venezuela. The integrity of the Colombian Republic was thus provisionally maintained.

JOSÉ ANTONIO PÁEZ, *Autobiografía de José Antonio Páez*, vol. 1 (1973); and GRACIELA SORIANO DE GARCÍA-PELAYO, *Venezuela, 1810–1830: Aspectos desatendidos de dos décadas* (1990).

INÉS QUINTERO

COSÍO VILLEGAS, DANIEL (*b.* 23 July 1898; *d.* 10 March 1976), Mexican intellectual figure and cultural entrepreneur. A graduate of the National Preparatory School and the National School of Law, he became a prominent student leader and began teaching before graduating with degrees in law and literature. He was a disciple of Pedro HENRÍQUEZ UREÑA and a political collaborator of José VASCONCELOS. He became one of the first members of his generation to study economics abroad. In 1938 he founded *El Trimestre Económico* and the leading publishing house Fondo de Cultura Económica, directing both until 1948. Known for his collaborative historical projects on the Porfiriato, he directed *Historia Mexicana* (1951–1961) and cofounded and directed the Colegio de Mexico, where he produced many distinguished disciples. He was awarded the National Prize in Letters in 1971, and was a member of the National College from 1951 until his death.

DANIEL COSÍO VILLEGAS, *Ensayos y notas,* 2 vols. (1966) and *Memorias* (1976); CHARLES A. HALE, "Review of *Memorias* by Daniel Cosío Villegas" in *Hispanic American Historical Review* vol. 58 (1978): 132–133; ENRIQUE KRAUZE, *Daniel Cosío Villegas: Una biografía intelectual* (1980); and GABRIEL ZAID, comp., *Daniel Cosío Villegas, imprenta y vida público* (1985).

RODERIC AI CAMP

COSTA, CLÁUDIO MANUEL DA (also Manoel; *b.* 5 June 1729; *d.* 4 July 1789), considered the father of Brazilian literature and its major neoclassic poet. He was born in Mariana, Minas Gerais, to a well-to-do family. After studying with the Jesuits in Brazil, he obtained a law degree in Coimbra, Portugal, in 1753. Returning to Brazil, he set up residence in Ouro Prêto, where he pursued a career as a lawyer and public servant. Through investments in gold mining and moneylending, he became one of the wealthiest men in the province. His collected poems were published as *Orbas* [*sic*] (1768), and he also wrote an epic poem on the history of his home town (published as *Vila Rica* in 1839). In 1789 he was arrested under the accusation of participating in a plot to declare Minas Gerais independent of the Portuguese crown (INCONFIDÊNCIA MINEIRA). After a month in jail, he compromised himself and several of his named co-conspirators. Broken and remorseful, he committed suicide. Without presenting serious documentation, some historians have tried to contest the official version of his death, accusing his jailer of murder.

SAMUEL PUTNAM, *Marvelous Journey* (1948), pp. 81–95; KENNETH R. MAXWELL, *Conflicts and Conspiracies: Brazil and Portugal, 1750–1808* (1973).

HEITOR MARTINS

COSTA, HIPÓLITO JOSÉ DA (*b.* 25 March 1774; *d.* 11 September 1823), journalist. Born in the colony of Sacramento, Brazil, where his father served in the royal troops, da Costa graduated with a degree in philosophy (1796) and law (1798) from the University of Coimbra. He began his public career under the protection of minister of the colonies Rodrigo de Souza Coutinho, who placed him in charge of a visit to the United States and Mexico in 1798, and appointed him director of Royal Press.

Da Costa undertook a voyage to England in 1802 with the aim of acquiring books, machinery, and other typographical equipment. When he returned, he was seized by the INQUISITION and accused of being a mason. He escaped to London (1805), where, in 1808, he founded the liberal newspaper *Correio Braziliense,* a publication that had a decisive influence at the time of Brazil's independence, even though it did not advocate separation from Portugal until February 1822. As a result of new freedoms of the press and the proliferation of numerous periodicals, da Costa believed that Brazil no longer needed news emanating from abroad. Publication of *Correio Braziliense* ceased in 1822. After independence, da Costa was appointed the Brazilian representative in London, but he died soon after his nomination.

MECENAS DOURADO, *Hipólito da Costa e o Correio Braziliense* (1957); CARLOS RIZZINI, *Hipólito da Costa e o Correio Braziliense* (1957).

LÚCIA M. BASTOS P. NEVES

COSTA, LÚCIO (*b.* 27 February 1902), Brazilian urban planner, best known for designing the city plan of BRASÍLIA. Born in Toulon, France, Costa was part of an extraordinary flowering of creative genius in Rio de Janeiro in the 1950s that included, among others, the architect Oscar NIEMEYER, the landscape architect Roberto BURLE MARX (Costa's neighbor), and the creators of BOSSA NOVA, such as Antônio Carlos JOBIM and Luís Bonfa. Twenty-six plans, some with elaborate models labored over for months by entire architectural firms, were submitted in the 1955 design competition for the new capital. Costa produced his plan in sixty-four hours. His only expenditures were for paper, pencils, and an eraser. Disillusioned by Brasília's failure to catalyze social change, as he and Niemeyer had hoped, Costa said, "You don't solve the social problems of a country by simply moving its capital, and in Brazil the main problem is the huge base of poor in the country."

ALEX SHOUMATOFF, *The Capital of Hope* (1980).

ALEX SHOUMATOFF

See also **Architecture.**

COSTA E SILVA, ARTUR DA (*b.* 3 October 1902; *d.* 17 December 1969), president of Brazil (1967–1969). Born in Taquarí, Rio Grande do Sul, Costa e Silva attended the Realengo Military Academy and graduated at the head of his class. As a young second lieutenant in 1922, he took part in the COPACABANA FORT REVOLT in Rio de Janeiro, for which he was imprisoned for six months. For supporting Getúlio VARGAS in the Revolution of 1930, Costa e Silva was named to a federal government post. During World War II, he served as an officer in the BRAZILIAN EXPEDITIONARY FORCE (FEB) in Italy, after which he joined a group of officers who removed Vargas from office in 1945. Costa e Silva became a brigadier general in 1952; six years later he was named a major general and commander of the second infantry division and of the armored vehicle division based in São Paulo.

He turned down President João GOULART's offer to become army chief of staff in 1961, but the following year he accepted command of the Fourth Army, based in northeastern Brazil. Costa e Silva played a key role in the March 1964 coup against Goulart, seizing the War Ministry Building in Rio, the armed forces' communication and bureaucratic center. The Supreme Revolutionary Command, which engineered the coup, named him head of the 200,000-man army. Two years later the Army High Command elected him to succeed fellow officer (and academy classmate) Humberto CASTELLO BRANCO as president.

Costa e Silva's presidency was marked by the imposition of authoritarian rule. In December 1968, he recessed the National Congress when it refused to waive immunity for a member perceived to have criticized the military. Costa e Silva then issued a series of Institutional Acts that expanded executive and military powers, limited media freedom, and suspended federal, state, and municipal elections. He justified his regime with an improving economy. The government cut taxes on Brazilian businesses, attracted foreign investment, and provided incentives to ranchers. The gross domestic product rose 11 percent in 1968 and the World Bank approved a $1 billion development loan, marking the beginning of the BRAZILIAN ECONOMIC MIRACLE.

In August 1969, while campaigning for a national referendum on revisions to the Constitution of 1967, Costa e Silva suffered an incapacitating stroke. A military junta composed of the three armed forces ministers assumed power, bypassed the constitutionally designated successor, Vice President Pedro Aleixo, and with the Army High Command named General Emílio Garrastazú MÉDICI in October 1969 to succeed immediately to the presidency. Costa e Silva died in Rio de Janeiro.

THOMAS E. SKIDMORE, *The Politics of Military Rule in Brazil, 1964–85* (1988).

ROSS WILKINSON

See also **Brazil: Revolutions.**

COSTA (ECUADOR), the coastal lowland region of Ecuador, comprising approximately one-quarter of the nation (roughly 27,000 square miles) in a strip ranging from 12 to 100 miles wide along the Pacific Ocean. The provinces of the *costa*—ESMERALDAS, Manabí, Los Ríos, Guayas, and El Oro—contain about half of the nation's population. The port city of GUAYAQUIL in Guayas is the nation's commercial center and largest city. Historically, the rivalry between the commercially oriented and politically liberal coast and the isolated and conservative sierra (site of the national capital of Quito) has shaped national politics. The *costa* developed close ties with international markets, and at various times was the world's leading producer of CACAO and bananas. It is culturally distinct—less Indian, traditional, Catholic, and provincial than the rest of Ecuador.

See LINDA ALEXANDER RODRÍGUEZ, *The Search for Public Policy: Regional Politics and Government Finances in Ecuador, 1830–1940* (1985), for a detailed analysis of political regionalism. Also valuable is OSVALDO HURTADO's interpretive *Political Power in Ecuador,* translated by Nick D. Mills, Jr. (1985). For a succinct summary of the major dimensions of Ecuadorian political economy, see DAVID W. SCHODT, *Ecuador: An Andean Enigma* (1987). On the geography of the *costa,* see PRESTON JAMES, *Latin America* (1986), or the classic survey by THEODOR WOLF, *Geography and Geology of Ecuador,* translated by James Flanagan (1933).

RONN F. PINEO

COSTA (PERU), one of the three principal geographic regions of Peru, with the selva and sierra. The costa is between the Pacific and the Andean mountains; it constitutes only 12 percent of the national territory but contains around 53 percent of the population—largely as a result of the massive migration from the less developed rural Andean interior during the second half of the twentieth century. Most of the coast is a desert where rainfall is scant due to the peculiarities of the HUMBOLDT CURRENT, but where numerous, fertile valley oases are watered by the fifty-two rivers that flow out of the Andes east to west, emptying into the Pacific. Historically, the coast, by virtue of its orientation toward Europe and the West, has tended to be more modernized and developed than the highland interior as well as more racially and ethnically mixed.

PETER K. KLARÉN

COSTA RICA. Costa Rica has grown and prospered in a manner so distinctive from that of other Latin American nations that its history warrants more extensive study than its small size and population would suggest. From an isolated and generally ignored colony of some sixty thousand inhabitants at the time of independence, it has developed into one of the most prosperous, educated, healthy, and democratic nations in Latin America. Its progress has been sustained and profound, without any great economic windfalls occasioned by the discovery and exploitation of such resources as petroleum or precious metals or precious stones. Its progress has come from the creativity, imagination, and common sense of its people, who have worked with a limited resource base and from a scant colonial material legacy of such items as infrastructure, wealth, roads, port facilities, and homes.

GEOGRAPHY
Costa Rica is the third smallest of the Central American republics (El Salvador and Belize have less land area) and is located wholly within the tropics (between 8° and 11° latitude). Despite its limited area of 19,575 square miles, Costa Rica contains a great variety of hot to moderate climatic zones because of its enormous variety of topography, coastlines on the Pacific Ocean and the Caribbean Sea, and variations in seasonal and annual precipitation.

The prevailing winds from the northeast that pass over the warm Caribbean waters account for the high annual rainfall along the Caribbean coast and the eastern slopes of the mountainous interior. Although there is a distinct rainy season in the humid tropical zone on the Caribbean side, it might be better designated the rainier season because there is substantial precipitation throughout the year. Much of the lowland area is tropical rain forest; at higher elevations dense vegetation and swift-flowing mountain streams are the norm. Along the Pacific coast and the western slopes of the mountains, there are pronounced rainy and dry seasons. The amount of precipitation increases as one moves from the northwestern region to the southwest. Guanacaste Province is a region of tropical dry forest and semiarid areas, whereas in the area around Golfito there is sufficient rainfall to sustain economically viable banana plantations.

Historically the country's most significant geographic feature has been the mountain ranges that run from the border with Nicaragua in the north to the southern border with Panama. The volcanoes not only add a dramatic element to the landscape but, when active, have had devastating effects on the surrounding areas. They also have benefited agricultural development by depositing rich volcanic soil at unpredictable intervals. The highest peaks are in the Talamanca Range in the southwestern part of the country.

The mountain valleys constitute the third major climate zone, which enjoys a moderate, springlike climate (*clima templada*). These valleys occur between 2,000 to 7,000 feet above sea level.

The heartland of Costa Rica is the great Central Valley and the Central Plateau (*meseta central*) within that valley. The principal cities of the early independence

San José, Costa Rica. © 1990 PETER MENZEL / STOCK, BOSTON.

period, San José, Cartago, Heredia, and Alajuela, were all on the *meseta central,* and the vast majority of the colonial population lived in these cities and their environs. The national culture, character, and values emanate from this central region. The Costa Ricans, then, are a mountain people who, in over a century and a half of independence, have gradually moved out from the heartland to occupy and develop the other regions of the nation. As they have adjusted to different climates and embraced other environments, their national culture has remained essentially that of the *meseta.* The national values of democracy, individual liberty, egalitarianism, peace, and universal education were fostered and inculcated in the *meseta* and then spread throughout the nation.

NATIONAL ORGANIZATION

With the triumph of San José over Cartago in 1823, Costa Rica turned its back on Mexico and Agustín ITURBIDE's imperial model for independence and embraced republicanism and the Central American Federation. It was still too early to clearly discern the emergence of a distinct Costa Rican nation, but the victory at Ochomogo by the combined forces of San José and Alajuela over those of Cartago and its ally, Heredia, marked an important milestone along the path to nationhood. Future development became more predictable with San José's victory in the War of the League (1835) over the other three cities of the *meseta.* San José became the undisputed capital of an emerging nation soon to break with the Central American Federation.

Costa Rica's relative stability was the reason that the province of Guanacaste aligned itself with Costa Rica rather than Nicaragua in 1824. The Federation approved the annexation. Juan MORA FERNÁNDEZ's long tenure as head of state (1824–1833) also reflected a growing cohesiveness in contrast to conditions elsewhere in Central America.

Braulio CARRILLO COLINA provided effective if somewhat arbitrary leadership for the consolidation of Costa Rican nationhood during his two periods as head of state (1835–1837 and 1838–1842). Carrillo took the lead in establishing San José as the permanent capital and in separating Costa Rica from the Federation (1838). He also fostered the cultivation of COFFEE, which became the principal national export and the mainstay of the national economy. It is difficult to overestimate the importance of coffee in Costa Rica's economic development and modernization. The manner in which Carrillo promoted the new crop also served to reinforce the existing positive land-tenure pattern in the *meseta.* He distributed coffee saplings to the peasant farmers as a means of providing them with a cash crop and the nation with its most significant export to date. This success confirmed in practice one of the major tenets of early liberal and republican dogma, that is, that more open trade and foreign capital—British capital was involved in the commercialization and shipping of coffee and in

supplying trees—would contribute significantly to economic development and should be encouraged.

The liberal-conservative conflict that raged throughout the rest of Central America afflicted Costa Rica in a very attenuated form. National leadership placed Costa Rican interests above party or ideological interests so that the country did not suffer from the same deep divisions as other Central American countries, and remained on the sidelines in inter–Central American conflicts.

The ultimate fate of the great liberal leader from Honduras, Francisco MORAZÁN, was determined by Costa Rican reluctance to be party to these inter–Central American disputes. After the disintegration of the Federation, Morazán attempted to use Costa Rica as his base for military operations to reclaim his presidency and restore the Federation. Morazán's ascendancy in Costa Rica lasted less than six months and ended with his execution there in September 1842.

Throughout the Carrillo period and the 1840s, coffee production expanded at a prodigious rate, and the road building that he initiated continued apace. The most important advances were related to the exportation of this new crop, particularly the improvement of the cart road to the major Pacific port, Puntarenas.

The expansion of coffee production in Costa Rica can be attributed to the initiative of those involved in the trade but also to the propitiousness of the setting. The moderate temperatures of the Central Valley together with rich volcanic soil and tropical sun without excess heat made for nearly ideal growing conditions. The predictability of the dry season provided a natural means of drying the husked beans in *beneficios* (processing plants) and made the trails to Puntarenas passable at the time that the dried beans were ready for market.

As coffee production expanded to meet the increasing external demand, there emerged a new coffee elite, which also manifested distinct Costa Rican traits. It was not a mere carryover from a colonial landholding oligarchy that introduced coffee production to its large estates, which was the case in several other Latin American nations. The coffee elite in Costa Rica was more commercial in origin and developed from early investment in processing, transporting, and marketing the bean. Some of its members were descendents of the colonial elite; others were foreign nationals who became involved in the trade and later invested in land and production (hence such surnames as Dent and Rohrmoser). Some were Costa Ricans of relatively humble background who prospered with the coffee boom in ancillary enterprises and then invested in land for coffee production.

Members of the coffee elite extended their land holdings and created relatively large estates. However, they did not do so to the exclusion of the peasant producers. The general scarcity of workers made the bargaining position of agricultural labor stronger than elsewhere in Central America. The larger-scale producers were dependent on the independent peasant farmers who would work for wages at harvest time. The patron-peon relationship did not involve the extreme exploitation common in so many other areas of nineteenth-century Latin America. Nonetheless, the new elite based on coffee became the dominant socioeconomic group and, as such, played a major role in the social, cultural, political, and economic development of the nation.

The political situation after the execution of Morazán was fluid until the presidency of Juan Rafael MORA PORRÁS (1849–1859), who reestablished republican forms despite being something of a caudillo. As chief executive, Mora emphasized order and had the support of much of the emerging coffee elite.

THE NATIONAL WAR AND
THE SENSE OF NATIONHOOD

The most dramatic events of Mora's presidency revolved around the military campaigns to repulse William WALKER's (1824–1860) invading forces. For Costa Ricans, this war against the filibusters contributed to their sense of nationhood in much the same way as the struggle for independence did in many other countries. In a sense, the NATIONAL WAR filled the void created by the absence of a war for independence and engendered the great national heroes, particularly the figure of Juan Santamaría (1831–1856).

Walker's ascendancy in Nicaragua (1855–1857) and his subsequent advance into the Guanacaste region of Costa Rica led President Mora to issue a call to arms to repel the invading forces. The Costa Rican forces that were organized on the *meseta* joined troops in Guanacaste and defeated the invading forces at Santa Rosa. The filibusters retreated to Nicaragua and were again defeated at Rivas (11 April 1856).

It was at Rivas that a simple soldier, Juan Santamaría, lost his life in a heroic and successful one-man attack that resulted in the fiery destruction of the filibusters' stronghold. Santamaría's sacrifice, coupled with his humble origin, made him a fitting hero for a nation that sought democratization and a greater spirit of equality among its people.

After the battle for Rivas, a cholera outbreak struck the Costa Rican forces, which then sought refuge in the Central Valley. The epidemic resulted in an estimated ten thousand deaths in a nation of approximately one hundred thousand inhabitants. This tragedy added to the indelible impression the National War left on Costa Rica and its people.

THE NEW LIBERALISM AND THE OPENING
TO THE CARIBBEAN

After a decade of military-political instability, then colonel and later general Tomás GUARDIA GUTIÉRREZ (1831–1882) seized power (1870). He remained the dominant figure in government until his death in 1882. Guardia, like several other Latin American presidents of the period, rationalized his departure from liberal principles by embracing positivist concepts. These authoritarian presidents maintained, and in the case of Guardia, even enhanced the mechanisms of republicanism, but they ruled by force of arms and personality. They placed great emphasis on economic development through modernization, particularly transportation infrastructure and trade expansion. Guardia's presidencies are somewhat ambivalently honored in Costa Rica because he contributed to political and economic development even though he relied on military power to govern.

He introduced the Constitution of 1871, which remained the fundamental law for over three-quarters of a century and in a sense beyond. When the Constituent Assembly met to write a new constitution following the 1948 revolution, it decided to discard the draft constitution presented by the revolutionary junta. The assembly chose to simply modify the 1871 Constitution. As a result, the 1949 Constitution bears a close resemblance to that formulated under Guardia.

The outstanding material achievement of Guardia's initiatives proved to be railroad construction. The project inspired and initiated but not completed by Guardia had immense implications for the future of the country. The major goal in contracting with the Keith brothers and Henry MEIGGS to build a railroad from the Central Valley to the Caribbean or Atlantic coast was to have a more direct, quicker, and less costly means of exporting coffee to European and North American markets. With the death of his brother, Minor Cooper KEITH emerged as the driving force for the project. The railroad, which finally became operational around 1890 after great expense and loss of life, brought several profound changes to Costa Rica. The most obvious difference was the connection between the heartland and the Atlantic coast, which facilitated new development along the whole course of the railway. In the space of just a few years, Puerto Limon on the Caribbean became the principal port.

The prevalence of endemic DISEASES, particularly yellow fever, malaria, and dysentery, in the hot, humid tropical lowlands created problems for the railroad builders that were as difficult to overcome as the mountainous and heavily forested terrain. The Costa Ricans living in the Central Valley and along the Pacific side of the mountains were reluctant to live and work along the notoriously unhealthy railroad route.

Minor Cooper Keith experimented with importing workers from Italy and China before finally finding the desired labor supply in the British West Indies, principally Jamaica. The Chinese and Italians became small but significant ethnic groups that contributed disproportionately to subsequent national development. The West Indian population became the principal population component of the Caribbean coastal area. This importation of workers gave the whole region a distinct character that has only been modified since 1945 with greater internal migration by the Afro–Costa Ricans to other regions and by people from other regions into Limon and the coastal area.

THE BANANA TRADE

The projected railroad from San José to Limon met many obstacles, not the least of which was the increasing financial burden. Keith came up with an idea that had long-term consequences of political, social, and economic importance: He began to cultivate bananas for export to the U.S. market.

The BANANA trade provided a means for exploiting the land grants conferred on Keith's railroad construction enterprise in order to subsidize the project. Banana production also provided a cargo for the ships that brought supplies for the railroad construction crews. In this way it partially resolved one of the problems inherent in building a railroad to connect the Central Valley to the Atlantic coast: construction had to proceed primarily from the coast inward because essential materials had to be imported. The principal potential export, coffee, could not reach the coast until the railway reached the Central Valley.

Keith's solution consisted of planting bananas along the right of way and then exporting them to an expanding U.S. market. The banana, which had elicited a favorable popular response from U.S. consumers at the 1876 Centennial Exposition, needed only refrigerated ships and regular sailings to reach a U.S. port from which the fruit could enter the already technologically advanced U.S. transportation system. By 1880 Costa Rica was developing a second major export that proved to be a consistent and significant source of revenue and foreign exchange from the late nineteenth century to the present.

The opening of the Atlantic coast area to banana cultivation intensified immigration from Jamaica. U.S. private investment and management coupled with a Jamaican labor force created an English-speaking enclave in the banana zone. Because the whole zone had previously been unexploited, the banana and railroad companies ultimately built the infrastructure, from hospitals and schools to wharfage and water-treatment facilities. This led to an impressive upsurge in Costa Rican contact with the outside world as these companies served as the catalysts for more rapid and predictable transportation to the coast and from Limon to Europe and North America. They introduced new technologies in communications as well.

Although the nation welcomed the material progress, the increased access to the outside world, and the new sources of revenues and foreign exchange, the fact that banana production led to an outwardly oriented, English-speaking enclave became a major political issue in the twentieth century. First, such reformers as Jorge VOLIO JIMÉNEZ (1882–1955) protested the enclave, and then mainstream political leaders such as Ricardo JIMÉNEZ OREAMUNO (1859–1945) and José FIGUERES FERRER (b. 1906) eventually enacted measures to integrate the enclaves into national life.

DEMOCRATIZATION AND EDUCATIONAL REFORM

When Costa Rica celebrated one hundred years of democratic government in 1989, it commemorated the watershed election in which President Bernardo SOTO ALFARO (1885–1889) and his hand-picked successor, Ascensión Esquivel Ibarra, accepted electoral defeat. The victor, José Joaquín Rodríguez Zeledón (1890–1894), and subsequent governments sometimes deviated from the democratic norm, but the all-important transfer of power based on a free election had taken place.

Soto, through his revered education minister, Mauro Fernández Acuña (1843–1905), made one of the most important advances for the consolidation of the democratic tendencies that had been present in Costa Rica since its beginnings. They established a system of free, compulsory public education in practice, not just in theory. The commitment to universal literacy has endured from the time of Fernández and contributed to sustained cultural, political, and economic progress in the twentieth century. Fernández's democratic proclivities manifested themselves when on the grounds that it was an unjustifiable expense for the benefit of the elite he closed the university until the state first had provided an elementary education for all.

THE AGE OF DON CLETO AND DON RICARDO

The period from 1906 to 1936 was dominated by two civilian presidents of unusual dedication and ability: Cleto GONZÁLEZ VÍQUEZ (1906–1910 and 1928–1932) and Ricardo Jiménez Oreamuno (1910–1914, 1924–1928, and 1932–1936). Although personalism and ephemeral party organizations characterized political activity, it remained civilian, peaceful, and civil throughout the period except for the Federico TINOCO GRANADOS (1870–1931) dictatorship (1917–1919).

González Víquez and Jiménez Oreamuno consolidated the civilian tradition. Both governed within the Constitution and presided over progressive, fiscally responsible administrations that continued to support popular education, civil rights, and economic expansion. During this period Costa Rica served as the site for the Central American Court of Justice and gained international recognition for its progressive and orderly ways.

Under the surface, however, there were growing problems of increased class distinction, rural poverty, and the concentration of economic power in the hands of the coffee elite and foreign enterprise. The United Fruit Company, which administered a virtual state within a state along the Caribbean coast, interfered less in Costa Rica than in several other Central American nations. However, the presence of an English-speaking enclave dominated by a foreign corporation met with increasing ambivalence despite its recognized contributions to national progress and well-being.

Alfredo GONZÁLEZ FLORES's presidency (1914–1917) and the organization of Jorge Volio Jiménez's (1882–1955) Reformist Party in the 1920s served as precursors of the social reform movements that would transform the national agenda for two decades beginning in 1940. Both recognized that the emerging middle sectors, the urban laborers, and peasants suffered from social injustice and lack of economic opportunity.

Congress chose González Flores as president after the 1914 election failed to produce a clear victor. Despite assuming power without a substantial political base, he attempted a fundamental reform by successfully sponsoring an income tax that placed a heavier burden on those of greater wealth. His position was further weakened by an attempt to control the off-year elections in order to secure greater congressional support for his economic reform program. When economic crisis struck as a result of market disruptions occasioned by World War I in Europe, González Flores was overthrown by his war minister, Federico Tinoco Granados.

Tinoco's repressive ways and the nonrecognition of his government by U.S. President Woodrow WILSON (1913–1921) led to ever more vociferous protest and armed rebellion. He resigned and went into exile in 1919.

Jorge Volio Jiménez became a "general" in the armed struggle against the Tinoco dictatorship after having been a reform-minded priest who identified with the plight of small, independent, but poor farmers. After Tinoco's fall he turned his talents to politics and organized the Reform Party, which championed popular causes. His ideas strongly influenced future generations. In exchange for the inclusion of some of his program in the platform of the National Republican Party (PRN), he supported the victorious candidacy of Ricardo Jiménez Oreamuno in 1924.

The more educated and better informed electorate searched for government programs that would improve their standard of living. Jiménez, with the support of Volio, advocated reforms in 1924, but his second term, like his first, was characterized by profound respect for democratic traditions and a concern for public works, but without major advances in social reform. He did, however, create a National Insurance Bank. In his third term Jiménez successfully sponsored the nation's first minimum wage and carried out a very modest program of land distribution in the Caribbean lowlands.

The Great Depression and the void left by the disappearance of the Reform Party presented an opportunity for the development of a new political movement that had profound impacts on the nation for decades to come. In 1931 a young law student, Manuel MORA VALVERDE organized a communist party, the Farmers and Workers Bloc (Bloque de Obreros y Campesinos). Mora and like-minded leaders such as the novelist Carlos Luis FALLAS SIBAJA and Jaime Cerdas Mora capitalized on the growing discontent and occupied a significant political space as an influential minority party. The communists' program emphasized realizable reforms, many of which were already commonplace in contemporaneous Europe and North America. By the mid-1930s they had demonstrated sufficient strength to have led a suc-

cessful strike in the banana zone (1934) and to have two representatives in Congress. By 1930 the population had reached one-half million and the personalistic politics of the period no longer commanded the allegiance of all the voters. The more organized and ideologically defined Bloque had demonstrated its growing appeal.

The National Republicans met the challenge presented by the communists by electing a no-nonsense anticommunist, León CORTÉS CASTRO, in 1936. Cortés won high marks as an administrator and for extending public works. However, his record on civil rights was widely questioned as were his allegedly pro-German sympathies. The protest against his high-handed dissolution of the Electoral Tribunal to deny the communists a seat in Congress extended far beyond the aggrieved party and included much of the political and intellectual leadership.

In 1940, the National Republican Party's candidate was Rafael Angel CALDERÓN GUARDIA (1940–1944). The opposition experienced difficulties in organizing behind a viable candidate when Ricardo Jiménez, elder statesman and three-time president, withdrew his candidacy charging President Cortés with obstructing the electoral process. The opposition finally supported Mora Valverde's unsuccessful candidacy.

SOCIAL REFORM AND POLITICAL REACTION
With the opposition in disarray and without a viable candidate, Calderón won an overwhelming victory that seemed to confirm the continuance of Cortés's policies. Calderón, however, broke sharply with the past and initiated a sweeping program of change and social progress and set in motion the conflicts that culminated in the 1948 civil war.

Calderón's inauguration marked the beginning of a tumultuous and decisive decade in Costa Rica. The events of the 1940s resulted in a new Costa Rica in which the democratic and egalitarian tendencies of the past reached a new level of definition and effectiveness; in which sustained economic development through diversification and modernization reached ever higher levels; and in which a national conscience formed in support of social justice. The decade of the 1940s served to break with the past and yet build on the very positive achievements of that past. The reform program elicited strong reactions that shook the nation to its very foundations.

There were many factors involved in shaping the Calderón administration. The president leaned on his friend and advisor, Víctor Manuel SANABRIA MARTÍNEZ, who ascended to the post of archbishop of San José in 1940. The two shared the conviction that the best answer to the communists' promise of a more just society was to be found in the social encyclicals of the Roman Catholic Church. The Franklin D. ROOSEVELT administration in the United States (the hegemonic power in Central America) favored welfare capitalism and assiduously courted the Latin American nations with the expectation of establishing Western Hemisphere solidarity for the Second World War. In response to the elite reaction against his reform program, Calderón took advantage of the wartime alliance between the United States and the Soviet Union to enlist the support of a renamed and supposedly democratic communist party (Popular Vanguard Party—PVP), which ostensibly accepted his social Christian approach to reform.

In this atmosphere of change, and with the disruptions and initiatives of wartime (price controls, intervention of enemy properties, financial and trade agreements with the Allies, a military training unit and intelligence operations from the United States), Calderón secured passage in Congress of his extensive reform program. Congress amended the Constitution to include social guarantees. The social security system included national health insurance as well as provisions for retirement and disability pensions. The labor code provided for the creation of a ministry of labor and a series of guarantees for workers, including the right to organize and strike, a minimum wage, protection against arbitrary dismissal, and obligatory collective bargaining.

Calderón, with support in Congress from his own majority National Republicans and the Popular Vanguard, passed extensive social legislation. The University of Costa Rica, the nation's first university in the twentieth century, was founded. Another bill provided for the distribution of uncultivated land to those who brought it under cultivation and for compensation if the land was privately held. Another program distributed shoes to school children.

This set of social programs, along with graft and mismanagement, elicited a strong response from much of the national elite, many of whom considered Calderón a traitor to his class. It also served to activate increasingly politicized members of the middle class who opposed Calderón because he was an oligarch and because his administration was fiscally irresponsible. They also opposed the communists because they were inherently undemocratic. These middle-class dissidents formed the Center for the Study of National Problems (1940) and Democratic Action (1944), which later coalesced to form the Social Democratic Party (1945).

In the 1944 election, the governing party selected Teodoro PICADO MICHALSKI (1944–1948) to confront the Democratic Party, newly reorganized to advance the candidacy of former president León Cortés. The campaign was vigorous, vehement, and sometimes violent. Picado won amid widespread charges of fraud and intimidation. Although he was on the defensive from the very beginning, Picado passed a progressive income tax. He hoped that electoral reform would diminish the growing discontent. It did seem to have a beneficial effect on the off-year election in 1946, but that proved to be little more than the calm before the storm.

During the next two years, Costa Rica suffered from acrimonious political confrontations that ran the gamut from street protests and gang clashes through press excesses and terrorism to attempts at and preparations for armed uprisings. On the electoral front, the opposition united behind the figure of the prominent liberal journalist Otilio ULATE BLANCO, leader of the National Union Party (PUN).

Among the dissidents who doubted the efficacy of the electoral reforms was José FIGUERES FERRER, who became more prominent and sought support nationally and internationally for arms to overthrow the "Calderónist-communist" regime. Upon entering into an alliance to overthrow dictatorship in the region by signing the Pact of the Caribbean, Figueres received assurance from the Guatemalan president Juan José ARÉVALO BERMEJO (1944–1948) that arms and men would be made available to him in the future.

When the election held on 8 February 1948 resulted in a provisional count showing Ulate victorious over Calderón, the governing coalition maintained its unity in Congress and voted to annul the presidential election. Both sides charged fraud; the flawed electoral apparatus had failed.

CIVIL WAR AND REVOLUTIONARY JUNTA

Although Archbishop Sanabria, along with business and political leaders, continued to seek a compromise to avoid armed conflict, events moved quickly to a bloody confrontation. Government forces repressed opposition leaders. Figueres, from his estate in the south, called on the opposition to mobilize for revolution. As Figueres's forces mustered at his estate, La Lucha, he called on Arévalo to send arms and men from Guatemala. On 10 March 1948, Figueres's Army of National Liberation seized several strategic objectives in the south. Picado, unaware of Figueres's international connections and therefore of his potential strength, reacted reluctantly and somewhat ambivalently to the uprising. He did not maintain decisive control over the small army under his command so that the initiative remained with the insurgents. As a consequence, the major force that confronted the rebels was made up of PVP volunteers.

After several bloody battles, the rebels were poised to move on San José. At this crucial juncture the progovernment forces, now split by mutual suspicions and distrust, welcomed the intervention of the diplomatic corps to bring about a negotiated peace. At this point Mora, who controlled the most numerous and reliable progovernment forces, met in secret with Figueres at the Alto de Ochomogo, just outside Cartago. With assurances from Figueres that the National Liberation would respect the social legislation and that there would be no reprisals against the progovernment supporters, Mora agreed to abide by the peace treaty negotiated by Picado with Figueres's representative Father Benjamin NÚÑEZ VARGAS.

Since the pretext for the rebellion had been Congress's annulment of the 1948 election, it was incumbent on the triumphant forces to recognize Ulate as president-elect. On 1 May, Ulate reached an agreement with Figueres under which he accepted that title. Figueres, who took the title of president of the Founding Committee of the Second Republic (Junta), organized the junta along the lines of a presidential cabinet, which then governed the nation for the next eighteen months. The victors recognized only the results of the 1948 presidential election; all other results remained annulled.

To the surprise of many within the former opposition, the junta consolidated rather than overturned the reforms of the previous eight years. It persecuted the PVP and Calderónist leadership, but enhanced their programs. However, Figueres gave them a social democratic orientation.

The most profound changes instituted by the junta were contained in the 1949 Constitution. The armed forces were abolished in favor of a national police force. The banking system was nationalized. The creation of an electoral tribunal as a fourth power within the government allowed Costa Rica to develop one of the world's fairest and most transparent systems for guaranteeing the validity of the exercise of suffrage. The junta also gave new impetus to the creation of cooperatives, the modernization of education, the extension of higher education, and the creation of autonomous institutions, such as the Costa Rican Insurance Institute (INS), which were created by the state but governed by an independent board of directors.

The social democratic orientation of the junta met with a strong negative response from Ulate's followers, the numerically dominant PUN members of the victorious coalition that had opposed Calderón. This political dissent even led to an abortive armed uprising headed by Figueres's defense minister, Edgar Cardona Quiros. PUN elected a clear majority in the Constituent Assembly, which then declined to ratify the draft document prepared for the junta, but instead updated the liberal constitution that had served the nation since 1871. The reformed constitution fell far short of the reforms that the junta espoused.

POLITICAL DEMOCRACY AND SUSTAINED GROWTH
After Ulate served his term, a new party committed to the ideals of the revolution, the National Liberation Party (PLN), successfully supported Figueres's candidacy. As the first president (1953–1958) elected under the new constitution, Figueres interpreted the great margin of victory that carried him to office as a popular mandate to implement the new party's social democratic program. From this election forward, the PLN has been the dominant political force in the nation and its principles have profoundly affected many aspects of national life. Its greatest strength has been a burgeoning, self-conscious middle class that transformed Costa Rica over the next generation into an unusually well-developed country, given its small population and limited resource base.

During the postwar period, Costa Rica sustained a remarkable rate of cultural and economic growth. Education on all levels reached all areas of the country; the arts flourished. Economic growth was fueled by increased productivity in traditional crops and by diversification into new crops and light industry. The expanding delivery system of medical care is rivaled in Latin America only by that of post-revolution Cuba. The rate of increase in living standards brought the nation nearly to the level of the industrialized nations in many areas, such as literacy and life expectancy.

This remarkable growth was accomplished in the face of rapid population increase. By 1960 Costa Rica had one of the highest rates of population increase in the world (estimated to be nearly 4 percent). It declined to somewhere between 2 and 2.5 percent by 1970 and has remained within that range since then. From an estimated population of one million in 1956, it had soared to 1,871,780 by the census of 1973, and by 1990 it was estimated to be just under three million.

The PLN provided the nation with vital and viable alternatives for social, economic, and political development that were neither communistic nor dominated by an oligarchy. It provided the country with a stable political environment that permitted it to survive the cold war with its political democracy intact as well as to sustain a high rate of economic development and diversification.

The permanent, highly organized, and ideological nature of the PLN also marked a turning point in political development. In the face of the PLN challenge, the ephemeral, personalistic groupings of the past could no longer compete. For the generation following Figueres's election, political contests pitted the PLN against anti-PLN coalitions supported by the hugely successful daily newspaper *La Nación* (founded in 1946). The Liberationists controlled the legislature for the most part, but the presidency alternated between them and the opposition. After Figueres's term, a PUN leader, Mario ECHANDI JIMÉNEZ (1958–1962), was elected with support from the still potent National Republicans. He was followed in office by Francisco ORLICH BOLMARCICH (1962–1966), one of the leaders in the 1948 uprising and a contemporary and close friend of Figueres. Continuing this alternation in power, José Joaquín TREJOS FERNÁNDEZ (1966–1970), a National Republican and long-time supporter of Calderón, was elected to the presidency in 1966 as the wounds from the confrontations of the 1940s began to heal. The PLN recovered the presidency in 1970, when Figueres won his second term. (The Constitution had been amended to prohibit second terms, but the prohibition did not apply to Figueres or Echandi.) When Daniel ODUBER QUIRÓS was elected (1974–1978) to succeed him, Costa Rican pundits began to speculate about the possible creation of a one-party state similar to Mexico.

However, in the 1978 campaign the PLN candidate, Luis Alberto MONGE ÁLVAREZ, met a revived coalition which demonstrated greater internal coherence than the previous challenges to its continued dominance. Calling itself simply Unidad, the anti-Liberation coalition nominated Rodrigo CARAZO ODIO (1978–1982), a former PLN leader, and won the election.

The Carazo presidency, however, did not live up to its promise. Concerns about the Sandinista revolution in Nicaragua, low coffee prices, and high petroleum costs plagued the administration. Cararzo failed to react quickly enough to the crisis, and the resultant inflation and excessive national debt broke the pattern of rapid and sustained development that had characterized Costa Rica for a generation. The Unidad coalition, however, laid the foundation for a second major party based on social Christian principles and less state intervention in the economy.

The PLN's Monge (1982–1986) defeated the discredited Unidad in the 1982 election but faced daunting tasks. Heavy debt coupled with American pressure to play a more active role in the U.S.-directed effort to bring down the Sandinista government in Nicaragua seriously crippled Monge's efforts to revive the economy and maintain political democracy and peace. Although avowing neutrality, the Monge adminstration was only partially able to avert American and internal pressures to aid the contras. The continual influx of Central American refugees, particularly from Nicaragua, placed an added economic and social burden on the Monge administration and those of his successors.

After leading a generational revolt within the PLN that culminated in his nomination, Oscar ARIAS SÁNCHEZ (1986–1990) defeated the leader of the unified party that had emerged from the Unidad coalition, Rafael Angel CALDERÓN FOURNIER. As president, Arias brought renewed vigor and vision to his party and nation. He went beyond Monge's neutrality to become the most prominent and successful leader seeking peace in Central America. He decreased the national debt through a series of initiatives. He asserted national interests despite American pressure and largely eliminated Costa Rica as a base for anti-Sandinista activities. His growing international stature, a result of being awarded the Nobel Prize for peace, helped Arias maintain an independent, pronegotiations stance that greatly contributed to increased stability in Central America.

The election of Calderón Fournier in 1990 marked a new milestone in national political development. Calderón Fournier and Arias represented the rise of a new generation of political leaders who were not involved in the 1948 civil war. They are the beneficiaries of the reforms that transformed the nation between 1940 and 1970, but they do not carry the scars and rancor of many of their predecessors. Calderón Fournier brought a more internally coherent major party to power, the Christian Social Unity Party (PUSC), which was based on the social Christian principles that had inspired the reforms of the early 1940s. The earlier insistence by the Center for the Study of National Problems on the need for per-

manent, ideologically based political parties led to the formation of the PLN. The PLN's success had created the necessity for a similarly coherent rival. As of the election of 1990, that necessity seemed a reality.

WATT STEWART, *Keith and Costa Rica* (1964); CARLOS ARAYA POCHET, *Historia de los partidos políticos: liberación nacional* (1968); JOHN PATRICK BELL, *Crisis in Costa Rica* (1971); BURT H. ENGLISH, *Liberación Nacional in Costa Rica* (1971); SAMUEL F. STONE, *La dinastia de los conquistadores* (1975); CHARLES D. AMERINGER, *Don Pepe* (1978); HUGO MURILLO JIMÉNEZ, *Tinoco y los Estados Unidos* (1981); RICHARD BIESANZ, KAREN ZUBRIS BIESANZ, and MAVIS HILTUNEN BIESANZ, *The Costa Ricans* (1982; rev. ed. 1988); CARLOS MELÉNDEZ, *Juan Santamaría* (1982); CAROLYN HALL, *Costa Rica: A Geographical Interpretation in Historical Perspective* (1985); LOWELL GUDMUNDSON, *Costa Rica Before Coffee* (1986); and MARC EDELMAN and JOANNE KENEN, eds., *The Costa Rica Reader* (1989).

JOHN PATRICK BELL

See also **Costa Rica: Political Parties.**

COSTA RICA: CONSTITUTIONS. The basic constitutional framework of Costa Rica has been established by documents of 1825, 1844 (as amended in 1847 and 1848), 1871, and 1949. However, constitutions of one sort or another were also written or rewritten in 1823, 1824, 1841, 1847, 1848, 1859, 1869, and 1917. Moreover, the existence of a Central American Federation Constitution of 1824 (amended in 1835) makes Costa Rican constitutional authority problematic until the 1840s at the very least. Finally, the earliest constitutional precedents date from both the CORTES OF CÁDIZ experiment of 1812 and the Independence-era pacts and statutes of 1821–1823; major codifications of Costa Rican civil law were undertaken in 1841 and 1886.

Political participation as voter, elector, or officeholder was severely limited by property, literacy, and gender qualifications in all constitutions prior to 1949. However, major electoral changes were made somewhat earlier, with direct elections after 1913, the secret ballot in 1928, an increasingly nonpartisan electoral machinery after the 1930s, a much more inclusive literacy and property qualification in practice after the 1890s, and the vote for women, finally, in 1949. While pre-1870 experiments with dual-chamber assemblies were undertaken, the Chamber of Deputies, or Assembly, legislated while a Senate was a more advisory, quasi-judicial body. However, the single-assembly model has long dominated. In this, as in the fairly rigid nineteenth-century stance on indirect elections with stiff requirements for a limited electorate, the influence of the Spanish constitutionalism of Cádiz would appear to be more directly relevant than the North American model of the time.

According to the Costa Rican authority Hernán G. Peralta, the constitutional tradition draws most heavily upon the 1821 "Pacto de Concordia," the 1825 Ley Fundamental, and the 1871 and the 1949 constitutions. The sequential relationship of Costa Rican constitutions can be summarized as follows:

1. The independence-related Pacto de Concordia (also Pacto Social Interino; 1 December 1821), reformed by political statutes of 17 March and 16 May 1823

2. The Central American Federation Constitution of 1824 (amended in 1835, largely irrelevant after 1838)

3. As a consequence of the 1824 document, the Ley Fundamental of 25 January 1825, formally abrogated by the Ley de Bases y Garantías of 1841

4. The Constitution of 9 April 1844, which reinstated much of the 1825 law, amended in various ways by new constitutions of 10 February 1847, 30 November 1848, 26 December 1859, and 15 April 1869

5. The Constitution of 7 December 1871, amended by its promulgator, General Tomás GUARDIA, in 1882, and suspended by the TINOCO dictatorship of 1917–1919

6. The Constitution of 7 November 1949, which continues in force.

The constitutional tradition in Costa Rica has, in general, opposed Central American union tendencies regardless of the local attitudes toward centralization or decentralization of government. Until the 1871 Constitution, the legislative branch held most power with various schemes to restrain the executive, particularly after dictatorships led by Braulio CARRILLO (1838–1842) and Juan Rafael MORA (1859).

Early in independent national life the supremacy of the legislative branch was extreme and a thin disguise for the power of municipal, localist authorities who doubled as deputies in early national assemblies. Carrillo defeated the most extreme of such tendencies—the rotation of the site of the capital—with the 1841 Ley de Bases y Garantías, which abrogated the 1825 Constitution. When Mora amassed great power in the late 1850s, in part as a consequence of his immense popularity as the victor over William WALKER in Nicaragua, constitutional changes were again instituted to annul his reelection (1859) and restrain like-minded future executives. With the revolt led by Guardia Gutiérrez in 1870, the pendulum swung sharply back toward presidentialism and against the rule of family-based cliques in the Assembly. Although Guardia briefly abrogated the 1871 Constitution as dictator (1877–1882), he reinstated the document, along with the total elimination of the death penalty, shortly before his death in 1882.

The framework of the 1871 Constitution survived until the civil war of 1948 and the new Constitution of 1949, although some major changes were made in the interim. The preeminence of the executive was clear throughout the early twentieth century, in regimes led by such figures as three-time president Ricardo JIMÉNEZ, by Cleto GONZÁLEZ, and by León CORTÉS, as well as in the controversial actions of president Rafael Angel CALDERÓN GUARDIA leading up to the conflict of 1948.

Only once was the Constitution of 1871 challenged directly prior to 1948: by the military coup and dictatorship of the Tinoco brothers, Federico and José Joaquín, in 1917. Their own constitution was short-lived, being abrogated in favor of the 1871 document with their downfall in 1919.

The document drawn up by the victors of 1948 remains in force today. While it was still largely presidentialist, efforts were made to avoid the worst of the earlier excesses. While no truly radical strengthening of the Assembly or the municipalities was attempted, each was recognized as an important seat of power. As a counterbalance to the perceived ills of presidentialism, the 1949 Constitution established the new category of "autonomous" or "decentralized" institutions in the public sector. The social security health system, the electrical and telecommunications services, and the national insurance institute, among others, were to be administered nonpartisanly, independent of executive branch control. While such control has been realized only partially, these agencies have become the largest employers and interest groups in the nation and, arguably, have provided an element of restraint on partisanship from the executive branch.

The 1949 Constitution also established a number of new departures. The social function of property and the need for state intervention in the economy were changes from earlier Liberal orthodoxy. As part of this thrust the banks were nationalized and a special one-time 10 percent tax on capital was levied to provide for reconstruction. The abolition of a standing army has often been credited to the authors of the 1949 Constitution, although professional military forces were few in number and had exerted little influence as a separate interest group for a long time. Most military figures leading revolts in the past—against Mora in 1859, by Guardia in 1871, or by the Tinoco brothers in 1917—did so at the behest of civilian forces against unpopular regimes. They acted as barracks commanders within an elite political contest with few troops and little in the way of institutional interests to defend.

Most important of the constitutional changes brought about in 1949 are the enfranchisement of WOMEN and the elimination of illiteracy and property qualifications for the vote. Likewise, the power of the independent Supreme Electoral Tribunal was strengthened significantly, as a consequence of the alleged fraud of 1948. The very visible success of this agency since then has been built upon similar, incremental reforms made since the 1920s, in reaction to the evident manipulation of votes by executives under the 1871 Constitution. Presidential reelection was also prohibited, putting to rest another of the means by which the executive controlled votes. This has led to a basically two-party or two-coalition alternation in power since 1948. Modern constitutional conflicts have been infrequent, although on the negative side, the political rights of those who lost in 1948 were denied them for some time thereafter. Nevertheless, perhaps the most serious and recurrent weakness of Costa Rican constitutionalism prior to 1948—the manipulation of electoral machinery and vote counting—appears to have been resolved by the 1949 Constitution.

On Costa Rican constitutionalism the authority is HERNÁN G. PERALTA, *Las constituciones de Costa Rica* (1962). Also useful is JORGE SÁENZ CARBONELL, *El despertar constitucional de Costa Rica* (1985). On the 1949 Constitution see OSCAR AGUILLAR BULGARELLI, *La constitucion de 1949: Antecedentes y proyecciones* (1973). On the disruptions of constitutional rule, see RAFAEL ORBREGÓN LORÍA, *Conflictos militares y políticos de Costa Rica* (1951); and on the legislature, his *El poder legislativo en Costa Rica* (1966). On the question of suffrage, see SAMUEL Z. STONE, *La dinastía de los conquistadores* (1975), and CLETO GONZÁLEZ VÍQUEZ, *El sufragio en Costa Rica ante la historia y la legislacíon*, 2d ed. (1978).

LOWELL GUDMUNDSON

See also **Central America: Constitution of 1824.**

COSTA RICA: POLITICAL PARTIES

National Liberation Party
Partido Liberación Nacional—PLN

The National Liberation Party became the dominant political party in Costa Rica with the election of José FIGUERES FERRER as president in 1953. Since that time a majority of the nation's chief executives have been PLN members, and the party generally has enjoyed a majority in the national legislature. Not only did the PLN achieve a dominant position in Costa Rican politics, but its organization and success induced a "new politics." No longer could informal, transitory groups form around a charismatic candidate to contest an upcoming election. To meet the challenge of the highly organized, ideologically coherent PLN, its opponents had to become more organized and present the electorate with specific programs and a greater degree of continuity.

The PLN was founded in October 1951 by a group of insiders of the National Liberation movement, which had supported the successful 1948 armed uprising and the resultant de facto government under Figueres Ferrer's presidency (1948–1949). They met at Francisco ORLICH BOLMARCICH's *finca*, La Paz. They wanted to convert the movement into a permanent, highly structured political party by capitalizing on the immense popularity of Figueres. Although many of the participants had been active in the Social Democratic Party, they recognized that its poor showing in the December 1948 election indicated the need to form a more broadly based party and to take advantage of the National Liberation label and its association with military victory, social justice, political renewal, and a greater political role for the middle class.

The PLN traces its origins to the formation of the Center for the Study of National Problems (1940), with its strong affinity for social democratic ideas. The Center merged with the Democratic Action group to form the Social Democratic Party (1945), which unsuccessfully presented Figueres as its candidate to lead the united opposition in the 1948 election. It was a party born of national crisis. The successful revolt of 1948 vaulted the founders of the movement into prominent positions in government. Figueres's decisive victory in the 1953 election assured a bright future for the PLN.

CARLOS ARAYA POCHET, *Historia de los partidos políticos: Liberacíon Nacional* (1968); JOHN PATRICK BELL, *Crisis in Costa Rica* (1971); BURT H. ENGLISH, *Liberación Nacional in Costa Rica* (1971); and CHARLES D. AMERINGER, *Don Pepe* (1978).

JOHN PATRICK BELL

COSTA RICA

Second Republic

The Second Republic is the name given to the government that resulted from the reorganization following Costa Rica's 1948 civil war. On 1 March 1948, outgoing Costa Rican president Teodoro PICADO MICHALSKI used his control over the Legislative Assembly (national congress) to annul the presidential election held in February, replacing the apparent winner, Otilio ULATE, with the defeated candidate, Rafael Ángel CALDERÓN GUARDIA. Reacting to this violation of the constitutional order, José FIGUERES FERRER (1906–1990), a little-known political activist, led a six-week War of National Liberation to restore legitimate government and enforce Ulate's claim to the presidency.

Raising a volunteer force and using arms supplied by antidictatorial exile elements in Guatemala, Figueres defeated the would-be usurpers and presided over the Founding Junta of the Second Republic for eighteen months (April 1948–November 1949). During its exercise of power, the Founding Junta abolished the national army and held elections for a constituent assembly for the purpose of drafting a new constitution. With the adoption of the Constitution of 1949, Figueres Ferrer and the Junta turned over the executive power to Ulate, beginning Costa Rica's Second Republic, a new political era characterized by free elections, stable government, diminished presidential authority, and a tilt toward socialism in economic and social affairs.

JOHN PATRICK BELL, *Crisis in Costa Rica: The 1948 Revolution* (1971); BERT H. ENGLISH, *Liberación Nacional in Costa Rica: The Development of a Political Party in a Transitional Society* (1971); CHARLES D. AMERINGER, *Don Pepe: A Political Biography of José Figueres of Costa Rica* (1978), and *Democracy in Costa Rica* (1982).

CHARLES D. AMERINGER

COTAPOS BAEZA, ACARIO (*b.* 30 April 1889: *d.* 22 November 1969), Chilean composer. Born in Valdivia, Chile, Cotapos was one of the group of authors, poets, composers, architects, and visual artists known as Los

Diez, the first group to comprise the Chilean cultural avant-garde. Initially self-taught, at the age of twenty-seven Cotapos moved to New York to study. For the ten years following, he counted among his associates Edgard Varèse, Aaron Copland, Henry Cowell, Ernest Bloch, and Darius Milhaud. In 1927, with Varèse and others, Cotapos founded the International Composers Guild, one of the first organizations with a mandate to perform new music. In 1927, Cotapos left New York for Paris and Madrid, where he composed a number of important works. Returning to his homeland in 1940, he served as secretary of the National Conservatory from 1940 to 1946. He was supervisor of the Instituto de Extensión Musical of the University of Chile from 1949 until his death in Santiago. His musical output includes works for voice, piano, orchestra, and chamber ensembles. Much of his music, characterized by a free and independent spirit, tends toward the dramatic and monumental.

Revista musical chilena (April 1961); JOHN VINTON, ed., *Dictionary of Contemporary Music* (1971); SAMUEL CLARO VALDÉS and JORGE URRUTIA, *Historia de la música en Chile* (1973); GERARD BÉHAGUE, *Music in Latin America: An Introduction* (1979); SAMUEL CLARO VALDÉS, *Oyendo a Chile* (1979); SAMUEL CLARO VALDÉS et al., *Iconografía musical chilena*, vols. 1 and 2 (1989).

SERGIO BARROSO

COTEGIPE, BARÃO DE (João Mauricio Wanderley; *b.* 23 October 1815; *d.* 13 February 1889), Brazilian politician. Cotegipe was identified with Bahian politics and slavocratic sugar interests throughout his life. After graduating from the Olinda Law Faculty in Pernambuco in 1837, Cotegipe set out on the path that eventually made him the archetypal imperial mandarin. He moved up steadily through the political ranks, holding a county judgeship and a variety of provincial elected offices before becoming a national deputy in the early 1840s. By 1856 he was a senator from Bahia, and a member of the cabinet. An important chieftain of the pro-slavery national Conservative Party, Cotegipe was himself a slaveowner and a holder of several SUGAR plantations, all inherited by his wife, a daughter of the Conde de Passé, perhaps the richest planter in Bahia Province. In 1875 Cotegipe, then serving as minister of finance, authored the landmark legislation (Decree no. 2687 of 6 November 1875) that created the agricultural credit guaranteeing 7 percent interest on all investments to create the modern sugar mill complex, or *engenho central*. In 1885 Cotegipe became prime minister. His Conservative government, finally facing up to the reality that slavery in Brazil could not continue forever, introduced the SARAIVA-COTEGIPE LAW of 1885 that freed all slaves over sixty-five years old, thereby immediately manumitting 120,000 older slaves. Typical of many imperial mandarins, Cotegipe was a poor businessman when it came to looking after his own interests and died

poor, months before the monarchy was overthrown by a discontented army.

SACRAMENTO AUGUSTO VICTORINO ALVES BLAKE, *Diccionario bibliographico brasileiro*, 7 vols. (1897); JOSÉ WANDERLEY PINHO, *Cotegipe e seu tempo: Primeiro phase, 1815–1867* (1937), and *História de um engenho do Recôncavo, 1552–1944* (1946); EUL-SOO PANG, *In Pursuit of Honor and Power: Noblemen of the Southern Cross in Nineteenth-Century Brazil* (1988).

EUL-SOO PANG

See also **Brazil: Second Empire; Slavery.**

COTO WAR (1921), an armed conflict between Panama and Costa Rica over the Coto, a region in Panama's Chiriquí Province along the Panamanian–Costa Rican border. The controversy began soon after independence from Spain. In 1911 the chief justice of the U.S. Supreme Court, Edward D. White, was asked to arbitrate. He rendered his decision in 1914, but Panama did not accept it, alleging that it favored Costa Rica. Hostilities broke out in 1921, when Costa Rica invaded the area. Panama recaptured the area easily. The conflict spread, however, when Costa Rica moved into the province of Bocas del Toro. Fearing that its interests might be threatened, the United States forced Panama to accept the White decision.

MANUEL OCTAVIO SISNET, *Belisario Porras o la vocación de la nacionalidad* (1972).

JUAN MANUEL PÉREZ

COTOCOLLAO, a large prehistoric habitation site located in the northwestern sector of the Ecuadorian capital of Quito. The site was occupied from approximately 1500 to 540 B.C., corresponding to the Late Formative Period in the chronological schema of Ecuadorian prehistory. The occupational levels at the site are capped by a thick layer of pumice and volcanic ash. This deposit may be associated with the eruption of Mount Pululagua, thought to have occurred around 500 B.C. Prior to the discovery of Cotocollao in the 1970s, little was known about the Formative Period in the northern highlands. Cotocollao has subsequently become the type site for the Late Formative archaeological phase in this region.

The Formative Period in Andean prehistory is defined by the appearance of pottery and incipient agriculture. These developments occurred at different rates in different areas. The earliest evidence of pottery in Ecuador is found on the coast where Valdivia ceramics have been dated to 3200 B.C. This tradition was eventually replaced by Machalilla Phase pottery around 2000 B.C. The Cotocollao ceramic assemblage exhibits decorative and morphological similarities with both Valdivia and Machalilla pottery, suggesting that connections existed between the highlands and the coast around the time of transition between these two coastal phases. The Cotocollao assemblage also evidences some stylistic affinities with ceramics from the southern highlands and the eastern slopes of Ecuador.

Distinctive vessel forms in the ceramic assemblage from Cotocollao include straight-walled, flat-bottomed bowls; stirrup-spout bottles; and strap-handled bottles. The latter form is typical of the Chorrera pottery horizon, which follows Machalilla and is found throughout much of Ecuador during the Late Formative Period. The most important diagnostic element of the Cotocollao assemblage is the decorated stone bowl. A ceremonial function is postulated for this artifact type on the basis of the technical expertise involved in its manufacture and the lack of apparent use wear. The stone bowls from Cotocollao are the earliest known in the northern sierra, and the Valley of Quito has been suggested as a possible locus of manufacture for these vessels.

The pattern of spatial organization identified at the site of Cotocollao involves the arrangement of household clusters around a village cemetery. The cemetery apparently served as the ritual focal point of the community. This is in contrast to the pattern described for Formative Period sites on the coast, where dwellings are typically arranged around a central public-ceremonial space. The cemetery at Cotocollao has produced one of the largest samples of prehistoric skeletal remains from the northern sierra. Analysis of the approximately 200 sets of remains from the site has provided important information on diet, disease, and demography for the Late Formative Period population. In addition to the osteological evidence, finds of carbonized beans and maize in the earliest levels at Cotocollao, together with the quantity of *manos* (pestles), *metates* (mortars), and hoes recovered at the site, indicate that agriculture was the primary means of subsistence for the inhabitants of this site.

The two basic reference volumes on Cotocollao are MARCELO VILLALBA, *Cotocollao: Una aldea formativa del Valle de Quito* (1988), and PEDRO PORRAS, *Arqueología de Quito* (1982). On the osteological materials from the site, see DOUGLAS H. UBELAKER, "Prehistoric Human Remains from the Cotocollao Site, Pichincha Province, Ecuador," in *Journal of the Washington Academy of Science* 70, no. 2 (1980): 59–74.

TAMARA L. BRAY

COTTON, a plant native to most of the warmer regions on earth, including the tropical and semitropical regions of the Americas. It was cultivated and woven into cloth by all three of the great pre-Columbian civilizations: the Mayas, the Aztecs, and the Incas. Long before European contact with the Americas, cotton had been introduced into Europe from the Middle East, and consequently was not particularly impressive to the newly arrived Spanish conquerors. Nevertheless, cultivation of cotton continued after contact, and contributed to a cottage textile industry in Spanish and Portuguese America during the colonial period.

The mechanization of the spinning and weaving processes during the industrial revolution of the eighteenth century increased production of cotton textiles enormously. In the mid-1700s both the Portuguese colony of Brazil and the British Caribbean islands exported large amounts of cotton fiber for the rapidly growing British textile industy. By 1800, however, the United States had replaced the Caribbean islands as the major transatlantic source of cotton, thanks to Eli Whitney's cotton gin.

After Independence, during the middle and late nineteenth century (the liberal/positivist period), many Latin American countries, particularly Mexico, Brazil, and Colombia, attempted to develop their own textile industries, and in conjunction with this effort they expanded cotton production. In addition, cotton became a very profitable export commodity for Latin American countries after the U.S. cotton industry was destroyed by the Civil War. By the end of World War I, textile manufacturing had been initiated in most Latin American countries, and most countries were producing cotton for domestic use, for export, or for both. Because cotton was intimately connected to industrialization and nascent capitalism, it produced a semiproletarian agricultural work force in many places. Accordingly, wage-earning cotton workers were often among the first agricultural laborers to organize unions.

Cotton again became important in the 1960s, when the United States and its ALLIANCE FOR PROGRESS encouraged the stimulation of nontraditional agricultural exports in Latin America. Cotton was a natural choice for Central Americans because improved pesticide technology made their Pacific coastal plain ideal for the crop. In Central America, access to credit and other incentives were available for those who would produce and export raw cotton. Consequently, Central American cotton production increased by 500 percent between 1961 and 1973. By 1977, Central America was the third largest producer of cotton for the world market, behind the United States and Egypt.

Vastly increased cotton production in Central America had disastrous economic effects for the poorest agricultural workers. Land that had previously been dedicated to subsistence farming of corn was turned over to cotton. This displacement contributed to the proletarianization process that was taking place among agricultural workers in much of Latin America during the 1960s and 1970s. Unfortunately for the peasants who had previously inhabited this cropland, cotton did not provide stable employment for wage laborers. Because of the mechanized nature of modern cotton production, labor demands are relatively low for much of the growing season. Consequently, most of these newly proletarianized agricultural workers were forced to migrate.

Cotton, both as an export commodity and as an input for domestic textile production, continues to be an important Latin American industry.

JOSÉ ROMERO LOZA, *Algodón en Bolivia*, 2d ed. (1978); BERTHA DODGE, *Cotton: The Plant That Would Be King* (1984); FORREST D. COLBURN and SILVIO DE FRANCO, "Privilege, Production, and Revolution: The Case of Nicaragua," *Comparative Politics* 17, no. 3 (1985): 277–290; ROBERT G. WILLIAMS, *Export Agriculture and the Crisis in Central America* (1986); BARRY CARR, "The Mexican Communist Party and Agrarian Mobilization in the Laguna, 1920–1940: A Worker-Peasant Alliance," *Hispanic American Historical Review* 67, no. 3 (1987): 371–404; DAWN KEREMITSIS, *The Cotton Textile Industry in Porfiriato Mexico* (1987); MICHAEL J. GONZALES, "The Rise of Cotton Tenant Farming in Peru, 1890–1920: The Condor Valley," *Agricultural History* 65, no. 1 (1991): 51–71.

RACHEL A. MAY

COUNCIL OF THE INDIES, central administrative and judicial institution for the Spanish Empire. In 1524 CHARLES I created the Council of the Indies as a judicial, legislative, and executive body responsible for the administration of Spain's New World empire. Located in Spain, and ultimately based in Madrid, it had jurisdiction over the Spanish colonies analogous to that of the Council of Castile over much of Spain. Thus the Council of the Indies initially had jurisdiction in legislative, financial, judicial, military, ecclesiastical, and commercial matters in the New World.

The council prepared all legislation related to administration, taxation, and, initially, defense of the New World; no major project could be undertaken without its approval. It corresponded directly with both civil and ecclesiastical officials in the New World and exercised patronage, except during the existence of the Cámara of the Indies, over both lay and clerical positions.

The Council of the Indies also had judicial responsibilities and sat as the final court of appeals for civil cases tried by the colonial AUDIENCIAS and for civil and criminal cases tried by the House of Trade. In addition, it held first-instance jurisdiction in cases concerning ENCOMIENDAS and those initiated in Spain which dealt with matters in the Indies. The council also arranged judicial reviews (*residencias*) of high-ranking colonial officials and special inspections (*visitas*) of colonial officials and districts. Finally, the council exercised censorship over all books dealing with the Indies and had to approve any papal decree prior to its transmission to the New World.

During the sixteenth century, the Council of the Indies was at the peak of its power. In the seventeenth century, however, favoritism and corruption led to a reduction of its authority in favor of both other tribunals and royal favorites. From 1600 to 1609 and 1644 to 1701, a subcommittee of the council known as the Cámara of the Indies handled its patronage responsibilities. In 1717 and from 1721 to 1808, the *cámara* again was charged with fulfilling the council's patronage responsibilities.

In its early years, the council had a president, four or five councillors, a crown attorney (*fiscal*), and various subalterns. Initially, the councillors were men trained in law (*ministros togados*). However, in 1626, PHILIP IV began naming some councillors without any training in law. These were called *ministros de capa y espada* to distinguish them from the *ministros togados*. The rights and responsibilities of the two groups were identical, with the important exception that *ministros de capa y espada* could not vote on judicial matters. By the end of the seventeenth century, the quality of the *ministros de capa y espada* had eroded significantly as the crown sold appointments and even named a nine-year-old boy as a reward for the services of his father. The dubious quality of the minister and the acknowledged inefficiency of the Council of the Indies at the close of the seventeenth century stimulated its reform and reduction of authority by PHILIP V in 1717.

When Philip V, the first Bourbon monarch in Spain, organized his government, he named a minister of the Indies (secretary of state for the Indies) with responsibility for American affairs in administration, war, finance, and commerce. A clarification in September 1717 left judicial matters, patronage (including making recommendations for high-ranking judicial and ecclesiastical appointments), and matters related to municipal government to the council. Although overshadowed by the minister, the council slowly increased its influence in the latter eighteenth century as its size increased in response to the growing population, wealth, and importance of the empire and as its ranks were increasingly filled with men who had personal experience in the New World. Declared equal in rank and prerogatives to the Council of Castile in 1773, the Council of the Indies enjoyed a renaissance of prestige and authority. From the 1773 decree to 1808, thirty-one of thirty-nine new *ministros togados* had American experience. When responsibility for both peninsular and American affairs was united in five ministerial portfolios organized by function rather than by territory in 1790, and the House of Trade was abolished in the same year, the Council of the Indies remained the only body in Spain devoted solely to American affairs.

The Cortes of Cádiz suppressed the council in 1812, but FERDINAND VII reestablished it in 1814, naming an unprecedented number of American-born ministers to its ranks in a modest effort to win favor in the New World. Belatedly, after the loss of Spain's colonies in the American mainlands, the council was finally abolished in 1834.

ERNESTO SCHÄFER, *El consejo real y supremo de las Indias*, vol. 1 (1935); CLARENCE H. HARING, *The Spanish Empire in America* (1947), pp. 102–118; MARK A. BURKHOLDER, *Biographical Dictionary of Councilors of the Indies, 1717–1808* (1986).

MARK A. BURKHOLDER

COUNTERINSURGENCY. Since achieving independence, many Latin American governments have fought to stave off challenges to their legitimacy from armed segments of their own population. When, in the decades following the Bolshevik Revolution of 1917, many of these uprisings acquired an ideological dimension, the United States became increasingly concerned about what it had heretofore regarded as an internal problem of the countries involved. This concern peaked in the late 1950s and early 1960s after Fidel CASTRO's victory in Cuba and Soviet Premier Nikita Khrushchev's declared support for wars of national liberation. Convinced that "the sweep of nationalism" presented "the most potent factor in foreign affairs today," and that insurgency had become the Communists' preferred method of expansion, U.S. President John F. Kennedy in 1961 made counterinsurgency the cornerstone of his strategic doctrine of Flexible Response for containing communism during the Cold War.

In concept, counterinsurgency was a twist on traditional U.S. policies that posited a middle path between reactionary dictatorship on the Right and COMMUNIST totalitarianism on the Left. With the focal point of the Cold War having shifted to the less developed countries, the United States promoted a variety of programs designed to allow Third World nationalists to realize their aspirations for social, economic, and political change through peaceful reform instead of violent revolution. Extensive economic assistance from international sources, both public and private, together with structural reforms and better management of resources within recipient countries, presumably would pave the way for economic development, social mobility, and, where it did not already exist, political democracy. To protect this liberal reform program from Communist subversion, the United States would encourage a government's military forces to engage in civic action projects that would improve local conditions while winning the allegiance of the people. Indigenous police and military forces would also take military action against hard-core insurgents whose ideological commitment prevented them from accepting peaceful reform as a legitimate approach to progress and stability.

President Kennedy, according to an official memorandum, observed that "the most critical spot on the globe nowadays is Latin America, which seems made-to-order for the Communists." Consequently, during his administration, the preponderance of U.S. counterinsurgency efforts took place within the Western Hemisphere, with special attention given to Guatemala, Venezuela, Colombia, Peru, and Bolivia. The ALLIANCE FOR PROGRESS (1961) offered a plan for long-term economic development and political stability, while civic action and counterguerrilla activities offered short-term responses to the Communist threat. Latin American military forces seeking instruction in this comprehensive approach could attend courses at the U.S. Army School of the Americas in the Canal Zone and receive training from U.S. military advisory groups and from small, highly skilled teams of Special Forces (Green Berets). Weapons and equipment for counterinsurgency could be procured through a military assistance program that

Kennedy reoriented from hemispheric defense to internal security.

The success of Latin American governments against leftist insurgencies in the 1960s seemed to prove the efficacy of the U.S. strategy. In reality, the failure of those insurgencies can be attributed not so much to U.S. assistance as to the inability to duplicate Cuba's *foco* model (the employment of a small armed band operating from a rural base to create the conditions for revolution) in other countries. Other factors were factionalism within guerrilla movements and the reformist or repressive responses of threatened governments.

After a brief hiatus, concern about Latin American insurgencies again mounted in Washington in the late 1970s, following the reemergence of leftist guerrillas in Guatemala and other countries and the success of the Sandinistas in Nicaragua. Compared with the insurgents of the 1960s, the new or rejuvenated movements placed greater emphasis on organization, received generous support from external sources, such as Cuba, and mastered the art of public relations directed at foreign agencies and public opinion, especially in the United States. The United States again assisted friendly governments seeking to suppress revolutionary movements, although the remembrance of Vietnam, a divided public, and an

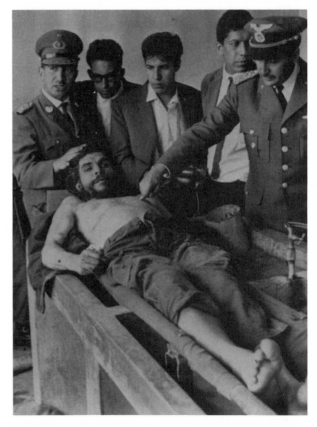

The corpse of Ernesto "Che" Guevara, Cuban insurgent, two days after he was killed by Bolivian rangers (1967). UPI / BETTMANN ARCHIVE.

emphasis on human-rights issues placed constraints on U.S. counterinsurgency efforts, for example, in El Salvador, a major recipient of Washington's largess.

Entering the 1990s, most leftist insurgencies in Latin America again seemed under control, Guatemalan National Revolutionary Unity (URNG) and, in Peru, Shining Path (Sendero Luminoso) being two exceptions. But the conditions that gave rise to insurgent movements have not been removed in most countries, and trafficking in narcotics has added a new dimension to the problem. Conversely, the demise of the Eastern bloc and the initiatives of several Latin American countries, including peace negotiations in El Salvador, have given rise to hopes that diplomacy might become an effective counterinsurgency tool. But if for some the trends seem hopeful, the fact that insurgencies have plagued Latin America for centuries adds a cautionary note regarding the future.

JOHN CHILD, *Unequal Alliance: The Inter-American Military System, 1938–1978* (1980); GEORGES FAURIOL, ed., *Latin American Insurgencies* (1985); ERNESTO CHE GUEVARA, *Guerrilla Warfare* (1985); ROY GUTMAN, *Banana Diplomacy: The Making of American Policy in Nicaragua, 1981–1987* (1988); BENJAMIN C. SCHWARZ, *American Counterinsurgency Doctrine and El Salvador* (1991); THOMAS P. WICKHAM-CROWLEY, *Guerrillas and Revolution in Latin America* (1992).

LAWRENCE A. YATES

See also **Guerrilla Movements; Revolutionary Movements** (under individual countries).

COURTS. *See* **Judicial Systems.**

COUTINHO, JOSÉ JOAQUIM DA CUNHA DE AZEREDO (*b.* 8 September 1742; *d.* 12 September 1821), bishop of Olinda (1794–1806) and author. A child of the late Portuguese ENLIGHTENMENT, Coutinho was born into a landowning family from the Rio de Janeiro captaincy. He graduated with a degree in canon law from Coimbra University in 1780. Twelve years later he was elected to the Royal Academy of Sciences. In 1798, he left Lisbon for Olinda, Pernambuco, where he founded a renowned seminary, whose "Estatutos" ("Ordinances") he wrote. Also serving as provisional head of Pernambuco's government, he took harsh measures against what he considered, given his enlightened outlook, abusive practices such as tax evasion, and private appropriation of funds from the royal treasury. By so doing, he offended powerful vested interests. In 1802, Coutinho was called back to Portugal, where he was nominated bishop of Elvas in 1806. He retired from his see in 1817, and was appointed the last general inquisitor of the realm the following year.

As an author, Coutinho was chiefly concerned with the economic policy of the crown. His *A Political Essay on the Commerce of Portugal and Her Colonies* was published in 1794, and was translated into English in 1801. Later, he wrote a number of important works in a polemic vein on religious and administrative matters. His physiocratic beliefs, shrouded in a conservative outlook, revealed his sympathies with the reform-minded officials of the times, but some extreme attitudes, such as the defense of the slave trade, kept him somewhat apart from the leading intellectuals of the period.

E. BRADFORD BURNS, "The Role of Azeredo Coutinho in the Enlightenment of Brazil," in *Hispanic American Historical Review*, no. 2 (1964): 145–160; SÉRGIO BUARQUE DE HOLANDA, "Apresentação," in *Obras econômicas de J. J. da Cunha de Azeredo Coutinho (1794–1804)*, edited by Sérgio Buarque de Holanda (1966); MANOEL CARDOZO, "Azeredo Coutinho and the Intellectual Ferment of His Times," in *Conflict and Continuity in Brazilian Society*, edited by HENRY H. KEITH and S. F. EDWARDS (1969); SEVERINO LEITE NOGUEIRA, *O Seminário de Olinda e seu fundador o bispo Azeredo Coutinho* (1985).

GUILHERME PEREIRA DAS NEVES

COUTINHO, RODRIGO DOMINGOS ANTONIO DE SOUSA (*b.* 3 August 1755; *d.* 26 January 1812), first count of Linhares (1808) and a Portuguese diplomat. From a noble family of important court and state functionaries, Coutinho was the son of Francisco Inocêncio de Sousa Coutinho, a governor and captain-general of Angola (1764–1772) and ambassador to Madrid (1774–1780).

After studying at the Nobles' College in Lisbon and at Coimbra University, Coutinho visited France and subsequently served at Turin as minister plenipotentiary from 1779 to 1796. In 1790 he published a discussion of the effects of the mining of precious metals on industry that implied the need for technological innovation in Brazil's MINAS GERAIS mining industry. Recalled to Lisbon in 1796 to succeed the deceased Martinho de MELO E CASTRO as state secretary for the navy and colonies, Coutinho developed the concept of a joint Luso-Brazilian imperial economic and political unit, declaring in 1798 that Portugal's vast overseas domains, especially those in the Americas, were the basis of the crown's power and that without them continental Portugal would be reduced to a province of Spain.

After a term as president of the treasury (1801–1803), Coutinho left Lisbon in October 1807 with the regent João and the court and government when the capital was transferred to Rio de Janeiro to escape French armies invading Portugal. In Brazil he served as secretary of state for foreign affairs and war (1808–1812) and advised the regent on the negotiations leading to the three Anglo-Portuguese treaties of February 1810, which opened Brazilian ports to international trade and committed the Portuguese never to establish a tribunal of the Inquisition in the New World.

MARQUEZ DO FUNCHAL, *O conde de Linhares: Dom Rodrigo Domingos António de Sousa Coutinho* (1908); MARIA BEATRIZ NIZZA

DA SILVA, "O império Luso-Brasileiro, 1750–1820," in *Nova história da expansão portuguesa*, edited by Joel Serrão and Antônio Henrique de Oliveira Marques, vol. 8 (1986); JOSÉ LUÍS CARDOSO, *O pensamento econômico em Portugal nos finais do século XVIII, 1780–1808* (1989).

DAVID HIGGS

See also **Inquisition: Brazil.**

COUTO, JOSÉ BERNARDO (*b.* 1803; *d.* 1862), Mexican jurist, politician, and writer. Couto studied jurisprudence and humanities at San Ildefonso, Mexico City. In 1827 he became a lawyer, and in 1828 served in the Veracruz legislature. He was counselor of state in 1842 and minister of justice in 1845. Couto was one of the Mexican commissioners during the peace negotiations with the United States in 1847–1848. A distinguished jurist, he was known for his radical anticlerical views in his youth, particularly because of his *Disertación sobre la naturaleza y límites de la autoridad eclesiástica* (1825). Decades later he retracted his anticlerical position in *Discurso sobre la constitución de la iglesia* (1857).

Couto was a supporter of the arts, particularly painting and sculpture, and served as president of the governing committee of the Academy of San Carlos. In addition, he was a writer of note, translating Horace, publishing various novels and volumes of verse, and contributing to the *Diccionario universal de historia y geografía*.

JOSÉ ROJAS GARCIDUEÑAS, *Don José Bernardo Couto* (1964); MARÍA DEL REFUGIO GONZÁLEZ, "Ilustrados, regalistas, y liberales," in *The Independence of Mexico and the Creation of the New Nation*, edited by Jaime E. Rodríguez O. (1989).

JAIME E. RODRÍGUEZ O.

COVARRUBIAS, MIGUEL (*b.* 22 November 1904; *d.* 4 February 1957), Mexican artist. Miguel Covarrubias was extremely multifaceted, particularly in artistic and cultural endeavors. A native of Mexico City, he was a caricaturist, set designer, book illustrator, cartographer, painter, writer, art historian, ethnologist, and anthropologist. His work on the Olmec civilization made a major archaeological contribution, and his innovative museum installations forever changed the way exhibitions are designed. Toward the end of his life, as director of dance at the Instituto de Bellas Artes, he created a nationalist dance movement that initiated what has been termed the golden age of modern Mexican dance.

In everything that Covarrubias accomplished he remained an artist. He possessed a rare intuitive ability to capture and synthesize at a glance the essentials of character or situation, as demonstrated by his famous caricatures for *Vanity Fair* and his illustrations for his first books, *The Prince of Wales and Other Famous Americans* (1925) and *Negro Drawings* (1927).

Covarrubias married Rosemonde Cowan, a dancer and choreographer, in 1930. She became his collaborator as researcher and photographer for his next two books, *The Island of Bali* (1938) and *Mexico South* (1946). In the early 1940s, they returned to live permanently in Mexico, where they entertained many of the major intellectual and show-business figures of the time.

As he matured, Covarrubias immersed himself in studies of early historical happenings, peoples, folklore, and civilizations, principally on the American continent and in Polynesia. He wrote and illustrated *The Eagle, the Jaguar, and the Serpent* (1954) and *Indian Art of Mexico and Central America* (1957).

Terence Grieder has said, "In some ways, Covarrubias was a man out of his age. The typical thought of his day took mathematical or statistical form rather than the pictorial form which was his, and incidentally the Renaissance way of expressing thought. But he typified the best of twentieth-century humanism: its fascination with the visual arts, its openness to other cultures, and its desperate and doomed struggle to preserve the humane virtues of the traditional societies against technocratic commercialism."

Miguel Covarrubias was the encyclopedic artist of Mexico's rebirth. When he died in Mexico City, he had won a lasting place as a distinguished artist, scholar, teacher, and advocate of Mexican cultural studies. His final gesture to the Mexican people was the gift of his extraordinary pre-Columbian collection to the National Museum.

TERENCE GRIEDER, "The Divided World of Miguel Covarrubias," in *Americas*, 23 (May 1971): 19–24; ADRIANA WILLIAMS, *Covarrubias* (1994).

ADRIANA WILLIAMS

CRABB, HENRY A. (*b.* 1827; *d.* 7 April 1857), filibuster. A schoolmate of William WALKER, a fellow filibuster, in Nashville, Tennessee, Crabb journeyed to California during the Gold Rush. After settling in Stockton in 1849, he led a brief expedition of adventurers to Nicaragua in 1855. Crabb returned to California the next year and married Filomena Ainsa, who came from a prominent Sonora, Mexico, family. Then, in 1857, he organized the American and Arizona Mining and Emigration Company in a bold attempt to colonize part of Sonora. Crabb outfitted a group of men and marched into Mexico. Ambushed on 1 April 1857 by Mexican troops and besieged for six days, Crabb and fifty-nine of his men were captured and brutally executed to serve as a warning to Americans that Mexico was not open to further colonizing ventures.

RUFUS KAY WYLLYS, "Henry A. Crabb—A Tragedy of the Sonora Frontier," *Pacific Historical Review* 9, no. 2 (June 1940):

183–194; JOE A. STOUT, "Henry A. Crabb—Filibuster or Colonizer?" *The American West* 8, no. 3 (May 1971): 4–9; DIANA LINDSAY, "Henry A. Crabb, Filibuster, and the *San Diego Herald*," *Journal of San Diego History* 19 (Winter 1973): 34–42.

IRIS H. W. ENGSTRAND

See also **Filibustering.**

CREEL, ENRIQUE CLAY (*b.* 30 August 1854; *d.* 17 August 1931), Mexican banker, governor of Chihuahua (1904–1911). Born in Chihuahua, Creel was the son of the U.S. consul there. He married the daughter of General Luis TERRAZAS and subsequently headed the financial and industrial enterprises of the Terrazas family. He was the leading Mexican banker of the prerevolutionary era and was a founder and manager of the Banco Minero de Chihuahua and several other banks. He also had widespread interests in food processing, mining, textiles, and manufacturing. He served as the most prominent Mexican officer or board member of several foreign corporations. Creel also entered politics, serving in Chihuahua's state legislature in 1882–1885 and 1897–1900. He was an alternate federal deputy from Chihuahua in 1892–1894 and a full deputy from Durango in 1900–1902 and from Chihuahua in 1902–1906.

In 1904 the governor of Chihuahua resigned in Creel's favor. Creel was elected on his own in 1907 and served to 1911. Creel was a member of the CIENTÍFICOS, a positivist group led by José Y. LIMANTOUR, the secretary of the treasury (1892–1911) under dictator Porfirio Díaz. As governor he tried to implement positivist principles by streamlining and modernizing state government, which caused protests from fiercely independent municipalities. While serving as governor, he was also Mexican ambassador to the United States (1907–1908) and secretary for foreign relations (1910–1911).

During the MEXICAN REVOLUTION, when he fled for his life, Creel suffered heavy financial losses. He returned to Mexico from exile in the early 1920s and served as a financial adviser to President Álvaro OBREGÓN SALIDO.

FRANCISCO R. ALMADA, *Gobernadores del Estado de Chihuahua* (1980), furnishes basic biographical information. MARK WASSERMAN, "Enrique C. Creel: Business and Politics in Mexico, 1880–1930," in *Business History Review* 59 (Winter 1985): 645–662, examines Creel's public and business career.

MARK WASSERMAN

CREELMAN INTERVIEW, an interview given by Mexican President Porfirio DÍAZ (1876–1880, 1884–1911) to the U.S. journalist James Creelman of *Pearson's Magazine* and published on 17 February 1908. It subsequently appeared in Spanish in the Mexico City newspaper *El Imparcial* on 3 March 1908. In it Díaz revealed his plans to retire from the presidency following the June 1910 election, when he would be eighty years old. He also called

for the formation of opposition political parties, which effectively had been banned during his thirty-year dictatorship.

The purpose of Díaz's statement most likely was to calm both external and internal criticism of his rule. Others claim that Díaz expected his offer to resign to be met with demands from his supporters that he remain in power. Finally, it may have been designed to bring into the open those who opposed him. Whatever the motive, Díaz made a mistake, as the interview stimulated long-dormant political activity in the country resulting in his overthrow in May 1911.

CHARLES C. CUMBERLAND, *Mexican Revolution: Genesis Under Madero* (1952); STANLEY R. ROSS, *Francisco I. Madero: Apostle of Mexican Democracy* (1955), esp. pp. 46–48.

DAVID LaFRANCE

CREOLE. In Spanish America, the term "creole" (*criollo*) refers to people of European descent, especially Spaniards who were born in the New World—in contrast to *peninsulares*, born in Europe. Because few Spanish women came to the colonies, creoles often were not exclusively of European descent. Nevertheless, they represented a privileged group that held much of the land and economic power in the colonies, although they often felt discrimination from Spanish-born *peninsulares* in political and economic privileges. Creoles occupied many of the positions in the bureaucracy and were legally equal to *peninsulares*, although a tendency under the Bourbons to appoint *peninsulares* to office heightened the rivalry between these two groups in the eighteenth century and contributed to independence sentiment. Creoles led the independence movements in the early nineteenth century and were the group that inherited political power in Hispanic America. They imposed a strong conservative legacy in their domination of the higher clergy, military officer corps, and the landowning and merchant elites, often in collaboration with foreign investors.

The term *criollo* or *créole* also was used in Portuguese and French colonies to indicate those of European descent, while in Brazil *criolo* defines a black person of African descent. In modern Latin America the term often refers to characteristics that are especially native or traditional to the country, for example, "creole cuisine."

In English-speaking areas, especially those once ruled by France or Spain, the term has been corrupted to mean not only those of French or Spanish descent but also those of mixed, often African, descent, as in the British Caribbean, Haiti, or Louisiana; and indeed, in modern times, it has come to be applied to virtually all the native inhabitants. In much of the Caribbean, it also often refers to the mixed European-African language spoken by natives of the former colonies.

Since the term is used in different ways in different

regions, the context of its use is important for understanding its precise meaning.

SEVERO MARTÍNEZ PELÁEZ, *La patria del criollo: Ensayo de interpretación de la realidad colonial guatemalteca* (1970); MARK A. BURKHOLDER and D. S. CHANDLER, *From Impotence to Authority: The Spanish Crown and the American Audiencias, 1687–1808* (1977); BARBARA LALLA and JEAN D'COSTA, *Language in Exile: Three Hundred Years of Jamaica Creole* (1990).

RALPH LEE WOODWARD, JR.

CRESPO, JOAQUÍN (*b.* 1845; *d.* 1898), Venezuelan president (1884–1886, 1892–1898). Crespo, a tough young *llanero*, joined the Liberal side in the FEDERAL WAR (1859–1863) and, as a loyal supporter of Antonio GUZMÁN BLANCO, became his minister of war (1877–1878). In 1879, as a reward for his loyalty to the dictator, Crespo was given the title "Hero of Duty Done." From 1884 to 1886 Crespo served as figurehead president for Guzmán Blanco, and in 1888 he ran unsuccessfully for president. From 1892 to 1894 he served as interim president after seizing power in a caudillo rebellion. His constitutional presidency (1894–1898) corresponded with an economic slump and with clashes with Great Britain over the border with British Guiana. Crespo is credited with initiatives to professionalize the national army. After his presidential term was completed, he led the forces of the new regime of General Ignacio Andrade against a rebellion headed by José Manuel ("El Mocho") Hernández. In one of its first engagements Crespo was killed in battle.

ROBERT L. GILMORE, *Caudillism and Militarism in Venezuela, 1810–1910* (1964); RAMÓN J. VELÁSQUEZ, *La caída del liberalismo amarillo* (1972); JUDITH EWELL, *Venezuela: A Century of Change* (1984).

WINFIELD J. BURGGRAAFF

CREYDT, OSCAR (*b.* 1907; *d.* ?) Paraguayan Communist leader. Born in San Miguel, in southern Paraguay, Creydt was the scion of a wealthy family, and although trained as a lawyer, he dedicated his life and fortune instead to organizing the Paraguayan Communist Party.

During the early 1920s, Creydt was a leading figure in the University Students Federation, and in the Consejo Mixto de Obreros y Estudiantes. This latter group (not more than fifty individuals) formed the basis for the Paraguayan Communist Party (PCP), founded in 1928 and brought into the Comintern four years later.

At this time, the PCP could count on little meaningful support in Paraguay, even within the labor unions. After the CHACO WAR (1932–1935), the Communists found many of their social programs "hijacked" by the nationalist Febrerista Party, and, at the same time, the PCP itself was forced underground. Creydt, however, proved to be a talented clandestine organizer. Through discipline and hard work, he drove out the

Trotskyists within the party and managed to weather the persecutions of the MORÍNIGO dictatorship (1940–1948).

In 1947, Creydt got his only opportunity for a measure of national power. A civil war had erupted, and the Communists forged an alliance with disaffected soldiers, Febreristas, and Liberals, which came critically close to defeating the rival Colorados. The strength of the PCP at this juncture surprised many observers, but Creydt, who felt that the political work was finally paying off, was not surprised. Nonetheless, the victory of the Colorados and the subsequent terror sent him and most party members into exile.

Creydt retained his hold on the secretary-general's post for many years. In the 1960s, younger Paraguayan Communists accused him of mimicking Stalin in fostering a cult of personality. The PCP split over this issue in 1968, with a substantial minority shifting to Creydt's old associate, Obdulio Barthe, who now adopted a pro-Beijing line. In an attempt to heal the breach, Creydt negotiated with the Maoists, but in the end this gesture resulted only in a split of his own pro-Moscow wing. Creydt himself was supplanted as party chief by the much younger Miguel Angel Soler, whose arrest (and probable murder) by General Alfredo STROESSNER's police in 1975 brought another round of factionalization from which the Communists did not recover.

OSCAR CREYDT, *Formación histórica de la nación paraguaya* (1963), pp. 48–55; PAUL H. LEWIS, *Paraguay Under Stroessner* (1980), pp. 32, 220–221; HUMBERTO ROSALES, *Historia del Partido Comunista Paraguayo (1928–1991)* (1991), *passim*.

THOMAS L. WHIGHAM

See also **Paraguay: Political Parties.**

CRIMINAL JUSTICE. Crime and violence were part and parcel of the conquest and settlement of the New World and persisted throughout the colonial era. Contemporary accounts are replete with references to crimes against property, crimes perpetrated by one individual on another, and, far less frequently, crimes against the state. Cases of robbery, assault, and homicide regularly reached colonial officials and provoked efforts to find and punish the perpetrators. Officials paid far less attention, however, to illegal physical and financial abuse of Indians and slaves. In urban centers, authorities devoted considerable effort to controlling crime and punishing criminals. In many rural areas, in contrast, much crime went unreported to royal bureaucrats in the AUDIENCIA's capital, and local officials meted out punishment. Indeed, the only types of crime that officials in rural communities had to report were homicides, aggravated assault, and sedition.

The most effective large-scale crackdown on crime took place in New Spain in the eighteenth century with the creation in 1710 of a new body, the ACORDADA, which actively pursued and punished criminals throughout the viceroyalty. An indication of the frequency of crime in late colonial New Spain can be found in the nearly forty-three thousand cases heard by a single judge of the *acordada* from 1782 to 1808.

Several types of officials shared responsibility for dealing with crime. Municipalities had *alguaciles*, sheriffs or constables who apprehended criminals and received as income a portion of the fines levied. In addition, the audiencias had ALGUACILES MAYORES who engaged in the same activities. Local magistrates (*alcaldes ordinarios*), provincial administrators (ALCALDES MAYORES and CORREGIDORES), and the regional high courts (*audiencias*) heard cases and pronounced sentences. Provincial administrators heard appeals from local magistrates; the *audiencias* heard appeals from both as well as from corporate bodies that enjoyed special judicial privileges (FUEROS). Viceroys and captains-general heard military cases, and ecclesiastical courts handled cases involving clerics. Appeals in criminal cases ended at the *audiencias*. In civil cases involving substantial sums of money, however, plaintiffs could appeal to the Council of the Indies.

Colonial judges invoked criminal statutes codified in the *Recopilación de leyes de los reynos de las Indias* (1681) and in Spanish legal compilations. These included the *Nueva recopilación de Castilla* (1659), the Laws of Toro (1505), and other legislation extending back to the SIETE PARTIDAS (1265). In addition, judges consulted local ordinances, viceregal decrees, and other legislation.

Interpersonal crime was commonplace and usually involved people who knew each other. The offenders, particularly those who used a deadly weapon such as a butcher or household knife, were usually young males, as were the victims. Most reported crimes against women, which included beating, stabbing, homicide, and sexual offenses, took place in the home.

Homicide was one of the few offenses that virtually all members of colonial society considered criminal. Consequently, records of homicides, although fragmentary, are more complete than those for any other crime. A review of these records for central Mexico reveals that rural homicide rates rose beginning in the late seventeenth century. Rural homicides usually took place after work and on Sundays.

The colonial authorities' toleration of crime and violence varied considerably over time. Behavior condoned during and immediately following the conquest of a region was often subsequently condemned and punished. The illegal branding and exportation of Indian slaves in Central America in the 1530s, for example, continued both because officials participated in the trade and because violators, on the occasions when they were punished, usually received light sentences. The race, class, and sex of the perpetrator and victim also affected the extent to which officials tolerated criminal activities and the vigor with which they pursued the perpetrators.

Spanish officials considered persons of mixed racial background to be of "vicious origins and nature," expected them to engage in crime and violence, and consequently were willing to tolerate a high level of criminality. When they finally took action against mestizos, mulattoes, and other *castas*, however, the punishment was apt to be severe and exemplary.

Legislation made Indians legal minors. From this paternalistic perspective, criminal behavior was expected as a result of their alleged lack of reason, and was not considered as serious as that of Spaniards. As a result, punishment was usually lenient.

A substantial body of royal and municipal legislation defined measures for controlling the behavior of black slaves. For example, blacks in Lima were subject to a curfew, forbidden to leave the city without official permission, and prohibited from carrying weapons. Punishments for violations were theoretically severe and included whipping of up to three hundred lashes, castration, exile, and hanging. In many cases, however, well-connected slave owners simply bribed the *alguaciles* to overlook the offense. The most common offense slaves committed was running away, but they also committed theft, assault, and murder with some frequency. The victims of slave theft were usually Spaniards or Indians, while victims of assault or murder were apt to be persons of color. Blacks were often victims of assault and murder committed by Spaniards.

As the colonial period progressed, the number of Spaniards in the lower and lower-middle classes increased. Many Spanish criminals came from these groups. A review of the cases of 958 prisoners sentenced to service in a presidio or garrison of New Spain or elsewhere in the empire in 1799 and 1800 revealed that 28 percent of the men were Spaniards, most of them from the lower or lower-middle class.

Much justice, particularly in rural areas, was handled informally. The *hacendado* or plantation owner often took it upon himself to discipline workers and to punish petty theft and assault. Urban residents, on the other hand, especially Spaniards and *castas*, were much more apt to be punished following formal proceedings.

While every group in colonial society was victimized by criminals, women were particularly ill served by the judicial system. Physical abuse, wife beating, rape, and kidnapping were the most common crimes against women; most occurred in the home and were committed by a member of the family or another person known by the victim. Frequently the husband was the perpetrator, lashing out at his spouse in anger over her conduct, especially her sexual conduct. Many, perhaps most, wives were reluctant to file charges, for fear of provoking even harsher abuse.

When a woman sought legal redress, she found that a male judge questioned her closely, in search of any sign of blemished reputation. A woman had to document her pure behavior, and if any stain was found, her husband's conduct was condoned. Not surprisingly, accused husbands routinely countercharged that their wives had engaged in misconduct.

Assailants were seldom punished for the rape or kidnapping of a single woman. Only when a married woman had been raped did colonial judges consider the offense a serious crime—not for its heinous nature but because it damaged the honor of the victim's husband. If convicted, the assailant often was temporarily exiled.

In cases of adultery, the cuckolded husband could legally murder his wife and her lover, but this form of retribution happened only among the lower classes. For an elite male to take this step would stain his honor by publicly proclaiming his wife's infidelity. If a wife murdered an adulterous husband, she could expect no mercy.

Colonial authorities employed various punishments, depending on the specific crime committed; the class, race, age, health, and sex of the perpetrator; the length of time spent in prison prior to sentencing; and prior criminal record. The one crime certain to result in a death sentence was sodomy. Otherwise, capital punishment was rarely employed, even for homicide, and *audiencia* judges examined the cases carefully for evidence of premeditation, treachery, or assassination. For the most part judges reserved death sentences for highwaymen who had robbed and killed their victims and rape-murderers.

Labor service in the presidios of Havana or Veracruz from one to a maximum of ten years was the usual punishment for homicide in Mexico during the eighteenth century. Animal rustling and robbery also merited presidio sentences; vagrancy was frequently punished by two to four years of labor on a royal ship. Indians were not sentenced to military service, and only rarely to ship duty.

Terms of service as convict labor for private employers were common in Mexico, and many male criminals found themselves working in *obrajes* (textile workshops). Whippings were common, administered for many crimes committed by Indians, black slaves, and *castas*. Spaniards alone were exempt from the lash. Although women were punished less rigorously than men, they were sentenced to labor in artisans' workshops or in private households.

Most criminal offenses were misdemeanors and punished accordingly. Temporary confinement prior to sentencing or minor punishment—for example, a small fine—accounted for the vast majority of the sentences handed down by the judge of the *acordada* in Mexico in the closing decades of colonial rule.

One feature of criminal justice in colonial Spanish America that deserves special notice is the use of pardons. From time to time, the crown declared general pardons in celebration of a coronation, a royal marriage, or the birth of a prince of princess. These resulted in numerous prisoners being released, although some crimes, such as robbery and fraud, were not covered by a pardon. A general pardon also reduced the number of unsolved crimes, for under the terms of the pardon,

criminals who turned themselves in were absolved. In addition, viceroys could grant clemency and commute sentences.

COLIN M. MAC LACHLAN, *Criminal Justice in Eighteenth-Century Mexico: A Study of the Tribunal of the Acordada* (1974); WILLIAM B. TAYLOR, *Drinking, Homicide, and Rebellion in Colonial Mexican Villages* (1979); GABRIEL HASLIP-VIERA, "Criminal Justice and the Poor in Late Colonial Mexico City," in *Five Centuries of Law and Politics in Central Mexico*, edited by Ronald Spores and Ross Hassig (1984); LYMAN L. JOHNSON, ed., *The Problem of Order in Changing Societies: Essays on Crime and Policing in Argentina and Uruguay, 1750–1940* (1990).

MARK A. BURKHOLDER

See also **Judicial System.**

CRIOULOS. *See* **African Brazilians: Color Terminology.**

CRISTÃOS NOVOS. *See* **Inquisition.**

CRISTERO REBELLION, a peasant uprising from 1926 to 1929, pushed Mexico to the brink of political chaos. The Cristeros generally saw the conflict as a religious war against the ANTICLERICALISM of the Mexican government.

This anticlericalism originated in northern Mexico, where North American–style entrepreneurs, Protestant converts, and ambitious politicians built a movement to transform their traditionally Catholic nation into a cen-

Priest and Cristero rebel awaiting execution by firing squad. ARCHIVO GENERAL DE LA NACIÓN, MEXICO.

ter of secular economic expansion. The movement's leading proponent, Plutarco Elías CALLES (president of Mexico, 1924–1928), placed rigid regulations on the church, including required registration of priests and the closing of church schools. The church responded with a strike—the cessation of religious services—which caused a panic among the faithful. In Jalisco and the surrounding states of central Mexico, this panic sparked a peasant rebellion.

Government claims that the rebels were superstitious tools of scheming priests were largely propaganda. Only about 45 of the 3,600 priests in Mexico supported the rebellion. The Cristeros were Indian and mestizo peasants whose motives for rebellion were mixed. Most acted to defend their faith against an expansive secular state, while others seized the opportunity to demand more extensive land reform.

The Mexican army's early victories obscured the depth of popular support for the rebels. By July 1927 approximately 20,000 rebels operated in small, uncoordinated guerrilla bands that lost several skirmishes but grew in numbers. The Cristeros moved to a new level of military action under the leadership of Enrique Gorostieta, a professional military officer who developed disciplined units to confront the army with conventional battlefield tactics. His attack on Manzanillo in May 1928 forced the federal army to bring in several regiments to avoid a major defeat.

The federal army mounted an offensive in Jalisco in December 1928, but the Cristeros simply left the area to escape the army's superiority in numbers and firepower. The frustrated soldiers attacked and looted the local villages, whose outraged inhabitants actually strengthened the Cristero base of support. Gorostieta's largest offensive climaxed at the Battle of Tepatitlán on 19 April 1929, when José Reyes Vega (one of the few Catholic priests active in the fighting) commanded a 900-man force that defeated a federal contingent more than three times its size.

By 1929 the fighting was stalemated. The Mexican government saw that a complete victory in the field was unlikely because of massive popular support for the rebels in their home districts. However, in spite of their 50,000 recruits, the Cristeros did not have the resources to overthrow the central government, which had the support of the United States.

The end of the revolt came from the outside. A reluctant but shaken Mexican government heeded the pleas of U.S. Ambassador Dwight MORROW and reached an agreement with representatives of the CATHOLIC CHURCH in Mexico and Rome. The government relaxed its clerical regulations, and on 21 June 1929 the Catholic clergy resumed public worship. By September of that year the Cristeros had disbanded.

JEAN MEYER, *La Cristiada*, 3 vols. (1973–1974), is fundamental. An abridged translation by Richard Southern is available under the title *The Cristero Rebellion: The Mexican People Between Church and State, 1926–1929* (1976). See also DAVID BAILEY, *¡Viva Cristo Rey! The Cristero Rebellion and the Church-State Conflict in Mexico* (1974); JIM TUCK, *The Holy War in Los Altos: A Regional Analysis of Mexico's Cristero Rebellion* (1982); ROBERT QUIRK, *The Mexican Revolution and the Catholic Church, 1910–1929* (1973), pp. 145–247; and RAMÓN JRADE, "Inquiries into the Cristero Insurrection Against the Mexican Revolution," in *Latin American Research Review* 20, no. 2 (1985): 53–69.

JOHN A. BRITTON

CRISTIANI, ALFREDO (*b.* 22 November 1947), elected president of El Salvador in 1989. His constitutional term of office ended in 1994. The scion of a family of coffee planters and a graduate of Georgetown University, Cristiani was elected president during El Salvador's civil war (1979–1992). Before his nomination as candidate for the presidency, he was a businessman with little political experience. Although his party, the National Republican Alliance (ARENA), was founded by Roberto D'ABUISSON, a cashiered army officer with alleged links to death squads, and represented the most conservative elements in Salvadoran society, Cristiani conveyed a moderate image. With his election ARENA won the presidency for the first time.

In November 1989 Cristiani had to face the first major crisis of his presidency, a guerrilla offensive that reached San Salvador. During the struggle for the capital, six well-known Jesuit priests were brutally murdered. The prosecution of the crime was seen as a test of the commitment of his administration to control the excess of the army. Two army officers were eventually convicted of the crime, but disagreements remained as to whether the investigation had uncovered the full extent of army involvement. The main priority of the Cristiani administration was to bring the civil war to a negotiated end. The negotiations between the government and the guerrillas, sponsored by the UNITED NATIONS, culminated with a cease-fire agreement signed 16 January 1992 by Cristiani and the leaders of the guerrilla forces in Mexico City. His administration advocated free-market economic policies. Despite criticisms of the way in which his administration implemented the peace accords, when Cristiani's term ended in 1994, opinion polls ranked him as the most popular politician in El Salvador, thanks in part to the pacification of the country and a healthy rate of economic growth.

There is no full biography. A profile was published in the *New York Times*, 21 March 1989. An excellent source for this period of Salvadoran history is the documents section of the journal *Estudios Centroamericanos*.

HÉCTOR LINDO-FUENTES

See also **El Salvador: Political Parties.**

CROIX, MARQUÉS DE (*b.* 1699; *d.* 1786), viceroy of New Spain (1766–1771). Born in Lille, France, Carlos Francisco de Croix rose to the rank of general within the

Spanish army. He was serving as captain-general of Galicia when he was designated viceroy of NEW SPAIN in 1766. His term overlapped the VISITA of José de GÁLVEZ (1765–1771), who had been sent by Charles III to inspect and reform the colony. Croix presided over the efficient expulsion of the JESUITS in 1767. He supported Gálvez's suppression of the resulting riots in Guanajuato and San Luis Potosí the following year. A staunch regalist in ecclesiastical matters, the viceroy successfully defied the Mexican INQUISITION when he was summoned before it. Croix undertook the colonization of Alta California in 1769 to defend the northern boundary of the empire. By the end of his term, four settlements had been founded. Croix urged the creation of the Interior Provinces jurisdiction in the north, which was accomplished five years after his departure. He sought improvement of the militias being formed in Mexico and encouraged the addition of regular Spanish army units to bolster the defense of the colony. He departed Mexico in 1771 to become captain-general of Valencia, where he died.

LUIS NAVARRO GARCÍA, "El virrey Marqués de Croix," in *Los virreyes de Nueva España en el reinado de Carlos III,* edited by José Antonio Calderón Quijano, vol. 1 (1967), pp. 161–381.

JOHN E. KICZA

CROIX, TEODORO DE (*b.* 30 June 1730; *d.* 8 April 1791), viceroy of Peru (1784–1790). Born in Lille, Flanders, into a military family, Croix went to America with his uncle, Carlos Francisco, who served as viceroy of New Spain (1765–1771) and, following his recall to Spain, as captain-general of Valencia. Not surprisingly, this powerful patronage brought Teodoro rapid promotion in the Mexican military hierarchy. He succeeded JÁUREGUI as viceroy of Lima as Peru began its slow economic and political recovery from the TÚPAC AMARU I rebellion, the administrative confusion associated with the *visita general* (general inspection), and the indebtedness of the exchequer in the early 1780s.

Although overanxious to protect the dignity of his office against the authority of the first generation of intendants (installed in 1784), Croix succeeded in overseeing a period of stable government and economic and fiscal growth. He succeeded in 1787 in persuading the crown to restore the superintendency of exchequer affairs to the viceroy, thereby undermining a key feature of the intendant system.

LILLIAN ESTELLE FISHER, "Teodoro de Croix," in *Hispanic American Historical Review,* 9 (1929): 488–504; RUBÉN VARGAS UGARTE, *Historia del Perú: Virreinato (Siglo XVIII) 1700–1790* (1956), esp. pp. 435–467; JOHN R. FISHER, *Government and Society in Colonial Peru* (1970), esp. pp. 54–70.

JOHN R. FISHER

CROWDER, ENOCH HERBERT (*b.* 11 April 1859; *d.* 7 May 1932), U.S. military officer and diplomat. After

graduating from West Point in 1881, Crowder received a law degree in 1886. In 1891 he joined the staff of the advocate general of the U.S. Army and went to the Philippines as judge advocate general during the SPANISH-AMERICAN WAR. During the U.S. provisional government of Cuba in 1906, Crowder served as president of the Advisory Law Commission that wrote legislation for Cuban elections, civil service, the courts, and local and provincial government. He chaired the committee that oversaw the Cuban elections in 1908 and established new electoral laws there in 1919. In 1921 he returned as the personal representative of President Warren Harding to help out following the crash of the economy after the DANCE OF THE MILLIONS. He strongly impressed on President Alfredo ZAYAS the need for honest government, and was successful in eliminating some corrupt practices. In 1922 he helped secure a $50-million loan for Cuba. From 1923 until his retirement in 1927, Crowder served as ambassador to Cuba.

DAVID HEALY, *The United States in Cuba, 1898–1902: Generals, Politicians, and the Search for Policy* (1963); ALLAN R. MILLET, *The Politics of Intervention: The Military Occupation of Cuba, 1906–1909* (1968); LOUIS A. PÉREZ, *Cuba Under the Platt Amendment, 1902–1934* (1986), and *Cuba: Between Reform and Revolution* (1989); LESLIE BETHELL, *Cuba: A Short History* (1993).

WADE A. KIT

CRUZ, ARTURO (*b.* 18 December 1923), banker, Nicaraguan ambassador to the United States (1981), former CONTRA leader. Born in Jinotepe, Cruz attended Georgetown University and earned degrees in economics from the School of Foreign Service (B.S., 1947; M.S., 1971). Cruz joined the Conservative Party at an early age and helped form the National Union of Popular Action in 1948. In 1954, he participated in an unsuccessful effort by young Conservatives to overthrow Anastasio SOMOZA GARCÍA, for which he was jailed for eleven months.

Cruz joined the INTER-AMERICAN DEVELOPMENT BANK as a finance officer in 1959. He was one of the architects of the CENTRAL AMERICAN COMMON MARKET in the early 1960s. In 1977, the Sandinistas convinced him to join a prestigious group of Nicaraguans, known as "The Twelve," which supported the revolutionary movement. Cruz was president of the Central Bank of Nicaragua from July 1979 to May 1980, when he became a member of the Governing Junta of National Reconstruction. In March 1981, the Sandinista government named him ambassador to the United States; he resigned at the end of that year. Cruz started to run for president against Daniel Ortega in 1984, but never registered as a candidate. In 1985, he helped found the Nicaraguan Opposition Union, the political arm of the counterrevolutionary force. He resigned his post in February 1987 and from 1990 to 1994 served as the alternate executive director of the Inter-American Development Bank's section for Central America.

LATIN AMERICAN STUDIES ASSOCIATION, The Electoral Process in Nicaragua (1984); LLOYD GROVE, "Arturo Cruz," in *Washington Post*, 19 February 1987, sec. B, pp. 1, 4; *The IDB Report* 17, no. 9–10 (1990): 6.

MARK EVERINGHAM

CRUZ, OSWALDO GONÇALVES (*b.* 5 August 1872; *d.* 11 February 1917), Brazilian pioneer in medicine and public health. Cruz's careers in medicine and public health were closely intertwined. As director of public health for the federal government between 1903 and 1909, he led the campaign to eliminate yellow fever, smallpox, and the plague from the federal capital of Rio de Janeiro. As director of the OSWALDO CRUZ INSTITUTE, he created the first important center in the country for microbiological research and tropical medicine.

The son of a doctor, Cruz obtained his medical degree at the Rio Medical School in 1892 and pursued further training in bacteriology in Paris between 1896 and 1899. On his return to Brazil in 1899 he joined the staff of the Serum Therapy Institute at Manguinhos, outside Rio, rising quickly to the position of director. In 1902, Cruz came to the attention of the newly elected president of Brazil, Francisco Rodrigues ALVES, who asked him to lead an ambitious campaign against yellow fever, smallpox, and the plague, all of which were epidemic in the federal capital.

The campaign was based on the newest techniques of the sanitation sciences, notably the destruction of mosquitoes and their breeding sites, fumigation of houses, and isolation of sick individuals. Despite considerable opposition from doctors, sections of the military, and the poor, who were the main targets of the campaign and who objected to its intrusive nature, Cruz and his teams of "mosquito killers" were successful in controlling the plague and yellow fever. However, resistance to compulsory smallpox vaccination meant that many people were not vaccinated; as a result, the city experienced a severe epidemic in 1908, with more than 9,000 deaths.

In 1909 Cruz resigned his position in public health in order to devote his attention to the Serum Therapy Institute, which was renamed the Oswaldo Cruz Institute in his honor. There he established the first modern school of experimental medicine in Brazil. In early 1916 Cruz retired to Petrópolis, where he died at the age of forty-three.

DONALD B. COOPER, "Oswaldo Cruz and the Impact of Yellow Fever in Brazilian History," in *Bulletin of the Tulane Medical Faculty* 26 (1967): 49–52; CLEMENTINO FRAGA, *Vida e obra de Osvaldo Cruz* (1972); NANCY STEPAN, *Beginnings of Brazilian Science: Oswaldo Cruz, Medical Research, and Policy, 1890–1920* (1976).

NANCY LEYS STEPAN

See also **Diseases.**

CRUZ, SERAPIO (*d.* 23 January 1870), Guatemalan military officer and revolutionary leader. Known by the nickname of "Tata Lapo," Cruz served under the command of José Rafael CARRERA in the Guatemalan revolt of 1837. Cruz broke with Carrera in 1848. Though a leader in the revolution of 1848, he refused to collaborate with the new liberal government and continued to resist until he reached an agreement with President Mariano PAREDES on 2 February 1849. Upon Carrera's return to power in August 1849, Cruz reestablished his relationship with Carrera. He was an important military leader at the BATTLE OF ARADA in 1851 and in the campaign against El Salvador in 1863. Carrera suspected Cruz of a plot against him in 1863 but retained Cruz's loyalty by promising to leave him the presidency. Infuriated by Carrera's deathbed designation of Vicente CERNA as his successor, Cruz launched a revolt in 1867 against Cerna's government. In a daring attack at Palencia, near the capital, early in 1870, he died, thus becoming one of the principal martyrs of the Liberal Reforma of 1871.

RODOLFO GONZÁLEZ CENTENO, *El mariscal de campo Don Serapio Cruz: Sus notables campañas militares*, 2d ed. (1985); RALPH L. WOODWARD, JR., *Rafael Carrera and the Emergence of the Republic of Guatemala, 1821–1871* (1993); WAYNE M. CLEGERN, *Origins of Liberal Dictatorship in Central America: Guatemala, 1865–1873* (1994).

RALPH LEE WOODWARD, JR.

CRUZ, VICENTE (*d.* 20 March 1849), one of the leading officers in José Rafael CARRERA's 1837 revolt in Guatemala. Once in control of Guatemala, Carrera appointed Cruz CORREGIDOR of the departments of Mita and of Guatemala. Cruz was Carrera's vice president in 1844–1848, and he exercised the office of president when Carrera stepped down briefly from 11 September to 31 October 1845 and again from 25 January to 4 February 1848. When Carrera resigned in August 1848, Cruz expected to succeed him. But because the legislature opposed Cruz, he resigned on 28 November 1848 and took up arms against the government. He accepted, however, the Convenio de Zacapa (2 February 1849) arranged by President Mariano PAREDES and returned to the government's army. Little more than a month later, he died fighting rebels led by Agustín Pérez.

For details on his career, see RALPH LEE WOODWARD, JR., *Rafael Carrera and the Emergence of the Republic of Guatemala, 1821–1871* (1993). On the death of Cruz, see FEDERICO HERNÁNDEZ DE LEÓN, *El libro de las efemérides*, vol. 5 (1963), pp. 455–459.

RALPH LEE WOODWARD, JR.

CRUZ DIEZ, CARLOS (*b.* 17 August 1923), Venezuelan artist. Born in Caracas, Cruz Diez studied at the Cristóbal Rojas School of Fine and Applied Arts. He began his career as a graphic designer, working as an art director at several advertising agencies. While his paintings display a taste for social realism with portrayals of daily life and common people, his graphic work reflects a

303

fascination with color. During a visit to Barcelona and Paris in 1955, he began experimenting with the kinetic possibilities of color in his series *Physichromies*. He returned to Caracas in 1957 and opened a studio of art and industrial design. Later he designed publications for the Venezuelan Ministry of Education and taught art history and design at the School of Fine Arts and Central University in Caracas.

Shortly after his solo show at the Museum of Fine Art in Caracas, he moved to Paris with his family (1960). Three years later he joined the Nouvelle Tendence group in Paris and his work began to appear in international group exhibitions: The Responsive Eye (New York, 1965) and Soundings Two (London, 1966). He won the grand prize at the Córdoba Bienal (Argentina, 1966), and the international prize of painting at the São Paulo Bienal (1967). His large chromatic works are in the Caracas international airport and the Guri Dam powerhouse.

ALFREDO BOULTON, *Cruz Diez* (1975); BÉLGICA RODRÍGUEZ, "Carlos Cruz Diez and the Transformable Work of Art" (Master's thesis, Courtauld Institute of Art, University of London, 1976), and *La pintura abstracta en Venezuela, 1945–1965* (1980).

BÉLGICA RODRÍGUEZ

CRUZ E SOUSA, JOÃO DA (*b.* 24 November 1861; *d.* 19 March 1898), Brazilian poet. Born in Santa Catarina to freed slaves, Cruz e Sousa became one of the most notable men of letters of his time. His protector, the former master of his parents, sent him through high school (1874) and tutorials. After brief experiences in teaching and journalism, Cruz e Sousa joined a touring dramatic troupe in 1881. His travels around Brazil revealed to him the abject conditions of his fellow blacks. From 1882 to 1889, he collaborated on a pro-republican, abolitionist periodical that he published. In 1884 he was appointed to a government post in a provincial city but was barred from assuming his duties because of his race. At that time he issued his first books of verse, which reflect the dominant realist rhetoric of the period. In 1890, he moved to Rio to work in journalism and later in the archives of the railroad company. He soon launched symbolism in Brazilian letters, becoming the leader of the new aesthetic movement.

Cruz e Sousa suffered several tragedies: two of his four children succumbed to tuberculosis while the two that remained died of other causes, his wife went mad, and he himself became consumptive. The poet retired to a country home in Minas Gerais but soon passed away. While personal misfortune is reflected in his verse, Cruz e Sousa's awareness of the condition of blacks is historically more significant. His leadership role in symbolism is outstanding and important in terms of black participation in elite cultural production.

RAYMOND SAYERS, "The Black Poet in Brazil: The Case of João da Cruz e Sousa," in *Luso-Brazilian Review* 15 (suppl.)

(1978): 75–100; DAVID BROOKSHAW, *Race and Color in Brazilian Literature* (1986).

CHARLES A. PERRONE

CRUZ UCLES, RAMÓN ERNESTO (*b.* 3 January 1903; *d.* 1985), lawyer, president of Honduras (1971–1972). After a thirty-year career in law, much of it as a district judge and legal expert in Honduras's border disputes with Nicaragua, Cruz was nominated by the National Party as a compromise candidate in 1962. The elections were scuttled in 1963 by the coup of Oswaldo LÓPEZ ARELLANO. Cruz was again nominated for president of Honduras by the National Party when General López stepped aside to permit elections in 1971. Cruz won a bare plurality (49.3 percent) and took office on 7 June 1971. During his brief eighteen months in office, he concentrated on foreign affairs, traveling widely and winning the return of the Islas de Cisne (Swan Islands) from the United States. This diplomatic master stroke, however, could not offset his rapid and total isolation from his own party. In the face of virtual economic collapse and the escalation of agrarian strife, cresting with the massacre of Olancho peasants at La Talanquera by angry cattle ranchers, President Cruz lost control. General López quietly removed him from office on 4 December 1972.

JAMES A. MORRIS, *Honduras: Caudillo Politics and Military Rulers* (1984).

KENNETH V. FINNEY

CUADRA, PABLO ANTONIO (*b.* 4 November 1912), Nicaraguan poet, essayist, journalist, playwright, professor, and director of the Nicaraguan Academy of the Language. Cuadra studied with the Jesuits and attended law school at the Universidad Nacional de Oriente y Mediodía. At age nineteen he cofounded the Vanguardia group and began his lifelong involvement in journalism. Through the years he edited and coedited several literary and political newspapers and journals: *Vanguardia* (1931–1933), *Trinchera* (1936–1939), *Cuaderno del Taller San Lucas* (1942–1944), *El Pez y La Serpiente* (1961–1979), *La Prensa Literaria* (1954–1987), and *La Prensa*, the influential newspaper he edited after Somoza forces assassinated its editor, Pedro Joaquín CHAMORRO, in 1978. Cuadra has been deeply involved in theater since 1936, when he founded the Lope Theater and wrote *Por los caminos van los campesinos*.

Cuadra's poetry and political ideology grew together. He participated in the original Sandinista struggle and published his first poems while still in school. At twenty-two he published *Poemas nicaragüenses* (1934), followed by *Cuaderno del Sur* (1934–1935), *Hacia la cruz del sur. Manual del navegante hispano* (1936), and *Canto temporal* (1943). In the 1940s, while teaching and traveling, Cuadra wrote some important essays: *Breviario imperial* (1940), *Promisión de México* (1945), and *Entre la cruz y la espada* (1946).

Upon his return to Nicaragua in 1950, he resumed his writing and his political commitment. He published *La tierra prometida* (1952) and *Libro de horas* (1954). Upon Somoza's assassination, Cuadra was persecuted and imprisoned, an experience he recorded in *América o el purgatorio* (1955). He was awarded the Central American Rubén Darío Prize in Poetry (1959) for *El jaguar y la luna* and Spain's Rubén Darío Prize for Hispanic Poetry (1964) for *Poesía: Selección (1929–1962)*. Some of his most important poetic contributions were written in the 1970s and 1980s. The lyrical rendering of the lives of ordinary people in *Cantos de Cifar y del Mar Dulce* (1971), *Tierra que habla* (1974), *Esos rostros que asoman en la multitud* (1976), *Siete árboles contra el atardecer* (1980), and *La ronda del año: Poemas para un calendario* (1988) reveal his profound humanism. His *Poesía selecta* (1991) contains an excellent introduction and biobibliography by the editor, J. E. Arellano.

The triumph of the Sandinista revolution did not end Cuadra's political marginalization. His commitment to human rights provoked the Sandinistas to close *La Prensa* in 1986. In the late 1980s and early 1990s, Cuadra firmly established his international status. He traveled and lectured abroad, was awarded Fulbright (1987) and Guggenheim (1989) fellowships, published his complete works, and participated in congresses on Latin American literature as well as on his own.

JOSÉ EMILIO BALLADARES, *Pablo Antonio Cuadra: La palabra en el tiempo* (1986); GREG SIMON, "Horizons: Nicaragua and Pablo Antonio Cuadra," in *Northwest Review* 26, no. 3 (1988): 58–64; ANGEL FLORES, ed., *Spanish American Authors: The Twentieth Century* (1992).

MARÍA A. SALGADO

CUARTELAZO, a barracks revolt. *Cuartelazos* have been one of the means frequently used by disaffected factions within Latin American society to change the government. The term is derived from the Spanish *cuartel* ("quarter" or "barracks"), so it refers very specifically to the use of a key garrison to begin a generalized military move against the government. The leaders often issue a *plan* or PRONUNCIAMIENTO outlining their goals. Mexican history in the nineteenth century is a particularly good example of the importance of the military revolt in dictating the rhythm and direction of political change. That country saw the issuing of over one hundred *planes* and many more attempted *cuartelazos*.

TODD LITTLE-SIEBOLD

CUAUHTEMOC (*b.* ca. 1494; *d.* 1525), last ruler of TENOCHTITLÁN-TLATELOLCO and leader of the final defense against the Spanish invaders. Nephew of Emperor MOCTEZUMA II, Cuauhtemoc was elected to the post of TLATOANI after CUITLAHUAC, Moctezuma's immediate successor, died of smallpox. Around twenty-five years old when he took power, Cuauhtemoc married a daughter of Moctezuma who was a widow of Cuitlahuac. Later baptized as Isabel Moctezuma, she wed three Spaniards in succession.

Though the Mexica under Cuauhtemoc put up a spirited resistance to Spanish attacks, lack of water and food, and mounting deaths from disease and combat took their toll. Abandoned by most of his allies, Cuauhtemoc finally embarked on 13 August 1521 with a large canoe-borne force (or, according to some indigenous accounts, in one canoe with a small number of companions), either to flee or to mount one last offensive. The *tlatoani*'s canoe was captured by the captain of one of the Spanish brigantines used in the siege, and though Cuauhtemoc is reported to have pleaded for death, he was instead brought as a prisoner before a jubilant Hernán CORTÉS.

Early in his captivity, Cuauhtemoc was pressed to reveal the location of the "lost" Mexica treasure by having his feet burned with hot oil. This torture led to nothing, and Cuauhtemoc remained a prisoner until October 1524, when Cortés took him and a number of other indigenous rulers on an expedition to Honduras to subdue Cristóbal de OLID, who had declared against the conqueror. Cortés and others seem to have feared that the Indian leaders might rebel if left behind, but the Spaniards soon came to suspect that Cuauhtemoc was somehow plotting an uprising. Accordingly, during Lent of 1525 Cuauhtemoc and two other rulers were convicted of treason and hanged from a *cieba* tree beside the trail to Honduras. As in the later Peruvian case of the captured Inca ATAHUALPA, who was executed on a similar charge, the conquerors became convinced that Cuauhtemoc had outlived his usefulness.

Though defeated in life, Cuauhtemoc, and not Cortés, ultimately triumphed as an important symbol of Mexican nationalism. Evidence of his heroic stature includes such work as the later-nineteenth-century libretto of the heroic opera *Guatimotzín* (ca. 1872), by Mexican composer Aniceto ORTEGA DEL VILLAR. By the twentieth century Cuauhtemoc's valor was celebrated in everything from post-Revolutionary murals to a statue gracing a *glorieta* (traffic circle) on Mexico City's Paseo de la Reforma, and even in the name of Cuauhtémoc CÁRDENAS, opposition presidential candidate in the election of 1988.

Many colonial chronicles, both indigenous and Spanish, contain information about Cuauhtemoc, including BERNAL DÍAZ DEL CASTILLO, *The Discovery and Conquest of Mexico*, translated by A. P. Maudslay (1956); DIEGO DURÁN, *The Aztecs: The History of the Indies of New Spain*, translated by Doris Heyden and Fernando Horcasitas (1964); FRANCISCO LÓPEZ DE GÓMARA, *Cortés: The Life of the Conqueror by His Secretary*, translated and edited by Lesley B. Simpson (1964); BERNARDINO DE SAHAGÚN, *Florentine Codex: General History of the Things of New Spain*, vol. 12, *The Conquest of Mexico*, translated and edited by ARTHUR J.

O. ANDERSON and CHARLES E. DIBBLE (1971); FERNANDO DE ALVA IXTLILXOCHITL, *Obras históricas*, 4th ed. (1985); and HERNANDO CORTÉS, *Letters from Mexico*, edited by Anthony Pagden (1986). Accessible syntheses can be found in MIGUEL LEÓN-PORTILLA, ed., *The Broken Spears: The Aztec Account of the Conquest of Mexico* (1992); PATRICIA DE FUENTES, ed. and trans., *The Conquistadors: First-person Accounts of the Conquest of Mexico* (1993); and ROSS HASSIG, *Mexico and the Spanish Conquest* (1993).

ROBERT HASKETT

CUAUTLA, SIEGE OF, the most famous engagement by the royalist armies against insurgents during the War of MEXICAN INDEPENDENCE. In early 1812, with 4,000 to 4,500 men, José María MORELOS fortified the town of Cuautla, south of Mexico City. Morelos had threatened Puebla and Toluca before Viceroy Francisco Javier VENE-GAS ordered Félix CALLEJA and the Army of the Center to march out of the Bajío provinces north of the capital and into the new center of insurgent activity. After destroying the rebel stronghold of Zitácuaro, Calleja arrived near Cuautla on 17 February 1812. As Morelos anticipated, the royalists lacked effective logistics and were short of munitions and provisions. Despite these difficulties, Calleja launched three frontal attacks that were repulsed by the insurgents. After this failure, Calleja called for reinforcements and commenced a formal siege, cutting off all communications, provisions, and water. After seventy-two days, during which the insurgents suffered starvation and disease, on May 2 1812, Morelos and some of his troops broke through the royalist lines and escaped. Although victory went to the royalists, the fame and glory went to Morelos.

LUCAS ALAMÁN, *Historia de México desde los primeros movimientos que prepararon su independencia en al año de 1808 hasta la época presente*, 5 vols. (1849–1852; repr. 1942); WILBERT H. TIMMONS, *Morelos: Priest Soldier Statesman of Mexico* (1963); ERNESTO LEMOINE VILLICAÑA, *Morelos: Su vida revolucionaria a través de sus escritos y de otros testimonios de la época* (1965); BRIAN R. HAMNETT, *Roots of Insurgency: Mexican Regions, 1750–1824* (1986).

CHRISTON I. ARCHER

CUBA. [Coverage begins with a three-part survey of Cuban political history. There follow a variety of entries on specialized topics: **Constitutions; Geography; Organizations; Political Movements; Political Parties; Revolutionary Movements; Revolutions;** and **War of Independence.**]

The Colonial Era (1492–1898)

CONQUEST AND COLONIZATION

Christopher COLUMBUS reached Cuba on 27 October 1492 and disembarked the next day in the port of Bariay, which he named San Salvador. Although impressed with its beauty, he lost interest in this land. He returned during his second voyage and sailed along the southern coast. He believed it to be part of the Asian continent, and not an island, and registered it as such on 12 June 1494. The conquest of America began in HISPANIOLA, and Cuba was of secondary importance. In 1504 King FERDINAND II asked Nicolás de OVANDO to verify that it truly possessed the riches attributed to it. Sebastián de Ocampo was charged in 1508 with measuring its perimeter, an undertaking concluded in July 1509, when Diego COLUMBUS became governor of Hispaniola. Diego Columbus arranged for the conquest of the island in order to satisfy royal desires and to secure the territories discovered by his father, assigning the task to Diego VELÁZQUEZ, whom he appointed as his ADELANTADO. The conquistador set out from Salvatierra de la Sabana, Spain, in 1510, accompanied by some 300 men. He disembarked on the southeastern coast between Guantánamo and Maisí, where he encountered a group of Indians led by Hatuey, a chief who had escaped from the abuses of the colonists in Hispaniola. The rebels resisted for some three months, but they were forced to flee to the mountains. Hatuey was captured and condemned to be burned at the stake.

Velázquez established his residence and organized the CABILDO in the indigenous region of Baracoa, which he named Our Lady of the Assumption. Then began excursions toward the west with the aim of subduing the inhabitants peacefully and avoiding the horrible consequences of the mistreatment in Hispaniola. Nevertheless, Francisco Morales dealt cruelly with the inhabitants of Maniabón and was dismissed. Pánfilo de NARVÁEZ proceeded with greater brutality but went unpunished, leading the massacre of Cuban Indians in the area of the Zaza River. From 1512 to 1515, seven settlements were established: Baracoa, Bayano, Trinidad, Sancti Spíritus, La Habana (Havana), Puerto Príncipe, and Santiago de Cuba. In 1515 the island was named Fernandina, but the customary name of Cuba was the one that later prevailed.

When Velázquez was appointed as Indian distributor in 1513, the period of mining ENCOMIENDAS began, opening the way for permanent settlement. The *encomiendas* became the most cruel form of SLAVERY. Indians were forced into intense labor, which was contrary to their social organization and traditions of production, and were annihilated. Through this exploitation of the Indians, there ensued a period of rapid growth, based on gold mining and agriculture on ESTANCIAS, allowing the first colonists to amass great wealth.

Velázquez did not content himself with Cuba. He knew of the existence of MOTECUHZOMA's empire and attained royal authorization to begin expeditions in Mexico. He sent the expedition that conquered Mexico under the command of Hernán CORTÉS. Cortés betrayed Velázquez and routed Pánfilo de Narváez, who was sent to subjugate him. When Velázquez died in 1524, the island of Cuba had entered a period of decline owing to the exhaustion of its gold and the depopulation begun with the conquest of Mexico. Once news of Mex-

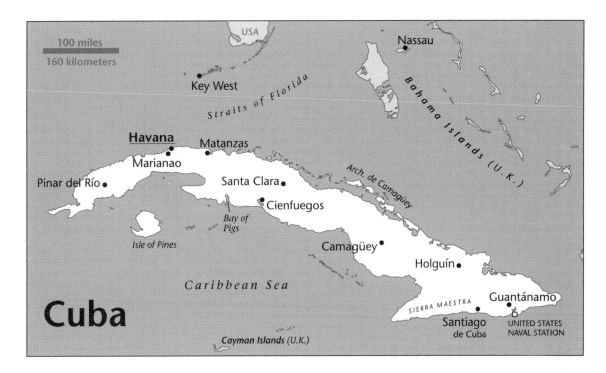

ico's riches spread, the exodus from Cuba increased, leading to more and more Indian uprisings. As towns became increasingly endangered, it became necessary to prohibit people from abandoning the island.

As a consequence of gold depletion, uprising, and the work of Fray Bartolomé de LAS CASAS, the NEW LAWS OF 1542, declaring the Indians to be free and subjects of the crown, were introduced. The colonists opposed the New Laws and managed to delay their implementation until 1553.

THE INTRODUCTION OF SLAVERY

The second half of the sixteenth century brought significant changes. The establishment of a system of annual fleets (1561), the introduction of African slaves, and the distribution of land by the *cabildos* (town councils) all contributed to the long-term settlement of the towns and to the creation of bases for systematic exploitation. Economic activities included the raising of livestock, the cultivation of tobacco, and, primarily in Havana, service industries, and military construction. Toward the end of the century another slave-based undertaking arose, sugar production.

For a long time, the principal business of Havana was to house the crews and passengers of the fleets and to repair and supply galleons for the ocean crossings. In 1553 the residence of the governor was moved from Santiago de Cuba to Havana, which was reorganized and transformed into a stronghold, with fortifications paid for by revenues from New Spain, assuring its supremacy. Slavery of blacks, who were known as "black earners," became the norm in the town. Slaves were used in all types of labor, including military construc-

tion and agriculture. The great majority of their earnings went to their owners.

The occupation of the western territories assumed the form of MERCEDES (land grants) or circular haciendas, overseen by the *cabildo* in Havana. The *mercedes* were of two types: *corrales*, dedicated to the raising of swine; and *hatos*, for livestock such as cows, oxen, horses, or mules. There were also *estancias* where minor crops were raised as well as gardens and cultivated plots surrounding the town. With some differences, the other *cabildos* functioned in the same manner. The so-called "ransom" (*rescate*) trade was practiced in the interior regions. This practice evaded the monopoly of the House of Trade in Seville by means of bartering goods, mainly leather and tobacco, for which ships from other European nations were brought in.

Despite the risk of attack to Cuba owing to continuing wars between Spain and other powers, as well as repeated menaces from corsairs and pirates, criollo society established itself during the seventeenth century. Cuba's strategic location made it a vital center of communication between Europe and America. While the fleet system continued, an economy existed in western Cuba that Manuel Moreno Fraginals has classified as service-production, split between shipbuilding and finished wood products. The need to supply the fleets and armadas stimulated both large- and small-scale operations, which coexisted with, and eventually displaced, extensive livestock raising.

The first half of the eighteenth century saw the establishment of the forms of land use that would come to characterize the Cuban agrarian structure. The bases for the development of slave plantations also took shape.

Landowners amassed wealth through the extensive exploitation of enormous livestock farms and the destruction or subdivision of the primitive haciendas. This made possible investments in sugar production, the most important of which was slave acquisition. The sparse population made it possible for small-scale white farmers, mostly from the Canary Islands, to settle on small plots. Some blacks also had access to land, due to the existence of legal means by which slaves could obtain their freedom. The population of free blacks grew, and they began to hold positions in the cities. The presence of these middle sectors prevented Cuba from following the same route as most colonies in the Caribbean. Although there were the so-called "black earners" and domestic slaves, slavery in Cuba on the whole was a rural phenomenon. Nevertheless, the average sugar mill in the Havana area relied on twenty to thirty slaves.

Spain's continual wars had numerous effects on Cuba. The WAR OF THE SPANISH SUCCESSION brought French squadrons accompanied by merchants and slaves. With the 1713–1714 Utrecht treaties' territorial concessions to the English, slaves began to arrive in greater numbers and under better conditions, and it became easier to thwart the Spanish commercial monopoly. The crown became more interested in exploiting Cuba's riches. With Cuban tobacco famous in Europe, a state monopoly company was established, which would sell all Cuban tobacco at a fixed price. This led to the 1717 uprising of Cuban tobacco growers, which forced a temporary suspension of the monopoly. An attempt to reimpose the monopoly led to a second uprising in 1720, after which it was agreed that the growers could sell surplus tobacco to Spain and its colonies after satisfying its quota for the Factoría (Royal Agency). A third uprising in 1723 was met with severe military force, resulting in some deaths, but free trade in tobacco was authorized.

Interest in land was growing, along with the hope of making a profit by selling it. A 1729 royal decree prohibited the municipalities from granting further *mercedes*. However, it was not ratified until ten years later. After that, land acquisition was accomplished through the so-called "*composición*," wherein lands were sold at auction to benefit the royal treasury.

By 1740 the SUGAR INDUSTRY had entered a crisis. In that year, a commercial monopoly was authorized under the control of the Royal Commerce Company of Havana. The monopoly adversely affected tobacco growers, imported goods became harder to find, and the cost of living went up. But the monopoly contributed to the growing predominance of the sugar industry and the slave plantation. Several thousand slaves were introduced, and the new oligarchy of criollos began to receive noble titles. There was a corresponding growth of cultural institutions, such as the Seminary of San Basilio el Magno, founded in Santiago de Cuba in 1722, and the University of Havana (1728). New urban centers arose, stimulating new civil and ecclesiastical construction. The first historians—such as Ambrosio Zayas Bazán, Pedro Agustín Morell de Santa Cruz, José Martín Félix de Arrate, and Ignacio José de Urrutia—appeared during this era.

The first direct offensive against Cuba by the English was the occupation of part of Guantánamo Bay in 1741. After failing to take Santiago de Cuba, they retreated after five months. In June 1762 an English squadron of more than 10,000 men arrived in Havana. Although fortified, the city had a weak point. The English took control of Las Cabañas, which allowed them to take the fort called El Morro. Despite strong resistance, the city was surrounded. It surrendered on 12 August. The substantial booty seized by the occupiers demonstrated the economic progress that Cuba had achieved. Although English domination technically extended throughout the territory under the jurisdiction of Havana, which comprised the western portion of the island, in practice it was limited to the area around the city itself.

Historians and ideologists from among the landowners, Francisco de Arango y Parreño foremost among them, have maintained that the English occupation provided a fundamental impulse to the Cuban economy. The historian Ramiro Guerra points out, however, that Havana was not a miserable outpost, but rather had already become a vital mercantile and cultural center, considered an emporium of wealth and one of the most important cities in the New World, with more inhabitants than Boston, New York, or Philadelphia. Later investigations have corroborated Guerra's assertion. Spain reclaimed Havana in 1763 in exchange for Florida, which was not productive and practically uninhabited.

After the occupation of the city, the new fortifications of La Cabaña, Atarés, and El Príncipe were built, as was a new arsenal. The economy revived and trade with other Spanish ports grew. Havana became one of the most important fortified cities in the world. The Royal Agency was reestablished and Cuban revenues began to increase. The Intendancy of Finance and Customs was organized. The 1778 regulation for free trade between Spain and the Indies raised the number of Spanish ports with which business could be conducted, authorized traffic between the colonies, reduced tariffs, and eliminated duties for ten years on some products, including Cuban sugar. During the U.S. War of Independence, France declared war on England. Spain supported France, and Cuba became a base of operations toward the reclaiming of Florida. In 1779 free trade with North America was authorized. It lasted four years and brought benefits to Cuba.

THE PLANTATION SYSTEM

The destruction of plantations and decline in the sugar trade during the Haitian Revolution were felt immediately in Cuba. Arango y Parreño saw the opportunity for Cuba to surpass the wealthy French colony in international trade. He received authorization for the free introduction of slaves and exemptions from start-up taxes for the new sugar mills. Institutions such as the Patriotic Society (1793) and the Royal Consulate of Agriculture, Industry, and Trade (1795) influenced economic transformation and cultural growth. With the decisive transformation of the sugar industry, the slave plantation began to flourish. The number and size of sugar mills increased. Cuba's participation in the international sugar trade increased dramatically. The open slave trade allowed for larger work forces and the regular replacement of slaves who had been worn out by the hard labor. Traders in black slaves amassed huge fortunes, which they reinvested in sugar. The population, particularly that of the slaves, grew rapidly.

In a relatively short time, Cuba surpassed Haiti as a supplier of sugar and significantly increased its production of coffee for export. In 1792 Cuba had 84,496 blacks in slavery—30 percent of its population. The slaves did not submit passively, and as their exploitation intensified, so did their struggle against it. Chained and fugitive slaves were a common sight. The free blacks did not show open resistance until 1795, when Nicolás Morales led a conspiracy in Bayamo demanding equal rights. He was discovered and executed.

High-ranking criollos did not make a stand for independence, but a group of well-to-do youths did try to achieve it. Joaquín Infante, Román de la Luz, and Luis Francisco Basave were tried for inciting rebellion in 1810. They were deported to Spain, but Infante escaped to South America, where he published the first plan for an independent Cuban constitution. José Antonio Aponte, a free black, organized a vast movement that spread to other regions and called for the abolition of slavery and the overthrow of the colonial regime. He and his principal collaborators were denounced and executed in 1812. The year 1820 saw the beginnning of a conspiracy inspired by movements on the Latin American continent. It was known as the Suns and Rays of Bolívar. The poet José María HEREDIA was involved before escaping to the United States. Francisco Agüero and Manuel Andrés Sánchez disembarked from an expedition originating in Jamaica and were captured and executed in Puerto Príncipe. The Black Eagle Conspiracy (1828), which had support in Mexico, was also uncovered.

From his professional chair at the Seminary of San Carlos, Félix VARELA Y MORALES influenced the thinking of many young people. He was elected representative to the Spanish Cortes in 1822, and he proposed a constitution of autonomy for Spain's overseas provinces. He wasn't able to set forth his plan for the abolition of slavery because he was forced to flee when FERDINAND VII was restored to the throne in 1823. From Philadelphia he published the periodical *El Habanero*, in which he openly promoted his ideas favoring independence. Brilliant intellectuals among his followers and supporters included José Antonio SACO, Domingo del MONTE, and José de la LUZ Y CABALLERO, all of whom powerfully influenced Cuban thought.

Several measures were stimulating economic development: the state monopoly on tobacco was eliminated, land granted by the *cabildos* (*mercedes*) was recognized, and an open market was decreed. In 1817 Spain was obliged to sign a treaty with England by which slave trading was outlawed. Although this treaty went into effect in 1820, it ended only legal slave trading; traffic in slaves continued and increased. White immigration to Cuba was encouraged, and new colonies were established in coastal areas. The prosperous economy and the racial imbalance created by the excessive increase in the slave population pitted the landowners against any pro-independence activity. Slave uprisings were repeatedly quelled. By 1827 the slave population had reached 286,946, some 40.7 percent of the total. Slaves and free blacks together accounted for 55 percent.

During the 1830s, use of the steam engine became common, large warehouses were constructed, and the first railroad was built (1837). But the colonial government was changing. In 1825 all-embracing powers had been granted to the captaincies general, and in 1837 it was agreed that the colonies would be ruled by special laws and would no longer have representatives in the Spanish Cortes.

With their exploitation intensifying, the slaves responded with uprisings in sugar mills and on coffee plantations. Whites lived in a state of terror. English abolitionists mounted an intense propaganda campaign. Outstanding among these were the consuls David Turnbull and Richard Madden. A vast conspiracy involving slaves and free blacks, which came to be called the Conspiracy of the Ladder (LA ESCALERA), was uncovered in 1843, and a cruel and violent reaction against all blacks ensued. Among those implicated in the conspiracy was the mulatto poet Gabriel de la Concepción VALDÉS (Plácido). White intellectuals were also accused, including Domingo del Monte and José de la Luz y Caballero. The landowners began to grow alarmed at the increase in the black population and sought the cessation of the SLAVE TRADE. Their most brilliant voice was José Antonio Saco, who denounced the regime in power and was exiled.

THE SYSTEM IN CRISIS

Although the plantation-based economy continued to grow and factories relied on work forces of slaves, the decline of slavery in general began to be apparent. The rate of growth in the slave population decreased abruptly. Owing to the difficulty of replacing worked-out slaves, intense research began into labor-saving techniques that would allow reductions in the size of the work force. Asian coolies were introduced and contracted laborers were recruited from Spain and the Canary Islands.

From early on, U.S. politicians had shown interest in Cuba. The 1823 MONROE DOCTRINE affirmed a U.S. right to annex Cuba, but European opposition inhibited attempts to do so. The first annexation attempt from within Cuba was markedly proslavery. With the prospect of abolition looming, the support of the southern U.S. states was sought. Between 1846 and 1848, the annexationists came together as the Havana Club, comprised of prominent landowners and intellectuals. In Puerto Príncipe a group led by Gaspar BETANCOUR CISNEROS (El Lugareño) also put out annexationist propaganda. Both of these groups created the Cuban Counsel in New York City in 1848. During that period, U.S. President Polk made attempts to purchase Cuba for $100 million.

Backed by the southern U.S. states and with important participation by North Americans, Narciso LÓPEZ led an expedition which managed to take the city of Cárdenas and fly the Cuban flag for the first time in 1850. He met with a lack of support and retreated. His next attempt, at Pinar del Río, also failed. The group was captured and condemned to death. The movements of Joaquín de Agüero in Puerto Príncipe (1851) and Isidro Armenteros in Trinidad met with similar fates. The executions of Ramón Pintó and Francisco Estrampes in 1855 put an end to armed attempts at annexation.

The landowners returned to reformism. In 1865 José Ricardo O'Farrill and Miguel Aldama organized the Reformist Party, whose mouthpiece was the periodical *El Siglo*. They proposed tariff reform, the cessation of the slave trade, representation in the Spanish Cortes, and the gradual abolition of slavery with compensation. The sugar mills had grown without restraint, and the introduction of new technologies reduced the need for slaves. Change and competition demanded new forms of organization.

In 1866–1867 the Board of Information on Reforms in Cuba and Puerto Rico, convened by Spain, met with Cuban reformers who sought gradual abolition with compensation, cessation of the slave trade, an immigration plan, free commerical exchange, and assimilation giving Cuba the character of a Spanish province. Spain responded with the application of a direct tax of 10 percent on revenue without eliminating tariffs, and it acceded to none of the other suggestions of the Board. This failure and the new tax led to a separatist rebellion (the GRITO DE YARA) on 10 October 1868. Led by Carlos Manuel de CÉSPEDES, the uprising started the TEN YEARS' WAR, at the end of which the situation in the country became critical. Many criollos lost their capital to the skyrocketing war taxes, which rose to 30 percent of the net yield. Areas that had seen combat were devastated.

The 1880 law calling for the establishment of a *patronato* (trusteeship) began a process of economic change that led to the social division of labor in the sugar industry, marking the transition from slave manufacture to capitalist industry. *Patronatos*, which offered monthly stipends and conditions for gaining freedom, replaced traditional slavery. The war contributed to the elimination of inefficient mills in the east and hastened the development of business districts. These economic changes made the atmosphere ripe for the effective abolition of slavery in 1886. With the abrogation that year of the *patronato* came a massive immigration of laborers from Spain for the sugar crops.

One consequence of the Pact of ZANJÓN, which put an end to the Ten Years' War, was a change in metropolitan policies that made possible the formation of political parties. Freedom of the press, assembly, association, and worship were also granted. Two parties developed: the Autonomist Party, which sought self-governance, and the Constitutional Union Party, which proposed some reforms but opposed independence. They represented the opposing interests of Cubans and Spaniards. The Autonomists, with Rafael Montoro, Eliseo Giberga, and Enrique José Varona among them, demanded civil and economic rights for Cubans equal to those that existed for Spaniards. Their few representatives to the Cortes repeatedly protested Cuba's wrongs and defended her interests. Among their ranks figured outstanding intellectuals and brilliant orators.

On the economic scene, the differential right of flags—a scale of tariffs, based on the national flag under which a ship sailed, that charged less from ships flying the Spanish flag—was suspended and the fiscal system was streamlined. Negotiations began toward the forging of treaties with the United States. Until 1890, relations with the United States were defined by policies that favored exports to that important market. The implementation of the McKinley Tariff Act (1890) placed this trade with the United States in danger. This act provided tax-free sugar imports to the United States in exchange for a reciprocal trade agreement. Financial corporations and political parties organized themselves into the Economic Movement. A treaty between Spain and the United States that favored raw sugar but not finished tobacco products was signed in 1891. The Wilson–Gorman Tariff Act in 1894 abrogated reciprocity, worsening the situation created by the crisis of 1893.

The Autonomists had not given up hope. A group of combatants from the Ten Years' War began to conspire. Upon being discovered in 1879, Guillermo Moncada, José Maceo, and Quintín Banderas led quick uprisings in the east, and another group rebelled in Las Villas. When Calixto GARCÍA arrived in 1880, the movement known as the Little War had already failed. Among its conspirators was José MARTÍ, who knew that the time was not ripe to renew the fight. There were, however, other isolated attempts. Between 1884 and 1886, Máximo GÓMEZ and Antonio MACEO conspired in a movement known as the Gómez–Maceo Plan. Maceo traveled to Cuba in 1890 and affirmed that the ideal of independence was still alive.

Among the émigrés in the United States led by José Martí, the Cuban Revolutionary Party was already forming. The party was officially announced on 10 April 1892, and Martí was named its representative. From the start, the group dedicated itself to raising funds and unifying Cubans to prepare for war. With the critical economic situation, the drop in the price of sugar, and the failure of the reform plan proposed by Overseas Minister Antonio Maura, armed struggle appeared to be the only option. A plan for simultaneous uprisings suffered a setback when arms in Fernandina were confiscated. Nevertheless, the plan went ahead with a limited uprising on 24 February 1895. When Maceo, Martí, and Gómez arrived, the War of Independence took shape. Martí's death in Dos Ríos did not deter the revolution. The invasion headed toward the west and developed into generalized war that cost Cuba large-scale destruction, numerous lives, and the impoverishment of the great majority of its inhabitants. When autonomy was finally declared in 1897, the course of events could not be altered. The U.S. Congress approved a joint resolution clearing the way for U.S. intervention in the war. Proposals and ultimatums were sent to Madrid, but rejected. In May 1898 U.S. troops were sent to Santiago de Cuba. With the aid of Cuban troops, the city was surrounded and taken. It surrendered on 16 July.

Negotiations between Spain and the United States began. The main concern was Cuba's debt of $500 million, which weighed heavily on its treasury. To this were added the costs of both wars of independence, expeditions, and diplomatic activities with Spain. With the signing of the Treaty of Paris, the island was freed of this heavy burden. Cuban independence began on 20 May 1902, three years after General John R. Brooke took charge of the government of Cuba.

FE IGLESIAS GARCÍA

See also p. 314 for bibliography.

The Republic (1898–1959)

THE EARLY YEARS

Cuba ceased being a Spanish colony, only to become a protectorate of the United States. After the devastating War of Independence, the country was left in a lamentable condition. The war destroyed the economic base and casualties claimed a large part of the population, owing especially to epidemics and famine brought about by the decrees of General Valeriano to relocate the rural population.

One of the first measures of the new military government was to proceed with the country's reconstruction. A public administration was organized and an educational system established. Measures were taken to strengthen the economic base of the island, and tariffs on U.S. goods were unilaterally reduced. Despite the approval of the Foraker Amendment in 1899, which prohibited concessions to U.S. firms for the exploitation of Cuban natural resources, U.S. investments were on the rise.

The general disarmament of the Cuban populace in January 1899 gave way to the dissolution of the Liberation Army. Tomás ESTRADA PALMA already had dis-

solved the Cuban Revolutionary Party in 1898. Even so, during the government of John R. Brooke, anti-annexationist sentiment was evident in Cuba. Brooke, who became known as a moderate, was replaced in less than a year by Leonard WOOD, who had annexationist ideas. But economic and political forces in the United States remained opposed to annexation.

A Constituent Assembly was convened in July 1900, and the Constitution of the Republic of Cuba was signed 21 February 1901. A commission was formed within the Assembly to deal with relations between Cuba and the United States. Criteria to define these relations was sought as an appendix to the constitution, but the U.S. government pushed instead for a congressional accord, proposed by Senator Orville Platt, creating the basis for them. Known as the PLATT AMENDMENT, its third article established the principle of U.S. intervention in the internal affairs of Cuba. One condition of its approval was the removal of occupying military forces. Despite strong opposition, a small majority of the commission approved the Platt Amendment on 12 June 1901.

Landowners and financial corporations advocated commercial reciprocity, which was of vital importance to reconstruction. A treaty to this effect was signed in December 1902 and approved by the U.S. Congress in December 1903. Cuban commodities received a tariff 20 percent lower than that of their counterparts from other countries, while the tariff on U.S. commodities was between 25 percent and 40 percent lower. This raised the value of U.S. exports to Cuba by 45 percent. The first elections were held on 31 December 1901. Tomás Estrada Palma was the sole candidate after Bartolomé Maso's withdrawal. On 20 May 1902 the Cuban flag was raised in El Morro and Leonard WOOD handed over the government to Estrada Palma, the new president, who returned from the U.S. upon his election.

The first years of the Republic were characterized by power struggles between liberals and conservatives. Despite the fact that almost all of the political leaders had been part of the struggle for independence, fraud, shady business deals, and dishonesty were rife among them. Estrada Palma, however, was one exception. Attempts to remain in power provoked political battles and power struggles that made consolidation difficult. Racial and labor disputes aggravated the unstable situation. From an economic viewpoint, the country was experiencing an accelerated process of reconstruction and population growth. Thousands of immigrants, primarily Spanish, who were attracted by employment possibilities, contributed to the latter. Agriculture relied more and more exclusively on sugar, due to the dependence on the U.S. market.

By 1905 U.S. companies owned twenty-nine sugar mills, which were responsible for 21 percent of Cuba's total production. The process of land acquisition by U.S. interests had begun with the first intervention, and by 1905 an estimated 13,000 U.S. colonists lived in Cuba, primarily on the Isle of Pines (now called the Isle of

Youth), whose status had not yet been determined. There were also U.S. investments in mining, tobacco, and the railroad. After World War I, control of the economy remained in the hands of U.S. monopolies, in alliance with the domestic bourgeoisie. The 1920–1921 crisis strengthened the financial domination of U.S. banks and further increased U.S. land holdings. Estrada Palma's reelection in 1906 produced an armed movement of liberals, led by José Miguel GÓMEZ. Unable to control the situation, the president requested U.S. intervention, and Charles E. MAGOON headed a provisional government from 1906 to 1909. To the already critical situation of a country in reconstruction were added the effects of the international economic crisis of 1907. There were numerous strikes centered on demands for better pay and an eight-hour workday.

José Miguel Gómez took power as elected president in 1909. Although he did not especially favor U.S. business, he ignored the hopes of Cubans and continued with the administrative corruption that had begun with Magoon. In 1912 there developed a racial movement opposed to the prohibition of organizations based on race, known as the Independents of Color. The movement's leaders, Pedro Ivonet and Evaristo Esternoz, perished in the struggle. U.S. troops landed, but the Cuban government opposed this intervention. That same year the lease turning over Guantánamo Bay to the United States for an indefinite period was signed.

The new president, Mario García MENOCAL (1913–1921), capitalized on the economic upswing that drove up sugar prices during World War I. Investments in sugar by U.S. monopolies, courted by the administration, continued to increase. Menocal was reelected through fraud, and the liberals returned to armed struggle in the 1917 movement known as La Chambelona. Again U.S. troops landed, and Enoch CROWDER was sent as a mediator. The U.S. government announced that it would not recognize a government that had taken power through violence, and the movement failed.

A HISTORICAL TURN

Following the war, Cuba experienced the "dance of the millions." An abrupt rise in sugar prices caused euphoria and speculation. But the subsequent rapid drop in the price by over 70 percent from 1920 to 1921 resulted in a grave crisis in which vast amounts of capital were lost and the domestic banking industry was broken. Small businesses went under, savings were lost, and thousands were left unemployed. The years 1920 to 1925 can be considered a period of consolidation of civil society and the national conscience, marking a historical turn. The crisis had demonstrated the consequences of such an extreme dependence on sugar and on the U.S. market. The loss of domestic capital in favor of that from the United States reinforced anti-imperialist sentiment throughout society. Likewise, General Crowder's intervention in internal affairs during the administration of Alfredo ZAYAS (1921–1925) accentuated an attitude of rejection of U.S. policies toward Cuba and deepened nationalist sentiment.

In 1923 movements with a new orientation appeared on the political scene, in which intellectuals, youth, and students seeking solutions for national problems took an active role. These movements distinguished themselves from the traditional political parties, which until then had been involved in a struggle for power and privilege. Among them was the Cuban Junta for National Renovation, led by the outstanding intellectual Fernando ORTIZ. Its manifesto highlighted national woes. Arising out of the so-called Protest of the Thirteen—a group of young intellectuals, led by Rubén Martínez Villena, who challenged the fraudulent business practices of the Zayas administration—was the Minorista Group (*Grupo Minorista*), which united the vanguard of the Cuban intelligentsia. The Veterans' and Patriots' Movement was organized, and the First National Congress of Women, proposing equality of civil and political rights and the protection of children, was celebrated. Merchants, industrialists, and financial corporations also organized in defense of their interests.

Students became an important force in political life. Their struggles for university reform began in 1922. Out of them arose the University of Havana Student Federation (FEU), of which Julio Antonio MELLA was an outstanding figure. The movement's strength earned it a participating role in the University Assembly, whose agenda was reform. With an anti-imperialist agenda, the First National Revolutionary Congress of Students was held in 1923. The Anti-Imperialist League, with Rubén Martínez Villena and Julio Antonio Mella at its forefront, was founded in 1925. That same year, the United States ratified the Hay–Quesada Treaty, which recognized Cuban sovereignty over the Isle of Pines. This treaty had been signed in 1904, and its ratification had been demanded by Cuban organizations ever since.

The labor movement was unified at the Third National Workers' Congress in 1925. The National Confederation of Cuban Workers (CNOC) also was formed, and a small group, including Carlos Baliño and Julio Antonio Mella, founded the country's first Communist Party in 1925. Outstanding social scientists such as Enrique José VARONA, Fernando Ortiz, Emilio ROIG DE LEUCHSENRING, and Ramiro GUERRA pointed out the evils of large landed estates, monoculture, foreign interests, and extreme dependence on the United States. Progressive intellectuals played an important role in public life; they also cofounded and taught at the José Martí Popular University.

The sugar industry had begun a modest recovery when the United States adopted a protectionist policy and raised the tariff on sugar. From 1926 to 1929 the price of sugar and volume of exports declined, resulting in a decrease in the value of the harvests. Beginning in 1929, the Great Depression caused an increase in U.S. protectionism, and Cuba was forced to reduce production. Exports in 1932 were only 18 percent of what they had been in 1922–1923. Cuban sugar's share in the U.S. market dropped from 52.2 percent in 1922–1926 to only 25 percent in 1933. A policy restricting sugarcane harvests was put into effect. The 1932–1933 harvest was half of what it had been in 1922. Sugar revenues dropped about 80 percent.

THE REVOLUTION OF 1930

The dictatorship of Gerardo MACHADO began with his triumph at the polls in 1924. His government promoted a demagogic program and practiced political assassination and repressed civil-rights movements. Two labor leaders, Enrique José Varona and Alfredo López, were slain and various communists jailed, Mella among them. He engaged in a hunger strike for nineteen days and, once freed, went to Mexico, where he was later assassinated.

Machado implemented his promised public-works plan, which turned into a very profitable business for him and his collaborators. With financing by Chase National Bank of New York and the Warren Brothers Company, both fronts for public officials, the cost of the central highway reached ten times its true value. U.S. investments in Cuba had increased from about $200 million in 1911 to $1.5 billion in 1927. Actual cash investments are thought to have been around $500 million. The rest were government subsidies, especially for the railroad, and reinvested dividends. Introduced in 1927 was a timid protectionist tariff reform which had no effect on U.S. interests but did aid the development of certain areas of production for the domestic market.

In order to remain in power, Machado applied what was known as "cooperativism," with the backing of a group of politicians. Opposition parties were prohibited. The 1901 Constitution was reformed in 1928, and the presidential term of office extended to six years. The only candidate in the 1928 elections, Machado served a second term from 1929 to 1935. Public reaction was immediate. The Great Depression further exacerbated political contradictions. Thus began the convulsive period known as the Revolution of 1930. Resistance against the dictatorship involved diverse organizations and various social strata and assumed various forms, including strikes, public demonstrations, and armed insurrections.

Martínez Villena organized a general strike in March 1930. In a student demonstration on 30 September, Pablo de la Torriente Brau was wounded and Rafael Trejo killed. In reaction to the repression, the student movement was radicalized. The Student Directorate was formed to fight the dictatorship. From this the Student Left Wing split off in 1931. The government intensified its repression, using regular police and military forces as well as paramilitary groups. The opposition parties set up underground organizations. One such group, the Revolutionary Union, was formed by Antonio Guiteras in 1932. It was anti-imperialist and oriented toward armed struggle.

At the height of the revolutionary movement in 1933, Sumner WELLES was appointed U.S. ambassador. His mission was to mediate between the dictator and the opposition. Negotiations were interrupted by the strikes in August, which began in the Havana bus system and developed into a general strike. The result was the overthrow of the dictatorship, and Machado fled to the Bahamas on 12 August 1933. The new president, Carlos Manuel de CÉSPEDES (Junior), was deposed in a 4 September military coup, dominated by then Sergeant Fulgencio BATISTA. An administration called the Pentarchy was formed, and on 10 September Ramón GRAU SAN MARTÍN assumed the presidency.

The so-called "government of a hundred days" had as its secretary of the interior Antonio Guiteras, who promoted various measures beneficial to the rank and file, including an eight-hour workday, a minimum wage, legalization of unions, restitution of the university's autonomy, and nationalization of labor—a work guarantee for Cubans that challenged the control of jobs by Spanish employers. But as chief of the army, Batista repressed the popular movements. Lack of unity among the forces that had overthrown the dictatorship made the situation very difficult for the government. Batista took advantage of these circumstances and led another military coup, deposing the new administration and installing Carlos MENDIETA as president. In order to strengthen his position, Batista obtained the abrogation of the Platt Amendment, and a new treaty of relations between Cuba and the United States was signed in 1934. A plan for sugar quotas was approved, and a new treaty of trade reciprocity reducing the tariff on sugar was signed. The number of favored U.S. products increased, and tariffs on several other Cuban products were reduced. This affected industries that had sprung up in the period of tariff reform. Labor and peasant struggles continued, and Antonio Guiteras formed Young Cuba, which advocated further armed conflict. A strike in March 1935 was put down violently, and on 8 May Guiteras was assassinated. These events brought to a close the Revolution of 1930.

CONSOLIDATION OF THE REPUBLIC

A series of ephemeral governments followed. A 1940 Constituent Assembly provided Cuba with one of the most progressive constitutions in Latin America, a sign of the maturity the republic had achieved. Elected president in 1940, Fulgencio Batista abandoned his populist policies. His party lost to Ramón Grau San Martín in 1944, thus beginning a period of governments of the Authentic Cuban (or Revolutionary) Party, which abandoned its nationalist program and became characterized by corruption, scandalous fraud, and the repression of workers and students.

Standing out during this period is the figure of Eduardo CHIBÁS. One of the original rank and file who had founded the Cuban People's Party, he launched an active campaign against the rampant political corruption.

His suicide in 1951 brought increased popularity to the party, which had been favored to win in the election of 1952. Batista aspired to the presidency with the United Action Party. Knowing that he would lose in the election, he led a 10 March 1952 military coup that deposed President Carlos PRÍO SOCARRÁS.

During World War II, the economic situation had improved. Harvests were brought in at profitable prices. But the 1950s saw a decline in sugar's share of the national product. Cuba began to nationalize the sugar industry and U.S. capital investment declined by $713 million. Sugar no longer yielded the tremendous profits it had in the early years, leading U.S. companies to sell their sugar holdings to Cuban interests. Although the overall economic pattern didn't radically change, a process of diversification had begun. Between 1947 and 1958 national revenues increased by 31 percent, the gross national product by 32.6 percent, and per-capita income by 27.2 percent, to one of the highest in Latin America. Production other than sugar increased 20 percent over the 1953 level, and the value of sugar harvests increased 27 percent from 1955 to 1958. Nevertheless, sugar's share in national revenues dropped to 28 percent and agricultural revenues in general dropped to 27.9 percent, indicating growth in other areas. These economic indicators can be misleading, however. Although attributed to economic factors, the 1959 Revolution in fact stemmed from the political crisis reflected in the hardships of the poorest Cubans.

The adoption of constitutional statutes in April 1952 unleashed a struggle for the implementation of the Constitution of 1940, which was joined by all levels of society. A group of young people from the Orthodox Party, led by Fidel CASTRO, attacked the Moncada military quarters in Santiago de Cuba on 26 July 1953. This offensive was a military failure: several of the insurgents were killed and a period of repression bringing about a national movement against the dictatorship followed. An underground struggle was organized in the cities, and in 1955 the popular movement obtained amnesty for Fidel Castro and his cohorts, who emigrated to Mexico. The student movement produced the Revolutionary Directorate, led by José Antonio ECHEVARRÍA. The underground organization, especially in Santiago de Cuba, organized by Frank PAÍS, aided the return from Mexico of Castro and others on the small yacht *Granma* on 2 December 1956. The guerrilla front dug in in the mountains of the Sierra Maestra. Camilo CIENFUEGOS and Ernesto ("Che") GUEVARA were the leaders of the invasion that moved through Camagüey and Las Villas. In 1957 a coalition comprised of the TWENTY-SIXTH OF JULY MOVEMENT, the Revolutionary Directorate, and the People's Socialist Party was born. Despite failures in the strike of 9 April and the attack on the presidential palace on 13 March, the conflict intensified. The war entered its final stage in November 1958, when strategic military points and important cities were occupied. December brought the decisive Battle of Santa Clara, and Batista fled at dawn on 1 January 1959. Attempts were made at establishing a government of compromise, but a general strike enabled the Rebel Army to take power.

RAMIRO GUERRA, *Historia de Cuba*, 2d ed. (1922–1925), *Manual de historia de Cuba* (1938), and *Azúcar y población de las Antillas* (1976); LELAND H. JENKS, *Our Cuban Colony* (1928); RAMIRO GUERRA et al., eds., *Historia de la nación cubana*, 10 vols. (1952); Havana, Oficina del Historiador de la Ciudad, *Revalorización de la historia de Cuba por los congresos nacionales de historia* (1959); OSCAR PINO-SANTOS, *Historia de Cuba: Aspectos fundamentales*, 2d ed. (1964); JULIO LE RIVERAND, *Economic History of Cuba* (1967), and *La república: Dependencia y revolución*, 3d ed. (1973); FERNANDO PORTUONDO DEL PRADO, *Estudios de historia de Cuba* (1973); JOSÉ LUCIANO FRANCO, *Ensayos históricos* (1974); *La república neocolonial* (Yearbook of Cuban Studies), 2 vols. (1975–1979); LIONEL SOTO, *La revolución del 33*, 3 vols. (1977); LOUIS A. PÉREZ, *Cuba: Between Reform and Revolution* (1988).

FE IGLESIAS GARCÍA

See also **Fleet System; Slavery; Tobacco Industry.**

Cuba Since 1959

After the victory of the TWENTY-SIXTH OF JULY MOVEMENT in 1959, Fidel CASTRO realized that to implement a revolution, he needed people with organizational skills who shared his radical views and had political experience. Among Cuba's active political groups, only the Communist Party had a mature worldview, including an anti-imperialist perspective. Revolutionary groups, including the Twenty-sixth of July Movement and the Communist Party, merged into the Integrated Revolutionary Organization (ORI) in 1961. In 1963 ORI became the United Party of the Socialist Revolution, and the new Communist Party of Cuba in 1965.

Many middle- and upper-class Cubans left the nation after Castro's takeover. Strong upper- and middle-class institutions no longer existed, nor did an independent economic base to foster counterrevolution. Castro worked to transform Cuba from an underdeveloped nation with a weak capitalist class, rampant inequality, and economic and political instability into a more socially and economically progressive classless country.

From the beginning of the new regime, education was deemed essential to economic and political development. A major literacy campaign begun in 1961 raised Cuba's literacy rate from 76 to 96 percent, the highest in Latin America. Revolutionary education stressed nationalism, Third World solidarity, and Marxism.

By the middle of 1961, after the CIA-sponsored BAY OF PIGS INVASION failed, and after Castro declared Cuba a Marxist-Leninist state, the bourgeois-democratic phase of the Revolution ended. Cuba nationalized the means of production, antagonizing the United States. On 4 February 1962, after the United States orchestrated the expulsion of Cuba from the Organization of American States, the Cuban government issued the Second Declaration of Havana, which called for revolution throughout Latin

America. By the late 1960s, after failing to incite insurrections in Bolivia, the Dominican Republic, Nicaragua, Panama, and Venezuela, Cuba realized that it could not foster revolution abroad. Castro and his comrades began to concentrate on domestic matters and to construct participatory democracy. They contended that popular democracy was not brought forth by the mere existence of easily violated constitutions or by political parties, but through democratic institutions, such as schools and hospitals, that serve all equally and without cost.

The Catholic church opposed the new political system. The government viewed the church as an undemocratic institution, but not one to be dismantled through legislation or persecution. Cuban law permitted freedom to practice religion. In 1960 a few priests accused of associating with the wealthy instead of helping the poor to whom the Revolution was dedicated, left the country. By 1961, the Marxist-Leninist direction of the Revolution frightened many Catholics, and church leaders voluntarily left the nation. The state pursued a policy of benign neglect toward the church, hoping it would disengage from politics and disappear. This resulted in a drop in regular church attendance from 17 percent of the population in the mid-1950s to 1 percent in the early 1990s. Castro attributed the defection from the church to a revulsion of the impoverished against the affluent. By 1970, the church had become more supportive of movements for social change in Latin America and entered into friendly dialogue with the Cuban government. Church-state relations improved during the 1980s. By 1991, increased accord with the church led the Cuban Communist Party to accept Roman Catholics as members.

While the church militated against Cuba's government, the United States authorized the CIA to destabilize it. The CIA plotted to assassinate Castro. The United States, intent upon destroying nationalist movements that threatened the repatriation of profits to its companies, tried to undermine the Revolution. In 1960 it launched an economic embargo calculated to ruin Cuba's economy. The embargo was still being enforced in 1995. The United States refused to resume diplomatic relations with Cuba, broken in 1961, unless the latter renounced socialism.

Soon after the start of the embargo and the Bay of Pigs confrontation, Cuba accepted Soviet missiles to increase security in the event of an attack by the United States. The Soviets acceded to U.S. pressure in 1962 and withdrew the weapons from Cuba. This left Cuba, which had been denied membership in the Warsaw Pact, somewhat unprotected.

In order to keep the Cuban economy afloat, between 1966 and 1970, Che GUEVARA's "new man" theory, emphasizing moral over material incentives for production, supplanted the Soviet development model. Cuba stressed capital accumulation and mass stabilization, and tried to abolish crass materialism. When these measures failed to yield significant advances by 1970, the

nation returned to a pragmatic approach to development and accepted the concept of a balance between moral and material incentives for workers.

In 1970, when Cuba did not produce the 10-million-ton quota of sugar it had set as a political and economic goal, Castro acknowledged that the nation had not elevated the living standard or accumulated capital during the 1960s, and insisted that more democratic consultations at lower levels were necessary to increase productivity. His public admissions of error enhanced his charismatic hold on the people. During the first fifteen years of the Revolution, Cuba was preoccupied with defending itself, developing a socialist economy, building schools and hospitals, and educating, housing, and feeding the people. Looking back over that period, Castro realized that he and his comrades were idealistic and arrogant, and that they had failed to institutionalize democratic revolutionary structures except on some local levels.

To establish more democratic practices, Cuba promulgated a new constitution in 1976. It established guidelines for citizens to elect leaders, granted Cubans the right to work free of exploitation, gave peasants access to land, eliminated high rents, made free education available to all, initiated free medical care and hospitalization, gave everyone the right to vacations, established universal sickness and accident insurance, guaranteed maternity leaves for women, provided equal pay for equal work, promoted racial equality, and defended the right to organize unions. The constitution institutionalized the Revolution as its provisions became reality. It reduced Castro's omnipotence a bit, and broadened the distribution of authority between the people and their government.

While Cuba prepared a new form of government, it became a role model for developing nations. In 1974, through the Nonaligned Movement, in which Cuba achieved a leadership position, Castro introduced the idea of establishing a new international economic order under which countries could defend their sovereignty over natural resources, maintain the right of national self-determination, and reform the international monetary system. Cuba also pursued diplomatic relations with as many states as possible, to create dialogues designed to prevent nuclear war. By 1990, Cuba had diplomatic ties with 120 countries, twice the number it had in 1959. The international positions it emphasized included Puerto Rican independence, the Panama Canal for Panama, the Falkland Islands for Argentina, a Palestinian homeland, and condemnation of colonialism and U.S. intervention in the Third World.

Until the late 1980s, Cuba strove to negate the idea that it was a Soviet surrogate. To questions of whether it traded dependence on the United States for similar reliance on the Soviet Union, Cuba answered that its economy did not respond directly to developments in the Soviet economy, as it had to developments in the United States; that whereas the United States had owned or controlled much of Cuba's economic infrastructure, the Soviets owned or controlled nothing in Cuba. Cuba admits that in the cold war it sided with the Soviet Union to gain assistance. Despite receiving huge Soviet subsidies, Cuba often disagreed with the Kremlin's foreign policies, such as its invasion of Afghanistan. Cuba rejected Soviet perestroika (restructuring) and glasnost (public openness), claiming that, in contrast with the Soviet Union, its Communist Party never became alienated from the people. While the Soviets fostered nonsocialist restructuring in the 1980s, Cuba pursued "rectification," which intensified centralization and moral commitment to the Revolution.

In 1975 Cuba, without consulting the Soviet Union, sent a battalion to Angola to support its black brothers and to resist invasion by two CIA-supported groups— that of Holden Roberto, who was also supported by the PRC and Zaire, and that of Jonas Savimbi, who also had the help of the PRC as well as South Africa. With the eventual aid of over 15,000 Cuban troops, Angola decisively defeated South African forces in 1988. Cuba was also involved in Ethiopia in an effort to maintain freedom there. These acts of solidarity in Africa brought Cuba closer to the Third World and stimulated national and racial pride at home.

During the 1980s Cuba backed revolutionary movements in Nicaragua, Grenada, and El Salvador, primarily by extending moral support and sending teachers and physicians to those countries. In 1983 the United States invaded Grenada and destroyed its socialist-oriented revolution. Washington hailed the Grenada adventure as a blow to Cuba and communism. Cuba believed it damaged U.S. prestige by letting the world see a bully commit a cowardly act. In 1990, after a decade of internal dissension and "low-intensity" conflict with the United States, Nicaragua's Sandinistas lost power in a free election. The inability of the revolutionary forces to retain power in Grenada and Nicaragua induced Cuba to support the negotiated peace that prevailed in El Salvador from 1992.

Solidarity extended by Cuba to progressive forces played a role in unifying leftist political groups in the Americas. Also, as a result of the Cuban Revolution, neo-Marxist ideas often replaced rigid orthodox European Marxist thought in Latin America. The area's intellectuals increasingly accepted the theories of Guevara, Castro, Lenin, and Antonio Gramsci, combining these with aspects of Indianism, existentialism, feminism, nationalism, and Christian social justice to produce systemic change.

While Cuba gained international stature, it began to solve its domestic problems by building new economic relationships within the socialist community. By the mid-1980s, 85 percent of Cuba's trade, mostly through credits, was with socialist nations. Its economy grew at a 4 percent annual rate for over a quarter of a century. It eliminated hunger and homelessness and attained the highest standard of living in Latin America for its population as a whole.

However, despite major infusions of Soviet aid, which did mitigate Cuba's financial difficulties, Cuba's foreign debt grew, as did that of the rest of Latin America, where "unequal exchange" increased tremendously. The area lost about $60 billion a year to wealthy industrialized states. Castro contended that the debt was politically, economically, and morally impossible to pay or collect. He proposed that the Latin American nations cancel their debts, both principal and interest. With the debt situation gone, he believed, a new international economic order could stimulate development.

Cuba's economic boom faded in the mid-1980s. In the early 1990s, with the collapse of the Eastern European socialist system, Cuba's ability to import goods fell 75 percent. The nation experienced low productivity, poor quality and distribution of goods, waste, and agricultural and industrial insufficiency. In this hardship era, or "special period," Cuba attempted to locate new markets and expand existing industries to increase the hard-currency income necessary to deal with the capitalist world.

As the economy deteriorated, the government, fearful of counterrevolution, cracked down on the few who urged a return to capitalism. Counterrevolutionaries, as well as socialist reformers, advocated economic changes and a more open society. They wanted a freer press, whereas the government required that all views in the nation's major newspaper, *Granma*, conform to those of the Communist Party. It declared this necessary to counter the persistent threat from the United States. Under socialism newspapers belong to the majority. The press could not oppose the majority. Opposition had to occur within revolutionary institutions. Despite considerable censorship, some intellectual and artistic expression was allowed in Cuba as long as it did not directly challenge the state.

Propaganda about lack of freedom and racial and sexual discrimination in Cuba often originates in the United States. Blacks, who make up about 58 percent of the population, have advanced steadily since 1959. Racial harmony is especially strong among Cubans born after the Revolution. Sexism has also diminished. In 1959, 9.8 percent of Cuban women held jobs, 70 percent of them as domestics. By 1990, women accounted for 38.7 percent of the work force, held 53.3 percent of the country's technical positions, and constituted 55 percent of its university students. By 1991 over half of the members of the executive committee of the National Assembly were women. Women have increasingly assumed public leadership positions. A feminist consciousness exists among most women and in a growing number of men.

In the course of building egalitarianism and homogeneity, Cuba borrowed the Italian thinker Antonio Gramsci's idea of unifying society by creating a revolutionary culture with mass appeal. Today, proportionately more

Cubans participate in cultural activities (including sports) than do the citizens of any other Latin American country. Artists, writers, and athletes are encouraged to put their talents at the service of the people. Cuba currently follows Western cultural traditions as well as its own folk culture. By the 1990s the nation had become a Latin American leader in cinema, literature, dance, music, and sports.

The Communist Party of Cuba, with over 600,000 members out of a population of 11 million, and Castro currently preside over the Revolution. The party occupies the majority of seats in the National Assembly even though it does not run candidates for office and is not a political party in the sense understood in the United States. Technically, it guides and serves as a counterbalance to the state; in reality, it governs state institutions.

Castro has prevented rivals from usurping his power. In the 1990s he displays greater maturity and more sophisticated statesmanship than he did in the 1960s. A two-level decision-making process exists in Cuba. On one level, Castro decides; on the other, the elected state apparatus and the Communist Party formulate policies. If Castro's decision does not concur, or cannot be reconciled with those of the government and the party, his word prevails.

Under Castro's direction Cuba has sought to eliminate excessive militarism, to terminate caudillismo, to reduce monoculture (e.g., sugar) and economic and political dependence, and to reinstitute constitutionalism. The military no longer runs Cuba but has an influential role in government. Cuba still functions under a caudillo, albeit one who has used his power not for the benefit of a small group but to help the majority for whom he has institutionalized positive social changes. Cuba no longer relies chiefly on sugar for foreign exchange. Industries such as fishing, nickel, citrus, and tourism now enhance trade.

H. MICHAEL ERISMAN, *Cuba's International Relations: The Anatomy of a Nationalistic Foreign Policy* (1985); SHELDON B. LISS, *Roots of Revolution: Radical Thought in Cuba* (1987); MORRIS H. MORLEY, *Imperial State and Revolution: The United States and Cuba, 1952–1986* (1987); MAX AZICRI, *Cuba: Politics, Economics, and Society* (1988); JOHN M. KIRK, *Between God and the Party: Religion and Politics in Revolutionary Cuba* (1989); JANETTE HABEL, *Cuba: The Revolution in Peril* (1991); THOMAS C. WRIGHT, *Latin America in the Era of the Cuban Revolution* (1991); CENTRO DE ESTUDIOS SOBRE AMÉRICA, ed., *The Cuban Revolution into the 1990s* (1992); SANDOR HALEBSKY and JOHN M. KIRK, eds., *Cuba in Transition: Crisis and Transformation* (1992); MARC FRANK, *Cuba Looks to the Year 2000* (1993); MARIFELI PÉREZ-STABLE, *The Cuban Revolution: Origins, Course, and Legacy* (1993); SHELDON B. LISS, *Fidel! Castro's Political and Social Thought* (1994).

SHELDON B. LISS

CUBA: CONSTITUTIONS. Since its independence from Spain, Cuba has had three constitutions. The first was drafted in 1901, immediately following the SPANISH-AMERICAN WAR, and reflected the new hegemonic role the United States played in Cuban affairs. The second, the Constitution of 1940, represented a thorough reworking of the Constitution of 1901 and reflected the strong sense of nationalism and liberalism that had begun to emerge in Cuban society in the 1930s. And while one of the goals of the revolution of 1959 was the enactment of a new constitution, the third constitution was not approved until 1976, seventeen years after Fidel Castro's forces entered Havana and established a new regime.

Enacted under the shadow of a just-terminated U.S. military occupation and the passage of the imperialistic PLATT AMENDMENT by the U.S. Congress, the Constitution of 1901 failed to fulfill the Cuban dream of a truly independent nation. While Cuba had successfully thrown off the yoke of Spanish imperialism, the United States more than filled that void; through the Platt Amendment, it delivered to Cuba conditions that limited independent action. The amendment limited Cuban authority to negotiate international treaties and to borrow money from abroad. The U.S. also claimed a coaling station on Cuban soil, and one clause of the amendment stated that "Cuba consents that the United States may exercise the right to intervene for the preservation of Cuban independence, the maintenance of a government adequate for the protection of life, property, and individual liberty. . . . " While nominally independent, Cuba was expected to incorporate the Platt Amendment into the drafting of the Cuban Constitution. Even efforts to modify the amendment were vetoed by the United States, and in the end Cuba was forced to incorporate the original U.S. version.

Not surprisingly, the Constitution of 1901 bitterly divided Cuban society, and while the Platt Amendment was abrogated by the United States in 1934, the fact that the first Cuban constitution had obediently followed the dictates of the U.S. government was not lost on future generations of Cuban nationalists. Support for the Constitution of 1901 was generally drawn along class lines, with the European upper class arguing that given U.S. support for Cuban independence against Spain, its northern neighbor had a legitimate role to play in Cuban affairs. The Cuban middle class, on the other hand, accepted the constitution as a distasteful inevitability, while working-class and poor Cubans, in general, believed that the Constitution of 1901 was a humiliating concession to the imperialist United States.

The effects of the Constitution of 1901 were immediately felt in Cuba, and a series of governments with little real power passed in and out of office under the watchful eye of the United States. Under the authority of the Cuban constitution, the United States intervened militarily from 1906 to 1909, sent troops to quell an uprising in 1912, and again deployed troops from 1917 to 1922. It was not until the collapse of the pro-U.S. dictator Gerardo MACHADO Y MORALES in 1933 that steps would be taken to draft a new constitution.

Cuba's second constitution would take years to draft, and both the amendments of 1934 and the Constitution of 1940 were an outgrowth of the political and economic crisis that swept the island in 1933. While Machado openly ruled as a dictator (he forced the Cuban Congress to extend his term of office), the island was crippled in the early 1930s by falling sugar prices. Growing unrest led Machado increasingly to employ brute force to maintain his rule. From Cuban students, influenced by the Russian and Mexican revolutions, came demands to reject U.S. political and economic control and to nationalize Cuban industry. From labor, both rural and urban, also came demands for nationalization as well as for higher wages and better social programs. Finally, even the army revolted, and hounded by the popular slogan "Cuba for the Cubans," the pro-U.S. Machado was forced to resign in 1933. During the 120-day reign of Ramón GRAU SAN MARTÍN, who replaced Machado and enjoyed widespread support, a number of revolutionary decrees were issued, some of which were included in the "provisional" Constitution of 1934. Many of the demands of the revolution of 1933, however, were not fulfilled, most prominent of which were demands to nationalize some of Cuba's largest industries. Even the mild reforms enacted by the amendments of 1934 were negated when the regime of Carlos MENDIETA Y MONTEFUR suspended constitutional guarantees.

Advocates of more far-reaching reforms found an unexpected ally in Fulgencio BATISTA Y ZALDÍVAR, the Cuban army officer who supported the U.S.-backed Mendieta as president in the wake of the revolution of 1933. Ever the pragmatist, Batista recognized the need for some type of reform, and the Constitution of 1940 was, on paper, a radical departure from Cuba's 1901 Constitution. Article 24, for example, acknowledged the right of the government to expropriate property "for reason of public utility or social interest," while Article 66 authorized the government to use all of its powers to "provide jobs for everyone." Articles also banned *latifundia*, allowed for state control of the sugar industry, and placed restrictions on foreign ownership of land. Labor was a particular beneficiary of the Constitution of 1940, whose pro-labor articles reflected the growing numbers and collective strength of the Cuban working class. Pro-labor provisions included the right to a job, the eight-hour workday, minimum wages, mandatory union membership, vacation pay, collective bargaining, and old-age pensions. The fact that these provisions were spelled out in the new constitution, however, did not mean that they were ever enacted; a much more militant political and economic movement would have to emerge to forge the hopes of the 1940 Constitution into reality. The Constitution of 1940 was nonetheless significant in two ways: it reflected in concrete form the aspirations of the revolutionary generation of 1933 and served as a rallying point of disappointed aspirations skillfully exploited by Fidel CASTRO in the 1950s.

While the Constitution of 1940 spelled out important reforms that were never carried out, the CUBAN REVOLUTION of 1959 enacted many of those reforms without embodying them in a new constitution. The constitution governing postrevolutionary Cuba was not to be enacted until 1976. With the victory of the TWENTY-SIXTH OF JULY MOVEMENT in 1959, the revolutionary government enacted the Fundamental Law, a provisional body of laws intended to guide the country until a permanent constitution could be drafted. Ignoring the Constitution of 1940, the Cuban government instead chose to govern by amending the Fundamental Law. Between 1959 and 1963 over one hundred new statutes were enacted, reflecting the rapid shift to the left that the Cuban government was then undergoing. These and other changes guided Cuba until the enactment of the Constitution of 1976.

The Constitution of 1976 reflected the Cuban government's commitment to a political and economic system modeled after the Soviet Union. To that end the constitution replaced previous civil law with "socialist" law. Marxism-Leninism was recognized as the state ideology and the Communist Party was made the only legal political party in the country (which in fact had already been the case for many years). While the Constitution defined state and political power as resting in the "dictatorship of the proletariat," power was actually concentrated in the bureaucratic class—not in the workers and peasants. The Council of Ministers was the "highest ranking executive and administrative organ" of the regime and was headed by a president (Fidel Castro) and vice president (Fidel's brother, Raúl CASTRO). The Council of Ministers was in theory accountable to the National Assembly. But given that the National Assembly met only a few days each year, real political power rested with Fidel Castro, much as it had with Batista before the 1959 revolution. A small step toward greater democracy was taken in 1993, when the first popular elections were held for the National Assembly. While no opposition was allowed to run candidates, voters were given the option to abstain from voting or to reject the Communist Party candidate on the ballot. While the vote was, not surprisingly, an overwhelming victory for Castro's government, neutral observers acknowledged that the 1993 election proved once again that Fidel Castro and his government still enjoyed widespread support among Cubans.

RAMÓN EDUARDO RUIZ, *Cuba: The Making of a Revolution* (1970); SAMUEL FARBER, *Revolution and Reaction in Cuba, 1933–1960* (1976); MAX AZICRI, *Cuba: Politics, Economics, and Society* (1988); LOUIS A. PÉREZ, JR., *Cuba: Between Reform and Revolution* (1988); SANDOR HALESKY and JOHN KIRK, eds., *Cuba in Transition: Crisis and Transformation* (1992).

MICHAEL POWELSON

CUBA: GEOGRAPHY. In 1993, Cuba had a population of 10,940,646; with its land mass of 44,218 square miles, this creates a population density of 247 people per square mile. It is the largest archipelago in the Antilles and is situated between the Straits of Florida on the north, the Caribbean Sea on the south, the Windward Passage on the east, and the Yucatán Channel on the West.

Cuba rests on a sea shelf that was formed by deep and calm seas and provides one of the richest ecological water habitats in the world. There are plentiful bays, estuaries, beaches, cliffs, and island keys. The terrain is mostly flat, with some hills. The highest point is Turquino Peak (6,560 feet), located in the Sierra Maestra in the eastern part of the island. The Sierra de Trinidad is located on the southern shore of the central section of the island.

Mineral deposits in Cuba include kaolin, nickel reserves in the northeast, copper, chromium, iron, manganese, and oil. The climate is tropical, with rain and intense heat from May to October. The annual mean temperature is about 72 degrees Fahrenheit, but can exceed 100 degrees in the summer. Annual rainfall averages 54 inches. From November to April the climate is fresh and dry. Only 22 percent of the annual rainfall occurs during the winter months, and it comes from cold air masses to the north. The eastern part of the island is most affected by the decline in temperature, with measurements as low as 34 degrees Fahrenheit.

Rivers that cut across Cuba are short due to the long and narrow formation of the island. The Cauto is the longest river, at 155 miles. Vegetation is highly *antropizada* mainly in the plains, the Zapata March, and the Guanahacabibes Peninsula. Many native species of flora and fauna are found in the mountain zones and the keys. The royal palm tree (*Roystonea regia*) is considered native to Cuba. Animals that are native to Cuba include the Santa María snake (*Epicrates angulifer*), the bat species *Philonycteris poeyi*, and the hummingbird species *Kellisuga relenae*. There are no large, dangerous animals native to Cuba.

The Cuba economy is based on agricultural production. Seventy-five percent of arable land is under cultivation: 30 percent is pasture, 23.5 percent is forest, 18 percent is devoted to sugarcane, 2 percent is in citrus groves, 1.7 percent is devoted to coffee and cacao, 1.5 percent to rice cultivation, and 1 percent to tobacco. In livestock, Cuba has 40 million poultry, 5 million head of cattle, and 100,000 head of oxen. The principal agricultural income producers are sugar and sugar derivatives, rum, tobacco, textiles, and construction materials. Tourism and biotechnical products have recently joined Cuba's traditional exports as commercial products. Cuba's main exports are sugar and its derivatives, minerals, fish and shellfish, citrus fruits, beverages, and tobacco. Cuba imports fuel, food, raw materials for industry, fertilizers, machinery, and equipment.

The Cuban population is multiethnic. Indigenous people initially mixed with the Spanish following the Conquest. But disease and mistreatment all but eliminated the Indian population. An imported laboring class consisted of African slaves and smaller groups of Chinese immigrants and indentured servants who arrived from the late eighteenth through early twentieth centuries. According to the 1981 census, the Cuban population is 66 percent white, 21.1 percent mulatto, and 12 percent black. The major migratory flows in the twentieth century occurred immediately after independence, when many Spanish sought jobs in the former colony, and after the 1959 revolution, when many Cubans emigrated for political, economic, and family reasons. The current rate of population growth is 1.66 percent annually, one of the lowest in the Western Hemisphere.

The employment rate is 36.4 percent of the total population. The annual death rate is 7.2 per 1,000 people, and the mortality rate for newborns is 9.4 deaths per 1,000, also one of the lowest in the world. The average life expectancy is 75.8 years. There are sixteen doctors for every 300 inhabitants of the island, and everyone over five years of age is educated.

The country is divided into fourteen provinces and the municipality of the Isle of Youth. The capital, Havana, has a population of 2,096,054 (1990 estimate). Other major cities are Santiago de Cuba (405,354), Camagüey (283,008), Holguín (228,052), and Guantánamo (200,381). Sixty-nine percent of the population is urban.

RAÚL BENAVIDES

See also **Explorers and Exploration.**

CUBA: ORGANIZATIONS

Club Femenino

The Club Femenino was formed in 1917 by a group of middle- and upper-class women to improve social conditions on the island and obtain suffrage for women. They advocated the elimination of prostitution, establishment of women's prisons and juvenile courts, improvement of educational opportunities for women, and improved job conditions for working-class women.

The Club Femenino joined with five other women's rights groups in 1923 to form the umbrella organization *Federación Nacional de Asociaciones Femeninas*. The First Annual Women's Congress, headed by Club Femenino member Pilar Morlon y Menéndez, invited all women's organizations throughout the country. The congress addressed issues as varied as female participation in government to the beautification of Havana. Many of its leaders joined with the Veterans and Patriots Organization in calling for "regeneration" of the government.

By 1925, the Second Congress promised success because President Gerardo MACHADO pledged support for women's suffrage. When he reneged on his promises and began massive repression of opposition groups, Club Femenino members, led by Hortensia Lamar, formed another coalition, the Women in Opposition to Machado, and participated with students and labor unionists in street protests. Lamar met with U.S. Ambassador Sumner WELLES to call for Machado's removal from office. President Ramón GRAU SAN MARTÍN granted suffrage during his brief tenure, but the issue remained uncertain until it became a part of the formal Constitution of 1940.

After gaining suffrage, the club continued pressing for education and social reform, joining other women's organizations in running night schools and free classes for working-class women. In 1934 they successfully pressured the government to implement a 1913 law offering free breakfasts to school children.

The success of Club Femenino came from working within a male-dominated system in a manner that did not threaten the political structure of the island.

An excellent book on the members and activities of the women's movement in this period is K. LYNN STONER, *From the House to the Streets: The Cuban Woman's Movement for Legal Reform, 1898–1940* (1991). Little else is available in English, but good sources for beginning a study are K. LYNN STONER, *Latinas of the Americas: A Source Book* (1989), and NELSON VALDÉS, *Cuban Women in the Twentieth Century: A Bibliography* (1978).

JACQUELYN BRIGGS KENT

See also **Feminism and Feminist Organizations.**

Committees for the Defense of the Revolution

Organization formed in Cuba on 28 September 1960 to combat counterrevolutionary activity through collective vigilance of the populace. One of many Cuban mass organizations, CDRs arose as a response to perceived internal and external threats to the CUBAN REVOLUTION. Early goals of the CDR included mobilization and unification of the people, and advancement of revolutionary ideals. Organized by neighborhood blocks, factories, labor unions, and state farms, their primary responsibilities involved community patrols and watchfulness against subversive activities.

With a membership of more than one-half million people by 1961, the function and scope of the CDRs gradually expanded to address other societal issues, such as public health, education, food distribution, conservation, the need for voluntary work, and community improvement. Throughout the 1960s, the CDRs acquired both legitimacy and permanent institutional status vis-à-vis the Cuban government and became an integral part of Cuban society. The organization was structured on three levels, with the block level being the most basic unit, followed by the district and national levels. Political autonomy, particularly on the local level, has been extremely limited, with policy and decision making instituted from the top echelons of the government and the Communist Party of Cuba. Leadership in the upper ranks of the CDR traditionally has been the domain of persons with strong party affiliations.

Membership in the CDR has fluctuated considerably, with the percentage of the adult population in its ranks rising from around 38 percent in 1963 to near 80 percent by the early 1970s. An easing of restrictions on membership led to the sharp increase in numbers, as did general changes in the association. While vigilance remained a priority, by the early 1970s the focus had shifted from counterrevolutionary to more common criminal activities. Criticized by its enemies as a totalitarian spy organization, the CDR nevertheless contributed to societal improvement in Cuba through participation in public-health programs, literacy campaigns, agricultural works, and construction.

JORGE I. DOMÍNGUEZ, *Cuba: Order and Revolution* (1978), pp. 208–209, 261–267; MARTA HARNECKER, ed., *Cuba: Dictatorship or Democracy?*, translated by Patrick Greanville (1979), pp. 56–70; RHONDA PEARL RABKIN, "The Cuban Political Structure," in *Cuba: Twenty-Five Years of Revolution, 1959–1984*, edited by Sandor Halebsky and John M. Kirk (1985), pp. 261–264.

D. M. SPEARS

Democratic Socialist Coalition

The Democratic Socialist Coalition was a broad alliance organized and controlled by Cuban dictator Fulgencio BATISTA Y ZALDÍVAR in the 1940s. The coalition consisted of Batista supporters, liberals, labor leaders, and the Cuban Communist Party. Formed in 1940, the coalition sought broad-based support for the election of Batista. In exchange for membership in the coalition, leftists received many favors from the Batista regime, including the appointment in 1942 of Communist Party member Juan MARINELLO as minister without portfolio in the Batista government. Marinello was the first member of a Communist organization in any Latin American country to become a government minister.

The coalition was used again in the elections of 1944, and again a Batista supporter ran for the presidency. But the opposition, led by Ramón GRAU SAN MARTÍN and his Auténtico Party, defeated the Batista candidate. Grau San Martín then turned on the leftists of the coalition who dominated organized labor, ousting its members from government positions. Those who participated in the Batista-controlled coalition were largely discredited among Cubans seeking sweeping reforms.

While leftist leaders in the coalition cynically lined up behind Batista, a revolutionary force, Fidel CASTRO's TWENTY-SIXTH OF JULY MOVEMENT, was formed with neither the knowledge nor the support of the Democratic Socialist Coalition, thus ensuring the coalition's isolation after the CUBAN REVOLUTION of 1959. The coalition members' lack of public credibility allowed Castro to dominate Cuba's labor unions, the Cuban Communist Party, and other organizations that comprised the Democratic Socialist Coalition.

RALPH LEE WOODWARD, JR., "Urban Labor and Communism: Cuba," in *Caribbean Studies* 3, no. 3 (1963): 17–50; RAMÓN EDUARDO RUIZ, *Cuba: The Making of a Revolution* (1970); SAMUEL FARBER, *Revolution and Reaction in Cuba, 1933–1960* (1976);

MARIFELI PÉREZ-STABLE, *The Cuban Revolution: Origins, Course, and Legacy* (1993).

MICHAEL POWELSON

Federation of Cuban Women
Federación de Mujeres Cubanas—FMC

The Federation of Cuban Women is the official governmental body overseeing women's issues. Founded in 1960 by Fidel Castro and directed by Vilma ESPÍN, the FMC sought to mobilize WOMEN following the 1959 CUBAN REVOLUTION. Called the "revolution within the revolution," the Cuban women's movement sent women into new regions of the country to teach the illiterate and nurse the ill. Women received professional training in traditional and nontraditional fields, and they were encouraged to participate in militia forces to respond to possible international threats. The FMC has pursued the objective of liberating women through revolutionary political activism, not through gender-based activism. It publishes *Mujeres* and *Muchachas.*

The FMC is not an autonomous organization; rather it is one of the popular-based institutions designed to convey government views to the populace and reflect women's needs to the government. This two-way communication was most evident at the FMC national congresses in 1962, 1974, 1980, 1985, and 1995. The FMC directly influenced the 1974 Maternity Law, the 1975 Family Code, the Protection and Hygiene Law, and the Social Security Law. By 1986 the FMC had established 838 child-care centers that supported 96,000 mothers.

Open to all women between the ages of fifteen and sixty-five, the FMC relies on modest membership dues for its financial sources. The group has various organizational levels (national, provincial, municipal, block, delegation, and individual), and its duties and responsibilities entail production, finance and transport, education, social work, ideological orientation, day care, and foreign relations.

The FMC has increased women's presence in the workforce, including managerial positions, and has raised the level of women's education. In 1986 women comprised 35 percent of the workforce and were concentrated in services, education, health, and technology. In 1981 the FMC formed the Commission for Coordinating Women's Employment to oversee what had been an unfavorable implementation of work laws regulating when and where women worked, maternity and hiring practices, and pay scales.

Over 50 percent of university students in Cuba are women. Eighty-five percent of all women have a ninth-grade education. Political ideology is provided at the Fe del Valle Cadre School for selected students, who are expected in turn to propagandize in their communities and work places.

The FMC has formed health brigades to conduct programs such as mother and infant care, environmental hygiene, uterine cancer diagnosis, and health education.

It has sponsored a vigorous sex education campaign and promoted birth control.

The FMC has encouraged women to stand for national elections in the municipal, provincial, and national assemblies, and it has gained governmental approval for candidates. Nevertheless, in 1985 women accounted for only 22.6 percent of administrative leaders, including the National Assembly (22.6 percent), provincial (21.4 percent) and municipal (11.5 percent) assemblies, Communist Party members (21.9 percent), and trade union leaders (40.3 percent).

Criticism of the FMC surfaced in the 1990 *llamamiento* (mass evaluation) of the Revolution. The major complaint concerned the excessive amount of time spent in meetings, work, and voluntary activities, which was made worse by the generalized complications in obtaining food and managing transportation. Also, scarcity of goods has forced many young women into prostitution, which the government has tacitly supported. The FMC's effort to convert women into productive and moral revolutionaries is being undermined by a declining economy.

K. LYNN STONER

Federation of Cuban Workers
Confederación de Trabajadores Cubanos—CTC

Cuba's primary labor confederation from its foundation in 1939 to the present has been the CTC. Communists under Lázaro PEÑA controlled this organization until 1946. The CTC claimed over 400,000 members by the early 1940s. Eusebio Mujal, an Auténtico (nationalist-revolutionary), became secretary general of the CTC in 1947. Under Mujal the CTC suppressed strikes, organized pro-government rallies, and repressed labor dissidents in exchange for government support. Union corruption became a serious problem. Despite shortcomings, the CTC continued to grow and by 1959 represented over 1 million Cuban workers.

Cuban labor history changed dramatically with the onset of the CUBAN REVOLUTION in 1959. Mujal fled the country and the CTC went into decline. It remained largely inactive during the first decade of the revolution. After 1970, however, the government revitalized the CTC in an effort to counter declining worker productivity and high absenteeism. The CTC undertook initiatives in worker education, grievance committees became more active, and workers on the factory level began to take part in production decisions. The election of union officers became more open and democratic. New unions formed, and CTC membership rose to include 94 percent of Cuba's work force.

MAURICE ZEITLIN, *Revolutionary Politics and the Cuban Working Class* (1967); RODOLFO RIESGO, *Cuba: El movimiento obrero en su entorno socio-político, 1865–1983* (1985); EFRÉN CÓRDOVA, *Castro and the Cuban Labor Movement: Statecraft and Society in a Revolutionary Period (1959–1961)* (1987); LINDA FULLER, "The State and the Unions in Cuba Since 1959," in *Labor, Autonomy, and the State in Latin America*, edited by Edward C. Epstein (1989), pp. 133–171.

STEVEN S. GILLICK

See also **Labor and Labor Movements.**

CUBA: POLITICAL MOVEMENTS, NINETEENTH CENTURY.

Cuban political attitudes in the nineteenth century were conditioned by a number of factors, particularly the hardening of Spanish colonial rule after the loss of the South American mainland colonies in 1825 and the development on the island of a prosperous SUGAR INDUSTRY (1790–1830) that depended on the importation of an increasing number of African slaves. As a result, during the first half of the century the majority of Cuba's population was black or mulatto. In those days, slaves represented a great asset but also a menace. In 1791 there had been a slave revolt in Haiti that had laid waste the island, wiping out its white planter class. Haiti's specter never ceased to haunt Cuban slave owners.

A land like Cuba, therefore, was not receptive to political extremism. When the sense of national identity matured among Cubans, a process that roughly coincided with the sugar revolution, some small groups, encouraged by events in continental Spanish America, began to consider seriously the prospect of independence. But the planter class and the leading intellectuals refused to support the movement. Although they, too, were disgruntled with the existing order, they favored evolution over revolution; and whenever they became too impatient with Spanish despotism, they sought to preserve their wealth by making Cuba one of the slave states of the United States. These two attitudes gave rise to the two major political movements of the first two-thirds of the century: reformism and annexationism.

Generally speaking, reformists opposed abolition of slavery, proposing instead that the slave trade be suppressed and white colonization promoted. Some, like José Antonio SACO, dreaded Cuba's absorption by the

United States, and others at times could live with it, but all of them dreamed about "building a fatherland," as José de la LUZ Y CABALLERO put it, and believed that Cuba was sufficiently rich and powerful to force Spain to make concessions.

Annexationism was basically supported by slave owners who feared that England would compel Spain to free the slaves in Cuba, although there were some who joined the movement for other reasons. Its influence pervaded the Cuban political milieu, either overtly or implicitly, until the eve of independence, but it reached its peak with the two futile attempts made in 1850 and 1851 by a former officer of the Spanish army, Narciso LÓPEZ, to carry the "annexationist revolution" into Cuba. In both cases López had U.S. backing.

Annexationism was little more than a dream after the U.S. Civil War, and the same fate befell reformism after the failure in April 1867 of the Junta de Información convened by the Madrid government to discuss the reforms that were necessary in Cuba. After this new setback, Cubans, who were then feeling the impact of an international economic crisis, began to think again that armed rebellion was the only way out of their predicament. And so it was that a group of planters and patriots rose up on 10 October 1868, the start of the TEN YEARS' WAR. The war was unsuccessful, but its consequences were lasting. It began the process of integration of all the various elements that made up Cuban society and solidified the nationalistic spirit that ultimately ignited the 1895–1898 war of independence. As far as Cuba is concerned, the history of the last third of the nineteenth century is the history of the rise and culmination of *independentismo*, the third great political movement of the period.

For a discussion of the subject in English, see HUGH THOMAS, *Cuba: The Pursuit of Freedom* (1971). Further details will be found in JOSÉ IGNACIO RODRÍGUEZ, *Estudio histórico sobre el origen, desenvolvimiento y manifestaciones prácticas de la idea de la anexión de la isla de Cuba* (1900); FRANCISCO FIGUERAS, *Cuba y su evolución colonial* (1959); RAMIRO GUERRA, *Guerra de los diez años, 1868–1878,* 2 vols. (1972); SERGIO AGUIRRE, "Seis actitudes de la burguesía cubana en el siglo XIX," in his *Eco de caminos* (1974); RAMIRO GUERRA, *Manual de historia de Cuba* (1975); and PEDRO ROIG, *La guerra de Martí* (1984).

JOSÉ M. HERNÁNDEZ

See also **Slave Trade; Slavery.**

CUBA: POLITICAL PARTIES

ABC Party
Partido ABC

The ABC Party was a prominent clandestine organization opposing the Gerardo MACHADO regime (1925–1933) in the early 1930s. Composed of intellectuals, students, and members of the middle class, the ABC

Political rally commemorating the birthday of José Martí, father of Cuban independence. © 1991 RICHARD BICKEL / BLACK STAR.

used the cellular concept for an underground organization. Each cell contained seven members who had no knowledge of the other cells. The directing cell was known as A, the second tier of cells was B, then C, and so on. In December 1932, the ABC issued its program manifesto, which opposed not only the Machado regime but also the circumstances that brought it into existence. ABC advocated the breakup of large landholdings, nationalization of public services, limitations on landownership by U.S. interests, and political liberty and social justice.

In late 1932, the ABC conceived a two-phased plan to eliminate Machado. Phase 1 succeeded when Senate president Clemente Vásquez Bello was assassinated in Havana. Phase 2, which contemplated blowing up all top government leaders during Vásquez Bello's funeral in a Havana cemetery, failed when the Vásquez Bello family requested that he be buried in the family plot in a Santa Clara cemetery. Machado's police then launched a manhunt for members of the organization, driving most of the ABC leadership into exile. In 1933, the ABC supported the mediation efforts of U.S. Ambassador Sumner WELLES to ease Machado out of the presidency and bring an end to the violence. Following Machado's resignation on 12 August, the group participated in the short-lived regime of Carlos Manuel de CÉSPEDES and later opposed the more radical regime of Ramón GRAU SAN MARTÍN (1933–1934). The ABC ceased to operate after those turbulent years, but many of its leaders came to occupy prominent positions in later administrations and exerted considerable influence until the 1950s.

HUGH THOMAS, *Cuba: The Pursuit of Freedom* (1971); JAIME SUCHLICKI, *Historical Dictionary of Cuba* (1988) and *Cuba: From Columbus to Castro*, 3d ed. (1990).

JAIME SUCHLICKI

Authentic Party
Partido Revolucionario Cubano [Auténtico]
Partido Auténtico—PA

After Fulgencio BATISTA had engineered the downfall of Ramón GRAU SAN MARTÍN and the thwarting of the 1933 revolution, the students who had supported Grau were angry and disillusioned. Many who desired to continue fighting formed the Auténtico Party in 1934. Their model was the party of Jose MARTÍ (the Partido Revolucionario Cubano of 1892). Leaders of the Directorio Estudiantil Universitario joined the new party and Grau San Martín was appointed president. The Auténtico program called for economic and political nationalism, social justice, and civil liberties.

Through the mid-1940s the Auténticos consistently opposed Batista and his puppet presidents. In 1944, Grau and the Auténticos were elected, during a period in which organized use of violence to achieve political power increased. To many Cubans in the late 1940s, the

Auténticos and Grau had failed to fulfill the aspirations of the anti-MACHADO revolution, especially with regard to administrative honesty. Eduardo CHIBÁS and others split from the party in 1947, forming the Partido del Pueblo Cubano (Ortodoxo). The failure of the Auténticos to bring profound structural, economic, and political changes to Cuba was perhaps the most important factor contributing to Batista's 1952 coup.

HUGH THOMAS, *Cuba: The Pursuit of Freedom* (1971); JAIME SUCHLICKI, *Historical Dictionary of Cuba* (1988) and *Cuba: From Columbus to Castro*, 3d ed. (1990).

JAIME SUCHLICKI

Autonomist Party
Partido Autonomista

After the end of the TEN YEARS' WAR (1878), Spain dismantled Cuba's colonial regime, took steps to reduce its insular army, and allowed Cubans to elect deputies to the Spanish CORTES. These reforms led to the formation of the Liberal or Autonomist Party, made up of reformist Cubans and some Spaniards, most of middle-class origin. Its platform differed little from traditional Cuban reformism. Essentially what it demanded was "the liberty of Cuba legally within Spanish nationality."

The Autonomist Party was the most critical movement in Cuba in the decade that followed the war, but it failed to make genuine headway. It was distrusted by conservative Spaniards, who thought that autonomy was merely the anteroom of independence. Spain, on the other hand, breaking the promises it had made when the war ended, never fully granted Cubans the same political rights that Spaniards enjoyed. There was no real freedom of the press and assembly on the island, and the property qualification was so high that black and poor Cubans could not vote. Furthermore, elections were manipulated whenever necessary. By 1892 the Autonomists were thoroughly disillusioned. They issued a manifesto to the nation warning that Spain's obduracy would force Cubans to make "radical decisions." Their more distinguished men began openly to back the course of revolution.

On the eve of the SPANISH-AMERICAN WAR, Spain finally established in Cuba a home-rule government led by Autonomists. But by then the 1895 war of independence had been raging in the countryside for three years, and the Autonomist government was caught in the middle of the conflict staged by Spain, the United States, the diehard Spaniards in Cuba, and the Cuban insurgents. A few days before the American declaration of war (25 April 1898), it sent a message to President William McKinley protesting American intervention in Cuba and claiming that Cubans had the right to govern themselves. Apparently, McKinley did not reply.

For an interesting non-Cuban view of the Autonomists, see J. C. M. OGELSBY, "The Cuban Autonomist Movement's Perception of Canada, 1865–1898: Its Implications," *The Americas* 48

(April 1992): 445–461; see also ANTONIO MARTÍNEZ BELLO, *Origen y meta del autonomismo, exégesis de Montoro* (1952).

JOSÉ M. HERNÁNDEZ

See also **Cuba: War of Independence.**

Communist Party
Partido Communista de Cuba—PCC

Founded in 1925, the Cuban Communist Party underwent many changes in perspective and political program, from operating as an openly revolutionary party in the 1920s and 1930s to its tactical alignment with the Batista regime in the 1930s, through its demise in the late 1940s and 1950s, and its revival in the 1960s and 1970s. While the party played a significant role in twentieth-century Cuba, and while it worked hard to organize Cuba's working class, the party's leaders failed to recognize the growing revolutionary movement within Cuba in the 1950s, which culminated in the overthrow of Fulgencio BATISTA Y ZALDÍVAR on 1 January 1959. In fact the CUBAN REVOLUTION, led by Fidel CASTRO, was carried out largely without the support of the Cuban Communist Party, and Castro and his followers maintained a distrust of most of the party's leaders throughout this revolutionary period. Only with the defeat of Batista and with Castro firmly in power did the remnants of the TWENTY-SIXTH OF JULY MOVEMENT seek to reorganize the Cuban Communist Party—on terms dictated by Castro and his close associates. One cannot ignore the influence of Moscow on the party throughout its history, which helps at least in part to explain why it increasingly took positions contrary to the principles of revolutionary socialism. The revolutionary movement in the Soviet Union peaked in the 1920s and declined in the 1930s—a pattern repeated in the early history of the Cuban Communist Party. And just as the Soviet Union in the 1940s and 1950s abandoned all pretense to international revolution in favor of cooperation and coalitions with bourgeois democracies and dictatorships, this can also be said for the Cuban Communist Party.

Inspired by the Bolshevik Revolution, Julio Antonio Mella founded the Partido Comunista de Cuba in 1925, and from its inception it was successful at organizing Cuban workers, especially those in Cuba's sugar and railroad industries. The party published a weekly newspaper, *El Comunista*, and by the late 1920s its organizing and propaganda efforts bore fruit when one of its members, César Vilar, was elected secretary-general of the Confederación Nacional Obrera Cubana (CNOC), the central labor federation of Cuba. In the early 1930s, the party instigated and led many successful strikes, including walkouts by textile, cigar, transportation, and sugar workers.

The sugar workers' strike of 1933 led to the overthrow of the dictatorship of Gerardo MACHADO. But the party opposed the strike, claiming it would prompt U.S. intervention. International politics may have also played a role in the party's rejection of the strike, since 1933 was also a time when the Stalin-dominated Communist International had concluded a truce with the United States culminating in the recognition of the Soviet Union by Cuba's powerful northern neighbor. The party continued to grow throughout the 1930s, despite the Batista dictatorship. Even a crackdown on the party and the CNOC by Batista in 1935 hardly deterred the growth of the Communist-led labor movement, and by 1938 the party had even agreed to support the Cuban dictator. In exchange Batista granted legal recognition to the party, now named Partido Unión Revolucionaria (PUR), and allowed the publication of the party's organ, *Hoy*, edited by Aníbal ESCALANTE.

This tactical alliance with the Batista dictatorship brought real benefits for the party; Batista's Ministry of Labor was dominated by party members; party candidates ran in, and won, elections; and its secretary-general, Blas ROCA played a prominent role in drawing up the section dealing with labor in the Constitution of 1940. Party membership increased from 90,000 in 1940 to 150,000 in 1946. In 1944 the name of the party was changed to the Partido Socialista Popular (PSP), once again reflecting Moscow's influence.

The postwar period saw the decline of the party, as divisions within the PSP were exploited by the government. The new Cuban minister of labor was a vocal anti-Communist, and in 1947 he removed PSP members from the Workers' Palace then under construction in Havana. That same year the government arrested hundreds of PSP members, shut down their radio stations, and censored their newspaper.

Despite Castro's later espousal of communism, neither he nor his Twenty-sixth of July Movement worked with the PSP in the years leading up to the ouster of Batista. In fact, the official position of the PSP was *not* to back Castro's growing revolutionary movement, although many individual PSP members worked in support of it. After the revolution the PSP merged with Castro's Twenty-sixth of July Movement and the Revolutionary Student Directorate in 1961 to form the Integrated Revolutionary Organizations (ORI), to be renamed the Communist Party of Cuba in 1965. Further evidence of Castro's mistrust of the old guard of the Communist Party is evidenced by the fact that the reconstituted party's first congress, promised for 1967, was not held until December 1975. It is ironic that while the PSP claimed to be a revolutionary party of the working class, it played no official, and only a weak unofficial, role in the most important revolutionary movement within Cuba during the twentieth century.

RALPH LEE WOODWARD, JR., "Urban Labor and Communism: Cuba," in *Caribbean Studies* 3, no. 3 (1963): 17–50; RAMÓN EDUARDO RUIZ, *Cuba: The Making of a Revolution* (1970); NELSON P. VALDÉS, *Ideological Roots of the Cuban Revolutionary Movement* (1975); SAMUEL FARBER, *Revolution and Reaction in Cuba, 1933–1960* (1976); LIONEL MARTIN, *The Early Fidel: Roots of Castro's Communism* (1978); IRVING LOUIS HOROWITZ, ed., *Cuban Com-*

munism, 4th ed. (1981); BARRY B. LEVINE, ed., *The New Cuban Presence in the Caribbean* (1983).

MICHAEL POWELSON

Cuban People's Party
Partido del Pueblo Cubano—PPC
Ortodoxo Party

The Ortodoxo Party was created in 1947 by a faction that broke with the ruling Auténtico Party over the issues of the 1948 presidential nomination and the corruption of the Ramón GRAU SAN MARTÍN administration (1944–1948). Its leader was the mercurial senator Eduardo CHIBÁS, a former student activist who had built a strong national following through his weekly radio broadcasts. He launched a national crusade against governmental corruption, promising to rescue the Cuban revolutionary tradition and to clean up Cuba's politics. Appropriately, he chose a broom as the party emblem. Under the slogan "vergüenza contra dinero" (honesty versus money), he entered the 1948 presidential race, and although he lost to the Auténtico candidate, Carlos PRÍO SOCARRÁS, he was able to attract nearly 20 percent of the vote.

Since Auténtico scandals continued, Chibás pressed onward with his often immoderate campaign, increasing his political strength and contributing powerfully to the final discrediting of the Prío administration. When he again ran for president in 1951, it appeared that this time he had a good chance of winning. A few months before the election, however, he shot himself at the end of one of his broadcasts. His suicide was apparently an ill-conceived attempt to regain popularity that he had momentarily lost as a result of a campaign miscalculation. It dealt a severe blow to the hopes of the party, for although his candidacy was eventually filled, the new candidate, Roberto Agramonte, was a colorless university professor who lacked his dynamism and oratorical skill. It also paved the way for Fulgencio BATISTA, who, three months before the election, staged his 10 March 1952 coup d'état, thereby putting an end to the political aspirations of all parties. Thus forced into the opposition, many Ortodoxos, especially the younger elements who made up the party's more radical left wing, chose revolution as the way to overthrow Batista's dictatorship. One of them was a young lawyer who was running for Congress—Fidel CASTRO.

In English see HUGH THOMAS, *Cuba: The Pursuit of Freedom* (1971); SAMUEL FARBER, *Revolution and Reaction in Cuba, 1933–1960* (1976); RUBY HART PHILLIPS, *Cuba: Island of Paradox* (1959). On the corruption of the Auténtico administrations see ENRIQUE VIGNIER and GUILLERMO ALONSO, *La corrupción política y administrativa en Cuba, 1944–1952* (1973); Chibás's life and work are studied by LUIS CONTE AGUERO, *Eduardo Chibás, el adalid de Cuba* (1955), probably the most extensive treatment of the subject thus far.

JOSÉ M. HERNÁNDEZ

CUBA: REVOLUTIONARY MOVEMENTS

Twenty-sixth of July Movement—J-26

The Twenty-sixth of July Movement overthrew Cuba's dictator Fulgencio BATISTA in 1958, in the first successful socialist revolution independent of the Communist Party. The founder and undisputed leader was Fidel CASTRO, born in Oriente province, cradle of José MARTÍ's struggle with Spain. Castro's caudillist movement centered on revolutionary symbolism and the personalities of its leaders: Ernesto ("Che") GUEVARA, Raúl CASTRO, and Fidel's alter ego, Celia SÁNCHEZ MANDULEY. Interested in winning and avoiding ideology, J-26 forged a guerrilla peasant army that became a social revolutionary force.

Typical of the J-26 leadership, Castro came not from the Communist Party tradition but from the antiimperialist Ortodoxo Party of Eduarde (Eddy) CHIBÁS, to whom Castro was protégé. By the time of Batista's coup in 1952, there was an Ortodoxo radical youth wing around Castro that formed a resistance nucleus. From the start, the movement's organization had a military hierarchy. The first general staff consisted of Castro, lawyer Melba Hernández, and Abel and Haydée SANTAMARÍA.

On 26 July 1953, a premature attack on the Moncada barracks in Santiago de Cuba resulted in Castro's imprisonment on the Isle of Pines, where the movement evolved its military organization. Returning from Mexican exile in 1956, a handful of J-26 members built a peasant rebel army in Oriente's Sierra Maestra. In "liberated territory," the prototype new Cuban society included agrarian reform, revolutionary justice, and indoctrination.

Debate continues over whether the J-26 leadership hid an original Marxist viewpoint or evolved it during the struggle. In April 1958, a failed general strike showed the ineptness of the moderate (*llano*) J-26 faction, and left the pro-Marxist Sierra Army and its rural guerrilla strategy dominant. In August, the Communists signed a secret pact that grudgingly acknowledged guerrilla warfare's benefits while Castro admitted Communist organizational superiority. After Batista's fall, a transitional period led to a new United Party of Cuban Socialist Revolution (PURSC).

The only evidence of J-26 ideology lies in various manifestos, beginning with that issued by Castro at the Moncada trial ("History Will Absolve Me"). All of them are typical Cuban leftist programs, stemming from antiimperialism agendas of the 1930s, agrarian reform, and industrialization. J-26's originality lay in its use of revolutionary symbolism (drawn from Cuban, French, and its own revolutionary history) and in its guerrilla strategy. In the 1960s and 1970s, Che Guevara and Fidel Castro opposed the orthodox Communist route of "peaceful transition" with their *foco* strategy of armed revolution.

ROBERT TABER, M-26 (1964); THEODORE DRAPER, *Castroism: Theory and Practice* (1965); JAIME SUCHLICKI, ed., *Cuba, Castro, and Revolution* (1972); TAD SZULC, *Fidel* (1984).

PAT KONRAD

CUBA: REVOLUTIONS

Cuban Revolution

On 1 January 1959, the guerrilla forces of the TWENTY-SIXTH OF JULY MOVEMENT, led by Fidel CASTRO, entered Havana, the capital of Cuba, signaling the collapse of the dictatorship of Fulgencio BATISTA. From a small group of radical students and professionals, Castro had organized in less than three years a successful revolutionary force that not only toppled the Batista regime but also challenged Cuba's powerful northern neighbor, the United States.

The roots of the Cuban Revolution can be traced to the TEN YEARS' WAR (1868–1878), in which Cuban nationalists unsuccessfully battled to end Spanish control of the island. Despite defeat, the war fueled the determination of many Cubans to end foreign domination of their homeland. With the renewal of the struggle for independence at the turn of the century, two significant events had a profound influence on later Cuban history. First, José MARTÍ emerged as the ideological and symbolic leader of an independent Cuba. Cuba's greatest poet and thinker, Martí exhibited a genius that served the independence movement well. Second, the United States intervened in the struggle in 1898, and rather than full independence, gave Cuba protectorate status. Although the United States certainly hastened the departure of Spain's army from Cuba, the newly independent nation had a new, and far mightier, imperialist power to contend with.

The PLATT AMENDMENT, passed by the U.S. Congress in 1901, granted the United States access to Cuban ports and the right to intervene both to preserve Cuban independence and to "protect life, property, and individual liberty." Although most wealthy Cubans accepted U.S. suzerainty, many labor leaders and intellectuals refused to believe that Cuba would enjoy full independence. In the aftermath of the SPANISH–AMERICAN WAR and the Platt Amendment, there emerged a nationalist revival with Martí as its symbolic leader. In 1933, with Cuba suffering under the brutal dictatorship of Gerardo MACHADO, a general strike called by the Communists (known as the Popular Socialist Party—PSP) revived nationalist sentiment and led to the overthrow of Machado.

After a period of political instability, Ramón GRAU SAN MARTÍN emerged as the head of the new revolutionary government. Under his direction, Interior Minister Antonio Guiteras Holmes introduced a series of long overdue reforms, including the eight-hour workday, a cut in utility rates, the rights of peasants to oc-cupy lands, and limits on foreign ownership of Cuban property. However, political infighting, U.S. opposition, and plots within the military led to Grau's resignation in January 1934. The failed revolution of 1933 proved to be a focus for Cuba's future generations, and the revolution of 1959 was clearly rooted in it.

Between 1934 and 1959, Fulgencio Batista was the de facto head of the Cuban government. Although he is most remembered as the dictator overthrown by Castro's forces, in the 1930s he was regarded as a reformer. Batista enacted many of the demands put forward in the revolution of 1933, including limits on women's work hours, a pension for veterans, expanded education, and guarantee of permanent land tenure to Cuba's medium-sized farmers. In 1939 Batista was confident enough of his power base to allow free elections, which he won, and in 1940 drafted a new constitution that guaranteed universal suffrage, freedom of political organization, mandatory public education, and a limit to foreign holdings. In addition, the death penalty was outlawed.

Between 1940 and 1952, Cuba had a series of constitutional governments, and each year brought greater prosperity for the working and middle classes. During this period, Cuban politics was dominated by the Authentic (Auténtico) Party, two of whose members, Grau (1944–1948) and Carlos PRÍO SACORRÁS (1948–1952), became president. In 1944 Batista retired to the United States.

Conditions in the rural areas remained static or declined, however. And because Cuba's principal source of income was agriculture, and the majority of its population continued to reside in the countryside, social, economic, and political tensions continued to brew outside the principal cities. Furthermore, the period leading up to the coup of 1952 was characterized by political cronyism, corruption, and incompetence. In 1946, charges of corruption led to a split in the Authentic Party ranks and the formation of the Orthodox (Ortodoxo) Party, which consisted of disgruntled professionals, intellectuals, and Cuba's growing middle class, all of whom considered themselves heirs to the 1933 revolution. Their slogan, "Honor Before Money," underscored their commitment to end corruption and cronyism in the government. Although not socialists, the Orthodox Party members resented the control exerted by U.S. business interests on the Cuban economy; many of its members advocated the nationalization of foreign-owned sugar plantations.

Elections were scheduled in 1952, and Fidel Castro ran for a seat in Congress as an Orthodox Party candidate. Although Batista, who had returned from exile, could not count on broad popular support, he knew he could amass the necessary cabal of cronies, army officers, and members of the national police to take control of the government. The coup of 1952 also had the implicit support of the Communists, who welcomed a return to political stability. The United States quickly recognized the new government, and despite scattered protests, there was little real resistance. However, although he had support from key power blocs, Batista was never able to legitimize his rule among the Cuban masses. Fidel Castro, deprived of his chance to serve in an elected position, recognized this, and immediately began the work of undermining the Batista regime.

Castro's earliest attack on the Batista government occurred on 26 July 1953, when Fidel, his brother Raúl, Ramiro Valdés, and others attacked the Moncada barracks in Santiago de Cuba. Although virtually all of the guerrillas were killed or captured, including the Castro brothers, the attack made Fidel a national figure. It was not the first time that a military defeat resulted in a political and propaganda victory for Castro. As a recent candidate of the Orthodox Party, he viewed the attack as the fulfillment "of what Martí wanted to do." At his trial, Fidel utilized his impressive oratorical skills to attack Batista's government and to call for the implementation of a constitutional government, agrarian reform, profit-sharing in key industries, and the confiscation of money gotten by corrupt politicians for political favors. Although he was certainly a reformist, Castro's program had little to do with Marxism-Leninism. Castro was jailed in 1953 and freed in a general amnesty in 1955. Fearing Batista's police, Fidel and his brother Raúl fled to Mexico City, where they formed the Twenty-sixth of July Movement with the intention of plotting the overthrow of the Batista regime. It was in Mexico that Castro joined forces with the Argentine revolutionary and Marxist Ernesto "Che" GUEVARA.

Castro's guerrillas were not the only organized force opposing the Batista dictatorship. The Revolutionary Directorate (DR), an offshoot of the University Students Federation (FEU), was an anticommunist urban-based guerrilla organization whose single goal was the ouster of Batista. Its leader, José Antonio ECHEVERRÍA, was killed, along with other DR leaders, during an attack on the presidential palace in March 1957. This greatly weakened both the DR and the noncommunist guerrilla opposition to Batista.

There were also efforts throughout the 1950s to bring a peaceful end to the Batista dictatorship. Among these groups, the Society of Friends of the Republic (SAR), which included representatives of the Authentic Party, students, and members of the opposition, attempted to engage Batista in a "civic dialogue." Not surprisingly, their efforts got nowhere, since SAR had no clear political agenda, and its members were willing to do no more than engage in dialogue with the dictator, in the naive hope of convincing him of the necessity for reform.

While opposition to Batista grew, relative economic prosperity and cordial foreign relations undermined the dictator's efforts to step up repression by claims of threats to national security. On 2 December 1956, Castro landed eighty-two guerrillas on the southeast coast of the island, making good on his promise to return to Cuba. Although Castro's forces were initially routed, he was able to regroup and, with his brother Raúl and Che Guevara, launch attacks on Batista's forces. The Twenty-

sixth of July Movement issued a manifesto, *Nuestro razón* (Our Purpose), which spelled out its political program. The manifesto attacked four aspects of Cuban political and economic life that needed thorough revision: the colonial mentality, foreign economic domination, corruption, and the military. The manifesto called for constitutional reforms, political pluralism, a "constructive friendship" with the United States, and an independent economy.

Castro's Twenty-sixth of July Movement also had an urban wing, which in 1958 called for a general strike. Although the liberals of the movement supported the strike, and Castro at first agreed, the Communists, including Guevara, considered the strike poorly planned and ill timed. After the strike proved to be a failure, Castro withdrew his support for it, thus undermining the influence of the noncommunists in the Twenty-sixth of July Movement. Officially, the PSP objected to Castro's tactics and believed them doomed to fail. Yet Castro appreciated their commitment to organization and their ability to follow commands. Once it was clear that Batista was doomed, PSP members increasingly backed Castro's Twenty-sixth of July Movement, and Castro in turn relied increasingly on Communists because of their loyalty and reliability.

The final blow to the Batista regime was a U.S.-imposed arms embargo in March 1958. The U.S. State Department, which distrusted Castro, saw no option but to halt arms shipments until government repression lessened. Underestimating Castro's strength, State Department officials hoped that a decrease in repression would quiet the Cuban middle class, which had long protested the excesses of the Batista regime. Further, Castro had the foresight to use respected, educated liberals of the Twenty-sixth of July Movement to speak to the world press and diplomatic community, thus giving the impression that his forces were fighting solely to end the Batista dictatorship, not to restructure Cuban economic and social life.

By the end of 1958, even some of Batista's officers were ambivalent about the dictator's future or, worse, openly supported the guerrillas. With declining support within the army, political and material isolation from the United States, and no popular base of support, Batista fled the country on 1 January 1959. Although Manuel URRUTIA LLEÓ was named the new president, Castro was clearly the true head of state. Once victorious, the revolutionaries worked to fulfill the promises of the revolution, including the nationalization of foreign-owned properties and a massive program of land redistribution. The United States officially objected to the programs of the new government, and privately plotted to overthrow the revolutionary regime. As with all revolutions, factions united against a common enemy before victory end up fighting each other for the right to control the new government. Castro and his Communist allies proved more than equal to the task, and within two years of the revolution, most of the noncommunists in the Twenty-

Cavalry by Raúl Corrales (1960). CENTER FOR CUBAN STUDIES.

sixth of July Movement had been removed from power, executed, or exiled. With the decline of the anticommunist faction in the new government and the increased hostility of the United States, Castro's programs grew increasingly radical: first nationalizing large landholdings, then medium-sized ones, and finally virtually all of the farms on the island.

U.S. hostility to the revolution peaked in April 1961 with the BAY OF PIGS INVASION. The invasion, a military and propaganda disaster for the United States, solidified Castro's grip on the Cuban government. In December 1961, eight months after the invasion, Castro declared himself a Communist. Although Castro's commitment to socialism has been the subject of intense debate, it is clear that Castro believed that only by endorsing communism and establishing a close relationship with the Soviet Union could Cuba hope to achieve the goals of nationalization and economic independence from the United States that had been the dream of so many Cubans since the Ten Years' War almost a century earlier.

ADOLFO GILLY, *Inside the Cuban Revolution*, translated by Felix Gutiérrez (1964); RAMÓN EDUARDO RUIZ, *Cuba: The Making of a Revolution* (1970); SAMUEL FARBER, *Revolution and Reaction in Cuba, 1933–1960* (1976); JUAN M. DEL AGUILA, *Cuba: Dilemmas of a Revolution*, rev. ed. (1988); HUGH THOMAS, *The Cuban Revolution* (1977).

MICHAEL POWELSON

See also **Castro, Raúl; Cuba: Constitutions; Cuba: Political Parties.**

Revolution of 1933

The revolution of 1933 resulted from the violent opposition of the Cuban people to President Gerardo MACHADO's attempt to perpetuate himself in power in 1928. Political dissent was further inflamed by the widespread misery caused by the economic collapse of 1929, and by the fact that the 1920s were for Cuba, as for the rest of Latin America, a period of unrest and transformation. A new and more radical type of nationalism appeared on the island; students and rising labor unions undertook to promote the creation of a new and different type of society; and new leftist political organizations arose to defend the rights of the masses. It was the concurrent action of these forces that metamorphosed the anti-Machado protest into a revolutionary upheaval.

From 1930 to 1933 Cuba was caught between the violent tactics of the opposition, spearheaded by the Student Revolutionary Directorate and a secret organization known as ABC, and the brutal repression of the government, supported by the army. The struggle seemed to have reached a stalemate when President Franklin D. ROOSEVELT, who needed political stability in Cuba in order to implement his New Deal Cuban policy, sent his trusted aide Sumner WELLES to Havana to seek a peaceful solution to the unrest. At first Welles acted as a mediator, but subsequently he pushed Machado toward making concessions, encouraged the opposition, and undermined the army's loyalty to the president. Machado was desperately trying to stand up to Welles's pressure when, in August 1933, a general strike paralyzed the nation. Fearing a U.S. intervention, the army moved against Machado, who fled the island.

Following the coup, the first in Cuban history, Welles moved to fill the resulting political vacuum with a hastily organized provisional government supported by the ABC and the majority of the opposition. But the new government proved unable to cope with the situation. In September the Student Directorate (which had rejected Welles's good offices) and other elements turned a mutiny of army sergeants led by Fulgencio BATISTA into a triumphant revolutionary takeover. The officers were removed from the army and replaced with sergeants, and the provisional government was unceremoniously supplanted with a new leadership headed by Ramón GRAU SAN MARTÍN, a physician and professor at the University of Havana.

For four months the revolutionaries struggled to push forward a radical and ambitious program of social and profoundly nationalistic reforms. But Welles thought that theirs was a "frankly communistic" government, and consequently Washington confronted it with a stern nonrecognition policy. This was far more than Grau San Martín and his colleagues could withstand, especially after Batista, who was less radical and more pro-American than the students, astutely withdrew his support from the government. On 15 January 1934, Grau San Martín resigned as president, thus ending the radical phase of the revolution.

Although the more advanced elements did not remain in power for long, the revolution of 1933 marked a turning point in the evolution of twentieth-century Cuba. It put new life into Cuban nationalism, helped to restrain U.S. influence on Cuban affairs, and opened the way for the enactment of new and progressive social legislation. Most of the trends that it initiated proved irreversible, and many of them were reflected and sanctioned in the Cuban Constitution of 1940. In many ways the type of society that existed in Cuba in 1958 grew out of the revolution.

The most comprehensive account in English of the revolution is LUIS E. AGUILAR, *Cuba 1933: Prologue to Revolution* (1972). See also JULES R. BENJAMIN, "The 'Machadato' and Cuban Nationalism, 1928–1932," *Hispanic American Historical Review* 55 (February 1975): 66–91; HARRY SWAN, "The Nineteen Twenties: A Decade of Intellectual Change in Cuba," *Revista/Review Interamericana* 8 (Summer 1978): 275–288; and JUSTO CARRILLO, *Cuba 1933: Students, Yankees, and Soldiers*, translated by Mario Llerena (1994). On the role of the students, see JAIME SUCHLICKI, *University Students and Revolution in Cuba, 1920–1968* (1969). In Spanish the reader may wish to consult RICARDO ADAM Y SILVA, *La gran mentira, 4 de septiembre de 1933* (1947); LIONEL SOTO, *La revolución del 33,* 3 vols. (1977).

JOSÉ M. HERNÁNDEZ

See also **Cuba: Political Parties.**

CUBA: WAR OF INDEPENDENCE (1895–1898), the culmination of the Cubans' struggle to gain their freedom from Spanish colonial rule. The armed separatists were committed to more than just independence. The CREOLE bourgeoisie was just as much the enemy of Cuba Libre as were the Spanish officeholders, and the revolutionaries recognized that inequity was not caused by Spanish political rule as much as by the Cuban social system. They believed that a transformation of Cuban society was the only remedy. Originally the war was primarily between the colony and the metropolis, but after 1896 the conflict expanded to become a struggle between the creole bourgeoisie and a populist coalition over competing claims of hegemony within the colony. The rebellion offered oppressed groups—poor blacks and whites, peasants and workers, the destitute and dispossessed—the promise of social justice and economic freedom.

Jose MARTÍ, the father of Cuban independence, Máximo GÓMEZ Y BÁEZ, Antonio MACEO, and other vet-

Combat in the mountain pass at Cubitas, Cuban War of Independence. CENTER FOR CUBAN STUDIES.

erans of the TEN YEARS' WAR coordinated the war effort-sin Cuba. On 24 February 1895, the insurrection began with the GRITO DE BAIRE (Declaration of Baire). On 24 March Martí presented the Manifesto de Montecristi, which outlined the insurgents' war policies: the war was to be waged by blacks and whites alike (participation of all blacks was deemed crucial for victory); Spaniards who did not object to the war effort were to be spared; private rural properties were not to be destroyed; and the revolution was to bring new economic life to Cuba. Martí said, "Cubans ask no more of the world than the recognition of and respect for their sacrifices."

Martí's death in 1895 did not stop the independence movement. In September representatives of the five branches of the Army of Liberation proclaimed the Republic in Arms. In July 1895 Gómez and Maceo sent orders to end all economic activity on the island that might be advantageous to the royalists. Defeat of the Spanish required destruction of the bourgeoisie's social and economic power, and so the insurrection became an economic war. The insurgents burned fields to stop sugar production. The population continued to support the rebellion despite its economic consequences, and the war did in fact destroy the Spanish bourgeoisie as a social class as well as end colonial rule.

Spanish authorities were stunned by the insurrection. They enlarged their army to 200,000 men and appointed General Valeriano WEYLER Y NICOLAU to bolster the war effort. He instituted the reconcentration policy under which the rural population was ordered to evacuate the countryside and relocate in specially designated fortified towns. Subsistence agriculture was banned and villages, fields, homes, food reserves, and livestock were all destroyed. Over 300,000 Cubans were relocated into these concentration camps. Mass deaths resulted because the municipal authorities were not prepared to assume the responsibility of caring for the internal refugees. The policy proved to be counterproductive. As a result of the camps, more Cubans supported the insurrection; also, in the United States and even Spain there was a strong public reaction against the Spanish policy.

The Spanish controlled the cities and attacked the peasants, while the Cubans controlled the countryside and attacked the planters. By the end of 1897, Cuban victory was inevitable. Weyler was incapable of expelling the insurgents from the western area of the island, and the Cuban elites were appealing to the United States to intervene and restore order. The explosion on 15 February 1898 of the U.S.S. MAINE, which had been sent to the Havana harbor to protect U.S. citizens, killed 260 enlisted men and officers. This tragedy provided the United States with an excuse to enter the war. On 25 April 1898, the U.S. Congress declared war against Spain, but the TELLER AMENDMENT stated that the United States would make no attempt to establish permanent control over the island. In June 1898 some 17,000 U.S. troops landed east of Santiago, Cuba. On 3 July the Spanish fleet was destroyed, and a few subsequent land victories prompted Spanish surrender on 12 August.

Although the Cuban forces were instrumental in the outcome of the war, they were excluded from the peace negotiations that resulted in the Treaty of Paris. The terms of the treaty, which permitted the United States to dominate Cuba, reflected the view that the quick victory over Spain was attributable solely to the United States. That view did not acknowledge that the Cuban struggle for independence had been depleting the crown's resources for several decades, especially in the preceding three years. On 1 January 1899, the Spanish administration retired from Cuba, and General John R. Brooke installed a military government, establishing the U.S. occupation of the island, which ended in 1902.

JULIUS W. PRATT, *Expansionists of 1898: The Acquisition of Hawaii and the Spanish Islands* (1936); HERMINIO PORTELL VILÁ, *Historia de Cuba en sus relaciones con los Estados Unidos y España* (1938); EMILIO ROIG DE LEUCHSENRING, *1895 y 1898: Dos guerras cubanas, ensayos de revaloración* (1945); MIGUEL VARONA GUERRERO, *La Guerra de la Independencia de Cuba, 1895–1898*, 3 vols. (1946); HERMINIO PORTELL VILÁ, *Historia de la guerra de Cuba y los Estados Unidos contra España* (1949); EMILIO ROIG DE LEUCHSENRING, *La guerra libertadora cubana de los treinta años, 1868–1898* (1952), and *La Guerra Hispano-cubanoamericano fué ganada por el lugarteniente general de Ejército Libertador Calixto García Iñiguez* (1955); FRANK FREIDEL, *The Splendid Little War* (1958); HUGH THOMAS, *Cuba, or the Pursuit of Freedom* (1971); JAMES D. RUDOLPH, *Cuba: A Country Study* (1985); LOUIS A. PÉREZ, JR., *Cuba: Between Reform and Revolution* (1988).

DAVID CAREY

See also **Spanish-American War.**

CUBAGUA, the smallest (10 sq. mi.) of the three Venezuelan islands that comprise the state of Nueva Esparta. Though deserted today, Cubagua enjoyed a brief, prosperous heyday in the early sixteenth century due to the pearl-rich oyster beds near its shores. The island group was discovered by Columbus during his third voyage and later visited by Alonso de OJEDA, who gathered numerous pearls near the islands of Margarita and Cubagua. In 1500 Ojeda founded a small colony on the island, the first Spanish settlement in Venezuelan territory. The oyster beds were not systematically exploited until 1519, when the Audiencia de Santo Domingo decided to use Indian slaves to dive for pearls. Cubagua grew rapidly. In 1526 it was incorporated as the Villa of Santiago and in 1528 became known as the city of Nueva Cádiz, which had a population of 1,000. Intensive exploitation quickly exhausted the oyster beds and, by the late 1830s, new and richer beds were being discovered elsewhere. By 1539, the island was abandoned and in 1541 it was destroyed by either a hurricane or a tidal wave.

JOAQUÍN GABALDÓN MÁRQUEZ, ed., *Descubrimiento y conquista de Venezuela: Textos históricos y documentos fundamentales* (1962); and ENRIQUE OTTE, *Las perlas del Caribe: Nueva Cádiz de Cubagua* (1977).

INÉS QUINTERO

CUBAN AMERICAN SUGAR COMPANY. Following the United States war with Spain, which ended in 1898, Cuban property owners reeled from debt. American businessmen, interested in investment possibilities, flocked to the island. American occupation enhanced business opportunities, and in 1899, R. B. Hawley organized the Cuban American Sugar Company and acquired both extensive tracts of land (77,000 acres) and important SUGAR mills in the Matanzas, Pinar del Río, and Puerto Padre regions.

Along with other American-owned companies, the Cuban American Sugar Company not only generated tremendous wealth for its investors but promoted the development of American enclaves, usually in towns surrounding the sugar mills. These areas grew into privileged neighborhoods inhabited by American technicians, chemists, agronomists, administrators, and their families. The area surrounding the company's mill in Puerto Padre consisted of six hundred homes, racially differentiated social clubs, and schools. The infrastructure was also well established. While creating exclusive neighborhoods for Americans living in the region, the company's enclaves also came to dominate the local political and economic life.

LOUIS A. PÉREZ, JR., *Cuba and the United States: Ties of Singular Intimacy* (1990).

ALLAN S. R. SUMNALL

See also **Spanish–American War.**

CUBAN INTERVENTION IN AFRICA. As part of its efforts to play a major role in Third World affairs, the Cuban government of Fidel CASTRO directly involved itself with military and diplomatic efforts on behalf of several African socialist movements. Cuba's ties to Africa, however, also heightened opposition to those movements and increased cold war tension between the United States and the Soviet Union.

Cuban interest in African anticolonial movements began soon after Fidel Castro came to power. Cuba sent military and medical supplies to the Algerian National Liberation Front and upon achievement of Algerian independence in 1962, Castro established a Cuban military mission in Algeria. He had sent a similar military mission to Ghana in 1961.

More substantial involvement in African affairs began in 1964, when Ernesto "Che" GUEVARA visited with leaders of progressive movements in the Portuguese colonies. A year later, Cuba began sending them military missions. The main recipient of Cuban military assistance was Angola's Popular Movement of Liberation (MPLA). Although there were several revolutionary movements in Angola, the MPLA received Cuban support because its socialist ideology most closely reflected that of the CUBAN REVOLUTION, whereas others emphasized tribalism and racism, or were pro-Western. Cuban support of African socialist movements in the early

1960s began to replace declining Soviet aid to these movements, and Cuba was openly critical of the USSR for its failure to offer more assistance. This point of contention even hindered Cuban-Soviet relations for a number of years.

The support of other governments for different Angolan movements prompted Cuba and the USSR to reconcile their differences and unite in their support of the MPLA. The United States, China, and South Africa supported the National Union for the Total Independence of Angola (UNITA) and the Liberation Front of Angola (FNLA). Although the United States charged that the Soviets were dictating Cuba's actions in Angola, scholarly research on the subject suggests that Cuba was largely acting on its own behalf in initiating aid to the MPLA.

Cuban involvement intensified after the breakdown of peace negotiations in Portugal in 1975. As fighting escalated, Cuba sent 230 military instructors to the MPLA. South Africa, meanwhile, began to train FNLA and UNITA troops in Namibia. When these troops failed to make consequential gains against the MPLA, South African forces intervened directly. South Africa sought to maintain instability in the region, which it hoped would guarantee the continued economic dependence of southern African nations on South Africa. South Africa was also encouraged by the United States. With strong anti-Communist rhetoric, South Africa cited the presence of Cuban troops as grounds both for delaying Namibian independence and for continuing its policy of apartheid.

Direct South African intervention in Angola changed the scope of the struggle there. It prompted the Organization of African Unity (OAU) immediately to condemn South Africa while simultaneously avoiding any judgment against Cuba or the Soviet Union. Nigeria's strong protest against South Africa, combined with praise of the Soviet and Cuban action in Angola, demonstrated that the struggle embodied more than an East-West competition at the international level. Nigeria had been one of the West's strongest allies in the sub-Sahara region, but here sided with anticolonialism and against racist South Africa.

Cuban military aid was crucial to an MPLA victory. By March 1976 some 24,000 Cuban troops were in Angola, a number that grew to nearly 40,000 by 1984. With this assistance the MPLA drove the South Africans out of Angola. Negotiations over Namibian independence had complicated the issue. Namibia (Southwest Africa before 1968) had been mandated to South Africa following Germany's defeat in World War I. After World War II, South Africa, having expanded its apartheid policies into the territory, refused to allow the United Nations to monitor its administration of the area. Although the United Nations nullified South African jurisdiction in 1966, resolution of the dispute came slowly. In the negotiations, South Africa linked Namibian independence to Cuban withdrawal from Angola. The Cubans, however, were unwilling to give South Africa the strategic geographic advantage that a removal of Cuban troops would cause. Moreover, as G. R. Berridge has pointed out, Cuba insisted that withdrawal had to be conducted in a way that emphasized a positive legacy of Cuban influence in African history. In 1988 a number of accords involving Cuba, Angola, Namibia, and South Africa were signed, with Cuba and Angola agreeing to remove Cuban troops by July 1991.

Cuba's presence in Mozambique was more subdued, involving by the mid-1980s seven hundred Cuban military and seventy civilian personnel. While Cuba's presence in Angola was vital in shifting the balance of power in southwest Africa, its presence in Mozambique was relatively insignificant.

In Ethiopia the Cubans also played a role, closely in concert with Soviet policy. Before 1974, both the USSR and Cuba had supported Ethiopia's adversary, Somalia. But in that year Ethiopia, suffering from much internal turmoil, began to move toward the Left. After Emperor Haile Selassie's overthrow in 1974, a bitter military struggle led to the victory of the socialist faction in 1977. Meanwhile, Cuba's former ally, Somalia, sponsored a revolutionary group in Ogaden, which had historically been a part of Ethiopia. As Ethiopia reshuffled its international alliances, Somalia found itself on the outside. Only two months after supplying aid to Somalia, in 1977, Cuba, in collaboration with Soviet policy, began sending arms and advisers to Ethiopia. After unproductive negotiations, Somalia broke relations with Cuba and sent its own troops into Ogaden. Cuba responded by sending 17,000 troops into war-torn Ethiopia, which by 1987 had established a Marxist-Leninist state and was suffering massive economic and social devastation, exacerbated by famine and drought. The end of the cold war resulted in foreign withdrawal from the area, leaving Ethiopia and Somalia to struggle with internal strife and continued economic and physical hardships.

Although Cuba's presence in Africa was beneficial to Angola, Ethiopia, and several other nations, there was a high cost in lives and material. Cuba had both gains and losses from its intervention in Africa. It greatly strengthened its ties to the Soviet Union, while further alienating it from the United States at a time when a willingness to normalize U.S.-Cuban relations had begun. In effect, it furthered Cuba's break with the West, solidifying its membership in the Soviet economic and political bloc.

ROBIN NAVARRO MONTGOMERY, *Cuban Shadow over the Southern Cone* (1978); BASIL DAVIDSON, *The People's Cause: A History of Guerrillas in Africa* (1981); CARMELO MESA-LAGO and JUNE S. BELKIN, eds., *Cuba in Africa* (1982); J. GUS LIEBENOW, *African Politics: Crises and Challenges* (1986); OWEN ELLISON KAHN, "Cuba's Impact in Southern Africa," in *Journal of Inter-American Studies and World Affairs* 29 (Fall 1987): 33–54; JUAN F. BENEMELIS, *Castro, subversión y terrorismo en Africa* (1988); LOUIS A. PÉREZ, JR., *Cuba: Between Reform and Revolution* (1988); G. R. BERRIDGE, "Diplomacy and the Angolan/Namibia Accords," in *International Affairs* 65, no. 3 (1989): 463–479; PHILIP BRENNER, et al., eds., *The Cuban Reader: The Making of a Revolutionary*

Society (1989); A. ADU BOAHEN, ed., *Africa Under Colonial Domination: 1880–1935* (1990); FESTUS UGBOAJA OHAEGBULAM, *Towards an Understanding of the African Experience from Historical and Contemporary Perspectives* (1990).

ALLAN S. R. SUMNALL

CUBAN MISSILE CRISIS. In mid-1962 the CIA and the U.S. military learned from photographs taken by U-2 spy planes of nuclear missile sites and Soviet nuclear-capacity bombers in Cuba. Eager to reaffirm U.S. dominance of the Western Hemisphere after the embarrassment of the failed BAY OF PIGS INVASION, President John F. Kennedy, on 22 October, denounced the existence of the missiles and demanded their immediate removal. The Soviets and Cubans argued that the missiles were for defensive purposes only. On 24 October 1962 Kennedy imposed a naval quarantine of Cuba. In response to this action, the Soviet ships that were on course for Cuba slowed down while Soviet premier Nikita Khrushchev began to consider a compromise.

Characteristic of the posturing of the two leaders, Kennedy refused to negotiate before the existing missiles were removed from Cuba, while Khrushchev stated that he would comply if the United States removed its missiles from Turkey. The Soviet leader in secret then proposed that he would remove the missiles if the U.S. agreed not to invade Cuba—an offer Kennedy decided to accept. However, the Soviets decided to withdraw the missiles and to permit a U.N. inspection team to supervise the process without consulting Cuba. This oversight infuriated Fidel CASTRO, who refused to permit the U.N. inspection, although the eventual removal of missiles was substantiated by U.S. surveillance flights over the island. Castro's exclusion from direct negotiations was an embarrassment to him and contributed to a rift in Soviet-Cuban relations. His rejection of U.N. supervision meant that the U.S. never had to acknowledge publicly its promise not to invade Cuba.

The literature devoted to the missile crisis and Cuba is vast. See HUGH THOMAS, *The Cuban Revolution* (1986), esp. pp. 607–641, and LOUIS A. PÉREZ, JR., *Cuba: Between Reform and Revolution* (1988), esp. pp. 477–480. Among more specific works, see DINO A. BRUGIONI, *Eyeball to Eyeball: The Inside Story of the Cuban Missile Crisis* (1991); LAURENCE CHANG and PETER KORNBLUH, eds., *The Cuban Missile Crisis, 1962: A National Security Archive Documents Reader* (1992); JAMES A. NATHAN, ed., *The Cuban Missile Crisis Revisited* (1992); ROBERT SMITH THOMPSON, *The Missiles of October: The Declassified Story of John F. Kennedy and the Cuban Missile Crisis* (1992).

MICHAEL A. POLUSHIN

See also **Communism; Soviet–Latin American Relations.**

CUCHUMATANES. The Sierra de los Cuchamatanes of Guatemala is the most massive and spectacular nonvolcanic region in all Central America. It lies at elevations ranging from 1,500 feet to more than 12,000 feet in the northwestern Guatemalan departments of Huehuetenango and El Quiché. The region's isolation and limited economic potential meant that MAYA peoples there survived the Spanish conquest and its destructive aftermath more resiliently than did native communities elsewhere in Latin America. The disruptions of the colonial period have had their modern-day equivalent in the form of violent civil war, the Cuchumatanes being the part of Guatemala hit hardest by counterinsurgency sweeps in the early 1980s. Remarkably, however, the Cuchumatán Maya endure, and culturally and demographically still constitute a visible, conspicuous element in the human landscape.

Two books by W. GEORGE LOVELL, *Conquest and Survival in Colonial Guatemala: A Historical Geography of the Cuchumatán Highlands* (1985, rev. ed. 1992) and *Conquista y cambio cultural* (1990), situate the Cuchumatanes in historical and geographical context. On the embattled Maya, see LOVELL's "From Conquest to Counter-Insurgency" in *Cultural Survival Quarterly* 9:2 (1985): 46–49; and "Surviving Conquest" in *Latin American Research Review* 23, no. 2 (1988): 25–57.

W. GEORGE LOVELL

CÚCUTA, CONGRESS OF. The constituent congress of GRAN COLOMBIA met at Cúcuta, on the border between Venezuela and New Granada, from May to October 1821. Though comprised only of representatives from Venezuela and New Granada, and not the present-day Ecuador, it confirmed the union of all sections of the former Viceroyalty of New Granada in a single independent republic. It adopted the first constitution, which was centralist in structure but typically liberal in providing for the separation of powers and a list of individual rights that did not, however, include freedom of religious worship. By separate enactments, the same congress adopted a first round of legal and institutional reforms that included abolition of the Inquisition and of various colonial taxes, and a free-birth law for the gradual elimination of slavery. To save time, it also elected the first president and vice president of the new nation: Simón BOLÍVAR and Francisco de Paula SANTANDER.

DAVID BUSHNELL, *The Santander Regime in Gran Colombia* (1954; repr. 1970), chap. 2; *Congreso de Cúcuta de 1821: Constitución y leyes* (1971).

DAVID BUSHNELL

CUENCA, the third largest city in Ecuador (1990 est. pop. 150,000) and capital of Azuay Province. Cuenca is located in the southern sierra of Ecuador, 8,500 feet above sea level, on the banks of the Tomebamba River. Pre-Incaic civilizations flourished in the region and attained their most highly developed cultural phase with the CAÑARI, known for their beautiful GOLDWORK. The Cañari had no centralized authority and were not able to defend themselves effectively against the invading INCAS, who came from Peru between 1463 and 1471. The Incas established a reputedly breathtaking city known as Tomebamba (Tumipampa) on the site of modern Cuenca. The nearby ruins of INGAPIRCA, on the great Incan highway, are the only Incan architectural monu-

Cuenca, Ecuador. LATIN AMERICAN LIBRARY, TULANE UNIVERSITY; PHOTO BY SIDNEY MARKMAN.

ments left in Ecuador today. The indigenous city was razed in 1557, when the Spanish conquerors arrived in the region after defeating the Incas. On the orders of Viceroy Gil Ramírez Dávlos, Fray Vicente Solano founded the city anew as a Spanish town, naming it Cuenca after a city in Spain.

During the colonial period, the Spanish built a picturesque tiled city, of which much architecture remains today. Cuenca became known for the devoutly religious and conservative character of its residents. The economy depended on agriculture and on the textile production of the indigenous peoples of the region. The population was not at first in favor of the independence movement; and indeed, after independence the local economy suffered due to the sudden rise in imports of British textiles. During the nineteenth century, the misnamed "Panama hat," woven of straw and formerly made on the Ecuadoran coast, made its way to the highlands and became the basis for the dominant cottage industry among local native people. These hats and other artisan productions are exported in great numbers today. The economy also depends on agriculture, cattle ranching, and leather processing.

For an excellent summary of what is known about the ancient history of Cuenca, see BETTY JANE MEGGERS, *Ecuador* (1966). For the transition from the colonial period to the modern, see SILVIA PALOMEQUE, *Cuenca en el siglo XIX: La articulación de una región* (1990).

CAMILLA TOWNSEND

See also **Textile Industry.**

CUERNAVACA, Mexican municipality and capital of the state of Morelos. With a population of nearly 400,000 (as of the late 1980s), it is located about 36 miles south of Mexico City at an elevation of 5,059 feet above sea level. Known as Cuauhnahuac (near the trees) in pre-Spanish times, it became the residence of the conqueror Hernán CORTÉS. Franciscan missionaries arrived in 1529.

In colonial times Cuernavaca was an important center of local indigenous government and the seat of a Spanish magistrate appointed by the administrators of Cortés's estate. The town's growing non-Indian population became enfranchised with the creation of a municipal government shortly before Mexican independence.

Cuernavaca was often involved in nineteenth-century politics; a junta held there in 1855 named Juan ÁLVAREZ as interim president of Mexico, and Emperor MAXIMILIAN von Hapsburg frequently vacationed there. In 1869 it became the capital of the new state of Morelos, and in 1891 its first bishop was consecrated. Railroads arrived in 1897, and Cuernavaca played a pivotal role in the Revolution of 1910.

During the 1920s a new highway to Mexico City enabled President Plutarco Elías CALLES and many of his

associates to commute easily to their vacation homes in Cuernavaca. In recent decades the city has continued to be a favored weekend retreat of Mexico City residents.

A scholarly treatment of the colonial period can be found in ROBERT S. HASKETT, *Indigenous Rulers: An Ethnohistory of Town Government in Colonial Cuernavaca* (1991). For a highly personal account of events in Cuernavaca during the Revolution of 1910, see ROSA E. KING, *Tempest over Mexico: A Personal Chronicle* (1970).

CHERYL ENGLISH MARTIN

CUERPO DE CARABINEROS, Chile's national police force, founded 1919. The *carabineros* used as their nucleus a mounted unit of the army originally created to maintain order particularly in the countryside. Although the force was under the authority of the Ministry of Interior, military laws and regulations governed its members. In 1927 at the behest of President Carlos IBÁÑEZ the *carabineros* were fused with various autonomous municipal police forces to create a very centralized national organization dedicated to enforcing the law throughout Chile. Considered highly professional and often serving as an unofficial auxiliary to the army, the *carabineros* joined the 1970 coup against the Allende government. Its then commander, César Mendoza, served as one of the members of the first post-Allende junta, and other officers held ministerial portfolios.

LUIS GALDAMES, *A History of Chile* (1941) pp. 383, 387, 436; FREDERICK M. NUNN, *Chilean Politics: The Honorable Mission of the Armed Forces* (1970), pp. 89, 149.

WILLIAM F. SATER

CUERVO, RUFINO JOSÉ (*b.* 19 September 1844; *d.* 17 July 1911), Colombian philologist. Rufino José Cuervo, born in Bogotá, was largely self-taught in his various specialties, which spanned ancient and modern languages and literature, including Native American tongues and American Spanish dialects. Among his earlier works are *Apuntaciones críticas sobre el lenguage bogotano* (1867–1872) and *Gramática de la lengua latina* (1876), a Latin grammar he wrote with Miguel Antonio CARO. Cuervo traveled extensively in Europe, and after 1882 settled permanently in Paris, where he taught at the Sorbonne and contributed to European specialized journals. He also produced, in collaboration with his brother Ángel, a historically important life of their father, *Vida de Rufino Cuervo y noticias de su época* (1946). Cuervo also undertook a massive *Diccionario de construcción y régimen de la lengua castellana* (1886–1893), which he completed only to the letter D.

LUIS LÓPEZ DE MESA, *Miguel Antonio Caro y Rufino José Cuervo* (1944); FERNANDO ANTONIO MARTÍNEZ, *Rufino José Cuervo* (1954).

DAVID BUSHNELL

CUESTAS, JUAN LINDOLFO (*b.* 6 January 1837; *d.* 21 June 1905), president of Uruguay (1899–1903). A veteran politician, Cuestas was president of the Senate between 1895 and 1898 and provisional president between 1898 and 1899. In his early career he subscribed to the collectivist Colorado group led by HERRERA Y OBES, which had overseen the transition from militarism to civilian government. As president of the Senate exercising executive power after the death of the constitutional president, he modified his politics in order to broaden his base of support within both the Colorado and the Blanco (National) parties. The preceding president, Juan Idiarte Borda, assassinated in 1897, had left a legacy of revolution in the Blanco Party, led by Aparicio SARAVIA. Cuestas made a pact with Saravia, accepting what amounted to a formula for cogovernment. In 1898, unable to assure his own election by the Parliament, he dissolved the assembly by decree and assumed dictatorial powers. During his provisional presidency, military and presumably collectivist factions attempted a coup d'état and an invasion, which ultimately failed. Cuestas's constitutional presidency deserves credit for bringing the peace and order so longed for. José BATLLE Y ORDÓÑEZ succeeded him as president, beginning a new era in Uruguayan politics and suppressing the cogovernment of Cuestas and Saravia.

EDUARDO ACEVEDO, *Manual de historia uruguaya: Desde el coloniaje hasta 1930* (1935), esp. pp. 241–298; ENRIQUE MÉNDEZ VIVES, *El Uruguay de la modernización* (1977), esp. pp. 87–95, 117–122.

FERNANDO FILGUEIRA

CUEVA, FRANCISCO DE LA (*b.* ca. 1501; *d.* 1576), Spanish governor of Guatemala. Cueva accompanied the expedition of Pedro de ALVARADO Y MESÍA to Guatemala (ca. 1524). Later, he married Alvarado's daughter Leonor, child of Alvarado's union with the Tlaxcalan princess Luisa Xicoténcatl.

Alvarado named Cueva acting governor and captain-general of Guatemala on two occasions. He was acting governor when news of Alvarado's death reached Guatemala in 1541. He was replaced by his cousin Beatriz de la CUEVA DE ALVARADO, who was Alvarado's second wife. After her death (10 September 1541), Cueva and Bishop Francisco MARROQUÍN were co-governors until a replacement, Alonso de Maldonado, was sent from Mexico, 17 May 1542.

MURDO J. MACLEOD

CUEVA DE ALVARADO, BEATRIZ DE LA (*d.* 10 September 1541), second wife of Pedro de ALVARADO Y MESÍA and the only female governor during the Spanish-American colonial period. Niece of the duke of Albuquerque, she married Pedro de Alvarado, her deceased sister's husband, in Spain in 1538, after receiving a pa-

pal dispensation, and accompanied him to Guatemala when he returned there as governor the following year.

When news of Alvarado's death arrived in Guatemala in June 1541, she demanded the governorship. Her cousin, the acting governor, Francisco de la CUEVA, gave it to her. The conquistador elite, already shocked by what it considered to be her excessive and sacrilegious mourning for her husband, resented her assumption of the governorship. She was killed on 10 September 1541 by the flood and mudslide that destroyed the city following rainstorms and earthquakes. Years later she was buried beside Alvarado in the cathedral of Antigua, Guatemala.

MURDO J. MACLEOD

CUEVA ENRÍQUEZ Y SAAVEDRA, BALTÁSAR DE LA (count of Castellar), viceroy of Peru (1674–1678). An experienced administrator, Castellar attempted to reform colonial administration and increase crown revenues by streamlining accounting procedures and investigating tax collectors and regional treasuries throughout the viceroyalty. Through his efforts, hundreds of thousands of pesos in back taxes and other revenues owed the crown were collected, many from the CONSULADO (merchant guild). His anticorruption campaign resulted in the public execution of two treasury officials and sanctions against many others, one of whom attempted to assassinate Castellar in 1675. Disgruntled treasury officials and members of the powerful *consulado* of Lima complained so strenuously to the crown that Castellar was removed from office in 1678.

See the excellent account of colonial administration in KENNETH J. ANDRIEN, *Crisis and Decline: The Viceroyalty of Peru in the Seventeenth Century* (1985), esp. pp. 184–189, which give details of Castellar's career. A more general discussion of colonial administration can be found in MARK A. BURKHOLDER and LYMAN L. JOHNSON, *Colonial Latin America* (1990).

ANN M. WIGHTMAN

CUEVAS, JOSÉ LUIS (*b.* 26 February 1933), Mexican artist. Cuevas's precocious talent became apparent in 1953, a crucial time in Mexican art when the hegemony of the Mexican School was in question. His pen and ink drawings of mad people, cadavers, freaks, and prostitutes brought him acclaim in 1954 at the Pan American Union under the tutelage of its director, José Gómez Sicre. Cuevas promoted himself with a publicity campaign that culminated in 1956 with his article "La cortina de nopal" (The Cactus Curtain) in the newspaper *Novedades*, in which he fulminated against the Mexican School. He initiated an expressive figurative and intimist drawing style based on monsters and the grotesque. His later work drew extensively from literary sources (Kafka, Dostoevsky, Quevedo) and from such artists as Van Eyck, Rembrandt, Goya, Dürer, Picasso, and OROZCO. He did several thematic series, which include *The Worlds of*

Kafka and Cuevas (1957), *Funerals of a Dictator* (1958), *The Spain of Franco* (1960), and *The Conquest of Mexico* (1961), as well as innumerable self-portraits. Cuevas has had a strong influence on neofigurative Latin American artists.

RALPH DIMMICK et al., trans., *Cuevas by Cuevas: Autobiographical Notes* (1965); CARLOS FUENTES, *El mundo de José Luis Cuevas*, translated by Consuelo de Aerenlund (1969); SHIFRA M. GOLDMAN, *Contemporary Mexican Painting in a Time of Change* (1981).

SHIFRA M. GOLDMAN

CUEVAS, MARIANO (*b.* 1879; *d.* 1949), Mexican historian. Born in Mexico City, Cuevas studied there until joining the Society of Jesus in Loyola, Spain, in 1893. From 1902 to 1906, Cuevas taught literature and history in Saltillo and Puebla, Mexico. He went on to study theology in St. Louis, Missouri (1906–1910). Cuevas was ordained a priest but continued to study archaeology, paleography, diplomacy, and historical methods. He spent most of the rest of his life researching and writing historical works. He published collections of documents as well as the results of his own investigations. His principal works include *Documentos inéditos del siglo XVI* (1914), *Cartas y otros documentos de Hernán Cortés* (1915), *Historia de la iglesia en México*, 5 vols., (1921–1928), and *La historia de la nación mexicana* (1940).

CARLOS GONZÁLEZ PEÑA, *History of Mexican Literature*, translated by Gusta Barfield Nance and Florence Johnson Dunstan, 3d ed. (1968); *Diccionario Porrúa de historia, biografía y geografía de México*, 5th ed. (1986).

D. F. STEVENS

CUGAT, XAVIER (*b.* 1 January 1900; *d.* 27 October 1990), Spanish musician and bandleader. Born near Barcelona, Spain, Cugat immigrated to Cuba with his family in 1904. At age six, he appeared as a guest violinist with the Havana Symphony and became a full-time member of that orchestra in 1912. Later that same year, he moved to the United States. Unable to find work as a classical musician, he drew caricatures of movie stars for the *Los Angeles Times* until Rudolph Valentino asked him to organize a band to accompany him in a film requiring tango music. He and his band, the Gigolos, appeared in several films of the 1940s and 1950s, making his name a household word. He introduced the rumba to American audiences in his movies and through his appearances at clubs like the Coconut Grove, the Hotel Chase, and Al Capone's Chez Paris in Chicago, and a ten-year run at the Waldorf Astoria. His full-time career as a big band leader spanned from the 1940s to the 1960s. In 1986, he formed his last band and began touring Spain. He was married and divorced five times and had no children.

Cugat wrote two books that best define his life, *I, Cugat* (1981) and *My Wives*. His work with his band is discussed in GEORGE T. SIMON, *The Big Bands*, 4th ed. (1981). The introduction and effects of Latin American music in the United States is the subject of JOHN S. ROBERTS, *The Latin Tinge: The Impact of Latin American Music on the United States* (1979).

JACQUELYN BRIGGS KENT

See also **Arnaz, Desi.**

CUIABÁ, capital of Mato Grosso State in central-west Brazil. This city lies in the geographical center of South America on the Cuiabá River, a tributary of the Paraguay River, and has a population of roughly 220,000 (1991). Cuiabá was founded in 1718 when the gold boom hit Mato Grosso, but its gold fields proved to be shallow, with most deposits lying within two feet of the surface.

Cuiabá persisted as a permanent settlement, unlike most boom towns, becoming the provincial capital in 1820. At times it has taken center stage in the land struggles between the ranchers and Amerindians of Brazil. In October 1991, Pope John Paul II met at Cuiabá with 160 Indian representatives who opposed a quincentennial celebration of Columbus's first voyage. Cuiabá continues to be an important commercial center for much of Mato Grosso's economy, including rubber manufacturing, cattle raising, tourism, and mining.

ROLLIE E. POPPINO, *Brazil: The Land and People* (1968); VIC BANKS, *The Pantanal: Brazil's Forgotten Wilderness* (1991).

CAROLYN E. VIEIRA

CUICUILCO, an archaeological site located at the southern end of the Valley of Mexico on the outskirts of Mexico City. Between 300 and 100 B.C. it was one of the largest and most influential communities in central Mexico. The site grew to cover 1.4 square miles and had a resident population of around twenty thousand people. A large circular temple platform 88 feet in diameter and 22 feet high was constructed as the center of ritual activity at the site. This was the first monumental temple platform to be constructed in the Valley of Mexico, predating similar constructions at TEOTIHUACÁN by several hundred years.

The Valley of Mexico appears to have been divided into several large chiefdom societies between 300 and 100 B.C. Cuicuilco was one of the largest of these, and a large portion of the southwestern Valley of Mexico was under its sociopolitical control. Teotihuacán in the northeast corner of the Valley of Mexico was Cuicuilco's primary political competitor during this period.

The site of Cuicuilco was dramatically destroyed around 100 B.C. by a volcanic eruption from Mount Xitle. The entire residential area was covered by a massive lava flow that encased the archaeological site in a thick layer of basalt. The destruction of Cuicuilco had immediate and dramatic repercussions throughout the Valley of Mexico. Teotihuacán emerged as the region's undisputed political leader and underwent accelerated growth as populations throughout the Valley of Mexico were resettled within its limits.

BRYON CUMMINGS, *Cuicuilco and the Archaic Culture of Mexico* (1933); WILLIAM SANDERS et al., *The Basin of Mexico: The Ecological Processes in the Evolution of a Civilization* (1979); JEFFREY PARSONS et al., *Prehistoric Settlement Patterns in the Southern Valley of Mexico: The Chalco-Xochimilco Region* (1982); DANIEL SCHAVELZON, *La pirámide de Cuicuilco* (1983).

KENNETH HIRTH

CUISINES. The cuisines of Latin America reflect the complexity and diversity of the history and culture of the region. Centuries of adaptations to the land have produced cuisines that are unique modifications of the food habits of Indians, Europeans, and Africans. Many of the staples upon which these cuisines are based have their origins in the early history of agriculture in Latin America. MAIZE, cassava, or MANIOC, and POTATOES, the three most important of these staples, remain essential in Latin American cooking today. They have also become central to the cuisines of many other regions of the world.

Maize was the most widely cultivated of the New World staples. Considered a miraculous food because of its yield, and a sacred food because of its ceremonial significance, it became the main component of a dietary complex that included varieties of beans, squash, CHILES, tomatoes, and fruits. Traditionally, maize was prepared by shucking the kernels, either by hand or by using the cob as a tool. In much of Mexico, so dependent on maize, it was then soaked or boiled in water and lime, which prepared the kernels for milling, often done with stone *metates*. More water was then added to the mixture, known as *nixtamel*, to give it the texture and consistency necessary for cooking. The result was *masa*, commonly used to make tortillas, a versatile food that has long been the basis of Mexican cuisine. Tortillas came in all shapes and sizes, determined by history and custom, and were common accompaniments to meals. Served as a bread, tortillas help to accent the classic dishes of Mexican cuisine, such as fish, meat, and poultry carefully prepared with *mole* or *adobo* sauce. When wrapped around meat, poultry, beans, or cheese, tortillas became the tacos, enchiladas, quesadillas, and burritos so commonly associated with Mexican cuisine today. Tamales, made from maize flour with salt and fat added, were more labor intensive and generally reserved for special occasions.

Mexican maize was almost as versatile when served as a liquid. *Atole* was a thin drink prepared from maize water. *Pozole* was a heartier beverage, at times served with chunks of meat or vegetables. *Pinole* was made from lightly toasted maize that was ground into a flour and then mixed with water. Maize also achieved a culinary complexity in other areas of Latin America. In the Andes, people ate *macha*, roasted maize flour; *cancu*, special loaves of maize bread; *humitas*, similar to Mex-

ican tamales; and *mote*, a maize gruel. In Colombia and Venezuela, *arepas*, a type of roasted maize bread served plain or stuffed, were favored over tortillas. In Brazil, maize was also prepared in many different ways, from *angu*, a cornmeal gruel, to *biscoitos de milo*, maize biscuits with sugar, eggs, fat, and a pinch of salt. Variations of these dishes were common through most of Latin America.

Maize, an Indian food associated with Indian agricultural and cultural practices, was often maligned by the Europeans for its bland taste and indigestibility, yet it was widely used. In the late sixteenth century, the popular writer GARCILASO DE LA VEGA noted that "with maize flour the Spaniards make little biscuits, fritters, and other dainties for invalids and the healthy. As a remedy in all sorts of treatment, experienced doctors have rejected wheat flour in favor of maize flour."

Cassava, called *yuca* in much of the Caribbean and *mandioca* (manioc) in Brazil, was a staple for many lowland peoples. It was similar to maize in that it required processing before eating. The most popular cassava contained hydrocyanic acid, removed by peeling and grating the root, then pressing out the poisonous juices. Gratings were then toasted and used for gruels and bread. *Pan de casabe* was described by some Europeans as "very white and savourie," but most Spaniards thought it tasteless and difficult to digest. In Brazil, *mandioca* achieved a special importance in the sixteenth-century diet as planters and explorers relied on it to provide cheap sustenance to Portuguese colonists, African slaves, and Indians. Bureaucrats encouraged its production, recognizing its centrality to Portuguese control over Brazil. In its most common form, it was a dried and toasted flour, known as *farinha* or *farofa*, eaten by rich and poor, though occasionally it emerged as *beijús*, tasty fritters for special occasions. Different types of *farinha*, used as thickeners, eaten as side dishes, or elaborately prepared with many different ingredients, are widely consumed in Brazil today.

Potatoes were the most localized of the three great staples. Found in the highlands of the central Andes, potatoes were a basic food source for the growing population of the Andean region. Variant soils, climatic conditions, and human experimentation had created a multitude of shapes, sizes, and colors of potatoes. Usually eaten boiled or in soups, potatoes were also frozen and dried to make *chuños*. Reverence for the potato is still seen in *papas a la huacaina*, a sturdy dish of potatoes (preferably those with yellow flesh), cheese, cream, peppers, and eggs.

Dozens of foods complemented the basic staples, some of them so widely consumed that during different times and places they almost achieved the status of staples. Grains, tubers, fruits, and vegetables such as quinoa, AMARANTH, chia, oca, ulluco, jicama, sweet potatoes, beans (kidney, tepary, lima, black, navy, wax, and others) pumpkins, chayotes, squash, peppers, tomatoes, avocados, pineapples, papayas, sapotes, soursops, guavas,

Open market in Bahia, Brazil. ROGÉRIO REIS / PULSAR IMAGENS E EDITORA.

and much more came in such abundance that early writers frequently talked about the profusion of food.

Beans deserve special mention, since they, along with grains and tubers, figured prominently in the cuisine, offering a solid basis for many dishes. Their importance in the diet continues today, and several of the traditional dishes of Latin America are based on beans. Frijoles, served in innumerable ways in Mexico but commonly mashed and mixed with fat, salt, and chilies, accompany many dishes. The Brazilian *feijão* can be cooked with coconut milk and vegetables, or served as the classic *feijoada completa,* a combination of beans and meats.

Meat was not absent from the diet of pre-Columbian peoples. The llama served the multiple purposes of transportation, wool, leather, fuel, and food. Llama meat was often eaten as CHARQUI, a type of jerky. In this sense, the llama was as important to highland Andean peoples as the camel was to nomads of the Arabian desert. The alpaca, better known for its fine wool, was also a source of meat. The *cui,* or small cavy, also known as *muca-muca* and *chucha,* was kept as a source of meat by households. Mesoamerican peoples did not have domesticated animals similar to the llama and *cui,* but they did keep ducks, turkeys, and dogs for the table. They were also hunters, and the iguana, peccary, tapir, coati, armadillo, rabbit, and deer, along with birds, fowl, and fish supplemented the diet. As Europeans were quick to point out, Indians also ate snakes, rats, lizards, insects, larvae, and lake scum—in other words, they effectively used their environment to enrich their diets and add diversity to their cuisines.

Foods introduced after 1492 altered the cuisines of the New World. The key European staples of wheat and rice challenged, and in some cases replaced, staples indigenous to the region. Introduced very early, wheat was the preferred food of Spaniards and Portuguese, who planted the crop wherever possible and relied on imported flour and hardtack when wheat could not be grown. Soon, the bakeries of cities produced several types of bread, some carefully refined and white, others dark and coarse with much of the bran remaining.

Rice also became important in local diets, often as a result of temporary shortages of more traditional foodstuffs. In the nineteenth and twentieth centuries, as larger populations sought new staples and as techniques for rice growing improved, Latin Americans ate more of it. IMMIGRATION affected the importance and method of consumption of rice. The arrival of large numbers of East Indian, Indonesian, Chinese, and Japanese immigrants led to increased consumption. While rice was prepared in many ways, a method common to many regions was to sauté the grains, often with a little onion, then cover with water and simmer. Examples of specialized techniques include *morisqueta* in Mexico, where rice is ground into a powder before cooking. Rice flour is also the basis for specialty drinks with sugar, honey, cinnamon, and other ingredients added.

The cultural and regional interplay of food staples in Latin America has not yet been sufficiently studied.

There is a disagreement among scholars about the ease with which European settlers adapted to a manioc-based cuisine in Brazil, thus reducing their reliance on imported foods. There are differing estimations of the importance of barley and wheat in the diet in regions with large Indian populations. In Cuba, at least according to Alexander von HUMBOLDT, Old World grains had "become articles of absolute necessity" for some by about 1800, displacing the traditional staples of maize, cassava, and bananas. Whereas some traditional foods fell out of favor, others increased in importance. Bananas (and plantains), introduced only in the sixteenth century, spread quickly through tropical and subtropical Latin America; eaten raw, boiled, fried, or dried, they were versatile, nutritious, and economical additions to the cuisine.

Meat was so abundant in the sixteenth century that it became a staple for many. Meat was usually prepared in one of the four ways common in fifteenth-century Spain: *asado* (roasted), *cozida* (stewed), *frita* (fried), and *empanada* (baked, at times breaded). Today, the classic meat dishes in the cuisine are roasted, often over an open fire. Examples range from the almost dainty Peruvian *anticuchos*, succulent beef hearts marinated and then grilled, to the spectacular Argentine *asado* and Brazilian *churrasco*, different cuts of meat cooked slowly over open fires. This type of cooking is far more popular than the old methods of *barbacoa* in Mexico or *pachamanca* in Peru, where food is placed over heated rock, then sealed with earth for slow baking, similar to the New England clambake. A fifth method of preparation was dehydrating and salting, already in use before 1492. With the abundance of meat and the development of long-distance trade in meat, preservation techniques became more elaborate. The cattle regions of plains and pampas produced charqui, *cecina*, *tasajo*, *carne seca*, and other types of dried, salted, and smoked meat.

In the cattle regions, beef was the mainstay of the cuisine, eaten three times a day. When meat was not available, animal fats generally were. Foods previously only boiled or roasted could now be fried, and indulgence in fried, fatty foods became commonplace by the eighteenth century. The abundance of animal fat quickly reduced the dependence on olive oil, reducing it to a secondary role in cooking by the end of the sixteenth century.

The emerging cuisines of Latin America depended on a combination of flavors, some pronounced, others subtle. Chilies assumed prominence in the colonial cuisines of Mexico, Peru, and Brazil, much more so than vanilla or any other indigenous flavoring. In addition, black pepper, citrus, ginger, anise, cinnamon, nutmeg, and more regionally specialized flavorings such as *azeite de dende*, characteristic of Bahian cooking, and cilantro (Chinese parsley), so widely used in Mexican food, became characteristic of Latin American cuisine. In this way, American, African, European, and later Asian foods and cooking techniques mixed to form the creole cuisines of Latin America.

Sugar, though lacking in nutritional value, was essential as a sweetener for chocolate, coffee, and tea, and as the principal ingredient of many diverse and creative foods. Sugar combined with all types of fruits and nuts yielded spectacular results. Cookbooks list innumerable recipes for *dulces* in Spanish America and *doces* in Brazil. Milk and eggs, other new ingredients in the cuisine, also became popular for desserts, especially flan, the caramelized custard common to Latin America. Chocolate, Latin America's gift to the desserts of much of the world, was consumed primarily as a beverage during its early history. In the nineteenth century its popularity increased as it took the form of modern milk chocolate. While still important as a beverage and dessert in Latin America, chocolate consumption there pales in comparison with that of many other regions of the world.

The encounter between different cultures established the basis for the cuisines of Latin America. Foods and methods of preparation that would endure into the twentieth century had already taken root by the end of the sixteenth century. Later external influences, especially those of France in the nineteenth century, affected cuisines but did not alter the basic foods and cooking techniques. The post–World War II global trends of commercialization, mass production, and food substitutes may ultimately change the cuisines of Latin America more profoundly than any other influences since the encounter.

EUGENIO PEREIRA SALAS, *Apuntes para la historia de la cocina chilena* (1977); AMANDO FARGA, *Historia de la comida en México* (1980); LUÍS DE CÂMARA CASCUDO, *História da alimentaçao no Brasil*, 2 vols. (1983), offers good introductions to the history of food in individual countries. For specific foods see NELSON FOSTER and LINDA S. CORDELL, *Chilies to Chocolate: Food the Americas Gave the World* (1992). Two good examples of the historical interpretation of individual foods are GILBERTO FREYRE, *Açúcar: Em tôrno da etnografia, da história, e da sociologia do doce no Nordeste canaviero do Brasil* (1969), and ALFREDO CASTILLERO CALVO, *El café en Panamá: Una historia social y económica* (1985). Early cookbooks, such as SIMÓN BLANQUEL, *Novísimo arte de cocina* (1831), and MARIANO RIVERA GALVÁN, *El cocinero mejicano*, 3 vols. (1831), are particularly valuable sources. For cookbooks in English see JONATHAN NORTON LEONARD, *Latin American Cooking* (1968), ELISABETH LAMBERT ORTIZ, *The Complete Book of Mexican Cooking* (1967), and MARY URRUTIA RANDELMAN and JOAN SCHWARTZ, *Memories of a Cuban Kitchen* (1992), which offer interesting cultural and historical insights.

JOHN C. SUPER

See also **Fruit Industry; Meat Industry; Nutrition; Sugar Industry.**

CUITLAHUAC (*b.* before 1467; *d.* 1520), Aztec ruler, son of Axayacatl and older brother of MOTECUHZOMA II. Cuitlahuac governed the disintegrating Aztec Empire for a brief period during the Spanish invasion. Ruler of the town of Iztapalapa and one of his brother's chief advisers, Cuitlahuac was already a seasoned warrior and statesman when the Spaniards entered Mexico. According to native histories, he advised Motecuhzoma against allowing Hernán CORTÉS and his army to enter TENOCHTITLÁN, the Aztec capital. When Cortés occupied the city, he imprisoned Cuitlahuac along with Motecuhzoma. After the AZTECS turned against the invaders and laid siege to their headquarters, Cuitlahuac gained release on the pretense that he would reopen the market to allow food to reach the invaders.

Following Motecuhzoma's death and the flight of the Spaniards and their allies from the city on the night of 30 June/1 July 1520, Cuitlahuac was elected to succeed his brother (according to some accounts he assumed this role even before Motecuhzoma's demise). His leadership of the resistance to the ensuing Spanish-led siege was short-lived. Within a few months of his accession, he died. His death is frequently attributed to smallpox, the first of many Old World infectious diseases to strike Mexico's native population, but the early sources do not state this explicitly. He was succeeded by his young nephew CUAUHTEMOC.

BURR CARTWRIGHT BRUNDAGE, *A Rain of Darts: The Mexica Aztecs* (1972); FERNANDO DE ALVA IXTLILXOCHITL, *Obras históricas*, 3d ed. (1975); MIGUEL LEÓN-PORTILLA, *The Broken Spears* (1992).

LOUISE M. BURKHART

See also **Mesoamerica.**

CUMANÁ the first permanent European-built settlement in Latin America. It was founded on the site of a FRANCISCAN monastery on the northeastern Venezuelan coast in 1520. The pearl beds of Margarita and Cubagua for a short period in the early sixteenth century sustained the small colony and Spanish commercial interests. The German banking house of Welser obtained a grant from the Spanish crown to explore the region and used Cumaná as one of its bases of operation. The only other commercial interest in the region during this period was slave raiding, which predictably resulted in a high level of Indian hostility from the early sixteenth century into the seventeenth century.

The region was characterized by a high level of strife, not just between Spaniards and Indians, but between Spaniards themselves. Jurisdictional disputes arose frequently between rival CONQUISTADORES as royal territorial authorizations often overlapped. By the end of the 1500s, Spanish control of the region had been established. Religious missions were created by the Franciscans in the early seventeenth century and the CAPUCHINS in 1650. Cumaná was an important port that was economically associated with the Caribbean colonies. It also was one of the major links in the Caribbean defense network. The colony was governed by a CAPTAIN-GENERAL from 1650 to 1830. Although econom-

ically focused on the Caribbean, it was Lima's central treasury that provided annual subsidies for the settlement. In the 1700s the Cumaná area supported a hide and cattle industry. Due to its coastal location and the nature of Spanish expansion, Cumaná's economic, political, and religious activities were directed toward the Caribbean rather than Caracas.

Today, Cumaná is the capital of the province of Sucre and functions as a minor seaport. Its economic and strategic importance declined, and its major commercial activities now center around resort hotels and sport fishing on the coast.

RAYMOND E. CRIST and EDWARD P. LEAHY, *Venezuela: Search for a Middle Ground* (1969); JOHN V. LOMBARDI, *Venezuela: The Search for Order, the Dream of Progress* (1982).

HEATHER K. THIESSEN

CUMBIA, a form of Latin American popular music originating on the Caribbean coast of Colombia. The name was originally applied to a traditional dance of the region as well as to the music of the dance and the musicians who play it. Perhaps derived from the Spanish fandango, the dance is performed by couples who form a circle around the seated musicians. Carrying lighted candles in their right hands, the women dance with shuffling steps while the men perform zigzagging steps around them. The partners pass each other back to back but rarely touch. A similar folk dance is performed in Panama.

Music for the *cumbia* was once purely instrumental, but lyrics were later introduced. The music is played by either of two ensembles. In one, the *caña de millo*, an open pipe with a single reed, is the melodic instrument; in the other, the *gaita hembra*, a vertical-duct flute, provides the melody. All other members of the ensembles play percussion instruments. Starting in the 1930s, the *cumbia* began to gain popularity in the interior of Colombia, and by the 1960s commercialized versions had spread to Peru, Mexico, and other Latin American countries.

GEORGE LIST, *Music and Poetry in a Colombian Village: A Tri-Cultural Heritage* (1983); THOMAS TURINO, "Somos el Perú: 'Cumbia Andina' and the Children of Andean Migrants in Lima," *Studies in Latin American Popular Culture* 9 (1990): 15–37.

HELEN DELPAR

See also **Music: Popular Music and Dance.**

CUMPLIDO, IGNACIO (*b.* 20 May 1811; *d.* 30 November 1887), Mexican publisher. Born in Guadalajara, Cumplido, the son of a doctor and medical school professor, grew up in Mexico City. While an employee at the National Museum, he began publishing newspapers. In 1829 he became the manager of the shop that printed *El Correo de la Federación*, soon followed by *El Fénix de la Li-*

bertad. In 1838 he went to the United States to buy the equipment necessary for a first-class printing establishment, but he lost everything when the French blockaded the port of Veracruz. Nevertheless, he continued to publish the most celebrated authors of the day in *El Museo Mexicano, La Ilustración Mexicana,* and other periodicals. Although associated with liberal politics, Cumplido was imprisoned in 1840 for printing José María GUTIÉRREZ ESTRADA's pamphlet advocating monarchy. Soon after he was named superintendent of prisons.

Cumplido is best known for founding *El Siglo XIX* on 8 October 1841; it became the foremost daily newspaper of nineteenth-century Mexico City and was published almost continuously through 1896. The list of its editors forms a who's who of Mexican intellectual life of the time and includes Guillermo PRIETO, Manuel PAYNO, Ignacio RAMÍREZ, Francisco ZARCO, Francisco Sosa, and Francisco BULNES. In 1842 he was elected to Congress first as deputy and then as senator, always giving his salary to charity. He founded a lithography school for orphans in his home. In 1847, during the war with the United States, Cumplido volunteered as head of a battalion of national guard and was subsequently promoted to captain.

In 1848 Cumplido went to Europe and purchased steam-powered presses. Following the FRENCH INTERVENTION, Cumplido became a member of the 1873 Ayuntamiento of Mexico City in charge of boulevards. It was his idea to plant trees on both sides of the Paseo de la Reforma in emulation of the Champs-Élysées.

RAMIRO VILLASEÑOR Y VILLASEÑOR, *Ignacio Cumplido: Impresor y editor jalisciense del federalismo en México* (1974).

BARBARA A. TENENBAUM

CUNA. *See* **Kuna.**

CUNDINAMARCA, a department in central Colombia comprising an area of 9,300 square miles. It had approximately 5.3 million inhabitants in 1985, most of whom lived in BOGOTÁ, which serves as both the departmental and the national capital.

Located between the MAGDALENA RIVER valley and the eastern plains region, Cundinamarca is varied in climate and terrain. The population is concentrated in high intermontane basins, the most important of which is the *sabana* (savanna) of Bogotá. Cundinamarca was a major center of Chibcha civilization, and Lake Guatavita, site of the Chibcha ceremony believed to have inspired the EL DORADO legend, is located here.

Cundinamarca's varied topography has encouraged agricultural diversification. During the mid-nineteenth century, TOBACCO and INDIGO grown in lowland areas near the Magdalena were important commercial crops. Cundinamarca also became a major COFFEE producer after 1870. In the coffee-growing areas of western Cundi-

namarca, such as Sumapaz, there was much agrarian unrest during the 1920s and 1930s and later much communist and guerrilla activity.

MICHAEL F. JIMÉNEZ, "Traveling Far in Grandfather's Car: The Life Cycle of Central Colombian Coffee Estates. The Case of Viotá, Cundinamarca (1900–30)," in *Hispanic American Historical Review* 69 (1989):185–219.

HELEN DELPAR

CÚNEO PERINETTI, JOSÉ (*b.* 11 September 1887; *d.* 19 July 1977), Uruguayan artist. Cúneo Perinetti studied at the Circle of Fine Arts in his native Montevideo; in Turin, Italy, with Leonardo Bistolfi and Anton Mucchi (1907–1909); and in Paris at the Académie Vity with the Spanish painter Hermenegildo Anglada Camarasa (1911). Early in his career, he painted naturalist gardens under the belated influence of the Italian Macchiaioli and the contemporary Spanish painter Santiago Rusiñol. Back in Uruguay, he painted landscapes in Treinta Tres Orientales. In 1917 he returned to Paris to study with Kees van Dongen. Upon his return to Uruguay, he began painting geometrical landscapes, including Uruguayan rural huts (*ranchos*) and Spanish colonial sites in the town of Maldonado, and portraits involving pure, extended areas of color. In the 1930s he started the series of his so-called moon landscapes, for which he is best known (*The Moon Over the Ranch*, 1934).

Cúneo Perinetti's work from this period is characterized by a low palette, thick pigment, and compositions based on diagonals and dynamic lines. Swirling strokes give the impression of dragging everything—trees, dwellings, earth—into a vortex. These turbulent paintings reveal the influence of Vincent van Gogh and Chaim Soutine. Oversized moons give his expressionistic landscapes a cosmic quality. He won gold medals at the National Salon in Uruguay in 1941, 1942, and 1949. In the late 1940s he turned once more to naturalist landscapes. Despite his long career he had little influence on subsequent Uruguayan artists.

JOSÉ PEDRO ARGUL, *El pintor José Cúneo: Paisajista del Uruguay* (1949); RAQUEL PEREDA, *José Cúneo: Retrato de un artista* (1988).

MARTA GARSD

CUNHA, EUCLIDES DA (*b.* 20 January 1866; *d.* 15 August 1909), Brazilian writer. Cunha began his career in 1888 as a journalist for the prestigious *A Província de São Paulo* after interrupting his studies at the Military Academy of Rio de Janeiro and resuming his military education at the Escola Superior de Guerra (Superior School of War) from which he would graduate in 1892 with an engineering degree. His fame as a writer began with the publication of his first articles, both titled "A nossa Vendéia" (Our Vendée), suggesting a comparison between the French Revolution of 1793–1796 and its Brazilian

341

counterpart, the messianic movement of 1874–1897 headed by Antônio CONSELHEIRO (Anthony the Counselor) in the northeastern backlands, (CANUDOS). Positive responses from readers and his own fascination with the subject prompted his newspaper to assign Cunha to cover the battles between the republican army and Antônio Conselheiro's followers. By the time he arrived at the war zone, the latter had crushed three military expeditions sent by local and federal governments. Thousands of republican soldiers had died and, baffled by the turn of events, government officials began to seek a plausible explanation for the series of defeats that had led the young and already fragile Brazilian republic into chaos and confusion.

During some thirty days spent in the battlefield, Cunha experienced scenes so tragic and horrifying that he was compelled to reevaluate his own view of the conflict. For Cunha, a confessed republican who had also been an ardent militant, it did not take long to realize that Canudos was not simply a clash involving primitive peasants and "civilized" men, but a brutal civil war.

Once home from the battlefield, Cunha began to write his most acclaimed book, *Os sertões* (*Rebellion in the Backlands*), a powerful account of the war at Canudos. In it he strives to show that a misunderstanding and a breakdown in communications were responsible for the war between the two groups. The republicans thought of Antônio Conselheiro's movement as a means to restore the monarchy with the help of the British crown. The poverty-stricken members of his flock believed, on the other hand, that they were fighting the forces of evil, Freemasonry, and heresy.

It may well be that no other Brazilian journalist before or since Cunha has acquired such a deep understanding of Brazil's tremendous social problems. His ambition in writing *Rebellion* was not only to analyze the war but also to provide an account of the formation of the national identity of Brazil. Thus, the book delves into geology, geography, sociology, anthropology, military and social history, literature, and philosophy. Cunha's language is precise, metaphorical, and, above all, oxymoronic. He takes liberties with the use of technical terminology to render clear, precise descriptions of the complex geography of Canudos.

Despite the reliable voice of the narrator at the beginning of *Rebellion,* when Cunha presents himself as an unbiased historian, the book is not a completely objective historical account of the war. A divergence between its literary achievements and its scientific accuracy is noticeable. In his quest for truth Cunha did some intriguing speculating and arguing, especially since he knew little of geology and botany and had never seen Canudos before the last thirty-five days of the war. While many are inclined to ascribe the difficulties in Cunha's book to his peculiar language, undoubtedly some of his theories, for example, on what he called "physical determinism" (the influence of the backlands upon the individual) and on genetic anthropology (de-

Euclides da Cunha. ICONOGRAPHIA.

generation of the white race through miscegenation), today sound arcane and obsolete, though expressed with vigor and intelligence. On the other hand, his sociological theory of cultural isolation is still viable.

Soon after its publication in 1902, *Rebellion* was enthusiastically received by critics and became a bestseller in Brazil. The success of the book guaranteed Cunha membership in the Brazilian ACADEMY OF LETTERS, which he joined in 1903. Following literary fame came opportunities to work with the Brazilian government. In 1906, after returning from an official trip to the Amazon, where he chaired a committee to survey the borders of northwestern Brazil, Cunha began to write a report that became his next most important book, *Contrastes e confrontos* (Contrasts and Comparisons), issued in 1907. Cunha spent the last two years of his life working on his third book, *À margem da história* (On the Margin of History), posthumously published in 1909. In this collection of essays he demonstrates his maturity as a writer and thinker, and replicates the artistic qualities of his masterpiece.

SAMUEL PUTNAM, " 'Brazil's Greatest Book': A Translator Introduction," in *Rebellion in the Backlands* (1945); OLÍMPIO DE SOUZA ANDRADE, *História e interpretação de "Os sertões"* (1960);

FREDERICK C. H. GARCIA, "Duas apresentaçoes de Euclides da Cunha," in *Luso-Brazilian Review* 7, no. 1 (1970): 23–34; WALNICE NOGUEIRA GALVÃO, ed., "Euclides, elite modernizadora e enquadramento," in *Euclides da Cunha* (1984); LUIZ COSTA LIMA, "Nos sertões da oculta mimesis," in his *O controle do imaginário* (1984); LEOPOLDO M. BERNUCCI, *História de un malentendido* (1989), esp. pp. 189–218.

LEOPOLDO M. BERNUCCI

CUNHA DOTTI, JUAN (*b.* 1910; *d.* 1985), Uruguayan poet. Born in Sauce de Illescas, Cunha left for Montevideo when he reached eighteen; his first book of poetry was published a year later. That volume, *El pájaro que vino de la noche* (1929), established his enduring fame through hermetic yet colloquial images that communicated well the nostalgia of the time for a less complicated and anguished existence. Other collections of poems—Cunha published twenty-six during his lifetime—demonstrated his agile versification skills in sonnets as well as free verse, in popular songs as well as difficult, esoteric verses. His poetry always registered subtle mutations of taste and concern with urgent social issues. During the 1940s he published little. Cunha's mature expression after 1951, in works such as *A eso de la tarde* (1961) and *Pastor perdido* (1966), communicates the poet's resentful solitude amid the silent streets and locked front doors of Uruguay's capital city. Additional works by Cunha include *Sueño y retorno de un campesino* (1951); *Hombre entre luz y sombra* (1955); and *Carpeta de mi gestión terrestre* (1960).

FRANSCICO AGUILERA and GEORGETTE MAGASSY DORN, *The Archive of Hispanic Literature on Tape: A Descriptive Guide* (1974).

WILLIAM H. KATRA

CUPISNIQUE CULTURE. In 1926 the Peruvian archaeologist Rafael Larco identified a distinctive cultural pattern that characterized the north coast of Peru during much of the second and first millennia B.C. While the Cupisnique culture was once considered to be simply a coastal variant of the CHAVÍN culture, it is now recognized as an independent cultural tradition that provided one of the sources of inspiration for the slightly later Chavín culture. Although the Cupisnique culture was originally defined on the basis of fine pottery from burials in the Cupisnique drainage and adjacent Chicama valley, late-twentieth-century research has favored a broader definition. As currently understood, the Cupisnique culture extended along the Peruvian coast from the Virú valley up to the Lambayeque drainage, and it maintained close relations with adjacent highland cultures and the occupants of the coastal valleys immediately to the north and south.

The center of Cupisnique culture was the rich but arid lands of the lower coastal valleys, and its economy was based mainly on irrigation agriculture and fishing. Besides numerous shoreline fishing villages and agricultural hamlets, there were larger centers where monumental architecture was built for civil ceremonial activities. The largest known Cupisnique sites, Purulén in the Zaña drainage and Caballo Muerto in the Moche valley, have numerous mounds suggesting a pattern of organization very different from that found on the central coast. Public constructions were built of stone or conical adobes and usually featured combinations of low tiered platforms, elaborate colonnades, massive central inset stairways, and sunken rectangular courtyards. In many cases the public architecture was decorated with painted or sculpted religious iconography featuring feline, ophidian, and avian imagery.

Much of the information on the Cupisnique culture derives from cemeteries excavated by Larco and others. People of the Cupisnique culture buried their dead in irregular oval pits dug into subsoil. The carved bone rings, shell ornaments, necklaces of semiprecious stones (including lapis lazuli from northern Chile) and shell, and high-quality anthracite mirrors that often accompanied the deceased suggest a special interest in personal adornment. Among the other items left in the tombs were pottery vessels, especially modeled or incised stirrup-spouted bottles, and, more rarely, carved bone tablets or spatulas believed to have been used to ingest hallucinogenic snuff during rituals. Among the most distinctive Cupisnique artifacts are elaborate stone mace heads, perhaps used as symbols of authority, and ceramic "stamps" or "seals," which may have been used for skin painting or decorating cloth.

Sometime after 500 B.C., the north coast became integrated into the Chavín sphere of interaction, and Cupisnique culture, while still distinctive, came to share features with cultures in central and southern Peru. When the Chavín sphere of interaction collapsed at approximately 200 B.C., the Cupisnique culture was replaced by a cultural pattern known as Salinar.

A more detailed discussion is in RICHARD L. BURGER, *Chavín and the Origins of Andean Civilization* (1992). A summary of RAFAEL LARCO's pioneering research is available in his essay "A Culture Sequence for the North Coast of Peru," in *The Handbook of South American Indians*, vol. 2, edited by Julian Steward (1946). For a widely available article on the excavations at Caballo Muerto, see THOMAS POZORSKI, "The Early Horizon Site of Huaca de los Reyes: Societal Implications," in *American Antiquity* 45 (1980): 100–110. The Huaca Lucia investigations are described in IZUMI SHIMADA, "The Batan Grande–La Leche Archaeological Project—The First Two Seasons," in *Journal of Field Archaeology* 8, no. 4 (1981): 405–446. One of the few detailed discussions of Cupisnique symbolism is LUCY SALAZAR-BURGER and RICHARD L. BURGER, "La araña en la iconografía del horizonte temprano en la costa norte del Perú," in *Beiträge zur Allgemeinen und Vergleichenden Archäologie* 4 (1983): 213–253.

RICHARD L. BURGER

See also **Chavín de Huántar.**

CURAÇAO, the largest of the islands of the Netherlands Antilles, with an area of 182 square miles and a population of 160,000 (1993 estimate). It is situated in the southern Caribbean Sea about 60 miles off the coast of Venezuela. As the yearly rainfall measures only 21 inches, the arid landscape is composed of barren hills, the highest of which is Mount Cristoffel, at 1,220 feet. The south coast has many deep inland bays, the largest of which is the Schottegat, Curaçao's major harbor. Willemstad, the capital of both the island and of the Netherlands Antilles, lies on the St. Anna Bay, a part of the Schottegat. The oldest part of the city still has a picturesque eighteenth-century appearance, with a fort that dates back to the seventeenth century.

The population is predominantly of African descent, with small European and Asian groups. Curaçao has the oldest continuously occupied Jewish communities in the Western Hemisphere, with its earliest settlement of 1651. The Mikven Israel synagogue, founded in 1732 in Willemstad, is the oldest synagogue in the Western Hemisphere. The oldest Protestant church still standing was built in 1764 as part of the fort. The newer section of the city is dominated by the Roman Catholic cathedral, and Catholicism is now the predominant religion of the island.

Curaçao was discovered by the Spanish navigator Alonso de OJEDA in 1499. In the following years, most of the Indians living on the island were taken by Spanish slave hunters to the island of Hispaniola. This practice ended when, under the leadership of Juan de AMPUÉS, the island was settled by the Spaniards in 1527. In 1634 the DUTCH WEST INDIA COMPANY sent a small fleet under the command of Johannes van Walbeeck, assisted by Pierre Le Grand, to take Curaçao and establish a naval base. Van Walbeeck conquered the island, and aside from two short periods (1800–1803, 1807–1816) during the Napoleonic wars of the early nineteenth century when the island was occupied by the British, Curaçao has been part of the Dutch realm ever since. Curaçao was a colony of the first and second Dutch West India Company until 1791, when it came under the direct control of the Dutch government. It remained a Dutch colony until 1954, when it became part of the self-governing Netherlands Antilles.

In the second part of the seventeenth century, the island was heavily involved in the SLAVE TRADE as one of the key markets of the West Indies. The economy of the island prospered for most of the eighteenth century. In the nineteenth century, economic conditions worsened. The establishment of the Shell Oil refinery for Venezuelan crude oil in the early twentieth century reversed this trend. By the 1950s, tourism and offshore banking also contributed to the island's prosperity. As a result of financial losses, Shell closed its operations in Curaçao in 1985. This was followed by U.S. legislation against offshore banking, a slump in the tourist trade, shrinkage of exchange reserves, and a sharp rise in unemployment.

RENE A. RÖMER, *Curaçao* (1981); TONY THORNDIKE, "Netherlands Dependencies," in *South America, Central America, and the Caribbean, 1991* (1990), pp. 429–443.

ALBERT GASTMANN

CURANDERO/CURANDEIRO, a folk healer. Terms such as *botánico, curioso,* or *empírico* are local variations. Folk healing is found in practically all Latin American cultures. Although its practice varies widely, the two major styles are American Indian and urban. The typical American Indian *curandero* is a shaman who bases his or her work on native beliefs, such as the idea that the soul can wander and be captured or that magical objects can be shot into the body. In addition to shamans, there are native specialists who prescribe herbal medicines, or set broken bones, or massage the body. The typical Indian *curandero*, whose work may seem exotic to non-Indians, follows a cultural pattern that is more orthodox than the eclectic, personal styles of most urban *curanderos*.

In the cities and towns of Latin America, religious ideas from all over the world have mingled to create a wide variety of urban folk-healing practices. The typical urban *curandero* is a healer who claims religious power and who uses techniques derived from different sources. Almost any religion or healing theory can be the basis for the urban *curandero*'s practice. Naturopathy, spiritism, spiritualism, Catholicism, Buddhism, African-American religions, homeopathy, and Indian traditions all have had roles in Latin American urban *curanderismo*. The synthesis of practices and beliefs is the rule rather than the exception. In spite of the variety, a specific region may be known for a particular type of *curanderismo*. For example, some cities in Brazil (Belém, São Paulo, Rio de Janeiro, Pôrto Alegre) abound in *Umbandista* curing; *Iquitos,* on the Peruvian Amazon, is known for healers who give their patients a hallucinogenic drug made from the *Banisteriopsis* vine; and healers on the north Peruvian coast conduct ceremonies in which the participants drink a potion derived from the San Pedro cactus.

The old American Indian traditions of folk healing were effective both psychologically and physiologically and have continued into the present. The high civilizations of the Andes and Mexico developed healing arts based on magic and medicinal knowledge. The AZTECS of central Mexico had both shamans and herbalists. Aztec herbal medicines were effective in correcting what was believed to be the cause of a disease. For example, if the healers felt that excess urine caused an illness, they prescribed an effective herbal diuretic. They used bleedings, baths, purges, dressings, plasters, and the extracts of plants, as well as magic. Aztec medicinal knowledge compared well with that of then-contemporary Europe. In Peru, INCA folk medicine men were low-level priests who divined the causes of illness and then provided cures. The ancient Peruvians developed extensive pharmacological knowledge. From skeletal remains and pottery drawings, we know that the ancient Peruvians also were excellent surgeons. The people from the PARACAS region of Peru performed a prodigious number of successful skull trepanations probably to relieve pressure on the brain due to war club injuries.

Today, Indian shamans are ritual specialists who claim to know about unseen, supernatural worlds. Male shamans are more numerous in Indian communities, but the office is open to women as well. Shamans may speak of a supernatural experience that has brought them the power to cure. They learn their profession from other shamans, and they may undergo a period of formal training, such as that given by the Ixil Maya shamans of Guatemala. In the regions where ancient civilizations once flourished, the profession of shaman may include such nonhealing services as priestly officiating. There is a tendency for shamans to deal more and more with the psychological components of illnesses as modern medicine becomes more successful in dealing with physical infections. Modern shamans often divide illness into a sorcery-caused type, which they will treat, and a natural type, which modern medicine and doctors treat.

Shamanic healing rituals have significant psychological effects. A belief in the shaman's magical power over animistic life forces supports the psychological component of shamanic work. Such a belief can be extended to include the power to harm or kill. Shamans often struggle on mythical battle lines between the good use of

their power, curing, and the bad use of it, sorcery. In their rituals they combat the sorcery caused by the enemies of the patient. Sometimes they become involved in countersorcery aggressions themselves. However, many shamans prefer to be called *curanderos* (healers) to highlight the positive, healing function of their work. They prefer not to be called *brujos* (sorcerers).

In many parts of Latin America, Indian shamans take hallucinogenic drugs to induce visions. Various plants, such as *Banisteriopsis*, *Virola theiodora*, *Nicotiana tabacum* (tobacco), and *Datura*, aid the shaman in seeing into the supernatural world. The drugs are seldom given to patients; they are used primarily by shamans to arrive at the correct diagnosis of a disease or the solution of a personal problem.

The early European medical traditions introduced into Latin America also were effective models of disease and healing. Humorial theories introduced by the Moors influenced Iberian medical concepts of the sixteenth century. These concepts entered Latin America with the missionaries, who founded hospitals and ministered to the Indians. Once the accepted knowledge of educated people, these traditions became the lore of the people of Latin America. Popular *recetarios* (home-care manuals) published in the sixteenth and seventeenth centuries contained medical information for home use and explained illness in humorial terms. The humorial qualities of wet and dry became less significant, and the qualities of hot and cold came to dominate Latin Amer-

Curandero performing healing ritual. Venezuela. LIBRARY OF CONGRESS; PHOTO BY MARIANO DÍAZ.

ican folk medicine. Many of today's folk-healing systems seek to maintain a balance between hot and cold essences in the body, particularly in reference to what is eaten. In Guatemala, for example, peaches, chocolate, and honey are thought to be "hot," while tomatoes, squash, and carrots are "cold." People are careful not to eat too much of one or the other type of food.

The modern urban *curandero* goes well beyond the common beliefs in hot-cold imbalances. He or she may perform psychic surgery, purification rituals, or other types of healings. He or she may treat magical illnesses, such as sorcery, *susto* (debilitating fright), or soul-loss, and "natural" illnesses, such as cancer, tuberculosis, and obesity. Each urban *curandero* seems to have a personal twist to what he or she does; idiosyncratic styles are prevalent. Urban *curanderos* diagnose illnesses by talking with the patient; by examining the patient's urine, iris, skin, hair, or personal object; or by using such instruments as stethoscopes and magnifying glasses. Urban *curanderos* are less socially involved with their patients than are shamans, and they seldom include the entire family in a treatment. Urban *curanderos* usually charge modest fees or accept only donations. Some religious groups in Latin America practice healing in larger group ceremonies. For example, the public attends Umbanda rituals in Brazil to obtain healing and spiritual benefits from possessed cult members.

RICHARD N. ADAMS and ARTHUR J. RUBEL, "Sickness and Social Relations," in *Handbook of Middle American Indians*, vol. 6, (1967), pp. 333–356; IRWIN PRESS, "The Urban Curandero," *American Anthropologist* 73, no. 3 (1971): 741–756; MARLENE DOBKIN DE RIOS, *Visionary Vine: Hallucinogenic Healing in the Peruvian Amazon* (1972); DOUGLAS SHARON, *Wizard of the Four Winds: A Shaman's Story* (1978); KAJA FINKLER, *Spiritualist Healers in Mexico: Successes and Failures of Alternative Therapeutics* (1985); MICHAEL F. BROWN, *Tsewa's Gift: Magic and Meaning in an Amazonian Society* (1986); JAMES DOW, *The Shaman's Touch: Otomí Indian Symbolic Healing* (1986); GEORGE M. FOSTER, "On the Origin of Humoral Medicine in Latin America," *Medical Anthropology Quarterly* 1, no. 4 (1987): 355–393.

JAMES DOW

CURITIBA, capital of the state of PARANÁ, Brazil. In 1991 Curitiba had an area of 171 square miles and a population of 1,313,094. Gold prospectors founded the settlement of Nossa Senhora da Luz dos Pinhais, which became the village of Curitiba in 1693. Until the end of the eighteenth century, the inhabitants lived on subsistence agriculture and marginal old gold sites. Progress came with cattle drives south to São Paulo's cattle market in Sorocaba and, in 1820, with the export of YERBA MATÉ through Paranaguá harbor. The village of Curitiba, the center of a community of large rural estates, was declared a city in 1842. After the territory of Paraná was separated from the province of São Paulo in 1853, Curitiba became the capital of the newly formed province. Together with the Indian and white populations, black and mulatto slaves constituted a significant work force, about 40 percent of the total population of Curitiba in the first half of the nineteenth century. In the second half of that century, European immigrants—primarily Germans, Italians, Ukrainians, and Poles—settled on the outskirts of the city, contributing their cultures to its development. At the beginning of the twentieth century, the city had acquired the features of a modern capital and had 30,000 inhabitants. In 1940 a Frenchman named Agache devised a plan to regulate the disorganized growth of the city. At the same time there was an expansion of coffee production, which resulted in increased wealth for the capital.

ERMELINO DE LEÃO, *Dicionário histórico e geográfico do Paraná* (1929); ALTIVA P. BALHANA, BRASIL PINHEIRO MACHADO, and CECÍLIA MARIA WESTPHALEN, *História do Paraná* (1969); LOUIS HENRY and ALTIVA PILATTI BALHANA, "La population du Paraná depuis le XVIII siècle," in *Population, revue bimestrielle de l'Institut national d'études démographiques* (Nov. 1975); JOSÉ FRANCISCO DA ROCHA POMBO, *O Paraná no centenario: 1500–1900*, 2d ed. (1980); MÁRCIA ELISA DE CAMPOS GRAF, "Economia e escravidão no Paraná" in *Boletim do Instituto histórico, geográfico e etnográfico do Paraná* 45 (1987); *Anúario estatístico do Brasil* (1990); *Sinopse preliminar do censo demográfico—1991* (1992).

MÁRCIA ELISA DE CAMPOS GRAF

See also **Brazil: Geography.**

CURRENCY (BRAZIL). Brazil has had a complex monetary history, notable for a variety of mediums of exchange, chronic currency shortages, and in recent times, periods of hyperinflation. Until 1942 the basic unit of account was the *real* (plural *réis*), or *milreis* (1,000 *réis*, written as 1$000). Its origin was in silver and billon (silver and copper alloy) coins first struck in Portugal in the 1300s, and the name was derived from a similar Castilian piece. In time, the value of all gold, silver, billon, and copper coinage, of which there were many types and denominations, was expressed as so many *réis*, but identified also by specific name and as multiples of smaller coins or divisions of more valuable ones. Copper coins as small in value as a single or one and one-half *réis* were coined until the 1680s. Silver coins included the *vintém* (20 *réis*), *tostão* (100 *réis*), and *meiotostão* (50 *réis*). The gold coins of the time were the *cruzado* (400 *réis*), *quarto de cruzado* (100 *réis*), and the *Portuguez* of 10 *cruzados*, or 4,000 *réis* (4$000). For large sums, such as the financial transactions of merchants and the state, the term *conto* (equal to 1,000 *milréis*) was employed (expressed as 1:000$000).

Early on, however, specie was used mainly in colonial ports. Cowrie shells (*zimbos*) and commodities (brazilwood, sugar, tobacco, cattle, cotton, cotton cloth or thread, even slaves) were customarily bartered for trade goods. Where coins were used, Spanish silver *pesos* were common. In the 1640s, during the era of West India

Company occupation of the northeast coast, the Dutch were the first to mint money (florins) for local use. Currency debasement was the rule in Portugal in the late seventeenth century, but following the establishment of colonial mints after gold was discovered in the interior of Brazil (1697 onward), a policy of "strong money" for the mother country was adopted. Gold and silver products of mints at Bahia and Rio de Janeiro were valued differently for Brazilian and Portuguese usage in order to limit the outflow of money from the colony. Gold *dobras*, *peças*, and *escudos*; silver *patacas* and *tostões*; and silver and copper *vintems* and *réis* were produced by these mints. Gold, in the form of bars or ingots and gold dust, was allowed to circulate as legal tender, but only in the region of the mines. Locally restricted currency issues were common in other provinces as well.

Following independence from Portugal (1822), currency shortages spawned widespread counterfeit copper coins. Paper money, in very limited use in the late eighteenth century in Portugal, was promoted by the establishment of the Bank of Brazil (1808–1829); 1853 onward) and by the founding of provincial banks throughout the nineteenth century. A national monetary system was established in 1833, but old coins continued to circulate along with new mintings; foreign coins, such as British sovereigns and U.S. dollars, were also permitted. After 1922 the national bank became the sole issuer of paper notes, and gold coins ceased to be struck.

In 1942 the *cruzeiro* (equal to 1$000 and divided into 100 *centavos*, with its symbol Cr$) succeeded the venerable *milreis*. Subsequent currency reform in 1965 created the *cruzeiro novo*. Since then monetary policies designed to reverse inflation have introduced frequent currency shifts, including the *cruzado* (1986), *cruzado novo* (1989), the return of the *cruzeiro* (1990), and the *cruzeiro real* (1993). Currency reform in 1994 restored the *real* (plural *réais*), first as a basic unit of account or Unit of Real Value (URV) pegged to the U.S. dollar (initially 647 *cruzeiros réais* = 1 URV). In mid-1994 the currency was renamed the *real* (R$).

M. B. LOPES FERNANDES, *Memória das moedas correntes em Portugal*, 2 vols. (1856–1857); S. SOMBRA, *História monetaria do Brasil colónial* (1938); JOÃO PANDIA CALOGERAS, *A política monetária do Brasil* (1960); AMARO CAVALCANTI, *O meio circulante nacional*, vol. 1 (1983); F. DOS SANTOS TRIGUEIROS, *Dinheiro no Brasil*, 2d ed. (1987).

CATHERINE LUGAR

CURUPAYTY, BATTLE OF, a major Paraguayan victory on 22 September 1866 during the WAR OF THE TRIPLE ALLIANCE. The Brazilian and Argentine expeditionary forces had been making steady, if very bloody, progress against the Paraguayans throughout 1866 and, by September, were approaching the fortress of Humaitá from the southwest. Hoping for real negotiations, or at least to buy time, Paraguayan President Francisco Solano López met with the Allied commander, General Bartolomé MITRE, at Yataity Corá.

Though this foray into diplomacy failed, it permitted López's British engineers time enough to construct a 2,000-yard line of deep trenches at Curupayty and to reinforce them with forty-nine cannon and Congreve rocket stands. Five thousand troops under the command of General José Eduvigis DÍAZ guarded this position, which the Allies assaulted in force on 22 September. Unknown to the advancing troops, their naval bombardment, which had begun in the morning, had been totally ineffectual, and when the 11,000 Brazilians and 7,000 Argentines came within range, Díaz poured concentrated blasts of grape and canister into them. The carnage was so dreadful that Mitre gave early orders for a general retirement.

The Allied dead numbered about 9,000, including the son of the Argentine vice president (Mitre's successor), Domingo Faustino Sarmiento. The Paraguayans lost only 50 men. As a result of this debacle, the Allies were unable to resume their advance into Paraguay for fourteen months.

CHARLES J. KOLINSKI, *Independence or Death! The Story of the Paraguayan War* (1965); *The Cambridge History of Latin America*, vol. 3 (1985), pp. 787, 790.

THOMAS L. WHIGHAM

CUYAMEL FRUIT COMPANY, a large banana-producing enterprise in Honduras founded by Samuel ZEMURRAY. After arriving in Puerto Cortés, Honduras, in 1905, Zemurray purchased the properties and concessionaire's rights of William F. Streich. In 1911, with plans of expanding beyond the Honduran northern coast, Zemurray incorporated Cuyamel, only to discover that Honduran president Miguel DÁVILA had negotiated a customs receivership agreement with the United States. The agreement provided Dávila with a loan from New York bankers, secured by a U.S. customs receiver, who would have restricted Cuyamel's duty-free imports. To protect his interests, Zemurray supported Manuel BONILLA CHIRINOS in a coup that ousted Dávila in 1911. In return, the new president granted Zemurray generous concessions. Zemurray turned to large-scale irrigation, flooding of inferior lowlands, and selective pruning that enabled Cuyamel to compete successfully against the UNITED FRUIT COMPANY (UFCO). In 1915, Zemurray expanded Cuyamel's holdings into the Motagua Valley along the disputed border between Honduras and Guatemala. In 1929, UFCO bought out Cuyamel for $31.5 million. The agreement also required Zemurray to retire from the banana industry. He returned to New Orleans as UFCO's largest shareholder, a position he subsequently used to take over the operations of that company.

CHARLES D. KEPNER and JAY H. SOOTHILL, *The Banana Empire* (1935); CHARLES M. WILSON, *Empire in Green and Gold: The Story of the American Banana Trade* (1947); STACY MAY and GALO

PLAZA, *The United Fruit Company in Latin America* (1958); THOMAS P. MC CANN, *An American Company: The Tragedy of United Fruit* (1976).

THOMAS M. LEONARD

CUYO, the historical region of western Argentina that comprises the present-day provinces of Mendoza, San Juan, and San Luis. The region was discovered and colonized by the Governancy of Chile, across the Andes, during the administration of García Hurtado de Mendoza, son of the Viceroy of Peru. Pedro de Castillo founded the towns of Mendoza in 1561 and San Juan in 1562. San Luis was founded in 1596 by Martín de Loyola. During its early decades Cuyo represented the eastern flank of Spanish colonization from central Chile, but isolation increasingly drove the outpost into the commercial and cultural spheres of Tucumán and Córdoba. Mules, hides, dried fruits, and wine were sent to Peru or traded in Tucumán and Córdoba, but scarcely in Santiago. Therefore, when the Viceroyalty of Río de la Plata was established in 1776, Cuyo became part of that colonial unit. Renowned for the quality of its agricultural products, Cuyo attracted Spanish, Italian, and Portuguese immigrants at the end of the nineteenth and the first half of the twentieth century. Wineries, fruit-export enterprises, a flourishing agricultural economy, natural gas, and an excellent university have made it the most dynamic and prosperous area of the Argentine Republic.

WILLIAM J. FLEMING, *Region Versus Nation: Cuyo in the Crosscurrent of Argentine National Development, 1861–1914* (1986).

CÉSAR N. CAVIEDES

CUZCO, a city and department in southeastern Peru. The estimated population of the city in 1985 was 236,000. Geographic diversity characterizes the region as high mountains descend into river valleys that flow to eastern, tropical lowlands. The range of elevations and temperatures creates many distinct ecological zones that influence the economic and social life of the region.

During its early history, the city of Cuzco was the religious and political center of the Inca Empire. Legend dates the founding of the city from the reign of MANCO CAPAC, who may have entered the area around 1200. Under the Inca royal family the city and the empire expanded, especially toward the end of the fifteenth century, when the influence of Cuzco extended north to Ecuador and south to Chile. Tribute was essential to the city's growth. From the lowland valleys came TOBACCO, coca, COTTON, chiles, and yucca; from the highlands, grains, wool, and tubers. Long river valleys, most notably that of the Urubamba, were major population and agricultural centers. Cuzco's location as a crossroad between north and south and highlands and lowlands helped it to emerge as an important economic and political center.

The city of Cuzco became more imposing as the wealth and power of the INCAS expanded. In addition to some 4,000 residential structures, granaries, and storage sheds, the city boasted magnificent religious and imperial structures, built of carefully shaped stones. Central to life in the city before the arrival of Europeans were the palaces of the former emperors and Coricancha (the Palace of the Sun). Many of the most important buildings were around the central square of Aucaypata. Just outside the city was SACSAHUAMÁN, a massive fortress or ceremonial structure of crafted walls made from rocks that weighed up to 300 tons each.

Inca dominance of Cuzco was challenged with the arrival of a small group of Spaniards on the coast of Peru in 1532. Led by Francisco PIZARRO, Spaniards entered Cuzco in November 1533, and declared it La Muy Noble y Gran Ciudad del Cuzco in 1543. Fighting among Spaniards and resistance from Indians slowed but did not prevent Spanish control of Cuzco. New buildings rose on the ruins of the old, at times made from the same stones and foundations of Inca structures. The center of the Inca city became the Spanish Plaza de Armas, the site of the seventeenth-century Cathedral and Jesuit Church of the Compañía, built on the Place of the Serpents.

Spanish owners of landed estates, mines, and textile factories, along with merchants, bureaucrats, and clerics, relied on Indian labor to generate the wealth of the city and region. Indian resistance continued to challenge Spanish control. Revolts in Cuzco in the eighteenth century, especially the revolt of (José) TUPAC AMARU II in 1780, had an influence beyond the region. By the time of this revolt, Cuzco had become a city of complex social and ethnic relationships, a distinctive culture that was the result of centuries of contact between Europeans and Indians. The culture of the old and the new, the Indian and the European, is more evident in Cuzco than in many other Latin American cities. Carleton Beals perhaps captured it best in his *Fire on the Andes* (1934) when he described Cuzco as "two cities, locked in deadly embrace of love and hate."

Cuzco's cultural history includes significant intellectual and artistic achievements. The University of San Ignacio (1622) gave way to the University of San Antonio Abad (1692), which continued as the intellectual center of the city into the twentieth century. In the eighteenth century, an outpouring of art distinguished the city. Cuzco also had writers who achieved fame, beginning with El Inca GARCILASO DE LA VEGA, best known for his *Comentarios reales* (1609). In the nineteenth century, Clorinda MATTO DE TURNER captured the memories of Cuzco in her writings and won international recognition for her *Aves sin nido* (1889), a portrayal of Indian struggles. Cuzco became the Andean center of INDIGENISMO, a complex intellectual and social movement that sought to understand, protect, and further the interests of the Indian peoples of the region.

Independence brought economic change to the city.

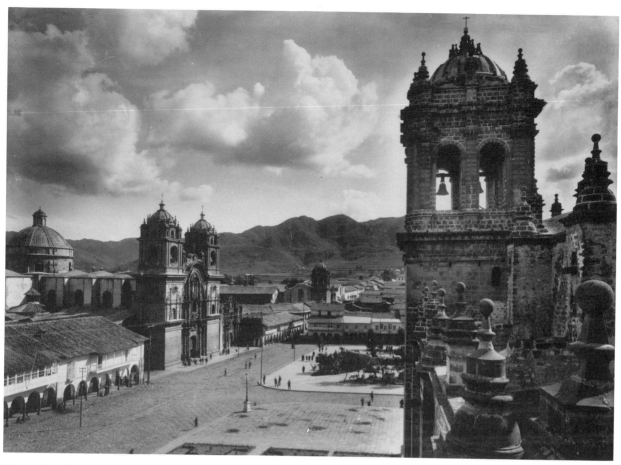

View of Clochers de Cuzco, Peru. In the foreground is the bell tower of the Cuzco cathedral. PHOTO BY MARTÍN CHAMBI. COURTESY OF JULIA CHAMBI.

The textile industry, so important during the colonial period, suffered as foreign cloth and garments entered the Peruvian market. But Cuzco still sat astride the old Lima-Potosí trade route and benefited temporarily from the PERU-BOLIVIA CONFEDERATION. With the confederation's collapse and the rise of the GUANO INDUSTRY, the coast emerged as the dominant economic region of the country. Population data demonstrate the extent of the collapse. The population of the city dropped from 40,000 in 1834 to 18,370 in 1876. Recovery came slowly, and by 1912 the city still claimed only 19,825 residents. Impetus for growth came from railroad links with the outside and new highway construction. Sicuani was the railroad terminal for Cuzco until the arrival of a railhead in Cuzco. The corvée known as the *Conscripción vial*, which required men aged eighteen to twenty and fifty to sixty to work on the roads, was reminiscent of colonial labor drafts in the Andes. Cuzco continued to ship out agricultural products and textiles along these routes as it had done in the past. A new direction for growth in the late nineteenth and early twentieth centuries was the *montaña*, the lower elevations around OLLANTAYTAMBO and MACHU PICCHU. By the 1920s the TOURISM potential of

these and other sites was recognized. This potential was realized beginning in the 1960s, as Cuzco and its many magnificent archaeological sites emerged as leading tourist attractions in the Andes.

The recent history of the city dates from the earthquake of 1950. The rebuilding that took place after the earthquake brought growth and expansion. Accelerated migration from rural areas added to the growth of the city. With the population increase came the *barriadas*, or *pueblos jóvenes*, the new communities common to the peripheries of all the major cities of Peru. Despite the physical and demographic changes, Cuzco still retains much of the past, evident in the carefully preserved monuments and architecture, and in the people, language, and culture of the city.

Much good writing has been done on the history of Cuzco. JOHN H. ROWE describes the architecture and pottery of the city in *An Introduction to the Archaeology of Cuzco* (1944). For Cuzco as the seat of the empire, see BURR CARTWRIGHT BRUNDAGE, *Lords of Cuzco* (1967); and JOHN HEMMING, *The Conquest of the Incas* (1970). VÍCTOR ANGLES VARGAS, *Historia del Cusco incaico*, 3 vols. (1988), narrates the early history of Cuzco in detail. PAULO O. D. DE AZEVEDO, *Cuzco, ciudad histórica: Continuidad y cambio* (1982), provides a brief historical overview with specialized attention to architecture and recent problems. JOSÉ TAMAYO HERRERA analyzes major changes in the city since independence in *Historia social del Cuzco republicano* (1978). He is also the author of *Historia del indigenismo cuzqueño* (1980), a social and intellectual history of Indianist movements in Cuzco. PIERRE L. VAN DEN BERGHE and GEORGE P. PRIMOV analyze the social, economic, and political structure of Cuzco in *Inequality in the Peruvian Andes: Class and Ethnicity in Cuzco* (1977).

JOHN C. SUPER

CUZCO SCHOOL OF PAINTING, the most distinctive major school of painting in Spain's American colonies, which evolved during the seventeenth and eighteenth centuries in the old INCA capital of CUZCO. Indian and MESTIZO artists transformed formal and iconographical types from European art to create a uniquely American style of religious painting, characterized by brilliant color, flattened space, and a strongly decorative aesthetic. Favorite subjects include anecdotal biblical narratives, hieratic figures of the Virgin and saints, and gaily dressed archangels, as well as brightly colored tropical birds and idealized imaginary landscapes without reference to local geography.

The origins of the school can be found in the many Flemish engravings and European paintings that were taken to Peru from Spain, as well as in works by European artists such as the Italian mannerist painter and Jesuit Bernardo Bitti, who was active in Peru and Bolivia between 1575 and 1610. The key figure in establishing the new style was the Indian painter Diego Quispe Tito (1611–after 1681), from a village outside Cuzco, whose uniquely American sensibility exerted a powerful effect on *cuzqueño* painting for over a century.

The popular style of painting that evolved in the eighteenth century from the work of Quispe and his immediate followers is frequently labeled "mestizo," a racial term that suggests a mixture of foreign and indigenous elements. From busy workshops in the prosperous city, painters such as Marco Zapata (active 1748–1764) produced sophisticated baroque compositions for major patrons and religious institutions while other, mostly anonymous painters worked in a more simplified, decorative style to service a vast market that stretched from Ecuador to Chile.

The principal study of viceregal painting in Cuzco is JOSÉ DE MESA and TERESA GISBERT, *Historia de la pintura cuzqueña,* 2d ed., 2 vols. (1982), which incorporates many earlier studies by this prolific Bolivian couple. GISBERT focuses on the distinct iconography of Andean painting in *Iconografía y mitos indigenas en el arte* (1980). Two of the most characteristic subjects of Cuzco painting are studied in the exhibition catalogue *Gloria in Excelsis: The Virgin and Angels in Viceregal Painting of Peru and Bolivia* (1986). Earlier, more general catalogues in English are LEOPOLDO CASTEDO, *The Cuzco Circle* (1976); and PAL KELEMAN, *Peruvian Colonial Painting* (1971).

SAMUEL K. HEATH

DAINZÚ, an archaeological site located 12 miles east of Oaxaca City, near the village of Macuilxóchitl, in Oaxaca, Mexico. Located on the eastern side and at the base of a large, loaf-shaped mountain spur rising from the floor of the Valley of Oaxaca, Dainzú was excavated by Ignacio BERNAL in the 1960s. Although the excavated remains are referred to as Dainzú and date from around the time of Christ, they actually are part of the site of Macuilxóchitl, which has both earlier and later occupations. The most spectacular of the excavated remains are some fifty carved stone slabs that form the vertical walls of a probable temple, called Building A, and are placed on both sides of the temple's stairway. Thought to represent ball players, many of the individuals portrayed on the slabs are attired in helmets and protective gear. They are shown in action and in dynamic positions with spherical objects (perhaps balls) in their hands. Most of the players are facing right, toward an important individual who faces them and stands on what is probably the top of a hill. Among the slabs depicting ball players are slabs carved with persons who may be priests, judging from their attire. Some scholars suggest that the carved stones form a ritual scene of calendrical significance associated with the BALLGAME. Others suggest that a battle scene is represented and that the individuals portrayed are soldiers. Down the slope from Build-

ing A are residences of the elite, one of which contains an elaborate tomb with a carved JAGUAR on its facade. A ball court, similar to those of YAGUL and MONTE ALBÁN, lies some distance away. It dates to the Postclassic period (*ca.* A.D. 900–1521), however, and therefore was built about 1,000 years after the stones were carved. Dainzú is important because the carved stones represent a unique style in the Valley of Oaxaca.

IGNACIO BERNAL and ANDY SEUFFERT, *The Ballplayers of Dainzú,* translated by Carolyn B. Czitrom (1979); GEORGE KUBLER, *Art and Architecture of Ancient America,* 3d ed. (1984), pp. 160–161; MARCUS WINTER, *Oaxaca: The Archaeological Record* (1989), pp. 55–56, 103–104.

MICHAEL D. LIND

DALTON GARCÍA, ROQUE (*b.* 14 May 1935; *d.* 10 May 1975), Salvadoran Marxist writer and activist. Born and educated in San Salvador, Dalton went to Chile to study law and there began his career as a poet, essayist, novelist, and biographer. Returning to El Salvador with strong leftist political leanings, he became part of the literary group known as the Committed Generation. His leftist views forced him into exile in 1961. After several years in Cuba, Dalton traveled extensively in Europe and became closely associated with the ideas of Che GUEVARA and Régis DEBRAY in defense of the Cuban Revolution. After returning clandestinely to El Salvador, where he was the effective founder of the leftist Armed Forces of National Resistance (Fuerzas Armadas de Resistencia Nacional), he was executed by members of the rival Revolutionary Army of the People (Ejército Revolucionario del Pueblo), from which his FARN had broken away, in San Salvador. In addition to his many poems and novels, Dalton wrote a biography, *Miguel Mármol: Los sucesos de 1932 en El Salvador* (1972).

ROQUE DALTON, *El Salvador* (1963); JAMES DUNKERLEY, *The Long War: Dictatorship and Revolution in El Salvador* (1982); LUIS GALLEGOS VALDÉS, *Panorama de la literatura salvadoreña del período precolombino a 1980* (1987), esp. pp. 342–355, and 429–431; JOHN BEVERLEY and MARC ZIMMERMAN, *Literature and Politics in the Central American Revolutions* (1990), esp. pp. 115–141.

RALPH LEE WOODWARD, JR.

See also **El Salvador: Revolutionary Organizations.**

DANCE. *See* **Music: Popular Music and Dance.**

DANCE OF THE MILLIONS, the phrase used to describe the boom-and-bust prosperity associated with the rapid rise and collapse of SUGAR prices in Cuba at the conclusion of World War I. The war stimulated an unprecedented demand for Cuban sugar and great business growth in Cuba from 1914 through the conflict's end. The U.S. price of sugar was fixed at 5.5 cents per pound during the war, which allowed for substantial profits and encouraged rapid expansion of sugar cultivation and speculation in Cuban land and other businesses. Although the entire economy expanded rapidly, speculators and investors also incurred heavy debts in their rush to join the rising prosperity. When price controls ended after the war, prices soared, driven upward by widespread speculation. Sugar reached a peak of 22.5 cents per pound in the United States by May 1920. By this time, however, European beet sugar had resumed production and the shortage of sugar that had stimulated the initial rise in prices no longer existed. Once it became apparent that there was a surplus of sugar, prices plummeted to less than 4 cents per pound by December 1920. The collapse of sugar prices caused widespread financial and business failure.

A similar surge in foreign investment and speculation in Colombia in the 1920s has also been called the Dance of the Millions by some writers.

HUGH THOMAS, *Cuba: The Pursuit of Freedom* (1971), pp. 525–563, provides a detailed description of the Cuban sugar boom of 1912–1920, and ROBERT F. SMITH, *The United States and Cuba: Business and Diplomacy, 1917–1960* (1960), describes its relation to the U.S. economy. See also LELAND HAMILTON JENKS, *Our Cuban Colony: A Study in Sugar* (1928). VERNON LEE FLUHARTY, *Dance of the Millions: Military Rule and the Social Revolution in Colombia, 1930–1956* (1957), pp. 30–35, describes the Colombian Dance of the Millions.

RALPH LEE WOODWARD, JR.

DANISH WEST INDIES, also known as the Danish Virgin Islands, an island group that includes the islands of Saint Croix, Saint Thomas, and Saint John. Denmark's first settlement on Saint Thomas in 1665 failed. In 1670 King Christian V established the Danish West India Company to resettle Saint Thomas. Settlers arrived in 1672, among them bondmen and convicts. The Company claimed Saint John in 1684 but did not occupy it until 1717. Denmark purchased Saint Croix from France in 1733.

A profitable plantation economy developed despite hardships. Generous land grants from the Danish West India Company attracted immigrants. Oddly, most settlers were not Danes but French, German, English, Dutch, and other foreigners. Plantations produced COTTON, INDIGO, TOBACCO, and especially SUGAR. Saint Thomas thrived as a trade center. Crown rule came in 1755 and brought increased prosperity. Once free of the Danish West India Company's monopoly, planters could sell their commodities at higher free-market prices.

Bondmen and convicts proved insufficient as plantation laborers, a situation that the colonists resolved by importing African slaves. The first slave ship brought 103 Africans in 1673. The slave population rose steadily and peaked in 1803 at 35,727. Africans soon vastly outnumbered Europeans. Reliance on slave labor, however, had its problems. A slave rebellion, provoked by the harsh slave code of 1733, rocked Saint John in November 1733. The abolition of the SLAVE TRADE in 1803 restricted the slave supply even though illegal imports continued. Meanwhile, sentiment in Denmark led the government to plan for gradual emancipation. In 1847 authorities passed a law of free birth and decreed the emancipation of all slaves in twelve years. Impatient slaves revolted in early July 1848, took over most of Saint Croix, and demanded immediate freedom. Governor-General Peter von Scholten complied, issuing an emancipation proclamation on 3 July 1848. The crown confirmed the action in September. Modest compensation to slave owners did not come until 1853.

Emancipation did not end labor unrest. To replace slave labor, authorities implemented the Labor Act of 1849, establishing a system of yearly contract labor. Opposition to the contract system led to violence in 1878. Protesters burned homes and shops in Frederiksted, and unrest spread into the countryside. Mary Thomas, dubbed "Queen Mary" by her followers, was one of the leaders of the uprising. The violence, which lasted several days, included the destruction of fifty-three plantations and cane fields. Three Europeans and seventy-four Africans died. Authorities later executed twelve protesters. On 1 October 1879 authorities abolished the Labor Act.

The United States had a long-standing interest in the Danish Virgin Islands. Efforts to purchase the islands failed in 1867 and 1902. Fearful that Germany would gain control over the islands during World War I, the United States forwarded a new proposal that was accepted in 1916. The United States paid $25 million for the islands, the most expensive land acquisition in its history. Formal transfer took place on 31 March 1917.

CHARLES C. TANSILL, *The Purchase of the Danish West Indies* (1932); DARWIN D. CREQUE, *The U.S. Virgins and the Eastern Caribbean* (1968); PEARL VARLACK, *The Virgins: A Descriptive and Historical Profile* (1977); WILLIAM W. BOYER, *America's Virgin Islands: A History of Human Rights and Wrongs* (1983); KAREN FOG OLWIG, *Cultural Adaptation and Resistance on St. John: Three Centuries of Afro-Caribbean Life* (1985).

STEVEN S. GILLICK

DANTAS, MANUEL PINTO DE SOUZA (*b.* 21 February 1831; *d.* 29 January 1894), prime minister of Brazil (1884–1885). One of the leading Liberal politicians of the last decades of the Brazilian Empire, Dantas began his career soon after finishing law school in 1851. He held a number of local and provincial political posts, including provincial president of Alagoas and of his native Bahia. At the same time he was a member of various sessions of the national Chamber of Deputies from 1852 to 1868 and was named minister of agriculture, commerce, and public works in the Zacarias de Góes cabinet in 1866. When that administration fell in 1868, Dantas retired temporarily from electoral politics.

Dantas gained his greatest recognition when he returned to politics as a senator in the 1880s. In a period when the abolition of slavery was increasingly seen as the nation's most pressing problem—it was abolished in 1888—the emperor asked Dantas in 1884 to form a new cabinet that would take steps toward emancipation. Moderate in his views, Dantas described the goals of his cabinet as "neither retreat, nor halt, nor undue haste." Nevertheless, the bill he presented, the central provision of which would free slaves over sixty years of age, set off a storm of opposition in Congress. After attacking the principle of liberating any slave without compensating the former master, his enemies finally forced Dantas's cabinet out of power in 1885. The Conservative ministry that followed then passed a watered-down version of Dantas's SEXAGENARIAN LAW that same year.

With the end of the Brazilian Empire in 1889, Dantas became director of the Bank of Brazil and then the Bank of the Republic, until his death.

ROBERT E. CONRAD, *The Destruction of Brazilian Slavery, 1850–1888* (1972); ROBERT BRENT TOPLIN, *The Abolition of Slavery in Brazil* (1972); EMÍLIA VIOTTI DA COSTA, "Masters and Slaves," chap. 6 in her *The Brazilian Empire: Myths and Histories* (1985).

ROGER A. KITTLESON

See also **Slavery, Abolition of.**

DARIÉ, SANDU (*b.* 1908), Cuban artist and art critic. Born in Romania, Darié studied law at the University of Paris. While there he continued to write art criticism for Romanian newspapers and contributed humorous sketches to the French press. Darié emigrated to Cuba in 1941 and embraced Cuban life and culture; he subsequently became a full citizen. In 1949 he had his first solo exhibit, at the Lyceum in Havana, and another showing in New York. He exhibited at shows in Brazil, Mexico, Italy, Argentina, and Japan, and has pieces in the permanent collection of the Museum of Modern Art in New York. Darié's work is uniquely interactive: through his transformable constructions, such as *Estructura espacial transformable* (1960), the viewer is able to participate in the creative process.

GOVERNMENT OF CUBA, *Pintores Cubanos* (1962) and *Pintores Cubanos* (1974); ADELAIDA DE JUAN, *Pintura cubana: Temas y variaciones* (1978).

KAREN RACINE

DARIÉN, the first Spanish settlement on the North American mainland, was established in 1510 when Martín Fernández de ENCISO captured an Indian village on the hot, swampy Caribbean coast of Panama, which he christened Santa María La Antigua de Darién.

Enciso was not an able leader, and one of his lieutenants, Vasco Núñez de BALBOA, soon took over control of Darién. Balboa established an agricultural economic base for Darién, worked by Indian labor, and the settlement thrived. In 1513, Darién served as the base for Balboa's expedition to find the "Southern sea," during which Balboa became the first European to set eyes on the Pacific Ocean.

Although the crown rewarded Balboa with the title of "*adelantado* of the Southern sea," his own father-in-law, Pedrarias Dávila, contested his control over the settlement. In 1517 Pedrarias beheaded Balboa and assumed control of Darién.

Darién suffered under Pedrarias's administration. In 1519, Pedrarias moved the Spanish population from the swamplands of Darién to the more healthful climate of Panama City. In 1524, Darién was formally abandoned.

MURDO J. MAC LEOD, *Spanish Central America: A Socioeconomic History, 1520–1720* (1973); RALPH LEE WOODWARD, JR, *Central America: A Nation Divided* (2d ed., 1985).

VIRGINIA GARRARD-BURNETT

DARÍO, RUBÉN (*b.* 18 January 1867; *d.* 6 February 1916), born Félix Rubén García Sarmiento in Nicaragua, he was the leading poet writing in Spanish between 1888 and 1916.

Life and Works Darío was born in Metapa (now Cuidad Darío). After his parents separated, he was reared by his great-aunt Bernarda Sarmiento Ramírez and her husband. He studied with the Jesuits and at the National Institute, reading the classics and publishing poetry from age twelve. By age fourteen he had joined the editorial staff of the local newspaper. In 1883 he traveled to El Salvador, where President Rafael Zaldívar enrolled him in school. Upon his return to Nicaragua (1884), he worked as a journalist and read voraciously at the National Library. In 1886 he moved to Chile. Through his friendship with the president's son, Pedro Balmaseda, he became immersed in French poetry, especially the Parnassians, which is the most salient influence in his *Azul*, a collection of short stories and verse, published in Valparaíso (1888).

In 1889, Darío returned to Central America and worked feverishly on his poetry and newspaper articles. The following year he married Rafaela Contreras. They moved to Costa Rica in 1891. In 1892 he was named secretary of Nicaragua's delegation to Spain's celebration of the fourth centennial of Columbus's voyage of discovery. Upon his return, he learned of his wife's death and was named Colombia's consul to Buenos Aires. He married Rosario Murillo in 1893, but left alone for Argentina via New York and Paris. In Paris he met Jean Moreas, Théodore de Banville, and Paul Verlaine, and in New York, José MARTÍ. In Argentina, Darío discharged his consular duties, wrote for *La Nación* and other newspapers, and became the leader of a group of young and brilliant writers. With one of them, the Bo-

livian Ricardo Jaimes Freyre, he founded the literary journal *Revista de América*.

In 1896 Darío took over the leadership of the *modernismo* group. That same year, he published *Los raros*—a collection of essays on American and European writers—and *Prosas profanas*—a book influenced by French Symbolism, although rooted in the Spanish classics. *Prosas*, a deliberate break with Romanticism, became Darío's most imitated work for its innovative form, musicality, beauty, and exoticism. In 1898, *La Nación* sent him to Spain to report on the aftereffects of the Spanish-American War. The results of this endeavor were later collected in *España contemporánea* (1901). While in Madrid he reaffirmed his leadership of modernism and met the younger poets, among them Antonio and Manuel Machado and Juan Ramón Jiménez. He also met Francisca Sánchez, the woman who became his lifetime companion and the mother of his son. In 1900 he moved permanently to Paris.

In 1905, Darío published *Cantos de vida y esperanza*. Its first poem, "Yo soy aquél . . .," rejected his previous "blue verse and profane songs," while continuing his revolutionary treatment of meter, rhythms, and poetic techniques. *Cantos* is perhaps Darío's most accomplished book. In it he also introduced a note absent from his earlier poetry: sociopolitical concerns for the future of Latin America and Hispanic culture. The Spanish defeat in 1898 and Theodore Roosevelt's policies in Central America had awakened Latin Americans to the fact that the United States could no longer be regarded as a trusted neighbor. Instead, it appeared as a menace capable of swallowing the southern half of the continent. *Cantos* manifests this new awareness and the new sense of allegiance to Spain as the mother country.

During the following years Darío maintained his residence in Paris, while visiting Spain and Latin America and publishing a number of important books: *El canto errante* (1907), *El viaje a Nicaragua* (1909), and *Poema del otoño* (1910). In 1911 he joined *Mundial* magazine in Paris. Its publishers took Darío on an advertising trip to the New World the following year. While in Buenos Aires, he wrote *Autobiografía*, a work serialized in *Caras y caretas*. He returned to Paris in 1913. When World War I erupted, Darío was ill and in serious economic straits, but he accepted another lecture tour throughout the Americas. He spoke at Columbia University in New York, where he contracted pneumonia. Taken to Nicaragua, he died in the city of León.

Significance By the time Darío published his first book, *Epistolas y poemas* (1885), at age eighteen, he was the leading Central American poet. Three years later, with the publication of *Azul*, he became the leading poet of the Hispanic world. It has even been said that Darío's poetry divides Hispanic literary history into "before" and "after." His renovation of poetic expression was so thorough that he is still a leading force. In his quest for poetry, he broke away from traditional conventions and maintained no allegiance to any one set of esthetic

Rubén Darío. ORGANIZATION OF AMERICAN STATES.

norms. He learned from the primitives and the standard-bearers of Golden Age poetics—Góngora, San Juan de la Cruz, Saint Teresa d'Ávila, Cervantes, Quevedo—as well as from Gustavo Adolfo Bécquer and the Romantics. To their invaluable lessons he added what he learned from the French Parnassians and Symbolists. He acknowledged his debt and achieved a style unequaled by any other Spanish poet of his day. His range of expression, his inventiveness, and his flawless rendering of music into words are still refreshingly new.

CHARLES D. WATLAND, *Poet-Errant* (1965); *Selected Poems of Rubén Darío*, translated by Lysander Kemp, prologue by Octavio Paz (1965, 1988); ENRIQUE ANDERSON IMBERT, *La originalidad de Rubén Darío* (1967); ÁNGEL RAMA, *Rubén Darío y el modernismo: Circunstancia socio-económica de un arte americano* (1970); GEORGE D. SCHADE and MIGUEL GONZÁLEZ-GERTH, eds., *Rubén Darío: Centennial Studies* (1970); RAYMOND SKYRME, *Rubén Darío and the Pythagorean Tradition* (1975); CATHY LOGIN JRADE, *Rubén Darío and the Romantic Search for Unity: The Modernist Recourse to Esoteric Tradition* (1983); ENRIQUE ANDERSON IMBERT, "Rubén Darío," in *Latin American Writers*, edited by Carlos A. Solé and Maria Isabel Abreu (1989), vol. 1, pp. 397–412.

MARÍA A. SALGADO

See also **Literature**.

DARTIGUENAVE, PHILIPPE-SUDRÉ (*b.* 1863), president of Haiti (1915–1922). Installed as president by the U.S. Marines, he was the first Haitian president since 1879 to be from the south of Haiti and the first mulatto. Dartiguenave supported the U.S. occupation and customs receivership, and relied on the U.S. authorities for financial advice. Contrary to popular opinion, however, he did not surrender absolute control of the island to U.S. interests. In 1922 the vote of the mulatto elite in the south prevented his reelection.

CYRIL L. R. JAMES, *The Black Jacobins*, 2d ed. (1963), is a classic study on Haitian history. A more recent analysis is MICHEL-ROLPH TROUILLOT, *Haiti: State Against Nation* (1990).

DARIÉN DAVIS

D'AUBUISSON, ROBERTO (*b.* 23 August 1943; *d.* 20 February 1992), Salvadoran army officer and political leader. Roberto d'Aubuisson was a career intelligence officer who left the service when a new reformist government seized power in El Salvador on 15 October 1979. An outspoken anti-Communist who opposed social reforms and called for a hard line against leftist rebels in the country's civil war, d'Aubuisson was widely believed to be responsible for human rights violations. His name was frequently associated with the activities of DEATH SQUADS, most notably the assassination on 24 March 1980 of San Salvador's archbishop Oscar Arnulfo ROMERO, as well as with coup conspiracies against the reformist junta.

Youthful and charismatic, d'Aubuisson sought a po-

litical following. He founded the right-wing Nationalist Republican Alliance (Alianza Republicana Nacionalista—ARENA) in 1981 and served briefly as president of the Constituent Assembly (1982–1984), but his higher ambitions were discouraged by the armed forces and by the administration of U.S. president Ronald Reagan, which feared that his reputation would jeopardize congressional support for military aid to El Salvador. Following his defeat by José Napoleón DUARTE in the 1984 presidential election, d'Aubuisson yielded his party leadership post to Alfredo CRISTIANI, a less controversial politician. D'Aubuisson's political influence endured. When Cristiani was elected president in 1989, many observers believed that the charismatic former party leader would wield the real power, but d'Aubuisson's death of cancer three years later at age forty-eight brought a premature end to his career.

There is no biography of d'Aubuisson. A number of press and magazine accounts are useful, among them the obituary in the *New York Times*, 21 February 1992, and CHRISTOPHER DICKEY, "Behind the Death Squads," in the *New Republic* (26 December 1983): 16–21. General works on the Salvadoran crisis are TOMMIE SUE MONTGOMERY, *Revolution in El Salvador: Origins and Evolution* (1982); ENRIQUE A. BALOYRA, *El Salvador in Transition* (1982); and RAYMOND BONNER, *Weakness and Deceit: U.S. Policy and El Salvador* (1984).

STEPHEN WEBRE

DAVIDOVSKY, MARIO (*b.* 4 March 1934), Argentine composer who became a naturalized U.S. citizen. Born in Médanos, province of Buenos Aires, he was a composition student of Guillermo Graetzer in Buenos Aires, where he developed an atonal, abstract lyricism in his compositions, such as String Quartet no. 1 (1954), *Noneto* (1957), and *Pequeño concierto* (1957). He then moved to the United States under a Guggenheim Fellowship and studied with Varèse, Babbit, Ussachevsky, Luening, and Sessions. He was associated with the Columbia-Princeton Electronic Music Center in New York from its inception and was an assistant director from 1965 to 1980. He became director in 1981. Davidovsky has been particularly interested in the combination of acoustic instruments and electronically produced sounds on tape. He is celebrated for his series of Synchronisms, including no. 1 for flute and tape (1963), no. 2 for flute, clarinet, violin, cello, and tape (1964), which was commissioned by the Fromm Foundation for the Tanglewood Festival, and no. 3 for cello and tape (1965). If some of his earlier pieces were somewhat exploratory, Davidovsky's style and personality emerged strongly in his Synchronisms no. 5 for percussion and tape (1969) and no. 6 for piano and tape (1971), which in 1971 was awarded the Pulitzer Prize. In 1974 the series was continued with Synchronisms no. 7 for orchestra and tape and no. 8 for violin and tape.

Davidovsky has produced a remarkable series for solo tape called Electronic Studies. The first dates from

1960, and the third (1965) was written as a homage to Varèse. Other important works include Transients for orchestra (1972) and String Quartet no. 3 (1976).

RODOLFO ARIZAGA, Enciclopedia de la música argentina (1971), p. 110; DAVID ERNST, The Evolution of Electronic Music (1977), pp. 128–129, 142; GÉRARD BÉHAGUE, Music in Latin America: An Introduction (1979), pp. 329, 338–339; New Grove Dictionary of Music and Musicians (1980).

ALCIDES LANZA

DÁVILA, MIGUEL R. (d. 1927), provisional president of Honduras (1907–1908), then elected president (1908–1911). Dávila, a member of the Liberal Party, headed a regime that exemplified the political instability prevailing in Central America at the beginning of the twentieth century. The legendary rivalry between the Nicaraguan dictator José Santos ZELAYA and Guatemala's Manuel ESTRADA CABRERA brought Dávila to power in 1907 when Zelaya engineered a coup against Estrada Cabrera's ally General Manuel BONILLA. During Dávila's term in office, Honduras participated in the 1907 Washington Conference sponsored by Mexico and the United States to restore stability to Central America. He had to deal with numerous rebellions organized by Honduran exiles. Dávila's regime ended in 1911 when Bonilla, financed by banana interests, took advantage of the tensions created by the renegotiation of Honduras's debt with the United States (part of Secretary of State Philander Knox's DOLLAR DIPLOMACY) to regain power.

There are no monographs on Dávila's presidency. For the Honduran context a standard source is RÓMULO ERNESTO DURÓN Y GAMERO, Bosquejo histórico de Honduras, 2d ed. (1956). A more analytical approach is in MARIO POSAS and RAFAEL DEL CID, La construcción del sector público y del estado nacional en Honduras, 1876–1979, 2d ed. (1983). The international rivalries of the period are detailed in DANA G. MUNRO, Intervention and Dollar Diplomacy in the Caribbean, 1900–1921 (1964).

HÉCTOR LINDO-FUENTES

DÁVILA ESPINOZA, CARLOS GUILLERMO (b. 15 September 1887; d. 19 October 1955), Chilean political figure and newspaper publisher. After serving as ambassador to Washington, Dávila continued his education in the United States. Dávila was one of three men who led the Socialist Republic of 100 Days. More conservative than his colleagues, he eventually replaced them until he too was deposed, this time by a military coup under the leadership of General Bartolomé Blanche Espejo. Following the socialist republic's fall, Dávila resumed his newspaper career, working in the United States and eventually acting as editor of the government-owned journal La Nación. Having served as Chile's representative to various international organizations, he subsequently became secretary-general of the Organization of American States, a position he held at the time of his death.

FREDERICK B. PIKE, Chile and the United States, 1880–1962 (1963), pp. 210–211; FREDERICK M. NUNN, Chilean Politics: The Honorable Mission of the Armed Forces 1920–1931 (1970), pp. 171–173.

WILLIAM F. SATER

See also **Chile: Socialist Republic of 100 Days.**

DAWSON AGREEMENT. The vehicle through which the United States granted Nicaragua a critical loan and recognition of its government in exchange for certain concessions. After the ouster of Nicaraguan dictator José Santos ZELAYA in 1909, the U.S. wanted to control Nicaragua's finances. The new Nicaraguan president, Juan ESTRADA, needed a loan, but the U.S. first wanted assurances that any Zelayista influences would be purged from the government—Zelaya had been vehemently antiforeign, and presumably any of his supporters would oppose foreign interests. In October 1910 the U.S. dispatched Thomas Dawson to Managua, to assist in the reestablishment of a constitutional government by ensuring that no Zelayistas maintained power and by preparing Nicaragua for new elections. The Estrada government signed the Dawson Agreement on 27 October. Dawson intimated that if the Nicaraguans did not accept the agreement, there could be outside interference if disorder were to reoccur.

The Dawson Agreement called for the destruction of Zelaya's monopolies, the establishment of a claims commission to compensate foreigners for losses incurred during the civil war, U.S. supervision of a customs receivership based on the Dominican Republic model, and the creation of a new constitution by the Constituent Assembly. The U.S. agreed to recognize the Estrada government and to reorganize Nicaragua's finances through a loan secured by customs revenues.

WILLIAM KAMMAN, A Search for Stability: United States Diplomacy Toward Nicaragua, 1925–1933 (1968), esp. pp. 12–13; LESTER D. LANGLEY, The Banana Wars: United States Intervention in the Caribbean, 1898–1934 (1985), esp. p. 65; RALPH LEE WOODWARD, JR., Central America: A Nation Divided (1985), esp. p. 196.

SHANNON BELLAMY

See also **United States–Latin American Relations.**

DAWSON ISLAND, Chilean land mass of about 8 square miles located in the central section of the Strait of MAGELLAN, where it takes a northwestern turn and travels away from the Seno del Almirantazgo. On the continental shore, and facing the northern tip of the island, lies Puerto del Hambre (Port Famine), the site where Pedro SARMIENTO DE GAMBOA tried unsuccessfully in 1584 to establish a permanent settlement. Wind-swept Dawson Island houses a detachment of the Chilean Marines, whose barracks held political prisoners during the first dictatorship of Carlos IBÁÑEZ DEL CAMPO (1927–1931) and during the early years (1974–1978) of General Augusto PINOCHET's rule.

CÉSAR N. CAVIEDES

DAZA, HILARIÓN (*b.* 14 January 1840; *d.* 27 February 1894), president of Bolivia (1876–1879). Born in Sucre, Daza was trained as a soldier and rose to the rank of colonel under Mariano MELGAREJO (1864–1871). In 1870 he defected to revolutionaries, who deposed Melgarejo on 15 January 1871. Gen. Agustín Morales, the leader of the revolution, died in 1872, and his civilian successors showed little ability to consolidate power. Daza, head of the elite Colorado battalion, seized power in 1876. In constant need of funds for his army, Daza imposed a new tax on the Chilean mining concessions along the Pacific coast (1878). This tax, which immediately provoked a Chilean attack against Bolivia's coastal territory, resulted in the WAR OF THE PACIFIC (1879–1884). Repeated Chilean victories led not only to Daza's downfall at the end of December 1879, but also to Bolivia's loss of the guano and nitrate-rich coastal area. Daza's major political accomplishment was the calling of the Constitutional Convention of 1878, whose work led to the adoption of the Constitution of 1880, the longest lasting in Bolivian history (1938). Daza was assassinated in 1894 in Uyuni by persons who claimed he was trying to regain the presidency.

HERBERT S. KLEIN, *Parties and Political Change in Bolivia, 1880–1952* (1969), pp. 14–19; ENRIQUE VIDAURRE RETAMOZO, *El presidente Daza* (1975).

ERWIN P. GRIESHABER

DE JESUS, CLEMENTINA (*b.* 1902; *d.* 1987), Brazilian samba singer who achieved national acclaim late in life. Born to a musical family in Valença, Rio de Janeiro State, Clementina, as she is called, was singing by age twelve with the Carnaval singing group Moreninha das Campinas. At fifteen, she frequented *samba de roda* sessions in the Oswaldo Cruz neighborhood, and later paraded with the Portela and Mangueira SAMBA schools. For most of her life, Clementina had to work as a maid to support herself, even though she was a superb samba vocalist and a living archive of old musical forms such as *lundu, jongo,* and *partido alto* (a type of samba). Finally, at the age of sixty she was "discovered" by critic-impresario Hermínio Bello de Carvalho, who arranged numerous concert appearances for Clementina. She performed on stage with the likes of classical guitarist Turíbio Santos and in 1963 starred with Paulinho da Viola, Araci Cortes, and several others in the musical *Rosa de ouro*. In 1970, when she was sixty-eight, Clementina recorded her first album, "Clementina, cade você?" (Clementina, Where Are You?), and was celebrated as a national musical treasure. Many leading Brazilian art-

ists, such as Milton NASCIMENTO, invited her to perform duets on their albums.

RITA CAÚRIO, *Brasil Musical* (1988).

CHRIS McGOWAN

DE LA HUERTA, ADOLFO (*b.* 26 May 1881; *d.* 9 July 1955), interim president of Mexico in 1920 and an important figure among the Constitutionalists during the MEXICAN REVOLUTION. De la Huerta was born to an important family of Guaymas, in the state of Sonora. His family supported his studies in Hermosillo, where he obtained a teaching certificate in music. In 1900 he abandoned a career in that field to maintain his family by working in a variety of bookkeeping posts. In 1908 he joined the Anti-Reelectionist Club, becoming secretary in 1910. In that year, however, his antigovernment activities cost him his managerial job. In 1911 he entered local politics, defeating Plutarco ELÍAS CALLES to become the local deputy to the state legislature.

Having joined the Constitutionalists under Venustiano CARRANZA on 20 February 1913, de la Huerta served as Carranza's *oficial mayor* (chief clerk) of government from 1915 to 1916. His other positions included interim governor of Sonora (1916–1917), consul general in New York City (1918), senator (1918), and governor of Sonora (1919–1920).

De la Huerta supported the opposition to Carranza that resulted in the Plan of Agua Prieta and, after Carranza's death, served as provisional president of the republic, from 1 June to 30 November 1920. On the election of Alvaro OBREGÓN he joined the cabinet as secretary of the treasury (1920–1923), but when Obregón supported Calles for the presidency, de la Huerta led the first major, and most important, rebellion against the post-Revolutionary government (7 December 1923). Despite the support of a large part of the army and the civilian political community, the rebellion failed, and de la Huerta went into exile in Los Angeles, where he survived by giving piano lessons until 1935.

President Lázaro CARDENAS appointed him inspector general of Mexican consulates in the United States, a post he held until 1946, when he retired. His son, Adolfo, also became a senator from his home state, and his brother Alfonso was a revolutionary general.

ADOLFO DE LA HUERTA, *Memorias* (1957); JOHN W. F. DULLES, *Yesterday in Mexico: A Chronicle of the Revolution, 1919–1936* (1961); and ALVARO MATUTE, *La carrera del caudillo: Historia de la Revolución, período 1917–1924* (1980).

RODERIC AI CAMP

DE LEÓN, MARTÍN (*b.* 1765; *d.* 1833), successful Mexican rancher, colonizer, and founder of Victoria, Texas. De León was born in Burgos, Tamaulipas, in Mexico, to Spanish parents. He became a muleteer and merchant, and in 1790 joined the Fieles de Burgos Regiment in

Nuevo Santander, reaching the rank of captain. He married Patricia de la Garza in 1795 and had ten children who became community leaders in Texas and northern Mexico. In 1824, De León founded the colony of Victoria on the Guadalupe River with forty-one Mexican families from Tamaulipas. De León's cattle raising made Victoria one of the most prosperous of the Texas colonies. He died in the cholera epidemic of 1833.

VICTOR M. ROSE, *Some Historical Facts in Regard to the Settlement of Victoria, Texas* (1883), repr. as *A Republication of . . . Victor Rose's History of Victoria,* edited by J. W. PETTY, JR. (1961); ROY GRIMES, ed., *300 Years in Victoria County* (1968); ARTHUR B. J. HAMMETT, *The Empresario Don Martín de León* (1973).

A. CAROLINA CASTILLO CRIMM

DE SOTO, HERNANDO. *See* **Soto, Hernando de.**

DEATH SQUADS. Death squads appeared in Latin America in the late 1960s as a consequence of increasing revolutionary activity. The aim of death squads is to destroy an opponent's infrastructure through terrorism. Although death squads exist on the left and on the right of the political spectrum, they are most often associated with extreme rightists. Members of right-wing death squads are often recruited from police and military forces, or from paramilitary organizations. Rightist death squads are usually financed by wealthy conservatives and work closely with repressive national governments and their security forces in an alliance that has allowed them to operate with impunity.

Death squads were originally associated mainly with political instability in Central America, but they have been increasingly active in South America too. In the late 1960s, the military government in Brazil gave covert approval for the use of death squads against real or suspected opponents of the regime. In the 1970s and early 1980s, death squads of both the Right and the Left operated in Argentina, but the military regime's use of death squads in its DIRTY WAR against suspected leftists was especially brutal. Victims of Brazilian and Argentine death squads included intellectuals, students, journalists, workers, priests and nuns, and common criminals. A recent trend in Brazil is the use of death squads by businessmen to murder orphaned street children.

The Andean countries of Colombia and Peru also have been plagued by death squads in the 1980s. In 1987 there were 137 active paramilitary death squads in Colombia. The most notorious in Colombia is the right-wing death squad MAS, or Death to Kidnappers. Formed in 1981, MAS has links to the drug cartels and the armed forces, and is believed to have committed some 500 murders by decapitation of peasants and left-wing leaders, including the country's only Indian priest. In 1987 priests advocating liberation theology were killed at the rate of one each month. The most famous case of right-wing death squad brutality was the October 1987 murder of presidential candidate Jaime Pardo Leal, who had identified retired and active military officers as ringleaders of Colombian death squads.

Peru's state-sponsored police antiterrorist unit Sinchis also has gained notoriety. Founded in 1984 to combat leftists, especially the Marxist group Sendero Luminoso (Shining Path), Sinchis has conducted summary executions of suspects with little fear of official condemnation. Sendero death squads are active, as are a variety of peasant groups who have committed retribution killings.

The most notorious death squads operated in Honduras, Guatemala, and El Salvador. The Honduran Anticommunist Movement, known by its Spanish acronym MACHO, appeared in 1982 and targeted liberal politicians, students, labor leaders, and Indians suspected of leftist tendencies. Emerging in the 1960s, the Guatemalan Organized National Anticommunist Movement murdered leftists and peasants suspected of being guerrilla sympathizers. Another Guatemalan group that appeared in the late 1970s, the Secret Anticommunist Army, specialized in the assassination of union leaders, students, politicians, and professionals who questioned the status quo. Until their exposure in the 1980s, urban death squads in Guatemala were controlled directly from the National Palace.

El Salvadorian death squads of the Left and Right have achieved special notoriety due to their violent acts. The Farabundo Martí Front for National Liberation (FMLN), a leftist organization, engaged in the murder of military and political leaders and their U.S. advisers, while rightist death squads retaliated by killing intellectuals, clerics, and anyone else suspected of supporting the FMLN. In 1966 police and army officers joined with the National Liberation Movement, an extreme-right political party, to create the Mano Blanca (White Hand) death squads. When Mano Blanca's close association with the government and the police became public and embarrassed the regime, it was replaced by OJO POR OJO (Eye for Eye). In 1977 the White Warriors Union became known for terrorism against Jesuits, and in 1980 the Maximiliano Hernández Martínez Brigade organized to assassinate Christian Democrat and Marxist leaders. Many of the recruits for El Salvador's death squads came from ORDEN, a paramilitary organization founded by ex-army major Roberto D'AUBUISSON. It is believed that D'Aubuisson and the death squads associated with ORDEN were responsible for the murders of Archbishop Oscar Arnulfo ROMERO, four American Maryknoll nuns, and a group of Jesuit priests in 1980. Though the precise number of deaths in Latin America attributed to leftist and rightist death squads is unknown, some place the death toll at more than 100,000.

PETER FLYNN, *Brazil: A Political Analysis* (1971); GARY E. MC CUEN, *Political Murder in Central America: Death Squads and U.S. Policies* (1984); REPORT OF THE ARCHDIOCESE OF SÃO PAULO, *Torture in Brazil* (1986); DAVID ROCK, *Argentina, 1567–1987: From Spanish Colonization to Alfonsín* (1987); AMNESTY INTERNA-

TIONAL, *El Salvador Death Squads, A Government Strategy* (1988); JAVIER TORRES, *The Armed Forces of Colombia and the National Front* (1990); MARTHA K. HUGGINS, ed., *Vigilantism and the State in Modern Latin America: Essays on Extra-legal Violence* (1991); DEBRAH POOLE and GERJERDO RENIKUE, *Peru: Time of Fear* (1992).

SONNY B. DAVIS

See also **Guatemala: Terrorist Organizations.**

DEBRAY, [JULES] RÉGIS (*b.* 2 September 1940), French intellectual and Marxist philosopher. Debray was Ché GUEVARA's most articulate interpreter, but after Guevara's death in the disastrous 1967 Bolivian revolution, he synthesized the Leninist traditional view of revolution and Guevarist *focoismo* (revolution from a rural guerrilla center, or *foco*).

Debray became a student of the French Communist ideologue Louis Althusser in the early 1960s. While traveling in revolutionary Latin America, he became convinced that only insurrection, conducted according to local conditions, could bring successful revolution. Debray's most influential book, *Revolution in the Revolution?* (1967), popularized the *foco* philosophy of Guevara.

Three years in a Bolivian prison (1967–1970) and Marxist successes achieved without *focoismo* caused Debray to admit strategic mistakes. Nonetheless, he never criticized Guevara, but did criticize Chilean president Salvador ALLENDE and Uruguay's urban guerrilla Tupamaros for not adhering to the Cuban position. Many insist that his novel of revolutionary alienation, *The Undesirable* (1975), is autobiographical.

LEO HUBERMAN and PAUL M. SWEEZY, eds., *Régis Debray and the Latin American Revolution* (1968); RICHARD GOTT, *Guerrilla Movements in Latin America* (1970); HARTMUT RAMM, *The Marxism of Régis Debray* (1978).

PAT KONRAD

See also **Communism.**

DEBRET, JEAN-BAPTISTE (*b.* 1768; *d.* 1848), French painter. Under the leadership of Joachim Lebreton (1760–1819), secretary of the fine arts class in the Institute of France, Debret left his country in 1816 and went to Rio de Janeiro with the French group known as the FRENCH ARTISTIC MISSION, which had been invited by the Portuguese government. The group was composed of Nicolas Antoine Taunay (1755–1830), a landscape painter; his brother, Auguste Marie Taunay (1768–1824), a sculptor; Auguste Henri Victor GRANDJEAN DE MONTIGNY (1776–1850), an architect; Charles S. Pradier (1768–1848), an engraver; Sigismund Neukomm (1778–1858), a composer; and François Ovide, a specialist in mechanics. Although Debret was classified as a history painter, his first works in Brazil were portraits of the royal family, decorative paintings for public festivities,

and stage settings for the Royal Theatre São João in Rio de Janeiro. It took ten years to establish the Brazilian Academy of Fine Arts, where the members of the French group were supposed to teach. Meanwhile, Debret taught his students in a private house.

Debret's best-known work is a series of drawings depicting Brazilian life and culture, which was published in three volumes in 1834 and 1839 under the title *Voyage pittoresque et historique au Brésil*. The drawings and the explanatory texts that accompany them may be considered the most striking documents on Brazilian daily life in the first decades of the nineteenth century. Following what he calls a "logical order," Debret began his book with descriptions of Indians belonging to several tribes. Although he had not traveled outside Rio de Janeiro,

Charrúa chief. Engraving by Debret. ICONOGRAPHIA.

Nègres scieurs de long, lithograph from Jean Baptiste Debret's *Voyage pittoresque et historique au Brésil*, vol. 2 (Paris, 1834–1839). BY PERMISSION OF THE HOUGHTON LIBRARY, HARVARD UNIVERSITY.

various travelers gave him the information he needed to represent the Indian way of life in the interior. No one better than Debret depicted slave life in Rio de Janeiro, and his drawings shocked the members of the Brazilian Historical and Geographical Institute because of their realism.

As a history painter, Debret also depicted historical events of the late colonial period: Her Royal Highness Princess LEOPOLDINA disembarking in Rio de Janeiro, the coronation of King JOÃO VI, the baptism of Princess MARÍA DA GLÓRIA, the oath to the Constitution, and the coronation of PEDRO I as emperor of Brazil.

AFONSO ARINOS DE MELO FRANCO, *Jean-Baptiste Debret: Estudos inéditos* (1974); AFFONSO DE ESCRAGNOLLE TAUNAY, *A missão artística de 1816* (1956).

MARIA BEATRIZ NIZZA DA SILVA

DEBT PEONAGE. Labeled "debt slavery" by those critical of it, debt peonage is a general term for several categories of coerced or controlled labor resulting from the advancement of money or goods to individuals or groups who find themselves unable or unwilling to repay their debt quickly. As a consequence they are obliged to continue working for the creditor or his assignees until the debt is repaid, and are often further coerced to borrow more or to agree to other obligations or entanglements. According to the traditional view, these individuals, once indebted, whether because of inadequate wages or employer fraud, were reduced to servitude and, in theory, to an inability to leave the workplace to which they have contracted.

Such peonages are usually found in societies with deep class or caste divisions in which elites, in spite of labor shortages, are able to restrict movement, sometimes by so-called vagrancy laws, and to control custom or law so that migration or flight, reneging on debts, and formal protest against conditions, are limited or prohibited. Some observers have associated debt peonage with paternalistic societies in which wage labor has not yet emerged as a dominant form.

In the aftermath of the Conquest and faced with the obvious and precipitous decline of indigenous populations, the European rulers of the new colonies abandoned the haphazard measures of the early years and sought more formal organization of the labor they required for commercial agriculture and mining. Where Indians survived, they usually retained at least initial access to the resources needed for their subsistence. Therefore, they resisted working for the intruders under the conditions offered, prompting the state and would-be employers to adopt coercive measures. These included Indian SLAVERY (abolished by about 1550 in the core areas of the empires) and African slavery, coerced wage labor (*repartimientos* or *mitas*), and debt peonage or servitude. Prohibitions against *adelantos* (advances) to Indians appear in the third quarter of the sixteenth century. Favorite spots to catch Indians were at the entrances to market towns or at church doors on days of obligatory attendance. Peonage of various kinds grew in the late seventeenth century and after as ENCOMIENDA and draft-labor systems declined, as the labor shortage caused by Indian population decline worsened, and as new haciendas and textile *obrajes* searched for a resident workforce. Slavery and forced labor continued on the empire's fringes, in the mining industry in Upper Peru that relied on *mitas* until independence, and on lowland plantations where black slavery predominated. As the population recovered and the economy and society stabilized, however, the general tendency favored labor mobilization and control to shift over time from more to less coercive forms, including debt peonage.

As it developed, colonial debt peonage embraced several systems of labor recruitment. In its seasonal form, recruiters advanced money or goods (*enganche*) to induce Indians and peasants, usually from the highlands, to go to the lowlands to work the harvest season on monocultural plantations. Advances of money or the goods to be worked on were also behind many of the "putting out" *derramas* or *repartos de efectos* of the eighteenth century.

In the highlands of Mesoamerica and the Andes, subsistence villages and nearby plantations often lived in symbiosis. It was to the large landowners' advantage to have a reliable workforce for which they were not responsible outside the planting, weeding, and harvesting seasons. The villagers found the large estate useful for providing cash for tribute and other obligations as well as for money purchases. Often the bond was many small

debts from landowners to peasants. Debt peonage, *mitas*, *derramas*, etc., continued from the colonial period into the twentieth century, although scholars now believe that colonial peonage, in most areas, was far from being as pervasive and dominant as once thought.

In the nineteenth and twentieth centuries debt peonage took new forms. In isolated or peripheral areas of the new nations, especially in semideserts or jungles, local landowners and political bosses became very powerful, and their mines or haciendas were able to recruit and control labor through the *tienda de raya*, a system characterized by the "company store" and the "running tab." In some places private police forces prevented escape; in others the national army or police cooperated by pursuing and punishing those who fled. Rubber plantations were especially notorious, and those of the Putumayo region in Colombia and Peru, and in Chiapas, Tabasco, and Campeche in Mexico were the scenes of scandalous brutalities, backed up by the indifference or cooperation of the government. While debt may have been the official excuse for detention of workers in these cases, conditions were more like chattel slavery backed up by brute force.

The abolition of SLAVERY in the nineteenth century created the problem of finding a substitute labor force, and debt was among the devices used. Sugar plantations in Cuba and the Dominican Republic used debt to finance COLONOS through the dead season and to pro-

Picking coffee at San Isidro, ca. 1875. Reproduced from Eadweard Muybridge, *Central America Album*, vol. 2. BOSTON ATHENAEUM.

vide them with funds to buy seed, equipment, and daily necessities while they awaited the *zafra* (harvest) on their rented parcels, some of which were large and prosperous. Variations of debt peonage still surface from time to time in the late twentieth century, especially in the poorer nations.

Academic debate has led to the abandonment of the old view that debt labor was monolithically exploitive and harsh. In the colonial period villagers sometimes preferred it to the difficulties of life in the village or *encomienda*. In the national period, loans from employers were one of the few opportunities for the poor to obtain money for improvements.

Where elites lost their cohesion and competed for scarce labor, and when rural police were few and ineffective, peons could shop around for bargains, flee from creditors with impunity, and thus had some bargaining power. One must conclude, then, that in its numerous forms and degrees of exploitation and servitude, debt peonage varied widely over time and space.

More recent research, for example, on north-central Mexico (the Bajío) and coastal Peru, has suggested a different picture, particularly for the nineteenth century. The need for wage income among the rural poor and their willingness to work in the cash sector increased dramatically as population growth and land loss in the late colonial and early national periods made subsistence more difficult and survival less certain. With pressures mounting and more and more families seeking employment, those able to obtain steady work and food at advantageous prices on the HACIENDAS and who were allowed to run up debts at the hacienda store, far from seeing their condition as "slavery," felt themselves a labor aristocracy, and their peers envied them as such. If the worker was dissatisfied with his or her situation or the hacienda with the worker, there were always large numbers of land-short, desperate peasants and "free" laborers ready to take their place. A feared punishment was expulsion from the property, and the haciendas made little effort to seek to bring back those who fled, even if they owed money.

Also, before the last quarter of the nineteenth century, employers and the state had such limited political control over the countryside that enforcing peonage on individuals or a population that actively resisted was almost impossible. Where—for example, in southern Mexico and Chiapas—planters depended on a seasonal labor force drawn from intact indigenous villages rather than on workers resident on the property, the Indians' attachment to their home communities made mobilization and control easier, but peonage remained largely voluntary.

The limit case for the severity of debt servitude, and one in which extraeconomic coercion did predominate, was the involuntary peonage enforced in late-nineteenth-century Guatemala. Under laws intended to provide workers for export coffee production, Guatemala's Indians faced the choice of "voluntary" contracts requiring several months' labor a year for very low wages on the export plantations or repeated stints of forced wage labor (*mandamientos*) demanded by the planters and mobilized by the state. The threat of direct coercion pushed individuals into the debt contracts that provided the only, and that imperfect, protection from such drafts.

Debt peonage, however, whether voluntary or involuntary, tended to be an expensive and unwieldy form of labor mobilization, requiring that employers carry on their books large amounts of "dead" capital committed as advances and in some cases to employ a number of recruiters and policing agents, all of which added to labor costs. By the early twentieth century, population growth in most areas of Latin America, together with declining resources available to rural populations and new "needs" that could be satisfied only with cash, were at once pushing and drawing more and more individuals into free labor, without need of large advances or debt coercion.

SILVIO ZAVALA, "Orígenes coloniales del peonaje en México," in *El trimestre económico* 10, no. 4 (1943–1944): 711–748; FRIEDRICH KATZ, "Labor Conditions on Haciendas in Porfirian Mexico: Some Trends and Tendencies," in *Hispanic American Historical Review* 54, no. 1 (1974): 1–47; KENNETH DUNCAN and IAN RUTLEDGE, eds., *Land and Labour in Latin America* (1977); ARNOLD J. BAUER, "Rural Workers in Spanish America: Problems of Peonage and Oppression," in *Hispanic American Historical Review* 59, no. 1 (1979): 34–63 (see also "Forum," a discussion of this essay, in 59, no. 2 [1979]: 478–489); PETER BLANCHARD, "The Recruitment of Workers in the Peruvian Sierra at the Turn of the Century: The Enganche System, in *Inter-American Economic Affairs* 33, no. 3 (1979): 63–83; HARRY CROSS, "Debt Peonage Reconsidered: A Case Study in Nineteenth-Century Zacatecas, Mexico," in *Business History Review* 53, no. 4 (1979): 473–495; DAVID MC CREERY, "Debt Servitude in Rural Guatemala, 1876–1936," in *Hispanic American Historical Review* 63, no. 4 (1983): 735–759; ROGER PLANT, *Sugar and Modern Slavery: A Tale of Two Countries* (1987).

DAVID MCCREERY
MURDO J. MACLEOD

See also **Sugar Industry.**

DECENA TRÁGICA, "the tragic ten days" of violence that erupted in Mexico City as a result of a revolt against the government of Francisco I. MADERO that began on 9 February 1913. The rebels, led by generals Félix DÍAZ, Manuel Mandragón, and Bernardo REYES, failed to take the National Palace but seized a strong position at LA CIUDADELA, the army's ammunition depot. General Victoriano HUERTA was appointed commander of the government forces.

For ten days artillery fire raked the capital, causing extensive damage and fueling cries for a settlement that weakened support for the already tottering Madero government. On 18 February troops loyal to Huerta, under the command of General Aureliano Blanquet, seized Francisco Madero, while Huerta arrested his brother Gustavo. With Madero effectively deposed, U.S. ambassador Henry Lane WILSON mediated talks between Huerta and Díaz, which led to the PACT OF THE EMBASSY recognizing Huerta as provisional president. Madero was assassinated four days later.

STANLEY R. ROSS, *Francisco I. Madero: Apostle of Mexican Democracy* (1955); KENNETH J. GRIEB, *The United States and Huerta* (1969); MICHAEL C. MEYER, *Huerta: A Political Portrait* (1972).

KENNETH J. GRIEB

DECOUD, HECTOR FRANCISCO (*b.* 1855; *d.* 1930), Paraguayan historian and journalist. Born in Asunción, Decoud was a mere youth when the disastrous WAR OF THE TRIPLE ALLIANCE began in 1864. Entering the army as a noncommissioned officer, he fought in several battles before being arrested, together with his mother, by the dictator Francisco Solano LÓPEZ. Though his imprisonment was brief, he was poorly treated, and this left him with a lifelong hatred of López, a hatred that was reflected in his historical writings.

After the war, Decoud dedicated himself to journalism, working for *La Regeneración* and other Asunción newspapers. In 1882, he was appointed district attorney, but he resigned that post the following year after having been elected a national deputy, a position he held until 1887.

Decoud found the time during subsequent years to produce many highly partisan historical works. He focused on the Triple Alliance War and on the figure of López, whom he regarded as the worst sort of tyrant. His many studies included *Sobre los escombros de la guerra: Una década de vida nacional, 1869–1880* (1925), *Guerra del Paraguay: La masacre de Concepción ordenada por el mariscal López* (1926), *La revolución del comandante Molas* (1930), and *Elisa Lynch de Quatrefages* (published posthumously in 1939). Decoud died in Asunción.

WILLIAM BELMONT PARKER, *Paraguayans of To-Day* (repr. 1967), pp. 305–306; JACK RAY THOMAS, *Biographical Dictionary of Latin American Historians and Historiography* (1984).

THOMAS L. WHIGHAM

DECOUD, JOSÉ SEGUNDO (*b.* 1848; *d.* 4 March 1909), Paraguayan statesman. Born into a prominent Asunción family, Decoud began his studies in the Paraguayan capital before moving on to the Colegio Nacional of Concepción del Uruguay, in Argentina. At the beginning of the 1860s, he transferred to the University of Buenos Aires, where he studied law. At the beginning of the WAR OF THE TRIPLE ALLIANCE in 1864, Decoud joined with his brother Juan Francisco and other Paraguayan exiles to found the Legión Paraguaya, a military unit that fought with the Argentines against Paraguayan President Francisco Solano LÓPEZ. An ardent Liberal, Decoud was anxious to see a constitutional regime es-

tablished in Paraguay. When the secret clauses of the Triple Alliance treaty were published, however, he denounced the territorial claims they made against Paraguay and resigned his position in the *legión*.

After the war, Decoud returned to Asunción, where he became editor of *La Regeneración* and a key member of the 1870 Constitutional Convention. Annoyed by infighting among the Liberals, he supported the rise of Conservative Cándido BAREIRO and, later, of generals Bernardino CABALLERO and Patricio ESCOBAR. From 1879 until the end of the century, he was a member of every cabinet except one and was generally regarded as the most influential politician in the country throughout this time. He provided the ideological argument behind Paraguayan conservatism, formulating the original party platform when the Caballeristas organized the Asociación Nacional Republicana (or Colorado Party) in 1887.

Decoud was also active in diplomatic and educational affairs. He attempted at one point to create new *colegios nacionales* in several communities of the interior, but his plans were vetoed at the last moment. His fluency in many languages and his superb private library made him the focus of much intellectual interest, not only for Paraguayans but also for foreign visitors to the Platine countries.

HARRIS G. WARREN, *Rebirth of the Paraguayan Republic: The First Colorado Era, 1878–1904* (1985), *passim*; CARLOS ZUBIZARRETA, *Cien vidas paraguayas*, 2d ed. (1985), pp. 195–197.

THOMAS L. WHIGHAM

DEGOLLADO, SANTOS (*b.* 1811; *d.* 1861), Mexican liberal general and cabinet minister. Degollado was born in the city of Guanajuato during the wars for Mexico's independence from Spain. Since his father was a supporter of the insurgency, the Spanish government confiscated his property. On the death of his father, an uncle took Degollado to Mexico City. In October 1828, Degollado moved to Morelia, where he took a job as a notary's clerk and studied in his spare time. Recognizing Degollado's organizational skills, the governor of Michoacán, Melchor OCAMPO, named him secretary of the Colegio de San Nicolás, and in 1846 Degollado served briefly as a substitute for Ocampo.

As a foot soldier, Degollado dedicated himself to the struggle against SANTA ANNA and rose through the ranks to general. After the triumph of the Revolution of AYUTLA (1854), he was elected to the Constitutional Convention of 1856–1857 as a representative of the state of Michoacán. In 1857, he was elected governor of that state but served only a few months before resigning to join the forces of Benito Juárez in the War of the REFORM. On 27 March 1858, Juárez named Degollado his minister of war and general of the federal army. Degollado also served briefly as minister of foreign relations during the first months of 1860. A talented and tireless organizer of armies, Degollado was notably less successful as their leader in battle. After his subordinate, Manuel Doblado, confiscated silver from British mine owners, Degollado took responsibility and promised repayment. Then, without authorization, he sought a negotiated settlement to the war, with a British official, George W. Mathew, as mediator. Juárez reacted to this step by removing Degollado from his command and replacing him with Jesús GONZÁLEZ ORTEGA, who led the army Degollado had organized to victory over the conservatives in late 1860. González Ortega paid homage to Degollado when the liberal army marched into Mexico City. Degollado received another command in Michoacán to pursue the guerrillas who had killed Melchor Ocampo, but he was ambushed, captured, and executed by the conservatives.

WALTER V. SCHOLES, *Mexican Politics During the Juárez Regime, 1855–1872* (1957); RICHARD N. SINKIN, *The Mexican Reform, 1855–1876: A Study in Liberal Nation-Building* (1979); *Diccionario Porrúa de historia, biografía y geografía de México,* 5th ed. (1986).

D. F. STEVENS

DEGREDADO, a "degraded" person, one who was convicted of crimes by royal and Inquisition courts and sent to the colonies or the galleys to serve the sentence. The Portuguese crown used this punishment to rid Portugal of petty criminals and social deviants. As they explored Africa and Brazil, Portuguese sea captains left *degredados* ashore to learn local languages and customs. Later, *degredados* figured prominently in the early colonization of Angola and Brazil. Although officials protested receiving *degredados* in Brazil, they themselves adopted the practice and sentenced Brazilian criminals and deviants to Africa, the galleys, or frontier outposts.

SÔNIA A. SIQUEIRA, *A Inquisição Portuguesa e a sociedade colonial* (1978); A. J. R. RUSSELL-WOOD, *A World on the Move: The Portuguese in Africa, Asia, and America* (1992).

ALIDA C. METCALF

See also **Inquisition: Brazil.**

DEIRA, ERNESTO (*b.* July 1928; *d.* 1986), Argentine artist. Born in Buenos Aires, Deira turned to pop art, expressionism, and informalism to define a style halfway between abstract and figurative painting. He studied with Leopoldo Torres Agüero and Leopoldo Presas in the 1950s. Early works were reminiscent of Goya's grotesque creatures. A member of the Argentine New Figuration group, in 1961 he received a fellowship from the Argentine National Fund for the Arts to study in Paris. In 1964 he won the Guggenheim International Award and two years later a Fulbright fellowship to study in New York City, where he was visiting professor at Cornell University.

Deira's work is characterized by gestural brushstrokes and harsh contrasts of color. He allowed paint to drip freely over the canvas to generate informalist structures which he accentuated with graphic signs and dribbles to define distorted figures. Some of his segmented figures, with exposed entrails, are erotic. His images became more serene after 1966, although they still tended toward ironic, nightmarish themes. In his later years he settled in Paris, where he died.

GILBERT CHASE, *Contemporary Art in Latin America* (1970), pp. 152, 155; FÉLIX ANGEL, "The Latin American Presence," in Luis R. Cancel ET AL., *The Latin American Spirit: Art and Artists in the United States, 1920–1970* (1988), p. 259; MIGUEL BRIANTE et al., *Nueva Figuración: 1961–1991* (1991).

MARTA GARSD

DEL PRADO, JORGE (*b.* 15 August 1910), leader of the Peruvian Communist Party for much of the twentieth century. Del Prado was born in Arequipa, where in 1928 he helped form the "Revolution Group" that united radical writers, artists, and union leaders. The group maintained close ties to the "Amauta Group" in Lima led by José Carlos MARIÁTEGUI. In 1929 he traveled to Lima, where he collaborated closely with Mariátegui during the rupture with Víctor HAYA DE LA TORRE and the APRA party and the creation of the Socialist Party that would soon become the Peruvian Communist Party (PCP). In the early 1930s, he worked in the mines of Morococha as a union organizer. In the following decades, he held many positions in the Communist Party. He was repeatedly imprisoned and exiled.

Since 1961, Del Prado has been the secretary-general of the Communist Party (referred to as the PCP-Unidad since the withdrawal of pro-China factions in 1964). In 1978 he was elected to the Constituent Assembly. In 1980 he was a candidate for vice president for the United Left (IU). He served three terms in the Peruvian Senate (1980–1985, 1985–1990, and 1990–1992). He has written almost a dozen books on the Peruvian left and on Mariátegui.

JORGE DEL PRADO, *40 años de lucha: Partido comunista del Perú, 1928–1968* (1968); CARLOS MILLA BATRES, *Diccionario histórico y biográfico del Peru, siglos XV–XX* (1986), pp. 186–187; ALBERTO TAURO, *Enciclopedia ilustrada del Perú* (1987), vol 5, pp. 1678–1679.

CHARLES F. WALKER

See also **Peru: Political Parties—Peruvian Aprista Party.**

DEL RIO, DOLORES (Dolores Asunsolo; *b.* 1905; *d.* 11 April 1983), Mexican stage and motion picture star. Born in Durango, Del Rio was discovered by the American director Edwin Carewe, who cast her in the silent film *Joanne* (1925) in Hollywood. She subsequently starred in various other silent and early sound Hollywood films, such as *Journey into Fear,* directed by Orson Welles. In 1942, director Emilio "El Indio" FERNÁNDEZ convinced her to return to Mexico and become a central part of his film team. Del Rio thus had major roles in the most acclaimed of Fernández's films: *Flor silvestre* (1943), *María Candelaria* (1943), *Bugambilia* (1944), and *Las abandonadas* (1944). In later years, she continued her career in both Hollywood and Mexico, receiving numerous acting awards in Mexico and elsewhere.

LUIS REYES DE LA MAZA, *El cine sonoro en México* (1973); E. BRADFORD BURNS, *Latin American Cinema: Film and History* (1975); CARL J. MORA, *Mexican Cinema: Reflections of a Society: 1896–1980* (1982); and JOHN KING, *Magical Reels: A History of Cinema in Latin America* (1990).

DAVID MACIEL

DELFIM NETO, ANTÔNIO (*b.* 1 May 1928), Brazilian minister of finance (1967–1974) and planning (1979–1985). Economist, professor, and legislator, Delfim Neto oversaw Brazil's substantial economic policy apparatus for two extended periods during the military regime of 1964–1985. Known as a pragmatist, he was professor of economics at the University of São Paulo (1952–1965), secretary of finance of the state of São Paulo (1966–1967), ambassador to France (1975–1978), minister of agriculture (1979), and federal deputy (1987–). From 1967 to 1974, Delfim Neto presided over the ECONOMIC MIRACLE, a period when Brazil experienced an average annual growth rate in excess of 10 percent. Building on economic stabilization and institutional reform (1964–1967) and with the backing of a strong military government, his policies stimulated the economy, in the presence of wage and price controls, through lower interest rates, loosening of credit, export promotion, expansion of public investment in transportation and energy, and strengthening of public administration. The period witnessed rapid expansion of production, while provoking criticism over the increasingly unequal distribution of income and controversy over manipulation of the price indexes in 1973 to mask rising rates of inflation.

Delfim Neto began his second period in power promising to avoid a recession while combating inflation. In spite of active management, inflation surged in 1980, and output fell markedly in 1981. After a slight improvement in 1982, a key election year in the redemocratization process, chronic problems in Brazil's balance of payments worsened into a debt crisis. The years 1983–1984 witnessed harsh stabilization and export-promotion programs that caused a major internal recession while generating a sizable trade surplus that mitigated the debt crisis and created the external preconditions for the Cruzado Plan of 1986. The plan was an attempt to fight inertial inflation by freezing prices; ending wage indexation; and generally deindexing the economy, including long-term contracts. Although it was unsuccessful, experience with the plan contributed to subsequent plans. Delfim Neto was elected to the nation's constituent assembly in 1986 and again in 1990.

ISRAEL BELOCH and ALZIRA ALVES DE ABREU, eds., *Dicionário histórico-biográfico brasileiro, 1930–1983*, vol. 2 (1984); LEÔNCIO MARTINS RODRIGUES, *Quem é quem na constituinte: Uma análise sócio-política dos partidos e deputados* (1987); WERNER BAER, *The Brazilian Economy: Growth and Development*, 3d ed. (1989).

RUSSELL E. SMITH

See also **Campos, Roberto (de Oliveira); Economic Development; Simonsen, Mário Henrique.**

DELGADO, JOSÉ MATÍAS (*b.* 24 February 1767; *d.* 12 November 1832), Salvadoran cleric and leader of the independence movement. Born in the provincial capital of San Salvador, Father Delgado became a champion of the Kingdom of Guatemala's independence from Spain and his province's separation from the overbearing influence of neighboring Guatemala. Trained in canon law and jurisprudence at the University of San Carlos in Guatemala, Delgado was part of a generation of discontented creoles who passed through the university in these years. The ENLIGHTENMENT ideas he learned at San Carlos and his provincial resentments of both Spanish and Guatemalan control over his native Salvador quickly bore fruit. Delgado, Manuel José ARCE, and other Salvadorans organized the uprising of 1811, in which they planned to seize the Spanish magistrate, the armory, and the treasury and gain independence. The conspiracy failed, as did a similar revolt in Nicaragua, in the face of strong royalist military action. The repression following these conspiracies helped to postpone independence for another decade but could not quell the unrest that was their root cause.

Delgado soon went to Guatemala to contact other independence activists and begin agitating for the establishment of a separate bishopric for El Salvador. By 1821 he was again in the thick of political intrigue. With many of the leading Liberals of the day, such as José Cecilio del VALLE, Pedro MOLINA, and José Francisco BARRUNDIA, Delgado played an instrumental role in convincing Captain-General Gabino GÁINZA to declare Central America's independence from Spain on 15 September 1821.

After the collapse of the Mexican Empire, Central America gained its independence in its own right, and Father Delgado presided over the assembly that promulgated the first constitution of the independent UNITED PROVINCES OF CENTRAL AMERICA in July of 1823. With union came the reward for Salvador's help in the cause of independence, the formation of a new bishopric of El Salvador in 1825, with Delgado as the first bishop. Seven years later he died while witnessing the bloodshed of the internecine fighting that would plague the former Kingdom of Guatemala for generations to come.

RAMÓN LÓPEZ JIMÉNEZ, *José Matías Delgado y De León, su personalidad, su obra y su destino: Un ensayo histórico* (1962); JOSÉ SALVADOR GUANDIQUE, *Presbítero y doctor José Matías Delgado: Ensayo histórico* (1962); RUDOLFO BARÓN CASTRO, *José Matías Del-*

gado y el movimiento insurgente de 1811 (1962); RALPH LEE WOODWARD, JR., *Central America: A Nation Divided*, 2d ed. (1985), esp. pp. 92–95.

TODD LITTLE-SIEBOLD

DELGADO CHALBAUD, CARLOS (*b.* 20 January 1909; *d.* 13 November 1950), president of Venezuela's military junta (1948–1950). Son of a famous Venezuelan general, Delgado received a degree in military engineering in France. Upon his return to Venezuela, he entered the army and rose rapidly in the officer ranks. From 1945 to 1948 he served as a member of the revolutionary junta and as war minister. After the 1948 military coup, Delgado, now a lieutenant colonel, served as president of the military junta until his assassination in 1950. One of the best-educated Venezuelan military men of his generation, he was regarded as a voice of political moderation among his army colleagues.

ANA MERCEDES PÉREZ, *La verdad inédita: Historia de la Revolución de Octubre revelada por sus dirigentes militares*, 2d ed. (Buenos Aires, 1953); WINFIELD J. BURGGRAAFF, *The Venezuelan Armed Forces in Politics, 1935–1959* (1972).

WINFIELD J. BURGGRAAFF

DELLEPIANE, LUIS J. (*b.* 26 February 1865; *d.* 2 August 1941), career army officer, engineer, minister of war (1928–1930). Dellepiane was born in Buenos Aires and attended the military college in his home city, graduating in 1884. A general by 1910, he established his reputation as the officer who did the most to foster the development of the engineering branch of the Argentine army. He was also closely involved in Argentine politics. Following the assassination of the Buenos Aires police chief, Dellepiane was named interim chief in 1909. During the quasi-revolutionary SEMANA TRÁGICA (Tragic Week) in Buenos Aires in 1919, President Hipólito YRIGOYEN (1916–1922) placed him in command of all military and civilian forces to restore order. Dellepiane's loyal service to Yrigoyen was later rewarded when he was appointed minister of war during Yrigoyen's second term (1928–1930). Concerned about rumors of a coup, Dellepiane advised Yrigoyen to arrest officers believed to be involved in the conspiracy. When he refused, Dellepiane resigned on 2 September 1930, just four days before elements of the army drove Yrigoyen from power. Dellepiane remained in retirement until his death.

ROBERT A. POTASH, *The Army and Politics in Argentina, 1928–1945: Yrigoyen to Perón* (1969); MARVIN GOLDWERT, *Democracy, Militarism, and Nationalism in Argentina, 1930–1966: An Interpretation* (1972).

PAUL GOODWIN

DEMOGRAPHY. *See* **Population.**

DENEVI, MARCO (*b.* 12 May 1922), Argentine writer. Born in Sáenz Peña, Denevi today is considered perhaps more a gadfly presence in Argentine literary circles than a major voice. His works are best known for the absurdist humor with which he narrates the seemingly trivial comedy of quotidian existence. This is the salient feature of *Rosaura a las diez* (1955), cast as detective fiction but with several features atypical of the classic genre that has had so much influence in Argentina. As a consequence, the novel deals more with *porteño* idiosyncrasies within a register of gritty neorealism than with the dynamics of the thriller. *Ceremonia secreta* (1955; *Secret Ceremony*, 1961), an expressionistic tale of fatalistic human rituals reminiscent of Roberto ARLT, won a prize from *Life en Español* magazine and was made into a movie (*Secret Ceremony*, 1967) with Elizabeth Taylor and Robert Mitchum, in which the shift from a Buenos Aires to a London locale deprives the story of any of its Argentine significance. *Falsificaciones* (1966) is a series of microtexts that are parables of human foibles, the dehumanization of modern social life, and the unknown lurking beneath the surface of routine existence. Denevi has written on Argentine national characteristics in *La república de Trapalanda* (1989).

JOSÉ MARÍA CARRANZA, "La crítica social en las fábulas de Marco Denevi," in *Revista Iberoamericana*, no. 80 (1972): 477–494; DONALD A. YATES, "Un acercamiento a Marco Denevi," in *El cuento hispanoamericano ante la crítica*, edited by Enrique Pupo-Walker (1973), pp. 223–234; IVONNE REVEL GROVE, *La realidad calidoscópica de la obra de Marco Denevi* (1974); CHRISTINA PINA, "Marco Denevi: La soledad y sus disfraces," in *Ensayos de crítica literaria año 1983* (1983), pp. 311–417; MYRON I. LICHTBLAU, "Narrative Perspective and Reader Response in Marco Denevi's *Rosaura a las diez*," in *Symposium* 40, no. 1 (1986): 59–70; GUILLERMO GOTSCHILICH REYES, "*Ceremonia secreta* de Marco Denevi: Enigma y ritualización," in *Revista Chilena de Literatura*, no. 33 (1989): 87–101.

DAVID WILLIAM FOSTER

DEPENDENCY THEORY, a concept that emerged from Latin American intellectual centers in the early 1960s as a critique of the development programs then advocated by policymakers in national and international institutions. While popularly accepted as a new development theory or paradigm, many scholars, such as Fernando Henrique Cardoso, Peter Evans, Theotonio Dos Santos, and Andre Gunder Frank, maintain that dependency theory offers an approach to the study of political development that is related to the Marxian tradition of dialectical analyses of historical structures and social processes within a dynamic global economy.

The central premise of the dependency conception of Latin American economic history is that underdevelopment was created by the expansion of European capitalism. The same process by which the developed world, the "core" countries of western Europe and North America, became developed and wealthy, is the same one by which Latin American countries on the "periphery" became dependent and impoverished. Since the conquest and colonization of the Americas, the Latin American economic system has provided imperial powers with the raw materials required for an expanding industrial base and with captive markets for their surplus products. Colonial policies fashioned a monocultural export orientation on Latin America that political independence in the early nineteenth century did not change. With the assistance of a domestic elite, commercial capital, followed by financial and manufacturing capital, penetrated the area, perpetuating the dependency of Latin American economies on the export of one or two primary commodities and the import of manufactured goods.

The inequitable terms of trade stifled industrial growth, for capital accumulation in a dependent country requires the continued acceptance of its primary materials in the developed world. A dependent country can grow and expand only as a reflection of the growth and development of the developed countries to which it is subordinated. While the developed countries can achieve self-sustaining growth, the economy of the dependent country, being oriented toward external markets that it cannot control, is exceptionally vulnerable to the periodic fluctuations in the international market.

Dependency analysts concluded that the solution to Latin American underdevelopment, countrary to the opinions of policymakers in Europe and North America, did not lie in increased penetration of Latin America by foreign capital. Whereas economic policymakers from the core countries advocated increased levels of foreign investment in Latin American industry as one of the solutions to underdevelopment and poverty, the dependency theorists argued that multinational industries would only strengthen the structure of international dependency, enrich the core, and impoverish the periphery. The immediate political implication of the dependency critique is that Latin America can only develop by severing its ties to the core and promoting self-sustaining economic growth through an industrialization program based on the expansion of the domestic market by agrarian reform and income redistribution.

Dependency theory provoked heated theoretical debates and inspired a wide range of empirical investigations. Charging that it was simply old Marxian wine in new Latin American bottles, critics (and some theorists) reduced it to simplistic hypotheses of external determination and domination by malicious foreign capitalists. Under continuous attack, dependency theory fell into disfavor in the 1980s, even though it had established itself as one of the primary lenses through which scholars view Latin American political economy. It compelled scholars to analyze the dynamic international forces that condition Latin American development and distinguish it from the processes by which western Europe and North America have developed. While dependency theory undermined the assumptions on which previous development studies were based, its implicit political agenda has been superseded by other models and approaches, such as post-imperialism and imperial industrialization.

ANDRE GUNDER FRANK, *Latin America: Underdevelopment or Revolution* (1969); THEOTONIO DOS SANTOS, "The Structure of Dependency," in *American Economic Review* 60, no. 2 (May 1970): 231–236; RONALD CHILCOTE and JOEL EDELSTEIN, *Latin America: The Struggle with Dependency and Beyond* (1974); FERNANDO HENRIQUE CARDOSO, "The Consumption of Dependency Theory in the United States," in *Latin American Research Review* 12, no. 3 (1977): 7–24; FERNANDO HENRIQUE CARDOSO and ENZO FALETTO, *Dependency and Development in Latin America* (1979); TULIO HALPERIN-DONGHI, " 'Dependency Theory' and Latin American Historiography," in *Latin American Research Review* 17, no. 1 (1982): 115–130; PETER EVANS, "After Dependency: Recent Studies of Class, State, and Industrialization," *Latin American Research Review* 20, no. 2 (1985): 149–160.

PAUL J. DOSAL

See also **Economic Development; Foreign Trade; Industrialization.**

DEPESTRE, RENÉ (*b.* 29 August 1926) Haitian poet, essayist and novelist. After the surprising sales of a first volume of poetry (*Étincelles*, 1945), Depestre participated in the movement to overthrow the Haitian president, Élie Lescot, in 1946. As a student in Paris (1946–1950), he collaborated with the Caribbean and African intellectuals—Aimé CÉSAIRE, Léopold Senghor, and Léon Damas—to found the NÉGRITUDE movement. Expelled from France for political activism in 1950, Depestre found asylum in Czechoslovakia as secretary to the Brazilian novelist Jorge AMADO. Years of wandering through South America finally brought Depestre to a long stay in Cuba (1959–1978).

Depestre's poetry ranges from a passionate yearning to affirm the humanity and freedom of Haitians to very personal love poetry and, at times, doctrinaire political verse. In early stories (*Alléluia pour une femme—jardin*, 1981), he created a unique blend of humor and eroticism to produce some of the most readable fiction in the tradition of "marvelous realism." His first novel, *Le mât de cocagne* (1979) (translated by Carrol F. Coates as *The Festival of the Greasy Pole*, 1990) deftly applied similar narrative elements to political satire of the François Duvalier dictatorship (1957–1971). With his second novel, *Hadriana dans tous mes rêves* (1988), Depestre continued to exploit his Haitian heritage by focusing on the tale of a young woman turned into a zombie on her wedding night in the lush tropical setting of Jacmel, where Depestre grew up. He returned to the erotic vein in the stories of *Érôs dans un train chinois* (1990).

Other works include: *Gerbe de sang* (poems, 1946); *Un arc-en-ciel pour l'occident chrétien* (poems, 1967), translated with an extensive introduction by Joan Dayan as *A Rainbow for the Christian West* (1977); *Bonjour et adieu à la négritude* (essays, 1980); and *Journal d'un animal marin: Choix de poèmes, 1956–1990* (1990). See also CLAUDE COUFFON, *René Depestre* (1986).

CARROL F. COATES

DERQUI, SANTIAGO (*b.* 19 June 1809; *d.* 5 September 1867), Argentine president. Trained as a lawyer, Derqui took an active role in the politics of his home province of Córdoba until, in the mid-1830s, it came firmly under the control of the dictatorship of Juan Manuel de ROSAS. He then joined the Unitarist general José María PAZ in the struggle against Rosas. After Rosas fell, Derqui served in the Constituent Convention of 1853 and collaborated with Justo José de URQUIZA in the government of the ARGENTINE CONFEDERATION. He succeeded Urquiza as president in 1860, just as rivalry between the Confederation and the secessionist province of Buenos Aires came to a head in armed conflict. Defeated, he resigned the presidency in November 1861.

WILLIAM H. JEFFREY, *Mitre and Argentina* (1952), pp. 141–158; JAMES R. SCOBIE, *La lucha por la consolidación de la nacionalidad argentina, 1852–1862* (1964); ANA ROSA FERÍAS DE FOULKES, *Después de la derrota—Derqui, desde el Pacto de San José de Flores hasta la batalla de Pavón (1859–1861)* (1970).

DAVID BUSHNELL

DESAGÜE, a drainage channel that was the greatest ENGINEERING project of colonial Spanish America. Designed to prevent the periodic flooding of Mexico City, the *desagüe* (with both open and tunneled sections) stretched from Lake Zumpango to the Tula River. Floods had plagued the capital since pre-Columbian times; colonial officials worked to maintain the Aztec system of dikes and causeways, but by the early seventeenth century it had become apparent that this was an inadequate solution. In 1607 the German-born engineer Enrico Martínez received approval for the construction of a drainage canal that would reduce water levels in the Valley of Mexico. Within a year, some 40,000 workers using hand tools had excavated 14 miles of channels, including a 4-mile tunnel that reached a depth of 175 feet.

Inaugurated on 17 November 1608, the *desagüe* soon proved to have numerous flaws, notably its inability to drain low-lying Lake Texcoco, the valley's largest body of water. The tunnel itself was too narrow and had poorly shored walls, and the entire system suffered from inattentive maintenance. As a result, the *desagüe* failed to prevent the great flood of 1629, which left parts of Mexico City inundated for five years. After this disaster, the authorities concentrated on converting the tunnel to open cut, removing obstructions from the channel, and increasing the *desagüe*'s capacity. But work proceeded sporadically, generally only in response to threats of severe flooding. In the end, the project outlasted the colonial government; construction was completed in the last two decades of the nineteenth century, at the cost of nearly 16 million pesos.

For a detailed study of the *desagüe* see J. IGNACIO RUBIO MAÑE, *El virreinato*, 2d ed., vol. 4 (1983). Much useful information can be found in CHARLES GIBSON, *The Aztecs Under Spanish Rule: A History of the Indians of the Valley of Mexico, 1519–1810* (1964). RICHARD EVERETT BOYER, *La gran inundación: Vida y so-*

ciedad en México, 1629–1638 (1975); and LOUISA HOBERMAN, "Bureaucracy and Disaster: Mexico City and the Flood of 1629," in *Journal of Latin American Studies* 6 (1974): 211–230, focus on the 1629 crisis. For the completion of the *desagüe*, see MOISÉS GONZÁLEZ NAVARRO, "México en una laguna," in *Historia mexicana* 4, no. 4 (April–June 1955): 506–522.

R. DOUGLAS COPE

DESCAMISADOS, a term translated literally as the "shirtless ones," first used in a pejorative manner by Argentina's mainstream press on 17 October 1945 to describe the lower-class supporters of Juan Domingo PERÓN. Workers had gathered by the hundreds of thousands in the Plaza de Mayo to protest, successfully, the arrest of Perón, a symbol of working-class aspirations. They embraced the label and transformed it into a badge of honor that signified both their poverty and hard work. Perón himself first used the word publicly at a rally of the Labor Party early in 1946. At the end of his speech, he tossed his jacket aside and rolled up his sleeves. He, too, would be a *descamisado*, and Eva, his wife, would become a symbol of both their dignity and their close identification with the regime. The attention given the *descamisados*, however, obscured the multiclass character of the Peronist movement.

SAMUEL L. BAILY, *Labor, Nationalism, and Politics in Argentina* (1967), p. 90; JULIE M. TAYLOR, *Eva Perón: The Myths of a Woman* (1979), chaps. 4 and 6; JOSEPH PAGE, *Perón: A Biography* (1983), pp. 136–137.

PAUL GOODWIN

D'ESCOTO BROCKMANN, MIGUEL (*b.* 5 February 1933), Nicaraguan priest active in the Sandinista revolution; foreign minister of Nicaragua (1979–1989). Born in California to Nicaraguan parents, D'Escoto was educated in Managua, California, and New York. He studied theology, education, and political economy and became a Catholic priest in the MARYKNOLL ORDER. During the 1960s, he worked first for Maryknoll in New York, then in the slums of Brazil and Mexico. Returning to his own country, he established the Nicaraguan Foundation for Integral Community Development in 1973. In 1975 he became an active supporter of the Sandinista movement. He was a leader of the Group of Twelve (*Los Doce*), which organized resistance to the SOMOZA government. When the Sandinistas came to power in 1979 he was named foreign minister, a post he held for ten years. In 1980 he became a member of the party's political group, the Sandinista Assembly.

The Vatican made known in 1980 its desire that priests not be involved in politics. This policy was relayed to D'Escoto; Ernesto Cardenal, the minister of culture; and two other priests who were participating in the Nicaraguan government at the time. D'Escoto and the others proposed that they take a leave of absence from the church and continue with their work in the

Los Descamisados. Supporters of Juan Perón greet their leader in the Plaza Retiro in Buenos Aires as he arrives from Chile, 1953. ARCHIVO GENERAL DE LA NACIÓN, BUENOS AIRES.

government. The Nicaraguan bishops accepted this compromise. Cardenal was subsequently expelled from the Jesuit order, but the Maryknollers did not expel D'Escoto. Throughout the 1980s, D'Escoto was a forceful spokesman for the Sandinista cause. Because of his fluency in English and his understanding of the political system of the United States he was particularly successful in communicating Sandinista positions to audiences in that nation.

TEOFILO CABESTRERO, *Un grito a Dios y al mundo* (1986); THOMAS P. ANDERSON, *Politics in Central America,* rev. ed. (1988).

DAVID L. JICKLING

See also **Nicaragua: Political Parties.**

DESEMBARGADORES, Brazilian high-court magistrates who were divided into *extravagantes,* unassigned judges who were appointed to cases on an as-needed basis, and *dos agravos,* or appellate judges. As a kind of traveling circuit judge in the colonies, the *desembargador* enforced royal policy and was regularly used as a judicial investigator in outlying areas.

Occupying the pinnacle of the Portuguese justice system was the Desembargo do Paço, which developed from an advisory committee to Dom João (1481–1495) into a fully institutionalized government board, established by the Ordenações Manuelinas of 1514. Although it could hear cases of special merit, its primary function was as an advisory board and council on all matters of justice and legal administration. It became a central organ in the bureaucratic structure of the Portuguese Empire. The Desembargo do Paço appointed royal magistrates, promoted them, and evaluated their performance through the *residência* (investigation) at the end of their tours of duty. It settled conflicts of jurisdiction between subordinate tribunals or magistrates and, on occasion, conducted special examinations (*devassas*). By custom, the Desembargo do Paço consisted of six magistrates, including one ecclesiastic trained in church law.

STUART B. SCHWARTZ, *Sovereignty and Society of Colonial Brazil* (1973).

ROSS WILKINSON

DESNOES, EDMUNDO PÉREZ (*b.* 2 October 1930), Cuban novelist, essayist, and poet. Desnoes was born and raised in Havana and lived in New York, where he attended college from 1956 to 1959. He then returned to Cuba, where he held several posts in national cultural institutions, such as editorial board member of the CASA DE LAS AMÉRICAS. In 1967 he and film director Tomás Gutiérrez Alea adapted his 1965 novel *Memorias del subdesarrollo* (*Memories of Underdevelopment*) into a highly successful film that brought him immediate recognition. Largely because of this adaptation, Desnoes became a prominent figure in the Cuban cultural world of the 1960s, but in subsequent years his importance diminished as his literary output failed to live up to its earlier promise. Other works by Desnoes include the novel *El cataclismo*, an essay "Lam: Azul y negro," and a controversial anthology of Cuban literature, *Los dispositivos en la flor* (1981).

PAOLO GASPARINI, *Para verte mejor, América Latina* (1972).

ROBERTO VALERO

DESSALINES, JEAN JACQUES (*b.* 1758; *d.* 17 October 1806), emperor of Haiti (1804–1806). In the early hours of an October morning in 1806, a fierce-looking black commander was trying to force his mount through a crowd of mutinous but stunned soldiers. Finally a shot rang out, the commander's horse rolled over, breaking and pinning the rider's leg, and with cries of anguish and curses rolling from the commander's lips, the stunned soldiers knew that their hated victim was mortal after all. They shot him to pieces and dragged his mutilated body from Pont Rouge to Port-au-Prince for public display. There but one person mourned his death—she was Défilée, an insane black woman. The object of her tears and flowers was the emperor, Jean Jacques Dessalines. No man in Haitian history has been more hated by his contemporaries or loved and respected by future generations of his countrymen than Dessalines.

Born on the Cormiers Plantation in northern Saint-Domingue, young Jean Jacques Duclos (later Dessalines) experienced many of slavery's horrors. Master Duclos sold both his parents and a favorite aunt to neighboring plantation masters, a clear violation of the Code Noir (1685), which mandated that slave families be kept intact. In the late 1780s a free black master named Dessalines acquired the now mature Jean Jacques Duclos. His new master often whipped him, leaving him only pain and a new last name. Small won-

der that Dessalines despised whites, mulattoes, and authority by the time of the Haitian Revolution.

When the revolution began, Dessalines may have been a maroon (slave fugitive), but runaway or not, he soon joined the black rebels. When Dessalines joined Toussaint L'OUVERTURE is unclear, but he became indispensable to the "Black Spartacus" once he did. With a viciousness rare in Toussaint's generals, he figured heavily in crushing the rebellion of Theodore Hedouville at Le Cap (1798), in defeating and punishing the mulattoes of South Province, led by André RIGAUD, during the War of the Knives (1799), in suppressing the rebellion of General Moyse (1801), and in opposing the expedition of French General Charles LECLERC (1802–1804). Clearly Dessalines was a gifted field commander, who earned the title of "Tiger."

But Dessalines's brutal manner and greed often tainted these achievements. At one time Dessalines had thirty plantations and an income so large that he refused to join the Moyse rebellion on the grounds that plantation division, one of its demands, threatened his economic interests. When Toussaint sent him to South Province as an occupation governor following the War of the Knives, the Tiger murdered hundreds of mulat-

Jean Jacques Dessalines. ORGANIZATION OF AMERICAN STATES.

toes. He also slaughtered practically the entire white population of Haiti in 1804. And he enforced *fermage* (system of forced labor and government management on plantations), introduced by Toussaint, with a severity seldom seen in any of the old colonial masters.

C. L. R. James is among those historians who emphasize that Dessalines acted largely on his own. But others, among them Hubert Cole, believe that Dessalines usually acted with Toussaint's knowledge and approval, the War of the Knives providing their best argument. The brutal Dessalines served as a sort of alter ego for the gentle Toussaint. While Toussaint might have found Dessalines useful on the battlefield, he absolutely believed him unfit to rule the emerging black state. Toussaint was right.

Dessalines carried Haiti to independence on 1 January 1804 and himself to the emperorship at his coronation on 8 October 1804. That France might once again attack Haiti was his abiding fear and, as Hubert Cole indicated, may have triggered his mass slaughter of all whites in mid 1804. But his furious behavior extended to the mulattoes also. He once quipped that he murdered any mulatto who looked white during the massacres of 1804. Later he mellowed with regard to the mulattoes and remarked that blacks and mulattoes should intermarry and obliterate race lines. But rationality soon gave way to another volcanic eruption of rage in Dessalines. When the mulatto Alexandre PÉTION refused to marry his daughter, Dessalines once again turned on them, and by the end of 1806 had planned their destruction. The Haitian national historian Thomas Madiou has treated Dessalines's social policies as those of a liberal. But other historians outside Haiti disagree. James Leyburn believes Dessalines brought social disaster on Haiti and fixed the caste system on the new state.

A reckless economic policy finally brought Dessalines down. He challenged mulatto land titles, put most of Haiti's able-bodied men under arms, enforced a harsh labor system, and neglected education. On 17 October 1806 most of Haiti rejoiced over his assassination.

W. W. HARVEY, *Sketches of Haiti* (1827); THOMAS MADIOU, *Histoire d'Haiti*, 4 vols. (1847–1904); C. L. R. JAMES, *The Black Jacobins* (1938); JAMES LEYBURN, *The Haitian People* (1944); HUBERT COLE, *Christophe: King of Haiti* (1967); THOMAS O. OTT, *The Haitian Revolution, 1789–1804* (1973); DAVID NICHOLLS, *From Duvalier to Dessalines: Race, Colour, and National Independence in Haiti* (1979).

THOMAS O. OTT

DESTERRO, NOSSA SENHORA DO. *See* **Florianópolis.**

DEUSTUA, ALEJANDRO O. (*b.* 1849; *d.* 1945), Peruvian philosopher, educator, politician, and lawyer. Born in Huancayo, Deustua initially was an exponent of the POSITIVIST school of thought prevalent in Latin America in the late nineteenth and early twentieth centuries. Subsequently he espoused idealist concepts developed by the European philosophers Karl Krause and his followers and Henri Bergson. This transition was not uncommon among Latin American intellectuals after the MEXICAN REVOLUTION. In his later works, *Ante el conflicto nacional* (1931) and *La cultura nacional* (1937), Deustua expressed the need for a renewed sense of humanist nationalism among the elites. Deustua was a founding member of the historical Civilista Party (1872), minister of justice (1895) and government (1902), senator for Lima (1901–1904), a diplomat, and president of San Marcos University (1928–1930). He died in Lima.

FREDERICK PIKE, *The Modern History of Peru* (1967).

ALFONSO W. QUIROZ

DEVIL'S ISLAND. *See* **French Guiana.**

DI CAVALCANTI, EMILIANO (*b.* 1897; *d.* 1976), Brazilian painter. In 1914 Di Cavalcanti initiated his artistic career with the publication of one of his drawings in a magazine entitled *Fon-Fon*. In 1916 he moved from Rio de Janeiro to São Paulo, where he studied law and worked as an illustrator and journalist. In 1918, one year after exhibiting a series of "antiacademic" Beardsley-inspired caricatures in São Paulo, he began studying painting with the German painter Elpons. His first exhibition of paintings took place in 1921. During this period, Di Cavalcanti, in collaboration with modernist PAULISTAS Anita Malfatti and Vítor BRECHERET, became one of the leaders of the Brazilian modernist movement. These three artists conceptualized and ultimately organized the 1922 Semana de Arte Moderna (MODERN ART WEEK), a week-long series of poetry, dance, and fine arts exhibitions. It coincided with the centenary celebration of Brazilian independence and is regarded as a watershed for Brazilian cultural expression.

Di Cavalcanti's first trip to Europe in 1923 introduced him to the European avant-garde in art and literature. While the cubism and surrealism of Picasso, Braque, Léger, and Matisse influenced his own painting greatly, he remained devoted to national themes such as the bohemian life in Rio de Janeiro, mulatto women, and Carnival. In his memoirs he affirmed that "the mulata for me is a Brazilian symbol. She is not black or white, neither rich nor poor. Like our people, she likes to dance, she likes music and soccer. . . . The mulata is feminine and Brazil is one of the most feminine countries in the world."

Upon his return to Brazil, he settled in Rio. Between 1927 and his return to Paris in 1935, Di Cavalcanti received a commission to prepare two wall panels for the João Caetano Theater. During this same period he exhibited in Rio de Janeiro and São Paulo. By the 1950s he had attained international recognition as one of the greatest modernist painters. In the second São Paulo

Di Cavalcanti paints a portrait of Marina Montini.
ICONOGRAPHIA.

Biennial in 1954, he won the highest honor, Best National Painter, and in the seventh São Paulo Biennial there was a special room devoted exclusively to an exhibition of his paintings.

LUIS MARTINS, *Emiliano Di Cavalcanti* (1953); EMILIANO DI CAVALCANTI, *Reminiscências líricas de um perfeito carioca* (1964); ARACY AMARAL, *Artes plásticas na Semana de 22: Subsídios para una história da renovação das artes no Brasil* (1992), esp. pp. 99–128, 246–248.

CAREN A. MEGHREBLIAN

DI TELLA, TORCUATO (*b.* 15 May 1892; *d.* 22 July 1948), Argentine entrepreneur. Until age thirteen Di Tella lived in Italy, at which time his family emigrated to Argentina. His entrepreneurial career was launched in 1910, when he linked his market study of the demand for dough-kneading machines to a mechanic who could build a machine capable of competing with imported technology. Operating from a converted garage, the

fledgling business, which would eventually operate under the name S.I.A.M. (Sección Industria Amasadoras Mecánicas), expanded rapidly over the next five years.

Di Tella's entrepreneurial career was interrupted by service with the Italian army in World War I. In 1919 he returned to Argentina, where he confronted a stagnant economy, sluggish market, and volatile labor force. The protectionist economic policies of the government and a labor policy that ranged from firing troublesome personnel to co-opting others through promotion allowed Di Tella to overcome the difficulties. With an unmatched ability to take advantage of every opportunity and to anticipate markets, he expanded his operations. Gasoline pumps were added to bakery machinery, and by the end of the 1920s S.I.A.M.'s success was symbolic of the emergence of industry in Argentina. Management became the province of the extended Di Tella family, which could be trusted to administer and operate the company. Di Tella expanded his operations to Brazil, Chile, Uruguay, and, for a while, London. By the end of the 1930s, S.I.A.M. had diversified into household appliances. Operating in the style of a *patrón*, Di Tella the man became "an integrating symbol for the company."

As a successful businessman, Di Tella was sought out

Torcuato Di Tella (right) talking with Minister of War Basilio Pertine during a visit to his factory in Avellaneda, November 1937. COLLECTION OF TORCUATO S. DI TELLA.

for a variety of national and international roles. He fought against the spread of Fascism, both in Italy and Argentina, wrote several books, represented Argentina at important international meetings, and between 1944 and 1948 was a professor of economics and industrial organization at the University of Buenos Aires. He was a patron of the arts and owner of an experimental dairy farm.

THOMAS C. COCHRAN and RUBEN E. REINA, *Entrepreneurship in Argentine Culture: Torcuato Di Tella and S.I.A.M.* (1962); GUIDO DI TELLA and MANUEL ZYMELMAN, *Las etapas del desarrollo económico argentino* (1967).

PAUL GOODWIN

DÍA, EL, an Uruguayan newspaper founded by the great Colorado Party political leader and two-time president, José BATLLE Y ORDÓÑEZ, on 16 June 1886. The newspaper was the vehicle through which Batlle formulated and publicized his political ideology of the welfare state and support for the working class, which propelled him to the presidency (1903–1907 and 1911–1915). In the 1940s and 1950s the newspaper was controlled by Batlle's sons, César and Lorenzo. Although they were more conservative than their father, the sons used the newspaper to promote Batlle's long-sought dream of a purely collegial executive system, which was finally adopted under the 1952 Constitution but abandoned in 1966. In 1966, Jorge PACHECO ARECO, editor of *El Día*, was elected vice president. When President Oscar GESTIDO died one year later, Pacheco became president.

El Día was the most influential newspaper in Uruguay for the first six decades of the twentieth century. During the military dictatorship (1973–1984), *El Día* remained a subdued but subtle voice of opposition to the regime by daily publishing a picture of Batlle with one of his pithy quotes about democracy or against dictatorship. The newspaper fell on hard times in the 1980s, with no major Colorado politician reflecting its legacy, and it ceased publication on 31 January 1991. Briefly resurrected, it again closed down.

ROBERTO B. GIUDICI and EFRAÍN GONZÁLEZ CONZI, *Batlle y el batllismo*, 2d ed. (1959); MILTON VANGER, *José Batlle y Ordóñez of Uruguay: The Creator of His Times, 1902–1907* (1963).

MARTIN WEINSTEIN

DIAGUITAS, sedentary agriculturalists dispersed in the transversal valleys of the Andean cordillera (northwest Argentina and north-central Chile), mid-first millennium to sixteenth century. Archaeological studies indicate that Diaguita culture in the region emerged in the transition from transhumant hunting and gathering to complete sedentary agriculture in the second half of the first millennium. Archaeologists detect three distinct periods in the material culture left by the Diaguitas in the following centuries until the mid-fifteenth century,

when they were first conquered by the INCA, and then by the Spanish in the sixteenth century.

When the Spanish first contacted the Diaguitas, they found evidence of Inca domination in clothing, beliefs, and technology. Archaeological findings suggest also that the Diaguita culture was at its apogee when Inca expansion to the south incorporated the Diaguitas in the mid-fifteenth century. At that time, the Diaguitas occupied the transversal valleys on both sides of the cordillera from present-day Aconcagua to Copiapó, where they grew corn, beans, potatoes, quinoa, squash, and, according to the climate, cotton, in irrigated valleys fertilized with sardine heads or llama and alpaca manure. They herded LLAMA and ALPACA for wool and for transport; hunted GUANACO, chinchillas, and fowl; and also fished to supplement their diet.

In each settlement consanguineous relations linked all members; communal lands were assigned by the chief to each nuclear family. Within each valley settlements were further organized according to moieties with one half near the coast and the other half near the cordillera. The relative isolation of each of the valleys allowed the development of notable political autonomy, and even different dialects.

The incorporation of the Diaguitas under Spanish colonial rule was achieved without major resistance, and Diaguita tribute was important in providing the foundation of the colonial settlements in the region established to supply the Potosí mines with mules, textiles, and food.

JULIAN H. STEWARD, ed., *Handbook of South American Indians*, vol. 2 (1946), pp. 587–597; JORGE HIDALGO L. et al., eds., *Prehistoria: Culturas de Chile desde sus orígenes hasta los albores de la conquista* (1989); GRETE MOSTNY, *Prehistoria de Chile* (1991), p. 117.

KRISTINE L. JONES

DIÁLOGOS DAS GRANDEZAS DO BRASIL, manuscript written in 1618 and attributed to Ambrósio Fernandes Brandão. The Dialogues were well known in manuscript form to the nineteenth-century scholars Francisco Adolfo de VARNHAGEN and João Capistrano de ABREU. Varnhagen made a copy of the manuscript in Leiden Library in 1874, and the Dialogues were printed in the *Revista do Instituto Arqueológico Histórico e Geográfico Pernambucano* between 1877 and 1887. Abreu tried to have them published in a volume in 1900, but the first edition did not appear until 1930 under the patronage of the BRAZILIAN ACADEMY OF LETTERS.

There are six Dialogues. In the first one, the two characters, Alviano and Brandônio, talk about natural products and their possible use for colonists, distinguishing between those that were the result of human efforts through agriculture and those that were a kind offering from nature. In the same Dialogue, Portuguese settlement is discussed and the northern captaincies are described. The second Dialogue is a scholarly dissertation on the torrid zone and on the human races, with special emphasis on the original inhabitants of Brazil. It ends with some considerations of diseases and of Indian and white medical practices. Social groups, sugar mills, agriculture, fishing and hunting, and Indian culture occupy the remaining Dialogues.

FRANCISCO ADOLFO DE VARNHAGEN, *História geral do Brasil*, 9th ed. (1975); JOÃO CAPISTRANO DE ABREU, *Ensaios e estudos: Crítica e história* (1st ser., 1975); AMBRÓSIO FERNANDES BRANDÃO, *Dialogues of the Great Things of Brazil*, translated and annotated by Frederick Holden Hall et al. (1987).

MARIA BEATRIZ NIZZA DA SILVA

DIAMONDS. *See* **Gems and Gemstones.**

DIANDA, HILDA (*b.* 13 April 1917), Argentine composer. Born in Córdoba, she studied under Honorio Siccardi and did postgraduate work in Europe (1958–1962) under Gian Francesco Malipiero and Hermann Scherchen. Dianda wrote some electroacoustic works at the Studío di Fonologia Musicale in Milan, Italy, and attended the new music summer courses in Darmstadt, Germany. Her early works have traces of moderated modernism—dissonant chords and jagged melodies—and a lyrical style. This is true of *Concertante* for cello and orchestra (1952) and *Poemas de amor desesperado* for voice and six instruments (1942). Later her style became more experimental, and she was one of the leading figures of the musical avant-garde in Argentina. Dianda participated in numerous international festivals, including Florence, Caracas, Rio de Janeiro, Madrid, Washington, D.C., Mexico, Zagreb, and Donaueschingen. Dianda has also written articles published in several publications around the world and one book, *Música en la Argentina de hoy* (1966). For several years Dianda collaborated as a composer-member and concert organizer with the Agrupación Música Viva in Buenos Aires. This organization, which also included composers Gerardo GANDINI, Armando Krieger, Antonio TAURIELLO, and Alcides Lanza, presented concerts in Buenos Aires consisting of their own compositions and contemporary music from other countries.

Other important compositions by Hilda Dianda are *Núcleos* for two pianos, vibraphone, xylorimba, eight percussionists, and string orchestra (1963); *Estructuras* nos. 1, 2, and 3 for cello and piano (1960); String Quartet no. 3 (1963–1964); *Percusión 11,* for eleven percussionists (1963); *Ludus* no. 1 for orchestra (1968); *Ludus* no. 2 for eleven performers (1969); *Idá-ndá's* for three percussionists (1969); *a7* for cello and five tapes (1966); *Resonancias* no. 3 for cello and orchestra (1965); *Resonancias* no. 5 for two choirs (1967–1968); *Ludus* no. 3 for organ (1969); *Impromptu* for string orchestra (1970); and *Cadencias* no. 2 for violin and piano (1986).

Fourth Inter-American Music Festival (1968), pp. 41, 67; RODOLFO ARIZAGA, *Enciclopedia de la música argentina* (1971), p.

117; JOHN VINTON, ed., *Dictionary of Contemporary Music* (1974), pp. 184–185; GÉRARD BÉHAGUE, *Music in Latin America: An Introduction* (1979), p. 336; *New Grove Dictionary of Music and Musicians* (1980).

ALCIDES LANZA

DIAS, ANTÔNIO GONÇALVES (*b.* 10 August 1823; *d.* 3 November 1864), Brazilian poet. An outstanding romantic poet, Dias was the founder of truly national Brazilian literature. Romanticism represented perfectly the ideals of freedom, patriotism, and nativism so fervent in Brazil in the time of Independence. These sentiments were well expressed by Dias, whose work dealt mainly with Brazil's landscape and Indians (Indianism). He wrote exultant hymns to the beauty of tropical nature. With great imagination he treated Indian themes. Besides being a lyric poet, he was a prose writer, historian, ethnologist, and dramatist.

Born in Caxias, Maranhão, Dias was the illegitimate son of a Portuguese shopkeeper and a Brazilian *cafuza* (of mixed Indian and African blood). When his father married another woman, the child was separated from his mother and taken to live with the new couple. After his father's death, he went to Portugal to study at the University of Coimbra, where he received a bachelor's degree in 1845. His years in Portugal were very valuable. In addition to university work, he studied languages and literature, wrote intensively, made contact with great writers, and was loved and admired. Because of economic difficulties, however, he returned to Maranhão. In 1846 he went to Rio, where he published *Primeiros cantos* (First Songs, 1847), which was favorably reviewed by Alexandre Herculano. Other publications followed, including *Leonor de Mendonça* (1847); *Segundos cantos* (Second Songs, 1848), which contains "Sextilhas de Frei Antão" (Friar Antão's Sextets), a poem in the Portuguese troubadour style; and *Últimos cantos* (Last Songs, 1851).

Besides teaching positions, Dias held important government posts in Brazil and Europe. He published in Leipzig the second edition of his poems, titled *Cantos* (Songs, 1857), as well as *Os timbiras* (The Timbiras, 1857), and *Dicionário da língua tupi* (Dictionary of the Tupi Language, 1858). Additional works by Dias include *Obras póstumas* (6 vols., 1868–1869) and *Poesia completa e prosa escolhida* (1959).

In 1858 Dias traveled to Brazil, but in 1862 he returned to Europe seeking a cure for his poor health. Feeling worse, he sailed again for Brazil; although his wrecked ship was rescued from sinking, because he was ill, he was the only passenger who perished.

RAYMOND SAYERS, *The Negro in Brazilian Literature* (1956); FRITZ ACKERMANN, *A obra poética de Antônio Gonçalves Dias*, translated by EGON SCHADEN (1964); DAVID T. HABERLY, "The Songs of an Exile: Antônio Gonçalves Dias," in *Three Sad Races: Racial Identity and National Consciousness in Brazilian Literature* (1983), pp. 18–31; ALMIR C. BRUNETI, "Antônio Gonçalves

Dias," in *Latin American Writers,* edited by C. Solé and M. I. Abreu, vol. 1 (1989), pp. 185–193.

MARIA ISABEL ABREU

DIAS, HENRIQUE (*d.* 8 June 1662), black military leader during the seventeenth-century Portuguese campaign against the Dutch occupation of northeastern Brazil. Although it is unknown whether or not he had ever been a slave, Henrique Dias was a free and literate man when he volunteered for service in 1633. At that time the Dutch were expanding their occupation of Pernambuco beyond the coastal towns of Recife and Olinda and would eventually overtake large portions of the northeastern captaincies.

Initially the captain of a small force, Dias later commanded over three hundred men of color, some of whom were slaves. By 1636 he was a master of the guerrilla tactics that were then the basis of the Luso-Brazilian strategy against the Dutch. His skills as a military tactician were evident in all of his engagements, which ranged from his participation in the defense of Salvador (the capital of Bahia) in 1638 to his role in the campaign to recover territory in Alagoas in 1639. Returning to Pernambuco in 1645, Dias resumed his part in the fight against the enemy, eventually traveling to Rio Grande do Norte, where he and his men took a Dutch fort in 1647. By 1648 he was in Olinda, where his fighting prowess contributed to the defeat of the enemy. Finally, he fought in the front lines in the recapture of Recife in January 1654.

Though subject to racist treatment during his long career, Dias received many honors for his service. In 1638, for example, King Philip IV awarded him a knighthood, a highly unusual status for a man of African descent. In Brazil, Portuguese commander the Count of Torre granted him a patent in 1639 that carried the title "Governor of All Creoles, Blacks, and Mulattoes." Finally, in March 1656, he traveled to Portugal, where, in an audience with the court, Dias requested and received the freedom of all slaves who had served in his *têrço* (unit) and the continued existence of his force, which was to have the rights and privileges of white units. Though he later died much as he had been born, in relative obscurity, his memory was preserved in the name given to all subsequent black militia companies. They were called the "Henriques."

The most extensive sources about the life of Henrique Dias are in Portuguese. See especially JOSÉ ANTÔNIO GONSALVES DE MELLO, *Henrique Dias: Governador dos pretos, crioulos, e mulatos do estado do Brasil* (1954). Many shorter sketches are available in English, but the older of these contain inaccuracies. The best is found in A. J. R. RUSSELL-WOOD, *The Black Man in Slavery and Freedom in Colonial Brazil* (1982), pp. 84–87 and 102–103. On the Dutch presence in Brazil, see CHARLES R. BOXER, *The Dutch in Brazil, 1624–1654* (1957).

JUDITH L. ALLEN

DIAS GOMES, ALFREDO (*b.* 1922), Brazilian playwright. Born in Bahia, Dias Gomes has tried and mastered all forms of drama, whether on the stage, radio, or television, and his theater has continued steadily to evolve. Always he has been both artist and social commentator. With his play *O pagador de promessas* (1960), Dias Gomes gained national prominence as a playwright. The central theme of the play is the tragic uphill struggle of the strong individual for true personal freedom in a capitalist society. This theme, a recurring one in Dias Gomes's theater, is closely related to two others: the problems of communication and intolerance, particularly religious intolerance, in modern society. The willful priest, every bit as intransigent as Zé, the title character, stands as the play's principal antagonist, and although Dias Gomes describes him as the symbol of universal rather than merely religious intolerance, the priest's attitude and actions constitute a rather caustic commentary on religious dogmatism. Yet another strength of the play is the adroitness with which the dramatist parallels the "Afro-Catholic syncretism" that characterizes the religious views of Zé and several other characters with a similar SYNCRETISM in setting and symbol. *O pagador,* then, with a compelling plot, a carefully elaborated classical structure, and a protagonist who is perhaps the most memorable character of all Brazilian drama, deservedly ranks as one of the best plays of that country's theatrical tradition.

It is in *O berço do herói* (1965) that the satiric humor and the expressionistic techniques introduced in *A revolução dos beatos* (1962) and *Odorico, o bem amado* (1962) find their fruition. The work concerns itself chiefly with the problem of true individual liberty in a capitalist society, much as does *O pagador.* Various critics, in fact, have stated that *O berço* is a very pessimistic answer to the questions concerning individual freedom and liberty that are raised in *O pagador.* Both heroes experience one phase of Calvary—Zé the journey with the cross and Jorge the trial. The similarity between the plays is such, in fact, that they seem to comprise a dramatic experiment in which the same set of basic ingredients is poured into two distinct molds—one tragic and the other burlesque. The play, although long banned, is perhaps the best satire to be found in the contemporary Brazilian theater.

Dias Gomes's sixth major play, *O santo inquérito,* was first presented in Rio in September 1966. Based on the life of Branca Dias, it is the only one of his works whose setting is in the rather distant past: the year 1750, in the state of Paraíba. The major concerns or themes, just as in *O pagador,* are individual freedom within a tightly structured societal boundary (i.e., the church), existential communication, and religious fanaticism. The INQUISITION is employed primarily as a metaphor to describe military and political repression in Brazil in the 1960s. Following *O santo inquérito* and representing yet another experiment in structure and technique is *Dr. Getúlio, sua vida e sua glória,* a piece in two acts in which verse and prose are mixed. It dramatizes the period of ultimate crisis in the life of the president-dictator Getúlio VARGAS—the crisis that precipitated his suicide in 1954.

In *Os campeões do mundo*, Dias Gomes tells the story of two lovers who are involved in terrorism during the World Soccer Cup in Rio in the 1970s. It is a story of political oppression and torture whose outcome is known to the public; the dialectic of how and why things happened takes precedence over plot. With little of the usual interest in the denouement, spectators can be more objective and better able to exercise critical judgment, which is the goal of the author.

LEON F. LYDAY and GEORGE WOODYARD, *Dramatists in Revolt: The New Latin American Theater* (1976), pp. 221–242.

RICHARD A. MAZZARA

See also **Literature: Brazil.**

DÍAZ, ADOLFO (*b.* 1874; *d.* 27 January 1964), president of Nicaragua (1911–1916, 1926–1928). Previously a secretary for La Luz and Los Angeles Mining Company, a U.S. firm based in BLUEFIELDS, the Costa Rican–born Díaz entered Nicaraguan politics during the Conservative overthrow of Liberal dictator José Santos ZELAYA in 1909. He served as a source of funds for the rebel leader Juan ESTRADA. After Zelaya's ouster, Estrada became president and Díaz, his vice president. On 8 May 1911, Estrada resigned in the face of a revolt led by Minister of War Luis Mena. Díaz succeeded to the presidency and quickly cultivated U.S. goodwill. One month into his presidency he signed a treaty with the U.S. that permitted the Nicaraguan government to negotiate a loan with U.S. private banks.

Díaz desired financial and political security, but his forging of closer ties between Nicaragua and the U.S. caused him to lose support at home. Mena declared that Díaz had sold out, and sought supporters in the National Assembly. In July 1912 Mena led a revolt against Díaz. Although Conservative Party leader Emiliano CHAMORRO defeated Mena, Díaz failed to control this tumultuous situation and finally turned to the U.S. for assistance. President William Howard Taft dispatched the marines on 4 August 1912.

Díaz was reelected president in 1926 after Chamorro's unsuccessful coup d'état. A reinstated national assembly acknowledged him as president, and the U.S. promptly recognized his government. The former Liberal vice president, Juan Bautista SACASA, however, claimed the presidency for himself, and with the support of José María MONCADA, rose against the Conservative administration. With the help of the U.S., Díaz was able to end the resulting civil war, and gain control of the government until 1928. During this period he cooperated with the U.S. in the development and training of the National Guard.

WILLIAM KAMMAN, *A Search for Stability: United States Diplomacy Toward Nicaragua, 1925–1933* (1968); LESTER D. LANGLEY,

The Banana Wars: United States Intervention in the Caribbean, 1898–1934 (1985); JAMES DUNKERLEY, *Power in the Isthmus: A Political History of Modern Central America* (1988).

SHANNON BELLAMY

DÍAZ, FÉLIX, JR. (*b.* 17 February 1868; *d.* 9 July 1945), Mexican general, diplomat, and politician. He was the son of Félix Díaz (1833–1872), a general and governor of Oaxaca (1867–1871), and a nephew of Porfirio DÍAZ, the dictatorial president. Díaz is best known for his role in the overthrow of President Francisco I. MADERO in February 1913 during the so-called DECENA TRÁGICA (tragic ten days).

Born in the city of Oaxaca, Díaz graduated from the National Military College with a degree in engineering in 1888. By 1909 he had become a brigadier general. He served as alternate federal deputy from Oaxaca (1894–1896) and Veracruz (1896–1900) and federal deputy from Veracruz (1900–1912). In 1902 he was a candidate for governor of Oaxaca, and in 1910 he served as that state's interim chief executive. He was a member of the Exploratory Geographic Commission (1901); consul general in Chile (1902–1904); inspector of police, Mexico City (1904); chief of the presidential staff (1909); and ambassador to Japan (1913).

Díaz was separated from the army and jailed by President Madero, who overthrew Díaz's uncle, Porfirio. Díaz initiated, along with generals Manuel Mondragón (1859–1922) and Bernardo REYES (1850–1913), the February 1913 rebellion against Madero that, when joined by federal army commander General Victoriano HUERTA, successfully ousted the president. Díaz subsequently lost the power struggle he waged with Huerta, briefly served as ambassador to Japan, and then went into self-imposed exile in Havana and New York. In 1916 he returned to Mexico to head the National Reorganizing Army against revolutionary chief Venustiano CARRANZA. He remained active against the Carranza regime until 1920, when he was again exiled until 1937. He died in Veracruz.

LUIS LICÉAGA, *Félix Díaz* (1958); PETER V. N. HENDERSON, *Félix Díaz, the Porfirians, and the Mexican Revolution* (1981); ALAN KNIGHT, *The Mexican Revolution*, 2 vols. (1986), esp. pp. 1:473–490, 2:375–392.

DAVID LaFRANCE

DÍAZ, GONZALO (*b.* 1947), Chilean artist. Throughout his career Díaz has addressed what he has termed the conceptualization of Chile as "cultural landscape" and the troubled status of painting in contemporary Chilean art. Born in Santiago, he studied art at the Escuela de Bellas Artes, Universidad de Chile, Santiago, from 1965 to 1969. Like the conceptually minded artists associated with the Avanzada, he was strongly affected by the institution of General Augusto Pinochet's military dictatorship in 1973. However, while most of the

Avanzada artists abandoned painting, Díaz remained captivated by its theory, practice, and history in the era of photography. In the late 1970s he began producing labyrinthine installations that incorporate paintings as well as objects. His painting *Historia sentimental de la pintura chilena* (1982) exemplifies his central thematic concerns: the troubled status of painting in contemporary Chilean art, which in the late 1970s and early 1980s was largely dominated by conceptual and photographic practices, and the relationship between painting and the construction of national identity. Díaz has taught at the Universidad de Chile (1969), the Universidad Católica (1974), and the Instituto de Arte Contemporáneo (1977–1986), all in Santiago.

ADRIANA VALDÉS, "Gonzalo Díaz," in *Contemporary Art from Chile,* edited by Fatima Bercht (1991), pp. 10–21; MARI CARMEN RAMÍREZ, "Blueprint Circuits: Conceptual Art and Politics in Latin America," in *Latin American Artists of the Twentieth Century* (1993), pp. 156–167.

JOHN ALAN FARMER

DÍAZ, JORGE (*b.* 1930) was born to Spanish parents in Rosario, Argentina, but raised in Chile. He graduated in architecture and first entered the theater as a scenographer. The Latin American playwright most closely associated with theater of the absurd, he achieved early success with *El cepillo de dientes* (1961), a two-character play that in language and structure epitomizes the clichés of contemporary life. Although his linguistic dexterity creates an illusion of vacuous and sterile relationships and the difficulties of authentic communication, his plays are underscored by a strong social and political reality. His early pieces played with language, time, music, humor, and the stultifying effects of bourgeois society.

In 1965 Díaz emigrated to Spain to escape the administrative responsibilities of ICTUS, a vanguard theater in Santiago. In Spain his plays became more aggressive, using mixed-media techniques to denounce greed and insensitivity, such as a massacre in a Brazilian *favela* and the ITT intervention in Chilean politics. After Franco's death in 1975 brought a new sense of freedom to the Spanish theater, Díaz began to experiment with two distinctly different styles, one focusing on the sociopolitical, the other more personal and intimate. He wrote about the archetypal qualities of sex and death, which he claimed was to write about life. Some plays were intended for a Madrid audience, others for Santiago. On two occasions Díaz has dramatized his compatriot, the Nobel laureate Pablo NERUDA, most recently in *Pablo Neruda viene volando* (1991). Díaz's trenchant style and playful language have earned him the epithet of "absurdist" writer, but he seeks only to express his view of contemporary human existence. Díaz is also a prolific writer of theater for children.

TEODOSIO FERNÁNDEZ, "Jorge Díaz," in *El teatro chileno contemporáneo (1941–1973)* (1982), pp. 153–67; TAMARA HOLZA-PFEL, "Jorge Díaz y la dinámica del absurdo teatral," in *Estreno* 9, no. 2 (1983): 32–35; GEORGE WOODYARD, "Jorge Díaz and the Liturgy of Violence," in *Dramatists in Revolt: The New Latin American Theater,* edited by Leon F. Lyday and George W. Woodyard (1976), pp. 59–76.

GEORGE WOODYARD

DÍAZ, JOSÉ EDUVIGIS (*b.* 1833; *d.* 7 February 1867), Paraguayan soldier. Born in Pirayú, Díaz entered the military at age nineteen and showed sufficient promise as a soldier to receive several important appointments by the early 1860s. He was police chief of Asunción when the WAR OF THE TRIPLE ALLIANCE broke out in 1864. One year later, Díaz participated in the Corrientes campaign, during which he caught the eye of President Francisco Solano LÓPEZ for having ferried 100,000 head of cattle to the Paraguayan lines with the Allied armies in close pursuit. Díaz rose quickly to the rank of general and fought in engagements at Corrales, Tuyutí, and Boquerón. His greatest achievement, however, came in September 1866, when his troops, defending reinforced trenchworks at CURUPAYTY, repulsed a massive Allied attack, killing 9,000 of the enemy and suffering almost no losses themselves.

For a short time, Díaz was feted as López's favorite, but in January 1867, while on a reconnaissance patrol along the Paraguay River, his canoe was hit by a Brazilian cannonball, which shattered his leg. Despite the ministrations of several army doctors, septicemia soon set in, and Díaz died at López's encampment at Paso Pucú.

CHARLES J. KOLINSKI, *Independence or Death! The Story of the Paraguayan War* (1965); CARLOS ZUBIZARRETA, *Cien vidas paraguayas,* 2d ed. (1985), pp. 164–170.

THOMAS L. WHIGHAM

DÍAZ, JOSÉ PEDRO (*b.* 1921), Uruguayan writer, literary critic, and educator. Uruguay's foremost critic of French literature, Díaz often writes about French as well as Uruguayan literature in the weekly *Correo de los viernes.* He is also one of Uruguay's most important novelists. His *Los fuegos de San Telmo* (1964), one of the best novels produced by the Uruguayan Generation of 1945, investigates the Italian origins of Uruguay's majority population. *Partes de naufragios* (1969) focuses on the complacent life in Montevideo of the 1930s and 1940s, a view that assumes ironic dimensions, given the productive and moral crisis affecting the country at the time of its publication. Also important are Díaz's conceptual essays treating the Spanish poet Gustavo Adolfo Bécquer (1953), the Uruguayan fantasy writer Felisberto HERNÁNDEZ, and the poet Delmira AGUSTINI.

FERNANDO AINSA AMIGUES, *Tiempo reconquistado: Siete ensayos sobre literatura uruguaya* (1977); MARIE JOHNSTON PECK, *Mythologizing Uruguayan Reality* (1985).

WILLIAM H. KATRA

DíAZ, PORFIRIO (*b.* 15 September 1830; *d.* 2 July 1915), president of Mexico (1876–1880 and 1884–1911). In recognition of his prominence in Mexican politics and government, the period from 1876 to 1911 is called the PORFIRIATO. Much of the literature written about Díaz during his presidency reflects the sycophantic adulation of his biographers, while that dating from the Revolution of 1910 has tended to castigate him as a repressive dictator. His life, of course, was more complicated.

Porfirio Díaz was born in the city of Oaxaca, the sixth child of a modest innkeeper and his wife. His father, José de la Cruz Díaz, died before Porfirio reached the age of three. His mother, Petrona Mori, was unable to keep the business going. As soon as he was old enough, Porfirio was sent to work for a carpenter, but he found time for his primary studies. At the age of fifteen, he began attending the seminary, apparently with the aid of his godfather, the canon and later bishop of Oaxaca, José Agustín Domínguez. Porfirio interrupted his studies to enlist in the national guard during the war of 1846–1847 with the United States but saw no fighting. After graduating in 1849, Díaz refused to be ordained and insisted on studying law at the Institute of Sciences and Arts, passing his first examination in civil and canon law in 1853.

With the triumph of the Plan of AYUTLA (1854), Díaz was named subprefect of Ixtlán, the beginning of his political career. He joined the Oaxaca national guard in 1856 and fought for the liberals during the War of the REFORM. He was promoted to the rank of brigadier general in August 1861. Elected to Congress that same year, he served only briefly.

Porfirio Díaz first achieved fame as a result of his crucial role in the victory against the invading French troops at Puebla on 5 May 1862. The following year he was twice captured but managed to escape and return to the struggle, sustaining guerrilla warfare against the occupying French army throughout 1866 and taking the city of Oaxaca on 31 October of that year. The following year he led his Army of the East to victory at Puebla on 2 April and drove the imperial army from the national capital on 21 June.

Díaz opposed President Benito JUÁREZ's *convocatoria* of 1867, which attempted to increase presidential power and alter the constitution by referendum. Díaz regarded the *convocatoria* as both unconstitutional and a personal affront. The legislature of Oaxaca lauded him in recognition of his efforts against the French, gave him the hacienda of La Noria, and supported him for the presidency of the republic. After Juárez's reelection (1867), Díaz resigned from the army and turned his attention to agriculture, his investment in the telegraph connecting Mexico and Oaxaca, and the presidential election in 1871. With another reelection of Juárez, Díaz rebelled. His PLAN OF LA NORIA claimed the election had been fraudulent and demanded that the presidency be limited to a single term. Díaz failed to dislodge Juárez, who died in mid-1872. Sebastián LERDO DE TEJADA, head of

the supreme court, ascended to the presidency and was soon elected to a four-year term. Díaz retired to his hacienda, made furniture, and prepared for another campaign.

Díaz rebelled against Lerdo in January 1876, charging that the elections scheduled for July of that year would be fraudulent. His PLAN OF TUXTEPEC retained the principle of no reelection and insisted on municipal autonomy. An expert in guerrilla warfare from his days fighting the French, Díaz designed a military strategy for the revolt that called for the use of hit-and-run tac-

President Porfirio Díaz at the horse races at the Hipódromo de Peralvillo, Mexico City, ca. 1903. LA FOTOTECA DEL INAH.

tics to force the government to diffuse its forces. Contrary to traditional histories, the "battle" of Icamole on 20 May did not indicate that Díaz's effort was crumbling. Although portrayed by Lerdo's government as a great victory over forces commanded personally by Díaz, the rebel leader was not present and his subordinate in charge of the encounter was under orders only to reconnoiter and skirmish with the enemy, not to engage in a decisive battle.

In any case, Lerdo's reelection prompted José María IGLESIAS to charge fraud and refuse to recognize the results. As head of the Supreme Court and next in line for the presidency, Iglesias tried to assume that office himself. Faced with the opposition of both Iglesias and Díaz, Lerdo resigned and went into exile. Díaz offered to acknowledge Iglesias as president if new elections could be held soon. Iglesias refused, but soon resigned when his forces were unable to stop Díaz's advance. After holding elections, Díaz took formal possession of the presidency on 5 May 1877 for a term to end on 30 November 1881.

Although the image of a repressive Díaz has been pervasive in the post-Revolutionary literature, his first term was notable for his efforts to conciliate his rivals and opponents as well as foreign governments. Díaz sent the proposal for no reelection to Congress and supported efforts to increase political competition for state and municipal posts as well. He attempted to divide and rule the economic elite by creating rivals for political power and expanding economic opportunities.

When the Grant administration in the United States attached conditions to its recognition of his government, Díaz arranged for payments on Mexico's debt. Rutherford B. Hayes soon succeeded Grant and raised the stakes, ordering U.S. troops to cross into Mexico in pursuit of raiders, bandits, and rustlers. Díaz ordered Mexican troops to resist any invasion, and only forbearance on both sides prevented a major escalation. Díaz defused the crisis by wooing U.S. investors (among them former president Grant) with concessions, thereby ending the clamor for intervention and achieving formal recognition of his government in 1878. To balance the tremendous weight of the United States, Díaz sought to renew ties to France and other European powers, using similar efforts to attract investment and diplomatic recognition.

At the end of his first term, Díaz made good on his promise and did not run for reelection; he accepted the post of secretary of development under President Manuel GONZÁLEZ and served as governor of the state of Oaxaca. In 1884, Díaz was again elected president, losing his antipathy to reelection in 1888, 1892, 1904, and 1910. He provided stable government, balanced the budget, and assured economic growth but increased Mexico's reliance on foreign capital and the subservience of Mexican capital and labor to foreign control. His power became dictatorial; he prevented the election of his opponents and muzzled the press. But if his skills

had been limited to repression, he would never have lasted as long as he did. Díaz blocked formation of political parties but encouraged rivalries between elite factions. The two major contenders for favor were the CIENTÍFICOS, led by his father-in-law, Manuel ROMERO RUBIO (and after his death by Díaz's finance minister, José Yves LIMANTOUR), and a cohort of military officers, led by Manuel González and later by Bernardo REYES. Recent research suggests Díaz was able to exercise a relative degree of autonomy from economic interests. He acted to limit the expropriation of Indian lands by surveying companies and was flexible in dealing with peasant and labor grievances until the turn of the century.

After 1900, the system began to fall apart as the result of economic depression, political organization, increasing nationalism, blatant repression, and the fundamental uncertainty generated by the president's age. Díaz was either unwilling or unable to maintain the complex system of rivalries and balancing of contending interests that had provided stability for decades. In 1908, in an interview with the U.S. newspaper reporter James CREELMAN, he appeared to announce that Mexico was ready for competitive elections and that he would not run for reelection in 1910. Later Díaz changed his mind, but not until after the published remarks had created a sensation.

As he neared the age of eighty, it was obvious to everyone else that Díaz could not remain president much longer. Every level of Mexican society clamored for more nationalistic policies, from the *científicos*, who resented the interventionism of the U.S. government and the increasing size and power of U.S. corporations, to the railroad workers and miners, who were paid half as much as foreigners for the same work. Díaz rejected economic nationalism, but U.S. interests saw him as increasingly anti-American while his domestic opponents accused him of selling out to the United States. Finally, Díaz lost power the way he first gained it, as a result of guerrilla warfare. On 21 May 1911, his representative signed the Treaty of Ciudad Juárez with Francisco MADERO. Díaz resigned the presidency on 25 May, and by the end of the month was on his way to exile in Paris, where he died.

The literature on Porfirian Mexico is voluminous, but there is no good, recent biography of Díaz. See the classic indictments by JOHN KENNETH TURNER, *Barbarous Mexico* (1910; repr. 1969); and CARLETON BEALS, *Porfirio Díaz, Dictator of Mexico*, (1932; repr. 1971). In Díaz's defense, see JORGE FERNANDO ITURRIBARRÍA, *Porfirio Díaz ante la historia* (1967). As a guide, consult THOMAS BENJAMIN and MARCIAL OCASIO-MELÉNDEZ, "Organizing the Memory of Modern Mexico: Porfirian Historiography in Perspective, 1880s–1980s," in *Hispanic American Historical Review* 64 (May 1984): 323–364. For an excellent historical summary, see FRIEDRICH KATZ, "Mexico: Restored Republic and Porfiriato, 1867–1910," in Leslie Bethell, ed., *The Cambridge History of Latin America*, vol. 5 (1986), pp. 3–78. On the restored republic and the Revolution of Tuxtepec, see LAURENS BALLARD PERRY, *Juárez and Díaz: Machine Politics in Mexico*

(1978). On Porfirian history, see DANIEL COSÍO VILLEGAS, *Historia moderna de México*, 9 vols. (1955–1972); DANIEL COSÍO VILLEGAS, *The United States Versus Porfirio Díaz* (1963); and FRANÇOIS-XAVIER GUERRA, *México, del antiguo régimen a la Revolución*, 2 vols., translated by Sergio Fernández Bravo (1988). Recent works on Díaz's role in land-tenure questions include DONALD F. STEVENS, "Agrarian Policy and Instability in Porfirian Mexico," *The Americas* 39, no. 2 (1982): 153–166; and ROBERT H. HOLDEN, "Priorities of the State in the Survey of the Public Land in Mexico, 1876–1911," *Hispanic American Historical Review* 70, no. 4 (1990): 579–608.

D. F. STEVENS

DÍAZ AROSEMENA, DOMINGO (*b.* 25 June 1875; *d.* 23 August 1949), Panamanian politician and president (1948–1949) and a member of one of the most prominent political families in the country. He spent many years in public service as a member of the Panama City Council and deputy to the National Assembly. After the revolution of 1931 Díaz Arosemena founded the Doctrinary Liberal Party, one of the many offshoots of the Liberal Party after the revolution. He was a candidate for president in the 1936 elections, one of the most hotly contested elections in the history of the country, but lost to the official candidate, Juan Demóstenes AROSEMENA. In 1948, Díaz Arosemena won the presidency with the backing of the country's major political forces. He died the following year.

ERNESTO DE JESÚS CASTILLERO REYES, *Historia de Panamá*, 7th ed. (1962); JOAQUÍN A. ORTEGA C., *Gobernantes de la República de Panamá, 1903–1968*, 3d ed. (1965).

JUAN MANUEL PÉREZ

DÍAZ CASTRO, EUGENIO (*b.* 1804; *d.* 11 April 1865), Colombian author noted for his novels and local-color sketches (*cuadros de costumbre*). Born in Soacha, Díaz studied in Bogotá's Colegio de San Bartolomé but spent most of his life in agricultural endeavors. When he was over fifty, he became acquainted with José María Vergara y Vergara, who published his sketches of rural life in Vergara y Vergara's literary magazine *El Mosaico*. Díaz also wrote three novels: *Manuela* (1858), *Los aguinaldos en Chapinero* (1873), and *El rejo de enlazar* (1873), only the first of which is well regarded. Set in 1856 in a small town near Bogotá, it is partly a romantic love story centered around the simple but sharp-witted Manuela. The novel also effectively portrays the ideological disputes of the era and points up the gulf between recently enacted reform legislation and the realities of rural Colombia.

EUGENIO DÍAZ CASTRO, *Novelas y cuadros de costumbre*, 2 vols. (1985); RAYMOND L. WILLIAMS, *The Colombian Novel, 1844–1987* (1991), esp. pp. 56–68.

HELEN DELPAR

DÍAZ DE GUZMÁN, RUY (*b.* ca. 1558; *d.* June 1629), known primarily for being the first creole historian of the Río de la Plata. Díaz de Guzmán was born in or near Asunción (modern Paraguay) and spent most of his early adult years fighting Indian wars and settling towns in the Río de la Plata, Paraguay, and Tucumán. Between the founding of Santa Fe in 1573, the recolonization of Buenos Aires in 1580, and the division of La Plata into two major jurisdictions in 1617, most littoral and interior towns had been permanently established. Díaz de Guzmán's history of the first half-century of Spanish rule is composed mainly of the accounts of town foundings and stories surrounding the early post-Conquest years. Known as the *Argentina Manuscrita*, it was first printed in 1835 and has had subsequent editions. Díaz de Guzmán died in Asunción. Ricardo Rojas (1882–1957), the Argentine writer and scholar whose pioneering *Historia de la literatura argentina* (4 vols., 1917) is a milestone in Argentine scholarship, traces influences of Díaz de Guzmán's history from the sixteenth to the twentieth century.

NICHOLAS P. CUSHNER

DÍAZ DE SOLÍS, JUAN. *See* **Solís, Juan Díaz de.**

DÍAZ DEL CASTILLO, BERNAL (*b.* ca. 1495; *d.* 3 February 1584), Spanish conquistador and author. In a passage from his *Historia verdadera de la conquista de la Nueva España* (True History of the Conquest of New Spain), Díaz establishes his birthplace as Medina del Campo and recalls his first journey to America in Pedro Arias de AVILA's expedition to the Darien in 1514. He subsequently participated in the explorations of the Yucatán by Francisco HERNÁNDEZ DE CÓRDOBA (1517) and of the Gulf of Mexico by Juan de GRIJALVA (1518), both of which preceded Cortés's conquest in 1519. After the Conquest, Díaz was awarded several *encomiendas* in Guatemala.

Like the other *encomenderos*, Díaz was adversely affected by a series of decrees in the mid-sixteenth century that eliminated *encomiendas* in perpetuity and personal services. However, his description of his poverty in the *Historia verdadera* should be taken as a rhetorical device. There are numerous documents that disprove his complaints about not having been sufficiently rewarded for his participation in the Conquest. Recently critics have insisted that his claims of "lacking letters" and his criticism of Francisco López de Gómara's elevated style in the *Historia de las Indias y la conquista de México* (1552) are a subterfuge to mask the fact that Bartolomé de LAS CASAS is the true target of his attacks. Díaz's and Gómara's styles are not as different as Díaz would lead us to believe; both cultivate a simple and clear language. Las Casas's condemnations of the colonial order, however, influenced the decrees against the *encomienda* system, and it was during the early 1550s that Díaz decided to write his *Historia verdadera.* He constantly revised the work until he finally finished it in 1568. The *Historia verdadera,* however, was not published until 1632. Although Díaz's expressed intent in writing the *Historia* was to better the lot of his children and grandchildren, his story is nevertheless a riveting account of the Conquest that ultimately constitutes a defense of the conquistadores. He died in Guatemala.

HERBERT CERWIN, *Bernal Díaz, Historian of the Conquest* (1963); BERNAL DÍAZ DEL CASTILLO, *The Discovery and Conquest of Mexico, 1517–1521,* translated and edited by A. P. Maudslay (1970); ROLENA ADORNO, "Discourses on Colonialism: Bernal Díaz, Las Casas, and the Twentieth-Century Reader," in *Modern Language Notes* 103 (March 1988): 239–258; and BERNAL DÍAZ DEL CASTILLO, *Historia verdadera de la conquista de la Nueva España,* edited by Carmelo Saenz de Santa María (1989).

JOSÉ RABASA

DÍAZ LOZANO, ARGENTINA (*b.* 15 December 1909), Honduran novelist. Born in Santa Rosa de Copán, Honduras, Díaz Lozano moved to Guatemala, the setting for many of her novels, in 1912. She studied at the University of San Carlos and became the first woman to graduate in journalism. A prolific writer (translated into French and English), she published her first novel at age seventeen and has received many awards for both her fiction and her journalism, among them the National Prize for literature in Honduras (1968) and awards from Guatemala, Brazil, and Italy. In 1957 ex-president Juan José Arévalo nominated her for the Nobel Prize in literature.

Her fiction belongs to the regionalist school predating the "Boom" of the 1960s in Latin American letters. Her novels focus on local themes, often exposing the plight of the poor, especially the tragic circumstances of Guatemalan Indians. Nevertheless, she shows little willingness to explore underlying issues of race, gender, and politics which might threaten the status quo. Her portrayal of women and Indians, while compassionate, essentially reflects the romantic and patronizing perspectives of the LADINO.

The best-known novels include *Mayapán: Novela histórica* (1950), translated by Lydia Wright (1955); *Y tenemos que vivir* (1961), translated by Lillian Sears as *And We Have to Live* (1978); and *Ha llegado una mujer* (1991), based on Eugene O'Neill's *Desire Under the Elms.* She is mentioned briefly in SEYMOUR MENTON, *Historia crítica de la novela guatemalteca,* 2d ed. (1985), and is exceedingly praised in JOSÉ FRANCISCO MARTÍNEZ, *Literatura hondureña y su proceso generacional* (1987).

ANN GONZÁLEZ

DÍAZ ORDAZ, GUSTAVO (*b.* 11 March 1911; *d.* 15 July 1979), president of Mexico (1964–1970). Díaz Ordaz was the last president to preside over a period of consistent, stable economic growth, but his administration was widely condemned for his handling of student unrest on the occasion of the 1968 Mexico City Olympics.

Díaz Ordaz was born in Chalchicomula, Ciudad Serdán, in the state of Puebla. His father was a government accountant, his grandfather was General José María Díaz Ordaz, and one of his direct ancestors was the conquistador and chronicler Bernal DÍAZ DEL CASTILLO. After studying in Oaxaca, he received his law degree from the University of Puebla on 8 February 1937. While still a student he had begun his public career, serving as a court clerk (1932). Upon graduation he became a prosecuting attorney, then a federal agent, and later director of the labor arbitration board in Puebla.

After serving briefly as vice rector of the University of Puebla (1940–1941), Díaz Ordaz became secretary-general of government in Puebla and then federal deputy from that state (1943–1946). He moved from the lower to the upper chamber, serving as senator (1946–1952), and then joined the government secretariat, first as director-general of legal affairs (1952–1956), then as *oficial mayor* (1956–1958), and, finally, as secretary of government (1958–1964) in the administration of Adolfo LÓPEZ MATEOS.

The successful PRI candidate for president in 1964, he held that office when the Olympic Games took place in Mexico City in the fall of 1968. His government then became entangled in a conflict with a student movement that, like such movements in many other countries, involved a number of issues. When students staged a demonstration in the Plaza of the Three Cultures in the Tlatelolco district, the government called out army troops, who fired on the demonstrators, leaving hundreds of students and bystanders dead. The repercussions of this event produced the generation of Mexican political and intellectual leaders of the 1990s, including former President Carlos SALINAS, and altered the relationship between intellectuals and the government. Even more, this event raised serious questions about the legitimacy of the Mexican political and economic model and introduced pressures for political liberalization, the effects of which were to be seen in the 1970s and 1980s, culminating in the 1988 presidential election.

Even before the debacle of 1968, Díaz Ordaz had discouraged the early efforts of PRI president Carlos A. MADRAZO to democratize the party in 1965. As a result of these political failures, the Mexican presidency suffered a loss of prestige. After his presidency, his successor appointed him ambassador to Spain (1977), but he was so unpopular, and the public outcry against him so intense, that he resigned the appointment before serving and remained out of the public eye until his death.

RICARDO COVARRUBIAS, *Los 67 gobernantes del México independiente* (1968); ROGER D. HANSEN, *The Politics of Mexican Development* (1971); SERGIO ZERMEÑO, *México: una democracia utópica* (1978); JUDITH A. HELLMAN, *Mexico in Crisis* (1983); KENNETH F. JOHNSON, *Mexican Democracy, A Critical View* (1984); and DANIEL C. LEVY and GABRIEL SZÉKELY, *Mexico: Paradoxes of Stability and Change* (1987).

RODERIC AI CAMP

DÍAZ SOTO Y GAMA, ANTONIO (*b.* 1880; *d.* 1967), leading precursor of the Mexican Revolution. With Camillo Arriaga and Ricardo FLORES MAGÓN, he founded the Club Liberal Ponciano Arriaga and was one of its four secretaries. This organization later served as an organizational base for the Liberal Party. Díaz Soto is also remembered for his lively participation in debates in the Chamber of Deputies in the 1920s and as one of the founders of the National Agrarian Party in 1920.

He was born into the middle-class provincial family of Conrado Díaz Soto and Concepción Gama, and graduated from the Scientific and Literary Institute of San Luis Potosí as a lawyer in 1900. He later taught at the National Preparatory School and University. While in exile for his opposition to Porfirio DÍAZ, he became a Liberal Party activist. During the MEXICAN REVOLUTION he supported Emiliano ZAPATA and, although he was named secretary of justice by the Convention government in 1915, he refused the post. In 1920, and again in 1927–1928, he gave his political support to Alvaro OBREGÓN. He ended his political career as vice president of the Mexican Democratic Party in 1945 and then returned to intellectual activities.

ANTONIO DÍAZ SOTO Y GAMA, "The Agrarian Movement in Mexico," in HUBERT C. HERRING et al., *The Genius of Mexico* (1976); and JAMES D. COCKCROFT, *Intellectual Precursors of the Mexican Revolution, 1900–1913* (1969).

RODERIC AI CAMP

DÍAZ VÉLEZ, JOSÉ MIGUEL (*b.* 1770; *d.* 1833), Argentine patriot. Born in Tucumán and trained as a lawyer, Díaz Vélez was military commandant of Entre Ríos province from 1810 to 1814. He later held various positions in Buenos Aires. In 1825 he was a member of a mission to Upper Peru that sought to treat with Simón BOLÍVAR concerning the future status of that region and collaboration in a possible war against Brazil. The mission was a failure, as Upper Peru was by then committed to becoming a separate nation-state and Bolívar proved ambivalent regarding an anti-Brazilian alliance. Díaz Vélez served in the Unitarist regime set up in Buenos Aires by Juan LAVALLE in 1828; when it collapsed, he emigrated to Uruguay, where he died at Paysandú.

JACINTO R. YABEN, *Biografías argentinas y sudamericanas*, vol. 2 (1938), pp. 294–295; THOMAS B. DAVIES, JR., *Carlos de Alvear: Man of Revolution* (1955, repr. 1968), pp. 63–83.

DAVID BUSHNELL

DICKMANN, ADOLFO (*b.* 1882; *d.* 1 September 1938), Argentine Socialist councilman and congressman. Born in Finland, Dickmann immigrated as a youth with his family to Entre Ríos Province, Argentina, in the late nineteenth century. After joining the Socialist Party in 1900, he received his degree in dentistry from the University of Buenos Aires in 1905 and established a practice in Morón in the province of Buenos Aires. He served first on the city council of Morón, and then in 1914 was elected to the provincial legislature, where he introduced legislation to create a provincial department of labor, to modify the tax on inheritances, and to regulate child and female labor.

In 1919, Dickmann was elected to the city council of the federal capital and then served three terms as a Socialist representative to the national Chamber of Deputies (1922–1926, 1926–1930, and 1932–1936). A prominent member of the Socialist delegation in the national Congress, he was associated with legislation intended to improve the management of municipal administration and to better the living and working conditions of employees, workers, and rural laborers. Himself a naturalized citizen, Dickmann wrote several works on immigration and nationalism as well as on tax policy, collective bargaining, and state control of the petroleum industry.

RICHARD J. WALTER

See also **Argentina: Political Parties.**

DICKMANN, ENRIQUE (*b.* 20 December 1874; *d.* 30 December 1955), Argentine Socialist congressman and party leader. Born in present-day Latvia, Dickmann settled in Argentina in 1890. He became a naturalized citizen in 1897 and graduated from the medical school of the University of Buenos Aires with a medal of honor in 1904. In 1905 he was appointed chief of the clinic in a local hospital. As with several other Socialists, however, he became better known as a politician than as a physician. He joined the Socialist Party in 1896 and soon became an important figure in that organization, serving as editor of the party newspaper, *La Vanguardia,* first in 1898 and then for several periods thereafter.

Dickmann was elected for the first time to the national Chamber of Deputies from the federal capital in 1914 and served in that body for more than three decades (1914–1916, 1916–1920, 1920–1924, 1924–1928, 1932–1936, 1936–1940, and 1942–1946). An energetic and outspoken legislator, Dickmann was a prominent figure in the Socialist bloc of deputies. He had a hand in most of the Socialists' initiatives of these years, ranging from measures to promote and protect the rights of workers, including women and children, to opposition to what the Socialists viewed as overly favorable concessions to foreign investors. In 1931–1932, Dickmann played an important role in helping to form a joint presidential ticket with the Progressive Democratic Party, one of the few instances when the Socialists agreed to participate in a political coalition. In the late 1930s and early 1940s, Dickmann was a vocal opponent of the rise of fascism in Europe and warned of its possible extension to and growing influence in Argentina. He was close to party founder Juan B. JUSTO and remained steadfast in his loyalty to the central party until the 1940s, when, contrary to the stance of most Socialists, he expressed sympathy with the goals and achievements of President Juan PERÓN (1946–1955). The author of numerous books, his best-known work is his autobiography, *Recuerdos de un militante socialista* (1949).

RICHARD J. WALTER

See also **Argentina: Political Parties.**

DICTATORS LEAGUE, a myth concerning four Central American dictators that was popularized during 1936 and 1937 by the growing hysteria over the rise of fascism in Europe. Rumors spread by exile movements and the press in Mexico, Costa Rica, and the United States presumed an alliance among the regimes of generals Jorge UBICO in Guatemala (1931–1944), Maximiliano HERNÁNDEZ MARTÍNEZ in El Salvador (1931–1944), Tiburcio CARÍAS ANDINO in Honduras (1933–1949), and Anastasio SOMOZA GARCÍA in Nicaragua (1937–1956). The similarities of the methods used by these personalistic caudillos and their prompt recognition of the Spanish regime of Generalíssimo Francisco Franco alarmed U.S. opinion makers and journalists. In fact, the dominance and actions of the Central American dictators reflected each country's domestic political situation, all the results of the global depression.

The dictators were rivals who contested supremacy in the isthmus for many years. The only cooperation among them was a mutual tolerance stemming from belated recognition that none was capable of overthrowing the others—a standoff that resulted in a tacit accord to stop aiding exiles from neighboring nations.

KENNETH J. GRIEB, ''The Myth of a Central American Dictators' League,'' in *Journal of Latin American Studies* 10, no. 2 (1978): 329–345; and *Guatemalan Caudillo: The Regime of Jorge Ubico, Guatemala, 1931–1944* (1979).

KENNETH J. GRIEB

DIEGO, ELISEO (*b.* 2 July 1920; *d.* 2 March 1994), Cuban poet and essayist. Diego was born in Havana, where he studied law for two years at the University of Havana. He was part of the editorial board of the literary publication *Clavileño* and was one of the founders of the influential magazine *Orígenes*, where his first poems and short stories appeared between 1944 and 1956. He taught English and served as inspector of English instruction for the Ministry of Education. In 1959 he earned a degree in education from the University of Havana. In 1962 Diego was put in charge of the Department of Children's Literature at the José Martí National Library in Havana, a post he occupied until 1970. He was secretary of public relations for the Cuban Union of Writers and Artists (UNEAC), and served on juries for several important literary contests in Cuba, including those of the UNEAC and the Casa de las Américas. He

traveled widely to represent Cuba officially at international cultural events.

In 1993 Diego was awarded Mexico's Juan Rulfo literary prize, among the most important in Latin America. One of the foremost Cuban poets of the century, Diego exerted great influence on the younger generation of Cuban poets, especially after the publication of his first book, *En la calzada de Jesús del Monte* (1949). There is one compendium of his poems in prose, essays, and short stories (*Prosas escogidas*, 1983) and another of his poetry up to 1983 (*Poesía*). Both were published in Havana in beautiful editions. Other works by Diego include *Entre la dicha y la tiniebla: Antología poética, 1949–1985* (1986), and *Veintiséis poemas recientes* (1986). His poetry has been translated widely. Diego died in Mexico City.

ROBERTO VALERO

DIEGO, JOSÉ DE (*b.* 16 April 1866; *d.* 16 July 1918), Puerto Rican poet. Born in Aguadilla, Puerto Rico, de Diego studied law at the University of Barcelona in Spain, where he began writing poetry and prose. After completing his degree in Havana in 1892, he returned to Puerto Rico and became a prosecutor, later serving as undersecretary of justice and government, congressional representative, and Supreme Court justice. A staunch autonomist, he advocated the primacy of the Spanish language and Puerto Rico's independence from the United States. He was Speaker of the House of Representatives from 1907 until his death, president of the Union Party from 1914 to 1916, and president of the Puerto Rico Athenaeum from 1916 to 1918. De Diego was famous as an orator and for his books of poetry, among them *Pomarrosas* (Rose apples, 1904), *Cantos de rebeldía* (Songs of rebellion, 1916), and *Cantos de Pitirre* (Songs of Pitirre, published posthumously in 1949). Patriotism, Puerto Rico's country life, Americanism, the Antilles, and romantic love are his major themes. He also published a volume of selected prose, *Nuevas campañas* (New campaigns) in 1916.

MARGOT ARCE DE VÁZQUEZ, *La obra literaria de José de Diego* (1967); CONCHA MELÉNDEZ, *José de Diego en mi memoria* (1966); DELMA S. ARRIGOITIA, *José de Diego: A Legislator in Times of Political Transition (1903–1918)* (1985).

ESTELLE IRIZARRY

DIESELDORFF, ERWIN PAUL (*b.* 10 June 1868; *d.* 3 November 1940), German-born coffee planter and merchant in the Alta VERAPAZ, Guatemala. A member of a wealthy Hamburg family active in trade with Central America, Dieseldorff worked for three years in his uncle's export firm in London before going to Guatemala in 1888 to search for investment opportunities. On the advice of relatives who had preceded him, he engaged in the production and export of COFFEE. He acquired properties from the Polochic River to the Petén and became the largest private landowner in Guatemala. His coffee business was vertically integrated with plantations that served different complementary functions. Dieseldorff had a lifelong interest in and wrote extensively about the MAYA and the MEDICINAL plants of the Alta Verapaz.

ERWIN P. DIESELDORFF, *Der Kaffeebaum* (1908), *Kunst und Religion der Mayavölker*, 3 vols. (1926–1933), and *Las plantas medicinales del Departamento de Alta Verapaz* (1940); GUILLERMO NÁÑEZ FALCÓN, "Erwin Paul Dieseldorff, German Entrepreneur in the Alta Verapaz of Guatemala, 1889–1937" (Ph.D. diss., Tulane University, 1970).

GUILLERMO NÁÑEZ FALCÓN

DIET. *See* **Cuisines; Nutrition.**

DIEZMO (tithe; in Portuguese, *dízimo*), an ecclesiastical tax of 10 percent levied on agricultural production. The tithe has biblical roots but came to be the standard level of support of the CATHOLIC CHURCH by the faithful. As the tithe was implemented in the Hispanic Americas it was levied only on agricultural and pastoral production: of a harvest of ten bushels of wheat, for instance, one bushel would be paid to the church; of ten lambs born in a given year, one would go to the church. Usually the tithe was paid on the raw material produced. Bulk wool was subject to the tithe, not woven cloth. Nevertheless, sugar was taxed, not cane. Generally all Christians were subject to the tithe. In Mexico, however, the practice evolved to require that natives pay only on three things (*tres cosas*): silk, wheat, and cattle. In other regions natives had to pay on all European products, but not on native goods, whereas in other regions they were fully liable.

The tithe could be collected directly by the ecclesiastical authorities, yet often the right to collect the tithe was rented to local contractors. By renting out the collection, the church received slightly less income, but with little or no delay. When the church collected the tithe directly, it often took quite a long time to complete collections for a given year, but it also gave the church more income and an opportunity to speculate in local commodity markets.

The tithe was used for the support of the ecclesiastical hierarchy under the local bishop or archbishop. According to the scheme under which the tithe was divided, one quarter went to the bishop and one quarter to the cathedral chapter. The remaining half was divided into nine parts, with two parts going to the king as patron, four to the local curates, and the remaining three divided equally between the local hospital and the cathedral for its upkeep.

The tithe in Brazil was controlled by the Portuguese crown. The right to collect and administer the tithe in Portuguese overseas possessions had been granted to the military-religious Order of Christ (Ordem de Cristo). Consequently, the tithe collected in Brazil was then sent to Portugal, where crown officials divided it, returning part to Brazil to support the local church.

JOHN F. SCHWALLER, *Origins of Church Wealth in Mexico: Ecclesiastical Revenues and Church Finances, 1523–1600* (1985).

JOHN F. SCHWALLER

DIOMEDE, MIGUEL (*b.* 20 July 1902; *d.* 15 October 1974), Argentine painter. Diomede was born in La Boca, an Italian bohemian neighborhood on the outskirts of Buenos Aires, where he lived and worked all his life, except for a short trip to Italy in 1954. A self-taught artist, he earned a living in humble jobs (street photographer, stevedore, hospital orderly, ship painter). He received several awards, including the first prize at the Salón de La Plata in Buenos Aires Province, 1957, and the bronze medal at the International Exhibition of Brussels, 1958. In 1959 he had a show at the Organization of American States in Washington, D.C. He became a member of the National Academy of Fine Arts in Buenos Aires in 1973. In 1974, two months before his death, he had a retrospective exhibition at the Galería LAASA in Buenos Aires.

The Argentine critic Damián Bayón called Diomede "one of the great melancholics," comparing his style to that of Eugenio Daneri. Diomede's work is marked by soft tones and large-scale composition. The elegance of his still lifes is immediately suggestive of the Italian Giorgio Morandi. He had a refined perception of reality and a soft sense of rhythm.

Museum of Modern Art of Latin America (1985); VINCENTE GESUALDO, ALDO BIGLIONE, and RODOLFO SANTOS, *Diccionario de artistas plásticos en la Argentina* (1988).

AMALIA CORTINA ARAVENA

DIRETÓRIO DOS ÍNDIOS (Indian directorate), a legislative code (1757–1798) that secularized the administration of Indian mission villages in Portuguese America. As part of the POMBALINE REFORMS, the Diretório initially sought to weaken Jesuit economic influence in the Amazon, but in 1758 the code was extended to all of Brazil. To replace the missionaries, local governors appointed lay directors who were to stimulate settled agriculture, encourage mixed marriages, and facilitate the adoption of the Portuguese language and customs. The code was strengthened by other decrees, such as the elevation of missions to the status of *vilas* (towns) in 1758 and the expulsion of the Jesuits in 1759. In practice, the directors frequently disregarded Diretório guidelines and, entitled to one-sixth of the villages' output, organized forced-labor drafts and abusive collecting expeditions for personal gain.

As a "civilizing" project, the Diretório failed miserably. It was, in effect, more interested in the exploitation of native labor than in the development of a social program. As a result, the Diretório period proved disastrous for the Indians, as village populations declined, communal lands were usurped, and ethnic identity became eroded. Repeated complaints of corruption and abuses led to the abolition of the Diretório in 1798.

COLIN MAC LACHLAN, "The Indian Directorate. Forced Acculturation in Portuguese America," in *The Americas* 28 (1972): 357–387, provides a detailed treatment, with particular emphasis on the Amazon. A more general discussion may be found in JOHN HEMMING, *Amazon Frontier* (1987).

JOHN M. MONTEIRO

DIRTY WAR, conflict between rightist governments and leftist opposition in Argentina, 1974–1983. The *guerra sucia* evolved out of confrontations—beginning with the *Cordobazo* (Córdoba insurrection) of May 1969—between the Right regimes of generals Juan Carlos Onganía, Roberto Marcelo Levingston, and Alejandro Lanusse and the Left opposition. The latter comprised industrial workers, university students, and young professionals frustrated with political stagnation and Argentina's economic decline. They were led by two armed factions: the Peronist MONTONEROS, Fuerzas Armadas Peronistas (Peronist Armed Forces), and Fuerzas Armadas Revolucionarias (Revolutionary Armed Forces) and the Trotskyite Ejército Revolucionario del Pueblo (People's Revolutionary Army). In the early 1970s the Left carried out numerous robberies, kidnappings, and assassinations, including that of former president and general Pedro Aramburu in 1970. Rightist strike forces retaliated. The *retorno* of Juan PERÓN in 1973 brought a brief hiatus as young radicals and the aging general sought to use each other for their own purposes. Perón's rejection of the Left, his death in 1974, and the disintegration of the successor regime (1974–1976) of his widow, Isabel PERÓN, unleashed unprecedented terror from the Right. The work of government death squads such as the "Triple A" (Alianza Anticomunista Argentina) was supplemented by antiguerrilla units of all three armed services. The dirty war reached its height between 1976, when Jorge Rafael VIDELA reinstituted direct military rule, and 1978, by which time the Left was in ruins and thousands of leftists were dead, in exile, or "disappeared."

Counterguerrilla operations included kidnappings, torture, rape, and murder. Detainees' families were denied information on the victims' fate; their mutilated bodies might (or might not) turn up months after their "disappearance." Accountability was avoided: operations were decentralized into autonomous commands, each with prisons, torturers, and graveyards. Prominent among the victims were journalists, trade unionists, intellectuals (Silvio Frondizi, Haraldo Conti, Rodolfo Walsh), clergy (Bishop Enrique Angelelli), and students; some persons were "disappeared" for no known reason. A disproportionate number were Jews. The future Nobel Peace Prize winner Adolfo PÉREZ ESQUIVEL survived kidnapping and torture. Some children born to women who were later murdered have been traced to military families to whom they were entrusted by their mothers' killers. The Mothers of the Plaza de Mayo, undeterred by obfuscation, indifference, and police brutality, focused international attention on Argentina through their demands to know the fate of their children or grandchildren. Most Argentines, however, were intimidated by the government terror.

Following the collapse of military rule in 1983, the National Commission on Disappeared People, headed by Ernesto Sábato, carried out a detailed public inquiry. Only in 1995 did some military officers begin to admit their direct involvement in the killings. The "dirty war" has been the subject of many Argentine films and novels. Lives lost to leftist violence in the early 1970s are estimated at several hundred; those "disappeared" in state-sanctioned terror total at least 13,000. The elected Radical government of Raúl ALFONSÍN (1983–1989) successfully prosecuted many leading military criminals; however, judicial foot-dragging and an amnesty (1990) by Alfonsín's successor, Carlos Saúl MENEM, left the rule of law in Argentina in question.

JACOBO TIMERMAN, *Prisoner Without a Name, Cell Without a Number* (1981); ARGENTINE NATIONAL COMMISSION ON DISAPPEARED PEOPLE, *Nunca más* (1984; *Never Again*, 1986); IAIN GUEST, *Behind the Disappearances: Argentina's Dirty War Against Human Rights and the United Nations* (1990); DONALD C. HODGES, *Argentina's "Dirty War"* (1991); FRANK GRAZIANO, *Divine Violence: Spectacle, Psychosexuality, and Radical Christianity in the Argentine Dirty War* (1992); and MARTIN EDWIN ANDERSON, *Argentina's Desaparecidos and the Myth of the "Dirty War"* (1993).

RONALD C. NEWTON

DISCÉPOLO, ENRIQUE SANTOS (*b.* 27 March 1901; *d.* 23 December 1951), Argentine radio commentator, movie director, and composer of tangos. Born in Buenos Aires and the brother of the neogrotesque dramatist Armando Discépolo, Enrique Santos was known as "Discepolín" to distinguish him from Armando. Discépolo participated fully in the enormous expansion of commercial popular culture based in Buenos Aires in the golden years following World War I and the 1930 watershed marked by economic collapse and the country's first fascist-inspired military dictatorship. A radio personality of considerable note and a successful movie director, Discépolo also wrote some of the most famous tangos of the period, compositions that have become an integral part of the classical repertoire: "¿Qué vachaché?" "Esta noche me emborracho," "¿Qué sapa, señor?" "Chorra," and, perhaps one of the most famous tango lyrics of all time, "Cambalache." The latter was banned by the military dictatorship in the late 1970s because of its harshly pessimistic tone, which was interpreted as socially disruptive.

HORACIO ARTURO FERRER and LUIS ADOLFO SIERRA, *Discepolín* (1965); NORBERTO GALASSO, *Discépolo y su época* (1967); HOMERO MANZI, *Discépolo* (1973); OSVALDO PELLETTIERI, *Tango (II)* (1976).

DAVID WILLIAM FOSTER

See also **Tango, The.**

DISEASES. Prior to the voyages of Columbus, the Americas constituted a relatively salubrious hemisphere, although the region was by no means disease free. The Indians suffered from some forms of trypanosomiasis—pinta to be sure, and perhaps yaws—but according to recent bioanthropological research, probably not syphilis. They had tuberculosis, hepatitis, and encephalitis, and a variety of intestinal parasites afflicted them as well. In certain locations, the distinctly American illnesses of Carrion's disease (Andean region) and American trypanosomiasis, or Chagas's disease, as it is more commonly known (tropical South and Central America), were in evidence.

In the past it has been argued that malaria and yellow fever were resident in the Western Hemisphere prior to contact with the wider world. But today, combined immunological, epidemiological, and etymological as well as historical evidence reveal these to be imported illnesses, as were a host of other maladies, including smallpox, chicken pox, measles, whooping cough, diphtheria, mumps, typhus, typhoid fever, scarlet fever, influenza, and bubonic plague, to name but a few of the most prominent of the diseases to which the Amerindians proved extraordinarily susceptible.

The Amerindians' pre-Columbian state of epidemiological grace is dramatic testimony to protracted isolation from the rest of the world. Beginning some 180 million years ago, long before humankind made its appearance on the globe, first South America and then North America broke free of Pangaea, the primordial supercontinent, gradually to work their way into their current locations. The animals that sailed with them presumably carried pathogens. But those were the days when reptiles—dinosaurs and the like—were dominant, and as they perished it is likely that most of their diseases perished with them.

Homo sapiens emerged some 40,000 years ago to spread out over the Old World as far as Siberia, and there is speculation based on genetic evidence that Polynesian voyagers in sea-going canoes may have reached the Americas. Certainly during the last ice age, when the oceans were low, other bold pioneers set out on the frozen tundra that formed a land bridge between Asia and Alaska. They probably crossed in small groups over millennia. About 10,000 years ago when the ice caps melted, the seas rose to seal off the Americas once again.

It might be supposed that the door had been opened for a sufficiently long time to admit pathogens into the region. But the pioneers who crossed the Bering Straits came as bands of hunter-gatherers whose restless lifestyle and small numbers were not supportive of most of the diseases that have more recently assaulted humans who became sedentary and crowded together. Moreover, the long trek through harsh weather presumably would have weeded out those who were ill. And finally, the new Americans arrived before humans had begun domesticating animals, a process that introduced literally hundreds of illnesses.

If the Amerindians were virginal in the face of Old World diseases, the Iberians who first reached the Americas had perhaps the most sophisticated immune systems of any people on earth. A series of invaders from the Romans to the Muslims had exposed the people of the peninsula to the diseases of vast empires extending throughout much of the Eurasian landmass. Also, their own exploration of the African coast as well as contact with the African slaves they brought back to Europe had exposed them to many of the diseases of that continent as well. The port cities of Iberia had long been the clearinghouse of diseases, and its towns and cities were open sewers abounding with disease-bearing rodents and insects, while the Iberians' lack of hygiene encouraged the presence of lice, fleas, and intestinal parasites.

We may never know with certainty what pathogens launched the first New World epidemic that was killing Arawaks in the Caribbean as early as 1493, but swine influenza has been put forth as a likely candidate. The *modorra* that assaulted Spaniards (and presumably Indians as well) on the Spanish Main a bit later on produced symptoms that suggest typhus. Smallpox had arrived in the Caribbean at least by 1518, swept through Mexico between the years 1520 and 1524, and then raced on to precede Pizarro into the land of the Incas. By 1554, it had penetrated southward as far as Chile to mount assaults on the Araucanians. Measles hammered the Caribbean in 1529 and then spread to Mexico and Central America. A pandemic in 1545 that the Aztecs called *matlazáhuatl* was probably typhus or influenza. Diphtheria was another important killer of the Indians, and there is evidence that bubonic plague as well may have visited the New World in the sixteenth century.

Vivax malaria probably arrived in the blood of the first Europeans, whereas the far more deadly falciparum malaria reached the Americas in the blood of African slaves. Yellow fever also rode the slave ships from Africa, but its debut was delayed until populations of its mosquito vector (which also required importation) and human hosts became sufficiently dense. The first recorded epidemic of yellow fever in the Caribbean is that which began in Barbados in 1647. Yellow fever is said to have occurred in Brazil between the years 1685 and 1694, to have disappeared until 1849, when it was omnipresent until the end of the century. Because survivors of yellow fever cannot host the disease a second

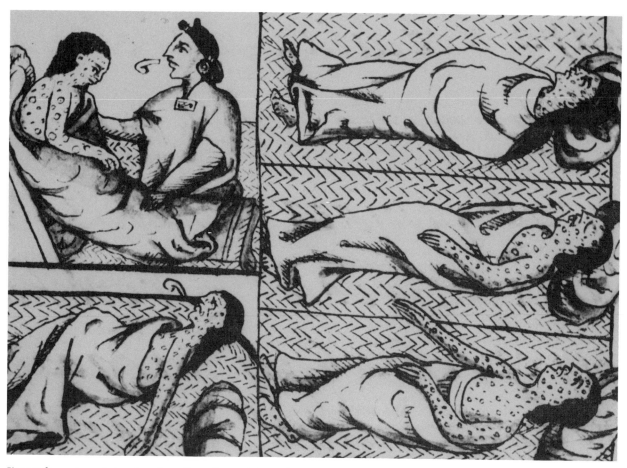

Sixteenth-century Aztec drawing of smallpox victims, from the Florentine Codex. BIBLIOTECA MEDICA LAURENZIANA, FLORENCE.

time, the significant numbers reported as resistant to the illness in both the 1685 and the 1849 epidemics suggest that yellow fever was in the country prior to 1685 and had returned prior to 1849.

It was this wave of African fevers coming hard on the heels of the Eurasian diseases that brought extermination to the Indians in the islands of the Caribbean and adjacent low-lying mainlands, and depopulation to the Amazon valley. In the higher elevations of the mainland, by contrast, the colder temperatures were not conducive to the mosquito vectors of yellow fever and malaria. Indian populations reeled under the onslaught of Eurasian illnesses but, without the added burden of the African plagues, ultimately recovered.

The African fevers afflicted whites to the same extent as they did Indians, while sparing blacks, who possessed both innate and acquired protection against them. The immunities of blacks to disease thus created an accelerating demand for African workers, and the ships that carried them also brought schistosomiasis, onchocerciasis, leishmaniasis, filariasis, hookworm disease, dengue fever, yaws, and a host of other African ailments, which settled onto the American tropics.

In fact, although the initial incursion of diseases in the Americas came from Europe, most of the illnesses reaching Latin America were African in origin until the closing of the slave trade in the nineteenth century. Smallpox epidemics traveled from Africa to Brazil and the Caribbean before subsequently fanning out to engulf the rest of Latin America. Yellow fever epidemics that continually battered the West Indies and coastal cities practically everywhere in the Americas continued to originate mostly in Africa, even though the disease had become endemic in the jungles of Central and South America.

Yet Africa cannot be blamed for Asiatic cholera, originating in India during the nineteenth century to sweep the globe in five pandemics. The Americas were hit by four of these; the first, in the 1830s, was limited to Cuba (and North America), but the remaining three devastated much of the Caribbean and Latin America, leaving hundreds of thousands of dead in their wake. The great epidemic of 1855–1856 in Brazil may have killed up to 200,000 individuals in that country alone, while in the Caribbean the disease rolled over island after island during the 1850s.

The last few decades of the nineteenth century and the first decades of the twentieth century saw the discovery of beriberi as a significant health problem in Cuba and especially in Brazil, but the turn of the century also brought with it dramatic advances against many old scourges. Carlos FINLAY and the Yellow Fever Commission of Walter REED unraveled much of the riddle of yellow fever's epidemiology and etiology, and yellow fever was stopped in Cuba. Subsequently, William Gorgas applied mosquito-control measures in Panama, which greatly facilitated the construction of the canal. In Rio de Janeiro, Oswaldo CRUZ led successful campaigns against bubonic plague (which had broken out in 1899) and yellow fever, and soon mosquito-control programs had curbed yellow fever almost everywhere in the hemisphere. Effective control of the mosquito vectors of malaria, however, had to await DDT, which was widely used only after World War II.

Programs funded by the Rockefeller Foundation were launched early in the twentieth century to combat such diseases as hookworm infection and yellow fever. These attempts fell far short of the ambitious goal of eradication but represented important steps in controlling such diseases. In the case of yellow fever, Rockefeller researchers in Brazil discovered that the disease was alive in the monkey inhabitants of the great South American rain forest. With this knowledge came the realization that yellow fever was really a disease of monkeys that incidentally infected humans, and since the monkeys could not all be killed, the disease could not be eradicated but only controlled.

Over the course of the nineteenth century, tuberculosis became an ever-increasing threat to the health of Latin Americans, especially those of African descent. The disease generated mortality rates as high as 1,000 per 100,000 population in cities such as Bahia and Havana. After the turn of the century, however, tuberculosis began to fade slowly and by mid-century it was no longer an important threat, at least until very recently when strains of tuberculosis resistant to antibiotics have become menacing worldwide, and other strains are taking advantage of compromised immune systems.

Modern medicine can claim no credit for the decline of tuberculosis in the hemisphere, but medicine has made considerable headway against neonatal tetanus (once a massive killer of infants) and childhood diseases ranging from diphtheria to rubella. Yet far too many Latin Americans have little or no access to modern medicine, and thus in many places the circumstances of poverty with attendant malnutrition intertwine with pathogens in synergystic fashion to produce very high levels of morbidity and mortality. Protein-energy malnutrition, especially kwashiorkor, affects the young, while a variety of deficiency diseases can be found in those of all ages. Nor has the hemisphere been freed from the threat of epidemic diseases both ancient and modern. Bubonic plague, which broke out in Ecuador during the first decade of the twentieth century, remained endemic there until well into the 1930s. In the late twentieth century, AIDS was widespread in Haiti and Brazil and threatened

to become a serious problem throughout the hemisphere. In 1994, Asiatic cholera once more returned to the Americas, spreading from Peru throughout the South American continent, in an epidemic that will probably kill thousands.

PERCY MOREAU ASHBURN, *The Ranks of Death: A Medical History of the Conquest of America* (1947); ERWIN H. ACKERKNECHT, *History and Geography of the Most Important Diseases* (1965); DONALD B. COOPER, *Epidemic Diseases in Mexico City, 1761–1813* (1965); LYEURGO DE CASTRO SANTOS FILHO, *História geral da medicina brasileira*, 2 vols. (1977); NOBLE DAVID COOK, *Demographic Collapse: Indian Peru, 1520–1620* (1981); KENNETH F. KIPLE, *The Caribbean Slave: A Biological History* (1984); ALFRED W. CROSBY, *Ecological Imperialism: The Biological Expansion of Europe, 900–1900* (1986); GUENTER B. RISSE, ''Medicine in New Spain,'' in *Medicine in the New World: New Spain, New France, and New England*, edited by Ronald L. Numbers (1987).

KENNETH F. KIPLE

DISTENSÃO, the policy of decompression, or political liberalization, pursued by the Brazilian regime of General Ernesto GEISEL during the late 1970s. Through a careful manipulation of the *distensão* process, the military government implemented democratic reforms.

In November 1974, President Geisel allowed an open election in which the opposition party, the Brazilian Democratic Movement (MDB), made substantial gains. The election results convinced Geisel that political liberalization would have to occur slowly in order to prevent the overthrow of his moderate military faction. To avoid future electoral surprises, President Geisel suspended Congress on 1 April 1977 for fifteen days and issued a decree providing for the indirect election of state governors and one-third of the federal senators. Ensured of keeping the government's party, the National Renovating Alliance (ARENA), in power, Geisel proceeded to dismantle components of the government's authoritarian structure.

Under the provisions of an executive-sponsored constitutional amendment in 1978, the regime stopped its censorship of the print media, reinstated habeas corpus for political detainees, and abolished the fifth INSTITUTIONAL ACT, thereby ending the president's authority to suspend Congress, remove congressmen, and deny citizens their political rights.

Although the government retained significant arbitrary powers during Geisel's term, the *distensão* period prepared the way for the opening to democracy under General João Batista FIGUEIREDO.

MARIA HELENA MOREIRA ALVES, *State and Opposition in Military Brazil* (1985); THOMAS SKIDMORE, *The Politics of Military Rule in Brazil, 1964–1985* (1988); ALFRED STEPAN, *Rethinking Military Politics* (1988).

MICHAEL POLL

See also **Abertura; Brazil: Political Parties.**

DITTBORN, EUGENIO (*b.* 1943), Chilean artist. Born in Santiago, Dittborn studied painting and printmaking at universities in Chile and Europe from 1962 to 1969. Like many Chilean artists of his generation, he rejects traditional painting and the conservative values he believes it embodies. In the 1970s Dittborn became a leading member of the Avanzada, a group of Chilean artists and critics who developed an artistic language of metaphor and analogy related to conceptual art, in part to criticize General Augusto Pinochet's military dictatorship. In 1983 he produced his first Pinturas Aeropostales (Airmail Paintings), the works for which he has become best known. Consisting of appropriated photographic images, as well as drawings, texts, and objects, applied to wrapping paper and—after 1988—synthetic nonwoven fabric, they are folded in envelopes and airmailed to exhibitions throughout the world. Quintessential examples of the political-conceptual art Dittborn helped pioneer, they address, among other issues, the peripheral condition to which Latin Americans are often subject. He lives in Santiago.

NELLY RICHARD, "Margins and Institutions: Art in Chile Since 1973," in *Art and Text* 21 (May–June 1986); GUY BRETT, "Eugenio Dittborn," and EUGENIO DITTBORN, "Correcaminos—Roadrunner," both in Guy Brett, *Transcontinental: An Investigation of Reality. Nine Latin American Artists,* edited by Elizabeth A. Macgregor (1990); GUY BRETT and SEAN CUBITT, *Camino Way: The Airmail Paintings of Eugenio Dittborn* (1991); MARI CARMEN RAMÍREZ, "Blueprint Circuits: Conceptual Art and Politics in Latin America," in Museum of Modern Art, *Latin American Artists of the Twentieth Century* (1993).

JOHN ALAN FARMER

DOBLES SEGREDA, LUIS (*b.* 17 January 1891; *d.* 27 October 1956), Costa Rican educator, writer, and diplomat. Born in Heredia, Dobles Segreda attended the Liceo de Costa Rica high school where he was taught by well-known intellectual Joaquín García Monge. In 1910 he became professor of Spanish at the Liceo and began writing articles for the *Havana Post,* as well as other newspapers, and founded, with others, the journal *Selenia.* Subsequently he taught at the Normal School in Heredia and in 1917 became its director. He received graduate degrees in education (1918), geography (1925), philology and grammar (1929), and literature (1930) from that school. He had studied English in his youth and in 1927 taught at Marquette University, and also at the Louisiana State Normal College. He was General Director (1927) and Minister of Education of Costa Rica in 1926–1928, 1930–1932, and 1936. Dobles Segreda served as minister plenipotentiary in Chile, Argentina, Spain, France, Belgium, and the Vatican. In 1927 he served on the municipal council of Heredia, his hometown, and was Costa Rica's delegate to the International Congress of Education in Paris. He wrote fifteen books about Costa Rica, among them *Por el amor de Dios* (1918), *Rosa mística: Historia y tradiciones* (1920), *El libro del héroe:*

Documentos históricos (1926), *Caña brava* (1926), and his nine-volume *Índice bibliográfico de Costa Rica* (1927–1935). He assembled a comprehensive collection of books about Costa Rica which the Library of Congress purchased in 1943 and microfilmed in 1995. Dobles Segreda wrote articles about education and language in the journal *Repertorio americano,* the newspaper *El Triunfo* (San José), and other major papers in Latin America. He served in Costa Rica's 1948 constitutional convention, published the newspaper *Fortín* (Heredia), and in 1950 again represented his country in Spain. He was a member of the Costa Rican Academy of Language and was awarded the Order of Isabel la Católica (Spain) and France's Legion of Honor. Dobles Segreda, one of the major Costa Rican intellectual figures of his times, died in Heredia.

ABDENAGO CORDERO, *Luis Dobles Segreda* (1985).

GEORGETTE MAGASSY DORN

DOBRIZHOFFER, MARTÍN (*b.* 7 September 1717; *d.* 17 July 1791), Austrian missionary active in Paraguay. Born in the Bohemian town of Friedburg, Dobrizhoffer studied philosophy and physical sciences at the universities of Vienna and Graz. In 1748, after joining the JESUITS, he was sent to the Río de la Plata region in Argentina, where he finished his education at the University of Córdoba. He then went to work for four years among the MOCOBÍ Indians of Santa Fe. From 1754 to 1762 Dobrizhoffer was stationed at the Jesuit settlements of Paraguay, at Santa María la Mayor on the Uruguay River, where he gained considerable fame as a learned man among his colleagues and among the GUARANI Indians.

In 1762, the royal governor at Asunción mandated the establishment of a new mission some fifty leagues to the west in the most inhospitable area of the Chaco. He ordered Dobrizhoffer to take charge of the mission, called Nuestra Señora del Rosario de Timbó. The Austrian's missionary goal there, the conversion of the "wild" ABIPÓN Indians, eluded him. After many bitter experiences, he abandoned Rosario de Timbó in 1765 and was reassigned to San Joaquín, in northern Paraguay.

With the expulsion of the Jesuits two years later, Dobrizhoffer returned to Vienna. There he attracted the attention of the empress Maria Theresa, who begged him to write an account of his life in the New World. These memoirs, published in 1783–1784 as *Geschichte der Abiponer,* constitute the most detailed examination we have of Indian–Caucasian relations in the eighteenth-century Chaco.

MARTIN DOBRIZHOFFER, *An Account of the Abipones: An Equestrian People of Paraguay,* translated by Sara Coleridge, 3 vols. (1822); EFRAÍM CARDOZO, *Historiografía paraguaya* (1959), pp. 344–351.

THOMAS L. WHIGHAM

See also **Missions.**

DOCE, LOS, the twelve Franciscan friars who arrived in New Spain in 1524: Martín de Valencia (their superior), Luis de Fuensalida, Francisco de Soto, Andrés de Córdova, García de Cisneros, Martín de Coruña, Juan Suares, Toribio de Benavente (MOTOLINÍA), Juan de Palos, Antonio de Ciudad-Rodrigo, Juan de Ribas, and Francisco Jiménez. While they were not the first clergy or even the first FRANCISCANS on the scene, their arrival represented the true beginning of the systematic Christianization program and the establishment of the Mexican church. Motolinía, the best-known member, wrote several important accounts of the indigenous society, and in general the prominence of these "Twelve Apostles" solidified the primacy of the Franciscan order in New Spain. From its privileged position, the order was able to obtain the best and most populous sites for its monasteries and to exert a great deal of influence on early colonial affairs, in part because a member of the order, Juan de ZUMÁRRAGA, was Mexico's first bishop.

Standard English-language accounts of the activities of the Franciscans (and other orders) in Mexico are JOHN LEDDY PHELAN, *The Millennial Kingdom of the Franciscans in the New World: A Study of the Writings of Gerónimo de Mendieta (1525–1604)* (1956); ROBERT RICARD, *The Spiritual Conquest of Mexico* (1966); and JOHN FREDERICK SCHWALLER, *The Church and Clergy in Sixteenth-Century Mexico* (1987). For a translation of Motolinía's work, see TORIBIO MOTOLINÍA, *History of the Indians of New Spain*, translated and edited by Elizabeth Andros Foster (1950). For an early history of the Franciscans in Mexico, consult GERÓNIMO DE MENDIETA, *Historia eclesiástica indiana* (1971). (Motolinía was Mendieta's mentor.)

ROBERT HASKETT

See also **Catholic Church; Missions.**

DOLLAR DIPLOMACY, a stratagem closely associated with the foreign policy of U.S. President William Howard Taft (1909–1913) and his secretary of state, Philander Knox. Dollar diplomacy was most clearly manifested in Latin America, especially Central America and the Caribbean, but the Taft-Knox team also labored hard to apply it to China. The proponents of dollar diplomacy intended to avoid direct military intervention to protect U.S. interests or to induce the stable political and social order necessary to establish a favorable environment for U.S. commercial and financial expansion. Their objective was to develop important U.S. political, economic, cultural, and strategic influence by substituting the power of U.S. capital and financial aid for more direct diplomatic or military pressure. These goals were pointedly expressed in 1911, when Knox declared: "It is rational to hold that a fatherland owes its children the duty of assuring them opportunity for self-advancement. The Department of State can help in this way by securing for our citizens equal and fair opportunity abroad commensurate with that which the National Government aims to secure for them at home." President Taft summarized his

administration's foreign policy when he explained in his final message to Congress on 3 December 1912, that "the diplomacy of the present administration sought to respond to modern ideas of commercial intercourse. This policy has been characterized as substituting dollars for bullets. It is one that appeals alike to idealistic humanitarian sentiments, to the dictates of sound policy and strategy, and to legitimate commercial aims."

U.S. economic and security interests were most evident in the small Central American and Caribbean island states, which were the chief targets of dollar diplomacy, although historians have traced implementation of the policy to Ecuador and Mexico as well. The U.S. government induced the Caribbean and isthmian governments to accept U.S. customs collectors, financial advisers, tax administrators, and economic consultants appointed with the cooperation of the State Department. Dollar diplomacy resulted in numerous military interventions, despite claims to the contrary, because it insisted upon a U.S. role in the financial and economic life of the republics around the Caribbean. U.S. Marines occupied Nicaragua, Haiti, and Santo Domingo for long periods and landed frequently in Cuba and Panama and on at least two occasions in Honduras.

The core idea behind dollar diplomacy was an old one: managing another society's political economy without recourse to a costly and bloody conflict. Early U.S. efforts to exert such influence in Mexico included the Corwin–Zamacona (1861) and the Corwin–Doblado (1862) loan treaties. These loans were to be used to pay the principal and interest on the outstanding Mexican debt to France, Great Britain, and Spain and thereby reduce the threat of European intervention in Mexico's LA REFORMA conflict. The U.S. Congress, however, rejected the loans, and the three European powers intervened.

U.S. officials and private parties had frequently compared the political and economic benefits and the costs of foreign and U.S. investment in Latin America, especially in the Caribbean–Central American regions, with alternative diplomatic-military activity. Emily Rosenberg has placed dollar diplomacy within a framework of liberal developmentalism that describes dollar diplomacy as merely one variation of numerous efforts to spread the American system abroad. For example, such considerations were common in the 1890s, when U.S. officials and private businessmen wished to replace British economic and financial involvement in Nicaragua's Mosquito region. Similar reasoning prompted President Theodore ROOSEVELT's decision to announce the policy that became known as the ROOSEVELT COROLLARY to the MONROE DOCTRINE. The Roosevelt administration assumed (as did the Taft administration) that financial and economic activity translated into political and strategic power. The U.S. government used the Roosevelt Corollary to claim a financial and economic supervisory authority over the economies of Latin American states. Under Taft and his successors, banks, financial institutions, humanitarian organizations, corporations, and other private agencies were selected as "chosen instruments" to advance U.S. objectives, but without formal involvement of U.S. institutions because that course would have been inconsistent with laissez-faire principles. This reservation changed over time, however. Simon G. Hanson has described the ALLIANCE FOR PROGRESS in the 1960s as a modern, unsuccessful, and formal U.S. governmental variation of that same policy outlook.

SCOTT NEARING, *Dollar Diplomacy: A Study of American Imperialism* (1925); DANA G. MUNRO, *Intervention and Dollar Diplomacy in the Caribbean, 1900–1921* (1964); ROBERT FREEMAN SMITH, "Cuba: Laboratory for Dollar Diplomacy, 1898–1917," *Historian* 28, no. 4 (1966): 586–609; EUGENE P. TRANI, "Dollar Diplomacy," and JOAN HOFF WILSON, "Economic Foreign Policy," in Alexander DeConde, ed., *Encyclopedia of American Foreign Policy*, vol. 1 (1978), pp. 265–274 and 281–291; EMILY ROSENBERG, *Spreading the American Dream: American Economic and Cultural Expansion, 1890–1945* (1982).

THOMAS SCHOONOVER

DOMADOR. In any ranching economy, certain skills are more highly esteemed because of their centrality to ranch work. Certainly, the broncobuster or *domador* held highest status. All GAUCHOS could ride reasonably well. But the *domador* could tame, often with brutal efficiency, any wild horse to the saddle. Injury or death to the animal was not uncommon. Because of the demand for his skills, the *domador* earned higher wages than the average ranch worker. By the late nineteenth century wild horses were scarce and mounts became more costly. Harsh, traditional taming methods gave way to gentler ones. The Argentine writer Ricardo GÜIRALDES provides a memorable literary portrait of the *domador* in his novel *Don Segundo Sombra* (1926).

RICHARD W. SLATTA, *Gauchos and the Vanishing Frontier* (1983), p. 43; *Cowboys of the Americas* (1990), pp. 74–75.

RICHARD W. SLATTA

DOMESTIC SERVICE. Domestic servants have always been important to Latin American society and its economy. In the colonial period the patriarchal household was the primary basis of juridical identity and social control in Spanish and Portuguese America, with all persons being controlled through the male head of household. The Spanish *casa poblada* (the home of the *encomendero*, required by law to include room for at least forty guests and military retainers) was literally viewed as the basis for Spanish civilization in the New World. In sixteenth-century Latin America domestic servants were found not only in the houses of *encomenderos* and *senhores de engenho* (Brazilian sugar planters), with as many as forty, but also in the houses of merchants and artisans, with the former having as few as one. In addition, Spanish and Portuguese law mandated that

women be maintained in a position of tutelage, which implied that most employment options for women prior to the end of the nineteenth century were domestic—in terms of where the work was executed, the type of labor demanded, and often the type of family relationship necessary to exercise a craft or trade.

The dominant race of domestic servants varied by location, depending upon the ethnic mix of the population, and also changed over time. However, Indians, slaves, freed slaves, persons of mixed races (*castas*), and white men and women were all part of the servant population in the sixteenth century. In Brazil, African and Indian slaves composed the servant population from the sixteenth through the eighteenth centuries. In Mexico, Indians were the dominant form of domestic labor in the sixteenth century, but blacks, slave and freed, became more important in the seventeenth century. By the eighteenth century, most Mexican domestic servants were *castas*. Spanish servants continued to be considered prestigious. Women seeking employment as wet-nurses in Mexico City frequently claimed Spanish blood—probably because of the idea that a baby would imbibe qualities of character common to an ethnic group along with its milk. In Brazil, although most domestic servants were Indian or African slaves and freed persons until the middle of the nineteenth century, there was a definite preference for mixed-blood or "whiter" servants.

Domestics in the colonial period are difficult to trace. The only relevant regulations specified that domestic servants were under the authority and responsibility of the head of the household in which they worked. The significance of domestic servants in colonial Latin America becomes most apparent through studies on household composition. Studies of eighteenth-century Caracas, Buenos Aires, Mexico City, and various areas in Chile and Brazil indicate the high proportions of dependent members of the household who were not part of the nuclear family and were generally regarded as servants. These *allegados* or *agregados* frequently contributed from 20 to 40 percent of household members. Orphaned relatives, "adopted children," manumitted children and women in Brazil, Indians captured in frontier wars, illegitimate ("natural") offspring of the head of the household, and the adolescent children of neighbors or kinfolk were natural components of the servant category and contributed to the personalized, paternalistic master–servant relationship, which also was often strengthened through ritual kinship. This characteristic of domestic servitude declined in the nineteenth century. At the same time, the association of domestic service with the lower end of the class/caste/color system that dominated Latin American society caused a gradual alienation between employers and servants as well as a loss of status for the occupation of domestic service.

In the nineteenth century the effects of urbanization and structural economic changes increasing the size of the middle class led to renewed demand for domestic servants in the urban areas of Latin America. At the same time, domestic service acted to continue preindustrial social and productive relationships and to reinforce the patriarchal household. The private home was seen as a "protected place for a woman to work" and a "guardian of moral virtue." Most domestic servants were migrants from nearby villages. In nineteenth-century Mexico City and in Argentina about 60 percent of women workers were domestic servants.

Female labor participation during industrialization has followed a U-shaped path, according to studies on Brazil, Mexico, Peru, and the United States. In these countries the high proportions of women working in the mid-nineteenth century were followed by dramatic declines in the ranks of working women from the 1890s to the 1930s. In this period domestic service declined as well, though less than other forms of female employment. In the period from 1940 to 1970 female employment expanded throughout Latin America in response to generally improved economic conditions and to the expansion of the service sector. Middle-class and upper-class women entered the white-collar sector, which enlarged the demand for domestic service. This contrasts strongly with the experience of the United States and

Europe, where domestic servants disappeared in this period. The difference in Latin America may be attributed to the much larger unskilled lower-class population, many of them rural migrants, desperately in need of jobs. Furthermore, with the continued use of domestics, upper-class and middle-class Latin American women were able to go to work without threatening the traditional patriarchal organization of the household.

Most domestic workers are recent migrants, frequently utilizing the "educational" and patronage advantages of a live-in domestic situation to provide them with a transition from the provinces. Nevertheless, the "mobility" experienced by domestic servants is not a move between types of employment, but rather a move as a domestic to a better neighborhood with a higher salary and more privileges. In the 1980s and 1990s the increased value of privacy, the growth of daycare and nursery schools, and improved technology in the middle-class home began to dampen the demand for full-time, live-in servants. More domestics were employed part-time for specific tasks—a change that has reduced the paternalistic privileges of the live-in situation as well as some of its oppressiveness in terms of hours and personal supervision. Although "casual" domestic labor was even less regulated and usually less secure than a live-in position, it did permit the domestic to acquire several employers.

Everywhere in Latin America domestic service has historically been the most important form of female employment. However, in part because of the colonial circumstances of conquest and caste/race relations, domestic service became an aspect of race and class subordination rather than the "stage-of-life" learning experience it usually was in pre-industrial Europe. In the sixteenth century many (perhaps half) domestic servants were male, and some were white. By the eighteenth century, most domestic servants were female and predominantly of mixed-blood or mixed-caste background, and those who were male were also of mixed blood or of slave status. Domestic service in the nineteenth and twentieth centuries has become an almost entirely female and lower-class occupation. One is tempted to write that the continued importance of domestic labor is an anachronism in the industrial age—a continuation of patriarchal employment practices and paternalistic educational methods. Ironically, in the twentieth century, the efforts to equalize employment benefits for women have led to a shrinkage of available industrial jobs and a greater willingness among lower-class women to become domestic workers.

An excellent source on domestic service in Latin America, both historically and today, is ELSA M. CHANEY and MARY GARCIA CASTRO, eds., *Muchachas No More: Household Workers in Latin America and the Caribbean* (1989). On Brazil, see SANDRA LAUDERDALE GRAHAM, *House and Street: The Domestic World of Servants and Masters in Nineteenth-Century Rio de Janeiro* (1988), and MARY KARASCH, "Suppliers, Sellers, Servants, and Slaves," in *Cities and Society in Colonial Latin America*, edited by Louisa

Mónica, a slave nurse, with Artur Gomes Leal, the child she nursed, ca. 1860. Recife. PHOTO BY JOÃO FERREIRA VILLELA. DOCUMENTATION INSTITUTE, JOAQUIM NABUCO FOUNDATION.

Schell Hoberman and Susan Migden Socolow (1986). An accessible article relating larger economic changes, women's employment opportunities, and domestic service is ELIZABETH JELIN, "Migration and Labor Force Participation of Latin American Women: The Domestic Servants in the Cities," in *Signs* 3, no. 1 (1977): 129–141.

ELIZABETH ANNE KUZNESOF

DOMÍNGUEZ, MANUEL (*b.* 1869; *d.* 1935), Paraguayan historian and essayist. Domínguez is widely regarded as the most important revisionist historian of Paraguay after Juan E. O'Leary. Born in the river port of Pilar toward the end of the WAR OF THE TRIPLE ALLIANCE, Domínguez grew up in an Asunción that had been terribly affected by the fighting. Despite these difficulties, he made major intellectual strides and ended up teaching subjects as varied as zoology, anatomy, and Roman history at the National College and serving as rector of the university. He also held various political and diplomatic posts for brief periods.

Domínguez was instrumental in introducing Auguste Comte's POSITIVISM to Paraguayan historical studies, which meant applying more scientific methods to research. Domínguez himself put theory into practice in his *El Chaco Boreal*, a work that defended Paraguayan claims to the Gran Chaco region. He also wrote an influential series of essays entitled *El alma de la raza*, which argued for a portrayal of Paraguayan history in strongly nationalist terms; the book likewise championed the figure of Marshal Francisco Solano LÓPEZ, who had led Paraguay into the earlier war. In this respect, Domínguez broke with the virulently anti-López diatribes of earlier historians, particularly Cecilio BÁEZ.

WILLIAM BELMONT PARKER, *Paraguayans of To-Day* (1921), pp. 299–302; JACK RAY THOMAS, *Biographical Dictionary of Latin American Historians and Historiography* (1984); CARLOS ZUBIZARRETA, *Cien vidas paraguayas*, 2d ed. (1985), pp. 225–228.

THOMAS L. WHIGHAM

DOMÍNGUEZ, MIGUEL (*b.* 20 January 1756; *d.* 22 April 1830), precursor of Mexican independence. A distinguished lawyer born in Mexico City, Domínguez was named *corregidor* of QUERÉTARO in 1802. His opposition to the Law of Consolidation of *vales reales* (royal bonds) (1805) gained him the enmity of Viceroy José de ITURRIGARAY, who had him replaced, although he was eventually restored to his post. With his wife, Josefa ORTIZ, he took part in the Querétaro conspiracy of 1810 against the colonial regime. When the plot was discovered, Domínguez, constrained by his office, locked his wife in their house and arrested some of the plotters. But she managed to notify others, causing Miguel HIDALGO to begin the revolution on 16 September. Domínguez was detained the same day; shortly thereafter he was released and restored to his post, although he was ousted again in 1820. He became a member of the Supreme Executive

Power in 1823. At the end of 1824, he became president of the Supreme Court, a position he held for the rest of his life. He died in Mexico City.

JOSÉ MARÍA MIGUEL I VERGÉS, *Diccionario de insurgentes* (1969), pp. 175–176; HUGH M. HAMILL, JR., *The Hidalgo Revolt*, 2d ed. (1970); *Diccionario Porrúa de historia, geografía y biografía de México*, 5th ed. (1986), vol. 1, p. 922.

VIRGINIA GUEDEA

See also **Academia Literaria de Querétaro; Allende, Ignacio; Ortiz de Domínguez, Josefa.**

DOMINICA, a small Caribbean island nation in the Lesser Antilles, located between Martinique and Guadeloupe in the chain of islands known as the Windwards. Dominica was sighted and named by Christopher COLUMBUS on 3 November 1493, but the island remained a stronghold of the native Carib peoples until the flow of European settlers to the area increased in the late seventeenth century. The island was one of the many smaller islands that Spain could not or chose not to exclude other European powers from seizing, so in the era of imperial rivalries Dominica became the target of competing French and British claims. After driving the CARIBS into the mountains, the French held most of the island until 1761. That year, however, the British seized the island as part of their effort to build an empire in North America, the Caribbean, and elsewhere during the SEVEN YEARS' WAR.

Under the British, Dominica became a classic slave society producing tropical agricultural products for export to Europe. The population of slaves and settlers skyrocketed. With the end of French efforts to claim the island in the first decade of the nineteenth century, coffee production was established as the first in a series of cash crops that would subject Dominica to cycles of economic boom and collapse. Around 1900 coffee and sugar gave way to cocoa, to be replaced by bananas in the middle of the twentieth century.

After the establishment of an elected assembly in 1763, Britain consistently dictated policy for the island, with minor changes in representation, until 3 November 1978, when Dominica gained its independence from Britain. The process toward autonomy had been a gradual one throughout most of the twentieth century, with increasing participation by Dominicans in self-rule and expanding suffrage.

ROBERT A. MEYERS, *Dominica* (1987); MICHEL-ROLPH TROUILLOT, *Peasants and Capital: Dominica in the World Economy* (1988).

TODD LITTLE-SIEBOLD

DOMINICAN REPUBLIC

HAITIAN RULE (1822–1844)

In 1822, under President Jean-Pierre Boyer, the Haitians began a twenty-two-year occupation of the eastern two-thirds of Hispanolia. Dominican historians have traditionally described this period as the nadir of their country's history because of the imposition of high taxes, a military draft, the confiscation of church lands, the destruction of the prevailing educational system, and efforts of Haitianization. Recently, revisionist historians have stressed some of the positive aspects of the Haitian occupation, such as the freeing of the Dominican slaves. There is no doubt, however, that a substantial part of the Dominican people desired the end of Haitian rule.

The fight for Dominican liberation was led by Juan Pablo DUARTE, who is regarded as "the father of his country" and its greatest national hero. He was ably assisted by Ramón Matias MELLA and Francisco del Rosario Sánchez, who are almost equally admired. On 27 February 1844, the Dominican Republic successfully proclaimed its independence from Haiti.

FROM SANTANA TO HEUREAUX (1845–1899)

Duarte's dream of establishing a liberal, democratic republic soon vanished with his permanent exile to Venezuela and his replacement by two caudillos (Pedro SANTANA and Buenaventura BÁEZ) who for decades battled each other to control the country. The instability produced by this struggle was aggravated by the threat of frequent armed incursions by Haiti. Since neither Báez nor Santana believed in the viability of the Dominican Republic, they searched for foreign protectors. Whereas Báez hoped for annexation by France or the United States, Santana looked for salvation to Spain, which reannexed its former colony of Santo Domingo in 1861. Most Dominicans objected to the reestablishment of Spanish control and commenced the War of Restora-

tion (of Dominican independence) on 16 August 1863, a conflict that resulted in Spain's permanent withdrawal from Santo Domingo in 1865. Báez's U.S. annexation scheme was almost realized in the 1870s, when the administration of President Ulysses S. Grant strove to carry it out. The determined resistance of Senator Charles Sumner of Massachusetts narrowly defeated the annexation treaty's passage in the Senate.

The frequent turmoil that had plagued the nation ever since it attained independence was suspended temporarily during the last two decades of the nineteenth century, when General Ulises HEUREAUX (1882–1899) clamped an iron dictatorship on the country. His rule was marked by assassinations, bribery, and secret police surveillance. Nevertheless, the stability of the political situation led to a flurry of foreign investments that resulted in the building of telegraph lines, railways, roads, and the first large sugar mills in the southern Dominican Republic.

INCREASED UNITED STATES DOMINATION (1900–1926)

Heureaux's assassination in 1899 resulted in renewed political and financial destabilization, which was instrumental in persuading the government of the United States to take over the receivership of Dominican customs (1905) under the ROOSEVELT COROLLARY of the Monroe Doctrine. Under the beneficent presidency of Ramón CÁCERES (1906–1911), the Dominican Republic experienced a brief spell of reform and modernization. Cáceres's assassination hurled the country into a new cycle of violence and financial indebtedness that persuaded President Woodrow Wilson to send in the U.S. Marines.

From 1916 to 1924 the Dominican Republic remained under the military control of the United States. The occupation resulted in improved roads, schools, and sanitation facilities as well as in the introduction of baseball, which became a national pastime. U.S. rule, however, also had its negative aspects, including the suppression of Dominican guerrilla activities, which was accompanied by incidents of torture. A pervasive attitude of racism on the part of the occupiers toward Dominicans created long-lasting resentments. Perhaps the worst legacy of the U.S. occupation was the creation of a Marine-trained National Guard under a commander in chief named Rafael Léonidas TRUJILLO MOLINA, who became the dictator of the Dominican Republic in 1930.

THE ERA OF TRUJILLO (1930–1961)
Trujillo followed in the footsteps of Báez, Santana, and Heureaux—he even patterned his uniforms after those worn by Heureaux. However, his regime was infinitely more encompassing than the governments of his three caudillo predecessors. Perhaps it would be more appropriate to compare him with his more famous contemporaries, Adolf Hitler and Joseph Stalin. In terms of cruelty, *Gleichschaltung* (conformity laws), secret police terror, genocidal massacres, and megalomania, Trujillo certainly held his own in comparison with the German and Soviet rulers. He differed from them, however, in one important aspect: whereas Hitler and Stalin were indifferent to the accumulation of personal wealth, Trujillo, the son of a lower-middle-class postal officer, was determined to amass one of the world's great fortunes. He turned the Dominican Republic into his personal fiefdom by taking possession of most of the land, many industries, and many export-import monopolies. It is estimated that by the time of his death in 1961, his personal fortune amounted to more than U.S. $800 million. Members of Trujillo's extensive family were given important government positions that they used to make their own fortunes.

Trujillo added another bloody chapter to the long history of hostilities between Dominicans and Haitians by ordering the execution of all Haitians who could be found on Dominican soil. In October 1937, approximately 25,000 Haitian women, men, and children were massacred at the dictator's request. Trujillo, whose maternal grandmother was Haitian, hoped to "whiten" his country by this measure.

Owing his meteoric military career to the U.S. occupation forces, Trujillo sought to ingratiate himself with his former superiors. Besides creating a George Washington and Marine Corps Boulevard in Santo Domingo, Trujillo made sure that his country's debt to the United States was paid in full, within a decade. With the exception of the final phase of his reign, Trujillo elevated the maintenance of good relations with the United States to the cardinal principle of his foreign policy. These efforts resulted in the Trujillo–Hull Treaty (1940), by which the United States gave up its right to collect Dominican customs duties.

When the United States became involved in World War II, the Dominican Republic was one of the first Latin American countries to declare war on the Axis. The products of the Dominican Republic's agro-industries, which Trujillo had done so much to develop in the 1930s, found a ready market in the United States during the war. Dominican coffee, tobacco, and cocoa were in high demand, and the Dominican Republic became the second largest sugar exporter (after Cuba) to the United States. In 1944, when Franklin D. Roosevelt and Winston Churchill called for worldwide adherence to democratic principles, Trujillo even allowed the formation of opposition parties. He crushed them ruthlessly in 1947, at the beginning of the cold war, during which the Dominican dictator posed as Latin America's champion of anticommunism. His anticommunist stance, as well as the administering of favors and outright bribes, assured him support from a powerful group of U.S. senators and congressmen. Most North American journalists lavished praise on Trujillo for establishing a stable government in his country.

The Dominican ruler reached the apex of his reign in 1955, when he celebrated the twenty-fifth anniversary of his seizure of power by arranging for a Fair of Peace and Brotherhood of the Free World at Santo Domingo. After that event, Trujillo's fortunes began to decline rapidly. The toppling of dictators all over Latin America with the encouragement of the administrations of Dwight D. Eisenhower and John F. Kennedy left Trujillo an isolated relic. On 14 June 1959, Dominican exiles, with the encouragement of President Rómulo BETANCOURT of Venezuela and Fidel Castro of Cuba, launched an abortive invasion of the Dominican Republic. Trujillo ordered the captured rebels tortured and then killed. In retaliation for Betancourt's sponsorship of the invasion, Trujillo sent agents to Venezuela who dynamited Betancourt's car and injured the Venezuelan president. Other Dominican agents participated in the assassination of Guatemala's president, Carlos CASTILLO ARMAS, in 1957. These actions resulted in the imposition of economic sanctions against the Dominican Republic by the Organization of American States (OAS).

In his desperation, Trujillo began to abandon his principle of never antagonizing the United States. The 1956 kidnapping and subsequent murder of Columbia University instructor Jesús de GALÍNDEZ, who had infuriated the Dominican dictator by publishing a book dealing with Trujillo's many crimes, lessened Trujillo's support in the U.S. Congress. Many congressional members were outraged by Trujillo's murder of the North American pilot who had flown the kidnapped professor to his death in the Dominican Republic. The United States imposed an arms embargo on the Dominican Republic that was followed by a special excise tax on the importation of Dominican sugar. The latter measure dealt a crippling blow to the Dominican economy. Isolated abroad and increasingly opposed at home, the aging dictator was ambushed and murdered along Santo Domingo's waterfront (Malecón) on 30 May 1961.

THE AFTERMATH OF TRUJILLO (1961–1965)

The murdered dictator left behind a dislocated economy and a large power vacuum that his favorite son, Rafael Leónidas Trujillo Martínez (Ramfis), and Trujillo's last puppet president, Joaquín BALAGUER, attempted to fill. While Ramfis was rounding up and torturing his father's assassins (they were all caught and killed, except for Luis Amiama Tío and General Antonio Imbert Barrera), Balaguer initiated some minor democratic reforms that failed to persuade the OAS to lift its economic sanctions. The reforms alarmed the late dictator's brothers, José Arismendi and Héctor Bienvenido, who tried to undo even these minor changes in order to preserve "Trujilloism with Trujillo." The protests of Santo Domingo's business community, backed by a show of force of U.S. naval units, persuaded the entire Trujillo clan to go into permanent exile on 20 November 1961. Before following suit, however, Balaguer formed and headed a seven-man Council of State. Consisting of members of the Dominican elite, this body was designed to preside over the country's transition to democracy until the national elections were held on 20 December 1962. These changes resulted in the lifting of sanctions by the OAS as well as a massive outpouring of economic and technical assistance by the United States.

The elections of 1962 proved to be a contest between two major parties: the conservative National Civic Union (UCN), which was backed by the elite, and the DOMINICAN REVOLUTIONARY PARTY (PRD), which had been founded in 1939 by anti-Trujilloist exiles and consisted largely of members of the middle and lower classes. The PRD was led by the prominent Dominican novelist Juan BOSCH, who won the presidential election. President John F. Kennedy, who was pleased by the outcome of the voting, invited the newly elected Dominican president to the White House and appointed his liberal speech writer, John Bartlow Martin, as ambassador to the Dominican Republic. The Kennedy administration's enthusiasm for Bosch soon vanished when the new president ignored the guidelines of the Alliance for Progress program and considered establishing diplomatic relations with Castro's Cuba. Elements of the Dominican armed forces, known as Loyalists and led by General Elías Wessín y Wessín, were well aware of the changed U.S. attitude toward Bosch, which enabled them to stage a successful military coup against Bosch in September 1963.

After Bosch's overthrow, the Dominican Republic was run by a triumvirate headed by business leader Donald Reid Cabral. The real power behind this civilian facade, however, was the military, which became so steeped in corruption and repression that the Dominican people revolted on 24 April 1965 in order to restore civilian rule under former president Bosch, who then was living in exile in Puerto Rico.

THE REVOLUTION OF 1965

The rebels of 24 April 1965 called themselves Constitutionalists because they advocated the reestablishment of a truly civilian, constitutionalist government headed by deposed president Juan Bosch. The Constitutionalists, who consisted of members of the PRD, some Christian Socialists, and part of the armed forces under Colonel Francisco Caamaño Deñó, stormed the National Palace and placed Reid Cabral under house arrest. When the people of Santo Domingo realized that the hated triumvirate had ended, they poured into the streets to support the Constitutionalists, who provided them with arms. General Wessín y Wessín, who headed those elements of the armed forces who called themselves Loyalists because they remained loyal to the triumvirate, unleashed the air force upon the defenseless population of the capital, which suffered thousands of casualties. He also sent heavily armed units backed by tanks across the Duarte Bridge, which spans the Ozama River. This river separated the Loyalist forces, headquartered at San Isidro Air Force base, from the Constitutionalists, who were concentrated in the old part of Santo Domingo (*zona colonial*). Armed with only light weapons and Molotov cocktails, the rebels were able to repel and defeat the Loyalists, capturing and disabling many armored vehicles.

With Caamaño's supporters on the verge of victory in the capital, the revolution threatened to spread to the rest of the country, a development that caused such panic at the U.S. embassy that Ambassador William Tapley Bennett informed President Lyndon Johnson that Communist-led hordes were committing atrocities and endangering the lives of U.S. citizens. On 28 April 1965, President Johnson sent tens of thousands of Marines (and, later, airborne units) into Santo Domingo, ostensibly to prevent a Communist takeover (a "second Cuba"), but in reality to obviate a Constitutionalist victory. On 29 April, the Constitutionalists formed a government with Caamaño as president. The Loyalists, too, formed a government, which was headed by General Antonio Imbert Barrera, one of the two surviving Trujillo assassins.

Johnson had been mistaken in his belief that U.S. intervention would put a quick end to the civil war. Instead, it lasted until 31 August 1965, when the Act of Dominican Reconciliation put an end to the conflict. This reconciliation pact called for the reintegration of the armed forces, the establishment of a temporary government, and the holding of national elections in June 1966.

THE ERA OF BALAGUER (1966–1978)

The ensuing electoral battle was fought between the PRD, once again led by Bosch, who had returned from exile, and the PR (Reformist Party), headed by Joaquín BALAGUER, who had founded that party in 1963 during his exile in New York City. Balaguer, presenting himself as the candidate who could bring peace and reconciliation to his nation, won 57 percent of the vote. He was reelected in 1970 and 1974, thus creating the era of Balaguer, which coincided with a dramatic increase in the world price for sugar, the Dominican Republic's main export. Balaguer used the impressive revenues derived from the sugar export boom to construct schools, hospitals, roads, bridges, and dams. He concentrated particularly on the countryside, where he gained much political support from segments of the peasantry. The Dominican president tried to reduce his country's dependence on sugar production by encouraging the tourist industry and by inviting foreign companies to explore the Dominican Republic's mineral resources (gold, silver, ferronickel, and bauxite).

The economic boom benefited the upper class and some strata of the bourgeoisie. It also produced much corruption, particularly among the top military leaders, many of whom became millionaires under Balaguer. Human rights violations constituted another negative aspect of the era. Especially in the 1970s, former leading Constitutionalists, Socialists, and Communists were murdered by a roving paramilitary gang known as La Banda (The Band), which was encouraged by the government. By 1978, as Balaguer was finishing his third consecutive term as president, his "economic miracle" was under assault by rising oil prices and the simultaneous decline in world demand for coffee, cocoa, and sugar. In June of that year, impoverished urban workers, ill-paid professionals, and disillusioned Dominicans everywhere put an end to twelve years of Balaguerism by voting in the PRD's candidate for the presidency, Antonio Guzmán Fernández.

THE PRD INTERLUDE AND THE
RETURN OF BALAGUER

During the electoral campaign, Guzmán had promised to bring about a change (*el cambio*) for all those Dominicans (the majority) who had been left out of the "economic miracle" of the Balaguer epoch. However, the continuing increase in the price of oil and the further decline in demand for the Dominican Republic's agricultural products prevented Guzmán from initiating the social reforms he had delineated during the campaign. The endemic political corruption continued under Guzmán. When the president learned that members of his immediate family were involved in a scandal, he committed suicide at the National Palace on 4 July 1982. His vice president, Jacobo Majluta Azar, served the remaining forty-three days of Guzmán's term. Although disappointed by Guzmán and Majluta, the Dominican voters showed that they still preferred the PRD to Balaguer's PR or Bosch's Party of Dominican Liberation (PLD, founded in 1973) when they elected the PRD's Salvador Jorge Blanco to the presidency in 1982.

Beset from the start by the Dominican Republic's enormous debt and the constantly falling world price

Loading docks at Santo Domingo. © 1984 MARTIN ROGERS / STOCK, BOSTON.

for sugar, Jorge Blanco was as unable as his predecessors to improve the lot of the average Dominican. Under pressure from the International Monetary Fund (IMF), the Dominican president trebled the price of subsistence items such as cooking oil, rice, and beans in April 1984. The resulting outbursts of popular fury were bloodily suppressed by the police and armed forces. When Jorge Blanco was accused of personal corruption (for which he was jailed in 1988 and tried in 1991), the Dominican people's disillusionment with the PRD was complete. In the 1986 electoral battle of three ex-presidents (Balaguer, Bosch, and Majluta), Balaguer (and his party, the Reformist Social Christian Party [Partido Reformista Social Cristiano—PRSC]) emerged as the winner.

The government formed by the nearly blind, seventy-eight-year-old president seemed like an apparition from the past: former president of the triumvirate Reid Cabral as foreign minister, General Wessín y Wessín as minister of the interior (and later head of the armed forces), and Imbert Barrera as army chief. Balaguer, in his fifth term as president, faced nearly insurmountable problems. His country's agricultural exports were selling as poorly as ever and the U.S. Congress made the situation worse by cutting the Dominican sugar quota. The poor infrastructure of the Dominican Republic was crumbling everywhere. Electric power outages of up to twenty hours a day wrought havoc with industry, hotels, restaurants, and homes.

Balaguer's answer to these problems was a gigantic building program that included the construction of apartments, bridges, and highways as well as an immense lighthouse monument at Santo Domingo honoring Columbus. The building boom relieved unemployment but, at the same time, increased the country's already staggering debt. It also fueled a fierce inflation that threatened not only the survival of the poor but also the viability of the middle class. As far as the observance of human rights was concerned, the record of Balaguer's fifth term compared favorably with his previous tenures as head of state.

During the presidential elections of 1990, the PRD no longer proved to be a major factor because it had split into two hostile groupings: a left wing under the former mayor of Santo Domingo, José Francisco Peña Gómez, and a conservative faction, calling itself La Estructura, under former President Majluta. In the ensuing electoral battle, known as the "battle of the octogenarians," Balaguer was pitted against his old nemesis, Juan Bosch. The incumbent president defeated his opponent by a thin margin; Bosch claimed that he was cheated out of victory by electoral fraud.

Balaguer entered his sixth term as president in an atmosphere of rapid economic deterioration. He soon faced massive demonstrations against the prevailing inflation, unemployment, and dearth of medical and educational facilities, as well as the collapsing infrastructure. Only through the mediation of the Roman Catholic church and his promise to step down as president in 1992 was Balaguer able to survive this crisis. (Although he remained in power through 1994 and was reelected.) After a temporary reprieve, a new crisis began building up during the summer of 1991, when severe power blackouts and continuing hyperinflation made life miserable for most Dominicans. Balaguer, at this point, apparently attempted to deflect attention from the domestic crisis by becoming embroiled in a bitter dispute with the Dominican Republic's old enemy, Haiti, over the expulsion of thousands of Haitians from Dominican soil.

The future holds awesome prospects for Balaguer and his successors. The present is bad enough. Of the 7 million Dominicans (1990), 4 million exist in poverty and 2 million are illiterate. Eighty percent of Dominican families earn less than U.S. $47 a month. By the year 2000, the capital, Santo Domingo, will have doubled its present population of 2 million. The entire country will contain 10 million people. There will be 8 million poor and 3 million illiterates. There will also be more pollution, more deforestation, more legal and illegal emigration, less agriculture, and less water. One wonders how any future government will be able to cope with such overwhelming problems.

SUMNER WELLES, *Naboth's Vineyard: The Dominican Republic, 1844–1924*, 2 vols. (1928); SELDEN RODMAN, *Quisqueya: A History of the Dominican Republic* (1964); HOWARD J. WIARDA, *The Dominican Republic: A Nation in Transition* (1969); FRANK MOYA PONS, *Manual de historia dominicana* (1977); IAN BELL, *The Dominican Republic* (1981); H. HOETINK, *The Dominican People, 1850–1900* (1982); HOWARD J. WIARDA and MICHAEL J. KRYZANEK, *The Dominican Republic: A Caribbean Crucible* (1982); JAN KNIPPERS BLACK, *The Dominican Republic: Politics and Development in an Unsovereign State* (1986); FRANK MOYA PONS, *El pasado dominicano* (1986); MICHAEL J. KRYZANEK and HOWARD J. WIARDA, *The Politics of External Influence upon the Dominican Republic* (1988); KAI P. SCHOENHALS, *Dominican Republic* (1990).

KAI P. SCHOENHALS

DOMINICAN REPUBLIC: CONSTITUTIONS.

Since 1844, the Dominican Republic has had twenty-five constitutions. This number may appear to be extraordinary for a relatively young republic; however, it does not seem so large when taking into account the fact that the country followed the Spanish American model, in which virtually every new regime writes its own constitution—even though few substantive changes are made—to give it independence and validity in a very unstable system. To complicate matters further, the Dominican Republic was controlled by Haiti from 1822 to 1844, by Spain from 1861 to 1865, and by the United States from 1916 to 1924. Thus its status as an independent republic was a major constitutional issue that needed to be addressed. In general, all the constitutions have guaranteed basic human rights and have appeared to be democratic and progressive. In reality, however, they have been more symbolic than functioning documents. Adherence to the spirit of the many constitutions was more in the breach than in the observance.

The first constitution after the country's liberation from Haiti, promulgated in 1844, represented a compromise between conservative and liberal factions but was rhetorically quite liberal. It called for a popularly elected government and specified powers of the Congress and judiciary. It forbade the suspension of the constitution. Roman Catholicism was declared the state religion (although other sects were free to worship), and slavery was abolished. Ten years later (June 1854) a more liberal constitution briefly replaced the 1844 document. After political unrest, however, the caudillo Pedro SANTANA (1844–1848, 1853–1856, 1859–1861) returned to power and in December 1854 changed the constitution to fit his autocratic governing style. This authoritarian document was reflected in several later constitutions from the 1850s to the 1870s. An exception was the Moca Constitution of 1858, a more politically progressive document, which was reinstated after the Spanish occupation. It provided for universal male suffrage and direct voting by secret ballot for all elective offices. Its liberal provisions were extended by the Constitutions of 1865 and 1866.

Early-twentieth-century constitutions were influenced by the U.S. Constitution. The main features of the Constitution of 1924, promulgated after the U.S. military authorities withdrew, were retained in subsequent documents until the era of Generalíssimo Rafael TRUJILLO (1930–1961). Trujillo's constitutions enunciated principles of civilian democratic rule and representative government, called for three equal and independent branches of government, and included provisions for human rights. But constitutional theory and political reality were two very different things. Trujillo, while ruling as autocratically and ruthlessly as any Caribbean dictator, was scrupulous about upholding the narrow letter of the law—with no intention of abiding by the spirit of the constitution. Indeed, if examined closely, his 1955 Constitution, for example, granted almost absolute power to the president.

After Trujillo was assassinated in 1961, a provisional

Council of State enacted a new Constitution of 1962, which remained in effect for less than a year. Its symbolic importance, however, was that it represented a continuation of *trujillismo.* Anti-Trujillo elements regarded it as a symbol of oppression and retention of privileges for the elites. It encountered bitter opposition from antidictatorial sectors and seemed strikingly unsuited to the needs of the impoverished country.

The reformist regime of Juan BOSCH (1963) enacted a far different constitution. The 1963 Constitution not only retained the most politically and socially progressive features of the 1962 Constitution but also explicitly committed the government to an active role in fostering socioeconomic development and laid the bases for a modern welfare state. Unfortunately, several constitutional provisions alienated powerful traditional elements in society. The Catholic church objected to the legalization of divorce and the new emphasis on secular education. The business community was alarmed over the emphasis on public rather than private economic interests. The landowners feared expropriation of their holdings, and the military feared a loss of power and subordination to civilian authority. These groups combined to overthrow Bosch in late 1963 and quickly restore the Constitution of 1962.

After the 1965 civil war, in which the United States intervened militarily, a compromise constitution was hammered out by a constituent assembly the following year. In essence the 1966 Constitution provides for modern progressive government and civil liberties but lacks the kind of social provisions that would alienate the traditional elites.

HOWARD J. WIARDA, *The Dominican Republic: Nation in Transition* (1969); THOMAS E. WEIL et al., *Area Handbook for the Dominican Republic* (1973); IAN BELL, *The Dominican Republic* (1981); JULIO BREA FRANCO, *El sistema constitucional dominicano,* 2 vols. (1983); JAN KNIPPERS BLACK, *The Dominican Republic: Politics and Development in an Unsovereign State* (1986).

WINFIELD J. BURGGRAAFF

DOMINICAN REPUBLIC: POLITICAL PARTIES

Dominican Revolutionary Party
Partido Revolucionario Dominicano—PRD

The PRD was founded in 1939 by Dominican anti-Trujilloist exiles for the purpose of toppling the Dominican dictator Rafael Trujillo. It established branches in Caracas, New York, and San Juan, Puerto Rico. Among its founders were Juan BOSCH, Juan Isidro Jiménes Grullón, and Angel Miolán. Shortly after Trujillo's assassination in May 1961, a PRD delegation led by Angel Miolán, Nicolas Silfa, and Ramon Castillo returned to Santo Domingo to participate in the now reviving political life that had been stifled for over three decades. In the first national elections (December 1962) after Trujillo's death, PRD candidate Bosch defeated his National

Civic Union (UCN) opponent. After only seven months in office, Bosch was toppled by a military coup. While the ensuing Triumvirate remained in power, the PRD spearheaded the opposition to a government that was dominated by UCN members and the military. During the revolution of 1965, the PRD led the struggle of the Constitutionalist cause.

In the first election (1966) after the end of the revolutionary and civil war of 1965, PRD candidate Juan Bosch was defeated by his Reformist Party (PR) opponent, Joaquín BALAGUER, who also won the presidential elections of 1970 and 1974. After Bosch broke with the PRD in 1973 in order to form his own political party, the Dominican Liberation Party (PLD), PRD party affairs were taken over by José Francisco Peña Gómez, who went on to become vice president of the Socialist International after the PRD, which considered itself a Social Democratic party, had become a member of that organization.

The PRD staged a political comeback in 1978, when its candidate, Antonio Guzmán Fernández, won the presidential election. That victory was followed in 1982 by Salvador Jorge Blanco's winning the presidency on behalf of the PRD. Thereafter, the PRD's fortunes declined as the party fragmented into diverse factions.

MICHAEL J. KRYZANEK, "Political Party Decline and the Failure of Liberal Democracy: The PRD in Dominican Politics," in *Journal of Latin American Studies* 9, pt. 1 (1977): 115–143; ANGEL MIOLÁN, *El Perredé desde mi ángulo* (1984).

KAI P. SCHOENHALS

DOMINICAN REVOLT (1965), the civil conflict spurred by the military's overthrow of Juan Bosch and the installation of a repressive puppet regime. The September 1963 coup that removed the democratically elected Bosch after a mere seven months in office brought to power a military-backed civilian triumvirate, headed by businessman Donald Reid Cabral, that embarked on a course of corruption and repression that reminded Dominicans of the dictatorship of Rafael Trujillo. On 24 April 1965, members of the Dominican Revolutionary Party (PRD), some Christian Socialists, disgruntled professionals, and dissident elements of the armed forces led by Colonel Francisco Caamaño Deñó, seized the government and arrested Reid Cabral. The Constitutionalists' appeal for the restoration of democracy and the return of the constitutionally elected President Juan Bosch from exile was met with enthusiasm from the Dominican populace but with consternation on the part of pro-Cabral elements among the armed forces and the U.S. embassy, represented by William Tupley Bennett.

The organizer of the coup against Bosch, General Elías Wessín y Wessín, ordered the bombing of Santo Domingo by his air force, which was followed by an attempted thrust into the old part of the capital. Not only were the Constitutionalists able to repulse Wessín's attack, but within a few days they were on the verge of victory. At this point U.S. President Lyndon B. Johnson ordered a massive armed intervention, ostensibly to rescue North American citizens and prevent a supposed Communist takeover, a "second Cuba," but in reality to obviate the return of Juan Bosch. There followed a bitter civil war between the Constitutionalists and Loyalists (loyal to Reid Cabral), with the supposedly neutral U.S. Marines and airborne units clearly siding with the forces of Wessín y Wessín. Contrary to Johnson's expectation of a brief skirmish, the conflict lasted the entire summer and resulted in thousands of Dominican casualties.

Johnson's intervention was criticized by Latin America's democracies (Mexico and Chile), which viewed his action as the end of Roosevelt's Good Neighbor Policy. The hemisphere's dictatorships, however, approved of the intervention and dispatched 500 Brazilian, Nicaraguan, Honduran, and Paraguayan soldiers to Santo Domingo to serve in an Inter-American Peace Force under U.S. General Bruce Palmer. A compromise settlement worked out by U.S. special envoy Ellsworth Bunker finally led to an end of the revolution and civil war on 31 August 1965. The Act of Dominican Reconciliation called for the creation of a provisional government, the reintegration of the country's armed forces, and the holding of national elections in June 1966.

DAN KURZMAN, *Santo Domingo: The Revolt of the Damned* (1965); TAD SZULC, *Dominican Diary* (1965); JOSÉ ANTONIO MORENO, *Barrios in Arms* (1970); ABRAHAM F. LOWENTHAL, *The Dominican Intervention* (1972); PIERO GLEIJESES, *The Dominican Crisis* (1978); HAMLET HERMANN, *Francis Caamaño* (1983).

KAI P. SCHOENHALS

DOMINICANS (Order of Preachers). The Dominican order was one of several religious orders important in colonial Latin America. Having been founded in medieval Europe as a means of combating heresy, it was particularly well suited to missionary activity in the Americas.

The Dominican order arrived in the New World in 1510 with a contingent of friars sent by the crown to Hispaniola. Although the FRANCISCANS, and others, had begun the early missionary work on the island, the Dominicans would leave a lasting impression. The order was chosen for two reasons. The Spanish crown had received disquieting rumors of the outbreak of heresy in the new colony, and there was a generally conceded need for more priests. The first contingent was organized by Friar Alonso Loaisa. Although some fifteen friars were chosen, only nine, led by Friar Pedro de Córdoba, sailed for the New World, arriving in Santo Domingo in September 1510.

The impact of the Dominicans on Hispaniola was dramatic. Well trained in theology, as expounded by the famous Dominican, Saint Thomas Aquinas, the friars began to attempt to reform Spanish society. They taught the doctrine of the equality of all human beings in the sight of God. In 1511, Friar Antonio de MONTESINOS began to rail in the pulpit against the system of forced Indian labor prevalent on the island. His sermons raised such ire in the colony that he was forced to return to Spain to defend his views. One settler, Bartolomé de LAS CASAS, deeply influenced by Montesinos, entered the Dominican order in 1523. Las Casas spent the remainder of his life continuing the struggle for social justice and for the protection of the American Indians, eventually becoming the bishop of Chiapas in Mexico.

The first contingent of Dominicans to arrive in Mexico after the Conquest came in 1526. The group of twelve friars, led by Friar Tomás Ortíz, suffered badly during the first year. Five of their number died, and four more were forced to return to Spain because of ill health, leaving only three friars: Domingo de Betanzos, Gonzalo Lucero, and Vicente de las Casas. Betanzos assumed leadership of the order in Mexico, overseeing its development until 1528, when seven more friars arrived.

In Mexico the Dominicans initiated their mission in the Valley of Mexico and surrounding regions. Their greatest efforts were made in the south, especially among the Mixteca and Oaxaca. In the south they had near complete autonomy. Some of the most impressive early churches were built by Dominicans, including Teposcolula, Yanhuitlán, and Cuilapán. Their devotion to Our Lady of the Rosary resulted in several magnificent works of ecclesiastical decoration, notably the Rosary chapel of the Church of Santo Domingo in Puebla.

The Dominicans were among the first orders to arrive in Peru. In 1529 a group of six Dominicans, led by Friar Reginaldo Pedraza, accompanied PIZARRO on his return to the New World as participants in his expedition. Five of the six died or abandoned the enterprise, leaving only Friar Vicente de Valverde to participate with Pizarro in the conquest. He was counted among the men of Cajamarca and rewarded with the bishopric of Cuzco, in reality all of Peru, for his efforts.

The formal establishment of the order in Peru occurred in 1540, when Friar Francisco Toscano arrived with twelve other friars. The order quickly established monasteries in both Lima and Cuzco. Their church and convent in Cuzco was built upon the sacred temple of the Sun, the Coricancha. At the same time, the Dominicans under Friar Alonso de Montenegro established themselves in the other Inca capital of Quito.

Although the Dominicans were deeply involved in missionary activity among the Indians, they also had close ties to the Spanish population. In the capital cities, the Dominican conventual churches were often among the most ornate and best endowed. Many Dominicans also participated in the literary life of the colonies. In Lima, Friar Diego de Ojeda (Hojeda) won great repute for his poetry, especially the sacred epic *La cristiada*.

The Dominicans played an important role in the study of native languages. The order was responsible for the production of one of the most popular early catechisms in Mexico. In 1548 and 1550 their *Doctrina cristiana* was published. Later, in 1565, Friar Domingo de la Anunciación published his *Doctrina christiana breve,* another key early catechism, this one written in both Spanish and NAHUATL, the Aztec language. Among early students of the indigenous cultures, Friar Diego Durán ranks as very important. In his *Historia de las indias de la Nueva España* he compiled much information about the ancient rites and culture of the Aztecs, acquired during his childhood in Texcoco, near Mexico City. In Peru the efforts of the Dominicans to study the native languages was represented by Friar Domingo de Santo Tomás who published the first grammar and a dictionary of Quechua in 1560.

In Europe the Dominican order participated in the Holy Office of the INQUISITION, but in the New World the Holy Office was organized under the monarch. The role played by the Dominicans was no greater than that of any other order. At the close of the sixteenth century one Dominican who had achieved some fame for his work in the Inquisition and for his skills as an historian was Friar Agustín DÁVILA Y PADILLA, author of the *Historia de la fundación y discurso de la provincia de Santiago,* a history of the Dominicans in Mexico.

As in other orders, by the end of the sixteenth century, nearly half of the membershp of local monasteries consisted of CREOLES. Another important faction within the order were PENINSULAR Spaniards who had entered the order in the New World, *hijos de provincia.* In order to cope with the competition for political power among these three groups, the Dominicans adopted the system known as the *alternativa* in their regular leadership elections. In this system, the leadership of local monasteries regularly rotated from peninsulars to creoles to *hijos de provincia.*

There were several Dominicans who became bishops during the colonial period. Some of the most famous of these include Friar Alonso de Montúfar, the second archbishop of Mexico and Friar Diego de Loaysa, first archbishop of Lima.

In Lima, during the seventeenth century a rich culture emerged out of the Dominican order. Saint Martín de PORRES (1579–1639) was the mulatto son of a local gentleman. He sought entry into the Dominican order, but due to his illegitimate birth and mixed ancestry he was denied. Through quiet determination de Porres continued his quest, until in 1603 he was admitted as a lay brother. He was canonized in 1962. Juan Macias (1585–1645) arrived in Lima as a begging orphan. After living in the streets for several years, Macias entered the Dominican order and gained great fame for his piety and the austerity of his prayer life. He was beatified in 1837. Saint ROSA DE LIMA (1586–1617) was born into polite Lima society. Although baptized as Isabel, as a child she took the name Rose of Saint Mary. She did not formally enter the Dominican order, but dressed as a Dominican tertiary. She lived her life in extreme austerity, devoting long hours to prayer and mortification. She was canonized in 1671. Saint Mariana de Jesús Pare-

des (1618–1645) also was a member of the Dominican order. Born in Quito, she was orphaned at age five. Raised by her older sister, she soon demonstrated a vocation for the contemplative life. Although she studied with the Jesuits, she entered the Dominican convent of Santa Catalina in Quito. When an epidemic threatened to destroy everyone in the city, she offered herself to God as a sacrifice. The pestilence stopped, and within a day of her vow she died. Canonization proceedings began immediately and met with success in 1950.

DANIEL ULLOA, *Los predicadores divididos: Los dominicos en Nueva España, siglo XVI* (1977); *Los dominicos y el Nuevo Mundo* (1988).

JOHN F. SCHWALLER

See also **Catholic Church.**

DONATÁRIOS, lord proprietors. In 1534 King JOÃO III made donatary grants of fifteen strips of land in Brazil to a dozen noblemen to encourage permanent settlement and better defense from pirates. The lord proprietors who received these grants were required to defend and settle the land at their own expense, to found and charter townships, administer justice, collect tithes, and license sugar mills. The *donatários* were similar to the proprietors of large land grants in English North America, although in the case of Brazil, most were absentee landlords. As a recipient of a captaincy, the *donatário* had extensive administrative, fiscal, and judicial powers over colonists. They were empowered to make land grants (*sesmarias*) to prospective settlers who arrived to form permanent settlements and establish sugarcane plantations and cattle ranches to export crops.

None of the *donatários* came from the high nobility, but they were all members of the Order of Christ. Some of the *donatários* were soldiers of fortune, like Duarte COELHO PEREIRA and Francisco Pereira Coutinho. Others were well educated, like the historian João de BARROS, or were government bureaucrats.

The original *donatários* of the captaincies around 1534 were:

João de Barros and Aires da Cunha	Pará
Fernão Alvares de Andrade	Maranhão
Antônio Cardoso de Barros	Piauí
Pêro Lopes de Sousa	Itamaracá, Santo Amaro, Santa Ana
Duarte Coelho Pereira	Pernambuco
Francisco Pereira Coutinho	Bahia
Jorge Figueiredo Correia	Ilhéus
Pêro do Campo Tourinho	Pôrto Seguro
Vasco Fernandes Coutinho	Espírito Santo
Pêro de Góis	São Tomé
Martim Afonso de Sousa	Rio de Janeiro, São Vicente

CARLOS MALHEIRO DIAS, ed., *História da colonização portuguesa do Brasil*, 3 vols. (1921–1926); ALEXANDER MARCHANT, *From Barter to Slavery: The Economic Relations of Portuguese and Indians in the Settlement of Brazil, 1500–1580* (1942); BAILEY W. DIFFIE, *Latin American Civilization: The Colonial Period* (1945), p. 642a, and *A History of Colonial Brazil, 1500–1792* (1987).

PATRICIA MULVEY

DONATARY CAPTAINCY SYSTEM. *See* **Captaincy System.**

DONOSO, JOSÉ (*b.* 5 October 1924), Chilean writer. Donoso is one of the most distinguished contemporary Latin American writers belonging to the generation of Gabriel GARCÍA MÁRQUEZ and Carlos FUENTES. Born in Santiago, Donoso began writing at the age of twenty-five. In 1951 he received a scholarship from the Doherty Foundation to study English literature at Princeton University. Upon returning to Chile he began a period of increased creative activity, writing short stories and publishing in 1955 his first book, *Veraneo y otros cuentos*, which won the Municipal Prize. His first novel, *Coronación* (1957) (*Coronation* [1965]) won the William Faulkner Foundation Prize for the Latin American Novel in 1962. He moved to Buenos Aires in 1958. Upon his return to Chile in 1960, he wrote for the weekly *Ercilla* and married María Pilar Serrano, a Bolivian painter. By the mid-1960s, Donoso was recognized as a major literary figure and was invited in 1965–1967 to the University of Iowa Writers' Workshop. He published his novels *Este domingo* (1966) (*This Sunday* [1967]) and *El lugar sin límites* (1966) (*Hell Has No Limits* [1972]) and a book of stories, *Los mejores cuentos de José Donoso* (1966).

In 1967 he left for Spain, eventually settling in Barcelona, where he published in 1970 what it had taken him eight years to write, *El obsceno pájaro de la noche* (*The Obscene Bird of Night* [1973]). This acclaimed novel placed Donoso among the top Latin American writers of his generation. There followed a series of outstanding novels: *Casa de campo* (1978) (*A House in the Country* [1984]), which won the Critics' Prize in Spain, *La misteriosa desaparición de la marquesita de Loria* (1980), *El jardín de al lado* (1981), and *La desesperanza* (1986) (*Curfew* [1988]), among others. In his 1972 *Historia personal del boom* (*The Boom in Spanish American Literature: A Personal History* [1972]) Donoso scrutinizes with humor and grace Emir RODRÍGUEZ MONEGAL's discussion of the publishing phenomenon of the 1960s. Donoso also created a series of masterful short story collections, among them *El charleston* (1960) (*Charleston and Other Stories* [1977]), *Tres novelitas burguesas* (1973) (*Sacred Families* [1977]), *Cuatro para Delfina* (1982), and *Taratuta* (1990). He has also written a book of poetry, *Poemas de un novelista* (1981) and dramatic versions of one of his short stories, *Sueños de mala muerte* (1985), and of his novel *Este domingo* (1990).

Donoso's fictional narratives stand out as the most important part of his production. His novels, *The Obscene Bird* and *House in the Country*, in particular, are the most valuable narratives of the contemporary period in Chile. They are also unique manifestations of the Spanish American novel, standing alongside García Márquez's *Cien años de soledad* (1967) and Carlos Fuentes's *Terra nostra* (1975). Donoso's literary expression represents the dark side of imagination, a grotesque recreation of myth, folklore, psychology, and the fantastic. The mixing of many voices constitutes the unmistakable stylistic feature of his narrative.

ALFRED J. MAC ADAM, *Modern Latin American Narratives: The Dreams of Reason* (1977); GEORGE R. MC MURRAY, *José Donoso* (1979); PHILIP SWANSON, *José Donoso: The Boom and Beyond* (1988); CEDOMIL GOIC, "José Donoso," in *Latin American Writers*, edited by Carlos A. Solé and María Isabel Abreu, vol. 3 (1989), pp. 1,277–1,288.

CEDOMIL GOIC

See also **Literature.**

DONOVAN, JEAN (*b.* 10 April 1953, *d.* 2 December 1980), U.S. Catholic lay missionary murdered in El Salvador. Donovan was born in Westport, Connecticut. Influenced by an Irish priest who had served as a missionary in Peru, she applied to and was accepted for the Salvadoran mission program of the Cleveland diocese. Sent to La Libertad, El Salvador, in 1979, she taught religion, hygiene, and nutrition and worked with a CHRISTIAN BASE COMMUNITY. Due to the escalation of the civil war, the Cleveland team soon joined MARYKNOLL nuns in transporting displaced peasants from war zones to Catholic refugee centers. On 2 December 1980, Donovan and her partner, Ursuline Sister Dorothy Kazel, picked up Maryknoll Sisters Ita Ford and Maura Clarke at the San Salvador airport. Their van was stopped by Salvadoran national guardsmen, who raped and murdered the four women. Their deaths and the cover-up of the crime by Salvadoran authorities shocked millions of North Americans and awakened them to the violent realities of El Salvador.

ANA CARRIGAN, *Salvador Witness: The Life and Calling of Jean Donovan* (1984); DONNA WHITSON BRETT and EDWARD T. BRETT, *Murdered in Central America: The Stories of Eleven U.S. Missionaries* (1988), pp. 189–252.

EDWARD T. BRETT

DORREGO, MANUEL (*b.* 11 June 1787; *d.* 13 December 1828), Argentine military officer in the independence struggle and Federalist leader. Though born in Buenos Aires, Dorrego was studying law in Chile when the revolution against Spain began. He actively embraced the patriot cause, first in Chile and then in his own country, joining the 1811 campaign to liberate what is now Bolivia. Later still he fought in Uruguay with the forces of Buenos Aires against those of the Uruguayan leader José ARTIGAS. He gained a reputation as quarrelsome and undisciplined, but he also took a principled stand against the centralism and monarchist intrigues of the government of Juan Martín de PUEYRREDÓN (1816–1819), which exiled him in 1817.

Dorrego spent three years in the United States, an experience that strengthened his Federalist convictions. After his return he held a number of military and other positions and became an active publicist in opposition to the Unitarist regime of Bernardino RIVADAVIA. At the collapse of Rivadavia's government in 1827, Dorrego became governor of Buenos Aires Province, in which capacity he brought to a close the war fought with Brazil over Uruguay, agreeing to accept Uruguayan independence. In December 1828 he was overthrown by Juan LAVALLE, who by executing Dorrego made him a martyr in the eyes of Federalists and unleashed a round of bloody reprisals and counterreprisals between the two parties.

A recent biography is MARCOS DE ESTRADA, *Una semblanza de Manuel Dorrego* (1985). See also the treatment in the biography by JOHN LYNCH of his party ally and successor, *Argentine Dictator: Juan Manuel de Rosas, 1829–1852* (1981).

DAVID BUSHNELL

DORTICÓS TORRADO, OSVALDO (*b.* 1919; *d.* 23 June 1983), president of Cuba from 1959 to 1976. Born in Cienfuegos, Dorticós Torrado graduated from the University of Havana Law School in 1941. He served as dean of the Cienfuegos Bar Association and subsequently as vice president of the Cuban Bar Association. After his release from a short imprisonment for anti-BATISTA activities, Dorticós joined Fidel CASTRO's TWENTY-SIXTH OF JULY MOVEMENT and soon became its Cienfuegos coordinator.

When President Manuel URRUTIA resigned on 17 July 1959, Dorticós ascended to the presidency, becoming at forty the youngest president in the nation's history. Real power remained in Castro's hands, but Dorticós nevertheless remained loyal, receiving additional appointments, including minister of the economy in 1976. He held positions in the National Assembly of the People's Power and Council of State, was vice president of the Council of Ministers, and was a member of the Political Bureau of the Central Committee of the Cuban Communist Party. Dorticós committed suicide in 1983.

JAIME SUCHLICKI, *Historical Dictionary of Cuba* (1988) and *Cuba: From Columbus to Castro,* 3d ed. (1990).

JAIME SUCHLICKI

DOS PILAS, an important archaeological site of the MAYA civilization located in the PETEXBATÚN region of the Petén rain forest of Guatemala. Archaeological and epigraphic research has shown that Dos Pilas was the capital of a Classic Maya state remarkable for its late and rapid trajectory of florescence, expansion, and violent collapse.

The major occupation at the site began in the seventh century, when outcast members of the royal family of the great city of TIKAL arrived at Dos Pilas and rapidly constructed the site center. From this new base, the first rulers concentrated their political and military efforts on defeating their relatives and rivals at Tikal. In the late seventh century, Dos Pilas defeated and sacrificed the king of Tikal, Shield Skull, enhancing the prestige of this newly created Maya polity. During the next century, the rulers of Dos Pilas successfully expanded their state across the Petexbatún region through royal marriages, alliance, and warfare. Even some large and ancient centers, such as SEIBAL, were subjugated. By A.D. 740, the kingdom of Dos Pilas controlled much of the Pasión River valley, one of the major trade routes of the Maya world. During this period of expansionism, the Dos Pilas center acquired great wealth and prestige, as reflected in its tombs and cave deposits, and its many stone monuments. The site's numerous sculpted stelae and its four hieroglyphic stairways present military themes in both text and imagery.

The fall of Dos Pilas was as rapid and dramatic as its rise. In A.D. 761, previously subordinate Petexbatún centers defeated the ruler of Dos Pilas. Archaeological remains corresponding to this date show that the site was besieged and destroyed. Evidence of the final years of the site includes concentric fortification walls around architectural complexes and impoverished occupation by small remnant populations. After the fall of Dos Pilas its Petexbatún kingdom fragmented into intensively warring smaller polities. This final violent period of Petexbatún history ended by A.D. 800 with the virtual abandonment of most of the region.

STEPHEN HOUSTON and PETER MATHEWS, "The Dynastic Sequence of Dos Pilas, Guatemala," in *Pre-Columbian Art Research Institute, Monograph 1* (1985); ARTHUR DEMAREST et al., eds., *Petexbatún Regional Archaeological Project Preliminary Report 3* (1991) and *Petexbatún Regional Archaeological Project Preliminary Report 4* (1992); ARTHUR A. DEMAREST, "The Violent Saga of a Maya Kingdom," in *National Geographic* 183, no. 2 (1993): 95–111.

ARTHUR A. DEMAREST

DOUBLE SIMULTANEOUS VOTE. *See* **Uruguay: Electoral System.**

DOWRY, an important gift given to a woman contributing to her support in marriage or convent life. Until the end of the nineteenth century, parents had an explicit legal obligation to endow their daughters to the best of their abilities. Other relatives or, sometimes, charitable institutions also gave dowries or contributed toward them. In the sixteenth, seventeenth, and eighteenth centuries in Latin America most women who married and practically all nuns received a dowry.

The law and practice of dowry came from Iberia to Latin America with the first Spanish conquistadores and Portuguese settlers. In sixteenth-century Iberia it was customary for both spouses to bring property to marriage; the bride's contribution was her dowry and her inheritance (after one or both of her parents died). The practice of dowry, practically a requisite for marriage in Latin America in the sixteenth and seventeenth centuries, declined throughout the eighteenth and nineteenth centuries and disappeared by the early twentieth. The practice of a dowry to enter a convent persisted longer, although the relative size of the dowry had decreased considerably by the end of the nineteenth century.

When it was given by parents, the dowry was an advance on their daughter's inheritance. Daughters always inherited in Latin America, since Spanish and Portuguese law dictated equally partible inheritance and made all children forced heirs. (They could not be disinherited except for extremely serious causes.) When an endowed woman's parents died, the value of her dowry was usually added to the share of their estate that went by law to their children (usually four-fifths in Spanish America, and two-thirds in Brazil). The division was made equally among all heirs, and the daughter (whether a married woman or a nun) received the difference between her dowry and her inheritance.

Within marriage, dowry functioned differently in Spanish America from the way it did in Brazil because the marriage systems were different. In Spanish America there were three main kinds of property in a marriage: the property the husband brought to marriage; the property the wife brought to marriage, called her dowry, though it might not be restricted to the actual dowry given by her parents but could also include inherited property, or the property she had retained as a widow; and the property acquired in the course of the marriage through the husband's administration of all the couple's property (*bienes gananciales*). Because a wife's dowry was meant to revert to her when her husband died, her dowry could not be alienated or mortgaged and served as a kind of insurance for the wife. A widow received her dowry back and retained half the *bienes gananciales*. Brazil, in contrast, had full community property within the marriage (unless a prenuptial contract established otherwise), so that a woman's dowry disappeared into the pool of property. When she became a widow, she retained half the couple's property, no matter what proportion each spouse had contributed.

The system of equally partible inheritance with forced heirship combined with dowries for daughters meant that Latin American women of the propertied class made large economic contributions to their marriage or to the convents they entered. Furthermore, the marriage regimes by which widows retained considerable property gave Latin American widows of the propertied class importance as economic actors. Nuns likewise had significant economic roles.

The Latin American dowry system is now well understood, but its actual practice throughout the history of Latin America has been studied only in some regions and time periods, and more extensively in regard to marriage than in regard to convents. The main finding about dowry at marriage is that the practice varied somewhat from region to region and everywhere declined over the centuries. In the sixteenth and early seventeenth centuries, there was a tendency for brides to contribute greater amounts of property to marriage than did their husbands. By the late eighteenth or early nineteenth century, it was husbands who usually contributed more property to marriage than their wives. Simultaneously, fewer parents gave dowries and many marriages took place without a dowry. In São Paulo not only were dowries fewer and smaller in relation to the daughter's inheritance as the centuries progressed, but the total divestment made by parents for their daughters' dowries in relation to the size of their estate dropped precipitously, and the contents of dowry changed from mainly means of production in the seventeenth century to mainly items for consumption in the nineteenth century.

The historical decline and disappearance of the practice of dowry was clearly related to changes in the roles of men and women and to alterations in marriage and the family which were a part of the general social changes experienced in the eighteenth and nineteenth centuries.

For marriage dowry see ASUNCIÓN LAVRIN and EDITH COUTURIER, ''Dowries and Wills: A View of Women's Socioeconomic Role in Colonial Guadalajara and Puebla, 1640–1790,'' in *Hispanic American Historical Review* 59, no. 2 (1979): 280–304; EUGENE H. KORTH and DELLA M. FLUSCHE, ''Dowry and Inheritance in Colonial Spanish America: Peninsular Law and Chilean Practice,'' in *The Americas* 43, no. 4 (1987): 395–410; and MURIEL NAZZARI, *Disappearance of the Dowry: Women, Families, and Social Change in São Paulo, Brazil (1600–1900)* (1991). For dowries in convents see SUSAN SOEIRO, ''The Social and Economic Role of the Convent: Women and Nuns in Colonial Bahia 1677–1800,'' in *Hispanic American Historical Review* 54, no. 2 (1974): 209–232; and ASUNCIÓN LAVRIN, ''Women in Convents: Their Economic and Social Role in Colonial Mexico,'' in *Liberating Women's History: Theoretical and Critical Essays*, edited by Berenice Carroll (1976).

MURIEL NAZZARI

See also **Marriage and Divorce; Women.**

DRAGO, LUIS MARÍA (*b.* 6 May 1859; *d.* 9 June 1921), Argentine jurist. A native of Buenos Aires, Drago was elected three times to the Chamber of Deputies and became one of Argentina's most eminent international jurists. In 1909, at the request of Britain and the United States, he arbitrated two major disputes between them; he also was a judge on the Permanent Court of International Justice (1912–1916). His major contribution was in the context of American international law and another important doctrine, the Drago Doctrine, which was a narrowing of the CALVO DOCTRINE. This contribution, made while he was minister of foreign affairs, was in response to armed European intervention against Venezuela. In 1902, three European states (Britain, Germany, and Italy) imposed a naval blockade in order to force their financial claims resulting from default on bonds. On 29 December 1902 Drago sent an official note to the heads of the American governments stating that such use of force was contrary to international law: "The collection of loans by military means implies territorial occupation to make them effective [and it is] the suppression or subordination of the governments." His note received strong support in Latin America and at the Second Hague Conference (1907), where the United States had his doctrine modified.

LUIS MARÍA DRAGO, "State Loans in Their Relation to International Policy," in *American Journal of International Law* 1, no. 3 (1907): 692–726, and HAROLD EUGENE DAVIS, JOHN J. FINAN, and F. TAYLOR PECK, *Latin American Diplomatic History: An Introduction* (1977).

LARMAN C. WILSON

DRAGO DOCTRINE, a principle of international law that rejects the right of a country to use military force against another country to collect debts. The doctrine was first enunciated on 29 December 1902 by Luis María DRAGO, Argentina's minister of foreign affairs, in a letter to the Argentine minister in Washington, D.C., in response to the naval blockade imposed on Venezuela by Germany, Great Britain, and Italy for the purpose of collecting debts incurred by the Venezuelan government with nationals of those countries.

Although based on the CALVO DOCTRINE, the Drago Doctrine goes further by rejecting the right of intervention and specifying that economic claims give no legal right to intervene militarily in another country. The Calvo Doctrine says, in essence, that investors have to accept the jurisdiction of the host country's laws and should not appeal to their own governments in case of any conflict in the enforcement of a contract. The Drago Doctrine stipulates that a nation, although it is legally bound to pay its debts, cannot be forced to do so.

The doctrine was innovative because it rejected categorically the right of military intervention or occupation of a country for the purpose of collecting debts. At the time, however, European powers were intervening and carving out empires everywhere and the United States had also joined the club of colonial powers after the SPANISH-AMERICAN WAR, and thus the doctrine was not readily accepted as a principle of international law. At the Second Hague Conference (1907) a toned-down form of the doctrine was adopted. The resolution declared illegal an intervention for the collection of debts, provided that the nation in question had accepted arbitration and the decisions adopted in that arbitration. Drago explained his doctrine extensively in two of his

books: *La República Argentina y el caso de Venezuela* (1903) and *Cobro coercitivo de deudas públicas* (1906).

ALFREDO N. VIVOT, *La Doctrina Drago* (1911); VICTORINO JIMÉNEZ Y NÚÑEZ, *La Doctrina Drago y la política internacional* (1927); EDWIN M. BORCHARD, "Calvo and Drago Doctrines," in *Encyclopaedia of the Social Sciences*, vol. 3 (1930); ISIDRO FABELA, *Las doctrinas Monroe y Drago* (1957).

JUAN MANUEL PÉREZ

DRAGÚN, OSVALDO (*b.* 1929), Argentine playwright, achieved international status with his *Historias para ser contadas* (1957), a group of brief and dehumanizing vignettes that capture a pithy social reality with sparse language, minimal plot and scenery, and often grotesque elements. Dragún, a native of San Salvador, Entre Ríos, lacked formal training in the theater but learned quickly by acting, directing, and writing for community theater groups. His career was launched with the independent group Fray Mocho in 1956 and the production of two historical plays that underscored individual and political freedom, *La peste viene de Melos* (1956) and *Tupac Amaru* (1957). The writers of Dragún's generation (including Roberto Cossa, Carlos GOROSTIZA, and Ricardo Halac) sought to interpret an Argentine reality that was chaotic under Juan Perón but even more anarchic after his demise. This "new realism" found expression in the aesthetics of the grotesque, an honored tradition in Argentina with its dehumanization of the individual. Dragún wrote many full-length plays, including *Y nos dijeron que éramos inmortales* (1963), a study of the illusions of alienated generations, and *Milagro en el mercado viejo* (1964), a Brechtian play about crime and betrayal. Of his twenty or so theater pieces, the most successful are *El amasijo* (1968), an absurdist rendering of two lonely individuals who regularly miss the opportunities life hands them, and *Arriba corazón!* (1986), an expressionist piece with autobiographical overtones. Dragún spent many years outside Argentina, primarily in Cuba, where he has been greatly involved with the International Theater School. In Argentina he was instrumental in creating the Teatro Abierto in 1981, a daring and ambitious presentation of twenty new plays, by various authors, structured to challenge Argentine political reality at its most vicious and repressive stage, the military dictatorship.

DONALD L. SCHMIDT, "The Theater of Osvaldo Dragún," in *Dramatists in Revolt: The New Latin American Theater*, edited by Leon F. Lyday and George W. Woodyard (1976): 77–94; BONNIE HILDEBRAND REYNOLDS, "Time and Responsibility in Dragún's *Tupac Amaru*," in *Latin American Theatre Review* 13, no. 1 (Fall 1979): 47–53; JACQUELINE EYRING BIXLER, "The Game of Reading and the Creation of Meaning in *El amasijo*," in *Revista Canadiense de Estudios Hispánicos* 12, no. 1 (Fall 1987): 1–16; AMALIA GLADHART, "Narrative Foregrounding in the Plays of Osvaldo Dragún," in *Latin American Theatre Review* 26, no. 2 (Spring 1993): 93–109.

GEORGE WOODYARD

DRAKE, FRANCIS (*b.* ca. 1545; *d.* 28 January 1596), English privateer who became, from 1570 to 1595, the central figure in attacks by privateers on the Spanish Indies. A maritime genius and fervent Protestant, Drake was a glorious hero to the English and a frightening monster in the eyes of the Spanish. He developed a coherent West Indian strategy to replace the established pattern of small, uncoordinated raids on the Spanish. Although Drake achieved much success, acquiring great booty and inflicting considerable damage to Spanish holdings, he failed to break Spain's monopoly on territorial possession in the Caribbean.

Originally an illicit trader, Drake was with John HAWKINS OF PLYMOUTH during the disastrous defeat at SAN JUAN DE ULÚA in late 1568. In 1571 he carried out reconnaissance activities and forged alliances with savage indigenous warriors, particularly on the Central American isthmus. A year later he led a voyage which attacked Nombre de Dios, Panama, and acquired a large booty of Peruvian treasure. After the English-Spanish peace of 1574, Drake remained active in the West Indies for eleven years, becoming the first captain to sail his own ship around the world (1577–1580).

In 1585, Drake resumed his naval efforts by carrying out a full-scale operation known as the Indies Voyage, with a fleet of over twenty sail, which aspired to attack Santo Domingo and Cartagena, Colombia, then Nombre de Dios and Panama (by land, in collaboration with runaway slaves), and, finally, Havana. In addition to establishing an English stronghold in the Indies, Drake hoped to disrupt the flow of Latin American resources, particularly Peruvian silver, to the Iberian Peninsula, thereby hindering Spain's military efforts in Europe. This plan proved to be too ambitious, however. After destroying much of Santo Domingo and Cartagena, Drake decided not to attack the isthmus, because of his depleted manpower, a result of shipboard health problems. When adverse weather also prevented him from attacking the Spanish treasure fleet, Drake sailed for home in June 1586. Despite its temporary successes and the great damage it caused Spain's possessions and prestige, Drake's Indies Voyage failed in its larger aims, for the Spanish maintained their territorial supremacy.

Spain's desire to destroy England's growing geopolitical power took the form of an enormous naval attack against England in 1588, in which Drake played a key role. Along with John Hawkins and others he contributed to one of the largest naval defeats in history, that of the Spanish Armada (1588). By 1595, however, the Spanish had clearly learned some lessons, particularly in regard to the activities of privateers. When another great fleet, under the direction of Hawkins and Drake, left England to attack Spain's possessions in the Indies, the Spanish were well prepared. They defeated the English at San Juan, Puerto Rico, and at Cartagena. Moreover, having established a more defensible harbor, Porto Bello, to replace Nombre de Dios, they emerged victo-

rious on the isthmus as well. Sir Francis Drake died shortly thereafter, off the coast of Veragua, Panama.

SIR JULIAN S. CORBETT, *Drake and the Tudor Navy*, 2 vols. (1898, repr. 1988); J. A. WILLIAMSON, *Sir John Hawkins: The Time and the Man* (1927, repr. 1970); A. E. W. MASON, *The Life of Sir Francis Drake* (1941, repr. 1950); J. A. WILLIAMSON, *Sir Francis Drake* (1951); GARRETT MATTINGLY, *The Armada* (1959); GEORGE M. THOMPSON, *Sir Francis Drake* (1972); J. H. PARRY et al., *A Short History of the West Indies*, 4th ed. (1987); JOHN SUGDEN, *Sir Francis Drake* (1990).

BLAKE D. PATTRIDGE

See also **Piracy.**

DROUGHT REGION (BRAZIL), area encompassing most of eight states in Northeast Brazil; defined politically as the *polígono das sêcas* or drought polygon. Historically the designation has had more to do with social structure, politics, and psychology than with climate; generations of Brazilians have been conditioned through political debate, essays, novels, songs, and films to define the Northeast interior and its social problems in terms of drought. Meteorologically, the droughts are produced by Caribbean and South Atlantic weather systems, the instability of which can cause wide variations in seasonal rainfall. However, the human effects of these poorly understood natural phenomena derive historically from the social and political structure of the region.

The droughts entered the historical record in 1584, when Friar Fernão CARDIM reported that over four thousand indigenes had fled from the interior to the Pernambucan coast because of a drought. The intermixture of meteorological, social, economic, and political factors in historical memory and contemporary perceptions has led to disagreement over the precise historical pattern of droughts, but most agree that severe droughts occurred in 1639, 1724–1725, 1736–1737, 1745–1746, 1777–1778, 1791–1793, 1825–1827, 1845–1847, 1877–1880, 1888–1889, 1906, 1915, 1936, 1953, 1958, and 1979–1983. The social and economic consequences of several of these earned them the label *grandes sêcas* (great droughts). The end of the great colonial northeastern cattle kingdoms, the "Leather Civilization," is traditionally marked by the *grande sêca* of 1793, and exceptionally severe droughts since that time tend to be associated with periods of economic and political stress or rapid change: the drought of 1825–1827 coincided with the political confusion of Brazilian independence and its aftermath; the drought of 1845–1847 accompanied the political and economic transformations of midcentury; the Empire of Brazil was ushered out by the drought of 1888–1889; the drought of 1958 accompanied the regional development crisis of the 1950s.

The worst drought in Brazilian history, which had a profound influence on the regional image and on the perception of and reaction to droughts in Brazil ever since, was the Great Drought of 1877–1880. This event followed two decades of population growth and incipient development spurred by an illusory cotton boom associated with the U.S. Civil War, then debt, retrenchment, and stress during the middle 1870s. Practical and psychological unpreparedness, combined with a lack of political and economic cohesion, led to at least a quarter of a million deaths, forced the permanent migration from the region of perhaps an equal number, and so profoundly dislocated the lives of survivors that its effects, on individuals, families, and the Northeast as a whole, were felt for generations thereafter. The crisis persuaded the imperial government to treat the droughts as a national problem for the first time, and added an important new factor to the Brazilian political equation. Politicians from the drought states, divided over other issues, unified to force central governments to issue drought aid.

Imperial funds injected into the Northeast provinces during the great drought of 1877–1880 and the decade following moved "drought fighting" into a central position in regional politics. The drought "solutions" that emerged—relocation of refugees, public works for emergency employment and infrastructure improvement, and hydraulic works—have persisted to the present time. The drought-fighting discourse that then engaged intellectuals contained enduring subthemes that help to explain why the region and the nation have never solved the social problems that underlie the climatic phenomena, such as the contention that the climate of the Northeast could somehow be restored through the building of large reservoirs and reforestation, or that the common people of the SERTÃO had been shaped permanently by the climate into an inferior race, incapable of rational, modern action.

After the establishment of the republic in 1889, the ill-managed projects initiated by the imperial government were reincarnated as a series of federal agencies: the Federal Institute of Anti-Drought Works (IFOCS), established in 1909, developed through a series of droughts, sharp regional pressure, and the politics of the VARGAS years into the National Department of Drought-Fighting Works (DNOCS) in 1949. The 1934 and 1946 Brazilian constitutions stipulated that fixed percentages of national, state, and municipal revenues be set aside for antidrought works and emergency relief for drought victims. While this financial obligation to the drought polygon is absent from the 1988 constitution, mounting a "permanent defense" against natural calamities is listed among the twenty-five enumerated responsibilities of the federal government.

In the 1950s, comprehensive regional planning began to replace the single-minded "hydraulic approach" that saw building reservoirs as the answer. The corruption and inefficiency revealed in DNOCS during the severe drought of 1958 discredited (but did not end) the drought-fighting approach and brought favor to the integrated regional-development approach embodied in the giant Superintendency for the Development of the Northeast (SUDENE). After 1958, the focus of DNOCS shifted from reservoir building to irrigation projects, which often forced peasants off their land in the fertile river bottoms. Since 1970 the favored solution to the problems of the drought region has been integration into the national economy, including improved transportation and renewed encouragement of outmigration to the more developed center-south and developing Amazon basin, while paying somewhat more, but still far inadequate, attention to basic social problems and sustainable development within the region. Near the end of the twentieth century, as overpopulation, economic and social exploitation, and an inadequate resource base continue to shape recurrent climatic episodes into social disasters, the social solution to the drought problem seems as remote as it was in 1877.

ANTHONY L. HALL, *Drought and Irrigation in North-East Brazil* (1978), and KEMPTON E. WEBB, *The Changing Face of Northeast Brazil* (1974), are geographical surveys with good historical and political background information. MANUEL CORREIA DE ANDRADE, *The Land and People of Northeast Brazil,* translated by Dennis V. Johnson (1980), is indispensable for any study of the Northeast. JOAQUIM ALVES, *História das Sêcas (séculos XVII a XIX),* is a scholarly survey from within the region, but limited to Ceará. The most complete account of any Brazilian drought is ROGER CUNNIFF, "The Great Drought: Northeast Brazil, 1877–1880" (Ph.D. diss., Univ. of Texas, Austin, 1970), complemented by GERALD GREENFIELD, "The Great Drought and Elite Discourse in Imperial Brazil," *Hispanic American Historical Review* 72 (1992): 375–400. ANTONIO MAGALHÃES and PENNIE MAGEE, "The Brazilian Nordeste (Northeast)," in *Drought Follows the Plow,* edited by Michael H. Glantz (1994), surveys developments in the drought area.

ROGER CUNNIFF

See also **Brazil: Organizations: Superintendencia do Desenvolvimento da Amazonia (SUDENE).**

DRUGS AND DRUG TRADE

DRUGS AND DRUG USE

Latin America is home to several important native drugs. The coca shrub (*Erythroxylon coca*), the basis for cocaine, grows in the Andean region. A variety of cactus, including the peyote cactus (*Lophophora williamsii*) and the San Pedro cactus (*Trichocereus pachanoi*), grown primarily in Mexico and on the west coast of South America respectively, have mescaline as their active principle. Various mushrooms, members of the *Stropharia* and *Psilocybe* genera, are found in Mexico and Central America and have psilocybin as their base.

The female hemp plant (*Cannabis sativa*), whose dried leaves and flowers are known as cannabis or marijuana, was introduced to North and South America in the sixteenth century by the Spanish and Portuguese, and to the Caribbean in the early eighteenth century by immigrants from India. The opium poppy (*Papaver somniferum*), from which heroin is distilled, was first planted in Latin America in Mexico in the early twentieth century.

The use of drugs by traditional Latin American societies can be traced to 3000 B.C. They were used in diverse cultural and religious activities, such as divination, meditation, and curing, and for relief from hunger and discomfort. Archaeological evidence suggests that the coca shrub originated on the eastern slopes of the Andes and spread by A.D. 500 to Panama. Once the mildly stimulant and medical properties of the leaves were known, they were collected, dried in the sun, and masticated and held in the mouth as a quid. An alkaline substance (usually ash from vegetables) was added to facilitate the release of their chemical properties. During the TIWANAKU Empire (A.D. 600–1200) coca was integrated into cultural and religious activities such as ritual nocturnal intoxication. Coca chewing was widespread during the INCA Empire from about 1400 to 1532 at all levels of society.

During Spanish colonial rule (1532–1825) in the Andean region, coca production and use by Indians continued, and the coca leaf was also chewed by the Spanish, primarily for medical reasons, despite attempts by the colonial administration at eradication and prohibition. The prohibition of the growth and trade of coca in the Spanish American Empire for political and humanitarian reasons was not successful, although the use of coca in shamanic activities was seen as fostering resistance to Spanish rule and the miserable conditions and high death rate of the workers in coca fields were condemned by Bartolomé de LAS CASAS.

In the late sixteenth century the crown accepted the fact that coca was an integral part of the Indian workforce and Viceroy TOLEDO regulated all aspects of the production and trade of the coca leaf in the *ordenanzas de la coca*. Production increased over time because of more widespread consumption in highlands farming communities and in mining areas. The cycles of boom and bust that afflicted the MINING industry affected the coca industry as miners depended on coca because of their difficult and demanding working conditions. The symbiotic relationship between coca production and mineral exportation continued after independence from Spain primarily in large haciendas in the Yungas region of Bolivia, one of the main coca-growing areas in the Andes until the boom in the 1970s.

After the Conquest, the coca leaf continued to play an important role in the cultural identity of AYMARA and Quechua Indians in the Andean highlands, or ALTIPLANO. Coca is still essential in many religious and nonreligious ceremonies for 3 million Andean Indians who, for example, use coca leaves in ritual exchanges between families or groups as part of systems of reciprocal labor or favors. The traditional use of coca continues also in communities of Amazonian Indians in Peru and Ecuador.

In addition to coca, traditional societies in Peru before and after the Conquest used a variety of different drugs.

Archaeological evidence allows us to reconstruct the use of the San Pedro cactus, various night-shade plants, and the willka shrub by the Mochica (100 B.C.–A.D. 700) and by the Nazca (A.D. 100–800). In both cultures psychotropic plants played an important part in shamanic activities. Their use continued after the Spanish Conquest despite attempts at prohibition, and Roman Catholic beliefs were eventually syncretized with their traditional use. The San Pedro cactus is still used among traditional societies in northern Peru to treat illness believed to be caused by witchcraft. In Peruvian Amazonian cities today, men and women use the plant hallucinogen ayahuasca in the diagnosis and treatment of witchcraft-related illness. Folk healers assemble groups of patients several times a week and administer the plant potion to allow their clients to obtain visions of the men and women who bewitched them.

Psychoactive substances have been used in Mesoamerica from Preclassic times (1650 B.C.) until the present. An examination of ancient MAYA art from Mexico, Guatemala, and Belize reveals the use of mind-altering mushrooms, toad venom, and the rhizomes of the common water lily. These substances, some of which are referred to in the POPOL VUH, influenced the ancient Maya religion, especially in divination and healing. The hallucinogenic mushrooms of pre-Columbian Mexico were called "god's flesh" by the AZTECS, who used at least four major hallucinogenic plants for ceremonies connected with human sacrifice, entertainment of guests at ceremonial feasts, and payment of tribute. The drugs were also used by the Aztecs for medical purposes and to give warriors courage to fight. The use of hallucinogens in Mexico and Central America continued despite their prohibition by the INQUISITION, which declared in 1620 that the use of the peyote cactus was the work of the devil, and peyotism eventually became fused with Christianity.

Marijuana is a relatively unimportant drug in most traditional Latin American cultures. Only in Jamaica and other Caribbean nations does the drug, usually referred to as ganja, have a significant role with certain societal groups, such as the Rastafarians.

THE DRUG TRADE

The Latin American drug trade is dominated by cocaine and to a lesser extent by marijuana and heroin. Since the rapid increase in demand in the 1970s, the production, refining, and trafficking of these drugs in a growing number of nations in the region have affected the economy, politics, social fabric, and relations with the United States, which is the primary market for drugs produced in Latin America.

Cocaine, one of thirteen alkaloids distilled from the coca plant, is produced exclusively in Latin America. While about 80 percent of the coca grows in the Bolivian Chaparé and the upper Huallaga Valley in Peru, coca production has spread to all neighboring countries, where it had not been planted traditionally and where the cocaine content is often lower. A small percentage of the coca production is exported legally to the United States for use in manufacturing Coca Cola, which requires de-cocainized leaves, and for pharmaceutical companies. Colombia has a dominant role in the cocaine trade, primarily because it has many processing laboratories and because it is strategically located between the main coca-producing nations and the routes through the Caribbean and Central America that lead to the lucrative U.S. and European markets. Brazil has also become an increasingly significant route for cocaine transshipment.

Marijuana has been exported to the United States since the nineteenth century, most of it coming from Latin America. While Mexico decreased its supply of the drug in the 1970s, Colombia and nations in Central America and the Caribbean increased production. Today, marijuana is most likely the largest cash crop in Jamaica and Belize.

During the 1980s Latin America became a significant source of heroin, supplying 40 percent of the U.S. market. Mexico's share of the U.S. market has increased from 10 to 15 percent in the 1980s to 30 percent in the 1990s. Production is increasing in Mexico and has spread to Guatemala and to the Cauca Valley in Colombia.

Drug production and processing have affected the economies of Latin American nations. Especially in the crisis decade of the 1980s, dollars earned in the drug trade became an important source of foreign exchange in the region's economies. It is probable that the difficult position of the Mexican economy became a major impetus for the drug trade, and it is alleged that the marijuana

trade in Jamaica kept that economy afloat in 1980 when the country was exceedingly short of foreign exchange. In the Andean region, coca dollars helped to weaken the impact of the decline in mineral prices. Estimates of annual profits made by cocaine traffickers range from $5 billion to $6 billion, and the reflow of coca money to producing countries ranges from approximately 10 to 20 percent. The drug industry is also an important source of employment in producing nations. In Bolivia, for example, it is estimated that cultivating coca, initial processing of coca paste, and refining and smuggling cocaine provide jobs for 10 percent of the economically active population.

The drug trade influences the politics of the region. In the absence of strong political support for the war on drugs weak central governments are only partially successful in implementing programs of drug eradication and interdiction. Some governments have demonstrated the political will to acknowledge and strike out against corruption but strong criminal syndicates threaten national sovereignty and institutions. In Colombia, where the Medellín cartel was weakened by the death of its leader Pablo Escobar in 1993, the Cali cartel emerged as the largest in the world in refining, smuggling, and distributing cocaine—until it, too, was weakened by the arrest of its leaders in 1995. The huge profits involved in the drug trade contribute to the weakening of the juridical system in some countries and have corrupted segments of the police and the armed forces. In some instances, narco-traffickers have been linked to terrorist activities. They threaten governments with occasional acts of ter-

Bolivian coca growers in Cochabamba demonstrating in response to U.S. intervention. © 1987 RICKEY ROGERS / BLACK STAR.

rorism and have reached agreements with the Shining Path in Peru and Colombian guerrillas to provide arms and money in exchange for protection of drug production and trade. Powerful political constituencies, such as the coca farmers in Bolivia and Peru, are well-organized pressure groups opposed to government programs of coca eradication and cocaine interdiction. Most Latin American nations have become involved in the transit of illegal drugs and are vulnerable to money laundering because of strict bank secrecy regulations and weak banking and criminal laws.

The social costs of the expanding drug production and trade in the region are reflected, for example, in the addiction to coca paste by a rapidly increasing number of abandoned children in Peru, Bolivia, and Colombia. Domestic demand-reduction programs in most Latin American countries indicate a growing awareness of drug abuse.

National and international efforts to deal with the drug crisis have had mixed results. Latin American governments have faced a dilemma pitting the economic benefits of the drug trade against its political and social costs. Most governments have favored demand-side solutions, such as treatment of addicts, education, and prevention programs. But the National Drug Control Strategy of successive U.S. governments has emphasized supply-side measures, such as border interdiction and suppression programs in the source countries. These efforts have had only limited success. For example, crop-eradication and crop-substitution programs in Bolivia and Peru have failed to significantly slow coca production because the income from coca, which has a high and stable rate of return, is far greater than the income from substitute crops, such as citrus fruit or macadamia nuts, and the programs have been violently resisted by coca growers. As part of President Bush's Andean Strategy, a multifaceted effort to reduce the flow of cocaine into the United States announced in 1989, Andean countries have promised to cooperate with the United States in enhancing their drug-fighting capabilities by training special police forces and getting the Latin American armed forces more involved in the drug war. However, because of the military's history of intervention into politics, Peruvian and Bolivian leaders have been reluctant to accept the militarization of the drug war and have called for a more economic approach to the problem. In the antidrug accord reached between the United States and six Latin American nations in San Antonio, Texas, in February 1992, the expanded role by South American militaries was shifted to the police. International organizations such as the Organization of American States and the United Nations favor a more equal distribution of supply and demand reduction. They provide a juridical framework for dealing with illegal drugs, but their authority is limited because international cooperation remains voluntary.

Ever since the beginning of large-scale drug trade in the 1970s, the Latin American traffickers have adjusted to antinarcotic efforts by spreading production and smuggling over the entire region, opening new markets, and recruiting new allies. Because of a wide range of political, social, and economic factors, the fight against drugs remains an extremely complex and difficult issue.

A good analysis of the use of drugs by pre-Columbian cultures and traditional societies is in MARLENE DOBKIN DE RIOS, *Hallucinogens: Cross-Cultural Perspectives* (1989). *Coca and Cocaine: Effects on People and Policy in Latin America* (1966), edited by DEBORAH PACINI and CHRISTINE FRANQUEMONT, deals with coca from an interdisciplinary perspective. On drug production and trade in Latin America and the relations between drugs and terrorism, see SCOTT B. MAC DONALD, *Dancing on a Volcano: The Latin American Drug Trade* (1988). A good survey of the dilemma of Latin American nations in their fight against drugs is RENSSELAER W. LEE, *The White Labyrinth: Cocaine and Political Power* (1990). On the socioeconomic and political impact of illicit drugs, see James PAINTER, *Bolivia and Coca: A Study in Dependency* (1994), part of a new series from the U.N. Research Institute for Social Development. For a critical assessment of U.S. policies, see Raphael PERL, ed., *Drugs and Foreign Policy: A Critical Review* (1994). For U.S. government views, see U.S. DEPARTMENT OF STATE, BUREAU OF INTERNATIONAL NARCOTIC MATTERS, *International Drug Control Strategy Report* (annual).

MARIA LUISE WAGNER

DRUMMOND DE ANDRADE, CARLOS. *See* **Andrade, Carlos Drummond de.**

DUARTE, AUGUSTO RODRIGUES (*b.* 1848; *d.* 1888), Portuguese-born history painter. Augusto Rodrigues Duarte came to Brazil in 1866 and entered the Imperial Academy of Fine Arts, where he studied under the painter Vítor MEIRELES. Upon completion of his academic training in the early 1870s, Duarte left Brazil to study in Paris. In 1874 he entered the atelier of the French history painter Jean-Léon Gérôme and shortly thereafter won a second prize in the Paris Salon. He was one of the few nineteenth-century painters in Brazil to portray the Indian as the subject of a monumental history painting, a role traditionally reserved for members of the royal family and military heroes.

His most important artistic achievement was the Indianist painting entitled the *Funeral of Atala*, which was exhibited at the 1878 Universal Exhibition in Paris. The subject matter of the work borrowed from Chateaubriand's 1826 novel *Les Natchez*. Duarte's paintings exhibit the influences of the European aesthetic formulas of impressionism, symbolism, and even art nouveau. Beyond history painting, he is also known for his landscapes and genre paintings. He was awarded the title of Knight of the Imperial Order of Roses at the 1884 academic exhibition, where he entered fourteen paintings.

Arte no Brasil, vol. 2 (1979), p. 516; CAREN MEGHREBLIAN, "Art, Politics and Historical Perception in Imperial Brazil, 1854–1884" (Ph.D. diss., UCLA, 1990).

CAREN A. MEGHREBLIAN

DUARTE, JUAN PABLO (*b.* 26 January 1813; *d.* 15 July 1876), leader of Dominican independence. While studying abroad in Europe, Duarte was influenced by the French romantic literary movement. With his homeland under Haitian occupation (1822–1844), the ideals of liberty and equality became of great importance to him. In 1838, Duarte and two others, Francisco de Rosario Sánchez and Ramón Mella, formed La TRINITARIA, a secret society whose goal was independence. The society proved very successful but resulted in Duarte's exile. After the Haitian president Jean-Pierre BOYER was overthrown in 1844, Duarte returned to Santo Domingo to take part in the formation of a new and independent government. Imbued with the ideals of the French Revolution, his idealism soon alienated him from the more militaristic leaders, and strongman General Pedro SANTANA jailed and ultimately exiled him once more. After a brief stay in Germany, Duarte spent fifteen years as a recluse in the jungles of Venezuela.

When Santana agreed to the country's reassumption of colonial status in 1864, Duarte returned to the Dominican Republic to take up the cause of independence again. Once more, however, Duarte was unable to participate in the provisional government of the Dominican Republic. It has been said of Duarte that he could inspire but not lead. He was exiled for the third time in 1865 and he returned to Venezuela, where he lived the rest of his life in poverty and obscurity. Like many great men, Duarte's significance and value was recognized only after his death. He is now considered the father of Dominican independence.

SELDEN RODMAN, *Quisqueya: A History of the Dominican Republic* (1964); HOWARD J. WIARDA, *The Dominican Republic: Nation in Transition* (1969); IAN BELL, *The Dominican Republic* (1981); HOWARD J. WIARDA and M. J. KRYZANEK, *The Dominican Republic: A Caribbean Crucible* (1982).

HEATHER K. THIESSEN

DUARTE, PEDRO (*b.* 1829; *d.* 1903), Paraguayan soldier and statesman. At the beginning of the WAR OF THE TRIPLE ALLIANCE, Duarte, a relatively obscure officer, was chosen as second in command of an expeditionary force sent south to attack Brazil. As the Paraguayans approached the Brazilian frontier in June 1865, their commander, Colonel Antonio de la Cruz ESTIGARRIBIA, split his forces, sending one column of 2,500 men under Major Duarte down the right bank of the Uruguay River, while he himself led the bulk of the troops down the left bank, toward the Riograndense town of Uruguaiana. The Argentines and Brazilians were waiting for both columns. Unable to secure help from Estigarribia and unwilling to consider withdrawal, Duarte was effectively isolated, and, on 17 August, at a spot called Yatai, 10,000 Argentine troops struck his column, annihilating almost everyone. Gravely wounded, Duarte was taken to Buenos Aires, where he spent the rest of the war as a prisoner. After the Allied victory in 1870,

he returned to Paraguay and subsequently served as minister of war and marine in the governments of Cándido BAREIRO, Bernardino CABALLERO, and Patricio ESCOBAR.

CHARLES J. KOLINSKI, *Independence or Death! The Story of the Paraguayan War* (1965); HARRIS G. WARREN, *Rebirth of the Paraguayan Republic: The First Colorado Era, 1878–1904* (1985), pp. 52, 65.

THOMAS L. WHIGHAM

DUARTE FUENTES, JOSÉ NAPOLEÓN (*b.* 23 November 1925; *d.* 23 February 1990), president of El Salvador (1980–1982, 1984–1989). A civil engineer trained in the United States, Duarte first became active in Salvadoran politics as a leader of the Christian Democratic Party (Partido Demócrata Cristiano—PDC), founded in 1960. Personable and skilled at organization, he developed a substantial political following, especially among urban and middle-class constituencies. He was elected mayor of San Salvador in 1964, and his six years in office witnessed a number of governmental reforms at the municipal level. Over the years he became the country's most successful opposition politician. In 1972, Duarte ran for president as the candidate of the National Opposition Union (Unión Nacional Opositora—UNO), a coalition that included the centrist PDC and two smaller leftist parties. Although the UNO claimed victory on the basis of the popular vote, the army tampered with the results and awarded the presidency to Colonel Arturo Armando MOLINA (1972–1977). Duarte joined with a faction of dissident officers in an unsuccessful coup d'état and was captured, tortured, and expelled from the country. He spent most of the 1970s in exile in Venezuela.

Duarte returned to El Salvador following the coup (15 October 1979) that overthrew the repressive regime of Molina's successor, General Carlos Humberto ROMERO. In spite of rapid political polarization, spreading civil warfare, and escalating human rights abuses by the military and right-wing DEATH SQUADS, Duarte joined the second provisional junta in March 1980 and became its president in December. His willingness to collaborate with the armed forces angered many of his former political allies and precipitated a split in the PDC, but he insisted that the junta's agrarian reform and bank nationalization measures justified his actions.

Ousted as provisional president in 1982 by the right-wing coalition that controlled the newly elected constituent assembly, Duarte returned to office as constitutional president in 1984 when he defeated his chief political rival, rightist demagogue Roberto D'AUBUISSON of the Nationalist Republican Alliance (Alianza Republicana Nacionalista—ARENA). As El Salvador's first elected civilian president in more than fifty years, Duarte sought to expand his reforms and to open a dialogue with the leftist rebels engaged in the country's

José Napoleón Duarte Fuentes, speaking at the Organization of American States in 1985. ORGANIZATION OF AMERICAN STATES.

five-year-old civil war. His options were limited, however, by a war-damaged economy heavily dependent upon aid from the United States, by the need to maintain the loyalty of the officer corps, and by the refusal of the Left to support his reforms or to participate in the political process.

Despite the optimism surrounding Duarte's first meeting with guerrilla representatives at La Palma in October 1984, little came of his efforts to forge a lasting peace. He lost more credibility when his government responded poorly to a major earthquake that struck San Salvador on 10 October 1986. Finally, terminal cancer, diagnosed in May 1988, compromised his effectiveness even further during his last year in office. His most significant achievement may have come in June 1989, a few months before his death, when he completed his term in office and transferred the presidency to a legally elected civilian successor, Alfredo CRISTIANI of ARENA.

Duarte's role in the Salvadoran crisis of the 1980s remains controversial. While personal ambition may have led him to cooperate with military-dominated regimes, for his own part, Duarte always insisted that he accepted office only because he understood that change in El Salvador was impossible without the support of the officer corps, the real power in the country. Rightists considered him a Communist because he supported reforms to benefit the poor, while his enemies on the left, many of them former allies and supporters, blamed him for the corruption, violence, and ineffectiveness that characterized his governments. Duarte was an outspoken anti-Communist, but he was also a critic of U.S. policies in Latin America and a well-known advocate of democracy and social justice. As such, his presence in office was essential both to the administration of Ronald Reagan and to the Salvadoran military. In spite of his chronic inability to restrain the excesses of the armed forces, Duarte helped guarantee continued approval of economic and military aid by the U.S. Congress.

On Duarte's early political career, see STEPHEN WEBRE, *José Napoleón Duarte and the Christian Democratic Party in Salvadoran Politics, 1960–1972* (1979). There is much detail on events of the 1980s in his autobiography, written with DIANA PAGE, *Duarte: My Story* (1986), and useful material also appears in JAMES DUNKERLEY, *Power in the Isthmus: A Political History of Modern Central America* (1988).

STEPHEN WEBRE

DUEÑAS, FRANCISCO (*b.* 1817; *d.* 31 March 1884), last Conservative president of El Salvador (1851–1854, 1863–1871). Francisco Dueñas studied law and was active in letters, education, and public service before seizing power in 1851 and again in 1863 with the assistance of Guatemala's Rafael CARRERA. As president, Dueñas strengthened the Salvadoran armed forces and enacted a new constitution (1864), which consolidated military and political power in his hands. He persecuted his political rivals and had a number of them killed, including his Liberal predecessor, Gerardo BARRIOS. The Dueñas regime created a stable environment for the growth of the coffee industry, which it encouraged with incentives similar to those more commonly associated with Liberal governments. Dueñas also promoted physical improvements in the country's infrastructure and in the capital city, San Salvador. Congress reelected Dueñas in 1870, but he lost the following year to a Liberal revolt under Santiago González. Dueñas spent much of his later life in exile. A pioneer coffee grower himself, he founded one of El Salvador's wealthiest and most powerful families.

JUAN J. CAÑAS, "Doctor Don Francisco Dueñas," in *San Salvador y sus hombres,* 2d ed. (1967); ENRIQUE CHACÓN, *El presidente Dr. Francisco Dueñas y su época* (n.d.).

STEPHEN WEBRE

DULLES, JOHN FOSTER (*b.* 25 February 1888; *d.* 24 May 1959), U.S. secretary of state from 1953 to 1959. Dulles's early Latin American experiences took place before World War I, when he represented the international law firm Sullivan and Cromwell. During the war, President Woodrow Wilson sent him on a mission to Costa Rica, Nicaragua, and Panama to insure the success of pro-Allied policies aimed at securing the Panama Canal. Dulles's most notable Latin American experience came in 1954, when at the Tenth Inter-American Conference at Caracas, he steered the approval of a resolution calling for action against subversive (i.e., Communist) movements in the hemisphere. Although not referred to specifically, Guatemala was Dulles's target; the U.S. Central Intelligence Agency directed the overthrow of the Jacobo ARBENZ administration in June 1954 because of alleged excessive Communist influence in government that resulted in policies antithetical to capitalism, including the expropriation of lands owned by the UNITED FRUIT COMPANY.

LOUIS L. GERSON, *John Foster Dulles* (1967); MICHAEL A. GUHIN, *John Foster Dulles: A Statesman and His Times* (1972); TOWNSEND HOOPES, *The Devil and John Foster Dulles* (1973).

THOMAS M. LEONARD

See also **Pan-American Conferences: Caracas Conference (1954)**.

DUPRAT, ROGÉRIO (*b.* 7 February 1932), Brazilian composer. Born in Guanabara, Rio de Janeiro, Duprat studied philosophy at São Paulo University. He also studied music theory, harmony, and composition with Olivier Toni and Cláudio SANTORO and cello with Varoli at the Villalobos Conservatory in São Paulo (1952–1960). From 1953 to 1963 he was a cellist with the São Paulo Municipal Orchestra and took summer courses at Darmstadt, Germany. He also studied electronic music at studios in Cologne, Paris, and Karlsruhe under Stockhausen, Ligeti, Boulez, and Pousseur. Duprat returned to São Paulo, where he cofounded the Estadual Orchestra and the São Paulo Chamber Orchestra; for the latter he was the director of an experimental music group. His early style was nationalist but later he turned to twelvetone, serial, and electronic music. In 1963 he formed the group Música Nova with Gilberto MENDES, Willy Correia de OLIVEIRA, and Damiano Cozzella, manifesting strict devotion to contemporary and avant-garde trends. He has composed music for television and collaborated with the musical group Tropicália; and he has also taught at the University of Brazil.

R. DUPRAT, "En torno al pronunciamiento" in *Revista musical chilena* xvii/86 (1963): 30, 33; JOHN VINTON, ed., *Dictionary of Contemporary Music* (1974); *New Grove Dictionary of Music and Musicians*, vol. 5 (1980).

SUSANA SALGADO

DURÁN, DIEGO (*b.* 1537; *d.* 1588), one of the more important chronicler/ethnographers who lived in sixteenth-century New Spain. A Dominican friar born in Seville and raised in Texcoco and Mexico City, Durán wrote a three-part work, *Historia de las Indias de Nueva España islas de tierra firme*, on the pre-Hispanic history,

religion, and calendar of the Aztecs, respectively. He based it on indigenous manuscripts—including the Crónica X, now lost—and hundreds of indigenous informants. He also had some assistants, probably monastery-trained Nahuas, who helped him gather, copy, and interpret information, and he interviewed Spanish eyewitnesses who had been on the scene of the Conquest. The three parts of the *Historia*, containing many descriptions not duplicated in any other chronicles, were written approximately during the period 1576–1581. Durán's goal, like that of many chroniclers of his time, was to improve the Christian instruction of the indigenous people by first gaining a better grasp of their beliefs.

There is a more vivid and human biographical sketch of Durán in FERNANDO HORCASITAS and DORIS HEYDEN's English ed. of two parts of Durán's *Historia*, the *Book of the Gods and Rites* and *The Ancient Calendar* (1971). The third part, *The Aztecs: The History of the Indies of New Spain* (1964), was also translated by Horcasitas and Heyden. In the *Handbook of Middle American Indians*, vol. 13, pt. 2, edited by Howard F. Cline (1973), J. BENEDICT WARREN explains the relationships between Durán's work and that of others who borrowed from him and/or consulted some of the same sources.

STEPHANIE WOOD

DURÁN, FRAY NARCISO (*b.* 16 December 1776; *d.* 1 June 1846), Franciscan missionary. Durán was born at Castellón de Ampurias in Catalonia, where he entered the FRANCISCAN order at Gerona in 1792. Ordained in 1800, Durán left Spain in 1803 for Mexico, arriving in the Alta California MISSIONS three years later.

Durán remained in the Alta California missions for forty years and died at the Santa Barbara mission in 1846. During most of this period (1806–1833) he was stationed at the San José mission in the San Francisco Bay region and at the Santa Barbara mission. In 1832 Durán became the *vicar forane* (foreign vicar) and ecclesiastical judge for Alta California. He was president of the missions from 1833 to 1838 and commissary prefect after 1838.

Durán tried to defend the missions against reforms initiated by Mexican politicians and was vocal in his criticism of these changes. For example, he criticized the emancipation of mission Indians in the late 1820s and early 1830s. Moreover, in the 1820s and 1830s he refused to take oaths of loyalty to Mexico. Despite his views, Durán, like the other Spanish-born Franciscans in Alta California, was not expelled. However, in 1833 the Mexican government sent Mexican-born Franciscans from the apostolic college in Zacatecas to staff its missions in the northern part of the province, which was especially sensitive politically because of the presence of the Russians at FORT ROSS north of San Francisco Bay.

MAYNARD J. GEIGER, O.F.M., *Franciscan Missionaries in Hispanic California, 1769–1848: A Biographical Dictionary* (1969).

ROBERT H. JACKSON

DURAND, OSWALD (*b.* 17 September 1840; *d.* 22 April 1906), Haitian writer, journalist, and politician. Durand began work as a tinsmith and studied at night. He became a lycée principal and went into politics in 1885. After being elected president of the Chambre des Députés in 1888, he traveled to France and was introduced to the "Société des Gens de Lettres" by François Coppée. Upon his death in 1906, he was given a state funeral and was praised as the greatest Haitian poet.

The poetry of Durand was often an erotic evocation of the women he loved (he was divorced for philandering by the poet Virginie Sampeur), but he also evoked simple people and the landscapes and traditions of Haiti. Some poems in Creole contributed to the recognition of the language's literary citizenship.

Other works include *Rires et pleurs* (1896); *Quatre nouveaux poèmes* (1900). *Mosaïques* and *Primes fleurs et ballades* are both unpublished.

NAOMI M. GARRET, *The Renaissance of Haitian Poetry* (1963), pp. 30–33; See also F. RAPHAËL BERROU and PRADEL POMPILUS, *Histoire de la littérature haïtienne illustrée par les textes*, vol. 1 (1975), pp. 322–396.

CARROL F. COATES

DURÃO, JOSÉ DE SANTA RITA (*b.* ca. 1722; *d.* 24 January 1784), Brazilian poet. Durão was born in Minas Gerais, Brazil, but left, never to return, at age nine. He grew up and was educated in Portugal, entering the AUGUSTINIAN ORDER in 1738 and earning a doctorate in theology from the University of Coimbra in 1758. After serving as a papal librarian in Rome, he returned to Portugal and served as a professor of theology at Coimbra before becoming prior of the Gration convent.

In 1781 Durão published his major work, *Caramuru*. Modeling himself on Luís de CAMÕES's *Os Lusíadas* with its celebration of Portuguese accomplishments in the Orient, Durão produced an epic poem in ten ottava rima cantos celebrating similar accomplishments in Brazil. As Camões had elaborated his narrative around Vasco da GAMA's voyage to India, Durão used the discovery of Bahia by Diogo Álvares CORREIA (1510) and Correia's subsequent adventures. Caramurú, or Dragon of the Sea, is Correia's Indian name.

Again like Camões, and contrary to the rationalism of the age, Durão endorsed the ideal of a Christian empire served by Portuguese conquests, but he accepted eighteenth-century natural law and viewed the savage as innately noble. His accurate descriptions of Brazilian nature, moreover, together with those of native life and customs, make him an important precursor of both literary nationalism and Indianism.

DAVID M. DRIVER, *The Indian in Brazilian Literature* (1942), pp. 34–40; ANTÔNIO CÂNDIDO, *Formação da literatura brasileira: Momentos decisivos*, 2d ed., vol. 1 (1964), pp. 183–193; CLAUDE L. HULET, "The Noble Savage in *Caramurú*," in *Homage to Irving A.*

Leonard, edited by Raquel Chang-Rodríguez and Donald A. Yates (1977), pp. 123–130.

NORWOOD ANDREWS, JR.

DURAZNO, department of central Uruguay with an area of 4,713 square miles and a population of 53,864 (1985). Most of the departmental territory extends between the rivers Negro and Yi, often called Uruguay's Mesopotamia. The capital is the city of Durazno (27,835 inhabitants in 1985), founded in 1821. The main activities of the department are farming, cattle raising, and shoe manufacturing. A large reservoir on the RÍO NEGRO provides irrigation for a good part of central Uruguay and electric energy for Greater Montevideo.

CÉSAR N. CAVIEDES

DUTARY, ALBERTO (*b.* 1932), Panamanian painter. Dutary studied at the Escuela Nacional de Pintura in Panama (1950–1952) and in Madrid, at the San Fernando Academy (1953–1955) and the Escuela Nacional de Artes Gráficas (1956–1958). From 1962 until 1992, he was art professor in private schools and at the University of Panama, where he became the first director of the Fine Arts Career Program in 1987.

A notable draftsman and figurative painter, his works from the 1960s, including the "Santos" series, combined the surface textures of Spanish informalism with dramatic ghostlike figures. He later turned to more realistic, and at times surrealistic, still lifes. In the 1970s, he focused on mannequinlike female figures that play with the concept of reality in paintings such as *Figuras frente a la Bahía* (1979).

STANTON LOOMIS CATLIN and TERENCE GRIEDER, *Art of Latin America Since Independence* (1966); X. ZAVALA CUADRA et al., "Alberto Dutary: Pintor panameño," in *Revista del Pensamiento Centroamericano*, no. 155 (April–June 1977): 1–9.

MONICA E. KUPFER

DUTCH IN THE CARIBBEAN. *See* **Suriname and the Dutch in the Caribbean.**

DUTCH IN COLONIAL BRAZIL. One of the great tragedies in the history of Brazil took place between 1624 and 1654 when the DUTCH WEST INDIA COMPANY attempted to occupy Portuguese America, with enormous loss of life and property and massive dislocation of populations. At least 10,000 Dutchmen, Germans, Frenchmen, and other Europeans in the service of the company lost their lives, as did a similar number of opposing Portuguese, Spaniards, and Italians. Untold numbers were maimed. In addition, at least a thousand Amerindians and possibly an equal number of blacks also died fighting for one side or the other. More than a thousand ships were captured or sunk during the thirty years of conflict. Several hundred sugar mills were destroyed, countless cane fields burned, and numerous oxen killed. Tens of thousands of inhabitants of northeastern and northern Brazil were uprooted and forced to march southward to Bahia or Rio de Janeiro, flee into the interior, or return to the Iberian Peninsula. The economy of northeastern Brazil was seriously disrupted, and many decades elapsed before parts of that region were restored to normalcy.

Initially, Dutch contacts with Portuguese America were peaceful. By the latter decades of the sixteenth century, despite Spanish Hapsburg prohibitions against foreign trade with Brazil, an increasing number of Dutch ships and crews were helping carry cargoes, especially TEXTILES, from Europe to Brazil, returning with SUGAR and BRAZILWOOD. By 1621 an estimated ten to fifteen ships were built annually by the Dutch solely for the Brazil trade. By that time, the Dutch controlled about one-half to two-thirds of the carrying trade between Portuguese America and Europe. The end of the twelve-year truce (1609–1621) between the Spanish Hapsburgs and the United Provinces of the Netherlands and the founding of the Dutch West India Company (1621) set the stage for a new Dutch activity in Portuguese America—military conquest.

BAHIA AND THE DUTCH, 1624–1627

In late 1623 and early 1624, twenty-six ships and 3,300 men left the Netherlands in a successful effort to capture the Brazilian capital, Salvador, in the captaincy of Bahia. By the time the Dutch troops reached the city's limits, Salvador's defenders had fled. However, the Portuguese soon rallied and succeeded in confining the invaders to the capital. In the meantime, a joint Spanish-Portuguese force of fifty-two ships and 12,566 men under Don Fadrique de Toledo y Osorio sailed from the Iberian Peninsula and recaptured the capital of Brazil (May 1625). Although the Dutch had been ousted from Brazil, they were able to capture a considerable amount of Portuguese shipping both off the coast of Brazil and in the Atlantic. In 1627, Piet Heyn twice sailed into Bahia's harbor and captured or destroyed dozens of ships. The following year Heyn captured the richly laden Spanish silver fleet in Cuba's Matanzas Bay, providing the Dutch West India Company with the wealth to make another attempt at conquest in Brazil.

THE DUTCH OCCUPATION OF BRAZIL, 1630–1654

In February of 1630, a Dutch West India Company fleet of sixty-seven ships and more than 7,000 men, under the command of Hendrick Corneliszoon Loncq, captured Olinda, Recife, and the island of Antônio Vaz in the sugar-rich captaincy of Pernambuco. Although most of the Portuguese defenders initially fled, the inhabitants of the captaincy were rallied by Matias de ALBUQUERQUE, brother of Pernambuco's lord-proprietor. Albuquerque and his forces were able to restrict the Dutch to their coastal positions and for the next two years successfully mounted a campaign of guerrilla warfare from the fortress called Arraial do Bom Jesus while awaiting a rescue armada from the Iberian Peninsula.

It was not until May 1631 that substantial reinforcements left Portugal for Brazil under the command of Biscayan Don Antonio de Oquendo. He landed troops in Bahia, but on his way to disembark additional troops in Pernambuco and Paraíba, he encountered a Dutch fleet of sixteen ships commanded by Adriaen Janszoon Pater. They fought to a draw. Although Pater was killed in the struggle, only 700 of Oquendo's men (including 300 Neapolitans) reached the Arraial do Bom Jesus. The remainder of Oquendo's fleet returned home, leaving the coastal waters of Brazil in Dutch hands. However, the Portuguese resistance continued to keep the Dutch fighting force of about 7,000 men hemmed in at Recife and forced the abandonment of Olinda in November 1631. Even though the Dutch erected a fort (Oranje) in the neighboring captaincy of Itamaracá to the north, Albuquerque's troops were able to prevent the Dutch from capturing the northern captaincies of Paraíba and Rio Grande do Norte and from occupying the *várzea*, the rich sugar lands of Pernambuco.

By mid-1632, the tide of war began to turn with the desertion to the Dutch side of the Pernambucan-born Domingos Fernandes Calabar. He knew the terrain intimately and directed the Dutch forces to the Portuguese weaknesses. In addition, substantial Dutch reinforcements arrived in Pernambuco. By mid-1633, the standoff between Albuquerque's troops and the Dutch had ended, and the latter were making major advances. The Dutch expanded into the sugar lands of Pernambuco and into the captaincy of Itamaracá. They also captured the fort of Reis Magos in the captaincy of Rio Grande do Norte. The Portuguese forces fought valiantly, but they were no match for the continuing reinforcements sent by the Dutch West India Company. By the end of 1634, the Dutch had occupied the Brazilian coastline from Rio Grande do Norte to Pernambuco's Cabo de Santo Agostinho. In addition, they continued to control the seas, thus largely cutting off resupply and export. By 1635, increasing numbers of Portuguese settlers were accepting Dutch offers of freedom of worship and security of their property in Pernambuco and in the three captaincies to the north.

Both sides employed Amerindian allies in the fighting. The majority of the Indians of northeastern Brazil allied themselves with the Dutch, though they made up only a relatively small percentage of the fighting forces of either side. The most famous of the Portuguese Indian allies was the Petiguar chieftain Dom Antônio Filipe Camarão, who was rewarded by the Hapsburg crown with a patent of nobility and a knighthood and commandery in the Order of Christ. The Portuguese and the Dutch also used African slaves in the war, at times promising freedom to those who took up arms. The most famous of the black leaders fighting for the Portuguese cause was Henrique DIAS, who was given a

Detail from *Garasu*, engraving by Franz Post. Reproduced from Kaspar van Baerle, *Rerum per Octennium in Brasilia* (Amsterdam, 1647). BY PERMISSION OF THE HOUGHTON LIBRARY, HARVARD UNIVERSITY.

patent of nobility by King Philip IV but who never received the knighthood in the Order of Christ he was promised and awarded.

In 1635 the Dutch captured three Pernambucan strongholds: the town of Porto Calvo, the Arraial do Bom Jesus, and Fort Nazaré on Cabo de Santo Agostinho. Control at these areas gave the Dutch access to major sugar-growing lands of the captaincy. Additional settlers accepted Dutch terms, but more than 7,000 inhabitants of the captaincy, including women, children, Indians, and black slaves and freedmen retreated southward under the leadership of Albuquerque. On their way south, they temporarily recaptured Porto Calvo, apprehending Calabar and executing him as a traitor. In September 1635, the first major Iberian reinforcements since 1631 left Portugal for Pernambuco. The 2,500 soldiers (Spaniards, Portuguese, and Neapolitans) were under the command of the Spaniard Don Luis de Rojas y Borgia, who led the war against the Dutch until he was killed in combat less than two months after his arrival. The Italian Giovanni Vincenzo de San Felice, count of Bagnuoli, who had arrived in Brazil with Oquendo's 1631 armada, succeeded Rojas. Bagnuoli accelerated the tactics of guerrilla warfare, as did the Dutch. The victims frequently were those who were trying to continue or revive sugar production under Dutch control and who were caught in the middle of a "scorched earth" policy adopted by both sides.

The Dutch West India Company, deeply in debt, in an attempt to bring peace to the region and restore sugar production, named Johan MAURITS, count of Nassau-

Siegen, as governor-general of Netherlands Brazil in 1636. He arrived in Recife on 23 January 1637, and his stay of just over seven years marked the height of Dutch power in Portuguese America. Soon after his arrival in Brazil, Maurits, commanding 3,000 European soldiers, 1,000 sailors, and 1,000 Indians, easily ousted Bagnuoli from Porto Calvo. He then pursued him southward to the Rio São Francisco. Hoping to make that river the boundary between Portuguese and Dutch Brazil, he laid waste to Alagoas, forcing Bagnuoli's troops to cross the São Francisco into the captaincy of Sergipe del Rey. The Dutch leader then returned to Recife, where he began rebuilding the city, connecting it to the island of Antônio Vaz, which became the new town of Mauritsstad.

Maurits also restored discipline and attempted to conciliate the Portuguese living under Dutch control and restore the economy of the region. He increased protection for the large number of Dutch JEWS, the great majority speaking Spanish or Portuguese, who had made a home in Brazil. A much smaller number of New Christians already living in the Northeast abjured the Catholicism forced upon their ancestors and openly proclaimed their Judaic heritage. Jews living in Dutch Brazil had their own synagogues. It is estimated that in 1645 the Jewish population under the protection of the Dutch West India Company was at its peak and numbered 1,450, a little less than half of the total white civilian population.

In order to gain easier access to African slaves, Maurits sent an expedition in 1637 that captured the Portuguese fortress and trading center of São Jorge da Mina (Elmina) on Africa's Gold Coast. Later that year he dispatched a Dutch fleet southward along the coast of Portuguese America to raid São Jorge de Ilhéus in the captaincy south of Bahia. Another expedition devastated Sergipe, forcing Bagnuoli to retreat to within forty miles of the Brazilian capital. To the north, the captaincy of Ceará was taken before year's end. In May 1638, a force of 4,600 Europeans and Indians, led by Maurits, attacked Salvador but was driven off by the town's defenders.

Toward the end of 1638, a large armada of forty-six ships and 5,000 soldiers under the command of Dom Fernão de Mascarenhas, count of Torre, left Portugal to reconquer the Brazilian Northeast. The voyage was a slow one, and more than 3,000 of the fighting men and sailors died en route to Brazil. Torre made what proved to be a costly decision by landing at the Brazilian capital rather than attacking Recife immediately. In Salvador the count organized an expedition to attack Recife. He dispatched bands of guerrilla fighters led by André Vidal de Negreiros, Camarão, and Dias overland to encourage the Portuguese settlers to revolt and to hem in the Dutch while he and the majority of his troops, loaded into eighty-seven ships, attacked by sea in late 1639. But unfavorable winds and strong ocean currents drove the count of Torre's armada northward past Recife. The Dutch fleet, which gave battle in January 1640, was relatively small, and the naval results were not decisive. But Torre's mission was a failure, and he was forced to put Luis Barbalho Bezerra and some 1,200 troops ashore near Cape São Roque to make the 1,200-mile trek through Dutch territory back to Bahia. En route, they joined up with the guerrilla fighters sent out from Bahia. Most of the armada was scattered, some ships making their way to northern Brazil, others to the Azores, while the bulk ended up in the Spanish Caribbean before attempting the return trip to the Iberian Peninsula.

The majority of Barbalho Bezerra's troops, after skirmishes with the Dutch and their Indian allies, reached Bahia. Both sides accused each other of atrocities, and a bitter war of reprisal followed. When fresh troops arrived from the Netherlands, an expedition led by Jan Corneliszoon Lichthart destroyed twenty-seven sugar mills in the environs of Salvador before it was driven off by the Portuguese defenders augmented by Barbalho Bezerra's men. On 1 December 1640, the Portuguese overthrew Hapsburg rule, and the eighth duke of Bragança became King JOÃO IV of Portugal. Most of Spain's enemies became Portugal's allies. A ten-year truce between Portugal and the Netherlands was signed on 12 June 1641. Although it took effect immediately in Europe, its implementation was delayed in the colonies. Maurits took advantage of the delay by occupying the captaincy of Sergipe del Rey and capturing São Luis do Maranhão. In 1641 he sent a force of twenty-one ships and 3,000 men (including 240 Indians) to Africa to capture Angola, Benguela, the islands of São Tomé and Ano Bom, and the fortress of Axim on the coast of Guinea. The Dutch West India Company had reached its territorial apogee.

King João IV found himself in a difficult position regarding the Dutch interlopers in Brazil since he needed Dutch help in Europe against King PHILIP IV of Spain. A number of influential Portuguese, including Padre Antônio VIEIRA, initially recommended that João IV give up claims to Dutch Brazil in exchange for further Dutch aid against Spain in Europe. However, there were others, such as Antônio Teles da Silva, governor-general of Brazil from 1642 to 1647, who clandestinely plotted to oust the Dutch and sent men and supplies to achieve this aim, especially after the departure of Maurits in 1644. Teles da Silva's envoy, the Paraíban-born military man André Vidal de Negreiros and Madeiran-born João Fernandes Vieira, a Portuguese planter living in Pernambuco under Dutch rule, secretly planned a revolt for 1645. Teles da Silva also covertly dispatched to Pernambuco experienced soldiers and leaders like Antônio Dias Cardoso, Henrique Dias, and Dom Antônio Filipe Camarão to join the revolt. Betrayal of the conspiracy forced Fernandes Vieira to begin the revolt prematurely, on 13 June 1645.

The Portuguese governor in Bahia used the pretext of helping the Dutch to send two Portuguese regiments under Martim Soares Moreno and Vidal de Negreiros to Pernambuco. The troops landed in Tamandaré. Salvador Correia de Sá, returning to Portugal with the sugar fleet from Rio de Janeiro and Bahia, was encouraged to attack Recife by sea. On 3 August 1645, at Monte das Tabocas, 30 miles from Recife, Fernandes Vieira and Dias Cardoso with 1,000 supporters defeated a Dutch contingent of 400 whites and 300 Indians. Ten days later, they joined up with the troops of Dias and Camarão. In the meantime, Moreno and Negreiros occupied the district of Serinhaém and captured the fort of Nazaré. On 16 August 1645, they joined Fernandes Vieira. The following day, another Dutch force was defeated at Casa Forte. However, Salvador de Sá failed to attack Recife by sea, and the sixteen caravels that had disembarked Portuguese troops at Tamandaré were defeated and destroyed by a Dutch fleet under Lichthart.

News of the Portuguese victories on land encouraged many of the settlers living under Dutch rule to join the revolt. In September 1645, the Portuguese insurgents recaptured much of the captaincy of Paraíba, the town of Porto Calvo, Fort Maurits on the Rio São Francisco, and Sergipe del Rey. By the end of 1645, the Dutch were confined to Recife and its environs, the islands of Itamaracá and Fernão de Noronha, and the coastal forts of Cabedelo and Reis Magos (Ceulen). The Portuguese had recovered most of Netherlands Brazil, including the best sugar-producing areas.

When news of these losses was relayed to the Netherlands, efforts were made by the Dutch West India Company to aid their beleaguered colony, but for a variety of reasons only twenty ships and 2,000 men were sent to Brazil by May 1646. In the meantime, King João

IV claimed no involvement in the rebellion and emphasized that he wanted nothing to interfere with Dutch support in the war against Spain. Gradually, however, he was won over to the cause of the Pernambucan rebels. In December 1646, he appointed Francisco Barreto de Meneses as commander in chief of all forces involved in the restoration of Pernambuco to Portuguese control. However, en route to Brazil near Bahia, Barreto was captured by the Dutch and imprisoned in Recife until he managed to escape early in 1648.

In the meantime, because of the arrival of Dutch reinforcements, the insurgents decided to regroup and abandoned Paraíba, Goiânia, and Itamaracá after destroying as much of the sugar-producing land as possible. The Dutch recaptured Fort Maurits—albeit temporarily—and in February 1647 a Dutch force of twenty-six ships and 2,400 men, led by the German Sigismund von Schoppe, occupied the island of Itaparica in Bahia's Bay of All Saints, holding it until 14 December. This action spurred King João IV to abandon all efforts at secrecy, and plans were made to send the Portuguese royal fleet to recapture the island. On 18 October 1647, an armada of fifteen ships and almost 4,000 men, commanded by Antônio Teles de Meneses, newly created count of Vila Pouca de Aguiar and governor-general of Brazil, sailed from Lisbon. The following month, a fleet of seven ships, commanded by Salvador de Sá, sailed for Rio de Janeiro to prepare an expedition for the recovery of Angola.

At the same time, the Dutch were preparing a fleet, under the command of Witte Corneliszoon de With, to capture Bahia and drive the Portuguese insurgents from Pernambuco. Internal rivalries in the Netherlands prevented de With from leaving until 26 December 1647. His fleet, slowed by bad weather and scattered by storms, began to arrive in Recife after mid-March of 1648, although the last of the ships did not reach port until late August. Many of his troops were in poor condition. After much debate, the Dutch decided to attack the insurgents by land rather than attack Bahia by sea. On 19 April 1648, at the site called Guararapes, more than 5,000 Dutch and their Indian allies under von Schoppe met a Portuguese force, estimated to be between 2,200 and 3,000, commanded by Francisco Barreto, which included regiments headed by Fernandes Vieira, Negreiros, Camarão, and Dias. The Portuguese emerged victorious and also forced the Dutch to abandon Olinda. In August the Portuguese were reinforced by another infantry regiment with recruits from Madeira and the Azores, under the leadership of Francisco de Figueiroa.

In the meantime, Salvador de Sá had left Rio de Janeiro with fifteen ships and some 1,500–2,000 men to regain Angola from the Dutch. On 24 August, Sá captured Luanda, and shortly thereafter Benguela and São Tomé were in Portuguese hands. However, the Dutch still controlled the seas off Brazil. In December 1648 a Dutch force sailed into the Bay of All Saints and remained there for a month attacking the Bahian RECÔN-cavo, destroying 23 sugar mills and capturing 1,500 chests of sugar while meeting little Portuguese resistance. Emboldened by this success, a Dutch army force of 3,500 left Recife on 17 February 1649 in an effort to avenge their loss at Guararapes a year earlier. Two days later, at the second battle of Guararapes, the Portuguese, led by Barreto and taking advantage of their superior knowledge of the terrain, gained another victory.

But the Dutch still ruled the seas. In fact, between 1 January 1647 and 31 December 1648, approximately 220 Portuguese ships were captured by the Dutch, most of the vessels being seized by ships fitted out by the Zeeland Privateering Board. To counter this superiority in sea power, the Portuguese organized a convoy system. The brainchild of Padre Antônio Vieira, the convoys were supplied by the newly organized (1649) monopoly called the Companhia Geral para o Estado do Brasil (Brazil Company), funded in large part by Portuguese New Christian investors, who were granted special privileges for their participation. In exchange for providing warships to escort merchant vessels to and from Brazil, the company was given the monopoly over the wine, flour, codfish, and olive oil entering Portuguese America. It was also given the right to levy taxes on such products as sugar, tobacco, cotton, and hides returning to Portugal.

Rivalries and disagreements among the seven provinces of the Netherlands over tactics regarding Brazil and Portugal hampered efforts to reverse Dutch losses in Portuguese America and West Africa, although the Dutch did recapture Ceará in April 1649. In May of that year, Admiral de With began an ineffectual blockade of Rio de Janeiro. Dutch forces in Recife continued to be hemmed in by land by the Portuguese insurgents. Since Recife had to be provisioned by the Netherlands, the besieged occupants were frequently close to starvation. Because of the dissension among the United Provinces, few supplies were being sent from Europe to feed the 4,000 white civilians and 3,000–4,000 troops living in Dutch Brazil. Discontent among the naval forces was so great that most of the Dutch warships returned home by the end of 1649 without authorization, leaving Recife largely unprotected by sea. However, because the Portuguese insurgents were almost equally short of supplies, a five-year stalemate ensued.

On 4 November 1649, the Brazil Company's first armada, composed of eighty-four ships, including eighteen warships, left Lisbon under the command of João Rodrigues de Vasconcelos e Sousa, count of Castelo Melhor, who was to replace the governor-general of Brazil. This expedition was probably strong enough to recapture Recife by sea, but a cautious King João IV did not want to expand the conflict. Futhermore, after the execution of King Charles I of England (30 January 1649), King João IV continued to back the royalist cause. In turn, the Puritan fleet under Admiral Robert Blake blockaded the Tagus in 1650. Blake hampered the second Brazil Company armada from going to America and captured most of the homeward-bound sugar fleet, upon which much of the Portuguese war effort against Spain was dependent.

Portugal's defensive posture in Brazil and Castelo Melhor's instructions not to risk a naval battle with the Dutch returned the mastery of Brazilian waters to the Dutch. Although naval losses continued, the Brazil Company was able to outfit a third armada of sixty ships, which arrived in Brazil in early 1652. Despite harassment by a small Dutch fleet, most of this armada reached Bahia safely. Shortly thereafter, the weakened Dutch fleet fled to Europe, thus enabling the Portuguese to regain control of Brazilian waters.

In June 1651 the ten-year truce between Portugal and the Netherlands expired. The United Provinces again were at odds with Amsterdam, which had commercial ties to Portugal and preferred peace to war. Even though João IV feared a Dutch blockade of the Tagus if he sent a Portuguese fleet to attack Recife, the outbreak of the First Anglo-Dutch War (May 1652) began to alleviate his fears. On 20 December 1653, the Brazil Company's fleet of seventy-seven ships, under the command of Pedro Jacques de Magalhães and Francisco de Brito Freire, arrived to blockade Recife while the Portuguese insurgents pressured the Dutch on land. On 26 January 1654, the Dutch surrendered and signed the capitulation of Taborda, giving up not only Recife and neighboring Mauritsstad but also the islands of Itamaracá and Fernão de Noronha and the captaincies of Paraíba, Rio Grande do Norte, and Ceará, all of which had been in Dutch hands at the time Recife surrendered. The Dutch, including 600 Jews still living under their control, were given generous terms. They were allowed three months to liquidate their assets or take their possessions with them and were provided with shipping to leave Brazil. On 28 January 1654, the victorious Portuguese insurgents, led by Barreto, entered Recife.

AFTERMATH OF THE DUTCH OCCUPATION

This evacuation did not end Portugal's problems with the Netherlands. A treaty between the Portuguese and the Dutch needed to be hammered out. Although the Dutch West India Company was virtually bankrupt, there was still talk in the Netherlands of declaring war on Portugal and blockading the Tagus River to prevent Brazilian sugar from arriving to pay for Portugal's continuing war with Spain. Various ultimatums were issued to King João IV and later to his widow, Queen Luisa de Guzmán. In November 1657, a Dutch fleet under Admiral Michiel Adriaanszoon de Ruyter, which was blockading the Tagus, captured twenty-one of the thirty-four ships in the returning Brazilian fleet. However, England and France could not stand by and see a weakened Portugal lose its struggle with Spain. A treaty between the Dutch and the Portuguese was finally signed on 6 August 1661, providing that the Portuguese would pay an indemnity of 4 million cruzados over sixteen years to compensate the Dutch for their loss of Brazil. A special tax was instituted to pay this indemnity, almost half of which was to be paid by the Brazilians themselves. This tax lasted throughout the colonial period and late into the reign of Emperor Dom PEDRO I (1822–1831) in an independent Brazil. A supplementary treaty of 1669 ensured that Portugal's part of the indemnity would be paid from Setúbal's salt duties. That part of the indemnity was not paid off until the early eighteenth century.

In the immediate aftermath of the restoration of northeastern Brazil to Portuguese control, old scores were settled as reprisals were carried out against Amerindians who had sided with the Dutch. Other problems festered. Animosity marked relations between the Portuguese who had lived under Dutch control and those who had fled the region and who now returned to recover their properties. Litigation over the ownership of sugar mills, houses, cane fields, and other properties dragged on for decades, leaving wounds that were slow to heal.

There is a vast literature on the Dutch presence in Brazil. The best guide to what was available by the mid-1940s is JOSÉ HONÓRIO RODRIGUES, *Historiografia e bibliografia do domínio Holandês no Brasil* (1949), which discusses in great detail the printed primary and secondary sources. The best account in English is CHARLES R. BOXER, *The Dutch in Brazil, 1624–1654* (1957). Among the most recent of Portuguese accounts is EVALDO CABRAL DE MELLO, *Olinda restaurada: Guerra e açúcar no Nordeste, 1630–1654* (1975), which includes previously unused sources from Spanish and Portuguese archives. Also of great value are JOSÉ ANTÔNIO GONSALVES DE MELLO, *Tempo dos flamengos: Influência da ocupação holandesa na vida e na cultura do norte do Brasil* (1947), and FRANCISCO ADOLFO DE VARNHAGEN, *Historia das lutas com os Hollandeses no Brazil desde 1624 a 1654* (1871). Gonsalves de Mello has also translated from the Dutch and annotated the important contemporary account of the sugar industry in Netherlands Brazil by ADRIAEN VAN DER DUSSEN, *Relatório sôbre as capitanias conquistadas no Brazil pelos Holandeses (1639): Suas condições econômicas e sociais* (1947). Also useful is HERMAN WÄTJEN, *Das Holländische Kolonialreich in Brasilien: Ein Kapitel aus der Kolonialgeschichte des 17. Jahrhunderts* (1921), which has been translated into Portuguese (1938).

There are a number of biographies of Portuguese and Brazilians involved in driving out the Dutch. GONSALVES DE MELLO has contributed a number of model monographs in honor of the 300th anniversary of the ouster of the Dutch: *Francisco de Figueroa: Mestre de campo do têrço das ilhas em Pernambuco* (1954); *Antônio Dias Cardoso: Sargento-mor do têrço de infantaria de Pernambuco* (1954); *Henrique Dias: Governador dos pretos, crioulos e mulatos do estado do Brasil* (1954); *D. Antônio Filipe Camarão: Capitão-mor dos Indios da costa do nordeste do Brasil* (1954); *Filipe Bandeira de Melo: Tenente de mestre de campo general do estado do Brasil* (1954); *Frei Manuel Calado do Salvador: Religioso da ordem de São Paulo, pregador apostólico por sua santidade, cronista da restauração* (1954); and *João Fernandes Vieira: Mestre-de-campo do têrço da infantaria de Pernambuco*, 2 vols. (1956). Also available is CHARLES R. BOXER, *Salvador de Sá and the Struggle for Brazil and Angola, 1602–1686* (1952). Other biographies include PEDRO CALMON, *Francisco Barreto: Restaurador de Pernambuco* (1940); BERNARDINO JOSÉ DE SOUSA, *Luiz Barbalho (1601–1644)* (1940); AFRANIO PEIXOTO, *Martim Soares Moreno: Fundador do Seará,* iniciador do maranhão e do pará, herói da restauração do Brasil, contra Franceses e Holandeses (1940); and FRANCIS A. DUTRA, *Matias de Albuquerque: Capitão-mor de Pernambuco e governador-geral do Brasil* (1976).

Biographies of some of the principal Dutch figures are also available: PIETER J. BOUMAN, *Johan Maurits van Nassau, de Braziliaan* (1947); W. J. VAN HOBOKEN, *Witte de With in Brazilië, 1648–1649* (1955). The role of Jews in Dutch Brazil is discussed by ARNOLD WIZNITZER, *Jews in Colonial Brazil* (1960). The diplomacy of the Dutch episode in Brazil is best handled in EDGAR PRESTAGE, *The Diplomatic Relations of Portugal with France, England, and Holland from 1640 to 1668* (1925).

FRANCIS A. DUTRA

See also **Trading Companies, Brazil.**

DUTCH–LATIN AMERICAN RELATIONS. Spain enjoyed complete control of the New World until the 1530s, when other European countries, particularly Portugal, began to challenge its supremacy. At that time the Dutch were waging a war of independence from Spain, and America served as a major theater of battle. In 1596 the Dutch allied with England and France against Spain in a war that ended with the Treaty of Antwerp (1609), which recognized the independence of the Netherlands. Almost from the beginning, the newly independent country made explicit its designs on the Americas, setting the stage for the raids, settlements, and commercial ventures of the seventeenth century.

More than any other European nation, the Dutch were violently anti-Spanish and vitally concerned with seagoing commerce; by this time they dominated the Atlantic sea-carrier routes and aggressively sought access to new markets. As early as 1605, the Dutch made raids on the South American mainland at Araya, where they captured the valuable salt pans and forced Spain into a defensive position. The Dutch, urged on by Calvinist refugee Willem Usselinax, began to consider permanent settlements in the West Indies to serve as trading outposts and bases for raids on the ships and towns of other powers. The earliest of these were established in 1624 near the mouth of the Orinoco at Essequibo and Berbice.

Events in Europe at this time also had an impact on Dutch activities in America: the House of Orange rose up and took the throne in the Netherlands; the twelve years' truce with Spain broke down in 1621; and in that same year the DUTCH WEST INDIA COMPANY got its charter. This last event was of paramount significance, for it established a permanent, highly capitalized, and centralized joint stock company able to mount an organized challenge to Spain in the New World. The West India Company turned its attention from the Caribbean toward Brazil and, in 1624, mounted an attack on the Portuguese at Bahia. Its success was short-lived, but in 1630 the Dutch took Recife, a little farther north, and held it long enough to establish plantation settlements. By this time, sugar and slaves were at the forefront of the Brazilian economy.

Led by Calvinist soldier and administrator Johan MAURITS, the Dutch in Brazil conducted scientific studies of their possessions, attempted to diversify the economy and build up a powerful sugar plantation and refinery complex. The Dutch captured Curaçao, Saint Martin, Saint Eustatius, and Saba in the 1630s, and they seized the coast of Angola in Africa to guarantee an adequate supply of slaves for their agricultural enterprises in the New World. Their sugar plantations in Brazil prompted the British and the French to try to emulate the Dutch success on their own islands in the Caribbean. Nevertheless, the Braganças in Portugal had declared independence from Spain in 1640 and, although the two countries were allies in Europe, in Brazil, war between Portugal and the Netherlands raged on. The Brazilians won a major victory at the battle of Guararapes in 1649 and drove the Dutch from Brazil entirely in 1654.

Although the Dutch remained powerful, the English and the French began to supersede the Dutch as Spain's main rivals in the New World in the latter part of the seventeenth century. The Dutch held on to their Caribbean island possessions and gained a foothold on the South American coast at Suriname in the 1630s; their pirates and ships continued to sail American waters and participate actively in the lucrative slave trade. Although the debate over the relative mildness or harshness of the European colonizers continues, many consider the Dutch to have been the most exploitative.

In the late twentieth century, the Dutch heritage was strongest in those Caribbean islands that were their former colonies—Aruba, Bonaire, Curaçao, Saint Martin, and Saint Eustatius—as well as mainland Suriname. These small nations continue to contribute to the overall diversity of life in the Caribbean as they struggle to find both their identities and their places in the world economy. Like so many others in their position, the former Dutch possessions turned to tourism as the major pillar of their national economies and attract thousands of visitors each year from North America, Europe, and Latin America.

Among the general works on the subject are J. H. PARRY and P. M. SHERLOCK, *A Short History of the West Indies*, 2d ed. (1956); CHARLES R. BOXER, *The Dutch in Brazil, 1624–1654* (1957); FRANKLIN KNIGHT, *The Caribbean*, 2d ed. (1990); and BONHAM C. RICHARDSON, *The Caribbean in the Wider World, 1492–1992: A Regional Geography* (1992). On slavery and the economy, see PHILIP D. CURTIN, *The Atlantic Slave Trade: A Census* (1969); GERALD CARDOSO, *Negro Slavery in the Sugar Plantations of Veracruz and Pernambuco, 1550–1680* (1983); and JOHANNES POSTMA, *The Dutch in the Atlantic Slave Trade* (1990). On piracy, military campaigns, and settlement, see ALEXANDER EXQUEMELIN, *The Buccaneers of America*, translated by Alexis Brown (original Dutch publication, 1678; 1969); CORNELIS GOSLINGA, *The Dutch in the Caribbean and on the Wild Coast, 1580–1680* (1971); DONAL SHOMETTE, *Raid on America: The Dutch Naval Campaign of 1672–1674* (1988); RAFAEL ABELLA, *Los piratos del Nuevo Mundo*, 2d ed. (1989); and JENIFER MARX, *Pirates and Privateers of the Caribbean* (1992).

KAREN RACINE

DUTCH WEST INDIA COMPANY (also Nederland-ische West-Indische Compagnie or WIC), a trading and colonizing company. The Dutch West India Company received its first charter from the States General of the United Provinces of the Netherlands on 3 June 1621 for trade and colonization in Africa and the Americas (along the Atlantic coast from Newfoundland to the Strait of Magellan as well as on the Pacific coast). Previously, commercial adventuring and the search for salt pans to supply the herring fisheries of the North Atlantic had led Dutch ships to Cape Verde and across the Atlantic to the Caribbean as interlopers in areas where Spain and Portugal claimed colonial hegemony. The WIC was founded in the year of the expiration of the Twelve Years' Truce (1621), an interruption in the eighty-year war of rebellion by the Spanish Netherlands against Hapsburg rule. Through its board of directors, the Heeren XIX, who represented bodies of investors in Amsterdam, Zeeland, the Maas, the Northern Quarter (West Frisian towns), and Friesland (including Groningen), the WIC adopted a more hostile policy toward Spain than had been desired by its veteran propagandist, William Usselinx (1567–1647). Buccaneering expeditions attacked Spanish shipping, and plans were made for extensive land conquest, beginning with a territory regarded as rich and vulnerable: Portuguese Brazil.

A first attempt to take Brazil, at Bahia in 1624–1625, was short-lived, but windfall wealth from the capture of the Spanish silver fleet at Matanzas (Cuba) by Piet Heyn in 1628 allowed the company to strike again in 1630 at the northeastern sugar capital of Pernambuco. At its height, under WIC governor Johan MAURITS (1637–1644), Dutch-occupied Brazil (New Holland) was an exemplary plantation colony: Dutch merchants financed the SUGAR INDUSTRY, supplied slave labor from newly secured African entrepôts on the Guinea coast south to Loango, and shipped the product to their refinery operations in the Netherlands. After being dislodged by Luso-Brazilian rebels in a protracted struggle (1645–1654), during a period of disputes over the extent of its trade monopolies and renewal of its charter as well as conflict with England, the WIC concentrated on its profitable slaving operations and trade and agricultural settlement in the Caribbean.

In Guiana, the "Wild Coast" between the Amazon and Orinoco rivers, French, English, and Dutch colonists fought for a piece of the Spanish American mainland. Sugar, coffee, cotton, and cocoa plantations thrived in the districts of WIC-administered outposts at Demerara, Essequibo, Berbice, and Suriname. In the Leeward Antilles, Saint Eustatius, Saint Martin, and Saba became subject to WIC control. A strategically located slave mart at Willemstad, Curaçao (in an island group including Bonaire and Aruba), flourished, especially between the 1670s and 1720, for successive holders of the Spanish ASIENTO until the contract passed to the WIC's chief rival, the Royal African Company.

Bankruptcy followed losses incurred during the Third Anglo-Dutch War (1672–1674), but the company reorganized in 1674 as the Second or New WIC under a smaller board, the Heeren X. Thus restructured, it enjoyed decades of prosperity in the eighteenth century based on slaving and the provisions trade in the Caribbean. Forced to relinquish most of its monopoly privileges after 1730, the conditions of free trade drove the company into insolvent obsolescence by 1791.

CHARLES R. BOXER, *The Dutch in Brazil, 1624–1654* (1957; repr. 1973); CORNELIS CH. GOSLINGA, *The Dutch in the Caribbean and on the Wild Coast, 1580–1680* (1971) and *The Dutch in the Caribbean and in the Guianas, 1680–1791* (1985); JOSÉ ANTÔNIO GONSALVES DE MELLO NETO, *Tempo dos flamengos: Influência da ocupação holandesa na vida e na cultura do norte do Brasil*, 3d ed. (1987); JOHANNES MENNE POSTMA, *The Dutch in the Atlantic Slave Trade, 1600–1815* (1990).

CATHERINE LUGAR

See also **Buccaneers and Freebooters; Slave Trade.**

DUTRA, EURICO GASPAR (*b.* 18 May 1883; *d.* 11 June 1974), president of Brazil (1945–1951). Son of merchant José Florêncio Dutra and Maria Justina Dutra, Dutra was born in Cuiabá, state of Mato Grosso. He married Carmela Leite, widow of Uchoa Cintra, on 19 February 1914; they had two children.

Dutra studied at the Escola Preparatória e Tática of Rio Pardo and completed his military studies at the Escola Militar do Brasil. After distinguishing himself during the Constitutionalist Revolution, Dutra became a general in 1932. In 1935 he was made commandant of Military Region I and put down the Communist rebellion of 27 November 1935 in Rio de Janeiro.

As minister of war (1936–1945) during the Getúlio VARGAS dictatorship, Dutra organized the BRAZILIAN EXPEDITIONARY FORCE (FEB), which saw combat in Europe during World War II. During this period, he actively participated in the Golpe Integralista (Integralist Coup) of 1937, for which he laid the groundwork. Dutra was also deeply involved in Vargas's nationalistic campaign to maintain Brazilian ownership of the nation's petroleum under the banner of "O petróleo é nosso" (the oil is ours).

In 1946 Dutra was elected president of Brazil and served until 31 January 1951. Not known as a charismatic figure, Dutra was respected for his honesty and ability to complete a full presidential term. Two Brazilian municipalities were named in his honor. Pursuing a close relationship with the United States, Dutra received President Harry S. Truman in Brazil, made an official visit to the United States, and broke relations with the Soviet Union. During his presidency, Dutra implemented a number of reforms in the federal government, including the establishment of the Tribunal Federal de Recursos, the Conselho Nacional de Economia, and the regional planning commissions.

IÊDA SIQUEIRA WIARDA

DUVALIER, FRANÇOIS (*b.* 14 April 1907; *d.* 21 April 1971), president of Haiti (1957–1971). A *noir* (black), Duvalier was born in Port-au-Prince; his father was an elementary schoolteacher and his mother a bakery worker. His formal education included elementary and secondary school at the Lycée Pétion and a medical degree from the École de Médecine the same year that the U.S. occupation (1915–1934) ended. After his internship, he worked in a clinic and in 1939 married Simone Ovide Faine, a mulatto (*mulâtresse*) nurse whose father was a merchant. They had four children, three daughters and a son—Jean-Claude.

In the 1940s, Duvalier became involved in the campaign against yaws (*pian*), a contagious tropical disease caused by a parasite, and then went on to direct training in the U.S. Army's malaria program. In the mid-1940s, he assisted Doctor James Dwinelle in the U.S. Army Medical Corps' yaws program. During this time he had a year's fellowship and studied public health at the University of Michigan.

Duvalier's ideas about race and politics and his literary and political activities were developed and took place both before and during his medical studies and working with yaws. In the 1920s, he became important in an ethnology movement as one of its three Ds, *les trois D*, later known as the *Griots*, and was a cofounder of its journal, *Les Griots*. This movement was based upon black nationalism (*noirisme*), *indigénisme*, and NÉGRITUDE, stressing African roots, including *voudon* (voodoo, VODUN). It opposed the control and rule of the mulattoes. Certain events also affected Duvalier's attitudes and values: the U.S. occupation; President Rafael TRUJILLO's anti-Haitian views and actions, particularly the 1937 massacre of Haitians in the Dominican Republic; foreign intervention; control of economic and political life by the mulattoes; army intervention in national politics; and the campaigns of the church against *voudon*.

François Duvalier became politically active in 1946, when presidential candidate Daniel Fignolé formed a new party and made him its secretary-general. After the army assured the election of President Dumarsais ESTIMÉ, in his "Revolution of 1946," he designed reforms that downgraded the mulattoes in government. President Estimé made Duvalier a part of his government, first as director of the yaws program, then as undersecretary of labor in 1948, which was followed the next year by minister of labor and public health. The growing rift between blacks and mulattoes resulted in Estimé's overthrow in 1950, and the army brought in General Paul MAGLOIRE, who lasted until 1956. There ensued great instability and virtual civil war, with five provisional governments, and then rule by a military council. In his 1957 campaign for president against Louis Déjoie, Duvalier called for honesty in government, stressed his background as a country doctor, and organized a paramilitary group to deal with his opponents. The army also "managed" this election, assuring the defeat of Fignolé (the U.S. embassy count showed a victory for Fignolé).

Presidential candidate Dr. François Duvalier, May 1957. AP / WIDE WORLD PHOTOS.

Once he was inaugurated as president at the age of fifty, Duvalier began the transformation of "cultural *négritude*" into "political *négritude*" by destroying his critics; neutralizing the army; Haitianizing the church; legitimizing *voudon* and making it an instrument of government; and establishing a black nationalist, xenophobic, and personalist regime. He became the state.

Duvalier first silenced the press and broadcasters, who were arrested, attacked, and killed; he then burned and bombed their offices and stations. The major instrument was the TONTON MACOUTES (in *créole*, bogeymen), who were officially recognized by the creation in 1962 of the *Volontaires de la Securité Nationale* (VSN). Second, he neutralized the army by transfers and by politicizing it, and he created a separate palace guard, which was quartered there with their arsenal located in the basement. At the same time he invited a U.S. Marine Corps mission to train the army as a means of showing U.S. support; but the mission (1958–1962), commanded by Colonel Robert D. Heinl, withdrew when the VSN replaced the army. Third, he took on the church in 1959, expelling high officials, including the archbishop; arresting members of the clergy; closing the seminary; and expelling the Jesuits. The Vatican responded by excommunicating him and his entire cabinet. Then he "Haitianized" the church by increasing the number of Haitian clergy until they were in the majority. (He reconciled with the church in 1966, mainly on his own terms.) He openly favored and practiced *voudon,* used some of its priests (*houngans*) as advisers, and always dressed in black.

What was unique about Duvalier's rule was that he controlled everything and almost everyone by making them responsible to him—loyalty was more important than competence. He and his family and closest advisers got a financial cut from all government enterprises, thus, it was "government by franchise."

In relations with the U.S., Duvalier played the anticommunist game in order to get aid, but when the administration of John F. Kennedy cut off most aid in 1963, he turned inward and toward Africa, stressing *négritude.* He invited and welcomed Ethiopia's Haile Selassie I with great fanfare and at great expense in 1966. Although a *noirist,* he really did not care about the black masses. After paving the way for naming his son Jean-Claude as his successor as "president for life," he died of natural causes at the age of sixty-four.

BERNARD DIEDERICH and AL BURT, *Papa Doc: The Truth About Haiti Today* (1969); FRANÇOIS DUVALIER, *Mémoires d'un leader du Tiers Monde* (1969)—although a public relations document, it has a useful vita plus many interesting photographs, showing "Haitianization" of the church plus apparent support of the church and the U.S. of his regime; HAROLD E. DAVIS and LARMAN C. WILSON, *Latin American Foreign Policies: An Analysis* (1975), chap. 10; LESLIE F. MANIGAT, *Ethnicité, nationalisme et politique: Le cas d'Haiti* (1975); ROBERT D. HEINL, JR., and NANCY G. HEINL, *Written in Blood: The Story of the Haitian People, 1492–1971* (1978), esp. chaps. 13–14; FRANCES CHAMBERS, *Haiti* (1983), an annotated bibliography (see esp. sections on History, Politics and Government, Law and Constitution, and Foreign Relations); BRIAN WEINSTEIN and AARON SEGAL, *Haiti: Political Failures, Cultural Successes* (1984), chaps. 2, 3, 5, and 7; JAMES FERGUSON, *Papa Doc, Baby Doc: Haiti and the Duvaliers* (1987), esp. chap. 2; PATRICK BELLEGARDE-SMITH, *Haiti: The Breached Citadel* (1990), esp. chaps. 3–5; and MICHEL-ROLPH TROUILLOT, *Haiti, State Against Nation: The Origins and Legacy of Duvalierism* (1990), chaps. 5–6.

LARMAN C. WILSON

See also **Duvalier, Jean-Claude.**

DUVALIER, JEAN-CLAUDE (*b.* 3 July 1951), president of Haiti (1971–1986). An unsuccessful law student and playboy, Duvalier became "president for life" upon the death of his father, François DUVALIER, but was only the titular head for the first few years, since decisions were made by a council of state appointed by his father before he died. This arrangement assured the continuation of *Duvalierisme.* The council members included his mother and his father's main advisers; Luckner Cambronne was the power behind the throne and also headed the Leopards, a counterinsurgency force created with U.S. aid in 1971. When Jean-Claude dismissed and exiled Cambronne in 1972, it marked the president's emerging control and influence.

Duvalier stated that his goal was to effect an "economic revolution" (he had little interest in NÉGRITUDE or *noirisme*), which he pursued by making some cosmetic and some real changes in reducing political repression. These changes plus some genuine economic incentives ended Haiti's isolation, brought about the resumption of U.S. aid, and attracted foreign investment and companies.

Duvalier's marriage in 1980 to a mulatto divorcée, Michèle Bennett, daughter of a wealthy exporter-importer, provoked criticism from the antimulatto blacks. Her life-style served as a catalyst—along with the corrupt and incompetent bureaucracy—for his downfall. Her shopping sprees in Paris and lavish parties in Haiti caused national revulsion, prompting riots and demonstrations, which began in rural cities in 1984. Supported by the church, these acts of opposition convulsed the country and led the U.S. to urge Jean-Claude's resignation and departure. He and his family along with several close advisers were flown out of Haiti on a U.S. cargo plane in early February 1986.

BRIAN WEINSTEIN and AARON SEGAL, *Haiti: Political Failures, Cultural Successes* (1984), esp. pp. 43–45, 57–61, 114–118; JAMES FERGUSON, *Papa Doc, Baby Doc: Haiti and the Duvaliers* (1987), esp. chaps. 3 and 4; PATRICK BELLEGARDE-SMITH, *Haiti: The Breached Citadel* (1990), pp. 97–98, 104–107, 123–126, 134–141, 186; MICHEL-ROLPH TROUILLOT, *Haiti, State Against Nation: The Origins and Legacy of Duvalierism* (1990), pp. 181–183, 200–219.

LARMAN C. WILSON

DZIBILCHALTÚN, an important and long-occupied Maya archaeological zone and site located 10 miles north of Mérida, Yucatán. Dzibilchaltún and nearby sites such as Komchen were populated as early as 800 B.C. The earliest occupants of northern Yucatán lived in small farming villages, and by around 500 B.C. there is good evidence for formally arranged, public buildings located near town centers. During the Late Formative period (ca. 300 B.C.–A.D. 250) the people of the Dzibilchaltún region were increasingly engaged in long-distance trade, and the production of salt may have provided them with a valuable resource for that trade. Ceramic and architectural similarities with Late Formative sites on the east coast of Yucatán (e.g., Cuello and CERROS) suggest maritime contacts.

During the period between 250 and 700, Dzibilchaltún and the surrounding area were sparsely populated for reasons that remain poorly understood. By 700, however, the site of Dzibilchaltún experienced rapid growth, becoming one of the largest centers in the Yucatán peninsula. An area covering 7.6 square miles with over 8,000 structures was occupied between 700 and 1000; population may have reached 25,000 or more at this time. Early in this period there are architectural similarities with Early Classic sites in the southern lowland (e.g., Uaxactun) because Dzibilchaltún architects revived an earlier style. There are also similarities with contemporary western Maya sites like PALENQUE. By around 830, the Puuc architectural style came to dominate Dzibilchaltún, and structures had veneer facings with geometric mosaics and three-dimensional masks.

By around 1000, Dzibilchaltún had lost its dominant position in the area and there was strong influence from CHICHÉN ITZÁ to the east. The resident population of Dzibilchaltún declined dramatically, and the site appears to have become a ceremonial center in the Late Postclassic period (ca. 1200–1540).

E. WYLLYS ANDREWS IV and E. WYLLYS ANDREWS V, *Excavations at Dzibilchaltún, Yucatán, Mexico* (1980); E. WYLLYS ANDREWS V, "Dzibilchaltún," in *Handbook of Middle American Indians*, suppl. 1, *Archaeology* (1981), pp. 313–341.

JANINE GASCO

E

EARTH SUMMIT, RIO DE JANEIRO (1992), the second of the major international conferences on the environment sponsored by the United Nations, the first having been held in Stockholm, Sweden, in 1972. Formally known as the United Nations Conference on Environment and Development (UNCED), the June event was popularly known as "Earth Summit" and "Eco 92." Some thirty thousand delegates from 178 nations, including 117 heads of state, attended. Other delegates included representatives of nongovernmental organizations, religious groups, and indigenous movements as well as business executives, educators, and students. Over eight thousand journalists covered the proceedings.

The conference produced an eight-hundred-page action plan entitled "Agenda 21," which outlined one hundred program areas for achieving sustainable development globally through the twenty-first century. Most of the document focuses on specific environmental problems, while lesser attention is paid to such issues as poverty, health, and politics. Two major conventions were signed: the UN Framework Convention on Climate Change (154 signatories) and the Convention on Biologic Diversity (153 signatories), the latter of which the United States refused to sign. The Authoritative Statement of Forest Principles constituted a third, nonbinding agree-

ment. The Rio Declaration on Environment and Development, containing guidelines for human behavior toward the environment, was also issued.

The conference received both praise and criticism. Most observers agreed that it definitively convinced world leaders of the potentially devastating consequences for the planet of not taking concerted action on environmental matters. However, many critics believed that population, poverty, and development issues received too little attention, and that the three major agreements lacked serious substance.

A vast amount of literature exists on the Earth Summit, particularly in article form. For book-length works on the subject, see DANIEL SITARZ, ed., *Agenda Twenty-one: The Earth Summit Strategy to Save Our Planet* (1993), and JOHAN HOLBERG, ed., *Making Development Sustainable: Redefining Institutions, Policy, and Economics* (1992). For the UN's official version of the conference, see UNITED NATIONS CONFERENCE ON ENVIRONMENT AND DEVELOPMENT, *The Earth Summit: The United Nations Conference on Environment and Development (UNCED)* (1993).

LAURA JARNAGIN

See also **Environmental Movements.**

EARTHQUAKES. Seismic activity of varying intensity is a common natural phenomenon in Latin America. Some occurrences have had profound long-term consequences. In 1773, massive destruction led colonial Guatemalans to move their capital from Antigua to its present site. Dissatisfaction with Anastasio Somoza's management of relief and reconstruction following the 1972 Managua quake turned many Nicaraguans against his government. In Peru, a 1970 earthquake-landslide eliminated the elite of Yungay more thoroughly and quickly than any social revolution. Preventing such hazards from persistently becoming disasters requires long-term planning. Appropriately, the United Nations late in 1987 designated the 1990s as the International Decade for the Reduction of Natural Hazards.

Protecting society against any hazard's impact requires understanding of that hazard. Nineteenth-century pioneers in seismology include James Alfred Ewing, who published "Earthquake Measurement" in 1883, and John Milne, who promoted the establishment of seismographic stations worldwide. Chile had a seis-

Earthquake in El Salvador, September 1986. © WESLEY BOCKE / PHOTO RESEARCHERS.

mograph in Santiago in 1850 and a national seismological service in 1908. The Organization of American States funded seismological surveys in Peru and Costa Rica in the 1970s. The Quito, Ecuador, astronomical observatory (1873) has a seismology department. Earthquake study institutes date from 1941 in Colombia and 1955 in Venezuela. Mexico's national seismological service is part of the Institute of Geophysics (1949) of the national university.

In the nineteenth century, Giuseppe Mercalli devised a Roman-numeral scale to measure the impact of an earthquake on an affected community. Later, Charles Richter developed an arabic-numeral scale based on the physical force at the epicenter. Scholars attempt to estimate numerical equivalents for descriptions that come from times before the existence of seismographic instruments.

Earthquakes and tsunamis with catastrophic impact occurred within the borders of present-day Chile in 1730 (Concepción), 1822 (Valparaíso), 1835 and 1837 (Concepción), 1868 (Arica and off the northern coast), 1877 (Iquique and Tarapacá), and in 1965 (without tsunami) in central Chile. More than 1,000 people died in each of the following: 1906 (Santiago and Valparaíso), 1922 (Copiapó), 1939 (28,000 in Chillán), and 1960 (Concepción). Especially strong earthquakes shook Peru in 1746 (Callao and Lima, with tsunami) and in 1868 (Chala, Arequipa, Moquegua, and Tacna). In colonial times, there were other significant quakes in Peru in 1604 (Arequipa), 1619 (Trujillo, Piura, Santa), 1658 (Trujillo), 1664 (Ica, Pisco), 1687 (Lima, Arequipa), 1699 (Lima), 1724 (Callao), and 1821 (Camaná, Ocoña, Caravelí). Five severe earthquakes occurred in the 1940–1950 period; three, between 1970 and 1974. Andean Argentina sustained considerable loss of life in 1861 (Mendoza) and 1944 (San Juan).

The Ecuadorian cities of Quito, Ambato, and Riobamba are situated in an earthquake-prone area. The quakes of 1575, 1640, 1645, 1698, 1755, 1797, 1859, 1868, 1949, and 1979 are regarded as especially devastating, most notably that of 1868, which also struck Guayaquil and Ibarra, and that of 1797. Within the boundaries of modern Colombia, there were earthquakes in 1644, 1785, and 1804. The May 1875 earthquakes in Cúcuta took thousands of lives. Severe damage resulted from the Colombian quakes of 1851, 1923, 1935, 1938, 1950, 1955, 1958, 1961, 1966, 1967 (especially), 1979, and 1983. In Venezuela, there are reports of severe quakes in Cumaná in 1530, Bailadores in 1599, and Caracas in 1641. The 1812 Caracas quake was the deadliest and most destructive of the colonial era. In the national period, heavy damage resulted from quakes in 1929, 1966, 1967 (especially), and 1981.

Colonial documents indicate more than a dozen earthquakes in the vicinity of Antigua, Guatemala, before the relocation of the city; those of 1717 and 1765 caused considerable damage. Colonial San Salvador experienced quakes in 1671, 1715, 1719, 1776, and 1798. Among the more significant twentieth-century Central American earthquakes were those in 1902 (Guatemala), 1910 (Costa Rica), 1917 (El Salvador), 1917–1918 (Guatemala), 1931 (Nicaragua), 1951 (Honduras), 1965 (El Salvador), 1972 (Nicaragua), 1973 (Costa Rica), 1976 (Guatemala), 1982 (El Salvador), 1983 (Costa Rica), 1986 (El Salvador), and 1991 (Costa Rica).

Mexico City and Jalisco endured earthquakes in 1611; Oaxaca, in 1701. The state of Guerrero had notable quakes in 1845, 1874, 1882, 1887, 1907, 1956, 1964, and 1979; Michoacán, in 1858, 1911, and 1981; southern Mexico, in 1962, 1973, and 1980. As one of the largest metropolitan population concentrations in the world, Mexico City suffered extreme casualties in the earthquake of 1985.

In 1692, Jamaica's capital, Port Royal, sank beneath the ocean during an earthquake; an earthquake damaged Kingston in 1907. Other significant quakes in the Greater Antilles were in 1766, 1775, and 1932 (Cuba); 1918 (Puerto Rico); 1751, 1770, 1842, and 1953 (Haiti); and 1691, 1751, 1842, and 1946 (Dominican Republic).

Social scientists began systematic studies of natural hazards only in the 1950s. Researchers consider such indicators as the impact of earthquakes on physical and mental health, disrupted infrastructures, simplified social relationships, exacerbation of inequities or inefficiencies, and retarded growth. Until the twentieth century, authorities had to depend on local resources for relief.

JOHN TOMBLIN, "Earthquakes, Volcanoes, and Hurricanes: A Review of Natural Hazards and Vulnerability in the West Indies," in *Ambio* 10, no. 6 (1981): 340–345; FREDERICK L. BATES et al., *Recovery, Change, and Development: A Longitudinal Study of the Guatemalan Earthquake* (1982); ANTHONY OLIVER-SMITH, *Martyred City: Death and Rebirth in the Andes* (1986); ENRIQUE SILGADO, *Terremotos destructivos en América del Sur, 1530–1894* (1989); BARBARA BODE, *No Bells to Toll* (1990); NATIONAL OCEANIC AND ATMOSPHERIC ADMINISTRATION, *Significant Earthquakes, 2000 B.C.–1990* (1992); LAWRENCE FELDMAN, *Mountains of Fire, Lands That Shake: Earthquakes and Volcanic Eruptions in the Historic Past of Central America, 1505–1899* (1993).

ROBERT H. CLAXTON

EASTER ISLAND, a Chilean possession in the South Pacific approximately 2,000 miles west of South America. This territory became part of Chile in 1888. This small isle, known for its monumental statues, was originally inhabited by a Polynesian people who were decimated by European diseases and forced work on Peru's CHINCHA ISLANDS, remained largely isolated. It attracted the attention of Chile, which coveted a Pacific enclave and saw Easter Island as both economically valuable and strategically important. After Chilean occupation, the land's economy remained primitive, from a lack of resources to support agriculture and an unwillingness by

Easter Island. SEBRA FILM.

the Chilean government to provide assistance. Easter Island's economy remained essentially pastoral until the development of jet aviation made the island a tourist attraction, thus diversifying its economic base.

JOHN DOS PASSOS, *Easter Island: Island of Enigmas* (1971); J. DOUGLAS PORTEOUS, *The Modernization of Easter Island* (1981).

WILLIAM F. SATER

EASTERN COAST OF CENTRAL AMERICA COMMERCIAL AND AGRICULTURAL COMPANY. The Eastern Coast Company metamorphosed from a speculative venture calculated to restore value to worthless MOSQUITO COAST securities (1833) into a legitimate colonizer. Its agent, Thomas Gould, in Guatemala seeking confirmation of spurious land titles, fortuitously obtained (1834), as one of several grants the state government of Mariano GÁLVEZ made for colonization under his development program (and to confine BELIZE within Anglo-Spanish treaty limits), all the public lands in the vast department of VERAPAZ. Critics immediately voiced sharp protests against sacrifice of Guatemalan interests by cession to foreigners of virtually all remaining public lands and natural resources within the state, by concession to alien colonists of privileges denied nationals, and by risk of state territory through affording aggressively expanding Belize an opportunity to incorporate adjacent English settlements.

Deterred from occupying coastal areas by the British government's stated intent to prevent any activity that might transgress Belize boundaries (which it refused to define), the company in 1836 established New Liverpool, an inland settlement on the Cajabón River near its confluence with the Polochic that failed miserably. Two years later a reorganized company negotiated revalidation of its Verapaz charter and cession of the port and district of SANTO TOMÁS on the Bay of Honduras. Projecting a deep-water port at Santo Tomás and an inland center on the Polochic River, it planned a huge agricultural development in Verapaz and a commercial empire embracing Central America and adjacent parts of Mexico. It introduced steamer service between IZABAL and Belize and briefly on the Polochic, and provided an iron bridge for the Motagua River crossing on the road between the Polochic and the capital.

A victim of underestimated difficulties, undercapitalization, mismanagement, and perhaps sabotage by employees, the company sought to avert forfeiture of its charter by selling to Belgian speculators 1 million acres of land to be selected from its Verapaz and Santo Tomás concessions. On arrival in Guatemala, the Belgian agents found the British company in disrepute and its land sale effectively invalidated by pending abrogation of its charters. They seized the opportunity to negotiate for themselves an independent cession of the port and district of Santo Tomás. Its concessions voided (1842), the British company ceased operation.

The episode is representative of the postindependence Latin American pursuit of foreign colonization as the most viable route to rapid population growth and development; the speculative, often fraudulent, Latin American enterprises that fueled British investment "bubbles"; the early appearance in Latin America of issues that have since accompanied "development" by international corporations; and the persistence after independence of colonial boundary and sovereignty disputes.

WILLIAM J. GRIFFITH, *Empires in the Wilderness: Foreign Colonization and Development in Guatemala, 1834–1844* (1965), gives fully documented coverage of the company's activity. JORGE LUIS ARRIOLA, *Gálvez en la encrucijada: Ensayo crítico en torno al humanismo político de un gobernante* (1961), criticizes the colonization grants and the company's operation as a threat to the integrity of Guatemala that, fortunately, failed. PEDRO PÉREZ VALENZUELA, *Santo Tomás de Castilla: Apuntes para la historia de las colonizaciones en la costa atlántica* (1956), includes the English and Belgian company projects but lacks essential documentation.

WILLIAM J. GRIFFITH

ECHANDI JIMÉNEZ, MARIO (*b.* 1915), president of Costa Rica (1958–1962). Mario Echandi, who received his law degree from the University of Costa Rica, first came to prominence in national affairs as the general secretary of the National Union Party (PUN), which backed Otilio ULATE BLANCO's successful presidential campaign (1948). Under Ulate, he served as ambassador to the United States (1950–1951) and as foreign minister (1951–1953).

While in the national legislature (1953–1958), he was a recognized leader of the opposition to President José FIGUERES FERRER's social democratic programs. His leadership in Congress served as a springboard for his political ascension.

With the support of the followers of Ulate and Rafael Angel CALDERÓN GUARDIA, Echandi led the PLN opposition to victory in the 1958 election. His administration emphasized fiscal restraint, the expansion of the highway network, and a program to foster industrial development. True to his conservative credentials, he opposed the proposed Central American Common Market. After his presidency Echandi remained a conservative leader, and in 1970 ran unsuccessfully for president against his old adversary José Figueres Ferrer.

FRANKLIN D. PARKER, *The Central American Republics* (1964); CHARLES D. AMERINGER, *Don Pepe* (1978); and HAROLD D. NELSON, ed., *Costa Rica: A Country Study* (1983).

JOHN PATRICK BELL

ECHAVE ORIO BALTASAR DE (*b.* ca. 1548; *d.* ca. 1623), painter. Echave was in New Spain by around 1573 and is the most important of the second generation of mannerist painters in colonial Mexico. It is not clear how much of his training was European, since he does not seem to have been famous when he arrived in the New World. In 1582 he married Isabel de Ibía, the daughter of the painter Francisco de Zumaya, reportedly an artist in her own right. Two sons, Baltasar and Manuel, were both painters. Among the works by Echave which survive is the earliest known copy of the Virgin of GUADALUPE, signed and dated 1606, and some of the panels from the RETABLO of Tlatelolco. Also attributed to Echave are the paintings of the retablo of XOCHIMILCO. Echave wrote a treatise on the Basque language, published in 1607.

JOSÉ GUADALUPE VICTORIA, *Un pintor en su tiempo, Baltasar de Echave Orio*, in press.

CLARA BARGELLINI

ECHEANDÍA, JOSÉ MARÍA DE (*d.* after 1833), governor of Alta California (1825–1831), in control of the southern part of the territory from 1832 to 1833. His most important policies concerned the Franciscan MISSIONS. He refused orders to expel the Spanish-born FRANCISCANS in 1828, because most of the missionaries were from Spain and the missions would thus have been left without priests. Echeandía also initiated a partial emancipation of more acculturated Indian converts living primarily in the southern missions, most of whom left the missions.

Internally, Echeandía faced several revolts, which he successfully repressed, but he took power in the south following a military uprising against then-governor Manuel VICTORIA. In foreign relations, Echeandía allowed the Russians at FORT ROSS to hunt for otters in Mexican waters. Wounded in an 1833 uprising, Echeandía returned to Mexico.

DAVID J. WEBER, *The Mexican Frontier, 1821–1846: The American Southwest Under Mexico* (1982).

ROBERT H. JACKSON

ECHENIQUE, JOSÉ RUFINO (*b.* 1808; *d.* 16 June 1887), president of Peru (1851–1854). Chosen by the national congress, he had been a counselor to President Ramón CASTILLA. But he was politically naive and chose anti-Castilla ministers and counselors, some of them reputedly dishonest. He accepted fraudulent claims against the public treasury, leading to a tremendous increase in the internal debt. In 1853 he secretly converted nearly half of this debt into claims on Peru's foreign debt. Intended to strengthen domestic public bonds weakened by speculation and embezzlement, the debt consolidation was funded by huge foreign loans backed by guano. A great scandal ensued, which combined with the outrages of his ministers, encouraged a popular revolution. During the rebellion, Echenique decreed abolition of black slavery, apparently to generate an army. His opponent, former president Castilla, duplicated this decree. In 1855 Echenique was forced into exile, first in Panama and then the United States. His successors continued the policy of linking the national debt to foreign trade.

DAVID WERLICH, *Peru: A Short History* (1978), pp. 83–84; PAUL GOOTENBERG, *Between Silver and Guano: Commercial Policy and the State in Postindependence Peru* (1989), esp. pp. 126–127.

VINCENT PELOSO

ECHEVERRÍA, ESTEBAN (*b.* 2 September 1805; *d.* 19 January 1851), Argentine poet and political essayist.

After five years of study in Paris, Echeverría returned to Buenos Aires in 1830 infused with the spirit of romanticism and liberalism. He soon gained recognition as the leading figure of a new generation of writers. Influenced by Victor Hugo and François René de Chateaubriand, Echeverría published *Elvira, o la novia de la Plata* (Elvira, or the River Plate Bride) in 1832 and then, in 1837, *La cautiva* (The Captive), a long narrative poem exalting the American scene. In 1838 Echeverría wrote "El matadero" (The Slaughterhouse), a classic short story denouncing the Juan Manuel de ROSAS dictator-

ship, but for political reasons the work was not published until 1871.

Although Echeverría was the first romantic poet in Hispanic America, his reputation rests as well on the impact of his political writings at a time when Argentina was under the iron rule of Rosas (1829–1852). In 1837 Echeverría organized the Asociación de Mayo, which espoused the principles of the May 1810 revolution upon which the nation had been founded and swore its opposition to Rosas. The aspirations of this association were codified by Echeverría and published in Montevideo in 1846 as the *Dogma socialista*. This document expounded the ideals of a free society and a national literature similarly free of traditional restraints. Its political and social implications for a new Argentina based on liberty and justice were quickly recognized.

RAFAEL ALBERTO ARRIETA, *Historia de la literatura argentina*, vol. 2 (1958), pp. 19–111; JULIO CÉSAR MORENO DAVIS, *Esteban Echeverría: Su vida y su pensamiento* (1972); SAÚL SOSNOWSKI, "Esteban Echeverría: El intelectual ante la formación del estado," *Revista Iberoamericana* 47, nos. 114–115 (1981): 293–300; EDGAR C. KNOWLTON, *Esteban Echeverría* (1985).

MYRON I. LICHTBLAU

See also **Literature: Spanish America.**

ECHEVERRÍA ÁLVAREZ, LUIS (*b.* 17 January 1922), president of Mexico (1970–1976). To the surprise of most analysts, Luis Echeverría, though a disciple of Gustavo DÍAZ ORDAZ, turned out to be a president in the populist mold, reintroducing, in certain respects, a style similar to that of Lázaro CÁRDENAS.

Echeverría was born in the Federal District, as were so many leading politicians of his and succeeding generations. He attended school in Mexico City and Ciudad Victoria, then, after graduating from the National Preparatory School, he enrolled in the National Law School in 1940, completing his degree in August 1945. He married the daughter of José Zuno Hernández, a former governor of Jalisco and a member of an important political family. A political disciple of Rodolfo Sánchez Taboada, the president of the PRI, he first held positions in the party, including press secretary, before following his mentor to the navy secretariat. In 1954 he became *oficial mayor* of public education, after which he attached himself to the career of another mentor, Gustavo Díaz Ordaz, as undersecretary of the government secretariat (1958–1963). Upon his mentor's nomination as the presidential candidate of the PRI, he replaced him as secretary, a position in which he remained from 1963 to 1969, when he resigned to become himself a presidential candidate. He was the last official party presidential candidate to come from this cabinet agency.

Echeverría's regime was characterized by greater levels of economic and political uncertainty than were those of his immediate predecessors. Early in his administration, he faced strong internal opposition within his own cabinet, led by Alfonso Martínez Domínguez, the head of the Federal District. Martínez Domínguez used a paramilitary force in a 1971 incident, after which the president removed him from office. Echeverría also faced—for the first time in many years—well-organized guerrilla opposition groups in urban and rural settings, most notably the band of Lucio Cabañas in Guerrero, which the army eventually eliminated.

On the economic front, Echeverría was responsible for the rapid growth of state-owned enterprises and the alienation of many elements of Mexico's private-sector leadership. He exacerbated divisions between the state and the private sector by nationalizing agrarian properties in northwest Mexico immediately before leaving office and by presiding over the first devaluation of the peso in many years. He left the presidency further delegitimized than when he took office, passing on to his successor, José LÓPEZ PORTILLO, a difficult set of problems.

After leaving the presidency in 1976, Echeverría served as ambassador to UNESCO (1977–1978), then briefly to Australia. He also directed a Third World studies institute upon his return to Mexico in 1979. He subsequently retired from all public activities.

YORAM SHAPIRA, *Mexican Foreign Policy Under Echeverría* (1978); MIGUEL BASAÑEZ, *La lucha por la hegemonía en México, 1968–1980* (1981); STEVEN SANDERSON, *Agrarian Populism and the Mexican State* (1981); JUDITH A. HELLMAN, *Mexico in Crisis* (1983); ROBERTO NEWELL and LUÍS RUBIO, *Mexico's Dilemma: The Political Origins of Economic Crisis* (1984); and DANIEL S. LEVY and GABRIEL SZÉKELY, *Mexico: Paradoxes of Stability and Change* (1987).

RODERIC AI CAMP

ECHEVERRÍA BIANCHI, JOSÉ ANTONIO (*b.* 16 July 1932; *d.* 13 March 1957), Cuban revolutionary. Born in Cárdenas, Matanzas, Echeverría was educated in primary school at the Colegio Hermanos Maristas de Cárdenas and graduated from high school in the same city. He entered the University of Havana School of Architecture in 1953, where he was elected president of the Federation of University Students (1954, 1955, and 1956). Echeverría, along with Fauré Chomón, founded the Revolutionary Directorate in 1956. In the same year he attended the Congress of Latin American Students in Chile. He and Fidel CASTRO were signers of the "Letter from Mexico." He participated in the organization that attacked the presidential palace in March 1957, and he directed the takeover of a Havana radio station, where he was killed in a gun battle with police.

MARÍA DEL CARMEN ALMODOVAR

ECKHOUT, ALBERT (*b.* ca. 1607–1610; *d.* ca. 1665), Dutch painter, noted for his portraits of the flora, fauna, and inhabitants of Brazil. Eckhout was born in Groningen in the Netherlands, the son of Albert Eckhout and Marryen Roeleffs. Eckhout and Frans POST were the most famous of the artists in the entourage of Johan MAURITS of Nassau while he was governor-general of Dutch Brazil from 1637 to 1644. Little is known of Eckhout's training, early career, and the reasons for his appointment, and it is not known exactly when he arrived in Brazil. Because some paintings attributed to Eckhout portrayed Chilean Indians and llamas and African peoples, plants, and trees, some have suggested that Eckhout might have been part of Hendrick Brouwer's expedition to Chile in 1643 or might have visited West Africa with the forces of Colonel Hans Coen that captured Elmina in 1637 or with those of Admiral Cornelis Jol and Colonel James Henderson that occupied Angola in 1641. Finally, it is uncertain when Eckhout returned to Europe or how long he remained in the service of Maurits. In any case, by 1645 Eckhout was back in Groningen. From at least 1648 to 1652 he lived in Amersfoort before moving to Dresden, where he spent ten years (1653 to 1663) as a painter at the court of the elector of Saxony, Johann Georg II. Eckhout is thought to have died in Groningen in 1665.

Relatively few of Eckhout's paintings were signed or dated. Although most were probably painted in Brazil, others were completed after his return to Europe. He seems to have made a large number of preliminary sketches while in Brazil. Moreover, other artists based their works on Eckhout's paintings and drawings. At times, it is not entirely clear which paintings are copies, which were made under his supervision, and which are his own. In addition, Eckhout's artwork was the basis for many of the woodcut illustrations of Caspar Barlaeus's *Rerum per octennium in Brasilia* (1647) and Johannes de Laet's *Historia naturalis Brasiliae* (1648). The latter included 533 woodcuts and published notes by the German naturalist, geographer, and astronomer Georg Marcgraf on the fauna and flora of Brazil, and a section on medicine by the Dutch physician Dr. Willem Piso, both of whom had served Maurits in Brazil. The basis for these woodcuts was more than 800 paintings, most of them probably by Eckhout. These works later formed part of the collection sold by Maurits to his cousin Friedrich Wilhelm, elector of Brandenburg. They have survived as the *Handbooks* (two volumes of watercolors), the *Theatri rerum naturalium Brasiliae* (four volumes, mostly oil paintings), and the *Miscellanea Cleyeri*. Formerly housed in Berlin, these collections disappeared during World War II. In 1977 they were rediscovered in Kraków, Poland.

Probably the most famous and valuable of Eckhout's paintings are his ethnographic works. Many were done in Brazil in 1641 and 1643 for Maurits, who later gave them to another cousin, King Frederik III of Denmark. They include life-size portraits of a Tapuya (Tarairiu) man, a Tapuya woman, a Tupinambá man, a mestizo man, a mameluco woman, an African man, an African woman, and a Tapuya dance. Both Alexander von HUMBOLDT and Emperor Dom PEDRO II of Brazil enthu-

Tupi Woman and Child, by Albert Eckhout, 1641. THE NATIONAL MUSEUM OF DENMARK, DEPARTMENT OF ETHNOGRAPHY.

siastically praised these paintings when they visited Copenhagen in 1827 and 1876, respectively. Eckhout is credited by scholars with having created the best and most numerous portraits of Brazil's plants, birds, fish, reptiles, mammals, and peoples during the first three centuries of Europe's presence there.

The standard study on Eckhout is THOMAS THOMSEN, *Albert Eckhout, ein niederländischer Maler und sein Gönner Johan Maurits der Brasilianer: Ein Kulturbild aus dem 17. Jahrhundert* (1938). Valuable for its reproductions is CLARIVAL DO PRADO VALLADARES and LUIZ EMGYDIO DE MELLO FILHO, *Albert Eckhout: Pintor de Maurício de Nassau no Brasil 1637–1644* (1981). There are numerous other studies, but the most important in English are PETER J. P. WHITEHEAD and MARINUS BOESEMAN, *A Portrait of Dutch 17th Century Brazil: Animals, Plants, and People by the Artists of Johan Maurits of Nassau* (1989), and the chapter by R. JOPPIEN, "The Dutch Vision of Brazil: Johan Maurits and his Artists," in *Johan Maurits van Nassau-Siegen, 1604–1679,* edited by E. van den Boogart (1979).

FRANCIS A. DUTRA

ECONOMIC COMMISSION FOR LATIN AMERICA AND THE CARIBBEAN (ECLAC), one of five commissions created after World War II as part of resolution 106 adopted in 1948 by the Economic and Social Council (ECOSOC) of the United Nations. The original title was Economic Commission for Latin America; "and the Caribbean" was added in 1984. The body is also known by its Spanish acronym CEPAL (Comisión Económica para América Latina y el Caribe). ECLAC was created to study and find solutions to Latin American and Caribbean development problems, particularly those derived from the international economy, and to design common regional efforts that contribute to worldwide and economic progress. Latin American and Caribbean members include Antigua and Barbuda, Argentina, Bahamas, Barbados, Belize, Bolivia, Brazil, Chile, Colombia, Costa Rica, Cuba, Dominica, Dominican Republic, Ecuador, El Salvador, Grenada, Guatemala, Guyana, Haiti, Honduras, Jamaica, Mexico, Nicaragua, Panama, Paraguay, Peru, Saint Kitts and Nevis, Saint Vincent and the Grenadines, Saint Lucia, Suriname, Trinidad and Tobago, Uruguay, and Venezuela, with Aruba, British and U.S. Virgin Islands, Montserrat, Netherlands Antilles, and Puerto Rico as associate members. Canada, France, Italy (since 1990), the Netherlands, Portugal, Spain, the United Kingdom, and the United States are members from the industrialized world.

The executive secretariat of ECLAC is headquartered in Santiago, Chile, with subregional offices in Mexico and Port-of-Spain, Trinidad, as well as offices in Bogotá, Brasília, Buenos Aires, Montevideo, and Washington; it forms part of the Secretariat of the United Nations and includes the Latin American Institute for Economic and Social Planning (ILPES) and the Latin American Demographic Center (CELADE). The commission meets every two years.

Several prominent Latin American economists have served as executive secretary, including Gustavo Martínez Cabañas (Mexico) 1949–1950; Raúl PREBISCH (Argentina) 1950–1963; José Antonio Mayobre (Venezuela) 1963–1967; Carlos Quintana (Mexico) 1967–1972; Enrique Iglesias (Uruguay) 1972–1985; Norberto González (Argentina) 1985–1987; and Gert Rosenthal (Guatemala) since 1986.

Since its founding, ECLAC has distinguished itself through its advocacy of specific economic remedies, which have evolved in response to the changing circumstances of both the regional and world economy. For example, under the leadership of Prebisch, it recommended import substitution, planning, and economic integration as components of a strategy to overcome underdevelopment. Today, however, it supports a more integrated approach, whereby technical progress, international competitiveness, and social equity are all considered essential for the region's sustainable development.

GERT ROSENTHAL, "ECLAC: Forty Years of Continuity with Change," in *CEPAL Review,* no. 35 (August 1988): 7–12; PEDRO

CASTRO SUAREZ, *Teorías del desarrollo: Crítica a la teoría de la CEPAL* (1992); ENRIQUE IGLESIAS, ed., *The Legacy of Raúl Prebisch* (1994).

ISAAC COHEN

ECONOMIC DEVELOPMENT. Latin America, a mosaic of highly diverse nations in terms of income, population, geography, ethnic composition, and natural resources, opened up to the global exchange economy after the Wars of Independence of the early 1800s. This essay examines the salient characteristics of Latin American economic development from Independence to the 1990s. Before describing the broad contours of this development, the immense diversity of the hemisphere, with a population of 445 million in 1991, is highlighted.

From 1820 to the present, Latin America has been marked by significant economic diversity. At the one extreme are three large countries: Brazil, the industrial giant, with 150 million inhabitants (population figures are for 1990) and a gross domestic product (GDP) equal to 38.8 percent of the regional total (GDP figures are for 1980–1989); Mexico, with 89 million inhabitants and 20.2 percent of GDP; and Argentina, with 32 million and 11.5 percent of regional GDP. At the other extreme are sixteen small states (in terms of GDP and market size): Bahamas, Barbados, Bolivia, Costa Rica, Dominican Republic, El Salvador, Guatemala, Guyana, Haiti, Honduras, Jamaica, Nicaragua, Panama, Paraguay, Suriname, and Trinidad and Tobago, each accounting for less than 1 percent of regional GDP. An intermediate group, in terms of market size, includes Chile, with 3.2 percent of regional GDP, Colombia (4.8 percent), Ecuador (1.5 percent), Peru (4.0 percent), Uruguay (1.1 percent), and Venezuela (7.2 percent).

Diversity also characterizes other aspects of Latin American economic development. Illiteracy rates (figures are for 1990) are unusually high in Haiti (47 percent), Guatemala (44.9 percent), and El Salvador (27 percent). In contrast, they are extremely low in Argentina (4.7 percent), Chile (6.6 percent), Costa Rica (7.2 percent), Uruguay (3.8 percent), and Cuba (6.0 percent). Life expectancy at birth in 1987–1992 ranges from a high of 76 years in Cuba to a low of 60 years in Bolivia. Infant mortality rates per thousand live births in 1982–1992 vary measurably, being highest in Haiti (93 deaths) and lowest in Cuba (10.2 deaths). Finally, the average income in 1990 of $1,946 conceals major differences among countries. Per capita income is highest in the Bahamas ($9,902) and lowest in Haiti ($324), and it is significantly below average in Bolivia ($870) and close to or above average in Argentina ($2,623), Brazil ($2,169), and Mexico ($1,980).

FROM INDEPENDENCE TO THE GREAT DEPRESSION
Latin America has immense natural riches, yet its long-term growth, although significant and uneven, has not been spectacular. The 1820–1930 period, which coincides with the rise and fall of laissez-faire liberalism, was one of immense change and progress. Each phase (genesis, growth, maturity, fatigue, and collapse) revealed vital elements of continental evolution. The genesis of laissez-faire liberalism (1820–1860) opened a new era as colonial trade restrictions were abolished and freedom of trade was introduced. The period of growth (1860–1900) in trade, consumption, investment, immigration, and modernization marked the golden age of Latin American prosperity. Maturity (1900–1914) brought unprecedented, though not always harmonious, institutional innovation in labor and capital markets, education, transportation, health, welfare, and political ideologies. During the phase of fatigue (1914–1930), it became evident that in spite of a remarkable degree of institutional transformation and modernization, the pluralistic—that is, affecting differently the poor, the middle classes, the rich, indigenous populations, immigrant groups, and so forth—unequal, and even inequitable nature of laissez-faire liberalism had contributed to an economic structure that left much to be desired. The collapse (1930–1938) of laissez-faire liberalism was precipitated by the Great Depression of the 1930s. Not surprisingly, instead of solving the remaining problems through "better" government, after 1930 most countries adopted public policies involving "more" government intervention.

The rate of increase in per-capita income is determined by forces shaping the growth of gross domestic product, on the one hand, and population, on the other. On the demand side, the spectacular growth and remarkable instability of exports from Latin America, which were composed of "primary" (that is, agricultural and mineral) products, played a pivotal role in shaping welfare as the continent was increasingly incorporated into the global production and exchange structure. Growth was both export-led and trade-facilitated.

Although generally described as "primary," all exports are "composite," meaning that they embody value added by other goods and service sectors. Most primary products, however, have their origin in and most value added by agriculture or mining. They are primarily resource based, being either land intensive, as with coffee (Colombia, El Salvador, Brazil), bananas (Guatemala, Costa Rica, Nicaragua, Panama), cotton (Peru), sugar (Cuba), wheat and maize (Argentina), meat and wool (Uruguay), and cocoa (Ecuador), or they are depletable, natural-resource intensive, as with silver (Mexico), copper (Chile, Venezuela), petroleum (Venezuela, Mexico, Peru), nitrates (Chile), and tin (Bolivia). To a lesser degree, they are labor or capital intensive. These "primary" exports are exposed to extreme price, quantity, and revenue fluctuations, thereby imparting a high degree of instability on aggregate demand. Business cycles became an integral part of hemispheric growth between 1820 and 1930. Export bonanzas spread unprecedented prosperity, but they were invariably followed by sharp contractions, causing acute despair through income and employment declines, financial panics, foreign exchange crises, and public and foreign debt defaults.

Export instability was caused not only by business cycles in developed, importing nations of Europe and North America but also by input-substituting and raw materials–saving technological progress (nitrate, rubber) and physical exhaustion (guano, nitrate, gold, silver, tin). Excessive dependence on volatile, natural resource–based exports emerged by the early 1900s as a structural "trade defect" of the laissez-faire era and as a symptom of the corresponding fatigue.

In addition to exports, government and private consumption and investment played a significant role in economic growth. Production of government services, usually referred to as government consumption, as well as labor income in public administration and defense and the size of the public sector underwent multiple transformations. As power was violently transferred from Spain, Portugal, and France to the newly independent states, there was a long period (1810–1870) of internal conflicts followed by the consolidation of national states. Although Mexico's experience of social upheaval and extended civil conflict was particularly intense, much of Latin America experienced internal conflicts, boundary disputes, and political instability during this era. Furthermore, beginning with Independence, a tradition of dictatorial, authoritarian *caudillista* regimes initiated a pattern of production of government services (and their consumption by the public) that was neither democratic nor representative. With the crown and the *peninsulares* gone, the collective services of public administration and defense served the interests principally of the elites and oligarchies, and later also the burgeoning native and immigrant urban middle classes. The Indian and ex-slave populations were largely ignored.

The production of public services, which took off during the golden age of exports (1860–1930), displayed an elite bias, a foreign bias, a trade-tax bias, and a credit bias. These policy biases contributed to a slowdown in overall economic growth, perpetuation of deep income inequalities, and inadequate development of efficient markets. The elite bias, which has its roots in the violent Conquest and exploitative colonial heritage, fostered policies that were both unequal and inequitable. Collective services, which guarantee basic human, political, and economic rights, and semipublic services, such as education, health, and welfare, were produced preferentially for the elites and the middle and upper classes of European ancestry. In the cities, the general level of public services, which was never high, was unable to solve severe problems of overcrowding, contaminated water, and inadequate sanitation and lagged behind the rapid growth of population. The degree of inequality, pluralism—that is, unequal benefits for the poor, the middle class, and the rich—and discrimination in availability and access to collective services was far less pronounced in newly settled, ethnically homogeneous Argentina and Uruguay than in ethnically heteroge- neous Brazil, the Andean countries, and Mesoamerica.

The foreign bias, which was a consequence of preferential treatment of foreign entrepreneurs, capital, labor, and government, reflected a hemispheric desire for global integration and related policies designed to stimulate an influx of foreign resources. Finally, the biases of excessive government dependence on volatile trade taxes and foreign and internal credits, although they initially contributed only to periodic revenue shortfalls, ultimately were responsible, with rising expenditures, for the pernicious secular public-sector deficits and inflationary tendencies in the region. These trends were reinforced by the post-1900 incorporation into the public sector of inefficient, deficit-ridden railroad, public-utility, and other large enterprises.

Even though the pre-1930 period is described as one of laissez-faire or free-trade liberalism, actual policies enforced political and economic stability by utilizing limited resources to serve the middle- and upper-income elites that controlled power. Pre-1930 liberalism involved a combination of laissez-faire in the export arena and *caudillismo-caciquismo* in government expenditures and public policy.

The growth of aggregate and per-capita consumption, and thus welfare, was impressive, especially between 1870 and 1930. The golden age of exports gave rise to a golden age of consumption sustained through domestic production and imports. Per-capita consumption may have increased as much as 5 percent annually during periods of export bonanza, although this average masks the fact that most growth in consumption affected the privileged classes, including the immigrants, and was negligible for the poor and the social outcasts. Private consumption in the age of *caudillista* liberalism was plural—that is, plentiful for the privileged rich; minimal for the poor, disenfranchised masses; and adequate for the emerging middle classes— and inequitable. It generated a boom in all activities that are necessary to satisfy food, shelter, and clothing needs, as well as a burgeoning demand for education, health, transportation, welfare, and personal services.

Capital accumulation accelerated in quantity and in quality in export activities, transportation, industry, and the service sectors of the rapidly growing primary and secondary cities. Construction of railroads, schools, palaces, hospitals, opera and theater houses, mansions, and harbors was phenomenal. Capital accumulation improved the infrastructure, which in turn facilitated both exports and local production of consumer, intermediate, and capital goods. Savings were provided by local enterprises, well-to-do households, governments, and foreigners. These savings, which were mostly British before 1914 and from the United States after that, financed direct investment and purchases of Latin American private and public debt. A synchronous and quite phenomenal growth of national and foreign banks, insurance companies, and trading houses led to improvements in money and capital markets.

On the supply side, the abundance of land, natural resources, immigrant labor, and foreign resources was particularly significant, especially after 1860. Pre-1930 growth was as much supply-facilitated as it was demand- or export-propelled. Seen from a supply perspective, economic development was eminently "inward-oriented," as witnessed by the phenomenal and unparalleled inflow of immigrants, financial and real capital, technology, institutions, and ideas, all of which were directed toward satisfying rapidly expanding public and private consumption and investment needs.

By 1930 more than 4 million immigrants, three-quarters of them Spanish and Italian, had settled permanently in Argentina. The concentration was densest in the littoral provinces, especially the Federal District. Likewise, Uruguay, with 600,000 permanent settlers, and southern Brazil, with 2 million, became southern European provinces, in terms of ethnicity. Cuba and Chile also benefited from significant levels of immigration. Labor markets included temporary immigrants (*golondrinas*), permanent settlers, and pioneering entrepreneurs. Immigrants dominated the cities, labor, the entrepreneurial class, and most economic activity in Argentina and Uruguay. In the Andean countries and Mesoamerica, immigrants were a small but powerful minority.

Latin America experienced a continuous process of largely natural, spontaneous industrialization between 1820 and 1930. In addition to receiving a big push from the rise in exports, income, and urbanization, industry also benefited from high import duties, wars, and recurrent balance-of-payments and foreign-credit crises. By 1925, industrial employment reached 4.5 million, accounting for 12.9 percent of total employment (32 million) and 35.4 percent of nonagricultural employment (12.5 million). Of this, 74.3 percent was artisanal. Factory employment totaled 1.1 million and ranged from 40 percent of industrial employment in Argentina to only 7 percent in Peru.

Traditional, vertically integrated, rural hacienda and urban home-based production of industrial commodities was increasingly replaced by specialized urban artisanal and factory production. Specialization, division of labor, and easy access to imported intermediate goods (raw materials) as well as capital goods and technology facilitated rapid growth in traditional textiles, food, beverages, tobacco, footwear, leather, wood, furniture, paper, and printing as well as in modern chemical, petroleum, nonmetallic ore, basic metal, and metal-transforming industrial production.

The agricultural bonanza; rapid development of the infrastructure; immigration of skilled laborers, managers, and entrepreneurs; and abundant foreign capital facilitated the early establishment in Argentina of a prosperous consumer, intermediate (used up in production of final consumer and capital goods), and capital-goods industrial sector. Processing of agricultural and mineral products for export and domestic consumption also led to the establishment of dynamic manufacturing nuclei in Cuba (sugar mills), Uruguay (packing plants, tanneries, woolen textiles), Chile (ore-dressing plants), Mexico (steel after 1903, textiles), and elsewhere. Growth of Brazil's industrial sector, the largest in Latin America with 1.2 million employed in 1930, concentrated in the Rio–São Paulo region, was facilitated by the export boom, urbanization, immigration, and financial development.

Even though industrial production flourished before 1930, especially in Argentina, Brazil, and Mexico and to a lesser extent in Colombia, Peru, and Chile, final consumption of industrial commodities remained highly concentrated. Industry largely catered to the affluent middle- and upper-income strata. Furthermore, with the possible exceptions of Argentina and Uruguay, the interaction mechanisms between industry and agriculture, education, health, transportation, finance, and commerce remained weak, unequal, and pluralistic. The splintered nature of the continental market hindered regional integration, unification, and cooperation, and thereby perpetuated dependence on imports such as iron and steel, which were necessary during the vast expansion of railroads.

In addition to industry, service activities and the demand for education, health, transportation, and personal services rose continuously. In 1925 approximately 8 million Latin Americans were employed in activities other than agriculture and industry, that is, primarily in services. Thus, even before 1930, urban Latin America contained a highly prosperous amalgam of modern commerce, transportation, communications, and finance and traditional personal, housing, and government services.

Rural employment, however, which absorbed 20 million people in 1925, remained dominant. In Argentina, Brazil, Uruguay, and Chile, especially, European immigrants entered the cities on the way to the rural countryside where they were settling. Pre-1930 urbanization was reinforced both by foreign immigrants and, especially after 1900, by a population exodus from rural areas.

A fatigue with laissez-faire liberalism gradually spread throughout Latin America after 1914, generated by pervasive inequalities and debilitating biases in government and private consumption, tangible and intangible investment, and the underlying *caudillista* mesoeconomic—that is, sectoral, group-based and -oriented, and semiaggregate—policies in education, health, transportation, agriculture, and even industry. Among the most prominent symptoms of fatigue were a slowdown in growth; unstable capital and foreign-exchange markets; separate and unequal markets, in terms of income and productivity, for skilled and unskilled labor; rising xenophobic sentiments; and gaping inequalities. These developments gave rise to rising skepticism and even animosity toward free and competitive markets and trade, private property and enterprise, and foreign capital. This in turn led to a contagious enthusiasm for nationalistic, statist, protectionist economic planning. The full magnitude of the fatigue with classical liberalism—largely induced by defective mesoeconomic policies—was concealed by export prosperity and limited natural population growth among the poor but then fully exposed by the Great Depression of the early 1930s.

FROM THE DEPRESSION TO THE PRESENT

The periods before and after 1930 contained fundamental similarities as well as differences in the nature of economic growth; that is, there was continuity as well as change.

The Great Depression of the 1930s led to the collapse of laissez-faire, free-trade liberalism and contributed to the genesis of structuralism. Structuralism marked a radically new phase of development as protection from imports replaced free trade. The government itself came to supplement and even replace private enterprise as producer and owner. Planning, regulation, and intervention superseded free and competitive national and international markets. Domestic production of previously imported commodities, generally described as import-substitution industrialization, emerged as inward orientation replaced the pre-1930 outward orientation of reliance on foreign trade, imports, and external forces. Structuralism, which evolved through the not always easily distinguishable phases of genesis (1930–1935), recovery (1935–1950), maturity (1950–1955), fatigue (1955–1980), and collapse (1980–1990), arrived and departed at different times and with unequal degrees of intensity in different countries.

Structuralism was born amid the cataclysmic collapse of export demand, imports, and capital inflows; the end of large-scale immigration; and widespread unemployment and unused capacity, which forced governments to implement deficit-spending fiscal policies. Furthermore, Latin America began to assemble an elaborate institutional apparatus of foreign exchange, import and price controls, development corporations and institutes, state-owned banking and other financial institutions, and social-security agencies as it embarked on a process of government-sponsored, artificial import-substituting industrialization. Even though laissez-faire trade policies were swept aside, the inherited pluralistic, inequitable *caudillista-caciquista* economic edifice was left almost intact.

The recovery to pre-1930 income levels (1935–1950) was facilitated by import difficulties during World War II and subsequent use of foreign exchange reserves accumulated during the war to augment necessary imports. As government ownership, intervention, and industrial promotion gained momentum, inflationary pressures, balance-of-payments disequilibria, and shortages in food, clothing, and other products became endemic. Persistent attacks against private property and enterprise, free-market forces, and trade created an environment that led to increasing displacement of natural, market-determined growth by artificial, government-directed growth. Government-sponsored modern enclaves arose in manufacturing and formal urban services. *Caudillista-caciquista* structuralism was born.

Increasingly, the call for "economic independence" accelerated the drive for import-substituting industrialization. The goals of price stability, balance-of-payments equilibrium, equitable distribution of income, and efficient utilization of resources were neglected, even abandoned, as excessive planning took hold of much of the continent (1950–1955). Mesoeconomic policies promoting large-scale, capital-intensive, state-owned industries led often to phenomenal increases in output but failed to generate those relative increases in industrial employment needed to remove poverty. A structuralist malaise set in as a result of discriminatory agricultural, financial, and trade policies, and of pluralistic health, education, welfare, transportation, and other mesoeconomic policies. Structuralism gave birth to a diverse interventionist state that solidified the inequitable, *caudillista* economic edifice. In the opinion of some, it unleashed conflicts that, instead of healing old wounds, increased the cleavages between nonwhites and whites, industry and agriculture, rural and urban, "haves" and "have nots."

In spite of considerable sustained growth, especially in Mexico and Brazil, a structuralist fatigue arose throughout the region between 1955 and 1980. This fatigue was the consequence of accelerated income growth that coincided with, and was marred by, rising budget deficits, severe sectoral imbalances, disintegration of money and capital markets, capital flight, two oil shocks, accelerating inflation, and falling economic independence. The increasingly complex network of interventionist institutions that embodied structuralist biases against free trade, markets, prices, and private enterprise and initiative gave rise to a host of nationalist, populist, and statist proposals. As Marxism, structuralism, populism, and dependency theories were gradually discredited by stagnation, hyperinflation, and political, economic and social chaos, the pendulum swung toward structural liberalism, or neoliberalism. Widespread institutional disintegration added to the fatigue of the 1960s, 1970s, and 1980s. It precipitated the celebrated shift to a neoliberalism based on freedom, equality, and cooperation.

Neoliberalism was first implemented in Chile after the fall of Salvador Allende's regime in 1973. It then spread during 1975–1993 to Uruguay, Argentina, Mexico, Brazil, Venezuela, and other countries.

Overshadowing, in terms of continuity and strength, these structuralist phases and their respective strategies, was the post-1930 population explosion. Propelled by stable fertility and sharply declining mortality rates, this growth differed from the immigration-induced population growth of the pre-1930 period. Immigration, which had been stimulated by impressive economic growth, came to a halt as exports, income, and output collapsed. It was replaced by an autonomous increase in population caused more by medical advances that reduced

Oil workers assembling pipes. Arauca, Colombia, 1988. PHOTO BY VICTOR ENGLEBERT.

mortality rates than by increases in income—even though these were generally significant between 1939 and 1980. Almost explosive population increases in excess of 3 percent annually occurred in Colombia (1960–1971), Costa Rica (1960–1970), Dominican Republic (1970–1982), Ecuador (1960–1981), El Salvador (1960–1982), Guatemala (1960–1982), Honduras (1960–1982), Mexico (1960–1982), Nicaragua (1960–1991), Paraguay (1971–1980), and Venezuela (1960–1982). Annual population growth exceeded 2.5 percent from 1960 to 1980, when it began a gradual decline. Only in Argentina, Barbados, Guyana, Haiti, Jamaica, Trinidad and Tobago, and Uruguay did population growth rates stay below 1.7 percent annually during 1960–1990. This population growth, which further encouraged rural to urban migration, was most pronounced among the poor, and it put enormous pressure on urban and rural infrastructures and on the supply of basic educational, water, sewage, electrical, health, and welfare services.

The Evolution of Production On the demand side, the importance of exports declined during the structuralist period. The forces behind this shift in aggregate demand also underwent a significant transformation. Be-

fore 1930 the natural forces of free global markets and competition largely determined the level, composition, rate of growth, and oscillations in aggregate demand and its export, public- and private-consumption, and private-investment components. From 1930 until the advent of structural liberalism (neoliberalism) the level and composition of aggregate demand were increasingly determined artificially by governmental actions shaping both domestic and external exchange relationships.

Latin America remained an important but declining global trading partner. When exports faced discrimination, all economic activities that added value to "composite export products" were also penalized. Imports confronted import quotas, multiple exchange rates, tariffs, and outright prohibitions.

Following their cyclical collapse during the Great Depression, both consumption and investment grew significantly until approximately 1980. Government consumption, expenditures, and the size of the public sector, all of which grew continuously under structuralism, underwent radically new transformations. Production of collective services showed strong protectionist, nationalistic, populist, and statist biases. In addition, government expanded its role in producing semipublic services and aggressively complementing or displacing private enterprise in the production of private commodities.

Furthermore, as revenues from export and import taxes and foreign capital inflows declined, government expenditures were financed by direct and indirect domestic taxes and, increasingly, by inflationary credit. This credit dependence established an inflationary bias of major, and in the 1980s catastrophic, proportions. The postindependence era of spectacular, though often cyclical growth in overall government consumption largely bypassed and ignored the Indians, blacks, and other residents of urban slums and the rural hinterland.

The rate of increase in private consumption of industrial, agricultural, and service composite commodities between 1935 and 1980 was significant. In some countries and during some periods it was phenomenal. Real per-capita consumption grew by 1.9 percent annually in 1961–1970 and by 3.4 percent in 1971–1980. It declined, however, during 1981–1990 at an annual rate of 1.1 percent. From 1971 to 1980 the annual rate of growth of real per-capita consumption was 5.6 percent in Brazil, 3.1 percent in Mexico, 5.0 percent in Ecuador, and 6.8 percent in Venezuela.

The level of, as well as the rate of increase, in private consumption was unequal, segmented, and pluralistic in most of Latin America. Rates of increase in consumption by the privileged upper- and middle-income groups may have been twice as high as the average figures cited above. In many countries the poorest households experienced negligible improvements in consumption and welfare. As the ECONOMIC COMMISSION FOR LATIN AMERICA (ECLA) pointed out in 1966, "one-half of the Latin American population—mainly the inhabitants of rural areas—absorbs less than 10 percent of the total available supply of manufactured products other than food." Furthermore, "in the higher income brackets *per capita* consumption of manufactures other than food would seem to be 8 times that of the middle income group and 48 times that of the lowest stratum" (*The Process of Industrial Development in Latin America*, pp. 123–124).

The enormous consumption inequalities between urban and rural areas and between rich, middle-class, and poor households, which characterized laissez-faire liberalism, persisted during the 1930–1980 period of artificial, government-sponsored, import substitution. As export surpluses evaporated, upper- and middle-income groups sustained their income and welfare levels through increased domestic production of composite commodities and policies that perpetuated their historically high shares in income and output. Much of the increased production of consumer commodities after 1930 was appropriated by the middle and upper classes (that is, the top 20–40 percent of households) while the bottom 40 percent (and as much as 60 percent in Bolivia and Guatemala) benefited very little from the prosperity induced by artificial industrialization. A fierce competition over sharing in consumption emerged not only between the rich and poor, but also among the rich. As middle and upper classes attempted to increase their private consumption, they often relied on competitive borrowing. With capital markets unable to accommodate the rising demand for credit by government and private households for consumption and by producers for investment purposes, an inflationary spiral was initiated in the 1940s that accelerated in the 1950s, 1960s, and 1970s and exploded to uncontrollable, destructive heights in the 1980s. Inflation, rather than serving as a safety valve, became a measure and expression of a process of disintegration and destruction.

"Inward-oriented" import-substituting industrialization policies profoundly changed Latin America's production structure. Especially in Brazil and Mexico, but also in medium-sized countries, the quantity, variety, and quality of consumer commodities produced experienced phenomenal increases. Furthermore, large complexes producing capital goods emerged in Brazil, Mexico, and Argentina.

Total hemispheric employment increased between 1925 and 1960 by 35.7 million persons. Of these, 12.2 million were absorbed by agricultural and 23.5 million by nonagricultural activities. The increase in industrial employment amounted to 5.3 million. Other urban activities, primarily services, absorbed 18.2 million. According to the ECLA, "one of the outstanding features of industrialization in Latin America is a marked failure to contribute sufficient employment to permit the absorption of the rapidly growing labour force" (p. 38). A takeoff in industrial employment failed to materialize. Latin America experienced rapid urbanization, service expansion, rural to urban migration, and even industrial-output growth, but not self-sustaining economic development.

Capital accumulation made significant but not always sustained strides. Highly advanced and diversified capital-goods sectors in Brazil and Mexico permitted them to catch up with Argentina. Capital formation suffered under structuralist policies of protection in medium and small countries as discrimination of the quasi-capital-goods export sector and an increased demand for imported capital goods led to severe foreign exchange shortages. Throughout much of Latin America, investment in inward-oriented industry and ancillary activities absorbed the lion's share of savings. The post-1973 petroleum-income bonanza greatly stimulated investment in Venezuela, Mexico, Ecuador, and Peru but derailed the secular growth of Brazil and other oil-importing countries. Furthermore, the first and second oil shocks caused a hemispheric capital flight of approximately $500 billion, which severely depleted investable resources. As investment was increasingly carried out by the public sector and financed by central-bank credit, inflation skyrocketed, reaching a rate of 1,186.3 percent in 1990. However, physical and human capital formation benefited almost exclusively the upper- and middle-income groups. Capital formation shaped overall prosperity but failed to allay poverty, inequality, and inequity.

Chaotic inflationary conditions in Chile, Brazil, Bolivia, Argentina, and Peru led to an abandonment of structuralist planning and the introduction of neoconservative policies of market deregulation, price stabilization, trade liberalization, and privatization of state enterprises beginning in the 1970s. As fiscal and monetary stability was restored, Latin America entered the 1990s experiencing phenomenal capital inflows and rising investment, income, industrial exports, and intraregional trade. However, Latin America is as economically divided today as it was at Independence or at the apogee of laissez-faire liberalism.

Rural Development and Land Reform According to structuralist theory, the perennial food deficit and rigidities in agricultural supplies were caused by the *latifundio-minifundio* land-tenure system. The strategy proposed to cure this agricultural structural defect was land reform. Incorporation of land into production through new settlements made a significant contribution to the output of agriculture until approximately 1940. With the collapse of exports in the 1930s, the exhaustion of new land, and the rise of urban middle classes, policymakers became concerned with the twin problems of food shortages and persistent rural poverty and inequality within the land-tenure structure.

During the age of structuralism, welfare of the rural population was shaped by two distinct, even opposite, trends. One school of thought argues that in some countries, on the one hand, as industry and the urban population attempted to maintain their income by increasing their share whenever gross domestic product shrank or remained static, agriculture and the rural hinterland were victimized through discriminatory price, credit, education, health, and other policies. As the pre-1930 export surpluses evaporated, rural agriculture was forced to transfer part of its income to the urban masses in Argentina, Chile, and elsewhere. On the other hand, with political power shifting from the shrinking rural population and the *latifundista* oligarchy to the growing urban population, middle classes, and industrial interests, demand for land tenure reform spread throughout Latin America. Structuralism aimed at redistributing power and resources from rural to urban regions and from the *latifundistas* to the peasantry.

The oldest and most extensive uncompensated land-tenure reform was implemented in Mexico. The resulting EJIDO system, which established plots of land under public title, was embodied in the 1917 Constitution. The reform was carried out, however, primarily in the 1930s under the CÁRDENAS administration. Mexico's rapidly modernizing, large-scale commercial farming, which was not reformed, has been dynamic and export oriented, while the *ejido,* which accounted for 69 percent of rural households in 1971, and non-*ejido* peasant farms have remained backward. Absence of title to the land, inadequate integration into the marketplace, small size, poor land quality, and inadequate credit have restricted rapid growth of output, productivity, and income of the *ejidos.* In spite of the relative backwardness of noncommercial farming, Mexican land reform, which improved the welfare of the rural population, did not significantly offset the overall impressive long-term growth in agricultural output and productivity.

A comprehensive land reform was implemented in Bolivia in the aftermath of the revolution of 1952. Semifeudal, inefficient haciendas, which encompassed entire indigenous communities, were expropriated. Eighty percent of the land was redistributed to the peasants, who had previously worked the land as small-scale producers, through allocation of individual property rights. The beneficiaries, who made up 50 percent of the rural population, increased output, efficiency, and productivity and gradually transformed previously discriminatory government policies in education, credit, transportation, and health. They also diversified into more lucrative coca production.

Land-tenure reform accelerated in the 1960s when it was advocated by the Alliance for Progress in an effort to contain the advance of Marxism. Concurrently, structuralists, dependency theorists, Marxists, and populists promoted land-tenure reform as a means of depriving landed oligarchies of their obstructive political power and of augmenting agricultural output through more efficient utilization of land, and as a necessary first step in improving the welfare of the peasantry.

Land-tenure reform spread to much of Latin America in the 1960s: Venezuela (1960); Colombia and Costa Rica (1961); Chile, Dominican Republic, and Honduras (1962); Peru (1963); Ecuador (1964); and Panama (1968). Radical land expropriation efforts began in Cuba in 1959, continued in Allende's Chile in 1970, and accelerated in Nicaragua following the Sandinista overthrow of the Somoza dynasty in 1979. Reform involving collective farming was implemented on sugar plantations in Cuba, Nicaragua, and Peru. The most common land reform involved the breakup of large estates into individual holdings, which represents the Bolivian experience, and conversion into cooperative farming. Organization of production in state farms emerged under the Marxist regimes in Cuba and Nicaragua.

Land reform in Peru was carried out in the coastal and highland regions, but not in the tropical forests. In 1969 the military government of Juan VELASCO ALVA-RADO started expropriating the most profitable coastal plantations producing sugar, cotton, rice, and corn. They were turned over in their entirety to workers for collective management. Beginning in 1981 the expropriated plantations were subdivided into individual holdings. Peasant resistance in the highlands against establishment of collective farms turned reform toward subdivision. The unfortunate coincidence of disastrous price, trade, financial, health, and fiscal policies contributed to the chaos and disintegration that gripped rural and urban Peru beginning in the late 1980s.

Along with structuralism, land reform lost its appeal because it failed to cure rural Latin America's seemingly intractable ailments of widespread poverty, plural—that is, unequal and separate—labor markets, pervasive income inequality, shrinking agricultural surpluses, low productivity, unrest, and violence. Many have concluded that only a composite rural-development strategy involving free and competitive markets; respect of property rights; natural changes in land tenure; and cooperative, progressive, rural-friendly governments will lead to integrated rural prosperity.

The annual reports on *Economic and Social Progress in Latin America* published by the Inter-American Development Bank provide detailed regional and country overviews and statistical information. The United Nations, its Economic Commission for Latin America and the Caribbean, and the World Bank annually publish numerous survey studies on Latin America. The most comprehensive analysis of the industrial sector up to 1965 is found in UNITED NATIONS, ECONOMIC COMMISSION FOR LATIN AMERICA, *The Process of Industrial Development in Latin America* (1966).

Valuable historiographical survey essays on Central and South America are in *The Cambridge History of Latin America*, edited by Leslie Bethell, 8 vols. (1984–1991). These essays contain comprehensive bibliographies.

Excellent reviews of long-term growth in Argentina, Brazil, Chile, Colombia, Cuba, Mexico, Peru, and Venezuela are found in LLOYD G. REYNOLDS, *Economic Growth in the Third World, 1850–1980* (1985).

Long-term, comprehensive analyses and quantitative information on individual countries are: CARLOS DÍAZ-ALEJANDRO, *Essays on the Economic History of the Argentine Republic* (1970); CELSO FURTADO, *The Economic Growth of Brazil* (1963); WERNER BAER, *Industrialization and Economic Development in Brazil* (1965) and *The Brazilian Economy: Growth and Development* (1983); MARKOS MAMALAKIS, *The Growth and Structure of the Chilean Economy: From Independence to Allende* (1976), *Historical Statistics of Chile*, 6 vols. (1978–1989), and, with CLARK REYNOLDS, *Essays on the Chilean Economy* (1965); CLARK W. REYNOLDS, *The Mexican Economy: Twentieth-Century Structure and Growth* (1970); and MATS LUNDAHL, *Peasants and Poverty: A Study of Haiti* (1979).

Comprehensive statistics in respect to income and employment trends by sector between 1950 and 1970 are in MARKOS MAMALAKIS, "Urbanization and Sectoral Transformation in Latin America, 1950–65," *Actas y Memorias del XXXIX Congreso Internacional de Americanistas* (*Lima, 2–9 de agosto de 1970*): *El Proceso de urbanización en América desde sus orígenes hasta nuestros días* (1972), and "Urbanización y transformaciones sectoriales en Latinoamérica (1950–1970): Antecedentes e implicaciones para una reforma urbana," in *Asentamientos urbanos y organización socioproductiva en la historia de América Latina*, compiled by Jorge E. Hardoy and Richard P. Schaedel (1977).

The notion of mesoeconomics is defined and used in MARKOS MAMALAKIS, "Sectoral Clashes, Basic Economic Rights, and Redemocratization in Chile: A Mesoeconomic Approach," in *Ibero-Americana, Nordic Journal of Latin American Studies* 22, no. 1 (1992), and "Sectoral Conflicts in the U.S. and the Soviet

Union: A Mesoeconomic Analysis," in *Eastern Economic Journal* 18, no. 4 (1992).

MARKOS MAMALAKIS

See also **Agriculture; Foreign Investment; Foreign Trade; Industrialization; Informal Economy; Privatization; Taxation.**

ECONOMIC DEVELOPMENT, THEORIES OF. This essay summarizes the orthodox, Marxist, structuralist (including dependency), structuralist liberal (including monetarist), and sectoral-clash theories of Latin American economic development. Each has made a unique contribution to shaping or explaining the Latin American paradigm.

ORTHODOX ECONOMIC THEORY

Among the many contributions of orthodox economics are the theories of Adam Smith, John Maynard Keynes, Robert Malthus, and David Ricardo. These theories, summarized below, have been singularly relevant to Latin America.

The theories of Adam Smith (1723–1790), author of *Wealth of Nations* (1776) and founder of economics, greatly influenced Latin American economic development theory during the age of laissez-faire (1860–1930) and neoliberalism (1973–). According to Smith, if individuals were left alone to pursue their self-interests, their behavior, as if guided by an "invisible hand," would maximize the welfare of their society. Furthermore, expansion of market size through free trade and minimal government intervention (laissez-faire) would increase productivity and income. Division of labor into specialized tasks would permit rapid technological progress and capital accumulation. According to Smith's law of absolute advantage, Latin America could benefit from engaging in trade by specializing in products which it could produce more efficiently than developed countries, such as agricultural and mineral products.

Mainstream economic theory based on these ideas has attributed rapid income growth during the 1870–1930 golden age of exports to the full incorporation of Latin America into the global production and exchange system. In this view, expansion in aggregate demand and its export component were matched by increases in the supply of natural resources, including land, labor (especially immigrant), and national and foreign capital. Free trade stimulated investment as well as the efficient allocation of resources. Access to vast global markets led to unprecedented increases in productivity, wages and real income through specialization in production, division of labor, rapid capital accumulation, and technological progress.

Latin American economic development has also been profoundly affected by the theories of John Maynard Keynes (1883–1946). Author of the classic work *The Gen-*

eral Theory of Employment, Interest, and Money (1936), Keynes established the macro approach to economic analysis. This emphasized the role of such aggregate variables as consumption, investment, saving, and government expenditure in the generation of income and employment. Especially during the Great Depression of the 1930s but also during subsequent cyclical downturns, Latin American governments have relied on government deficit spending, the favorite Keynesian tool for generating full employment and stimulating growth. The subordination of monetary to fiscal policy, which dominated much of Latin American economic policy from 1930 to 1990, reflected ideas advanced by Keynes. The heavy reliance on deficit spending and the ensuing uncontrolled inflation, which characterized most Latin American economic development from the 1960s to the 1980s, can be seen as governmental loss of control over the fiscal and monetary tools advocated by Keynes.

Latin America failed to sustain its pre-1930 prosperity because of the adoption of inward-oriented economic policies that violated the comparative advantage and exportable surplus (vent for surplus) principles of international trade and the marginalist rules of an efficient allocation of resources. When regional ties to global markets were cut off by industrialization strategies of import substitution, it became difficult to achieve specialization, division of labor, and the reduction of production costs owing to greater output (increasing returns to scale). Furthermore, according to orthodox economics, increasing ownership and market intervention by government created unprecedented distortions, allocational inefficiencies, inequality, and, ultimately, stagnation through price controls, barriers to trade, stifling bureaucracy, and massive budget deficits.

The views of Robert Malthus (1766–1834) on population have also found some support as an explanation of Latin American economic development. Malthus argued that economies ultimately suffer from stagnation because population grows at a geometric progression (2, 4, 8, 16, 32, 64) while natural resources and the food supply grow only at an arithmetic progression (2, 4, 6, 8, 10, 12). This principle gained particular relevance in explaining the post-1930 experience, which saw economic growth, but frequently at a rate below population growth. The net result, in this view, was economic growth plus increasing inequality.

Malthusians also attach great significance to the different levels of population growth among the rich and poor. Population growth has been highest among the poorest sectors, which tend to live outside the formal economy and are often indigent. But contrary to the theories of Malthus, low productivity and income among the poor cannot be attributed to overall scarcity of natural resources, including land, and to inadequate supplies of food. Instead, poverty persists among plenty because these households face formidable artificial mesoeconomic—that is, sectoral, group-based and -oriented—institutional barriers that limit their access to the continent's abundant natural resources and to the food, shelter, education, health, and other commodities produced with their help. Mesoeconomic—that is, agricultural, industrial, and service—growth has been too sluggish to significantly reduce poverty. Furthermore, mesoeconomic, that is, sectoral, constitutions (sets of rules) in education and health have favored the middle- and upper-income households, thus perpetuating inequality. Remedial strategies include population control, to which many in Latin America object, and removal of barriers to mobility through improved access to health, education, and government-sponsored self-help programs.

At the other extreme, population growth has been slow and, thus, of little consequence among the rich. With income growth disproportionately benefiting the middle- and upper-income groups, distributional inequality has been solidified.

The theory of comparative advantage developed by David Ricardo (1772–1823), an English classical economist, has also influenced economic policy, especially during the age of structural liberalism (1973–). According to his law of comparative advantage, if England can produce both cloth and wheat more efficiently than Argentina but can produce cloth more efficiently than wheat, then England should specialize in the production of cloth, in which it is most efficient, and leave the production of wheat to Argentina. Then, by engaging in trade, England and Argentina would have more of both cloth and wheat.

The late-twentieth-century wave of free trade agreements implemented in Latin America reflects the lasting appeal of Ricardo's ideas. The North American Free Trade Agreement (NAFTA) between Mexico, Canada, and the United States, which was implemented on 1 January 1994, provided the nucleus of a free trade system that most Latin American nations aspired to join. Numerous subregional agreements were in operation in the 1990s, and a free trade area consisting of the entire Western Hemisphere was viewed as a possibility. However, both during the pre-1930 age of laissez-faire and the post-1973 era of structural liberalism, expansion of free trade on the basis of absolute and comparative advantage has failed to equalize incomes and significantly reduce poverty and inequality. The failure of the pre-1930 laissez-faire policies to lead to rapid growth, modernization, democratization of government, economic stability, and improved distribution of income gave rise to the laissez-faire fatigue of the 1920s and its rejection in the 1930s.

MARXISM

Marxism represents a unique ideology both in terms of the diagnosis it offers and in its revolutionary strategy for overcoming Latin American underdevelopment. Marxists argue that underdevelopment, poverty, and stagnation are the direct consequence of exploitation of labor by monopoly capital. Class struggle, they contend, has dominated Latin American economic development, with global, regional, and national repercussions. The orthodox Marxist view envisages a class struggle primarily between industrial capitalists and the proletariat in advanced stages of development. In Latin America, however, Marxism has developed a basic regional version emphasizing a different form of class struggle, which focuses on a rural struggle between the landowning capitalist class (*latifundistas*) and a peasant "proletariat" consisting of landless workers and small landowners (*minifundistas*). Stagnation prevails because the landowning class transfers its earnings to the cities or abroad rather than reinvesting them in rural modernization programs that could benefit the poor. These Marxists propose a radical land reform aimed at expropriating private landholdings and destroying the power of the landowning class. Such radical land-reform strategies have been implemented in Cuba under Fidel Castro, in Chile under Salvador Allende, and in Nicaragua under the Sandinistas. This Marxist rural-exploitation theme has enjoyed significant appeal among the rural poor.

Latin American Marxists also argue that another aspect of class struggle has been the presence of foreign-owned enclaves producing mineral or agricultural products for export. This struggle has touched nitrate and oil fields; copper, tin, silver, and gold mines; coffee, banana, sugar, and cotton plantations; and cattle ranches. Foreign capitalists exploit these quasi-colonies by repatriating profits and paying subsistence wages to local laborers. This system, it is argued, condemns Latin America to the paralysis of underdevelopment and exploitative dependence on foreign capital, labor, technology, and markets, which must be eliminated by nationalization of natural resources by the state. According to many Marxists, only expulsion of foreigners, as in Castro's Cuba or Allende's Chile, can put Latin America's fabulous natural resources to the service of the Latin American people. Foreign, private ownership, which Marxists consider as a second, major factor responsible for underdevelopment, can be exorcised only through confiscation and excision. In practice, widespread populist, nationalist, and statist antiforeign and anticapitalist sentiment in much of Latin America has to varying degrees provided fertile ground for adoption, if not of the whole package of Marxism and socialism, then at least its strategy of state ownership and exploitation of mineral resources, even by virulently anti-Communist regimes. In 1937 Standard Oil Company of Bolivia became the first major North American company in Latin America to be nationalized. President Lázaro CÁRDENAS nationalized the entire oil industry through the famous expropriation decrees of 18 March 1938. Venezuela nationalized its entire oil industry in 1975.

Most Marxists further contend that "unequal exchange" between labor and capital and ruthless exploitation of labor are facilitated by monopolistic, largely foreign-owned financial capital, which caters to the needs of capitalists in both the goods (industrial, mining, agricultural) and service (trade, transportation, health, information, communication) sectors. Nationalization and state ownership and control of the financial sector and capital markets are seen as means to destroy monopoly financial capitalism and end labor exploitation. Similar arguments are advanced with respect to class struggle in industry, public utilities, and urban services.

With the sudden collapse of the Soviet Union and the severe problems faced by the Cuban experiment, the appeal of Marxism has suffered a precipitous decline.

STRUCTURALISM

The structuralist school is most closely associated with the economic development ideologies of Raúl PREBISCH, one of the most prolific and innovative economic thinkers and public servants of the twentieth century in Latin America. It was given significant institutional credibility by the ECONOMIC COMMISSION FOR LATIN AMERICA (ECLA), which was established by the United Nations. Prebisch was the first director of the ECLA. (The name was later changed to the Economic Commission for Latin America and the Caribbean [ECLAC].) Other structuralist thinkers include Celso FURTADO (Brazil), Aníbal PINTO (Chile), and Juan Noyola (Mexico).

Prebisch argued that the world is divided into the "center," which is industrial, rich, dynamic, technologically advanced, homogeneous, unionized, and an exporter of industrial goods, and the "periphery," which is agricultural, poor, backward, heterogeneous, an exporter of primary commodities, with an abundant, nonunionized supply of unskilled labor. (Hans Singer developed, independently, the same theme.)

Within this center-periphery framework, structuralism maintains that the responsibility for the underdevelopment of the periphery rests squarely on the shoulders of the center. External rather than internal forces controlling the destiny of the region have resulted in persistent backwardness. The Latin American periphery has suffered from deteriorating terms of trade, in which the region's primary exports, for which demand is limited, contend with industrial exports from the center, for which demand is unlimited, leading to a perniciously unequal exchange relationship.

Adoration and glorification of industry form a second critical pillar of structuralism. Structuralist industrialization, however, differs from the natural, free, and outward-oriented industrialization of Adam Smith, promoting instead import-substituting industrialization, i.e., local production of otherwise-imported products.

Structuralists look to the state to defend and promote the neglected interest of the periphery by not only providing services but also becoming a producer of private commodities. The state would assure an abundant supply of food by carrying out land-tenure reform. It was expected to overcome the government's excessive dependence on export and import taxes through revenues from income taxes and surpluses of successful state enterprises. It would cure the problems of low rates of saving and conspicuous consumption through high public-sector saving. It would replace the unreliable and defective free-market exchange and allocation mechanism with a system of government controls and planning. And it would fill the alleged gap in private, national entrepreneurship, initiative, and risk taking through creation, management, and ownership of technologically advanced enterprises.

Structuralism is a "supply-side" ideology. Unlike the classical theory, which emphasizes such macroeconomic variables and defects as low savings due to low profits and diminishing returns on land, the structuralist supply-side economics are mesoeconomic, i.e., sectoral, in nature. It identifies three critical supply-side defects. First is that of "trade rigidity," which gives rise to the export-based import rigidity, i.e., inadequate exports as well as imports, and the foreign-exchange constraint, i.e., a shortage of foreign currency. Second is the "food-deficit defect," which results from an agricultural supply rigidity, i.e., inadequate supply of food, caused by the *latifundio-minifundio* land-tenure system. And third is the "industrialization defect." Industrialization under high protectionist walls is necessary but also inefficient, pushing up costs and creating rigidities throughout the economy, i.e., universal product shortages.

Structuralism, by emphasizing supply-side factors, offers an alternative to the monetarist explanation of inflation. It sees the money supply, without which inflation cannot materialize, as merely a veil. Structuralists explain inflation in terms of the underlying factors that lead to money-supply increases. These, which are structural in nature, include the export, saving, agricultural, tax revenue, and industrial-supply rigidities. Inflation occurs because monetary authorities, in an effort to prevent stagnation and unemployment, accommodate the cost-induced price increases by augmenting the supply of money.

Structuralism has undergone a variety of transformations, but two major strands are discernible. The first proposes policies of limited protection, mild inflation, selective government promotion of industry, and cooperation with capitalists, a strategy that governments adopted in the depths of the Great Depression of the 1930s. The second strand embraces increased planning, widely expanded state ownership, radical government intervention in markets, and increased use of inflationary central-bank credit. This approach was implemented in Peru under Juan Velasco (1968–1975) and Alan García (1985–1990), in Chile under Salvador Allende (1970–1973), and in Nicaragua under Daniel Ortega and the Sandinistas (1979–1990), demonstrating its partial compatibility with Marxism.

Early, mild structuralism, implemented before Prebisch's ideology was formulated in the 1940s, emerged in response to the fatigue with laissez-faire policies that spread after 1900 and especially during the Great Depression. De facto structuralism grew out of the unprecedented shock of complete export collapse in the 1930s and the effort, albeit aborted, to catch up with the North American and European giants of the center. After giving rise to significant growth, especially in industrial output, extreme structuralism contributed to the hyperinflation, disintegration, and chaos of the 1980s. By failing to generate sustainable growth, eliminate poverty, or improve the distribution of wealth, it gave rise to the structuralist fatigue of the 1970s and 1980s. However, even now there are many supporters of neostructuralism.

The dependency approach enjoyed immense popularity among members of the academic, intellectual, and policy-making community in Latin America during the late 1960s and early 1970s. Its ideas are best understood as a highly heterogeneous reformulation of structuralism. The reformulation was performed in light of the failure, according to dependency thinkers, of structuralism's specific import-substitution industrialization and overall inward-oriented development strategies to solve the problems of dependency and achieve both growth and equity. A valuable contribution of the multidisciplinary dependency literature is seen to be, according to its followers, its emphasis on the complex interaction mechanisms between the social, political, and economic dynamics of the dominant countries of the developed center and those of the dependent, underdeveloped countries of the Latin American periphery. These mechanisms, it is argued, perpetuate the dependency and underdevelopment of Latin America. Among its most celebrated thinkers, André Gunther Frank, Theotonio Dos Santos, and Aníbal Quijano believe that dependency can be overcome only through a socialist revolution, while Fernando Henrique Cardoso, Enzo Faletto, Celso Furtado, and Aldo Ferrer argue that the dependency problem can be cured by means of social, political, and economic reform rather than by the destruction of the capitalist system.

STRUCTURAL LIBERALISM

The extensive post-1973 implementation of structural, neoliberal public policies reflected a profound ideological and strategic shift away from structuralist planning. This ideological paradigm is structural in that it considers the highly visible structural defects of export dependence, rigid agricultural supplies, unstable public finances, and industrial inefficiency as causes of income stagnation and inequality, poverty, balance-of-payments disequilibria, unemployment, and even inflation. It considers these, however, only as proximate, not as the true causes. Its diagnosis of the fundamental, original causes of economic malaise is distinctly liberal in that it attributes stagnation, inflation, and inequality to inadequate, inefficient, and excessive government intervention pursued by Marxism, structuralism, and other ideologies. The villain of underdevelopment, the structural liberals contend, is the predatory state.

National savings are low because real interest rates are negative, state enterprises generate deficits rather than surpluses, and foreign saving (loans and grants) too often is readily available at concessional terms. Neoliberals hold deficit spending and anti-private-sector and anti-free-market government policies responsible for the approximately $500 billion of capital flight. General government as well as public-sector deficits are caused largely by excessive transfers to privileged households and the insatiable appetite for transfers by inefficient state-owned enterprises. Furthermore, discrimination, state ownership, and excessive legislation and intervention of the agricultural, transport, health, education, welfare, and industrial sectors turn them rigid and unresponsive to Latin America's needs, in particular those of the rural and urban poor.

According to the disciples of structural liberalism, these interlocking structural defects, which led to economic as well as social ossification, are imposed on, not inborn to, Latin America. They are caused by the crowding out of free and competitive markets and of private ownership by central planning and state ownership. They are a byproduct of abandoning the pivotal principles of consumer sovereignty and full respect of human, political, and economic rights in favor of the Marxist-socialist principles of state ownership of the means of production and excessive intervention, control, and central planning in production and exchange. However, it should be noted that human and political rights have also been repeatedly violated by regimes espousing neoliberal principles, as under Augusto Pinochet in Chile.

Privatization and liberalization are considered to be tools necessary to remove the structural defects. Liberalization, that is, the introduction of free and competitive markets, increases sectoral and aggregate production efficiency and accelerates growth. By facilitating maximum domestic and international mobility of labor, capital, and commodities, it maximizes the welfare that can be gained through division of labor, specialization, and exchange. Furthermore, this school argues, liberalization promotes consumer welfare by eliminating all market controls and discrimination based on nationality, nature of product, income, age, gender, and regional or ethnic origin of the economic agents.

As a complement to liberalization, privatization is seen as maximizing output and welfare by transferring decision-making responsibility from the centralized state to individual households and enterprises. Individuals are sovereign both in selling services and in purchasing commodities for consumption or further transformation. Liberalization and privatization, along with regulation, enable the introduction and implementation of nondiscriminatory rules for producers and consumers alike.

The paradigm of structural neoliberalism was formulated and implemented by Roberto CAMPOS in Brazil, giving rise to the ultimately ephemeral "Brazilian miracle," Alejandro Vegh Villegas in Uruguay, Sergio De Castro and Hernan Büchi in Chile, and Carlos SALINAS DE GORTARI, Pedro Aspe, and Gil Díaz in Mexico. The Chicago School of liberalism, represented by Milton Friedman and the CHICAGO BOYS, provided vital support and encouragement to various experiments throughout Latin America. Their monetarist views, which are also identified with International Monetary Fund (IMF) stabilization policies, maintain that inflation is a purely monetary phenomenon that emerges when the supply of money grows more rapidly than the supply of goods. In turn, increases in money supply are attributed to public-sector deficits financed by new money printed by the central bank. If inflation and money supply increases are to be arrested, public-sector deficits must first be eliminated.

Monetarism can be interpreted as a subset of structural liberalism or as a short-term strategy confined strictly to the financial domain. As an ideology, it provides theoretical justification for monetary policies strictly controlling the supply of money that can be relied upon to support deficit spending. As a strategy, it aims at monetary and price stabilization through draconian cuts in public deficits and rates of growth in money supply.

Monetarism arose in response to the needs of transition from structuralism to neoliberalism. It has been implemented in economies that display such structuralist fatigue symptoms as hyperinflation, excessive intervention, production and trade stagnation, and inefficient state ownership. As a strategy of last resort that often involves shock treatment, it aims at price stability. Often carrying an enormous cost in terms of foregone production, welfare, and employment, it is sustainable only if accompanied by liberalization, privatization, and other liberal reforms of the economic structure. Monetarism is seen by some as a vital, albeit limited, element of a liberal ideology and strategy of comprehensive modernization. None of the late-twentieth-century neoliberal experiments has as yet been successful in eradicating poverty and eliminating the appallingly uneven income distribution in Latin America.

SECTORAL CLASH

According to the theory of sectoral coalitions and clashes, formulated by Markos Mamalakis, the genesis, growth, maturity, fatigue, and collapse of the pre-1930 laissez-faire era are largely attributable to *caudillista-caciquista* mesoeconomic—i.e., sector-oriented—governmental policies, rather than inadequate macroeconomic policies of government. Mesoeconomic policies have failed to promote enlightened education, health, and welfare services that could have facilitated integration of poor households into modern production, thus eliminating poverty and equalizing income.

Similarly, the genesis, growth, maturity, fatigue, and collapse of post-1930 structuralism are attributed to domestic mesoeconomic governmental policies of industrial dominance; discrimination against agriculture, exports, and financial services; and the perpetuation of education, health, and welfare services that largely neglect the poorest 40–60 percent of households. This guarantees the perpetuation of poor people's misery. Meanwhile, the siphoning off of agricultural, financial, and export trade sectoral surpluses into industry, government, and other state-owned enterprises by those in power prevents the rapid overall growth to lift the poor out of poverty. Many of these policies stem from populist, nationalist, and structuralist ideas. Ultimately, inadequate cooperation, harmony, and integration between sectors precipitate hyperinflation, stagnation, and even social and political upheaval.

Lacking appropriate enlightened mesoeconomic educational, health, welfare, and other policies, even late-twentieth-century neoliberalism has been unable to achieve sustainable growth, eradicate poverty, reduce inequality, preserve the environment, and attain integration into the global economy. Through the application of enlightened social policies and the elimination of unequal treatment of sectors, growth would accelerate and inequality lessen.

The standard reference for the classical school remains ADAM SMITH, *An Inquiry into the Nature and Causes of the Wealth of Nations,* edited by Edwin Cannan (1976). Equally relevant to the Latin American experience is THOMAS R. MALTHUS, *An Essay on the Principle of Population* (1798). A valuable introduction to economic theories relevant to Latin America is found in JOSEPH A. SCHUMPETER, *History of Economic Analysis* (1954).

The classic documents of structuralism are H. W. SINGER, "The Distribution of Gains Between Investing and Borrowing Countries," in *American Economic Review: Papers and Proceedings* 40, no. 2 (May 1950): 473–485; and RAÚL PREBISCH, "Commercial Policy in the Underdeveloped Countries," in *American Economic Review: Papers and Proceedings* 49, no. 2 (May 1959): 251–273.

A comprehensive survey of the literature on the theories of structuralism and dependency, internal colonialism, and marginality is CRISTÓBAL KAY, *Latin American Theories of Development and Underdevelopment* (1989).

The theory of sectoral clashes and coalitions is presented in MARKOS MAMALAKIS, "The Theory of Sectoral Clashes," in *Latin American Research Review* 4, no. 3 (1969): 9–46, and "The Theory of Sectoral Clashes and Coalitions Revisited," in *Latin American Research Review* 6, no. 3 (1971): 89–126. The notion of "mesoeconomics" is defined and utilized in MARKOS MAMALAKIS, "Sectoral Clashes, Basic Economic Rights, and Redemocratization in Chile: A Mesoeconomic Approach," in *Ibero-Americana, Nordic Journal of Latin American Studies* 22, no. 1 (1992), and "Sectoral Conflicts in the U.S. and the Soviet Union: A Mesoeconomic Analysis," in *Eastern Economic Journal* 18, no. 4 (Fall 1992).

Alternative reviews of the ideologies of Latin American economic development are in CHARLES A. HALE, "Political and Social Ideas," in *Latin America: Economy and Society, 1870–1930,* edited by Leslie Bethell (1989); and ALBERT O. HIRSCHMAN, "Ideologies of Economic Development in Latin America," in *Latin American Issues: Essays and Comments,* edited by Albert O. Hirschman (1961), pp. 3–42.

MARKOS MAMALAKIS

ECONOMIC INTEGRATION. The economic integration of Latin America—either of the entire region (as was agreed to in 1967 but never realized) or subregions—was advocated by the United Nations Economic Commission for Latin America in the late 1940s and thereafter. The UN body, under Raúl PREBISCH and others, saw economic integration as a means of promoting development, especially industrialization.

The first concrete step toward economic integration came in 1958 when Costa Rica, El Salvador, Guatemala, Honduras, and Nicaragua signed the Multilateral Treaty on Central American Free Trade and Economic Integration, providing for a limited and gradual approach to the economic merger of the five countries (see CENTRAL AMERICAN COMMON MARKET). Costa Rica did not ratify the agreement. In early 1960 some signatories expressed dissatisfaction with integrative programs. El Salvador, Guatemala, and Honduras concluded a more ambitious agreement, the Treaty of Economic Association, which prompted another round of negotiation. The main result was the General Treaty of Central American Economic Integration (1960). It provided for an expanded and much accelerated approach to regional economic merger and established a modest institutional structure. Also in 1960, the Central American countries concluded the agreement establishing the Central America Bank for Economic Integration. (Costa Rica signed and ratified the agreements only in 1963.)

During the 1960s, under the General Treaty, intra–Central American trade expanded several hundredfold, industrialization increased, capital flowed in, and the region experienced both economic development and growth; however, the all-important agrarian sector was all but ignored by the integration effort, a serious flaw. Functioning of the Central American Common Market was seriously interrupted by the 1969 war between El Salvador and Honduras and came to a virtual halt as political violence consumed the region in the 1970s and 1980s.

In 1960, Mexico plus most of the South American countries concluded the Treaty of Montevideo, creating the LATIN AMERICAN FREE TRADE ASSOCIATION (LAFTA). LAFTA's modest goals were to be achieved through annual negotiation, over an extended period of time. The overall objective was to realize free trade among the member countries for most, but not all, products; there was no provision for a common external tariff on imports into the free-trade area.

Despite these limited goals, LAFTA members experienced difficulty meeting treaty commitments from the outset. Eventually, they totally failed to do so. In 1980 the LAFTA countries signed a new agreement establishing the Latin America Integration Association, an even looser and less demanding arrangement than LAFTA. Bilateral, rather than regional, agreements were emphasized. The 1980 agreement achieved no more, perhaps less, than the Treaty of Montevideo. A more recent and geographically reduced trade liberalization effort by some Latin American countries was MERCOSUR. Its prospects were difficult to assess.

The most ambitious and far-reaching effort at economic integration came in 1969 with the creation of the ANDEAN GROUP, or Andean Common Market, by Bolivia, Chile, Colombia, Ecuador, Peru, and Venezuela. Their Andean Pact set the following objectives: a virtually free market among the member countries, a common external tariff, allocation of certain industries among the member countries, special provisions for the less-developed members (as did the LAFTA and Central American agreements), and restrictions on foreign investment. The agreement also established a significant institutional structure, including a quasi-supranational Junta. Restrictions on foreign investment were detailed in decision 24, which declared certain sectors of the economy off-limits to foreign owners and otherwise phased out foreign investment.

The Andean Common Market achieved some of its objectives; however, both economic and political factors prevented full implementation. Deadlines were repeatedly set back and requirements downgraded. Chile withdrew in 1976 when its military government adopted an economic approach at odds with that of the integration effort. By the early 1980s, forward momentum for the remaining members had all but halted.

Each of the Latin American economic integration efforts encountered problems. Among the commonest were a lack of political will, instability in some member countries, conflict among some members, complaints on the part of less-developed members, unwillingness on the part of the more-developed countries to make sacrifices to benefit the less-developed, and competition among member countries for developed resources.

A totally different sort of economic integration effort is the North American Free Trade Agreement (NAFTA), which joins Mexico, the United States, and Canada into a single market after a transition period. Several Latin American countries desire to join in this arrangement or to conclude a free-trade agreement with the United States.

MIGUEL S. WIONCZEK, ed., *Latin American Economic Integration* (1966); WALTER KRAUSE and F. JOHN MATHIS, *Latin America and Economic Integration* (1970); DONALD H. MC CLELLAND, *The Central American Common Market* (1972); EDWARD S. MILENKY, *The Politics of Regional Organization in Latin America: The Latin American Free Trade Association* (1973); WILLIAM P. AVERY, "The Politics of Crisis and Cooperation in the Andean Group," in *Journal of Developing Areas* 17 (January 1983): 155–183; G. POPE ATKINS, *Latin America in the International Political System*, 2d ed. (1989).

JAMES D. COCHRANE

See also **Organization of Central American States (ODECA).**

ECOPETROL. Empresa Colombiana de Petróleos, Colombia's national oil company, was created in accor-

dance with Law 165 of 1948. It has supervised the country's oil industry since the reversion of the De Mares concession—controlled for thirty years by a former subsidiary of Exxon, the Tropical Oil Company—to the national government on 25 August 1951. From its original base in Barrancabermeja (department of Santander), in the area of the concession, Ecopetrol has expanded its operations into the Llanos and Magdalena Valley. In contrast to the more familiar Latin American pattern, it has pursued its goal of oil development through a policy of close cooperation with foreign oil companies and multinational corporations, as illustrated by its entering into "association" contracts with several of the latter in the 1980s.

HARVEY KLINE, *Colombia: Portrait of Unity and Diversity* (1983); RENÉ DE LA PEDRAJA, *Energy Politics in Colombia* (1989).

PAMELA MURRAY

ECUADOR

Conquest Through Independence

When the Spanish armies of Sebastián de BELALCÁZAR invaded the north Andes in 1533, the region had already undergone fifty years of turmoil. The INCA Empire (Tawantinsuyu) had not incorporated the region's six independent indigenous chiefdoms until 1495, and the subsequent succession struggle between ATAHUALPA and HUASCAR had only prolonged the period of disorder.

THE ERA OF CONQUEST

The Spanish overthrow of the Inca state brought additional problems, as the distribution of Native American towns as grants of ENCOMIENDA precipitated squabbles among the conquistadores that developed into civil strife. In 1534 the Spanish leader Francisco PIZARRO tried to consolidate political control by establishing for the region a governorship that extended from Popayán in the north to Loja in the south, and from the eastern cordillera of the Andes to the Pacific. Nevertheless, the persistent civil wars among the conquistadores prolonged the political turmoil in the region until 1563, when the crown formed in the city of Quito an *audiencia* (high court) that had jurisdiction over the old governorship, the northwestern province of Atacames, and the eastern provinces of Quijos, Macas, Mainas, and Jaén de Bracamoros. After consolidating their political power, the Spaniards began laying the foundations of a stable society and a colonial economy based on the production of woolen textiles.

By the late sixteenth century, the *audiencia* district of QUITO was linked to a prosperous, integrated network of regional economies extending throughout the Viceroyalty of Peru. While silver MINING formed the link between Spain's Andean colonies and the international economy, numerous smaller regional markets evolved to supply foodstuffs, textiles, labor, and alcoholic beverages for the burgeoning mining zones. Quito's textile economy occupied a central place in these emerging secondary regional markets. Local elites used the fertile lands in the narrow Andean valleys and the extensive stretches of *páramo* pasturelands to establish an extensive network of OBRAJES (textile mills) in the provinces from Otavalo in the north to Riobamba in the south. These mills supplied woolens to markets in Peru and New Granada (Colombia) in return for specie, which the Spanish elite used to purchase the luxury goods needed to maintain a comfortable European life-style.

THE ERA OF PROSPERITY: 1570–1690

The inability of Spanish textile manufacturers to supply the growing demand for cloth in the mining and urban centers of South America led to the founding of numerous *obrajes* in the Audiencia of Quito. The rich agricultural and grazing lands in the Ecuadorian Andes, stocked with Spanish merino sheep, and the dense Native American population supplied the raw materials, foodstuffs, and labor to support the growing *obraje* sector. By the mid-seventeenth century more than 10,000 workers annually were producing 230,000 yards of the region's famous *paño azul* (blue cloth) and an additional 470,000 yards of *bayetas* and *jergas* (coarser woolens), fetching over 3 million pesos in the marketplaces of Peru and New Granada. Throughout the seventeenth century the woolen textile industry served as the foundation of the audiencia's economic prosperity.

The Textile Boom The first Spaniards to establish cloth manufactures were the region's *encomenderos*, who sought viable sources of income from the indigenous communities. Placer mining deposits were quickly exhausted, so the original European settlers began to found textile mills, called *obrajes de comunidad*, on their grants as money-making enterprises. The profits from the mills were used to pay the Native American communal tax levies, the salaries of the local priest and *corregidor* (magistrate), and an annual pension for the *encomendero*. Although legally owned by the indigenous Amerindian community, the *obraje* was, in reality, treated by the local Spanish *encomendero* as his own personal property. The mills grew into extremely large operations, often employing more than 200 laborers from the local Andean villages. By the early seventeenth century, the *encomenderos* had founded fourteen *obrajes de comunidad* scattered throughout the Ecuadorian highlands, and there were two additional mills in Otavalo owned directly by the crown.

The crown and the Audiencia of Quito issued numerous laws regulating the operation of the *obrajes de comunidad*—laws that ultimately undermined their profitability. To curb the local power of the *encomenderos*, the crown first began appointing special administrators to run the mills. When these officials too often proved corrupt and inept, the audiencia leased to local elites the right to run the *obrajes*, but this change provided no

improvement. In addition, deducting the salaries of the local priest, magistrates, and workers drained the profits. The crown also set abnormally high tribute rates for the Andean villagers to encourage them to work in the *obrajes*, but these rates were so exorbitant that the mills seldom met more than half the communal tax assessment. As a result, the crown had sold these large and increasingly unprofitable mills to private owners by 1728.

From the early seventeenth century on, the most lucrative and productive *obrajes* were privately owned. The crown demanded that all *obrajeros* (mill owners) purchase a license, which gave them the right to operate their enterprises, recruit wage laborers, and in some cases to employ slaves or receive allotments of *mitayos* (corvée workers). The largest and most profitable *obrajes* tended to be located on rural estates, with medium and small-scale mills found on modest rural holdings or on the outskirts of towns. Entrepreneurs founded most of the mills in the provinces of Quito, Latacunga, and Riobamba, which possessed the fertile land and Amerindian laborers needed for the industry's growth. Early in the century the crown had licensed only 41 private mills, but by 1690 the number of legal operations had grown to more than 100—an indication of the profitability of the private cloth industry.

Colonial Society With the prosperity of the textile industry a small, tightly knit network of peninsular (European-born) and creole (American-born) families made substantial fortunes based on ownership of *obrajes* and land. The greater profitability of larger, integrated estate complexes organized around *obrajes* only concentrated more economic and social power in these elites. Some wealthy and powerful families even acquired noble titles and entails. Regardless of whether they secured titles, however, most consolidated their social position through intermarriage and alliances with powerful peninsular bureaucrats and nouveau riche merchants. By the late seventeenth century, important families—the Villacis, Sánchez de Orellana, Guerrero, Pérez Ubillus, Larrea, Maldonado, Monteserín, Ramírez de Arrelano, Galarza, Londoño—were related through a complex nexus of business and family connections, which they used to dominate the audiencia district.

Despite the devastating effects of European epidemic diseases, the Amerindian population of the north-central highlands began to expand during the seventeenth century. Most of this increase was apparently the result of migrations from adjacent frontier zones in the north and south. Highland communities had long sent colonists to those regions to gain access to their resources, and refugees from the Inca and Spanish conquests had also found havens there. These colonists and refugees evidently returned later to the north-central highlands to repopulate the Andean communities hard hit by epidemic diseases. After returning, these migrants formed the core of the labor force for the *obrajes* in the late sixteenth century, and their integration into

CÍVDAD
LACÍVDADÍAVDÍENCÍA
DE QVITO

Colonial Quito. Reproduced from Guamán Poma de Ayala, *El primer nueva corónica y buen gobierno* (ca. 1615). COURTESY OF THE ROYAL LIBRARY, COPENHAGEN.

the Spanish textile economy was a major reason for its success.

Despite their importance to the *obrajes*, the Native Americans suffered ongoing abuses in the mills. Wages remained low, and owners often paid their workers in overvalued cloth rather than in specie. Likewise, *socorros* (supplies) of foodstuffs were often inedible, overpriced, and distributed at *haciendas* several miles away. Workers were also beaten, forced to work long hours, and often bound to the *obrajes* through DEBT PEONAGE. *Obrajeros* even coerced the wives and children of laborers into service in the mills. Amerindian laborers tolerated these abysmal working conditions only because their wages helped defray the heavy taxes levied on their village communities. For the Native Americans the prosperity of these sweatshops brought heavy burdens and few tangible benefits.

ECONOMIC CRISIS AND CHANGE: 1690–1809
By the 1690s, the prosperity of the woolen textile industry had begun to erode. A gradual decline of the mining economy in Peru and Bolivia lessened the demand for

cloth in Lima, the most lucrative market for the *quiteños*. In addition, the growth of textile mills in closer proximity to the mines provided more competition amid the mining decline. By the 1690s, a number of droughts, earthquakes, and epidemics, which accounted for the death of nearly one-third of the Amerindian labor force in the audiencia district, ended the period of relatively cheap labor for mill owners.

Decline of the Textile Industry According to contemporaries, the crucial blow to the local textile economy came with the influx of cheap, high-quality European cloth, first brought by French traders during the WAR OF THE SPANISH SUCCESSION (1700–1716). As the Spanish crown began liberalizing trade regulations after ending the system of GALEONES and *flotas* (see FLEET SYSTEM) in 1740, the importation of foreign cloth increased, which further restricted the market share available to Quito's *obrajes*. As a result, the prices for *quiteño* cloth fell dramatically, and the net output of the region's *obrajes* dropped by some 50 to 75 percent during the eighteenth century.

The rigid organizational structure of the textile business frustrated efforts by the *obrajeros* to compete with foreign imports. By licensing elite-run enterprises and providing the legal mechanisms to recruit laborers, the crown had created an oligopoly in the audiencia that nurtured selected producers. Most of the successful mill owners flourished in this protected environment by establishing family-run enterprises that linked the clothing mills to food-producing estates and sheep ranches. Such rural estate complexes integrated the key elements of production in one enterprise, thus reducing the problem of cash outlays needed to pay for labor and raw materials. These textile mills, however, used no sophisticated machinery capable of lowering the unit cost of production, a principal advantage associated with modern factory production. Instead, the *obraje* absorbed many of the functions of the market, supplying the capital, labor, and raw materials needed for production.

This organizational structure had served mill owners well in the protected colonial markets of the sixteenth and seventeenth centuries, but it made it impossible for them to increase the quality of their cloth or to lower prices to compete with European imports. In short, by liberalizing trade policies and allowing the importation of relatively cheap European cloth, the crown effectively ended the oligopolistic arrangement responsible for the prosperity of Quito's mills.

The influx of European cloth drove the *quiteños* from the lucrative Lima market. Large mill owners in Quito had traditionally transported their higher-quality cloth to the viceregal capital, where they exchanged it for specie, Peruvian products, and European wares. The earnings from these transactions could be substantial, since the *obrajeros* controlled the sale of their own woolens and the importation of much European merchandise into the district. Although the northern trade to

New Granada maintained greater vigor during the eighteenth century than earlier, it offered more modest profits. New Granada's merchant houses purchased mostly cheap, lower-quality cloth while also taking charge of introducing European goods into the audiencia. As a result, the loss of the Lima market curtailed the long-term profits of Quito's textile producers.

The Results of the Decline in Textiles The diminishing demand for local textiles from the 1690s onward prompted a slow agrarian decline in much of the north-central highlands. Most agrarian enterprises there had organized the abundant land and labor resources in the rural zones to export textiles, not food or livestock. Geographical barriers and high transport costs limited the ability of most *hacendados* to change over from exporting textiles to selling their bulk crops in distant colonial markets. Attempts to find a suitable cash crop usually proved impracticable, and only the largest estates of the religious orders or the wealthy elites could muster the political clout and economic resources needed to profit from textile production.

The decline of the *obrajes* had negative repercussions also on regional commerce and state revenues. The sale of woolens had financed the importation of European luxury goods and provided the specie for domestic enterprise, regional trade, and the fiscal needs of the colonial state. As cloth exports declined, however, so too did imports, commerce, and government tax receipts. As a result, the decline in the textile sector prompted an overall economic recession, which in turn led to a marked shift in the socioeconomic structure of the audiencia of Quito.

The Rise of the Southern Highlands As the *obraje* economy in Quito declined, there emerged a prosperous cotton and woolen textile industry centered in the province of Cuenca. This industry was concentrated in the Amerindian villages of the south, where merchants from Lima organized a cottage, or putting-out, system of manufacturing. The merchants usually supplied the raw cotton and wool, while the villagers—many of them women—used traditional Andean methods of spinning and weaving to produce cheap, light cloth. The Andean villagers could supplement their income from agriculture by participating in this vibrant cottage industry. The Lima merchants then used their commercial connections to market these *tocuyos* or *lienzos* (cottons) and *bayetas* (woolens) at considerable profit in the cities and mining centers of northern Peru.

The Spanish agricultural economy of the southern highlands also experienced steady growth during the eighteenth century. The prosperity of most Spanish estates depended on the demand for agricultural products in local highland markets, Guayaquil, and northern Peru. Some Spanish landowners also prospered by selling abundant supplies of a local tree bark called *cascarilla*, which was rich in QUININE. The Spanish landlords seldom participated in the cottage textile industry, but the trade in coarse cloth undoubtedly stimulated the local agrarian economy and promoted the introduction of European luxury items.

In the early nineteenth century, the textile business in the southern highlands began to decline. The diminished productivity of the Peruvian mines and the disruptions of the independence era led to a falloff in demand for southern Ecuadorian cloth. As a result, Lima's merchants began abandoning the industry, and textile exports dropped rapidly. The cottage industry system was simply too limited in scale and lacking in capital to survive without its merchant backers. The Amerindian villages suffered most from this decline. The Spanish estates, which were less directly connected to the local textile trade, continued to experience modest prosperity.

The Coastal Export Boom The export economy of the coast did not begin to prosper until the crown allowed free trade within the empire between 1778 and 1789. Along the extensive river system of the coastal plain, Spanish elites established increasing numbers of plantations to produce CACAO for export to markets in South America, Mexico, and Europe. From the 1780s to 1810, cacao production increased nearly 300 percent. The fertile coastal soils also yielded copious amounts of tobacco, sugar, and hardwoods, but the cultivation and export of cacao became the economic core of the coastal economy until cacao exports began to decline markedly by the 1840s.

Large and medium-size plantations growing cacao developed rapidly in the late eighteenth century, particularly in the parishes of Baba, Babahoyo, Palenque, and Machala. Abundant rainfall, a hot climate, and cheap transportation along the river system in these zones contributed to the expansion of cacao cultivation. These cacao zones produced the only major export crop in the Audiencia of Quito capable of generating large amounts of hard currency in the colonial and international markets. By the nineteenth century, this export crop had finally begun to ease the specie shortage accompanying the decline of Ecuador's textile trades.

Although it was the cacao plantations that linked the productivity of the coast to the international economy, the outside merchant houses were often the ones to reap the largest profits from the export trade. The coastal planters lacked access to credit and did not have the commercial connections of the large mercantile companies based in Lima, Mexico City, and Spain. These outside merchant companies also profited from introducing European wares. The concentration of land in the hands of a small elite also guaranteed that only a very few *costeños* (coastal residents) would benefit from the export bonanza.

Colonial Society Although the elites of the north-central highlands remained powerful during the eighteenth century, the long-term decline of the textile industry undermined their economic position. Estates became ever more heavily encumbered, which prompted the elite to petition (successfully) to have the interest rate on all *censos* (loans and liens held by the church) lowered from 5 to 3 percent by 1755. Rural landowners also tried marketing foodstuffs and commodities such as *aguardiente* (cane liquor) to compensate for declining textile sales, with only limited success. By the late eighteenth century, only the largest estate complexes (owned by the clergy and the wealthiest elite families) had the scale, access to credit, and marketing connections to prosper.

A network of landowners and merchants came to dominate the socioeconomic life of the southern highlands. Powerful families such as the Valdivieso, Veintimilla, Otando, Bermeo, Crespo, and Ochoa owned large estates and maintained their wealth and status through skillful business and marriage connections. This elite was active in the economic life of the province, buying and selling luxury imports, land, and urban properties throughout the late colonial period. Business and family ties also linked the powerful families of Cuenca and Loja to their counterparts in northern Peru and the coast. In fact, land ownership became a powerful asset after the commercial and industrial downturn by the early nineteenth century.

The rapidly expanding coastal economy allowed greater social mobility than could occur in the more established social hierarchies of the highlands. Within a short time, however, a few powerful families began consolidating their control over the best cacao lands. In the 1780s, for example, just five plantation owners accounted for more than 40 percent of the new cacao trees along the coast; and one man, Silvestre Gorostiza Villamar, planted more than 90,000 trees in Machala. Indeed, by the independence era, five landowners—Martín de Icaza, Domingo Santísteban, Josefa Pareja, Francisco Vitores, and General Juan José Flores—controlled over 25 percent of the total cacao production. These wealthy planters and the leading mercantile families made considerable fortunes and formed the new political elite along the coast during the late colonial and independence periods.

The decline of the *obraje* economy and the rising importance of the southern highlands and the coast had a profound effect on the Amerindian population. Many Andeans had already left their traditional ethnic communities to participate in the regional market economies, working in Spanish *obrajes* and *haciendas* and in the chief cities. By the eighteenth century, large numbers of Indians had migrated from the depressed provinces of the north-central highlands to regions of greater economic opportunity.

The first of these movements promoted the development of the southern highlands until the cottage textile industry declined by the early nineteenth century. The pattern of migration began shifting to the coast in the late eighteenth century and continued to attract large numbers of migrants until the export market for cacao declined by the 1840s. In short, the regional economic realignments during the late colonial period encouraged major demographic movements that reflected the diminished economic opportunities for Amerindians in the highlands.

The Bourbon Reforms and Political Unrest By the seventeenth century, Ecuadorian elites had gained considerable influence over local government—even over the Audiencia of Quito. This trend gained momentum only when the crown began selling appointments to important bureaucratic offices: the royal treasury in 1633, *corregimientos* (magistracies) in 1678, and *audiencia* judgeships in 1687. By the early eighteenth century, the institutions of royal government had a well-deserved reputation for representing local over imperial concerns.

This pattern of local control began to shift during the eighteenth century. The crown enacted policies permitting the influx of European cloth without consulting the Audiencia of Quito, which proved powerless to resist them. In addition, the metropolis began to impose stricter control over the local royal government by ending the sale of offices after 1750 and enforcing the more efficient collection of local taxes. In 1765, for example, the viceroy of New Granada, Pedro de Messía de la Cerda, transferred control over the sales tax and the *aguardiente* monopoly from local tax farmers to the royal treasury. When the audiencia proved unable to convince the crown's agents in Bogotá to reverse this unpopular measure, a popular revolt—supported by all social classes in the capital city—overthrew the royal government. In fact, a popular coalition ruled the city until internal dissension and the arrival of royal troops a year later ended the affair. The failure of this revolt left the citizenry deeply divided and pessimistic about their ability to influence important crown policies.

A decade after this turbulence, the Madrid government dispatched a special inspector-general, José García de León y Pizarro, as president-regent (a newly created office of presiding officer) of the Audiencia of Quito. García Pizarro was an influential protégé of the minister of the Indies, José de Gálvez, who implemented a far-reaching set of reforms aimed at increasing state power and raising taxes. The keystone of these reforms was the creation of a militia system and a new fiscal bureaucracy, which the president-regent controlled by appointing kin, friends, and a few loyal allies among the creole elite. García Pizarro then used this regalist state bureaucracy to raise unprecedented amounts of tax revenue. In the depressed north-central highlands, for example, state income rose from more than 860,000 pesos in the period 1775–1779 to nearly 2.5 million pesos in the next five years.

Despite these successes, prominent citizens charged that García Pizarro and his group had ruled despotically in Quito, intimidating the local aristocracy and the church, extorting bribes, selling public offices, and using the militia to enforce his corrupt designs. A long, acrimonious investigation, which continued until 1790, uncovered startling abuses by the bureaucracy, but the crown imposed no punishments. Most of García

Pizarro's clan and allies were transferred, but taxes remained high and government abuses continued. Throughout the remainder of the colonial period, many among the elite remained discontented and disillusioned with the colonial government and the crown.

Discontent also spread to the Indian and mestizo populations as high taxes and the economic depression of the north-central highlands led to hardship in many communities. Periodic uprisings against escalating taxes, poor working conditions on Spanish estates and *obrajes*, and dishonest government officials broke out during the eighteenth century. Revolts in Otavalo (1777), Guano (La Matriz, 1778), Ambato (1780), Alausí (1781), Chambo (1790), and even the larger insurrections in Guamote and Columbe (1803) caused considerable loss of life and property, but they never spread like the great rebellions of Upper Peru in the 1780s. In Ecuador the Spanish authorities always managed to combine brutal repression with judicious concessions to restore order.

THE MOVE TO INDEPENDENCE: 1809–1830

A serious challenge to Spanish power occurred in 1809, after the abdications of Charles IV and Ferdinand VII, when *quiteño* elites formed a *junta* (provisional government) under the leadership of the marqués de Selva Alegre. Dissension within the *junta* and its failure to gain widespread popular support, however, led to its downfall within three months. In 1810, when royalist troops feared a new uprising, most of the rebel leaders were summarily executed in their jail cells. Popular outrage at this massacre prompted the establishment of another popular *junta* in 1810, which ruled until a new president, Toribio Montes, and a royal army extinguished the popular government two years later.

The defeat of these *juntas* in Quito discouraged any new movements for independence, until discontent in Guayaquil in 1820 led the coastal elites to rise. Like the Quito revolts, however, this movement did not spread beyond the coast, and formal independence for the entire audiencia district did not come until the insurgent armies of Antonio José de SUCRE won the Battle of PICHINCHA in 1822. For the next eight years Ecuador remained a province of the independent republic of GRAN COLOMBIA (Colombia, Venezuela, and Ecuador). Finally, in 1830 Ecuador withdrew from that union to become an independent republic.

Although the number of historical studies on the Andes during the colonial period has increased dramatically, few have dealt specifically with Ecuador. The best work on bureaucratic politics remains JOHN LEDDY PHELAN, *The Kingdom of Quito in the Seventeenth Century* (1967). For Native American rebellions see SEGUNDO E. MORENO YÁÑEZ, *Sublevaciones indígenas en la Audiencia de Quito: Desde comienzos del siglo XVIII hasta finales de la colonia*, 3d ed. (1985). Landholding among the clergy is treated in NICHOLAS P. CUSHNER, *Farm and Factory: The Jesuits and the Development of Agrarian Capitalism in Colonial Quito, 1600–1767* (1982). Two influential works on the export boom along the Ecuadorian coast are MICHAEL T. HAMERLY, *Historia social y económica de la antigua provincia de Guayaquil, 1763–1842*, 2d ed. (1973; 1987), and MARÍA LUISA LAVIANA CUETOS, *Guayaquil durante el siglo XVIII: Recursos naturales y desarrollo económico* (1987). Disease and population patterns are the subject of SUZANNE AUSTIN ALCHON (née BROWNE), *Native Society and Disease in Colonial Ecuador* (1992). Some major articles on landholding patterns, the transfer of land from Andeans to Spaniards, and the early *obrajes* include CHRISTIANA BORCHART DE MORENO, "Composiciones de tierras en la Audiencia de Quito: El valle de Tumbaco a finales del siglo XVII," *Jahrbuch für Geschichte von Staat, Wirtschaft und Gesellschaft Lateinamerikas* 17 (1980): 121–155, and "La transferencia de la propiedad agraria indígena en el corregimiento de Quito hasta finales de siglo XVII," *Caravelle* 34 (1980): 5–19; SEGUNDO E. MORENO YÁÑEZ, "Traspaso de la propiedad agrícola indígena a la hacienda colonial: El caso de Saquisilí," *Jahrbuch für Geschichte von Staat, Wirtschaft und Gesellschaft Lateinamerikas* 17 (1980): 97–119; and JAVIER ORTIZ DE LA TABLA DUCASSE, "El obraje colonial ecuatoriano: Aproximación a su estudio," *Revista de Indias* 149–150 (1977): 471–541. The best survey of the *obraje* economy is ROBSON BRINES TYRER's "The Demographic and Economic History of the Audiencia of Quito: Indian Population and the Textile Industry, 1600–1800" (Ph.D. diss., Univ. of California, Berkeley, 1976). A significant study of Amerindian migration is KAREN M. POWERS, "Indian Migration and Sociopolitical Change in the Audiencia of Quito (Ecuador)" (Ph.D. diss., New York Univ., 1990). Other important dissertations are MARTIN MINCHOM's "Urban Popular Society in Colonial Quito, c. 1700–1800" (Ph.D. diss., Univ. of Liverpool, 1984) and ROSEMARY D. F. BROMLEY's demographic work "Urban Growth and Decline in the Central Sierra of Ecuador" (Ph.D. diss., Univ. of Wales, 1977). Two fine published master's theses for the Facultad Latinoamérica de Ciencias Sociales (FLACSO) in Quito are SILVIA PALOMEQUE, *Cuenca del siglo XIX: La articulación de una region* (1990), and GALO RAMÓN VALAREZO, *La resistencia andina: Cayambe, 1500–1800* (1987).

KENNETH J. ANDRIEN

See also **Quito Revolt of 1765; Textile Industry.**

Since 1830

Since independence, Ecuador has faced two fundamental obstacles to development: geographic fragmentation and limited natural resources. Geography, which has been a major barrier to national integration, fostered political, social, and economic division. Regionalism, the political expression of the division and isolation imposed by geography, has been a significant and enduring factor in Ecuadorian politics. The development of divergent economic and social systems on the coast and in the highlands resulted in antagonistic political attitudes and interests.

The demise of Spanish authority plunged the country into a crisis of legitimacy. The ruling elite failed to reach a consensus that would have allowed them to resolve their conflicts amicably. To curb the tendencies toward fragmentation, strong national leaders resorted to force to maintain power. From 1830 to 1992 only twenty presidents completed their constitutional terms of office. There have been only three periods (1921–1925, 1948–

Ecuador

1	BOLÍVAR
2	CHIMBORAZO
3	COTOPAXI
4	IMBABURA
5	LOS RÍOS
6	TUNGURAHUA
7	ZAMORA-CHINCHIPE

GALÁPAGOS ISLANDS
approx. 600 miles west of Ecuador
Isabela I.
San Salvador I.
Santa Cruz
Santa María I.
(same scale as main map)

1961, and 1979–1992) when several presidents were elected, completed their terms, and transferred power to other elected chief executives. Ecuador is an extreme example of the crisis that engulfed most of Spanish America in the post-Independence period.

CHARACTERISTICS OF ECUADORIAN POLITICS
Historically, a small elite has dominated effective political participation in Ecuador. Large landowners, wealthy businessmen, professionals, and high-ranking military men were the principal power contenders in the nineteenth century. Despite the trend toward greater political participation that emerged in the twentieth century, the elite continue to dominate Ecuadorian politics. Literacy requirements denied the vote to large segments of the population until 1979. As the nineteenth century progressed, ideologies grew in importance in national and regional politics. The coast became the home of liberalism, while the highlands were the stronghold of conservatism. The development of political parties dedicated to implementing these competing worldviews had little effect on the manner in which national leaders governed.

Both liberals and conservatives responded in similar ways to the challenges of ruling a divided country. The characteristic features of Ecuadorian politics—regionalism, authoritarianism, militarism, and personalism—provide coherence and continuity to the nation's chaotic political history.

From independence, regionalists struggled to receive adequate representation in national government, to obtain a significant share of national revenues for their areas, and to maintain local autonomy. During the nineteenth century, Ecuador endured four civil wars that threatened to dismember the country. Although Ecuador was, in theory, a constitutional republic, force became the accepted method of transferring or retaining power. All eleven constitutions promulgated during the period provided for elected officials. Political reality, however, was quite different. Elections were generally held not to select a president but to ratify or legalize the power of a person who gained office through force. In such cases, elections were usually preceded by the writing of a new constitution. In other instances, the government controlled elections to ensure the victory of its official candidate. In either situation, disappointed presidential contenders often violently challenged the outcome.

The use of force was not limited to military politicians: Generals Juan José FLORES (1830–1834, 1839–1845), José María Urvina (1855–1856), Francisco ROBLES (1856–1859), and Ignacio VEINTIMILLA (1876–1883) relied on armed might either to bring them to power or to help them retain it, as did the leading civilian politicians. The two great nineteenth-century statesmen Vicente ROCAFUERTE (1835–1839) and Gabriel García Moreno (1861–1865, 1869–1875) achieved power through armed conflict and then relied on force to remain in office.

A pattern of authoritarian politics developed in Ecuador. Liberals, conservatives, and opportunists relied on controlled elections, press censorship, and extralegal coercion to limit the opposition. A close relationship between authoritarianism and militarism emerged. The willingness of many groups to use force to attain political goals meant that national leaders, whether civil or military, had to rely on the army for support. The system favored strong and ruthless chief executives, whether civilian or military. The pressures of war, economic decline, and political instability led to the rise of powerful individuals who could circumvent legal structures. Individual leaders, rather than political parties or institutions, governed the country. The failure to develop strong political institutions meant that men, rather than ideas or abstract political principles, shaped political movements. Individuals with strong personalities and political ambition took control of existing political parties or formed their own organizations.

During the twentieth century, groups such as the liberals, conservatives, socialists, and social democrats attempted to replace personalist politics by creating effective mechanisms for selecting candidates and developing programs. However, the traditional patterns of social and political relations retarded the formation of a modern political structure. The most enduring personalist movement in Ecuadorian politics, *velasquismo*, led by José María VELASCO IBARRA, remained an important force into the 1970s. Although the movement's leader served as president on five different occasions (1934–1935, 1944–1947, 1952–1956, 1960–1961, 1968–1972), it failed to develop an institutional structure that could function in the absence of Velasco Ibarra.

COASTAL LIBERAL DOMINANCE

In the late nineteenth century expanding CACAO exports provided Ecuador with its first period of sustained economic prosperity since the decline of sierra textile production in the colonial period. Cacao growers and exporters financed the successful liberal revolution of 1895, which shifted the balance of political power to the coast. The liberals, who retained power until 1925, used growing government revenues to form a secular, activist state. The liberal development program sought to remove obstacles to social and economic progress and to foster national development.

Although the liberals were successful in defeating the conservatives and fostering modernization through an ambitious public works program, they were less successful in establishing a mechanism for the peaceful transfer of power. The liberal triumph did not herald a change in Ecuador's political culture. Personalism and regionalism remained crucial factors. The emergence of an activist state in Ecuador provided a new arena for regionalist struggles, while two men, Eloy ALFARO and Leonidas PLAZA GUTIÉRREZ, dominated the first decades of liberal rule. Their rivalry was a major cause of the turbulence that lasted until 1916. The death of Alfaro in 1912 as the result of an abortive rebellion allowed Plaza to initiate the process of strengthening political institutions and to accomplish the peaceful transfer of power in the period 1916–1924.

SIERRA DOMINANCE

The combined effects of unsound liberal fiscal practices and the economic crisis resulting from a decline in the value and volume of cacao production ended the political stability established by Plaza. Since the government received the majority of its revenue from customs receipts, cacao exports were the primary determinant of government income. As the scope of government activity expanded after 1896 to meet the growing demands for material progress, liberal administrations relied on loans from Guayaquil banks to cover perennial budget deficits. The symbiotic relationship between successive liberal administrations and coastal banks angered sierra regionalists, who viewed the relationship as proof that coastal exporting interests controlled the country. As the economy deteriorated, Quito journalists and politicians were increasingly vocal in their criticism of the "corrupt coastal banking oligarchy." A few of these critics courted young army officers, arguing that only the military could save the country from disaster by returning political control to the sierra. In July 1925, a group of these military officers overthrew the government. In the period 1925–1931, military-backed governments, acting on the advice of a team of foreign advisers led by Princeton economist Edwin W. KEMMERER, implemented a number of reforms that restructured the nation's banking and fiscal systems. A major objective of the reforms was to eliminate the budget deficits that had characterized liberal administration by centralizing tax collection and disbursement. Ecuadorians, however, found it easier to enact laws than to implement them. Many of the institutional and procedural changes proved incapable of maintaining fiscal integrity during a period of economic, social, and political stress.

The severe economic dislocations of the 1930s exacerbated Ecuador's perennial problems of insufficient government revenues and chronic political instability.

Modern Quito. © PETER MENZEL / STOCK, BOSTON.

President Isidro AYORA's ouster in 1931 ushered in the most turbulent period in the country's history. Between 1931 and 1948 nineteen men served as chief executive; none completed his term of office. The period witnessed the rise of populist politics and the loss of half of the territory to Peru. Political stability would not be restored until the country entered a second period of economic expansion based on a new agricultural export, bananas.

THE POSTWAR ERA

Banana exports underwrote a twelve-year period of political stability in which three presidents Galo PLAZA LASO (1948–1952), José María Velasco Ibarra (1952–1956), and Camilo PONCE ENRÍQUEZ (1956–1960) completed their constitutional terms. The export boom allowed expanded government investments in economic and social infrastructure and promoted population movement from the sierra to the coast. When the economy deteriorated in the 1960s, however, the weakness of the political system resurfaced; no president completed his term of office during the next decade, and for three years the country was ruled by a military junta (1963–1966).

The 1970s were a period of rapid economic growth based on the export of petroleum, which fostered the emergence of a relatively autonomous state. From 1972 to 1979 Ecuador was governed by two moderate military juntas. Although these military governments, like their 1960s counterparts, sought to implement socioeconomic reforms, economic inequity and political underdevelopment continued to characterize Ecuador in the 1980s.

RETURN TO CIVILIAN RULE

The return to civilian rule in 1979 with the inauguration of President Jaime ROLDÓS AGUILERA initiated a new state of Ecuadorian political development. Although Roldós was a member of Asaad BUCARAM's populist Concentration of Popular Forces (CFP), he and his Christian Democratic running mate, Osvaldo HURTADO, represented a new generation of politicians who stressed programmatic rather than personalist concerns. They supported the modernization of the political system through the expansion of the electorate, issue-oriented campaigning, and the development of modern political parties.

During the 1978 campaign, Roldós and Hurtado issued a twenty-one-point program, which was later elaborated in the January 1980 five-year National Development Plan. The plan proposed using petroleum revenues to promote national agricultural and industrial production through investment in economic and social infrastructure. Hydroelectric, transportation, and communication projects; agricultural credits; and rural education were priorities. In addition, the government proposed to improve tax collection, to promote national integration, and to expand the political and economic participation of the lower socioeconomic groups.

The ambitious reform program failed when Asaad Bucaram withdrew his support and assumed leadership of the anti-Roldós congressional majority. Congress thwarted the efforts of the Roldós administration to contain deficit expenditures and to introduce a national development strategy, which included educational and agrarian reform. With the fall of petroleum prices in

453

1980 and a burgeoning public debt, the administration was forced to implement an austerity program and to abandon its efforts to introduce structural reforms. The worsening economic situation eroded public support for the government. Labor, the economic elite, and politicians on the right and left became increasingly strident in their criticism of the government.

In May 1981, Osvaldo Hurtado inherited a deteriorating economic and political situation when Jaime Roldós was killed in a plane crash. His administration faced a series of political and economic crises that threatened to provoke military intervention. Hurtado managed to preserve civilian rule by forming an unstable center-left coalition within Congress. With this uncertain support, the administration was unable to pass reform legislation, but did manage to restrain public spending. The energies of the executive branch were consumed in managing the country's finances, including renegotiating the foreign debt and maintaining fiscal austerity. The political costs of the austerity program were high, particularly in 1983, when the worsening economic crisis resulted in a sharp devaluation of the sucre and a burst of inflation. The economic decline had begun to moderate by the 1984 presidential campaign.

The 1984 presidential election was the first in which illiterates were to vote. The campaign highlighted a central weakness of the Ecuadorian political system: highly factionalized politics that promoted unstable coalitions and personalism. Nine presidential candidates and seventeen political parties participated in the elections. In the first electoral round, Rodrigo BORJA CEVALLOS, founder of the center-left party Izquierda Democrática (ID), barely beat the right-wing Social Christian León FEBRES-CORDERO. However, in the runoff, populist appeals and regional rather than ideological factors determined the outcome: Febres-Cordero edged out Borja.

The election of Febres-Cordero was less a reflection of the general appeal of the coalition of right-wing parties that endorsed his candidacy than a protest vote against the economic problems that crippled the Roldós and Hurtado administrations. Febres-Cordero took office with a Congress controlled by the opposition. Of the thirteen parties represented in Congress, the four rightist parties elected sixteen of the seventy-one congressmen. His neoliberal economic program, which failed to control inflation or end the nation's economic recession, sparked an upsurge in political confrontation and violence, including abortive coup attempts and clashes between students, labor, and guerrillas and the government. The situation was exacerbated by declines in the price of petroleum and disruptions in exports when earthquakes damaged the trans-Amazonian pipeline. A series of confrontations between Febres-Cordero and Congress led to the censoring of a number of administrative officials for corruption and abuse of civil rights. Economic uncertainty fueled capital flight and the depreciation of the sucre.

The 1988 presidential election was won by Rodrigo Borja, whose campaign called for a mixed economy, the rescheduling of the nation's foreign debt based on its real value, and an end to the free-market, neoliberal economic program of Febres-Cordero. During the campaign Borja stressed the need to reduce unemployment through tax incentives to companies and public works projects, to increase the minimum wage, to promote social welfare, and to reform public finances.

Unlike Roldós, Hurtado, and Febres-Cordero, Borja took office with significant congressional support; Izquierda Democrática elected twenty-nine of the seventy-one deputies, and Borja had the support of other major parties. Despite this advantage, he faced a difficult economic situation, including a large public-sector deficit, high unemployment, unresolved foreign debt negotiations, and high inflation. During his first year in office he introduced minidevaluations of the sucre; increased taxes, the minimum wage, and prices for electricity, gasoline, and basic foods; and imposed import restrictions. Although the program fell short of the recommendations of the World Bank, which included elimination of public subsidies, sharp cuts in public expenditures, the privatization of state enterprises, and the freezing of interest rates, the gradualist approach satisfied neither labor nor business. Borja's limited austerity policies had a high political cost, including strikes and the reemergence of a highly fragmented political system.

In the 1990 congressional elections, the president's party lost sixteen of its thirty seats. None of the twelve parties represented in the legislature achieved a majority, returning Ecuador to government by unstable coalition. Labor unrest and confrontations between the legislature and the other branches of government, including impeachment proceedings against a number of Borja's ministers, increased in 1991.

Confrontations between the Congress and the Borja administration continued in 1992 as politicians positioned themselves for the presidential elections. As in the 1980s, the 1992 campaign was dominated by bitter personal rivalries and a fragmented party system. Sixto Durán-Ballén defeated Jaime Nebot Saadi in a runoff election. Durán-Ballén, a founder of the Partido Social Cristiano with León Febres-Cordero, broke with the party when Jaime Nebot Saadi was selected to run for president in the 1992 elections. He and his supporters from the Partido Social Cristiano formed the Partido Unidad Republicana as a vehicle to support his candidacy. Although Sixto Durán-Ballén won the election, his party secured only twelve seats in the seventy-seven-seat legislature. Twelve parties elected representatives to Congress. Durán-Ballén and his vice president Alberto Dahik, whose Partido Conservador Ecuatoriano won five legislative seats, formed a minority government.

The new government faced the difficult task of implementing tough austerity measures and structural economic reforms in a country with a highly inequitable distribution of income, where living standards have fallen steadily throughout the 1980s. Durán-Ballén's program, which included the privatization of state-owned industries, a sharp reduction in the public-sector payroll, and policies to stimulate foreign investment, threatened a number of important groups. Despite repeated efforts to establish and maintain coalitions with other parties including the Partido Social Cristiano, which held twenty legislative seats, the administration was unable to avoid the legislative gridlock and repeated votes of censure that have crippled Ecuadorian governments since 1979.

LUIS ROBALINO DÁVILA, *Orígines de Ecuador de hoy*, vols. 1–8 (1967–1970); JOHN D. MARTZ, *Ecuador: Conflicting Political Culture and the Quest for Progress* (1972); JOHN SAMUEL FITCH, *The Military Coup d'État as a Political Process: Ecuador, 1948–1966* (1977); OSVALDO HURTADO, *Political Power in Ecuador* (1980), esp. pp. 43–311; LINDA ALEXANDER RODRÍGUEZ, *The Search for Public Policy: Regional Politics and Government Finances in Ecuador, 1830–1940* (1985); JOHN D. MARTZ, *Politics and Petroleum in Ecuador* (1987); DAVID W. SCHODT, *Ecuador: An Andean Enigma* (1987); FRANK MACDONALD SPINDLER, *Nineteenth-Century Ecuador: A Historical Introduction* (1987); MARK J. VAN AKEN, *King of the Night: Juan José Flores and Ecuador, 1824–1964* (1989).

LINDA ALEXANDER RODRÍGUEZ

ECUADOR: CONSTITUTIONS Ecuador's present constitution was adopted by popular vote on 15 January 1978 (43 percent yes; 32 percent no; 23 percent spoiled ballots) and went into effect in August 1979. It is the nation's seventeenth since Ecuador became independent in 1830, but few have touched the lives of most of the population. The impact on the political process has been greater, however, as institutional rules and procedures have been altered through the years.

The 1830 charter, which brought together the departments of Quito, Guayaquil, and Cuenca in a confederation, was replaced five years later by a more centralized constitutional system. This, in turn, was supplanted in 1843 by the "Charter of Slavery" imposed by Juan José FLORES, who, having begun his second term as president in 1839, sought to enshrine his personalist rule through a constitution that granted him dictatorial powers while stressing separation of church and state. It was replaced following his ouster from power in 1845, and in 1861 another constitution provided for direct popular suffrage and recognized Catholicism as the state religion. Eight years later Gabriel GARCÍA MORENO decreed a new document, known as the "Black Charter," which further enhanced the role of the Roman Catholic church by giving it unchallenged control over education. The secular authority of the church was underlined by the requirement that citizenship be denied to non-Catholics.

The Constitution of 1897, adopted after Eloy ALFARO led the Liberals to power, reversed the position of Catholicism and broadened the recognition of individual rights; the death penalty was abolished and religious freedom was made explicit. In 1906 Alfaro convened a Constituent Assembly to draft a new document that explicitly called for separation of church and state while extending the constitutional commitment to the protection of basic civil rights and privileges.

Women acquired the right to vote in the Constitution of 1929—the first such action in Latin America. It was also a document that, in reaction against presidential excesses, provided Congress with powers that virtually crippled the central government. Any minister could be dismissed through a vote of no confidence, and presidential authority was severely restricted. Reorganization of Congress included the establishment of both regional and functional representation. Thus there were, among others, senators for industry and for agriculture from both the coast and the highlands. Representatives of labor and of the armed forces were also included. Overall, traditional elites benefited from the introduction of functional senators chosen by leaders of Ecuador's major interest associations.

Ecuador's fourteenth and fifteenth constitutions were promulgated in 1945 and 1946, at a time when José María VELASCO IBARRA had returned to power and was seeking to legitimize and restructure the nature of executive rule. The second of these survived until the convening of a Constituent Assembly in 1966 following the resignation of a military junta. It resulted in the sixteenth constitution, promulgated on 25 May 1967, which took effect upon the inauguration of Velasco Ibarra to his fifth term on 1 September 1968. It created a large number of new autonomous state agencies outside the budgetary and administrative control of the chief executive; regional interests were also strengthened at the expense of the central government through a decentralized system of disbursing taxes. When Velasco was forced out of office in 1972, the 1967 constitution was set aside.

When the military junta decided in 1976 to move toward the reestablishment of elected government, it named a commission to study the question of constitutional forms. The commission eventually drew up two choices for submission to a plebiscite: a revision of the 1945 constitution and a new charter. The second was chosen by nearly 75 percent of the electorate and, with minor adjustments, has been in effect since the reinauguration of civilian government in August 1979. Perhaps the most striking change was the extension of suffrage to illiterates for the first time. In addition, the bicameral legislature became a unicameral body from which functional representatives were excluded. Four economic sectors were specified: public, private, mixed public-private, and communitarian. There was controversy over the communitarian, which was viewed by traditional elites as a threat to private property. In practice this would prove to be a misplaced concern.

New electoral regulations accompanying the 1978 Constitution introduced a double round of presidential elections, so that the eventual victor would enter office with a clear majority. There were also efforts to regulate political parties in order to minimize the degree of fragmentation which had long been prevalent. Among other things, parties failing to poll 5 percent of the vote in two consecutive elections would lose official recognition by the Supreme Electoral Tribunal.

The new constitution was viewed as a reflection of the reformist mood which gripped Ecuador in the 1970s, underlined by the emergence of a new generation of political leaders to replace Velasco, Camilo Ponce Enríquez, Galo Plaza Lasso, Otto Arosemena Gómez, and Carlos Julio Arosemena Godoy. In practice it has encouraged popular electoral participation and some opening of the system, but not to such an extent that traditional elitist attitudes and interests have been threatened. While there have been three successive constitutional periods since the armed forces relinquished power, each has been plagued by instability, intransigent opposition, congressional obstructionism, and judicial timidity in the face of partisan attacks. Thus the constitutional structures, while more consistent with a modernizing nation, have not significantly encouraged a maturation of the political process in Ecuador.

GEORGE I. BLANKSTEN, *Ecuador: Constitutions and Caudillos* (1951); ALBERT WILLIAM BORK and GEORG MAIER, *Historical Dictionary of Ecuador* (1975); HOWARD HANDELMAN and THOMAS G. SANDERS, eds., *Military Government and the Movement Toward Democracy in South America* (1981); OSVALDO HURTADO, *Political Power in Ecuador*, translated by Nick D. Mills, Jr. (1980); JOHN D. MARTZ, *The Politics of Petroleum in Ecuador* (1987); DAVID W. SCHODT, *Ecuador, an Andean Enigma* (1987).

JOHN D. MARTZ

ECUADOR: GEOGRAPHY. The country's borders have been in doubt during most of the nation's life. When it seceded from Gran Colombia in 1830, the new nation claimed 282,972 square miles. Two years later with the incorporation of the Galápagos Islands the figure increased to 285,944 square miles. Colombia and Peru disputed Ecuador's claim to much of this territory, however. Border incidents became a frequent source of friction among the three nations. Ecuador and Colombia finally settled their boundary conflict in 1916; an agreement with Peru has proved more difficult to achieve.

Most of the area claimed by both Ecuador and Peru was in the Oriente, the lands east of the Andes. Ecuador failed to occupy the region effectively. In contrast, Peru advanced steadily into the disputed territory. By 1892 the southern republic had occupied 46,772 square miles of the contested area and claimed another 154,600 square miles. After two wars and decades of conflict, Ecuador and Peru seemingly agreed to a firm border in 1942 by signing the Protocol of Rio de Janeiro. The agreement reduced Ecuador to approximately 105,800 square miles. President José María Velasco IBARRA repudiated the accord in 1960 claiming that it had been imposed by force of arms. The issues remain unsettled and border clashes continue in the region.

The twin cordilleras of the Andes, which traverse the country from north to south, divide mainland Ecuador into three distinct geographic zones. These great mountain ranges include among their high peaks Mount Chimborazo (20,561 feet above sea level), Cotopaxi (19,347 feet), Cayambe (18,996 feet), and Antisana (18,228 feet). They partition the country into the Oriente, or eastern region, the Sierra, or highland region, and the Costa, or coastal region.

The Oriente contains approximately 46 percent of the national territory. It extends from the foothills of the eastern cordillera to the lower regions of the AMAZON basin. Most of the area is a single floodplain covered with tropical woodlands and rain forest. This hot and humid region has a heavy annual rainfall that ranges from 71.4 inches in the south to 166.6 inches in the north. Median temperatures range from 73°F to 80°F. The Oriente has an excellent system of navigable rivers, but they flow southeastward, away from the heavily settled parts of Ecuador into Brazil and the Atlantic.

The Oriente is sparsely populated and, until recently, produced nothing of sufficient value to attract large-scale settlement or investment. Only since the 1960s with the discovery of petroleum has the region begun to enter the mainstream of national political and economic life. Previously the area did not command national attention unless a border dispute became the subject of intense diplomatic activity or exploded into open conflict. Since most of the Oriente's tiny population consisted of Indians with no political power, the national government could avoid committing its scarce development capital to the area. Even if sufficient capital had existed, the contemporary level of technology could not develop the area efficiently. The cost of exploiting the Oriente remained prohibitive, even after World War II, when scientific advances removed many barriers. Circumstances changed in the late 1960s because of the growing world demand for energy, dwindling petroleum reserves, and the rise of OPEC. At that time significant petroleum deposits were confirmed in the Oriente's Aguarico basin. The increase in the world market price of oil made the cost of developing the area acceptable. The Oriente is currently an important focus of national concern and government development policy.

The highlands, sandwiched between the Cordillera Occidental and the Cordillera Oriental, comprise about a quarter of the nation's territory. This central zone is divided into a series of narrow basins formed when lava flows linked the Andean ranges. The eleven basins between 7,029 feet and 9,075 feet—Tulcán, Ibarra, Quito, Ambato, Riobamba, Alausí, Cañar, Cuenca, Jubones, Loja, and Macará—are isolated from each other as the sierra is from the Oriente or from the coast. Each basin varies from mountainous to slightly rolling terrain and, in most, there are deep valleys cut by streams. The rivers that drain the region are not navigable in the highlands. All the basins are densely populated, with most of the land exploited either for subsistence agriculture or for livestock.

Temperatures range from below freezing above the permanent snow line (about 16,689 feet) to a pleasant 71° F in the subtropical valley. Sierra agriculture varies with altitude. Most basins contain four climatic zones. The *páramos,* a barren windswept region above 10,065 feet, are used for pasture and to grow potatoes and other native tubers. The *altiplano,* which lies between 8,052 feet, and 10,065 feet, is suitable for grain cultivation and pasture. The growing season, however, is short and frequent frosts endanger even hearty crops. Annual rainfall in the *páramos* and the *altiplano* is about 40 inches. The temperate valley, at elevations from 6,039 feet to 8,052 feet, is devoted to a variety of temperature crops. The average yearly rainfall of 20 inches is supplemented by the runoff from higher altitudes. Located at elevations between 3,018 feet and 6,039 feet are tropical valleys that produce vegetables, cotton, sugarcane, citrus fruits, as well as the highland staples: potatoes and grains.

The productivity of the sierra varies. Centuries of continuous cultivation by primitive methods have eroded and depleted soils. The fertility of the Ambato and Riobamba basins suffers because the soil is of recent volcanic origin and does not retain moisture. In contrast, the Cuenca basin, with ample rainfall and one of the least porous soils in the highlands, enjoys much greater agricultural potential. Slightly less favorable conditions exist in Quito; the rolling hills in the southern part of the basin are the site of extensive grain cultivation and livestock raising.

The coastal, or littoral, region of Ecuador encompasses approximately 69,300 square miles of plain, hills, and Andean piedmont. It is bounded by the Pacific Ocean on the west and by the Andes on the east. About half of the region is a low alluvial plain known as the Guayas lowlands; it lies below 990 feet and varies in width from 19 to 111 miles. The littoral region also contains two hilly areas: the foothills of the Andes that rise to an altitude of 1,617 feet and the hilly region that extends west of Guayaquil to the coast and northward.

The natural vegetation of the coast reflects the decrease in rainfall from north to south. While there are two rainy seasons at the Colombian border, most of the littoral has a single rainy season that becomes shorter as it moves south. The rain FORESTS of the north give way to semideciduous forest and tropical woodlands in the south. Along the Santa Elena peninsula and in the extreme south only xerophytic shrubs can survive without irrigation. In the east, however, the foothills of the Andes receive enough precipitation to support rain forest.

The littoral region is very productive. Coastal soils are generally fertile, well watered, with a temperature that averages between 73° F and 77° F. While a wide variety of fruits and vegetables are grown for local consumption, coastal agriculture is oriented primarily toward an export market. The Guayas lowlands, which extend north and southwest of Guayaquil, possess ideal conditions for tropical agriculture. Navigable rivers provide the region with access to the sea. As a result, the Guayas basin be-

came the country's primary producer of agricultural exports including cacao, bananas, and coffee. Since these products constituted Ecuador's most important exports for most of the national period, the coast and its major port, Guayaquil, dominated the country's economy.

The GALÁPAGOS ISLANDS, or the Archipiélago de Colón, are a group of volcanic islands about 600 miles due west of the mainland. The islands suffer from a scarcity of water, and consequently they are thinly populated and of little economic value. However, the wide variety of exotic fauna and flora that survives makes the Galápagos interesting to scientists and to tourists. The waters surrounding the archipelago are excellent fishing grounds that Ecuadorians have only recently begun to exploit.

LILO LINKE, *Ecuador: Country of Contrasts,* 3d ed. (1960, reissued 1981).

LINDA A. RODRÍGUEZ

ECUADOR: ORGANIZATIONS

Ecuadorian Confederation of Class-Based Organizations
Central Ecuadoriana de Organizaciones Clasistas—CEDOC

CEDOC (originally the Ecuadorian Confederation of Catholic Worker Organizations) was founded in 1938 as a Catholic labor federation. It is the oldest labor federation in Ecuador. Conservative, sierra-based, and linked with the ruling elite, CEDOC favored employee-employer harmony under capitalism. CEDOC appealed to artisans who rejected the anticapitalist positions taken by the rival CTE (Confederation of Workers of Ecuador). CEDOC broke ties with the Catholic church in 1955 and moved toward a philosophy of Christian humanism. By the 1970s CEDOC had evolved into a much less conservative organization. After 1971 CEDOC began to cooperate with the CTE in the United Workers Front (FUT).

For a concise and highly perceptive summary see RICHARD LEE MILK, "Ecuador," in *Latin American Labor Organizations,* edited by Gerald Michael Greenfield and Sheldon L. Maram (1987), pp. 289–305. See also Milk's 1977 Indiana University dissertation, "Growth and Development of Ecuador's Worker Organizations, 1895–1944," which provides the best general account of Ecuadorian labor. PATRICIO YCAZA, *Historia del movimiento obrero ecuatoriano,* 2d ed. (1984), also contains much worthwhile information.

RONN F. PINEO

Workers Confederation of Ecuador
Confederación de Trabajadores del Ecuador—CTE

Ecuador's largest union federation. In 1944 elements of the radical labor movement reached an agreement with leading politician José María VELASCO IBARRA: labor supported Velasco's return to power and he permitted the legal founding of the CTE. The CTE organized principally coastal workers from the more advanced sectors of the economy. It frequently provided important support for populist and reform-oriented politicians. Led at different times by both socialists and communists, the CTE has historically been the most staunchly militant of Ecuador's labor federations. As a result, it has repeatedly been the target of vigorous government repression. The CTE has also often been harmed by bitter left-wing factional disputes. Prior to the 1970s, the CTE was usually openly hostile to its key rival labor federation, the generally more conservative Ecuadorian Confederation of Class-Based Organizations (CEDOC). Since 1971, however, the CTE and CEDOC have sometimes cooperated in the United Workers Front (FUT).

For a concise and highly perceptive analytical summary, see RICHARD LEE MILK, "Ecuador," in *Latin American Labor Organizations*, edited by Gerald Michael Greenfield and Sheldon L. Maram (1987), pp. 289–305 See also Milk's 1977 Indiana University dissertation, "Growth and Development of Ecuador's Worker Organizations, 1895–1944," for the best general account of Ecuadorian labor. PATRICIO Y ICAZA, *Historia del movimiento obrero ecuatoriano*, 2d ed. (1984), also contains much worthwhile information. For the broader political economic context see OSVALDO HURTADO, *Political Power in Ecuador*, translated by Nick D. Mills, Jr. (1985).

RONN F. PINEO

ECUADOR: POLITICAL PARTIES

Overview

The history of Ecuadorian political parties is consistent with the instability, rampant partisanship, and opportunistic factionalism of the political system. The parties also reflect the stark regionalism of the nation that is seen in the contrast between the two historic parties, the Conservatives and the Radical Liberals. In their early years these parties represented divergent interests. Conservatives favored church involvement in national affairs and an active role for the state; Liberals preferred to minimize the role of the church while favoring regional interests and a weak central government. These two views were personified by the rule of two major figures: Gabriel GARCÍA MORENO and Eloy ALFARO.

García Moreno, who came to power in 1861, established Latin America's most theocratic state. During his time in power Catholicism became the state-sanctioned religion, a concordat with the Vatican ceded national control over education, and governmental centralization was promoted. For the first time the administration of the state was rationalized. Conservative domination continued following García Moreno's assassination in 1875, but political dialogue was further polarized with the rise of the Radical Liberal Party (Partido Liberal Radical—PLR), officially organized in 1878 by José Ignacio de VEINTIMILLA. The Liberals provided the base

for Alfaro's 1895 revolution, which initiated a lengthy period of Liberal domination. Although Marxist organizations were later established—notably the Partido Socialista Ecuatoriano (Ecuadorian Socialist Party—PSE) in 1926 and the Partido Comunista Ecuatoriano (Ecuadorian Communist Party—PCE) five years later—the Liberals and Conservatives retained hegemonic influence until the last Liberal government, that of Carlos ARROYO DEL RÍO, was overthrown in 1944. Meanwhile, populism had become an important force in party politics, exemplified in its most extreme form by José María VELASCO IBARRA, the first of whose five nonconsecutive administrations began in 1934.

The Velasquista movement survived until the end of Velasco's fifth and final government in 1972, and disappeared following the death of the octagenarian caudillo in 1979. Avowedly anti-party in outlook, Velasco organized his followers during campaigns, inspiring them with fiery oratory and his uniquely austere charisma. Once in office, however, the electoral organization soon disintegrated while his maladroit administrative style nourished the civil turmoil which encouraged all but one of his presidencies to be overthrown. Despite the many twists and turns of his rhetoric through the years, Velasco customarily responded to vested economic and business elites while effectively discouraging the emergence of well-organized, mass-based political parties.

During the period of military rule (1972–1979) a new generation of leaders began to emerge. There arose a new set of parties ranging across the ideological spectrum while showing attention to rationalized organization and to the winning of enduring popular support. Notable in this regard were Izquierda Democrática (Democratic Left—ID) and Democracia Popular (Popular Democracy—DP), each of which participated in the 1978 elections and subsequently built further popular strength. The ID, true to its label as a party of the democratic Left, espoused social and economic reforms via a strong government backed by broad-based support. Led by Rodrigo BORJA, the ID increased its strength until he won the presidency on his third attempt, in 1988.

The Christian democratic DP, originally a small group of academics and intellectuals, entered an electoral alliance in 1978 that brought its leader, Osvaldo HURTADO LARREA, to the vice presidency. When President Jaime ROLDÓS AGUILERA was killed in a 1981 plane crash, Hurtado succeeded to the presidency and, despite strong partisan opposition, preserved constitutional legitimacy. Since leaving office he has been an influential national figure, although the DP has not returned to power on its own. It advocates a moderate reformist program broadly similar to that of the ID, with which it sometimes cooperates. Together they are often in bitter conflict with rightist forces. The latter won national power in 1984 with the coalition Frente de Reconstrucción Nacional (National Reconstruction Front—FRN) backing the fiery populist León FEBRES-CORDERO, who pulled together a revived Partido Social Cristiano (Social Christian Party—PSC) along with the remnants of the Conservative and Radical Liberal parties. Febres left office badly discredited, thus helping to pave the way for Borja's win in 1988. By the 1990s Ecuadorian conservatism was resurgent, representing a powerful and well-financed current in national politics.

Populism is also an important factor in party politics. In 1978 it helped bring Roldós a smashing victory with the Concentración de Fuerzas Populares (Concentration of Popular Forces—CFP). The party later fragmented, and Abdalá Bucaram Ortiz, brother-in-law of Roldós and nephew of the CFP's former caudillo, Asaad BUCARAM, has risen to power in Guayaquil. His own personal vehicle, the Partido Roldosista Ecuatoriano (Ecuadorian Roldosist Party—PRE) has become an important voice for lower-class demands from the coastal areas, and the quixotic and erratic Bucaram ran second to Borja in 1988. The party is largely personalist, and although it is well organized on the coast, it is weak in the highlands.

By the 1990s the party panorama, while different from that of a generation earlier, still showed the characteristics of immaturity. Granted an increase in organizational structures and greater concern with doctrinal and programmatic matters, the impact of powerful personalities remains critical. Unbridled partisanship and short-term opportunism are very much present, and the party system is still traditionalist. Much greater growth will be necessary before the parties become as modern and rational as in most of Ecuador's South American neighbors.

DAVID CORKILL and DAVID CUBITT, *Ecuador: Fragile Democracy* (1988); OSVALDO HURTADO, *Political Power in Ecuador*, translated by Nick D. Mills, Jr. (1980); JOHN D. MARTZ, *The Politics of Petroleum in Ecuador* (1987); LINDA ALEXANDER RODRÍGUEZ, *The Search for Public Policy: Regional Politics and Government Finances in Ecuador, 1830–1940* (1985); DAVID W. SCHODT, *Ecuador, an Andean Enigma* (1987).

JOHN D. MARTZ

Concentration of Popular Forces
Concentración de Fuerzas Populares—CFP

The Concentration of Popular Forces has been the leading populist political party of Ecuador since 1946. It generally favors an agenda of socioeconomic reform. Founder Carlos Guevara Moreno finished third in the presidential balloting in 1956. Asaad BUCARAM ELMHALIN (1921–1981), twice mayor of Guayaquil, followed as CFP leader. Bucaram was a leading presidential contender twice: in 1972, when the military canceled the elections; and in 1978, when the military disqualified him on the grounds that his parents were Lebanese. In 1978 Bucaram's nephew-in-law, Jaime ROLDÓS AGUILERA, took Bucaram's place, campaigning under the slogan, "Roldós to govern, Bucaram to power." Roldós led the CFP to victory over conservative Sixto Durán Ballén of the Social Christian Party (PSC) in the runoff election

of 1979. Bucaram became leader of the National Chamber of Representatives, but soon broke with Roldós over the president's austerity program. Roldós left the CFP and formed a new party, the People, Change, and Democracy (PCD) in 1980.

For an excellent overview of modern Ecuadorian political economy, see DAVID W. SCHODT, *Ecuador: An Andean Enigma* (1987). For a focused treatment of the recent transition to elected government, see the analysis offered in CATHERINE M. CONAGHAN, *Restructuring Domination: Industrialists and the State in Ecuador* (1988). AMPARO MENÉNDEZ-CARRIÓN, *La conquista del voto en el Ecuador: De Velasco a Roldós* (1986), examines the party's popular basis of support. JOHN D. MARTZ provides an insightful treatment of the Bucaram/Roldós feud in *Politics and Petroleum in Ecuador* (1987).

RONN F. PINEO

Conservative Party
Partido Conservador

One of Ecuador's two historic political parties, the Partido Conservador emerged informally in the 1860s during the dictatorship of Gabriel GARCÍA MORENO and was officially founded in 1883. Consistent with the tenets of García Moreno, the party staked out a position as the unyielding champion of Catholic church interests, as well as of public education and many other secular matters. Advocates of a strong central government, the Conservatives remained influential during the long period of Liberal hegemony (1895–1944).

Traditionally the vehicle for the political expression of conservative interests in general and of highland landowners' interests in particular, the party enjoyed renewed influence during the 1956–1960 presidency of Camilo PONCE ENRÍQUEZ. It then began to decline, and was notably weakened by introduction of universal suffrage in 1978. Even before then, however, its progressive wing had split off in 1964 to form Democracia Popular (Popular Democracy—DP). In 1978 and 1984 the Conservatives joined rightist coalitions while running their own congressional slate. They placed ten members in Congress in 1978 but only two in 1984. By the 1990s they had lost these seats, the party was moribund, and former followers had gone over to the Social Christians.

GEORGE I. BLANKSTEN, *Ecuador: Constitutions and Caudillos* (1951); JOHN D. MARTZ, *Ecuador: Conflicting Political Culture and the Quest for Progress* (1972).

JOHN D. MARTZ

Democratic Alliance
Alianza Democrática—ADE

The ADE, an ad-hoc, wide-ranging political coalition, was formed in 1944 to support exiled populist José María VELASCO IBARRA's bid to remove the government of Carlos Alberto ARROYO DEL RÍO (1940–1944). The coalition, led by Francisco Arízaga Luque, brought together Socialists, Conservatives, independents, and Communists, joined only by their shared dissatisfaction with Arroyo del Río. Arroyo had earned the enmity of Ecuadorians by presiding over the nation's disastrous defeat in a war with Peru. In January 1942 Arroyo del Río agreed to the Rio Protocol, whereby Ecuador surrendered 80,000 square miles of territory in Amazonia to Peru. The Democratic Alliance, assisted by elements within the military, overthrew Arroyo del Río in May 1944. Velasco Ibarra returned from exile and claimed the presidency. In May 1964 various conservative groups briefly revitalized the ADE as part of a failed effort to force out the military government of Ramón CASTRO JIJÓN (1963–1966).

DAVID W. SCHODT, *Ecuador: An Andean Enigma* (1987), provides a summary overview of political economy. JOHN D. MARTZ, *Ecuador: Conflicting Political Culture and the Quest for Progress* (1972); and GEORGE I. BLANKSTEN, *Ecuador: Constitutions and Caudillos* (1964), offer accounts of the return of Velasco Ibarra.

RONN F. PINEO

See also **Ecuador–Peru Boundary Disputes.**

Democratic Left
Izquierda Democrática—ID

The Democratic Left, the political party of President Rodrigo BORJA CEVALLOS and of Vice President Luis Parodi Valverde (1988–1992), generally favors moderate reform. It began as a splinter party in 1970, breaking off from the Radical Liberal Party (PLR). In 1984 ID presidential candidate Borja lost the national runoff election to conservative Guayaquil businessman León FEBRES-CORDERO (1984–1988) of the National Reconstruction Front. In 1988 Borja defeated former Guayaquil mayor Abdalá Bucaram Ortiz of the Ecuadorian Roldosist Party (PRE): Bucaram carried the coast, but Borja took the sierra. Although Borja campaigned on a platform of liberal-left policies, in office he dealt with Ecuador's continuing economic crisis by adopting an austerity program, devaluing the sucre, increasing taxes, and loosening price controls on basic necessities. In foreign affairs, Borja changed course from the previous administration and reopened relations with Sandinista Nicaragua.

For an excellent overview of modern Ecuadorian political economy, see DAVID W. SCHODT, *Ecuador: An Andean Enigma* (1987).

RONN F. PINEO

Radical Liberal Party
Partido Liberal Radical—PLR

One of Ecuador's two historic political parties, known officially as the Radical Liberal Party (Partido Liberal Radical—PLR), the Liberals were officially organized by Ignacio de VEINTIMILLA in 1878 and convened the first party assembly two years later. First seizing power through the 1895 revolution led by its renowned leader Eloy ALFARO, the PLR remained the dominant force in national politics until 1944, when its last president, Carlos ARROYO DEL RÍO, was ousted. The PLR, originally firmly committed to church-state separation, to public education, and to promotion of external trade and commerce, gradually grew more conservative as these issues became less salient to the nation.

In the 1950s, despite their support for the administration of Galo PLAZA LASSO, the Liberals progressively declined. The party's last serious bid for national power came in 1968 when its venerable leader, Andrés F. CÓRDOVA, ran for the presidency and was narrowly defeated by José María VELASCO IBARRA. During the 1970s the PLR was weakened by internal schisms, most notably that of younger militants who founded the Izquierda Democrática (Democratic Left—ID). In 1978 the Liberal old guard made a final electoral effort but was rebuffed. Since that time the PLR has sought legislative and electoral coalitions with other parties and leaders. Its congressional representation had dropped to three by 1990, and the PLR had become irrelevant to national politics as newer parties emerged to engage the electorate.

GEORGE I. BLANKSTEN, *Ecuador: Constitutions and Caudillos* (1951); JOHN D. MARTZ, *Ecuador: Conflicting Political Culture and the Quest for Progress* (1972).

JOHN D. MARTZ

ECUADOR: REVOLUTIONS

Revolution of 1895

The liberals were brought to power in Ecuador by an uprising that followed the resignation of the progressive president Luis CORDERO in the face of a conservative-inspired rebellion. The provisional government lost control as the country disintegrated into warring factions, with insurrections in Ambato, El Oro, Guayaquil, Latacunga, Los Ríos, Manabí Province, and Quito. Coastal liberals saw an opportunity to achieve national supremacy by inviting Eloy ALFARO to return from exile and assume command of their forces. With the support of other *guerrilleros*, including Leonidas PLAZA, Alfaro's coastal *montoneras* decisively defeated government troops in August 1895. Alfaro first assumed power and then called an assembly that wrote a new liberal constitution and elected him interim president in October 1896. The triumphant liberals, who dominated national politics until 9 July 1925, stressed the necessity of establishing a secular state to promote social and economic development and modernization.

LUIS ROBALINO DÁVILA, *Orígenes del Ecuador de hoy*, vol. 7 (1969); LINDA ALEXANDER RODRÍGUEZ, *The Search for Public Policy: Government Finances in Ecuador, 1830–1940* (1985), esp. pp. 44–52, 88–92; FRANK MAC DONALD SPINDLER, *Nineteenth-Century Ecuador* (1987), esp. pp. 147–169.

LINDA ALEXANDER RODRÍGUEZ

Revolution of 1925

The coup of 9 July 1925 was the first institutional intrusion of the military into politics. The young officers, who believed they represented national rather than regional interests, justified their actions in a twelve-point reform program. The coup followed an extensive campaign by sierra publicists and politicians who portrayed the professional military as the only body that could free the government from the domination of a corrupt coastal oligarchy. These critics argued that the government was the captive of Guayaquil bankers and that the professional military was being dishonored and compromised by corrupt political officers who supported liberal governments. The reforms advocated in the name of national unity and rehabilitation actually were used by sierra (conservative) politicians to return political control to Quito.

LUIS ROBALINO DÁVILA, *El 9 de julio de 1925* (1973); LINDA ALEXANDER RODRÍGUEZ, *The Search for Public Policy: Regional Politics and Government Finances in Ecuador, 1830–1940* (1985), esp. pp. 118–133.

LINDA ALEXANDER RODRÍGUEZ

ECUADOR–PERU BOUNDARY DISPUTES. From their foundation the nations of Ecuador and Peru have disputed the demarcation of their common border. The chief point of contention is control over 120,000 square miles of mostly uninhabited AMAZON jungle between the Marañón–Amazon and the Putumayo rivers. The nations appeared to have settled the issue as early as December 1823 in the Mosquera–Galdiano Agreement, a document that reaffirmed the 1809 colonial boundary between the viceroyalties of PERU and NEW GRANADA. However, in 1827 Peru attacked Ecuador, then part of the nation of Gran Colombia. In 1829 Gran Colombia defeated Peru at the battle of Tarqui, and Peru signed the Treaty of Girón. In September 1829 the two nations agreed to the Treaty of Guayaquil, also known as the Larrea–Gual Treaty, which again designated the boundary as that of the former viceroyalties. The Pedemonte–Mosquera Protocol of August 1830, designed to implement the prior treaties, granted Ecuador access to the Amazon River.

In 1857 Ecuador attempted to retire its debt to Great Britain by issuing bonds for Amazonian territory still under dispute. Peru objected, and war followed. In the Treaty of Mapasingue (January 1860), victorious Peru secured considerable Ecuadorian concessions. However, the treaty was ratified by neither nation. In August 1887 the two nations signed the Espinoza–Bonifaz Arbitration Convention, calling for the intercession of the king of Spain; his decision was to be binding and without appeal. The García–Herrera Treaty of May 1890 divided the disputed zone in half. Again, however, neither nation ratified the treaty. Finally, in 1924 Peru and Ecuador signed a protocol naming the United States as

arbiter, and in 1933 both nations formally requested that President Franklin D. ROOSEVELT intercede. In 1936 the two nations agreed to a protocol resolving the matter. However, the ensuing talks broke off in 1938.

It fell to military power, not diplomacy, to determine the boundary. Of the two nations, Ecuador's position has historically been weakened by its failure to establish a physical presence in the disputed area. Peru, on the other hand, has been more effective in settling the region. In 1935 Colombia ceded to Peru territory that Ecuador continued to claim. After Ecuadorian efforts to provoke an incident, in 1940 Peruvian troops massed along the southern border. Argentina, Brazil, and the United States offered joint mediation, but border skirmishes flared in 1941 and rapidly escalated into a serious military engagement. Nevertheless, Ecuadorian president Carlos Alberto ARROYO DEL RÍO maintained his troops in Quito, guarding his presidency against internal enemies. As a result, Ecuador was powerless to respond to Peru's July 1941 invasion of the rich, densely populated coastal province of El Oro. Ecuadorian forces lacked basic supplies; in all respects they were woefully unprepared for the conflict. Peru had an air force of 25 planes and troops numbering from 5,000 to 10,000; Ecuador had neither an air force nor antiaircraft weapons, and its troops totaled only from 635 to 1,600.

Ecuador retreated headlong before the Peruvian advance. The civilian population of El Oro did almost nothing to oppose the invading army, and some 20,000 refugees streamed into GUAYAQUIL. Ecuador suffered some 150 killed and wounded; Peru, about 400. Peru seized the province of El Oro and began to move on Guayaquil, Ecuador's most important port. As Peru bombed coastal towns and advanced, troops in Guayaquil designated as frontline reinforcements mutinied. Ecuador sought peace talks. Following negotiations, Ecuador and Peru agreed to a military pullback and in January 1942 signed the Rio Protocol. Both nations ratified the accord. During the discussions, the United States, Argentina, Brazil, and Chile—mediators and later guarantors of the agreement—were preoccupied with World War II. They made it plain to Ecuador that if it refused to sign, they would withdraw from the talks, leaving Ecuador to deal with the victorious and still menacing Peru. Ecuador surrendered two-thirds of the disputed Amazonian territory: some 80,000 square miles of uninhabited lands and an additional 5,000 square miles of settled territory. Ecuador also lost its outlet to the Amazon River. Still, if Ecuador had not signed, it stood to lose a great deal more. Following the agreement, Peru withdrew from El Oro.

In 1951 new problems arose when the discovery of the Cenepa River in the Amazon complicated the final demarcation of the border. In August 1960 populist Ecuadorian president José María VELASCO IBARRA declared the Rio Protocol null and void and the Ecuadorian Supreme Court later followed suit. Ecuador has since continued to regard the settlement as invalid. Problems persist along the frontier. In 1981 and 1995 brief clashes led to several deaths.

For the most evenhanded treatment of this disputatious matter, see DAVID HARTZLER ZOOK, JR., *Zarumilla–Marañón: The Ecuador–Peru Dispute* (1964). Brief overviews of the issues are in JOHN D. MARTZ, *Ecuador: Conflicting Political Culture and the Quest for Progress* (1972); and GEORGE I. BLANKSTEN, *Ecuador: Constitutions and Caudillos* (1964).

RONN F. PINEO

See also **Zarumilla, Battle of.**

EDER, SANTIAGO MARTÍN (*b.* 24 June 1838; *d.* 25 December 1921), Colombian agricultural entrepreneur. Born in Mitau, in present-day Latvia, Santiago emigrated in 1851 to the United States to join his brother Henry, who was engaged in various mercantile activities in California, Panama, and Chile. His Harvard law education sustained his later activities as U.S. consul in Buenaventura, but his family's commercial relations shaped his life.

In 1864 Eder purchased La Rita and La Manuelita plantations near Palmira to develop export agriculture. After spotty success with tobacco, indigo, coffee, and sugar, Eder devoted himself to the general economic development of the Cauca Valley. His investments in the Buenaventura-Cali railroad, the Cauca steamship company, and various banks in Cali placed him at the fore of regional developers. Eder's son Charles married the daughter of Italian entrepreneur Ernesto Cerruti and assumed control of the family's Cauca properties. Another son, Phanor, became active in international commerce and law. The Manuelita mill, completely modernized by 1903, became the country's leading producer of domestically consumed refined sugar.

PHANOR J. EDER, *El fundador: Santiago M. Eder* (1959); CARLOS DAVILA L. DE GUEVARA, *El empresariado colombiano: Una perspectiva histórica* (1986), pp. 52–67.

DAVID SOWELL

EDUCATION. Education in Latin America today is largely a product of what the Spanish began in the colonial period. Prior to their arrival there were no schools comparable to what existed in Europe at the time. Indigenous people learned from their parents and acquired skills through a system of apprenticeship. The first schools established in the sixteenth century were aimed at Christianizing the local population. These were established by the Catholic Church, particularly the Dominican and Jesuit orders, who worked largely with children of privileged families. JESUITS opened and staffed numerous schools and colleges, wrote about historical matters and the various regions of the empire, and came to dominate the intellectual life of the times. The order administered ranches and forest rights, and used their considerable resources to train peasants in horticulture, weaving, reading, and writing. By the sev-

enteenth century there were universities in Santiago de Chile, Córdoba, La Plata, Cuzco, and Quito, most of which trained clergy as well as some doctors and lawyers. By the eighteenth century chairs of classical and Indian languages were added to natural science and after the expulsion of the Jesuits for fear of their dominance in the New World, higher education exhibited a new secularism that reflected the philosophy and influence of the ENLIGHTENMENT.

The dominance of scholasticism was being challenged by a new introduction of science and the empirical method. The effort to rationalize the doctrines of the church by wedding philosophy and theology yielded to the new ideas which rejected the notion of using reason to justify faith. When the Jesuits departed, they left a legacy of some twenty-five institutions of higher education in Latin America. The importance of some of these continued for at least two centuries. While most of the population during the colonial period could neither read nor write, the cultural life of the times produced a number of celebrated intellectuals. Among these notables may be included Fray Bartolomé de LAS CASAS (1474–1566), author of *History of the Indies,* and Bernal DÍAZ DEL CASTILLO (1492–1584), known for his *True History of the Conquest of New Spain.*

After the Independence movement the CATHOLIC CHURCH remained a dominant influence in education but gradually this control was eroded by the demands of citizens for a more enlightened intellectual atmosphere and by the end of the century secularism dominated schooling in the area. Major advances in education were made particularly in Argentina, Chile, and Uruguay, where a combination of citizen demand and the need for more technical training eroded the rigidity of church doctrine. Under President Domingo SARMIENTO, Argentina became the educational leader in Latin America. But the introduction of more scientific studies at the expense of humanism also brought an increase in state control of education. Idealism was replaced by POSITIVISM and the curriculum no longer required Latin. In Mexico President Benito Juárez's educational reform commission, influenced by Comte's philosophy, aimed at a new way to train elites. In Argentina the Escuela Normal de Panana, created in 1870, provided a training ground for the new leaders of society. By the end of the nineteenth century secularism had overtaken Catholic control in all of Latin America and was codified by the Argentine law of 1884, which settled the matter.

What appeared at the end of the nineteenth century was a varied system of education that reflected diverse European influences. Argentina was influenced by the British system, Chile by the German, and many other Latin American countries by the French. National governments established ministries of education to run the schools, and a system of hierarchical levels of administration created a pattern that is only now being seriously challenged. Though LITERACY grew, the rigid class divisions that characterized Latin American society remained. Both internal as well as external developments helped to influence change in early-twentieth-century schooling. In Córdoba in 1918 the new middle classes succeeded in making the university more democratic by including research and student participation in university affairs. Here, too, improved teaching and a new curriculum was influenced by radical ideas inspired by the Mexican and Russian revolutions. Militant student strikes led by the student union incited an examination reform, an end to nepotism, and social accountability.

This new radicalism was reflected in Mexico during the 1930s, when left-leaning teachers were urged to become social reformers by playing a role in rural uplift. They were asked to help the peasants struggle for land and to help the workers struggle for wages. President Lázaro CÁRDENAS demanded a school in every village; while the program proved successful in Oaxaca, in other areas teachers often faced popular indifference and even hostility. Despite these changes all over Spanish America, a centralized and standardized form of primary education persisted and was promoted from the 1930s onward. Municipalities lost control of schools to the ministries of education, which assumed control of teacher recruitment, training, and placement and inspection. This policy was justified in the name of using education to develop the nation and establish national identity. Despite these national efforts, fully half the population of Latin America remained illiterate in 1964. In all countries after World War II the attraction of education was a force that increased enrollments substantially, and resources were poured into schools.

In Brazil there were 2.1 million students in 1932, with 2 million in primary schools, 103,000 in secondary, and 22,000 in higher education. By 1985 there were 30 million students, with 1.5 million in higher education. While questions of enrollment, resources, and national development are still important concerns of educators and politicians in Latin America, the more recent global competitive environment has added new dimensions to traditional views of education.

Global political and economic changes have altered traditional views of education in Latin America and throughout the world. The increasing interdependence of trade, commerce, and finance now challenges the conventional view of education as an exclusive function of sovereign states and leads to a reassessment of the broader objectives of education in an internationally competitive environment. Organizations such as the UNITED NATIONS, the ORGANIZATION OF AMERICAN STATES, and the Organization for Economic Cooperation and Development routinely play significant roles as advisors and consultants to national ministries. This development has brought about the inclusion of new educational concepts, such as gender issues, environmental problems, human rights, the cultural integrity of indigenous people, and the disparity between the technical and scientific work forces in poor versus developed economies. With these increased demands have come the recognition that government resources are inadequate. International lending institutions such as the International Monetary Fund and the World Bank insist that officials find ways to curtail expenditure, increase taxes, and consider user fees and more privatization of schooling.

The South Commission (1990), for example, pointed to the widening "knowledge gap" between developed countries and the third world. In their report, they found that "unless the South learns to harness the forces of modern science and technology, it has no chance of fulfilling its developmental aspirations or its yearning for an effective voice in the management of global interdependence." The information age, with its requirements for technical and scientific workers, demands a more competitive population six to fifteen years old than was ever required in the past. Latin American ministries of education are now called upon to emphasize basic science and mathematics preparation as never before.

This emphasis is not just for an elite, but rather for a much wider population of children. *The World Education Report* issued by UNESCO in 1993 calls for making education for all a universal reality, not just a universally recognized right. Many nations have moved forward in providing primary schooling for most of their eligible population (see table 1; percentages greater than 100% indicate that some students enrolled in primary school are either younger or older than the usual age range). However, Bolivia, El Salvador, Guatemala, and others have not succeeded in providing even this minimal level of education for all children. At the secondary level, usually considered appropriate for ages twelve to seventeen, no country in Latin America reported very high enrollment ratios. Cuba led the list with 85 percent, followed by Argentina, Chile, and Uruguay, but many countries barely had a third of eligible students enrolled. Other statistics underline the severe diversity that characterizes educational attainment in Latin America. The illiterate population of persons over fifteen years of age rises from single-digit percentages in Argentina, Costa Rica, and Uruguay to very high rates in Guatemala and Nicaragua. Countries with the highest college and university enrollment ratios have the smallest number of illiterates, and those countries with the lowest ratios have the highest rates of illiteracy. These national figures do not reveal the kinds of disparities between rural and urban areas or among marginalized indigenous populations.

More important, perhaps, than the numbers of children receiving instruction is the changing philosophical outlook of government, from a traditional acceptance of exclusive governmental responsibility to a broader social mandate for meeting educational needs that includes the family, the workplace, the media, and other community organizations. The traditional role of schooling as an instrument for molding social personality and work-force training for human capital are being eroded by a new focus on alternate agencies of education.

The Chilean Ministry of Education enunciated a pro-

463

TABLE 1   Educational Indicators in Latin America

	Primary School Enrollment as a Percentage of Population Age 6–11		Secondary School Enrollment as a Percentage of Population Age 12–17		University Enrollment as a Percentage of Population Age 20–24	Illiteracy Rate as a Percentage of Population Age 15 and Older
	1965	1985	1965	1985		
Argentina	101	108	28	70	43.4 (1991)	4.7 (1990)
Bolivia	73	91	18	37	22.2 (1980)	22.5 (1990)
Brazil	108	104	16	35	11.7 (1991)	18.3 (1990)
Chile	124	109	34	69	23.3 (1991)	6.6 (1990)
Colombia	84	117	17	50	13.7 (1989)	13.3 (1990)
Ecuador	91	114	17	55	29.0 (1987)	12.7 (1990)
Paraguay	102	101	13	31	8.2 (1990)	9.9 (1990)
Peru	99	122	25	65	35.6 (1990)	14.9 (1990)
Uruguay	106	110	44	70	32.0 (1991)	3.8 (1990)
Venezuela	94	108	27	45	29.5 (1990)	11.9 (1990)
Costa Rica	106	101	24	41	27.6 (1991)	7.2 (1990)
Cuba	121	105	23	85	20.9 (n.d.)	6.0 (n.d.)
Dominican Republic	87	124	12	50	18.6 (1985)	16.7 (1990)
El Salvador	82	70	17	24	16.1 (1991)	32.7 (1990)
Guatemala	50	76	8	17	8.6 (1986)	44.9 (1990)
Haiti	50	78	5	18	1.2 (1985)	47.0 (1990)
Honduras	80	102	10	36	9.1 (1991)	26.9 (1990)
Mexico	92	115	17	55	15.2 (1990)	25.8 (1990)
Nicaragua	69	101	14	39	10.4 (1985)	42.5 (1971)
Panama	102	105	34	59	21.3 (1989)	11.2 (1990)

SOURCE: WORLD BANK, *Development Data Book*, 2d ed. (n.d.); UNESCO, *Statistical Yearbook* (1993); UNITED NATIONS DEVELOPMENT PROGRAMME, *Human Development Report (1993)*.

gram in 1992 to improve the quality of primary schools by inviting the community to participate actively in the education of their children. Some educators see this development as an opportunity for greater democratization whereby citizens help establish their own priorities. The International Institute for Educational Planning sponsored a study of decentralization in Latin America in which the older view of exclusive governmental responsibility is altered by the need for broader citizen participation in education. This trend is also evident in the development of rural women's education in the Andean subregion, as reported by the International Bureau of Education. It is increasingly recognized that the rights of indigenous people have been neglected in many countries, and that they have legitimate cross-national concerns that need to be addressed by local and international agencies. In Peru, for example, the 1979 Constitution established that peasant and native communities are autonomous in their organization and community work, although these populations do not feel that they have equal rights to education, health, and other government services. Efforts are currently under way to institute bilingual schools, train teachers in their native language, and provide expanded instruction for the indigenous population.

By the 1960s and 1970s a new genre of educational criticism had emerged in North and South America, taking as its starting point the apparent inability of governments to make schools alter social injustice and poverty. Critics such as Everett Reimer, Paulo Freire, and Ivan Illich carefully detailed the ways that schools served to perpetuate privilege in general and specifically in Latin America. They concluded that the formal school system could not be saved and instead called for a whole new "informal" system that would educate children outside the regular classroom.

JOHN JOHNSON, *Political Change in Latin America* (1958); HAROLD R. W. BENJAMIN, *Higher Education in the American Republics* (1965); PAULO FREIRE, *Pedagogy of the Oppressed* (1968); EVERETT REIMER, *School Is Dead: Alternatives in Education* (1970); JOSEPH MAIER and RICHARD W. WEATHERHEAD, eds., *The Latin American University* (1979); MARY KAY VAUGHAN, *The State, Education and Social Class in Mexico, 1880–1928* (1982); UNITED NATIONS, *Convention on the Rights of the Child* (1989); SOUTH COMMISSION, *The Challenge to the South* (1990), pp. 227–228; WORLD CONFERENCE ON EDUCATION FOR ALL, Meeting on Basic Learning Needs (1990); *World Declaration on Education for All* (conference in Jomtien, Thailand, 1990); CHILEAN MINISTRY OF EDUCATION, "Programme to Improve the Quality of Primary Schools in Poor Areas," in *Bulletin of the Major Project of Edu-*

cation in Latin America and the Caribbean, no. 27 (1992): 30–31; BEATRICE EDWARDS, "Linking the Social and Natural Worlds: Environmental Education in the Hemisphere," in *La Educación,* no. 115 (1993); INTERNATIONAL BUREAU OF EDUCATION, *Innovation and Information* (December 1993): 4; NELLY STROMQUIST, "The Political Experience of Women: Linking Micro and Macro-democracies," in *La Educación,* no. 116 (1993); UNESCO, *Statistical Yearbook* (1993); WORLD BANK, *Development Data Book,* 2d ed., n.d.; UNITED NATIONS DEVELOPMENT PROGRAMME, *Human Development Report* (1993); INTERNATIONAL INSTITUTE FOR EDUCATIONAL PLANNING, *IIEP Newsletter XII,* no. 1 (1994); BRITISH COMPARATIVE EDUCATION SOCIETY, Conference on Education Beyond the State, September 1994.

JOSEPH DI BONA

See also **Universities.**

Nonformal Education

Nonformal education includes a range of organized instructional activities that usually occur outside of the formal educational system. Popular, alternative, adult, experimental, and grass-roots education are terms that have been used to describe recent nonformal educational activities in Latin America.

While many examples can be found in early Latin American history, including the creative educational programs sponsored by religious institutions and the *Sociedad económica de amigos del país,* the term "nonformal education" more appropriately refers to twentieth-century educational activities. The activities were at times linked to traditional educational institutions, but they usually relied on different methods and served different populations.

Mexico, which initiated many educational innovations outside of the traditional school setting during the colonial period, was often at the forefront of educational experimentation in the twentieth century. It was one of the first countries to have a "popular university," established by intellectuals and educators in 1912, to educate workers. Popular universities followed in many countries, most notably the GONZÁLEZ PRADA POPULAR UNIVERSITIES in Peru, which offered courses in culture, health, and vocational training. Mexico was also the initiator of another, more comprehensive program of grass-roots education in the 1920s. Under the leadership of José VASCONCELOS, the famous cultural missions program sought to transform rural life in Mexico. Interdisciplinary teams of teachers, health professionals, and technical workers traveled to remote villages for short periods to teach and to promote social change. Variants of the Mexican cultural missions were adopted in other Latin American countries (the socio-pedagogical missions of Uruguay, for example) and in Spain during the early 1930s. In addition, rural schools, emphasizing technical and vocational training along with academic subjects, had appeared in many Latin American countries by the 1930s.

These activities set precedents for broadening the scope of nonformal educational activities during the 1940s. In response to development needs and the inadequacy of formal educational systems, individuals and groups created new methods of attacking the massive social problems of illiteracy, unemployment, and malnutrition. Experimental programs sought to improve the education, health, and welfare of the poor. At times these programs were comprehensive national efforts, designed to increase literacy and basic skills in the hopes of integrating marginal populations into a national polity and economy; at other times they were grass-roots movements, emerging from individuals, communities, and religious organizations.

Extension education, though a part of formal educational and governmental organizations, has long supported nonformal, alternative educational activities. Extension programs that emphasized social development rather than simple cultural diffusion became an avowed aim of Latin American universities, especially after the Córdoba Reforms of 1918 initiated efforts to make universities more socially responsible. During and after World War II international and national development agencies relied on extension to promote development. One of the earliest of these was the Inter-American Cooperative Food Production Service in Peru, started in 1942 by the Institute of Inter-American Affairs, and designed to increase food and fiber for domestic and international markets. Through agent contact with farmers, youth, and women's organizations, and diffusion of in-

Thirteen-year-old Rafael teaching a man to read and write, April 1961. MARIO GARCÍA JOYA.

465

formation, all essential to extension programs, most Latin American ministries of agriculture had tried to initiate some type of agricultural extension program by the late 1950s.

Population increases and social and economic needs led to the rapid increase of nonformal education in the 1960s. Brazil offers an example of the range and diversity of programs that were established for literacy (Fundação Movimento Brasileiro de Alfabetização), vocational training (Serviço Nacional de Aprendizagem Comercial and Serviço Nacional de Aprendizagem Industrial), using television for primary education (Fundação Centro Brasileiro de Televisão Educativa), university extension (Centro Rural Universitário de Treinamento e Ação Comunitaria), and for merging religious beliefs and social action (Comunidades Eclesiais de Base).

As popular education became recognized as an agent of social change, reform and revolutionary movements employed it as a method of achieving their objectives. The Cuban literacy crusade of 1961 set the standard and was imitated by other countries in Latin America and Africa. Important theoretical and practical work came from Paulo FREIRE and Ivan Illich. Freire developed a program for literacy and *conscientização* (critical consciousness) that influenced many grass-roots educational efforts around the world. Ivan Illich, recognizing the inability of Latin American nations to provide traditional education to all, stressed the need for flexible, alternative education. More recently, new methods and educational programs have been created in many Latin American countries to address the growing number of "street children." New pedagogies, adapted to the complex cultural milieu of street life, are a part of programs that provide shelter, food, clothing, health care, and job training to street children. These programs, like those before them, are based on the conviction that traditional educational institutions are no longer capable of addressing the changing needs of Latin America.

THOMAS J. LA BELLE, *Nonformal Education and Social Change in Latin America* (1976) and *Nonformal Education in Latin America and the Caribbean: Stability, Reform, or Revolution* (1986), provides a good introduction to the diversity of programs and philosophies; CARLOS ALBERTO TORRES, *The Politics of Nonformal Education in Latin America* (1990) analyzes adult education; ADRIANA PUIGGRÓS, *La educación popular en América Latina: Orígenes, polémicas y perspectivas* (1984), gives a theoretical overview of the history of popular education; and MYLES HORTON and PAULO FREIRE, *We Make the Road by Walking* (1990), compare experiences in nonformal education.

JOHN C. SUPER

See also **Universities.**

Pre-Colombian Education

The AZTEC, INCA, and MAYA of ancient America had formal educational systems. Although the Inca and Maya generally restricted formal training to the nobil-

ity, the Aztecs educated the children of each *calpulli* in Tenochtitlán. The Aztecs established two schools, one for the nobility and the other for commoners. Noble Aztec boys received training to become political leaders or priests in the *calmecacs* that were attached to their temples. Since the Aztecs dedicated each *calmecac* to a different Aztec deity, training varied from school to school, but officials in all *calmecacs* dealt severely with their pupils. They ordered serious offenders, such as drunkards, to be shot with arrows or to be burned to death. Harsh punishments helped train future political and military leaders to endure pain in battle or in ritual bloodletting ceremonies.

By the age of fifteen, sons of Aztec commoners were given a military education in the *telpochcalli*, or "young men's house." School officials trained the boys to use weapons and to capture victims because, if needed, every young adult male went to war. These young men also performed manual labor, such as tending fields, which strengthened their bodies and helped them develop stamina and self-discipline.

The Aztecs insisted that all children, including girls, between the ages of twelve and fifteen train in the *cuica-*

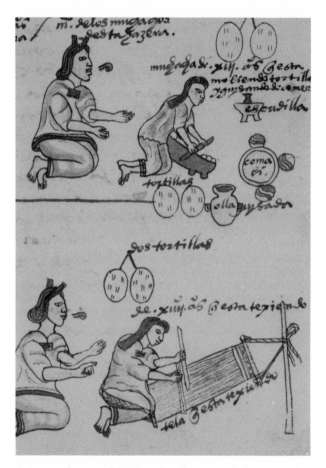

Aztec mother teaching her daughter to grind corn and to use the loom. Reproduced from *Codex Mendoza* (ca. 1540). COURTESY OF BODLEIAN LIBRARY, OXFORD, U.K.

calli, or "house of song" for a few hours each evening. They memorized songs and poetry that told them of their past and helped them understand what their relationship with their various gods should be. Although some daughters of the nobility were sent to temples to train as priestesses, most mothers taught their daughters skills, such as spinning cotton or grinding MAIZE on the *mano* and *metate,* that would enable them to be efficient housewives.

Much like the Aztecs, the Inca educated men and women of the nobility in Cuzco at the Coricancha. Garcilaso de la Vega wrote that Inca Roca, the sixth Inca and first "emperor," felt "it was proper that the sons of common people should not learn the sciences, and that these should be restricted to the nobility." The Inca expected children of commoners to begin serving the empire at an early age in order to help their families meet their quota for the Inca. Instruction would have interfered with service time.

Amautas, philosophers held in high esteem, taught schools for the Inca nobility and for the sons of rulers the Inca conquered. They focused on religious instruction, principles of government administration, Inca history, public speaking, the use of the QUIPU, and the official language, Quechua. The entire course of elite instruction culminated in a military-style examination (the *huarachicoy*). Inca officials collected a select number of girls—chosen for their beauty, pleasant dispositions, or good figures—as *acllas* (the chosen ones). For five years, *mamaconas* (cloistered women dedicated to the services of their gods) taught young girls between the ages of eight or nine and fourteen the arts of brewing *chica* (maize beer) and weaving fine textiles, after which a select few were sent to Cuzco, where the Inca assigned some to a cloistered religious life in the temples or redistributed others as wives to relatives of the Inca or neighboring lords.

The Maya, much like the Inca, educated their nobility. The sons of Maya lords and priests learned to read hieroglyphic texts or to study the movement of the stars and planets under the direction of priests. Much learning may also have occurred at the village warrior houses, where young men gathered to play ball and lived together until marriage. Sons of commoners spent most of the day with their fathers helping them in the cornfields or with other work, while daughters remained at home with their mothers, who taught them spinning, weaving, and other household tasks.

FRIAR DIEGO DE LANDA, *Yucatán Before and After the Conquest* (1566; repr. 1978); FATHER BERNABÉ COBO, *History of the Inca Empire* (1657; repr. 1988); HUAMAN POMA, *Letter to a King,* translated by Christopher Dilke (1978); FRANCES F. BERDAN, *The Aztecs of Central Mexico* (1982); FRAY BERNADINO DE SAHAGÚN, *Florentine Codex,* vols. 2, 3, 4, 8, 9, 10 (1982); BRIAN FAGAN, *The Aztecs* (1984); NANCY FARRISS, *Maya Society Under Colonial Rule* (1984); R. TOM ZUIDEMA, *Inca Civilization in Cuzco* (1990).

CAROLYN JOSTOCK

EDWARDS, AGUSTÍN (*b.* 17 June 1878; *d.* 1941), Chilean politician, financier, and writer. At age twenty-two, Edwards became one of the youngest members in Chile's House of Representatives. At the same time he became active in the Edwards Bank of Valparaíso. Elected vice president of the House and president of the Ministry of Finance in 1902, he negotiated a peace treaty with Bolivia and initiated the construction of a railroad from Arica to La Paz. In 1906 he began his diplomatic career, serving successively in Italy, Spain, and Switzerland. Upon his return to Chile, he served as finance minister under President Pedro MONTT. During World War I he was named envoy to Great Britain in charge of diplomatic and financial affairs and, in 1920, became special envoy to the Court of St. James. In 1921 he was named representative to the League of Nations. He received many honors in Chile and Europe.

While living abroad Edwards studied newspaper and magazine production, then utilized this knowledge in Chile, where he founded the newspaper EL MERCURIO and several magazines, including *Zig-Zag.* In the financial domain, he reorganized the Edwards Bank, founded several companies, and was involved in nitrate mining. In 1925 he resolved a conflict with Bolivia and reestablished peace. Among his writings are his *Memoria sobre el plebiscito tacneño* (1926), in which he opposes a plan to allow Tacna and Arica to determine their nationality; *My Native Land* (1928), a cultural history of Chile; *Peoples of Old* (1929), on the Araucanian Indians; *The Dawn* (1931), on Chilean history from Independence (1810) to the first elected president (1841); and *Cuatro presidentes de Chile* (1932), on the period from 1841 to 1932.

VIRGILIO FIGUEROA, *Diccionario histórico, biográfico y bibliográfico de Chile,* vol. 2 (1974), pp. 20–25.

BARBARA MUJICA

EDWARDS, JORGE (*b.* 29 July 1931), Chilean writer and diplomat. Considering his writing merely a pastime, Edwards entered the diplomatic corps in the late 1950s. His early books include two collections of stories, *El patio* (1952; The Patio) and *Gente de la ciudad* (1961; City People). His first novel, *El peso de la noche* (1965; The Weight of Night), a semifinalist in the Seix Barral literary contest, was followed by another collection of stories, *Las máscaras* (1967; The Masks). In 1970 the ALLENDE government sent Edwards to Havana to open a Chilean embassy. In spite of the official nature of his assignment, Edwards maintained contact with vehement critics of the Castro government such as José Lezama Lima and Heberto PADILLA. After retiring from the diplomatic corps, he wrote *Persona non grata* (1973), a scathing indictment of the Castro regime as well as of other authoritarian systems. Attacked by both the extreme Left and the extreme Right, the book launched Edwards's international literary career. *Persona non grata* was banned in Chile by the PINOCHET regime and boycotted by several European and American publishers. After a new edition was published in Spain, Edwards brought suit against the government to allow its sale in Chile. Although he lost, the case drew attention to his cause. Edwards's other books are less overtly political. They include *Desde la cola del dragón* (1977; From the Dragon's Tail), a collection of essays on Chilean culture; *Los convidados de piedra* (1977; The Stone Guests), a novel about the bourgeois intellectuals of his generation who became revolutionaries; *El museo de cera* (1981; The Wax Museum), a historical fantasy about a conservative aristocrat who tries to stop time; *La mujer imaginaria* (1985; The Imaginary Woman), another novel, *El anfitrión* (1987; The Host), a kind of Chilean Faust story; *Adiós poeta* (1990; Goodby, Poet), a memoir about Edwards's experiences with Pablo NERUDA; *Cuentos completos* (1990; Complete Stories); and *Fantasmas de carne y hueso* (1993; Flesh and Blood Ghosts), stories that draw on Edwards's experiences as a diplomat and writer.

EMIR RODRÍGUEZ MONEGAL, "Joseph K en la Habana: A propósito de *Persona non grata*," in *Plural* 39 (1974): 77–82; MARIO VARGAS LLOSA, "Un francotirador tranquilo," in *Plural* 39 (1974): 74–77; M. MOODY, "Jorge Edwards, Chile y *El museo de cera*," in *Chasqui* 14 (1985): 37–42; FERNANDO ALEGRÍA, *Neuva historia de la novela hispanoamerican* (1986), pp. 371–391; T. RODRÍGUEZ ISOBA, "*La mujer imaginaria*: Una reflexión de Jorge Edwards sobre la historia chilena reciente," in *Epos* 4 (1988): 225–239; GUILLERMO GARCÍA CORRALES, "Entrevista con Jorge Edwards: Una reflexión sobre su literatura y el momento político chileno," in *Confluencia* 6 (1990): 85–92; JOSÉ OTERO, "Subjetividad y mito como modos narrativos en *Persona non grata* de Jorge Edwards," in *Confluencia* 5 (1990): 47–53; BENJAMÍN ROJAS PIÑA, "*El anfitríon* de Jorge Edwards: Reescritura de mitos en el contexto de la dictadura y el exilio chilenos," in *Chasqui* 21 (1992): 77–91; BARBARA MUJICA, "Haunted by the Past," in *The World and I* (August 1993): 339–345, and "Persona Gratíssima," in *Americas* (May–June 1993): 24–29.

BARBARA MUJICA

EDWARDS BELLO, JOAQUÍN (*b.* 10 May 1887; *d.* 1968), Chilean journalist and novelist. A prolific writer and memorialist, Edwards Bello created an extensive commentary on Chilean life from a personal perspective. As a *criollista*, he was interested in creating an autochthonous literature, using South American subjects and a literary style free of European influences. He was a harsh critic of Chilean society and its decadence. In many newspaper columns and in novels such as *El inútil* (1910), *El roto* (1920), and *La chica del "Crillón"* (1935) he studied, from a naturalist perspective which underlined the grotesque in everyday life, the human and social weaknesses of the system.

JULIO ORLANDI ARAYA, *Joaquín Edwards Bello: Obras, estilo, técnica* (1958).

S. DAYDÍ-TOLSON

EDZNÁ, site in northern Campeche, Mexico, first known for its complex Late Classic MAYA architecture. Investigations at the site center and in the surrounding area by Mexican and American archaeologists have demonstrated that Edzná was a large urban center occupying an area of perhaps 6.8 square miles during some time periods. The first known occupation occurred during the Middle Preclassic period (ca. 400–300 B.C.), when the site apparently was sparsely occupied, followed by a surge of development and population during the Late Preclassic period.

Edzná functioned as a major center from about 150 B.C. to A.D. 200, possibly the period of its greatest extent and population. An ancient, complex hydraulic system was constructed during that time. Thirty-one canals and twenty-five reservoirs made possible collection of rainwater and had a storage potential of more than 71 million cubic feet. They may have provided the Preclassic and later Classic city with water reserves for the dry season because there is little or no surface water available in the area. Edzná was occupied, at a lesser level, during the Protoclassic and Early Classic periods, until a second population and development surge in Late Classic times. Its final period of occupation, during the Terminal Classic period, ended by approximately 900.

In the 1980s investigations by Antonio Benavides Castillo, under the auspices of Mexico's Instituto Nacional de Antropología e Historia, focused on the site center. Excavations revealed new information about the Large Acropolis and the Small Acropolis. Of particular interest is a large modeled stucco mask associated with a structure buried inside a later building on the Small Acropolis. Its style and associated artifacts date the mask to the Protoclassic period or earlier. In a brief discussion of the known carved stelae from Edzná, Benavides Castillo notes that two date to Baktun (between A.D. 41 and 435).

RAY T. MATHENY, DEANNE L. GURR, DONALD W. FORSYTH, and F. RICHARD HAUCK, *Investigations at Edzná, Campeche, Mexico*, vol. 1, pt. 1, *The Hydraulic System*, and pt. 2, *Maps* (1983); GEORGE F. ANDREWS, *Edzná, Campeche, Mexico: Settlement Patterns and Monumental Architecture* (1984); ANTONIO BENAVIDES CASTILLO, "Edzná, Campeche, Mexico: Temporade de campo 1989," in *Mexicon* 12, no. 3 (May 1990): 49–52.

RAY T. MATHENY

EFFECTIVE SUFFRAGE, NO REELECTION, a slogan (*sufragio efectivo, no reelección* in Spanish) characterizing much of the philosophy of the political movement in Mexico that led to the overthrow of long-time president and dictator Porfirio DÍAZ (1876–1880, 1884–1911) and marked the beginning of the MEXICAN REVOLUTION of 1910. The idea of a free vote with no possibility of reelection was most thoroughly explored in revolutionary leader Francisco I. MADERO's (1873–1913) book, *La sucesión presidencial de 1910* (1908), written in reaction to Díaz's multiple reelections to the presidency through largely fraudulent means. Madero also named his anti-Díaz political party the Anti-Reelectionist Party. No re-election, as opposed to effective suffrage, became a principle of the postrevolutionary political system, enshrined in the Constitution of 1917. It was breached only once, in the 1920s, when Alvaro OBREGÓN (1880–1928) maneuvered to have himself chosen president a second time.

CHARLES C. CUMBERLAND, *Mexican Revolution: Genesis Under Madero* (1952), pp. 55–61; STANLEY R. ROSS, *Francisco I. Madero: Apostle of Mexican Democracy* (1955), pp. 50–64.

DAVID G. LaFRANCE

See also **Mexico: Constitutions, Political Parties, Revolutionary Movements.**

EGAÑA FABRES, MARIANO (*b.* 1 March 1793; *d.* 24 June 1846), Chilean lawyer, diplomat, and intellectual. The son of Juan EGAÑA, from whom he inherited his strong intellectual streak, Mariano Egaña qualified as a lawyer in 1811, and held office briefly in the patriot governments of 1813–1814. Like his father, he was confined to Juan Fernández (an island prison for exiled political prisoners) during the Spanish reconquest (1814–1817). In 1824 he was sent as Chilean envoy to London. His credentials were not accepted because Britain had not yet recognized Chile's independence, so Egaña settled in Paris. He returned to Chile in 1829. It was as a result of his initiative that Andrés BELLO (1781–1865), a prominent Venezuelan intellectual, was offered government employment in Chile.

In the new Conservative regime of 1830, in which he was a key figure, Egaña served as minister of finance (1830), of the interior (1830), and of justice (1837–1841), as well as senator (1831–1846). He was a leading influence on the drafting of the Constitution of 1833, though his more reactionary proposals (such as indefinite re-eligibility of presidents and hereditary senators) were excluded. Egaña's death (he collapsed and died in the street) had a great impact on Santiago. His book collection, the best in Chile, was bought by the state for the National Library.

SIMON COLLIER, *Ideas and Politics of Chilean Independence, 1808–1833* (1967); MARIANO EGAÑA, *Documentos de la misión de Mariano Egaña en Londres, 1824–1829* (1984).

SIMON COLLIER

EGAÑA RISCO JUAN (*b.* 31 October 1768; *d.* 20 April 1836), Chilean patriot and intellectual. One of the most learned men of his time and place, Juan Egaña Risco was born in Lima, the son of a Chilean father. He studied at San Marcos University, Lima, from which he graduated in 1789, the year he moved to Chile. An active patriot after 1810, he was a member of the first national congress (1811), for which he was banished to Juan Fernández (an island prison for exile of political prisoners) during the Spanish reconquest (1814–1817). He served several times in the congresses of the 1820s, but his moment of greatest influence came in 1823, when he was the principal author of the idiosyncratically conservative constitution of that year. It proved unworkable and was swiftly abandoned. Egaña's cast of mind was conservative, moralistic, and steeped in admiration for classical antiquity, the Inca empire, and China. Several volumes of his writings were published in London in the 1820s, and another volume in Bordeaux in 1836.

RAÚL SILVA CASTRO, *Egaña en la Patria Vieja, 1810–1814* (1959); SIMON COLLIER, *Ideas and Politics of Chilean Independence, 1808–1833* (1967), chap. 7.

SIMON COLLIER

EGAS, CAMILO ALEJANDRO (*b.* 1895; *d.* 1962), Ecuadorian artist. Egas was born in Quito and attended the Academy of Arts in that city. A disciple of Paul Bar and Víctor Puiz, he won first prize in a national competition in celebration of Ecuadorian independence (1909). With the aid of an Ecuadorian government grant he studied at the Academy of Rome (1918) and the following year continued his studies at the Academy of San Fernando in Madrid. On another trip to Europe, he met Picasso in Paris, where he studied at the Colorrossi Academy (1922). Egas exhibited at the Salon des Indépendents and Salon d'Automme (Paris, 1924–1925). His expressionist paintings of Ecuadorian Indians frequently depict women in mourning or tragic instances (*Desolation*). In 1929 he received an appointment to teach painting at the New School for Social Research and in 1935 became the director of the school's painting department, a position he held until his death. In 1938 he collaborated on a mural project for the Ecuadorian Pavilion at the New York World's Fair. Egas was influenced by the surrealist exiles in New York in the 1940s and by Mexican muralist José Clemente OROZCO. He died in New York.

Arte Ecuatoriano, vol. 2 (1976), pp. 246–247; DAWN ADES, *Art in Latin America: The Modern Era, 1820–1980* (1989).

MARTA GARSD

EGERTON, DANIEL THOMAS (*b.* 1800; *d.* 1842), English painter. One of the first traveling painters to arrive after Mexican independence, when the borders were opened to non-Hispanics, Egerton remained in Mexico from 1829 to 1836. Europeans came to Mexico moved by curiosity about its natural wonders, exoticness, and legendary mineral wealth, which explains the predominance in their work of landscapes, both rural and urban, popular sites, folkloric scenes, and representations of pre-Columbian ruins.

Returning to London, Egerton published *Vistas de México* in 1840. The twelve plates that illustrate the book, stone lithographs retouched with watercolors, are accompanied by brief textual explanations in which scientific and folkloric information are mixed, indicating the fascination of Europeans with the exotic aspects of Mexico. In this publication, which focuses primarily on the images, Egerton depicts a series of cities: some characterized by their agricultural and commercial wealth, such as Puebla and Guadalajara; others as mining centers, such as Zacatecas; and still others as supply points, such as Aguascalientes. These works inspired Egerton to produce oil paintings on the same themes.

At the end of 1840, Egerton returned to Mexico and took up residence in Tacubaya (Mexico City), where both he and his wife were murdered in 1842. The murderers' cases were extensively publicized in 1844.

MANUEL ROMERO DE TERREROS, *Paisajes mexicanos de un pintor inglés* (1949); JUSTINO FERNÁNDEZ, *Artistas británicos en México* (1968).

ESTHER ACEVEDO

EGUREN, JOSÉ MARÍA (*b.* 7 July 1874; *d.* 29 April 1942), Peruvian poet. Eguren began writing poetry at the height of the Spanish American *modernismo* movement at the turn of the century. Ironically, however, he is the one Peruvian poet to break out of the mold and bring Peruvian poetry into the twentieth century. Both in personality and poetry, he was radically different from such contemporaries as José Santos CHOCANO. In fact, Eguren was something of a recluse, and in his poetry he created imaginary worlds in which to cocoon himself. Steeped in French symbolism, his poetry at first blush seems to imitate the *modernistas* because of certain typical motifs, among them, mystery, love, and dreams, but his language is a storehouse of creativity that had tremendous influence on later Peruvian poets. His works also lead Peruvian poetry into the modern age in their themes of alienation, skepticism, and imitation of earlier forms.

Eguren produced three books of poetry: *Simbólicas* (1911), *La canción de las figuras* (1916), and *Poesías* (1929). Lyrical, telluric, symbolic, and imaginative, his poetry enriches the Spanish language with regionalisms, archaic terms, neologisms, and even foreign and invented words. Inspiration, for instance, is allegorized in the form of a small girl with a blue lamp who leads the poet into the spheres of the imagination and the spiritual. In his later poetry, Eguren draws on the work of the European vanguard in his use of metaphor and dream imagery.

JAMES HIGGINS, "The Rupture Between Poet and Society in the Work of José María Eguren," *Kentucky Romance Quarterly* 20, no. 1 (1973): 59–74, and *The Poet in Peru* (1982); PHYLLIS W. RODRÍGUEZ-PERALTA, *Tres poetas cumbres en la poesía peruana: Chocano, Eguren y Vallejo* (1983); RENATO SANDOVAL BACIGALUPO, *El centinela de fuego: Agonía y muerte en Eguren* (1988).

DICK GERDES

EICHELBAUM, SAMUEL (*b.* 14 November 1894; *d.* 4 May 1967), Argentine playwright and short-story writer. When he was only twelve years old, Samuel Eichelbaum left the town of his birth, Domínguez, Entre Ríos Province, to travel to Rosario, where he tried to interest theater companies in producing his *sainete Un lobo manso* (1906). Although this early attempt met with rejection, it exemplifies his lifelong dedication to the THEATER. Eichelbaum's work reflects characters who are archetypes within Argentine society, yet critics frequently recognize in his works the presence of Dostoyevsky, Ibsen, and Strindberg rather than any direct influence from other Argentine writers. His plays are rooted in introspection, as for example in *Dos brasas* (1952); through a seemingly psychoanalytic approach to drama he explores the self and the nature of conflicts between the conscious and unconscious. Other major themes include the importance for Argentina of both rural and urban areas, the strength of women, individual tragedy found at all socioeconomic levels, and the need to survive as an individual against all adversity. The theater of Eichelbaum is clearly distinguished by the intellectual capacity of the characters and their ability to think and reason, as expressed through dialogue.

Although few of his plays are political in nature, Eichelbaum does direct his attention to social problems. In *El dogma* (1922) he alludes to the role of Jewish activists in the labor movement, and in *Nadie la conoció nunca* (1926) there is a reference to attacks on Jewish neighborhoods after the workers' strikes of 1910 and 1919 (the latter known as *La Semana Trágica*). More than twenty years later, *Un patricio del 80* (1948), written in collaboration with Ulises Petit de Murat, was subject to official opposition because it was considered to imply criticism of Perón's interest in supporting foreign exploitation of Argentine natural resources.

Un guapo del 900 (1940), Eichelbaum's best-known and most commercially successful play, explores the moral codes of the *guapo*, a bodyguard to a political boss. Individual freedom of choice and sacrifice are bound to machismo and self-destruction in the search for dignity among the lower classes of Argentine society. As in other plays, Eichelbaum concentrates on the internal turmoil of his characters and the psychological processes guided by honor and individuality that lead to sorrowful outcomes.

JORGE CRUZ, *Samuel Eichelbaum* (1962); PANOS D. KARAVELLAS, *La dramaturgia de Samuel Eichelbaum* (1976); MARTA LÍA GODOY FROY, *Introducción al teatro de Samuel Eichelbaum* (1982); ULISES PETIT DE MURAT, *Samuel Eichelbaum* (1986).

DANUSIA L. MESON

EISENHOWER–REMÓN TREATY (1955), one of a series of accords (signed 25 January) redefining the status of the Panama Canal Zone. According to this agreement the United States gradually relinquished privileges gained in the HAY–BUNAU–VARILLA TREATY of 1903, an accord already revised, in particular through the HULL–ALFARO TREATY of 1936, in which the United States relinquished its protectorate over Panama.

The Eisenhower–Remón Treaty addressed the economic issues related to the status of U.S. citizens of the Canal Zone, a source of constant irritation to Panamanians, who considered the zone a colonial enclave. Although it did not alter U.S. sovereignty over the zone, the treaty increased the annual payment to Panama to $1,930,000, granted Panama the right to tax the income of Canal Zone employees who were not U.S. citizens, and modified the zone boundaries. Commissary and post exchange (PX) privileges of U.S. citizens in the zone were limited to those citizens who actually worked for the canal, and Panama gained the right to impose import duties on some goods entering the zone. These provisions increased the share of zonian business controlled by Panamanian firms. The United States also relinquished its control of sanitation in Panama City and Colón, and its exclusive rights to construct transisthmian railroads and highways. Panama granted the United States a fifteen-year lease on 19,000 acres of land outside the zone for military exercises.

The treaty was supplemented by a Memorandum of Understandings Reached, pledging the establishment of a single wage level for all Canal Zone employees and equal employment opportunities for Panamanian citizens in zone posts, thereby eliminating the privileged status of U.S. citizens in the zone.

J. LLOYD MECHAM, *A Survey of United States–Latin American Relations* (1965); WALTER LA FEBER, *The Panama Canal: The Crisis in Historical Perspective* (1978).

KENNETH J. GRIEB

EJIDOS, collectively held farming lands. *Ejidos* remain a prominent feature of the Mexican countryside. These lands are legally inalienable and are held in usufruct in individual parcels by the families represented on local *ejido* committees. In traditional Iberian usage, *ejidos* were held collectively by rural towns and villages and dedicated to common livestock grazing. These practices overlapped considerably with Aztec landholding patterns and in Mexico trace their formal existence to a 1573 law of King PHILIP II regarding the establishment of Indian towns. In independent Mexico liberal doctrines of political economy frowned on corporately held property, so *ejidos* were officially abolished by laws of the reform period (LA REFORMA) and the Constitution of 1857, though many survived the nineteenth century. *Ejidos* were revived in somewhat altered form by the agrarian thinkers of the Revolution of 1910, their formal existence ensured by the Constitution of 1917 and subsequent legislation. By 1970 some 170 million acres of land were held as *ejidos* in Mexico. In keeping with the Mexican government's neo-liberal project of the early

1990s, Article 27 of the 1917 Constitution has been altered to allow private sale of *ejido* plots by individual farmers, thus throwing into doubt the future of the institution.

GEORGE M. MC BRIDE, *The Land Systems of Mexico* (1923, repr. 1971); EYLER N. SIMPSON, *The Ejido: Mexico's Way Out* (1937).

ERIC VAN YOUNG

EL BAÚL, a Late Classic (A.D. 600–900) center of the Cotzumalhuapan culture in the department of Escuintla, on the Pacific coast of Guatemala. The site is one of six architectural centers clustered on the rich cacao lands. Located near mountain corridors, these centers were strategically situated for coastal, piedmont, and highland trade. El Baúl is famous for its carved stelae and boulders, and sculptures in the round executed in a Mexican-derived Cotzumalhuapan style. The site also has an Izapan-style monument, Stela 1, dated A.D. 36, and a decapitated potbelly sculpture from 500–200 B.C.

The mapped portion of El Baúl has an acropolis, 83 feet high and 660 feet with four courts, a ball court, and twenty-two platforms. Some of the earthern structures have ramps. Pavements, staircases and drains are of stone.

There are twenty-eight Cotzumalhuapan-style monuments on the site. The themes of the sculptures are ritual scenes involving humans. Some include cacao imagery, reinforcing the idea that the elite of El Baúl were involved in the production and distribution of the crop. Other scenes show ball players and confrontation scenes between older and younger individuals. The death theme is represented by death's heads and figures in the round with closed eyes and crossed arms. Tenoned heads of serpents were architectural decorations. There are individual boulder sculptures of gods, one of which, the "Dios del Mundo," is used in present-day Maya ritual. There also are portraits of rulers. Speech scrolls, elements of dress, and glyphs indicate the art is of Mexican derivation.

The ethnic group associated with the art of El Baúl is thought to derive from southern Mexico. The style is found for 90 miles along the Pacific coast and perhaps as much as 30 miles into the mountainous interior of Guatemala.

JOHN ERIC SIDNEY THOMPSON, *An Archaeological Reconnaissance in the Cotzumalhuapan Region: Excuintla, Guatemala,* Carnegie Institution of Washington Publication 574, Contribution to American Anthropology and History no. 44 (1948); MICHAEL D. COE, "Cycle 7 Monuments in Middle America: A Reconsideration," in *American Anthropologist,* 59, 4 (1957): 597–611; LEE PARSONS, *Bilbao, Guatemala: An Anthropological Study of the Pacific Coast Cotzumalhuapa Region,* Publications in Anthropology (Milwaukee Public Museum) 11 and 12 (1967–1969).

EUGENIA J. ROBINSON

See also **Mescamerica.**

EL CERREJÓN, area of Colombia's La Guajira peninsula, known for its rich coal deposits. Discovered in 1865 by an engineer named John May (probably of British origin), the Cerrejón deposits did not draw much attention until the outbreak of World War II, with its accelerating demand for fossil fuels. In 1941 demand for coal motivated the Colombian government to sponsor a geologic study of the deposits. Yet coal production began only in the late 1970s in response to the energy crisis produced by the rising oil prices of those years. From 1976, coal production has proceeded under the auspices of Carbocol, the state coal company, which expects to reap the benefits of the vast coal reserves concentrated in the North Cerrejón region, with the technical assistance of Intercor, a subsidiary of Exxon.

HARVEY KLINE, ''The Coal of 'El Cerrejón': An Historical Analysis of Major Colombian Policy Decisions and MNC Activities,'' in *Inter-American Economic Affairs* 35, no. 3 (1981):69–90; RENÉ DE LA PEDRAJA, *Energy Politics in Colombia* (1989).

PAMELA MURRAY

EL DORADO, the European legend of great South American wealth associated with the Muisca (Chibcha) traditions of a chieftain who covered himself in gold dust before immersing himself in the waters of Lake Guatavita, north of Bogotá.

The European legends of El Dorado, ''Land of Cinnamon,'' became a central element in the lore of Spanish and English exploration and conquest in northern South America in the sixteenth century. The El Dorado fantasy had both Indian and Spanish origins. On one hand, Indian informants repeated rumors of the pre-Columbian Muisca rite of accession to political leadership in which the chieftain of Guatavita, covered with gold dust, dipped himself in the sacred lake and shed his gold covering while attendants and spectators threw golden offerings into the water. The extant artistry of indigenous Colombian goldsmiths and native practices of body painting have lent credence to this account. On the other hand, the conquistadors Gonzalo JIMÉNEZ DE QUESADA, Sebastián de BELALCÁZAR, and Nicolás FEDERMANN, all of whom met in Muisca territory in 1539, and their chroniclers, including Gonzalo Fernández OVIEDO, Pedro de CIEZA DE LEÓN, Juan de CASTELLANOS, and Fray Pedro Simón, embellished the myth to explain feats of conquest and to enliven their narratives.

Over the course of the sixteenth century and into the eighteenth, the legend was transformed from that of the golden man of Guatavita to a golden land in northeastern South America, which is what attracted Walter Raleigh in 1595 and 1617–1618. The persistent association of the legend with Guatavita, however, led to several attempts between 1562 and 1913 to drain the lake and expose its alleged hidden treasure.

Three useful and accessible examinations of El Dorado are WALKER CHAPMAN, *The Golden Dream: Seekers of El Dorado* (1967); VICTOR W. VON HAGEN, *The Golden Man: The Quest for El Dorado* (1974); and JOHN HEMMING, *The Search for El Dorado* (1978). A strong critique of the Guatavita version is found in DEMETRIO RAMOS PÉREZ, *El mito del Dorado: Su génesis y proceso* (1973).

LANCE R. GRAHN

EL INCA. *See* **Garcilaso de la Vega, El Inca.**

EL MIRADOR, a very large Late Formative MAYA site in the northern part of Petén, Guatemala, near the Mexican border. Its inaccessibility has limited research, but evi-

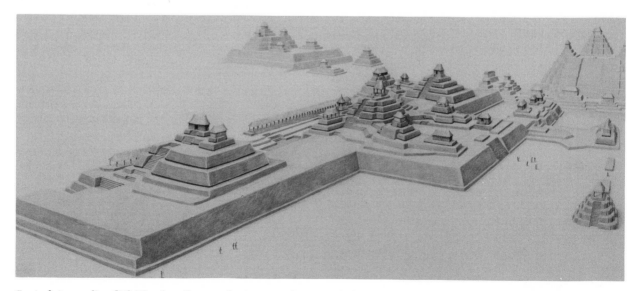

Central Acropolis of El Mirador, Guatemala. Late Preclassic period, ca. 150 B.C. Drawing by Terry Rutledge. © EL MIRADOR PROJECT, COURTESY OF RAY T. MATHENY / BRIGHAM YOUNG UNIVERSITY.

dence now shows that the site was occupied in the Middle Formative Period, grew to prominence and power during the Late Formative, and declined in the Protoclassic—ultimately relinquishing its power by A.D. 300 to TIKAL, 40 miles south. The site was superficially reoccupied during the Late Classic Period. Like Tikal, El Mirador derived its importance from its domination of transpeninsular trade routes and control of portages between the Gulf drainage and the Caribbean drainage.

The architecture of El Mirador is of the grandest scale. In the central area of the site, to the east, the Danta complex includes a multitiered grouping of platforms and truncated pyramids on a basal platform nearly 1,000 feet square. The summit of the crowning pyramid rises 230 feet above the ground. Danta is both the tallest Maya structure and the Maya structure of greatest volume.

About one mile to the west, and linked to the Danta complex by a *sacbe* (causeway), are several additional large-scale architectural groupings. Next in size to the Danta complex is El Tigre, whose tallest pyramid stands 180 feet high. Some 400 yards south of El Tigre, the Monos group includes a pyramid 130 feet high.

Construction utilizes cut-stone facings on rubble cores, and there are substantial remains of extensive stucco decoration of the exterior surfaces. Excavation of Structure 34 uncovered large masks of modeled stucco adjacent to the plastered front steps. Groupings of pyramids on large basal platforms are frequently in triples, with two smaller pyramids flanking the front plaza of the largest structure. Structures are linked by walls and causeways, and the region around the site center is dotted with *bajos* (lowlands), which flood seasonally.

RAY T. MATHENY, ed., *El Mirador, Petén, Guatemala: An Interim Report* (1980); SYLVANUS G. MORLEY and GEORGE W. BRAINERD, *The Ancient Maya,* 4th ed. (1983), esp. pp. 296–300.

WALTER R. T. WITSCHEY

EL MORRO CASTLE (Castillo de los Tres Reyes del Morro) is the monumental fortress that dominates the narrow entrance to Havana's vast harbor. Designed by the famed military engineer Bautista Antonelli, it was completed in 1590. The exterior walls blend with massive rocks on the elevations overlooking the port from the east and still stand as an impressive symbol of Hapsburg and Bourbon authority. Throughout the colonial period, El Morro functioned as a prison and as the key strong-point in Havana's defense complex. To close off Havana harbor to pirates and invaders, authorities on several occasions laid a huge iron chain or cable across the water from El Morro to the smaller western fort of Salvador de la Punta. When El Morro fell to a British land and sea attack on 31 July 1762, the city of Havana was doomed. For most of the next year, the Cuban capital remained in British hands. After the Treaty of Paris was signed in 1763, El Morro's defenses were again strengthened, financed by the *situados* (subsidies) from Mexico. Other Cuban fortresses, including the impressive one built in Santiago in 1633, also bear the name El Morro.

J. H. PARRY and P. M. SHERLOCK, *A Short History of the West Indies,* 3d ed. (1971); VICENTE BÁEZ, ed., *La enciclopedia de Cuba: Arquitectura, Artes Plásticas, Música,* vol. 7 (1974), pp. 5–9; LEVÍ MARRERO, *Cuba: Economía y sociedad,* vol. 2 (1974), pp. 406–409

El Morro. © FRITZ HENLE / PHOTO RESEARCHERS, INC.

and vol. 6 (1978), pp. 112–119; ALLAN J. KUETHE, *Cuba, 1753–1815: Crown, Military, and Society* (1986).

LINDA K. SALVUCCI

EL NIÑO, a warm current that temporarily raises the surface-water temperature off the Peruvian and Ecuadorian coasts around Christmas, hence the name ("the child"). Occasionally, especially warm waters disrupts the food chain significantly. Notably strong El Niño episodes have occurred in 1541, 1578, 1614, 1624, 1652, 1701, 1720, 1728, 1763, 1770, 1791, 1804, 1814, 1828, 1845, 1864, 1871, 1877–1878, 1884, 1891, 1899, 1911, 1918, 1925–1926, 1941, 1957–1958, 1972–1973, 1982–1983, and 1991–1992. Observers have noted "teleconnections," such as drought in central Chile and northeast Brazil and heavy rain in Peru and Ecuador, during strong El Niño years. The research of Sir Gilbert Walker (1868–1958), Jakob Bjerknes (1897–1975), and the 1985–1995 Tropical Ocean and Global Atmosphere (TOGA) study have contributed to a comprehensive explanation for El Niño events and their global implications.

WILLIAM H. QUINN et al., "Historical Trends and Statistics of the Southern Oscillation, El Niño, and Indonesian Droughts," in *Fishery Bulletin* 76, no. 3 (July 1978): 663–678; KEVIN HAMILTON and ROLANDO R. GARCÍA, "El Niño / Southern Oscillation Events and Their Associated Midlatitude Teleconnections, 1531–1841," in *Bulletin of the American Meteorological Society* 67 no. 11 (November 1986): 1354–1361; M. H. GLANTZ et al., eds., *Teleconnections Linking Worldwide Climate Anomalies: Scientific Basis and Societal Impact* (1991).

ROBERT H. CLAXTON

See also **Fishing Industry.**

EL PARAÍSO (Chuquitanta), a Late Preceramic-period monumental site on the central coast of Peru. Among the many archaeological treasures of the desert coast of Peru are massive stone and adobe architectural complexes, which served as ceremonial or administrative centers, dating to the Late Preceramic and Initial (early ceramic) periods (ca. 2000 B.C.–1400 B.C.). Among the most impressive of these is the El Paraíso site, a complex of eight or nine stone buildings covering about 125 acres in the Chillón River valley north of Lima. The site, which was occupied between 1800 and 1500 B.C., has been investigated by the archaeologists Frédéric Engel (mid-1960s) and Jeffrey Quilter (mid-1980s).

El Paraíso is the largest of the early monumental sites of the Peruvian coast. Complexes of rooms that make up the site are constructed of fieldstone laid in clay; walls were often covered by clay plaster, now disintegrated. The two largest architectural units are 1,320 feet long and parallel to each other, about 594 feet apart. The area between these units may have been a plaza. Other room complexes are smaller; the presence of architectural units and public spaces of different sizes suggests that a variety of ceremonial, administrative, and residential activities were carried out at the site.

Quilter and colleagues focused their research on recovering food remains from residential areas of the site. They found that fish was the most important animal consumed along with a variety of cultivated and wild plant foods. Cotton remains were abundant at the site—the Late Preceramic of the Peruvian coast is traditionally called the Cotton Preceramic—and researchers propose that El Paraíso controlled and developed cotton production in the Chillón-Rímac region.

FRÉDÉRIC-ANDRÉ ENGEL, "Le complexe précéramique d'El Paraíso (Pérou)," in *Journal de la société des américanistes* 55 (1966):43–95; JEFFREY QUILTER, "Architecture and Chronology at El Paraíso, Peru," in *Journal of Field Archaeology* 12 (1985):279–297; JEFFREY QUILTER, BERNARDINO OJEDA E., DEBORAH M. PEARSALL, DANIEL H. SANDWEISS, JOHN G. JONES, and ELIZABETH S. WING, "Subsistence Economy of El Paraíso, an Early Peruvian Site," in *Science* 251 (1991):277–283.

DEBORAH M. PEARSALL

EL SALVADOR is a city-state that developed around its capital, San Salvador. About 50 miles wide and less than 200 miles in length along a volcanic chain paralleling the Pacific coast, it is Central America's only state without a Caribbean shoreline. It is bounded on the west and northwest by Guatemala, on the north and east by Honduras, and on the east by the Gulf of Fonseca, which it shares with Honduras and Nicaragua. Much of the population lives in valleys at altitudes between 2,000 and 3,000 feet above sea level. El Salvador's fertile valleys and coastal plain have determined much of its modern history, as agroexports have been responsible for both the enrichment of a small landed oligarchy and the impoverishment of the rural masses.

The smallest of the Central American states in area (8,416 square miles), its population of 5.2 million (1990 estimate) makes it the most densely populated country in Latin America (642 per square mile) and second only to neighboring Guatemala in total population among the states that formerly comprised the Kingdom of Guatemala. Its population grew especially during the twentieth century, when after rising at a rate of about 1.5 percent in the nineteenth century its annual growth rate increased to more than 3 percent.

THE COLONIAL PERIOD

Although Mayans inhabited El Salvador before its conquest by Pedro de ALVARADO in 1524, Nahuatl peoples from Mexico were also important, and the aggressive and industrious Pipiles have, at least in the country's mythology, been given credit for Salvadorans' tendency toward greater industry and aggressiveness than other Central Americans.

Throughout most of the colonial period San Salvador was part of the province of Guatemala, within the Kingdom, or Captaincy-General, of Guatemala and Viceroy-

Estimated Population of El Salvador

Year	Population	Density (per sq km)
1821	248,000	11.8
1850	366,000	17.4
1900	800,000	38.0
1950	1,860,000	88.4
1980	4,525,000	215.1
2000	6,739,000	320.3

SOURCES: Ralph Lee Woodward, Jr., "Crecimiento de población en Centroamérica durante la primera mitad del siglo de la independencia nacional," in *Mesoamérica* (Antigua Guatemala) 1 (1980): 219–231; James W. Wilkie, ed., *Statistical Abstract of Latin America*, vol. 28 (1990), pp. 9, 114, 122.

alty of New Spain. It was subdivided into *alcaldías mayores* centered on the towns of San Salvador, San Miguel, San Vicente, Santa Ana, and Sonsonate.

In the eighteenth century, the rise of INDIGO production under the impetus of Bourbon economic policy brought changes to El Salvador that would lead to its emergence as a separate political unit. The establishment of the intendancy of San Salvador in 1786, although it remained within the Kingdom of Guatemala, marked the beginning of Salvadoran nationalism, a sentiment encouraged by several of its intendants, who defended and promoted Salvadoran economic interests. Smaller indigo planters chafed under the economic dominance of Guatemalan merchant capitalists, who financed the export trade, while the Salvadoran clergy objected both to the anticlericalism of the Bourbons and to the conservative ecclesiastical hierarchy in Guatemala City. They demanded a separate diocese for San Salvador, which remained under the jurisdiction of the bishop of Guatemala.

In Guatemala, the 1773 earthquakes had destroyed the capital city (Antigua Guatemala), resulting in a decision to move to a new site (present-day Guatemala City). Disruption of the kingdom's capital coincided with the rise of Salvadoran indigo as the leading agroexport of the kingdom and caused many Salvadoran creoles to favor, unsuccessfully, moving the capital to San Salvador, thus heightening their rivalry with Guatemala City.

These issues became more acute at the close of the colonial period when severe economic decline troubled the kingdom. Regional separatism and resentment toward conservative Guatemala made San Salvador a hotbed of liberalism in the nineteenth century. An abortive independence attempt in 1811, led by Father José Matías Delgado, reflected that sentiment but was crushed by military force from Guatemala under the command of a new intendant, José de AYCINENA, scion of the most powerful Guatemalan merchant family. This defeat intensified Salvadoran resentment toward Guatemala.

INDEPENDENCE TO 1900

Independence from Spain came fairly suddenly on 15 September 1821, when a meeting of notables in Guatemala City endorsed the Mexican creole Agustín de Iturbide's Plan of IGUALA. Officials in San Salvador accepted and proclaimed this act on 21 September, and on 29 September, Salvadoran creoles met and issued their own declaration of independence from Spain, but they resisted incorporation into Iturbide's Mexican Empire and sought to end El Salvador's subordination to Guatemala. In the resulting military conflict, San Salvador surrendered in 1823 after a long siege by a Mexican-Guatemalan force led by Vicente Filísola, but in the meantime the Mexican Empire itself collapsed. Salvadorans now successfully led the movement to declare Central America independent of Mexico on 1 July 1823, as El Salvador became an autonomous state in the United Provinces of the Center of America.

The deep animosities that developed in the independence process and the strong differences between the liberal and conservative approaches to national development plagued the administration of the new federal president, a Salvadoran military officer named Manuel José ARCE, elected under the Constitution of 1824. The takeover of the federal government by Guatemalan conservatives led to civil war from 1826 to 1829, principally between El Salvador and Guatemala, although Hondurans and Nicaraguans were also involved. Liberal victory, under the leadership of a Honduran general, Francisco MORAZÁN, restored Salvadoran importance in the Central American federation, and San Salvador became its capital in 1835, after having first moved from Guatemala to Sonsonate in 1834.

The Pipil Indian area of El Salvador, however, resisted development efforts, taxes, and reforms that threatened their lands and customs. Under the leadership of Anastasio Aquino, a violent Indian uprising threatened the stability of the government in 1833. Although Morazán's forces were able to suppress this uprising, it weakened the liberals considerably. On the heels of that revolt came a similar but successful peasant uprising in Guatemala which toppled the liberal government of that state and led to the collapse of the federation when the Guatemalan caudillo Rafael CARRERA defeated Morazán decisively at Guatemala City in March 1840. Conservative strength in Nicaragua and Costa Rica sealed the doom of the federation as each of the individual states began to go its separate way. Carrera's iron rule in Guatemala from 1839 to 1865 dominated El Salvador through much of the mid-nineteenth century, curtailing the liberal and unionist strength there, but El Salvador was the last of the Central American states to declare itself formally a separate, sovereign republic (1856).

The rise of General Gerardo BARRIOS ESPINOSA after 1858 marked liberal resurgence in El Salvador. Barrios had commanded the Salvadoran forces in the united Central American effort to drive the U.S. filibuster

William Walker from Nicaragua (1856–1857). Upon his return to El Salvador from that campaign, he failed in an 1857 attempt to unseat President Rafael CAMPO, but the following year he regained influence during the administration of Miguel Santín Castillo. He became acting chief of state in 1858 and again in 1859–1860; as president of El Salvador in 1861 he consolidated his political and military strength and began to initiate liberal economic and anticlerical reforms. The immediate result was an invasion by Rafael Carrera in 1863, which Barrios repulsed at Coatepeque on 24 February of that year, but Carrera returned later in the year to defeat Barrios and place the more conservative Francisco DUEÑAS in power (1863–1871). Nevertheless, many of the economic reforms begun by Barrios continued, and the process of liberalization once more accelerated under the rule of Santiago González (1871–1876) and Rafael Zaldívar (1876–1885).

Liberal Party dominance from 1871 to 1944 brought remarkable changes to El Salvador. Independence from Guatemalan intervention was achieved with the defeat and death of the invading army of the Guatemalan liberal caudillo Justo Rufino Barrios at Chalchuapa in 1885. Barrios was trying to restore the Central American union under his military leadership, and although El Salvador had traditionally favored union, its antipathy toward Guatemala outweighed unionist sentiment.

The Salvadoran governments that followed, concentrated on economic development as they facilitated the expansion of coffee exports by the planter elite at the expense of peasant land and labor. Indigo exports had continued to be important for El Salvador, but the development of aniline coal-tar dyes diminished its importance after 1860. The loose, volcanic soil in the tropical highlands of the country produced high-quality coffee and enabled a few planters to become dominant in economic and political affairs. Under their leadership, El Salvador became highly dependent on international markets for coffee. They modernized its transportation system and capital city, and gained control over more rural land for coffee production. In the early twentieth century this "coffee prosperity" gained El Salvador a reputation as the most progressive of the Central American states. With new ports and railways, it also became the first nation in Central America to have paved highways, and the city of San Salvador grew impressively in size and economic activity. A stronger military force maintained the liberal oligarchy, often referred to as the "fourteen families," although there were always more than that. Between 1913 and 1927 members of these families, notably the Meléndez and Quiñónez, presided over governments that were generally more stable than those in the neighboring states.

THE EARLY TWENTIETH CENTURY
Spanish colonialism had left a heritage of a small elite ruling a servile mass, and feudal traditions persisted well into the twentieth century. The principal features of the Salvadoran social structure, however, are especially related to the rise of coffee cultivation and the emergence of a dominant oligarchy in the late nineteenth and early twentieth centuries. Expansion into other agroexports, the rise of manufacturing, and the growth of the military officer corps, especially since 1950, expanded and diversified this elite to more than 250 families. Moreover, the modernization of the economy contributed to the growth in San Salvador of a significant middle class, which played a growing role in the intellectual, political, and cultural development of the country. The vast majority of the population, however, remained poor, uneducated, and lacking in economic opportunity. The widening gulf between urban modernization and rural backwardness, and between rich and poor, is perhaps nowhere so obvious in Latin America as in El Salvador. These serious social and economic inequities worsened in the late twentieth century as rapid population growth exceeded economic growth. Modernization sometimes obscured the growing social inequities that were aggravated by rapid population growth. While San Salvador became a modern urban center, rural poverty and malnutrition soared.

Challenges to the liberal oligarchy began to appear in the 1920s, especially as articulated by the Salvadoran intellectual leader Alberto MASFERRER, who founded the Labor Party in 1930. There was also the Communist Party of El Salvador, organized in 1925, reflecting more radical opposition, among whom the most outspoken

Outdoor market in San Salvador. © 1990 OWEN FRANKEN / STOCK, BOSTON.

representative was Agustín Farabundo MARTÍ. The economic hardships occasioned by the international depression following 1929 intensified the problems and encouraged labor organization and agitation. Yet the victory of the Labor Party candidate, Arturo ARAÚJO, a progressive member of the planter elite, in the election of 1930 came as a surprise to the oligarchy, who were unprepared to make concessions to social democracy, land reform, and improved health and education along the lines Masferrer had advocated. Following nearly a year of chaotic government and massive labor demonstrations, the army intervened and ousted Araújo in favor of his vice president, General Maximiliano HERNÁNDEZ MARTÍNEZ of the Liberal Party, on 2 December 1931. Martí and the Communists then led a rural revolt in January 1932, but in a struggle that essentially pitted peasant machetes against army machine guns, the result was a massacre of between 10,000 to 30,000 peasants, followed by repression and establishment of a military dictatorship that would last until 1944.

The 1932 massacre (MATANZA) was a watershed in Salvadoran history, for it marked the end of a period of relatively tolerant civilian oligarchical rule and the growth of labor organizations. The elite, frightened by the 1932 peasant uprising, became reactionary and relied on a repressive military to defend it from the masses, whose economic situation steadily deteriorated. Even after the end of Hernández Martínez's fascist-type dictatorship in 1944, the military continued to rule the country. The 1932 revolt also marked the end of identifiable Indian communities and culture in most of El Salvador, for the massacre had especially concentrated on Indians. Culturally, the remaining Indians quickly adopted mestizo dress and life-styles.

While coffee continued to be the primary export of the country, after World War II there was considerable expansion of other agroexports—cotton, sugar, rice, and beef—as the planter class expanded its holdings along the Pacific coastal plain. This expansion of agroexports enriched the elite, but in a period when the population was expanding rapidly, it also caused poverty among rural peasants who were forced off their land and into unemployment or jobs paying very low wages. Production of corn, beans, and other staples, forced onto the poorest land, could not keep pace with the expanding population, and in the latter half of the twentieth century, El Salvador became one of the most poorly nourished countries in the world.

Profits from agroexports and a growing awareness of the limitations of El Salvador's small area combined with its rapid population growth encouraged investment in manufacturing and service industries in San Salvador from the 1950s forward. The establishment of the CENTRAL AMERICAN COMMON MARKET in 1960 contributed notably to industrial expansion as trade among the Central American states rose through the following two decades and was especially beneficial to Salvadoran industry. While much of this development came from

the same families who had developed the agroexports, foreign investment and multinational corporations also became important to the Salvadoran economy for the first time.

POST 1950

Following the relatively peaceful overthrow of Hernández Martínez in 1944 by a combination of students, workers, and progressive military officers, a more open political climate had returned to El Salvador. Although military men continued to head the government, there was greater tolerance for political parties and labor unions, and the urban middle class became politically active. New parties replaced the long monopoly of the Liberal Party, which now disappeared, having been discredited by its association with the Hernández Martínez dictatorship. Yet the military-dominated Party of Democratic Revolutionary Unification (PRUD), with the support of the coffee elite, maintained power until 1961. Then the new but similar Party of National Conciliation (PCN), dominated by General Julio Rivera, replaced it and ruled until 1979.

Notable during this period, however, was the growth of broader-based popular parties, especially the Christian Democrats (PDC) and the Social Democrats (MNR). Under the dynamic leadership of a U.S.-trained civil engineer, José Napoleón DUARTE, the PDC was effective in the 1960s in organizing students and workers and in gaining support from Catholic clergy and laypeople. Duarte won election as mayor of San Salvador in 1964, but the 1969 war with Honduras interrupted the Christian Democratic surge.

The "FOOTBALL WAR", so called because rioting between rival Honduran and Salvadoran fans at a June 1969 World Cup playoff match touched it off, had much more fundamental causes. Border disputes had occurred between the two states since colonial times, but more serious were the trade imbalances in their common market relations. Honduran imports exceeded exports and Salvadoran manufactured goods damaged Honduran infant industries. Most serious, however, was the basic social inequity and overpopulation in El Salvador, causing massive emigration into Honduras. The Salvadoran immigrants threatened Honduran jobs, wages, land, and businesses. Large Honduran landholders led a campaign against the Salvadoran immigrants that gained widespread popular support among the Honduran working class, who felt threatened by the Salvadorans. A Honduran agrarian reform law of April 1968 displaced thousands of Salvadoran squatters and increased tensions leading to the riots.

The war itself, which began on 14 July when Salvadoran troops invaded Honduras, was briefly but costly. The Honduran air force inflicted serious damage to Salvadoran port installations at Acajutla and elsewhere. The Organization of American States arranged a cease-fire on 18 July and Salvadoran troops withdrew on 3 August, but a peace treaty was not finally agreed upon until 1980. The war was a setback to the Central American economic integration movement. In El Salvador it led to a resurgence of the military, which placed patriotism in support of the war effort ahead of the grim socioeconomic realities of the country.

Returning refugees from Honduras put an even greater strain on El Salvador's land-poor population, and there was widespread opposition to the government by 1972. An opposition coalition, the National Union of Opposition, with Duarte at the head of the ticket and Guillermo Ungo of the MNR as the vice presidential candidate, appeared to win a majority in the election of that year. Yet the government declared the PCN candidate, Arturo MOLINA, victorious and drove Duarte and Ungo into exile. Repressive, reactionary rule followed. El Salvador became notorious for human rights violations as the tide of civil disorder and dissent continued to rise.

The Sandinista success in ending the Somoza dynasty in neighboring Nicaragua in July 1979 and the rising popular opposition to the PCN government of Carlos Humberto ROMERO prompted a military coup in October 1979 that sought conciliation with the opposition but was primarily concerned with preserving the power and prestige of the military. Resignation of nearly all the civilians on the junta, including Guillermo Ungo, over continued military repression precipitated a new crisis in January 1980. The PDC now collaborated with the military to form a new junta, and Duarte became its chief later in the year. Under Duarte's leadership, and with strong United States backing, the government tried to restrain the military repression and to begin socioeconomic reform, including an agrarian reform plan. But Duarte appeared impotent as the real power remained with the military chiefs. Political assassinations by the Right, including those of the outspoken Catholic archbishop Oscar ROMERO, several PDC leaders, and four U.S. Catholic churchwomen, were common in 1980, while on the Left guerrilla organizations, headed by the Farabundo Martí National Liberation Front (FMLN) launched a civil war against the government. A new political party, the National Republican Alliance (ARENA) consolidated right-wing opposition behind the leadership of the charismatic Major Roberto D'AUBUISSON, who had been linked to death squad assassinations, including that of Archbishop Romero.

United States military aid to the government became an element of rising importance in this escalating civil war. With American assistance, the junta held a free election for a constituent assembly in 1982. Leftist parties did not participate, and the PDC won a plurality, but a coalition of the rightist ARENA and PCN held a commanding majority. The convention elected D'Aubuisson as its head, but United States pressure prevented his selection as provisional president of the country, and under the constitution that was drafted in 1983, Duarte won a decisive victory in the presidential election of 1984.

During his five-year term, Duarte could not revive the sagging economy. As a signatory to the Central American Peace Accord of 1987 (the Arias Plan), he agreed to seek peace with the guerrilla forces but had made little progress, and his country continued to be torn by violence and civil war. In June 1988 he entered a hospital in the United States for treatment of stomach cancer. (He died in 1990.)

The failure of the Christian Democrats to bring peace or economic recovery, and widespread criticism of corruption among Christian Democratic bureaucrats, allowed the consolidated neoliberal ARENA to win a decisive victory in 1989. An earthquake that destroyed much of San Salvador in 1986 had further eroded PDC strength. Under D'Aubuisson's leadership, ARENA skillfully organized rural and urban voters into a powerful political force, capitalizing on national exhaustion with the violence and fear of the extreme Left. The inherent conservatism of a portion of the peasant class was successfully exploited, as D'Aubuisson's 1982 victory in congressional elections had reflected. Moreover, the close association of ARENA leaders with the military gave that party a significant advantage that helps to explain its success in rural areas. ARENA's 1984 presidential candidate—an affable sportsman named Alfredo CRISTIANI, who was much more acceptable to the U.S. Congress than the tainted D'Aubuisson—thus swept to victory. After tortuous negotiations, a peace accord was reached with the FMLN at the end of 1991. Demobilization of armed forces proceeded slowly and was marked by mutual distrust. Outside economic aid brought only limited recovery as the country gradually fell out of the limelight of international attention by the mid-1990s.

Christianity has long played an important role in the "Land of the Savior." The strong anticlericalism that characterized the liberal period in nineteenth- and early-twentieth-century El Salvador, however, greatly weakened the Roman Catholic church, removing it from its close relationship with the government and reducing the number of clergy in the country, thereby reducing its influence in the countryside. In the mid-to-late twentieth century, however, a rejuvenated Catholic clergy once more became important in mobilizing the Salvadoran people for political change. They were a force in the Christian Democratic Party, but El Salvador has also been a place where the theology of liberation has been important in the radicalizing of political opinion. From parish priests through the hierarchy, the Catholic church has played an important part in the struggle to curb the terrible violations of human rights that have afflicted El Salvador, and as a result has often been a victim, as in the murder of six prominent Jesuits at the University of Central America in San Salvador on 16 November 1989. At the same time, as in Guatemala, there has been astonishing increase in converts to Pentecostal Protestant sects in the country, as these groups have gained among those who seek religion outside the framework of political controversy. In fact, Protestants have been important in building the more conservative, or apolitical, constituency that is reflected in ARENA's rise to power.

PHILIP L. RUSSELL, *El Salvador in Crisis* (1984), offers a useful summary of Salvadoran history, as does ALASTAIR WHITE, *El Salvador* (1973), although the latter is useful primarily for its description of the 1960s. DAVID BROWNING, *El Salvador: Landscape and Society* (1971), is a superb study of the role of land tenure and use in Salvadoran history, and in the process describes the basic structure of Salvadoran socioeconomic history. MARÍA LEISTENSCHNEIDER and FREDDY LEISTENSCHNEIDER, *Gobernantes de El Salvador (biografías)* (1980), provides useful biographical sketches of El Salvador's chiefs of state. For the nineteenth century, see HÉCTOR LINDO-FUENTES, *Weak Foundations: The Economy of El Salvador in the Nineteenth Century, 1821–1898* (1990); JAMES DUNKERLEY provides the best overview of twentieth-century El Salvador within the context of Central American history in *Power in the Isthmus* (1988); his *Long War, Dictatorship, and Revolution in El Salvador* (1982), focuses especially on the recent history of that country. THOMAS P. ANDERSON, *Matanza: El Salvador's Communist Revolt of 1932* (1971), details the events surrounding the 1932 revolt at the beginning of the Hernández Martínez dictatorship, when modern Salvadoran history is often said to have begun. PATRICIA PARKMAN, *Nonviolent Insurrection in El Salvador: The Fall of Maximiliano Hernández Martínez* (1988), studies his fall from power. WILLIAM H. DURHAM, *Scarcity and Survival: Ecological Origins of the Soccer War* (1979), is one of the most valuable studies of the social and economic situation in mid-twentieth-century El Salvador. STEPHEN WEBRE, *José Napoleón Duarte and the Christian Democratic Party in Salvadoran Politics, 1960–1972* (1979), describes the political history of El Salvador at a critical point; SARA GORDON RAPOPORT, *Crisis política y guerra en El Salvador* (1989), is especially useful for the 1972–1979 period. ENRIQUE A. BALOYRA, *El Salvador in Transition* (1982), and TOMMIE SUE MONTGOMERY, *Revolution in El Salvador: Origins and Evolution* (1982), are among the most useful items in the more plentiful literature on the early 1980s. For a more detailed bibliography, see RALPH L. WOODWARD, JR., comp., *El Salvador* (1988).

RALPH LEE WOODWARD, JR.

See also **Central America; Coffee Industry; United States–Latin American Relations.**

EL SALVADOR: CONSTITUTIONS Although it was part of the Kingdom of Guatemala during the colonial period, the region of modern-day El Salvador began to act with increasing independence in the late eighteenth century. Salvadorans came to resent the power and status of Guatemalans and were quick to adopt a liberal, progressive attitude as a counterweight to the latter's conservatism. In general, Salvadorans and their constitutions have been among the most consistently liberal in Central America and have been the most active advocates of isthmian attempts at unity and federation. However, the constitutions of El Salvador have followed a Napoleonic pattern in being documents designed and decreed from above with the intent of creating a smoothly functioning, just society. Accordingly, the documents often bear little resemblance to the society they are intended to govern and have been modified frequently, because they have no roots in tradition. The student of legal and constitutional history must therefore proceed with caution and skepticism, for the documents may say one thing but translate into action quite differently.

Since 1824, El Salvador has had twenty-three constitutions, some of them virtually identical except for a few key clauses.

CONSTITUTION OF 1824

Central America achieved its independence from Spain without bloodshed and immediately consolidated its gains with a liberal constitution based on both the 1812 Cádiz Constitution of Spain and that of the United States. The 1824 Constitution provided the structure of the federation and its component parts. In it the newly named Federal Republic of El Salvador consisted of five states, each with its own assembly and head of state. The federation had a congress and a president, but both the states and the federation were granted the rights to raise armed forces and taxes, wherein lay the basis for much future disunity. The 1824 Constitution abolished SLAVERY and recognized Catholicism as the official, exclusive religion. In general, it was a powerfully worded document that could not overcome the divisive forces arrayed against it. A Salvadoran-based attempt to revamp the constitution (1835) granted freedom of religion and introduced more parliamentary-style forms of government but proved insufficient to prevent the total breakdown of Central American unity in 1838.

Following this disruption, El Salvador and its politicians continued to hope for isthmian federation and provided a haven for other Central Americans of similar sympathies. Both in 1898 and 1921, representatives of the dream of federation met in San Salvador to draft constitutions for the United States of Central America and the Republic of Central America.

CONSTITUTION OF 1886

After decades of struggle between liberals and conservatives (never as violent in El Salvador as elsewhere in Central America), a series of strong liberal presidents established a new governmental ethos epitomized in the Constitution of 1886. President Francisco Menéndez was the primary architect behind this liberal-idealist document, which guaranteed the free expression of ideas, regular elections with universal suffrage for literate males, and similar tenets of political liberalism. This constitution contained a clause precluding successive terms in office, a process of alternating presidencies that became a respected and honored tradition in El Salvador which was not challenged until the period of Maximiliano HERNÁNDEZ MARTÍNEZ in the 1930s.

Despite its high ideals, the liberal Constitution of 1886 did not guarantee equality in practice. For instance, the titles to recently expropriated communal lands of the

Indian communities were legally turned over to their new entrepreneurial owners. Also, there were no provisions for taxation and public works, and urban development was placed above the welfare of the rural areas. Furthermore, political participation and the control of the emerging state remained in the hands of a very few elite families with access to education and financial resources. With a few modifications, the Constitution of 1886 survived until 1939 and served as the inspiration for the democratic movement of 1944.

CONSTITUTION OF 1939

The more authoritarian Constitution of 1939, initiated by General Maximiliano Hernández Martínez, was a thoroughly twentieth-century document that introduced the idea of state intervention to El Salvador. Under its provisions the state had the exclusive right to regulate money, mail, telegraph, telephone, and radio services. The government recognized an obligation to protect and promote small businesses and credit institutions and to offer some workers' protection. This constitution also gave the military courts jurisdiction over civilians charged with rebellion and extended the presidential term from four to six years, with no provision for reelection. The 1939 constitution and Hernández Martínez's dictatorship together spawned a military-civilian coup in 1944, but the trend toward government interventionism continued unchecked and actually extended its scope.

CONSTITUTIONS OF 1950 AND 1962

The constitutions of 1950 and 1962 are virtually identical, except for a few changes in wording and the location of specific clauses. Their major social concerns, which were concentrated on urban areas, allowed for the existence of muted political opposition. Women were granted the vote, and the right of the people to insurrection was guaranteed in principle. The army, renamed the Armed Forces, was held to a limit of 3,000 men, a figure that did not include the security forces. The constitutions of 1950 and 1962 revealed lofty ideals but also laid bare the apprehensions of the ruling powers, who wanted to orchestrate and manage social change from above.

Salvadoran constitutional history reveals some striking consistencies throughout the nineteenth and twentieth centuries; indeed, much of the wording is retained from one version to another. The Constitution of 1983 drew much inspiration from its predecessors of 1962 and 1950, which in turn owed a debt to those that had gone before. The various constitutions all share a desire for improvements in the general welfare and for isthmian union, but they suffer from fear of the dislocations that such changes necessarily imply.

GOVERNMENT OF EL SALVADOR, *Independencia: Objetivos y constitución* (n.d.); *Constitución política de la República de El Salvador* (1886); *Constitution of the Republic of El Salvador* (1950); *Constitution of the Republic of El Salvador* (1962); *Constitución política de la República de El Salvador* (1980), and *Proyecto político de la nueva constitución política de El Salvador* (1983).

JULIO ALBERTO DOMÍNGUEZ SOSA, *Génesis y significado de la Constitución de 1886* (1958); RICARDO GALLARDO, ed., *Las constituciones de la República Federal de Centro-América* (1958), *Las constituciones de El Salvador* (1961); SEMINARIO DE HISTORIA CONTEMPORÁNEA CENTROAMÉRICA, *El constitucionalismo y la vida institucional centroamericana* (1964); THOMAS KARNES, *The Failure of Union: Central America, 1824–1975* (1976); MARIO RODRÍGUEZ, *The Cádiz Experiment in Central America, 1808 to 1826* (1978); MARIA LEISTENSCHNEIDER and FREDDY LEISTENSCHNEIDER, *Períodos presidenciales y constituciones federales y políticas de El Salvador* (1980); RALPH LEE WOODWARD, JR., *Central America: A Nation Divided,* 2d ed. (1985).

KAREN RACINE

EL SALVADOR: ORGANIZATIONS

Nationalist Democratic Organization
Organización Democrática Nacionalista—ORDEN

ORDEN, Spanish for "order," was a paramilitary vigilance organization in El Salvador during the 1960s and 1970s. Founded in about 1964 by National Guard commander José Alberto Medrano, ORDEN sought to indoctrinate peasants in anticommunism, mobilize support for the governing National Conciliation Party, and police the countryside for suspected subversives. In return for protection and benefits, ORDEN members engaged in domestic espionage and the physical harassment of enemies of the regime, and they played a major role in the political violence of the 1970s. Most of ORDEN's estimated 100,000 members, however, probably joined only for self-protection. When a power struggle in 1970 led to Medrano's ouster, the Salvadoran army assumed control of ORDEN, and the president of the republic became its titular head. The provisional junta that replaced president Carlos Humberto ROMERO dissolved ORDEN in November 1979.

Good discussions of Salvadoran politics in the 1960s and 1970s are in JAMES DUNKERLEY, *Power in the Isthmus: A Political History of Modern Central America* (1988), and SARA GORDON RAPOPORT, *Crisis política y guerra en El Salvador* (1989).

STEPHEN WEBRE

EL SALVADOR: POLITICAL PARTIES

Farabundo Martí National Liberation Front
Frente Farabundo Martí para la Liberación Nacional—FMLN

The FMLN was the insurgent alliance in El Salvador during the civil war of the 1980s. It took its name from Agustín Farabundo MARTÍ (1893–1932), an early leader of the Salvadoran Communist Party.

The FMLN was a unified command structure created

in October 1980 to coordinate the military and political activities of five separate leftist guerrilla organizations. Its leaders were Marxist-Leninists seeking to make the front a vanguard revolutionary party governed by the principle of democratic centralism. However, the armed groups that made up the FMLN continued to maintain ties with their own political parties and mass movements, and doctrinal disputes were common, especially over revolutionary strategy and tactics.

The oldest and largest of the FMLN member movements, the Farabundo Martí Popular Liberation Forces (Fuerzas Populares de Liberación Farabundo Martí—FPL), founded in 1970, advocated "prolonged popular warfare" inspired by the Vietnamese example, while the other groups favored insurrectionist tactics. The member groups also disagreed on the relative importance of political organizational activity. For example, the People's Revolutionary Army (Ejército Revolucionario del Pueblo—ERP), organized in 1972, emphasized the military struggle, while the National Resistance Armed Forces (Fuerzas Armadas de Resistencia Nacional—FARN), which had split from the ERP in 1975, stressed the cultivation of popular mass movements and attempts to penetrate the government's armed forces by appealing to disaffected offices. Such internal quarrels occasionally resulted in violence. In April 1983, for example, a debate within the FPL over strategy led to the brutal murder of Commander Mélida Anaya Montes (Ana María) and to the apparent suicide of the group's founder and leader, Salvador Cayetano Carpio (Marcial).

In spite of the failure of its "final offensive," launched on 10 January 1981, the FMLN was able to survive as a fighting force, and in 1985 may have had some 8,000 combatants in the field, compared with the government's 50,000. Although never much larger than this and not always unified, the FMLN maintained a strong base of occupied territory in the northern provinces, especially Chalatenango and Morazán, from which it repeatedly struck at military and economic targets.

Although Cuban president Fidel CASTRO may have taken a personal role in bringing about the front's formation in 1980, Soviet and Cuban material support appears never to have been as significant as claimed by the United States. Support by the Sandinista regime in nearby Nicaragua was probably more important, but that government's electoral defeat in February 1990, along with the declining prestige of revolutionary socialist movements worldwide, left the FMLN increasingly isolated.

In May 1990, the FMLN entered into a series of United Nations–sponsored direct talks with the Salvadoran government aimed at achieving a cease-fire and reintegrating the insurgents into national political life. From the beginning, however, these discussions bogged down over guerrilla insistence on the reform of the government's armed forces. Demobilization began after the 1991 peace accord, and the FMLN began to move warily into the political arena.

TOMMIE SUE MONTGOMERY, *Revolution in El Salvador: Origins and Evolution* (1982); JAMES DUNKERLEY, *Power in the Isthmus: A Political History of Modern Central America* (1988).

STEPHEN WEBRE

National Conciliation Party
Partido de Conciliación Nacional—PCN

The National Conciliation Party was the official party in El Salvador during the 1960s and 1970s. Founded in September 1961, it represented military and business interests and was also a vehicle for the personal ambitions of army officer Julio Adalberto RIVERA, who had seized power in a coup d'état on 25 January. The party strongly opposed communism and Cuban influence in Central America and was an enthusiastic supporter of U.S. policy in the 1960s. Although its natural constituency was the conservative Salvadoran landowning class, early PCN leaders were pragmatists. Their modernizing agenda and occasional populist rhetoric led to defections on the right, which by the early 1970s forced the PCN to abandon reformist initiatives and to adopt a more openly repressive style. PCN elements controlled the armed forces and the electoral machinery for almost twenty years. Consecutive PCN presidents of El Salvador, all military officers, included Rivera (1962–1967), Fidel SÁNCHEZ HERNÁNDEZ (1967–1972), Arturo Armando MOLINA (1972–1977), and Carlos Humberto ROMERO (1977–1979). Following Romero's ouster in the coup d'état of 15 October 1979, the PCN survived as a minority opposition party.

STEPHEN WEBRE, *José Napoleón Duarte and the Christian Democratic Party in Salvadoran Politics, 1960–1972* (1979); SARAH GORDON RAPOPORT, *Crisis política y guerra en El Salvador* (1989).

STEPHEN WEBRE

National Republican Alliance
Alianza Republicana Nacional—ARENA

ARENA is a conservative political party in El Salvador. Founded in September 1981, chiefly by former army officer Major Roberto D'AUBUISSON, who was reputed to have links to right-wing DEATH SQUADS, ARENA champions private property and opposes land reform. Although founded to preserve the power of the ruling obligarchy, it has proved popular with a wide spectrum of the Salvadoran people. The first test of ARENA's popular appeal was the March 1982 election of members of a constituent assembly. Although its chief opponent, the Christian Democratic Party, won more seats in the assembly, ARENA, which was second in the balloting, was able to create a majority by forming coalitions with other conservative parties. D'Aubuisson was elected speaker of the assembly and prevented from becoming provisional president only by pressure from the United States, which feared his extremist views.

D'Aubuisson resigned as speaker in December 1983

to become ARENA's candidate in the March 1984 presidential election. In the first round of the multiparty election, Christian Democrat José Napoleón DUARTE and d'Aubuisson came in first and second; Duarte won the May runoff by 54 percent to 46 percent. In 1988 d'Aubuisson stepped down as party head and was replaced by Alfredo CRISTIANI, a wealthy coffee grower and industrialist. D'Aubuisson, however, continued to be regarded as the spiritual leader of ARENA until his death in 1992.

Profiting from public dissatisfaction with the handling of the civil war against leftist rebels and the country's economic collapse, ARENA gained exactly half the seats in the sixty-member national assembly elected in March 1988 and was able to dominate the assembly with the aid of its conservative allies. Cristiani ran as the party's candidate for president in March 1989 and won on the first ballot with 53.9 percent of the vote. The ARENA government appeared to have a close working relationship with the military.

The prestige of Cristiani was increased by the success of peace talks with the leftist rebels in December 1991 and the termination of the civil war. In the presidential elections of March 1994, ARENA ran San Salvador mayor Ernesto Calderón Sol, who won almost 50 percent on the first ballot and easily won election in the runoff. The party continued to dominate the national assembly.

ENRIQUE BALOYRA, *El Salvador in Transition* (1982); THOMAS P. ANDERSON, *Politics in Central America*, rev. ed. (1988), pp. 112–123.

THOMAS P. ANDERSON

EL SEÑOR DE LOS MILAGROS

EL SEÑOR DE LOS MILAGROS (Lord of Miracles), the most popular religious procession in Peru. It is based on a painting of the crucified Christ done by an anonymous black slave in Lima around 1650. After the wall on which the image was painted remained intact following the earthquake of 1655, the painting was perceived to be miraculous and devotion to the "Holy Christ of Miracles" spread rapidly. A copy of the painting was first taken out in procession in October 1687, following another earthquake. By the eighteenth century it had become the most popular procession in Lima. It continues to be held in October. The original painting is on permanent display in the church of the order of Nazarenes, and the Confraternity of the Bearers of the Lord of Miracles is the largest and most important in Peru. Although the devotion has not lost its original popular character, by the late twentieth century Peruvians of all social classes have come to accept the devotion as part of their Peruvian identity.

RUBÉN VARGAS UGARTE, *Historia del Santo Cristo de los Milagros*, 3d ed. (1966); MARÍA ROSTWOROWSKI, *Pachacamac y el Señor de los Milagros* (1992).

JEFFREY KLAIBER

EL SEÑOR DE LOS TEMBLORES (Lord of Quakes), one of the principal objects of devotion in Cuzco. It is a carved image of the crucified Christ, popularly believed to have been sent as a gift by Charles V but most probably fashioned by local artists. Originally known as the Lord of a Good Death, after the earthquake of 1650 the figure became known as the Lord of Quakes. Since 1741, its procession has taken place on Monday of Holy Week. Over time the image of Christ has become so darkened by the smoke and heat of the candles that accompany it in procession that it now appears to be an Indian or a black Christ. Declared the patron of Cuzco, the image is housed in the cathedral. The procession, accompanied by city officials, is a major tourist attraction.

VÍCTOR ANGELES VARGAS, *Historia del Cusco* (1979), vol. 2, bk. 1, pp. 129–131; JESÚS LÁMBARRI, "Imágenes de mayor veneración en la ciudad del Cusco," in Banco de Crédito, *Escultura en el Perú* (1991), pp. 251–255.

JEFFREY KLAIBER

EL TAJÍN, the most important archaeological city of northeastern Mexico. Characterized by highly distinctive architecture and art dating from about A.D. 250 to 1100, the city is situated near the Totonac Indian town of Papantla in the state of Veracruz. It covers approximately 2,400 acres, spilling out of a steep-sided mountain valley in the Tecolutla River basin.

At the center of the city are numerous multistory stone temples, palaces, ball courts, plazas, and terraces. Many buildings are constructed with the hallmark triangular "flying cornices" and rectangular niches on walls or stairways. Exterior surfaces, sealed with thick layers of high-quality stucco, were painted, most often red or blue, and many interior surfaces were decorated with murals. Some structures had massive flat roofs indicating a near-modern skill at pouring concrete. The maximum expression of this style is the centrally located Pyramid of the Niches, a seven-tiered temple, 69 feet high.

Sculpture at the site is abundant and ornate. It is executed in a unique double outline style embellished with diverse scroll elements. The large carved panels of the South Ball Court constitute one of the most elaborate depictions known of the rites associated with the cults of the planet Venus and the ritual drink pulque. There are at least fifteen ritual ball courts in the city, many with sculptures, making it one of the greatest concentrations in Mexico. The Building of the Columns, built atop the extensive acropolis known as Tajín Chico, enclosed an extraordinary entrance portico of carved columns depicting the sacrificial rites of a major ruler named 13 Rabbit.

El Tajín was the metropolitan center of a significant coastal culture that influenced, and at times ruled, broad areas, including parts of the adjoining highlands. Much of the relevant chronological data for interpreting the city comes from closely related SANTA LUISA. Comparative studies of art motifs suggest that El Tajín influ-

El Tajín. PHOTO BY ENRIQUE FRANCO TORRIJOS.

enced distant ruling groups, including some well beyond the northern Mesoamerican frontier.

The art of El Tajín is examined in MICHAEL KAMPEN, *The Sculptures of El Tajín, Veracruz, Mexico* (1972); JOSÉ GARCÍA PAYÓN, *Los enigmas de El Tajín* (1973); S. JEFFREY K. WILKERSON, "In Search of the Mountain of Foam: Human Sacrifice in Eastern Mesoamerica," in *Ritual Human Sacrifice in Mesoamerica*, edited by Elizabeth H. Boone (1984); and "El Tajín, Great Center of the Northeast," in METROPOLITAN MUSEUM OF ART, *Mexico, Splendors of Thirty Centuries* (1990). Architecture is reviewed in S. JEFFREY K. WILKERSON, *El Tajín: A Guide for Visitors* (1987); and chronology in S. JEFFREY K. WILKERSON, "Man's Eighty Centuries in Veracruz," in *National Geographic Magazine* 158, no. 2 (August 1980): 202–231.

S. JEFFREY K. WILKERSON

See also **Totonacs.**

ELCANO, JUAN SEBASTIÁN DE (*b.* ca. 1476, *d.* 4 August 1526), Spanish navigator. Elcano was born in Guetaria, Vizcaya. He completed the first circumnavigation of the world by sea, at a time of intense rivalry between Spain and Portugal over the spice trade. In 1519 he joined the expedition of Ferdinand MAGELLAN to the Orient via South America; it entered the Pacific in November 1520. When Magellan was killed in the Philippines in 1521, Elcano, one of his captains, assumed leadership of the expedition. The only remaining ship, *Victoria*, sailed for Spain via the Cape of Good Hope (May 1522). After a voyage fraught with deprivation and sickness, Elcano

and the seventeen other surviving men reached Spain in September 1522. As chief navigator and guide of an expedition to claim the Molucca Islands for Spain in June 1525, Elcano died en route in the Pacific.

CARLOS MARTÍNEZ SHAW, ed., *El Pacífico Español: De Magallanes a Malaspina* (1988); MAURICIO OBREGÓN, *La primera vuelta al mundo: Magallanes, Elcano y el libro de la nao Victoria* (1984).

HILARY BURGER

ELECTRIFICATION is regarded as the pacesetter for economic and social advancement in most developing countries. Electric utilities in Latin America are rapidly expanding their installed capacity and undergoing change, assisted by loans from the World Bank and INTER-AMERICAN DEVELOPMENT BANK.

Total net electricity consumption in Latin America

TABLE 1   Net Electricity Consumption in Latin America, 1980s   (Billion Kilowatt-hours)

Country	1980	1985	1989
Argentina	36.8	40.4	42.9
Brazil	122.4	170.6	244.3
Colombia	15.7	27.4	34.8
Mexico	59.6	82.5	105.5
Venezuela	27.7	42.8	54.6
Other	68.8	78.5	95.7
Total	331.0	442.2	577.8

has been growing at almost 7 percent annually since 1985, reaching 577.8 billion kilowatts in 1989. Brazil was responsible for most of this growth, doubling its electricity consumption from 1980 to 1989 (see table 1).

Hydropower represents the largest single supply source for electricity in Latin America. In 1989, 61 percent of all electricity supplied came from hydropower. Brazil has always dominated hydroelectric generation in Latin America and accounted for 60 percent (211.2 billion kilowatt-hours) of the total hydro generated in 1988. Brazil encouraged electricity-intensive industries such as aluminum smelters to use relatively cheap hydropower, and many industries substituted electricity for imported oil. By the early 1990s, hydro provided almost 90 percent of all electricity generated in Brazil.

In 1988, hydro provided 55 percent of the electricity generated in Venezuela. Ecuador also depends on hydropower from the Paute River for 80 percent of its electricity. Mexico, on the other hand, receives 20 percent of its electricity from hydro and 59 percent from oil. In 1988, petroleum, natural gas, and coal burned in thermal plants generated 36 percent of the electricity consumed in Latin America in 1988 (see table 2), while geothermal and other sources provided 3 percent. Geothermal development proceeded rapidly during the 1970s and 1980s in Mexico and El Salvador, but remains relatively insignificant.

TABLE 2   Net Electricity Generation by Type in Latin America, 1988   (Billions of Kilowatt-Hours)

Country	Thermal	Hydro	Nuclear	Other	Total
Argentina	26.4	15.7	5.5	0.0	47.6
Brazil	15.0	211.2	0.3	12.7	239.2
Colombia	8.4	29.0	0.0	0.0	37.5
Mexico	81.3	19.3	0.0	4.3	104.9
Venezuela	24.9	30.0	0.0	0.0	54.4
Other	55.8	46.9	0.0	1.0	103.7
Total	211.3	352.1	5.8	18.0	587.3

Like most developing countries, those of Latin America have substantial potential to increase the efficiency of their power systems. Subsidized electricity prices reduce the incentive for energy conservation. Distribution and transformation losses have been increasing to 21.5 percent in 1987. The Inter-American Development Bank is financing electric system upgrades to reduce power outages and losses in Jamaica and Bolivia, among other countries.

Most electricity generation, transmission, and distribution in Latin America is the responsibility of government ministries and corporations, except for self-generation by industrial facilities. Bolivia, Costa Rica, Ecuador, El Salvador, Guyana, Honduras, Mexico, Nicaragua, Panama, Paraguay, Uruguay, and most Carib-

Power plant in Paraíba, Brazil, ca. 1950s. ORGANIZATION OF AMERICAN STATES.

bean islands have centralized public utilities. Self-generation at aluminum factories, cement plants, sugar mills, and other industrial facilities assist the centralized power sector in Belize, the Dominican Republic, French Guiana, Haiti, Jamaica, and Suriname. Decentralized electric sectors exist in Argentina, Brazil, Colombia, Guatemala, Peru, and Venezuela.

The failure of most state-owned utilities in Latin America to generate sufficient revenues to cover normal expansion has combined with their nations' overall debt problems to place utilities in a precarious position with respect to meeting growing demands. Some countries are now permitting private power generation for distribution by the central grid (Mexico, Argentina, and Costa Rica) and others are discussing privatization as an option (El Salvador, Venezuela, and Brazil).

Chile has privatized its electricity sector, keeping only 10 percent of the previously public entity under public ownership. The process was scheduled for completion in 1992 at a cost of $27 million. The U.S. AGENCY FOR INTERNATIONAL DEVELOPMENT has encouraged El Salvador to follow Chile's lead and return its distribution companies to the private sector.

Regional cooperation has developed despite political differences. Grid interconnections exist in Central America, between Mexico and the United States, and in parts of South America. Paraguay has been exchanging electricity with Brazil and Uruguay since 1971 and with Argentina since 1973. Mexico has been selling power from its geothermal plants in Baja California to San Diego (California) Gas and Electric. Further cooperation is likely in the future. In February 1990, Venezuela and Guyana signed an agreement to interconnect their electricity grids. Venezuela will supply up to 70 percent of Guyana's electricity requirements by 1995, mostly from the Raúl Leoni hydroelectric complex at Guri. In March 1989, Venezuela and Colombia agreed to extend the Maracaibo grid into eastern Colombia.

Rural electrification continues to be an important issue in Latin America, despite the fact that 60 percent of the population live in urban areas. The availability of reliable electric power can substantially increase the ability of rural areas to produce for outside markets. Many countries have found it excessively expensive to extend the central power grid to small, dispersed load centers. As a result, many governments are working with international aid agencies to develop decentralized power, such as mini- and micro-hydroelectric facilities, photovoltaic, and wind.

MOHAN MUNASINGHE, Rural Electrification for Development: Policy Analysis and Applications (1987); LEE CATALANO, ed., International Directory of Electric Utilities (1988); LATIN AMERICAN ENERGY ORGANIZATION, Energy Balances for Latin America and the Caribbean (1988); U.S. DEPARTMENT OF ENERGY, 1989 International Energy Annual (1991).

MINDI J. FARBER

See also **Energy; Itaipú Hydroelectric Project.**

ELETROBRÁS, the state-owned electric power holding company in Brazil. After World War II, Brazil's need for power expanded faster than the ability of its private power companies to produce it. By the 1960s, more than half the electricity consumed in Brazil was generated by Rio Light and São Paulo Light, two subsidiaries of Toronto-based Brazilian Traction, Light, and Power. In addition to this Canadian firm there were small local generating companies throughout the country. Each produced a different voltage of power, a legacy that continues to this day.

In 1962, Eletrobrás (Centrais Elétricas Brasileiras, S.A.) was set up to develop and enforce a national electric ENERGY policy for Brazil. After 1964, the military gave Eletrobrás the authority to implement the objective of national electric energy self-sufficiency. The American Foreign Power Company, for instance, sold its Brazilian subsidiary to Eletrobrás. Rio Light and São Paulo Light agreed to turn over its operations to Eletrobrás in phases. By the early 1970s, Eletrobrás emerged as the unchallenged holding company of Brazil's electric generators and distributors, taking over small local state corporations and expanding their activities.

Eletrobrás built two of the world's largest hydroelectric power stations—Itaipú, on the Brazilian-Paraguayan border in the south, and Tucuruí, in the north. It also built the nuclear power stations Angra I and Angra II, in collaboration with Westinghouse and with KWU-Siemens of Germany.

JUDITH TENDLER, Electric Power in Brazil: Entrepreneurship in the Public Sector (1968); A energia elétrica no Brasil: Da primeira lâmpada à Eletrobrás (1977); LUIZ PINGUELLI ROSA, ed., Energia e crise (1984).

EUL-SOO PANG

ELHUYAR, JUAN JOSÉ DE (b. 15 June 1754; d. 20 September 1796), Spanish chemist and mineralogist and director of mines in NEW GRANADA (1783–1796). Born in Logroño, Spain, to Juan D'Elhuyar and Ursula de Zubice, Juan José de Elhuyar studied medicine in Paris from 1772 to 1777. After he returned to Spain, the Ministry of the Navy sent him and his younger brother Fausto de ELHUYAR in 1778 to study at the Mining Academy of Freiberg. Elhuyar's main objective was to learn better techniques for manufacturing cannon, but he also studied geology, metallurgy, and chemistry and visited many mining operations in Central Europe. Back in Spain the two brothers isolated tungsten and published Análisis química del volfram y examen de un nuevo metal que entra en su composición (1783).

In late 1783 Minister of the Indies José de GÁLVEZ selected Elhuyar as director of mines for New Granada, a position he occupied for the remainder of his life. He adapted the baron von Born's barrel method for amalgamating silver ores to local conditions and worked to raise the technological level of the Mariquita silver district. Elhuyar also developed a means for isolating platinum and carried out geological explorations. His work met resistance from both colonial officials and the mine operators. He died in Bogotá.

ARTHUR P. WHITAKER, "The Elhuyar Mining Missions and the Enlightenment," in *Hispanic American Historical Review* 31, no. 4 (1951):557–585; STIG RYDÉN, *Don Juan José de Elhuyar en Suecia y el descubrimiento del tungsteno, 1781–1782* (1963); and BERNARDO J. CAYCEDO, *D'Elhuyar y el siglo XVIII neogrnadino* (1971).

KENDALL W. BROWN

ELHUYAR Y ZÚBICE, FAUSTO DE (*b*. 11 October 1757; *d*. 6 January 1833), Spanish scientist and director general of the Mining Tribunal of New Spain (1788–1821). A native of Logroño, Spain, Elhuyar was educated in Paris and at the famous Mining School of Freiberg, Germany (1778–1781, 1787), and taught mineralogy at the Patriotic Seminary of Vergara, Spain (1782–1786). He and his brother Juan José discovered tungsten in 1783 while experimenting with wolframite.

In July 1786, while Elhuyar was in Austria to recruit mining experts for service in Spanish America and to study the Baron Ignaz von Born's method of amalgamating silver ores, Secretary of the Indies José de Gálvez appointed him director general of the Mexican Mining Tribunal. According to Walter Howe, "the renaissance of the Tribunal may be said to have begun with Elhuyar's arrival" in 1788. As director general he was an influential and energetic advocate for the MINING INDUSTRY, but his bureaucratic service hindered the promise of his early scientific achievements. Elhuyar established a school of mines in 1792, the first secular academy in the Spanish colonies. With Mexican independence, Elhuyar returned to Spain in 1821 and served as director general of mining, until his accidental death in 1833.

The most thorough treatment of Elhuyar's early years is ARTHUR P. WHITAKER, "The Elhuyar Mining Missions and the Enlightenment," in *Hispanic American Historical Review* 31, no. 4 (1951): 557–585. WALTER HOWE, *The Mining Guild of New Spain and Its Tribunal General, 1770–1821* (1949), details his labors in Mexico.

KENDALL W. BROWN

ELÍAS DOMINGO (*b*. 19 December 1805; *d*. 3 December 1867), Peruvian plantation owner and statesman.

Born to aristocratic parents in the Ica Valley, the winegrowing center of the southern coast, he was educated in elite Peruvian schools and in Spain and France. On returning home he married Doña Ysabel de la Quintana y Pedemonte, sister of the new archbishop of Lima. Beginning as a merchant and lender, he later became one of the largest landowners in the coastal valleys of Peru. He owned more than 600 slaves by 1850 and cultivated wine, *pisco*, and cotton on his plantations. Elías soon became politically active. A convinced liberal, he strongly favored free trade, and by 1843 he had formed a partnership with Ramón CASTILLA. After Castilla became president in 1845, Elías joined his council of state, a three-member body of presidential advisers who by serving as liaisons with the national congress, held a great deal of power. A philanthropist, he donated large sums to found a high school, the Colegio de Nuestra Señora de Guadalupe, which became the source of liberal thought in Peru for decades. Elías also sought to preserve black slavery in Peru.

A major scandal erupted when he tried to bypass the prohibition against the African slave trade with a purchase in Colombia. The purchase included children, who under Peruvian law were free. In 1849 he designed a law to regulate the importation of indentured Asian labor. When José Rufino ECHENIQUE became president in 1851, Elías strenuously opposed his debt consolidation program because it would overburden the state, and he called the program a fraud. Echenique resorted to censorship and terrorism to stop his opponents, and Elías rebelled. Soon he joined forces with the popular uprising led by Castilla. Returning to the private sector, probably by 1859, he converted most of his remaining vineyards to cotton and focused completely on international cotton commerce. His efforts in this trade foundered on inadequate marketing techniques, and by the time of his death his cotton empire was in ruins.

FREDRICK B. PIKE, *The Modern History of Peru* (1967), esp. pp. 101–102, 105; PETER BLANCHARD, *Slavery and Abolition in Early Republican Peru* (1992); ALFONSO QUIROZ, *Domestic and Foreign Finance in Modern Peru, 1850–1950* (1993).

VINCENT PELOSO

See also **Plantations.**

ELÍO, FRANCISCO JAVIER (*b*. 4 March 1767; *d*. 4 September 1822), last viceroy of the Río de la Plata. Born in Navarre, Spain, he began his military career as a lieutenant in the defense of Oran and Ceuta in North Africa. Elío was sent to the RÍO DE LA PLATA in 1805 with the rank of colonel, to command the BANDA ORIENTAL. Shortly after the first English invasion (1806), Viceroy Santiago de LINIERS Y BREMOND named Elío interim governor of MONTEVIDEO. After the second English invasion (1807), he became one of Liniers's chief opponents and assumed the post of viceroy. After Liniers's successor, Cisneros, was relieved of his post by the CABILDO ABIERTO in May 1810, Elío returned to Spain and convinced the Regency Council to appoint him viceroy. The junta established in Buenos Aires refused to recognize his appointment, however, so he governed from Montevideo until he was forced from power by an antiroyalist uprising in the Banda Oriental. Elío returned to Spain in 1812 and became involved in Spanish political life. He was executed at Valencia.

SOCIEDAD RURAL ARGENTINA, *El virreinato del Río de la Plata, 1776–1810* (1976); GUILLERMO F. DE NEVARES, *Como se desintegró el virreinato del Río de la Plata y se consolidó Brasil* (1987).

SUSAN SOCOLOW

ÉLITE (HAITI), a social class of Haiti. The *élite* of Haiti find their cultural traditions in the *gens de couleur* (mulattoes) of colonial Haiti (Saint-Domingue). The *gens de couleur* established individual status on the basis of the number of slaves owned, European education, orthodox Catholicism, and especially skin tone. The lighter one's complexion, the higher one's social position. This class, which makes up about 2 percent of the Haitian population, survived the Haitian Revolution (1789–1804) and has generally controlled Haitian politics since independence.

Even though the *élite* promoted white French values through their political and social domination of Haiti, there are notable individual exceptions. Alexandre PÉTION, who ruled the Republic of Haiti from 1807 to 1818, supported black culture and economic patterns. But in the twentieth century the *élite* has run afoul of rising black political control and cultural nationalism. Black Haitians have often resented *élite* attitudes toward their culture and the stain of collaboration the *élite* gained by supporting the U.S. occupation of Haiti (1915–1934).

In 1957 François "Papa Doc" DUVALIER (1957–1971) launched a campaign of extermination against the *élite*. Claiming that they were whites with black skins, he had thousands of them murdered while he convinced the masses that he was the reincarnation of Jean-Jacques DESSALINES. "Papa Doc" argued that he was completing the Haitian Revolution by destroying the *élite*. The *élite* survived because Duvalier abandoned his policy of mulatto extermination.

The elite enjoyed a resurgence of power after the death of Papa Doc. Under the rule of his son, Jean-Claude Duvalier (1971–1986), and under military rule, the government promoted its restoration. Jean-Bertrand ARISTIDE (1990–1991; 1995–), on the other hand, has publicly stated his opposition to the *élite*.

CYRIL L. R. JAMES, *The Black Jacobins* (1938); JAMES LEYBURN, *The Haitian People* (1941); THOMAS OTT, *The Haitian Revolution, 1789–1804* (1973), and "Haitian National Consciousness and the Revolution," in *Journal of Great Lakes History* 1 (1976): 71–78; DAVID NICHOLLS, *Haiti in Caribbean Context* (1985).

THOMAS O. OTT

ELIZAGA, JOSÉ MARÍA (*b.* 27 September 1786; *d.* 2 October 1842), Mexican pianist, organist, and composer. Piano study in his native Morelia and in Mexico City prepared Elizaga for a position as assistant organist in the Colegio de San Nicolás in Morelia (1799). Among his piano pupils was Doña Ana María Huarte, the future wife of emperor Agustín de ITURBIDE; he eventu-

ally became music director of Iturbide's imperial court (1822). Elizaga started his own music publishing business and in 1825 founded a conservatory that later formed the basis of the National Conservatory of Music. He served as *maestro de capilla* of the Guadalajara cathedral from 1827 to 1830 and retired to Morelia in 1842. His works include sacred music for orchestra and chorus, two didactic music treatises, and *Vals con variaciones* for piano.

ROBERT STEVENSON, *Music in Mexico: A Historical Survey* (1952).

ROBERT L. PARKER

ELIZONDO, SALVADOR (*b.* 19 December 1932), Mexican poet and author. This notable figure in Mexican letters had an eclectic interest in poetry, film, essays, and fiction that has given him a well-deserved reputation for experimental work.

Born in Mexico City of wealthy parents, Elizondo resided for several years in Europe, where he studied in Paris and Cambridge, as well as the University of Ottawa, Canada, and Mexico's School of Philosophy and Letters of the National University (1952–1953). As a fellow at the Center for Mexican Writers, he wrote *Farabeuf* (1965), which received the distinguished Villaurrutia Prize in 1965. He cofounded the magazine *S. Nob*, an exploration of eroticism in Mexican letters, and served as editor in chief of *Estaciones*. Twice a Guggenheim fellow (1968–1969 and 1973–1974), he was considered a leader in the Nuevo Cine group. He conducted the "Contextos" radio program for the National University (1968–1978) and wrote for *Vuelta* in the 1980s.

SALVADOR ELIZONDO, *Salvador Elizondo*, 2d ed. (1971); ROSS FRANK LARSON, *Fantasy and Imagination in the Mexican Narrative* (1973); HERIBERTO GARCÍA RIVAS, *Historia de la literatura mexicana*, 4 (1974); and SALVADOR ELIZONDO, *Camera lucida* (1983).

RODERIC AI CAMP

EMBOABA, a term used in MINAS GERAIS during the early eighteenth century to refer to an outsider or to a non-PAULISTA. The origin of the word is disputed, with the most likely interpretation being that it derived from the TUPI-GUARANI name of a bird whose feathered legs reminded some of the Portuguese style of wearing knee-high boots with the trousers tucked in.

The term is most commonly associated with the Guerra dos Emboabas (War of the Emboabas). The discovery of gold in the mining zone bounded by Ouro Prêto, São João del Rei, and Sabará during the last decade of the seventeenth century led to an immediate gold rush. Control of the mining zone was cause for a dispute that can best be seen as two distinct conflicts between Paulistas and non-Paulistas, the first in 1706–1707 and the second in 1708–1709. While the period of actual fighting was relatively short and produced few casualties, the Guerra dos Emboabas is important on two levels. The first was the displacement from the core gold-mining zone of the discoverers and initial settlers, the Paulistas, by those who later flooded into the zone from other areas. The other was the disagreement over the philosophy that was to govern the exploitation of gold. The Paulistas and allied royal authorities wanted controlled and gradual exploitation. The victory of the *emboabas* ensured a mass influx of settlers and a loss of royal control as well as the withdrawal of Paulistas to outlying areas of the mining zone.

The defeat of the Paulistas forced a reappraisal of Portuguese policy in the area. It was clear that the mining zone could not be closed for gradual development, so royal authorities turned to other measures to maintain control. Generally, this meant imposing royal authority on the mining camps. In 1709, São Paulo and Minas de Ouro were made into a separate captaincy that survived until 1720, when another uprising led to the separation of Minas Gerais as a distinct captaincy. That same year the first OUVIDORES (royal judges) in the area were created and the governor authorized to establish the first towns and militia units.

MANOEL S. CARDOZO, "The *Guerra dos Emboabos,* Civil War in Minas Gerais, 1708–1709," in *Hispanic American Historical Review* 22 (August 1942): 470–492; FRANCISCO DE ASSIS CARVALHO FRANCO, "Paulistas e emboabas," in *IV Congresso de historia nacional, Annais,* vol. 3 (1950), pp. 63–168; CHARLES R. BOXER, *The Golden Age of Brazil: 1695–1750* (1964).

DONALD RAMOS

EMERALDS. *See* **Gems and Gemstones.**

EMIGRATION within and out of Latin America has been on the rise since the Second World War. Millions have crossed borders within Latin America and millions more have moved farther north to the United States, Canada, and Europe. Yet, there remains much controversy and misunderstanding over the determinants and consequences of this massive out-migration. Among the most ill-understood and contested issues are: the causes for emigration, the socioeconomic backgrounds of migrants, and the impacts of emigration on labor-exporting societies.

While this essay will concentrate on labor emigration from Latin America to the United States, it should be noted that there are massive, highly institutionalized border migrations linking countries such as Bolivia and Argentina and Colombia and Venezuela. Since the late 1960s the Latin American continent has also witnessed repressive, authoritarian regimes and civil unrest, which has led to the displacement of large numbers of refugees into neighboring countries as well as to the United States, Canada, and Europe.

According to a myth popular throughout the hemisphere, most emigrants are peasants recently displaced from their land by commercial agriculture. Yet research conducted in countries such as Mexico, Colombia, and the Dominican Republic reveals a far more complex situation. Migration is a highly selective phenomenon that commonly finds landless households able to afford only internal migration into a regional or national city. By contrast, small and medium producers often dispatch select household members into border and transcontinental migration streams. These latter types of households share the goal of maintaining a rural base while exploiting opportunities in diverse economic sectors and labor markets.

No doubt, even more challenging to conventional wisdom is the finding that many emigrants from Latin American countries, other than Mexico, do not have rural backgrounds at all. Rather, they are long-term urban residents employed prior to emigration in relatively skilled jobs. For example, the first wave of Puerto Ricans who arrived in the United States in the 1950s were primarily urban dwellers with stable histories of employment. It was not until the 1960s that unskilled laborers came to constitute the bulk of Puerto Rican emigrants. Research on emigrants from countries, such as the Dominican Republic and Colombia, that have contributed to the post-1960 wave of immigration also demonstrates a clear pattern of urban-based emigration involving workers who have been employed in skilled and semiskilled jobs.

To account for this pattern of labor emigration we must examine those development policies that have come to threaten the socioeconomic viability and security of Latin America's middle sectors. Many labor-exporting countries, such as the Dominican Republic, have sought to benefit from the comparative advantage they possess within the international division of labor by making their large stock of cheap, underutilized labor available to foreign investors. While export-oriented industrialization has brought some employment benefits to Latin America's unskilled and semiskilled work force, it has had a far less salutary impact on the middle sectors. Since foreign investors commonly import their own materials, capital goods, and management, there is little demand for local inputs. Thus, one effect of foreign-dominated export industrialization is that Latin American entrepreneurs have often experienced a reduction in access to, and participation in, the economic opportunities generated by industrialization. Furthermore, due to its low-wage structure, the export-oriented sector has not appreciably increased the domestic market for products or goods offered by the middle class. Finally, the low-wage sector has had an especially depressive impact on wages for the lower middle class and upper working class. Their workplace demands and potential agitation tend to be muted by the fear that dissatisfied workers could easily be replaced by the large mass of more poorly paid workers.

Emigration to the United States, then, cannot be reduced to such simple and unicausal notions as rural displacement and the existence of a reserve army of unskilled workers nor to "push" or "pull" factors. Rather these factors are all implied as the economies of the United States and Latin American countries have become increasingly interdependent. Both domestic and foreign investments in agriculture, and the subsequent rural displacement to national centers, have resulted in a large supply of cheap domestic workers needed to lure export-oriented industrialization to Latin America. These developments have contributed, in turn, to the constriction of internal markets available to middle-strata populations in these developing countries. While alternatives may be limited for these groups at home, there are growing opportunities in a U.S. economy whose service and manufacturing sectors continue to experience deskilling, loss of union jobs, and a move toward subcontracting. These are trends that create a demand for cheap, compliant labor—attributes fostered by the legal vulnerability of new immigrants and their lack of familiarity with U.S. institutions.

As the description of the socioeconomic background of Latin American emigrants makes clear, empirical research challenges the conventional wisdom which holds that Latin American countries are underdeveloped due to a lack of well-trained, highly skilled workers. On the contrary, many of these developing countries are investing precious resources in the training of professionals, managers, and other skilled workers for export abroad. Of course, the other face of this conundrum is the belief that through remittances and eventual return, absent compatriots will continue to contribute to the development of their home countries.

Before considering whether these development objectives have been realized, it should be noted that these expectations reflect a notion of emigrants as being ethnically, socially, and economically tied to their countries of origin. This contrasts with a widely held conception in the United States that all immigrants are eager to assimilate and settle permanently. Unlike earlier waves of emigrants from Europe, today's "new immigrants" are constructing transnationalized lives. The economic opportunities they exploit and social identities they adopt are not limited by place but rather are multiple and stretch across national borders.

Remittances are one of the dominant ways in which emigrants personally bind "host" and "home" communities. And what may be dubbed "the people's foreign aid" has occasioned great expectations on the part of labor-exporting governments and some international agencies. At the national level, remittances are a bounty of hard currency that can be used to purchase needed foreign components and supplies, and that can be spent locally to generate jobs. Where the promise of remittances has fallen far shorter is in the anticipation that they would promote local investment in commercial agriculture and in urban enterprises—perhaps even mitigating emigration pressures. Research points to a very different outcome, however, with remittances often be-

ing invested in prestigious, imported durables, thus minimizing local job multipliers. Moreover, remittances are often used to speculate on and inflate land and housing prices. Rather than helping to rehabilitate foundering Latin American rural economies, all too often remittances encourage farming families to purchase their food and to abandon plots previously used to raise crops for home consumption and sale. There is a growing consensus that emigration actually reinforces the disruption of agrarian economies through the further reduction of local food production, the increase in the price of staples, and the decline in the demand for hired hands.

The hope that returnees might be agents for national development has also proved illusory. The literature suggests that deskilling rather than skills acquisition often occurs among middle-sector emigrants. Moreover, when skills have been acquired abroad, they often do not match the labor demand in the home country. Finally, there is often a marked redundancy in the types of businesses returnees establish. The investment in small businesses such as gas stations, restaurants, and groceries leads to saturated markets, small profits, and little job creation. Indeed, there is evidence that many returnees fail at their attempts to secure a middle-class standard of living at home and are forced to emigrate again.

While emigration from Latin America to the United States is selective and draws disproportionately from the better-educated, more economically secure sectors of urban and rural economies, there are indications that less skilled workers are gradually emigrating, as well. This occurs as emigrants create their own transnational social networks, which provide information, loans, employment, and housing for less-advantaged compatriots. We can anticipate a growing and more diversified emigration from Latin America in coming decades. This will be the case as increasing numbers of job seekers encounter saturated domestic markets with little capacity for job creation at home alongside established networks capable of linking them to labor markets and communities in the United States.

ADRIANA MARSHALL, "Structural Trends in International Labor Migration: The Southern Cone of Latin America," in Mary Kritz et al., eds., *Global Trends in Migration* (1981), pp. 234–258; ROBERT PASTOR, ed., *Migration and Development in the Caribbean* (1985); ALEJANDRO PORTES and ROBERT BACH, *Latin Journey* (1985); DOUGLAS MASSEY et al., *Return to Aztlán* (1987); PATRICIA PESSAR, *When Borders Don't Divide* (1986); EUGENIA GEORGES, *The Making of a Transnational Community* (1990); SHERRI GRASMUCK and PATRICIA PESSAR, *Between Two Islands* (1991); DEMETRIOS PAPADEMETRIOU and PHILIP MARTIN, *The Unsettled Relationship* (1991).

PATRICIA PESSAR

See also **Asylum and Refugees.**

EMPARÁN, VICENTE (*b.* January 1747; *d.* 3 October 1820), the last Spanish general of Venezuela. With the rank of rear admiral, Emparán left the Spanish Royal

Navy for his first major appointment in America as naval commander at Puerto Cabello, on the Venezuelan coast. In 1792 he was appointed governor of CUMANÁ, a post he held for twelve years. Emparán returned to Spain briefly in 1808 and was appointed captain-general of Venezuela. When he returned to Venezuela in May 1809, he was confronted with the conspiratorial movements of late 1809 and early 1810. News of French advances in Spain prompted the agitators to convoke a meeting with Emparán on 19 April 1810. By popular demand, Spanish authority was renounced and the Junta Suprema de Caracas was formed to take over the government, thereby effectively declaring Venezuela's independence. Emparán was taken prisoner and later exiled to Philadelphia. He returned to Spain in 1810.

HÉCTOR GARCÍA CHUECOS, *La capitanía general de Venezuela* (1955); INSTITUTO PANAMERICANO DE GEOGRAFÍA E HISTORIA, *El 19 de abril de 1810* (1957); ANGEL GRISANTI, *Emparán y el golpe de estado de 1810* (1960).

INÉS QUINTERO

EMPHYTEUSIS, LAW OF, a measure granting long-term rights of access to and exploitation of land that was the state's property. The law of emphyteusis (enacted in 1826) was used in Argentina in the 1820s by Bernardino RIVADAVIA in an effort to populate the vast interior of the fledging republic. The government could lease land to private individuals or companies for a rent equal to 8 percent of the assessed value of pastureland and 4 percent of that of cropland. The system did not function well and did not produce the results Rivadavia had hoped for. In the first place, assessments of the land were made by the people who were going to rent it, and thus were undervalued. Second, the law did not specify how much land a person could rent out. Since it imposed no limitations, it contributed to a large extent to the formation of LATIFUNDIOS. The law benefited only land speculators, who obtained large tracts for practically no cost at all.

EMILIO ÁNGEL CONI, *La verdad sobre la enfiteusis de Rivadavia* (1927); JUAN CARLOS RUBINSTEIN, *Filiación histórica y sociopolítica de la enfiteusis rivadaviana* (1984).

JUAN MANUEL PÉREZ

EMPRESA PETROLERA FISCAL, state-owned oil company organized in 1946 in Peru. The origins of Empresa date back to 1934, when the government of Oscar Raimundo BENAVIDES first established a petroleum department. The department's holdings and operations expanded during the 1930s; by 1938 it constituted the fourth largest oil producer in the country, though it languished during the Manuel PRADO and José Luis BUSTAMANTE y Rivero governments of the 1940s. Production eventually picked up, reaching 607,000 barrels by the late 1950s and 1.4 million barrels by the late 1960s.

The company was reorganized as PETROPERÚ by the administration of Juan VELASCO after it seized power in 1968 and nationalized the International Petroleum Company.

ROSEMARY THORP and GEOFFREY BERTRAM, *Peru 1890–1977: Growth and Policy in an Open Economy* (1978).

PETER F. KLARÉN

ENCARNACIÓN, port city of Paraguay on the PARANÁ RIVER (1982 population 27,632). Founded in 1615 by Jesuits from the Itapúa mission and a significant center of christianized GUARANÍ Indians, it is today the capital of the department of Itapúa. For a long time it was the outpost of Paraguayan resistance against expanding Argentine interests in the area of MISIONES, but now it is an active center of trade with the nearby Argentine city of Posadas. Its surroundings are actively farmed by the descendants of German, Slavic, and Japanese settlers, who raise cotton, tobacco, yerba maté, and citrus fruit. A university and radio station maintain a high cultural level for the population.

TOMÁS L. MICÓ, *Antecedentes históricos de Encarnación de Itapúa* (Asunción, 1975).

CÉSAR N. CAVIEDES

ENCILHAMENTO, a horse-racing term that refers to the stock-market boom in Brazil, especially in Rio de Janeiro, between 1889 and 1893. The abolition of slavery in Brazil in 1888 and the desire to attract immigrants and foreign investment demanded a greatly enhanced national banking system. To placate exslaveowners, ease the transition to wage labor, and take advantage of unusually abundant and interested European capital markets, the last imperial ministry began in July 1889 to lend funds and liberalize BANKING and currency issue laws. This ignited an explosion of national and foreign investments in banks, railways, and many other activities. The Rio stock market saw more activity in the second half of 1889 than it had in its previous history. Although much of the dealing was speculative and even fraudulent, as was depicted in the Viscount of Taunay's novel *O Encilhamento*, there were authentic efforts to create enormous corporations.

The demise of the empire on 15 November 1889 and the rise of the republic did not stop the dealing. The republican minister of finance, Rui BARBOSA, relaxed corporation laws and awarded generous government concessions to buy friends for the new regime and promote a laissez-faire state. Although European interest in Brazil waned in 1890, Brazilian investors continued to speculate. Mammoth investment banks created vast corporations.

The investors in the Encilhamento were behind President Deodoro da FONSECA's closing of Congress in November 1891. Opponents of the investors backed

490

Marshal Floriano PEIXOTO's overthrow of Fonseca twenty days later. Peixoto began attacking some of the key bankers, whom he considered enemies of the republic. The stock boom fizzled in early 1893 and ended with the defeat in 1893–1894 of the naval revolt the financiers had supported.

BARBARA LEVY, "O Encilhamento," in *Economia brasileira: Uma visão histórica*, edited by Paulo Neuhaus (1980); LUIZ ANTONIO TANNURI, *O Encilhamento* (1981); GUSTAVO HENRIQUE BARROSO FRANCO, *Reforma monetária e instabilidade durante a transiçao republicana* (1983); STEVEN TOPIK, "Brasil's Bourgeois Revolution," in *The Americas* 48 (October 1991): 245–271.

STEVEN TOPIK

ENCINA, FRANCISCO ANTONIO (*b.* 10 September 1874; *d.* 23 August 1965), Chilean deputy and intellectual. An attorney by education, Encina wrote the twenty-volume *History of Chile to 1891* describing the nation's past from precolonial days to 1891, as well as numerous monographs. A believer in the ideas of Joseph-Arthur Gobineau, he, like his contemporary Nicolás Palacios, argued that Chileans were a combination of Araucanian Indian and German *conquistador*. This genetic mixture, Encina believed, handicapped Chileans who, while biologically predisposed toward being warriors, were ill prepared to compete in the world of commerce. Though entranced by racist philosophies, Encina presciently recognized the need for Chile to diversify and modernize its economy by encouraging land reform, industrialization, and the teaching of technical skills.

CHARLES C. GRIFFIN, "Francisco Encina and Revisionism in Chilean History," in *Hispanic American Historical Review* 37, no. 1 (Feb. 1957): 1–28; RICARDO DONOSO, *Francisco A. Encina, simulador*, 2 vols. (1969–1970).

WILLIAM F. SATER

ENCINAS, JOSÉ ANTONIO (*b.* 1886; *d.* 1958), a prominent leader of the INDIGENISTA movement of early-twentieth-century Peru. As a land commissioner, in 1918 he drew up a program to help native Peruvians regain lands that had been stolen by white aristocratic lawyers. After the revolutionary military government of Juan Velasco Alvarado issued the Agrarian Reform Law of 24 June 1969, AGRARIAN REFORM officials turned to some of Encinas's findings to guide them in organizing the formation of agrarian reform zones. The section of the law creating peasant cooperatives reflected in part the writings of Encinas.

THOMAS M. DAVIES, JR., *Indian Integration in Peru, 1900–1948* (1974); JOSÉ TAMAYO HERRERA, *Historia del indigenismo cuzqueño: Siglos xvi-xx* (1980).

VINCENT PELOSO

See also **Agrarian Reform.**

ENCISO, MARTÍN FERNÁNDEZ DE (*b.* ca. 1470; *d.* ca. 1528), a lawyer and central figure in an early sixteenth-century Vasco Núñez de BALBOA venture. In the first years of the sixteenth century, Diego de NICUESA, a wealthy resident of Hispaniola, and Alonso de OJEDA, a prospector on the island, submitted to the Spanish crown a plan to divide the entire coast of South America into two governing areas. Ojeda would receive a concession to settle and exploit an area from Coquibacoa to the Gulf of Urabá in modern Colombia, and in return the crown would receive a fixed percentage of the settlement's profits. The crown sealed this contract in 1508.

After it became clear that Pizarro's first attempt at colonization in 1509 had failed, Ojeda contracted with a lawyer named Martín Fernández de Enciso to travel to present-day Central America in relief of PIZARRO. In return he promised Enciso the position of *alcalde mayor* (governor) in the new colonies. On 13 September 1510 Enciso's party sailed from Hispaniola with 152 new settlers bound for Urabá. Lacking supplies and facing innumerable difficulties, Pizarro's group was wandering hopelessly in Darién when Enciso's ships arrived in late September bearing supplies.

Meanwhile, Vasco Núñez de Balboa had secretly boarded Enciso's ship in Hispaniola to avoid creditors and bailiffs who were pursuing him for outstanding debts. On discovering the stowaway's presence aboard his ship, Enciso declared his intention to abandon Balboa on a deserted island. However, Balboa's popularity grew among the other passengers, who disliked the petty and temperamental Enciso. Once Enciso's group encountered the Pizarro contingent, despite the latter's protestations and a release order from Ojeda, Enciso forced them to stay in Urabá, hopeful that they would contribute to his pursuit of wealth.

As the expedition unfolded, it became clear that Enciso had many shortcomings as a frontier commander and lacked real authority, for Ojeda's poor health meant that he no longer really controlled the venture. Thus, the popular Balboa emerged from this power struggle as the natural leader of the early settlements in northern South America. Although Enciso's group took Darién (probably in November 1510), Balboa and his supporters forced them to leave the colony, thus triggering a series of events which led to Balboa's later execution.

Balboa erred in permitting Enciso to return to Hispaniola because he thereafter cleverly pursued legal action against Balboa. Contending that the king had given the territory to Ojeda, Enciso maintained that the area was therefore rightfully theirs. Enciso eventually returned to Spain, where he vociferously protested Balboa's actions and supposed abuses. He joined others opposing Balboa by incessantly pushing these charges until finally Balboa was beheaded in 1519.

Somewhat later, Enciso helped lead an ill-fated expedition to Cenu, in northwestern South America. This attempt to secure wealth, like the first, failed, and Enciso again returned to Spain. Enciso is remembered primarily for his role in the Balboa story.

HUBERT HOWE BANCROFT, *History of Central America*, vol. 1 (1883); KATHLEEN ROMOLI, *Balboa of Darién: Discoverer of the Pacific* (1953); MARTÍN FERNÁNDEZ DE ENCISO, *A brief summe of geographie* (1932, repr. 1967).

BLAKE D. PATTRIDGE

See also **Explorers and Exploration.**

ENCOMIENDA, the right to control the labor of and collect tribute from an Indian community, granted to subjects, especially the first conquerors and their descendants, as a reward for service to the Spanish crown. Unlike the Spanish peninsular version of the *encomienda*, the grant in the New World did not give the grantee, or *encomendero*, legal right to own land. It also did not give *encomenderos* legal jurisdiction over the natives, although many *encomenderos* assumed that right. In return the *encomendero* promised to settle down and found a family in the nearest Spanish town, or *villa*; to protect the Indians; and to arrange for their conversion to the Roman Catholic faith.

In the Antilles the institution was firmly established under Governor Nicolás de OVBANDO. Hernando CORTÉS granted the first *encomiendas* in Mexico, and Francisco PIZARRO did so in Peru. In the sixteenth century, *encomiendas* ranged in size from as many as 23,000 heads of households (Cortés's personal *encomienda*) to a few hundred in some areas of Central America and Peru.

Although there were never enough such grants to reward all those who felt they deserved one, the *encomienda* proved a useful institution, from the crown's point of view, in the first two or three decades after the discovery and conquest of the New World kingdoms of Mexico and Peru. It placed hundreds and sometimes thousands of Indians under the control of individual Spaniards at a time when a bureaucracy had not yet been established. The *encomenderos* put the Indians to work mining gold and silver; building houses, town halls, and churches; cultivating indigenous and imported crops; herding animals; and transporting goods.

Control of Indian labor became the basis of the fortunes of the *encomendero* elite, who became wealthy by selling provisions to arriving Spanish immigrants and by renting them stores and homes that had been built with the Indian labor they controlled. They invested revenues generated by their *encomienda* laborers in stock-raising enterprises. Some even became silent partners with merchants involved in lucrative import and export activities. Their wealth and their status as first- and second-generation conquerors gave them the leisure and respect that enabled them to exercise an early monopoly of the town councils. As councilmen they set prices for basic goods and services as well as the standards of morality and sanitation for the Spanish community. They screened applicants for formal citizen

status in the town and gave out house lots and suburban lands for kitchen gardens and orchards. They also were empowered to grant lands further afield. Their wealth, political power, influence, and prestige as conquerors and first settlers (later transferred to their descendants) made them almost omnipotent and, as such, independent of the wishes of the crown.

To counter their power, the crown began to issue protective legislation, such as the Laws of Burgos (1512) and the New Laws (1542). One provision of the latter abolished *encomiendas* at the death of the current holder. The resulting widespread protest throughout Spanish America along with a rebellion and civil war in Peru forced the crown to back down in the short run, but they also strengthened its resolve to break the power of the *encomendero* elite. It eventually did so by regulating the amount of tribute that the Indian population had to deliver; by abolishing personal, unpaid service by the Indians to the *encomendero*; by creating a loyal royal bureaucracy; and by fostering the rise of an independent class of Spanish farmers that would counterbalance the *encomendero* class. It was the landowners (and the mine owners) who eventually displaced the *encomenderos* at the top of the colonial social pyramid.

The connection between the *encomienda* and the hacienda, or large landed estate, has been the subject of debate. Some have argued that the hacienda developed directly from the *encomienda*. This was the case when and where *encomenderos* used their positions of authority—on the town council, for example—to grant themselves land parcels (*mercedes*) from among the lands once used by their Indian charges. However, such cases were relatively few in number.

Far more often, other scholars contend, haciendas developed independently of *encomiendas*. Like the *encomenderos*, many individuals who received land grants were given parcels from among those that had been abandoned by Indians because of either death or flight. However, the owners of these parcels depended on the *repartimiento* or *mita* (rotating draft of forced Indian labor) system that had been instituted after the crown prohibited the use of free personal services by the *encomendero* around the middle of the sixteenth century. These small enterprises were expanded over the years by the obtaining of additional land grants, by usurpation of Indian lands, by *composición* (obtaining legal title to untitled land by paying a fee to the royal treasury), by purchase, and by long-term lease to become the nuclei of what someday would be large estates, or haciendas.

The task of collecting tribute and overseeing the Indian communities was given to the *corregidor de indios*, a district administrator or governor, who was part of the bureaucratic apparatus established by the crown to regain control of the New World kingdoms from the all-powerful *encomenderos*. Except in peripheral areas of the Spanish New World Empire, like Paraguay, the *encomienda* had become by the start of the seventeenth century little more than a prestigious claim to a government pension, divorced of any direct control over the Indians.

c. h. haring, *The Spanish Empire in America* (1947); charles gibson, *Spain in America* (1966); james lockhart, "*Encomienda* and *Hacienda*: The Evolution of the Great Estate in the Spanish Indies," in *Hispanic American Historical Review* 49, no. 3 (1969): 411–429; and robert g. keith, "*Encomienda, Hacienda,* and *Corregimiento* in Spanish America: A Structural Analysis," in *Hispanic American Historical Review* 51, no. 3 (1971): 431–446.

Susan E. Ramírez

ENDER, THOMAS (*b.* 3 November 1793; *d.* 28 September 1875), Austrian painter known for his landscapes of Brazil. In 1816 Thomas Ender won the Imperial Court Gold Medal for landscape painting from the Vienna Academy of Art, whose curator, Prince Otto von Metternich, purchased the work and named the young artist part of a scientific expedition to Brazil he was organizing and partly financing. The group, assembled to accompany Hapsburg princess leopoldina to Rio de Janeiro to join her husband, the future emperor pedro i, was to explore the flora and fauna of Brazil. Setting sail in March 1817, Ender spent an entire year documenting not only the natural beauty of the country but its people as well.

Upon his return to Vienna, Ender delivered a total of 782 works to the Imperial government. These watercolors and sketches remain one of the most beautiful and evocative sources of information on the nature of Brazilian life and society and are monuments of watercolor landscape art. The trip to Brazil greatly influenced Ender throughout his career as he became chamber painter to Archduke Johann of Austria in 1829 and professor of landscape painting at the Vienna Academy.

joão fernando de almeida prado, *Thomas Ender: Pintor austríaco na côrte de D. João VI no Rio de Janeiro* (1955); lygia da fonseca fernandes da cunha, *Thomas Ender: Catálogo de desenhos* (1968).

Gloria Kaiser

ENERGY. Latin America is rich in energy resources, but these resources are unevenly distributed among the countries. Petroleum dominates commercial energy pro-

duction and consumption at every level throughout Latin America. The region is also richly endowed with natural gas and hydroelectric power potential, and Colombia and Venezuela have begun to develop their coal reserves for export.

Development of Latin American energy resources has come at great expense. Brazil is a prime example, with over 40 percent of public investment in the early 1980s accounted for by domestic energy investment. Foreign debt mounted during the 1970s and 1980s as the World Bank, inter-american development bank, and other lenders injected much needed capital into grandiose petroleum, gasohol, nuclear, and hydroelectric projects. Oil price fluctuations eroded the ability to repay these debts, causing many to rethink the approach to development of Latin American energy resources.

ENERGY CONSUMPTION

While the rest of the world is dependent on oil for 40 percent of its primary energy needs, Latin America and the Caribbean are dependent on oil for a disproportionate share of their energy needs, almost 60 percent in 1989. The degree of dependence on oil among the smaller countries is more pronounced. For the Caribbean islands, oil represents 76 percent of their total primary energy requirements.

Total primary energy consumption for Latin America and the Caribbean in 1989 equaled 18.45 quadrillion Btu, of which oil consumption represented 10.88 quadrillion Btu. Hydropower is the second most important source of energy consumption (20 percent), followed by natural gas (16 percent) and coal (5 percent) (see table 1).

Most of the region's energy is consumed in Brazil (29 percent) and Mexico (26 percent). Mexico is the region's largest and least efficient consumer of petroleum, using 32 percent of the petroleum available in 1989. Brazil relies more on hydropower as a commercial source of energy than does any other major country in Latin America.

The primary determinants of increased energy consumption in developing countries are population growth, income growth, industrialization, and urbanization, each of which requires more energy services. Increases in energy prices tend to reduce the rate of

Table 1   Primary Energy Consumption in Latin America, 1989 (Quadrillion Btu)

Country	Petroleum	Natural Gas	Coal	Net Hydro	Net Nuclear	Total
Argentina	1.02	0.73	0.03	0.17	0.06	2.01
Brazil	2.68	0.10	0.40	2.20	0.02	5.40
Colombia	0.41	0.17	0.11	0.30	0.00	0.99
Mexico	3.49	0.93	0.21	0.20	0.00	4.83
Venezuela	0.78	0.82	0.01	0.31	0.00	1.91
Other	2.50	0.28	0.08	0.45	0.00	3.31
Total	10.88	3.03	0.84	3.63	0.07	18.45

TABLE 2 Primary Energy Production in Latin America, 1989
(Quadrillion Btu)

Country	Crude	Natural Gas	Coal	Net Hydro	Net Nuclear	Total
Argentina	1.00	0.69	0.01	0.16	0.06	1.92
Brazil	1.29	0.14	0.14	2.20	0.02	3.78
Colombia	0.89	0.18	0.40	0.30	0.00	1.78
Mexico	5.51	1.42	0.23	0.20	0.00	7.36
Venezuela	4.27	0.99	0.02	0.31	0.00	5.58
Other	1.37	0.37	0.06	0.46	0.00	2.27
Total	14.33	3.79	0.86	3.63	0.07	22.69

growth in energy demand, as occurred during the early 1980s. Latin American energy demand surged in the late 1980s, increasing at an annual rate of 2.9 percent. Most of the growth was in hydroelectric, natural gas, and coal demand.

COMMERCIAL ENERGY PRODUCTION

Latin America has been a producer of surplus energy throughout the twentieth century. The region will likely remain a net exporter into the twenty-first century despite the fact that the rate of growth in energy production has fallen below that of energy consumption. Venezuela is a member of OPEC and must abide by its production quotas. (Ecuador withdrew from OPEC in 1992.)

Most Latin American countries exercise strong, monopolistic control over energy development. The lack of competition has negative effects on energy resource management. In Brazil, Mexico, and Venezuela, state control of oil and gas exploration and production sectors is absolute. In other countries, private sector participation is strictly controlled.

Oil and Gas. In 1989, Latin America produced 22.69 quadrillion Btu of primary energy (petroleum, natural gas, coal, hydropower, and nuclear) while consuming only 18.45 quadrillion Btu. Petroleum production of 14.33 quadrillion Btu represented 63 percent of total energy production. (See table 2)

Latin America had 125.1 million barrels of conventional crude oil reserves as of 1 January 1990. Venezuela and Mexico together account for 92 percent. Venezuelan reserves are the seventh highest in the world. Mexico's reserves are slightly smaller than Venezuela's. Mexico is the world's fifth largest oil exporter. Nine other countries (Bolivia, Brazil, Chile, Colombia, Argentina, Ecuador, Guatemala, Peru, and Trinidad and Tobago) have oil reserves of varying sizes which may not be considered significant by world standards.

Natural gas reserves are also dominated by Venezuela and Mexico, which account for 74.5 percent of the 233.7 trillion cubic feet in Latin America as of 1 January 1990. Nearly all current gas production is associated gas, and production levels have been restrained by oil production levels. These two countries are Latin America's largest producers and marketers of gas. Brazil has

a huge natural gas resource that is being underutilized. At present, natural gas meets only 2 percent of the country's energy requirements, mainly due to lack of infrastructure.

Intraregional oil and gas trade has become common in Latin America. Petroleum dominates intraregional trade in northern Latin America, while natural gas is more popular in the south. Argentina renewed a twenty-year agreement to import 2.19 billion cubic meters of natural gas annually from Bolivia. Brazil signed a deal with Bolivia whereby 1.28 billion cubic meters of gas will be burned annually in the thermal power plant to be built at the Bolivian border town of Puerto Suárez, and the electricity will be sent to the Brazilian state of Mato Grosso do Sul.

Bolivia and Argentina have turned to Chile, also in need of gas. Argentine-Chilean negotiations over routing, volume, price, and pipeline construction delayed bidding until November 1991. Bolivia entered the Chilean scene, offering alternative supply to mining complexes in northern Chile. However, any deal may founder due to the lack of diplomatic relations between Bolivia and Chile.

Coal. Recoverable coal reserves in Latin America were estimated to be 17.2 billion short tons in 1989. Colombia's reserves represent 62 percent of Latin America and the country produced 46.5 percent of the region's total. Colombia has the largest export coal mine in the world, the open-cast El Cerrejón. The mine has been exporting one million tons of coal per month since the mid 1980s.

Brazil, Chile, Mexico, and Venezuela are investing to spur bituminous coal production. In 1988, these four countries imported half as much coal as their mines produced, much of it from Colombia. Coal use in Brazil is very low despite substantial resources, due to poor quality. Mexico has offered to invest in the mining of Colombian coal, which would be used in Mexican power generation.

Hydropower. Hydropower represents the largest single supply source for electricity in Latin America. In 1989, 61 percent of all electricity supplied came from hydropower. Several Latin American nations have pursued development of hydro resources as a means of reducing their dependence on oil imports. Brazil, Argentina, Colombia, Venezuela, and Paraguay all have large shares of hydropower in their electricity generation. Hydro incurs high capital costs long before electricity begins flowing, and these projects accounted for sizable proportions of these countries' foreign and domestic debts.

The ITAIPÚ plant on the Paraná River along the Paraguay-Brazil border has the largest hydro capacity in the world , at 11.7 megawatts. Brazil underwrote all the construction costs and purchases all electricity generated. Despite supplying 24 percent of current primary energy needs and nearly 90 percent of its electricity, Brazil has exploited less than 20 percent of the country's estimated hydro potential. Another 12 percent is under construction or planned through 2000.

Nuclear. Nuclear-generated electricity provides less than one percent of Latin America's primary energy. Argentina has the longest experience with nuclear power; its 344-megawatt Atucha 1 heavy-water reactor has been operational since 1974. But by 1984, Atucha 1 was operating at half capacity, unable to compete with cheaper hydroelectricity. Work on Atucha 2 continued to be delayed. Brazil brought its 626-megawatt Angra dos Reis 1 plant into operation in 1981. Work on two additional units was delayed.

Construction on Mexico's first reactor, the 650-megawatt Laguna Verde, began in 1970, but it never went into operation. Uramex, the state-run mining company that had begun exploiting uranium reserves, closed in 1985. Mexico's nuclear program calling for twenty reactors by the year 2000 was canceled during the 1980s, after it was estimated that the program ac-

counted for more than half of the public sector debt attributable to the energy sector. Nuclear power in Latin America does not appear to have much of a future.

Traditional Fuels. Wood and agricultural-animal wastes are used in the rural sectors and account for an estimated 800,000 barrels per day of oil equivalent. Firewood provided as much as half of the region's energy in 1945. It continues to be used by rural populations in residential applications.

Sugarcane waste (bagasse) has become a significant source of energy for sugar mills producing their own electricity and steam. Bagasse is used in independent facilities, isolated from electricity grids, in Belize, Brazil, Mexico, Cuba, the Dominican Republic, Jamaica, and other Caribbean islands.

Renewables. The island nations of the Caribbean face pronounced isolation problems. Regional solutions, such as electricity interconnections or cross-border road networks are not viable. Caribbean islands are ideal candidates for smaller scale renewable energy applications. Geothermal, wind, biomass, and photovoltaic technologies have been demonstrated with the assistance of international agencies.

The tectonic regions of Mexico, Central America, and the Caribbean offer ample geothermal resources. El Salvador has exploited geothermal resources since 1975. Mexico is operating geothermal wells in Baja California, exporting half the output to southern California utilities. Guatemala is planning to build a 15-megawatt geothermal plant.

In addition to funding geothermal development in Central America, the Inter-American Development

Power plant. SOLOMON CYTRYNOWICZ / PULSAR IMAGENS E EDITORA.

Bank has financed wind power in Barbados, bagasse cogeneration studies in Guyana, biogas from chicken manure in Guatemala, microhydro in Brazil, and photovoltaic cell production in Mexico.

Alcohol Fuels. The alcohol fuel program, seen at one time as the savior of Brazil, was moribund by August 1990. Heavy subsidies on alcohol have cost Brazil $7 billion, since being introduced fifteen years ago in an effort to reduce the country's heavy dependence on imported oil. Removal of subsidies would mean that the 4.5 million owners of alcohol-fueled cars would be grounded. Production of alcohol fuel costs twice as much as gasoline. Excessive production costs are blamed on bureaucratic bungling, greedy sugarcane producers, corruption, and the vested interest of PETROBRÁS, the monopoly distributor of alcohol fuel.

Sales of alcohol-fueled vehicles in Brazil fell from 85 percent of total vehicle sales in 1985 to less than 5 percent in July 1990. Fuel production is not expected to meet demand, and imports will be required if rationing is to be avoided. In 1989, 29 distilleries closed down, and ten more closed during the first half of 1990. Guatemala also has a small alcohol fuel program.

DEVELOPMENT AND COOPERATION

In order to develop an energy infrastructure that will sustain economic growth, the countries of Latin America will have to attract new investment. World Bank lending for energy projects in 1990 totaled $3 billion. Of that, $1 billion went to Latin America. Two-thirds of the bank's lending goes directly to utilities to reinforce internal electric transmission systems. The balance goes to coal and oil-gas projects.

The U.S. Trade and Development Program has been operating in the private and public sectors of Latin America since the 1980s. Recent energy funding is almost exclusively oil and gas. The U.S. AGENCY FOR INTERNATIONAL DEVELOPMENT energy programs are limited and small, except for Central America. Their period of active involvement in large thermal and hydroelectric projects was in the 1960s and 1970s, particularly in Brazil.

The Inter-American Development Bank has allocated an average of 27.6 percent of its loans ($10.97 billion) to energy projects from 1961 through 1987. In 1988, $405 million were lent for energy, of which 88 percent were for electric projects. A small portion of the Caribbean Development Bank's loans are for energy.

Regional cooperation is being promoted as the best way to develop Latin American energy resources. In the past, the joint energy option was for costly, controversial, and time-consuming hydroelectric projects. Cross-border hydro projects account for 25 percent of Latin America's generating capacity and much its crippling debt. Grandiose schemes financed by the World Bank, the Inter-American Development Bank, and the United Nations have fallen out of favor. For example, Argentine President Carlos Saúl MENEM shelved the Yacireta

Dam on the Paraná River between Paraguay and Argentina, after receiving approval for an Inter-American Development Bank loan of $250 million.

Latin America will look to its own regional organizations specifically established to assist in energy development: the Organization of Latin American States for Energy Cooperation, the Regional Electrical Intergration Commission, and the Latin American State Oil Company Assistance Organization.

H. JEFFREY LEONARD, *Natural Resources and Economic Development in Central America* (1987); LATIN AMERICAN ENERGY ORGANIZATION, *The Foreign Debt of the Energy Sector of Latin America* (1989); ROBERTO SMITH-PERERA, *Energy and the Economy in Venezuela* (1988); RENÉ DE LA PREDRAJA TOMAN, *Energy Politics in Columbia* (1989); DEREK BAMBER, "Brazil: Coping with the Conflict," in *Petroleum Economist* 57 (October 1990), 13–17; D. V. HUDSON, *Renewable Energy Supply Systems for Use In Latin America* (1990); MUDASSAR IMRAN and PHILLIP BARNES, "Energy Demand in the Developing Countries," in *World Bank Staff Commodity Working Paper* (1990); "Latin America: Governments Eyeing Gas and Oil Deals," in *Petroleum Economist* 57 (May 1990): 142; U.S. DEPARTMENT OF ENERGY, *The Report on the Western Hemisphere Energy cooperation Study* (1990); "South America: International Gas Deals as Far Away as Ever," in *Petroleum Economist* 58 (March 1991): 18–50; U.S. DEPARTMENT OF ENERGY, *1989 International Energy Annual* (1991).

MINDI J. FARBER

See also **Electrification.**

ENGENHO, an agricultural establishment with machinery for refining sugar from sugarcane; such a facility typically includes a mill for milling cane as well as cauldrons and distilleries for preparing sugar. Begun in São Vicente and in Pernambuco in the 1500s, sugar production later expanded to Bahia, Rio de Janeiro, and other coastal areas. Profitable sugar production attracted the Dutch, who dominated the Brazilian Northeast until their expulsion in 1654.

The *engenho* first used two and later three wheels in milling. The first *engenhos* were run by animal power, then water power, and eventually steam. The designation *engenho* initially referred to the production unit where the milling of cane and the preparation of sugar took place. This term was eventually extended to encompass the entire agrarian structure, including the cultivation of cane, manioc, corn, rice, and beans in addition to the preparation of food, the weaving of cotton and wool, and manufacturing, processing, and various other services not exclusively related to agriculture.

Seen by some as a self-sufficient establishment, the *engenho* was a complex hierarchical, social, and economic unit involving field and domestic slaves, qualified salaried workers, tenants, and resident farmers in a network of kinship and nonkinship dependencies, at the center of which was the patriarchal figure of the *senhor do engenho.* As the sugar economy expanded in colonial Brazil, the *engenho* absorbed increasing num-

Engenho at Pernambuco. Reproduced from Blave, *Geographia*, vol. 2 (Amsterdam, 1662). COURTESY OF THE JOHN CARTER BROWN LIBRARY AT BROWN UNIVERSITY.

bers of African slaves and free cane farmers. In the aftermath of slavery, cane growers working under a variety of labor arrangements became the principal suppliers of cane to the *engenhos*.

CAIO PRADO, JR., *The Colonial Background of Modern Brazil* (1971); AUGUSTE DE SAINT-HILAIRE, *Viagem pelas províncias do Rio de Janeiro e Minas Gerais* (1975); RUY GAMA, *Engenho e tecnologia* (1983); STUART B. SCHWARTZ, *Sugar Plantations in the Formation of Brazilian Society: Bahia, 1550–1835* (1985).

NANCY PRISCILLA SMITH NARO

See also **Plantations; Sugar Industry.**

ENGINEERING, a discipline that puts scientific knowledge to practical use by utilizing natural resources for the material benefit of society. Throughout history, engineering has enabled the building of structures, the manipulation of natural energy sources, and the creation of new technologies. There are at least thirty-five subfields of engineering. Among the most notable are civil, mechanical, electrical, materials, mining, chemical, petroleum, metallurgical, and geologic, which deal with renewable and nonrenewable resources. Scientific discoveries of the nineteenth and twentieth centuries opened up the new subfields of electronic, computer, genetic, nuclear, environmental, biomedical, and aerospace. Most engineering projects, such as building a bridge or a pipeline, involve several of these fields.

Precolonial Engineering Precolonial engineers contributed much to Latin American civilization. The Maya mastered the principles of stress to construct corbeled arches (vaults) in their palaces, and raised lofty pyramids that supported temple structures, such as that of the Temple of the Giant Jaguar in TIKAL, Guatemala. In South America, the Inca constructed the great sawtoothed fortress of SACSAHÚAMAN near Cuzco, Peru, and

the 2,250-mile road system that stretched from Quito to Santiago. Such engineering feats attest to the human ingenuity of the pre-Columbian era.

Colonial Engineering In colonial times, the Spanish and Portuguese government built massive public works projects, such as ports, roads, forts, granaries, mines, public buildings, churches, towns, and cities to reflect the flavor of European metropolitan life. The churches of the San Franciscan Order and Jesuit missions in the Old and New Worlds look much alike. Engineering made possible the perpetuation of metropolitan civilization in town squares throughout the colonies.

The Twentieth Century The region's most impressive engineering achievement of this century was the Panama Canal, a man-made waterway that connects the Caribbean Sea and the Pacific Ocean. Opened in 1914, the canal is 50.72 miles long and cost the United States and France $639 million to build. The United States alone invested $352 million, four times the cost of the Suez Canal. The building of the canal was also costly in terms of human lives lost to yellow fever and other tropical diseases. The canal has six locks at three separate locations. The locks are flooded to lift ships, which are then pulled through the canal by trains on either side of its banks. At its widest the canal is 163 square miles (Gatun Lake); the narrowest point is 300 feet wide.

Latin America's modern era is characterized by the positivist credo of "order and progress." Material progress and social order were made possible by engineering. The new railroads and telegraphic lines crisscrossing the Andes and connecting Rio to the mountains beyond Petrópolis and the interior provinces to the great harbors of Buenos Aires, Santos, and Veracruz, ushered Latin America into the twentieth century. The rail line between Rio and São Paulo, Brazil, that passed through the Paraíba Valley was essential for the growth of the coffee economy. One of the most technically difficult railway engineering achievements was the building of the MADEIRA-MAMORÉ RAILROAD in the Amazon.

The CANANEA copper mine in northern Mexico was Latin America's largest at the end of the nineteenth century; by 1915, CHUQUICAMATA, Chile, located 8,860 feet above sea level, had replaced it as the world's largest open-pit COPPER mine. Carajás, in southern Pará, Brazil, is the world's largest iron ore mine, with 18 billion metric tons of confirmed reserve. Seven times the size of Switzerland and five times that of Texas, Carajás is connected to the port of São Luís, Maranhão, via 540 miles of railroad through the tropics. The rail line was the first in Latin America designed with environmental protection as a primary goal.

The two hydroelectric power plants on the Paraná River are a testimony to the achievements of modern integrated civil engineering technologies. The ITAIPÚ dam is a binational project, built, owned, and operated by Brazil and Paraguay. Constructed between 1975 and 1982, the dam houses eighteen turbines generating 12,600 megawatts. Some 100,000 workers were involved in building the dam, which is 5 miles wide and 643 feet high and is the world's largest hollow gravity dam. Brazil and Paraguay spent over $15 billion to complete the power station. Downriver, Argentina is building its own binational hydroelectric dam with Paraguay for geopolitical reasons. The Yacyretá dam began in 1974 and was not completed as of 1994 due to the political instability in Argentina during the 1970s and 1980s. Argentina and Paraguay began to discuss the project in 1955, but construction was delayed because of corruption and lawsuits. The first stage of power generation is targeted at 4,140 megawatts and the eventual completion cost is expected to exceed $20 billion.

The Rio–Niterói bridge in Brazil is among the world's most notable bridges. During the heyday of Brazil's miracle years (1968–1973), the military government, as a modernizing technocratic regime, dedicated itself to economic and material progress. The urban congestion of Greater Rio required a rapid transportation system that would connect Rio de Janeiro and Niterói, across the Guanabara Bay. The Rio–Niterói Bay Bridge spans 45,604 feet and opened for traffic in 1972.

Argentina, Brazil, and Chile possess the engineering capabilities required to build defense industries. During the 1960s and 1970s all three countries were denied access to the world arms market and became self-sufficient in small arms, munitions, and motor vehicles, as well as aircraft, ships, tanks, armed personnel carriers, and a line of rockets and missiles. By 1990, Brazil had emerged as the seventh largest arms maker in the world.

It is the knowledge, talent, and vision of engineers that make such benefits possible. The training of engineers at university in Latin America, however, is a relatively new phenomenon: it was the military schools that pioneered engineering studies. Late in the nineteenth century, military engineers began to study POSITIVISM. By the early twentieth century, economics and sociology were added to the military engineering curriculum. The notion that a better society could be "engineered" or built by technical and scientific education and by emphasizing material progress became the harbinger of Latin America's modernization and planning processes. Prior to 1930, Latin America's economic planners and professors came from the region's major engineering schools.

With the help of professionals from the international engineering community, Latin America has entered the nuclear age. In Brazil two nuclear power plants, Angra I and Angra II, were built by Westinghouse and a West German company (Siemens, AG) respectively. Siemens, AG, also built Argentina's first nuclear power plant in the late 1960s. Later Atocia II was built by Canada and Germany. A third plant, to be built at Embalse, was contracted to Canada and Italy in 1972. In Brazil, nuclear energy is developed, supervised, and managed by Nuclebrás. In Argentina, the parallel organization is CNEA (National Council of Atomic Energy). In both countries, the navy played a key role in nuclear technology and development. Even today, many Latin American economists are trained as undergraduates in one of the disciplines of engineering. The field of business management has also been influenced by engineering. Industrial engineering or commercial engineering combines business management with the exacting technical skills of engineering design and construction.

CHARLES GIBSON, *The Aztecs Under Spanish Rule* (1964); DAVID MCCULLOUGH, *The Path Between the Seas: The Creation of the Panama Canal, 1870–1914* (1977); PINO TUROLLA, *Beyond the Andes* (1980); JACQUES SOUSTELLE, *The Olmecs: The Oldest Civilization in Mexico* (1984); JOSÉ MARIA GONÇALVES DE ALMEIDA, JR., ed., *Carajás: Desafio político, ecologia e desenvolvimento* (1986); JOSÉ O. MALDIFASSI and PIER A. ABETTI, *Defense Industries in Latin American Countries: Argentina, Brazil, and Chile* (1994); GUSTAVO LINS RIBEIRO, *Transnational Capitalism and Hydropolitics in Argentina: The Yacyretá High Dam* (1994).

EUL-SOO PANG

See also **Mining; Nuclear Industry; Railroads.**

ENLIGHTENMENT, THE. Historical opinion on the role of the Enlightenment in Ibero-America was for a long time paradoxically united in that two different groups, each proceeding from wholly different premises, saw little of the light of the eighteenth century in the Hispanic and Portuguese worlds.

Catholic traditionalists, vociferously captained by the Spanish polymath Marcelino Menéndez y Pelayo (1856–1912) and loudly heard in Spain till the demise of Franco, gloried in what they saw as scant Hispanic involvement in a movement that to them was both repugnant and dangerous. Viewing the same complex history from beyond the Pyrenees or from overseas, many of the self-styled "lights" of Paris and their heirs saw little of their own brand of enlightenment and ample justification for the famous jeer of the encyclopedist Nicolas Masson: Has any good thing ever come out of Spain?

It would be misleading to say that either of these two views was entirely wrong. Certainly enlightenment in the Iberian world did not flourish from the beginning. The ideas and attitudes clustered around scholasticism long remained powerful. They continued to be intellectually satisfying to most Hispanic people well into the nineteenth century, and they were closely identified with strong vested interests. Yet, in spite of all these reservations, it is clear that Hispanic and Portuguese intellectual life did change in the course of the eighteenth century. Moreover, this change was instigated by an active, articulate minority that perceived the possibility of a different world but that, with few exceptions, remained emphatically Hispanic and Portuguese in fundamental outlook. The key point seems to be that all but a few reformers retained some aspect or form of Catholicism.

The most clear-cut of the changes was the entry of modern science. Its presence in Ibero-America can first be seen in the work of a few lonely pioneers. One was Carlos de SIGÜENZA Y GÓNGORA in Mexico, who as early as 1681 criticized scholasticism, explained comets in Copernican terms, and showed familiarity with the works of René Descartes and Pierre Gassendi. Another pioneer was Pedro de Peralta BARNUEVA Y ROCHA in Peru.

More appreciable change came a generation later, perhaps from about 1720 on. Over the next half century, the freely circulated works of such authors as the Spanish reformer Benito Jerónimo FEIJÓO Y MONTENEGRO, the Portuguese João Baptista da Silva Leitão de Almeida Garrett and Luis Antonio Verney, and the Italian Antonio Genovesi; the "Port Royale" logic of Antoine Arnauld; and the works of "Lugdenensis" (Antoine de Montazet, archbishop of Lyon) all advocated mathematical education and set forth new scientific ideas drawn from Descartes, Gassendi, Locke, Newton, and others.

In the eighteenth century, the INQUISITION was no longer an effective block against new scientific ideas. Control of the book trade was ineffective; much seminal scientific work was never on the index of proscribed works; and popularized or adapted versions of new discoveries and ideas were found in numerous legally circulated books. Poverty and poor communications constituted far more significant obstacles.

Frequently, new works and ideas became known through the scientific and technical missions that came to America. Groups led by Charles-Marie de La Condamine; Aimé Jacques BONPLÁND; Thaddeus, Baron von Nordenflycht; Helm; Anton Zaccarias; Thaddeus Haenkes; and Alexander, Baron von HUMBOLDT as well as José Celestino MUTIS, Hipólito Ruiz, José Pavón, José Longinos, and Alessandro MALASPINA, to cite only the best known, traveled extensively and had free interchange with local scholars. The travelers had new books and scientific apparatus; they knew the latest scientific gossip; and they generated immense interest.

New ideas and innovative organizations received strong official backing after CHARLES III came to the Spanish throne in 1759. The king's ministers, many of the officials he appointed, and the policies they put into action had clear ties to the Enlightenment. The attempts to rationalize administration, centralize authority, update law codes, collect accurate demographic and economic information, and improve the economy—to somehow manage Spain and its empire into a prosperous, well-ordered, and unified state—paralleled similar attempts all over Europe.

All these factors came together in the last third of the eighteenth century. There were numerous changes in university and in some seminary and convent school curricula that provided more training in mathematics and modern physics. The hitherto dominant training in Aristotelian logic and scholastic metaphysics, though hotly defended, was gradually reduced and made available only to those preparing for the clergy. The gradualness of this process and the determination—based partly on prudence but also on conviction—to preserve fundamental Catholic values must be emphasized.

The crown demanded and won significant changes in the teaching of law and some aspects of theology. Spanish law replaced Roman law as the dominant subject of study, and canon law strongly emphasized the *regalias*, the rights of the crown over the church. The most dramatic manifestation of this matter was the repression of the JESUITS and the proscription of their doctrines. A more constructive approach sought to use the critical study of church councils and ecclesiastical history to strengthen the position of the crown and the bishops against the papacy. This new approach to ecclesiastical history went hand-in-hand with a shift in emphasis toward dogmatic theology at the expense of speculative scholasticism.

In many respects, more up-to-date education exemplified the Enlightenment's preoccupation with useful projects. There were numerous attempts to develop the economy by official action, including encouraging private enterprise. The inmates of asylums and orphanages were put to work, *cabildos* (town governments) and *intendants* (provincial governors) saw to it that land was paved and drained. Newly founded economic societies discussed schools and new crops.

Just as the presence of the Enlightenment is in dispute among historians, so too is its outcome. Many have discerned its most clear impact in the WARS OF INDEPENDENCE, in which they clearly see the influence of the political writings of the Baron de Montesquieu, John Locke, Gaetano Filangieri, Emmerich von Vattel, Samuel von Pufendorf, Thomas Jefferson, and other theorists of natural law. But traditionalists do not see this. For them, the wars of independence are conservative movements based on the scholastic natural law of Francisco Suárez and Saint Thomas Aquinas.

Resolution of this problem seems to depend on how one sees the wars of independence. If they were the culmination of a developmental era, then the question of sources is all-important. If, however, independence came more from the collapse of the Spanish throne than from any process of colonial maturation, then the effects of the Enlightenment are to be seen not so much in the wars of independence as in the tumultuous struggles of the nineteenth century.

Indispensable for seeing the spectrum of views on the Enlightenment in Latin America are ARTHUR P. WHITAKER et al., *Latin America and the Enlightenment* (1961), and A. OWEN ALDRIDGE, ed., *The Ibero-American Enlightenment* (1971). A useful bibliography on the Enlightenment as well as other aspects of the Bourbon period is JACQUES A. BARBIER and MARK A. BURKHOLDER, "Colonial Spanish America: The Bourbon Period," in *The History Teacher* 20, no. 2 (1987): 221–250. On university curricula see JOHN TATE LANNING, *The Eighteenth-Century Enlightenment in the University of San Carlos de Guatemala* (1956). For a model treatment of a scientific expedition see ARTHUR R. STEELE, *Flowers for the King: The Expedition of Ruíz and Pavón and the Flora of Peru* (1964). For two representative and differing treatments of the Enlightenment in specific areas see JOSÉ CARLOS CHIARAMONTE, *La Ilustración en el Río de la Plata* (1989), and JUAN MANUEL PACHECO, S.J., *La Ilustración en el Nuevo Reino* (1975). O. CARLOS STOETZER, *The Scholastic Roots of the Spanish American Revolution* (1979), presents the case for the continued influence of scholasticism.

GEORGE M. ADDY

See also **Bourbon Reforms; Catholic Church: The Colonial Period; Universities.**

ENRÍQUEZ, CARLOS (*b.* 3 August 1901, *d.* 2 May 1957), Cuban artist. Born in Santa Clara, Cuba, Enríquez was sent by his parents to the United States to study engineering, but upon his arrival he instead entered the Pennsylvania Academy of Fine Arts. He was expelled from the school because of his rebellious personality and returned to Cuba. During a 1930–1934 sojourn in Europe, he became particularly attracted to the art of El Greco, Zurbarán, Velázquez, and Goya. During the 1930s he incorporated political and historical themes in his paintings. He won a prize at the National Salon in Havana in 1938.

His paintings depict nature in a state of turmoil, an effect achieved by swirling forms, translucid planes, and overlapping figures (*The Rape of the Mulattas*, 1937). Sensualism and the female body, to which he alluded even in the shapes of animals and vegetation, are characteristic of his work (*Cuban Outlaw*, 1943).

JOSÉ GÓMEZ SICRE, *Pintura cubana de hoy*, English text by Harold T. Riddle (1944), pp. 79–87; ADELAIDA DE JUAN, *Pinturas cubana: Temas y variaciones* (1980), pp. 71–74.

MARTA GARSD

ENRÍQUEZ, MANUEL (*b.* 17 June 1926; *d.* 26 April 1994), Mexican violinist, composer, and music administrator. At age six Enríquez began violin study with his father in Ocotlán, Jalisco, and continued with Ignacio Camarena in Guadalajara. He directed the Guadalajara Symphony (1949–1955). A scholarship to the Juilliard School of Music (1955–1957) allowed him to study violin with Ivan Galamian and composition with Peter Mennin. With a Guggenheim Fellowship in 1971 he researched folk music in Spain and the same year enrolled in the Columbia-Princeton Research Center for Electronic Music. His music, written largely in nontraditional graphic notation, embraces, at times, serially recurring patterns of pitch, rhythm, and timbre, and free sections in which some elements of chance are left to the performers. He deliberately avoids nationalistic references. Enríquez taught composition at the National Conservatory of Mexico and has directed both the Carlos Chávez Center for Music Research and the music department of the National Institute of Fine Arts.

GÉRARD BÉHAGUE, *Music in Latin America: An Introduction* (1979).

ROBERT L. PARKER

ENRÍQUEZ DE ALMANSA, MARTÍN (*b.* ca. 1508; *d.* 1583), viceroy of New Spain (1568–1580) and of Peru (1580–1583). Although from a noble family of Castile, Enríquez did not inherit a title and little is known of his early life. Appointed viceroy of New Spain at the age of sixty, he brought a strong rule to the colony in the aftermath of the Cortés-Ávila conspiracy. He was authoritarian and at times bad tempered, but he was also just and kindly toward the Indians. He refused to grant colonial demands for a total war against the wild CHICHIMECS of the north. That and his imposition of the detested ALCABALA (sales tax) made him unpopular. A wise administrator, he is generally credited with having raised the prestige of the viceroy's office. He reluctantly accepted the viceroyalty of Peru in 1580 and died in Lima three years later.

ANTONIO F. GARCÍA-ABÁSOLO GONZÁLEZ, *Martín Enríquez y la reforma de 1568 en Nueva España* (1983).

STAFFORD POOLE, C.M.

ENRÍQUEZ DE GUZMÁN, ALONSO (*b.* ca. 1501; *d.* ca. 1549), author of a picaresque account of Peru's conquest and civil wars. Born in Seville and related to one of Spain's most powerful noble families, he married Constanza de Añasco at eighteen. Duels and nighttime escapades led to difficulties with city authorities. He left to fight in the Italian campaigns and, later, to become a courtier in the service of the emperor, from whom he repeatedly requested induction into the Order of Santiago. He was inducted into the order in 1529.

Enríquez de Guzmán sailed without license to the Indies and convinced the Audiencia of SANTO DOMINGO to appoint him to an administrative position in Santa Marta, but news of Peruvian gold led him to South

America's western coast in 1534. He planned to get rich and return to Seville to enjoy his wealth. He was in Lima in August 1535 and continued to Cuzco. Diego de ALMAGRO invited him on the Chilean venture, but he remained in Cuzco, and fought during the great native uprising of MANCO INCA.

When the Chilean expedition returned, Enríquez de Guzmán helped the Almagrists retake Cuzco from the Pizzarists, for which he received ample reward. During the battle of Las Salinas, Almagro left him in charge of Cuzco, where the victorious Hernando PIZARRO captured him. Barely escaping with his life by offering ransom, Enríquez de Guzmán was returned to Spain (1539) and jailed, but connections at court led to his freedom. He became an older companion for young Prince Philip. Offered a military command by the duke of Alba, he fought in Germany against Lutherans (battle of Mühlberg).

Enríquez de Guzmán left two important manuscripts: a rambling autobiography, *Libro de la vida y costumbres de don Alonso Enriques, caballero...* (The Life and Acts of Don Alonso Enríquez de Guzmán, A Knight of Seville ...), and a poem on the death of Diego de Almagro. Originally believed to be more fictional than true, the work reveals upon careful reading that the Peruvian sections at least are largely accurate.

RAUL PORRAS BARRENECHEA, *Los cronistas del Perú (1528–1650)* (1962, 1986), pp. 153–163; JAMES LOCKHART, *Spanish Peru, 1532–1560: A Colonial Society* (1968), pp. 40–41.

NOBLE DAVID COOK

ENRÍQUEZ GALLO, ALBERTO (*b.* 24 July 1894; *d.* 13 July 1962), military figure and president of Ecuador (nonelected 1937–1938). Born in Tanicuchi, León, Enríquez graduated from the Colegio Militar Eloy Alfaro in Quito (1912). He served as minister of defense from 1935 to 1937, using his position to reform and professionalize the military. Promoted to general in 1937, Enríquez took over the presidency in October, when the military ousted interim president Federico PÁEZ (1936–1937).

Enríquez's administration undertook a broad-based reform of juridical, educational, administrative, and financial structures and legislation. His government also enacted a number of social reforms, including an advanced labor code and laws to protect children. Enríquez relinquished power to Manuel María Borrero after calling the Constituent Convention of 1938. Ten years later (1948) he was an unsuccessful presidential candidate of the liberal socialist coalition. He served as senator for the province of Pichincha from 1956 until 1960.

ENRIQUE AYALA MORA, ed., *Nueva historia del Ecuador: Época republicana,* vol. 10 (1983), esp. pp. 103–104; LUIS CRISTÓBAL CABEZAS, *50 años de vida política y anecdótica del Ecuador* (1986), esp. pp. 32–34.

LINDA ALEXANDER RODRÍGUEZ

ENSENADA, CENÓN DE SOMODEVILLA, MARQUÉS DE LA (*b.* 2 June 1702; *d.* 2 December 1781), secretary of state of Spain (1743–1754). Termed the "secretary of everything," by a contemporary because he was secretary of state, finance, war, marine affairs, and the Indies, Ensenada was the most powerful minister in Spain during the early reign of FERDINAND VI. Early in his bureaucratic career he specialized in naval administration, and once in office he became firmly committed to increasing Spain's naval power. In an effort to increase the crown's revenues from the Indies trade, he encouraged the use of register ships rather than fleets and imposed strict trade regulations. However, Ensenada is best known for his domestic fiscal reform policies, which included a proposed single tax on income, based on ability to pay and applicable to all citizens. A ministerial power struggle in 1754 brought about his dismissal and exile.

FELIPE ABAD LEÓN, *El Marqués de la Ensenada: Su vida y su obra,* 2 vols. (1985).

SUZANNE HILES BURKHOLDER

ENTRADA, an armed expedition, or literally "entry," into the Brazilian wilderness in search of Indian slaves, gold, or trade. In the Northeast, *entradas* sought Indian slaves for sugar plantations and domestic service in the sixteenth century. In Amazonia they pursued slaves, nuts, spices, wood, and herbal drugs in the sixteenth, seventeenth, and eighteenth centuries. In southern Brazil, *entradas,* along with the larger BANDEIRAS, forcibly relocated thousands of Indians to Portuguese towns in the seventeenth century and searched for gold in the eighteenth century. These long expeditions charted much of the Brazilian west and led to the discoveries of gold, emeralds, and diamonds in the interior.

JOHN HEMMING, *Red Gold: The Conquest of the Brazilian Indians* (1978); JOHN M. MONTEIRO, "From Indian to Slave: Forced Native Labour and Colonial Society," *Slavery and Abolition* 9 (1988): 105–127.

ALIDA C. METCALF

See also **Slavery.**

ENTRE RÍOS, province of northeastern Argentina (1991 population 1,022,865) located between the URUGUAY and PARANÁ rivers, whose capital city is Paraná (1980 population 161,638). Owing to its swamps, it was a neglected territory during colonial and early republican times, and most efforts toward colonization and settlement were directed at central Paraguay and the plains of SANTA FÉ, west of the Paraná River. The drive to populate Entre Ríos began after the city of PARANÁ was safely established at its present site in 1883. Secondary centers in the province, such as Diamante, Concórdia, Concepción del Uruguay, and Monte Caseros, grew as supporters of the mainly agrarian activities of Entre Ríos. The province's main commodities are flax (main national product, grown on 1,150,000 acres), corn (500,000 acres), rice (145,000 acres), and peanuts. In the southern segment of Entre Ríos, sunflower and wheat are important crops, but the volume of production does not compare with that of other agricultural regions of the country. Husbandry comprises more than 3 million cattle, 4 million sheep, and 1.3 million hogs, most of them processed in the packing plants of Paraná, Concepción del Uruguay, and Gualeguaychú.

MANUEL E. MACCHI, *Entre Ríos: Síntesis histórica* (Concepción, 1977).

CÉSAR N. CAVIEDES

ENVIRONMENT AND CLIMATE. The physical environment of Latin America is varied, complex, and frequently spectacular. Extending over 6,000 miles from north to south, Latin America encompasses environmental conditions from the northern subtropics to the sub-Antarctic. Within this size and diversity there are broad subdivisions.

RELIEF

Mexico continues the surface forms and geology of North America southward to about 20° N, and includes the Pacific and Gulf coastal plains, the upland Mexican plateau at around 8,000 feet, and its peripheral mountain chains. Beyond the Isthmus of Tehuantepec, the circum-Caribbean region consists of the limestone lowland of Yucatán, the rugged east-west mountain ranges of Central America and the Greater Antilles, and the volcanic axes of the Isthmus of Panama and the island arc of the Lesser Antilles.

South America, the largest of the structural elements, itself has three broad subdivisions. Half its area is occupied by the Guiana and Brazilian shields, north and south of the Amazon, and the Patagonian plateau. These geologically ancient and eroded uplands have limited surface relief, but in Brazil substantial scarplike edges form barriers along the Atlantic coast.

On the western margins the ANDES extend for over 5,500 miles as a series of parallel mountain ranges of over 10,000 feet, rising to 22,800 feet. They divide Pacific from Atlantic drainage, and their rugged topography is a major obstacle to east-west movement. Within the Andes small valleys and upland basins above 10,000 feet have provided important niches for human settlement.

The shields and Andes restrict coastal lowlands, and there are few good harbors. However, between these uplands stretch the broad plains of the ORINOCO, AMAZON, and PARANÁ-PARAGUAY-LA PLATA river basins. Despite their size, these major rivers have not created arteries of communication into the interior; elsewhere waterfalls, rapids, and shoals limit navigation.

CLIMATE

Although three-quarters of the region are within the tropics, there is considerable climatic diversity, in response to the influence of latitude, altitude, and, on the Pacific coast, cold ocean currents. Humid tropical climates have average monthly temperatures above 64°F and annual rainfall above 80 inches, with little seasonality; the savanna-type climate has less (30 to 60 inches) and more seasonal rain. The former occurs in Amazonia, the Guianas, the Colombian and Ecuadorian Pacific lowlands, and the circum-Caribbean, and the latter in southern Mexico and the region surrounding the Amazon basin. Markedly contrasting dry conditions exist in northern Mexico, Patagonia, the CHACO, and the arid coastlands of Peru and north Chile, while in northeast Brazil, low, strongly seasonal rainfall may extend into periodic drought. In the mountains, altitude and latitude give a vertical zonation with tropical to cold conditions in Mexico and the central Andes and tundra conditions, with glaciers and permanent snow, in the far south. More restricted but distinctive climates occur in the mediterranean area of central Chile and the subtropical conditions of the pampas, with winter and summer average temperatures of 50°F to 82°F and relatively low (20 to 40 inches) but year-round rainfall.

ALTITUDE

Altitude plays a critically important role in the control of temperature in Latin America, especially in tropical areas, and many different temperature regimes can express themselves over relatively short distances in highland areas. For the most part, highland locations near the equator manifest no real seasonal differences in temperature, although they do show considerable temperature change from day to night. As one moves away from the equator, however, there is an increasingly greater change in temperature from one season to the next. Also, the altitudinal zonations of temperature vary with latitudinal location as well as with their position on the east- or west-facing slope; therefore, altitudinal zonations are not given definite limits. The recognition of the importance of altitudinal zonation goes back at least to the colonial period as the basis for the growing of crops; indigenous peoples too incorporated such insights. It is known that the Incas traditionally moved peoples from one part of their empire to another, but they would always ensure that they stayed at approximately the same altitudinal position.

Many different zonation patterns have been used in the literature, but the traditional folk classification has been the most widely accepted. It divides the highlands into five zones or *tierras*, each one defined by prevailing temperature regimes, dominant vegetation (although the type of vegetation is also influenced by rainfall regimes), and typical crop complex. The *tierra caliente* is the region that lies between sea level and about 2,500 to 3,000 feet. Daytime temperatures usually reach 85° to 90°, and mild temperatures (70° to 75°) prevail at night;

rarely will temperatures drop below 50°, and there is no threat of frost at any time. The *tierra templada*, considered the most ideal for human occupation and highly desired by the Spaniards, lies between 2,500 and about 6,000 feet. This area typically experiences mild, pleasant days of 75° to 80°, although the mercury will rise to a hot 90° to 95° at higher altitudes during the warmer months. Nighttime temperatures fall to 60° to 70°, with a rare frost, especially during the cooler months as one moves north or south from the equator. The *tierra fría* defines altitudes between 6,000 and 12,000 feet, and occurs throughout the Andes and in some higher elevations in Mexico and Central America. It is known for its mild daytime temperatures (75° to 80°) and cold nights (50° to 55°), with frost very common in cooler months away from the equator and at higher elevations. The *tierra helada* lies above 12,000 feet in the Andes, between the daily frost line and the boundary of permanent snow (about 15,000 feet), and is typified by low-growing bunch grasses. The mountain peaks with year-round permanent snow are classified *tierra nevada* and are above the vegetation zone.

The *tierra helada*, located above the tree line and below the zone of permanent snow, is a bitterly inhospitable cold desert dominated by highland meadows that provide pasturage for a number of native species (e.g., deer, vicuña, and guanaco) and domesticated animals. These grasslands are referred to as the *páramo* in the damper highland areas between Costa Rica and northern Peru, but they are replaced by *puna* in the dry highland AL-TIPLANO region between Central Peru and northern Chile. The *páramo* is typified by a dense tussock grassland with concentrations of woody vegetation in sheltered areas, while the drier *puna* is dominated by a more xerophytic grassland that includes ichu, a type of poor-quality bunch grass, and tola, a resinous bush that thrives in areas of low temperature and rainfall. In both areas, the use of fire and the cutting of trees have tended to expand the grasslands into lower elevations.

SOILS AND VEGETATION

Poor latosols and podzolic soils, which are strongly weathered and leached, cover almost half the continent. Though they may carry luxuriant vegetation, they have limited nutrients and do not long sustain cultivation. In mountain areas steep slopes and erosion inhibit soil formation. Within such zones tracts of better soils exist, but the most productive soils are the black earths of the pampas and the *terra roxa* formed on volcanic material in south Brazil.

Vegetation cover reflects the influence of relief, geology, and climate. The three major but internally varied forms are forest, savanna, and desert. Forest cover ranges from the evergreen rain FOREST of Central America and Amazonia, surrounded by tropical seasonal forest, to the temperate woodlands of southern Chile. The savannas and grasslands occupy almost one-fifth of the area, grading from the woodland-grass scrubland of the Brazilian *campos* and Venezuelan LLANOS to the PAM-PAS grassland. One-quarter of the vegetation is dryland, including the thorn scrub of north Mexico, Patagonia, Chaco, and the Brazilian SERTÃO and the barren ATACAMA DESERT. In the mountains, altitude modifies cover from tropical forest to *puna-páramo* grassland and bare rocks.

ENVIRONMENT AND PEOPLE

Though the environment can be summarized in these broad terms, to do so would mask much local diversity, in that individual countries have conditions ranging from arid to humid or temperate to tropical. There are "negative" environments that have been inimical to settlement because of ruggedness, aridity, cold, or soil poverty, or because episodic hazards such as earthquakes, volcanoes, frost, drought, hurricanes, and EL NIÑO put life and economic activity at risk. Conversely, the forest, fertile soils, ecological niches in the mountains, precious and base metals in the sierras and shields, and, more recently, lowland petroleum deposits have attracted people and development.

ERNST JOSEF FITTKAU et al., eds., *Biogeography and Ecology in South America* (1969); WERNER SCHWERDTFEGER, ed., *Climates of Central and South America* (1976); TOM L. MARTINSON and GARY S. ELBOW, eds., *Geographic Research on Latin America: Benchmark 1980* (1981), esp. pp. 22–33 and 269–311; and GHILLEAN T. PRANCE and THOMAS E. LOVEJOY, eds., *Amazonia* (1985); PRESTON JAMES and CLARENCE MINKEL, *Latin America*, 5th ed. (1986); ARTHUR MORRIS, *South America*, 3rd ed. (1987); ROBERT WEST and JOHN AUGELLI, *Middle America: Its Lands and Peoples*, 3rd ed. (1989); CÉSAR CAVIEDES and GREGORY KNAPP, *South America* (1995).

JOHN P. DICKENSON

ENVIRONMENTAL MOVEMENTS. During the 1980s environmental matters gained strong currency in Latin America, especially with the proliferation of democracies throughout the region. By the 1990s nongovernmental environmental organizations numbered in the thousands. Some had their beginnings in the late 1960s or early 1970s, but most appeared in the 1980s.

Beginning in the 1980s, Latin American environmental issues were usually related to development, whether the subject be deforestation, industrial pollution, sanitation, transportation, indigenous populations, public education, or animal rights. Poverty itself was considered a major environmental concern, since the poor placed serious strains on natural resources for their livelihood in the absence of more environmentally sound alternatives. In short, environmental issues had strong political and economic implications and thus provoked much controversy.

The United Nations chose to hold its second major international conference on development and the environment in a Latin American setting (Rio de Janeiro) in 1992. (The first conference had taken place in Stockholm in 1972.) One objective of the 1992 conference was to establish a financial mechanism for industrialized nations to aid Third World environmental programs. It was suggested that developed countries should pay an "ecological debt" to Latin American nations and transfer pollution control technologies without charge.

Most international attention to Latin America's environmental problems tended to focus on global warming as it related to the destruction of tropical forests, especially in the Amazon and Central America. Brazil received much adverse attention in late 1988 when Chico MENDES FILHO, an Amazon rubber tapper and political activist, was murdered at the behest of a local rancher. Mendes's political success in the Brazilian Congress had resulted in legislation rendering the rancher's property worthless, so Mendes Filho was killed in revenge.

Tropical forests, however, had always been relatively underpopulated. A far greater number of Latin Americans were adversely affected by urban pollution problems, especially deficient sewage treatment (São Paulo and Rio de Janeiro, Brazil) and smog (Mexico City and Santiago, Chile).

While Latin America's environmental problems remained widespread and serious in the mid-1990s, progress was being made on some fronts. For instance, Cubatão, the Brazilian city once called the most polluted site on earth, reduced petrochemical and fertilizer pollutants to a fraction of their former levels with the assistance of a World Bank loan. The health indicators for the city's inhabitants improved dramatically, and lush vegetation reappeared in once-decimated areas.

Green Politics   The importance of environmental issues in Latin American politics was undeniable by the late 1980s. In Mexico, for example, President Carlos SALINAS DE GORTARI chose to seize the environmental initiative and pursue "preemptive reforms" rather than wait for grassroots mobilization and pressures. Salinas declared the health of the Mexican people to be a greater priority of his administration than development. His words were followed with substantive actions: $2.5 billion was budgeted to improve Mexico City's air quality, a major petroleum refinery operated by Pemex (Mexico's state-owned oil company) was closed, unleaded gasoline was introduced, and 3,500 city buses were replaced. As a result, Salinas was awarded the United Nations–backed United Earth Association award in 1991, a move applauded by many of Mexico's environmental groups.

Meanwhile, the intensity of international attention to the Amazon provoked a political backlash. In 1990 the state of Amazonas readily elected a governor whose platform was blatantly anti-environment; he had declared that since there were no healthy trees in the Amazon, people should use them up before the termites did. Subsequently, some military officers and conservative civilian politicians accused international environmentalists of threatening Brazil's national sovereignty and security.

While some Latin American countries had "green" political parties by the 1990s, they were relatively small and their political impact limited. Most were not formally linked to the European-based international "green movement."

The State and the Environment.   Cabinet-level environment posts (either ministries or secretariats) were created in many but not all Latin American countries in the 1980s and early 1990s. They were notably lacking in Central America, except for Guatemala. Some of the agencies were exclusively environmental ministries (Brazil and Argentina) while others combined environmental matters with such development-related areas as natural resources (Venezuela and Colombia) or urban planning and development (Uruguay and Mexico). Often, these new entities represented an upgrading of earlier, less powerful government agencies with environmental mandates.

Environmental legislation varied markedly throughout the region in the early 1990s. Some countries had fairly comprehensive laws and policies, while others lacked them almost totally. Even where such measures existed on paper, implementation and enforcement were difficult or sometimes even impossible; frequently the measures were simply ignored.

Debt-for-Nature Swaps.   In the 1960s and 1970s, Latin American governments contracted foreign public and private loans for development projects. When the world's economy entered recession in the early 1980s, these loans quickly became unserviceable. Several contentious years of debt negotiations followed, but by the late 1980s more creative approaches to the problem had emerged. One such idea was the debt swap, whereby a country's debt paper could be purchased at a fraction of its original worth on secondary markets and then utilized in that country for approved projects, including those related to the environment. Projects for such swaps were further encouraged in the Enterprise for the Americas Initiative of 1990, promoted by U.S. President George Bush. It was difficult, though, for environmental groups to raise substantial amounts of capital for such undertakings. Nevertheless, a few debt-for-nature swaps have occurred, most notably in Bolivia, Ecuador, and Costa Rica.

In the early 1990s, debt-for-nature initiatives included a project by Argentina's National Development Bank for natural grassland and forest preservation in the ecologically sensitive Patagonia region. There was also a swap proposal from the Central American Bank for Economic Integration to create a trust fund that could be tapped by Central American environmental organizations and university groups.

Debt swaps, however, could be politically sensitive issues. Mexico refused to participate in debt swaps instigated by third parties because it was unwilling to cede national territory and sovereignty to such ventures. Instead, it invented a variation on the debt swap theme by contracting a loan from the World Bank to purchase its own debt. This in turn created a $150 million fund for reforesting 173,000 acres of Mexico City with 200 million trees. In Brazil, the Collor administration reversed the policy of its predecessor and accepted debt-for-nature swaps in principle. This added to the criticism within Brazil that the country was losing control over the Amazon.

Development Versus the Environment. At the root of many Latin American environmental issues in the early 1990s were government development policies and objectives. Past development strategies of the 1960s and 1970s were often identified as the source of many of the most serious environmental problems of the 1980s and 1990s. By the 1990s new development projects were more likely to be scrutinized and criticized, often under the concept of sustainable development. Ecuador and Guatemala, for example, faced serious choices between opening new areas to petroleum production or forgoing same in favor of conserving the biologically diverse and unique areas involved.

The environmental movement in Latin America is just beginning to receive systematic scholarly attention, and sources remain scarce. Two of the few monographs covering the region as a whole are DAVID A. PRESTON, ed., *Environment, Society, and Rural Change in Latin America: The Past, Present, and Future in the Countryside* (1980), and DAVID GOODMAN and MICHAEL REDCLIFT, eds., *Environment and Development in Latin America: The Politics of Sustainability* (1991). Another recent scholarly effort to survey the Latin American environmental movement is the entire issue of *Latin American Perspectives* 19, no. 1, issue 72 (1992). Latin America often receives attention in works with broader, global themes, such as the WORLD COMMISSION ON ENVIRONMENT AND DEVELOPMENT, *Our Common Future* (1987). Articles with regionwide foci include EDUARDO GUDYNAS, "Environment and Sustainable Development in Latin America: The Challenge to Recover 'El Dorado,'" in *International Transnational Associations* 4 (1989): 197–199, and SCOTT WHITEFORD, DAVID WILEY, and KENNETH WYLIE, "In the Name of Development: Transforming the Environment in Africa and Latin America" in *Centennial Review* 35, no. 2 (1991): 205–219. Other articles often focus on a specific country or theme, such as STEPHEN P. MUMME, "System Maintenance and Environmental Reform in Mexico: Salinas's Preemptive Strategy," in *Latin American Perspectives* 19, no. 1, issue 72 (1992): 123–143. An indispensable source for updated information on environment-related developments throughout the world, usually organized on a country basis, is the Bureau of National Affairs's biweekly *International Environment Reporter: Current Reports.*

LAURA JARNAGIN

ERÁRIO RÉGIO, the Royal Treasury of Portugal. Its creation, on 22 December 1761, and the extinction of the Casa dos Contos were key measures of the reform program of the Marquês de POMBAL to overhaul the fiscal bureaucracy. In the reorganized exchequer, four departments, staffed by trained accountants and reporting to the treasurer-general, supervised the income and expenditures of the crown with respect to the geographical divisions of Portugal and its empire: (1) the Court (the heartland) and Estremadura; (2) other provinces and Azores and Madeira; (3) Africa, Maranhão, and Bahia; and (4) Rio de Janeiro, East Africa, and Asia. Headed initially by Pombal himself, succeeding treasurers-general included other eminent statesmen: the Marquês de Angeja, the Marquês de Ponte de Lima, and Rodrigo de SOUSA COUTINHO. With the passage of the court to Rio in 1808, the treasury was recreated in the colony. Subsequently abolished in 1832 in Portugal, in Brazil after independence (1822) the colonial department was superseded by the Tesouro Publico in 1824.

RUY D'ABREU TORRES, "Erário Régio," in *Dicionario de Historia de Portugal,* edited by Joel Serrão, vol. 2 (1965), pp. 67–68.

CATHERINE LUGAR

ERCILLA Y ZÚÑIGA, ALONSO DE (*b.* 1533; *d.* 1594), Spanish poet. Although he was in Latin America for only a short period, Alonso de Ercilla can be considered one of the first writers of the New World. In *La* ARAUCANA (1569, 1578, 1589), an exemplary Renaissance epic poem based on his brief experience as a soldier fighting the Araucanian Indians in southern Chile, he combines the imagination of the poet with the observations and

Alonso de Ercilla y Zúñiga. Engraving by Juan Moreno Sepata. Reproduced from Blave, *Geographia,* vol 2. (Amsterdam, 1662). COURTESY OF THE JOHN CARTER BROWN LIBRARY AT BROWN UNIVERSITY.

commentaries of the historian. He began writing the poem during the campaign, but he completed it years later in Spain, adding several passages about other important Spanish triumphs in Europe. Dedicated to King Philip II, in whose court he served from an early age, *La Araucana* praises the glories of the empire while also offering a sympathetic and admiring view of the Araucanians. Lacking an individual hero, the poem stresses the valiant defense by the Indians against the Spanish invasion and even criticizes some aspects of the war.

ALONSO DE ERCILLA Y ZÚÑIGA, *La Araucana*, edited by Marcos A. Morínigo and Isaías Lerner (1979); and ISAÍAS LERNER, "Don Alonso de Ercilla y Zúñiga," in *Latin American Writers*, edited by Carlos A. Solé and Maria Isabel Abreu, vol. 1 (1989), pp. 23–31.

S. DAYDÍ-TOLSON

ERRÁZURIZ ECHAURREN, FEDERICO (*b.* 16 November 1850; *d.* 12 July 1901), president of Chile (1896–1901). Son of former president Federico ERRÁZURIZ ZAÑARTU, Errázuriz was a lawyer by education and a farmer by profession. He entered politics in 1876, serving three terms as a deputy. Although he served as a minister in José Manuel Balmaceda's government (1886–1891), he joined the Congressionalist forces in the 1891 Revolution. Reelected to the chamber of deputies, he later became a senator. Errázuriz apparently spent heavily— probably over a million pesos—to win the presidency in 1896. Despite this sum, he barely defeated his opponent, the highly principled Vicente Reyes, who possessed neither Errázuriz's funds nor his political connections.

Despite these inauspicious beginnings, Errázuriz did manage to resolve the nation's frontier problems with Argentina over the Puna de Atacama, preserve Chile's territorial gains from the War of the Pacific, and personally intervene to avoid war with Argentina. In 1899 he met with the president of Argentina at the Strait of Magellan, where they declared that their two nations would never fight each other.

Errázuriz's fellow countrymen seemed less pacific, however, attacking the partially paralyzed and increasingly ill president. Forced by poor health to turn over his government in 1900 to his vice president for four months, Errázuriz returned to rule, but in May 1901 he again transferred power to the vice president. Errázuriz died before completing his term of office.

JAIME EYZAGUIRRE, *Chile durante el gobierno de Errázuriz Echaurren, 1896–1901* (1957); LUIS GALDAMES, *A History of Chile* (1941), pp. 366, 406, 444.

WILLIAM F. SATER

ERRÁZURIZ VALDIVIESO, CRESCENTE (*b.* 1839; *d.* 1931), archbishop of Santiago, Chile (1918–1931), during a period when the Catholic church distanced itself from its traditional alliance with the Conservative Party and accepted the separation of church and state.

Born in Santiago, Errázuriz was educated as a diocesan priest but subsequently joined the Dominican Order (1884–1911). Also trained in law, he worked as a journalist directing both *El Estandarte Católico* and *La Revista Católica,* and became one of Chile's best-known historians.

In 1918 the seventy-nine-year-old Errázuriz was named archbishop of Santiago after then President Juan Luis SANFUENTES, with the support of the Senate, convinced the Vatican that the appointment was essential for the maintenance of good relations with the new Liberal government. Throughout his term as archbishop, Errázuriz played a major role in the modernization of the church, as well as the maintenance of its influence with Chilean society. He believed that unless the church was adaptable, its power would be diminished. He was also concerned about the direct involvement of priests in politics, and in 1922 he issued a decree forbidding it. While Errázuriz did not himself support the separation of church and state, he pragmatically participated in the drafting of the relevant parts of the 1925 Constitution that mandated it. This document ended government involvement in the appointment of priests, as well as state subsidies for church purposes.

BRIAN H. SMITH, *The Church and Politics in Chile: Challenges to Modern Catholicism* (1982); HANNAH W. STEWART-GAMBINO, *The Church and Politics in the Chilean Countryside* (1992).

MARGARET E. CRAHAN

ERRÁZURIZ ZAÑARTU, FEDERICO (*b.* 25 April 1825; *d.* 20 July 1877), president of Chile (1871–1876). A lawyer, Errázuriz became president after serving numerous terms as a national deputy, provincial governor, and cabinet minister. Errázuriz broke with the Conservative Party when it opposed his attempts to secularize the cemeteries, permit non-Catholics to marry, and exempt non-Catholics from having to attend religious courses in public schools. After 1873, Errázuriz led a coalition known as the Liberal Alliance, which consisted of members of the Radical and Liberal parties.

Although Errázuriz was the first president to serve only one term, his administration nevertheless implemented numerous reforms, among which were those that limited the power of the state, altered voting procedures, and modernized the penal and mining codes. His term began during a period of prosperity, that allowed Errázuriz to finance railroad construction and purchase ironclads for the navy. However, a fall in metal prices as well as a decline in copper and silver production limited Chile's economic growth, devastated the national economy, and ushered in a period of budget deficits and trade imbalances.

ALFONSO BULNES, *Federico Errázuriz Zañartu: su vida* (1950); LUIS GALDAMES, *A History of Chile* (1941), pp. 314–319.

WILLIAM F. SATER

ERRO, ENRIQUE (*b.* 14 September 1912; *d.* 10 October 1984), Uruguayan politician and trade unionist. A journalist employed by *La Tribuna,* Erro was a founding member of the Uruguayan Press Association. He was subsequently a member of the House of Representatives (1953–1966), minister of industry and labor (1959–1960), and a senator (1971–1973).

Ideologically Erro followed the principles of a Latin American "Patria Grande"—the name of his slate of candidates within the Frente Amplio (Broad Front) in the 1971 elections—and a popular, revolutionary nationalism. He served on the Anti-imperialist Committee and was a member of the Blanco party. Erro was a founder of the Unión Popular in 1962, later formed a coalition with the Socialist party, then joined the newly founded Frente Amplio in 1971.

From 1973 to his death, Erro rejected all negotiations with the military regime and called for abstention from the 1980 constitutional referendum and the 1982 elections. He denounced Uruguayan human rights violations before European governments and the U.N. Commission on HUMAN RIGHTS.

ROBERTO GILARDONI and LUIS IMAS, *Biografía de Enrique Erro: Su vida, su lucha, su obra* (1988); NELSON CAULA, *Erro,* 3 vols. (1989–1990).

DIETER SCHONEBOHM

ESCALADA, ASUNCIÓN (*b.* 1850; *d.* 1894, Paraguayan educator. At the time of Escalada's birth in the mid-nineteenth century, education in Paraguay was almost entirely limited to male students; women were rarely permitted to take part in education except occasionally at the primary level. Escalada dedicated her career to opening Paraguayan education to women at all levels.

The WAR OF THE TRIPLE ALLIANCE (1864–1870) provided Escalada and other women with an opportunity to teach when so many male teachers were called to the front. She herself worked at a small primary school in the interior hamlet of Atyra. During the final stages of the fighting, however, Escalada was forced to abandon the town and accompany her grandfather, the noted Argentine educator Juan Pedro Escalada (1777–1869), on the tragic retreat to CERRO CORÁ.

After the war, Escalada convinced the new provisional government to fund the Escuela Central de Niñas, which she directed until 1875. This institution served as the model for the Colegio Nacional de Niñas, the best-known school for young women in today's Paraguay.

Aside from her efforts in education, Escalada was also instrumental in fomenting culture and the arts in the country, donating time and money to advance the career of guitarist Agustín BARRIOS and many others. She died in Buenos Aires.

CARLOS R. CENTURIÓN, *Historia de la cultura paraguaya,* 2d ed., 2 vols. (1961); CHARLES J. KOLINSKI, *Historical Dictionary of Paraguay* (1973), p. 91.

THOMAS L. WHIGHAM

ESCALANTE, ANÍBAL (*b.* 1909; *d.,* 11 August 1977), secretary-general of the Partido Socialista Popular (Cuban Communist Party—PSP) and editor of the party's organ *Hoy.* Born in Oriente Province into an affluent family, Escalante graduated with a degree in law from the University of Havana in 1932, the same year he joined the Communist Party. During that year Escalante founded *Hoy,* the official organ of the Cuban Communist Party. He was the paper's editor from 1938 into the early 1960s as well as the party's elected representative in the lower house of the Cuban Congress from 1948 to 1952.

Escalante survived the Batista dictatorship and the CUBAN REVOLUTION of 1959 to play a key role in the reformed Communist Party under the leadership of Fidel CASTRO. In 1961 he was given the task of merging Castro's own TWENTY-SIXTH OF JULY MOVEMENT with the Revolutionary Student Directorate and the Cuban Communist Party. Escalante attempted to forge a single party, the Integrated Revolutionary Organizations, modeled after the Soviet Communist Party. Perceived as a threat to Castro's power, he was dismissed from the National Directory in 1962 and was forced out of Cuba that same year. After a brief exile, Escalante returned to Cuba in 1964, and once again became active in politics.

In 1968 Escalante, along with other members of the old PSP, was accused of forming a "microfaction" within the new, ruling Cuban Communist Party (PCP), and was sentenced to fifteen years in prison for "attempting to destroy the unity" of the Cuban Revolution. He died in Havana.

RALPH LEE WOODWARD, JR., "Urban Labor and Communism: Cuba," in *Caribbean Studies* 3, no. 3 (1963): 17–50; RAMÓN EDUARDO RUIZ, *Cuba: The Making of a Revolution* (1970); SAMUEL FARBER, *Revolution and Reaction in Cuba, 1933–1960* (1976).

MICHAEL POWELSON

See also **Cuba: Political Parties.**

ESCANDÓN, ANTONIO (*b.* 1824; *d.* 1877), Mexican entrepreneur. The younger brother of the notorious Mexican moneylender Manuel ESCANDÓN, he was born in Puebla. He married Catalina Barrón, daughter of Eustaquio Barrón, another influential moneylender of the period. Escandón spent the years of the French Empire in Europe trying to raise funds for building a railroad from Mexico City to Veracruz, a project that was completed in 1873.

Escandón is also noteworthy for his commitment to the beautification of Mexico City following the fall of the empire. He believed that the national government should make the newly renamed Paseo de la Reforma into a Mexican version of the Champs-Élysées with streets intersecting to form traffic circles. In 1877, to celebrate the completion of the railroad, Escandón presented the city with a statue of Christopher Columbus that still stands in the second *glorieta* (traffic circle) on the Paseo. Ironically, he died in Europe, on a train en route from Seville to Córdoba.

LUIS GARCÍA PIMENTEL, *El monumento elevado en la ciudad de México a Cristóbal Colón* (1872); BARBARA A. TENENBAUM, "Development or Sovereignty: Intellectuals and the Second Empire, 1861–1867," in *The Intellectuals and the State in Mexico*, edited by Charles Hale et al. (1991).

BARBARA A. TENENBAUM

ESCANDÓN, JOSÉ DE (*b.* 1700; *d.* 1770), founder of Nuevo Santander. Born in Soto la Marina, Santander, Escandón came to New Spain in 1715 and settled in Querétaro, where he participated in numerous campaigns against the northern Indian tribes, the most notable of which being the pacification of the Sierra Gorda. In response to Indian attacks around Nuevo León and the threat of English and French expansion from Florida and Louisiana into Texas, the viceroy, the first Count of Revillagigedo, selected Escandón to conquer and settle the region around Tamaulipas and both sides of the lower Rio Grande. In 1749, after extensive planning and exploring, Escandón led a colonizing force of over 3,000 people to Tamaulipas and established twenty-one Spanish and Tlaxcalan communities and fifty-seven Franciscan and three Dominican missions. To pacify rebellious tribes in the area, he granted land and agricultural supplies to them and assigned Tlaxcalan instructors to their communities. The new region, Nuevo Santander, became one of the most successful colonies on New Spain's northern frontier and the birthplace of the Texas cattle industry.

LAWRENCE FRANCIS HILL, *José de Escandón and the Founding of Nuevo Santander: A Study in Spanish Colonization* (1926); JOHN FRANCIS BANNON, *The Spanish Borderlands Frontier*, 2d ed. (1974), pp. 139–140; OAKAH JONES, *Los Paisanos: Spanish Settlers on the Northern Frontier of New Spain* (1979), pp. 65–72.

AARON PAINE MAHR

ESCANDÓN, MANUEL (*b.* 1808; *d.* 7 June 1862), Mexican entrepreneur. Son of an Asturian merchant and a mother linked to the military and agricultural families of Jalapa, Veracruz, Escandón was born in Orizaba, Veracruz. Educated partly in Europe, he returned to Mexico in 1826 and moved to the capital in the early 1830s. By 1833, he was operating an important stagecoach line from Veracruz to Mexico City and had become involved in political wheeling and dealing through his relationships with prominent generals like Antonio López de SANTA ANNA, Mariano ARISTA, and others. Escandón quickly took advantage of the precarious financial situation of the Mexican treasury by lending money to the

government and by agreeing to provide important services to it. In 1848 he purchased the French-owned Cocolapam textile mill in Orizaba and gained even greater wealth after he and a consortium purchased the British-owned Real del Monte silver mines just before it hit a bonanza. By 1853 he and other moneylenders offered to found Mexico's first bank, but were turned down by Treasury Minister Antonio de HARO Y TAMARIZ.

During the last years of his life Escandón turned his attention to building a railroad from Mexico City to Veracruz, a project his younger brother Antonio completed in 1873.

MARGARITA URÍAS HERMOSILLO, "Manuel Escandón: de las Diligencias al Ferrocarril, 1833–1862," in *Formación y desarrollo de la burguesía en México: Siglo XIX*, edited by Ciro F. S. Cardoso (1978); BARBARA A. TENENBAUM, *The Politics of Penury: Debts and Taxes in Mexico, 1821–1856* (1986).

BARBARA A. TENENBAUM

ESCOBAR, LUIS ANTONIO (*b.* 14 July 1925; *d.* 11 September 1993), Colombian composer and diplomat. Born in Villapinzón, Escobar studied at the Bogotá Conservatory (1940–1947). In 1947 he received a scholarship to study with Nicholas Nabokov at the Peabody Conservatory in Baltimore. He attended composition courses at New York's Columbia University (1950–1951) and took classes with Boris Blacher at the Berlin Hochschule für Musik (1951–1953) and the Salzburg Mozarteum (1951). Upon his return to his native land he was named secretary of the National Conservatory, where he taught harmony, composition, and instrumentation. Escobar received several awards, including the National Prize (1955) for his *Sinfonía Cero* and two Guggenheim fellowships. In 1960 the New York City Ballet commissioned his *Preludios para percusión*. Escobar presented his *Pequeña sinfonía* at the Third Latin American Music Festival, held in Washington, D.C., in May 1965. He was appointed director of musical programs for television in Colombia and served on the national board of the Colombian National Orchestra. He was also chairman of the National Music Council and director of the cultural division of the Ministry of National Education. Escobar also served as consul (1964–1966) and second secretary (1967–1970) of the Colombian embassy in Bonn, West Germany. He died in Miami while serving as Colombia's cultural chargé d'affaires.

Composers of the Americas, vol. 8 (1962), pp. 65–70; JOHN VINTON, ed., *Dictionary of Contemporary Music* (1974); GÉRARD BÉHAGUE, *Music in Latin America* (1979); *New Grove Dictionary of Music and Musicians*, vol. 6 (1980).

SUSANA SALGADO

ESCOBAR, PATRICIO (*b.* 1843; *d.* 19 April 1912), president of Paraguay (1886–1890) and soldier. Born in San José, Escobar entered the army just before the outbreak of the WAR OF THE TRIPLE ALLIANCE and rose in rank from private to general during the course of the conflict. Like his mentor, the cavalry general Bernardino CABALLERO, Escobar remained loyal to the cause of President Francisco Solano LÓPEZ and doggedly resisted the Brazilians until he was captured at CERRO CORÁ, the war's last battle.

Returning to Paraguay after several years' captivity, Escobar attached himself to Caballero and to Conservative figures associated with President Cándido BAREIRO. After Caballero's accession to the presidency in 1880, Escobar received the portfolio of war minister. Six years later, he himself succeeded to the highest office and generally continued the conservative, paternalistic policies of his friend and predecessor, though Escobar was perhaps more tolerant of opposition criticism. He opened the National University in 1889 and helped to expand the Paraguay Central Railway and other public works. In partisan politics, Escobar collaborated in the organization of the Asociación Nacional Republicana (or Partido Colorado), one of the country's two traditional parties. Unfortunately, his administration was also marked by corruption.

Stepping down from office in 1890, the by-now-wealthy Escobar continued to influence Paraguayan politics through various surrogates and intrigues. He died in Asunción less than two months after the death of Caballero.

HARRIS G. WARREN, *Rebirth of the Paraguayan Republic: The First Colorado Era, 1878–1904* (1985); CARLOS ZUBIZARRETA, *Cien vidas paraguayas*, 2d ed. (1985), pp. 202–205; *The Cambridge History of Latin America*, vol. 5 (1986), pp. 475–496.

THOMAS L. WHIGHAM

ESCOBEDO, MARIANO (*b.* January 1826; *d.* 1902), Mexican Liberal army commander. Born in Galeana, Nuevo León, Escobedo fought as an ensign in the national guard against U.S. forces in 1846–1847, becoming a lieutenant in 1852. He supported the Plan of AYUTLA and fought under Santiago VIDAURRI in 1854–1855. He became a lieutenant-colonel in the cavalry in 1856. During the Civil War of the Reform (1858–1861), he again fought alongside Vidaurri in the north central states. During the FRENCH INTERVENTION, he fought at Puebla in 1862 and 1863, when he was captured.

Escobedo opposed Vidaurri's defection to the empire in 1864. He played the major role in the resurgence of Liberal forces in late 1865, capturing MAXIMILIAN, Miguel MIRAMÓN, and Tomás MEJÍA at Querétaro in 1867 and convening the summary military tribunal that sentenced them to death. A close friend of Sebastián LERDO, he became a senator in September 1875 and minister of war in 1876. He fought against Porfirio DÍAZ in the rebellion of Tuxtepec (1876) and conspired to restore Lerdo in 1877–1878. He was a federal deputy at the time of his death.

BRIAN HAMNETT

ESCOCESES, Scottish rite Masonic lodges. Introduced into Mexico in 1817 or 1819 by Spanish officers, the *escoceses* had earlier been established by these officers in the peninsula during the war against NAPOLEON. In 1821 the last Spanish ruler of New Spain, Juan O'Donojú, provided great impetus for the expansion of the *escocés* lodges. His physician, Manuel Codorniu, founded the newspaper *El Sol*, which became the organ of the group. Some Mexican deputies to the Spanish Cortes also joined lodges in the Peninsula, emerging as the nucleus of the *escoceses* after 1822. The lodge rapidly became a clandestine political organization. In 1825 some members splintered, founding the "populist" YORKINOS (York rite Masons), while the *escoceses* became the "aristocratic" party. Vice President Nicolás BRAVO, Grand Master of the *escoceses*, ultimately led a revolt against the government in January 1828. When the lodges were banned, the *escoceses* formed another secret group known as the *novenarios*, which continued to function as a political organization for some time.

LUIS J. ZALCE Y RODRÍGUEZ, *Apuntes para la historia de la masonería en México*, 2 vols. (1950); VIRGINIA GUEDEA, "Las sociedades secretas durante el movimiento de independencia," in *The Independence of Mexico and the Creation of the New Nation*, edited by Jaime E. Rodríguez O. (1989), esp. pp. 45–62.

JAIME E. RODRÍGUEZ O.

See also **Masonic Orders.**

ESLAVA Y LAZAGA, SEBASTIÁN DE (*b.* January 1685; *d.* 21 June 1759), military figure and viceroy of the New Kingdom of Granada (1740–1749). Born in Navarra, he studied at the Real Academia Militar in Barcelona and entered active military service. He reached the rank of lieutenant general of the royal armies.

PHILIP V named Eslava, brother of Rafael de Eslava, former president of the Audiencia of Santa Fe (1733–1737), the first viceroy of the reconstituted viceroyalty of New Granada in 1738. Unlike his predecessor, Jorge de VILLALONGA (1719–1724), Eslava put the colony on a firm footing. He disembarked at Cartagena de Indias in April 1740 and, because of the hostilities with England, stayed there throughout his tenure. English Admiral Edward Vernon's failed attempt to capture Cartagena (1741) made heroes of Eslava and the naval commander Blas de Lezo, a judgment widely supported by modern Colombian historiography. The pressures of wartime rule, however, took their toll; in 1742 the viceroy began to lobby the crown for reassignment. He subsequently declined the promotion to viceroy of Peru in favor of returning to Spain. Eslava served with distinction in New Granada until his appointment as captain-general of Andalusia and the arrival of his replacement, José Alonso Pizarro (1749–1753). He served as minister of war from 1754 to 1759.

Eslava apparently left no *relación de mando* (end-of-tenure report), but an important defense of his administration by Antonio de Verástegui can be found in GERMÁN COLMENARES, ed., *Relaciones e informes de los gobernantes de la Nueva Granada,* vol. 1 (1989). See also SERGIO ELÍAS ORTIZ, *Nuevo Reino de Granada: El virreynato,* pt. 1, 1719–1753, in *Historia extensa de Colombia,* vol. 4, pt. 1 (1970).

LANCE R. GRAHN

ESMERALDAS, one of Ecuador's most isolated and sparsely populated areas, visited by Francisco PIZARRO during one of his early expeditions to South America. The province is located on the northwest coast of Ecuador and shares its northern border with Colombia. Lured by stories of gold and emeralds, a few hardy Spaniards returned to the area, administered by the Audiencia of Quito. They established the city of ATACAMES, originally a native settlement, as the capital of the Atacames government, as the province was then known.

Historians hypothesize that blacks arrived in Ecuador in 1553, when a slave ship ran aground along the southern coast of the province. Alonso de Illescas, a former slave, governed a territory of free black survivors of the shipwreck so effectively that the province was almost completely outside of Spanish domination for about sixty years. Many of the shipwrecked blacks intermarried with natives. Seventeenth- and eighteenth-century migrations of blacks brought to work the mines in the Barbacoas area of Colombia swelled the black population of Esmeraldas. Today, the majority of Ecuador's black population (500,000) resides in the province and maintains traditional customs such as the MARIMBA dance and a form of oral literature known as the *décima.*

Pedro Vicente Maldonado, perhaps the province's most renowned citizen, worked as a geographer and assisted the French Geographic Mission, headed by Charles-Marie de la Condamine, during its travels throughout the province in the mid-1730s. Appointed governor and captain-general of Atacames and Esmeraldas in 1738, Maldonado had ambitious plans to build roads and a shipyard, but died in 1748 of a tropical fever before he could carry them out.

Two years before Antonio José de SUCRE ALCALÁ led his troops to victory in the battle of PICHINCHA in 1822, a group of stalwart Esmeraldas residents in Ríoverde declared independence from Spain. The movement quickly spread to neighboring towns, but this early revolutionary attempt was put down by government troops sent from Quito.

Following the murder of former president Eloy ALFARO and his supporters in 1912, Esmeraldas's black population again controlled much of the province, fending off well-armed government troops with machetes and sticks. The Concha War, essentially a skirmish protesting the second administration of President Leonidas PLAZAS GUTIÉRREZ, lasted from 1913 to 1916 and resulted in great loss of life.

More recently, the province has experienced a number of periods of growth and expansion, beginning with the export of cacao, the rubber and balsa wood boom during the two world wars, record exports of BANANAS from 1948 to 1968, and the opening of the country's largest oil refinery during the 1970s. Yet despite these

Zambo Chieftans of Esmeraldas. Mulatto noblemen in the service of King Felipe II. Oil on canvas, Adrian Sánchez Gálquez, 1599. MUSEO DE AMÉRICA, MADRID.

intermittent booms, the province remains both geographically and politically isolated from the mainstream of Ecuadorian life.

THEODORO WOLF, *Geografía y geología del Ecuador* (1892); NORMAN E. WHITTEN, JR., *Class, Kinship, and Power in an Ecuadorian Town: The Negroes of San Lorenzo* (1965); ALFREDO PAREJA Y DIEZ CANSECO, *Ecuador, la república de 1830 a nuestros días* (1979); SABINE SPEISER, *Tradiciones afro-esmeraldeñas* (1985); KAREN M. GREINER and JOSÉ G. CÁRDENAS, *Walking the Beaches of Ecuador* (1988), esp. 31–120.

KAREN M. GREINER

ESPAILLAT, ULISES FRANCISCO (*b.* 1823; *d.* 25 April 1878), president of the Dominican Republic (29 May–5 October 1876). A white *criollo* (creole) whose Spanish parents belonged to an old, well-established family, Espaillat was born in Santiago de los Caballeros, the main city in the fertile Cibao Valley in the north. A pharmacist by profession, he was an intellectual and a patriot who became involved in politics in an effort to stabilize and unify the country after the *restauración* from Spain in 1863. He served as vice president in the provisional governments of General José Antonio Salcedo (1863–1864) and General Gaspar Polanco (1864–1865).

Espaillat was an honest and liberal nationalist (author of the liberal constitution of 1858). Elected president in the spring of 1876 with the strong support of General Gregorio LUPERÓN, Espaillat appointed the best people to his cabinet (Luperón was minister of war) and stressed honesty, a balanced budget, and the end of foreign entanglements. His financial reforms were unpopular and the military, used to regular pay-offs, opposed his efforts to create a professional army. Two former presidents, Buenaventura BAEZ (1856–1857, 1865–1866, and 1868–1873), and Ignacio María González (1874–1876) organized uprisings against him. The capital, Santo Domingo, fell to supporters of González in October 1876; Espaillat took refuge in the French embassy and in December returned to his home in the Cibao.

JOSÉ GABRIEL GARCÍA, *Compendio de la historia de Santo Domingo, 1865–1880*, vol. 4 (1906); SUMNER WELLES, *Naboth's Vineyard: The Dominican Republic, 1844–1924*, vol. 1 (1966), chap. 6; FRANK MOYA PONS, *Manual de historia dominicana* (1978), pp. 384–387.

LARMAN C. WILSON

ESPEJO, ANTONIO DE (*b.* 1538?; *d.*?), Spanish explorer. From Córdoba, Spain, Espejo was a lay officer of the INQUISITION and a wealthy cattleman, with properties in Querétaro and Celaya, Mexico. In 1582–1583 he financed and led an expedition with the Franciscan friar Bernadino Beltrán to New Mexico and Arizona. The men hoped to rescue Fray Agustín Rodríguez, who had remained in New Mexico after having accompanied Francisco Sánchez Chamuscado from Mexico in 1581.

The small force left Santa Bárbara in New Biscay in 1582 and traveled north, up the Rio Grande valley. After learning of Rodríguez's death, Espejo decided to prospect for mines and went west to Acoma, Zuni, and Hopi, and then southwest into Arizona, where he found evidence of mineral deposits. After a failed mutiny at Zuni in 1583, Beltrán and the rebels went back to Santa Bárbara. Espejo, however, turned north and east from the Rio Grande, and returned to New Biscay by way of the Pecos River valley. An account of his experiences, published in 1586, contributed to a knowledge of and interest in New Spain.

JUAN GONZÁLEZ DE MENDOZA, *Historia de las cosas más notables,* (Madrid, 1586); GEORGE P. HAMMOND and AGAPITO REY, *The Rediscovery of New Mexico, 1580–1594* (1966).

RICK HENDRICKS

ESPELETA Y GALDEANO DICASTILLO Y DEL PRADO, JOSÉ MANUEL DE (*b.* June 1742; *d.* 23 November 1823), captain-general of Cuba (1785–1789), VICEROY of New Granada (1789–1797).

Born in Barcelona of Basque parentage, Espeleta came to Havana in 1779 as colonel of the Regiment of Navarre. During the AMERICAN REVOLUTION, he commanded the advance on Pensacola from Mobile (1780–1781). Later, after serving with distinction as captain-general of Cuba, he was promoted to viceroy of NEW GRANADA. An enlightened, effective administrator, Espeleta ranked among the best of New Granada's viceroys. He faced the monumental tasks of soothing the political tensions that had lingered since the COMUNERO REVOLT (1781) and reducing the colonial debt through curtailing the size of the army and eliminating unproductive programs.

He was acutely embarrassed when Antonio NARIÑO published the *Declaration of the Rights of Man and the Citizen*, obtained from his own personal library. Replaced by Pedro Mendinueta y Muzquiz at the end of his term, Espeleta returned to Spain, becoming governor of the Council of Castile and captain-general (1797–1798) and, later, councillor of state (1798), captain-general of Catalonia (1808), and viceroy of Navarre (1814–1820).

ERIC BEERMAN, "José de Espeleta," in *Revista de historia militar* (Madrid) 21, no. 43 (1977):97–118; ALLAN J. KUETHE, *Military Reform and Society in New Granada, 1773–1808* (1978); F. DE BORJA MEDINA ROJAS, *José de Espeleta, gobernador de La Mobila, 1780–1781* (1980).

ALLAN J. KUETHE

ESPERANZA COLONY, frontier settlement in Santa Fe Province, Argentina. SANTA FE was among the first Argentine provinces to attract European settlers to cultivate marginal public lands in frontier areas during the early national period. In 1856 Aarón CASTELLANOS brought 840 colonists to establish a colony at Esperanza, 20 miles from the city of Sante Fe, capital of the province. During the first four years, very little was produced due to the lack of agricultural experience of the Swiss and Northern Italian colonists, whose hardships were exacerbated by drought, the visitation of locusts, Indian attacks, and intermittent warfare between political factions over national unification. Esperanza, San Carlos, and other early colonies settled by European immigrants grew wheat, for the most part, which helped satisfy the demand for flour by the burgeoning number of immigrants arriving in Rosario and Buenos Aires. After 1862 Esperanza thrived, expanded, and became a prototype for many successful agricultural colonies which played an important role in the economic development of Argentina. The area of Santa Fe settled by agricultural colonists became known as the "pampa gringa" because of the large number of northern Italian settlers.

WILLIAM PERKINS, *Las colonias de Santa Fe: Su orígen, progreso, y actual situación* (1964); JAMES R. SCOBIE, *Revolution on the Pampas: A Social History of Argentine Wheat, 1860–1910* (1964).

GEORGETTE MAGASSY DORN

ESPÍN DE CASTRO, VILMA (*b.* 1930), Cuban revolutionary and feminist. Vilma Espín was part of the underground resistance that fought to overthrow Fulgencio BATISTA and offered intelligence assistance to Fidel CASTRO's 26 July 1952 attack on the Moncada Barracks. She studied chemical engineering at the University of Oriente, graduating in 1954, and then attended the Massachusetts Institute of Technology. She left her studies to join Castro's movement in the Sierra Maestra mountains in 1956, where she married Raúl CASTRO. After the overthrow of Batista's government, Espín rode into Havana with the triumphant revolutionary army. She became president of the new Federation of Cuban Women in 1960. In 1969 she became director of industrial development in the Ministry of Food Industries, and in 1971 she was named president of the Institute of Child Care. Espín joined the Central Committee of the Cuban Communist Party in 1965. She became a member of the Council of State in 1976 and of the Politburo of the Communist Party in 1986. She was removed as a member of the Central Committee in 1989.

K. LYNN STONER

See also **Cuba: Organizations; Cuban Revolution.**

ESPINOSA, JOSÉ MARÍA (*b.* 1796; *d.* 1883), Colombian artist. Born to an aristocratic and distinguished creole family in Bogotá, Espinosa began studying painting with artist Pablo Antonio García, but the revolution of July 1810 against Spain interrupted his training. He served in the army until independence was achieved in 1819 and then published his account of his experiences fighting under General Antonio NARIÑO from 1813 to 1816 in *Memorias de un abandero.* While on the southern campaign, he was taken prisoner and drew caricatures of fellow prisoners as well as landscapes and battle scenes.

At the conclusion of the war, Espinosa returned to Bogotá and took his position in the social and political life of the new republic. He painted many portraits of the heroes of the independence struggle, and of Bolívar in particular, in a style that marked a transition from the colonial to the republican period.

GABRIEL GIRALDO JARAMILLO, *La miniatura, la pintura y el grabado en Colombia* (1980).

BÉLGICA RODRÍGUEZ

ESPINOSA Y ESPINOSA, (JUAN) JAVIER (*b.* 20 January 1815; *d.* 4 September 1870), president of Ecuador (1868–1869). During Gabriel GARCÍA MORENO's domination of Ecuador (1861–1865, 1869–1975), Espinosa briefly served as figurehead president. The son of Quito notables, his prior government experience had been limited to a few relatively minor posts. Espinosa selected for his cabinet a group of moderate Liberals and Conservatives, a move that outraged García Moreno; he had fully expected to control Espinosa. In August 1868 a violent earthquake devastated the northern sierra, leveling the cities of Ibarra and Otavalo. Espinosa appointed García Moreno to oversee aid and reconstruction. These chores (and, critics allege, the theft of charity funds) kept the former president preoccupied for a time. However, in 1869, as Ecuador prepared to hold elections for a new presidential term, García Moreno staged a coup, removed Espinosa, and returned to office. Espinosa died in Quito.

On nineteenth-century Ecuadorian politics, see OSVALDO HURTADO's interpretive *Political Power in Ecuador,* translated by Nick D. Mills, Jr. (1985); and FRANK MAC DONALD SPINDLER's descriptive *Nineteenth Century Ecuador: An Historical Introduction* (1987). For a brief analysis of Ecuadorian political economy in the nineteenth century, consult DAVID W. SCHODT, *Ecuador: An Andean Enigma* (1987).

RONN F. PINEO

See also **Carbo y Noboa, Pedro José.**

ESPÍRITO SANTO, a small mountainous state (1993 population 2,429,000) located on the coast of Brazil, northeast of Rio de Janeiro, whose capital is Vitória. The original Indian inhabitants were the Papanazes, who were forced out by the Goaytacazes and the Tupiniquins. The first Europeans to settle in the area were a band of Portuguese who accompanied the DONATÁRIO Vasco Fernandes Coutinho in 1535. The captaincy of the state had been granted to Coutinho by the Portuguese crown to honor his services in India. He founded Vila

Velha, the first capital of the captaincy of Espírito Santo, from which the state gets its name.

The early history of Espírito Santo was marked by frequent warfare against the Indians, the English, and the French. Coutinho's successor, D. Simom de Castello-Branco, was murdered by Tamayo Indians. In 1592 the state was attacked by the English pirate Thomas Cavendish, who was successfully defeated by the Portuguese and their Indian allies. Some sugar plantations flourished in the seventeenth century, when the Dutch also invaded the captaincy.

The first gold extracted from Minas Gerais was displayed in Espírito Santo in 1695. This gold arrived via the Rio Doce as a gift to the Capitão Mor from Antônio Rodriguez Arzam. Henceforth Espírito Santo would be linked to Minas Gerais via trade, first to the goldfields of the eighteenth century and then to the iron ore deposits of the twentieth century.

The year 1830 marked the beginning of the national government's colonization efforts in the state. Immigrants who have settled in Espírito Santo include Germans, Italians, and Poles. These immigrants shaped the primarily agricultural nature of the state, whose people, nicknamed *capixabas*, cultivate coffee. In 1991 Albuino Azeredo, was the first black to become governor of the state.

ROBERT SOUTHEY, *History of Brazil*, 3 vols. (1819; repr. 1969); *Brazil A/Z: Enciclopédia alfabética em um único volume* (1988).

SHEILA L. HOOKER

See also **Mining.**

ESQUILACHES (Escuilaches), a secret, antigovernment group of students, primarily from the School of Law of the University of San Carlos in Guatemala, who mildly protested Jorge UBICO's anti-Communist massacre of 1934 and his repressive regime. From this group, led by Mario MÉNDEZ MONTENEGRO, Hiram Ordóñez, and Manuel Galich, came many of those who in the 1940s organized the resistance to the Ubico regime that led to its downfall in 1944.

Galich says the group was named after Fausto Squillace (Squillach), the early-twentieth-century Italian sociologist, but others have suggested that the group took its name from the 1766 Esquilace Revolt in Spain, a popular uprising in opposition to Bourbon attempts to change local customs and dress habits, especially as proposed by a foreign adviser, the Italian Marquis de Squillace. The group was sometimes compared to earlier Freemason groups in its conspiratorial political role.

MANUEL GALICH, *Del pánico al ataque* (1949; 2d ed. 1977), pp. 41–49.

RALPH LEE WOODWARD, JR.

ESQUIPULAS, the destination of religious pilgrims, Indian and Ladino, throughout Central America. Famous since the late sixteenth century as the site of the venerable Black Christ, the town is located in the department of Chiquimula in southeastern Guatemala. The Guatemalan sculptor Quirio Cataño (*d.* 1620) carved the dark brown statue from wood in 1594, and miracles were soon attributed to it. The beautiful church that houses the statue was founded in 1737. Those devoted to the cult of the Black Christ arrive every day of the year, but on 15 January, the day of the Christ of Esquipulas, the town is in full celebration. Pilgrims arrive to attend mass, to burn candles or incense in front of images of the saints, to obtain edible white clay tablets said to harbor curative powers, or to contemplate the Black Christ. The Black Christ of Esquipulas has long served as a religious symbol for Central America in much the same way as the Virgin of GUADALUPE has served for Mexico.

JUAN PAZ SOLÓRZANO, *Historia del Señor Crucificado de Esquipulas*, 2 vols. (1914–1916); JOSÉ LUÍS GARCÍA ACIETUNA, *Esquipulas: Reseña histórica del culto del Señor Crucificado que se venera en este santuario; origen de la imagen y las romerías; crónicas, leyendas y tradiciones: documentación histórica desde los tiempos de la colonia hasta nuestros días* (1940); VITALINO FERNÁNDEZ MARROQUÍN, *Remembranzas de Esquipulas* (1972).

MICHAEL F. FRY

ESQUIPULAS II, the 1987 accord based on a peace plan of Oscar ARIAS SÁNCHEZ, president of Costa Rica, and a proposal for a Central American parliament by Marco Vinicio CEREZO ARÉVALO, president of Guatemala. It was signed by the five Central American presidents on 7 August 1987. The provisions were designed to promote national reconciliation, cessation of hostilities, democratization, free elections, cessations of assistance to irregular forces, nonuse of national territory by irregular forces attacking other states, and international and national verification. Five mechanisms were created to implement the plan: a national commission of reconciliation in each country, an executive commission of the five foreign ministers, a Central American parliament, an International Commission of Verification and Follow-up, and yearly presidential summit commissions.

The plan was met with worldwide acclaim and earned Oscar Arias the Nobel Peace Prize, but U.S. president Ronald Reagan strongly resisted and criticized it. The U.S. government even took a variety of steps that appeared designed to undermine the peace process. Esquipulas II was supported by the United Nations specifically through the creation of the United Nations Organization in Central America (ONUCA), with the support of Canada, Spain, and West Germany. The role of the United States, Cuba, and the Soviet Union in the region was reduced.

In the months immediately after the signing of the agreement, some initial advances were made. A meeting between the Guatemalan government and the URNG (a guerrilla group) was held, a meeting between

Salvadoran president José Napoleón DUARTE and the FMLN-FDR (an opposition party and guerrilla group coalition) took place, and contacts between the Sandinista government in Nicaragua and the contras were made.

Esquipulas II contributed to the holding of democratic elections in El Salvador, Guatemala, Honduras, and Nicaragua and to ending the armed hostilities in Nicaragua (1990) and El Salvador (1992).

MARCO VINICIO CEREZO ARÉVALO, "Esquipulas II, tres años después," in *Panorama centroamericano (Pensamiento y acción)* no. 19 (1990): 3–11; FRANCISCO ROJAS ARAVENA, Ponencia presentada a seminario *Esquipulas: El camino de la paz* (Guatemala, 1990); JOHN A. BOOTH and THOMAS W. WALKER, *Understanding Central America*, 2nd ed. (1993); HOWARD H. LENTNER, *State Formation in Central America: The Struggle for Autonomy, Development, and Democracy* (1993).

DAVID CAREY, JR.

See also **Contadora**

ESQUIÚ, MAMERTO (*b.* 11 May 1826; *d.* 10 January 1883), Argentine Catholic spokesman and bishop of Córdoba. The son of a devout family of farmers in Callesita, Catamarca Province, at the age of ten he entered the FRANCISCAN order. He taught at the Franciscan convent school in Catamarca and for much of his career was closely associated with Catholic educational institutions. Also a noted preacher, he first gained national renown for a sermon he delivered on the occasion of the swearing of allegiance to the 1853 Constitution. Esquiú criticized the liberalism that permeated many provisions of the Constitution, but he called on Argentines to obey it in a spirit of submission to the constituted authorities.

Esquiú at various times was a member of deliberative assemblies in his native province, even as he became increasingly disillusioned with the factional wrangling and civil warfare that afflicted the country as a whole. He spent the years 1862–1875 in Bolivia (except for one brief trip to Peru and Ecuador), where he again earned prominence as a Catholic educator and publicist. For the final years of his life he was mainly in Argentina, despite his dismay over political and cultural trends there. Nevertheless, in view of his prestige among Argentine Catholics and his reputation as "orator of the Constitution," Esquiú was nominated as archbishop of Buenos Aires (which he refused) and bishop of Córdoba (which he reluctantly accepted). From the time he took over the Córdoba diocese in January 1881 until his death, he set an example of apostolic simplicity and tireless energy in service to his flock. Though he was never formally canonized, his biography appears in a series of "Popular Lives of Saints" published in 1977. He died in Suncho, Catamarca province.

JOHN J. KENNEDY, *Catholicism, Nationalism, and Democracy in Argentina* (1958), pp. 91–97; DAVID PEÑA, *La materia religiosa en la política argentina* (1960), pp. 181–210; JUAN ALBERTO CORTÉS, *Fray Mamerto Esquiú* (1977).

DAVID BUSHNELL

ESQUIVEL, MANUEL AMADEO (*b.* 2 May 1940), prime minister of Belize (1984–1989). Born in Belize City, Esquivel was educated at the Jesuit-run St. John's College. He received a bachelor's degree in physics from Loyola University of New Orleans and did postgraduate work at New York University. Returning to Belize in the early 1970s, he taught at St. John's until 1984.

A founding member of the UDP, an alliance of three former opposition parties, he served as party chairman from 1976 to 1982 and party leader after 1982. After two terms on the Belize City Council (1974–1980) he was appointed to the Belize Senate in 1979. In 1984 the United Democratic Party (UDP), led by Esquivel, won a landslide victory in national elections, capturing twenty-one of twenty-eight seats in the House of Representatives. With this majority, Esquivel became Belize's second prime minister.

During a five-year administration, in which he also served as minister of finance and defense, Esquivel's sound fiscal management and encouragement of foreign investment in tourism, agriculture, and manufacturing helped invigorate the economy. He achieved balance of payments surpluses for four consecutive years and left foreign exchange reserves at record levels. Despite these economic successes, the UDP was accused of selling out the country to foreign investors. A split in party ranks in 1989, allegations of ministerial corruption, and a series of contested party caucuses contributed to the party's narrow loss in the elections of 1989.

Just four years later, on 30 June 1993, in a stunning upset, Esquivel led his United Democratic Party to a narrow victory in the general elections. The UDP captured sixteen of twenty-nine seats in the new parliament. On 3 July 1993, Esquivel took the oath of office and began his second term as prime minister. Esquivel began to implement some of his campaign promises including free education for Belizeans from primary school to university level and an investigation into alleged registration of illegal immigrants. He faced a gauntlet of difficult problems including high unemployment and a rising tide of urban violence brought on by the drug trade.

"The Comet of Belize, Manuel Esquivel," in *New York Times Biographical Service* 15, no. 12 (1984): 1589–1590; PERCY C. HINTZEN and W. MARVIN WILL, "Esquivel, Manuel," in *Biographical Dictionary of Latin American and Caribbean Political Leaders* (1988), pp. 147–148; "1989/90 Budget Speech Presented by the Prime Minister and Minister of Finance and Defense, Rt. Hon. Manuel Esquivel," 9 March 1989 (pamphlet in the National Archives, 26–28 Unity Blvd., Belmopan, Belize).

BRIAN E. COUTTS

See also **Price, George.**

ESTADO DA INDIA. *See* **Portuguese Trade and International Relations.**

ESTADO NOVO (New State), Brazil's fascist-inspired dictatorship. On 10 November 1937, President Getúlio VARGAS overthrew the constitutional government that he had helped to establish in 1934, replacing it with a totalitarian regime that would continue in power until 1945. The coup d'état was justified as an emergency measure prompted by fear of class warfare and a Communist takeover in Brazil. This threat was trumped up, however, as was the document, the so-called COHEN PLAN, that Vargas and his supporters brought forth as evidence for the Communist plot. Created by the Integralists, the Cohen Plan was crafted to play on anti-Semitism, xenophobia, and fear of communism, all of which flourished in Depression-era Brazil.

The Estado Novo constitution allowed for both executive and legislative branches, but Vargas actually ruled by decree. Political parties were banned, as were, by extension, elections, the Congress, and politics. Vargas and his advisers, many of them supporters of the Revolution of 1930 from Vargas's home state of Rio Grande do Sul, created a highly centralized state whose main goal was domestic industrialization. Vargas himself was a populist and successfully co-opted much of the working class by placing all labor unions under a single national umbrella. These antidemocratic moves were accepted by an urban industrial class that found its wages, and education, and health standards rising rapidly.

Although based on European fascist models, the Estado Novo did not have an absolute or clear ideology. After flirting economically and politically with the Axis Powers, Brazil linked itself to the United States in 1939, eventually joining the Allies in World War II and sending troops to Italy in 1942. The defeat of FASCISM, and the increasing inability of the regime to pay for the benefits it had granted to the urban working class, led the armed forces to overthrow Vargas and the Estado Novo in October 1945. On December 2, seven years after the establishment of the Estado Novo and fifteen years after Vargas first took national power, democratic rule returned to Brazil.

THOMAS SKIDMORE, *Politics in Brazil, 1930–1964: An Experiment in Democracy* (1967), esp. pp. 3–53; ROBERT LEVINE, *The Vargas Regime: The Critical Years, 1934–1938* (1970); EDGARD CARONE, *O Estado Novo (1937–1945)* (1988).

JEFFREY LESSER

ESTANCIA (livestock ranch), the most important socioeconomic institution on the PAMPA. GAUCHOS considered the pampa's resources to be in the public domain, available to all. But *estancias* developed during the eighteenth century, when large ranchers began to extend their control over land, water, and cattle. Larger ranches traditionally had a central ranch house, usually topped by a tower (*mirador*) from which to spot Indian raiders. A modest bunkhouse and kitchen served the workers. Ranchers divided their ranges into many units, each under the charge of a manager.

By the nineteenth century, large, extensive *estancias* dominated the countryside. Wealthy ranchers built veritable castles that dominated their rural estates. Small ranchers often had to rent their land. Because of the vast distances between towns on the plains, many ranches included a PULPERÍA, a combination general store and tavern.

The *estancia* and *pulpería* were the most important institutions in the rural Río de la Plata. In economic terms, the ranches provided employment for gauchos and generated great wealth from livestock and agriculture. The *estancia* had political importance because ranch owners and managers often served as justices of the peace and dominated local politics. In cultural terms, ranches served as important settings for movies, novels, and poetry in the gauchesque genre.

JONATHAN C. BROWN, *A Socioeconomic History of Argentina* (1979), pp. 123–145; RICHARD W. SLATTA, *Gauchos and the Vanishing Frontier* (1983), pp. 69–72.

RICHARD W. SLATTA

ESTANCO, ESTANQUERO. The *estanco,* or *estanco de tabacos,* was the state tobacco monopoly introduced into Spanish America in the second half of the eighteenth century, starting with Peru in 1752. It was easily the most profitable of the imperial monopolies. In 1824 in newly independent Chile, the *estanco* was farmed out to the Valparaíso trading house of Portales, Cea, and Company, which agreed to assume responsiblity for a £1 million loan secured in London in 1822 by the Bernardo O'HIGGINS government. When payments on the loan were not met, the government rescinded the contract in 1826, to the considerable resentment of Diego PORTALES, a partner in the trading house. Portales and several like-minded associates (some connected with the *estanco* contract) formed a political group that demanded a stronger government and an end to the liberal approach favored by the regimes of the 1820s. The *estanqueros,* as these politicians became known, took a leading role in the Conservative capture of power in 1829–1830, following which Portales became the most powerful figure in Chile.

SIMON COLLIER

ESTEBAN (Estevan; *d.* May 1539), guide/explorer of New Spain. Esteban, a black Arab from the Atlantic coast of Morocco, traveled across Florida, Texas, and northern Mexico from 1527 until 1536 with his owner and Andrés Dorantes, Alvar Núñez CABEZA DE VACA, and Castillo Maldonado, all fellow survivors of Pánfilo de Narváez's ill-fated expedition to Florida. He was then purchased by the viceroy of New Spain, Antonio de MENDOZA, who was eager to take advantage of his knowledge of the largely uncharted north country. In 1539, Esteban guided Franciscan friar Marcos de NIZA in his search for the SEVEN CITIES OF CÍBOLA. The travelers departed from San Miguel de Culiacán in Sinaloa, Mexico, where they had been accompanied by Francisco Vásquez de CORONADO, governor of the province of New Galicia. On the journey north into Sonora, Arizona, and New Mexico, Esteban and a number of Indian allies ranged far ahead of Niza, sending back reports of their progress. Esteban apparently angered the PUEBLO INDIANS by demanding women and turquoise. He was killed at Hawikuh, the southernmost of the six Zuni pueblos.

Niza's report of his travels with Esteban helped persuade Vásquez de Coronado to launch his 1540 expedition to find the great cities and untold riches implied in Niza's descriptions. Among the Zunis, Esteban is known as an ogre kachina, or evil spirit.

CYCLONE COVEY, *Cabeza de Vaca's Adventures in the Unknown Interior of America* (1983); CLEVE HALLENBECK, *The Journey of Fray Marcos de Niza* (1987).

RICK HENDRICKS

See also **Explorers.**

ESTIGARRIBIA, ANTONIO DE LA CRUZ (mid-1800s), Paraguayan soldier. When the WAR OF THE TRIPLE ALLIANCE began in 1864, Estigarribia was one of the most highly respected officers in the Paraguayan army. He had been an adviser to war minister Francisco Solano LÓPEZ during the 1859 mediation of a dispute between Buenos Aires and the Argentine Confederation, and, thanks to Solano López's sponsorship, was promoted to full colonel and given command of a major Paraguayan column.

In mid-1865, Estigarribia and his force crossed the Alto Paraná into Brazil as part of a coordinated attack on Corrientes and Río Grande do Sul. As Estigarribia's troops moved south, they destroyed town after town in Brazil, but they also began to lose touch with their own supply bases. After taking the town of São Borja, Estigarribia split up his forces, sending Major Pedro Duarte and 2,500 men down the right bank of the Río Uruguay while he continued with the main body of 8,000 men down the left bank to the town of Uruguaiana. In early August, he occupied the town and awaited news from Duarte. The news was not good: on 17 August Duarte's entire command was obliterated in an Allied attack, leaving Uruguaiana surrounded and Estigarribia without much chance of resupply.

The Paraguayan colonel debated for some time what his next move might be. He was completely cut off and without clear instructions from López. Finally, on 18 September, he agreed to generous Allied terms for surrender, which stipulated that the rank and file would be treated as prisoners of war and that his officers would be allowed to take up residence in any of the Allied nations but not to return to Paraguay.

Estigarribia, whose action was bitterly denounced by López, chose to go to Rio de Janeiro. He then dropped from sight except for a brief, pathetic moment in March 1869, when he petitioned the Brazilian emperor to offer his services as a guide for the armies then advancing into the Cordillera of central Paraguay.

CHARLES J. KILINSKI, *Independence or Death! The Story of the Paraguayan War* (1965), pp. 100–108; LEANDRO APONTE B., *Hombres, armas y batallas* (1971), pp. 89–91.

THOMAS L. WHIGHAM

ESTIGARRIBIA, JOSÉ FÉLIX (*b.* 21 February 1888; *d.* 5 September 1940), president of Paraguay (1940) and soldier. Born at Caraguatay, Estigarribia came from a poor but distinguished family of Basque extraction. His ancestors included Colonel Antonio de la Cruz ESTIGA-

José Félix Estigarribia. ORGANIZATION OF AMERICAN STATES.

RRIBIA, who had surrendered his army at Uruguaiana during the WAR OF THE TRIPLE ALLIANCE.

Young José Félix passed his early years in the countryside, and there was reason to think he might choose farming as a career. In 1903 he enrolled in the Agricultural School at Trinidad and then moved on to attend the Colegio Nacional at Asunción. The revolutions of the first decade of the new century, however, propelled Estigarribia into the ranks of the army. In 1911, he was sent to Chile for further military training, from which he returned two years later, becoming a first lieutenant in 1914. Estigarribia remained loyal to the government during the disturbances of 1921–1922, a fact that provisional president Eusebio AYALA never forgot. As a partial reward, the young captain was sent to France for further military study under Marshal Foch. When he returned to Paraguay in 1927, he became chief of the general staff.

During Estigarribia's absence, the dispute with Bolivia over the CHACO REGION had provoked a series of ugly incidents. These, in turn, developed into a full-scale war by 1932. In August of that year Estigarribia was given command of 15,000 men, with which he forged a powerful fighting force.

Estigarribia gained a legendary status in the Chaco. Though his troops were regularly outnumbered by the Bolivians, still they boasted certain advantages over their counterparts from the Altiplano: they were closer to home bases, they were more accustomed to the terrain and climate, and, in Estigarribia, they had a commander who had a clear goal, who was a master tactician, and who understood his men. Over the next three years, Colonel Estigarribia went from victory to victory fighting on some of the roughest land in South America. After his exhausted troops gained the foothills of the Andes in 1935, a truce was signed. It was affirmed three years later in a boundary treaty generally favorable to Paraguay.

Meanwhile, President Eusebio Ayala had been removed by restive army officers and young radicals. Ayala's ally Estigarribia went on an extended tour abroad, teaching for a time at the Montevideo War College. In 1938 he became ambassador to Washington, and in 1939, though still in the United States, he ran unopposed as the Liberal candidate for president. When he returned for his inauguration at Asunción, however, Estigarribia discovered that radicals were demanding more far-reaching action than the Liberal program called for. Compromising, the new president proposed a semiauthoritarian constitution that had socialist, democratic, and fascist elements. Despite some inner doubts as to the wisdom of this document, Estigarribia ruled under it as dictator. Two months after its ratification, he died in an airplane crash outside Asunción. By executive decree, the Chaco hero was posthumously promoted to field marshal.

HARRIS G. WARREN, "Political Aspects of the Paraguayan Revolution, 1936–1940," *Hispanic American Historical Review* 30 (February 1950): 2–25; PABLO MAX YNSFRÁN, ed., *The Epic of the Chaco: Marshal Estigarribia's Memoirs of the Chaco War, 1932–1935* (1950); MICHAEL GROW, *The Good Neighbor Policy and Authoritarianism in Paraguay* (1981), esp. pp. 50–58.

THOMAS L. WHIGHAM

ESTIMÉ, DUMARSAIS (*b.* 1900; *d.* 20 July 1953), president of Haiti (1946–1950). A native of Verrettes and a former mathematics teacher at the Lycée Pétion, Estimé was a member of the National Assembly and secretary of education before becoming president. He came to power on 16 August 1946 with the support of elite blacks (members of the Noiriste Party) who had been excluded from government under the regime of Élie LESCOT.

Lasting until 10 May 1950, Estimé's government also drew support initially from young radicals and Communists who looked forward to a social revolution that would benefit Haiti's black masses, both workers and peasants. Although it never went far enough to satisfy leftist desires, the government did make use of its popular mandate to carry out genuine reforms. In addition to granting greater liberty of speech and the press, Estimé established a populist and nationalist program that embraced inclusion of blacks in the state patronage system; support for unions; social legislation recognizing workers' rights; public education; attempts to curb U.S. economic control of the country, in part by breaking up the STANDARD FRUIT Company's monopoly on banana production; and the agreement with the Export-Import Bank to finance the Artibonite Valley irrigation project. Estimé also encouraged development of Haiti's tourist industry by granting credits to the hotel business and investing millions of dollars in an international fair celebrating the founding of Port-au-Prince (1949). He was exiled to the United States and died in New York City.

RAYFORD W. LOGAN, *Haiti and the Dominican Republic* (1968); DAVID NICHOLLS, *From Dessalines to Duvalier: Race, Colour and National Independence in Haiti* (1979), and "Haiti Since 1930," in *The Cambridge History of Latin America*, vol. 7, edited by Leslie Bethell (1990), pp. 545–577.

PAMELA MURRAY

ESTÍPITE. *See* **Churrigueresque.**

ESTRADA, CARLOS (*b.* 15 September 1909; *d.* 7 May 1970), Uruguayan composer, conductor, and teacher. Born in Montevideo, Estrada studied there with Adelina Pérez Montero (piano), Carlos Correa Luna (violin), Father Pedro Ochoa (Gregorian chant), and Manuel Fernández Espiro (harmony, counterpoint, and composition). In 1938 he traveled to Paris and attended classes at the National Conservatory given by Jean-Jules Aimable Roger-Ducasse and Henri Busser (composition), Noel Gallon (counterpoint and fugue), and Albert

Wolff, Paul Paray, and Philippe Gaubert (conducting). Contrary to the prevailing Uruguayan nationalist style, Estrada utilized modal harmonic systems and neoclassical forms, with a strong influence, initially, from the French school. In 1936 he founded the Orquesta de Cámara de Montevideo.

In the early 1940s Estrada began to work in the major forms, composing the oratorio *Daniel* (1942) and incidental music for Paul Claudel's play *L'Annonce faite à Marie* (1943). He premiered and conducted his first symphony in Paris in 1951, and his string quartet no. 1, a SODRE Composition First Award, was premiered at the First Latin American Music Festival of Montevideo in 1957.

Estrada was director and professor of harmony and composition at the National Conservatory of Montevideo (1953–1968) and also taught at the Institute of Musicology (University of Montevideo School of Humanities). He founded the Municipal Symphony Orchestra in 1959 and conducted it until 1970; he also conducted several European orchestras. The French government honored Estrada by making him Officier de l'Académie and Chevalier des Arts et Lettres. He died in Montevideo.

Composers of the Americas, vol. 16 (1970); JOHN VINTON, ed., *Dictionary of Contemporary Music* (1974); *New Grove Dictionary of Music and Musicians*, vol. 6 (1980); SUSANA SALGADO, *Breve historia de la música culta en el Uruguay*, 2d ed. (1980).

SUSANA SALGADO

ESTRADA, JOSÉ DOLORES (*b.* 16 March 1792; *d.* 12 August 1869), Nicaraguan general and hero of San Jacinto. Born in Nandaime to an agricultural family descended from the Gonzalo de Sandoval group of conquistadores, Estrada showed an affinity for the military at an early age. During the independence movement, Estrada accompanied Argüello but achieved real fame only decades later, when he led a dramatic victory against the filibuster forces of William WALKER and Byron Cole. The battle of San Jacinto (14 September 1856) was fought on an old hacienda near Tipitapa. There 160 men led by Estrada barricaded themselves in the house and fought the North Americans bravely. Their successful effort convinced other Central Americans that Walker could indeed be beaten, and Estrada and his forces quickly became symbols of nationalism and patriotism.

ILDEFONSO PALMA MARTÍNEZ, *La guerra nacional* (1956); FRANCISCO PÉREZ ESTRADA, *José Dolores Estrada: Héroe nacional de Nicaragua* (1970); MARCO ANTONIO SOTO V., *La guerra nacional de Centroamérica*, 2d ed. (1975); ERNESTO DE LA TORRE VILLAR, ed., *La batalla de San Jacinto, Nicaragua, 1856* (1987).

KAREN RACINE

ESTRADA, JOSÉ MANUEL (*b.* 1842; *d.* 1894), Argentine writer, law professor, director of the Argentine Colegio Nacional and congressman. As a member of the so-called Generation of 1880, Estrada typifies the polyfaceted man of letters in Argentine public and intellectual life in Buenos Aires, where he was born. In addition to serving as rector of the Colegio Nacional, an institution that has traditionally provided secondary-school training to the brightest of the nation's youth, Estrada played an energetic role in the burgeoning area of cultural journalism. He was the founding editor of the *Revista Argentina*, an excellent example of the sort of comprehensive cultural publications of the period that contributed to a sense of sophisticated nationalism by serving as a forum for the exchange of ideas among privileged literati, most of whom had ties to the economic boom of the late nineteenth century. This exchange was abetted by the way in which such publications functioned as a channel for the intensive Western intellectual production of the day.

Estrada is notable for his identification with a conservative Catholicism that was opposed to what he viewed as an immoral and tyrannical capitalist expansion at the expense of traditional values. Estrada's antiliberalism is typified by his early *El catolicismo y la democracia* (1862) and in his work as leader of the high orthodox Unión Católica. His *Lecciones sobre la historia de la República Argentina* (1868), based on his lectures as a law professor, constitute a notable example of his overarching conservative Catholic point of view and typify the sort of grandiloquent rhetoric customarily found in militant writings of those who sought to shape national consciousness. Estrada died in Asunción.

ROBERTO F. GIUSTI, "Preliminary Study," in José Manuel Estrada, *Antología* (1941); ALBERTO CASAL CASTEL, *La actualidad de José Manuel Estrada* (1942).

DAVID WILLIAM FOSTER

ESTRADA, JOSÉ MARÍA. (*d.* 13 August 1856), acting president (1854) and president (1855–1856) of Nicaragua. President Fruto CHAMORRO turned over the presidency to José María Estrada on 27 May 1854 in order to give full attention to leading the Legitimist (Conservative) army against the Democratic (Liberal) insurgents headed by Máximo JEREZ. Estrada had earlier served as foreign minister and as a member of the Assembly. After Chamorro died (12 March 1855), the Assembly authorized Estrada to continue in office. When Granada fell to William WALKER, Estrada opposed the Walker-backed government of Patricio RIVAS, repudiating the treaty of 23 October 1855. He established a government first at Masaya, then at Somotillo, and later at Matagalpa, allying himself with the conservative governments of the other Central American states against Walker in the NATIONAL WAR. Democratic guerrillas attacked and killed Estrada at El Ocotal.

FEDERICO HERNÁNDEZ DE LEÓN, *El libro de las efemérides: Capítulos de la historia de la América Central*, vol. 3 (1930), pp. 283–287; ANDRÉS VEGA BOLAÑOS, *Gobernantes de Nicaragua: Notas y documentos* (1944), pp. 194–222; JOSÉ DOLORES GÁMEZ, *Hi-*

storia de Nicaragua desde los tiempos prehistóricos hasta 1860, en sus relaciones con España, México y Centro-América (1975); E. BRADFORD BURNS, *Patriarch and Folk: The Emergence of Nicaragua, 1798–1858* (1991).

RALPH LEE WOODWARD, JR.

ESTRADA, JOSÉ MARÍA (*b.* 1810?; *d.* 1862?), Mexican painter. Born in Guadalajara, Estrada signed his paintings sometimes as José María Estrada and sometimes as José María Zepeda de Estrada, which has caused some confusion about his work. He studied under José María Uriarte, director of painting at the Academy of Guadalajara, who had received his education at the Academy of Mexico City. Estrada did not, however, follow the path of academic painters. Specializing in portraits, he painted in a style typical of his native state of Jalisco. His portraits are enchanting and are characterized by meticulous detail, with subjects in sober dress, their faces in three-quarter position, and their hands always holding a fruit, a kerchief, or a fan. Estrada used unadorned backgrounds to emphasize his subjects, and his colors tended toward the cool end of the spectrum. Unlike his adult subjects, he portrayed children full-bodied.

Estrada's compositional style was typical of popular painters who paint what they know, as opposed to painting what "should be seen" according to the rules of illusionist perspective imposed in the academies. He also painted dead children, a custom common in traditional painting. Estrada died in Guadalajara.

LEOPOLDO ORENDAÍN, *José María Zepeda Estrada* (1950) and *Apundes sobre la pintura tapatía* (1967); JOSÉ GUADALUPE ZUNO, *José María Estrada* (1957).

ESTHER ACEVEDO

ESTRADA, JUAN JOSÉ (*b.* 1865; *d.* 1947), provisional president of Nicaragua (29 August 1910–9 May 1911). Estrada, governor of the Caribbean department of Mosquitia, launched an uprising against President José Santos ZELAYA, whose government fell in 1909. He continued the revolt against Zelaya's successor, José Madriz, and in 1910 established a provisional government at BLUEFIELDS, where he received assistance from U.S. marines. Madriz turned over power to Estrada's brother, José Dolores ESTRADA, on 20 August 1910, and Juan José Estrada formally became provisional president on 29 August. A new Constituent Assembly unanimously elected him for a two-year term on 31 December 1910, but the real power rested with General Luis Mena, who commanded the military. Under pressure, Estrada resigned on 9 May 1911, turning power over to his vice president, Adolfo DÍAZ.

JOSÉ JOAQUÍN MORALES, *De la historia de Nicaragua de 1889–1913* (1963); CHARLES E. FRAZIER, *The Dawn of Nationalism and Its Consequences in Nicaragua* (1972).

RALPH LEE WOODWARD, JR.

ESTRADA CABRERA, MANUEL (*b.* 21 November 1857; *d.* 24 September 1924), president of Guatemala (1898–1920). In 1898 Estrada Cabrera secured the Guatemalan presidency following the assassination of his protector and predecessor, President José María REYNA BARRIOS. A Quetzaltenango lawyer of limited ability and humble parentage, Estrada Cabrera has been described as one of the strangest personalities who ever raised himself to great power. Even though he served the Reyna Barrios administration (1892–1898) as minister of the interior and justice and first designate (vice president), upon his ascendency to the presidency as the constitutionally recognized presidential successor, Estrada Cabrera was largely regarded as an undistinguished rural politician. The violence of Reyna Barrios's assassination, however, proved to be a fitting introduction to Estrada Cabrera's twenty-two-year reign of terror, which still ranks as the longest uninterrupted rule in Central American history. The president's renowned tendencies toward cruelty and corruption, combined with his legendary resourcefulness and invulnerability undoubtedly contributed to the longevity of his administration.

Like the father of Guatemalan liberalism, the revered Justo Rufino BARRIOS (1873–1885), Estrada Cabrera was

Manuel Estrada Cabrera. LIBRARY OF CONGRESS.

a typical Latin American CAUDILLO. Careful to cultivate the support of the coffee elite and dedicated to the Positivist watchwords of "order" and "progress," the dictator guided Guatemala on a course common in Latin America in the latter half of the nineteenth century. Throughout his presidency, Estrada Cabrera fostered the creation of a society typified by large landed estates, forced labor, an export-oriented economy, and highly centralized political power. Latin American caudillos rarely delegated political authority to subordinates and Estrada Cabrera was no exception to this rule. According to Dana G. Munro, a U.S. State Department representative in the first quarter of the twentieth century, the dictator "had no friends or personal followers except the army officers and government officials who supported his regime" and these only "for the sake of the license and graft" that he permitted.

During the Estrada Cabrera presidency, the exploitative and exclusive nature of Guatemalan society became increasingly obvious. Instead of real development, what emerged was a landed oligarchy, engaged primarily in the production of coffee, that utilized its economic might to construct a state that protected its dominant social and political status. Although economic growth and modernization proceeded at a moderate pace during the first two decades of the twentieth century, political and social problems associated with increased economic activity, lack of development, and the altered fabric of Guatemalan society arose. Significant among these were the rapid growth of the capital's middle class, the emergence of a significant labor element, and a vocal and politically conscious student population, all of which were refused a forum for political expression, not to mention an equitable share in the profits of the republic's lucrative coffee industry. The cumulative effect of these forces, augmented by the extremely repressive nature of Estrada Cabrera's administration, presented the republic with a rare opportunity to implement real and significant reform.

In late 1917 and 1918 general disenchantment with the political and economic status quo of the Estrada Cabrera regime was accelerated by a series of devastating earthquakes that left much of Guatemala City in rubble. Estrada Cabrera's apathetic response to the earthquakes, coupled with the student protests of the same years, aroused a heretofore unknown reaction in the capital. Awakened by the students' commitment to reform, other sectors of society, notably the Roman Catholic church, an incipient urban middle class, organized labor, and eventually the military and the landed elite, pledged their support to a new unified political coalition, the Unionist Party, to oppose the dictator. By April 1920, the president's inability to adapt to the republic's changing political and social conditions and the coalition's commitment to the dictator's unconditional surrender, prompted the Guatemalan National Assembly to impeach a physically weakened and politically alienated Manuel Estrada Cabrera.

DANA G. MUNRO, *Intervention and Dollar Diplomacy in the Caribbean, 1900–1921*, (1964); CHESTER LLOYD JONES, *Guatemala: Past and Present* (1966); RAFAEL ARÉVALO MARTÍNEZ, *¡Ecce Pericles! La tiranía de Manuel Estrada Cabrera en Guatemala*, 3d ed. (1983); DAVID MC CREERY, "Debt Servitude in Rural Guatemala, 1876–1936," in *Hispanic American Historical Review* 63 (1983): 735–759; JIM HANDY, *Gift of the Devil: A History of Guatemala* (1984); RALPH LEE WOODWARD, JR., *Central America: A Nation Divided* (1985); MARY CATHERINE RENDON, "Manuel Estrada Cabrera, Guatemalan President, 1898–1920" (Ph.D. diss., Oxford Univ., 1988); WADE KIT, "Precursor of Change: Failed Reform and the Guatemalan Coffee Elite, 1918–1926" (Master's thesis, Univ. of Saskatchewan, 1989).

WADE A. KIT

ESTRADA PALMA, TOMÁS (*b.* 9 July 1835; *d.* 4 November 1908), Cuban patriot and politician, president of Cuba (1902–1906). Born in Bayamo, Tomás Estrada Palma grew up in Oriente, the center of Cuba's protracted struggle for independence. He was sent by his family to study in Havana and then pursued a law degree at the University of Seville in Spain. A family crisis required Estrada to return home and assume administration of the family estate before he had finished his studies; nevertheless, he retained his passionate belief in the value of education and tried to set up rural schools for the benefit of his community.

As a young and progressive man, Estrada Palma participated in the TEN YEARS' WAR (1868–1878), joining the rebels in 1868 and quickly rising to the rank of general. In 1876 Estrada was elected president of the Republic in Arms but fell prisoner to the Spanish the following year. He was transported to Spain and released in 1878, when the PACT OF ZANJÓN ended the war. Estrada then moved to Paris, where he began a discussion group for political exiles and took an interest in the intellectual life of Europe.

Estrada Palma left Europe for America in the late 1880s, passing through New York, where he visited José MARTÍ, and continuing on to Central America. He settled in Honduras, where he met and married Genoveva Guardiola, the daughter of the Honduran president. At the insistence of Martí, Estrada moved his family to New York, where the two expatriates formed the Cuban Revolutionary Party in 1892. Following Martí's death in battle in 1895, Estrada Palma reluctantly accepted the title of provisional president of Cuba after the defeat of Spain. He was elected president in his own right in Cuba's first independent election for the office, held in 1902.

A decent, honest, and hardworking man, Estrada Palma's accomplishments as president were manifold: expanded public education; a treaty of reciprocity with the United States; the completion of a national railroad; and the repayment of debts and reconstruction after a decade of war. His reputation, however, has suffered from his preference that the island remain a protectorate of the United States rather than a fully independent state.

Estrada's decision to employ government resources to support his reelection efforts in 1905 prompted the opposition Liberal Party to boycott the proceedings. In the ensuing crisis, Estrada invited in a U.S. military force, which remained on the island from 1906 until 1909. Estrada resigned in 1906 and returned to his humble family plot.

PÁNFILO D. CAMACHO, *Estrada Palma, el gobernante honrado* (1938); FERMÍN PERAZA SARAUSA, *Diccionario biográfico cubano*, vol. 14 (1968); ALLAN REED MILLETT, *The Politics of Intervention: The Military Occupation of Cuba, 1906–1909* (1968); LUIS AGUILAR, *Cuba 1933: Prologue to Revolution* (1972); and LOUIS A. PÉREZ, JR., *Cuba Under the Platt Amendment, 1902–1934* (1986).

KAREN RACINE

ESTRADA DOCTRINE, precept formulated in a 27 September 1930 note sent by Mexican foreign minister Genaro Estrada to Mexican diplomatic representatives throughout the world. Recent revolutions in Argentina, Bolivia, Peru, and Central America had presented the Mexican government with the question of recognizing a number of de facto regimes. Given Mexico's problems in obtaining diplomatic recognition from the United States and other powers during its own revolutionary period, it was understandable that the Mexican government would be sympathetic to the plight of other revolutionary governments. Accordingly, Estrada asserted that Mexico would "not make any declarations regarding recognition because it considers that such a policy is an insulting practice which, in addition to offending the sovereignty of other nations, places them in a position of having their internal affairs judged by other governments."

The Estrada Doctrine was received enthusiastically by many Latin Americans who felt that the region had been unfairly discriminated against by the great powers through the selective application of de jure recognition. With the exception of the Franco regime in Spain, Mexico has been remarkably consistent over the years in adhering to the Estrada Doctrine.

JOHN W. F. DULLES, *Yesterday in Mexico: A Chronicle of the Revolution, 1919–1936* (1961), esp. pp. 497–498; *Enciclopedia de México*, edited by JOSÉ ROGELIO ÁLVAREZ (1987), esp. vol. 5, p. 2,596.

RICHARD V. SALISBURY

ETCHEPAREBORDA, ROBERTO (*b.* 19 December 1923; *d.* 10 April 1985), Argentine historian, educator, and diplomat. Born in Milan, Italy, where his father was serving as an Argentine diplomat, Etchepareborda was educated in Europe and Argentina. As a prominent figure of the Radical Party, he was a member of the City Council of Buenos Aires (1958–1962), over which he later presided. In 1962 President Arturo FRONDIZI, a short time before he was deposed by a military coup, appointed Etchepareborda his foreign minister. From 1962 to 1964 Etchepareborda served as Argentina's ambassador to India. He was also director of the National Archives and a member of the Argentine Academy of History, as well as of similar academies in other American countries and in Spain. He was professor (1966–1971) and president (1971–1973) of the National University of the South in Bahía Blanca, Argentina, and in the 1970s and 1980s he taught at the University of North Carolina in Chapel Hill, and at the School of Advanced International Studies of Johns Hopkins University, and American University, both in Washington, D.C. In 1974 he held a Wilson Fellowship at the Woodrow Wilson International Center for Scholars, also in Washington. From 1979 to 1984 he was director of the Department of Cultural Affairs of the Organization of American States. An authority on Argentine political and diplomatic history, his most important works are: *Hipólito Yrigoyen: Pueblo y gobierno*, a twelve-volume compilation (1956); *Tres revoluciones: 1890, 1893, 1905* (1968), for which he received the National Book Award in 1970; *Rosas: Controvertida historiografía* (1972); and *Zeballos y la política exterior argentina* (1982). From 1981 until his death he was a contributing editor of the *Handbook of Latin American Studies*.

CELSO RODRÍGUEZ

EUCEDA, MAXIMILIANO (*b.* 1891; *d.* 1987), Honduran portrait painter. Born in Caridad, Honduras, near Tegucigalpa, Euceda, like other members of Honduras's Generation of '20, studied art in Spain, where he was especially influenced by the naturalism and realism of Romero de Torres. Euceda returned to Honduras in 1927, and gave art lessons until 1940, when he joined the staff of the newly formed Escuela Nacional de Bellas Artes in Tegucigalpa, where he taught for several decades thereafter. He and Carlos ZÚÑIGA FIGUEROA were especially important in training the generation of Honduran painters that emerged in the 1940s.

J. EVARISTO LÓPEZ R. and LONGINO BECERRA, *Honduras: 40 pintores* (1989).

RALPH LEE WOODWARD, JR.

EXALTADOS, advocates of republicanism, federalism, and political egalitarianism in an important political movement in Brazil during the late 1820s and the 1830s. Inspired by the Jacobin ideas of the French Revolution, the *exaltados* ("enthusiasts") were strongly anti-Portuguese and generally xenophobic. Their program and the use of the popular press, open public meetings, and street action—all innovations in Brazilian politics—generated strong support from urban elements, including artisans and shopkeepers, many of them mulattoes and all having socioeconomic grievances. Various developments, including the death of PEDRO I, the introduction of federalism in 1834, and increasing fears of social anarchy, deprived the *exaltados* of their political viability.

RODERICK BARMAN

EXPLORERS AND EXPLORATION

Brazil

The beginnings of the European unveiling of Brazil trace back to 1500. In mid-November 1499, Vicente Yáñez Pinzón, a former lieutenant of Christopher COLUMBUS, sailed from Palos in southern Spain and proceeded southwest from the Cape Verde Islands. Late in January 1500 he made a landfall, presumed to be along the present state of Pernambuco, and sailed north and then northwestward along the littoral of South America until he returned to the Caribbean. A month later Diego de LEPE, a kinsman of Yáñez Pinzón, replicated his predecessor's voyage and is believed to have entered the Genipapo River (later called the Pará), which bounds the southern extremity of the island of Marajó at the mouth of the Amazon. Spain did not pursue the discovery claims of these two Andalusians because much of the coast they traversed belonged to Portugal by the terms of the Treaty of TORDESILLAS (1494).

The first Portuguese encounter with the Brazilian littoral occurred on 22 April 1500, when Pedro Álvarez CABRAL, commander of the squadron sent from Lisbon to Calicut, India, to follow up the achievements of Vasco da GAMA, made contact with the Brazilian Indians near the future harbor of Porto Seguro. There the first mass was said on Brazilian soil. Cabral took possession of the unexpected land, thought to be an island, and his lieutenants wrote King MANUEL I concerning Brazil's promise as a haven for distressed ships engaged in sailing to and from India and as an opportunity for evangelization.

How extensive Cabral's find was became apparent when Gonçalo Coelho returned to Lisbon two years later. In 1501 Coelho was sent to Brazil by the king to determine the extent of Cabral's discovery. With three ships he not only examined the coast of the new land between the future states of Pernambuco and Rio Grande do Sul but also named outstanding landmarks in accordance with prominent church days when headlands, bays, river estuaries, and other features were first observed (for example, Cape São Roque, Cape São Agostinho, the São Francisco River, All Saints Bay, Rio de Janeiro, and São Vicente). The earliest map to include the Brazilian littoral incorporated the findings of the Coelho expedition. Prepared by an unknown cartographer, that planisphere was sent secretly by an Italian diplomat stationed in Lisbon, Alberto Cantino, to his patron, the duke of Ferrara, in 1502.

As the full extent of the seacoast of the new land gradually became known, the names attached to it evolved. Originally called the Island of Vera Cruz (be-

cause Cabral, like all navigators of his time, was convinced by medieval geographers that apart from Europe, Asia, and Africa, the land masses of the world consisted exclusively of islands), Brazil was successively termed the Land of the Holy Cross, the Land of Parrots, and, by about 1510, the Land of Brazilwood, after the red dyestuff that became Brazil's first significant export to Europe. That commodity, together with parrots, monkeys, and other exotica, remained Brazil's principal attraction during the first three decades of the sixteenth century while Portugal was establishing its empire in the East. Meantime, a series of navigators in Spain's service, including Juan Díaz de SOLÍS, discoverer of the Río de la Plata; the circumnavigator Ferdinand MAGELLAN; and Sebastian CABOT, seeker of the "city of the Caesars" in Paraguay, sailed along the Brazilian littoral but made no contribution to an understanding of Brazilian geography. It was the intrusions by French competitors, seeking brazilwood and Indian alliances, that compelled the Portuguese crown to device the captaincy system during the 1530s to promote the settlement and defense of Brazil.

That approach failed to secure Portugal's hold upon Brazil, and it was followed with the establishment of royal government after 1549, but it was not until the first decades of the seventeenth century that Portugal's control over Brazil's north coast as far as the Amazon was assured. As the early captaincies were being established, the full extent of the world's greatest river was revealed by a Spanish contingent led by Francisco de ORELLANA in 1541–1542. Orellana was a lieutenant of Gonzalo PIZARRO, governor of Quito (Ecuador), who led a large expedition eastward from the city of Quito in February 1541, seeking what Indian informants assured him was the "land of cinnamon." As the expedition encountered increasing difficulties, he sent Orellana ahead with fifty to sixty men in two brigantines to forage for food and to seek verification of the land's existence. Instead of returning to the Pizarro camp, Orellana sailed the length of the Amazon (February to August 1542), which he named after a serious encounter with Omagua Indians led by female warriors whose fighting ability seemed to confirm the substance of a widely believed medieval legend.

In 1616, Portuguese forces asserted their claim to one of the major estuaries of the Amazon when they founded the fortress of Santa Maria de Belém do Grão Pará. From this base, a series of patrols eliminated groups of forest-dwelling European competitors in the lower Amazon during the next decade and a half.

During the 1630s the human and natural resources of the Amazon were more closely scrutinized by Portuguese based at Belém and Spaniards from Quito. In 1636 Luís Figueira, a veteran north-coast Jesuit missionary, traveled throughout the lower reaches of the Amazon as far as the Rio Xingu. Figueira's reflections on the Amazon's material and spiritual promise were published in Lisbon in 1637, four years before the appearance of an even more impressive assessment of the river by another Jesuit, the Spaniard Cristóbal de Acuña, author of *Nuevo descubrimiento del gran río de las Amazonas* (1641).

Although Madrid acted promptly to suppress *Nuevo descubrimiento* because it revealed weaknesses concerning Spanish defenses in the interior of South America, it could not undo the damage caused by the action of a Portuguese captain, Pedro Teixeira. Teixeira was directed by the Portuguese governor of the Captaincy of Pará to return to Spanish territory two Franciscan missionaries who had descended the river in 1637. His massive party, some 2,000 people, was clearly intended to send a message to Spanish authorities in the Viceroyalty of Peru. After delivering his charges to Quito, Teixeira headed back to Belém. When he reached the confluence of the Napo and Aguarico rivers (16 August 1639), Teixeira, apparently pursuant to his superior's secret instructions, formally asserted Portugal's possession of the entire Amazon Valley. Although that act was in clear violation of the Treaty of TORDESILLAS, it served as a basis for Portugal's and later Brazil's claims to legal possession of the Amazon region.

While missionaries, traders, and Indian slavers were assessing the resources of the Amazon, other Portuguese, joined by Indian-whites (MAMELUCOS) and supported by Indian guides, bearers, foragers, and canoe paddlers, were exploiting the resources inland from the coastal captaincies of Pernambuco, Bahia, and especially São Vicente (the future state of São Paulo) and Spanish Paraguay. These roving teams, known as BANDEIRAS, began their quest in the 1590s and continued until the early decades of the eighteenth century to search the backlands for precious wealth, gems, and minerals, and to pay their expenses by the enslavement of indigenous peoples. Among their accomplishments were the destruction of two entire fields of missions planted by Paraguay-based Jesuits in what is today western São Paulo, Paraná, and Rio Grande do Sul, between 1628 and 1640, the discovery of labyrinthine river systems permitting passage between the seacoast and the remote interior, and the discovery of fluvial gold in a half dozen captaincies between the 1690s and the 1730s. The essential linkage between important southern rivers, such as the Tietê, Paraná, and Paraguay, and the northern rivers, including the Mamoré, Guaporé, Madeira, and Amazon, was demonstrated by the most famous of all of the *bandeiras*, that supposedly led by Antônio Rapôso TAVARES, veteran *bandeirante* captain, between 1648 and 1651. His expedition traversed 8,000 miles between São Paulo, western Brazil (Mato Grosso), the Andes, and the length of the Amazon.

Three outstanding assessments of Brazil's human and natural resources were published between 1587 and 1711. Two were by Portuguese secular authors, the other by an Italian-born Jesuit. They include Gabriel Soares de SOUSA's *Tratado descritivo do Brasil* (1587), Ambrósio Fernandes Brandão's *Diálogos das grandezas do Brasil*

(1618), and Giovanni António Andreoni, S.J., *Cultura e opulencia do Brasil por suas drogas e minas* (1711). Although each is richly informative, none was composed by a scientist. The first scientists (and artists) to describe Brazil's physical and human resources appeared during the Dutch occupation of the Northeast (1630–1654). Most noteworthy was Georg Marcgraf, botanist, zoologist, mathematician, and astronomer, and coauthor with Willem Piso of the seminally important *Historia naturalis brasiliae* (1648), and two famous landscape painters, Frans POST and Albert ECKHOUT.

No significant advances were made toward the classification of Brazil's flora and fauna and the exploration and mapping of the seacoast and interior between the departure of the Dutch and the mid-eighteenth century. The signing of the Luso-Spanish boundary treaties of 1750 and 1778 led to the dispatch to Brazil of small groups of artists, architects, astronomers, cartographers, engineers, and naturalists. Among them were António Giuseppe Landi, architect and naturalist who labored in the Amazon, and Ricardo Franco de Almeida Serra, who with António Pires da Silva Pontes confirmed the connection between the Branco, Rupununi, and Essequibo rivers. They were followed by the so-called Portuguese Humboldt, Alexandre Rodrigues Ferreira, a Bahian-born naturalist who spent nearly a decade in the Amazon and in Mato Grosso (1782–1792) collecting flora and fauna specimens and recording observations that unfortunately never were published. More successful was Fr. José Mariano da Conceição Velloso, a Minas Gerais-born Franciscan friar who compiled the eleven-volume *Flora fluminense* and found a publisher in Paris (1790).

Oddly, when the French-born naturalist Auguste de Saint-Hilaire accompanied Marshal Andoche Junot, the commander of the French army of occupation, to Lisbon in 1808 and encountered the prints of Conceição Velloso's work, he resolved to proceed to Brazil to undertake his own botanical investigations. Between 1816 and 1821, Saint-Hilaire traveled extensively throughout central and southern Brazil. Beginning in 1830, he published nine volumes of his botanical observations.

Saint-Hilaire was only one of a group of foreign scientists and travelers to examine the Brazilian landscape during the period when JOÃO VI resided in Brazil (1807–1821). Others included the mineralogist John Mawe, the first foreigner to see and write about the remains of the gold diggings in Minas Gerais. In 1817 a group of Austrian scientists arrived in honor of Brazil's new queen, Maria Leopoldina. Among them were Johann Emanuel Pohl, a botanist and mineralogist; and Johann Natterer, a zoologist at the Imperial Zoological Gardens and a horticulturist, specialist in flower painting, and taxidermist. Natterer spent nineteen years collecting specimens and returned to Vienna only in 1835 to found a special museum dedicated to Brasiliana. By then Pohl had already published his encyclopedic *Plantarum Brasiliae* (Vienna, 1827–1831). Two other scientists were sent by the queen's grandfather, the king of Bavaria, to identify

Brazilian resources. They were Johann Baptist von Spix and Karl Friedrich Philip von Martius. Spix was the curator of the Munich Museum, and the youthful Martius already had an enviable reputation as one of Europe's leading young botanists. Together they traveled overland from central Brazil to the Amazon gathering specimens and providing some of the best quality ethnographic observations on Brazil since the early seventeenth century. Apart from their popular travel account, their *Flora Brasiliensis* (37 folio vols. 1840–1906) was one of the towering descriptions of the uniqueness and richness of Brazil.

An avid naturalist, Georg Heinrich von Langsdorff originally went to Brazil as its first Russian consul general from 1813 to 1820. He returned to the country in 1822 as head of a scientific expedition that included artists Moritz Rugendas and Adrien Taunay. The group went to Minas Gerais in 1824, traveled from São Paulo down the Tietê River in 1825, and in 1827–1828 visited Bororo Indian groups. Next, they descended the Arinos and Tapajós, but Langsdorff contracted malaria and purportedly went insane.

Englishman Henry W. Bates explored Brazil from 26 May 1848 to June 1859, collecting over 3,000 new species of insects and other specimens. He began on the lower Amazon and Tocantins rivers and then went up the Solimões. He returned to Belém and settled for three years at Santarém. Sailing up the Amazon again, he spent four and a half years based in Ega (present-day Tefé) before returning home, publishing *The Naturalist on the River Amazon* (1863), and becoming the first paid secretary of the Royal Geographical Society (1864). In 1865, Swiss-born Harvard University professor Jean Louis Rodolphe Agassiz headed an expedition up the Amazon, traveling from Manaus to the Solimões River. Members of the party measured Indians on the Amazon, Tapajós, Içá, Jataí, and Branco rivers, while a team of geologists worked in Minas Gerais. In 1867, Sir Richard Burton, then serving as British consul in Santos, ventured to northern Minas Gerais and descended the São Francisco River, encountering Xavange, Xikriabá, and Karirí Indians at São João dos Indios.

Brazilian explorers too made important contributions to the exploration and description of their country. Antônio Gonçalves DIAS, head of the ethnographic section of the Imperial Scientific Commission, went to Ceará in 1858–1859 and wrote a Tupi dictionary after studying the POTIGUAR Indians. The next year he spent six months on the Amazon visiting the Mawé, Mundurukú, and Mura Indians. His romantic poems inspired the Indianist literary movement. In 1862 José Vieira Couto de Magalhães visited the Xavante, Karajá, and Tupi-speaking Anambé, collecting Tupi legends. He founded Isabel College on the upper Araguaia River for Indian children and established forts and steamship navigation on the Araguaia and Tocantins. His journal, *Viagem ao Araguaya* (1863), and his *O selvagem* (1876), discussed methods of acculturation for the Indians.

In 1871 João Barbosa Rodrigues went to Pará and Amazonas on behalf of the imperial government to conduct scientific studies. He identified many new species of palms and orchids, and published accounts of the Tembé in Pará, the Mundurukú, and Mawé of the Tapajós River, and the Tukâno of the Solimões in Alexandre Jose de Mello Moraes, ed., *Revista da Exposição Anthropologica Brazileira*, published as part of the Anthropological Exhibition in Rio de Janeiro, organized by Ladislau Neto in 1882. In 1884 he founded the botanical gardens of Amazonas in Manaus, which also contained important ethnographic collections. In 1884 he and his wife Constança contacted the Crishana (present-day Waimiri) tribe of the Jauaperi tributary of the lower Rio Negro, described in *Io Jauapery: Pacificaçao dos Crichanás* (1885).

One of the greatest Brazilian explorers of the twentieth century, Cândido Mariano da Silva RONDON, began his career by setting up telegraph lines throughout Amazonia from 1890 to 1915. In 1910 he was made head of the newly created Indian Protection Service and embarked on an exploration of the rivers in present-day Rondônia. In 1913–1914 he traveled with former U.S. President Theodore ROOSEVELT down the Dúvida (now Roosevelt) River. From 1927 to 1930 he surveyed all of the frontiers and led a mixed boundary commission in 1934–1938 on the Brazilian-Colombian border.

According to John Hemming, the exploration of the Amazon and contact with the indigenous peoples there often brought diseases and devastation to those areas. Nevertheless, the exploration of the Amazon and other parts of Brazil has proceeded inexorably throughout the twentieth century, as its vast territory fascinates the adventurous and those looking for new sources of wealth.

Bibliography appears below, following "Spanish America."

DAURIL ALDEN

See also **Dutch in Colonial Brazil; French in Colonial Brazil; Portuguese Empire.**

Spanish America

The voyage of Columbus sailing under the flag of Castile in 1492 is commonly seen as the beginning of the European exploration of Latin America, even though others, like Saint Brendan and Leif Eriksson, may have arrived centuries before. The European "Age of Discovery" began in 1433 when Portugal sent a succession of captains down the western and southern coasts of Africa in search of a maritime route to the East and access to its spices and silks. Columbus had unsuccessfully sought Portuguese patronage for his plan to reach the East by sailing west, but he found support in Castile, where FERDINAND II OF ARAGON and ISABELLA I OF CASTILE agreed to finance his voyage.

Christopher COLUMBUS (Cristóbal Colón) sighted land on 12 October 1492. During his first voyage he

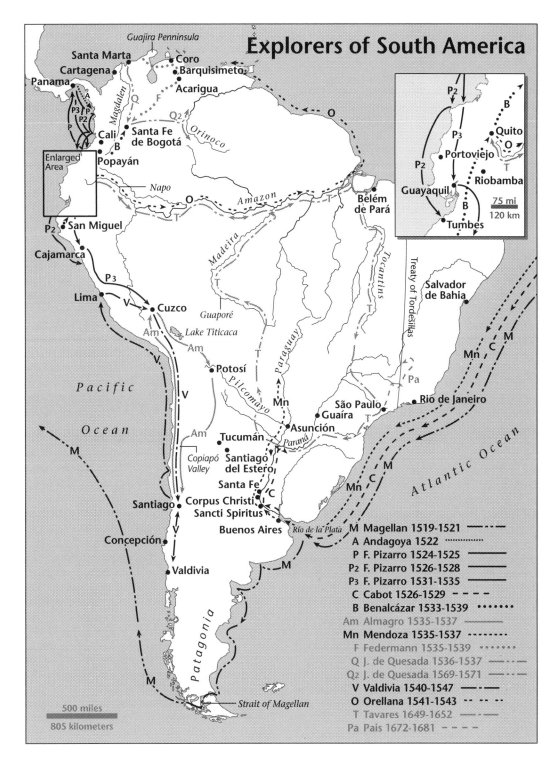

Explorers of South America

Guajira Peninsula

Santa Marta
Cartagena
Panama
Coro
Barquisimeto
Acarigua
Cali
Santa Fe
de Bogotá
Popayán
Enlarged
Area
Napo
San Miguel
Cajamarca
Lima
Cuzco
Guaporé
Lake Titicaca
Potosí
Tucumán
Copiapó
Valley
Santiago
del Estero
Santa Fe
Santiago
Corpus Christi
Sancti Spiritus
Concepción
Buenos Aires
Río de la Plata
Valdivia
Patagonia
Strait of Magellan

Pacific
Ocean

Magdalen
Orinoco
Amazon
Madeira
Guaporé
Paraguay
Pilcomayo
Paraná
Tocantins
Treaty of Tordesillas

Belém
de Pará
Salvador
de Bahia
São Paulo
Guaíra
Asunción
Río de Janeiro

Atlantic Ocean

Inset (Enlarged Area):
Quito
Portoviejo
Riobamba
Guayaquil
Tumbes
75 mi
120 km

500 miles
805 kilometers

M **Magellan 1519-1521** — · — · —
A **Andagoya 1522** ···············
P **F. Pizarro 1524-1525** ——————
P2 **F. Pizarro 1526-1528** ——————
P3 **F. Pizarro 1531-1535** ——————
C **Cabot 1526-1529** – – – –
B **Benalcázar 1533-1539** ●●●●●●●
Am **Almagro 1535-1537** ——————
Mn **Mendoza 1535-1537** ·········
F **Federmann 1535-1539** ·········
Q **J. de Quesada 1536-1537** —·—·—
Q2 **J. de Quesada 1569-1571** —··—··—
V **Valdivia 1540-1547** —·—·—
O **Orellana 1541-1543** ·· — ·· —
T **Tavares 1649-1652** ——·——·—
Pa **Pais 1672-1681** – – – –

explored the northeast corner of Cuba and the island of Bohio, which he rechristened La Isla Española, later to be known as Hispaniola. Following Columbus's discoveries, the Spanish and Portuguese crowns asked Pope ALEXANDER VI to draw a LINE OF DEMARCATION dividing future discoveries between them. On 7 June 1494, both powers signed the Treaty of TORDESILLAS, which established a line 370 leagues west of the Azores (cutting through present-day Brazil), giving Portugal all lands to the east and Spain those to the west. Columbus completed three more voyages from 1493 to 1504 in which he explored the Caribbean, established a settlement in Hispaniola at Isabela (later moved to Santo Domingo, the oldest European city in the Western Hemisphere), and made the first formal landing on the land mass of South America. Following up on these voyages, Alonso de OJEDA sailed on May 1499 and along with Juan de la Cosa and Amerigo VESPUCCI explored along the Caribbean coast of modern-day Venezuela (Dragon's Mouth) as far as the Guajira Peninsula of present-day Colombia. Pedro Alonso (Peralonso) NIÑO and Cristóbal Guerra sailed from Paria to Cape Codera, and Vicente Yáñez PINZÓN in his controversial voyage traveled around the Bulge of Brazil, discovering the mouth of the Amazon. When Amerigo VESPUCCI participated in an exploration of the Brazilian coast (10 May 1501 to 7 September 1502), he understood that this area was not the extreme shore of Asia, but a world unto itself—a New World.

The next phase of the European exploration of the Western Hemisphere began when Juan de la Cosa captured Darién, Panama, during his 1504 voyage. From that year until 1530, Darién-Panama and Hispaniola-Cuba would become the launching sites of many expeditions to Mexico and Central and South America. In 1508, Pinzón and Juan Díaz de SOLÍS presumably reconnoitered the coast of Yucatán while Sebastián de Ocampo circumnavigated Cuba, and Juan PONCE DE LEÓN occupied present-day Puerto Rico. The following year Juan de Esquivel and Pánfilo de NARVÁEZ explored Jamaica, Ojeda explored the Caribbean coast of Colombia, and Diego de NICUESA sailed around the Caribbean coast of neighboring Panama. In September 1513, Vasco Núñez de BALBOA discovered the Pacific Ocean; that same year Ponce de León sailed up the Atlantic coast to the Gulf side of present-day Florida. On 8 October 1515, Solís sailed to Brazil, then south to the estuary of the Río de la Plata. Diego de VELÁZQUEZ, governor of Cuba, dispatched first Francisco HERNÁNDEZ DE CÓRDOBA (1517) and then Juan de GRIJALVA (1518) to search for new discoveries. Hernán CORTÉS set sail on 18 February 1519, at the same time that Pedro Arias de ÁVILA (Pedrárias Dávila) was supervising the founding of Nombre de Dios and Panama City (15 August 1519) as terminal points of an interoceanic road, the overland forerunner of the Panama Canal. By 21 April 1519, Cortés had arrived on the Mexican mainland and founded the city of Veracruz. In mid-May 1519, Cortés renounced his position as the agent of Velázquez; he arrived in the center of the Aztec confederacy, TENOCHTITLÁN (modern Mexico City), on 8 November 1519 and conquered it for Spain on 13 August 1521.

Following the fall of the rich empire of Tenochtitlán, Europeans learned of the wealth available to those courageous enough to risk their lives in the New World. From 1521 to the 1550s, Spaniards could explore largely without fear of interference from other European powers. During these decades, Cortés traversed Pánuco (north of Veracruz), Cristóbal de OLID traveled through Michoacán, Nuño de GUZMÁN pillaged Nueva Galicia, and Francisco de MONTEJO struggled for Yucatán. Meanwhile, Pedro de ALVARADO went to Guatemala and Olid led an expedition to Honduras.

At the same time, Spain never abandoned its hope of finding an easy way to Asia. While Cortés was conquering Mexico, Ferdinand MAGELLAN left Spain on 20 September 1519 to search for the connecting strait between the seas and reach the East. He sailed to Brazil, entered the strait that now bears his name on 21 October 1520, and arrived in the present-day Philippines on 18 March 1521, where he was killed in an encounter with indigenous tribes. Juan Sebastián EL CANO (del Cano) continued the voyage and arrived at the Spice Islands (Ternate and Tidore) on 8 November 1521. Sebastián CABOT, originally dispatched as a follow-up to Magellan, became diverted at the Río de Solis (Río de la Plata). He founded Sancti Spíritus on 19 May 1528 and explored the Paraná and Paraguay rivers as far north as the junction with the Pilcomayo River, at present-day Asunción. In 1535, Simón de Alcazaba Sotomayor entered the Strait of Magellan and explored Patagonia, and the following year Pedro de MENDOZA founded Puerto de Santa María del Buen Aire (present-day Buenos Aires), while Juan de AYOLAS sailed up the Paraná and built the settlement and fort of Corpus Christi near modern-day Santa Fe on 15 June 1536. He continued beyond the junction of the Paraná and Pilcomayo to Corumbá on 2 February 1537 and was exploring the region near present-day Bolivia when he was killed by Indians. Juan de Salazar de Espinosa founded Nuestra Señora de la Asunción on 15 August 1537.

While these men searched the southern Atlantic and Pacific, Cortés began the exploration of the northern Pacific and on 3 May 1535 discovered the Bahia de Santa Cruz (present-day La Paz, Baja California). In 1542, Juan RODRÍGUEZ CABRILLO sailed from Acapulco and explored the western shore of Baja California as far north as the present California-Oregon border. He died at sea, leaving Bartolomé Ferrelo to pilot the ships home.

While Spain explored Mexico and the Pacific Ocean, it was also marching south from Panama toward the wealthy empire described to Balboa. In 1522, Pascual de ANDAGOYA explored the coast of northwestern Colombia, and Pedro Arias de Ávila founded Natá on the western edge of the Bay of Panama on 20 May 1522. Gil González Dávila progressed farther up along the Pacific coast of Costa Rica around Lake Nicaragua, and in 1525, Francisco HERNÁNDEZ DE CÓRDOBA explored Nicaragua, initially as the agent of Árias.

The exploration of the INCA Empire proceeded in several phases. Francisco PIZARRO and Diego de ALMAGRO participated in a voyage of exploration and reconnaissance from 1526 to 1528. Subsequently, Pizarro sailed to Spain to secure the rights to the conquest of this new territory from Charles V, which he received in the Capitulation of Toledo in 1529. Upon his return to Panama, Pizarro launched the conquest of Peru in January 1531. He arrived by sea and overland marched to Tumbes, which he regarded as the gateway to the Inca Empire. On 16 May 1532, Pizarro marched inland and founded San Miguel in July. He arrived in Cajamarca on

15 November, taking the Inca emperor ATAHUALPA prisoner the next day. Almagro arrived in mid-February 1533, and Atahualpa was tried and executed on 26 July 1533. Pizarro and Almagro traveled along the Inca highway, arriving in Cuzco on 14 or 15 November 1533. On 18 January 1535 Pizarro founded a new capital, La Ciudad de los Reyes (present-day Lima), near the coast. In 1545 silver was discovered in Potosí, located in present-day Bolivia.

Not all explorers went to Peru, however. Juan de AMPÍES sailed from Santo Domingo and founded Coro, Venezuela, on 26 July 1527. On 24 February 1529, Ambrosio Alfínger, a factor of the WELSER banking family, took over the colony in payment of debts owed by the Spanish crown. On 1 September 1530, he led an expedition west across Lake Maracaibo and founded the city of the same name. On 12 September 1530, Nicolás FÉDERMAN, Alfínger's deputy, explored south of Coro to the east of Maracaibo as far south as Acarigua and Barquisimeto. Diego de Ordás explored the Orinoco River Basin from its mouth in 1531–1532 as far as the cataracts of Ature, the precursor of many searches for EL DORADO. On 5 August 1532, Pedro de Heredia sailed from Spain, founding Cartagena, Colombia, the following year. Gonzalo JIMÉNEZ DE QUESADA led an expedition from Santa Marta on 5 April 1536. He followed the Magdalena River first to La Toro, then proceeded over the Andes and founded the city of Santa Fé de Bogotá on 6 August 1538.

The Spaniards also continued north from the Caribbean. Lucas VÁSQUEZ DE AYLLÓN established San Miguel de Gualdape in the vicinity of Sapelo Sound in present-day Georgia, the first European settlement in the United States, in 1526. Two years later, Panfilo de Narváez led a disastrous expedition to Florida, from which only four members, including the African slave ESTEBAN and Alvar Núñez CABEZA DE VACA, ultimately reappeared in Mexico in July 1536 after years spent wandering among the Indians. Fray Marcos de NIZA and Esteban went north in an unsuccessful search for the rumored SEVEN CITIES OF CÍBOLA, with only Fray Marcos returning with tales of golden villages. In 1540, Francisco Vázquez de CORONADO hunted for those cities, traveling as far as present-day Kansas. His lieutenant, García López de Cárdenas, discovered the Grand Canyon, but Coronado found no gold. Nor did Peruvian conquistador Hernando de SOTO, who explored the southeast of the United States from 1539 to 1543, discovering the Mississippi River.

Most explorers searched for territories like Mexico and Peru that they could claim for the crown and themselves. Some went north, like Sebastián de BELALCÁZAR, who left San Miguel in October 1533, arriving in Riobamba on his march toward present-day Quito. (The Incas, hearing of his approach, burned the city and fled with Atahualpa's treasure.) Belalcázar entered Quito at the end of 1533, but used Riobamba as his headquarters until Quito was rebuilt. As they searched for the trea-

sure, Belalcázar and his assistant Juan de Ampudia then founded Guayaquil, Portoviejo (1534), Popayán (1536), and Cali (1537). Following the conquest of Peru, Gonzalo PIZARRO went to Quito as governor in December 1540. Two months later, joined by his kinsman Francisco de ORELLANA, Pizarro set out to explore lands to the east. When the expedition failed, Orellana sailed down the Napo River, entering the Amazon on 11 February 1542. He returned to the Paria Peninsula at Cubagua on 9 September 1542 after six months exploring the Amazon.

Almagro left Cuzco on 3 July 1535 to seek his fortune southward, toward present-day Chile. By March 1536, his party had marched through the Andes and had arrived at the valley of Aconcagua. Almagro became dissatisfied and returned to Peru to contest Pizarro's possession of Cuzco. After the death of Almagro, the exploration of Chile was undertaken by one of Pizarro's lieutenants, Pedro de VALDIVIA. He arrived via the coastal route at the present-day valley of the Copiapó River, and marched farther south, founding present-day Santiago on 12 February 1541. In 1543, Diego de Rojas left Cuzco to search for a province between Chile and the Río de la Plata. He reached Tucumán but died enroute, and Francisco de Mendoza then commanded soldiers on the march to the original settlement of Sebastián Cabot on the Paraná. Valdivia returned to Chile as governor in April 1549 and founded numerous cities, including Concepción (1550) and Valdivia (1551), before he died in December 1553. Juan Francisco de AGUIRRE crossed the Andes in 1552 and founded the Argentine city of Santiago del Estero in 1553.

By the 1550s, Spain was no longer alone in the New World, and its exploration would often come in response to foreign threats to its sizable possessions, which included the entire Caribbean and the Western Hemispheric mainland from Zacatecas, Mexico, to Valdivia, Chile, and Patagonia, Argentina. During the centuries that followed, Spain went north through present-day Mexico into Texas, the Southwest, and California; took possession of the Philippines; explored the Amazon, Paraguay, and Argentina; but lost almost all of the Caribbean and the opportunity to claim much of present-day Brazil.

Once silver mines were discovered in Zacatecas, Mexico, in 1546, explorers were eager to march farther north, often accompanied by priests who established missions (*reducciones*) along the way. Francisco de Ibarra founded Durango in 1563. Two years later, Pedro MENÉNDEZ DE AVILÉS led an expedition to fight the French in Florida. In 1565, he founded present-day Saint Augustine, the oldest European city in the United States, and the following year members of his group founded Santa Elena in present-day South Carolina. Juan PARDO marched from that colony to present-day North Carolina, and in 1573, Pedro Menéndez Márquez explored the Chesapeake Bay area. But the Spanish soon lost the area north of Saint Augustine to British attack.

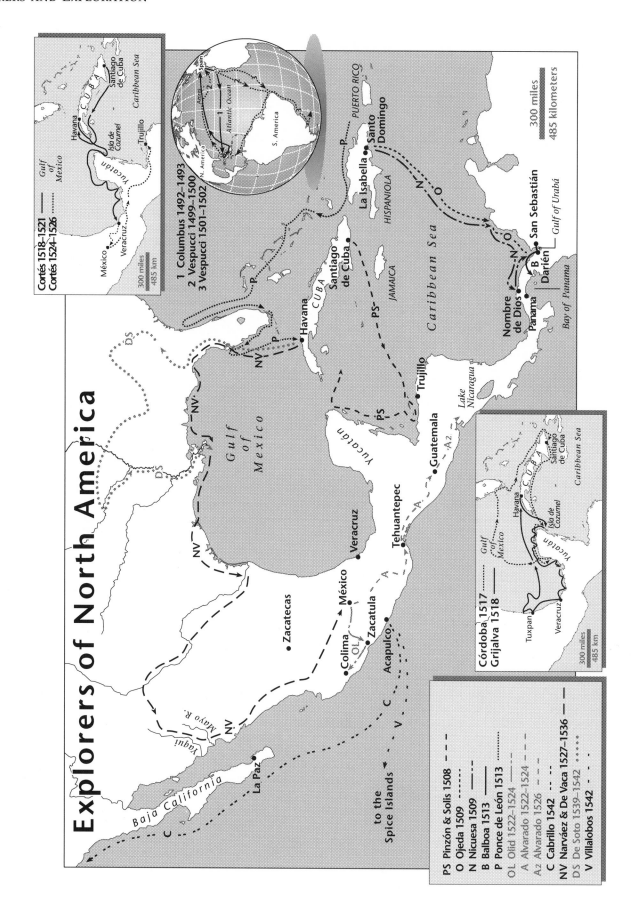

Explorers of North America

Cortés 1518–1521 ———
Cortés 1524–1526 ·········

1 Columbus 1492–1493
2 Vespucci 1499–1500
3 Vespucci 1501–1502

Córdoba 1517 ·········
Grijalva 1518 ———

PS Pinzón & Solís 1508	– – –
O Ojeda 1509	·········
N Nicuesa 1509	– ·· –
B Balboa 1513	———
P Ponce de León 1513	·········
OL Olid 1522–1524	– – –
A Alvarado 1522–1524	– – –
A2 Alvarado 1526	– – –
C Cabrillo 1542	– ·· –
NV Narváez & De Vaca 1527–1536	———
DS De Soto 1539–1542	·········
V Villalobos 1542	– · –

to the
Spice Islands

The Spanish continued exploring northern Mexico. In 1581, Fray Augustine Rodríguez and Captain Francisco Sánchez Chamuscacho led an expedition into New Mexico, as did Antonio de ESPEJO the next year. In 1598, Juan de OÑATE crossed the Rio Grande at El Paso and marched to San Gabriel, founding San Juan de los Caballeros. Later, as governor, Oñate descended the Colorado River to the Gulf of California (1604–1605). His successor, Pedro de Peralta, founded Santa Fe in 1610, two years after the French founded Quebec and three years after the British built Jamestown. Spaniards traversed the Pimeria Alta (present-day northern Sonora and southern Arizona), founding Sinaloa (1593) and settlements along the Mayo (1614), Yaqui (1617), and Sonora (1636) rivers.

In October 1560, Pedro de URSÚA and Lope de AGUIRRE began to sail down the Amazon. By 1 July 1561, Aguirre entered the North Atlantic, the second successful transcontinental crossing of the river. The Portuguese quickly wrestled with the Spanish for control of the Amazon. In January 1616, the Portuguese entered the mouth of the Amazon and constructed Fort Presepio, the precursor of present-day Belém (Pará). In 1622, Luis Aranha de Vasconcelos explored the eastern third of the river, mapping the lower Amazon as it split into two branches. In 1638, Pedro Teixeira arrived in Quito from Belém with orders to establish a Portuguese settlement west of the Line of Demarcation.

In the march northward from Mexico, Fray García de San Francisco y Zúñiga founded the Misión de Nuestra Señora de Guadalupe in El Paso del Norte in 1659. Fray Damián Mazanet built Misión San Francisco de los Tejas near the banks of the Trinity River in 1690. In 1718, Misión San Antonio de Valero (the Alamo) was founded, followed by Misión San José in the San José Valley in 1720.

The exploration of the Southwest continued under the leadership of the Jesuit father Eusebio KINO. In 1700, he founded the Misión San Xavier del Bac in Tucson, Arizona, and in March 1701, he discovered that present-day Baja California was a peninsula, not an island. In 1706, Governor Francisco Cuervo y Valdes founded Albuquerque and Juan de Ulibarri explored the area of the upper Arkansas River. Spanish explorers of the Midwest, however, now faced a conflict with the French, who had become established since the explorations of Marquette and Joliet in 1673 and LaSalle in 1685–1687.

In the eighteenth century, Spaniards explored and colonized present-day California in response to news of Russian threats to their control of the area. In 1769, Captain Gaspar de PORTOLÁ and Fray Junípero SERRA led an expedition to Alta California and founded San Diego. By 1782, Serra had founded eight more missions, including Misión San Gabriel Arcángel in Los Angeles (1771). Juan Bautista de ANZA commanded an expedition from Fort Tubac, Arizona, to San Francisco Bay and founded that city on 4 July 1776, while Fray Francisco Atanasio Domínquez and Fray Silvestre VÉLEZ DE ESCA-LANTE explored Arizona, New Mexico, Colorado, and Utah. With the founding of Misión Santa Bárbara in 1786, the Spanish completed their exploration of the Western Hemisphere.

The best general surveys are EDWARD J. GOODMAN, *The Explorers of South America* (1972); SAMUEL ELIOT MORISON, *The European Discovery of America*, vol. 2 (1974); JOHN HEMMING, *Red Gold: The Conquest of the Brazilian Indians, 1500–1760* (1978); J. H. PARRY, *The Discovery of South America* (1979); MANUEL LUCENA SALMORAL, coord., *Historia general de España y América*, vol. 7 (1982); *Cambridge History of Latin America*, vols. 1–2 (1984); BAILEY W. DIFFIE, *A History of Colonial Brazil, 1500–1792* (1987); JOHN HEMMING, *Amazon Frontier: The Defeat of the Brazilian Indians* (1987); FRANCISCO MORALES PADRÓN, *Historia del descubrimiento y conquista de América*, 5th ed. (1990).

For specific topics, see PETER GERHARD, *A Guide to the Historical Geography of New Spain* (1972); DANIEL BOORSTIN, *The Discoverers* (1991); *The Christopher Columbus Encyclopedia*, 2 vols. (1992); MANUEL BALLESTEROS GAIBROIS, ed., *Cronicas de América* (1992).

For the best map collections, see FELIPE FERNÁNDEZ-ARMESTO, ed., *The Times Atlas of World Exploration* (1991); and HANS WOLFF, ed., *America: Early Maps of the New World* (1992).

BRIAN LORDAN

EXTRACTIVE RESERVES, tropical forest areas set aside as a public trust for sustainable development by local residents, which first appeared in Brazil in 1990 with the formation of the 1,250,000-acre Chico Mendes Extractive Reserve. The idea is said to have originated in 1985 at the first national conference of Brazilian rubber tappers.

This meeting, held in Brasília, formally united the tappers with environmentalists who were interested in saving the Amazon rain forest from destruction by loggers and builders of roads and dams. Struggling to protect their livelihood against encroaching cattle ranchers, miners, and land-hungry settlers, the tappers had already formed cooperatives like the Projeto Seringueiro of Acre, in order to strengthen their bargaining power with rubber merchants and to pool resources for food production, education, and health care. Whereas the environmentalists envisioned the establishment of pristine national parks, the tappers sought support for their cooperatives.

An anthropologist named Carlos Teixeira is said to have coined the term "extractive reserves," which appeared as a positive alternative to conventional economic development strategies and promised to save both the forest and the way of life of those who exploited its abundance in the least destructive manner. The details of the concept were elaborated in a 1987 agrarian reform law.

The idea helped consolidate support for rain forest protection in Brazil and abroad. Nongovernmental agencies, already enamored of sustainable development schemes in other contexts, embraced the idea, as did politicians, human and cultural rights groups, and ecologists. In other Latin American countries, where tropical forests formerly had been preserved as national parks and Indian reservations, new campaigns were inspired by the Brazilian model. As in Brazil, anthropologists and environmentalists joined with organic rural workers, such as resin tappers in Honduras and nut gatherers in Peru, to establish extractive reserves. In Costa Rica, foreign pharmaceutical companies encouraged establishing reserves in order to protect potential medicinal resources from being destroyed. Extractive reserves have been debated in Belize, Bolivia, Colombia, Ecuador, Mexico, and Venezuela. Ironically, the movement became even stronger after Francisco "Chico" MENDES FILHO, a leader among Brazilian rubber tappers and a principal force behind the 1985 conference, was assassinated in December 1988. In March 1990, the first extractive reserve was established to honor him.

Some criticisms of the reserves have emerged. As a protective entitlement, they are said to interfere in the free flow market forces and to block economically depressed Latin American nations from fully exploiting their natural resource wealth. Some supporters of the reserve concept believe they ultimately will fail, given the great pressures for change facing Latin Americans, and they advocate more diversified strategies for the protection of the forest and its people. Lines on the map, they say, will not be able to stop the in-migration of masses of hungry settlers, exploitation by debt-ridden governments, and entrepreneurs anxious to capitalize on forest resources.

MARY HELENA ALLEGRETTI, "Extractive Reserves: An Alternative for Reconciling Development and Environmental Conservation in Amazonia," in *Alternatives to Deforestation: Steps Toward Sustainable Use of the Amazon Rain Forest*, edited by Anthony B. Anderson (1990), pp. 252–264; ANDREW REVKIN, *The Burning Season: The Murder of Chico Mendes and the Fight for the Amazon Rain Forest* (1990); DANIEL C. NEPSTAD and STEPHAN SCHWARTZMALL, eds., *Extractive Reserves Examined—Non-Timber Products from Tropical Forests: Evaluation of a Conservation and Development Strategy* (1992); SUSAN E. PLACE, ed., *Tropical Rainforests: Latin American Nature and Society in Transition* (1993).

CLIFF WELCH

See also **Forests; Rubber Gatherers' Unions.**

FABELA ALFARO, ISIDRO (*b.* 29 June 1882; *d.* 12 August 1964), Mexican public figure and international jurist who contributed numerous works on international politics and law and taught international law for many years at the National University. With expertise in international arbitration from his long career in foreign relations, he was appointed a judge of the International Court of Justice, The Hague (1946–1952).

Fabela was born in Atlacomulco, in the state of México, which subsequently produced many leading political figures. He was the son of Francisco Trinidad Fabela and Guadalupe Alfaro. In 1909, Fabela was one of the founders of the Ateneo de la Juventud, which included José VASCONCELOS and Antonio CASO Y ANDRADE. He began his public career in Chihuahua in 1911 and became a federal deputy under Francisco MADERO in 1912–1913. Under Venustiano CARRANZA he served as secretary of foreign relations (1914–1915), after which he held a variety of diplomatic posts, eventually representing Mexico in 1937–1940 at the International Office of Labor. He governed his home state of Mexico from 1942 to 1945.

FEDRO GUILLÉN, *Isidro Fabela* (1970?); BALDOMERO SEGURA GARCÍA, *Antología del pensamiento universal de Isidro Fabela* (1959); MICHAEL C. MEYER, "A Venture in Documentary Publication: Isidro Fabela's *Documentos Históricos de la Revolución Mexicana*," in *Hispanic American Historical Review* 52 (1972): 123–129.

RODERIC AI CAMP

FABINI, [FÉLIX] EDUARDO (*b.* 18 May 1882; *d.* 17 May 1950), Uruguayan composer and violinist. Born in Solís de Mataojo, Lavalleja, Fabini studied violin with Romeo Masi at the Conservatorio La Lira in Montevideo; he also received instruction under Virgilio Scarabelli and Manuel Pérez Badía. At the age of eighteen Fabini entered the Royal Conservatory in Brussels and enrolled in the classes of César Thomson (violin) and Auguste de Boeck (composition). In 1904 he was awarded the first prize with distinction in violin. Upon his return to Uruguay he gave recitals and performed chamber music in Montevideo. During his years in Brussels Fabini began to compose works for piano and guitar based on tunes, rhythms, and dances from the folk traditions of his homeland. With Alfonso BROQUA and Luis CLUZEAU-MORTET, he became a major exponent of musical nationalism in Uruguay. His best-known work is the symphonic poem *Campo*. Premiered by Vladimir Shavitch on 29 April 1922, it is considered Uruguay's major nationalist work of the period. Richard Strauss conducted it in Buenos Aires in 1923. *Campo* and *La isla de los ceibos* (1924–1926), another symphonic poem, were recorded by RCA Victor in the United States. *Mañana de Reyes* (1936–1937), *Melga sinfónica* (1931), and the ballet *Mburucuyá* (1933) completed Fabini's symphonic production. He also composed several *tristes* for piano and voice. He died in Montevideo.

ROBERTO E. LAGARMILLA, *Eduardo Fabini: Músico nacional uruguayo* (1954); *New Grove Dictionary of Music and Musicians*, vol. 6 (1980); SUSANA SALGADO, *Breve historia de la música culta en el Uruguay*, 2d ed. (1980).

SUSANA SALGADO

FACIO BRENES, RODRIGO (*b.* 23 March 1917; *d.* 7 June 1961), perhaps the most influential social and political thinker in twentieth-century Costa Rica. Facio, son of a Panamanian immigrant father, served as both national deputy (1948–1949) and rector of the University of Costa Rica (1952–1961), whose main campus today bears his name.

Facio earned his law degree in 1941, at the age of twenty-four, with the thesis *Estudio sobre economía costarricense* (1942), which was to have enormous influence on subsequent generations. He had already organized the Law Students Cultural Association in 1937 and was a key figure in the Center for the Study of National Problems (1940). This group became, after 1945, the Democratic Action and Social Democratic parties, which led eventually to the formation of the National Liberation Party after its victory in the 1948 civil war. He was an assembly deputy in 1949 and, subsequently, a director and vice president of the Central Bank. After many years of working with party leader José FIGUERES FERRER, Facio broke with him out of anger at not being chosen to succeed Figueres as the presidential candidate for 1962. He left Costa Rica to work for the Inter-American Development Bank. He drowned soon afterward in El Salvador.

Facio's other major historical works are *La moneda y la banca central en Costa Rica* (1947) and *La federación de Centroamérica: Sus antecedentes, su vida y su disolución* (1957).

Basic sources on Facio include JORGE ENRIQUE ROMERO PÉREZ, *La social democracia en Costa Rica* (1982); RAÚL HESS ESTRADA, *Rodrigo Facio, el economista* (1972); and CARLOS MOLINA, *El pensamiento de Rodrigo Facio y sus aportes a la ideología de la modernización capitalista en Costa Rica* (1981).

LOWELL GUDMUNDSON

FACIO SEGREDA, GONZALO (*b.* 28 March 1918), Costa Rican ambassador to the United States on three occasions, former president of congress, minister of justice, and foreign minister.

Gonzalo "Chalo" Facio was appointed ambassador to the United States in 1990 by the newly inaugurated president of Costa Rica, Rafael Angel CALDERÓN FOURNIER (*b.* 1949). His credentials included nearly one half-century of prominence in political, cultural, and economic affairs. His most salient contributions have been in international affairs.

Born in San José, Facio entered the national scene while he was still in law school and was a founding member of the Center for the Study of National Problems (March 1940). He graduated from the University of Costa Rica in 1941. During the social reform–oriented government of Rafael Angel CALDERÓN GUARDIA (1940–1944), the Center developed a social democratic alternative to the Calderón-led alliance between the National Republican Party and a communist party, the Bloque de Obreros y Campesinos (BOC), which was renamed the Popular Vanguard Party (PVP) in 1943.

He entered the direct action group under the leadership of José FIGUERES FERRER, which paved the way for the armed uprising that overthrew the Teodoro PICADO MICHALSKI administration (1944–1948) after the disputed election in February 1948. After the successful revolt, Figueres appointed Facio minister of justice in the Founding Junta of the Second Republic (1948–1949), where he played an active role in suppressing communists and Calderónist leaders who had held high-level positions in the previous two administrations (1940–1948) through the establishment of special courts, such as the Court of Immediate Sanctions, which tried public officials who served between 1940 and 1948 for offenses committed, and the Court of Probity, which intervened the property of public officials who served during that same period. The decisions of these courts could not be appealed.

After the return to constitutional government in 1949, he worked actively with Figueres to form the National Liberation Party (PLN), which represented the ideological position of the junta and the revolutionary movement that brought it to power. With Figueres's election to the presidency in 1953, Facio served as president of congress (1953–1958). He served as foreign minister under Figueres in his third presidency (1970–1974) and also under Daniel ODUBER QUIRÓS (1974–1978). Facio later broke with the PLN and became active in the Unidad coalition that elected Rodrigo CARAZO ODIO (1978–1982) and Rafael Angel Calderón Fournier (1990–1994) to the presidency.

Facio has also been active in business, professional, and academic affairs and has served as an officer and board member for several organizations. He has published numerous articles on national and international politics. He holds a doctorate in law from New York University.

For Facio's role in the formation and early years of the National Liberation Party see BURT H. ENGLISH, *Liberación Nacional in Costa Rica* (1971). He figures prominently in CHARLES D. AMERINGER's *Don Pepe* (1978). For his role in the events surrounding the 1948 revolution, see JOHN PATRICK BELL, *Crisis in Costa Rica* (1971).

JOHN PATRICK BELL

See also **Costa Rica: Political Parties.**

FACÓN, a long, swordlike knife, the GAUCHO's favorite and most dangerous weapon. Worn thrust through the back of the gaucho's broad, leather belt (*tirador*), the *facón* could easily inflict death in a duel. When dueling, a gaucho wrapped his poncho around one arm as a shield. Knife fights became storied events in gauchesque literature, like José Hernández's *Martín Fierro* (1872–1879) and Eduardo Gutiérrez's *Juan Moreira* (1879). Government officials repeatedly outlawed the dangerous weapon, but gauchos rejected firearms in favor of the *facón* through the twentieth century. They generally used smaller *facones* for eating, skinning animals, and fashioning equipment out of leather.

MADALINE WALLIS NICHOLS, *The Gaucho* (1968), p. 13; EZEQUIEL MARTÍNEZ ESTRADA, *X-Ray of the Pampa* (1971); RICHARD W. SLATTA, *Gauchos and the Vanishing Frontier* (1983); *Cowboys of the Americas* (1990), p. 150.

RICHARD W. SLATTA

FACTOR. In the late Middle Ages, merchants in foreign countries often grouped themselves into a community enjoying mutual protection and sometimes special privileges vis-à-vis local authorities. The head of such a foreign merchant group or colony was termed the "factor" and the community the "factory." Bruges, for example, in the fourteenth and fifteenth centuries, was the site of Portuguese and Castilian factories through which much of those nations' trade with northern Europe was channeled.

When the Portuguese began their expansion down the west coast of Africa, they adapted and made use of this system by establishing fortified warehouses and administrative offices through which they dealt with the native merchants. Such factories (*feitorias*) were established at Arguin in 1451 and at São Jorge de Mina in 1481.

Similarly, shortly after the discovery of Brazil in 1500, the merchant group that had leased the trade rights from the king established a factory there (1504) in order to have a place to store the dyewood awaiting shipment to Portugal. While claims have been made for the existence of Portuguese factories at various points along the coast in the period 1502–1534, according to the historian Rolando Laguardia Trías there was only one indisputable factory in Brazil before the arrival of Martim Afonso de SOUSA, and until recently it was thought to have been located at Cabo Frio. Trías, however, gives good reasons for thinking that it was actually situated on an island in GUANABARA BAY (Rio de Janeiro). In 1516, with expiration of the royal lease and the crown's resumption of direct control over Brazilian trade, this factory was moved north to Itamaracá near the present-day town of Igaraçu, both because better quality BRAZILWOOD was found there and because the site was closer by ship to Lisbon.

História naval Brasileira, vol. 1 (1975), pp. 254–256; JOHN VOGT, *Portuguese Rule on the Gold Coast, 1469–1682* (1979); A. H.

DE OLIVEIRA MARQUES, *Ensaios de história medieval Portuguesa*, 2d ed. (1980), pp. 164–166, 178–179.

HAROLD B. JOHNSON

FACTORY COMMISSIONS, BRAZIL, unofficial shop-floor committees of rank-and-file workers formed to bargain directly with employers. As early as the 1910s, industrial workers in São Paulo organized informal shop-floor committees, known as *comissões de fábrica*. Women textile workers pioneered this form of organizing in response to their exclusion from the male-dominated anarchist unions of their day. When the women's independent factory commissions initiated successful strike movements (e.g., São Paulo's General Strike of 1917), anarchist activists moved to incorporate the *comissões* in their union structures.

Male and female Brazilian workers were drawn to these shop-floor commissions because unions were often quite weak in the first half of the twentieth century. The local *comissões* offered workers not only an ongoing organization that they controlled, but also a form of local microunionization that survived government and industrialist repression of labor and leftist leadership cadres.

The factory commissions initially served as a tool that groups without access to power in anarchist and socialist unions (e.g., women) used to bargain with their employers. With the establishment of a corporatist industrial-relations system in the 1930s and early 1940s, male and female workers throughout Brazil were forced to rely on their own factory-level organizations because the state-sponsored *sindicatos* did not effectively support workers' demands.

Factory commissions took on the leadership of Brazil's labor movement at various times. In 1945–1947, workers who were organized in such commissions launched widespread strike movements throughout the country. In the early and mid-1950s, men and women who were organized in separate commissions took control of government-sponsored *sindicatos*. The commission structure became increasingly important during the 1964–1985 military dictatorship. Once again, by relying on nominally democratic, local organizations such as the *comissões*, industrial workers could maintain a de facto union structure even during a period of intense government repression.

The founders of the Brazilian Workers Party (Partido dos Trabalhadores—PT) relied on the factory-commission experience in the late 1970s and the 1980s. Metalworkers in São Paulo's industrial suburbs organized *comissões* within their factories as the bases for direct negotiations with their employers and eventually for establishing new, highly representative unions.

For an analysis of the development of factory commissions in the 1910s and their continued importance to workers throughout the 1950s, see JOEL WOLFE, *Working Women, Working Men: São*

Paulo and the Rise of Brazil's Industrial Working Class (1993). On commissions in the 1945–1950 period, see RICARDO MARANHÃO, Sindicato e democratização: Brasil, 1945–1950 (1979). A detailed study of the commission structure in the founding and ongoing operation of the Workers Party is presented in MARGARET E. KECK, The Workers Party and Democratization in Brazil (1992).

JOEL WOLFE

FACUNDO. See **Quiroga, Juan Facundo.**

FADO, the national song of Portugal. The fado is a folk music and dance form embodying the popular customs, poetic traditions, and cultural heritage of the Portuguese people. The fado, derived from the Latin *fatum* meaning fate, expresses the melancholic nature of destiny. Themes of the fado range from the travails of unrequited love to the matador's anxiety before a bullfight. Plaintive descriptions of lonely moonlit rivers and desolate cobblestone streets imbue this music with a sense of *saudade*, a Portuguese word referring to the yearning for the unattainable. Although some musicologists contend that the fado is entirely of Brazilian origin, research suggests that its roots include Provençal poetry, Moorish culture, and medieval troubadour songs.

Since achieving national popularity in the mid-nineteenth century, the fado has been associated with two principal styles: the fado of Lisbon, sung in cafes and taverns, and the University of Coimbra fado, performed by strolling student troubadours extolling their masculinity. Accompanied by the twelve-string Portuguese lute and the Spanish six-string guitar, singers of the fado, or fadistas, deliver their lyrics with a great sense of tragic drama. Whether sung in modern fado houses or on concert stages in Europe and America, the fado offers a chronicle of Portuguese history and culture.

RODNEY GALLOP, "The Fado: The Portuguese Song of Fate," *Musical Quarterly* 19 (1933): 199–213; MASCARENHAS BARRETO, *Fado: Origens liriicas e motivacao poetica* (1961); MARVINE HOWE, "Fado in Portugal," *Saturday Review* (September 12, 1970): 49, 108; DAVID P. APPLEBY, *Music of Brazil* (1983).

JOHN COHASSEY

FAGES, PEDRO (b. 1734; d. 1794), Spanish soldier and explorer. Fages, a native of Guisona, Catalonia, joined the Barcelona-based CATALONIAN VOLUNTEERS in 1767 and participated in the Sonora Expedition of 1767–1771 in Mexico. In 1769 Visitador General José de GÁLVEZ ordered him and twenty-five Catalonian Volunteers to join Governor Gaspar de PORTOLÁ's California expedition. Between 1769 and 1774, Fages participated in the founding of San Diego, the march to Monterey that named many sites in California, and the discovery of San Francisco Bay. Nicknamed "The Bear" ("El Oso"), Fages was the European discoverer of the Central and San Joaquín Valleys. In 1774 he wrote A Historical, Political, and Natural Description of California, an important ethnographic account of the area featuring references to its flora and fauna. Between 1774 and 1778, Fages commanded the Second Company of Catalonian Volunteers in Guadalajara. In 1776 he married Eulalia Callis, daughter of Agustín Callis, captain of the First Company of Catalonian Volunteers. In 1778 Fages served in Sonora, where in 1781 he commanded troops in the Colorado River campaign against the Yuma Indians who had destroyed a Spanish outpost at the confluence of the Colorado and Gila Rivers. In 1782 he was the first European to reach San Diego by crossing the Colorado River. He served as governor of California from 1782 to 1791, a generally peaceful time of mission building. Fages died in Mexico City.

DONALD A. NUTTALL, "Pedro Fages and the Advance of the Northern Frontier of New Spain, 1767–1782" (Ph.D. diss. University of Southern California, 1964); JOSEPH P. SÁNCHEZ, *Spanish Bluecoats: The Catalonian Volunteers in Northwestern New Spain, 1767–1810* (1990).

JOSEPH P. SÁNCHEZ

FAGOAGA Y LIZAUR, JOSÉ MARÍA (b. 1764; d. 1837), Mexican politician. Fagoaga was born in Villa de Rentería, Guipúzcoa, Spain, of a distinguished family, and educated in Mexico City. A determined autonomist, he was in contact with like-minded individuals, among them the marqués de San Juan de Rayas and Jacobo de VILLAURRUTIA. Fagoaga held several important posts, including magistrate of the criminal chamber (1808–1812) and member of the Ayuntamiento of Mexico (1812). As a member of the secret society of Los GUADALUPES, he aided the insurgents and later took part in the electoral processes established by the Constitution of Cádiz. He was elected to the Provincial Deputation in 1813 and in 1820 and served as deputy to the Cortes in 1814 and in 1820. Well known for his dissatisfaction with the colonial regime, Fagoaga was imprisoned and prosecuted in 1815. He was deported to Spain, but returned in 1821, in time to sign the Declaration of Independence and to become a member of the Provisional Governing Junta. He was one of the founders of the Scottish rite Masonic lodges, the *escoceses*, and he distinguished himself as a parliamentarian. In 1822 Fagoaga was one of the deputies imprisoned by Agustín de ITURBIDE. When the Spanish were expelled in 1827, he was forced into exile. Although Fagoaga subsequently returned to Mexico, he no longer participated in politics. He died in Mexico City.

Diccionario Porrúa de historia, geografía y biografía de México, 5th ed. (1986), vol. 1, pp. 1,049–1,050; VIRGINIA GUEDEA, *En busca de un gobierno alterno: Los Guadalupes de México* (1992).

VIRGINIA GUEDEA

See also **Peimbert, Margarita; Peña, Antonia; Sánchez de Tagle, Francisco Manuel.**

FAJARDO, FRANCISCO (*b*. ca. 1524; *d*. 1564), conquistador in Venezuelan territory. Fajardo was the son of a Spanish male and a female Indian chieftain of the Guaquerí tribe. He undertook various expeditions from Margarita Island to the mainland beginning in 1555 and in 1557 obtained authorization from the governor of El Tocuyo to rule and settle the coast. During a 1559 expedition, Fajardo headed inland and reached as far as the Valley of La Guaire, site of present-day Caracas. He returned to the coast, where he founded the settlement of El Collado. On a second expedition to La Guaire Valley, Fajardo discovered gold in Teque Indian territory. When the governor learned of the discovery Fajardo was stripped of his authority and sent to El Collado as its chief justice. In his place, Pedro Miranda was sent to exploit the gold, but he quickly alienated the local *cacique*, Guacaipuro. There followed a series of clashes in which Fajardo aided the Spanish forces despite his dispute with the governor. By 1562 the Indians had driven the Spanish from the valley and forced Fajardo to abandon El Collado. As Fajardo was provisioning yet another expedition in the settlement of CU-MANÁ in 1594, he was arrested by the local chief justice. Though the charges are unclear, he was tried and sentenced to death. In retaliation, his followers on Margarita Island went to Cumaná and seized the chief justice, Alonso Cobos, whom they tried before the Audiencia of Santo Domingo, where he too was sentenced to death.

JESÚS ANTONIO COVA, *El capitán poblador margariteño Francisco Fajardo* (1954); JUAN ERNESTO MONTENEGRO, *Francisco Fajardo: Origen y perfil del primer fundador de Caracas* (1974); GRACIELA SCHAEL MARTÍNEZ, *Vida de Don Francisco Fajardo* (1975).

INÉS QUINTERO

See also **Conquistadores.**

FALCÓN, JOSE (*b*. 1810; *d*. 1883), Paraguayan archivist, historian, and government official. Born in Asunción in the year of Platine independence, Falcón was well placed to participate in many key events during his country's formative years. Educated in the capital, he lived in seclusion in the far south of the country with his wealthy *hacendado* uncle during the dictatorship of José Gaspar FRANCIA. In 1844, President Carlos Antonio LÓPEZ chose Falcón as Paraguay's first foreign minister. In this capacity, he convinced foreign powers—especially Brazil, Britain, and the United States—to recognize Paraguay's independence. After stepping down from the foreign ministry, Falcón served successively as justice of the peace, criminal court justice, and, finally, director of the national archive (from 1854), which he organized along modern European lines.

When Francisco Solano LÓPEZ succeeded to the presidency in 1862, he named Falcón to the posts of interior minister and foreign minister. Falcón also remained director of the archive, which he had to move several times during the WAR OF THE TRIPLE ALLIANCE (1864–1870) as Brazilian forces advanced into Paraguay. He also witnessed some of the worst scenes of the war, notably the massacres at San Fernando, where many of his colleagues in government were executed on López's orders.

Falcón's fortunes improved after the war. He again occupied many official posts: senator, high court justice, president of the Asunción city council, and, once again, foreign minister. He helped to establish the Colegio Nacional in 1877. During the mid-1870s he went to Argentina to negotiate boundary agreements with that country.

During his thirty-six years of government service, Falcón kept copious notes, which he always meant to weave into a series of historical studies and memoirs. Although evidently these were never published, they are available in manuscript in the Manuel Gondra Collection in the Nettie Lee Benson Library at the University of Texas, Austin.

JUSTO PASTOR BENÍTEZ, *Carlos Antonio López (Estructuración del estado paraguayo* (1949), pp. 245–246; HARRIS GAYLORD WARREN, *Paraguay and the Triple Alliance: The Postwar Decade, 1869–1878* (1978); ANDREW R. NICKSON, *Historical Dictionary of Paraguay* (1993).

THOMAS L. WHIGHAM

FALCÓN, JUAN CRISÓSTOMO (*b*. 1820; *d*. 29 April 1870), Venezuelan president (1863–1868). Born in Coro (now Falcón) Province to a wealthy landowning family, Falcón participated in the civil wars of the mid-nineteenth century and rose to the rank of general. He was the outstanding commander of the Federalist armies in Venezuela's bloody FEDERAL WAR (1859–1863) and, as a reward for leading the victorious forces, he was named provisional president in 1863. Falcón's five years in office were marked by administrative ineptitude, corruption, civil turmoil, and rebellion. Uninterested in the day-to-day operations of government, he spent long periods of time in his home province of Coro. In 1868 a temporary coalition of liberals and conservatives raised the banner of the Blue Revolution and drove the largely discredited president into exile, from which he never returned.

ROBERT L. GILMORE, *Caudillism and Militarism in Venezuela, 1819–1910* (1964); GUILLERMO MORÓN, *A History of Venezuela*, edited and translated by John Street (1964); JOSÉ LUIS SALCEDO BASTARDO, *Historia fundamental de Venezuela*, 3d rev. ed. (1972).

WINFIELD J. BURGGRAAFF

FALKLAND ISLANDS, an archipelago of two large and some 200 small islands with a surface area of 4,620 square miles located about 300 miles east of the South

American mainland. From the capital of Port Stanley, the islands are administered as a British crown colony with local self-government.

The early history of discovery and settlement is confusing and often contradictory. Discovery is claimed by Spain (hence Argentina) in 1520, and by Great Britain in 1592. French, Spanish, and British settlers came to the islands in the late eighteenth century; so did American seal-hunters. The British took the islands in 1833 and have maintained control over them since that date, except for the brief period in April–June 1982 when the Argentines recovered them by force and held them until they were defeated by the British. The dispute over the islands' sovereignty continues to be a major issue in the relations between Britain and Argentina.

JULIUS L. GOEBEL, *The Struggle for the Falkland Islands* (1927); LAURIO H. DISTEFANI, *Malvinas, Georgias y Sandwich del Sur ante el conflicto con Gran Bretaña* (1982); LOWELL S. GUSTAFSON, *The Sovereignty Dispute over the Falkland (Malvinas) Islands* (1988); WAYNE S. SMITH, ed., *Toward Resolution? The Falklands/Malvinas Dispute* (1991).

JACK CHILD

See also **Vernet, Louis.**

FALKLANDS/MALVINAS WAR, a long-standing dispute between Argentina and Great Britain that led in 1982 to the most serious outbreak of interstate conflict involving a Latin American nation since the CHACO WAR of the 1930s. The historic causes of the 1982 war go back to eighteenth-century disputes between Spain and Great Britain over settlement and possession of the islands. In 1833, shortly after Argentina gained independence from Spain, the British expelled the remaining Argentine settlers and began their period of continuous occupation of the islands. During his first administration (1946–1955) Argentine president Juan Domingo PERÓN focused on the Malvinas issue in an appeal to Argentine nationalism, linking it to the Argentine Antarctic claim and his plan to create a "greater Argentina." In 1965 a United Nations resolution called on both parties to resolve the issue peacefully, but meaningful negotiations were blocked by the islanders themselves, who strongly preferred to remain under British administration.

For many years the Argentine military had contingency plans for an invasion of the islands, and in early 1982 these plans were activated when a number of circumstances convinced the ruling military junta, headed by Army Commander General Leopoldo F. GALTIERI,

Raising the Argentine flag on Las Malvinas/Falkland Islands, April 1982. WOLLMANN / GAMMA.

that the time was right. These circumstances included the fact that the junta was losing control over Argentina and was seeking some cause to unite the country under its leadership; the coming of the symbolic 150th anniversary of British possession; a diminishing British military and financial commitment to its South Atlantic possessions; geopolitical links to Argentina's Antarctic and BEAGLE CHANNEL interests; and, finally, a jurisdictional incident involving the Argentine scrap metal dealer Constantino Davidoff on the island of South Georgia in March 1982.

Argentina "recovered" the islands on 2 April 1982 with an amphibious task force of 5,000 men that overwhelmed the small Royal Marine garrison after a short firefight. The British military and civilian authorities were expelled via Montevideo, and the approximately 2,000 islanders were placed under the authority of the Argentine military governor. International reaction reflected shock and surprise that possession of a few seemingly unimportant islands could have led to the invasion. Most of Latin America supported Argentina's position on the sovereignty issue, although not necessarily the use of force. The UN Security Council quickly passed a resolution favorable to Britain, which then promptly mounted a naval task force that set sail on 5 April 1982. In Argentina there was euphoria over the recovery of the islands, and for a while it seemed that the junta had achieved its objective of distracting most Argentines from the abuses and failures of their government.

The first military action after the invasion of the FALKLAND ISLANDS took place on the island of South Georgia in late April as the ships of the British task force neared the operational area. On 25 April the British retook South Georgia, damaging and capturing an Argentine submarine in the process. For the next three weeks the war was fought in the air and sea around the Falkland Islands as the British prepared for their landing on the islands. In the principal air and naval actions, the Argentines lost a cruiser and numerous aircraft; the British lost two destroyers, two frigates, and a landing ship. After the sinking of the cruiser *Belgrano*, with a loss of over 300 lives, the Argentine ships stayed in port or close to shore, and most of the fighting was undertaken by the Argentine Air Force.

The ground war began with the British amphibious landing at San Carlos on 21 May. The British crossed East Falkland and hit weak Argentine defensive positions around the capital of Port Stanley. Although some regular Argentine Army and Marine units fought effectively, the majority of the Argentine infantry were recruits with little training and poor leadership who resisted only briefly before falling back to Port Stanley and eventually surrendering on 14 June 1982.

The war cost the Argentines 746 killed, 1,336 wounded, and 11,400 imprisoned (the remaining force at the time of surrender). The British suffered 256 killed and 777 wounded. In addition, three Falkland Island civilians were killed in the final assault on Port Stanley. The political consequences of the war included the strengthening of British Prime Minister Margaret Thatcher's Tory Party and her subsequent reelection. In Argentina there was strong resentment of the military's misjudgment and deception; the junta was dismantled and Argentines inaugurated an elected civilian president, Raúl ALFONSÍN (1983–1989), in December 1983. Full diplomatic relations between Argentina and Great Britain remained broken for eight years. For the 2,000 Falkland islanders the war meant that their status as British subjects was secure, at least for the midterm, although their lives had been altered by both the war and the large and expensive garrison the British now felt obliged to keep on the islands. Postwar disputes over control of foreign fishing vessels and reports of possibly substantial oil fields in the waters surrounding the Falkland Islands have added resource issues to this long-standing dispute between Argentina and Great Britain. One final consequence of the war was that any hope for an amicable settlement of the Falklands/Malvinas sovereignty dispute was set back for many years to come.

MAX HASTINGS and SIMON JENKINS, *The Battle for the Falklands* (1983); OSCAR RAÚL CARDOSO et al., *Malvinas: La Trama Secreta* (1983); ALBERTO R. COLL and ANTHONY C. AREND, eds., *The Falklands War: Lessons for Strategy, Diplomacy, and International Law* (1985); RUBÉN O. MORO, *The History of the South Atlantic Conflict* (1989); LAWRENCE FREEDMAN and VIRGINIA GAMBA-STONEHOUSE, *Signals of War: The Falklands Conflict of 1982* (1990).

JACK CHILD

See also **British–Latin American Relations.**

FALLAS SIBAJA, CARLOS LUIS (*b.* 21 January 1909; *d.* 6 May 1966), the best-known and most widely translated Costa Rican author, primarily through his classic work *Mamita Yunai* (1941). Fallas was an indefatigable labor organizer and politician who played a key role in the formation of the Communist Party in 1931 and in the Atlantic Coast banana workers' strike of 1934. Often writing from an autobiographical perspective in his novels, Fallas had worked as a youth of sixteen in the banana plantations of Límon province and on the docks of the port of Limón, loading the fruit. He knew first-hand the oppressive and absurd conditions suffered by local residents at the hands of the UNITED FRUIT COMPANY and corrupt local politicians.

Fallas returned to his native Alajuela in the Central Highlands in 1931 and joined in the newly formed Communist Party as a leader of his fellow shoemakers in that city. The court system "exiled" him to Limón in 1933 for an incendiary speech; he then took up the task of organizing the banana workers, whose 1934 strike was by far the largest labor mobilization in Costa Rican history to that date. He was imprisoned briefly but later served as national deputy (1944–1948) before assuming a major military leadership role on the losing side of the 1948 civil war. He was again jailed and spent a year in prison, being the last prisoner released owing to his refusal to request a pardon from the Figueres-led junta. Over the next nearly twenty years Fallas led the fight to regain formal political rights for the defeated Communist Party, serving finally as *regidor* of the San José municipal government (1966).

Although he completed only eight years of formal schooling, Fallas could count on a rich store of life experiences. His *Mamita Yunai* emerged from a report on the manipulation of the 1940 presidential voting in the Talamanca region in far southeastern Costa Rica. Likewise, his other major novels (*Marcos Ramírez*, 1952; *Gente y gentecillas*, 1947) are based on working-class life in his home town. Fallas received recognition abroad for his literary achievements long before local cultural authorities would challenge political conventions at home. *Mamita Yunai* was widely read, and the novel *Marcos Ramírez* won a William Faulkner Foundation Prize in 1963. Fallas was officially declared Benemérito de la Patria on 14 November 1967, but his life and work still remain polemical subjects in Costa Rica.

Basic sources on Fallas include MARIELOS AGUILAR, *Carlos Luis Fallas: Su época y sus luchas* (1983); and VICTOR MANUEL ARROYO, *Carlos Luis Fallas* (1977).

LOWELL GUDMUNDSON

FAMILY. It would be difficult to overemphasize the role of the elite family in the organization of the colonial economy (production and distribution) and in the development of political institutions in Latin America. One explanation is that both Spain and Portugal established the family as the appropriate institution for purposes of settlement, land distribution, and political power. For example, Spain preferred to award ENCOMIENDAS (grants of Indian labor) to married men (who were, preferably, married to Spanish women). These ENCOMENDEROS (who also received a seat on the city council) were required to establish a CASA POBLADA, a house on the town square of the Spanish seat of government large enough to house thirty-five people and to supply horses and arms sufficient for seventeen men. One result of this policy was that many of the *encomendero's* Spanish relatives or friends migrated and became a part of his effective extended family and business arrangements.

In Brazil the DONATARIO system that originally was intended to facilitate settlement and development also resulted in the dominance of the original grantee and his relatives. Land grants were based on the productive potential (capital, slaves) of the petitioner and led to a system of LATIFUNDIA, in which a small group of families had effective control over production. In the same way, the Brazilian city councils were made up of *homens boms* (good men). "Good men" were defined as married

men of property, legitimate birth, and clean blood (i.e., no Jewish or Moorish background and no history of vile occupations, such as merchant). "Good men" were "elected" by the "good men" already serving on the council. Thus the hierarchy reproduced itself. The city councils had unusual importance in Brazil because there were so few crown administrators. Many villages were literally hundreds of miles from the residence of any official. The "royal judges" constantly traveled between towns and villages, attempting to provide some semblance of law. But much of this was completely ineffective, and only the power of the dominant families and their personal "armies" determined what could happen within a settlement.

In terms of economic development, the elite family was essential. Neither the Spanish nor the Portuguese crown provided much in terms of resources to build public buildings, roads, or port facilities. Nor did they provide armies separate from the colonial militias. Instead, it was the elite families who organized contributions of building materials, slave labor, and other materials for these projects. True, the Indians in REPARTIMIENTO labor in Spanish America also worked and often died working on public projects, but the labor of these Indians was directed through elite Spanish *encomenderos*, who organized the gathering of appropriate materials. For Brazil these tasks were always performed by the slaves of elite families who contributed their labor for the cause.

Elite families in Latin America intermarried with each other, creating within politically defined regions clusters of kin who controlled both politics and the local economy. In addition, the inherited Iberian trait of "patriarchalism," enforced through law and tradition, gave the male head of lineage authority over his kindred throughout the colonial period. By the nineteenth century, it was the domestic group, rather than the kindred, that was dominated by the patriarchal figure.

Inheritance was the major means of property distribution until the end of the nineteenth century, when limited partnerships and incorporation laws were passed. In the absence of limited liability, prudence dictated that business partners also be cousins or brothers-in-law. Furthermore, most elite men established their households and businesses with the help of their wife's DOWRY until the nineteenth century, when other factors such as education became more important and the dowry gradually disappeared.

Indigenous families in Latin America went through an exceedingly difficult period in the sixteenth century, when from 40 to 90 percent of them died, mostly of European diseases brought in by the conquistadores. The recovery of these populations involved substantial miscegenation with Europeans and Africans, as well as the forced coresidence of tribes (*congregación*) formerly hostile to each other. Indigenous families utilized the European institution of ritual kinship to reestablish ties of reciprocity and exchange in their shattered communities. This means of "family creation" was also adopted by African slaves brought in from diverse areas of Africa, who sometimes also viewed those who traveled in the same slave ship as members of their family.

In religious and legal terms the Latin American family system was based on European categories. Kinship was bilateral, with kin counted on both the maternal and the paternal side. It was also widely extended, with kinship recognized to the seventh or tenth degree. Ritual kinship (COMPADRAZGO in Spanish) had substantial importance as both a means of recognizing reciprocal obligations and as a category that required church dispensation for MARRIAGE to take place. It could also be used to reinforce a kin relationship or to formalize a patron-client relationship, and was highly significant as a means of expanding kindred on an interclass basis. Divorce and remarriage had been common among the pre-Hispanic cultures of Latin America. While the Catholic church sometimes allowed "separation of bed and board" in exceptional circumstances, remarriage was never permitted in colonial Latin America. Furthermore, spouses were legally required to cohabit.

The average household in eighteenth- and nineteenth-century Latin America was relatively small (between four and six free members), both in urban and rural areas, with more affluent households generally being larger. This picture is similar to that of Europe over three centuries. What was unexpected, however, was the evidence that household size in Latin America increased significantly in both the rural and urban areas during the nineteenth century as the domestic unit expanded its productive capacity and oriented itself toward the marketplace. Just as families played an important role in the development of roads and other infrastructures and were important sources of credit, so also the early stages of commercialization and INDUSTRIALIZATION were almost always organized through the household. The low levels of liquid capital, the precarious condition of markets, and poor communications all meant that factories developed very slowly and that, for a long time, households followed a mixed economy of subsistence and market production. At a later stage in industrialization, the participation of the household and family in the exchange economy ceased to be a matter of choice. Capitalism overpowered prior modes of production as the economy took on an export character.

From the late eighteenth century until at least 1870, commercialization and protoindustrialization in Latin America were characterized by urban communities with 25 to 45 percent female-headed households. In some cases they were more common than couple-headed or single-male–headed households. This is particularly startling, for the female-headed household has never been the modal type in published studies of European or American communities, nor have female-headed households typically been portrayed as exceeding 10 to 15 percent of total households in a comparable historical period elsewhere. The high frequency of the female-headed household in eighteenth- and nineteenth-century Latin America appears to have been related to the peculiar characteristics of the changes in modes of production in Latin America and to the development of protoindustrial households based on domestic industry.

The prevalence of this form of household in nineteenth-century Latin America suggests much greater autonomy for women of all classes than had been perceived previously. It indicates that the nineteenth-century domestic unit was determined more by the productive organization of the household than by consumption, sexual ties, or affective needs. The reproductive unit (a mother with her children) was generally retained, but stable couple units were notable by their absence, particularly among the urban lower classes.

Female-headed households in the early nineteenth century were predominantly lower-class and involved in such occupations as subsistence agriculture (in the rural areas), textile or cigarette manufacture, and services such as laundering, ironing clothes, or preparing food to sell in the street. Many female-headed households were created through the dissolution of consensual unions that had been organized around the domestic mode of production in agriculture. The commercialization of agriculture resulted in a change in productive patterns and the migration of many men to areas of agricultural employment, leaving women and children either to continue subsistence agriculture or to migrate in search of better opportunities in urban areas. In the nineteenth century, development efforts tended to victimize the lower-class family, as they still do today.

Another dimension of eighteenth- and nineteenth-century household organization was the presence of nonrelated members (*allegados, agregados*), particularly in lower-class or female-headed urban households, often comprising up to 30 percent of household members. Accepting *allegados* into a household appears to have been a major strategy to alleviate financial difficulties in periods of urbanization and economic change for both family and nonrelated members. In some cases the nonrelated members may simply have been boarding with a family, either paying money or providing services such as housework, child care, water carrying, and the like. Housing shortages also accounted for some of this development. Still another dimension of the presence of nonrelated members in the household was the expansion in this period of the workshop attributes of the household. It became common to include apprentices, clerks, cashiers, and other helpers involved in the productive side of the household in its residential arrangements. Elite families also commonly incorporated *agregados* (including orphans, relatives, Indian captives in Brazil, and others) into their households, where they generally functioned as domestic servants.

Today, families in urban working-class communities depend on wages for support, though these are often uncertain and frequently insufficient to cover the needs of the household. Consequently household members try to acquire access to auxiliary resources, including extra employment benefits, state services, nonmonetary inputs from home production, and benefits from wider exchanges among kin or neighbors. In addition, the household often has multiple earners as well as earners with multiple employment.

Positive mechanisms utilized by poor households to defend themselves against inadequate wages and poor access to social services have been characterized as "family survival strategies." In the case of female-headed families, the increase in poor households headed by women is directly related to processes of modernization, including internal and international migration, mechanization of agriculture, the development of agribusiness, URBANIZATION, overpopulation, lower-class marginality, and the emergence of a class system of wage labor. Female-headed households are not only more likely to be poor than are other households, but they are also less likely to be employed in formal-sector jobs and, therefore, are frequently excluded from other benefits associated with employment.

In twentieth-century rural communities, household size, the organization of household labor, the use or sale of household production, and the overall mode of production continue to be closely related. Important strategies for survival and social mobility among peasant families include marriage, fertility, inheritance, and migration. Among Peruvian peasant families, it is common for the youngest son to inherit the parents' house, living with them in their declining years and taking over the farm after their deaths by purchasing the inheritance shares from his siblings. In some areas, the migration of adult children to new farmlands (in order to avoid extreme parcelization of properties) has been succeeded, as lands become unavailable, by migration to urban areas for employment, as well as by rural wage labor. Diverse family survival strategies involving several workers and types of relations (wage laborer, sharecropper, unpaid family laborer, estate tenant) are commonly joined for mutual benefit. Thus, while proletarianization makes labor more of an individual enterprise, it may still be strongly oriented toward family goals.

Often scholars of the family have assumed an "ideology of solidarity and cooperation within the family." Recent studies, although acknowledging that such an ideology exists, have emphasized that it is important to know how economic changes affect power relations within the household and family. For example, the proletarianization of rural labor in Brazil may have resulted in a decline in the solidarity of the lower-class rural family. This occurs because the husband cannot fulfill his role as provider and because the redefinition of wage labor tasks by gender has forced women and young girls into the most intensive, seasonal, and the lowest-paying jobs. Women give their entire wage to the household, but the older sons resist, paying only room and board, and the husband keeps drinking money. Many women resent having to accept wage labor and prefer to care for their houses and their families themselves. In addition, women's labor is often used to facilitate the entrance of children into the labor force. People sometimes ask whether the contemporary family in Latin America has declined in importance as compared to the colonial period. While modernization has definitely changed the definitions and roles of the family, in 1995 the family and kin network continue to be the primary units on which individuals depend for support, regardless of their class. In that regard, the Latin American family will always be critical.

GILBERTO FREYRE, *The Masters and the Slaves,* translated by Samuel Putnam (1933); *Journal of Family History,* special issues on Latin America: 3, no. 4 (1978), 10, no. 3 (1985), and 16, no. 3 (1991); ELIZABETH KUZNESOF, "Household and Family Studies," in K. Lynn Stoner, ed., *Latinas of the Americas: A Source Book* (1989), pp. 305–388; RAMÓN A. GUTIÉRREZ, *When Jesus Came, the Corn Mothers Went Away: Marriage, Sexuality and Power in New Mexico, 1500–1846* (1991).

ELIZABETH KUZNESOF

See also **Marriage and Divorce.**

FANGIO, JUAN MANUEL (*b.* 24 June 1911; *d.* 17 July 1995), Argentine race car driver. Born in Balcarce, 220 miles south of Buenos Aires, of recent Italian ancestry, as a teenage soccer player Fangio received the lifetime nickname "el Chueco" because of his bow legs. While working as a mechanic in a shop he partially owned, he ran in unsanctioned races beginning in 1936, then inaugurated his official career in 1938, winning for the first time in 1940. Except for four years during World War II, he raced continuously: open road, dirt track, and Grand Prix, joining the European circuit in 1948. He retired after finishing fourth in the French Gran Prix in 1958. Overall he won 102 of 186 international races he entered, 24 of 51 linked to the Driver's World Championship, a competition he captured five times (1951, 1954–1957), along with the affection of Argentines. Accused by some of being too cooperative with Juan and Evita Perón, he nonetheless avoided persecution and maintained heroic status among his countrymen. A 1941 tango, revived as late as the 1980s, labeled Fangio "the king of the steering wheel" and "the champion of champions"; a 1980 survey designated him "the greatest sportsman in Argentine sports history." Other drivers considered him talented and uncompromising, but always helpful and never deliberately dangerous or mean. The Centro Tecnológico-Cultural and Museo del Automovilismo Juan Manuel Fangio opened in Balcarce in 1986.

MIGUEL ANGEL MERLO, *Las tuercas calientes* (1976); JUAN MANUEL FANGIO and ROBERTO CAROZZO, *Fangio: Cuando el hombre es más que el mito* (1986); ANTONIO EMILIO CASTELLO, "Juan Manuel Fangio," in *Todo Es Historia,* 23, No. 265 (1989): 65–69; JUAN FANGIO and ROBERTO CAROZZO, *Fangio: My Racing Life* (1990); STIRLING MOSS with DOUG NYE, *Fangio: A Pirelli Album* (1991).

JOSEPH L. ARBENA

FAORO, RAYMUNDO (*b.* 27 April 1925), Brazilian jurist and essayist. Born in Rio Grande do Sul of Italian forebears, Faoro received his law degree in 1948 and practiced law in Rio de Janeiro. From 1977 to 1979 he was president of the Ordem dos Advogados (Brazilian Bar Association) during the military dictatorship. Faoro secured the reinstitution of habeas corpus and helped restore a constitutional regime through public advocacy and political journalism.

Faoro published his best-known book, *Os donos do poder* (The Masters of Power), in 1958, but it had a greater impact during the dictatorship, when it appeared in a revised and much-expanded edition in 1975. Faoro was the first to apply Weberian analysis to Brazilian history, and his book has joined a short list of celebrated essays on the nature of Brazilian society. *Donos* surveys the national experience, focusing especially on the political estate (*estamento*). For Faoro, this group controlled the state, which he saw as fundamentally unaltered from its Portuguese prototype.

Regarding civil society, Faoro broke with conventional historiography, which viewed nineteenth-century Conservatives as owners of large estates. Faoro viewed them rather as controllers of "mobile wealth," that is, slaves and credit. It was not Conservatives but Liberals, he held, who predominated among *latifundists*, merchants and creditors allied with the political estate after independence in 1822. Excepting the early Empire (1831–1837) and the Old Republic (1889–1930), when relative decentralization strengthened landed elites, the political estate and its commercial allies succeeded in dominating civil society through a centralized state.

According to Faoro, the political estate has shaped the stratified character of Brazilian society, and has been impervious to the needs of the people as well as inattentive to the demands of powerful economic interests. The state dominates civil society, but the ruling estate has no clear national project.

Donos is most obviously Weberian in its interpretation of bureaucracy, offering an explanation of the enormous power of the contemporary Brazilian state, authoritarian and heavily engaged in parastatal enterprises when the second edition appeared. The work challenged dominant Marxist currents, among which Nicos Poulantzas's interpretation of the "exceptional capitalist state" and its "relative autonomy" was then most popular in Brazil.

RAYMUNDO FAORO, *Machado de Assis: A pirâmide e o trapézio* (1974) and *Os donos do poder,* 2d ed. (1975); RICHARD GRAHAM, "Os donos do poder," in *Hispanic American Historical Review* 58, no. 3 (1978): 528–530; JOSEPH L. LOVE, "Machado de Assis," in *Hispanic American Historical Review* 58, no. 4 (1978): 753–755.

JOSEPH L. LOVE

FARIÑA NÚÑEZ, ELOY (*b.* 25 June 1885; *d.* 1929), Paraguayan writer. Probably the most respected author in Paraguay during the first quarter of the twentieth century, Fariña Núñez was born in the tiny hamlet of Hu-

maitá, site of a major battle during the disastrous WAR OF THE TRIPLE ALLIANCE some seventeen years earlier. Perhaps owing to the isolated position of his hometown, Fariña Núñez chose to go to Argentina for his education. He graduated from the Colegio Nacional of Corrientes and later studied law at the University of Buenos Aires.

Fariña Núñez spent most of his adult life in Buenos Aires, where he worked as a clerk in the internal revenue administration. His true love, however, was literature and his prime subject Paraguay. In 1913, when the Buenos Aires daily *La Prensa* opened a literary competition, Fariña Núñez won it with a short story entitled "Bucles de oro" (Golden Curls). He later published volumes of poetry (*Canto secular; Poesias escojidas*), miscellaneous prose (*Las vértebras de Pan; La mirada de los muertos; Cuentos guaraníes*), philosophical treatises (*Conceptos estéticos; Asunción; Crítica*), an essay in economics (*El estanco del tabaco*), and even a novel on Graeco-Egyptian life and customs (*Rhódopis*). His death at age forty-four robbed Paraguayan letters of one of its chief practitioners.

WILLIAM BELMONT PARKER, *Paraguayans of To-Day* (1921), pp. 31–32; CARLOS ZUBIZARRETA, *Cien vidas paraguayas,* 2d ed. (1985), pp. 273–275.

THOMAS L. WHIGHAM

FARQUHAR, PERCIVAL (*b.* 19 October 1864; *d.* 4 August 1953), American entrepreneur and railroad magnate. Born in York, Pennsylvania, Farquhar graduated from Yale University in 1884 with a degree in mechanical engineering. His Latin American business ventures began in Cuba shortly after the end of the Spanish-American War. There he profited from connections with U.S. occupation officials, purchased the Havana tram system, and electrically equipped it at the turn of the century. Beginning in 1900 he organized, along with Sir William Van Horne (of Canadian Pacific fame), the construction of the Cuba Railroad across the eastern half of the island.

In 1904 Farquhar purchased a Guatemalan concession to build a railroad connecting United Fruit Company lands and the Caribbean port of Puerto Barrios. With Indian draft labor, the line was completed in 1908. In the meantime, Farquhar had moved to Brazil, where he resided for the rest of his life. He invested in public utility companies in Rio de Janeiro and Salvador, managed the construction of port facilities in the north of the country, and directed the construction of the Madeira-Mamoré Railroad through the Amazon jungle. He also created and presided over the Brazil Railway Company, a syndicate that in 1912 controlled one-half of all Brazilian railroad mileage.

Farquhar spent the last decades of his life building and managing the steel plant at Itabira, Minas Gerais. From the start, this project faced fierce opposition from

Brazilian nationalists. President Getúlio VARGAS nationalized Itabira in 1942, making it part of the COMPANHIA VALE DO RIO DOCE. Farquhar died in Rio de Janeiro.

CHARLES GAULD, *The Last Titan: Percival Farquhar: American Entrepreneur in Latin America* (1964); STEVEN TOPIK, *The Political Economy of the Brazilian State, 1889–1930* (1987); TODD A. DIACON, *Millenarian Vision, Capitalist Reality: Brazil's Contestado Rebellion, 1912–1916* (1991).

TODD DIACON

See also **Railroads.**

FARRELL, EDELMIRO (*b.* 12 August 1887), Argentine general, ally of Juan PERÓN, and leader of a military junta (1944–1946). Farrell rose to prominence as part of a military *golpe* (coup) that seized power on 4 June 1943. A fervent nationalist, Farrell joined with Juan Perón and other army officers in the Group of United Officers (GOU). Influential among Argentina's officer corps, the GOU promoted anticommunism and economic nationalism. When factionalism pushed General Arturo Rawson, the *golpe*'s organizer, from command, Farrell became the minister of war (1943) under General and acting President Pedro Pablo RAMÍREZ (1943–1944) immediately after the *golpe*.

Factional disputes worked in favor of Farrell, who became president in 1944. As the junta's leader, Farrell allied with Juan Perón in efforts to establish a popular base for the military government. Farrell closed his term in power by supervising the national elections of 24 February 1946, which resulted in the election of Juan Perón as president.

ROBERT A. POTASH, *The Army and Politics in Argentina, 1928–1945: Yrigoyen to Perón* (1969) and *The Army and Politics in Argentina, 1945–1962: Perón to Frondizi* (1980).

DANIEL LEWIS

FARROUPILHA REVOLT, or Ragamuffin War (1835–1845), uprising in Brazil's southernmost province of Rio Grande do Sul, the longest and most dangerous of the five major regional revolts that shook Brazil during the REGENCY (1831–1840). First ridiculed as *farrapos*, or "ragamuffins," for their characteristic fringed leather garb, the rebels adopted the name as a banner of pride and defiance. Political and economic grievances fueled the rebellion. Complaints that the distant central government neglected the province's needs, undervalued its military sacrifices, and pursued policies that discriminated against its pastoral products generated intense regionalism and pressure for decentralization and increased autonomy. Attempts by unpopular imperial officials to strengthen central control and extreme interparty rivalry brought matters to the breaking point, dividing coastal cities from cattle ranchers of the interior. The revolt was cast in the rhetoric of radical liberalism and republicanism and attracted the participation of Italian exiles Giuseppe GARIBALDI and Luigi Rossetti.

The revolt began on 20 September 1835, under the capable leadership of rancher Bento Gonçalves da Silva. The rebels quickly captured the provincial capital of Pôrto Alegre but lost it in June 1836 to legalist forces, which controlled the coastal zone for the remainder of the conflict. When the Regency did not answer their demands, rebels met in the interior town of Piratini and declared an independent republic in September 1836, electing Bento Gonçalves provisional president. Imperial forces had little military success against the rebels in the interior, where most of the fighting occurred. Bento Gonçalves was captured in October 1836 but escaped the following year, lending the revolt renewed energy. The rebels received arms, supplies, and financial support from Uruguay's caudillo leader José Fructuoso RIVERA, who, along with some Riograndenses, had designs of forming a new state uniting Uruguay, Rio Grande do Sul, and the Argentine provinces of Entre Ríos and Corrientes. Rio Grande was a natural extension of the pastoral culture to its south, its ranchers had many ties across the border, and it had long been entangled in the political unrest of the Río de la Plata.

The Farrapos' successes influenced the outbreak of the SABINADA REVOLT in Bahia in 1837, and rebels proclaimed a second independent republic in Santa Catarina in 1839, following an expedition across Rio Grande's northern border. That republic fell four months later and the tide of battle turned against the rebels, who were beset by factionalism and shortages of supplies. On the imperial side, bungling, troop shortages, and conflicts of authority hampered efforts to suppress the uprising.

In 1842 Brazil's most formidable nineteenth-century military commander, Luis Alves de LIMA E SILVA, barão de Caxias, took over command of the legalist forces and administration of the province. The following year the rebels drew up a moderate constitution for the republic, retaining slavery, Catholicism as the official religion, and providing for indirect elections. The political skill of the barão de Caxias and his military victories in Caçapava, Bagé, and Alegrete gradually brought the province back under imperial control. His generous peace, which included freedom for slave soldiers, brought the conflict to an end in February 1845.

Subsequent disruption of Brazil's trade with the Río de la Plata due to renewed instability there, together with new Brazilian duties on jerked beef imports, alleviated Rio Grande's economic grievances by easing competition, at least temporarily. The extent to which the rebellion was separatist or federalist is still a matter of debate. In subsequent years, Riograndenses stressed the revolt's federalist and republican strains, seeing in it antecedents of the federalist republic of 1889.

DANTE DE LAYTANO, *Historia da República Riograndense, 1835–1845* (1936); MOACYR FLORES, *Modelo político dos farrapos* (1978); SPENCER L. LEITMAN, *Raízes socio-econômicas da guerra dos Farrapos* (1979); WALTER SPALDING, *A revolução farroupilha*, 2d ed. (1980).

JOAN BAK

FASCISM. The fascist movement in Latin America is not easily equated with such movements in Europe or elsewhere. European fascism emerged before 1914 amid the alienation caused by rapid industrialization. At first an intellectual mood comprising rejection of positivism, liberalism, and (in the arts) bourgeois formalism, it grew mightily owing to the psychic and social mobilization, military experience, sacrifice, and disillusionment of WORLD WAR I. Its salient characteristics were charismatic leadership; rituals, costumes, and symbols; an ethic of voluntarism, struggle, and instinct; nationalisms that sought to restore folk communities (often mythologized); and the belief that social justice could be achieved only through those folk communities. It comprised a youth revolt and the project of creating a moral, integral New Man. It rejected Marxism and class-based politics as well as bourgeois parliamentarism and democratic institutions generally. In power, fascists proved incompetent and corrupt; some movements (as in Italy) resorted to irredentism and foreign conquest to sustain revolutionary élan. Fascist leadership was middle class; however, mass followings were built among war veterans, uprooted and alienated individuals, and preexisting labor organizations disillusioned with or forcibly wrenched away from Marxism. In central and eastern Europe, fascism was markedly racist and anti-Semitic. In Hitler's Germany the genocidal "Final Solution" was the consequence.

Latin American movements called "fascist" lack many of these attributes; their closer affinities are with populism and authoritarian nationalism. Populist movements emerged before 1914 from the conjunction of increased rural-urban migration and the ambitions of reformist, upper-status politicians (such as Guillermo Billinghurst in Peru and José BATLLE Y ORDÓÑEZ in Uruguay); they arose in part from the "ruralization" of the cities, that is, transplantation of the personalistic patron-client relationships of the countryside. The context of these movements was municipal politics and the content pragmatic, not ideological, issues. Between the world wars the several strains of Latin American populism embraced nationalism, seeking to establish the idea of national identity ("peruanidad," "Mexicanidad"), to create integrated modern nation-states, and to make the state—not low-level clientelism—the vehicle for social justice. This inclusive nationalism embraced, if only rhetorically, hitherto repressed or marginalized peoples; it denounced as "vendepatrias" (those who sold out their country) those elite groups that had collaborated in the annexation of Latin America's economies to the European- and U.S.-dominated world trade system.

When in the crisis-ridden 1930s the military seized power in several countries, some military politicians (such as Luis Miguel SÁNCHEZ CERRO in Peru) combined traditional repression with expedient labor alliances, trading public works projects, housing, and beneficial legislation for political support. Others (such as José Félix URIBURU in Argentina) envisioned the military corporation as the only competent, dedicated agent of national integration, a concept adumbrated by the Brazilian *tenentes* ("lieutenants"; see TENENTISMO), restless, nationalistic young officers who staged the first of a series of minor revolts in July 1922. Although the utility of such projects in thwarting opposition Marxists or Apristas (in Peru) was obvious, they proved unpopular at the time, even among the military; but they would reappear in various guises after 1945.

In the early 1930s a number of fascist groups were founded in emulation of those in Antonio de Salazar's Portugal, Benito Mussolini's Italy, and José Antonio Primo de Rivera's Spain. "Mediterranean" fascisms, which evoked past imperial grandeur and drew strength from conservative Roman Catholicism, were preferable to German NAZISM, which harbored strains of irreligion and "Aryan" racial exclusivism. Among rightist intellectuals, particularly in Colombia, corporatism became fashionable; it also figured in the theorizing of Catholic intellectuals who, reacting against the anticlericalism of the Spanish Republic (1931–1936) and the outrages of the Civil War (1936–1939), promoted clerical fascism in the style of Engelbert Dollfuss's Austria or the Spanish CEDA (Confederation of Autonomous Rightist Organizations) of J. M. Gil Robles. Following General Francisco Franco's triumph in 1939, Spain's Nationalist regime promoted the doctrine of "hispanidad" throughout Latin America; it, too, enjoyed a vogue.

The most important Latin American fascist movements of the 1930s were the Brazilian Integralistas and the Chilean Nacistas—both of which staged abortive putsches in 1938, then went into decline—the Mexican Sinarquistas; factions among the Bolivian veterans of the disastrous CHACO WAR (1932–1935), some of whom later helped form the Movimiento Nacional Revolucionario (MNR); and a congeries of authoritarian nationalist groups in Argentina. The latter, unable to gain either a mass following or the unconditional backing of the traditional right, specialized in street fighting and anti-Semitic terrorism. They later attached themselves to Peronism; notwithstanding the vicissitudes of Peronism itself, anti-Semitic violence has remained the hallmark of the Argentine right.

The seeds—and charismatic leaders—were present, yet none of these movements developed into a full-fledged European-style fascism. This can be explained in part by the Axis defeat in 1945, in part by socioeconomic and political factors. The former include the inherent difficulties of creating national identities in societies still

543

strongly rooted in primary local, or ethnic solidarities, much less of mobilizing those societies; and the fact that although European capitalists had sheltered within their respective fascisms and supported them, many Latin American capitalists chose to work within foreign systems. Political factors include the emphasis in populist regimes on redistributive—rather than ideological—politics; and the postwar success of Christian Democratic parties (as in Chile and Venezuela), which offered to conservative electorates nonviolent modernizing alternatives to Marxism. In regimes slow to modernize, the Right retained its privileges through traditional means, which did *not* include the mobilizations characteristic of fascism. In regimes fractured or paralyzed by modernization—as in Argentina, Brazil, Chile, and Uruguay in the 1970s, and in Central America in the 1980s—the new military relied on state terror to suppress dissent rather than on demagogy to mobilize and deflect it.

The fundamental structure of fascism is sometimes taken to be an authoritarian, centralized state apparatus sustained ideologically by nationalism, economically by state capitalism, and socially by a dependent syndically organized mass following. If so, five regimes since the 1930s—Getúlio VARGAS's Brazil, especially after 1937; Juan PERÓN's Argentina; the Bolivia of the MNR after 1952; Fidel CASTRO's Cuba since 1959; and the Mexico of the PRI since 1928—merit possible inclusion under the fascist rubric. The first two—which were characterized also by charismatic leadership, ritual, and (in Argentina) anti-Semitism—most closely approximated European fascisms. In Brazil, regimes subsequent to Vargas's death in 1954—particularly the military regimes from 1964 to 1983—have dismantled the mass base of *varguismo*; Argentine Peronism, however, despite its vicissitudes during intervening years, retains some of its earlier dynamic. Bolivia's MNR leadership was uncharismatic; its social mobilization was incomplete and was soon reversed by the military. Cuba's Castro has proven an effective leader; the Cuban people have been mobilized for nationalistic or social justice purposes. However, the regime's affirmation of egalitarianism and rejection of irrationalisms and of capitalism place it outside the fascist category. Mexico's leadership is uncharismatic by design; in recent decades the practice of revolutionary nationalism and populism has drifted far apart from the rhetoric. Even the latter may disappear altogether as the NORTH AMERICAN FREE TRADE AGREEMENT was implemented after 1 January 1994.

A revival of Latin American fascism is possible, perhaps in response to the swallowing up of national economies in globalization; violence will undoubtedly remain endemic. Elites appear, however, to have learned from the fascist experience that it is easier to create caudillos than to dismiss them, easier to mobilize masses than to demobilize them.

JOHN D. WIRTH, *The Politics of Brazilian Development, 1930–1954* (1970); ALISTAIR HENNESSY, "Fascism and Populism in Latin America," in *Fascism: A Reader's Guide, Analyses, Interpretation, Bibliography,* edited by Walter Z. Laqueur (1976); JAMES D. COCKCROFT, *Mexico: Class Formation, Capital Accumulation, and the State* (1983); FREDERICK C. TURNER and ENRIQUE MIGUENS, eds., *Juan Perón and the Reshaping of Argentina* (1983); CARLOS WAISMAN, *Reversal of Development in Argentina: Postwar Counterrevolutionary Policies and Their Structural Consequences* (1987); MAX AZICRI, *Cuba: Politics, Economy, and Society* (1988); T. HALPERIN DONGHI, *La historia contemporánea de América Latina,* 2d ed. (1988).

RONALD C. NEWTON

See also **Caudillismo; Military Dictatorships.**

FAVELA, an urban shantytown in Brazil, often either perched precariously on a steep hillside or occupying low-lying, humid river lands, vulnerable to heavy rains and flooding. Individual houses are typically constructed from scrap wood, corrugated metal, or cement blocks. As squatter settlements without official recognition, *favelas* are deprived of city services such as water, sewage, and electricity, and they lack municipally sponsored schools and health clinics. One or two spigots

A favela. PHOTO BY JUCA MARTINS / PULSAR IMAGENS E EDITORA.

located on the outside perimeter may supply residents with water, carried home in cans, for cooking or washing. Dwellers pay high prices for illegal electricity hookups. Although outsiders have frequently condemned *favelas* as lawless places, sociologists have demonstrated that *favelas* can become communities, displaying the range of solidarities and conflicts that the word "community" implies. Some *favelas* have persisted for decades, their residents even resisting attempts to forcibly remove them to more remote sites.

The first *favela* arose in the Morro da Providência, near the Ministry of War in Rio de Janeiro, when disabled soldiers returned home after the CANUDOS expedition in 1897. The soldiers doubtless named the settlement after Mount Favela, a point near Canudos that had figured prominently in battle strategies. As Rio de Janeiro expanded to the southern seaside suburbs in the early twentieth century, hillside *favelas* replaced the razed slums of the central city known as *cortiços*, or beehives.

To an extent, *favela* is a regional term most commonly used in the center-south of Brazil. In the Northeastern city of Recife, for example, similar neighborhoods are referred to as *mucambos*, a term that once referred to slave quarters or runaway-slave settlements.

JANICE E. PERLMAN, *The Myth of Marginality: Urban Poverty and Politics in Rio de Janeiro* (1976).

SANDRA LAUDERDALE GRAHAM

FAZENDA, FAZENDEIRO, a plantation, large farm, or ranch; a planter, owner of a *fazenda*, great landholder, or, until slavery's abolition in 1888, a slave owner. *Fazendas* were large rural properties with a house and outbuildings as well as land divided into agricultural production units that could include coffee, cattle, food crops, and occasionally sugarcane. On some *fazendas* there were processing units for coffee, sugar, and manioc in addition to grazing areas and forested reserves. Although resident free farmers were part of a *fazenda's* labor force, these establishments largely operated with slave labor, which was utilized in all aspects of domestic and field production and, where available, in processing units for coffee, sugar, manioc, corn, and beans.

STANLEY J. STEIN, *Vassouras, a Brazilian Coffee County, 1850–1900* (1970); ROBERT G. KEITH, ed., *Haciendas and Plantations in Latin American History* (1977).

NANCY PRISCILLA SMITH NARO

See also **Plantations.**

FEBRES-CORDERO RIBADENEYRA, LEÓN (*b.* 9 March 1931), president of Ecuador (1984–1988). Born in Guayaquil, Febres-Cordero began his education in his native city and completed his secondary education in the United States. He studied mechanical engineering at the Stevens Institute of Technology in New Jersey. Returning to Guayaquil in 1956, he developed a successful business career, working as a mechanical engineer, manager, and executive in a variety of public and private enterprises, including the Exportadora Bananera Noboa S.A. He was active in a variety of business and civic organizations, serving terms as president of the Guayaquil Chamber of Industries in the 1970s, the National Federation of Chambers of Industries of Ecuador, and the Association of Latin American Industries.

Febres-Cordero entered politics in the 1960s as deputy to the Constituent Assembly (1966–1967), and senator and president of the Economic and Financial Commission of the National Congress (1968–1970). He was principal spokesman for rightist critics of the military juntas that ruled Ecuador from 1972 to 1979 and led the opposition to the Constitution of 1979. Elected deputy to Congress in 1979 as a candidate of the Social Christian Party, he emerged as the leading critic of the governments of Jaime ROLDÓS AGUILERO (1979–1981) and Osvaldo HURTADO LARREA (1981–1983), and a staunch defender of coastal business interests.

Febres-Cordero won the 1984 presidential election as the candidate of the Frente de Reconstrucción Nacional, a coalition of rightist parties. His administration sought to restructure the Ecuadorian economy by reducing government regulations, freeing exchange rates, promoting the export of manufactured items, and encouraging foreign investment. His ability to implement his neoliberal reform program was undermined by an opposition congress and a deteriorating economy. Falling petroleum prices and the subsequent loss of oil revenues after the destruction of the trans-Amazonian oil pipeline forced the administration to adopt austerity measures that quickly alienated labor and opposition political parties. The administration's problems mounted when it failed to control burgeoning budget deficits or to shield the working classes from the impact of the austerity program. Although Febres-Cordero completed his presidential term, his dictatorial style provoked a series of constitutional crises and increased political violence.

HOWARD HANDELMAN, "The Dilemma of Ecuadorian Democracy. Part III: The 1983–1984 Presidential Elections," in *UFSI Reports* 36 (1984); RAMIRO RIVERA, *El pensamiento de León Febres-Cordero* (1986); DAVID W. SCHODT, *Ecuador: An Andean Enigma* (1987), esp. pp. 157–168.

LINDA ALEXANDER RODRÍGUEZ

FEDERAL WAR (VENEZUELA, 1859–1863), the most significant civil strife in Venezuela since the War of Independence. When the consensus among the political elite that had dominated the republic dissolved after 1830, a prolonged period of political instability ensued. Several factors led to war, including social problems inherited from the struggle for independence, tensions among the diverse economic and political groups, a succession of armed movements in rural areas, and hopes for change in the centralist-federalist model of government adopted in 1830. The Conservative Party, under the leadership of Jose Antonio PÁEZ (until his defeat in August 1849), advocated a strong central government. Its supporters consisted of the commercial elite concentrated in Caracas. The Liberals, on the other hand, argued for greater regional autonomy. Their ranks consisted mostly of the remnants of the old landed aristocracy and new groups that arose as a result of the privileges and land grants bestowed upon them for their role in the wars of independence.

After José Tadeo MONAGAS was driven from power by the March Revolution of 1858—in which both Liberals and Conservatives participated—a new regime was set up under General Julián CASTRO. This government did not satisfy the aspirations to power of many Liberals, however, and the members of the Conservative Party fended off Liberal opposition until Castro issued a decree on 7 June 1858 expelling the most prestigious liberal leaders from the country.

The political conflict resulted in diverse armed uprisings, an atmosphere of profound political confusion, and the adoption on 31 December 1858 of a new fundamental charter produced by both Conservatives and Liberals (except for those in exile). Since this charter did not authorize the adoption of a federal system, federalists in exile began plotting a revolution to drive the Conservative majority from power.

On 20 February 1859 in the city of Coro, the federalists took over the military headquarters, proclaiming the creation of a federation, the abolition of the death penalty, universal suffrage, and political pluralism. This was the start of war. Fighting broke out in various parts of the country, and the war went on for four years until, in April 1863, the signing of the Treaty of Coche put an end to it.

After the war, there was no modification of Venezuela's economic or social structure. However, it did result in the establishment of a federal system that in the 1990s still underpinned the national Constitution. It also produced a *caudillo*-centered political system that was dominated by the Liberal Party, the political victor of the war.

JOAQUÍN GABALDÓN MÁRQUEZ, *Documentos políticos y actos ejecutivos y legislativos de la Revolución Federal desde el 20 de febrero de 1859 hasta el 18 de marzo de 1864* (1959); LISANDRO ALVARADO, *Historia de la Revolución Federal en Venezuela* (1975); and ADOLFO RODRÍGUEZ, *Exequiel Zamora* (1977).

INÉS QUINTERO

FEDERALISM, a constitutional system in post-Independence Latin America and, often, still a hotly debated political issue. Formally, it denoted a type of government in which power was explicitly divided between central (national) and regional (state or provincial) authorities. As such it bore resemblance to the system incorporated in the United States Constitution and, to a lesser extent, certain ancient and modern European models. It was first adopted by several Latin American countries during the independence movement, for example, in Venezuela in 1811 in the constitution of the so-called First Republic.

Critics of federalism, of whom the most prominent was Simón BOLÍVAR, condemned it as a dangerously weak system and as a foreign construct ill suited to the historical traditions and circumstances of Latin America. In its most common guise, it took provinces that in the colonial regime had enjoyed no administrative autonomy and suddenly equipped them with their own executive, legislative, and judicial branches that shared power with organs of the national government; sometimes these provinces, improvised as "sovereign" entities, did not even have enough qualified individuals to fill the offices created. However, federalism was a response to genuine regional loyalties and interests repressed or at least denied institutional expression during the colonial period. Moreover, federalism as a technique for dividing and thus curbing the power of government was compatible with the liberal ideology of individual rights that most Latin American leaders following independence professed to one degree or another.

The identification of federalism with political liberalism was perhaps clearest in Mexico, where it became a central dogma of the Liberal Party and of its twentieth-century revolutionary heirs. Thus the three constitutions under which Mexico has been governed for most of its national history—those of 1824, 1857, and 1917—all gave the country a federalist organization. This did not prevent the eventual emergence of a national presidency stronger than that in the U.S. model of federalism; yet the states have retained a distinct role in Mexican politics and government.

Federalism has been equally characteristic of the system of government in Argentina, where initially it was associated not with liberals but with traditionalist forces, especially in the interior provinces. These provincials distrusted the reforming tendencies of the liberal UNITARIOS, whose greatest strength was in the national capital, Buenos Aires. In the end, however, all factions came to accept the federalist Constitution of 1853. It was the country's first truly effective constitution and, though briefly replaced by the Peronista Constitution of 1949, is today the oldest Latin American constitution anywhere in force. Brazil, too, has been formally a federation most of the time since the adoption in 1891 of its first republican constitution, which closely followed the U.S. model even in the use of the name *Estados Unidos do Brasil* (United States of Brazil).

The countries mentioned, Latin America's three largest, are the only ones that still have a strictly federal constitution. The smaller countries, such as the individual Central American republics, Paraguay in South America, and the Dominican Republic in the West Indies, have never adopted anything other than a unitary organization. The other Latin American nations commonly experimented with federal or quasi-federal forms of government at different times in the nineteenth century. Colombia, under its Constitution of 1863, adopted the most extreme version of federalism ever known in Latin America, whereby the various states even had their own armies and postage stamps. Colombia turned to strict centralism with its Constitution of 1886, but in its current charter (that of 1991) included such measures of partial decentralization as the popular election of departmental governors. Still other countries that have opted for constitutional centralism have likewise retained particular features typical of federalism, and in the same way federalist charters (among them the Argentine constitution) commonly have included centrist provisions allowing the national president or congress to "intervene" in the government of the provinces or states when specified conditions arise.

L. S. ROWE, *The Federal System of the Argentine Republic* (1921); MIRON BURGIN, *Economic Aspects of Argentine Federalism, 1820–1852* (1946); CHARLES A. HALE, *Mexican Liberalism in the Age of Mora, 1821–1853* (1968); JORGE CARPIZO, *Federalismo en Latinoamérica* (1973); HELEN DELPAR, *Red Against Blue: The Liberal Party in Colombian Politics, 1863–1899* (1981), esp. chap. 5; FRANK SAFFORD, "Politics, Ideology, and Society in Post-Independence Spanish America," in *Cambridge History of Latin America*, edited by Leslie Bethell, vol. 3 (1985); NETTIE LEE BENSON, *The Provincial Deputation in Mexico: Harbinger of Provincial Autonomy, Independence, and Federalism* (1992).

DAVID BUSHNELL

See also **Constitutions** under individual countries.

FEDERALIST WAR (1898–1899), the conflict in Bolivia that marked the end of the hegemony of the Conservative (or Constitutionalist) Party run by the Sucre-based SILVER-mining oligarchy and the beginning of the predominance of TIN-mining interests based in La Paz. In 1898 a constitutional crisis developed when Sucre delegates to Congress forced through a bill that made their city the permanent site of the national government. The La Paz delegates stormed out and began a revolt, coordinated by the rival Liberal Party. The Liberals also were able to engineer an uprising of the AYMARA Indians of the ALTIPLANO under the leadership of Pablo ZÁRATE WILLKA. The rebel army led by Liberal José Manuel Pando and composed of Liberals, La Paz Federalists, and, most importantly, the Aymaras, was able to defeat the federal army under Conservative president Sévero FERNÁNDEZ ALONSO near La Paz in 1899. After the rebel victory, however, the Indians turned against all whites in the largest nineteenth-century Indian rebellion in Bolivia. Only a combined effort of the creoles was able to contain the incipient caste war. In the aftermath, Zárate Willka and other Indian leaders were executed, La Paz

became the de facto capital of Bolivia, and the Liberal Party began its twenty-year reign.

The definitive work is RAMIRO CONDARCO MORALES, *Zárate, el "Temible" Willka: Historia de la rebelión indígena de 1899,* 2d ed. (1983).

ERICK D. LANGER

See also **Bolivia: Political Parties.**

FÉDERMAN, NICOLÁS (*b.* 1505/09; *d.* 21/22 February 1542), German conquistador. Born Nikolaus Federmann, probably in the free imperial city of Ulm, Féderman worked for the Welsers, a German commercial house. The Welsers had authorization for a trading depot in Santo Domingo by 1526, and in 1528 their agents in Seville signed an agreement with Spanish officials to conquer and settle Venezuela. Féderman was one of several Germans sent to explore, conquer, govern, and exploit the commercial possibilities of the Venezuelan concession.

In his *Historia indiana* Féderman recounts how he crossed the Atlantic to Santo Domingo in 1529 and reached Coro, Venezuela, the following January. In July the ailing governor, Ambrosio Alfinger (Ambrosius Dalfinger), retired to Santo Domingo, leaving him in charge. Féderman boldly organized a successful six-month expedition into the interior, returning to Coro on 17 March 1531. Alfinger, now recuperated, banished him for four years for this unapproved expedition.

In Augsburg in 1532, Féderman shrewdly composed his *Historia indiana,* touting his exploits and the richness of Venezuela, with an eye on his employers, the Welsers. The *Historia,* with its keen analysis of Indian life and warfare, had its desired effect. Féderman signed a contract with the Welsers, and the Council of the Indies made him governor and captain-general of Venezuela.

After his return to Coro, Féderman and Jorge Espira (Georg Hohermuth) organized a two-pronged conquest of the Chibcha (MUISCA) Indians of highland Colombia, where some legends located El Dorado. Espira was to approach from the east by crossing the llanos, and Féderman was to enter from the west by moving up the Magdalena River, but the plan went awry. Espira left Coro in 1535 and spent three ruinous years before struggling back without having penetrated Chibcha territory.

In the meantime, Féderman secured the western boundary of the Welser concession, but then rival and vastly superior forces from Santa Marta blocked movement up the Magdalena. He returned to Coro, where, to avoid an unexpected *residencia* (impeachment), he suddenly resumed his expedition. Following the route taken by Espira, he traversed the Venezuelan and Colombian llanos, always keeping the Andes to the west in view. The two expeditions never met.

Upon finding gold, Féderman turned west and climbed the Andes, but discovered that Gonzalo JIMÉNEZ

DE QUESADA and his expedition from Santa Marta had arrived two years earlier (1537) and had already conquered the Chibchas. Then a group from Popayán, led by Sebastián de BELALCÁZAR, appeared. Each conquistador claimed the Chibcha territory, but they agreed to journey to Spain together to resolve the dispute there. Before departing, Féderman accepted seven shares of any future booty taken by the Jiménez group and the *encomienda* of Tinjacá. Most of his men joined Jiménez's forces and helped them establish new cities and colonize central Colombia. They sold their horses and armament at great profit to Jiménez's men, who were in desperate need of these resources.

Back in Flanders in 1540, Féderman disagreed with the powerful Welsers over his accomplishments and was jailed. Petitions to the Council of Flanders were to no avail. Desperate for a way out, Féderman denounced the Welsers before the Council of the Indies for defrauding the royal treasury. Since the council wanted to separate the Welsers from their Venezuelan concession, the case was transferred to the council's jurisdiction in Spain and Féderman was brought to Valladolid, where he died. The Welsers pursued their Venezuela claim before the council until 1557, when the bankruptcy of Philip II led them to abandon it.

An excellent survey of the German effort to conquer Venezuela and Colombia is JUAN FRIEDE, *Los Welser en la conquista de Venezuela* (1961). See also JOSÉ IGNACIO AVELLANEDA NAVAS, *Los compañeros de Féderman. Cofundadores de Santa Fé de Bogotá* (1900). Féderman's own account of his accomplishments down to 1532 is found in his *Historia indiana* (1958). In English a lively read is JOHN HEMMING, *The Search for El Dorado* (1978).

MAURICE P. BRUNGARDT

FEIJÓ, DIOGO ANTÔNIO (baptized 17 August 1784; *d.* 10 November 1843), Brazilian statesman and regent. Feijó's upbringing, career, style of life, and outlook personified the nativist, anti-Portuguese current in Brazilian affairs in the years after independence. A foundling, born in São Paulo, Feijó was educated for the priesthood and ordained in 1808. A deputy from São Paulo province to the Lisbon Cortes in 1822, he made his mark in the Chamber of Deputies elected in 1826 and 1830 as a prominent opponent to PEDRO I.

Absent from Rio de Janeiro, Feijó played no role in the crisis preceding Pedro I's abdication in April 1831. In July 1831, he accepted the key portfolio of justice. Defeating several armed risings and organizing the National Guard, Feijó served as bulwark of the new regime. Losing patience, he resigned in July 1832. He was a prime mover in the ensuing and abortive parliamentary coup, designed to turn Brazil into a federation of states. Despite this failure, Feijó remained the preeminent figure in liberal, nativist politics, becoming senator from Rio province in 1833. In the elections for a single regent, instituted by the constitutional amendment enacted in 1834 (the Ato Adicional), he was the MODERADO

party candidate and gained a plurality of votes cast. Worsening health and his own doubts about his suitability delayed his taking office until 12 October 1835.

Feijó's two years as regent proved as barren as he had feared, due in part to his foes' unrelenting hostility but also to his intransigence, belligerence, and, above all, failure to take drastic action against regional revolts. Reduced to impotence, he resigned on 18 September 1837. He stayed active in politics but no longer played a central role. Despite a paralytic stroke in 1840, Feijó actively supported the São Paulo revolt of 1842. Deportation to Espírito Santo and then a trial before the Senate probably hastened his death.

OCTAVIO TARQUINO DE SOUSA, *História dos fundadores do império*, vol. 1, *Diogo Antônio Feijó* (Rio de Janeiro, 1957); NOVELLI JÚNIOR, *Feijó: Um paulista velho* (Rio de Janeiro, 1966).

RODERICK J. BARMAN

FEIJÓO, BENITO JERÓNIMO (*b.* 8 October 1676; *d.* 26 September 1764), Benedictine monk who popularized modern European ideas in Spain and the colonies. Feijóo studied in Galicia and Salamanca before becoming professor of theology at the University of Oviedo. Through reading foreign works, Feijóo became aware of his country's intellectual backwardness, which he attempted to correct with his nine-volume collection of essays, *Teatro crítico universal* (1726–1739) and five volumes of *Cartas eruditas y curiosas* (1742–1760). The wide range of subjects he covered included literature, art, philosophy, natural science, mathematics, geography, and history.

Feijóo questioned contemporary medicine, exaggerated devotion to the saints, and religious superstition. He tried to persuade his countrymen that scientific progress need not undermine religious belief. Although his enlightened skepticism aroused controversy, he remained devoted to the Catholic faith and found favor with FERDINAND VI, who silenced his critics with a royal order in 1750. While few of Feijóo's ideas were new, many were relatively unknown in eighteenth-century Spain and its colonies. His writings enjoyed enormous popularity at home and, in part because of his favorable view of creoles' abilities, in the Indies.

UNIVERSITY OF OVIEDO, *P. Feijóo y su siglo*, 3 vols. (1966); RAMÓN OTERO PEDRAYO, *El padre Feijóo: Su vida, doctrina e influencias* (1972).

SUZANNE HILES BURKHOLDER

FEITOR. *See* **Factor.**

FEITORIA. *See* **Fleet System: Colonial Brazil.**

FELGUÉREZ, MANUEL (*b.* 12 December 1928), Mexican artist. Born in San Agustín Valparaíso, Zacatecas, Felguérez is one of the most important exponents of abstract art in Mexico. From 1947 to 1952 he lived in Paris, studying at the Academy of the Grande Chaumière; he also studied sculpture with Ossip Zadkine and Constantin Brancusi. Upon his return to Mexico City in 1953, he studied with Francisco Zúñiga. Felguérez's work includes a number of highly abstract sculptures, stained glass, and murals that he created with found objects. Most of his geometric paintings preserve figurative elements pointing to the dualism between order and disorder that characterizes his entire oeuvre. Felguérez has also worked as a set designer for such plays as *La lección* (1961) and *La ópera del orden* (1961), directed by Alexandro Jodorowsky. His work has been the subject of numerous individual and group exhibitions in Mexico and Europe.

MANUEL GARCÍA PONCE, *Felguérez* (1976); *Manuel Felguérez: Muestra antológica* (1987).

ILONA KATZEW

FÉLIX, MARÍA (*b.* 8 April 1914), Mexican film actress. Born near Alamos, Sonora, as a young girl Félix moved to Guadalajara, where she completed her early schooling. She made her film debut in 1942 in the classic *El penon de las ánimas*. One year later, she starred in *Doña Bárbara*, a screen adaptation of the famous Venezuelan novel. The character Félix portrayed in that film epitomized the dominant, self-assured, strong-willed, and seductive heroine that became the actress's screen persona. Among her greatest and best-known films are *Enamorada* (1947), *La diosa arrodillada* (1947), *Maclovia*

María Félix with Pedro Infante in *Tizoc* (1956). ARCHIVO GENERAL DE LA NACIÓN, MEXICO.

(1948), *Río escondido* (1949), *Doña Diabla* (1951), *El rapto* (1954), *Tizoc* (1957), *La cucaracha* (1959), and *Juana Gallo* (1961). The Mexican film academy awarded Félix the Ariel for best actress for the films *Enamorada, Río Escondido,* and *Doña Diabla.* Known as "La Doña," Félix is a living legend and symbol of Mexican beauty, femininity, and strength, and is arguably the greatest screen presence of twentieth-century Mexican cinema.

LUIS REYES DE LA MAZA, *El cine sonoro en México* (1973); E. BRADFORD BURNS, *Latin American Cinema: Film and History* (1975); CARL J. MORA, *Mexican Cinema: Reflections of a Society: 1896–1980* (1982); and JOHN KING, *Magical Reels: A History of Cinema in Latin America* (1990).

DAVID MACIEL

FEMINISM AND FEMINIST ORGANIZATIONS. The rise of a feminist consciousness in Latin America has been obscured by historiographic assumptions about Latin American society, cultural Catholicism, and stereotypic ideas of "Latin" femininity as well as by ahistorical assertions that feminist thought in the "Third World" is derivative rather than sui generis. The historical record belies these assumptions.

THE NINETEENTH CENTURY:
CITIZENSHIP AND EDUCATION
The issues of full citizenship for women and access to education for girls were addressed in the immediate aftermath of the WARS OF INDEPENDENCE. An 1824 petition presented to the government of Zacatecas, Mexico, states: "Women also wish to have the title of citizen . . . to see themselves counted in the census as 'La ciudadana.'" In Argentina, the Society of Beneficience was created in 1823 to establish public elementary schools for girls.

Women who founded girls' schools were among the first voices calling for women's rights in Latin America. Nisia Floresta Brasileira Augusta, who took a patriotic name (Nisia of the Majestic Brazilian Forest) to illustrate her claim to full citizenship, translated Mary Wollstonecraft's *A Vindication of the Rights of Women* into Portuguese in 1832 and sold out two printings. She wrote numerous articles on the education of women, published in *O Liberal*, and ran a girls' school from her home.

The periodical or political journal has a long history as a central forum for the public debate of women's issues in Latin America. Argentine writer Juana Manuela GORRITI founded *La Alborada del Plata* (1850), which engaged in the intense international debate surrounding women's role in the modern state. Juana Manso, while in exile from Argentina in Brazil, founded *O Jornal das Senhoras*, which dealt primarily with female education and politics. Similar journals appeared in Mexico (*La Semana de las Señoritas Mejicanas* [1851–1852]), Cuba (*Album Cubano de lo Bueno y lo Bello,* founded in 1860 by Gertrudis GOMÉZ DE AVELLANEDA),

Peru and Bolivia (*El Album*, 1860s), and elsewhere. The linkage of the ideas of independence, the emancipation of slaves, and the drive for political and economic modernity with full citizenship for women permeates the writings of these early feminists, as in the 1869 speech by Cuban patriot Ana Betancourt de Mora to a constituent assembly of male patriots: "Citizens: . . . you have emancipated men of servitude. . . . [Now] the Cuban male . . . will also dedicate his generous soul to women's rights."

By the latter half of the nineteenth century, arguments for women's equality were cast in terms of progressivism and the hope of a better life in the New World. The first issue of *O Sexo Feminino*, edited by Francisca Motta Diniz and "dedicated to the emancipation of women," appeared in Campanha, Minas Gerais, Brazil, on 7 September 1873, Brazil's independence day, as a symbol of patriotism—one of the hallmarks of Latin American women's movements. *O Sexo Feminino* declared: "It will be seen that America will give the cry of independence for women, showing the Old World what it means to be civilized, that women are as apt for education as young men." *La Mujer*, published in Chile in the 1890s, was committed to the idea that "woman is the basis of universal progress."

The emergence of women novelists, poets, journalists, and political activists and the development of a shared feminist consciousness in Latin America are directly linked to trends that combined to produce a modernization process in certain nations. Feminists found their voice—and their audience—in Argentina, Uruguay, Chile, and Brazil, states that received thousands of European immigrants and that had significant social and political reform movements, as well as in Mexico and Cuba, countries that experienced major social upheavals.

It was female schoolteachers who formed the nucleus of the first women's groups to articulate what may be defined as a feminist critique of society, that is, to protest the pervasive inequality of the sexes in legal status, marriage, access to education, and political and economic power. The teachers represented a new group in Latin American society—the educated middle sector—that included skilled workers, clerks, and government employees as well as educators. These groups were in touch with one another through their institutions of learning and through professional associations, forums where they could share their common experiences.

In Mexico, poet and educator Rita Cetina Gutiérrez, Cristina Farfán de García Montero, and several primary schoolteachers formed in 1870 La Siemprevivia, a female society dedicated to overcoming women's unequal status and to fighting social problems by improving hygiene and by educating mothers in nutrition and child care. By founding a publication to espouse their ideas and by opening schools to train a new generation, the members of La Siemprevivia employed tactics used by earlier advocates of women's rights; the critical change was that their activities were collective, not individual.

In South America a collective female critique of discriminatory practices based on gender occurred at a series of scientific congresses held between 1898 and 1909. Men and women delegates presented papers on health care, hygiene, the welfare of mothers, and botanical research. The divisive issue proved to be female education: Should women have equal access or be educated only in "suitable" professions, such as primary teaching? The women delegates were indignant that the debate should be cast in these terms and broadened the discussion into a wide-ranging attack on the pervasive inequality of the sexes within their societies.

THE EARLY TWENTIETH CENTURY: SUFFRAGE
In the following decades, women called numerous conferences to discuss these issues. In 1910, the date of the centennial celebration of Argentine independence, the first Congreso Femenino Internacional convened in Buenos Aires with more than 200 women from Argentina, Uruguay, Peru, Paraguay, and Chile in attendance. The congress was organized by the National Women's Council with Cecilia Grierson presiding. Sponsoring groups included the Association of University Women, the National Argentine Association against the White Slave Trade, the Socialist Women's Center, the Association of Normal School Teachers, the Women's Union and Labor Group, and the National League of Women Freethinkers.

The wide differences in political orientation among the women at the Congreso Femenino reflected the enormous political diversity of Buenos Aires, Montevideo, São Paulo, Santiago, and Lima at the time. Many of the reformist women belonged to the Argentine Socialist Party; others rejected the Socialist platform as too concerned with class and labor and aligned themselves with the anarchists, whose platform called for a complete reform of the bourgeois household. The loyalties of others lay with the Argentine Radical Party, a more traditional form of political opposition. Topics addressed ranged from international law, particularly as it related to the rights of married women to retain their citizenship, to health care and the problems of the married working woman, to equal pay for equal work. A resolution was passed commending the government of Uruguay for the enactment in 1907 of the first divorce law in Latin America.

Universal suffrage was part of the Socialist Party platform and women's suffrage was an issue of debate at women's congresses in Latin America in the first half of the twentieth century. In 1916 two feminist congresses were convened in Mexico to discuss the future role of women in post-Revolutionary Mexico and to attempt to influence the Mexican Constitutional Convention then meeting in Querétaro. On its promulgation in 1917, the Mexican Constitution was hailed as the most advanced social and political document of its day; political rights, including the right to vote, were granted "to all Mexi-

Natercia da Silveira speaking at a rally celebrating the approval of women's suffrage in Rio Grande do Norte, 1928. ICONOGRAPHIA.

can citizens." Women, however, were excluded from the category of citizen.

The history of feminism in Peru offers an example of a woman's movement in a country where a strong middle class had not developed by the early twentieth century and the secularization of schools had not occurred. María Jesús Alvarado Rivera, who studied at feminist thinker and author Elvira García y García's private secondary school for girls, founded Evolución Femenina in 1914 to discuss "the woman question." The core group of members had all attended the Congress Feminino Internacional in 1910. The conservatism and class bias of the Peruvian political milieu is apparent in the women's nine-year campaign not for access to government positions but merely for the right of women to be appointed as directors of the powerful private charitable organization Sociedades de Beneficencia Pública.

In the 1920s and 1930s, a number of national and international women's conferences met to discuss civil, legal, and educational reform; suffrage; and the rights of working women. In 1922, with the example of U.S. women's successful drive for suffrage (1920) and in the wake of World War I, the war to "make the world safe for democracy," 2,000 women from throughout the hemisphere convened in Baltimore and formed the Pan-American Association for the Advancement of Women. Veterans of the scientific congresses, such as Amanda Labarca of Chile and Flora de Oliveira Lima of Brazil, were among the Latin American delegates, as was a

rising generation of feminist leaders that included Elena Torres, who was at that time designing the radical rural education program in post-Revolutionary Mexico; Sara Casal de Quirós of Costa Rica; and Bertha LUTZ, founder of the Liga para a Emancipação Intelectual Feminina in Rio de Janeiro in 1920. Lutz's vision contrasts with that of the Peruvian women: "In Brazil the true 'leaders' of feminism . . . are the innumerable young women who work in industry, in commerce, in teaching."

In the 1920s Cuban women were heavily involved in the effort to establish democratic practices and social equality in their newly independent nation. In 1923 the CLUB FEMININO DE CUBA (1917) formed the Federación Nacional de Asociaciones Femeninas, an umbrella group of thirty-one women's organizations, led by Pilar Morlon de Menéndez, to plan the First National Women's Congress, held in Havana on 1–7 April 1923. Government officials were invited to the event in an effort to influence national reform policy. A Second Congress met in Havana in 1925 to call for social equality between men and women, protection of children, equal pay for equal work, equality of the claims of illegitimate children, elimination of prostitution, and a prohibition against the unequal treatment of women.

In Mexico, Sofia Villa de Buentello organized a Congreso de Mujeres de la Raza in July 1925. The ideological splits that were to characterize the women's movement in the hemisphere in later decades were manifest at the congress. Irreconcilable differences emerged between the socialist left, led by Elvia Carrillo Puerto and Cuca García, who insisted on the economic basis of women's problems, and conservatives and moderates, led by Sofia Villa, who believed female inequality to be rooted in social and moral conditions.

In Argentina, feminists Alicia MOREAU DE JUSTO and Elvira Rawson joined with a broad umbrella of reformist groups, including the conservative Catholic women's trade union, to support passage of protective legislation for women industrial workers in 1924. Encouraged by this success, the National Feminist Union and the Women's Rights Association formed a coalition to push a comprehensive reform of the Civil Code through the legislature in 1926. The reform granted married women civil rights equal to those of adult men; mothers parental rights over their children; and married women the right to enter professions, make contracts, and dispose of their earnings without spousal permission. In order to maintain the coalition, the Argentine National Council of Women agreed not to connect the reform to the divisive issue of women's suffrage.

In 1928 Cuban women's associations, including the Alianza Femenina Cubana and the Club Femenino de Cuba, hosted women from all over the hemisphere who came to Havana as unofficial delegates to the Sixth International Conference of American States. By the end of the conference, the women had presented an equal rights treaty for the consideration of the governments of the hemisphere and successfully lobbied for the creation of an officially designated body, the Inter-American Commission of Women (IACW), charged with the investigation of the legal status of women in the twenty-one member states. The use of the transnational forum for the discussion of women's issues proved particularly efficacious for Latin American women, who often found it difficult to create sympathetic political space in their own communities. Bringing international attention to an issue was a political strategy that Latin American feminists helped to pioneer, and it was one that would serve them well over time.

The enactment of women's suffrage should not be viewed as a signpost that the women's program had triumphed: The meaning of the vote and the reasons women's suffrage was enacted in a particular nation at a particular time vary greatly. In Brazil, Uruguay, and Cuba, the enactment of women's suffrage was the result of years of hard work and carefully planned campaigns by groups of women who were prepared to act when a political opening occurred. When the Brazilian Revolution of 1930 brought a reformist government to power, the Federação Brasileira pelo Progresso Feminino, led by Bertha Lutz and Carlota Pereira de Queiroz, presented the leaders with a platform of thirteen principles that included women's suffrage and equality before the law. In Cuba numerous women's organizations, including the Alianza Nacional Feminista, the Partido Nacional Sufragista, and the Partido Demócratica Sufragista were in the forefront of groups fighting for political reform and were poised to demand the extension of the franchise to women when the new provisional constitution was drafted in 1934.

The 1920s and 1930s saw the emergence of the first generation of educated, urban women. This was notably so in Cuba, Argentina, Uruguay, and Chile, where the number of women attending post–grade-school institutions was nearly equal to that of male students, if teacher preparation is included in the count. New associations of women seeking broad-based reform, inclusive of women's suffrage, appeared in the 1930s. One example is the *Movimiento Pro-Emancipación de la Mujer Chilena* (MEMCH, 1935–1953), established by Chilean university women under the leadership of lawyer Elena Caffarena. Journals such as Nelly Marino Carvallo's *Mujeres de América* (1930–1935, Buenos Aires) appealed to an international audience and carried articles written by Bolivian, Paraguayan, Peruvian, and Uruguayan women as well as Argentines.

Women leaders also emerged within the political left, though their politics as spokeswomen on behalf of their own sex often put them in sharp conflict with their male comrades, as illustrated by the career of Patricia Galvão, known as Pagú, who joined the Partido Comunista Brasileira (PCB) in 1930. Pagú shared the scorn of most radical women for bourgeois feminists, but she had a feminist vision of her own. In her novel *Parque industrial* (1933), she described the sexual discrimination and du-

ress experienced by female industrial workers. While her Marxist analysis of labor and call for revolution were orthodox enough, Pagú had the temerity to link the issue of sexual inequality with that of racism in the Brazilian work force. The leadership of the PCB was outraged by the sexually explicit descriptions in the book and even more so by Pagú's daring to address the taboo subject of race: the party demanded that the book be suppressed.

In Mexico, women loyal to the Revolutionary Party were deeply disappointed when reformist president Lázaro CÁRDENAS (1934–1940) failed to fulfill his campaign promise to "reform the constitution to grant equal rights." At the Eighth International Conference of American States at Lima in 1938, it was the Mexican delegation to the IACW, led by Amalia González Caballero de CASTILLO LEDÓN, which successfully lobbied for passage of the Declaration in Favor of Women's Rights. The resolution established the precedent for incorporation of the phrase "the equal rights of men and women" into the charter draft of the United Nations in San Francisco in October 1945.

DEMOCRACY AND SOCIAL JUSTICE

During World War II and its immediate aftermath, many women's groups were incorporated into established political parties, often in "women's sections." Those who maintained their autonomy took on patriotic nomenclature and sought to draw on their wartime loyalty to demand full citizenship in the late 1940s. Incorporation, combined with the repression of women's associations involved in community action in many areas of the hemisphere, effectively muted a separatist woman's politics in the 1950s.

Taking their political cue from the Cuban revolutionary experience, women who joined the revolutionary left in the 1960s adopted a class analysis that repudiated "feminism" as bourgeois and divisive to the cause. LIBERATION THEOLOGY, the other potent social critique to emerge in Latin America in the 1960s, retained a traditional view of women. But it was from this generation of women activists—the most highly educated generation of women in Latin American history—that the feminists of the 1970s emerged, giving up not a whit of their commitment to radical social change but adding to it a new brand of gender analysis. By 1985 these feminists had developed a stinging critique of the traditional left within their own communities, challenged the "First World" view of European and U.S. feminists, and contributed organizational models, political strategies, and a new understanding of grass-roots social movements to global feminism.

In 1975 the Conferencia Mundial del Año Internacional de la Mujer convened in Mexico City to draw up the World Plan of Action for the United Nations Decade for Women 1976–1985. It was at the sessions of the Tribune of Non-Governmental Organizations, where representatives of voluntary associations and individuals could speak, that Latin American women made their presence felt. The majority of the 6,000 women who attended the Tribune were from North, Central, and South America; 2,000 were from Mexico alone. The lines of debate that were to dominate the first half of the UN Decade emerged in the confrontation between Betty Friedan and Domitila Barrios de Chungara, who came to Mexico to represent the Housewives Committee of Siglo XX, an organization of Bolivian tin miners' wives.

By 1977 the incorporation of a feminist political critique was visible in the new women's movement in many areas of Latin America. Over the next decade newsletters, feminist journals, and women's movement periodicals appeared, indicating the presence of women's groups in every region of the continent. One of the earliest and most notable is *fem*, produced since 1976 by a collective editorship, Nueva Cultura Feminista, in Mexico City. The subjects addressed provide a microcosm of the concerns of Mexican feminists over the years: abortion, work, sexuality, feminism, language, family, education, mothers and children, women writers, the history of women in Mexico, and women in the struggle for social justice. *MUJER*/Fempress, published monthly in Santiago, Chile, carries articles by correspondents in every country in the hemisphere. In 1984 the independent women's studies group, Grupo de Estudios sobre la Condición de la Mujer en Uruguay, began publication of *La Cacerola* (referring primarily to the banging of casseroles with spoons as part of demonstrations against the military regime). In Peru the Centro de Flora Tristán publishes *VIVA*; Movimiento Manuela Ramos (Manuela Ramos signifying ''everywoman'') issues pamphlets on health and community resources: *Mujer y Sociedad* addresses the politics of violence in the nation and in the home. Brazilian women have been leaders in the innovative use of film and have succeeded in incorporating the concerns of the women's movement into popular telenovelas such as *Malu mujer*. Since the late 1980s new journals have continued to appear: *Feminaria* in Buenos Aires and *Enfogues de Mujer*, published by the Grupo de Estudios de la Mujer Paraguaya.

In July 1981, 250 women from Brazil, Chile, Colombia, Ecuador, Mexico, Panama, Peru, Puerto Rico, the Dominican Republic, and Venezuela met in Bogotá at the Primero Encuentro Feminista Latinoamericano y del Caribe. The *encuentros feministas* have since convened in Peru (1983), Brazil (1985), Mexico (1987), and Argentina (1990), where upwards of 2,000 women attended.

Since the mid-1980s a number of women's studies programs have been instituted in Latin America. Almost without exception, the programs grew out of independent feminist study groups and women's community action collectives that are only now finding an institutional home. These include the Programa Interdisciplinario Estudios de la Mujer (PIEM) at El Colegio de México, the Programa Interdisciplinario Estudios de la Mujer (PIEM) at La Universidad Autónoma de Costa Rica, and Carreras de Posorado Interdisciplinaria

de Especialización de Estudios de la Mujer (CIEM) at La Universidad de Buenos Aires.

Strategies developed by Latin American women activists over the past century have been widely adopted in other areas of the world. The Organizaciones de Trabajadores del Hogar de América Latina y el Caribe, founded in 1988 by women household workers, is a model for similar organizations in Africa and Asia. International Day Against Violence Against Women, observed on 25 November, was initiated by Latin American feminists at the IV Encuentro Feminista in Mexico to commemorate the deaths by torture of six Dominican peasant women at the hands of military troops; in 1992 the United Nations declared 25 November a global day of protest against violence directed at women.

In February 1993 the Programa Interdisciplinario de Estudios de Genero (PRIEG), the women's studies program instituted at the Universidad de Costa Rica in 1987, hosted the V Congreso Interdisciplinario y Internacional de Mujeres. Although the 2,000 participants represented women's organizations from throughout the world, the organization and the content of the program were telling indicators of the breadth and depth of feminist thought in Latin America in the 1990s. The concerns included women and the environment, heterosexual AIDS, GENDER AND SEXUALITY, indigenous women and peoples, feminism and democratic practice. These matters of urgent concern in Central America and elsewhere in Latin America dominated the week-long event, which culminated in a march from the university campus to the Plaza de la Democracia to celebrate ''Women's Rights/Human Rights.''

ASUNCIÓN LAVRIN, *The Ideology of Feminism in the Southern Cone, 1900–1940* (1986); MARIFRAN CARLSON, *¡Feminismo! The Woman's Movement in Argentina from Its Beginnings to Eva Perón* (1988); JANE S. JAQUETTE, ed., *The Women's Movement in Latin America: Feminism and the Transition to Democracy* (1989); SONIA E. ÁLVAREZ, *Engendering Democracy in Brazil: Women's Movements in Transition Politics* (1990); JUNE E. HAHNER, *Emancipating the Female Sex: The Struggle for Women's Rights in Brazil, 1850–1940* (1990); SEMINAR ON FEMINISM AND CULTURE IN LATIN AMERICA, *Women, Culture, and Politics in Latin America* (1990); SHIRLENE ANN SOTO, *Emergence of the Modern Mexican Woman: Her Participation in Revolution and Struggle for Equality, 1910–1940* (1990); FRANCESCA MILLER, *Latin American Women and the Search for Social Justice* (1991); and K. LYNN STONER, *From the House to the Streets: The Cuban Woman's Movement for Legal Reform, 1898–1940* (1991).

FRANCESCA MILLER

See also **Women.**

FERDINAND II OF ARAGON (*b.* 10 March 1452; *d.* 23 January 1516), king of Aragon (1479–1516), king of Castile and León (1474–1504); king of Sicily (1468–1516); king of Naples (1504–1516).

The son of John II of Aragon and his second wife,

Juana Enríquez, Ferdinand was king of Sicily and heir apparent to the throne of Aragon when he married his cousin, ISABELLA I OF CASTILE, on 19 October 1469. The terms of the marriage treaty, which were critical for a smooth transition, stipulated that Ferdinand would respect Castilian customs and appointments, reside in Castile, pursue the reconquest of Moorish territory, and cosign with Isabella all public decisions.

The news of this union was ill received at home and abroad. Although John II of Aragon had sought the Castilian alliance, the king of Castile, Isabella's half-brother Henry IV, disowned her in 1470 when he heard about the marriage and recognized his own daughter, Juana, as heir. Louis XI of France and Afonso V of Portugal, who also sought a marriage alliance with Castile, were against the union as well. Finally, an important group of Spanish grandees opposed the alliance, which as they correctly feared would strengthen the crown's authority.

In the civil war of succession following Henry IV's death (1474), Ferdinand played a critical role in assuming command of his wife's troops, planning campaigns, importing Aragonese military experts, and securing the support of powerful Castilian relations. By 1479, peace was restored and Ferdinand claimed the throne of Aragon. To complete the unification, he led a series of campaigns that resulted in the conquest of Granada (1492). In that same year, after much persuasion Ferdinand and Isabella became the financial backers of COLUMBUS's expedition.

In his native kingdom, Ferdinand perpetuated Aragonese constitutional traditions, implicitly rejecting a political or administrative union of the two crowns, and ended a protracted civil war in Catalonia. Ferdinand's particular expertise was, however, foreign, not domestic, policy. In the latter he usually acted in concert with Isabella.

Under Ferdinand, Castile abandoned her traditional alliance with Aragon's old enemy, France, and forged closer relations with Portugal. Ferdinand committed Castile to a threefold foreign policy: containment of France, domination of the western Mediterranean, and war against Islam and the Turks. The Spanish dominance in Italy was testimony to the success of Ferdinand's ambitions there. He also pioneered a new European diplomatic system by establishing five resident embassies—in Rome, Venice, London, Brussels, and Vienna—which were staffed by university-trained lawyers or clergy. Typically, diplomatic advances were accompanied by important marriage alliances. Ferdinand's daughter Catherine married Arthur, the heir to the English throne (1501) and later became the first wife of Henry VIII; another daughter (Isabella) married the Portuguese king, Manuel (1490); Juana, through whom the succession would continue, married Philip, the archduke of Austria (1496); and a son married Margaret, the daughter of Maximilian I (1497).

In 1504, the year Ferdinand conquered Naples, Isa-bella died and Ferdinand was demoted from king of Castile to regent for Queen Juana, then in residence at the court of Burgundy. With his position threatened, Ferdinand sought French support and by the Treaty of Blois (1505) arranged to be married to the niece of the French king, Germaine de Foix. This alliance served to strengthen the ties between the Castilian nobility and the future heir to that country's throne. Upon the arrival in Spain of his son-in-law, Philip, Ferdinand agreed to retire to Aragon (1506). His retirement was cut short in that same year by the death of the archduke Philip and his daughter Juana's madness, which rendered her unfit to rule and left Ferdinand once again administrator of Castile in 1510. Spain's last territorial acquisition under Ferdinand was the incorporation of Navarre (1515), which he justified through Isabella's claims to the throne.

W. H. PRESCOTT, *History of the Reign of Ferdinand and Isabella the Catholic of Spain* (1837); JAIME VICÉNS VIVES, *Historia crítica de la vida y reinado de Fernando II de Aragón* (1962); LUIS SUÁREZ FERNÁNDEZ and M. FERNÁNDEZ ÁLVAREZ, *La España de los Reyes Católicos (1474–1516)* (1969); J. N. HILLGARTH, *The Spanish Kingdoms, 1250–1516*, vol. 2, *1410–1516: Castilian Hegemony* (1978).

SUZANNE HILES BURKHOLDER

FERDINAND VI OF SPAIN (*b.* 17 September 1713; *d.* 10 August 1759), king of Spain (1746–1759). Ferdinand's ascent to the throne marked the end of the pro-Italian policy of his stepmother, Isabel (Elizabeth) Farnese, and the inauguration of policies determined by his Portuguese wife, Barbara of Braganza, and his three chief advisers, the marqués of ENSENADA, José de Carvajal, and Francisco de Rávago (the king's confessor). Ferdinand was well intentioned but had little interest in politics and experienced lapses into insanity. Thus, during his reign the government of Spain was entrusted to his ministers.

In foreign policy, Ensenada and Carvajal advocated peace and neutrality and sought to keep Spain out of hostilities brewing between France and England, with Ensenada hoping to maintain peace by adopting a pro-French stance and Carvajal favoring England. Under their joint leadership the Spanish state became an instrument of reform and, to a degree, modernization, as it pursued tax reform and investment in public works.

A colonial conflict with Portugal over its Uruguayan capital of Colônia do SACRAMENTO, the death of Carvajal (1754), and the machinations of an anti-Ensenada faction ended Ferdinand's first ministry. The second, no less marked by internal divisions, ended tax reform and replaced single register ships (an important commercial innovation of 1740) with the old fleet system. After the death of his wife (17 August 1758) Ferdinand went into a terminal state of mourning. His refusal even to sign documents brought the government to a halt until his death a year later.

CIRIACO PÉREZ BUSTAMANTE, "El reinado de Fernando VI en el reformismo español del siglo XVIII," in *Revista de la Universidad de Madrid* 12 (1954): 491–514; MANUEL TUÑÓN DE LARA, ed. *Historia de España*, vol. 7, *Centralismo, ilustración, y agonía del Antiguo Régimen (1715–1833)* (1980), esp. pp. 199–213; JOHN LYNCH, *Bourbon Spain, 1700–1808* (1989).

SUZANNE HILES BURKHOLDER

FERDINAND VII OF SPAIN (*b.* 14 October 1784; *d.* 29 September 1833), king of Spain (1808–1833). The early years of Ferdinand's life were marked by fear and rebellion against his parents, CHARLES IV and Queen María Luisa, and their chief minister, Manuel de GODOY, who excluded the young prince from participation in government and even threatened him with disinheritance. Ferdinand's rebellion was manifested in intrigues with NAPOLEON I as early as 1807. During the peak of Godoy's unpopularity, the young prince of Asturias became a symbol for those disaffected with the regime of Charles IV. After the riots at Aranjuez by supporters of the prince (1808), Charles IV abdicated in his son's favor. Nevertheless, Ferdinand, like his father and Godoy, remained Napoleon's pawn and spent the first years of his reign a captive in France during the Peninsular War (1808–1814).

Restored to the throne after signing a treaty of alliance with Napoleon (1813), Ferdinand returned to Spain and repudiated the work of those who had governed in his absence, especially the liberal CORTES OF CÁDIZ (1810) and the CONSTITUTION OF 1812. Ferdinand treated the liberals, including Americans, as traitors, and revived royal absolutism. Equally shortsighted in his colonial policy, he tried to recover the colonies and restore their traditional obedience to the crown through military force. He restored the COUNCIL OF THE INDIES but abolished the ministry of the Indies and reassigned its agenda to the ministries of war and finance.

Ferdinand's return to absolutism was supported by the church and wealthy landowners. Although he governed through ministers, his regime was unstable: during the first part of his reign (1814–1820) his ministers served an average of six months. In 1820 an army revolt forced Ferdinand to accept the constitution; thereafter, the revolutions at home and in the colonies were inextricably linked in his mind. In 1823, when Louis XVIII sent an army to restore Ferdinand's authority, the Spanish king once again revoked the constitution and embarked upon a policy of absolutism and repression.

Despite being unable to produce a male heir in four marriages, Ferdinand passed over his brother, Don Carlos, in favor of his daughter, the future Isabella II. His death thus provoked what became known as the Carlist wars, between the supporters of Isabella and those of Don Carlos. Ferdinand never abandoned the illusion that he could recover Spain's lost colonies—by 1824 only Cuba, Puerto Rico, and the Philippines remained—and died without recognizing their independence.

Portrait of Ferdinand VII by Goya. LIBRARY OF CONGRESS.

MIGUEL ARTOLA, *La España de Fernando VII* (1968); JOSÉ FONTANA, *La quiebra de la monarquía absoluta* (1971).

SUZANNE HILES BURKHOLDER

FERNANDES, FLORESTAN (*b.* 22 July 1920), Brazilian sociologist and reformer who founded the São Paulo school of sociology, which studied capitalist modernization in Brazil. Fernandes began his career with theses on social organization and war among the TUPINAMBÁ Indians (1949, 1952). In the 1950s, after establishing himself at the University of São Paulo, he turned to topics in folklore and race relations. A UNESCO-sponsored project, conducted in collaboration with Roger Bastide and others, resulted in *Relações raciais entre negros e brancos em São Paulo* (1955; Race Relations Between Blacks and Whites in São Paulo), the first of his several revisionist studies of race relations in the context of São Paulo's twentieth-century transition to a competitive, class society, including *The Negro in Brazilian Society* (1964; English trans. 1969). Fernandes influenced a generation of sociologists, including Fernando Henrique CARDOSO and Octávio IANNI, through his studies of slavery and race relations. Fernandes was purged from the University of São Paulo in 1969 and exiled. Upon his return to Brazil, he wrote an analysis of Brazil's transition to modern capitalism, *A revolução burguesa no Brasil: Ensaio de interpretação sociológica* (1975; The Bourgeois

Revolution in Brazil). In the 1980s he published treatises on political redemocratization, and in 1986 was elected to the Constituent Congress by the socialist PARTIDO DOS TRABALHADORES (Workers' Party).

OCTÁVIO IANNI, ed., *Florestan Fernandes* (1986), is an anthology of Fernandes's writings. MARIA ANGELA D'INCAO, ed., *O saber militante: Ensaios sobre Florestan Fernandes* (1987) is a collection of critical studies of Fernandes's thought that includes a useful bibliography. RICHARD M. MORSE, "Manchester Economics and São Paulo Sociology," in *Manchester and São Paulo: Problems of Rapid Urban Growth,* edited by John D. Wirth and Robert L. Jones (1978), pp. 7–34, is a study of the São Paulo school of sociology. CARLOS GUILHERME MOTA, *Ideologia da cultura brasileira, 1933–1974* (1977), provides an overview of São Paulo cultural debates.

DAIN BORGES

FERNANDES, MILLÔR (*b.* 1924), Brazilian humorist, poet, playwright, and artist. Brazilian society and politics are favorite themes of Fernandes's highly original and satirical views, and most of his works underscore his keen ability to expose the incoherence of everyday life. He often highlights his writings with his own illustrations. His critical but extremely creative irreverence is also found in his "fables"—*Fábulas fabulosas* (1964) and *Novas fábulas fabulosas* (1978)—and in his protest theater—*Liberdade, liberdade* (1965). Fernandes has published frequently in newspapers and journals (such as *O Cruzeiro, Tribuna da Imprensa, Correio da Manhã, Pif-Paf*), is an important contributor to *Veja,* and has worked in radio and television. His works of art have been exhibited in the major cities of Brazil. Fernandes has also translated drama, of special note being his translations of works by Shakespeare, Molière, Brecht, and Synge. He is perhaps Brazil's most famous humorist.

GUSTAVO A. DORIA, "Sobre Millôr Fernandes," in *Revista de teatro* no. 453 (January–March 1985): 29–31; JOSÉ LUÍZ FIORIN, "Millôr e a destruição da fábula," in *Alfa: Revista de lingüística* 30–31 (1986–1987): 84–94; ANN WITTE, "Feminismo e antifeminismo em Leilah Assunção e Millôr Fernandes," in *Dactylus* 9 (1988–1989): 15–20.

GARY M. VESSELS

FERNÁNDEZ, EMILIO "EL INDIO" (*b.* 26 March 1904; *d.* 6 August 1986), Mexican film director. Beginning his studies in the military academy, by the mid-1920s Fernández was in Hollywood, learning the craft of filmmaking. In the next decade, he returned to Mexico and worked as an actor in cinema. He debuted as a director with *La isla de la pasión* in 1941. Among his most celebrated films are *María Candelaria* (1943), *Bugambilia* (1944), *Flor silvestre* (1944), *Pueblerina* (1946), *Enamorada* (1946), *Río escondido* (1946), *Salón México* (1954), and *La red* (1954). His films won numerous national and international awards and brought Mexican cinema to the attention of both Mexican and foreign audiences.

Through a nationalistic and artistic treatment of subjects, Fernández extolled the beauties and virtues of Mexico and its people, particularly the *campesino* and the Indian. Fernández is not only one of Mexico's leading directors but a major figure of world cinema.

LUIS REYES DE LA MAZA, *El cine sonoro en México* (1973); E. BRADFORD BURNS, *Latin American Cinema: Film and History* (1975); CARL J. MORA, *Mexican Cinema: Reflections of a Society: 1896–1980* (1982); and JOHN KING, *Magical Reels: A History of Cinema in Latin America* (1990).

DAVID MACIEL

FERNÁNDEZ, JUAN (*b.* ca. 1530; *d.* 1599), Spanish navigator and discoverer of the JUAN FERNÁNDEZ ISLANDS. Actively engaged in navigation between Peru and Chile by 1550, Fernández theorized that Chile could be reached much more quickly by sailing further offshore, west of the HUMBOLDT CURRENT. Testing this theory, he discovered the islands that later bore his name, about 400 miles west of VALPARAÍSO, Chile, on 22 November 1574. He reached Chile only thirty days after leaving CALLAO, Peru, a voyage that formerly took three months or more. Although MAGELLAN may have seen these islands earlier, Fernández's sighting gave them navigational significance and greatly improved communications between Lima and Chile. His efforts to colonize the islands failed, but his leadership in the Peru-Chile trade earned him recognition in 1589 as "chief pilot of the South Sea." Minor difficulties with the INQUISITION earned him the nickname "El Brujo" (the sorcerer). In 1592 he retired to his Chilean estate of Rautén, where he lived until his death seven years later.

BENJAMÍN VICUÑA MACKENNA, *Juan Fernández, historia verdadera de la isla de Robinson Crusoe* (1883), esp. pp. 7–94; JOSÉ TORIBIO MEDINA, *El piloto Juan Fernández, descubridor de las islas que llevan su nombre, y Juan Jufré, armador de la expedición que hizo en busca de otras en el Mar del Sur* (1918; 2d ed. 1974); RALPH LEE WOODWARD, JR., *Robinson Crusoe's Island: A History of the Juan Fernández Islands* (1969), esp. pp. 3–14.

RALPH LEE WOODWARD, JR.

See also **Explorers.**

FERNÁNDEZ, MAX (*b.* 1943), founder and leader of Civic Solidarity Unity (Unidad Cívica Solidaridad—UCS) and president of the Bolivian National Brewery (CBN). Very little is known about Fernández's background except that he was born in Quillacollo, Cochabamba, and worked as a delivery man for the brewery he now owns. In 1985 Fernández purchased a majority share of the stock of the CBN and has since developed a significant empire. The U.S. embassy accused him of making his fortune trafficking drugs, but that allegation has not been substantiated.

With considerable support in the La Paz, Beni, Pando, and Cochabamba departments, Fernández became a serious contender in the 1993 elections. His populist style of campaigning, which included donating everything from hospitals to soccer balls, endeared him with marginal sectors of the Bolivian electorate. Fernández has also managed to destroy all competition to his beer factory and has announced plans to build new factories in Beni and Santa Cruz.

Fernández has run the UCS in an authoritarian manner and, in classic populist style, control over his political party has been determined by his capacity to deliver prebends. He has named the party leadership; in fact, no assemblies or elections have been held to elect the governing body of the UCS. Most striking, however, is Fernández's rather unappealing personality. He lacks charisma, speaks lower-class Spanish, and is unable to articulate any party platform. To overcome these shortcomings, Fernández has hired prominent members of the major political parties who generally present UCS campaign promises.

A pragmatic entrepreneur, Fernández is generally perceived as a man of action and few words. Most appealing to the working classes is Fernández's innovative employer-worker relations at his brewery. Workers in the CBN enjoy high wages and other benefits not available to blue-collar employees elsewhere in the private or public sector.

Dozens of dissidents from major and minor parties have flocked to the UCS. Fernández parlayed a fourth-place finish in the 1993 elections into an alliance dubbed the "governability pact" with the victorious National Revolutionary Movement. The UCS was granted the ministry of defense in exchange for support in Congress for the MNR.

EDUARDO A. GAMARRA, "Crafting Political Support for Stabilization: Political Pacts and the New Economic Policy in Brazil," in *Democracy, Markets, and Structural Reform in Latin America,* edited by William C. Smith, Carlos H. Acuña, and Eduardo A. Gamarra (1994), and "Market-Oriented Reforms and Democratization in Bolivia," in *A Precarious Balance,* edited by Joan M. Nelson, vol. 2 (1994).

EDUARDO A. GAMARRA

See also **Bolivia: Political Parties.**

FERNANDEZ, OSCAR LORENZO (*b.* 4 November 1897; *d.* 27 August 1948), Brazilian composer, best known for his art songs. His first works, written between 1918 and 1922, were principally songs and piano compositions, but in the early 1920s he became interested in the nationalist movement and began to write works based on Brazilian subjects. In 1924 he was appointed professor of harmony at the National Music Institute and in 1936 established the Brazilian Conservatory, which he directed until his death in 1948.

In 1946, in recognition of the importance of the work of Heitor Villa-Lobos, Fernandez wrote an article, "A contribuição harmonica de Villa-Lobos," which stressed the innovative quality of the harmonic practices of Villa-Lobos. Fernandez shared with him an interest in the Indian melodies collected by explorer Roquette Pínto and in the use of native percussion instruments in orchestral composition. Fernandez's principal contribution to the emerging nationalist movement in music in Brazil was his ability to capture authentic elements of the Afro-Brazilian tradition in art songs and operas based on folk songs. He is best known as the composer of "Batuque," a movement from the suite "Malazarte," taken from an opera of the same title. This piece has been frequently arranged for various band and orchestral ensembles.

OSCAR LORENZO FERNANDEZ, "A contribuição harmonica de Villa-Lobos," *Boletín latino-americano de música* 6 (April 1946); VASCO MARIZ, *A canção brasileira,* 5th ed. (1985).

DAVID P. APPLEBY

FERNÁNDEZ ALONSO, SÉVERO (*b.* 15 August 1849; *d.* 12 August 1925), president of Bolivia (1896–1899). Born in Sucre, Fernández Alonso was a SILVER-mine owner, lawyer, and minister of war (1892–1896). He was the last president of the Conservative oligarchy that ruled Bolivia in the last two decades of the nineteenth century. Despite his efforts at conciliation with the rival Liberal and Federalist parties, the FEDERALIST WAR (1898–1899) broke out during his presidency and effectively ended Conservative Party hegemony. Unable to fashion a compromise between the Sucre-based Conservatives and the northern Federalists, Fernández Alonso personally led the national army in an effort to crush the rebellion by the La Paz-based Federalists and Liberals. By remaining in Oruro with his army and vacillating in his attack on the city of La Paz, Fernández Alonso assured the military defeat of his government and the rise to power of the Liberal Party.

The best and most detailed summary of Fernández Alonso's term is in RAMIRO CONDARCO MORALES, *Zárate, el "Temible" Willka: Historia de la rebelión indígena de 1899,* 2d ed. (1983).

ERICK D. LANGER

See also **Bolivia: Political Parties.**

FERNÁNDEZ ARTUCIO, HUGO (*b.* 1912; *d.* 1974), Uruguayan professor and publicist, was political editor of *El Día* from 1941 to 1966. In 1966 he supported the presidential campaign of Oscar GESTIDO and became director of the University of Uruguay's Vázquez Acevedo Institute. Fernández Artucio gained public recognition through a series of interviews on the "Espectador" radio station in 1940, in which he revealed a Nazi plot to overthrow the Uruguayan government. His findings helped a parliamentary investigation commission, established in 1940, to analyze NSdAP (Nationalsozialistische Deutsche Arbeiter-Partei) activities in Uruguay and to prepare legal action against its members.

HUGO FERNÁNDEZ ARTUCIO, *Nazis en el Uruguay* (1940) and *The Nazi Underground in South America* (1942). See also ROQUE FARAONE, *El Uruguay en que vivimos, 1900–1968*, 2d ed. (1968); MARTIN H. J. FINCH, "Three Perspectives on the Crisis in Uruguay," in *Journal of Latin American Studies* 3 (November 1971): 173–190.

DIETER SCHONEBOHM

FERNÁNDEZ CRESPO, DANIEL (*b.* 1901; *d.* 1964),

Uruguayan educator and political leader of the National (Blanco) Party. Fernández Crespo was born in a rural area of the department of San José. He received his teaching degree and worked in education until 1932. His political career included his election to the town council of Montevideo in 1928, five terms as representative (1931–1950), senator in 1950, and national adviser in 1954. Between 1959 and 1963 he presided at the departmental council of Montevideo and at the National Council of Government, a nine-member committee established in 1952 to institutionalize coparticipation in the exercise of executive power. He was also active as a sports director, being associated with the Liverpool soccer club and the Aguada basketball club. Concerned especially with social problems, he personified the popular forces of nationalism in an urban setting, in which the Colorado Party and particularly BATLLISMO usually predominated. In 1958, after ninety-three years of government controlled by the Colorado Party, the National Party triumphed in the general elections as well as in those in Montevideo.

ANGEL COCCHI, *Nuestros partidos*, 2 vols. (1984); JUAN CARLOS PEDEMONTE, *Los presidentes del Uruguay* (1984).

JOSÉ DE TORRES WILSON

See also **Uruguay: Political Parties.**

FERNÁNDEZ DE CABRERA BOBADILLA CERDA Y MENDOZA, LUIS GERÓNIMO (Conde de Chinchón;

b. 1590; *d.* 28 October 1647), viceroy of Peru (1629–1639). The fourth conde de Chinchón and member of the Council of State (Aragon and Italy) and War assumed his viceregal duties on 14 January 1629. Reputed to be penurious, austere, and abstemious, Chinchón focused much of his attention on fiscal matters, especially new taxes imposed during his tenure, such as the MEDIA ANATA, UNIÓN DE ARMAS, MESADA ECLESIÁSTICA, and COMPOSICIÓN *de pulperías* (bar taxes). He also vigorously pursued donations from individuals and communities throughout the viceroyalty to meet exigencies in Spain. In fact, during the eleven years he was in office, Chinchón remitted over 4 million ducats to Spain despite the fall in silver production at POTOSÍ. Fortunately, silver strikes at Cailloma and Pasco in part made up for the drop in output in Upper Peru.

Militarily, the viceroy strengthened the fortifications at Callao, built two new vessels for the Pacific fleet, reinforced garrisons in Chile, and counteracted both the Dutch corsairs plying the Pacific coast and Portuguese encroachments on the eastern part of Peru. When the usefulness of QUININE for treating malaria was discovered in the Loja province of Ecuador in 1630, the viceroy enthusiastically endorsed its effectiveness, but when word reached Rome, church officials there called it a "pact of the Peruvians with the devil." In Lima, Chinchón certified guilds for hatmakers, tailors, ironworkers, locksmiths, and potters. Known for his social conscience, Chinchón vigorously defended Indian rights and provided basic necessities for newly arrived slaves and for orphans and abandoned children. Evidently, too, he had a strong sense of religious and moral propriety: during Lent he ordered men and women separated in the churches of Lima. Relieved of his duties on 18 December 1639, he returned to Spain, where he died.

MANUEL DE MENDIBURU, ed., *Diccionario histórico-biográfico del Perú*, vol. 3 (1932).

JOHN JAY TePASKE

FERNÁNDEZ DE CASTRO ANDRADE Y PORTUGAL, PEDRO ANTONIO (Conde de Lemos; *b.* 1635?;

d. 6 December 1672), viceroy of Peru (1667–1672). The tenth count of Lemos, Pedro Fernández de Castro was born in Spain and was only thirty-three when he assumed his post in Lima in November 1667. Upon arrival his most immediate task was quelling a civil war in the mining area of Laycacota in the province of Paucarolla, where armed bands led by the Salcedo brothers, Gaspar and José, terrorized other miners. In 1668 Lemos personally led a force of soldiers and militia into the mountains to put down the revolt, ruthlessly executing forty-two rebels. Returning to Lima in 1669 after visiting Chucuito and Cuzco, Lemos attached himself to the JESUITS, supporting their MISSIONS in the interior at Mojos and on the Marañon River and the construction of a sumptuous new chapel for their church of Nuestra Señora de los Desamparados, dedicated in June 1672. At the same time the viceroy sponsored construction of a new convent for female penitents and the Betelmite Indian Hospital of Santa Ana. An outspoken critic of the forced labor system (MITA) that supplied workers for the silver mines at Potosí, Lemos advocated its elimination but was successful only in reducing the number of *mita* Indians by half to approximately 2,000 annually.

Devout, fervent, and somewhat pompous, Lemos loved the panoply surrounding rites and ceremonies, ordering thirty masses each for the forty-two rebels he executed and elegant celebrations whenever religious or state occasions called for them. After only five years in office, Lemos suddenly fell ill and died at the age of thirty-eight.

JORGE BASADRE, *El Conde de Lemos y su tiempo* (1945); ROBERT R. MILLER, ed., *Chronicle of Colonial Lima: The Diary of Josephe and*

Francisco Mugaburu, 1640–1687 (1975); MANUEL DE MENDIBURU, ed., *Diccionario histórico-biográfico del Peru*, vol. 3 (1978), pp. 223–236.

JOHN JAY TePASKE

FERNÁNDEZ DE CÓRDOBA, DIEGO (marqués de Guadalcázar; *b.* 1578; *d.* 1630), viceroy of Mexico and Peru. Born in Seville, Guadalcázar served as VICEROY of New Spain from 1612 until 1621, when he moved to Peru, serving as viceroy there until 1629. During his reign in New Spain he was noted for the establishment of the *tribunal de tributos* (tribute court) and for two important public works projects: the continuing effort to drain the Valley of Mexico and the construction of the castle of San Diego in Acapulco.

In Peru, Guadalcázar put down a civil war in Potosí between the "Vicuñas" (CREOLES) and "Vascongados" (PENINSULARS). A Dutch fleet threatened the coast in 1624–1625, forcing the viceroy to fortify the coastal towns of the kingdom. Because the mercury mines at Huancavelica continued to pose health problems to the Indian miners, Guadalcázar eliminated nighttime mine activity and reduced the number of Indians assigned to the mines in the MITA. He sought to improve communications through the construction and maintenance of bridges. Rather than depend on a legal adviser, he took an active role in supervising law suits dealing with Indians. Although he, like his predecessor, attempted to deal with the issue of the Potosí *mita*, no concrete changes were implemented. He died in Córdoba, Spain.

MANUEL DE MENDIBURU, *Diccionario histórico-biográfico del Perú*, 8 vols. (1874–1890).

JOHN F. SCHWALLER

FERNÁNDEZ (HERNÁNDEZ) DE CÓRDOBA, FRANCISCO (*b.* 1475?; *d.* June 1526), conqueror of Nicaragua. (He is not to be confused with Francisco HERNÁNDEZ DE CÓRDOBA [*d.* 1518], a conquistador of the Yucatán.) Fernández de Córdoba was a Spanish soldier of fortune who came to Panama sometime between 1514 and 1517. In the service of Pedro Arias de ÁVILA (Pedrarias Dávila), he was captain of the guard at Panama City in 1519. Pedrarias sent him to Nicaragua in 1523 to check the pretensions of Gil GONZÁLEZ DÁVILA. There Fernández founded the cities of GRANADA and LEÓN in 1524, as well as the village of Bruselas, the first European settlement in what is today Costa Rica. He also tried to take control of the territory of Honduras and to establish a kingdom independent of Pedrarias, perhaps in alliance with Hernán CORTÉS. Learning of this in 1525, Pedrarias came to Nicaragua and captured Fernández. After a speedy trial, in which Fernández was convicted of treason, he was beheaded in León in late June 1526. The Nicaraguan unit of currency, the córdoba, is named for him.

CARLOS MELÉNDEZ CHAVERRI, *Hernández de Córdoba: Capitán de conquista en Nicaragua* (1976); JOHN H. PARRY and ROBERT G. KEITH, *New Iberian World: A Documentary History of the Discovery and Settlement of Latin America to the Early Seventeenth Century*, (1984), vol. 3, pp. 86–101; vol. 4, pp. 19, 27, 30.

RALPH LEE WOODWARD, JR.

See also **Explorers.**

FERNÁNDEZ DE LIZARDI, JOSÉ JOAQUÍN (*b.* 15 November 1776; *d.* 21 June 1827), Mexican writer. Born in Mexico City, Fernández de Lizardi began his education in Tepozotlán, where his father was a physician. He later went to Mexico City for further education and in 1793 entered the Colegio de San Ildefonso. After abandoning his studies in 1798 at his father's death, Fernández de Lizardi held various bureaucratic positions and initially opposed the independence movement, a stance that he soon reversed in support of Iturbide. As a journalist he is most remembered for the newspaper *El Pensador Mexicano* (The Mexican Thinker [1812–1814]), which he founded when the Spanish Constitution of 1812 established freedom of the press. His writings reflect the Mexican social milieu at the time of the country's struggle for independence. His special concern was the place of Spaniards born in the New World. Because of newspaper censorship, he resorted to fiction and wrote *El periquillo sarniento* (The Itching Parrot [published serially 1816; complete version published posthumously 1830–1831]). This picaresque tale is recognized as the "first" Spanish-American novel. It achieves compositional complexity and development, and it treats contemporary New World themes. Fernández de Lizardi wrote three other novels—*Noches tristes y día alegre* (Sad Nights and Happy Day [1818, 1819]), *La Quijotita y su prima* (Quijotita and Her Cousin [1818]), and *Don Catrín de la Fachenda* (written about 1819, published posthumously in 1832)—before he returned to journalism and pamphleteering in 1820. By 1822 Fernández de Lizardi became disenchanted with Iturbide and began to advocate liberal causes, and his modest social position became increasingly precarious. He died of tuberculosis in Mexico City.

JEFFERSON REA SPELL, *Bridging the Gap: Articles on Mexican Literature* (1971), esp. pp. 97–292; LUIS ÍÑIGO MADRIGAL, "José Joaquín Fernández de Lizardi," in his *Historia de la literatura hispanoamericana. Vol. 2, Del neoclasicismo al modernismo* (1987), pp. 135–144; NANCY VOGELEY, "José Joaquín Fernández de Lizardi," in *Latin American Writers*, edited by Carlos A. Solé and Maria Isabel Abreu, vol. 1 (1989), pp. 119–128.

DANNY J. ANDERSON

See also **Literature.**

FERNÁNDEZ HIDALGO, GUTIERRE (b. 1553; *d.* after 1620), Spanish composer. Born in Andalusia, Fernández Hidalgo arrived at New Granada (Colombia) in 1584 as the *maestro de capilla* of the Bogotá cathedral. He became sixteenth-century America's most eminent composer. As chapelmaster, Fernández Hidalgo asked the Bogotá bishop to require the seminarians of the newly founded Seminario Conciliar de San Luis to sing under his direction every day at cathedral services. In 1585 he was appointed rector of the seminary, but a dispute with his students over his demanding teaching style led him to leave Bogotá in 1586. He moved to Quito, where he was music director at the cathedral and seminary until 1589. Again, he proved too demanding for his subordinates. On 13 July 1591, he was appointed *maestro de capilla* of the Cuzco cathedral, where he conducted the cathedral choir and taught polyphony and counterpoint while composing in his free time. In 1597 he accepted a new assignment with a better salary, as *maestro de capilla* of the La Plata cathedral (present-day Sucre, Bolivia). He remained there, presumably, until his retirement in 1620. It is believed he died in Cuzco.

Fernández Hidalgo was technically and stylistically the best representative in America of the Spanish polyphony initiated by Tomás Luis de Victoria, Cristóbal de Morales, and Francisco Guerrero. Among his works are nine Magnificats for four and six voices, ten four-voice psalms, three Salve Reginas for four and five voices, and *villancicos*, motets, and hymns.

ROBERT STEVENSON, *The Music of Peru* (1950), and *Renaissance and Baroque Musical Sources in the Americas* (1970); JOSÉ IGNACIO PERDOMO ESCOBAR, *El archivo musical de la catedral de Bogotá* (1976); *New Grove Dictionary of Music and Musicians*, vol. 6 (1980).

SUSANA SALGADO

FERNÁNDEZ MADRID, JOSÉ (*b.* 19 February 1789; *d.* 28 June 1830), president of the United Provinces of New Granada. Born in Cartagena and trained in law and medicine, José Fernández Madrid was a prominent figure of New Granada's intellectual scene in the last years of colonial rule. A leading spokesman for the federalist cause in the independence movement, he was made president of the United Provinces in 1816, shortly before its final collapse. During the Spanish reconquest he was exiled from New Granada. He lived for a time in Havana, but at his death in London was serving as envoy of Gran Colombia to England and France. Fernández Madrid is further remembered as a noted journalist and author of poetry and drama.

CARLOS MARTÍNEZ SILVA, *Biografía de don José Fernández Madrid*, edited by Luis Martínez Delgado (1935); IGNACIO ARIZMENDI POSADA, *Presidentes de Colombia 1810–1990* (1989), pp. 31–32.

DAVID BUSHNELL

FERNÁNDEZ OREAMUNO, PRÓSPERO (*b.* 18 July 1834; *d.* 12 March 1885), president of Costa Rica (1882–1885). Born in San José, Fernández studied there and in Guatemala. His presidency marked a watershed in Costa Rican history, ending the political domination by the "coffee barons" and ushering in fifty years of steady progress toward democracy. Following Costa Rica's first brush with dictatorship under Tomás GUARDIA GUTIÉRREZ (1870–1882), a new generation of Costa Ricans, constituting a fiercely democratic emerging middle class, undertook to extend the suffrage and eliminate the influence of the Catholic church.

Identifying with this rising group, Fernández sponsored educational reform and tough anticlerical laws. He enacted the Liberal Laws of 1884, which established free, compulsory education, expelled the JESUITS, made marriage a civil contract, legalized divorce, and secularized cemeteries. Fernández died during a military campaign against the Guatemalan caudillo Justo Rufino BARRIOS, but he had set the course for the so-called generation of 1889 that dominated Costa Rican affairs until the mid-1930s. The Legislative Assembly awarded him the Benemérito de la Patria in 1883.

CARLOS MONGE ALFARO, *Historia de Costa Rica* (1948); SAMUEL STONE, *La dinastía de los conquistadores* (1975); CHARLES D. AMERINGER, *Democracy in Costa Rica* (1982).

CHARLES D. AMERINGER

FERNÁNDEZ RETAMAR, ROBERTO (*b.* 9 June 1930), Cuban essayist and poet. Fernández Retamar was born in Havana and received a doctorate in philosophy and literature in 1954. In 1951 he was awarded the National Poetry Prize for his book *Patrias*. He studied linguistics in Paris (1955) and London (1956). After returning to Cuba in 1958, he wrote using the pseudonym David for the underground revolutionary publication *Resistencia*. After the Cuban Revolution of 1959, he continued his academic career until the following year, when he was named cultural adviser for the Cuban embassy in Paris. He was elected coordinating secretary of the Cuban Union of Writers and Artists (UNEAC).

As of the mid-1990s, Fernández Retamar was a frequent representative of Cuba in international cultural activities and was active also in his own country's cultural affairs. His essays are among the best examples of revolutionary aesthetics in literature that Cuba has produced. Among his best-known works are his collection of poems *Cuaderno paralelo* (1973) and the essay *Para una teoría de la literatura hispanoamericana* (1977). Other works include *Entrevisto* (1982).

ROBERTO VALERO

FERNÁNDEZ Y MEDINA, BENJAMÍN (*b.* 31 March 1873; *d.* 1960), Uruguayan writer and diplomat. Born in Montevideo, Fernández y Medina held a large number of posts in public administration, especially in the diplomatic corps. He was secretary to the chief of police in Montevideo in 1897 and prepared a draft of the Police

Codes. He was a member of the Departmental Commission on Elementary Instruction in the capital in 1898 and became the first official of the Interior Ministry in 1905 and chief official in 1906. During the second presidency of José BATLLE Y ORDÓÑEZ, he was appointed undersecretary of foreign affairs. He later joined the Foreign Service and was appointed plenipotentiary minister in Germany and Holland in 1916. In 1917 he took up the same post in Spain, which was expanded to include Portugal. He later was transferred to Cuba and Mexico and retired from the diplomatic corps on 26 December 1935.

ARTURO SCARONE, *Uruguayos contemporáneos* (1937).

JOSÉ DE TORRES WILSON

FERNANDINI, EULOGIO E. (*b.* 13 September 1860; *d.* 24 December 1947), a pioneering Peruvian mine owner and cattleman who upgraded his MINING operations during the COPPER boom of 1897–1898. Importing an entire mill in parts on muleback, he built a highly modern smelter. Like his peers, he relied on local capital and initiatives. When copper prices and technology attracted foreign investment, Fernandini fought to maintain his independence, but CERRO DE PASCO CORPORATION drove out local business. Cerro spent massively on improvements and government contracts. By World War I, Fernandini was a minor shareholder in Cerro, to which he supplied food. In the 1920s and 1930s he turned to gold mining in the Andes.

ROSEMARY THORP and GEOFFREY BERTRAM, *Peru, 1890–1977: Growth and Policy in an Open Economy* (1978); FLORENCIA E. MALLON, *The Defense of Community in Peru's Central Highlands* (1983), esp. pp. 136–137, 172–173.

VINCENT PELOSO

See also **Mining.**

FERNANDO DE NORONHA, an island 200 miles northeast of Cape São Roque, Brazil. Covering 10 square miles and supporting a population of 1,340 (1985 est.), the island, of volcanic origin, is dominated by a 1,050-foot peak and is known for interesting wildlife.

Discovered about 1503 by Fernando de Noronha, a Portuguese participant in the dyewood trade, the island later became a dependency of PERNAMBUCO and in 1942, together with neighboring islets, a territory of Brazil. Strategically positioned off the bulge of Brazil, the island suffered several attacks, none of them successful, in the seventeenth and eighteenth centuries. It served as a penal colony in the 1700s and continued to receive a few political prisoners as late as the 1980s. During 1957–1962, the United States Air Force used the island as a tracking station for guided missiles based at Cape Canaveral, Florida. The Brazilian military currently controls the territory, and the population consists primarily of fishermen or civilian employees of the military. In 1989, surrounding waters were declared a Marine National Park.

CARA SHELLY

FERRÉ AGUAYO, LUIS ANTONIO (*b.* 1904) businessman, politician, and leading advocate of Puerto Rican statehood. Born into a wealthy Cuban family in 1904, Ferré spent his early years achieving commercial success. Through ventures such as the Puerto Rican Cement Company of Ponce, his hometown, Ferré added significantly to his family's fortune. His experience in business convinced him that Puerto Rico's future rested in North American–style capitalism. He became a leader of Puerto Rico's statehood movement and closely allied himself with the mainland Republican Party.

In 1951 Ferré was elected to Puerto Rico's constitutional convention. After 1952 Ferré and his brother-in-law, Miguel A. García Méndez, assumed leadership of the Republican Statehood Party (PER). Business successes such as the Puerto Rican Cement Company and philanthropic endeavors such as Ponce's art gallery brought Ferré widespread respect. While cultivating friendships among Eisenhower Republicans, Ferré appealed to the Puerto Rican working and middle classes by touting the economic benefits of statehood. Although badly losing the 1956 gubernatorial election to his rival, Luis MUÑOZ MARÍN, Ferré continued to develop a mass following. His defeat notwithstanding, PER demonstrated respectable electoral strength in urban centers such as San Juan, where a new middle class was taking shape. Ferré again ran for governor in 1964, but lost to Muñoz's handpicked successor, Roberto SÁNCHEZ VILELLA.

In the 1967 plebiscite regarding Puerto Rico's status, Ferré led an alliance favoring statehood, the United Statehooders, and gained a respectable 38.9 percent of the vote. Again displaying urban electoral muscle in San Juan and Ponce, the statehooders had high hopes for the 1968 elections. They were not disappointed. Ferré and the statehooders organized a new party, the New Progressive Party (PNP), under whose banner Ferré won a narrow victory in the November 1968 gubernatorial race. Ferré served only one term as governor, but remained a leading PNP personality. He maintained close contacts with Republican presidents Nixon, Ford, and Reagan, and in November 1991 received the Medal of Freedom from President George Bush.

ARTURO MORALES CARRIÓN, *Puerto Rico: A Political and Cultural History* (1983); ANNE NELSON, *Murder Under Two Flags: The U.S., Puerto Rico, and the Cerro Maravilla Cover-up* (1986); FRANKLIN W. KNIGHT, *The Caribbean: The Genesis of a Fragmented Nationalism*, 2d ed. (1990).

JOHN J. CROCITTI

561

FERREIRA, BENIGNO (*b.* 18 February 1840; *d.* 24 November 1920), president of Paraguay (1906–1908) and soldier. Born in Limpio, Ferreira moved with his family to Argentina at an early age. He studied law at the University of Buenos Aires, where he affiliated with a group of radical Paraguayan emigrés opposed to the government of Carlos Antonio LÓPEZ and his son, Francisco Solano LÓPEZ. With the outbreak of the WAR OF THE TRIPLE ALLIANCE in 1864, Ferreira helped convert this group into the Legión Paraguaya, which fought alongside the Argentines in their invasion of Paraguay. With the defeat of Solano López in 1870, Ferreira's prospects should have dramatically improved, but the chaos of the postwar era meant that he had to limit himself to temporary alliances with various political patrons. He was interior minister under Salvador Jovellanos and later vice president of the Partido Liberal.

During most of the late nineteenth century Ferreira was back in exile in Buenos Aires, but after the successful Liberal revolt of 1904, he was recalled to Asunción. Though he was without major popular support, he nonetheless was appointed president two years later. New revolts that threatened to oust him from that position quickly coalesced into full-scale civil war. In July 1908, having had little chance to do anything with his presidency, Ferreira was forced from office, and from Paraguay, this time for good. He died in Buenos Aires.

CARLOS ZUBIZARRETA, *Cien vidas paraguayas*, 2d ed. (1985), pp. 210–213; *The Cambridge History of Latin America*, vol. 5 (1986), pp. 475–496.

THOMAS L. WHIGHAM

FERREIRA ALDUNATE, WILSON (*b.* 1919; *d.* 1988), a Blanco (National Party) senator and presidential candidate and an outspoken critic of the military dictatorship that controlled Uruguay from 1973 to 1984. Wilson, as he was known by friend and foe alike, was a charismatic political leader and a modern caudillo within the National Party. His faction, Por la Patria, was the highest vote getter within the party in the 1971 and 1984 elections.

Ferreira was from a ranching family. He began his political career first as a deputy and then as a senator (1967–1972). He also served as minister of agriculture under a Blanco government in 1963. He was a presidential candidate in the 1971 elections and received more votes than any other candidate, but his party lost the presidency because the Colorado Party's candidates received more total votes than the Blanco candidates. Some observers believe that the Blancos did, in fact, receive more votes but that the Colorados and conservative Blancos, together with the military, were not prepared to see Ferreira as president.

After the military coup in 1973, Ferreira went into exile in Buenos Aires. He was an outspoken critic of the regime and fled to London after barely escaping with his life in June 1976, when two fellow exiled politicians were kidnapped and murdered. Ferreira testified before the U.S. Congress later that year and was a valuable voice in achieving a cutoff of military aid to the Uruguayan dictatorship. While in exile he continued his criticism of the regime and let his supporters know that he was opposed to the military's 1980 constitutional project. With his image enhanced by the defeat of the proposed constitution in a plebiscite, Ferreira's faction proved the most popular in the internal party elections permitted by the military in 1982. It was clear at this point that if the military allowed a free presidential election, Ferreira would emerge the victor. By early 1984, with the military convinced it had to exit politics but unwilling to accept the possibility of a Ferreira presidency, the generals released from prison Liber SEREGNI, leader of the leftist political coalition known as the Frente Amplio (Broad Front). The strategy was to relegalize the Left so that its followers would not support Ferreira in an upcoming election.

By this time Ferreira had returned to Buenos Aires. Sensing that events were outracing him, he returned to Montevideo on 16 June 1984. He was promptly arrested and incarcerated in a remote military installation in the interior, where he remained until several days after the November elections. The military, the Colorado Party, and the Frente Amplio had agreed to the elections in negotiations known as the Pact of the NAVAL CLUB. Not unexpectedly, with Ferreira excluded from running, the Colorados won the presidential election. Ferreira supported the incoming Julio María SANGUINETTI administration but favored some accounting for the military's human-rights abuses. Nevertheless, two years later, when a constitutional crisis seemed probable over the military's refusal to participate in civilian trials concerning abuses during the dictatorship, Ferreira reluctantly supported an amnesty law. Some felt he did this so that the military would permit him to run in the November 1989 presidential elections. Ferreira was diagnosed with cancer in 1987, however, and died the next year. There was a massive turnout at his funeral, as Uruguayans buried their last modern caudillo.

WILSON FERREIRA, *El exilio y la lucha* (1986); MARTIN WEINSTEIN, *Uruguay: Democracy at the Crossroads* (1988).

MARTIN WEINSTEIN

See also **Caudillismo; Uruguay: Political Parties.**

FERREIRA DA SILVA, VIRGOLINO. *See* **Lampião.**

FERRER, RAFAEL (*b.* 1933), Puerto Rican artist. Ferrer, a native of Santurce, studied literature and music at Syracuse University. He received art training from Eugenio Fernández Granell at the University of Puerto Rico in 1953. A resident of the mainland United States since 1966, Ferrer has taught at the Philadelphia College of

Art (1967–1977), the School of Visual Arts in New York (1978–1980), and the Skowhegan School of Painting and Sculpture in Skowhegan, Maine (1981). During the late 1960s and early 1970s, he created conceptual art pieces, installations, and mixed-media sculptures and contributed to the development of process art and body art. His more recent paintings and mixed-media sculptures evoke the Caribbean through expressionistic means. His work has been included in numerous solo and group exhibitions throughout the United States.

CONTEMPORARY ARTS CENTER (Cincinnati, Ohio), *Deseo: An Adventure* (1973); LAGUNA GLORIA ART MUSEUM (Austin, Texas), *Rafael Ferrer: Impassioned Rhythms* (1986); BRONX MUSEUM OF THE ARTS (Bronx, N.Y.), *The Latin American Spirit: Art and Artists in the United States, 1920–1970* (1988).

MIRIAM BASILIO

FERRERA, FRANCISCO (*b.* 1794 or 1800; *d.* 1851), president of Honduras (1841–1845). Ferrera was born in Cantarranas (later renamed San Juan de Flores), Honduras. Orphaned at an early age, he was educated by the village priest, José León Garín.

Ferrera rose to prominence when he laid siege to the fortresses on Honduras's north coast that Honduran conservatives had seized with aid from Spanish Cuba in 1831. He served as vice chief of state under Governor Joaquín RIVERA (1833–1836) and then rose to power as he led conservative Honduran and Nicaraguan forces against Francisco MORAZÁN's Central American government in 1839, forming an alliance with José Rafael CARRERA in Guatemala. Although he suffered reverses at Morazán's hand, notably at Espíritu Santo (5–6 May 1839) and at San Pedro Perulapán (25 September 1839), he became identified with the separation of Honduras from the Central American federation. Elected president by the National Assembly on 30 December 1840, he took office on 1 January 1841 as Honduras's first constitutional president. Ferrera served two two-year terms, until 1 January 1845, and was closely allied with Guatemala's Carrera and El Salvador's Francisco MALESPÍN, who assisted him in resisting the liberal forces of José Trinidad CABAÑAS. Ferrera was elected to a third term in 1847, but declined to serve; however, he did continue to be the country's dominant caudillo as minister of war and as armed forces chief until 1848.

RAMÓN ROSA, "Francisco Ferrera," in *Oro de Honduras, antología*, 2 vols. (1948), vol. 1, pp. 25–31; PAULINO VALLADARES, *Hondureños ilustres en la pluma* (1972), pp. 31–33; HARVEY K. MEYER, *Historical Dictionary of Honduras* (1976), p. 133; RAÚL A. PAGOAGA, *Honduras y sus gobernantes* (1979); RALPH LEE WOODWARD, JR., *Rafael Carrera and the Emergence of the Republic of Guatemala, 1821–1871* (1992).

RALPH LEE WOODWARD, JR.

See also **Central America.**

FERREZ, MARC (*b.* 7 December 1843; *d.* 12 January 1923), Brazilian-born portrait and landscape photographer. The son of a French sculptor who arrived in Brazil with the 1816 FRENCH ARTISTIC MISSION, Ferrez studied in Paris before returning to Rio de Janeiro to apprentice as a photographer with Franz Keller at the German-owned Leuzinger Studio. After a fire destroyed his first studio, he returned to Paris to order new equipment manufactured to his design to allow him to produce panoramic views. His most lasting photographs have as their subjects what he considered the wonders of the Brazilian landscape: natural features, such as mountains, waterfalls, and jungles, and man-made feats of engineering, such as railroads, bridges, and urban buildings. Ferrez also photographed members of the indigenous Botocudo tribe while serving as a member of the American Charles Fredrick Hartt's 1875–1876 geological and geographic expedition to the interior of the province of Bahia. Following late-nineteenth-century custom, he posed his Indian subjects against artificial backdrops. Highly skilled at neutralizing the effects of ship movement, Ferrez was named "photographer of the Royal Navy" by Emperor PEDRO II. Photographic historians consider him to be the equal of such late-nineteenth-century master photographers as William Henry Jackson (1843–1942) and Eadweard Muybridge (1830–1904). Ferrez's grandson, Gilberto Ferrez, a leading collector and scholar, has devoted his life to publishing and publicizing his grandfather's work.

BORIS KOSSOY, *Origens e expansão da fotografia no Brasil—Século XIX* (1980); RAINER FABIAN and HANS-CHRISTIAN ADAM, *Masters of Early Travel Photography* (1983); GILBERTO FERREZ, *A fotografia no Brasil, 1840–1900* (1985); PEDRO VASQUEZ, *Fotógrafos pioneiros no Rio de Janeiro* (1990).

ROBERT M. LEVINE

See also **Photography.**

FICHER, JACOBO (*b.* 15 January 1896; *d.* 9 September 1978), Argentine composer, violinist, and conductor. Born in Odessa, Ukraine, Ficher came from a musical family. He began violin lessons when he was nine years old with Pyotr Solomonovich Stolyarsky and M. T. Hait. He entered the St. Petersburg Imperial Conservatory at sixteen and studied under S. Korguyev and Leopold Auer, finishing his studies in 1917. In a violin competition he won the position of leader of the Petrograd State Opera Orchestra but declined the assignment. In 1923 he immigrated to Argentina, where he became active in the musical life of Buenos Aires. In 1929 he was a founding member of the Grupo Renovación, which was committed to the study and promotion of new styles of composition; he was also one of the founders of the Argentine Composers' League (1947). Ficher taught composition at the University of La Plata as well as at the National Conservatory of Buenos Aires, the Municipal Conservatory, and the Instituto Superior de Arte of the TEATRO COLÓN.

Ficher received numerous awards, including the Municipal Prize for his String Quartet no. 1 (1929), for the symphonic poem *Sulamita* (1931), and for his Sonata for Piano (1943); the Coolidge Prize for his String Quartet no. 2 (1937); and the first prize from the Comisión de Cultura de Buenos Aires for his Third Symphony (1940). Ficher's Concerto for Violin and Orchestra received honorable mention from the Free Library of Philadelphia (1942); his String Quartet no. 4 (1953) received the López Buchardo Prize; and his Seventh Symphony (1960) won first prize in an Argentine competition to celebrate the sesquicentenary of the May Revolution. The Indianapolis Orchestra commissioned the Suite for Strings (1954), which was performed under maestro Fabian Sevinsky. Ficher also composed two operas, *El oso* and *Pedido de mano*, both based on libretti by Anton Chekhov with Russian and Spanish texts, four ballets, several choral works, eight symphonies, concerti, piano works, and music for stage and film. He died in Buenos Aires.

Composers of the Americas, vol. 2 (1956); B. ZIPMAN, *Jacobo Ficher* (1966); *New Grove Dictionary of Music and Musicians*, vol. 6 (1980).

SUSANA SALGADO

FICO. *See* **Brazil: Independence Movements.**

FIERRO RIMAC, FRANCISCO (*b.* 1803; *d.* 1879), Peru's foremost painter of everyday life and prevailing customs (*costumbrista* painter). A mulatto, Fierro Rimac was born into a humble Lima family. Most of what is known about "Pancho Fierro," as he was called, is contained in a letter by Peruvian author Ricardo PALMA dated 1885. Fierro Rimac was self-taught and began his career as an artist drawing maps and painting coats of arms of Peruvian cities. Among his popular subjects were ZAMBOS (natives of Indian and black origin), artisans, water carriers, street vendors, fishermen (*Stream Fishermen*, 1850), dances, and bullfights (*Juanita Breña Challenging a Bull with a Cloak*, 1821). He painted the mentally ill living in the streets of Lima and left some of the earliest images of the *tapadas* (Peruvian women wearing a unique costume consisting of a cloak that covers the bust and most of the head, leaving only one eye uncovered). He also designed street posters advertising bullfights and decorated walls with *costumbrista* scenes, allegories, and bucolic landscapes, none of which have survived.

An intuitive and talented colorist, Fierro Rimac worked primarily in watercolor, favoring small formats. His drawing was rudimentary; he did not use perspective. His work has been compared to some of Goya's *The Caprices* because of his caricaturesque style and his penchant for writing comments on drawings.

JUAN E. RÍOS, *La pintura contemporánea en el Perú* (1946); DAWN ADES, *Art in Latin America: The Modern Era, 1820–1980* (1989), pp. 84–85.

MARTA GARSD

Danza de Pallas. Watercolor by Pancho Fierro. COLECCIÓN DEL BANCO DE CRÉDITO DEL PERÚ; PHOTO BY DANIEL GIANNONI.

FIESTAS, a Spanish term whose meaning ranges from private celebrations to nationwide fetes, from saint-day parties to the commemoration of national independence. Community holidays, especially civic and religious celebrations, serve as an occasion for social interaction, political negotiation, historical lessons, and turning-the-world-upside-down mimicry. Above all, fiestas serve as an occasion for the enjoyment of family, friends, compatriots, and coreligionists. The most dramatic Latin American celebrations contain a popular element—drawn from the indigenous peoples, blacks, mixed-ethnic groups, and European traditions—that often overwhelms official, sanctioned affairs. CARNIVAL, for example, has become a Brazilian cultural expression that long ago surpassed in popularity and participants the Ash Wednesday initiation of Roman Catholicism's Lenten period.

One description of fiestas in Latin America classifies them as civic, religious, and commercial holidays. Commemoration of independence serves generally as the most significant holiday in each of the region's nations (see the following list), although it might be joined by an additional political anniversary. Two examples of the latter are the CINCO DE MAYO holiday that celebrates the victory of the Mexican army over invading French troops (5 May 1867), and 26 July, which marks Fidel Castro's first (and unsuccessful) revolutionary effort in

1953 to seize power in Cuba, provided the name of his guerrilla movement, and commemorates his fellow rebels who died in the effort.

Independence Fiestas

Haiti	1 January
Dominican Republic	27 February
Paraguay	14–15 May
Cuba	17 May
Venezuela	5 July
Argentina	9 July
Colombia	20 July
Peru	28 July
Bolivia	6 August
Ecuador	10 August
Uruguay	25 August
Brazil	7 September
Costa Rica	15 September
El Salvador	15 September
Guatemala	15 September
Honduras	15 September
Nicaragua	15 September
Mexico	15–16 September
Chile	18 September
Panama	3 November

Because Roman Catholicism served as one instrument of conquest and acculturation in Latin America, church holidays of this religion have the most general participation. Jewish, Protestant, and African-derived religious holidays are also celebrated throughout the region. The most impressive celebrations during the colonial years occurred on Corpus Christi and Holy Week, climaxing with Easter services. In the last century the Christmas holiday has emerged as more popular, with the suppression of many public aspects of the Corpus Christi and Holy Week festivals. In the Antilles, the circum-Caribbean region, and Brazil, Carnival has generally emerged as one of the most significant holidays. Of special importance throughout Latin America are the celebrations of the manifestations of virgins and saints. The best-known and most widely celebrated of these are the Virgin of GUADALUPE, the patron of Mexico, on 12 December, and Santa ROSA DE LIMA, the first saint of South America, on 30 August. Other feasts mark the church's holy days of obligation. Such fiestas include the Feast of Christ of Esquipulas, called the Black Christ festival, in Guatemala (15 January) and the festival of Santiago (Saint James the Greater), the patron saint of Chile (25 July).

Commercial and special fiestas include those holidays created to honor special groups, such as Mother's Day

"Feasting the Dead" in Copacabana, near Lake Titicaca, Bolivia. CARL FRANK / PHOTO RESEARCHERS, INC.

and Teacher's Day. Others are attempts to revive, expand, and popularize celebrations to promote TOURISM. For example, Mexico's Day of the Dead fiestas in Pátzcuaro, Michoacán, resulted from the deliberate plans of the national tourism department. Carnival in several Caribbean nations today has taken on the character of a spectacle intended primarily for tourists. However commercial these events, they demonstrate what government officials want outsiders to recognize as typical of their culture.

Associated with most Latin American fiestas are special customs, artifacts, foods, band music, dancing, and fireworks. Gifts have become associated with special holidays—helmets at Corpus Christi, *matracas* (rattles) during Holy Week, and candy skulls at the Day of the Dead. Holiday cuisine ranges from special meals (for example, *chiles en nogada*, a green, stuffed chile pepper in a white cream sauce with red pomegranate seeds that displays the colors of the national flag for Mexican Independence Day), to preparations for religious feasts (for example, the Virgin's Tears, made from beet juice, for Holy Week; special egg-yolk bread made for the Day of the Dead; Three Kings Bread, a kind of sweet bread eaten on 6 January that has a ring baked in it to bring good luck to the person who finds it), to special beverages for holidays (Noche Buena beer brewed only during the Christmas holidays; *cuba libre*, a rum-and-cola drink, for national independence day; *chicha*, hard cider made from apples or grapes; and wine for Chile's major holidays).

The parades and processions often display visual lessons in social prominence and hierarchy through the order of march, the inclusion of different groups, and the nature of floats. Individuals find it necessary to participate as members of a residential, occupational, ethnic, or religious group. Fiesta organization in the past reflected these same groupings, with perhaps the religious confraternities (COFRADÍAS) dominant in the colonial years, occupational and ethnic associations slightly superior in the nineteenth century, and residential groups emerging as more important in the twentieth century. Displaying these groups during fiestas, while portraying social hierarchy, demonstrates and reaffirms the solidarity of the society.

Fiestas also mark individual rites of passage, including birth, christening, saint day, *quincinera* (fifteenth birthday for girls), marriage, and death. The nature of these fiestas varies from family to family and differs by religion. Nevertheless, the nature of the family holiday, its proper celebration, remains the province primarily of the leading (or centralizing) woman.

LAWRENCE URDANG and CHRISTINE N. DONOHUE, eds., *Holidays and Anniversaries of the World* (1985); PATRICIA QUINTANA with CAROL HARALSON, *Mexico's Feasts of Life* (1989); WILLIAM H. BEEZLEY, CHERYL E. MARTIN, and WILLIAM E. FRENCH, eds., *Rituals of Rule, Rituals of Resistance: Public Celebrations and Popular Culture in Mexico* (1994).

WILLIAM H. BEEZLEY

FIGARI, PEDRO (*b.* 29 June 1861; *d.* 24 July 1938), Uruguayan painter. Born in Montevideo, Figari had no formal art training in his youth but later studied drawing and painting with Godofredo Sommavilla in Montevideo and with Virgilio Ripari in Venice (1886). His astonishing artistic career did not begin until 1921, at age sixty, when he had his first exhibition in Buenos Aires at the Galería Müller. In 1925 he moved to Paris, where he remained for nine years. In the seventeen years following his first exhibition in Buenos Aires he turned out some 3,000 cardboard designs consisting of social topics, landscapes, colonial patios, folk dances, black country women, horses, and GAUCHOS. His style displays an inner dynamism deriving from rapid strokes and a poetic vision of color. He received the grand prize at the Centennial of Uruguayan Independence Exhibition in Montevideo, and the gold medal at the Ibero-American Exhibition, Seville, Spain, both in 1930. He was one of the founders of Uruguay's school of arts (1898), as well as a founding member of the Sociedad Amigos del Arte in Buenos Aires (1924). Figari was the author of several books, including *Art, Aesthetics and the Ideal* (1912), in which he developed ideas taken from Herbert Spenser, and *La historia Kiria* (1930), the description of a Uruguayan utopia.

VICENTE GESUALDO, ALDO VIGLIONE, and RODOLFO SANTOS, *Diccionario de artistas plásticos en la Argentina* (1988).

AMALIA CORTINA ARAVENA

FIGUEIREDO, AFONSO CELSO DE ASSIS (*b.* 31 March 1860; *d.* 11 July 1938), Brazilian politician and man of letters. The son of a prominent Liberal politician and nobleman, the viscount of Ouro Prêto, Figueiredo left his native Minas Gerais to study in São Paulo. After earning a doctorate in law in 1881, he quickly embarked on his political career, winning election to the parliament four times. In contrast to his father, he showed himself to be reform-minded, most notably supporting proposals for the gradual abolition of slavery in Brazil.

Although he had embraced republican ideas as a student, Figueiredo had become a strident monarchist by the time his father headed the final cabinet of the Brazilian Empire in 1889. When the empire gave way to the new republic late in that year, Figueiredo chose to follow his father into European exile. Upon his return he practiced and taught law, and dedicated himself to political journalism and other writings. Although he also produced poetry and novels, his greatest literary fame came from his nonfiction works. Figueiredo's historical memoirs, *Oito anos de Parlamento* (1981), and biography *Visconde de Ouro Prêto* (1935), are important sources for the study of politics in the late nineteenth century. By far his most widely read literary work was *Porque me ufano do meu país* (1900, 1943), a celebration of all things Brazilian. Hailed by many as a model of civic pride, this book gave rise to the term *ufanismo* (facile, unthinking patriotism).

Honored by France with the Legion of Honor and by Pope Pius X with the title of count, Figueiredo became a central figure in Brazil's literary and intellectual organizations. One of the founding members of the Academia Brasileira de Letras, he served as president of the Instituto Histórico e Geográfico Brasileiro from 1912 until his death.

ROBERT E. CONRAD, *The Destruction of Brazilian Slavery, 1850–1888* (1972); EMÍLIA VIOTTI DA COSTA, *The Brazilian Empire: Myths and Histories* (1985).

ROGER A. KITTLESON

FIGUEIREDO, JACKSON DE (*b*. 9 October 1891; *d*. 4 November 1928), Brazilian writer and Catholic layman who founded the Centro Dom Vital, a major center for orthodox Catholic thought.

Born in Aracajú, Sergipe, Figueiredo was an atheist who converted to Catholicism in 1918 and thereafter dedicated his life to church affairs. Influenced by nineteenth-century and contemporary European conservatives, he saw in Catholicism "the most fundamental element of Brazilian heritage," which could serve as a bulwark against the forces of disorder.

In 1922 he founded the Centro Dom Vital in Rio de Janeiro. It became the Catholic hierarchy's vehicle to mobilize opinions among educated Brazilians and advocated liturgical piety, theological thought, personal austerity, and conservatism. Figueiredo used the Centro to spark a powerful Catholic political movement that sought to regenerate the country morally. His political passion and intolerance, however, contrasted with his private gentleness and bohemianism. He died in Barra la Tijuca.

ROBERT M. LEVINE, *Historical Dictionary of Brazil* (1979); *Latin American Politics: A Historical Bibliography* (1984).

ROSS WILKINSON

FIGUEIREDO, JOÃO BATISTA DE OLIVEIRA (*b*. 15 January 1918), president of Brazil (1979–1985). At the time of his inauguration, Figueiredo was largely unknown to the public, though he had been an early conspirator in the 1964 military coup that overthrew President João GOULART. After the coup, he rose to the rank of general and served as chief of the Military Cabinet, secretary-general of the National Security Council, and head of the National Intelligence Agency (SNI).

Born in Rio de Janeiro, Figueiredo grew up in the town of Alegrete in Rio Grande do Sul. His father, General Euclides Figueiredo, commanded anti-Getúlio VARGAS troops during the 1932 São Paulo Rebellion. João Batista chose a military career, graduating first in his class at the numerous military schools he attended, including the military academy at Realengo, where he graduated as a cavalry officer in 1937. One brother, General Euclides de Oliveira Figueiredo, also followed a military path. Another brother, Guilherme de Figueiredo, is a well-known playwright and essayist.

The last of the post-coup military presidents, Figueiredo supervised the transition to civilian rule. Bridging the gap between hard-liners and moderates, he continued the cautious relaxation (*distenção*) of military rule begun by Ernesto GEISEL and completed the process of opening the political system (*abertura*). Under Figueiredo, prisoners who lost their political rights (*cassados*) were granted amnesty. His government abandoned the two-party system and promoted the creation of multiple parties. In 1982, Figueiredo allowed direct elections of state governors for the first time since 1965. Figueiredo tried to foster a populist image, but resorted to the hard line when necessary, as he did in the 1979 labor strikes.

Figueiredo left politics with the return to civilian rule in 1985. According to 1993 opinion polls, Brazilians rated Figueiredo's presidency high. Though mentioned as a possible candidate for the 1994 presidential elections, Figueiredo claimed little enthusiasm for the idea.

Although there is no biography of Figueiredo available in English, a number of works address his administration. THOMAS E. SKIDMORE, *The Politics of Military Rule in Brazil, 1964–1985* (1988), devotes chap. 8 and part of chap. 9 to the subject. RONALD M. SCHNEIDER, *Order and Progress: A Political History of Brazil* (1991), also discusses the Figueiredo government.

SONNY B. DAVIS

FIGUERES FERRER, JOSÉ (*b*. 25 September 1906; *d*. 8 June 1990), president of Costa Rica. José Figueres, "Don Pepe," presided over the Costa Rican nation on three separate occasions: once as head of a junta government (8 May 1948 to 8 November 1949) and twice as constitutional president (1953–1958 and 1970–1974). He was one of Costa Rica's most important political figures, setting the economic and social course of his country following the 1948 civil war and creating the National Liberation Party (PLN), Costa Rica's dominant political party after 1953. Moreover, during the 1950s and 1960s, he stood almost alone as the champion of democracy and economic and social reform in Central America and the Spanish-speaking Caribbean.

Born in rural San Ramón shortly after his parents had emigrated from Spain, Figueres had little formal education beyond the secondary level. He came to the United States in 1924 intending to study electrical engineering at the Massachusetts Institute of Technology, but he never matriculated. Instead, with the Boston Public Library as his classroom, he acquired the social democratic philosophy that guided his future political career. In 1928, he returned to Costa Rica to become a farmer-entrepreneur on a *finca* (ranch) he named La Lucha Sin Fin (The Endless Struggle), where he raised

Costa Rican presidential candidate José Figueres Ferrer shows broom to indicate that he swept away the opposition in the 1970 election. AP WIDE WORLD.

cabuya (a Central American agave) and built a factory to manufacture rope and bags from the homegrown fiber. La Lucha was the model for Figueres Ferrer's later national programs, wherein he developed the region, creating new jobs and skills and providing an array of benefits and social services. In 1942, Figueres Ferrer's life changed abruptly when he was expelled from the country in a dispute with President Rafael Ángel CALDERÓN GUARDIA.

Figueres criticized Calderón publicly for failing to prevent a riot in San José after an Axis submarine had attacked Puerto Limón. Calderón Guardia, for his part, accused Figueres of revealing military secrets and of participating in a scheme to shelter the properties of German and Italian residents of Costa Rica. When Figueres returned from exile in Mexico two years later, he was greeted as a hero who had opposed the authoritarian Calderón.

During his exile, Figueres and other Caribbean exiles developed the CARIBBEAN LEGION, a plan to rid Costa Rica (and the entire region) of tyranny. Figueres put his plan into operation in March 1948, when Calderón tried to steal the presidential election from the clear winner, Otilio ULATE BLANCO. Though most politicians hoped for a peaceful solution to the crisis, Figueres and Calderón were on a collision course. With a citizen-volunteer army and the help of his Caribbean allies, Figueres waged a successful six-week "war of national

liberation," and took control of the nation as head of the Founding Junta of the Second Republic in May.

During the eighteen months that the junta governed, Figueres made fundamental changes in the life of the nation. He abolished the army, nationalized the banking system, imposed a 10 percent tax on wealth, and held elections for a constituent assembly to draft a constitution. The new constitution (1949) embraced Figueres's socialist tendencies, providing for government regulation of the private sector and creating "autonomous institutions" to perform the economic and social functions of the public sector. With the constitution in place, Figueres turned over the presidency to Ulate.

In 1953, Figueres became constitutional president himself and resumed where he left off four years earlier. Figueres expanded the role of government through the creation of additional autonomous institutions to provide such services as the production and distribution of electrical energy, banking, health care, insurance, and telephones. He established the National Council of Production to stimulate agriculture and business through credits, price supports, and marketing facilities.

Despite the economic growth and social progress that Costa Rica experienced under Figueres, his presidency was not tranquil. The Figueres era was particularly troubled by foreign policy. Costa Rica's safe democracy attracted political exiles from throughout the region, and Figueres openly opposed the dictatorships of Anastasio SOMOZA in Nicaragua, Rafael TRUJILLO in the Dominican Republic, Fulgencio BATISTA in Cuba, and Marcos PÉREZ JIMÉNEZ in Venezuela. Though he made promises of military support to his Caribbean allies that he could not keep, he collaborated closely with Venezuelan exile Rómulo BETANCOURT and sought to influence U.S. policy against the dictators.

In 1954, Costa Rica was the only country to boycott the inter-American conference in Caracas, and in the same year Figueres aided Nicaraguan exiles in an attempt to overthrow Somoza. Figueres supplied arms to Fidel CASTRO after 1956. On two occasions, the dictators retaliated. In 1948, while Figueres was heading the junta, and again in 1955, Somoza sponsored "exile" invasions of Costa Rica. Both times, Figueres, with no army, appealed to the ORGANIZATION OF AMERICAN STATES for help. Though the OAS came to his rescue, it pressured him to expel the so-called Caribbean Legion from Costa Rica and to enter into agreements to reduce tensions in the region.

The U.S. State Department labeled Figueres a "troublemaker" in the 1950s, but during the 1960s, in the context of the CUBAN REVOLUTION, the attitude changed. The Central Intelligence Agency sought his assistance in covert action against Trujillo and secretly funded his efforts to strengthen the democratic Left. Figueres had criticized Castro in April 1959, advising him to remain on the side of the United States in the cold war, and he became an avid supporter of President John F. Kennedy and the ALLIANCE FOR PROGRESS. After Kennedy's assassination, Figueres's role in international affairs diminished. His decline was especially steep after 1967, when it became known that he had collaborated with the CIA.

With Figueres barred by the constitution from succeeding himself in 1959, and the party badly split in choosing a candidate, the PLN lost the presidential election. It did manage to reunite for victory in 1962, but lost again four years later, convincing Figueres to run in 1970.

Figueres's second presidency was no less controversial than his first, but had fewer accomplishments to claim. Needing to recharge the economy, Figueres established trade and diplomatic relations with the Soviet Union and proposed the creation of an international financial district in Costa Rica. Both measures bedeviled his presidency. There were street demonstrations against any sort of relations with the Soviet Union, and militant right-wing groups used the situation to agitate. The plan for the international financial district brought Robert VESCO to Costa Rica. Though Figueres argued that Costa Rica needed capital, Vesco's reputation as a swindler and his holdings in Figueres's La Lucha caused a crippling scandal. Figueres believed that he was acting in the best interests of his country, but the principal achievement of his second presidency was that its shortcomings paved the way for a new generation of PLN leaders to take charge.

During the remaining years of his life, Figueres permitted the institutions and party that he had created to take shape without him. Because of a near-even division in Costa Rica between pro-Liberation and anti-Liberation sentiment, an informal two-party system evolved through the process of coalition politics. Figueres himself enhanced his country's democratic traditions and formalized the nation's general commitment to economic and social well-being, which enabled Costa Rica to avoid the bloodshed of Central America in the 1980s.

ARTURO CASTRO ESQUIVEL, *José Figueres Ferrer: El hombre y su obra* (1955); ALBERTO BAEZA FLORES, *La lucha sin fin* (1969); JOHN PATRICK BELL, *Crisis in Costa Rica: The 1948 Revolution* (1971); BERT H. ENGLISH, *Liberación Nacional in Costa Rica: The Development of a Political Party in a Transitional Society* (1971); CHARLES D. AMERINGER, *Don Pepe: A Political Biography of José Figueres of Costa Rica* (1978).

CHARLES D. AMERINGER

FIGUEROA, GABRIEL (b. 26 April 1908), Mexican film photographer. Figueroa learned his trade in Mexico and in Hollywood. He was the principal photographer of *Allá en el Rancho Grande* (1938). Since then, he has filmed over 200 features for Mexican, North American, and European directors. Noted particularly for his work with black and white film, Figueroa was called "the greatest muralist of Mexico" by Diego RIVERA. His aesthetic style is characterized by contrasts of darkness and light and by the use of panoramic shots. He has worked for such acclaimed directors as Emilio Fernández, Luis Buñuel, John Ford, and John Huston. Figueroa has received more Ariels from the Mexican film academy than any other photographer in Mexican cinema. In addition, he has been awarded major international prizes in Venice, Cannes, Prague, Madrid, and San Francisco. In 1971 he received the National Award for the Arts in Mexico.

LUIS REYES DE LA MAZA, *El cine sonoro en México* (1973); E. BRADFORD BURNS, *Latin American Cinema: Film and History* (1975); CARL J. MORA, *Mexican Cinema: Reflections of a Society: 1896–1980* (1982); and JOHN KING, *Magical Reels: A History of Cinema in Latin America* (1990).

DAVID MACIEL

FIGUEROA, JOSÉ (d. 1835), governor of Alta California (1833–1835). General Figueroa was one of the most important Mexican governors of the territory. In 1833 he initiated a new emancipation of a limited number of Indian converts living in Franciscan-run MISSIONS. That same year he also established Indian towns at three sites in the southern part of the territory—the San Juan Capistrano mission, the Las Flores rancho, and the San Dieguito rancho—with the hope of creating stable Indian villages with formal municipal governments. This scheme, however, failed when the Spanish government secularized the missions.

Figueroa also cooperated in implementing the secularization of the missions ordered by the Valentín GÓMEZ FARÍAS government by way of a bill signed on 17 August 1833, working with local politicians to craft the secularization decree to benefit the elite of the territory. On 9 August 1834, Figueroa approved the secularization plan. Prominent CALIFORNIOS received appointment as *mayordomos* of the former missions, many using their positions to enrich themselves. Most of the converts still living in the missions were not legally emancipated.

After Figueroa died in office in 1835, a period of political chaos followed, and in 1836 local politicians seized control of the government.

DAVID J. WEBER, *The Mexican Frontier, 1821–1846: The American Southwest Under Mexico* (1982).

ROBERT H. JACKSON

FIGUEROA, PEDRO JOSÉ (b. 1780; d. 1838), Colombian artist. Son of a wealthy Bogotá family and descendant of a notable group of seventeenth-century Colombian painters, Figueroa began his studies with Peruvian painter Pablo Antonio García (1744–1814). During the war for independence in Colombia, he painted scenes of some of the battles as well as at least ten portraits (1819–1822) of Simón Bolívar. He served as director of the construction of the Church of Las Nieves in Bogotá and painted the *Holy Trinity* mural for the Bogotá cathedral. He painted many portraits of influential Colombians including archbishops. Figueroa established a studio for his pupils, among whom were his sons José Celestino and José Miguel y Santos.

GABRIEL GIRALDO JARAMILLO, *La miniatura, la pintura y el grabado en Colombia* (1980); DAWN ADES, *Art in Latin America* (1989).

BÉLGICA RODRÍGUEZ

FIGUEROA ALCORTA, JOSÉ (*b.* 20 November 1860; *d.* 27 December 1931), president of Argentina (1906–1910). With his presidency began the process of evolution toward a true democracy in Argentina. With the support of the followers of Bartolomé MITRE and Carlos PELLEGRINI, Figueroa Alcorta confronted head-on the old system created by Julio Argentino ROCA ("El Zorro"), president (1880–1886 and 1898–1904) and the most important political figure in Argentina since the 1890s. Figueroa Alcorta intervened in the provinces seven times and in the process dismantled the Roquista political machinery in the interior of the country. Figueroa Alcorta also confronted Congress, another Roquista stronghold. When Congress refused to consider Figueroa Alcorta's budget proposal and other measures, he closed it down on 25 January 1908. If President Roque SÁENZ PEÑA (elected to office in 1910) was able to implement political reforms later on, it was because Figueroa Alcorta had already purged the system.

ALFREDO DÍAZ DE MOLINA, *José Figueroa Alcorta: De la oligarquía a la democracia, 1898–1928* (1979).

JUAN MANUEL PÉREZ

FIGUEROA GAJARDO, ANA (*b.* 19 June 1907; *d.* 8 April 1970), Chilean career diplomat, journalist, women's rights activist. After graduating from the Instituto Pedagógico, Universidad de Chile, in 1928, Figueroa was a high-school teacher and principal. In 1946 she attended Columbia University and a summer institute at Colorado State University. From 1947 to 1949, she was general supervisor of the Chilean high-school system. In 1948 she became president of the Federación Chilena de Instituciones Femeninas (FECHIF) and was appointed director of the Chilean Women's Bureau. In 1950 she served as Chilean delegate to the Inter-American Commission of Women; from 1950 to 1952 she was the Chilean minister plenipotentiary to the Third General Assembly of the United Nations; and from 1952 to 1959 she served on the Security Council, UNESCO, and the UN Commission on the Juridical and Social Condition of Women. From 1950 to 1967, Figueroa was the first woman to serve as director-general of the International Labor Organization. She was also on the board of directors of the international YWCA.

INTER-AMERICAN COMMISSION OF WOMEN, *Libro de oro* (1980).

CORINNE ANTEZANA-PERNET
FRANCESCA MILLER

See also **Feminism and Feminist Organizations.**

FIGUEROA LARRAÍN, EMILIANO (*b.* 1866; *d.* 16 May 1931), lawyer, politician, diplomat, and president of Chile. A member of the Partido Democrático, he served as president twice. Following the death of President Pedro MONTT, he occupied the Moneda as interim president from September through December 1910, until the election of Ramón Barros Luco. He was elected to the presidency in 1925, following President Arturo Alessandri Palma's second resignation. His naive attempts to govern, however, were frustrated by the maneuverings of the minister of war, Carlos IBÁÑEZ DEL CAMPO, and in April 1927 Ibáñez forced him to resign his office. Figueroa later represented Chile as ambassador to Peru.

LUIS GALDAMES, *A History of Chile,* translated and edited by Isaac J. Cox (1941; repr. 1961); FREDERICK M. NUNN, *Chilean Politics, 1920–1931* (1970).

WILLIAM F. SATER

FILIBUSTERING, the process by which groups of men left U.S. territory on private military expeditions intended to liberate, subjugate or annex foreign—often Latin—nations or colonies. Persons engaged in such enterprises were known as "filibusters." Filibustering violated international law and several statutes, most particularly the Neutrality Act of 1818. The term "filibuster" came into English-language currency during the second half of the nineteenth century. It is derived from the Dutch *vrijbuiter* (freebooter) and related to the Spanish *filibustero* and French *flibustier.*

During America's early national period, filibuster plots and invasions were directed primarily against Spanish territory in North America. Then, in the late 1830s and early 1840s and the Fenian excitement of the late 1860s, filibustering focused upon Canada. But filibustering had its greatest impact in the 1850s, when thousands of U.S. residents, including many immigrants, joined filibuster units that invaded Mexico, the independent states of Central America, several South American countries, and the Spanish possession of Cuba. Although filibustering was never an exclusively U.S. phenomenon, it came to be identified within the international community as a dangerous manifestation of U.S. IMPERIALISM to the degree that during the nineteenth century it seriously complicated U.S. diplomacy with Mexico, Central America, the major European powers, and other governments.

William Walker's filibusters fighting against Central American troops at Rivas, Nicaragua. Reproduced from *Leslie's Illustrated Weekly Newpaper* (17 May 1856). COURTESY OF HARVARD COLLEGE LIBRARY.

The most significant filibustering expeditions of the 1850s were the 1850 and 1851 expeditions of Narciso LÓPEZ against Cuba, and William WALKER's 1853–1860 invasions of Mexico, Nicaragua, and Honduras. Walker succeeded in conquering Nicaragua and ruling it for parts of 1855–1857. Other significant expeditions of the decade included Californian Joseph Morehead's invasion of Mexican Sonora in 1851, Alexander Bell's expedition to Ecuador the same year, French adventurer Count Gaston Raoul de RAOUSSET-BOULBON's expeditions to Mexico from California in 1852–1854, Henry L. KINNEY's conquest of San Juan del Norte (GREYTOWN), Nicaragua, in 1855, and Henry A. CRABB's thrust into Sonora in 1857. Some filibustering expeditions, such as former Mississippi governor John A. Quitman's conspiracy to invade Cuba in 1853–1855 and the plot of the Knights of the Golden Circle to attack Mexico in 1860, aborted at the last moment.

The filibustering expeditions of the 1850s caused extensive destruction and many deaths in the countries victimized and contributed to a legacy of anti-Americanism throughout Mexico, Central America, and parts of South America. The Latins resented the inability—sometimes perceived as refusal—of the U.S. government to enforce its own neutrality laws effectually. None of the filibustering expeditions achieved permanent success, however, and many of the adventurers died during their campaigns. López, Raousset-Boulbon, Crabb, and Walker were all executed after being captured.

Filibustering continued to have an impact upon U.S. relations with Latin nations in the late nineteenth and early twentieth centuries. Several U.S.-based expeditions attacked Mexico in that period, and filibustering played a salient role in U.S. disputes with Spain over Cuba that triggered the Spanish-American War, such as the VIRGINIUS AFFAIR of 1873. Filibustering diminished dramatically after World War I.

HARRIS G. WARREN, *The Sword Was Their Passport: A History of American Filibustering in the Mexican Revolution* (1943); ROBERT E. MAY, *The Southern Dream of a Caribbean Empire, 1854–1861* (1973); JOSEPH A. STOUT, *The Liberators: Filibustering Expeditions into Mexico, 1848–1862 and the Last Thrust of Manifest Destiny* (1973); WILFRIED S. NEIDHARDT, *Fenianism in North America* (1975); CHARLES H. BROWN, *Agents of Manifest Destiny: The Lives and Times of the Filibusters* (1980).

ROBERT E. MAY

See also **United States–Latin American Relations.**

FILÍSOLA, VICENTE (*b.* ca. 1789; *d.* 23 July 1850), captain-general of Guatemala (12 June 1822–4 July 1823). Born in Rivoli, Italy, Filísola emigrated to Spain at a young age and began his military career. By 1810 he had attained the rank of second lieutenant and had received honors for his valiant fighting. He was sent to Mexico with royalist forces in 1811, but by 1815 he had become a close friend of Agustín de ITURBIDE. In 1821 he gave his support to Mexican independence, proclaimed in Iturbide's PLAN OF IGUALA. At the head of four thousand men, he was the first insurgent leader to enter Mexico City on 24 September 1821, securing it for Iturbide's triumphal entry. Iturbide promoted him to brigadier general and gave him the title of Knight of the Imperial Order of Guadalupe, then sent him on a mission to Central America. There he was to keep order while the region decided on annexation to Mexico. On 4 November 1822, after most of Central America had voted in favor of union with the Mexican Empire, Filísola published a decree splitting the captaincy-general of Guatemala into the three commandancies-general of Chiapas, Sacatepéquez, and Costa Rica, with their capitals at Ciudad Real, Nueva Guatemala, and León respectively. Later that month, on Iturbide's orders, he led about two thousand men against San Salvador, the only major city to resist union with the Mexican Empire. After routing Manuel José ARCE's troops, he entered the city on 9 February 1823. Upon learning of Iturbide's overthrow, he returned to Guatemala and convoked a congress of the provinces. Believing the basis for Mexican annexation to be gone, he accepted their declaration of independence.

After returning to Mexico, Filísola fought as a division general in the TEXAS REVOLUTION in 1835 and ended his career as president of the Supreme Court of War. He also wrote extensively. He published his two-volume *Memorias para la historia de Tejas* in 1848–1849, and conducted a lively polemic with José Francisco BARRUNDIA. Most of the documents ended up in Central America and were burned, but Filísola's biographer, Don Jenaro García, was able to obtain copies of Filísola's papers from one of his descendants and published them in two volumes as *La cooperación de México en la independencia de Centro América* (1911). Filísola died in Mexico during a cholera epidemic.

ALEJANDRO MARURE, *Bosquejo histórico de las revoluciones de Centroamérica desde 1811 hasta 1834*, 2 vols. (1834–1837), pp. 92–110, 113; HUBERT HOWE BANCROFT, *History of Central America* Vol. 8, *The Works of Hubert Howe Bancroft* (1887), pp. 56–57, 62–64; PEDRO ZAMORA CASTELLANOS, *Vida militar de Centro América*, 2 vols. (1966–1967), pp. 120–125; LUIS BELTRANENA SINIBALDI, *Fundación de la república de Guatemala* (1971), pp. 42–45.

PHILIPPE L. SEILER

See also **Central America, United Provinces of.**

FINCA, Spanish term for farm or other rural estate. In Guatemala and other Central American states, it usually refers to a coffee plantation.

RALPH LEE WOODWARD, JR.

FINLAY, CARLOS JUAN (*b.* 3 December 1833; *d.* 20 August 1915), a Cuban physician and epidemiologist. After earning his medical degree at Jefferson Medical College in Philadelphia, Finlay pursued additional studies in Havana and Paris before beginning his medical practice in Cuba. He represented the Cuban government to a commission from the United States that arrived on the island in 1879 to study the transmission of yellow fever. In 1881, Finlay concluded that a mosquito, known as the *Aëdes aegypti*, was the carrier of the disease, but his theory was largely ignored by the medical community until 1900, when U.S. General Leonard Wood ordered Walter REED to test Finlay's theory. Reed's experiments in Havana confirmed Finlay's findings, a discovery that led to the eradication of yellow fever in much of the tropics. Unfortunately, Reed, rather than Finlay, has received most of the credit for the elimination of yellow fever.

L. O. HOWARD, *The Yellow Fever Mosquito* (1913); JAMES H. HITCHMAN, *Leonard Wood and Cuban Independence, 1898–1902* (1971); HERMIO PORTELL-VILA, *Finlay: Vida de un sabia cubano* (1990).

THOMAS M. LEONARD

See also **Diseases.**

FISHING INDUSTRY. The commercial fisheries of the Latin American region are an important source of edible (seafoods) and nonedible (fish meals and oils) fishery products for the world market. In addition, the diversity of habitat found in the region, as well as the close proximity to rich oceanic fishing grounds of the Pacific and Atlantic oceans, allows for a complement of species that rivals or surpasses that for any other region in the world. Latin America accounts for approximately 18 percent of the total world landings (catches) of marine and freshwater fishery products. Landings from Latin American flagged vessels totaled 16 million metric tons in 1990, which represents an increase of 80 percent from just a decade earlier. This increase in landings has been fueled by a growing demand for seafood products in regional markets such as the United States, Japan, and Europe, which have become increasingly dependent on Latin American sources of fishery products.

Fishery landings within Latin America vary greatly by region. The Central American region represents 10 percent of the total annual landings for Latin America, whereas the Caribbean region lands less than 5 percent of the total. The South American countries bordering the Pacific Ocean account for approximately 80 percent, while the South American region that borders the Atlantic Ocean lands the remainder. The top ten producing countries in descending order of importance (volume) are Peru, Chile, Mexico, Brazil, Argentina, Ecuador, Venezuela, Cuba, Panama, and Uruguay. The combined production of Peru and Chile alone accounts for three-fourths of the total annual landings from the entire Latin American region.

Fishery production in the Latin American region targets both freshwater and marine species. However, less than 5 percent of the total annual landings are freshwater species, which includes predominantly characins (tetras) and cichlids (tilapias), although some salmonids (trout and salmon), cyprinids (carps and minnows), and catfish are also produced. South American countries that border the southern Pacific Ocean produce large quantities of relatively low-valued, pelagic, finfish species, which are used to produce primarily industrial fishery products. For example, Peru and Chile land vast quantities of jack and chub mackerels, pilchards, anchoveta, and herring, which are used predominantly in the production of fish meals and oils, although some may be utilized as low-valued products for human consumption. Uruguay and Argentina are major producers of hake, a groundfish species that is utilized for human consumption.

Countries located in the northern region of South America, such as Venezuela and Brazil, land a more diverse, subtropical complement of higher-valued, pelagic and near-shore species destined almost entirely for human consumption, including large quantities of shrimp, weakfish, tuna, sardines, croakers, and mollusks. In the Caribbean region, the fisheries are further characterized by many high-valued, tropical, finfish and shellfish species such as shrimp, snapper, grouper, spiny lobster, tuna, oysters, conch, and octopus. These species are caught in the Gulf of Mexico, Caribbean Sea, and the Gulf of California, as well as in the near-shore waters of the Pacific Ocean. Such high-valued species are destined for export to lucrative foreign markets. Mexico, however, does land significant quantities of relatively low-valued pilchard and chub mackerel due to its access to their main fishing grounds in the Pacific Ocean. In addition, Cuba's large distant-water fleet has historically landed substantial quantities of chub mackerel, jack mackerel, and herring—low-valued species which have been utilized as a source of protein for the domestic market.

A variety of fishery commodities are produced from the complement of species landed by the commercial fishing industries of Latin America. Of the total annual volume of all Latin American fishery commodities, 70 percent are comprised of inedible or industrial products, such as oils, fats, meals, and solubles. Latin America provides approximately 40 percent of the total world supply of these commodities. The remaining 30 percent of Latin American fishery products are destined for human consumption. Of these edible products, 80 percent are produced from finfish species and 20 percent are crustaceans, mollusks, and other invertebrates. Latin America produces about 5 percent of the world's annual supply of edible finfish products and approximately 10 percent of the world's supply of shellfish and other invertebrates.

The value of fishery-product exports from Latin American countries is approximately ten times the value associated with fishery product imports. As such, a sizable trade surplus is created by the commercial fishing industries in the Latin American region. This is especially true for South America, where import values are less than 10 percent of the export values. Chile, Peru, Ecuador, Argentina, and Brazil are the leading exporters of fishery products in the region. Mexico, Panama, and Costa Rica are the leading exporters for the Central America region. Cuba and the Bahamas are the export leaders for the Caribbean region.

The commercial fishing fleets associated with each Latin American country vary greatly in terms of numbers and size of vessels. For example, the Caribbean nations typically employ smaller vessels suitable for plying near-shore waters. In contrast, the fleets for Peru and Chile are comprised of large-capacity vessels capable of pursuing the pelagic stocks in distant waters and staying at sea for many days. Although many small vessels and artisanal boats exist in virtually every Latin American country, the five countries with fleets possessing the largest number of documented (non–flag of convenience) vessels are, in descending order of fleet capacity (gross tonnage), Mexico, Chile, Argentina, Cuba, and Peru. Many of the Cuban vessels are part of the large, distant-water fleet that was created with Soviet technical assistance and subsidies. Unless special provisions or joint-venture agreements prevail, individual country fleets must honor territorial jurisdiction over fishing rights claimed by most countries in the region. These territorial limits came into existence during the 1970s and extend 200 miles seaward from shore.

Although Latin America historically has been an important source of numerous wild-caught finfish and shellfish species, the region has more recently developed an important aquaculture industry. Ecuador has become a world leader in the production of farm-raised shrimp, and Chile has developed one of the world's largest salmon-farming industries. Chile is also a major source of cultured scallops. Other species cultured in the Latin American region include oysters, catfish, ornamental fish, tilapia, rainbow trout, conch, and seaweeds.

South America, Central America, and the Caribbean (1986); D. JACOBSON and D. WEIDNER, *Soviet-Latin American Fishery Relations*, U.S. Department of Commerce, National Marine Fisheries Service, Office of International Affairs, Division of Foreign Fisheries Analysis, International Fishery Report IFR/89/39 (1989); UN, ECONOMIC COMMISSION FOR LATIN AMERICA AND THE CARIBBEAN, *The Water Resources of Latin America and the Caribbean: Inland and Marine Fishing and the Water Resource* (1992); and *Statistical Yearbook for Latin America and the Caribbean, 1992* (1993); UN, FOOD AND AGRICULTURAL ORGANIZATION, *Yearbook of Fishery Statistics: Catches and Landings*, vol. 72 (1993) and *Yearbook of Fishery Statistics: Commodities*, vol. 73 (1993); U.S. DEPARTMENT OF COMMERCE, NATIONAL OCEANIC AND ATMOSPHERIC ADMINISTRATION, *World Fishing Fleets*, vol. 4 (1993).

CHUCK ADAMS

FLAG RIOTS. *See* **Panama Canal: Flag Riots.**

FLEET SYSTEM

Colonial Brazil

Unlike the *carrera de Indias* elaborated by Castile during the first half of the sixteenth century, which restricted all shipping between Spain and its colonies to a highly regulated system of fleets, voyages during the sixteenth century between Portugal and Brazil took place largely at will. Two factors contributed to this difference: the small size (60–160 tons) of most of the caravels used in the Brazil trade; and complications arising from the variety of departure points in Portugal, such that many ships left from small ports (for example, Viana and Aveiro), and the numerous ports of arrival in Brazil, especially after the establishment of the donatary captaincies in the period 1534 –1536. Neither characteristic was conducive to organizing shipping in fleets.

Individual ships could put out at any time, the only requisite being that they have a proper license and pay the duties demanded by the crown. Throughout the sixteenth century these unprotected ships were often attacked by corsairs and pirates. Finally, in 1592, the crown levied a 3 percent ad valorem duty on merchandise to pay for an armada of twelve warships intended to ward off attacks, but the merchant vessels themselves were still not organized into fleets. The CONSULADO, as the tax was called, produced considerable revenue for the crown, but the escort system itself did little to protect shipping. In fact, 83 percent of the ships sailing in the years from 1647 to 1648 were lost to pirates, a situation that finally led the distraught king to prohibit the sailing of SUGAR ships as long as the Dutch remained strong at sea.

Ultimately it was Father Antônio VIEIRA, a Jesuit with long experience in Brazilian affairs, who came up with a solution to the piracy problem. In 1649 he proposed the establishment of a company, the Companhia Geral do Comércio, modeled upon Dutch precedents. It would regulate shipping between Portugal and Brazil by organizing it into two fleets per year, each to be protected by an escort squadron of eighteen galleons. To defray the cost, the company was granted monopoly rights over four essential imports into Brazil—wine, flour, oil, and codfish—and one lucrative export, brazilwood. The resulting system proved reasonably satisfactory. In most years after 1650 escorted fleets of ships left Rio de Janeiro about the end of March, stopped in Bahia in April to pick up the ships waiting there, and arrived in Lisbon in July and August. Departure times from Lisbon were less regular: sometimes in the late fall, sometimes in the early spring. Though the company

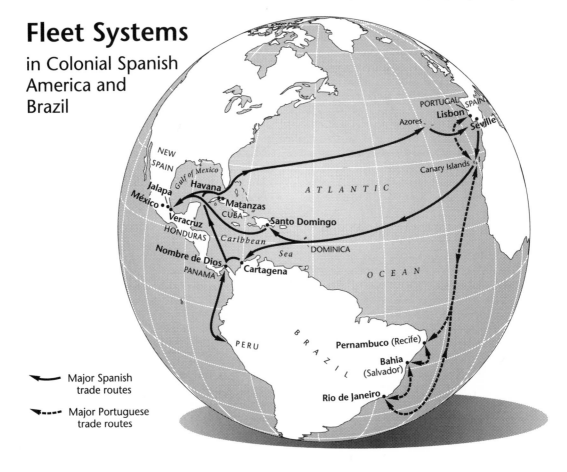

Fleet Systems
in Colonial Spanish America and Brazil

— Major Spanish trade routes

▼---- Major Portuguese trade routes

was dissolved in 1720, the fleet system it had created continued under the control of the CONSELHO DA FAZENDA (Ministry of the Treasury) until it was abolished by the marquês of POMBAL in 1765.

During the eighteenth century this fleet system, created largely to protect the sugar trade, was complemented by additional fleets that served other specialized companies: the Companhia Geral do Comércio do Grão Pará e Maranhão (1755–1778), created to develop the economy of the northern region; and the Companhia Geral do Comércio de Pernambuco and Paraíba (1759–1779), intended to revive the sugar industry of Pernambuco and Paraíba. While they lasted, these companies and their fleets monopolized shipping to and from the ports of Belem de Pará, São Luis de Maranhão, and Pernambuco, leaving the older fleet system created in 1649 to control the shipping from Rio and Bahia until its extinction in 1765.

C. R. BOXER, "Padre Antônio Vieira, S. J., and the Institution of the Brazil Company in 1649," in *Hispanic American Historical Review* 39 (1949): 474–497; JOEL SERRÃO, ed., *Dicionário de história de Portugal,* vol. 1 (1963), pp. 637–644; MANUEL NUNES DIAS, *A Companhia Geral de comércio do Grão Pará e Maranhão* (1971); and LESLIE BETHELL, *The Cambridge History of Latin America* (1984) vol. 1, pp. 441–508.

H. B. JOHNSON

See also **Commercial Policy; Companies, Chartered.**

FLEET SYSTEM (FLOTA)

Colonial Spanish America

The definitive organization of Spain's Indies trade into a structure characterized by the dispatch from Seville of regular merchant convoys, protected by warships, dates from 1564. Its origins lie, however, in the first half of the sixteenth century, when the CASA DE CONTRATACIÓN arranged for armed patrols both along the coast of Cuba and in the maritime triangle between Andalusia, the Canaries, and the Azores to counter attacks on shipping from foreign navies and French and Barbary corsairs. From 1543 until 1554 a single annual fleet sailed from Seville to the Caribbean, dividing in the vicinity of Dominica into two groups destined for Cartagena–Nombre de Dios and Santo Domingo–Veracruz.

In 1554 the crown ordered that two fleets a year, protected by warships, should sail for America. Prolonged hostilities with France, however, followed by increasing Dutch and English attacks on shipping, delayed the practical introduction of the new system until 1564. From this date two annual fleets were to sail for America: the first, known as the *flota* would leave in April for Veracruz, the principal port of the viceroyalty of New Spain, accompanied by a few vessels destined for the Caribbean islands and Honduras; it would be followed in August by the GALEONES, which traded indirectly

with Peru via the Isthmus of Panama. The departure dates from Seville were designed to enable the respective fleets to winter in their Indies ports before meeting in Havana during March and April for repairs and revictualing, and leaving together for Spain in time to get out of the Gulf of Mexico before the onset of the hurricane season in August.

This idealized structure was vulnerable to many imponderables, including adverse weather, piracy, warfare, the availability of cargoes, ships, and capital, commercial confidence, and bureaucratic incompetence. The synchronization of the returning fleets was frequently not achieved. Moreover, from as early as 1580 there was a clear shift toward biennial departures from Seville, and in the seventeenth century the gaps were often of several years' duration, particularly in periods of international warfare. Other problems included widespread fiscal fraud to avoid payment of the AVERÍA. Nevertheless, the system functioned effectively within its somewhat narrow terms of reference, the principal purpose of which was to protect the convoys from attack and thereby bring back to Spain the American silver destined for both the crown and merchants. The treasure of the *flota* was lost only once, in 1628, when the Dutch privateer, Piet Heyn, captured it at Matanzas, on the north coast of Cuba, provoking the bankruptcy of the crown and the onset of a prolonged period of commercial depression.

Although with this exception the fleet system functioned effectively in its prime task of protecting transatlantic trade, it also had the negative effect of constricting trade, both geographically and structurally, and failing to provide the commercial flexibility necessary to respond to the changing needs of American consumers and producers, particularly in the late-seventeenth and early eighteenth centuries. The CONSULADO (guild) of Mexico City, incorporated in 1592, whose merchants controlled the Veracruz trade fairs (and, in the eighteenth century, those held inland at Jalapa) had a powerful vested interest in preserving its monopoly control, and indeed, in tolerating scarcity of (and high prices for) imported goods, notwithstanding the consequential growth of contraband. Although the *galeones* were replaced by register ships in 1740, the New Spain *flotas* survived until 1776, and a further thirteen years were to pass before New Spain was finally incorporated into the free trade system introduced in 1778 in most other ports of Spanish America.

D. A. BRADING, *Miners and Merchants in Bourbon Mexico, 1763–1810* (1971); KENNETH R. ANDREWS, *The Spanish Caribbean: Trade and Plunder, 1530–1630* (1978); GEOFFREY J. WALKER, *Spanish Politics and Imperial Trade, 1700–1789* (1979); LUTGARDO GARCÍA FUENTES, *El comercio español con América, 1650–1700* (1980); FERNANDO SERRANO MANGAS, *Los galeones de la Carrera de Indias, 1650–1700* (1985).

JOHN R. FISHER

See also **Commercial Policy; Piracy.**

FLORENTINE CODEX. *See* **Sahagún, Bernardino de.**

FLORES, department in southern Uruguay not far from Montevideo. It was founded in 1885 to commemorate General Venancio FLORES, born in Trinidad, the capital of the department. The small territory of 1,982 square miles has 24,745 (1985) inhabitants engaged mostly in raising sheep and in garden agriculture.

CÉSAR N. CAVIEDES

FLORES, JUAN JOSÉ (*b.* ca. 1800; *d.* 1 October 1864), president of Ecuador (1830–1835, 1839–1845). Born in Puerto Cabello, Venezuela, Flores received little formal education before he was swept into the WARS OF INDEPENDENCE, first in a royalist army and then in the patriot forces of BOLÍVAR. He received rapid promotions: to colonel in 1821 and to general in 1826.

Assignment to the command of the difficult royalist region of Pasto (southern Colombia) prevented Flores from fighting in the campaigns to liberate Ecuador and Peru. In 1826 he assumed authority over the department of Ecuador and soon exercised authority over most of the territory later to comprise the Republic of Ecuador. Marriage to the aristocratic Mercedes Jijón y Vivanco facilitated his rise to regional prominence. Flores, who came to favor monarchism, urged Bolívar to convert GRAN COLOMBIA (Venezuela, New Granada, and Ecuador) into a monarchy.

In May 1830 an extraordinary assembly of officials and citizens in Quito decided to separate Ecuador from GRAN COLOMBIA and named General Flores supreme civil and military commander. He was elected president soon after the assassination of General Antonio José de SUCRE, which removed his only serious competitor for leadership.

Though endowed with a lively intelligence, Flores was poorly prepared intellectually to provide wise leadership. He attempted to make up for his shortcomings by engaging tutors, such as the poet José Joaquín OLMEDO, but his basic inclinations remained those of a military man. As president he tried unsuccessfully to incorporate the Cauca region into Ecuador, but he defended Ecuadorian independence from New Granada and helped establish the Carchi River as the northern border. In domestic matters Flores pursued liberal policies by restricting the privileges of the clergy, creating a public education system with special schools for Indians, and reforming tax laws.

These reforms, along with treasury deficits and other financial problems, aroused opposition to the foreign-born president. Publishers of the anti-administration newspaper *El Quiteño Libre* organized a violent uprising that Flores quelled only after agreeing to allow Vicente ROCAFUERTE, a rebel leader, to succeed him to the presidency in 1835.

During Rocafuerte's administration (1835–1839),

Flores exerted much influence as commander-in-chief of the armed forces, and he arranged his own reelection to the presidency in 1839. When his policy of cordiality toward opponents failed, Flores secretly decided to convert Ecuador into a monarchy. In league with Andrés SANTA CRUZ of Peru, he sought to monarchize Peru and Bolivia, too. He had himself reelected president in 1843 under the new, authoritarian constitution. He secured the backing of Spain to erect a throne in Quito, but an uprising in 1845 sent him into exile.

In Spain, Flores received official but secret support for an armed expedition to seize power and, presumably, to erect a monarchy in Ecuador. Public reports of the expedition, however, forced its abandonment before it could depart Spanish shores.

General Flores returned to Spanish America in 1847 and spent the next thirteen years conspiring in various countries to regain power. His plots seriously undermined the Ecuadorian government but did not topple it. Finally, in 1860, with Ecuador in near anarchy, the struggling regime of Gabriel GARCÍA MORENO invited Flores to return to the country, to take command of the army, and to put down the opposition to the government.

Playing the role of senior statesman thereafter, Flores was elected president of a constituent congress in 1860 and helped draft the conservative Constitution of 1861. He supported a fruitless effort by the president to secure French backing for yet another monarchical scheme. As general in chief of the armed forces, Flores was a mainstay of the administration and was expected by many to succeed to the presidency in 1865.

When New Granada threatened Ecuador's independence in 1863, General Flores, though in poor health, led a poorly equipped army to defend the northern border. Subsequently he helped crush a rebel invasion near Guayaquil but fell ill and died aboard a warship invoking the "Supreme God of Battles."

PEDRO FERMÍN CEBALLOS, *Resumen de la historia del Ecuador desde su origen hasta 1845*, vols. 4–5 (1870); ELÍAS LASO, *Biografía del General Juan José Flores* (1924); LUIS ROBALINO DÁVILA, *Nacimiento y primeros años de la República* (1967); GUSTAVO VÁSCONEZ HURTADO, *El General Juan José Flores: La República, 1830–1845* (1984); and MARK J. VAN AKEN, *King of the Night: Juan José Flores and Ecuador, 1824–1864* (1989).

MARK J. VAN AKEN

FLORES, LUIS A. (*b.* 1899; *d.* 1969), Peruvian politician, lawyer, and diplomat. Born in Ayabaca, Piura, he is best known for his leadership of the Revolutionary Union, a radical nationalist party adopted by Colonel and President Luis SÁNCHEZ CERRO (1931–1933). Flores had been imprisoned during the LEGUÍA regime but became deputy for Lima during the term of the Constituent Assembly (1931–1936). After the assassination of Sánchez Cerro in 1933, Flores assumed the leadership of the Revolutionary Union and espoused overt fascist principles, tactics, and organization, modeled after Benito Mussolini's party. Flores sought popular support and battled COMMUNISM and populist *aprismo*. In the 1936 presidential elections, which were annulled by President Oscar BENAVIDES, Flores finished second behind the candidate supported by the Aprista Party. Flores was subsequently exiled by Benavides but returned to become senator for Piura (1947–1948) and ambassador to Italy (1948–1950) and Nicaragua and Paraguay (1956–1962). He died in Lima.

STEVE STEIN, *Populism in Peru: The Emergence of the Masses and the Politics of Social Control* (1980).

ALFONSO W. QUIROZ

See also **Fascism.**

FLORES, VENANCIO (*b.* 18 May 1808; *d.* 19 February 1868), Uruguayan military and political leader (Colorado Party). Flores was born in the town of Porongos, today called Trinidad. He took part in the campaign to free Uruguay from Brazil in 1825. He was political chief of the department of San José and military commander of that department at the outbreak of the GUERRA GRANDE (1839–1852). A rising figure in the Colorado Party, he was appointed political chief of Montevideo and minister of war and the navy in 1852. Upon the resignation of President Juan Francisco GIRÓ in 1853, Flores formed a triumvirate with General Juan Antonio LAVALLEJA and General Fructuoso RIVERA in an attempt to avoid another outbreak of civil war. When these two men died, both of natural causes, Flores became a preeminent figure in his party.

Political hostilities and a popular disdain of the caudillo tradition that he represented led Flores to withdraw to the Entre Ríos province of Argentina (1857–1863). While there, he played an active role in the civil wars of that country, supporting the Liberal Party led by Bartolomé MITRE. When Mitre became president of Argentina in 1862, Flores gained his support and that of Emperor PEDRO II of Brazil for his campaign to win back the government in Uruguay. The leaders of these two powerful, neighboring countries, who were already planning what would come to be called the WAR OF THE TRIPLE ALLIANCE against Paraguay, were motivated by their need for the port of Montevideo. This was especially true for Brazil.

Calling his revolution the "liberation crusade," in memory of the 1825 campaign of that name, Flores began his assault against National Party President Bernardo Prudencio BERRO in 1863, and, with the help of an army of 5,000 Brazilian soldiers who entered Uruguayan territory, marched into Montevideo triumphantly in February 1865. Immediately, Argentina, Brazil, and Uruguay made public the treaty of the Triple Alliance, which committed them to fighting Paraguay to the end. Under the leadership of Francisco Solano LÓPEZ, Paraguay had become an important economic and military

power, which made the War of the Triple Alliance (1865–1870) one of the bloodiest in the history of South America. Although scholars disagree on the total casualties, they agree that Paraguay suffered huge demographic losses.

Returning to Uruguay from the war in 1866, Flores resigned in 1868 and called for new elections. Flores was slain four days later by unknown assassins.

ALFREDO LEPRO, *Años de forja* (1962); JOSÉ PEDRO BARRÁN, *Apogeo y crisis del Uruguay pastoril y caudillesco* (1974); WASHINGTON LOCKHART, *Venancio Flores, un caudillo trágico* (1976).

JOSÉ DE TORRES WILSON

See also **Uruguay: Political Parties.**

FLORES DA CUNHA, JOSÉ ANTÔNIO (*b.* 5 March 1880; *d.* 4 November 1959), Brazilian politician. Born to an oligarchical family from Santana do Livramento, Rio Grande do Sul, Flores was an important political figure in the three decades following the Revolution of 1930. He was educated at the São Paulo Law School from 1898 to 1902, and completed his studies at the Rio de Janeiro Law School in 1903.

Flores was among the dissident oligarchs who supported the revolution against the dominant oligarchies of São Paulo and Minas Gerais. Indeed, his support of Getúlio VARGAS was crucial to the overthrow of the First Republic and Vargas's seizure of power. However, as governor of Rio Grande do Sul and a senator in the 1930s, he staunchly defended federalism and worked to limit the centralization of political power under Getúlio Vargas's regime (1930–1945). His federalist stance, often backed by his threat to use the nation's largest state militia, made him too dangerous for Vargas to ignore. After a near outbreak of civil war in 1937, Flores was exiled to Uruguay until 1942. When he returned to Brazil, he was imprisoned.

Flores saw reaction against centralization as the only means of assuring oligarchical elites political space in the post-1930 world. Despite his support for the Revolution of 1930, Flores gradually distanced himself from Vargas after 1935. As governor of Rio Grande do Sul from 1935 to 1938, he was a major force in the continuing influence of traditional politicians and regionalism after 1930. In 1945, Flores joined the National Democratic Union Party (UDN), which opposed Vargas, and he supported the military's successful ouster of the dictator. In 1950 he was elected to Congress on a UDN ticket. In 1955 he broke with the UDN because he opposed its *golpistas*, who had conspired to mount a coup against the government. He lost his final campaign for office in 1958, completing his term in Congress in January 1959. Flores died in Rio Grande do Sul.

JOHN W. F. DULLES, *Vargas of Brazil* (1967); ROBERT M. LEVINE, *The Vargas Regime: The Critical Years, 1934–1938* (1970); JOSEPH L. LOVE, *Rio Grande do Sul and Brazilian Regionalism: 1882–1930*

(1971); CARLOS E. CORTÉS, *Gaúcho Politics in Brazil: The Politics of Rio Grande do Sul, 1930–1964* (1974); THOMAS E. SKIDMORE, *Politics in Brazil, 1930–1964: An Experiment in Democracy* (1986).

BRIAN OWENSBY

See also **Brazil: Political Parties; Brazil: Revolutions.**

FLORES JIJÓN, ANTONIO (*b.* 23 October 1833; *d.* 30 August 1915), president of Ecuador (1888–1892). Born in Quito, Antonio was the son of Juan José FLORES, Ecuador's first president. Antonio Flores Jijón completed his secondary education in Paris. In 1845, he entered the University of San Marcos in Lima, where he completed a law degree and joined the faculty.

Flores Jijón returned to Ecuador with Gabriel GARCÍA MORENO (president, 1860–1865) in 1860. Thereafter, he represented Ecuador in various diplomatic posts in Colombia, France, England, the Vatican, Peru, Spain, and the United States.

An unsuccessful candidate for the presidency in 1875, he opposed the government of General Ignacio de VEINTIMILLA (1876–1883), for which he was exiled. He lived in New York from 1878 to 1883, then returned to Ecuador in 1883 to participate in the ouster of Veintimilla and in the writing of a new constitution. During the José María Plácido CAAMAÑO presidency (1883–1888), Flores Jijón represented Ecuador in Europe, and in fact was in Paris in 1888 when he was elected president.

During his term, Flores Jijón sought to implement a progressive program with the support of moderates within the conservative and liberal parties. His government emphasized improved and expanded public education and public works, respect for civil liberties, and administrative, financial, and tax reforms. His accomplishments in the area of public finances included the suppression of the tithe, a renegotiation of the internal and external debt, reform of the customs tariff, state monopolies, and taxes on real estate. Many of his initiatives met strong opposition from conservatives and the clergy. After completing his term in 1892, Flores returned to Europe. He died in Geneva.

LUIS ROBALINO DÁVILA, *Orígines del Ecuador de hoy: Diez años de civilismo*, vol. 6 (1968); CARLOS MANUEL LARREA, *Antonio Flores Jijón* (1974); FRANK MAC DONALD SPINDLER, *Nineteenth-Century Ecuador* (1987), esp. pp. 126–137.

LINDA ALEXANDER RODRÍGUEZ

FLORES MAGÓN, RICARDO (*b.* 16 September 1874; *d.* 21 November 1922), Mexican journalist and revolutionary. Born in San Antonio Eloxochitlán, Oaxaca, Flores Magón was the second of three sons; his older brother, Jesús, was born in 1872, and his younger brother, Enrique, in 1877. In 1900 he founded the newspaper *Regeneración* to oppose the tyranny of the government of Porfirio DÍAZ. Flores Magón was arrested in May 1901 and *Regeneración* was suppressed soon after, closing in September 1901. He became a writer for Daniel Cabrera's *El Hijo del Ahuizote* until its demise early in 1903. Arrested again, Flores Magón was prohibited from publishing in Mexico. In January 1904 he and his brother Enrique entered the United States at Laredo, Texas, and went to San Antonio, where they renewed the publication of *Regeneración*. They settled in Saint Louis between 1905 and 1906 to escape harassment from local legal authorities along the border and to join revolutionary and radical labor groups. Persecution—including activities of local spies, police seizure of the printing press, and imprisonment of local partisans of a revolutionary exile group Flores Magón had founded in Saint Louis—eventually forced them to move to Los Angeles, where they established a new organ, *Revolución*. Arrested in August 1907, Flores Magón was tried in Arizona in 1909, sentenced to eighteen months in the Florence territorial prison, and released in August 1910.

When World War I began in 1914, Flores Magón, now an anarcho-Communist and pacifist, was a vociferous critic. Arrested on 22 March 1918 and charged with sedition, he was eventually found guilty of violating the Espionage Act of 1917. Sentenced to twenty-one years at McNeil Island, he was transferred in November 1919 to Leavenworth penitentiary because of failing health. On the morning of 21 November 1922, Flores Magón was found dead in Cell House B at Leavenworth. Although several radical scholars claim that he was murdered, the most likely explanation is that he died of natural causes, probably a heart attack.

Photo of Ricardo Flores Magón signing document as brother Enrique looks on. ARCHIVO GENERAL DE LA NACIÓN, MEXICO.

An excellent current biography of Flores Magón is WARD S. ALBRO, *Always a Rebel: Ricardo Flores Magón and the Mexican Revolution* (1992). For a general study of the *magonistas* see W. DIRK RAAT, *Revoltosos: Mexico's Rebels in the United States, 1903–1923* (1981).

W. DIRK RAAT

See also **Revoltosos.**

FLORES MALDONADO MARTÍNEZ Y BODQUÍN, MANUEL ANTONIO

FLORES MALDONADO MARTÍNEZ Y BODQUÍN, MANUEL ANTONIO (*b.* 27 May 1723; *d.* 20 March 1799), VICEROY of New Granada (1776–1782) and of NEW SPAIN (1787–1789).

Born in Seville, Flores pursued a naval career, holding the rank of lieutenant general of the Royal Armada at the time of his assignment to NEW GRANADA in 1776. An enlightened man, strongly interested in science, he was an efficient, perceptive administrator. He urged Regent Visitor GUTIÉRREZ DE PIÑERES to show restraint when imposing administrative and fiscal reforms, at least until the armed forces could be readied to discourage potential unrest, but his warnings went unheeded. While Flores was on the coast commanding the viceregal defenses during the War of the AMERICAN REVOLUTION, the COMUNERO REVOLT (1781) swept the interior, compelling him to order nearly a battalion of coastal troops to Santa Fe to bolster royal authority.

Becoming severely ill with arthritis, he resigned and was replaced by Cartagena's governor, Juan Pimienta. Flores later brought enlightened rule to New Spain, but, his health again failing him, he was soon replaced by the Segundo Conde de Revillagigedo. He died in Madrid.

JOSÉ ANTONIO CALDERÓN QUIJANO, ed., *Los virreyes de Nueva España en el reinado de Carlos IV*, vol. I (1972), especially pp. 1–80; ALLAN J. KUETHE, *Military Reform and Society in New Granada, 1773–1808* (1978); JOHN LEDDY PHELAN, *The People and the King: The Comunero Revolution in Colombia, 1781* (1978).

ALLAN J. KUETHE

FLORIANÓPOLIS

FLORIANÓPOLIS, coastal port and capital of the state of Santa Catarina, was founded in the late seventeenth century and became the provincial capital in 1823 under its original name, Destêrro. In 1893 Custódio José de MELO led a short-lived naval revolt against President Peixoto at Rio de Janeiro and ordered Captain Frederico de Lorena to set up the rebel government seat at Destêrro. That year the city was renamed after president Floriano PEIXOTO. From then on, the main thrust of the civil war moved from Rio Grande do Sul to Santa Catarina.

As of 1991 the population of Florianópolis was about 178,400. The city lies on Santa Catarina Island, between Baía Norte and Baía Sul. Pointe Hercílio Luz, one of the longest steel suspension bridges in Brazil, is one of two that connect the island and the mainland. Since 1983 it has been closed to traffic. Its natural beauty and forty-two beaches have made Florianópolis a popular tourist resort.

JOSÉ MARIA BELLO, *A History of Modern Brazil, 1889–1964*, translated by James L. Taylor (1966).

CAROLYN E. VIEIRA

FLORIDA, presidio with mission provinces. The name of Florida, which Juan PONCE DE LEÓN gave to the land he discovered in 1513, was once applied by Spain to all of eastern North America from Tampico to the Gulf of Saint Lawrence. For half a century, hurricanes and Indian hostility defeated one expedition after another: those of Ponce de León (1521); Lucas VÁSQUEZ DE AYLLÓN (1526); Pánfilo de NARVÁEZ, whose story was told by Álvar Núñez CABEZA DE VACA (1528); Hernando de SOTO (1539); Luis Cáncer de Barbastro (1549); and Tristán de LUNA Y ARELLANO (1559). In 1565 PHILIP II responded to the appearance of French forts along the strategic Gulf Stream by naming a new *adelantado,* the Asturian admiral Pedro MENÉNDEZ DE AVILÉS, who drove the French from Florida and established a number of fortified settlements. Most of these succumbed to Indian attacks, often provoked by the raids of hungry soldiers on native granaries. One of these, SAINT AUGUSTINE, survived, thanks to a set of royal subsidies (the *situado*) that maintained the presidio, guaranteed the cooperation of chiefs, and supported a growing number of FRANCISCANS.

The missionaries proved their value to the crown by adding an Indian hinterland, province by province: first the Timucuans of the east coast and the Saint Johns River, divided into saltwater and freshwater districts; then the Guales of the Georgia coast; then the Timucuans of central and western Florida; and finally the APALACHES, west of the peninsula and close to the Gulf. At their greatest extent the provinces included some 26,000 Christian Indians.

Spanish and Indian relations passed through several distinct stages: alliances for defense and exclusive trade aimed against foreign interlopers; conquest by the Gospel; uprisings provoked by interference in their political, social, and economic affairs; conquest by the sword; and, finally, the institutionalization of demands on Indian commoners through the *sabana* system (the communal planting of maize fields for chiefs and other leaders), the *repartimiento* (a labor levy for public works), and the *servicio personal* (the diversion of the labor levy to private use). As a result of war, famine, and introduced diseases, each province experienced a decrease in population that increased the burden of supporting the area's chiefs, soldiers, missionaries, and settlers on the natives who were left.

During the first half of the seventeenth century, Spanish soldiers were busy combating Dutch and French enemies, salvaging wrecks, and putting down uprisings, while friars baptized thousands of plague victims

Indians storing their crops in public granary, Florida 1564. DeBry after LeMoyne, *Grandes Voyages*. LIBRARY OF CONGRESS.

and extended the mission frontier. Opportunities for a provisioning trade with Havana led to the opening of new ports on the Gulf and the expansion of ranching and agriculture. This economic development was interrupted by the onset of yellow fever, which attacked Spaniards and Indians alike, followed by epidemics of smallpox and measles. A 1656 rebellion in central Florida, harshly punished, led to the virtual desertion of the province of TIMUCUA. By the 1660s, Florida was a hollow peninsula.

Exterior threats to the captaincy general then began to escalate. Pirates from English Jamaica sacked Saint Augustine in 1668. Traders from Carolina fomented wars among southeastern Indians by exchanging firearms for slaves. And buccaneers seconded La Salle's venture into the Gulf by raiding western ports. The crown reacted by strengthening the defenses of Saint Augustine. The price was high, for the construction of the stone Castillo de San Marcos, coupled with neglect of defenses in the provinces, led to wholesale flight—the commoner's form of resistance. Spain had just responded to French intrusion in the Gulf by establishing a new presidio at PENSACOLA in 1698, when the WAR OF THE SPANISH SUCCESSION (1701–1714) forced the French and Spanish colonies into an alliance. Carolina seized the opportunity to attack Florida. From Charleston, Colonel James Moore led two

invasions of Florida, destroying Saint Augustine and GUALE in 1702 and depopulating Apalache in 1704. Indian raids finished off Timucua in 1706. Eighteenth-century Pensacola, Saint Augustine, and the trading post of San Marcos de Apalache were without a hinterland. The wild cattle of abandoned ranches attracted fugitive slaves and nonaligned Indians. By 1763, when the colony changed hands after the SEVEN YEARS' WAR, these frontiersmen and women were ready to meet the British as the Seminoles (from the Spanish *cimarrón*, for "runaway").

VERNE E. CHATELAIN, *The Defenses of Spanish Florida, 1565 to 1763* (1941); JOHN JAY TE PASKE, *The Governorship of Spanish Florida, 1700–1763* (1964); MICHAEL V. GANNON, *The Cross in the Sand: The Early Catholic Church in Florida, 1530–1870* (1965); EUGENE LYON, *The Enterprise of Florida: Pedro Menéndez de Avilés and the Spanish Conquest of 1565–1568* (1976); JOHN H. HANN, *Apalachee: The Land Between the Rivers* (1988); DAVID J. WEBER, *The Spanish Frontier in North America* (1992); AMY TURNER BUSHNELL, *Situado and Sábana: Spain's Support System for the Presidio and Mission Provinces of Florida* (1994).

AMY TURNER BUSHNELL

FLORIDA, EAST, remnant of the Spanish BORDERLANDS. In 1763, when Great Britain acquired the Florida peninsula from Spain and eastern Louisiana from France, the combined territory was divided at the Chattahoochee River into two colonies: East and West Florida. During the American Revolution, Bernardo de GÁLVEZ captured West Florida, and by the Treaty of Paris of 1783, Spain recovered East Florida, to the chagrin of southern loyalists. Both colonies were military governorships, accountable politically to the captaincy general of Cuba and spiritually to the bishopric of New Orleans.

Outlawry was the immediate problem in East Florida. Havana used the presidio as a dumping ground for criminals, and armed bandits mounted slave and cattle raids across the Florida-Georgia border. Settlement was perceived as the solution. For lack of Spanish Catholics, Spain invited British Protestants to take an oath of loyalty and stay. Soon the gates were opened to American backwoodsmen, who avoided the plantations along the Saint Johns River and took the high road from Saint Marys, Georgia, to the Alachua prairie, where they could range their cattle.

Religion took a back seat to trade. The handful of Irish priests who came to convert Protestants reported little success. The FRANCISCANS did not return to the friary, which the British had used for barracks, and the southeastern Indians wanted no more missions. To keep the Indians peaceful, Governor Vicente Manuel de Zéspedes renewed the exclusive franchise of the English firm of Panton, Leslie, and Company, a measure that ran counter to the rising sentiment for free trade in both the British and Spanish empires and was heartily disliked by the Americans. The grievances that prompted the East Florida settlers to rebel in 1795 centered on this issue, which grew worse as Spain declined in sea power. In 1806 only five of the forty-two ships entering the Saint Augustine harbor came from the closest Spanish port of Havana.

When Napoleon's efforts to enforce his continental blockade turned Spain into a battleground and its king into a puppet, the Spanish Empire in America began to dissolve. American settlers in West Florida twice declared sections of their colony republics and turned them over to the United States. East Florida's Patriot Rebellion, during the War of 1812, was a similar bid for annexation. The patriots took the plantations along the Saint Johns but did not attempt the formidable defenses of Saint Augustine. The rebellion fell apart, disowned by President James Madison. Then the Creek War of 1813–1814 conclusively ended dreams of an Indian buffer state under British sponsorship.

In 1817 Sir Gregory MacGregor, a Scot, made one final attempt at an independent republic in the name of the republics of Venezuela, New Granada, Mexico, and Buenos Aires, but with the backing of merchants in Savannah and other U.S. ports. Leading a force recruited chiefly in Georgia, he captured the Amelia Island port of Fernandina, sister city in smuggling to Saint Marys and home of 40 percent of East Florida's civilian population. When East Florida's Anglo settlers failed to flock to his

Republic of the Floridas, MacGregor left. The French corsair Louis Aury, with a force of free black Haitians, opened the port to privateers and slave traders, triggering a peacekeeping intervention by U.S. forces. General Andrew Jackson sparked a series of international incidents in 1817 and 1818, when he crossed the border of West Florida to capture Pensacola, then entered East Florida to execute two British subjects trading with the Seminoles.

Having lost an empire, Spain lost the will and the means to maintain a lone military colony on the North American mainland. The ADAMS–ONÍS TREATY in 1819 transferred ownership of East and West Florida to the United States. Two years later, when the treaty was ratified, the flag of Spain came down from the Castillo de San Marcos.

REMBERT W. PATRICK, *Florida Fiasco: Rampant Rebels on the Georgia-Florida Border, 1810–1815* (1954); HELEN HORNBECK TANNER, *Zéspedes in East Florida, 1784–1790* (1963); PABLO TORNERO TINAJERO, *Relaciones de dependencia entre Florida y Estados Unidos (1783–1820)* (1979); DAVID BUSHNELL, *La República de las Floridas: Texts and Documents* (1986); DAVID J. WEBER, *The Spanish Frontier in North America* (1992).

AMY TURNER BUSHNELL

FLORIDA, SPANISH WEST (1783–1821). From 1513 to 1763, Florida was merely La Florida and included both SAINT AUGUSTINE and PENSACOLA. After acquiring La Florida in 1763, the British created East Florida and West Florida. West Florida extended from the Apalachicola and Chattahoochee rivers on the east to the Mississippi and from the Gulf of Mexico, Lakes Borgne, Pontchartrain, and Maurepas, and the Iberville River to 31 degrees north latitude. In 1764, the British moved the northern boundary to 32 degrees, 28 minutes north latitude. Except for Canada, West Florida was the largest British colony on the North American mainland.

By 1781, Bernardo de GÁLVEZ's victories during the American Revolution had brought West Florida under Spanish control. This fact was formalized in the Treaty of Paris (1783). From 1783 until 1821 West Florida belonged to Spain. At its peak (1783–1798) West Florida included Pensacola (the capital) and Mobile, Baton Rouge, Natchez, Nogales (Vicksburg), and Chickasaw Bluffs (Memphis). Unfortunately for Spain, however, the United States gnawed at West Florida until by 1813 it was reduced to an area perhaps half its original size, if that. Of its major cities only Pensacola remained under Spanish control.

Spain appointed military officers to govern West Florida, including several Irishmen in the Spanish service, such as Col. Arturo O'Neill, who ruled from 1781 to 1793. Because of the need for English-speaking priests, another Irishman, Father James Coleman, served as Pensacola's parish priest from 1794, and then as vicar-general and ecclesiastical judge of West Florida (1806–1822). Economically, Spanish West Florida was not a

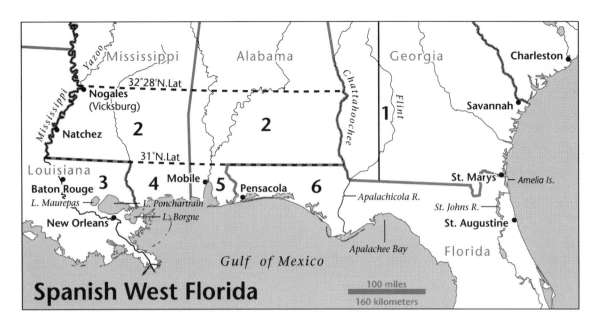

Spanish West Florida

1 Lower part of western boundary line of U.S., proposed by Spanish Count de Aranda, 1782.

2 Area added to British West Florida in 1764; given to U.S. by Great Britain in Treaty of 1783; in dispute between U.S. and Spain, 1783–1795; ceded by Spain to U.S. in Treaty of 1795; Mississippi Territory, 1798; western "half" included in State of Mississippi, 1817.

3 U.S. claimed area as part of Louisiana Purchase, 1803–1810; Republic of West Florida, September–December 1810; occupied by U.S., December 1810 and included in Orleans Territory; made part of State of Louisiana, 1812.

4 U.S. claimed area as part of Louisiana Purchase, 1803–1810; U.S. jurisdiction extended over area in 1811; became part of Mississippi Territory, 1812, and State of Mississippi, 1817.

5 Claimed by U.S. as part of Louisiana Purchase, 1803–1810; U.S. extended jurisdiction over area in 1811; included in Mississippi Territory in 1812, but Mobile was not occupied by U.S. until April 1813; incorporated into Alabama Territory, 1817, and State of Alabama, 1819.

6 Invaded by U.S. in 1814, 1816 and 1818; Spain ceded area to U.S. in Adams–Onís Treaty of 1819; formally occupied by U.S., 1821; part of Territory of Florida, 1822–1845, and State of Florida, 1845.

glowing success. It depended upon lumber, naval stores, indigo, tobacco, and the fur trade, the latter largely controlled by Scotsmen, for its limited income. Thus it required the annual government subsidy, the *situado*, for its economic support.

Following the disasters of the Napoleonic era (1807–1815), Spain was unable effectively to control the Floridas and in 1819 negotiated their transfer to the United States by means of the ADAMS–ONÍS Treaty. In 1821, Andrew Jackson reached Pensacola and formally accepted what was left of Spanish West Florida from Col. José de Callava, the last Spanish governor.

JAMES A. SERVIES, *A Bibliography of West Florida*, 3 vols. (1982); JACK D. L. HOLMES, "West Florida, 1779–1821," in *A Guide to the History of Florida*, edited by Paul S. George (1989), pp. 63–76; and WILLIAM S. COKER and JERRELL H. SHOFNER, *Florida, 1492–1992* (1992).

WILLIAM S. COKER

FLORIDABLANCA, CONDE DE (*b.* 21 October 1728; *d.* 30 December 1808), secretary of state in Spain (1776–1792). As secretary of state, Floridablanca was a conservative reformer and devoted servant of absolutism. After 1776, when he was appointed *fiscal* (crown attorney), his power and influence over the king, CHARLES III, were unparalleled, and he was accused of ministerial despotism by his opponents. The outbreak of the French Revolution (1789) horrified Floridablanca, and he tried to prevent revolutionary ideas from entering Spain.

Floridablanca found it impossible to sanction his monarch's approval of Louis XVI's acceptance of the French constitution. His inability to compromise on this issue resulted in his dismissal from office on 28 February 1792. Retirement in Murcia was interrupted by arrest and confinement to a fortress in Pamplona while his enemies investigated him for abusing his former powerful position.

In 1794 Manuel de GODOY, CHARLES IV's minister, released Floridablanca and allowed him to return to Murcia. He was recalled to government service as president of the central junta meeting at Aranjuez (1808) but died shortly after the group fled to Seville in the wake of the Napoleonic invasion of Spain.

CAYETANO ALCÁZAR MOLINA, *El Conde de Floridablanca: Su vida y su obra* (1934); A. FERRER DEL RÍO, ed., *Obras originales del conde de Floridablanca, y escritos referentes a su persona* (1952); RICHARD HERR, *The Eighteenth-Century Revolution in Spain* (1958), esp. pp. 239–268; ANTONIO RUMEU DE ARMAS, *El testamento político del conde de Floridablanca* (1962).

SUZANNE HILES BURKHOLDER

FLORIT, EUGENIO (*b.* 15 October 1903), Cuban-Spanish poet. Florit was born in Madrid and lived in Spain until 1918, when his family moved to Havana. He received a law degree from the University of Havana in 1926. In 1936 Florit befriended the Spanish poet Juan Ramón Jiménez. In 1940 he moved to New York to work for the Cuban consulate there. From 1945 to 1969 he taught at Barnard College, then part of Columbia University, and during summers, at Middlebury College, Vermont. He was the first codirector and later the director of the New York literary magazine *Revista Hispánica Moderna*. Florit edited and introduced such anthologies of poetry as *La poesía hispanoamericana desde el modernismo*, on which he collaborated with the eminent critic José Olivio Jiménez. In 1982 he moved to Miami, where he continues to reside.

As of the mid-1990s, Florit was one of the best-known living Cuban poets. His work is noted for its muted tones, religious—almost mystical—themes and its mastery of traditional poetic forms. *Asonante final* (1955) and *Doble acento* (1937) are two of the most important of his books. Florit has also been an excellent translator of American poets.

LUIS GONZÁLEZ DEL VALLE and ROBERTO ESQUENAZI-MAYO, eds., *Obras completas*, 5 vols. (1991).

ROBERTO VALERO

FLOTA. *See* **Fleet System.**

FLOWERY WARS, a term derived from the NAHUATL *xochiyaoyotl* (flower-war) referring to the semiritual battles between the Aztec and other states of ancient Mexico for purposes other than conquest. Contenders fought at a prearranged site and used tactics that demonstrated individual skills. Flowery wars provided military training and offered both sides an opportunity to capture prisoners for religious sacrifice. Such captures, once thought to have been the wars' primary purpose, are now seen as a minor one. More important were the strategic functions: to test the relative military strength of the contending forces, to keep one opponent occupied so that Aztec forces could concentrate on defeating

another, and to intimidate potential enemies through a display of military strength. The earliest recorded flowery wars were between the AZTEC and Chalco in the fourteenth century. Later and more deadly ones include many between the Aztec and the Valley of Puebla states in the late fifteenth and early sixteenth centuries.

The best treatment is in ROSS HASSIG, *Aztec Warfare* (1988), which deals with flowery war in the context of Aztec warfare in general. Other studies include FREDERIC HICKS, "'Flowery War' in Aztec History," in *American Ethnologist* 6 (1979): 87–92; and BARRY ISAAC, "The Aztec 'Flowery War': A Geopolitical Explanation," in *Journal of Anthropological Research* 39 (1983): 415–432.

FREDERIC HICKS

FONSECA, GONZALO (*b.* July 1922), Uruguayan sculptor. Born in Montevideo, as a child Fonseca traveled widely with his family and was particularly impressed by visits to museums and archaeological sites in Europe. He was carving in stone by the age of fifteen and entered the school of architecture at the Universidad de la República Oriental del Uruguay, Montevideo, in 1939. He abandoned his academic studies in 1942 for painting and shortly thereafter joined the studio of the artist Joaquín TORRES GARCÍA. While a member of the Taller Torres García (TTG), Fonseca began to study pre-Columbian art and architecture, and painted several constructivist murals in Montevideo. During the first half of the 1950s, he traveled throughout the Mediterranean region. He settled in New York City in 1958 and began making reliefs in cement and wood that featured semiabstract motifs and objects; in the aggregate, these function as symbols or, almost linguistically, as signs. In 1959 he completed a glass mosaic for the New School for Social Research. A one-man exhibition of his work was held in 1962 at the Portland Art Museum in Oregon.

In the mid-1960s, Fonseca began to carve quasi-architectural stone sculptures that simultaneously evoke ancient ruins, ritual fetishes, and mysterious games. He designed a cement *Tower* for the 1968 Olympic Games in Mexico City. In 1971 the Jewish Museum in New York City mounted an exhibition of his work; that same year he began to divide his time between New York and Italy, where he could create large-scale marble sculptures at his studio near Carrara. Fonseca represented Uruguay in the 1990 Venice Biennale.

GONZALO FONSECA, *Gonzalo Fonseca: Recent Works* (1962) and *Gonzalo Fonseca: XLIV Biennale di Venezia* (1990); MARI CARMEN RAMÍREZ, "Re-positioning the South: The Legacy of El Taller Torres-García in Contemporary Latin American Art," and CECILIA BUZIO DE TORRES, "Gonzalo Fonseca," in Mari Carmen Ramírez, ed., *El Taller Torres-García: The School of the South and Its Legacy* (1992), pp. 261–266, 353–354; FLORENCIA BAZZANO NELSON, "Joaquín Torres-García and the Tradition of Constructive Art," in Waldo Rasmussen et al., eds., *Latin American Artists of the Twentieth Century* (1993); pp. 80–82.

JOSEPH R. WOLIN

FONSECA, GULF OF. This large bay on the Pacific coast, named after Queen ISABELLA of Spain's counselor, Juan RODRÍGUEZ DE FONSECA, is partitioned among El Salvador, Honduras, and Nicaragua; the lion's share pertains to Honduras. In 1849, Ephraim George SQUIER, partly with an eye toward securing a Pacific terminus for the Honduras Interoceanic Railroad, persuaded Honduras to cede Tigre Island to the United States. British consul-general Frederick CHATFIELD sought to preempt this cession by occupying the island. The upshot was the signing of the CLAYTON-BULWER TREATY in 1850. The insular security afforded by the port Amapala has made it a favorite launch site for Honduran insurrectionists since independence.

KENNETH V. FINNEY

FONSECA, HERMES RODRIGUES DA (*b.* 12 May 1855; *d.* 9 September 1923), president of Brazil (1910–1914). The nephew of Manoel Deodoro da FONSECA, the republic's first president, Marshal Fonseca advanced his army and future political career by adroitly quelling a cadet rebellion during the 1904 Vaccine Revolt (an uprising by citizens opposed to forced vaccination against smallpox). Nominated as war minister in 1906, Fonseca championed efforts to modernize the army, outlining recruitment reforms, sending officers to study in Germany, and staging large-scale maneuvers. His victory as the conservative Republican Party's candidate marked the republic's first hotly contested presidential campaign.

The marshal's presidency was equally tumultuous. In his first week, the government was forced to negotiate an end to the CHIBATA Revolt, in which rebel sailors protesting barbarous corporal punishment commandeered newly purchased battleships and threatened to bombard Rio de Janeiro with impunity. This conflict was followed by Fonseca's "salvationist" campaigns, or his frequent use of federal troops to interfere in conflicts between political parties at the state level. After his presidential term Fonseca became a controversial military spokesman. President Artur BERNARDES arrested Fonseca in 1922 after the marshal openly advised an army colonel not to obey government orders to intervene in Pernambucan politics. The marshal argued ironically that the army should not be politicized. His arrest precipitated the first *tenente* (lieutenant) revolt in 1922, a coup intended to reinstate Fonseca as president. Shaken by imprisonment and weakened by inveterate smoking, Fonseca soon died of a stroke.

Sources in English on Hermes are piecemeal at best. The marshal's unique role in politics is touched on in JOSEPH L. LOVE, *Rio Grande do Sul and Brazilian Regionalism, 1882–1930* (1971). FRANK D. MC CANN highlights Fonseca's role as a military reformer in "The Nation in Arms: Obligatory Military Service during the Old Republic," in *Essays Concerning the Socioeconomic History of Brazil and Portuguese India,* edited by Dauril Alden and Warren Dean (1977), pp. 211–243. The most complete account of Fonseca's life to date is a hagiography written by his son: HERMES DA FONSECA FILHO, *Marechal Hermes: Dados para uma biografia* (1961).

PETER M. BEATTIE

FONSECA, JUAN RODRÍGUEZ DE (*b.* 1451; *d.* 4 March 1524), head of the CASA DE CONTRATACIÓN, the Spanish House of Trade. Born in Seville to a noble family, Fonseca came to Queen ISABELLA's court as a page, became a priest and royal chaplain, and in 1514 the bishop of Burgos. He was entrusted with diplomatic missions, administering the sale of indulgences and the outfitting of Christopher COLUMBUS's second voyage in 1493. In 1503 he was instrumental in establishing the Casa de Contratación, which, merging into the COUNCIL OF THE INDIES set up in 1524, was to retain exclusive control of the Indies trade for nearly 300 years. In 1518 Fonseca fitted out Ferdinand MAGELLAN's fleet. Reputedly tight-fisted, arrogant, and impatient, he was at odds with Columbus and, later, Hernán CORTÉS. He presided over the 1512 Junta of Burgos, which was concerned with the theology of the rights of the Indies. He died in Burgos.

QUINTIN ALDEA VAQUERO et al., *Diccionario de Historia Eclesiástica de España* (Madrid, 1972); MANUEL GIMÉNEZ FERNÁNDEZ, *Bartolomé de Las Casas,* 2 vols. (Madrid, 1984); HELEN NADER, "Fonseca," in *The Christopher Columbus Encyclopedia,* edited by Silvio A. Bedini (1992).

PEGGY K. LISS

FONSECA, MANOEL DEODORO DA (*b.* 5 August 1827; *d.* 23 August 1892), a career army officer who became the first president of the Brazilian republic (1889–1891). Born in Alagoas, in Brazil's poor Northeast, Fonseca and his seven brothers all followed family tradition and entered the army. He helped subdue the liberal PRAIEIRA REVOLT in Pernambuco in 1848, and served in the WAR OF THE TRIPLE ALLIANCE (1864–1870), achieving the ranks of brigadier general in 1874 and marshal in 1884. Through personal bravery and steadfastness, he became one of the most popular and respected army officers under the empire. Fonseca was a major figure in the so-called MILITARY QUESTION, a series of political conflicts during the 1880s between members of the armed forces and representatives of the imperial government that served gradually to weaken the imperial government.

Although not a republican by conviction, Fonseca was persuaded to join and lead the military movement that brought about the overthrow of the monarchy on 25 November 1889 and the proclamation of a republic that afternoon. A successful revolt toppling the monarchy would not have been possible without the support of influential senior career officers like Fonseca, who assumed the position of provisional president of the new republic. Elected to a four-year term as president of the republic by the Constituent Congress in February 1891, he continually clashed with this largely civilian body that often protested what it perceived as infringements on civil liberties by military men. Unable to adjust to the give-and-take of politics and lacking political sophistication and astuteness, Fonseca judged legislative opposition to his policies to be personal insults and unconstitutionally dissolved Congress early in November 1891. A few weeks later, he was forced out of office by dissatisfied military factions, notably members of the navy. His resignation as president late in November 1891 permitted the vice-president, Marshal Floriano PEIXOTO, to assume office and reconvene Congress. Fonseca died several months later.

JUNE E. HAHNER, *Civilian–Military Relations in Brazil, 1889–1898* (1969).

JUNE E. HAHNER

FONSECA AMADOR, CARLOS (*b.* 23 June 1936; *d.* 8 November 1976), Nicaraguan leader and cofounder of the Sandinista National Liberation Front. Born in the city of Matagalpa, Fonseca was an illegitimate son of Fausto Amador. His father was administrator of Anastasio Somoza García's rural properties in the department of Matagalpa. The family had a stable, middle-class lifestyle that enabled Fonseca to enter law school at the National Autonomous University in León in 1954. He immediately became involved in student politics and began studying the writings of Augusto César SANDINO. He joined a Conservative Party youth organization but left after a few months, complaining that it was "too perfumed." He then became a member of the Nicaraguan Socialist Party. In 1957 Fonseca toured eastern Europe and the Soviet Union as a delegate of the General Union of Nicaraguan Workers. After his return in 1958, the Socialist Party published the pamphlet "A Nicaraguan in Moscow," a compendium of Fonseca's impressions of the Communist world. Fonseca increased his activities in the student opposition to the Somoza regime and participated in the unsuccessful attempt, launched from El Chaparral, Honduras, to oust the dictatorship in June 1959. He recognized the futility of agitating within the restrictive ideology of the Socialist Party, and in 1960 started the New Nicaragua Movement, the basis for the creation of the Sandinista National Liberation Front in July 1961.

Fonseca was the principal thinker behind the revolutionary organization, but he was not a Marxist-Leninist theorist. Rather, he carefully refined Sandino's eclectic ideology in order to build popular support for revolution. From the early years of the Sandinista guerrilla army in Río Coco, Fonseca accepted the necessity of cooperating with diverse urban and rural social groups. The strategy of armed struggle through the gradual accumulation of forces was borrowed directly from Sandino.

Fonseca was captured by the National Guard in 1964 and deported to Guatemala. He returned clandestinely and participated in the failed attack at Pancasán in 1967. Two years later he was arrested for bank robbery in Costa Rica and spent more than a year in jail. Freed after Sandinistas hijacked a jetliner, Fonseca spent the early 1970s shuttling between Nicaragua and the safety of Cuba. He was responsible for developing the main objectives of the Sandinista program that guided the revolutionary government in the 1980s.

In November 1976 Fonseca was killed by the National Guard near Matagalpa. He is still considered the most important historical figure of the Sandinista National Liberation Front. After the victory over SOMOZA in 1979, his body was exhumed and reburied in the Plaza of the Revolution in Managua, where a monument was erected in his memory.

VICTOR TIRADO LÓPEZ, TOMÁS BORGE, and HUMBERTO ORTEGA, *Carlos Fonseca siempre* (1982); CARLOS FONSECA, *Obras*, 2d ed., 2 vols. (1985); DONALD HODGES, *The Intellectual Foundations of the Nicaraguan Revolution* (1986); STEVEN PALMER, "Carlos Fonseca and the Construction of Sandinismo in Nicaragua," in *Latin American Research Review* 23, no. 1 (1989): 91–109.

MARK EVERINGHAM

See also **Nicaragua: Political Parties.**

FONSECA E SILVA, VALENTIM DA (Mestre Valentim; *b.* 1750; *d.* 1813), Brazilian sculptor, wood-carver, and architect. Although he was born in Minas Gerais, Mestre Valentim lived most of his life in Rio de Janeiro. The mulatto son of a Portuguese diamond contractor and black mother, he was orphaned at a young age. While studying wood carving under the Portuguese master craftsman Luis da Fonseca Rosa, he began to receive numerous commissions for candelabras, altarpieces, statuary, and other religious decorative work for churches throughout the city.

Mestre Valentim's best-known commissions include the carvings for the Church of Santa Cruz dos Militares, the carving and main altar in the Church of São Francisco de Paula, and the chapel of the novitiate in the Church of the Third Order of Carmo.

Beyond religious wood carvings, Mestre Valentim was the first in Brazil to apply enamel to metal. He also devoted himself to secular projects such as public fountains and architectural design. His masterpiece, the plans for the Passeio Público, was undertaken in collaboration with the painter Leandro Joaquim and the designers Francisco dos Santos Xavier and Francisco Xavier Cardoso Caldeira. Viceroy Luiz de Vasconcellos commissioned the public park as part of the government's attempt at the beautification of Rio de Janeiro.

Arte no Brasil, vol. 1 (1979), esp. pp. 246–254.

CAREN A. MEGHREBLIAN

FONTAINEBLEAU, TREATY OF (1807), a secret agreement between Spain and France regarding the partition

585

of Portugal. In the Treaty of Fontainebleau, CHARLES IV and NAPOLEON I outlined a proposed conquest and partition of Portugal by Spain and France as part of Napoleon's ongoing attempt to isolate England. Consisting of twenty-one articles, seven of which were secret, the treaty divided Portugal into three parts. The north would go to the king of Etruria, the grandson of Charles IV; the central provinces to Napoleon, until a general peace could be concluded; and the south, the Algarve, to Manuel de GODOY, Charles's first minister. At the conclusion of the peace, Charles IV would be recognized as emperor in Spanish America. The treaty also allowed a French army of 25,000 men and 3,000 cavalry to cross Spain into Lisbon with a 40,000-troop reserve just north of the Spanish-French border at Bayonne, in case of English intervention. The treaty was signed 27 October 1807, nine days after a French army crossed into Spain and began its march on Lisbon.

Although this treaty permitted French soldiers on Spanish soil legally, it was never published, and the terms of the division of Portugal remained unfulfilled. The Treaty of Fontainebleau ultimately led to the Napoleonic occupation of Spain, the capture of Charles IV, and the designation of Napoleon's brother Joseph BONAPARTE as ruler of Spain.

MANUEL DE GODOY, *Memorias*, 2 vols. (1956); CARLOS SECO SERRANO, *Godoy: El hombre y el político* (1978); DOUGLAS HILT, *The Troubled Trinity* (1987).

SUZANNE HILES BURKHOLDER

FONTANA, LUCIO (*b.* 19 February 1899; *d.* 7 September 1968), Argentine sculptor. Born in Rosario, Sante Fe Province, the son of Italian parents, Fontana went to Italy when he was six. He studied at the Brera Royal Academy in Milan, graduating in 1922. The following year he returned to Argentina. In the mid 1920s he was back in Milan studying under Adolfo Widt. After that he lived several years in Paris. Fontana's repertory of forms includes figures that produce a sense of wonder and fascination in the viewer. His sculptures are in various museums and collections in Argentina and Europe. He wrote a series of manifestos on "spatialism," asserting the need to integrate all the physical elements (color, sound, movement, and space) in an ideal material unity. He died in Varese, Italy.

VICENTE GESUALDO, ALDO BIGLIONE, and RODOLFO SANTOS, *Diccionario de artistas plásticos en la Argentina* (1988).

AMALIA CORTINA ARAVENA

FOODS. *See* **Cuisines; Nutrition;** and individual foodstuffs.

FOOTBALL WAR, the name popularly given to the war between El Salvador and Honduras (14–18 July 1969), so called because the immediate provocation was violence surrounding soccer playoffs between the Salvadoran and Honduran national teams. The real causes

Salvadoran forces raise flag after capturing Nueva Ocotepeque, 18 July 1969. AP / WIDE WORLD.

lay much deeper, and although the war was brief, it had a lasting impact on Central America.

Domestic problems in both countries, as well as Honduras's dissatisfaction with its position in the Central American Common Market, led to growing tensions between the two neighbors, but the most serious issue was demographic. Since the 1920s, immigrants had left crowded El Salvador to settle in Honduras, which was much less densely inhabited. Many Salvadoran peasants squatted on public lands along the frontier between the two countries, sometimes remaining there for generations without formal title. During the 1960s, as relations worsened, Salvadorans living in Honduras were often the victims of harassment. In 1969, when Honduran president Oswaldo LÓPEZ ARELLANO attempted to distribute to Honduran peasants government-owned lands already occupied by Salvadorans, the result was a massive exodus back to El Salvador. Returning peasants carried tales of atrocities, which were widely believed.

Mob violence at the soccer games played in San Salvador and Tegucigalpa in June 1969 brought calls for action on both sides of the border. The pressure on Salvadoran president Fidel SÁNCHEZ HERNÁNDEZ was particularly intense, coming from military officers anxious for larger budgets and modern equipment and from conservative opponents of land reform, who feared that the repatriation of so many peasants in an already crowded country would lead to greater agitation from the Left. On 26 June, Sánchez Hernández severed diplomatic relations with Honduras, and on 14 July, Salvadoran troops marched into Honduran territory.

The fighting itself lasted only four days. Salvadoran ground troops advanced rapidly, seizing Nueva Ocotepeque and Santa Rosa de Copán along the western border and seeking to position themselves in the east for an assault on Tegucigalpa. But Honduras had air superiority and successfully bombed Salvadoran fuel storage facilities. Finally, on 18 July, under pressure from the United States and the ORGANIZATION OF AMERICAN STATES, El Salvador agreed to a cease-fire. The two countries did not agree to final peace terms until 1980. The number of war-related deaths is frequently reported as 2,000, many of them Honduran civilians. Long-term effects included the crippling of the CENTRAL AMERICAN COMMON MARKET and the aggravation of the impending social crisis in El Salvador. The return of thousands of landless peasants created demands that contributed to the failure of the political system in the 1970s and the onset of civil war in the 1980s.

The standard work on the war itself is THOMAS P. ANDERSON, *The War of the Dispossessed: Honduras and El Salvador, 1969* (1981). For its causes and consequences, see MARCO VIRGILIO CARÍAS and DANIEL SLUTZKY, eds., *La guerra inútil: Análisis socioeconómico del conflicto entre Honduras y El Salvador* (1971), and WILLIAM H. DURHAM, *Scarcity and Survival in Central America* (1979).

STEPHEN WEBRE

FORAKER ACT, legislation that created a civilian government in PUERTO RICO to replace the military regime that had governed the island since its conquest by U.S. military forces during the SPANISH-AMERICAN WAR (1898–1899). Introduced in 1900 by U.S. Senator Joseph B. Foraker of Ohio, the bill allowed only limited participation by Puerto Ricans. The governor, cabinet, and all judges of the Supreme Court were to be appointed by the president of the United States, a lower house of thirty-five delegates was to be elected by Puerto Ricans. In addition, the Foraker Act provided for Puerto Rico's commercial integration with the United States through the extension of U.S. currency for Puerto Rican coins. In sum, it formalized the colonial relationship that had emerged between the United States and the Puerto Rican people, among whom the act was highly unpopular. In 1917, largely due to skillful Puerto Rican diplomacy, the U.S. Congress passed the Jones Act, which granted Puerto Rico a bill of rights and full citizenship, thus mitigating the effects of the Foraker Act.

RAYMOND CARR, *Puerto Rico: A Colonial Experiment* (1984); FRANKLIN W. KNIGHT, *The Caribbean: The Genesis of a Fragmented Nationalism,* 2d ed. (1990).

PAMELA MURRAY

FORASTEROS, indigenous peoples and their descendants who lived outside of the *reducciones* (settlements) to which they or their ancestors had been assigned by Viceroy Francisco de TOLEDO Y FIGUEROA in his 1570s efforts to stabilize and exploit the indigenous labor force of the Andes. Under the *reducción* system, *originarios* (native-born members of those new communities) owed taxes and labor service to the state; because these levies were not assessed against *forasteros,* many individuals migrated, trading access to their community's resources for freedom from its tribute requirements. Regional demographic, migration, and labor patterns produced numerous types of *forasteros* with varying degrees of integration into rural society, mining and urban centers, and economic and political systems. *Forasteros* became a major force in the transformation of indigenous society under colonial rule. Numerous efforts to control indigenous migration and exploit the *forasteros* ended in failure, but in the early eighteenth century many *forasteros con tierra* (those with land) were redefined as taxpaying members of the communities in which they had access to land.

For a study of the *forasteros* and their impact on colonial society see ANN M. WIGHTMAN, *Indigenous Migration and Social Change: The Forasteros of Cuzco, 1570–1720* (1990). Various aspects of indigenous migration are presented in DAVID J. ROBINSON, ed., *Migration in Colonial Spanish America* (1990), esp. the chapters by NOBLE DAVID COOK, BRIAN EVANS, KAREN POWERS, EDDA O. SAMUDIO A., and ANN ZULAWSKI.

ANN M. WIGHTMAN

FORBES, JOHN MURRAY (*b.* 13 August 1771; *d.* 14 June 1831), U.S. diplomatic and commercial agent. Originally assigned to commercial posts in Europe, in 1820 Forbes was appointed by the State Department to serve as commercial attaché in Buenos Aires, where he remained until his death. His public and private correspondence provides an eyewitness account of the turbulent period following Argentine independence. Forbes described the anarchy among the independent Río de la Plata republics, including rivalry among contending provincial rulers, the presidency of Bernardino RIVADAVIA, and the rise to power of Juan Manuel de ROSAS, all part of the ongoing conflict between Buenos Aires and the provinces over the issue of national consolidation. Forbes also followed events in the rest of South America, and was particularly observant of the British presence in the Río de la Plata region.

JOHN MURRAY FORBES, *Once años en Buenos Aires, 1820–1831* (1956); HAROLD F. PETERSON, *Argentina and the United States, 1810–1960* (1964).

HILARY BURGER

FORBES, WILLIAM CAMERON (*b.* 21 May 1870; *d.* 24 December 1959), businessman and presidential adviser. Forbes, born in Milton, Massachusetts, graduated in 1892 from Harvard, where he later coached football. In 1894 he took a position at a Boston brokerage firm. He was named a life partner in the family investment house in 1899.

In 1904, President Theodore ROOSEVELT appointed Forbes to the Philippines Commission. He served there in various capacities, including governor-general, until 1913. The following year, he was appointed receiver of the Brazil Railway Company, which had operations in five South American countries.

Forbes was sent back to the Philippines in 1921, as part of a commission to study the future of U.S. relations there. The commission concluded that it would be a mistake to withdraw from the islands at that time. Later, Forbes wrote a history of the Philippines (1929).

In 1930, Herbert Hoover appointed Forbes to head a commission to advise him on U.S. policy regarding Haiti. There had been anti-American demonstrations in 1929 and expressions of discontent with the continued American military occupation of Haiti. Hoover wanted assistance in settling civil disturbances and in assessing the continued occupation.

Some of the commission members wanted the troops pulled out immediately. However, a majority, including Forbes, recommended a phased withdrawal to be completed no later than 1936, and they recommended that all services run by Americans be Haitianized.

RAYFORD W. LOGAN, *Haiti and the Dominican Republic* (1968), pp. 138–140; ROBERT M. SPECTOR, *W. Cameron Forbes and the Hoover Commissions to Haiti (1930)* (1985).

CHARLES CARRERAS

FOREIGN DEBT. From the time of independence the Latin American nations have accumulated large foreign debts, most of them the result of loans to the respective governments. The size of these debts and the difficulties in their repayment led to repeated debt crises during the nineteenth and twentieth centuries, generally coinciding with international economic recessions. The most recent Latin American debt crisis, which began in 1982, has been the largest and most devastating in its impact on the economies and societies of the region. The nature of this crisis can best be understood in the light of the long, complex history of foreign debt in Latin America. It is important to note, however, that the changing nature of financial instruments and markets over time has modified the character of foreign debt.

Foreign debt is the result of the contracting by domestic agencies or residents (public or private) of loans abroad (short or long term). In the Latin America of the nineteenth and early twentieth centuries, most such loans were taken by national, provincial, and municipal governments in the form of bonds payable in gold and issued on international capital markets, first in London and Paris, later in other European stock markets, and, after the turn of the century, in the United States, especially on the New York Stock Exchange. The bulk of Latin American foreign debt was, therefore, in the form of long-term public external liabilities. The bonds usually paid between 4 and 7 percent annual interest and were amortized over ten to thirty years, depending on the loan contract. In more recent decades, external bond issues have declined in importance for Latin American governments, which have taken a larger number of direct loans from European, U.S., and Japanese commercial and investment banks. At the same time, private companies have gone abroad for short- and long-term loans. A brief review of the historical experience illustrates the changing nature of these loans over time, as well as changes in volume of the debt, interest rates, and impact of the debt service on the Latin American economies.

Latin America's first foreign loans were negotiated in 1822–1825 by the founding fathers of the newly independent nations. Simón Bolívar, José de San Martín, Bernardo O'Higgins, and Bernardino Rivadavia negotiated loans with British bankers for their respective governments of Gran Colombia, Peru, Chile, and Buenos Aires (see Table 1). Most of these loans were used to finance the acquisition of military equipment and warships for the new nations. In this sense the loans were not unproductive but contributed to the consolidation of the Latin American independence movements. However, as a result of an international trade crisis in 1825–1826, most of the debtor governments were obliged to suspend payments, giving rise to the first Latin American debt crisis.

For a quarter of a century all the Latin American nations except Brazil remained in default on their external debts, a situation that provoked conflicts with European creditors and cut off the flow of foreign capital until the

TABLE 1 Latin American Government Issues Floated in England, 1822–1825

Year and Borrower	Nominal Value (£)	Price to Public	Interest Nominal %	Interest "Real" %	Sums Realized (£)	Bankers
1822						
Chile	1,000,000	70	6	8.6	700,000	Hulletts
Colombia	2,000,000	84	6	7.1	1,680,000	Herring, Powles & Graham
Peru	450,000	88	6	6.8	396,000	Thomas Kinder; Everett, Walker & Co.
1824						
Brazil	1,200,000	75	5	6.7	900,000	Fletcher, Alexander & Co.; Thomas Wilson & Co.
Buenos Aires	1,000,000	85	6	7.0	850,000	Barings
Colombia	4,750,000	88	6	6.8	4,203,750	Goldschmidts
Mexico	3,200,000	58	5	8.6	1,856,000	Goldschmidts
Peru	750,000	82	6	7.3	615,000	Frys & Chapman
1825						
Brazil	2,000,000	85	5	5.9	1,700,000	Rothschilds
Central America	163,000	73	6	8.2	118,990	Barclay, Herring, Richardson & Co.
Mexico	3,200,000	89	6	6.7	2,872,000	Barclay, Herring, Richardson & Co.
Peru	616,000	78	6	8.2	480,480	Frys & Chapman

Summary by State

State	Total Value of Bonds Issued in London, 1822–1825 (£)
Brazil	3,200,000
Buenos Aires	1,000,000
Central America	163,300
Chile	1,000,000
Colombia	6,750,000
Mexico	6,400,000
Peru	1,816,000
Total	20,329,300

1850s. The nation that suffered most as a result of the debt moratorium was Mexico. As a result of its war with the United States (1845–1847), the Mexican government was obliged to use the indemnity payments received in exchange for California and the other territories ceded to the United States to pay British bondholders. Subsequently, as a result of Benito Juárez's suspension of payments on the foreign debt in 1861, Britain, France, and Spain occupied the port of Veracruz. The French troops remained and conquered the nation, establishing the empire of MAXIMILIAN (1863–1867). International debt politics in nineteenth-century Latin America were thus enmeshed with imperialist adventures and wars.

After 1850 the economic situation of Latin America improved, largely because of rising exports in primary goods and minerals: coffee, sugar, leather, wool, silver, guano, and nitrates. As a result, Latin American governments once again became good credit risks and were able to negotiate approximately fifty foreign loans in the two decades preceding the international economic crisis of 1873 (see Table 2). Although some of these loans were used for military purposes, as had been the case in the Latin American loan boom of the 1820s, now a greater portion was utilized for financing public works, including state railways in Peru, Chile, Brazil, and Argentina. As the second loan boom gathered strength, the smaller

Latin American republics entered the fray and took numerous loans, many of which were highly speculative, in London and Paris. By 1873 the boom had run its course and the subsequent economic crisis caused a new debt crisis as Peru, Costa Rica, the Dominican Republic, Paraguay, and Bolivia suspended payments.

In the 1880s the larger Latin American nations participated in a new rush of foreign loans that was combined with the first major wave of direct foreign investment in mines, haciendas, railways, and urban infrastructure. In this regard it is worth pointing out that, according to the standard economic definition, government loans constitute a different type of foreign investment, one generally defined as portfolio investment. The largest debtor of the 1880s was Argentina, which took a grand total of fifty loans by national, provincial, and municipal government entities. The not unsurprising result was the financial crisis of 1890, known in England as the Baring crisis because the banking house of BARING BROTHERS was the major creditor of the Argentine government.

In the years preceding World War I virtually all Latin American nations again approached the international capital markets for public loans; as a result, by 1914 the combined foreign debts of the Latin American governments approached $2 billion. During the war, there was no suspension of payments; on the contrary, various Latin American countries were able to repatriate a portion of their foreign debts as a result of the extraordinary wartime export boom that provided them with substantial revenues. Nevertheless, after the war and the profound economic crisis of 1920–1921, most Latin American leaders began to turn to the United States for financial assistance. As a result, New York bankers agreed to provide a considerable number of loans to most of the governments of the region (see Table 3).

The loan expansion of the 1920s lost strength in 1928 and collapsed after the crash of 1929. During the first years of the Great Depression, most Latin American nations continued to pay a part of the interest on their foreign debts, but as the economic crisis deepened and

TABLE 2   Foreign Loans to Latin American Governments, 1850–1875

Country	Total No. of Loans	Nominal Value (£ thousands)	Purpose		
			Military (%)	Public Works (%)	Refinance (%)
Argentina	7	13,488	20	68	11
Bolivia	1	1,700	——	100	——
Brazil	8	23,467	30	13	57
Chile	7	8,502	37	51	12
Colombia	2	2,200		9	91
Costa Rica	3	3,400	——	100	——
Ecuador	1	1,824	——	——	100
Guatemala	2	650	——	77	23
Haiti	1	1,458	——	——	100
Honduras	4	5,590	——	98	2
Mexico	2	16,960	70	——	30
Paraguay	2	3,000	——	80	20
Peru	7	51,840	10	45	45
Santo Domingo	1	757	——	100	——
Uruguay	1	3,500	——	——	100
Venezuela	2	2,500	——	30	70

Combined Subtotals by Subperiods

Years	Total No. of Loans	Nominal Value (£ thousands)	Purpose		
			Military (%)	Public Works (%)	Refinance (%)
1850–1859	9	10,862	——	32	68
1860–1869	20	56,705	41	12	47
1870–1875	22	73,270	——	60	40

SOURCES: Corporation of Foreign Bondholders, *Annual Report* (1873–1880); C. Fenn, *Fenn's on the Funds* (1883); I. Stone, "The Composition and Distribution of British Investments in Latin America, 1865–1913" (Ph.D. diss., Columbia University, 1962).

TABLE 3 Foreign Loans to Latin American Governments, 1920–1930 (in thousands of U.S. dollars)

Country	No. of Loans	Nominal Value	Purpose		
			Public Works	Refinance	Other
Argentina	25	419,418	124,995	281,301	19,122
Bolivia	3	66,000	43,000	23,000	——
Brazil	36	641,318	247,514	246,821	145,983
Chile	18	342,538	200,446	52,092	90,000
Colombia	21	179,775	146,185	8,750	21,840
Costa Rica	3	10,990	9,800	1,190	——
Cuba	5	155,973	40,000	79,000	36,973
Dominican Republic	2	20,000	15,000	5,000	——
El Salvador	3	21,609	——	21,609	——
Guatemala	3	9,465	4,950	4,515	——
Haiti	2	18,634	——	18,634	——
Panama	2	20,500	4,500	12,000	4,000
Peru	7	110,314	60,366	49,948	——
Uruguay	5	70,388	70,388	——	——

SOURCES: A. Kimber, *Kimber's Record of Government Debts* (1929, 1934); Corporation of Foreign Bondholders, *Annual Report* (1928–1935); Foreign Bondholders Protective Council, *Annual Report* (1934, 1936).

TABLE 4 Long-Term Foreign Debt (Private and Public) of Latin American Countries

Country	(in millions of U.S. dollars)			
	1970	1980	1985	1990
Argentina	5,171	16,774	41,902	48,731
Barbados	13	98	355	504
Bolivia	471	2,274	4,066	3,858
Brazil	5,132	57,500	91,915	90,432
Chile	2,568	9,398	17,628	14,619
Colombia	1,580	4,604	11,141	15,803
Costa Rica	246	2,112	3,836	3,380
Dominican Republic	353	1,473	2,842	3,534
Ecuador	242	4,422	7,354	10,030
El Salvador	176	659	1,660	1,924
Guatemala	120	831	2,272	2,306
Guyana	83	598	780	1,663
Haiti	40	242	522	745
Honduras	109	1,165	2,278	3,284
Jamaica	982	1,496	3,188	3,907
Mexico	5,966	41,215	88,448	81,161
Nicaragua	147	1,661	4,892	8,067
Panama	124	2,271	3,320	3,988
Paraguay	112	780	1,638	1,753
Peru	2,655	6,828	10,223	13,236
Trinidad and Tobago	101	712	1,299	1,853

SOURCE: World Bank, *World Debt Tables, 1992–1993,* vol. 2, Country Tables (The World Bank, Washington D.C., 1993).

international trade plummeted, one nation after another confronted rising fiscal deficits. As a result, several nations defaulted on their external debts—first Bolivia, Chile, and Peru in 1931 and 1932, soon followed by Brazil and most of the other nations of the region. Only Argentina, the Dominican Republic, and Haiti did not suspend payments during the 1930s.

This new and widespread debt crisis led to prolonged renegotiations with bankers and investors, beginning with several accords in the 1930s to maintain partial debt service, but it was not until the end of World War II that most foreign debts were restructured. In some cases, such as Mexico and Brazil, the creditors (under heavy pressure from the U.S. government) accepted steep reductions of the real value of the debts. In others, like Argentina, all debts were paid off in gold.

During the 1950s and early 1960s most Latin American nations received little in the way of foreign loans, although they became associates of the International Monetary Fund (IMF) and the International Bank for Reconstruction and Development, or World Bank (WB),

innovative multilateral institutions designed to stabilize and coordinate international capital flows. However, by the mid-1960s new economic development programs that required heavy injections of external capital led most Latin American governments to negotiate a rising level of loans from those multilateral agencies as well as the recently created Inter-American Development Bank (IDB). Most of the loans from the IMF were used to cover deficits in the balance of payments, whereas the WB and IDB loans went basically to economic infrastructure closely linked to industrial and agricultural projects and to growing state enterprises in petroleum, electricity, steel, nuclear energy, and telecommunications.

While loans from multilateral financial agencies were dominant until the early 1970s, after the oil crisis of 1973 the private banks of the United States, Europe, and Japan began to channel a much larger flow of loan capital to virtually all the Latin American nations, providing money for both public and private enterprises. As can be observed in Table 4 (which covers only public-sector loans), the big jump in foreign indebtedness came in the

Más economía-ficción

Cartoon of man representing Mexico noosed by foreign debt entitled *More Economic Fiction*. Tag hanging from rope reads, "external debt." Cartoon by Rius, originally published in the magazine *Proceso*, Mexico. Reproduced from *Rius en proceso*. MEXICO CITY: REVISTA PROCESO, CISA, SA DE CV 1983.

1970s, the biggest debtors clearly being Brazil and Mexico, followed at some distance by Argentina, Peru, and Chile.

By the late 1970s, the debt service had become so considerable that many Latin American governments began to take new loans simply to cover interest payments, a bad omen and historically a sign of an imminent debt crisis. A sharp drop in petroleum prices in early 1982, combined with international monetary instability and a decline in world trade in 1980–1982, led to a new crisis. As sources of funds dried up in the foreign capital markets and hard currency fiscal revenues dropped, many governments of the region could no longer meet their debt payments. The outbreak of the debt crisis was signaled most clearly in the announcement by Mexican Finance Secretary Jesús SILVA HERZOG in August 1982 of his government's temporary suspension of payments on external debt. The upheaval that this decision caused in international money markets led to the first renegotiating program between Mexico and the creditor banks, but at first there was much doubt about whether an agreement could be reached—indeed, there was concern that a world financial crash might result from the Latin American debt crisis.

Over several years many Latin American nations were forced temporarily to suspend payments on their debts, each time provoking a minor financial panic. Simultaneously, the IMF and the large international banks pressured Latin American financial authorities to impose drastic austerity programs. Government deficits were gradually cut, but at the expense of economic growth. In fact, the 1980s proved to be a decade of negative growth, resulting in the loss of an important part of the socioeconomic advances of the previous two decades. In particular, working sectors suffered a steep decline in real wages at the same time that educational and health services deteriorated in quantity and quality. As a result, the living standards of the vast majority of Latin Americans fell significantly, provoking social and political discontent.

By the late 1980s some countries began to experience a slight improvement that made possible more solid debt renegotiations. In the case of Mexico, after various complex renegotiations a package deal was signed between the government and foreign bankers in 1989 to stabilize the Mexican debt. In the early 1990s other nations were in the process of drafting similar far-reaching agreements. It is not known whether the Latin American nations will become involved in a future loan boom. Given the relative scarcity of local capital, in part due to the huge volume of capital flight, it is likely that a new period of loan expansion will be initiated at some future date, although the dangers of contracting a large volume of foreign loans should now be more evident.

CHERYL PAYER, *The Debt Trap: The IMF and the Third World* (1974); BARBARA STALLINGS, *Banker to the Third World: U.S. Portfolio Investment in Latin America, 1900–1986* (1987); STEPHANY GRIFFITH JONES, ed., *Deuda externa, renegociación y ajuste en la América Latina* (1988); LUIS DE SEBASTIÁN, *La crisis de América Latina y la deuda externa* (1988); CARLOS MARICHAL, *A Century of Debt Crises in Latin America: From Independence to the Great Depression, 1820–1939* (1989).

CARLOS MARICHAL

See also **Foreign Investment; Foreign Trade.**

FOREIGN INVESTMENT. In the colonial period, capital came to the New World as human capital in the form of the knowledge and skills of immigrants; physical capital, or the animals and tools and equipment that they brought with them; and financial capital. Funds transferred from the mother country to Latin America for running the colonies provided resources which, after independence, were obtained from sales of bonds by the newly formed national governments.

BRITISH INVESTMENT

Latin American nations obtained from Great Britain both recognition of their independence and funds in exchange for improved access to their markets. The increased trade provided information to the British on profitable investments, which consequently increased. British holdings in Latin America in 1913 comprised about one-fifth of her overseas capital and were roughly equal to British investment in the United States. The behavior of British investment, the most important in Latin America before World War I, was indicative of the operation of all foreign investment in the region.

Mexico, Central America, Colombia, Venezuela, Peru, Chile, Argentina, and Brazil obtained loans in the British market before 1826. The loans often were guaranteed by customs receipts. Not all of the funds raised went to the governments that issued the loans, high commissions often having been charged by middlemen with political connections to place the loan. At various times, blockades of ports and armed intervention were used to obtain repayment of loans. In addition, some investments in mining companies turned out to be unsuccessful.

Latin American nations were politically unstable during the first decade after independence. Loans were limited until the 1850s, when new government issues were floated and railroad investment began. British loans were concentrated in transportation and public utilities, and particularly to enterprises whose obligations were guaranteed by a provincial or national government.

From 1825 to 1913, portfolio investment (in bonds) was larger than direct investment (in equities), because of the large share of government loans absorbed by the British market. However, the portfolio share fell from almost 80 percent in 1865 to less than 55 percent in 1913, when corporate securities accounted for 30 percent of portfolio investment. The British invested in public utilities, especially transport and light and power companies. Beginning in the 1890s, they also invested in financial, land, and investment companies. Their investment was concentrated in Argentina, Brazil, and Mexico.

British investors accepted a lower rate on loans to Latin America than on funds invested in Europe because they invested in risky manufacturing ventures in Europe, whereas in Latin America the natural monopoly of railroads and public utilities promised safer returns. Moreover, although in 1865 almost all direct private investment (excluding government loans) was in ordinary shares, by 1913 they constituted just a bit over 40 percent, with preference shares rising from 1 to 15 percent and debentures and mortgages growing from 12 to 44 percent.

Foreign investment in RAILROADS was especially important; by promoting exports, the railroads contributed to increased foreign exchange earnings and export-oriented economic development. Foreign-owned railroads, however, were as extortionate in their rates abroad as they had been in their home countries, and Latin Americans demanded that they be regulated or nationalized. Increasingly harsh regulation led foreign investors to stop investing in railroads. Conflicts over the railroads and the competition from other nations for funds made Latin America a less important destination for European capital by 1913.

U.S. INVESTMENT

Both the rise of the U.S. as a creditor nation and its proximity to Latin America led to the emergence of the U.S. as the dominant source of foreign capital for the twentieth century, accounting for over 60 percent in the 1980s. Western European corporations provided 25 percent. Japanese investment in Latin America, mostly in manufacturing, became noticeable in the 1950s and increased along with its trade surpluses.

U.S. investments in Latin America in 1897 were concentrated in railroads (42 percent), MINING and smelting (26 percent), and AGRICULTURE (19 percent). U.S. multinational corporations undertook investment to secure supplies and improve their competitive position in domestic and world markets. Latin America's changing economic structure led to a shift of foreign investment. By 1950 the share of U.S. funds in transport and communication and in mining and smelting had fallen to half the 1897 level, while investment in oil had risen to 28 percent and in manufacturing to 17 percent. In 1982, 16 percent was in PETROLEUM (reflecting the nationalization of the Venezuelan oil industry), 48 percent in manufacturing, 16 percent in finance, and 9 percent in trade. In 1992, 46 percent was in finance, insurance, and real estate; 9 percent in banking; 30 percent in manufacturing; and 5 percent in oil.

FORMS OF FOREIGN INVESTMENT

Foreign investment took increasingly varied forms. Direct investment, which was 75 percent of the total in 1900–1913, rose to 92 percent in 1914–1920 but fell to 15 percent in 1954–1980. Portfolio investment fluctuated widely, providing 25 percent in 1900–1913 but rising to 58 percent in 1954–1980. Suppliers' credit was not important until World War II; in the 1950s and 1960s, however, it rose to 6 percent of total private investment but fell to less than 1 percent of the total in 1976–1980, for an average of 1 percent for 1954–1980. Government loans, holdings of which fell during the Great Depression, rose to 50 percent of the total for 1939–1953 and then fell to 26 percent for 1954–1980.

The debt crisis of the early 1980s led to a net transfer abroad of $221.3 billion. The consequent fall in economic capacity led to a decline of Latin America's share in world trade to under 4 percent, just one-third of its 1950 share. To reverse this trend, Latin American nations restructured their debt and opened their financial markets. Increasingly deep discounts in the secondary market for debt issues from 1987 to 1989 led, in some cases, to the swapping of government debt for equity (attractive because the debt was accepted at close to par for conversion purposes), while commercial debt was reduced under the Brady Plan. Initiated by the U.S. in March 1989, the plan facilitated private debt forgiveness in exchange for International Monetary Fund (IMF) and World Bank debt guarantees and greater Latin American fiscal, monetary, and international commercial reforms. Consequently, the private sector increased its share in total investment from 57 percent in 1983 to 62 percent in 1990, although this was still below the 1970s level of 64 percent.

The improved economic climate for investment in the late 1980s revived foreign interest in Latin American stocks, which were increasingly purchased through foreign investment funds. In some cases, Latin American nations restricted the share of a domestic company that might have been owned by foreign investors. In others, trusts were established to hold accounts receivable, mortgages, and export income to guarantee the servicing of securities. Other investment techniques made it possible to acquire nonvoting shares previously restricted to domestic owners. Perhaps the most important of the innovations was American Depositary Receipts, which eased acquisition of foreign assets. ADRs are usually issued when foreign shares have been deposited with the bank's overseas branch or custodian. The bank obtains dividends on these stocks, pays foreign withholding taxes, and pays the net dividends in dollars to the receipt holders.

In 1991 Latin America obtained roughly $40 billion in new private capital flows. Private borrowing—private bonds, commercial paper, certificates of deposit, trade financing, and term bank lending—provided 39 percent; ADRs and other funds supplied 16 percent; and other direct foreign investment—in part resulting from privatization of government enterprise—accounted for 35 percent. The largest developing-nation corporations financed more of their growth from external sources during the 1980s than developed nations at similar stages of development. In the 1980s, the controlling interest of privately owned firms held a higher proportion of the total voting shares than was the case with firms in the U.S.; the former are not expected to relinquish control by opening their capital to outsiders.

THE ROLE OF FOREIGN INVESTMENT

Foreign direct capital stock has been estimated at almost 12 percent of GNP, or 4 percent of capital stock—close to $200 per capita for 1982. The largest per capita foreign investments were in Trinidad and Tobago (oil refineries), Panama (the canal), Barbados, Venezuela, Jamaica, Uruguay, Argentina, and Guyana. Latin American nations that frequently had excluded some areas of their economies to foreign capital had lower per capita foreign direct capital stock. The relatively small proportion of foreign direct capital in the overall total stems from the large amount of domestic capital in the rural areas and from the limitation of foreign capital to investment in raw materials, in production of goods previously sold by a foreign enterprise, and in areas where foreigners have proprietary technology.

Foreign investment often went into mines and other raw materials because the capital requirements of the ventures were too large for local capitalists. Foreigners, having far more funds available, could invest in capital-intensive ventures as one of many such investments that they made in several nations. In Latin America, often the government alone had sufficient funds to risk investment in mining or oil. Foreign investment in banks had the advantage of serving firms from the home country with branches or subsidiaries in Latin America, facilitating their investment and trade.

Investment was tied to the growth of multinational corporations, which raised the issue of whether those firms were run for the benefit of the nation in which the affiliates were located or for that of the parent firm or nation. One practice raising this issue was that of multinational corporations adjusting their accounting records of intrafirm sales from affiliates in one nation to affiliates in another (transfer pricing) so as to minimize their overall tax burden. Favoritism for foreign employees of multinational corporations gave rise to successful demands after World War II that jobs be increasingly reserved for Latin American nationals and that they be trained for the more skilled jobs and for managerial positions.

Opponents of foreign investment objected to its use of capital-intensive production methods. They regretted the displacement of labor-intensive artisan production. An extension of this argument was that foreign techniques and foreign goods replaced local culture and products.

When foreign firms borrowed funds on Latin American markets, they were perceived as crowding out local borrowers. It was feared that foreign capital would dominate individual industries and sectors. This led to restrictions on the quantity of foreign investment and on the sectors in which it was invested. At the same

time, remittances of profits and capital were limited in order to alleviate strains on the balance of payments. ANDEAN PACT nations forged stringent common policies for foreign capital, requiring foreign investors to reduce their ownership in local enterprises to a minority share over a fifteen-year period. Since there was strong world competition for investment funds, such restrictions in Latin America contributed to a sharp fall in the share of foreign capital going there.

When a foreign investor bought out an existing firm, rather than investing in a new one, it was criticized for weakening the domestic entrepreneurial class and for not increasing the capital assets of the economy. The exports from U.S. majority-owned affiliates in Latin America were one-quarter of those in other developing nations because sales in the highly protected Latin American markets were more profitable than exports. But the proportion of manufactured exports to total exports of the Latin American affiliates was above the proportion for the developing-nation average.

Those favoring foreign investment stated that some foreign corporations provided services such as housing and community health and social welfare programs, as well as promoted economic development. Traditional proponents of foreign capital argued that foreigners provided capital and technology unavailable within Latin American nations, without which some domestic investments would not be possible. Some of the resentment of foreign capital was eased by stipulations that unless oil and pharmaceuticals utilized concessions and produced patented items within a few years, the concession or patent would be void.

The increasing number of suppliers of capital and technology, and the growing sophistication of Latin American negotiators, made it possible to unbundle technology. Instead of seeking a single supplier to provide the technology for all parts of a process, Latin Americans broke the process into its component parts. Several suppliers who could provide the technology for some, if not all of these process segments, were invited to bid for contracts, which greatly reduced cost.

At the same time, fears that foreign trade and investment would lead to domination by foreign nations were somewhat mitigated by the distinction made between the interests of a foreign corporation and that of its government. In the early twentieth century, the U.S. took measures to encourage and protect American investment abroad. Multinational corporations sometimes were accused of meddling in Latin American politics and bribing governments, with their greater financial strength giving them an unfair advantage over Latin American firms attempting to use the same strategy. According to Albert O. Hirschman, "Internal disputes over the appropriate treatment of the foreign investor have gravely weakened, or helped to topple, some of the more progressive and democratic governments which have held power in recent years in such countries as Brazil, Chile, and Peru" (*How to Divest*, p. 8). Paul E.

Sigmund states that broader political interest in good foreign relations not only led to U.S. acceptance of Latin American nationalization of U.S. property but also to establishment of economic boycotts by the U.S. government that harmed U.S. firms (*Multinationals*, p. 304). Further easing concern about the impact of foreign investment is the indication that in 1973–1986 foreign investment was most likely to go to nations with democratic political regimes, especially those with IMF support. It has also been pointed out that domestic firms faced with foreign competition either improve their competitive performance or fail. For all these reasons, restrictions on foreign investors were eased in the 1980s.

Experience with export processing zones contributed to the creation of the North American Free Trade Agreement (NAFTA) between Canada, Mexico, and the U.S. in 1994. It was generally believed that the agreement would be extended to other Latin American nations. The pact provided for foreign investment, thus consolidating the opening of the Mexican economy in the 1980s, which had included reducing barriers to trade, eliminating red tape, and extinguishing unprofitable government enterprises in nonstrategic sectors. Similar measures favoring investors were enacted in most Latin American nations, but more slowly in Brazil, which attracted less multinational investment than countries with stronger economic reforms or oil exports.

CLEONA LEWIS, *America's Stake in International Investments* (1938); IRVING STONE, "British Long-Term Investment in Latin America, 1865–1913," in *Business History Review* 42, no. 3 (Autumn, 1968): 311–339; ALBERT O. HIRSCHMAN, "How to Divest In Latin America, and Why," in *Essays in International Finance*, no. 76 (1969); IRVING STONE, "British Direct and Portfolio Investment in Latin America Before 1914," in *Journal of Economic History* 37, no. 3 (September 1977): 690–722; PAUL E. SIGMUND, *Multinationals in Latin America: The Politics of Nationalization* (1980); RHYS JENKINS, *Transnational Corporations and Industrial Transformation in Latin America* (1984); JOHN H. DUNNING and JOHN CANTWELL, *IRM Directory of Statistics of International Investment and Production* (1987); DENNIS T. OFFICER and J. RONALD HOFFMEISTER, "American Depositary Receipts: A Domestic Alternative for International Diversification," in *The Handbook of International Investing*, edited by Carl Beidleman (1987); LAURA RANDALL, *The Political Economy of Venezuelan Oil* (1987); BARBARA STALLINGS, *Banker to the Third World: U.S. Portfolio Investment in Latin America, 1900–1986* (1987); EVA PAUS, "Direct Foreign Investment and Economic Development in Latin America: Perspectives for the Future," in *Journal of Latin American Studies* 21, pt. 2 (May 1989): 221–239.

MELISSA H. BIRCH, "Changing Patterns of Foreign Investment in Latin America," in *Quarterly Review of Economics and Business* 31, no. 3 (1991): 141–172; PETER J. WEST, "Latin America's Return to the Private International Capital Market," in *CEPAL Review*, no. 44 (1991): 59–78; GUY P. PFEFFERMANN and ANDREA MADARASSY, *Trends in Private Investment in Developing Countries, 1992*, International Finance Corporation, Discussion Paper 14 (1992); AJIT SINGH and JAVED HAMID, *Corporate Financial Structures in Developing Countries*, International Finance Corporation, Technical Paper 1 (1992); UNITED NATIONS, *World Investment Report* (1992); MANUEL PASTOR, JR., and ERIC HILT, "Private Investment and Democracy in Latin America," in *World Development* 21, no. 4 (1993): 489–507; and JOHN H. WELCH, "The New Face of Latin America: Financial Flows, Markets, and Institutions in the 1980s," in *Journal of Latin American Studies* 25, no. 1 (1993): 1–24.

LAURA RANDALL

See also **Economic Development; Foreign Debt; Foreign Trade; Industrialization.**

FOREIGN TRADE, the exchange of goods and services among countries. Countries trade with one another to obtain goods and SERVICES that are of better quality than, less expensive than, or simply different from, those produced at home. Since Independence, Latin American foreign trade has been characterized first by freedom and unprecedented prosperity (1820–1930), then by protectionism (1930–1973), and increasingly since 1973 by trade liberalization. To many observers, foreign trade and external factors have played a central role in shaping the region's development. To others, foreign trade and external factors have played, at best, a supplementary, secondary role to the dominant internal forces.

THE YEARS OF PROSPERITY (1820–1930)
The foreign trade of most Latin American countries increased gradually between 1820 and 1860 as colonial restrictions were abolished and political stability in the region increased. Exports and imports rose sharply during the so-called golden age (1860–1910). The speed of trade expansion slowed down, however, between 1910 and 1930, as rich mineral deposits were exhausted and the best lands had been incorporated into agriculture. The period 1820–1930, which is often described as one of free trade, laissez faire, or outward orientation, also included instances of protectionism associated with import duties imposed because of low administrative collection costs.

Most of the products exported from Latin America between 1820 and 1930 have been described as "primary," that is, originating in agriculture or mining. All of them were "composite" in that they embodied not only value from agriculture and mining but also value added by manufacturing and services, such as trade, transportation, finance, and insurance.

Latin American foreign trade exploded after 1860 owing to a convergence of favorable supply-and-demand factors. As the industrial revolution transformed Britain, Germany, France, and the United States, there emerged a strong demand for raw materials. Furthermore, Britain abolished tariffs protecting domestic agriculture. A synchronous technological revolution, which brought the invention of the steam engine, propeller, and metal hull, precipitated an unprecedented reduction in maritime transportation costs. Consequently, agricultural or mineral products from distant Latin America could now compete with those from the Caribbean and the more industrialized countries. Furthermore, rapidly rising incomes pushed up the demand for food, other consumer products, and raw materials. Unable to meet rapidly rising demand internally, Europe and North America increasingly turned to Latin America for supplies of more, better, and less expensive agricultural products and raw materials.

The Latin American response to the rising external appetite for its exports was swift and often massive. As a consequence, by the middle of the nineteenth century, Argentina had become a major exporter of meat and hides, Cuba of sugar, Brazil of coffee, Venezuela of cacao, Peru of guano, and Chile of copper and wheat, which went to California during the gold rush years. Supplies of agriculture- and mining-based exports increased as new land was incorporated into production in Argentina, Uruguay, Brazil, and Chile. Export growth was facilitated by successive waves of immigrants, especially from southern Europe, into these regions. In addition, recurrent export bonanzas attracted large investments, first by the British and subsequently by the Americans, in agriculture, mining, railroads, public utilities, and industry. They also made it easier for Latin American governments to borrow in the capital markets of Europe and the United States.

The impact of free, and rapidly growing, foreign trade on Latin American incomes was considerable but uneven. According to estimates by Angus Maddison, by 1929, real per-capita gross domestic product (GDP) in dollars at 1965 factor cost had reached $908 in Argentina. This was almost double the income level of Japan ($485), about half that of the United States ($1,767), and over 80 percent of the income in the United Kingdom ($1,105). Per-capita incomes were, however, lower in other countries: Brazil ($175), Chile ($580), Colombia ($236), Mexico ($252), and Peru ($177).

By 1913, according to Maddison, exports of Latin American countries had reached levels close to or even higher than those in the rest of the world. Average Latin American per-capita exports, expressed in U.S. dollars at then-current prices and exchange rates, were $31.90 (Argentina, $66.70; Brazil, $13.30; Chile, $41.20; Colombia, $6.80; Cuba, $66.70; Mexico, $9.90; Peru, $9.70; Uruguay, $61.60; and Venezuela, $10.90) as compared to an average for developed countries of $37.30 (France, $33.40; Germany, $35.90; Japan, $6.90; Netherlands, $67.00; United Kingdom, $56.00; and United States, $24.50), $0.70 for China, and $2.60 for India. For Latin America, agriculture- and mining-based exports provided both an engine and a handmaiden for growth and prosperity. The outflow of exports raised welfare through an inflow of imports, immigrants, capital, institutions, and ideas. Latin America, Europe, and North America achieved an unprecedented degree of interdependence. Latin America supplied the agricultural and mineral primary commodities; Europe and the United States provided the industrial ones.

Latin American countries remained, however, highly dependent on one, or a few, export products, as the following figures of their percentage of total exports in 1929 reveal: Argentina (wheat, 29.2; maize, 17.6; frozen, chilled, and tinned meat, 12.8; linseed oil, 12.6), Brazil (coffee, 71.0), Chile (nitrates, 42.1; copper, 40.4), Colombia (coffee, 60.6; petroleum, 21.3), Cuba (sugar, 79.5), Mexico (silver, 20.6; other minerals, 47.0), Peru (petroleum, 29.7; copper, 22.4; wool, 21.0; sugar, 11.5; lead, 5.1), Uruguay (wool, 30.7; frozen, chilled, and tinned meat, 30.2; hides and skins, 12.7), and Venezuela (petroleum, 74.2; coffee, 17.2).

Between 1900 and 1930 agriculture-based products dominated exports from Colombia (coffee), Paraguay (quebracho, other timber), El Salvador (coffee), Brazil (coffee), Argentina (wheat, maize), Guatemala (coffee, bananas), Costa Rica (coffee, bananas), Cuba (sugar), Nicaragua (coffee, bananas), Uruguay (meat, wool), Ecuador (cacao), and Panama (bananas). Mining-based products dominated exports from Venezuela (copper, petroleum), Mexico (petroleum, silver), Chile (nitrates, copper), and Bolivia (tin). Peru exported both mineral (petroleum) and agricultural (cotton) products.

In the eyes of many, however, foreign trade was by no means an unmitigated blessing for the region before 1930. Demand for and prices of primary exports fluctuated wildly, unleashing large shocks that Latin America could not always master. Because cyclical booms were followed regularly by precipitous declines, export revenues, exchange rates, capital inflows, trade-based tax revenues, and domestic income experienced unprecedented instability. Exhaustion of rich mineral deposits and fertile agricultural lands exposed the region's excessive dependence on primary commodities with uncertain growth potential. Finally, some perceived that the benefits from trade accrued primarily to the workers and (foreign) capitalists of isolated production areas (enclaves), without a lasting and positive impact on the majority of the population. Not even the worst of the prognoses, however, anticipated the calamitous collapse of foreign trade between 1929 and 1932 (see Table 1).

THE YEARS OF PROTECTIONISM (1930–1973)
The Great Depression of the 1930s reduced the demand for primary export products, caused a decline in the relative prices of primary exports with respect to industrial imports, and suddenly stopped capital flows from Europe and the United States to Latin America. According to figures compiled by Angus Maddison, between 1929 and 1932 the average export volume for Argentina, Brazil, Chile, Colombia, Cuba, Mexico, Peru, and Venezuela fell by 35.8 percent, the average purchasing power of exports by 55.1 percent, the average import volume by 65.9 percent, and GDP by 18.5 percent. Chile suffered the most, with export volume declining by 71.2 percent, purchasing power of exports by 84.5 percent, import volume by 83.0 percent, and GDP by 26.5 percent. After initial adherence to old policy weapons and gold-standard rules, Latin America responded to the collapse of foreign trade with new approaches, such as

TABLE 1   Value of Latin American exports, 1913–1985 (US$ million, current)

	Argentina	Brazil	Chile	Colombia	Cuba	Mexico	Peru	Uruguay	Venezuela	Total
1913	510.3	315.7	142.8	33.2	164.6	148.0	43.6	71.8	28.3	1,458.3
1929	907.6	461.5	282.8	123.5	272.4	284.6	116.8	92.0	149.3	2,690.5
1930	517.0	317.8	37.1	163.8	167.4	216.3	83.8	87.8	139.0	1,730.0
1931	428.0	241.1	19.7	102.2	118.9	166.7	49.2	45.2	113.3	1,282.3
1932	331.4	178.1	34.3	66.3	79.9	97.3	37.1	27.4	93.2	945.0
1933	357.4	224.3	51.9	61.1	85.0	103.8	46.1	40.3	114.3	1,084.0
1934	426.0	287.5	93.7	94.2	107.5	178.4	71.2	49.6	166.0	1,474.1
1935	500.5	271.9	95.7	80.6	127.8	209.3	75.0	76.9	182.2	1,619.9
1936	537.4	321.9	113.1	90.1	155.1	215.9	83.5	72.3	193.2	1,782.5
1937	757.9	350.5	192.3	104.5	185.9	247.7	93.3	78.1	253.8	2,264.0
1938	437.9	296.3	138.8	91.4	144.6	186.3	77.2	58.9	267.5	1,698.8
1950	1,178.0	1,359.0	281.0	394.0	642.0	532.0	193.0	254.0	929.0	5,762.0
1973	3,266.0	6,199.0	1,231.0	1,177.0	1,410.0	2,261.0	1,112.0	322.0	4,680.0	21,658.0
1985	8,396.0	25,639.0	3,823.0	3,552.0	8,567.0	22,108.0	2,996.0	855.0	12,272.0	84,626.0

SOURCE: Angus Maddison, "Economic and Social Conditions in Latin America, 1913–1950," in *Long-Term Trends in Latin American Economic Development*, edited by Miguel Urrutia (1991), p. 3.

exchange controls, quantitative and bilateral trade restrictions, debt delinquency, and debt renegotiation with much larger write-offs than in the past.

The role of foreign trade was further reduced as a consequence of the protectionist, inward-oriented policies advocated after 1950 by Raúl PREBISCH, the ECONOMIC COMMISSION FOR LATIN AMERICA, and their structuralist theory of development. Import-substitution policies, which promoted domestic production of previously imported industrial commodities, frequently resulted in the neglect of exports. This exacerbated the isolation of Latin America from the rest of the world. According to Maddison, the average ratio of merchandise exports to GDP at current prices for Argentina, Brazil, Chile, Colombia, Mexico, and Peru declined from 22.1 percent in 1929 to 9.1 percent in 1973. In contrast, the average ratio of merchandise exports to GDP for France, Germany, the Netherlands, the United Kingdom, and the United States increased from 15.8 percent to 19.2 percent during the same period.

Latin America's share in value of world exports experienced a sharp decline, from 10.9 percent in 1950 to a meager 3.9 percent in 1992. Between 1950 and 1990, Argentina's share declined from 1.92 to 0.37 percent, Brazil's from 2.22 to 0.95 percent, Cuba's from 1.10 to 0.20 percent (in 1980), and Venezuela's from 1.91 to 0.53 percent. The decline in the relative importance of Latin America in world exports coincided with the widespread implementation of protectionist policies of import substitution. In contrast, between 1950 and 1990 the share of West Germany in the value of world exports increased from 3.29 to 12.39 percent, and that of Japan from 1.37 to 8.69 percent. Similarly, Latin American imports as a percentage of world imports declined from 8.10 in 1950 to 2.82 in 1990. The introduction of neoliberal policies of trade liberalization, privatization,

and stabilization, beginning with Chile in 1973, has contributed to a slight increase in the relative importance of Latin America in world imports and exports since 1989.

At least in part, the post-1930 decline in the relative importance of Latin America in world trade can be explained by its continued dependence on primary exports and the decline in their prices relative to industrial imports. As the figures presented in Table 2 reveal, the principal export commodities of most Latin American countries in 1985 were of agricultural and mineral origin. According to Richard Lynn Ground ["The Genesis of Import Substitution in Latin America," in *CEPAL Review*, no. 36 (December 1988): 179–203], Latin America's merchandise, or net barter, terms of trade fell from 100.0 in 1928 to 51.8 in 1933, reaching a level of 63.6 percent in 1987. (The merchandise, or net barter, terms of trade measure the relative movement of export prices against that of import prices. The merchandise terms of trade index is calculated as the ratio of a country's index of average export prices to its average import price index. Numbers above 100.0 are favorable, and those below 100.0 are unfavorable, relative to the base year.) After a sharp deterioration during the Great Depression, the merchandise terms of trade of Latin America recovered by 1950 (93.6 percent), declined in the 1960s (49.2 percent in 1965), rose again in the 1970s (76.7 percent in 1980), only to retreat in the 1980s (62.1 percent in 1986).

As a consequence of the Great Depression and the popularity of protectionist ideologies, most Latin American countries increased nominal tariffs after 1930. By the years 1960–1965, average nominal tariffs had risen to 148.8 percent in Argentina, 85.0 percent in Brazil, 89.0 percent in Chile, and 139.0 percent (1972–1977) in Uruguay. Nominal tariffs on consumer goods were even higher, reaching 235.0 percent in Argentina (1960–1965) and 204.0 percent in Chile (1960–1965). The 1930–1973

TABLE 2   Principal export commodities of nineteen Latin American countries, 1985

Country	Commodity	Value (US$)	Total export revenues (%)
Argentina	Wheat	1,133.2	13.5
	Corn	766.1	9.1
Bolivia	Natural Gas	372.6	59.8
	Tin	186.7	29.9
Brazil	Soybeans and Products	2,540.0	9.9
	Coffee	2,369.0	9.2
Chile	Copper	1,761.0	46.1
Colombia	Coffee	1,784.0	50.2
	Fuel Oil	408.8	11.5
Costa Rica	Coffee	15,644.0	32.2
(M. Colones)	Bananas	10,706.0	22.1
Dominican Republic	Sugar	190.1	25.9
	Ferronickel	120.7	16.4
	Doré	113.6	15.5
	Cocoa Beans and Products	64.8	8.8
	Coffee	57.6	7.8
Ecuador	Crude Petroleum	1,824.7	62.8
	Bananas	220.0	7.6
El Salvador	Coffee	1,131.4	66.9
(M. Colones)			
Guatemala	Coffee	450.8	42.5
(M. Quetzales)	Cotton	71.6	6.8
Haiti	Coffee	226.4	26.0
(M. Gourdes)	Bauxite (1982)	74.6	8.6
Honduras	Bananas (1984)	464.5	31.1
(M. Lempiras)	Coffee (1984)	338.2	22.7
Mexico (B. Pesos)	Petroleum	3,799.0	66.6
Nicaragua	Cotton	1,344.8	34.1
(M. Córdobas)	Coffee	1,198.4	30.4
Panama	Bananas	78.1	23.3
(M. Balboas)	Shrimp	59.8	17.8
Paraguay	Cotton	47,281.0	48.9
(M. Guaraníes)	Soybeans	32,134.0	33.2
Peru	Copper	464.2	15.6
	Petroleum Products	418.1	14.1
	Zinc	268.9	9.1
	Crude Petroleum	227.3	7.7
Uruguay	Wool	163.8	19.2
	Meat	117.9	13.8
Venezuela	Petroleum	77,599.0	84.3
(M. Bolívares)			

SOURCE: James W. Wilkie et al., eds., *Statistical Abstract of Latin America*, vol. 30, pt. 2 (1993), Table 2402, p. 747.

period of protectionism and import-substitution industrialization has been gradually replaced by a new era of neoliberal trade liberalization.

Even though the 1930–1973 period is generally described as the age of import-substitution industrialization and inward-oriented, protectionist development, it also contained the seeds of trade-liberalization efforts. Initially, such efforts were largely cornerstones of the region's integration schemes aimed at promoting import substitution by enlarging the size of the market. The LATIN AMERICAN FREE TRADE ASSOCIATION (LAFTA), which was launched in 1961, brought together Argentina, Brazil, Chile, Colombia, Ecuador, Mexico, Paraguay, Peru, and Uruguay, which were joined later by Bolivia and Venezuela. In 1980 Lafta was transformed into the Latin American Integration Association (LAIA), as a result of the Treaty of Montevideo. Subregional groupings gave rise to the CENTRAL AMERICAN COMMON

MARKET (CACM) in 1960, the ANDEAN PACT (ANCOM) in 1969, and the Caribbean Community and Common Market (CARICOM) in 1973. For the most part, these schemes lacked a clear commitment to free trade and made little progress.

THE YEARS OF LIBERALIZATION (1973–)

As part of far-reaching liberalization policies, Argentina, Bolivia, Brazil, Guatemala, Jamaica, Mexico, Nicaragua, Paraguay, Peru, and Uruguay have reduced tariffs, simplified tariff structures, and dismantled nontariff measures. Import licenses, quantitative restrictions, import prohibitions, discretionary licensing, additional taxes, and surcharges have been abolished or significantly reduced in Argentina, Bolivia, Brazil, Chile (where quantitative restrictions were prohibited by law), Colombia, Costa Rica, Jamaica, and Peru. Substantial reductions in tariffs and simplification of the tariff structure have been introduced in Argentina, Bolivia, Brazil, Chile, Costa Rica, Honduras, Jamaica, Mexico, Nicaragua, Peru, and Venezuela. By the years 1978–1981, average nominal tariffs had been reduced to 34.4 percent in Argentina, 10.0 percent in Chile, 28.0 percent in Colombia, 16.8 percent in Costa Rica, and 11.5 percent in Mexico.

The widespread adoption of neoliberal philosophies of trade liberalization, privatization, and stabilization has strengthened efforts to form or revive subregional trade blocks. The NORTH AMERICAN FREE TRADE AGREEMENT (NAFTA) between the United States, Mexico, and Canada was approved in 1994. The Southern Cone Common Market (MERCOSUR) movement started in July 1990, when Argentina and Brazil agreed to the elimination of tariff barriers between them by December 1994. This agreement, which was extended to Paraguay and Uruguay on 26 March 1991, calls for free intra-Cone movement of products by December 1995. The Andean Group, the Central American and Caribbean countries, Chile, and Mexico have either implemented agreements or renewed efforts to establish free-trade areas, common markets, or customs unions.

The value of Latin American exports reached $123 billion in 1990. The share of nonfuel primary composite commodities (food, live animals, beverages, tobacco, crude materials, and vegetable oils) in total exports had declined from 65.8 percent in 1970 to 41.2 percent in 1990. The growth of merchandise trade during 1970–1992 is presented in Table 3.

Exports of manufactures in 1990 were $40.6 billion, or 32.9 percent of total exports, up from 10.9 percent in 1970. Exports of machinery and transportation equipment, which were dominated by internal-combustion piston engines and passenger motor vehicles, equaled $13.9 billion, or 11.2 percent of total exports, up from 2.3 percent in 1970. These originated mainly in Brazil and Mexico. Exports of basic manufactures were $14.6 billion, or 11.8 percent of total exports, up from 4.4 percent in 1970. The principal exports of basic manufactures consisted of iron and steel, which originated mainly in

Brazil, Mexico, and Argentina. Other important exports were leather from Argentina, Uruguay, and Brazil; textile yarn from Brazil, Mexico, Peru, and Argentina; nonmetallic mineral manufactures from Brazil, Mexico, and Colombia; and paper and paperboard from Brazil, Chile, and Mexico. In 1990 exports of chemicals, principally from Brazil, Mexico, and Argentina, reached $7.0 billion, or 5.7 percent of total exports, up from 2.7 percent in 1970. Brazil and Mexico were the major exporters of plastics.

Brazil accounted for 90 percent of all Latin American exports of footwear in 1990. Brazil and Colombia accounted for more than 60 percent of the region's exports of textile clothing, although Argentina, Barbados, Colombia, Costa Rica, the Dominican Republic, El Salvador, Guatemala, Guyana, Haiti, Honduras, Jamaica, Mexico, Panama, Paraguay, Peru, and Uruguay also produced large volumes.

Brazil, Mexico, and Argentina accounted for more than 80 percent of the region's foreign exchange earnings from manufactured exports. Other countries have achieved in recent years a significant growth of their manufactured exports. Chemical elements and compounds have been exported from Trinidad and Tobago; plastics from Colombia, Uruguay, and Venezuela; other types of chemicals from Chile, Peru, Trinidad and Tobago, and Uruguay; clothing and textile yarn from Peru; plumbing, heating, and lighting equipment from Chile and Venezuela; and iron and steel from Colombia, Trinidad and Tobago, and Venezuela.

High-technology products (i.e., products having high research-and-development costs relative to total production costs) have grown at the impressive long-term annual rate of 20 percent. By 1989, Latin America's exports of high-technology products (chemicals and pharmaceuticals; plastic materials; nonelectrical and electrical machinery; transport equipment; and professional, scientific, and controlling instruments) reached $17.6 billion, with Brazil and Mexico accounting for 90 percent of the total. By the late 1980s high-technology export products represented 50 percent of Latin America's manufacturing exports.

The post-1930 policies of protectionism and import-substitution industrialization drastically changed the relative income position of most Latin American countries. While per-capita income (real per-capita GDP in dollars at 1965 factor cost) of the export-oriented Japanese economy increased nearly twelvefold between 1913 ($332) and 1985 ($3,952), and that of the United States more than tripled (from $1,358 to $4,569), that of Argentina less than doubled (from $790 to $1,417). Per-capita income in Brazil, which increased almost tenfold between 1913 ($118) and 1985 ($1,114), Chile ($1,137), and Venezuela ($1,199) has come close to that of Argentina. Recent trade liberalization schemes aim at accelerating the region's growth of income through closer integration into international trade. Foreign trade, however, cannot alone be expected to solve Latin America's

TABLE 3 Growth of merchandise trade, Latin America, 1970–1992

| | Merchandise trade (Million US$) | | Average annual growth rate (%) | | | | Terms of trade (1987 = 100) | |
| | Exports 1992 | Imports 1992 | Exports | | Imports | | 1985 | 1992 |
			1970–1980	1980–1992	1970–1980	1980–1992		
Argentina	12,235	14,864	7.1	2.2	2.3	−1.7	110	110
Bolivia	763	1,102	−0.8	6.1	7.3	0.1	167	53
Brazil	35,956	23,115	8.5	5.0	4.0	1.5	92	108
Colombia	6,916	6,684	1.9	12.9	6.0	0.2	140	79
Costa Rica	1,834	2,458	5.2	5.2	4.2	3.9	111	85
Chile	9,646	9,456	10.4	5.5	2.2	3.5	102	118
Dominican Republic	566	2,178	−2.0	−2.2	1.3	2.5	109	113
Ecuador	3,036	2,501	12.5	4.8	6.8	−2.0	153	91
El Salvador	396	1,137	1.3	−0.4	4.6	−2.9	126	65
Guatemala	1,295	2,463	5.7	0.0	5.8	−0.1	108	79
Honduras	736	1,057	3.8	−0.8	2.1	−0.8	111	79
Jamaica	1,102	1,758	−1.7	1.1	−6.8	2.0	95	96
Mexico	27,166	47,877	13.5	1.6	5.5	3.8	133	120
Nicaragua	228	907	0.8	−4.8	0.1	−4.1	108	75
Panama	500	2,009	−7.3	2.0	−5.1	−3.0	130	93
Paraguay	657	1,420	8.3	11.4	5.3	5.4	108	88
Peru	3,573	3,629	3.3	2.5	−1.7	−1.6	111	86
Trinidad and Tobago	1,869	1,436	−7.3	−2.4	−9.6	−9.7	156	100
Uruguay	1,620	2,010	6.5	2.9	3.1	1.3	89	97
Venezuela	13,997	12,222	−11.6	0.6	10.9	−0.6	174	157
World	3,575,198	3,785,925	4.0[a]	4.9[a]	4.0[a]	4.9[a]	—	—
Latin American & Caribbean	127,605	149,330	−0.1[a]	2.9[a]	3.6[a]	0.6[a]	114[b]	95[b]

[a] Weighted average.
[b] Median value.
SOURCE: World Bank, *World Development Report 1994: Infrastructure for Development* (1994), pp. 186–187.

multiple problems of poverty, inequality, and underemployment.

Much of the statistical information with respect to the evolution and impact of foreign trade before 1950 was obtained from ANGUS MADDISON, "Economic and Social Conditions in Latin America, 1913–1950," in *Long-Term Trends in Latin American Economic Development*, edited by Miguel Urrutia (1991), pp. 1–22. Statistics were also obtained from the *Statistical Abstract of Latin America*, vol. 30, pt. 2, edited by James W. Wilkie et al. (1993). Most of the information on manufactured exports was obtained from MONTAGUE J. LORD, "Latin America's Exports of Manufactured Goods," in Inter-American Development Bank, *Economic and Social Progress in Latin America* (1992), pp. 191–279.

The *Handbook of Development Economics*, vol. 2, edited by HOLLIS CHENERY and T. N. SRINIVASAN (1989), contains articles with excellent information and bibliographies on Latin America. Particularly valuable are chapters on primary exporting countries by Stephen R. Lewis, Jr., on import substitution by Henry Bruton, and on outward orientation by Bela Balassa. The *CEPAL Review*, published by the United Nations Economic Commission for Latin America and the Caribbean, contains numerous, highly informative articles pertaining to foreign trade.

An empirical and theoretical analysis of foreign trade is in MARKOS MAMALAKIS, "The Export Sector, Stages of Economic Development, and the Saving-Investment Process in Latin America," in *Economia Internazionale* 23, no. 4 (1970): 283–307. A brief description of the staples theory as well as its application to Argentina is in CARLOS F. DÍAZ ALEJANDRO, *Essays on the Economic History of the Argentine Republic* (1970). Díaz Alejandro also examines the impact of free trade and protectionist trade regimes on development in Argentina.

A description of the mineral theory of growth and an application to Latin America is in MARKOS MAMALAKIS, *The Minerals Theory of Growth: The Latin American Evidence* (1978). The mineral case of guano is examined in JONATHAN V. LEVIN, *The Export Economies: Their Pattern of Development in Historical Perspective* (1960). The case of Chilean nitrate is examined in MARKOS MAMALAKIS, "The Role of Government in the Resource Transfer and Resource Allocation Processes: The Chilean Nitrate Sector, 1880–1930," in *Government and Economic Development*, edited by Gustav Ranis (1971).

MARKOS J. MAMALAKIS

See also **Caribbean Common Market; Economic Development.**

FORESTS. The forests of the Neotropic plant realm, which corresponds roughly to modern Latin America, had been reduced in area by the last glacial epoch and were once again on the advance as the first humans entered the region. For them this was a strange biotic world. South America had evolved largely in isolation from the other continents, and its myriad species were mostly unique to it. Tropical and subtropical evergreen forest covered the Caribbean coast and highlands of Mesoamerica and northern South America, the Pacific coast of modern Colombia and Ecuador, the vast basin of the Amazon, and the coast of modern Brazil. On the rain-shadowed inland slopes of these regions, evergreens were replaced by deciduous trees. A broad swath of what is now Brazil's Northeast and Center-West and northern Argentina was covered with forests habituated to dry seasons, wildfire, and aluminum-toxified soils. In southern Brazil and along the southernmost Andes there are forests of araucaria, cyprus, and beech that display a close relationship to the forests of Australia and New Zealand.

The first human groups to arrive in the Western Hemisphere preferred open country, gallery forests, flood plains, and estuaries, where hunting and fishing were most productive. As they came to adopt agriculture, however, the forest necessarily became their principal resource. The technique of slash-and-burn farming offered extremely high yields for low labor input. It could be practiced even on poor soils and proved, at low levels of human population density, relatively stable. The continued burning of forest over a period of several thousand years, however, probably modified forest composition even where it did not eliminate it. In a few areas, notably highland Mesoamerica and northwestern South America, slash-and-burn farming had to be replaced by more laborious irrigation systems, representing a more permanent replacement of forest.

The European invasion of the Neotropic realm marked the beginning of extreme modification and degradation of its forests. Slash-and-burn could now be practiced with iron tools that made weeding easier, thereby encouraging the exploitation of cleared patches until soils were eroded and forests could not reestablish themselves. Most critically, the Spanish and Portuguese brought with them cattle, sheep, and horses and a social tradition that favored their maintenance in large numbers, unintegrated with farming. Cattle replaced farmers as soon as soils degraded, and their continued grazing prevented trees from returning. Fertile forest soils located near seaports were given over to plantation crops, especially sugarcane. The forests were mined for the large quantities of fuelwood needed by the sugar mills. Some of the smaller Caribbean islands lost nearly all of their forests to the plantations. Other colonial activities, especially gold and silver mining, deforested limited areas.

The eighteenth and nineteenth centuries witnessed the growth of forest extraction, as New World populations grew once again and as urban and industrial demand increased in Europe and the United States. Dyewoods had been exploited since the earliest days of colonization. Numerous exotic products were sought in the forest—sarsaparilla, supposedly a remedy for syphilis; quinine, decidedly a remedy for malaria; along with medicinals, orchids, pelts, chicle, tannins, resins, feathers, balsams, and essences. Hardwoods suitable for fine cabinetry were logged in lowlands close to sizable streams and harbors. Most important of all was wild RUBBER, for which the market grew rapidly from the 1840s onward.

The installation of railroads made possible in some areas a fuller exploitation of highland timber resources. Brazilian araucaria forest, one of the few homogeneous and, therefore, easily exploitable forests in South America, was nearly eliminated. Railroads extended the range of plantation agriculture and encouraged the inflow of small farmers seeking subsistence or cash crops for the city market. The penetration of forests was greatly accelerated in the 1960s and 1970s, as heavy road vehicles became common and governments invested more and more in road and bridge building in the interior.

Government policy and foreign capital have been blamed for the heedless destruction of the forest. Frontier expansion was politically advantageous: it reduced the pressure for land reform; created grateful constitu-

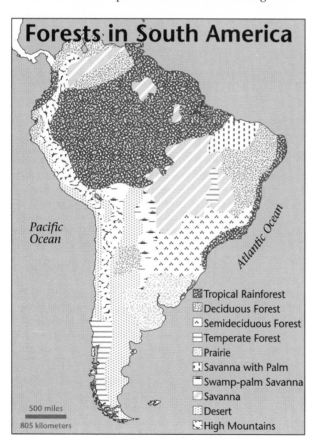

Forests in South America

Pacific Ocean

Atlantic Ocean

500 miles
805 kilometers

- Tropical Rainforest
- Deciduous Forest
- Semideciduous Forest
- Temperate Forest
- Prairie
- Savanna with Palm
- Swamp-palm Savanna
- Savanna
- Desert
- High Mountains

Défrichement d'une forêt (Destruction of a Forest). Reproduced from Johann Moritz Rugendas, *Malerische Reise in Brasilian* (Paris, 1835). BY PERMISSION OF THE HOUGHTON LIBRARY, HARVARD UNIVERSITY.

encies; and fortified sovereignty in border areas. Timber and cattle grazing have attracted foreign capital, and foreign markets have been a principal motive for government incentives. In Central America, for example, the forest has been largely replaced by pasture for cattle grazing. However, products such as timber and beef are also important inputs to the growing economies and populations of Latin America. Wood fuel and charcoal remain important sources of energy, not only in households, but even in modern sectors, such as Brazil's steel industry. Furthermore, long-term inflation has enhanced the speculative value of rural properties. Pressure on the forest, therefore, has continued regardless of government policies.

Conservationism is hardly practiced in forestry. The introduction of the chain saw has greatly increased the speed of timber felling, but the industry is in most places undercapitalized. Fifty to a hundred trees of lesser value may be destroyed to obtain one specimen. This waste is partly the result of the extraordinary richness of species of the tropical forest. Unfortunately, this same complexity makes it unlikely that even rationally logged forests will grow back to resemble their original state. Reforestation has taken place on a scale still insufficient to meet requirements for industrial raw materials such as plywood, chipboard, and paper pulp. Nearly all of the plantings are of fast-growing exotic species, especially eucalyptus and pines, not of species that would contribute to the restoration of native ecosystems. Large-scale reforestation has relied heavily on tax incentives, which are unpredictable.

A conservationist impulse has been present in at least a few Latin American countries since the turn of the century and even before. Since the 1970s and 1980s consciousness of the scientific, tourist, and economic values of the forests has grown and an environmental movement of considerable dimension has spread, favored by a renewed democratic political climate. Large areas of forest have been set aside as reserves and national parks, and conservationist laws have been strengthened. The conservationist practices of native peoples and forest dwellers have been given more attention, and many are beginning to understand and act upon the global implications of nature protection. It remains to be seen whether this new consciousness will be effective in protecting remaining forest resources.

FRANCES FLICK, *The Forests of Continental Latin America* (1952); E. J. FITTKAU et al., eds., *Biogeography and Ecology of South America* (1969); JAN DE VOS, *La paz de Dios y del rey: La conquista de la Selva Lacandona (1525–1821)* (1980); ANTÔNIO ELIO BRAILOVSKY, "Política ambiental de la generación del 80," in *Tres estudios Argentinos,* by Nora L. Siegrist de Gentile et al. (1982); ALFRED CROSBY, *Ecological Imperialism* (1986); SILVIA RODRÍGUEZ C. and EMILIO VARGAS M., *El recurso forestal en Costa Rica: Políticas púb-*

licas y sociedad, 1970–1984 (1988); JAN DE VOS, Oro verde: La conquista de la Selva Lacandona por los madereros tabasquenos, 1822–1949 (1988); RODOLFO CONTRERAS M., Más allá del bosque (1989); JAMES J. PARSONS, Hispanic Lands and Peoples, edited by William M. Denevan (1989).

WARREN DEAN

See also **Agriculture: Environmental Movements; Lumber Industry; Mining.**

FORNER, RAQUEL (b. 22 April 1902; d. 10 June 1988), Argentine painter. Born in Buenos Aires, Forner studied at the National Academy of Fine Arts in Buenos Aires, graduating in 1923, and with Othon Friesz in Paris (1929–1930). In 1932 she helped found the first private school of fine arts in Buenos Aires. She became a member of the Royal Society of Arts (England) in 1951 and received the National Prize for painting (Buenos Aires, 1942) and the grand prize at the First American Biennial of Art (Córdoba, Argentina, 1962). Through her encounter with the surrealists in Paris, Forner discovered the cosmic character of experience and endeavored to give it structural expression. In later years her paintings focused on a science-fiction interpretation of the cosmos, as exemplified in Black Astrobeings. From the technical point of view her compositions are highly unusual in structure; color plays a secondary role, inclining toward the monochromatic. Forner's work reflects the image of the human soul amid the complexity of the world.

Museum of Modern Art of Latin America (1985); VICENTE GESUALDO, ALDO BIGLIONE, and RODOLFO SANTOS, Diccionario de artistas plásticos en la Argentina (1988).

AMALIA CORTINA ARAVENA

FORT ROSS, Russian outpost in Spanish California. Beginning in the first decade of the nineteenth century, representatives of the Russian-American Company in Alaska visited Spanish Alta CALIFORNIA in search of both grain for the Alaskan colonies and sea otters and fur seals. In 1811 the company's directors approved a plan to establish an agricultural colony north of the Spanish territory in Alta California. Accordingly, in March 1812, Ivan Kuskov established Fort Ross on the coast some eighteen miles north of Bodega Bay. By 1820, Fort Ross had a population of 273, including Russians, creoles of mixed Russian-Aleut ancestry, Aleuts from Alaska, and local Kashaya Pomo and Coast Miwok tribes.

The agricultural operation at Fort Ross and at several farms established in the Bodega Bay area proved disappointing, never reaching expected production levels, but the hunt for fur-bearing marine mammals was somewhat more successful. Between 1824 and 1834 the company exported 1,822 pelts from mature otters, 94 from pups, and 2,669 fur-seal pelts. In 1841 the company sold Fort Ross to John Sutter, a Swiss entrepreneur who in the mid-1830s established a farming and ranching operation at the confluence of the San Joaquin and Sacramento rivers.

PETR A. TIKHMENEV, A History of the Russian-American Company, edited and translated by Richard A. Pierce and Alton S. Donnelly (1977); GLENN J. FARRIS, "The Russian Imprint on the Colonization of California," in DAVID HURST THOMAS, ed., Columbian Consequences. Vol. 1, Archaeological and Historical Perspectives on the Spanish Borderlands West (1989), pp. 481–497.

ROBERT H. JACKSON

FORTALEZA, capital of the state of CEARÁ in Brazil. On the northern coast of the Brazilian bulge, the city has a population of about 1,763,546 (1989 est.). Ceará's principal commercial center, Fortaleza is a port of call for European and North American lines and for coastal steamers. The harbor, previously an open roadstead (less sheltered harbor), is now protected by a breakwater with port facilities at the Ponta de Mucuripe, 3.6 miles to the east. Chief exports include sugar, cotton, hides, carnauba wax, and other agricultural products of the region.

Originating in the early seventeenth century as a village adjoining a Portuguese fort, hence its name, the settlement was occupied by the Dutch in the mid-1600s. Fortaleza became the capital of the captaincy of Ceará in 1810, receiving city status and designation as the provincial capital in 1823.

Fortaleza's population swelled during northeastern Brazil's periodic droughts as SERTANEJOS (inhabitants of the backlands) flocked to cities in search of work or relief. The capital was often ill equipped to meet such crises. During the drought of 1877–1879, the provincial administration in Fortaleza, overwhelmed by problems in the city, stopped sending aid to the interior.

Sertanejos sometimes manifested antagonism toward the government at Fortaleza. In 1914, followers of Padre Cícero Romão Batista, a priest in Joaseiro (now JUAZEIRO DO NORTE) popular among the sertanejos, marched on Fortaleza. Governor Marcos Rabelo, striving to avert bloodshed, entrusted the state government to federal authorities.

RALPH DELLA CAVA, Miracle at Joaseiro (1970).

CARA SHELLY

See also **Messianic Movements: Brazil.**

FORTS AND FORTIFICATIONS: BRAZIL. See **Santa Cruz, Fortaleza de.**

FORTS AND FORTIFICATIONS: SPANISH AMERICA. Almost from the outset of the Spanish occupation of the Americas, raids by English, French, Dutch, North African, and other competitors made the construction of coastal and port defenses essential. By the 1540s, certain strategic ports had become fortified centers: SANTO DOMINGO, Hispaniola, and SAN JUAN, PUERTO RICO—the centers of Spanish power in the islands; CARTAGENA—guardian of northern South America and the approaches to the Isthmus of Panama; Nombre de Dios and later PORTOBELO at the isthmus; SAN JUAN DE ULÚA at Veracruz—the key and entry to Mexico; and HAVANA—the strategic center and rendezvous point for the convoys returning to Spain. Additional secondary fortifications in Yucatán, Florida, Central America and the islands were designed to deter raiders and foreign settlers. The early defenses were quite simple—keep and bailey forts armed with a few iron or bronze culverins and smaller cannon. But the capture of Havana by French raiders in 1555 underscored the need for stronger fortifications and garrisons. In the late sixteenth and the seventeenth centuries, beginning with Sir Francis DRAKE's circumnavigation (1577–1580), English, French, Dutch, and buccaneer raiders plundered Spanish commerce and ports along the Pacific coasts and forced Spain to fortify CALLAO, PANAMA CITY, ACAPULCO, and other towns.

In the Caribbean and Gulf of Mexico, the construction of massive fortifications designed by Spanish and Italian military engineers incorporated revolutionary architectural changes stemming from European advances. In 1563 the engineer Francisco Calona began the redesign of Havana's fortifications to incorporate modern bastions, gun platforms, thick vaults, and a dry moat. These improvements gave defenders the best possible field of fire against enemy attackers as well as protection against the intense cannonades of besieging forces. The capture of the fortress of San Juan de Ulúa and the town of Veracruz (1568) by John HAWKINS, and Drake's Caribbean raid (1585–1586), during which he took Santo Domingo and Cartagena, caused Philip II to dispatch the well-known Italian engineer Juan Bautista Antoneli to design modern fortifications at San Juan de Ulúa and to survey the defenses of the Caribbean. Antoneli's proposals led to the construction of an expensive but fairly effective system of fortifications that in the case of Havana resisted capture for nearly 200 years until 1762. Indeed, renewed assaults by Drake and Hawkins in 1595 against improved fortifications failed at San Juan, Puerto Rico, and at Cartagena, where yellow fever, malaria, dysentery, and other tropical diseases forced the besieging force to desist. Drake went on to devastate Nombre de Dios at the isthmus, after which the town was abandoned permanently in favor of Portobelo.

After the Treaty of London in 1604, European competitors occupied vacant American territories that were excellent staging points for more serious attacks. Also, small forces of marauding BUCCANEERS, often supported by European allies, plundered Spanish fortified ports. They massacred the garrison of Portobelo in 1668 and managed to capture many Spanish port towns and fortifications. On several occasions, buccaneer forces crossed the isthmus, captured Spanish shipping, and attacked the poorly fortified Pacific ports of Central America, Mexico, and Peru. Although the major Caribbean fortifications should have been impregnable against such raiders, problems with manpower in the garrisons and failures to maintain expensive works, artillery, and magazines presented opportunities for successful lightning attacks.

With the decline in revenues during the seventeenth century, hastily recruited Spanish American militiamen lacked the resolve to defend fortifications against the implacable buccaneers. Campeche fell in 1672, and in 1683 a buccaneer force assaulted the fortress of San Juan de Ulúa and captured Veracruz. They pillaged the town, killed 300 of the 6,000 inhabitants, and even threatened to massacre the entire populace if a ransom was not paid. With the arrival of the annual Spanish fleet, Mexican militia forces from Puebla, Orizaba, Jalapa, and Córdoba reoccupied the town to find buildings gutted and the corpses of people and animals rotting in the streets. In the aftermath of this disaster, the Mexican authorities convened special tribunals to investigate and punish military officers who had failed to defend the fortifications.

Although international treaties gradually brought the buccaneers under control, the Spaniards were slow to improve their defensive fortifications. In April 1697, a French force of seven warships escorted by frigates and bomb vessels—more than 4,000 soldiers and seamen—surprised Cartagena, which was considered to be impregnable. Spanish cannon mounted on weak cedarwood carriages proved no match for the effective artillery fire of the attackers. The undermanned forts capitulated on 3 May, and the French sacked the city, holding wealthy residents for ransom. Fortunately for the defense of Spanish American possessions, the nadir had been reached. Compelled by the increasing ability of enemies to mount larger amphibious attacks against fortified ports, the eighteenth-century Spanish Bourbons invested heavily to upgrade and modernize the fortifications at Havana, Cartagena, Veracruz, Panama, and elsewhere. Critics argued that a defensive strategy centered upon a few major strongholds provoked enemies to direct their attacks against weaker secondary targets. But Spain improved its defenses to the point that would-be opponents no longer challenged fortifications without significant planning and much larger forces. Beyond looking after its own defensive works, the Viceroyalty of NEW SPAIN provided *situados* (financial subsidies) to improve and maintain Havana, Santo Domingo, and the Florida fortifications.

Spanish preoccupation with the upgrading of Caribbean defenses coincided with the possibility of large amphibious attacks by Britain during the succession of eighteenth-century wars. In the WAR OF JENKINS'S EAR (1739–1748), a major assault in 1741 by forces commanded by Admiral Edward Vernon and Brigadier-General Thomas Wentworth failed to capture Cartagena, which had been upgraded and modernized by the engineer Juan de Herrera y Sotomayor. Despite successful at-

605

tacks upon outlying forts, the 14,000 British regulars, Anglo-American militiamen, and some companies of black troops succumbed to tropical diseases as the siege progressed. Finally, Vernon abandoned Cartagena to attack Santiago de Cuba and the isthmus, but the expedition found no easy targets. In the end British forces lost more than 10,000 troops and many seamen. Spain's best defensive use of fortifications was to hold besiegers in place until yellow fever, malaria, and dysentery took hold. While Vernon misjudged the strength of improved Spanish fortifications, it was also obvious that Britain now possessed the logistical and marine strength to assault coastal defenses and even to undertake invasions inland against Spanish American provinces.

In 1762, during the Seven Years' War, Britain used its marine ascendancy to dispatch a force of thirty-five ships and an army of 14,000 troops—regular infantry, American provincials, black companies, and slaves. Arriving at Havana in June, the British caught the Spaniards completely off guard. On this occasion, the formidable fortifications of EL MORRO and the almost impenetrable seaward and landward defenses of Havana were insufficient to deter invasion. Striking quickly against disorganized defenders, the British stormed El Morro, which had been weakened by heavy fire from siege batteries set up ashore and by cannonades from the warships. The Spaniards hoped to prolong the siege until tropical diseases and the advancing hurricane season forced the British to desist, but full cooperation between the besieging army and navy units corrected earlier weaknesses from Vernon's day. Ha-

vana surrendered and was occupied for ten months until the Peace of Paris.

The fall of Havana, the strategic key to the Spanish Caribbean, caused repercussions that altered all aspects of defense planning. Not only were fortifications strengthened, but Spain introduced a military reform program designed to overcome deficiencies in the garrisons. Aware that Britain might contemplate an invasion of Mexico, the Spaniards spent five years (1770–1775) constructing a new fortress at Perote, inland from Veracruz, to protect against a surprise coup de main. Situated in the healthy uplands, this fortress was designed to impede the march of an enemy army on unfortified Mexico City. An invader would require heavy siege artillery, munitions, supplies, and sufficient troops to besiege a fortress distant from the coast. While Perote was not tested in the colonial period, its existence permitted Mexican viceroys to remove unacclimatized soldiers from garrison duty in the fortifications of Veracruz. According to most plans, potential invaders were to be bottled up on the coast until yellow fever destroyed their capacity to fight.

During the late-eighteenth- and early-nineteenth-century wars against Britain, Spanish forces and fortifications helped to defeat British attacks at San Juan, Puerto Rico (1797), and deterred invasion plans for Mexico in the period from 1805 to 1807. While the fortress of San Juan de Ulúa remained the last bastion of Spanish power in Mexico until 1825, it did not help Spain to reoccupy the viceroyalty. Through the nineteenth century, many of the fortifications became infa-

El Morro appears to the left of La Fortaleza on San Juan Bay. LIBRARY OF CONGRESS.

mous prisons and penitentiaries rather than serving as sentinels to protect strategic ports against foreign intrusions.

The best study on the early period in English is PAUL E. HOFFMAN, *The Spanish Crown and the Defense of the Caribbean, 1535–1585: Precedent, Patrimonialism, and Royal Parsimony* (1980). JOHN H. PARRY, *The Spanish Seaborne Empire* (1966), presents a good general survey, as does ARTHUR P. NEWTON, *The European Nations in the West Indies, 1493–1688* (1933). For maritime attacks on Spanish possessions in the Pacific, see PETER T. BRADLEY, *The Lure of Peru: Maritime Intrusion into the South Sea, 1598–1701* (1989). CLARENCE H. HARING, *The Buccaneers in the West Indies in the Seventeenth Century* (1910), provides a good survey of their raids on Spanish fortifications, as does the more recent work by JUAN JUÁREZ MORENO, *Corsarios y piratas en Veracruz y Campeche* (1972). For the eighteenth century, British attacks on Spanish fortifications are examined in RICHARD PARES, *War and Trade in the West Indies, 1739–1763* (1936); DAVID SYRETT, comp., *The Siege and Capture of Havana, 1762* (1970); and RICHARD HARDING, *Amphibious Warfare in the Eighteenth Century: The British Expedition to the West Indies, 1740–1742* (1991). For specific studies on the histories of fortifications see JOSÉ ANTONIO CALDERÓN QUIJANO, *Historia de las fortificaciones en Nueva España* (1953), and GUILLERMO LOHMANN VILLENA, *Las defensas militares de Lima y Callao* (1964).

CHRISTON I. ARCHER

See also **Armed Forces; Militia in Colonial Spanish America.**

FORTUNY, JOSÉ MANUEL (*b.* 22 March 1916), Guatemalan Communist leader. Fortuny was born in Cuilapa in the department of Santa Rosa to a middle-class family. He studied law at the University of San Carlos but never graduated. Beginning in 1938 he worked as a journalist, and the following year he began to write poetry and theatrical works for radio. In 1940 he won a national poetry prize. Until 1942 he was a journalist with the radio news program *Diario del Aire,* directed by the novelist Miguel Angel ASTURIAS.

Fortuny began his political career in the student struggle against the dictator Jorge UBICO (1931–1944) and participated in the revolution of October 1944. From 1945 to 1949 he was a representative to the National Constituent Assembly and to the Guatemalan Congress. He founded the leftist Popular Liberation Front (FPL) in 1944 and served as secretary-general to both the FPL and the Revolutionary Action Party (PAR) in 1947. In that same year he formed a faction within the PAR called the Democratic Vanguard, which gave rise in 1949 to the Guatemalan Communist Party (PCG), renamed the Guatemalan Labor Party (PGT) in 1952. He was the secretary-general of this group until 1954.

Fortuny played a key role in the administration of President Jacobo ARBENZ (1951–1954) as the president's friend, personal adviser, and member of the so-called "kitchen cabinet," writing many of his speeches. After the North American intervention and the fall of Arbenz, Fortuny went into exile. He continued as leader of his party, and between 1971 and 1974 lived clandestinely within Guatemala. He later moved to Mexico City and went to work for the newspaper *Uno Más Uno.* In the 1990s he remained a Marxist and followed the moderate evolution of the former Italian Communist Party.

RONALD M. SCHNEIDER, *Communism in Guatemala, 1944–1954* (1958); STEPHEN SCHLESINGER and STEPHEN KINZER, *Bitter Fruit: The Untold Story of the American Coup in Guatemala* (1982); PIERO GLEIJESES, *Shattered Hope: The Guatemalan Revolution and the United States, 1944–1954* (1991).

VÍCTOR ACUÑA

See also **Guatemala: Political Parties.**

FRANCIA, JOSÉ GASPAR RODRÍGUEZ DE (*b.* 6 January 1766; *d.* 20 September 1840), dictator of Paraguay (1814–1840). One of three major nineteenth-century rulers of Paraguay, Francia was viewed by his elite contemporaries and traditional historians as a ruthless dictator who isolated Paraguay from outside contact and whose iron rule destroyed all who opposed him—foreigners, intellectuals, and the Paraguayan elite. Revisionist historians perceive him as an honest, populist ruler who promoted an autonomous, social revolution within Paraguay and encouraged the economic development of the country.

Born in Asunción to a Brazilian military officer and his elite Paraguayan wife, Francia earned a doctorate in theology in 1785 at the University of Córdoba, Argentina. He then taught theology at Asunción's Real Colegio y Seminario de San Carlos. Upon his dismissal for his liberal ideas on religion and politics, he turned to law. He never married and did not use his political opportunities to amass wealth. He gained political experience by serving on the municipal council of Asunción from 1807 to 1809 and won enough respect for his legal and administrative knowledge to be given the responsibility of defining the qualifications for participation in the revolutionary junta. Eventually dominating the junta, he espoused Paraguayan independence from both Spanish and Argentine hegemony and wrote the first constitution of Paraguay, which the Congress adopted in October 1813. The dual consulship of Colonel Fulgencio YEGROS and Francia soon failed. Francia's popularity, personality, and political ability led the National Congress of 1814 to elect him supreme dictator. Even though there were periods of shared power as well as self-imposed exile between 1811 and 5 June 1816, when the Popular Congress elected him perpetual dictator, Francia was the most powerful and popular politician for the first twenty-nine years of Paraguayan independence.

Francia destroyed the traditional power of the Spanish elite and the church, strengthened the military, and appealed to the peasants. He did not abolish the municipal councils in small towns but did terminate those in Asunción and Villa Rica that were controlled by the elite. He promoted state-operated cattle ranches and

José Gaspar Rodríguez de Francia. BENSON LATIN AMERICAN COLLECTION, UNIVERSITY OF TEXAS AT AUSTIN.

state commerce, which competed with the private ES-TANCIAS and mercantile houses and undermined the elite's ability to increase its wealth. Francia dominated the operations of the Roman Catholic church by collecting tithes, paying the clergy's salaries, and constructing churches. Although he closed the seminary at which he had once taught, between 1815 and 1840 he had at least ten new churches constructed and increased the number of priests in the villages.

To promote the nation's self-sufficiency, Francia encouraged greater utilization of state lands through government enterprises and low rents for small farmers who produced food for local consumption. He promoted internal trade, controlled external commerce and immigration, increased industrial production in both the private and public sectors, improved communications and transportation, and reduced taxes. To limit government costs, he maintained only a small bureaucracy. His frugality and careful attention to detail resulted in governmental fiscal surpluses. A paternalistic ruler, Francia supported religious celebrations and paid

for pauper burials and the care of orphans. The state helped pay soldiers' debts, provided food for indigent prisoners, and aided foreign exiles.

To maintain internal security, suppress banditry, protect against Indians, and define the nation's boundaries, Francia built border forts and established garrisons at the northern border with Brazil at the Apa River, in the south at Pilar on the Argentine border, and in the southeast, which expanded control over the Misiones region. To end Paraguayan political independence, Francia sought Argentine recognition and free trade on the border along the PARANÁ RIVER. When Argentine caudillos disrupted trade between 1817 and 1822 and Buenos Aires refused to recognize Paraguayan independence, Francia closed Paraguay's borders in 1819 and again between 1823 and 1840, redirecting Paraguayan external trade through the department of Itapúa (Encarnación) to Brazil and Uruguay. The conduct of trade down the Paraná, although regulated by Francia, never entirely ceased, because small boats were able to get through Pilar to Corrientes. By maintaining neutrality in Río de la Plata affairs and using Brazilian commercial interests to balance Argentine political demands, Francia assured Paraguayan independence.

In contrast to other Spanish-American states after independence, Francia's government was stable, efficient, and honest. At his death Paraguay possessed a prosperous, independent national economy and a centralized political system. His economic and political power and willingness to use force created critics among the elite and laid the basis for autocratic rule in Paraguay. Even though military officers and civilians maneuvered for power after his death, the peaceful transfer of government that occurred testifies to the strength of his administration. A dedicated nationalist, popular with the masses, Francia was a dictator whose paternalistic policies benefited a large majority of Paraguayans.

The two major monographs are RICHARD ALAN WHITE, *Paraguay's Autonomous Revolution, 1810–1840* (1978), which views Francia's rule as having fomented a social revolution, and JOHN HOYT WILLIAMS, *The Rise and Fall of the Paraguayan Republic, 1800–1870* (1979), a revisionist interpretation, which assesses Francia as one of the three major nineteenth-century dictators to rule Paraguay. JULIO CÉSAR CHAVES, *El supremo dictador* 4th ed. (1964), is a well-researched, multi-archival political study examining Francia sympathetically within the context of Paraguayan history. RAUL DE ANDRADA E SILVA, *Ensaio sobre a Ditadura do Paraguai, 1814–1840* (1978), analyzes the social and economic system of eighteenth- and nineteenth-century Paraguay under Francia. JOSÉ ANTONIO VÁZQUEZ, *El Doctor Francia visto y oido por sus contemporáneos* (1975), is an excellent collection of 465 documentary excerpts on Francia, beginning with his youth and proceeding chronologically to his death.

VERA BLINN REBER

FRANCISCANS, men and women affiliated with a far-reaching tradition within the Roman Catholic Church, who embrace a life that may involve a state of consecration, or the taking of vows, and that follows one of several interpretations of the thirteenth-century Rule set down by Saint Francis of Assisi. The largest single branch of the Franciscans, the Order of Friars Minor (OFM), shares company with other members of the Franciscan family, such as the CAPUCHIN FRIARS, the Conventual friars, numerous branches of religious sisters, the Third Order of Saint Francis, and an assortment of lay associations. The term "Franciscan," especially in the history of Latin America, is most popularly employed in reference to the Friars Minor, the primary focus of the present article.

Saint Francis received approval of a rule in 1209 from Pope Innocent III, officially founding the Friars Minor as an order of mendicants; its members voluntarily relinquish all rights to the ownership of property and live solely from alms. The Franciscan habit, a brown tunic with a hood and a rope belt ending in three knots to signify the three vows of poverty, chastity, and obedience, is universally recognized. Franciscan men and women have been at work in Latin America since the beginning of European contact; their legacy of evangelization is pervasive, and the Franciscan presence in Latin America remains strong. From the second voyage of Columbus on, Franciscans made their way to the Americas in the rush to spread the Christian message. They founded their first MISSIONS in the Antilles, from which expeditions to the mainland were undertaken.

In Mexico, a group of reformist, millenarian Franciscans dominated the first generation of missionaries, seeing the newly found territories as inviting the dawn of a radical new social order, the kingdom of God on earth. The responsibility for building this new order, they believed, sat squarely on their shoulders, and the extreme zeal with which they undertook its realization has been alternately lauded and criticized.

In 1522 Emperor Charles V responded to requests from Hernán Cortés to send Franciscans to Mexico to undertake the systematic conversion of the natives. Thus began a steady stream of missionaries from Spain and other countries, the most notable among the first arrivals being Fray Pedro de GANTE, a Belgian who worked tirelessly among the poor and who established schools, chapels, and health facilities for the Indians. He was joined in 1524 by a group of friars known as "The Twelve," a name that symbolically connected the missionaries to the twelve Apostles. These friars firmly implanted Franciscanism, with its emphasis on poverty, communal living, and the passion of Christ, as the primary Christian force among the newly converted in Mexico. They battled, at times fiercely, with civil and church authorities over control of native populations. The first bishop of Mexico, Juan de ZUMÁRRAGA, himself a Franciscan friar, defended with a great sense of urgency the idea that the friars had primacy in all matters. By learning the native language and by instilling confidence in the church as the organizing principle of society, the friars met with success in their catechetical efforts. Accounts of mass baptisms found their way into early Franciscan accounts; the friars often recalled their exhaustion at administering the sacraments in towns near and far. By the mid-sixteenth century, the friars were organized into administrative units, or provinces, extending south from the central valley of Mexico to the Yucatán and Central America, north to Guadalajara, and eventually into the south and west of what is now the United States. Missionary colleges to train friars for work in the farthest reaches of New Spain were established in the seventeenth century in Querétaro, Mexico City, and Zacatecas. Friars were trained to teach not only Catholic doctrine but also those arts, crafts, and agricultural techniques considered beneficial to Christian living.

Policies of the ruling Bourbon dynasty in the mid- to late eighteenth century, aimed at centralizing the church under tighter royal regulation, had profound effects on the friars. The crown secularized, or turned over to clergy not affiliated with a religious order, most properties and parishes that had come under the friars' corporate control over the course of two and a half centuries. Though the friars maintained certain principal monasteries, the decree of secularization forced them to abandon much of their pastoral work. By the period of independence in the 1820s, their numbers had declined sharply.

Franciscan involvement in South America parallels that in New Spain, with missionaries taking part in the evangelization program from the early colonial period. Friars arrived in Peru in 1532, embarking on a program of conversion and beginning the construction of churches, hospitals, and schools throughout the region, including present-day Bolivia, northern Argentina, and Chile north of the Bío-bío River. Their first foundation in Ecuador, in Quito, dates to 1534. The symbolism of sending twelve friars into a new region was repeated in 1542, lending the name "Twelve Apostles" to one Peruvian province. As at New Spain, missionary colleges served to train friars for the more remote areas; only the JESUITS had as extensive a network of missions in South America, and once the Jesuits were expelled (Brazil, 1760; Spanish America, 1767), the friars took over these South American missions as well as the ones in New Spain. The annals of the Franciscans show that their missionary activities in South America met with varying degrees of success. The Friars Minor were much less active in what is now Colombia and Venezuela; those areas were dominated by their fellow Franciscans of the Capuchin branch.

Instability wrought by the Wars of Independence in the 1820s, combined with the already weakened state of the order resulting from eighteenth-century royal decrees aimed at curbing their power, made the Franciscans particularly vulnerable to attack from emerging social and political forces unfriendly to the clergy. The story of each individual country differs in the nineteenth century, but it is safe to conclude that the friars suffered persecutions of some type in nearly every locale. Over the course of the nineteenth century, the number of friars in Latin America declined, beginning with the flight of the Spanish Franciscans back to Europe after independence. The resuscitation of the order in the twentieth century likewise differs from one region to another. The most often cited catalyst for this rejuvenation, in any event, is the 1891 papal encyclical *Rerum Novarum* of Leo XIII, which brought to the fore the need for social action of a type reminiscent of the Franciscan spirit.

JOHN LEDDY PHELAN, *The Millennial Kingdom of the Franciscans in the New World* (1956); LEÓN LOPETEGUI and FÉLIX ZUBILLAGA, *Historia de la Iglesia en la América Española* (1965); ROBERT RICARD, *The Spiritual Conquest of Mexico,* translated by Lesley Byrd Simpson (1966); *New Catholic Encyclopedia* (1967); FRANCISCO MORALES, ed., *Franciscan Presence in the Americas* (1984); *The Americas: A Quarterly Journal of Inter-American Cultural History* (published by the Academy of American Franciscan History).

BRIAN C. BELANGER

FRANCO, GUILLERMO (active mid-1800s), Ecuadorian military and political figure. Following the ouster of Juan José FLORES in 1845, Ecuador entered a period of extreme political instability that culminated in the country's splintering into four regions in 1859. General Franco assumed leadership of Guayaquil on 6 September 1859 and signed a treaty with Peru conceding El Oriente to that nation in return for recognition of his presidency of Ecuador. As a result of this agreement, he lost popular support on the coast. The following year, in September 1860, Franco's forces were defeated by the army of the provisional government commanded by former president Juan José Flores. Franco fled into exile.

LUIS ROBALINO DÁVILA, *Orígenes del Ecuador de hoy,* vol. 6 (1967), esp. pp. 217–261; FRANK MAC DONALD SPINDLER, *Nineteenth-Century Ecuador* (1987), esp. p. 51.

LINDA ALEXANDER RODRÍGUEZ

FRANCO, HERNANDO (*b.* 1532; *d.* 28 November 1585), Spanish-born composer who, after his training in the Segovia cathedral and brief service in Guatemala, was brought to Mexico by Spanish patron Arévalo Sedeño. Music flourished under his direction at the Mexico City cathedral from 1575 until financial problems prompted his resignation in 1582. He returned to the post as conditions improved, but died shortly thereafter. His sacred music style incorporates the alternation of simple unison and intricate polyphonic part singing in a manner typical of the cathedral practice that existed during his apprentice and journeyman years in Spain.

ROBERT STEVENSON, *Music in Mexico: A Historical Survey* (1952).

ROBERT L. PARKER

FRANCO, ITAMAR AUGUSTO CAUTIERO (*b.* 28 June 1931), president of Brazil (1992–). Franco was born on board the ship *Itamar,* along the coast of Bahia. His mother, Italia Cautiero, who had just lost her husband, a public-health doctor in the interior of that state, was returning with her children Augusto and Matilde to raise them in Juiz de Fora, Minas Gerais. Although his birth certificate gives Salvador, Bahia, as the birthplace, Franco has always considered himself a Mineiro, and many of his initial curricula vitae, once he was elevated to the presidency, erroneously gave Juiz de Fora as his birthplace. His cultural background and his accent are Mineiro, and he was influenced by such nationally known Mineiro politicians as José Maria Alkimin, Bias Fortes, Carlos Luz, and former presidents Juscelino KUBITSCHEK and Tancredo NEVES.

Franco attended Colégio Granbery, a school established by American Methodist missionaries at the turn of the twentieth century. During a later visit to the school, then Vice President Franco declared that it was to his mother, to Granbery, and to the local engineering school that he owed his moral, intellectual, and professional training. As an engineering student from 1950 to 1955, he was twice elected president of the academic center and demonstrated great debating skills while advocating student concerns.

Two years after graduating, Franco ran for city councilman on the Brazilian Labor Party (PTB) slate and was defeated. Four years later he also lost an election for deputy mayor. He finally succeeded in becoming mayor as a candidate on the Brazilian Democratic Movement (MDB, later PMDB) slate. His administration was marked by public works and major improvements that changed the face of the city. While mayor, he married journalist Ana Elisa Surerus. The marriage lasted nine years and the couple had two daughters.

In 1975 he ran successfully for a seat in the federal Senate, where he served until he ran for vice president in 1990. When President Fernando COLLOR DE MELLO resigned from office because of malfeasance, Franco served as interim chief executive and then as president from 29 December 1992 on.

His cabinet reflected his nationalistic tendencies and his penchant to trust old and intimate friends. He postponed a number of initiatives that had been undertaken by his predecessor, notably in the area of privatization. His works include *O negro no Brasil atual* (The Blacks in Today's Brazil, 1980), an attempt at a sociological interpretation, and *Trabalho parlamentar* (Parliamentary Work, 1984), detailing his years in the senate.

IÊDA SIQUEIRA WIARDA

FRANCO, RAFAEL (*b.* 1897; *d.* 1973), Paraguayan president (1936–1937), CHACO WAR military figure, and founder of the Partido Revolucionario Febrerista, or Febrerista Party.

In December 1928 Paraguayan forces led by Major Rafael Franco, a relatively unknown army officer, launched an unprovoked attack against Bolivian-held Fortín Vanguardia in the disputed CHACO region. This incident, though successful in its immediate aim, was repudiated by the Asunción government, which was seeking a diplomatic solution to the conflict. Now regarded as an uncontrollable hothead, Franco lost his command, only to be recalled in 1932 when the border dispute gave way to open war. Franco's military exploits in the conflict were noteworthy, though hardly more so than his open political maneuvering against the Liberal regime of Eusebio AYALA. With the conclusion of the fighting, Franco, now a colonel, made his own position clear: on 17 February 1936, he led the armed forces in a mutiny that swept Ayala from office and installed the colonel as dictator.

Franco had no intention of ruling in the manner of previous dictators. He announced a reform program that focused on land redistribution, workers' rights, and statist politics. Before he could implement these plans, his regime was overthrown in August 1937 by military leaders loyal to the Liberal Party. Franco went into exile, though he remained influential in revolutionary circles within Paraguay.

From exile, the former colonel organized the Febrerista Party, a curious movement that drew support from students, workers, some military officers, and both left- and right-wing ideologues. The Febreristas burst onto the Paraguayan political scene in 1946, when dictator Higínio MORÍNIGO invited Franco to return to the country to participate in a coalition government. This coalition failed to materialize, however, and one year later the situation degenerated into civil war with the Liberals, Communists, and Franco's Febreristas on one side and the Colorados (and the majority of the military) on the other. Franco commanded the rebel forces in the fighting but, after a short time, had to accept defeat and exile once again.

The Febreristas retained some of their influence in Paraguay, though, as the years went by, the movement abandoned its earlier radicalism and adopted a social democratic line. Franco returned several times from exile at the behest of Alfredo STROESSNER (president 1954–1989); the Febrerista Party was permitted, in a limited way, to contest several elections after 1964, with the understanding that they would present little more than token opposition to the governing Colorados. Franco accepted this as a necessary compromise, but his own death in 1973 left the Febreristas without viable leadership.

HARRIS GAYLORD WARREN, "Political Aspects of the Paraguayan Revolution, 1936–1940," in *Hispanic American Historical Review* 30: 1 (1950), pp. 2–25; PAUL H. LEWIS, *The Politics of Exile: Paraguay's Febrerista Party* (1968); JOSÉ CARLOS MARCET, *Antecedentes, desarollo y resultado de la Guerra del Chaco* (1974).

MARTA FERNÁNDEZ WHIGHAM

See also **Paraguay: Political Parties—Febrerista Party.**

FRANCO, WELLINGTON MOREIRA (*b*. 19 October 1944), Brazilian politician. Moreira Franco entered Brazilian politics in the early 1970s, just as the military regime, which had controlled the federal government since 1964, began to liberalize national political life in a process known as ABERTURA. While serving as a federal deputy for the state of Rio de Janeiro (1975–1977), mayor of the city of Niterói in the state of Rio de Janeiro (1977–1982), and governor of the state of Rio de Janeiro (1986–1990), he became well-known for his vocal advocacy of the return to and consolidation of democratic political processes. During his mayoral and gubernatorial tenures, Moreira Franco sought to build grassroots support through government-sponsored projects in the areas of social welfare and political participation.

Born in the northern city of Teresina, Piauí, Franco moved to Rio de Janeiro in 1955, where he was trained in economics and public administration at the Universidade do Brasil (1966); the Pontífica Universidade Católica of Rio de Janeiro (1968); and the École Pratique des Hautes Études in Paris. A member of the opposition Brazilian Democratic Movement (MDB) during the 1970s, Franco joined the Social Democratic Party (PDS) in 1980. The PDS candidate for governor of the state of Rio de Janeiro in 1982, he was narrowly defeated. He later joined the Brazilian Democratic Movement Party (PMDB), which supported him during his successful 1986 gubernatorial bid.

WELLINGTON MOREIRA FRANCO, *Rio, a nosso desafio* (1982); "Franco, Moreira," in *Dicionário histórico-biográfico brasileiro, 1930–1983*, vol. 2 (1984), edited by Israel Beloch and Alzira Alves de Abreu, pp. 1,356–1,357; and WELLINGTON MOREIRA FRANCO, *Em defesa do Rio* (1991).

DARYLE WILLIAMS

See also **Brazil: Political Parties.**

FRAY BENTOS, capital city of the Department of Río Negro (1985 population 22,150) in western Uruguay, founded as Independencia on the banks of the URUGUAY RIVER in 1859. In 1861 the name was changed in honor of a hermit who had lived on that site during the eighteenth century. In 1859 Jorge Gilbert built a meatpacking plant, the first in Uruguay to can beef following the procedure invented by Julius Liebig in Germany. The plant does not operate any longer; today hides and wool are the department's main exports.

CÉSAR N. CAVIEDES

FREDONIA, REPUBLIC OF (a.k.a. Fredonian Rebellion), brief revolt by Anglo-American adventurers in East Texas that took place from December 1826 to January 1827. Land speculator Haden Edwards antagonized settlers when he claimed that those who could not prove ownership of their land had to pay him for it under terms of his 1825 contract with the Mexican government. Settler protests led the government to revoke the contract and order his expulsion. On 16 December 1826, during Edwards's absence from Texas, his brother Benjamin led about thirty armed men into Nacogdoches and proclaimed the Republic of Fredonia. Unable to muster support from local Cherokees and Anglo-Americans, the group fled to the United States on the approach of Mexican military forces. The incident heightened Mexican government unease with continued Anglo-American immigration.

EUGENE C. BARKER, *The Life of Stephen F. Austin: Founder of Texas, 1793–1836*, 2d ed. (1969), esp. pp. 148–177.

JESÚS F. DE LA TEJA

FREDRICKS, CHARLES DEFOREST (*b.* 1823; *d.* 1894), one of the New World's first successful commercial photographers. By 1843, when Fredricks traveled to Latin America, he was already a master of the daguerreotype process, which had been introduced in France just four years earlier. He spent nine years traveling on the Orinoco and Amazon rivers in Venezuela and Brazil, where he recorded the images of indigenous tribes and documented local scenes in coastal cities from Recife to Buenos Aires. He is said to have exchanged a daguerreotype portrait of a local caudillo for a live jaguar, which he kept as a pet. Familiar with Cuba—where as a boy he had been sent from New York to learn Spanish—in 1855 he opened a photographic studio in Havana, C. D. Fredricks y Daries, on Havana Street. His scenes, very similar to the works of the French-born lithographer Pierre Toussans Fredorie Mialhe, seek to memorialize urban architectural monuments, not to capture everyday life. Fredricks visited Cuba occasionally but mostly left his studio in the hands of Cuban employees.

ROBERT M. LEVINE, *Cuba in the 1850s: Through the Lens of Charles DeForest Fredricks* (1990).

ROBERT M. LEVINE

See also **Photography.**

FREE BIRTH LAW (known also as the Rio Branco Law, after its principal sponsor, Visconde de RIO BRANCO, and as the Law of the Free Womb), a decree passed by the Brazilian Parliament in September 1871 that declared free all children henceforth born to slave women. Enacted after five months of tempestuous and impassioned debate, the law marked a watershed in the history of Brazilian SLAVERY. The freedom of these children was carefully circumscribed, however, for they remained under the custody of their mother's master, who could elect to release them at age eight and be indemnified by the state or retain their labor until they reached majority at age twenty-one. Emancipation of the newborn combined with the earlier suppression of the Af-

rican slave trade by the QUEIRÓS LAW in 1850 was intended to force the eventual end of slavery in Brazil by depriving future slaveowners of fresh supplies of slaves, either imported or native-born. The law carried further provisions: (1) an emancipation fund from which to sponsor a limited manumission of adult slaves, and (2) a slave's right to accumulate savings and purchase freedom at a fixed price or in exchange for labor (not to exceed seven years).

Although the standard view locates the law in a series of steps that inevitably led to the final abolition of slavery, other scholars have emphasized that planters and politicians responded out of fear of perceived slave restiveness and a complete collapse of slaveowning authority. The bill simultaneously sought to buttress the position of landowners and placate a restless rural labor force by making individual freedom more accessible. Conservatives and liberals who joined to pass the law refused to give it teeth, leaving the law's execution in the arbitrary hands of planters. The lawmakers had acted cautiously and out of fear; the controversial law satisfied no one.

ROBERT CONRAD, *The Destruction of Brazilian Slavery, 1850–1888* (1972), esp. pp. 90–117; WARREN DEAN, *Rio Claro: A Brazilian Plantation System, 1820–1920* (1976), esp. pp. 125–129, 135; SANDRA LAUDERDALE GRAHAM, "Slavery's Impasse: Slave Prostitutes, Small-time Mistresses, and the Brazilian Law of 1871," in *Comparative Studies in Society and History* 33, no. 4 (1991): 669–694.

SANDRA LAUDERDALE GRAHAM

See also **Golden Law; Sexagenarian Law.**

FREE TRADE ACT, measure signed on 12 October 1778 that crowned CHARLES III's work to modernize Spanish mercantilism through commercial deregulation. Preceded by piecemeal reforms for the Caribbean islands (1765), Yucatán (1770), Santa Marta and Riohacha (1776), and Buenos Aires, Chile, and Peru (2 February 1778), it extended imperial free trade to all of the American empire except Venezuela and Mexico and opened thirteen Spanish ports to the colonial trade. For Spanish exports, licensing procedures were simplified and ad valorem tariffs replaced levies based on weight and volume. Duties on imports into Spain varied, totaling 4 percent for most, and 5.5 percent for SILVER. Venezuela, where the CARACAS COMPANY commanded influence, and Mexico, whose commercial strength threatened to overwhelm the other colonies, were not brought under the act until 1788–1789, except for tax rates. Meanwhile, tonnage limits constricted Spanish exports to Veracruz. Imperial trade increased impressively following deregulation, although it waned during the wars of the French Revolution and NAPOLEON.

JOHN R. FISHER, *Commercial Relations Between Spain and Spanish America in the Era of Free Trade, 1778–1796* (1985); JOSEP

FONTANA and ANTONIO MIGUEL BERNAL, eds., *El "comercio libre" entre España y América (1765–1824)* (1987).

ALLAN J. KUETHE

FREEDPERSONS. *See* **Manumission.**

FREI MONTALVA, EDUARDO (*b.* 16 January 1911; *d.* 22 January 1982), president of Chile (1964–1970). Frei was born in Santiago and entered politics as a law student, founding what later became the Christian Democratic Party. After graduation from the Catholic University of Chile (1933) he specialized in labor law, then turned to editing a newspaper in the nitrate region of Tarapacá, in Chile's extreme north. He entered the Chamber of Deputies in the late 1930s, eventually becoming minister of public works in the government of President Gabriel GONZÁLEZ VIDELA (1946–1952). For some years he represented the province of Santiago in the Chilean Senate, running unsuccessfully for president in 1958. In 1964, however, he ran again, this time in a two-way race, and defeated Socialist Salvador ALLENDE, who was also supported by the Chilean Communists.

Frei's campaign came at a time when the prestige of the Cuban Revolution was at its height in Latin America, and Allende its chief beneficiary in Chile. The Christian Democrats neutralized the appeal of the Left by conceding profound changes were needed to address inequality and injustice, but proposed to implement them without tampering with the country's historic commitment to the rule of law and due process (Frei's successful slogan was "A Revolution in Liberty"). Frei defeated Allende by a decisive majority, but one that

Eduardo Frei Montalva after his election, 1964.
PHOTOGRAPHIC ARCHIVE, UNIVERSIDAD DE CHILE.

owed much to the tacit support of the Chilean Right, which chose not to run a candidate of its own.

During Frei's presidency serious efforts were made at agrarian reform, tax reform, and the nationalization of the COPPER INDUSTRY. The Right managed to obstruct some of Frei's legislative projects in Congress, often joining hands with the Left, for whom they were too conservative. Meanwhile, the Christian Democratic youth movement was pulling Frei's own party to the left, even imposing a candidate of their own, Radomiro Tomic, for the 1970 presidential elections. The result was a three-headed race in which Socialist Salvador Allende emerged with a slight plurality.

At the time of Allende's election Frei predicted that the former's Socialist-Communist government (Popular Unity) would end in "blood and horror." At first these concerns were dismissed even by members of his own party. However, three years later, Chilean society was polarized to the point of civil war. The stalemate was broken by an exceptionally bloody military coup, which produced a sixteen-year political "recess," in which the country was ruled by the iron-handed Army commander General Augusto PINOCHET UGARTE. Frei's remaining years were spent resisting Pinochet and helping to rebuild the Christian Democratic Party. He also served on the Brandt Commission and other international bodies.

EDUARDO FREI MONTALVA, *Aun es tiempo* (1942); *Chile desconocido* (1942); *La verdad tiene su hora* (1955); and *Pensamiento y acción* (1958); LEONARD GROSS, *The Last, Best Hope: Eduardo Frei and Christian Democracy in Chile* (1967).

MARK FALCOFF

FREIRE, GILBERTO. *See* **Freyre, Gilberto.**

FREIRE, PAULO (*b.* 19 March 1921), Brazilian educator and philosopher. After studies in law and philosophy, Freire became a teacher with a special interest in grammar and linguistics. Between 1947 and 1959 he instructed adult illiterates as director of the Department of Education and Culture of the Social Service in Pernambuco. In 1959 Freire completed his doctoral thesis on teaching adult illiterates and was appointed professor of history and philosophy of education at the University of Recife. In 1963, after successfully leading literary efforts in his native state, Freire was placed in charge of a national literacy campaign by the GOULART government, which initiated training programs in almost all the state capitals. When this government fell prey to a military coup in April 1965, Freire, along with many others, was jailed, stripped of his citizenship rights, and finally sentenced to exile. Freire resettled in Chile, where for five years he worked as a UNESCO consultant with the Agrarian Reform Training and Research Institute. While in exile, he led a national literacy campaign that won Chile a UNESCO award, and he wrote his first two books, *Pedagogy of the Oppressed* (1970) and *Education for Critical Consciousness* (1973), which describe his practice and theory of literacy education.

After a year's stay at Harvard University, in 1970 Freire took a position as educational consultant to the World Council of Churches in Geneva. In 1971 he established the Institute for Cultural Action, which fostered experimentation with Freire's method of conscientization. From this position he took part in literacy education in a number of developing countries. *Pedagogy in Process* (1975) describes his literacy efforts in Guinea-Bissau.

With other political exiles, Freire was permitted to return to Brazil in June 1980 after President FIGUEIREDO granted amnesty to Brazilian exiles and dissenters. He has since devoted himself to educational projects throughout the world. Especially through *Pedagogy of the Oppressed,* which has been translated into numerous languages, Freire is one of the most influential educators of the twentieth century.

IRA SHORE and PAULO FREIRE, *A Pedagogy for Liberation: Dialogues on Transforming Education* (1987); PAULO FREIRE and ANTONIO FAUNDEZ, *Learning to Question: A Pedagogy of Liberation,* translated by Tony Coates (1989); JOHN ELIAS, *Paulo Freire: Pedagogue of Liberation* (1993).

JOHN ELIAS

FREIRE SERRANO, RAMÓN (*b.* 29 November 1787; *d.* 9 September 1851), Chilean patriot, supreme director of Chile (1823–1826, 1827). Freire enlisted in the patriot army in 1811 and fought with great valor in many actions of the Chilean WARS OF INDEPENDENCE. (During the restored colonial regime of 1814–1817 he served in Admiral William BROWN's corsair squadron.) In 1819 he was named intendant of Concepción. The desperate conditions in that war-ravaged southern province turned Freire against the Bernardo O'HIGGINS government. His PRONUNCIAMIENTO was the main cause of O'Higgins's downfall (January 1823). Freire was the inevitable successor. During his supreme directorship, he expelled the Spanish troops still holding out on the island of Chiloé (January 1826). In domestic affairs, Freire's liberalism allowed politicians a free rein; their failure to organize stable institutions made this a frustrating period. Freire soon had enough. In July 1826 he resigned, returning to power briefly in 1827 to restore order after a military mutiny.

Early in 1830 Freire once again took up arms, to oppose the Conservative seizure of power then well under way. His small army was defeated at the battle of LIRCAY (April 1830), after which he was arrested and exiled to Peru. From there, in mid-1836, he led an expedition to Chile in the vain hope of overthrowing the Conservatives. He was captured, put on trial, and exiled to Australia. (Diego PORTALES wished to have him shot, but did not get his way.) By the end of 1837 Freire was living in Tahiti (where he is said to have befriended

Queen Pomaré). In 1839 he settled in the Bolivian port of Cobija. The amnesty of 1841 enabled the general to return at last to his native land: the remaining years formed a quiet coda to an adventurous life.

JULIO ALEMPARTE, *Carrera y Freire, fundadores de la república* (1963).

SIMON COLLIER

FRÉMONT, JOHN CHARLES (*b.* 21 January 1813; *d.* 13 July 1890), U.S. Army officer, explorer, and politician. A native of Savannah, Georgia, Frémont gained renown in part through the political influence of his father-in-law, Senator Thomas Hart Benton of Missouri, and the literary skills of his wife, Jessie Benton Frémont. He rose from an obscure position with the U.S. Army's Corps of Topographical Engineers to fame as a western explorer during two expeditions to the Rocky Mountains (1842) and Oregon and CALIFORNIA (1843–1844).

In 1845–1846, at a critical point in U.S.-Mexican relations (see MEXICAN-AMERICAN WAR), Frémont returned to California with another military expedition. There he clashed with the Mexican authorities, took a leading part in the BEAR FLAG REVOLT, and cooperated with Commodore Robert Stockton in the U.S. conquest of California. A dispute with Brigadier General Stephen W. KEARNY ended with Frémont's court martial for mutiny and insubordination.

Though restored to duty by President James Polk, Frémont resigned his military commission and moved to California, where he supervised gold mining on his Mariposa estate. He served briefly as U.S. senator from California (1850–1851), became the first presidential candidate of the Republican Party in 1856, and was again the center of controversy during a short term as a major general in the Union Army during the Civil War. After losing the Mariposa estate in 1864, Frémont attempted to restore his fortune through land, mining, and railroad speculations in Arizona, where he was also territorial governor (1878–1881).

A heroic and popular figure during the 1840s, Frémont epitomized the U.S. expansionist spirit; but an impulsive, imprudent nature tarnished his early exploits and later thwarted his ambitions for wealth and high office.

The basic biography is ALLAN NEVINS, *Frémont, Pathmarker of the West,* new ed. (1955). His career as an explorer is documented in DONALD JACKSON and MARY LEE SPENCE, ed., *The Expeditions of John Charles Frémont,* 3 vols. (1970–1984). For his military role during the Mexican-American War, see NEAL HARLOW, *California Conquered: War and Peace on the Pacific, 1846–1850* (1982).

KENNETH N. OWENS

FRENCH ARTISTIC MISSION, the forerunner of the BRAZILIAN ACADEMY OF FINE ARTS in Rio de Janeiro. In 1808, fleeing the Napoleonic invasion of the Iberian

Peninsula, Portuguese Emperor Dom JOÃO VI (1767–1826) transferred the court from Lisbon to Rio de Janeiro. Upon the arrival of the Portuguese court in Brazil, the emperor contracted a group of French artists to organize an art academy in Rio de Janeiro along the lines of the French Academy. French painters, sculptors, architects, musicians, and engineers of the Missão Artística Francesa arrived in Rio de Janeiro in 1816. The original group included the painter Jacques Lebreton (1760–1819), the landscape painter Nicolas Antoine Taunay (1755–1830), the sculptor Auguste Marie Taunay (1768–1824), the history painter Jean-Baptiste DEBRET (1768–1848), the architect Auguste Henri Victor GRANDJEAN DE MONTIGNY (1776–1850), the engraver Charles Simon Pradier (1786–1848), and the composer Sigismund Neukomm (1778–1858). Their goal was the establishment of what João VI called the Royal School of Sciences, Arts, and Crafts. The Royal School would elevate Brazil, then the seat of the Portuguese Empire, and imbue it with European, specifically French, culture.

Having received training in the French Academy, the artists implanted French-inspired artistic and pedagogic models. They replaced the isolated attempts by the Jesuit fathers in the colonial period to encourage artistic teaching. They replaced the colony's religious baroque styles with French secular neoclassicism, an aesthetic orientation that endured through much of the First and Second Empires. This cultural transformation corresponded to the political and social changes that accompanied the royal family's arrival in Brazil: the opening of ports to world trade, the lifting of limitations of manufacturing in the colony, the establishment of military academies, the creation of a national library, and the introduction of the printing press.

Financial and political disruptions, coinciding with the personal crises of some of the artists, delayed the formal inauguration of the Royal School until 1820. The school underwent a number of name changes until 1824, when it was changed to the Imperial Academy of Fine Arts, the name it held until the fall of the Second Empire in 1889.

The original artists of the mission served as mentors for the first generation of academically trained Brazilian artists. Jean-Baptiste Debret chronicled the events of the colony with his royal family portraits and coronation paintings. His students, Simplicio Rodrigues de Sá, Manoel de ARAUJO PÔRTO ALEGRE, and José Correia de Lima, continued his aesthetic influences. The legacy cast a shadow long after Debret returned to France in 1820. Dom PEDRO I named Simplicio de Sá court painter, and Pôrto Alegre became the Academy's fifth director in 1854.

AFFONSO DE ESCRAGNOLLE TAUNAY, A missão artística de 1816 (1956); CAREN ANN MEGHREBLIAN, "Art, Politics, and Historical Perception in Imperial Brazil, 1854–1884" (Ph.D. diss., University of California at Los Angeles, 1990).

CAREN A. MEGHREBLIAN

FRENCH COLONIZATION IN BRAZIL. Brazil was the first region in the Americas frequented by the French, who competed with the Portuguese from 1504 to 1615. Brazil was a port of call en route to the East Indies, and it abounded in profitable resources, including logwood (used to dye Rouen cloth).

Normans and Bretons supported the TUPINAMBÁ tribes against their enemies and the encroaching colonization by the Portuguese. French sailors visited the coast, establishing posts where they traded with the indigenous population. The sailors used their compatriots, who had been adopted by the Indians, as guides and interpreters. The Norman Binot Palmier de Gonneville made the first confirmed voyage to Brazil in 1504, reaching the coast at 26 degrees south latitude and proceeding to just north of the equator. On his return voyage, near the island of Jersey, he was attacked by Breton pirates. All his cargo was lost, but Essomericq, an Indian whom Gonneville had brought with him, was baptized and was married to a cousin of the family. The descendants of that union took an interest in Brazil and appealed for missionaries from France. The two resulting French colonization efforts failed: La France Antarctique (1555–1560) founded by Nicolas Durand de VILLEGAIGNON, and La France Equinoxiale (1612–1615).

In the sixteenth century the French heavily fortified the "island" of Brazil, challenging the growing monopoly of the Portuguese. Francis I supplied the funding for the competition of empires. Between 1526 and 1529 the Verrazano brothers, discoverers of New York Harbor, made three voyages to Brazil. In 1550, Rouen honored Henry II with a Brazilian festival, including dozens of French sailors and Indians. Churches near Dieppe and houses in Rouen have stained glass windows and sculptures representing ships, the lumber trade, and the native peoples of America.

Shipwrecked on the Brazilian coast, the German Hans Staden later attested that the natives, who had been rumored to be cannibals, were actually friendly. The Indians at Cape Frio were on good terms with the French, those at Pôrto Seguro with the Portuguese. In 1551, Guillaume le Testu of Le Havre explored as far as the Río de la Plata. English and Norman merchants contracted to trade jointly with Brazil. The French, English, and Dutch all opposed the Catholic powers of the South. The French court took an interest in Brazil, as did businessmen, humanists, and Protestants. A manual compiled by Cordier, a Rouen merchant, set forth French and Brazilian words, but made no reference to any hostile terms.

Villegaignon's project prospered despite internal problems. In 1565, maritime insurance in Rouen had an 18 percent premium for Brazil and 17 percent for the Roman port of Civitavecchia. Between 1560 and 1610 an estimated 500 French ships sailed to Brazil. But in the meantime, the Portuguese began an all-out conquest. The unsubjugated Indians fled to the north, accompanied by the French.

Vaux de Claye opened the Amazon coast for trade in 1579. In 1612, La Ravardière and Rasilly established "Equinoxial France" at Maranhão with Saint Louis (São Luís) as capital. The French Capuchin friars made known the plight of the Indians, and when the Portuguese attacked Saint Louis in 1615, the French fled. Later, they would aid the DUTCH in their attempts at colonization in Brazil.

Thereafter the French shifted their enterprises to the Guianas. France and Brazil contested the frontier until World War I, and in 1711 René Duguay-Trouin, corsair of Louis XIV, actually attacked Rio de Janeiro. In the nineteenth century, however, French visits to Brazil were strictly scientific and commercial.

CHARLES ANDRÉ JULIEN, Les français en Amérique (1946) and Les débuts de l'expansion et de la colonisation françaises (1947); SAMUEL ELIOT MORISON, The European Discovery of America, vol. 2 (1974); BRASÍL, SERVIÇO DE DOCUMENTAÇÃO GERÁL DA MARINHA, História naval brasileira, vol. 1 (1975); MICHEL MOLLAT and JACQUES HABERT, Giovanni et Girolamo Verrazano, navigateurs de François ler (1982); FRANK LESTRINGANT, Le Huguenot et le sauvage (1990); PHILIPPE BONNICHON, Los navegantes franceses y el descubrimiento de América (1992).

PHILIPPE BONNICHON

FRENCH GUIANA, country on the northeast coast of South America between Suriname and Brazil and the only French territory in South America. A Département d'Outre-Mer (overseas department—DOM) of France since 1946, La Guyane, as it is officially called in French, encompasses some 35,600 square miles of a narrow coastal savanna (where most of the inhabitants live and work) and an extensive and largely unsettled wilderness interior. The extraordinarily diverse population of 98,000 (1990) is overwhelmingly black or racially mixed but not homogeneous culturally: Creoles are fragmented into locally born, Haitians, French Antilleans, Brazilians, Dominicans, Maroons, Colombians, Surinamers, and more. The remaining perhaps 20 percent is made up of whites, mostly metropolitan French, as well as of Chinese, Lebanese, Hmong (Laotians), Javanese, Vietnamese, and various Amerindian groups. Although it is potentially rich in gold, timber, bauxite, and fish, French Guiana has a standard of living that is the result of massive subsidies from France meant to extend metropolitan social and economic benefits to this distant but integral part of France. The official language is French, though a number of other languages are regularly used by various ethnic groups. The predominant religion is Roman Catholic, but various ethnic groups have their own faiths.

Although the French had been around the Guianas since the fifteenth century, it was not until 1664 that a permanent French colony was established at CAYENNE, the present capital. Amerindian attacks and rivalries among the Spanish, French, Dutch, and English made successful colonization precarious at best. In the late seventeenth and again in the early nineteenth centuries Cayenne was briefly occupied by the Dutch and the Portuguese, respectively. During the eighteenth century the colony was under French control but never grew in population or wealth, as did neighboring Dutch Suriname and the French Antillean colonies of Haiti, Martinique, and Guadeloupe.

French Guiana was chronically short of capital investment (in labor, particularly African slaves), of settlers (who might have established plantations and farms), and of technology (to build the water control systems needed for agriculture to prosper). One result was that plantation agriculture barely established itself. A number of plans were made to overcome labor deficiencies in the eighteenth and nineteenth centuries; all were disappointments, especially those aimed at recruiting large numbers of French farmers. The plantation economy prospered briefly in the early nineteenth century, when SLAVERY was reimposed in 1802 after a short period of emancipation during the Revolution. COTTON, SUGAR, and annatto were exported, as were some spices and hardwoods; both sugar and cotton lost out to international competition by mid-century. Slavery was finally abolished in 1848, and the former slaves moved from plantations and onto wilderness lands as private cultivators, further weakening the plantation sector. Some Asians were imported as contract laborers to replace slaves, but this failed to stop the steady decline of the plantation sector and the small white planter class. By the twentieth century there was no locally born, white planter elite left, in contrast with Martinique and Guadeloupe.

The postemancipation developments of greatest import were not related to plantation agriculture. First, a gold rush lasting from the 1870s until the Great Depression made gold the major export, pushed the center of economic activity into the interior and away from the coast, and enticed the immigration of fortune seekers from many parts of the world.

The wealth extracted was allowed to leave the colony, and never served as the basis for reinvestment, development, and local productivity, although it did encourage the survival of a myth of great wealth in the interior.

The second development involved immigration of inmates from overcrowded French prisons. Intended originally to populate the colony with prisoners who would be given land and a chance at a new life through small-scale farming, the scheme degenerated rapidly into the transformation of Guyane into a penal colony during the reign of Napoleon III. This innovation has given French Guiana its international reputation as Devil's Island. Devil's Island, one of the milder prison camps, achieved notoriety due to the incarceration in 1895 of Captain Alfred Dreyfus, whose plight was publicized in Emile Zola's famous open letter "J'accuse." The prison complex on the coastal islands and mainland was shut down in the late 1930s but did not officially close until 1947.

Agriculture continued to decline, and by 1942 was unable to produce enough food to feed the local population. In 1946, the colony's status was changed to that of DOM. The economic benefits of that change have raised the standard of living while, paradoxically, the local level of productivity has declined. As an integral part of France, Guyane is more dependent on public subsidies now than before. Unemployment runs at about 25 percent. Average per capita income is about U.S. $2,800, placing French Guiana in the middle income range of Caribbean countries.

Political parties in French Guiana tend generally to debate the degree of local autonomy that might be desirable within French nationality. The independence movement is minuscule, less than even that of Martinique and Guadeloupe, in part a result of having accepted settlers and refugees from throughout the former French empire who are particularly pro-French and loath to loosen their bonds to France. "Decolonization through integration" of former colonies into the French state continues to be French policy supported by most Guianese.

Today, French Guiana is particularly important to the French because of the huge space station and rocket-launching facilities at Kourou, begun in the 1960s, which services the European Community.

JEAN-CLAUDE MICHELOT, *La Guillotine sèche: Histoire du bagne de Cayenne* (1981); PIERRE PLUCHON, LOUIS ABENON, et al., eds., *Histoire des Antilles et de la Guyane* (1982); JEAN-CLAUDE GIACOTTINO, *Les Guyanes* (1984); NEUVILLE DORIAC, *Esclavage, assimilation et guyanite* (1985); ANNE-MARIE BRULEAUX, RÉGINE CALMONT, and SERGE MAM-LAM-FOUCK, eds., *Deux siècles d'esclavage en Guyane Française, 1652–1848* (1986); KENNETH BILBY, "The Remaking of Aluku: Culture, Politics, and Maroon Ethnicity in French South America" (Ph.D. diss., Johns Hopkins University, 1990).

ROSEMARY BRANA-SHUTE

See also **Slave Trade; Slavery; Abolition of.**

FRENCH INTERVENTION (MEXICO), the protracted attempt from 1862 until 1867 by the Second Empire under NAPOLEON III to establish military supremacy in Mexico in order to maintain the Mexican Empire as a counterbalance to U.S. expansion. Napoleon III resuscitated earlier Bourbon aspirations to hegemony over Hispanic dominions and thereby gain access to bullion supplies. The intervention was not motivated by the demands of French industry or commerce, in spite of significant growth in the 1850s. In fact, it was unpopular in business circles. The French were, however, interested in the construction of an interoceanic canal across the Isthmus of Tehuantepec. Prince Louis Napoleon Bonaparte had been interested in such schemes while a political prisoner at Ham in the early 1840s.

French diplomats and a handful of Mexican monarchists mooted the idea of a European monarchy as a solution to Mexico's post-Independence instability. Predominant mid-nineteenth-century racism encouraged the belief that Mexicans were incapable of governing themselves. Napoleon III adopted the idea already given some prominence in France that France as the senior "Latin" state should have a role in Latin American affairs. A "Latin" bloc in Europe and America could hold back the Slavs and Anglo-Saxons. Foreign monarchs had already ascended thrones in Belgium and Greece, and two American countries, Canada and Brazil, were constitutional monarchies. Napoleon III was not fully briefed on Mexican affairs and erroneously believed there to be significant support there for a monarchy. He was, however, careful not to alienate Great Britain, which had its own commercial interests in Latin America.

The intervention went far beyond the initial tripartite (Great Britain, France, Spain) debt-collecting mission of January 1862. The scheme had precise political objectives that corresponded to a specific phase in French foreign and colonial policy and should be viewed in the context of expansion in Algeria and Indochina. Marshal François BAZAINE, a veteran of the Algerian campaigns, was the commander who led the French forces, which included Algerian and Egyptian soldiers.

The fortuitous occurrence of the American Civil War (1861–1865) enabled the intervention to take place without effective American challenge. Napoleon, however, mistakenly believed that the Confederate states would endure, thus allowing the extension of pro-French monarchies into Central and South America. But imperial Brazil showed little interest in Napoleon's plan, and the JUÁREZ regime determined to resist the French to the end. Overconfidence caused the French disaster at PUEBLA on 5 May 1862, which delayed the capture of Mexico City until 10 June 1863.

In the meantime, Napoleon embarked upon the process of establishing a Mexican empire with the Hapsburg archduke MAXIMILIAN as emperor. The Fontainebleau Instructions of 3 July 1862 provided for both protection of the Catholic church and consolidation of Liberal disamortization policies (state policy of transferring ecclesiastical and Indian properties to private ownership, in accordance with the LEY LERDO of 25 June 1856). Napoleon wanted a liberal empire legitimized by elections and supported by moderates. Conservatives and the Mexican hierarchy, however, had no sympathy for the liberalism of either French military commanders or Maximilian. General Élie-Frédéric Forey established the ASSEMBLY OF NOTABLES, which in July 1863 invited Maximilian to assume the throne.

When Bazaine replaced Forey as supreme commander in October 1863, there were 40,000 French troops in Mexico. Bazaine's coolness toward the Conservative regency established by Forey lasted until Maximilian's arrival in June 1864. Bazaine advised Napoleon of the difficulty of establishing a Mexican imperial army on European lines, but in the military campaign to hold

Forey's arrival at the Plaza of Independence, 1863. Contemporary drawing by Durand. BIBLIOTECA NACIONAL, UNIVERSIDAD NACIONAL AUTÓNOMA DE MÉXICO.

down Mexico, Bazaine benefited from a unified command. The French formed a *contre-guérilla* unit to combat Juarista bands that were attacking supply lines in the Veracruz hinterland. Guanajuato fell on 8 December 1863, and Bazaine entered Guadalajara on 5 January 1864. The fall of Durango (4 July 1864), Saltillo (20 August), and Monterrey (26 August) were the high points of the campaign in the north. In October 1864 Juárez was forced into Chihuahua, where he remained until December without being forced out of the country. Liberal guerrilla bands operated behind French lines.

The growth of Prussian power on the European continent and the ending of the U.S. Civil War encouraged Napoleon to press for the evacuation of French forces, leaving only the Foreign Legion. This made the formation of a Mexican army urgent. The French army had always been relatively small as a result of domestic opposition to the Mexican "adventure." Maximilian refused to leave with the French. He had decided to commit himself to a last stand in order to try to save the empire. This decision threw him into the arms of the Mexican Conservatives, whom he had largely abandoned since June 1864. The urgent task of forming an imperial army was left to the Conservative generals Miguel MIRAMÓN, Tomás MEJÍA, and Leonardo MÁR-

QUEZ. Bazaine departed with the last French troops. In eight weeks, 28,000 troops left Veracruz, one-tenth of the entire French army.

JACK AUTREY DABBS, *The French Army in Mexico, 1861–1867* (1963); ALFRED J. and KATHRYN A. HANNA, *Napoleon III and Mexico: American Triumph over Monarchy* (1971).

BRIAN HAMNETT

FRENCH–LATIN AMERICAN RELATIONS. France became involved in the discovery, conquest, and colonization of Latin America as early as 1504, when its ships began to prowl the coasts of Brazil looking for dyewoods to trade. France did not view itself as bound by the Treaty of Tordesillas, for as King François I remarked, "I should very much like to see the passage in Adam's will that divides the New World between my brothers, the Emperor Charles V and the King of Portugal." Although from 1532 to 1550 the Portuguese drove the French from their outposts in northern Brazil, in 1555 a French expedition founded a Huguenot colony, France d'Antarctique, on an island in the harbor of Rio de Janeiro, that lasted until 1566–1567. In 1594 another French mission established a settlement, this time in the Bay of Maranhão (São Marcos Bay) that was destroyed in 1614–1615.

In 1624 merchants from Rouen established a trading post on the coasts of Tierra Firme known as Guiana. Other Frenchmen followed and in 1643 founded Cayenne, today the capital of FRENCH GUIANA. Cayenne was occupied by the Dutch in 1664 but awarded to France by the Treaty of Breda (1667), which gave France a legal presence it had never obtained in Brazil. The Dutch were driven out in 1676, and the area around Cayenne has remained under French control ever since. From 1624 to the present, settlement in French Guiana has centered around Cayenne and adjacent coastlands. Agriculture and forest products have anchored the economy for 300 years. The inhabitants, mostly creoles of African and European descent, have been citizens of France since 1877, and French Guiana has been a *département* of France since 1946. From 1852 to 1939 it was a penal colony and received 70,000 convicts at Devil's Island and other points. Since 1968 French Guiana has hosted the rocket-launching program of the European Space Agency. The population of about 100,000 (1992) remains highly dependent on France.

Although the French pirate François Le Clerc destroyed Yaguana, the forerunner to PORT-AU-PRINCE, in 1553, it was not until the seventeenth century that the French would become active in the Caribbean. In 1635 Pierre Belain d'Esnambuc conquered the island of MARTINIQUE for France, while Jean du Plessis did the same for Guadeloupe during that year. Martinique became a great sugar producer and France assumed sovereignty over the island in 1674. Many important contributors to French and international culture were born there, including the Empress Josephine and the revolutionary theoretician Frantz Fanon. In 1946 both Martinique and Guadeloupe became overseas *départements* of France. Jacques Jean David Nau, known as L'Ollonais from his French birthplace, grew up in the Caribbean and became a buccaneer on the island of Tortuga, terrorizing the Spaniards with his atrocities, including the sack of Maracaibo (1667), from 1653 until 1671.

In 1641 other buccaneers established themselves on the northwestern shores of HISPANIOLA. In 1664 Louis XIV claimed settlements there for France and gave control over them to the French West India Company, a title that was sustained by the Treaty of Ryswick in 1697. French settlers founded Port-au-Prince in 1749. The Treaty of Aranjuez (1777) determined the boundary between that territory, known as Saint Domingue, and the Spanish part known as Santo Domingo. On 14 August 1791, the slaves in Saint Domingue revolted, and three years later they murdered 800 white planters, prompting many to flee to other French islands. In 1800 the leader of the revolt, Toussaint L'OUVERTURE, took control over Saint Domingue, which the following year promulgated its first constitution. Although the French tried to recapture their part of the island with twenty thousand troops in 1802, the nation of Haiti proclaimed itself independent in 1804 and was recognized as such by France in 1825.

French activity sparked Spanish exploration in many parts of the present-day continental United States. For example, Admiral Pedro Menéndez de Avilés defeated the French settlement at Fort Caroline prior to establishing Saint Augustine in 1565. French explorations of the Midwest under Jacques Marquette and Louis Joliet in 1673 and Chevalier Robert La Salle in 1685–1687 halted Spanish incursions into the area. The French gave possession of LOUISIANA to Spain in late 1762, but in 1800 Napoleon I demanded that the territory be returned. In 1803 it was sold to the United States as the Louisiana Purchase.

French military technology and practice had a decided impact on the Spanish American officers who fought the wars of independence, including Simón Bolívar. The copying of French uniforms in the nineteenth century was such that when Argentine intellectual and politician Domingo Fausto Sarmiento joined Justo José de Urquiza's troops to oust Juan Manuel de Rosas from power, he was attired as a French officer. French immigrants came to northern Argentina after independence and by the 1830s had set up sugar refineries, known as *ingenios,* while others went to central Argentina, especially Buenos Aires province. French merchants were active in Mexico, Chile, and Peru during the nineteenth century. In that period, the French occasionally meddled in Latin American affairs, usually in Mexico where a series of inept ministers only worsened relations. In 1838 they bombarded Veracruz in hostilities dubbed the PASTRY WAR because France was demanding reparations for damage to the shop of a French baker. During the same year they sought to extend their trade and power in the Río de la Plata area and to show their displeasure at the Rosas regime by organizing an ineffective blockade on Buenos Aires in the 1830s. However, the worst example of French interference in Latin American affairs came with the ill-fated "French Empire" in Mexico.

In late 1861 France, Britain, and Spain agreed to force Mexico to pay outstanding debts by blockading the port of Veracruz in December. Britain and Spain bowed out once they learned that the French intended to invade Mexico and establish an empire there. French forces suffered a humiliating defeat at the battle of PUEBLA (5 May 1862) but took Mexico City in June 1863. Hapsburg prince Ferdinand MAXIMILIAN, younger brother of Emperor Franz Joseph, accompanied by his Belgian wife, Charlotte, arrived in Mexico in June 1864 and became Emperor and Empress Maximiliano and Carlota of Mexico. Maximilian was too liberal for his clerical supporters and became heavily dependent on French troops, which deserted him soon after the U.S. Civil War ended and French emperor Napoleon III faced a growing challenge across the Rhine from Otto von Bismarck's Prussia. Empress Carlota traveled to Europe in the summer of 1866, hoping to restore the commitment of Napoleon III and secure the intervention of the pope. These efforts failed (and cost Carlota her sanity), leaving Maximilian to be captured and executed on 19 June 1867.

The most enduring consequence of this French fiasco has been the term LATIN AMERICA. French publicists coined the phrase in an effort to justify Napoleon's intervention by claiming a kinship among the peoples who spoke languages derived from Latin.

The Mexican adventure was the last major French enterprise in Latin America. Subsequently, French influence has been felt chiefly in the financial and cultural spheres. In the nineteenth and twentieth centuries, France has been among the major investors in Latin America. In 1900 France had $600 million invested in Latin America, twice as much as the United States but less than one-third of Britain's total. By 1970, French investment in Latin America totalled about $540 million, well below the U.S., British, and German figures.

France also played an important part in the evolution of Latin American culture. ENLIGHTENMENT ideology and the example of the French Revolution helped spark the revolutions of 1808–1826; when King João VI wished to invite an artistic mission to visit Brazil in 1816, he sought a French one (see FRENCH ARTISTIC MISSION). Virtually every Latin American capital was remade in the late nineteenth century to look like Baron Georges-Eugène Haussmann's Paris, with its wide boulevards. In Argentina, French intellectual Paul Groussac was influential in improving education and enhancing the role of the National Library, of which he became the director. The impact of French socialist theories was felt in Latin America into the twentieth century, as were the works of Charles Maurras from the 1930s on FASCISM. Especially important is the respect accorded to existentialist works by Jean-Paul Sartre and Albert Camus along with French cinema in the post-World War II era. Although its cultural prestige in Latin America has declined somewhat in the twentieth century, those countries with large European immigrant populations still regard Paris as the source of cultural trends and fashion.

For books from a French perspective, see FERNANDO CAMPOS HARRIET, *Veleros franceses en el Mar del Sur, 1700–1800* (1964); W. ADOLPHE ROBERTS, *The French in the West Indies* (1971); and CARL LUDWIG LOKKE, *France and the Colonial Question: A Study of Contemporary French Opinion, 1763–1801* (1976). For a more Latin American focus, see PIERRE CHAUNU, *L'Amérique et les Amériques* (1964); ALFRED JACKSON HANNA and KATHRYN ABBEY HANNA, *Napoleon III and Mexico: American Triumph over Monarchy* (1971); YUYU GUZMÁN, *Estancias de Azul y pobladores franceses en la zona rural de Azul* (1976); and ANGEL SANZ TAPIA, *Los militares emigrados y los prisioneros franceses en Venezuela durante la guerra contra la revolución: Un aspecto fundamental de la época de la preemancipación* (1977); NANCY NICHOLS BARKER, *The French Experience in Mexico, 1821–1861: A History of Constant Misunderstanding* (1979).

JOHN MCNEILL

See also **Mexico: 1810–1910.**

FRENCH WEST INDIES. In 1625 French settlement began on SAINT CHRISTOPHER (Saint Kitts), which was shared with the British. In 1635 the first settlers appeared on MARTINIQUE AND GUADELOUPE, supported by the Company of the Islands of America, which had been chartered by the French crown to provide *engagés* (white indentured labor) and free settlers and missionaries in return for fees payable in tobacco and cotton. The company went bankrupt for lack of government and merchant support, and the colonies were sold to private investors. Under the new owners, Martinique, Guadeloupe, Marie Galante, Désirade, the Iles des Saintes, Grenada, and part of St. Kitts emerged as plantation colonies worked by African slaves. In the western Caribbean, the French planted sugar in the unoccupied western end of Hispaniola. On the mainland of South America, they sank roots at CAYENNE.

By the 1660s, the colonies were prospering sufficiently to attract the attention of the French government. Jean-Baptiste Colbert, minister of trade, arranged to repurchase the colonies in 1664; set up the French West Indies Company to control and tax trade with the colonies; built slave trading forts in West Africa; forced the withdrawal of Dutch merchant competitors from the French West Indies by 1678; and forced Spain to accept French plantations on St. Domingue. Colbert also institutionalized the *exclusif,* which forbade colonial trade with non-French territories, as well as any trade or industry in the colonies that might compete with metropolitan merchants and manufacturers. The colonies were limited to producing the raw materials needed by French industry, and to consuming French products.

The colonies did not have local assemblies or councils empowered to make laws. The Council of State in France passed colonial laws and appointed all colonial officials. The intendants were French; the governors answered to the governor-general in Martinique.

In the eighteenth century, French losses to Britain included St. Kitts (1713) and Grenada (1763). SAINT BARTHÉLÉMY went to Sweden in 1784, returning to France in 1877. France acquired SAINT LUCIA in 1763 and TOBAGO in 1783, then lost them to the British in 1815.

The end of plantation SLAVERY began in the French colonies in 1793 with the massive slave rebellion on Saint Domingue, which succeeded in ending both slavery and French rule in what was renamed HAITI. In 1794, the French Revolutionary government declared the end of slavery in all French colonies. In 1802 Napoleon reimposed slavery on the remaining Caribbean possessions.

Martinique and Guadeloupe, important producers of sugarcane, used slave labor imported from Africa. However, French farmers began growing sugar beets, thereby lowering demand for cane sugar. Abolition came finally in 1848.

Planters received compensation for lost slaves and help in acquiring 70,000 indentured laborers from India. Former slaves received limited political rights (e.g., universal male suffrage in 1848). Sugar and its by-products continued to dominate the island economies through much of the twentieth century. FRENCH GUIANA experienced a gold rush at the turn of the twentieth century, and today exports jungle hardwoods. From the 1850s until 1947, French Guiana also functioned as a penal colony.

French Guiana, with an area of 36,400 square miles, consists of low coastal plains and tropical rain forests. Guadeloupe and its dependencies cover 700 square miles of coastal plains and interior volcanic mountains. Martinique, with similar topography, covers 440 square miles. By 1990 the population of Guadeloupe was 342,000, that of Martinique was 340,000 and that of French Guiana was 98,000. French Guiana was the most ethnically heterogeneous.

The Caribbean Départements d'Outre-Mer (DOMs) were created in 1946. One consequence has been the significant decline of agriculture in all three; their economies are dominated by the administrative and service sectors. As integral parts of France, they are provided with all the government services available in mainland France. French Guiana provides the French, and through them the European Community, with the space and missile complex at Kourou. TOURISM is increasingly important to the economies of the two island territories. Unemployment is significant, over 25 percent, in all three territories but is offset by welfare programs and subventions from France that yield living standards that are among the best in the Caribbean.

The dominant political issue facing the three territories today is their political relationship with France. Virtually all political parties support the present relationship with France, although they differ on how much local autonomy is desirable. The several small independence parties are electorally insignificant but add to the ongoing debate.

PHILIP P. BOUCHER, *Les Nouvelles Frances: France in America, 1500–1815. An Imperial Perspective* (1989); ROBERT ALDRICH and JOHN CONNELL, *France's Overseas Frontier; Départements et Territoires d'Outre-Mer* (1992). For recent developments, see the essays on the Western Indian DOMs in the annual *Latin American and Caribbean Contemporary Record* (1983–).

ROSEMARY BRANA-SHUTE

See also **Slave Revolts; Slave Trade; Slavery; Sugar Industry.**

FRESNO LARRAÍN, JUAN FRANCISCO (*b.* 26 July 1914), archbishop of Santiago, Chile (1983–1990), during the last years of the military government of General Augusto PINOCHET.

Born in Santiago, Fresno was educated in the diocesan seminary and at Gregorian University in Rome, where he received a bachelor's degree in canon law. Ordained on 18 December 1937, he served in the influential posts of vice rector of the minor seminary in San-

tiago and as an adviser to the reformist lay group CATHOLIC ACTION, which was particularly active in Chile from the 1940s into the 1960s. In 1958 Pope Pius XII named him bishop of the recently created diocese of Copiapó, and in 1967 Pope Paul VI named him archbishop of the more important archdiocese of La Serena.

Fresno participated in the Second Vatican Council (1962–1965), supporting greater involvement of the Catholic church in social justice activities. He also influenced the deliberations of the second CONFERENCE OF LATIN AMERICAN BISHOPS (CELAM) in 1968, which translated into Latin American terms the general mandates of Vatican II to promote peace, justice, and human rights.

On 3 May 1983 he was named archbishop of Santiago and two years later was elevated to the rank of cardinal. While he had publicly justified the coup that brought Pinochet to power in 1973, ten years later he engaged in negotiations to speed the return of elected government. In addition, he traveled widely to generate pressure within and without Chile to encourage Pinochet to resign. While his efforts were not successful, they did contribute to the ultimate defeat of Pinochet in a 1988 plebiscite and to the return of democratic government in 1990. On 30 March 1990 Fresno resigned as cardinal archbishop of Santiago.

BRIAN H. SMITH, *The Church and Politics in Chile: Challenges to Modern Catholicism* (1982).

MARGARET E. CRAHAN

FREVO, frenetic carnival dance MUSIC of northeastern Brazil. The *frevo* first appeared around the turn of the twentieth century among newly formed carnival clubs of black and mestizo urban workers in Recife, Pernambuco. The acrobatic dance steps done to the *frevo* developed largely from the CAPOEIRA (an Afro-Brazilian athletic dance), and the music itself grew out of the marches and polkas of military-style marching bands that accompanied CARNIVAL parades. The *frevo* quickly became a mainstay of the Recife carnival, and several distinct substyles developed, including the *frevo de rua*, instrumental street music played by marching bands; *frevo de bloco*, played by small string and percussion ensembles with a female chorus; and *frevo canção*, middle-class sentimental songs involving a lead singer, a chorus, and a brass, woodwind, and percussion band. City-sponsored competitions take place each year in Recife, and numerous recordings have been released. Beginning in the 1950s, *frevo* was incorporated into the carnival of Salvador, Bahia, by *trios elétricos* (electric trios) using electric guitars and drums. This electric *frevo baiano* (Bahian *frevo*) entered mainstream Brazilian popular music in the 1970s and 1980s via such pop star luminaries as Caetano VELOSO and Moraes Moreira. Alceu Valença and other northeastern popular musicians have added Recife-style *frevos* to their repertoires.

VALDEMAR DE OLIVEIRA, *Frevo, capoeira e passo* (1971); FRED DE GÓES, *O país do carnaval elétrico* (1982).

LARRY N. CROOK

FREYRE, GILBERTO (DE MELLO) (*b.* 15 March 1900; *d.* 18 July 1987), pivotal Brazilian cultural historian and essayist of the 1930s. His historical essay *Casa-grande & senzala* (*The Masters and the Slaves,* 1933) popularized Franz Boas's anthropological concept of culture as an antidote to pessimistic race science. Freyre argued that Brazil's "mixture" was psychic and cultural in addition to racial. Modern Brazilians were not doomed racial mongrels but rather the fortunate heirs of the colonial plantation's fusion of Portuguese, Indian, and African culture. This energetic and erotic essay became a bestseller. It eventually inspired CARNIVAL samba pageants (1962) as well as nationalist political propaganda. For example, the claim that Brazil was a model of racial harmony became a theme of Brazilian diplomatic initiatives. Many of the ideas of *Casa-grande & senzala* and its two sequels, *Sobrados e mucambos* (*The Mansions and the Shanties,* 1936) and *Ordem e progresso* (*Order and Progress,* 1959), established themes for the next generation of social scientists in Brazil. These included the centrality of the patriarchal family as a social institution, Brazil's historical formation as a slave society, the sugar plantation as an institution, and the importance of folkways, especially those related to the house, food, and healing.

Outside of Brazil, Freyre's ideas had their greatest repercussion in the United States, where his studies at Baylor (1918–1920) and Columbia (1920–1922) universities, bohemian life in New York, and travels in the South had refined his sense of Brazil's uniqueness. In the 1940s scholars influenced by Freyre, such as Frank Tannenbaum, challenged Americans to measure themselves against the model of race relations presented in *Casa-grande & senzala.* Their debates developed into the contemporary fields of comparative race relations and comparative history of slavery. Freyre's impact was not limited to the United States. *Casa-grande & senzala* was translated into at least six languages. Freyre lectured, visited universities, and received honors throughout the world, including an honorary British knighthood in 1971.

Freyre's history of Brazil took a nostalgic and regional perspective, centering on the rise and decline of the sugar plantations of the Northeast. According to *Casa-grande & senzala,* Brazil was founded in a burst of energy by the "miscible" Portuguese, who were culturally suited to the task of building a multiracial tropical colony. During three centuries of near isolation from Portuguese government, Brazil's "patriarchal" society centered around the self-sufficient plantation big house. In its kitchens and bedrooms, a cultural and sexual fusion of peoples was accomplished. The result was a culturally "Oriental" society, in which the Jesuit religious order was the only disciplined, "European" coun-

Gilberto Freyre late in his life. PHOTO BY CLAUS C. MEYER / PULSAR IMAGENS E EDITORA.

terweight to patriarchal whims. Plantation paternalism harmonized Brazilians and encouraged racial democracy; but plantation SLAVERY, "like a great economic God," divided Brazilians into masters and slaves and encouraged authoritarianism.

Sobrados e mucambos chronicles the decline of this order. Upon the arrival of the exiled Portuguese king in 1808, Brazil centralized, urbanized, and "re-Europeanized." During the nineteenth century, plantation families moved from country big house to city mansion. Once there, urban social institutions—doctor, street, and school—destroyed patriarchalism. The woman and the child emerged as individuals, free from the father's tutelage. Ultimately, "white" planter fathers acceded to the marriage of their daughters to mulatto men of talent, forming a multiracial, "semipatriarchal" establishment. *Ordem e progresso* argues that the abolition of slavery in 1888 and the overthrow of the emperor in 1889 completed the dissolution of patriarchy. From 1890 forward, republican Brazil cast about for identity, having symbolically rejected its father. By 1914 the institutions of the republic had begun to forge a modern order that could accommodate the challenge of the "social question" of the working class while preserving the legacy of racial harmony.

A political interlude from 1946 to 1950 marked a watershed in Freyre's career. Previously, he had been secretary to the governor of Pernambuco (1926–1930) and had briefly gone into exile in 1930. During the dictatorship of Getúlio VARGAS, his sponsorship of two Afro-Brazilian congresses in 1934 and 1937 and the audacious reputation of *Casa-grande & senzala* placed him under political suspicion. With the fall of Vargas, Freyre was elected to the 1946 Constituent Assembly and the Chamber of Deputies by a União Democrática Nacional (UDN) coalition. While in congress, Freyre championed cultural causes, including the chartering of the Instituto Joaquim Nabuco de Pesquisas Sociais in Recife, which eventually became his institutional base. In 1949 he was Brazilian delegate to the General Assembly of the United Nations. Freyre left political office in 1950, but he remained an active voice in Brazilian politics, now generally from the right. He contributed to the platforms of the pro-government Aliança Renovadora Nacional (ARENA) in the 1960s and 1970s.

After 1950 Freyre proposed the creation of a discipline of "Lusotropicology" that would study common aspects of the adaptations of Portuguese culture and rule to tropical colonies in Brazil, Africa, and Asia. Because Lusotropicalism appeared to embrace a defense of modern Portuguese colonialism in Africa, many other currents of social science in Brazil avoided it. Lusotropicalism never became a widespread intellectual movement. Furthermore, during the 1960s and 1970s, historians revised and criticized Freyre's descriptions of the supposedly benign components of slavery and race relations. Cultural anthropologists in the 1980s looked back to the insights of his early work but not to Lusotropicology.

Freyre's presence in Brazilian intellectual life was not confined to his roles as anthropologist, historian, or politician; he was also a distinctive literary voice. In the 1920s he urged the literary avant garde of his native Recife to explore regionalist themes in contrast to the futurist avant garde of São Paulo. Later, he published a sequence of two "semi-novels," *Dona Sinhá e o filho padre: Seminovela* (*Mother and Son,* 1964) and *O outro amor do Dr. Paulo* (1977), that portray the traditional family relations and religiosity of the Brazilian Northeast. It was the style of his historical essays, however, that was his major contribution to Brazilian prose. He sometimes invoked Proust as his model for the autobiographical tone and nonlinear style of *Casa-grande & senzala;* other critics have detected a baroque aesthetic with Brazilian roots.

GILBERTO AMADO et al., *Gilberto Freyre: Sua ciência, sua filosofia, sua arte* (1962), a collection of interpretive essays; THOMAS E. SKIDMORE, *Black into White: Race and Nationality in Brazilian Thought* (1974; rev. ed, 1993), on racial ideology in Brazil; EDSON NERY DA FONSECA, *Um livro completa meio século* (1983), a study and reference guide to *Casa-grande & senzala.* For criticism, see THOMAS E. SKIDMORE, "Gilberto Freyre and the Early Brazilian Republic: Some Notes on Methodology," *Comparative Studies in Society and History* 6, no. 4 (1964): 490–505; CARLOS GUILHERME MOTA, *Ideología da cultura brasileira (1933–1974),* 4th ed. (1978); and LUIZ A. DE CASTRO SANTOS, "A casa-grande e o sobrado na obra de Gilberto Freyre," *Anuário Antropológico /83* (1985), pp. 73–102, a review of critiques. Recent evaluations of Freyre's legacy include RICHARD M. MORSE, "Latin American Intellectuals and the City, 1860–1940," *Journal of Latin American Studies* 10, no. 2 (1978): 219–238; GILBERTO FELISBERTO VASCONCELLOS, *O xará de Apipucos* (1987); ROBERTO DA MATTA, "A originalidade de Gilberto Freyre," *BIB: Boletim Informativo e Bibliográfico de Ciências Sociais* 24 (1987): 3–10. There is self-analysis in GILBERTO FREYRE, *Como e porque sou e não sou sociólogo* (1968); and *Tempo morto e outros tempos: Trechos de um diário de adolescência e primeira mocidade, 1915–1930* (1975), memoirs in the form of an edited diary.

DAIN BORGES

See also **Literature; Race and Ethnicity.**

FRÍAS, ANTONIO (*b.* 13 October 1745; *d.* 1824), Argentine-born astronomer. Frías was born in Santiago del Estero and entered the Society of Jesus in 1764, just three years before the Jesuits were expelled from the Río de la Plata. Exiled, he sailed on the *Venus* to the Papal States, where he was ordained to the priesthood. Frías became interested in astronomy as a seminarian and retained the interest throughout his life. He worked under the Jesuit astronomer and mathematician Roger Boscovich. Frías conducted research in the observatory of Brera, near Milan, and published his findings in the *Efemeridi astronomiche* of Milan. He left several unpublished manuscripts, which today are in the Jesuit archive of the Colegio Salvador in Buenos Aires. He died in Milan.

FRANCISCO TALBOT, "Otro astrónomo argentino. Antonio Frías, S.J., 1745–1824," in *Estudios* (Buenos Aires) 18 (1920): 346–349.

NICHOLAS P. CUSHNER

FRIGERIO, ROGELIO (*b.* 1914), Argentine industrialist, journalist, and politician. Born in Buenos Aires, Frigerio achieved business success in textiles, mining, and agriculture. He served as editor and political director of the newsmagazine *Qué Sucedió en Siete Días,* director of the Center for National Research (1956–1988), and secretary for Economic-Social Relations of the Nation (1958). In 1959 he became economic counselor to the presidency. As Arturo FRONDIZI's closest advisor, Frigerio was responsible for the accord between Frondizi's INTRANSIGENT RADICALS (Unión Cívica Radical Intransigente) and Juan D. PERÓN (then in exile), which had provided

Peronist voting support for Frondizi's presidential victory in 1958. Frigerio influenced Frondizi's industrial strategy for national economic independence, which required large-scale involvement, on favorable terms, of foreign capital and technology. The strategy—particularly as it affected the PETROLEUM INDUSTRY, which Frondizi had until shortly before defended as the cornerstone of economic nationalism—outraged nationalists; moreover, it failed to achieve the intended results.

The president's attempt to bring the Peronist remnant into a permanent Radical-led coalition aroused increasing opposition among military anti-Peronists; in late March 1962 Frondizi was ousted by a military coup—the first of many as Argentina descended into chaos in the 1960s and 1970s. Once in power, the military charged Frigerio and his associates with "economic crimes." Thereafter, Frigerio remained close to Perón, but stayed out of public life until the 1980s. He became affiliated with the Movement for Integration and Development after 1975, and in 1983 he made an unsuccessful run for the presidency.

Frigerio has published a score of books on politics and political economy, including *Los cuatro años (1958–1962)* (1962), *Petroleo y desarrollo* (1962), *Historia y política* (1963), *Crecimiento económico y democracia* (1963; 2d ed., 1983), *Estatuto del subdesarrollo: Las corrientes del pensamiento económico argentino* (1967; 3d rev. ed., 1983), *Síntesis de la historia crítica de la economía Argentina* (1979), and *Diez años de la crisis Argentina: Diagnóstico y programa del desarrollismo* (1983).

RONALD C. NEWTON

See also **Argentina: Political Parties.**

FRIGORÍFICOS (refrigerated meat-packing plants). On the traditional ESTANCIA, workers killed cattle for their yield of hides, tallow, and dried meat. By the early nineteenth century, the processing of cattle moved from the plains to SALADEROS, meat-salting plants. During the 1880s, *frigoríficos* began replacing *saladeros*. At the meatpacking plants, workers butchered animals and packed the meat for shipment in refrigerator ships to Europe. The *frigoríficos* required higher-quality meat, so ranchers introduced blooded bulls from Europe and planted alfalfa for feed to improve their stock. The British controlled the packinghouses of Buenos Aires until the early twentieth century, when the Chicago "beef trust" sup-

Argentine workers processing meat for export, 1920. ARCHIVO GENERAL DE LA NACIÓN, BUENOS AIRES.

planted them. Meat packing remains an important industry in Argentina and Uruguay.

DAVID ROCK, *Argentina, 1516–1987*, rev. and enl. ed. (1987).

RICHARD W. SLATTA

FRISCH, A. (*b.* ca. 1825), pioneer of anthropological PHOTOGRAPHY. Frisch journeyed from Europe to the upper Brazilian Amazon region, especially on the Solimões River in the early 1860s to record the indigenous population. He posed them as noble savages, sometimes contriving or alternating backgrounds so that his subjects appeared as living sculptures. His works were displayed at the Paris Universal Exposition of 1867 before any other photographer recorded images of the indigenous populations of North America, the Far East, or Africa. Little is known about Frisch's life. He did not stay in Brazil, but contracted with the Leuzinger Studio in Rio de Janeiro to sell his prints.

ROBERT M. LEVINE

FRONDIZI, ARTURO (*b.* 27 October 1908; *d.* 18 April 1995), president of Argentina (1958–1962). Born in Paso de los Libres, Corrientes Province, Frondizi trained as a lawyer and received his degree from the University of Buenos Aires in 1930. He became active in politics as a member of the Radical Party. He served as a national deputy representing Buenos Aires (1946–1951). In 1951, he ran as the Radical Party's vice-presidential candidate.

Although the Radicals lost the election, Frondizi became one of the Peronist regime's more influential opponents. His speeches and publications concerning domestic development of Argentina's oil reserves won him support among nationalists. After the military coup and President Juan PERÓN's resignation in September 1955, Frondizi moved to take control of the Radical Party. His competition with Ricardo BALBÍN, the party's 1951 presidential candidate, split the Radicals into two groups: the Radical Civic Union of the People (Unión Cívica Radical del Pueblo), which followed Balbín, and the Intransigent Radical Civic Union (Unión Cívica Radical Intransigente).

When the military scheduled elections in February 1958, Frondizi ran for president. With the Peronist Party banned from participating, he tried to attract Peronist supporters with a prolabor, proindustry and anti-United States campaign. While the strategy helped him defeat Balbín, it put his administration between pro-Peronist unions and the anti-Peronist military. Conditions in late 1958 and 1959 forced him to abandon his populist rhetoric and adopt austere economic measures to control inflation and attract investment. Organized labor called strikes and demonstrations against the new regime. By 1962, his actions had cost him support among the voters and the military. With popular unrest rising and economic conditions worsening, the military moved against him in March 1962.

Frondizi retired from active politics until the 1970s, when he abandoned the Radical Party to become the leader of the conservative Movement of Integration and Development (Movimiento de Integración y Desarrollo). Later, he headed the right-wing National Movement (Movimiento Nacional) coalition.

ARTURO FRONDIZI, *Petróleo y política: Contribución al estudio de la historia económica argentina y de las relaciones entre el imperialismo y la vida política nacional* (1955); ROBERT A. POTASH, *The Army and Politics in Argentina, 1945–1962: Perón to Frondizi* (1980); DAVID ROCK, *Argentina, 1516–1987: From Spanish Colonization to Alfonsín* (1987), pp. 337–342.

DANIEL LEWIS

See also **Argentina: Political Parties.**

FRONDIZI, RISIERI (*b.* 20 November 1910), Argentine philosopher and author. Born in Posadas, Misiones Province, and brother of President Arturo FRONDIZI, Risieri Frondizi studied at the National Secondary Teaching Institute and then accepted a teaching position at the University of Tucumán (1938–1946). He continued his training abroad while writing and translating the works of George Berkeley, Alfred North Whitehead, and others. He received a masters degree in philosophy from the University of Michigan in 1943 and a doctorate from the National University of Mexico in 1950. For political and intellectual reasons, he accepted positions at universities in the United States and Puerto Rico.

Through his research and writing, he gained an international reputation as an expert in the study of individuals within society and of the nature of value and value judgments. His work includes *Substancia y fundación en el problema del yo* (1952), published in 1970 as *El yo como estructura dinámica*. After the 1955 overthrow of Juan PERÓN, Frondizi returned to Argentina and became rector of the University of Buenos Aires in 1957. After political events forced him from his university position, he returned to his research and writing.

Reflections on Frondizi's thought and impact appear in *El hombre y su conducta: Ensayos filosóficos en honor de Risieri Frondizi* (1980). For an example of his work, see *The Nature of the Self* (1953).

DANIEL LEWIS

FRUGONI, EMILIO (*b.* 30 March 1880; *d.* 28 August 1969), Uruguayan lawyer, professor, writer, and founder of the Uruguayan Socialist Party. Frugoni promoted Marxist and socialist ideas in highly regarded works such as *Socialismo, batllismo y nacionalismo* (1928), *La revolución del machete* (1935), *Ensayos sobre marxismo* (1936), and *Génesis, esencia y fundamentos del socialismo* (1947).

Frugoni was a supporter of Colorado Party president José BATLLE Y ORDÓÑEZ, whose first term from 1903 to 1907 marked an end to the country's long civil wars and the beginning of peace, prosperity, and undisputed Colorado control of government. Frugoni supported Batlle's important moral legislation (permitting divorce and ending the death penalty), state enterprises (strengthening of the state-owned Bank of the Republic and the Montevideo Electric Power System), support of labor (police neutrality in strikes and the promotion of an eight-hour work day), public works, and school construction. He also approved of Batlle's opposition to the church and to intransigent conservatism. In 1910 he supported the government against the threat of the "October Revolution" led by Nepomuceno Saravia, son of Aparicio SARAVIA, the famous Nationalist (Blanco) Party caudillo, and Basilio Muñoz, military commander of the Radicals.

Beginning in 1904 Frugoni promoted the formation of a Socialist Party that would constitute the country's workers as a political force. The Socialist manifesto that he authored in 1910 supported the constitutional order, in contrast to the Anarchists' destabilizing politics. As Socialist deputy to the national congress (1911–1914), he again collaborated with Batlle, who had been elected to a second presidential term, by authoring several important legislative projects aimed at socioeconomic reform on behalf of the working class. Frugoni's Socialist Party never came to rival the country's two traditional parties; it did not attract a significant working-class membership, perhaps due to the successes of Batlle's Colorado Party in implementing the greater part of its social program.

In subsequent years Frugoni was dean of the National University (1933). While serving as Uruguay's ambassador to the Soviet Union (1945–1948), he wrote *La esfinge roja* (1948), which praised the significant transformations of that nation but raised a voice of alarm about its denial of individual rights in favor of an omnipotent state. Between 1900 and 1959 he published twelve collections of lyrical poetry.

MILTON I. VANGER, *The Model Country: José Batlle y Ordóñez of Uruguay, 1907–1915* (1980).

WILLIAM H. KATRA

See also **Uruguay: Political Parties.**

FRUIT INDUSTRY. Nineteenth-century improvements in transportation technology allowed tropical fruits to become a profitable Latin American export for the first time in the 1860s. BANANAS were, and continue to be, the most profitable of the fruit exports; their commercial cultivation has been largely confined to the Caribbean Basin (including Central America and the northern coast of Colombia) and Ecuador. In addition to bananas, other tropical fruits are exported from the Caribbean Basin and Mexico, and grapes and other fruits are increasingly important to Chile's export economy.

Bananas were first exported to the Gulf coast of the United States in small quantities by shipping companies that occasionally bought the fruits from small independent producers in the Caribbean. In the 1870s the Costa Rican banana industry got off the ground as a subsidiary of the U.S.-based Tropical Trading and Transport Company. At the same time a Boston sea captain, Lorenzo Baker, began to import bananas to New England; this was to become the basis of the BOSTON FRUIT COMPANY. In 1899 the two companies merged to form the UNITED FRUIT COMPANY. United Fruit was eventually organized as a vertical monopoly which included plantations, rail and sea transportation, and even a supermarket chain.

United Fruit and its major competitors, STANDARD FRUIT and CUYAMEL FRUIT COMPANY, were often deeply involved in the politics of the countries in which they operated, especially in Central America. The fruit companies operated on larger budgets than did any of the Central American republics, and the companies were able to buy off both politicians and mercenary soldiers to influence politics in their favor. Their power challenged the sovereignty of the Central American republics.

Although the fruit companies were in many ways model employers, paying higher wages than other agricultural enterprises and providing benefits such as schools and health care for employees, their power came to be resented among Latin Americans.

During the 1960s disease and political problems decreased the profitability of Caribbean-grown bananas. Although still an important industry, bananas do not dominate the economies and politics of the Caribbean Basin as they once did.

Ecuador is now Latin America's largest exporter of bananas. Although the United Fruit Company started operations in Ecuador in 1933, the fruit industry did not expand significantly until after World War II. Unlike the industry in the Caribbean Basin, the Ecuadorian banana industry has been dominated by small and medium-sized producers who sell their produce to the large corporations. They have accordingly avoided many of the political problems experienced in the Caribbean Basin.

Chilean grape exports are important to the modern Spanish American fruit industry. Since the 1970s Chile has successfully experimented with exports of citrus fruits and kiwi.

Since the late 1960s exports of tropical fruits such as mangoes, papayas, passion fruit, and guava have become increasingly important in Spanish America, especially for Mexico, although none have threatened the dominance of the banana.

THOMAS MC CANN, *An American Company: The Tragedy of United Fruit*, edited by Henry Scammell (1976); THOMAS L. KARNES, *The Standard Fruit and Steamship Company in Latin America* (1978); JOSÉ ROBERTO LÓPEZ, *La economía del banano en Centroamérica* (1986); CARLOS LARREA M., MALVA ESPINOSA, and PAOLA SYLVA CHARVET, *El banano en Ecuador: Transnacionales, modernización y subdesarrollo* (1987); STEPHEN SCHLESINGER and STEPHEN KINZER, *Bitter Fruit: The Untold Story of the American Coup in Guatemala*, 3d ed. (1990).

RACHEL A. MAY

FUENTES, CARLOS (*b.* 11 November 1928), Mexican writer, major literary figure, and spokesman not only for his country, but for all of Latin America. A prolific writer of novels, short stories, plays, and essays that possess intellectual brilliance and a powerful style, Fuentes is also a pioneer in narration and structure. A highly visible figure, he has been the subject of several television documentaries and interviews.

Son of Mexican diplomat Rafael Fuentes Boettiger and Berta Macías Rivas, Fuentes was born in Panama City and attended elementary school in Washington, D.C., and secondary schools in Buenos Aires and Santiago, Chile. He studied law at the Institut des Hautes Études Internationales (Geneva) and received a law degree from the National University of Mexico. He was named secretary to the Mexican delegation of the International Law Commission of the United Nations (Geneva) in 1950. He launched his literary career in 1954 with a collection of short stories, *Los días enmascarados* (Masked Days) and his first novel, *La región más transparente* (1958; *Where the Air Is Clear*, 1960) which brought him immediate recognition.

From 1956 to 1959 Fuentes served as director of international cultural relations at the Mexican Ministry of Foreign Affairs. In 1962 he published one of his major works, *La muerte de Artemio Cruz* (1962; *The Death of Artemio Cruz*, 1964), a novel that vividly depicts the corruption of the MEXICAN REVOLUTION through the portrayal of a man in his last twelve hours of agony, during which he relives twelve crucial moments of his life. The main themes of his novella *Aura* (1962), found in most of Fuentes's works, are time, history, identity, desire, and civilization. *Cambio de piel* (1967; *A Change of Skin*, 1968) received the Biblioteca Breve prize in Barcelona the same year it was published. In an important book of literary criticism, *La nueva novela hispanoamericana* (1969; The New Latin American Novel) Fuentes analyzed the internationally acclaimed group of Latin American writers of the 1960s. While serving as ambassador to France (1974–1977), he published his essay *Don Quixote; or, The Critique of Reading* (1976), arguably the best guide to a full understanding of Fuentes's ideas.

Fuentes's most ambitious novel, *Terra nostra* (1975), published in English under the same title in 1976, is a powerful epic illustrating how the discovery of America provided a second opportunity for utopia that was defeated by human events. Among the many literary accolades Fuentes has received are Mexico's Javier Villaurrutia Prize (1975), the Rómulo Gallegos Prize of 1977 in Caracas for *Terra nostra*, and in 1987 Spain's prestigious Cervantes Prize. *Burnt Water* (1980) is a collection of Fuentes's best short stories written between 1954 and 1980. They depict the Spanish and Indian past with force and nostalgia. In *Cristóbal Nonato* (1987; *Christopher Unborn*, 1989), the tone is similar to that of *Terra Nostra*, offering an apocalyptic vision of Mexico's future in which he uses humor, as well as his trademark remarkable play of words.

During the 1992 year of the quincentenary of the meeting of the Old World with the New, Fuentes narrated a popular television series, *The Buried Mirror*, on the epic of "encounter" of the European and the indigenous world of Hispanic America. He continues writing, delving into Mexico's past, defining Mexico's national identity, and serving as Mexico's goodwill ambassador.

HELMY F. GIACOMAN, ed., *Homenaje a Carlos Fuentes: Variaciones interpretivas en torno a su obra* (1971); ROBERT BRODY and CHARLES GROSSMAN, eds., *Carlos Fuentes: A Critical View* (1982); WENDY B. FARIS, *Carlos Fuentes* (1983); IVAR IVASK, ed., *World Literature Today* ("Carlos Fuentes" issue) 57 (Autumn 1983); ANA MARÍA HERNÁNDEZ DE LÓPEZ, ed., *La obra de Carlos Fuentes: una visión múltiple* (1988).

MARTHA PALEY FRANCESCATO

See also **Literature.**

Carlos Fuentes. PHOTO BY LOLA ÁLVAREZ BRAVO.

FUENTES, MANUEL ATANASIO (*b.* 1820; *d.* 2 January 1889), Peru's foremost statistician of the era, he also was an acute observer of Lima in the mid-nineteenth century. A census taker, journalist, administrator, social commentator, satirist, historian, and folklorist, he also delivered expert opinion on legal and medical questions. Fuentes drew notice as a journalist in the 1840s, when he began writing on the everyday life and customs of Lima. A traditionalist who feared that guano excesses would destroy Peru's subsistence highland village economy and thus alter traditional highland culture, Fuentes sought to awaken intellectuals to thinking about the primacy of Andean culture. He also documented the size and variety of the artisan population of Lima in *Guía histórico-descriptiva administrativa, judicial y de domicilio de Lima* (1860), a study carried out after the artisan uprisings of 1858. Between 1858 and 1878 he produced a series of statistical studies based on painstaking research. His voluminous *Estadística general de Lima* (1858) listed data on every aspect of urban life: population, architecture, customs, and industry. He updated this survey four times and issued editions in French and English. He also wrote street guides and almanacs on Lima. As a public administrator, he directed the organization of a new faculty of political science and administration at the National University of San Marcos, a task undertaken at the behest of President Manuel Pardo, and he undertook the country's first scientific national census (1876).

PAUL GOOTENBERG, *Imagining Development: Economic Ideas in Peru's "Fictitious Prosperity" of Guano, 1840–1880* (1993), esp. pp. 64–71; ALFONSO W. QUIROZ, *Domestic and Foreign Finance in Modern Peru, 1850–1950: Financing Visions of Development* (1993).

VINCENT PELOSO

FUENTES Y GUZMÁN, FRANCISCO ANTONIO DE

(*b.* 9 February 1642; *d.* 1 August 1699), Central American historian, poet, bureaucrat, and soldier. He was born in Santiago de los Caballeros (now Antigua), Guatemala; little is known about his early life. At age eighteen he was named *regidor* of his native city, and later first (and then second) *alcalde* of Santiago de Guatemala. He also held the post of *alcalde mayor* in the town of Totonicapán and the province of Sonsonate. In the army he attained the rank of captain. Among his poems are "El Milagro de América" and "La vida de Santa Teresa de Jesús."

The work for which Fuentes y Guzmán is remembered today is his monumental history of Guatemala, the full title of which is *Recordación florida: Discurso historial y demostración natural, material, militar, y política del reyno de Guatemala.* He embarked on the project with a number of aims in mind. First, he wanted to take advantage of the deteriorating documents still at his disposal, especially those pertaining to the Spanish conquest of Guatemala. Second, he hoped to fulfill a request of the crown to provide a detailed history of the region. Finally, Fuentes y Guzmán hoped to answer some of the criticisms directed at Bernal DÍAZ DEL CASTILLO, a lieutenant under Cortés whose own *True History of the Conquest of New Spain* drew attacks from many Spaniards and creoles. Fuentes y Guzmán was a great-great-grandson of Díaz and thus

may have hoped that writing the *Recordación florida* would clear his family's name.

The *Recordación florida* covers the history of Guatemala from antiquity to the end of the seventeenth century, and includes detailed studies of the topography, climate, population, minerals, and natural resources of the kingdom. In addition to published materials, Fuentes y Guzmán relied on documents stored, and long ignored, in the capital city, as well as on information he gathered as *alcalde* of Totonicapán.

Although by the standards of the day his work was a model of scholarship, Fuentes y Guzmán reflected many of the biases held by his contemporaries. In his work Spaniards were invariably depicted as heroes; Indians, generally as slothful and immoral. Amid sound scholarship Fuentes y Guzmán included fantastic stories and doctored historical fact in order to portray the conquistadores in the most favorable light. Nevertheless, the *Recordación florida* continues to be a standard work for scholars of the pre-Columbian and colonial periods in Guatemala. Its contributions on the religion, geography, history, and natural sciences of the region are still significant today. The writing is first rate, reflecting the highly educated and erudite individual who wrote the first secular history of the kingdom of Guatemala. Fuentes y Guzmán died in Santiago de Guatemala.

FRANCISCO ANTONIO FUENTES Y GUZMÁN, *Recordación florida: Discurso historial y demostración natural, material, militar, y política del reyno de Guatemala,* 2d ed., 3 vols. (1932–1933) and *Obras históricas de Francisco Antonio de Fuentes y Guzmán* (1969); MURDO MAC LEOD, *Spanish Central America: A Socioeconomic History, 1520–1720* (1973).

MICHAEL POWELSON

FUEROS, local laws and privileges extended to towns, provinces, or particular groups such as the clergy or military. In Spain, the term *fueros* is commonly associated with the constitutional liberties of non-Castilian provinces and towns that each new king promised to maintain before he could be formally recognized as monarch. These local and provincial privileges limited the authority of the king in matters of taxation and military recruitment and protected the authority of local elites. In Aragon, for example, *fueros* ensured the perpetuation of aristocratic privilege in the guise of territorial autonomy. Not until the reign of PHILIP V were the *fueros* of Aragon and Valencia (1707) and Catalonia (1714) abolished.

Ecclesiastical and military *fueros* constituted corporate privileges that provided the protection of these two areas of law. In the New World, militia members granted the *fuero militar* were exempt, together with their families, from trial in civil courts and certain forms of taxation.

JOHN H. ELLIOTT, *Imperial Spain, 1469–1716* (1963); HENRY KAMEN, *Spain, 1469–1714* (1983).

SUZANNE HILES BURKHOLDER

FUJIMORI, ALBERTO KEINYA (*b.* 28 July 1938), Latin America's first head of state of Japanese origin (nisei). Born in Lima of Japanese immigrants who arrived in Peru in 1934 and worked as farm laborers, Fujimori was raised in a working-class neighborhood and educated in Peru's public school system. After attending the National Agrarian University (La Molina) and receiving a degree in agricultural engineering, he pursued graduate study in France and in the United States, where he received a master's degree in mathematics from the University of Wisconsin at Milwaukee. Upon his return to Peru he became a professor at La Molina and was elected rector (president) of the university. He also hosted a successful television talk show on public issues, which made him widely familiar.

In 1989 Fujimori and a group of professionals, small businessmen, and evangelical Protestants organized a political party named Change 1990 (Cambio 90). He ran for the presidency in April 1990 and finished the first electoral round a surprising second, with 24.6 percent of the vote; in the second round, in June, he easily won with 56.5 percent, and was inaugurated for a five-year term on 28 July 1990.

Fujimori presided over major initiatives to bring the economy back from the brink of disaster, to dramatically reduce the threat posed by generalized political violence, and to recentralize government authority in a new constitution. His drastic economic shock program caused inflation to drop from record highs of 7,650 percent in 1990 to about 20 percent by 1994 (138 percent in 1991, 57 percent in 1992, and 40 percent in 1993). Economic liberalization reduced the number of government employees by over 400,000, induced net capital inflows of over $2 billion, and generated economic growth of 7–8 percent by 1993–1994, although over half the population remained below the "critical poverty" line. Fujimori's campaign against political violence was less successful during his first two years in office, but then achieved rapid success after the capture of the principal leaders and master computer file of Shining Path and the Tupac Amaru Revolutionary Movement (MRTA) by police intelligence, beginning in September 1992—political violence in 1994 was less than 25 percent of the 1992 levels.

In a surprising move supported massively by the populace, Fujimori suspended Congress and the judicial branch in a self-coup (*autogolpe*) on April 5, 1992. Over the next eighteen months, he masterminded new elections for a Constituent Assembly/Congress (January 1993) and referendum approval for a new constitution (53 percent yes, 47 percent no) that recentralized executive authority, set up a smaller and unicameral Congress, established the death penalty for terrorism, and allowed for reelection of a sitting president. In October 1994, Fujimori announced that he would be a candidate again; the next year he succeeded in becoming Peru's first president to be elected for two successive terms.

FOREIGN SERVICE INSTITUTE, *Summary Statistics on Peru (1990–1991)* (1992); CYNTHIA MCCLINTOCK, "Peru's Fujimori: A Caudillo Derails Democracy," in *Current History* 92 (March 1993): 112–119.

DAVID SCOTT PALMER

See also **Peru: Revolutionary Movements.**

FUNAI. *See* **Brazil: Organizations: National Indian Foundation.**

FUNDO, a Chilean landed estate that often includes ranching and farming. A benign climate and good soils made the narrow, central valley of Chile a rich agricultural and grazing region. Since the colonial era, a small number of landowners has controlled most of the arable lands. During the seventeenth century, *fundos* produced mostly food for local markets and cattle for tallow exports to Peru. *Fundos* began growing wheat at the end of the century, but the small internal market limited production.

Authorities differ slightly on the definition and size of a *fundo*, but they agree that large estates dominated the Chilean countryside. During the latter half of the nineteenth century, some subdivision of agricultural lands took place. The resulting CHACRAS, or *minifundios* (tiny plots), seldom included enough land for profitable farming or grazing. The twentieth century witnessed a rise both in land concentration and in the gulf between

Alberto Fujimori after swearing in new cabinet members, 7 April 1992. AP WIDE WORLD.

Chile's landed oligarchy and the rural masses. Not until the frustrated attempts at land reform under Salvador ALLENDE (1970–1973) was the position of large *fundo* owners challenged. His overthrow and death removed for a time threats to the Chilean rural elite.

BENJAMÍN VICUÑA MAC KENNA, *A Sketch of Chili* (1866); ARNOLD J. BAUER, *Chilean Rural Society from the Spanish Conquest to 1930* (1975); BRIAN LOVEMAN, *Struggle in the Countryside: Politics and Rural Labor in Chile, 1919–1973* (1976).

RICHARD W. SLATTA

See also **Estancia; Hacienda; Latifundia.**

FUNDO LEGAL, a minimum endowment of corporate lands for indigenous communities of Latin America from the sixteenth through the nineteenth centuries officially recognized to ensure their survival and viability as sources of agricultural goods and human labor. The sizes of central area pueblos were subject to legal guidelines. In 1567 the area of a *fundo* was 500 *varas* (1,375 feet) in each cardinal direction; in 1687, 600 *varas* from the last house in town; and in 1695, 600 *varas* from the parish church. Other factors in *fundo* size were the availability of resources and the density of population. The larger allotment seems to have overlapped with the concept of the EJIDO (commons), better known today yet fairly rare in many colonial indigenous towns, at least in central New Spain.

The legal endowment (not given the name *fundo legal* until the late eighteenth century) is best studied in Mexico. Stephanie Wood critiques old assumptions about the allotment in "The *Fundo Legal* or Lands *Por Razón de Pueblo*: New Evidence from Central New Spain," in *The Indian Community of Colonial Mexico,* edited by Arij Ouwensel and Simon Miller (1990).

STEPHANIE WOOD

FUNES, GREGORIO (*b.* 25 May 1749; *d.* 10 January 1829), Argentine priest and statesman. Funes was born in Córdoba, educated at the College of Montserrat, and continued his studies at the University of San Carlos, where he received his doctorate in 1774. He studied in Spain at the University of Alcalá de Henares, where he received a law degree in 1778. After returning to Córdoba, he became dean of the cathedral in 1804 and was elected rector of the University of Córdoba (1808). Having become familiar with and sympathetic to the ideas of the Spanish Enlightenment while in Spain, he declared his support for the May Revolution in 1810.

The *cabildo* of Córdoba elected him representative to the Congress of the United Provinces of the Río de la Plata, where he became an ardent spokesman for the interior provinces, which felt alienated from Buenos Aires. In 1811, he supported a freedom of the press law, and in 1816, following the uprising of José Gervasio Artigas's supporters in Córdoba, Funes became governor of the province. A staunch supporter of public education, he

was elected senator in General Juan Gregorio de Las Heras's national congress in 1820. In 1823 he edited the periodical *El Argos de Buenos Aires,* and in October of that year the minister of Colombia named him agent of that country in Buenos Aires, a post linking him to Simón Bolívar and Antonio José de Sucre, through whom he was offered the deanship of the cathedral of La Paz, Bolivia. Funes accepted Bernardino Rivadavia's reforms but protested what he thought were his anticlerical excesses. The best-known of his scholarly works is *Ensayo de la historia civil del Paraguay, Buenos Aires y Tucumán* (1816–1817). In 1825 he published *Examen crítico de la constitución religiosa para el clero.* He was elected deputy to the Constitutional Assembly in 1826, participating in the deliberations and in the formulation of a new constitution. Funes died in Buenos Aires.

GUILLERMO FURLONG CARDIFF, *Bio-bibliografía del dean Funes* (Córdoba, 1939); RICARDO LEVENE, *A History of Argentina* (1963).

NICHOLAS P. CUSHNER

FÚRLONG CÁRDIFF, GUILLERMO (*b.* 21 June 1889; *d.* 21 May 1974), Jesuit priest and prolific historian of Argentina and America. Fúrlong was born in the rural region just south of Rosario in Santa Fe Province, Argentina. He was educated in British schools before enrolling in the Jesuit Colegio de la Inmaculada in Rosario. He entered the Jesuit order at fourteen and traveled to Spain two years later. In 1911 Fúrlong moved to the United States and eventually obtained a Ph.D. from Georgetown University. He returned to Argentina and taught Greek and Latin in the Seminario Pontificio de Buenos Aires from 1913 to 1916, and then taught the English language and Argentine history at the Colegio del Salvador.

From 1922 to 1926 Fúrlong traveled to Europe and visited the principal archives of Spain, France, Belgium, England, and Germany. On his return, he continued at the Colegio del Salvador of Buenos Aires, punctuating his teaching with visits to libraries and archives in Montevideo, Chile, and Bolivia. He explored both official and well-known archives as well as little-known and previously closed archives, in the process bringing to light important new sources and manuscripts. Fúrlong's initial studies concentrated on the early missionary efforts of the Jesuits in Argentina. Subsequently, he published works on the cultural achievements of colonial Argentine society in general, covering topics such as architecture, mathematics, printing presses, music, the role of women, philosophy, and others. In 1969 he drew upon his forty years of research and incomparable archival experience to publish the comprehensive *Historia social y cultural del Río de la Plata, 1536–1810.*

For a complete bibliography of Fúrlong's work see A. R. GEOGHEGAN, *Bibliografía de Guillermo Furlong, S.J.* See also JORGE LARROCA, *El Padre Furlong, Proletario de la Cultura* (1969).

J. DAVID DRESSING

FURTADO, CELSO (*b.* 26 July 1920), public administrator, economic development theorist, economic historian, and educator. Born in Pombal, Paraíba, Brazil, Celso Furtado received an M.A. from the University of Brazil (1944) and a Ph.D. from the University of Paris (1948). As director of the Economic Development Division of the United Nations ECONOMIC COMMISSION FOR LATIN AMERICA (ECLA) from 1949 through 1953 in Santiago, Furtado argued that developing Latin American economies required agrarian reform and import-substituting industrialization. In 1953 he was given the chance to advance these ideas when he became head of a Joint Study Group established by ECLA and the Brazilian National Bank for Economic Development. The group's seven-year plan for Brazil, reported in 1956 and 1957, became the structure of President Juscelino KUBITSCHEK's economic development program.

After teaching at Cambridge (1958) and returning to Santiago, Furtado joined forces in Brazil with the Working Group for the Development of the Northeast. Furtado prepared a plan calling for colonizing frontier areas, boosting electricity supply, changing the agrarian structure, industrialization, and creating the Development Superintendency for the Northeast (Sudene). Sudene was established in 1959, with Furtado serving until 1964 as its superintendent. In 1961, at Furtado's prompting, President Jânio QUADROS initiated a system of fiscal incentives to encourage Brazilian companies to invest in the Northeast. In July 1961, Furtado met with U.S. President John Kennedy and, by some accounts, persuaded him that the Northeast could be a showcase for the ALLIANCE FOR PROGRESS. In 1962, the U.S. AGENCY FOR INTERNATIONAL DEVELOPMENT pledged $131 million to develop the region.

Late in 1962, President João GOULART named Furtado Brazil's first minister of planning. The Goulart administration's attempts to slow inflation through fiscal reform failed, and in June 1963 Furtado resigned. Ten days after seizing power in 1964, Brazil's generals included Furtado on the list of those deprived of their political rights, causing him to leave the country.

Furtado was a visiting professor at Harvard, Cambridge (1973–1974), and Columbia (1977), a professor at the Sorbonne (1965–1979), and in 1980 became director of research at the College for Advanced Studies in the Social Sciences at the University of Paris. His principal books include *Formação econômica do Brasil* (1959; *The Economic Growth of Brazil*, 1963), *Formação econômica da América Latina* (1969; *Economic Development of Latin America*, 1970), *Teoria e política do desenvolvimento econômico* (1967), and *Um projeto para o Brasil* (1968).

DAVID DENSLOW

See also **Brazil: National Bank for Economic Development; Brazil: Organizations: Development Superintendency for the Northeast.**

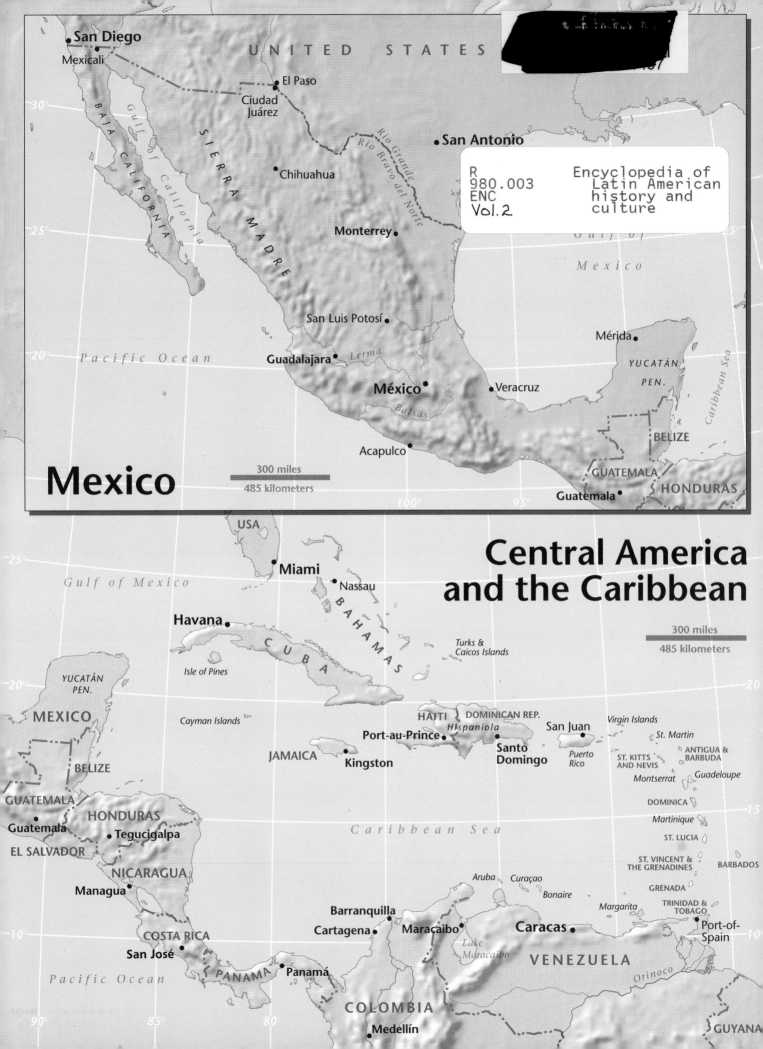

Mexico

San Diego
Mexicali

UNITED STATES

El Paso
Ciudad
Juárez

Chihuahua

Rio Grande
Rio Bravo del Norte

San Antonio

BAJA CALIFORNIA

Gulf of California

SIERRA MADRE

Monterrey

Gulf of Mexico

30°
25°
20°

Pacific Ocean

San Luis Potosí

Guadalajara
Lerma

México

Veracruz

Mérida

YUCATÁN
PEN.

Caribbean Sea

Balsas

Acapulco

300 miles
485 kilometers

BELIZE

GUATEMALA

Guatemala

HONDURAS

100°
95°

Central America
and the Caribbean

USA

Miami

Nassau

25°
20°
15°
10°

Gulf of Mexico

Havana

CUBA

Isle of Pines

BAHAMAS

Turks &
Caicos Islands

300 miles
485 kilometers

YUCATÁN
PEN.

MEXICO

Cayman Islands

HAITI
Hispaniola

DOMINICAN REP.

San Juan

Virgin Islands
St. Martin

BELIZE

Port-au-Prince

Santo
Domingo

Puerto
Rico

ANTIGUA &
BARBUDA

GUATEMALA

JAMAICA

Kingston

ST. KITTS
AND NEVIS

Montserrat

Guadeloupe

Guatemala

HONDURAS

DOMINICA

EL SALVADOR

Tegucigalpa

Caribbean Sea

Martinique

ST. LUCIA

NICARAGUA

ST. VINCENT &
THE GRENADINES

BARBADOS

Managua

Aruba
Curaçao
Bonaire

GRENADA

Margarita

TRINIDAD &
TOBAGO

COSTA RICA

Barranquilla

Maracaibo

Caracas

Port-of-
Spain

San José

PANAMA

Panamá

Cartagena

Lake
Maracaibo

VENEZUELA

Pacific Ocean

COLOMBIA

Orinoco

GUYANA

Medellín

90°
85°
80°